International Business

Environments and Operations

SEVENTH EDITION

▲

Addison-Wesley Publishing Company

Reading, Massachusetts · Menlo Park, California · New York
Don Mills, Ontario · Wokingham, England · Amsterdam · Bonn
Sydney Singapore · Tokyo · Madrid · San Juan · Milan · Paris

International Business

Environments and Operations

SEVENTH EDITION

John D. Daniels
Indiana University

Lee H. Radebaugh
Brigham Young University

Executive Editor:	Michael Payne
Senior Sponsoring Editor:	Beth Toland
Associate Editor:	Janice Jutras
Development Editor:	Cindy Johnson
Managing Editor:	Kazia Navas
Senior Production Supervisor:	Loren Hilgenhurst Stevens
Senior Production Coordinator:	Beth F. Houston
Production Services:	Jane Hoover, Lifland et al., Bookmakers
Copy Editor:	Laura Michaels, Mountainview Publications
Art and Design Manager:	Karen Rappaport
Art Development Editor:	Meredith Nightingale
Prepress Buying Manager:	Sarah McCracken
Technical Art Buyer:	Joseph Vetere
Art Editor:	Loretta Bailey
Illustrator:	Maryland CartoGraphics, Inc.
Text Design:	John Kane, Sametz Blackstone Associates
	Corey McPherson Nash
Cover Design Director:	Peter M. Blaiwas
Cover Design:	Corey McPherson Nash
Senior Marketing Manager:	David Theisen
Marketing Manager:	Craig Bleyer
Senior Manufacturing Manager:	Roy Logan
Compositor:	American Composition & Graphics, Inc.
Printer:	R. R. Donnelley & Sons Company

Photo Credits: Part 1: fabric photo by F. Khoury, © The Textile Museum, Washington, D.C., 1976.26.6, gift of Jerome A. and Mary Jane Straka; inset photo © 1993 R. Pharaoh, International Stock. Part 2: fabric photo by F. Khoury, © The Textile Museum, Washington, D.C., 1983.71.6, gift of Ralph S. Yohe; inset photo © M. and E. Bernheim, Woodfin Camp and Associates. Part 3: fabric photo by F. Khoury, © The Textile Museum, Washington, D.C., 91.146; inset photo © Paula Lerner 1990, Woodfin Camp and Associates. Part 4: fabric photo © The New England Quilt Museum; inset photo © Dario Perla 1982, International Stock Photo. Part 5: fabric photo by F. Khoury, © The Textile Museum, Washington, D.C., 1961.39.10, Arthur D. Jenkins collections; inset photo © Tom Stoddart/Katz Pictures 1990, Woodfin Camp and Associates. Part 6: fabric photo © Ruth Hollos, Bauhaus-Archiv, Berlin; inset photo © Chuck O'Rear, Woodfin Camp and Associates. Part 7: fabric photo by Mark Sexton, Peabody Museum, Salem, Mass.; inset photo © Robert Frerck 1980, Woodfin Camp and Associates.

Library of Congress Cataloging-in-Publication Data

Daniels, John D.
    International business : environments and operations / by John D.
Daniels, Lee H. Radebaugh. — 7th ed.
        p.   cm.
    Includes bibliographical references and index.
    ISBN 0-201-56626-5
    1. International business enterprises.   2. International economic
relations.   3. Investments, Foreign.   I. Radebaugh, Lee H.
II. Title.
HD2755.5.D35   1994
658.1'8—dc20   94-1384
                                                              CIP

Reprinted with corrections January, 1996.

5 6 7 8 9 10-DOW-9796

About the Authors

John D. Daniels

John D. Daniels, Professor of International Business at Indiana University, received his PhD at the University of Michigan. His dissertation won first place that year in the award competition of the Academy of International Business. Since then he has been an active researcher, publishing six books and over seventy articles and professional papers in such leading journals as the *Academy of Management Journal, California Management Review, Columbia Journal of World Business, Journal of International Business Studies,* and *Strategic Management Journal.* On its thirtieth anniversary in 1994, *Management International Review* referred to him as "one of the most prolific American IB scholars." He has served on the editorial board of eleven journals and has been a fellow of the Academy of International Business since 1985. Professor Daniels's international qualifications go well beyond his academic research. He has worked and lived a year or longer in seven different countries, worked shorter stints on six continents in another twenty-seven countries, and traveled in many more. His foreign work has been a combination of private sector, governmental, teaching, and research assignments; thus he is able to combine academic rigor with practical applications in this text. He has served as president of the Academy of International Business and as chairperson of the international division of the Academy of Management. He is director of the Center for International Business Education and Research (CIBER) at Indiana University.

Lee H. Radebaugh

Lee H. Radebaugh is the KPMG Peat Marwick Professor of Accounting at Brigham Young University and co-director of the BYU–University at Utah Center for International Business Education and Research. He received his MBA and doctorate from Indiana University. He taught at the Pennsylvania State University from 1972 to 1980. He has also been a visiting professor at Escuela de Administracion de Negocios para Graduados (ESAN), a graduate business school in Lima, Peru. In 1985, Professor Radebaugh was the James Cusator Wards visiting professor at Glasgow University,

Scotland. He was associate dean of the Marriott School of Management from 1984 to 1991. His other books include *International Accounting and Multinational Enterprises* (John Wiley & Sons, 3rd edition) with S. J. Gray, *Introduction to Business: International Dimensions* (South-Western Publishing Company) with John D. Daniels, and seven books on Canada-U.S. trade and investment relations, with Earl Fry as co-editor. He has also published several other monographs and articles on international business and international accounting in journals such as the *Journal of Accounting Research,* the *Journal of International Business Studies*, and the *International Journal of Accounting.* His primary teaching interests are international business and international accounting. He is an active member of the American Accounting Association, the European Accounting Association, and the Academy of International Business, having served on several committees as the president of the International Section of the AAA and as the secretary-treasurer of the AIB. He is also active with the local business community as president of the World Trade Association of Utah and member of the District Export Council.

Contents

Each part opener
displays fabric from
one of seven major regions
of international business.
Part 1 shows a 19th-century
Japanese Furisdoe kimono.

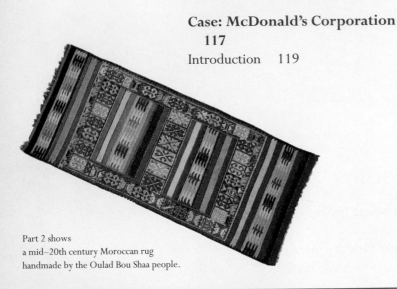

Part 2 shows
a mid–20th century Moroccan rug
handmade by the Oulad Bou Shaa people.

Part 3

Theories and
Institutions:
Trade and
Investment

Chapter 6
Governmental Influence on Trade   202

Chapter 7
Economic Integration and Cooperative Agreements   239

Chapter 8
Foreign Direct Investment   282

Part 3 shows fabric from the Ica valley of Peru.

Part 4

World Financial
Environment

Part 4 shows a mid–19th century American quilt from
New Hampshire in the variable star pattern.

Part 5

The Dynamics
of International
Business-
Government
Relationships

Part 5 shows a double saddlebag
from Shiraz (Qashqai), Iran.

Part 6

Corporate
Policy and
Strategy

Part 6 shows a German tapestry
by Ruth Hollós, circa 1926.

Part 7

Functional
Management,
Operations, and
Concerns

Part 7 shows a Maori feather cloak, circa 1930.

Preface

The Mystique of Seven

Few texts (or their authors) have the vitality to reach a seventh edition; thus, for us this book is a cause for celebration. This edition also has symbolic significance because of the universal mystique of the number seven. The ancients spoke of seven seas and seven wonders of the world. Greek mythology included the legend of seven heros against Thebes. Judaic tradition established the holiness of the seventh day. Christianity speaks of seven seals and seven pillars of wisdom, and Islam considers seventh heaven to be the highest abode of bliss. Currently U.S. geography books divide the world into seven continents. The world's largest oil companies are known as the Seven Sisters, and the most highly industrialized countries are known as the Group of Seven, or the G-7 countries.

Enhancements for the Seventh Edition

To help guide us in the preparation of this seventh edition, we queried people who have taught international business courses in a variety of institutions. Based on their familiarity with the sixth edition, we asked what topics should be added, deleted, or emphasized to a different degree. We asked how materials could be better presented. We asked what additional enhancements would best assist in teaching the course. We were gratified that so many professors took the time to give us constructive suggestions.

Although there were too many suggestions to detail them all here, the major ones for the text are as follows:

- Update examples and add new cases
- Simplify the presentation by using more tables and figures
- Help students identify where places are geographically by maintaining the large number of maps
- Use maps to a greater extent to convey information other than simply location
- Provide a framework for understanding and analyzing ethical issues

- Illustrate the countervailing forces that create uncertainties in international business management
- Integrate more coverage of the cultural environment as it affects business operations
- Incorporate examination of historically planned (transitional) economies into the general framework of political and economic discussions
- Present more examples of small company operations in international business
- Speculate more about the future

And, for the Instructor's Resource Manual, suggested improvements include:

- Update the section on audio-visual materials
- Furnish a completely new multiple-choice test bank
- Suggest supplementary reading materials to complement each chapter
- Add creative learning ideas that instructors may use

We have implemented each of these suggestions in the seventh edition. A description of the major content and pedagogical features follows. The enhancements to the ancillary package, cases, and art are described later in this preface.

Content   Major content changes to the seventh edition are as follows:

- Chapter 1 outlines the context for examining the countervailing forces that mold international business decisions: global versus multidomestic practices, company versus country competitiveness, and sovereign versus cross-national directives.
- Chapter 2 (formerly Chapter 3) has a new section on the causes of cultural difference and change and a discussion of the implications of recent ethnic unrest.
- Chapter 3 expands on the first half of Chapter 2 of the sixth edition by including more coverage of public sector influences on business and on the use of legal experts in conducting business abroad.
- Chapter 4 examines the economic issues discussed in the sixth edition's Chapter 2 and integrates the discussion of changes in historically planned economies that formerly appeared in Chapter 10.
- Chapter 5 (formerly Chapter 4) expands the coverage of the explanation of trading patterns.
- Chapter 6 (formerly Chapter 5) summarizes the outcome of GATT's Uruguay Round agreement.
- Chapter 7 includes a new section on regional trade in North America, especially the North American Free Trade Agreement.
- Chapter 8 (formerly Chapter 6) now discusses foreign direct investment patterns.
- Chapter 9 has a new section on the financial institutions that are instrumental in foreign-exchange trading, especially banks. In addition, the discussion of countertrade has been moved to Chapter 14, in the discussion of payments for exports.
- Chapter 10 covers important developments in China: the conversion of the renminbi to a floating currency and of the swap centers to foreign-exchange trading centers connected to the country's emerging banking system.

- Chapter 11 (formerly Chapter 16) has been moved forward to open a three-chapter sequence on the interrelationships of international businesses and governments.
- Chapter 12 now discusses issues concerning the loyalty of MNEs to their home countries.
- Chapter 13 expands the coverage of the bargaining school and dependencia theories of foreign direct investment.
- Chapter 14 separates the discussion of export and import strategies from that of global sourcing and production strategies, which was handled in the same chapter in the sixth edition. It examines the strategic and tactical issues involved in exporting and importing and provides a framework for small businesses.
- Chapter 15 has been retitled "Collaborative Strategies" to reflect its broader coverage of more than strategic alliances.
- Chapter 16 (formerly Chapter 17) has expanded coverage of hetarchies and of companies with mixed needs for integration and local responsiveness.
- Chapter 17 (formerly Chapter 18) now reflects the international alternatives within each of five product orientations.
- Chapter 18 expands on the sourcing and production strategies that were discussed in Chapter 14 of the sixth edition. There is more discussion of global sourcing, integrated manufacturing strategy, and quality and quantity standards, especially ISO 9000.
- Chapter 19 includes a new case, "Daimler-Benz and a U.S. Listing," which describes a foreign company's use of American Depositary Receipts to gain access to U.S. capital. The chapter also focuses more strongly on culture as an influential variable on accounting standards.
- Chapter 20 is a combination of Chapters 9 and 20 of the sixth edition. It discusses capital markets from the standpoint of companies rather than from a detailed institutional point of view.
- Chapter 21 has new coverage of the forms of expatriate allegiance.

Features   Each chapter now has a feature called "Ethical Dilemmas." Given the interest in ethics for international business, we considered writing a separate chapter on the topic; however, we quickly realized that ethics permeates every aspect of international business. Thus after introducing a framework in Chapter 1, we include a section in each of the other chapters that deals with ethical issues related to that chapter's content. For example, Chapter 16's "Ethical Dilemmas" covers control issues in the context of relativist versus normativist approaches to ethics.

In this edition, each chapter also has a section called "Countervailing Forces," which highlights the environmental conditions that pull companies in opposite directions. Countervailing forces add complexities to decision making in international business. The strength of one force relative to another will influence the choices available and the decisions made by companies competing internationally. Again, a framework for these sections is introduced in Chapter 1, and every chapter after that has a section related to its content.

We have retained a popular feature from the sixth edition, "Looking to the Future." In some earlier editions we discussed the future in a separate, end-of-book chapter; however, much of the material was too far removed from the topics to which it related. Each chapter now ends with a section that relates its content to future scenarios of which students should be aware.

Our Approach to Teaching International Business

Since the first edition of this text we have started each revision with a "zero budget," that is, planning anew rather than depending on what we had written before. There has been nothing that could not be altered, no matter how much effort went into writing it originally. This approach undoubtedly helped us avoid overlooking the multitude of environmental changes that are the norm for international business. At the same time, we have agreed that our text should have strong theoretical underpinnings that are probably unaffected by international occurrences. We are fortunate that these give our text continuity and a backdrop against which we are able to explain recent global changes that are likely to be familiar to students.

We have started each edition with the same question to guide us: *What should be taught in a first course in international business when some of the students will thereafter have little or no direct classroom exposure to the subject, and others will use the course as background for more specialized studies in the area?* We continue to feel strongly that introductory students should be exposed to all the essential elements of international business. But what are these essential elements? Our queries indicated a near consensus that our coverage should continue to be as broad as possible. The pervasive feeling is that the field will continue to evolve too rapidly for anyone to know for sure what the future essentials will be. It is far better, our respondents reasoned, to risk covering too many things than to risk the omission of emerging issues and approaches that may well turn out to be essentials by the time students enter the workplace and need to be informed citizens. Such a broad coverage is a challenge.

The text has expanded and contracted throughout its lifetime in response to new information and because of added features, as well as to our efforts to avoid an explosion in length. In this edition we have essentially maintained the length and presentation of the sixth edition but have substituted two new chapter topics for old ones and made a few changes in the order of the chapters. The basic content of the parts and their order of presentation are as follows: (1) an overview of the means of conducting international business, with an emphasis on what makes international different from domestic; (2) the effects of the social systems within countries on the conduct of international business; (3) the major theories explaining international business transactions and the institutions influencing those activities; (4) the financial exchange systems and institutions that measure and facilitate international transactions; (5) the dynamic interface between countries and companies attempting to conduct foreign business activities; (6) the alternatives for overall corporate policy and strategy that accommodate global operations; and (7) the management of and concerns about international activities that fall largely within functional disciplines.

Our viewpoint, exemplified throughout the text, is that of real-world managers rather than the social science disciplines from which international business draws its theoretical underpinnings. For example, as we talk about trade policy, we discuss not only the effects of different policies on national objectives but also the courses of action that companies and industries can and do take in order to influence policy making and to react to policies that are implemented.

Why Students Will Learn Well by Using This Book

Our objective still is to provide more breadth and depth of coverage than any of the other international business texts do, while at the same time taking care not to overwhelm students.

Visuals   Many new charts and figures have been added to clarify the discussions (the total is now 117). The accompanying captions will aid students in grasping materials rapidly. Color is now used throughout as a learning aid. For example, Map 2.4 in Chapter 2 shows countries colored to coincide with cultural clusters, and Figure 2.2 uses shades of color to demonstrate when companies need to be most aware of foreign cultures. The part openers have photographs that highlight seven major regions of international business, set against a backdrop of fabric from that region.

Integrated case methodology   We provide detailed cases to begin and end each of the twenty-one chapters. Eleven of the cases are entirely new; all others have been updated. Forty-one of the forty-two cases are real; all but one of those are identifiable situations.

The opening cases are designed to accomplish two objectives: (1) build the interest of the students so that they are motivated to read what is coming in the chapter, and (2) introduce problems and situations that will be explained further by theories and research findings presented within the chapter. For instance, the first chapter begins with a case dealing with the Walt Disney Corporation's decision to build a European theme park (Euro Disney) and the subsequent operation of that park. Almost all students should have some familiarity with and/or interest in this topic. Elements of the case are integrated into the chapter as examples to illustrate what makes international business different from its domestic counterpart and what types of adjustments Disney and other international businesses have to make. The closing cases are designed to serve a different purpose from the opening ones. They present situations for which students must analyze possible actions based on what they have learned in the chapter. In other words, the opening cases should enhance interest and the recall of essential facts; the closing cases should enhance the development of critical reasoning skills to apply the essential facts to necessary decision making.

Real-world examples   We have also continued the extensive use of updated real-world examples throughout the text to illustrate diverse approaches that individuals, companies, industries, and countries have taken in specific situations. (Examples of approximately 650 *different* companies are cited.) These examples not only help enliven the presentation, they also provide a practical and concrete counterpoint to the general discussion, which will help students understand the key concepts. Also, because most global employment growth has recently come from smaller companies and because students often think erroneously that international business is the domain of large enterprises, we have included many more examples about small companies. For example, Chapter 1 explains that small companies account for 20 percent of U.S.-manufactured exports. Further, two of the new cases, "Snider Mold Co. and NAFTA" and "Grieve Corporation," deal specifically with small businesses.

Study Support   To further emphasize key ideas (and to encourage students not to direct their study efforts too much to illustrative data), we continue to include the marginal notes that first appeared in the fourth edition. These notes highlight the text's major points in the margin for easy reference. They have been fully revised for this edition for the sake of emphasis and clarity. We have also highlighted new terms when they are introduced and included them in the expanded glossary. Chapter objectives are outlined clearly at the beginning of each chapter, and the summary's bulleted list recaps each chapter's major points.

An ample list of endnotes to aid students and instructors in digging deeper on the various subjects completes each chapter. Although we have omitted names of authors (except classics such as David Ricardo) within the text so that students would not think they had to remember those names, we reference approximately 1300 *different* contributors. Three indexes—subject, author, and company—are carryovers from earlier editions. A glance at these and the endnotes will show that the content is up-to-date, worldwide, and easy to access. There is also a map index keyed to the full-color atlas that appears between Chapters 1 and 2; this index includes a pronunciation guide for country names.

Maps   The maps for the sixth edition were well received, and we have retained the full-color atlas as a reference for students. All other maps are placed adjacent to relevant text material. We have added many maps (for a total of 54 of them) and have illustrated more types of information via maps. For example, a map that accompanies the new case on Blockbuster Video shows VCR equipment by region, and a new map in the revised case on Source Perrier shows bottled water consumption by region.

We feel strongly that there is a need to improve students' geographic literacy without having them resort to the rote memorization of maps. A poll conducted by the Gallup Organization asked for the locations of sixteen seemingly not too obscure places on a world map: for example, the United States, Central America, France, Japan, and the Pacific Ocean. No nationality scored very well. Swedes did the best but averaged only 11.6 correct answers, or 70 percent. Regardless of nationality, people were better able to locate places closer to them. For example, respondents in Sweden scored higher than those in the United States at locating the six European countries on the list; but U.S. respondents scored better than Swedes in finding the United States, Canada, Central America, Mexico, and the Pacific Ocean. The Gallup/National Geographic poll also indicated possible differences among countries in educational philosophy, such as emphasis on rote memorization of information versus the use of tools to find information. For example, Swedes scored higher than any other group on factual geographic information, such as locating countries without an index and knowing population figures. However, U.S. respondents placed more emphasis than those of any other nationality on tool skills, including the importance of using computers and knowing how to interpret maps, such as by estimating distances from map scales. Because of these two approaches, we have included two types of maps. Those within the chapters are not indexed and are aimed primarily at presenting information of an interpretive nature. The full-color atlas is indexed so that students may look up locations.

Regrettably, we cannot present maps from all national perspectives; however, students should be aware that maps do differ among countries. An obvious difference is in the portrayal of disputed territories. Furthermore, most people put their own countries toward the middle, from west to east, of a flat map projection. They also divide global segments differently. For example, in the United States students are taught that there are seven continents and that the Western Hemisphere is divided into two continents at the border between Panama and Colombia. But the International Olympic Committee uses a flag with five rings to symbolize the five continents of the world. And Panamanians are taught that North and South America are divided between Costa Rica and Panama. In most other Latin American and Caribbean countries, students learn that the Western Hemisphere contains only one continent, America, with several subcontinental segments. Most people within these countries refer to everyone living in the Western Hemisphere as Americans and to people from the United States as either *estadounidenses* or *norteamericanos*— Spanish for "United Statesians" and "North Americans," respectively.

Maximizing the Learning Environment

A highly competitive set of ancillaries is available to adopters of this text.

Instructor's Manual The Instructor's Manual contains many valuable materials for faculty. Suggestions are made for games, exercises, and projects suitable for classroom use, and a list of key articles that are useful in preparing for lectures or discussions is included. Chapter outlines, lecture support, and discussions of introductory and end-of-chapter cases have been revised for each chapter. Study questions complement the multiple-choice questions in the Test Bank and may be copied and distributed to students to help them focus on key elements for each chapter. There is a section called "Sources of Information," which may be copied and distributed to students for their general information or to help them in preparing research reports.

Test Bank   The Test Bank for the seventh edition is completely new. Each multiple-choice question has the correct answer and the text page on which the answer is found. The questions are organized in sections that correspond to each chapter's learning objectives. Discussion questions that may be used either in essay exams or in class discussion are included in the Instructor's Resource Manual. The Test Bank includes 35–55 questions per chapter, and all have been reviewed and edited from a student's perspective. Misleading words and phrases, "all of the above" and "none of the above" answers, and trivia-type questions have been eliminated.

Test Generator   The Test Generator for IBM computers allows faculty to personalize exams and easily add, edit, or delete questions from the Test Bank. The order of questions may be scrambled, and multiple versions of a test may be prepared. Answer sheets are generated for each test designed.

Videos   The Instructor's Resource Manual includes a completely updated section on audio-visual materials. This provides brief descriptions of approximately 300 videotapes, as well as information on where they may be purchased, rented, or borrowed.

A video collection, International Business Video Library Volume III (1995), is available to adopters. It consists of twelve segments, including six topics that are new for Volume III. Detailed summaries of each tape are provided in the Instructor's Resource Manual.

Transparencies   A collection of 92 color acetates presents a selection of figures, tables, and charts from the seventh edition. Over 150 transparency masters are included with the Instructor's Resource Manual.

"Global Access," an international business newsletter   This newsletter, featuring interviews with IB scholars, case updates, sources of audio-visual materials, teaching tips for IB faculty, and other articles of interest, is published twice annually for adopters of Addison-Wesley international business, finance, and marketing textbooks.

Both of us have diverse functional backgrounds, and we represent a gamut of opinions on the proper role of business and government in international affairs. In order to develop better coherence among the chapters, we read, criticized, and contributed to each other's work. John D. Daniels was charged with Chapters 1, 2, 5, 6, 8, 11, 12, 13, 15, 16, 17, and 21; Lee H. Radebaugh was charged with Chapters 3, 4, 7, 9, 10, 14, 18, 19, and 20. We welcome your comments and suggestions for the next edition.

J.D.D.
Bloomington, Indiana
L.H.R.
Provo, Utah

Acknowledgments

We have been fortunate since the first edition to have colleagues who have been willing to make the effort to critique draft materials, react to coverage already in print, advise on suggested changes, and send items to be corrected. Because this book is the cumulation of several previous editions, we would like to acknowledge everyone's efforts. However, many more individuals than we can possibly list have helped. To those who must remain anonymous, we offer our sincere thanks.

Since 1992, several people have taken part in our market research and have helped us to keep tabs on the changing nature of the international business field. We would like to thank them for their help:

Golpira Eshegi	Bentley College
John Reed	Clarion University
David Grisby	Clemson College
Robert Spagnola	Colorado State University
Suhail Abboushi	Duquesne University
Jeffrey Rosensweig	Emory University
Thomas Becker	Florida Atlantic University
Charles Newman	Florida International University
Victor Cordell	George Mason University
Kamal Elsheshai	Georgia State University
John McIntire	Georgia Tech University
Keun Lee	Hofstra University
Ann Hackert	Idaho State University
Khairy Tourk	Illinois Institute of Technology
Alberto Ottaviani	Iona College
Robert L. Thornton	Miami University
Kenneth R. Tillery	Middle Tennessee State University
Patrick Bourman	National University
Fairalee Winfield	Northern Arizona University

Ann Marie Francesco	Pace University
Gregory Stephens	Texas Christian University
Douglas Ross	Towson State University
Hoon Park	University of Central Florida
George Gore	University of Cincinnati
Jack Nedell	University of Oregon
Denise Dimon	University of San Diego
Gerald Cox	University of Texas
Jerry Ralston	University of Washington
Scott Kramer	University of Wisconsin
Peggy Chaudrey	Villanova University

Special thanks go to the faculty members who made detailed comments that contributed to the planning of this and previous editions:

Craig Woodruff	American Graduate School of International Management
Ann Perry	American University
Moonsong David Oh	California State University at Los Angeles
Ralph Gaedeke	California State University at Sacramento
Eldridge T. Freeman, Jr.	Chicago State University
Jean J. Boddewyn	City University of New York
Lucie Pfaff	College of Mt. St. Vincent
Urnesh C. Gulati	East Carolina College
George Sutija	Florida International University
Robert L. Thornton	Miami University of Ohio
Phillip D. Grub	George Washington University
Fernando Robles	George Washington University
Michael J. Hand	United States Department of Commerce
Charles Mahone	Howard University
Victor E. Childers	Indiana University
Paul Marer	Indiana University
John Stanbury	Indiana University, Kokomo
Miriam K. Lo	Mankato State University
Arvind K. Jain	Concordia University
Heidi Vernon-Wortzel	Northeastern University
Lee C. Nehrt	Ohio State University
Refik Culpan	Pennsylvania State University, Harrisburg
William A. Stoever	Seton Hall University
Thomas H. Bates	San Francisco State University
Leslie Jankovich	San Jose State University
Jeffrey T. Doutt	Sonoma State University
Van Wood	Texas Tech University

John Thanapoulos	University of Akron
Peter Walters	University of Arkansas, Little Rock
Kang Rae Cho	University of Colorado, Denver
Robert Grosse	Instituto de Empresa, Madrid
Duane A. Kujawa	University of Miami
Klaus Sinai	University of Portland
Arnold Stebinger	University of South Carolina
Mark E. Mendenhall	University of Tennessee, Chattanooga
Karin Fladmoe-Lindquist	University of Utah
Richard W. Moxon	University of Washington
Jerry Ralston	University of Washington
Scott Kramer	University of Wisconsin, Madison

Several typists and graduate students gave us needed assistance during the preparation of this edition, and without this anonymous support we could not have made the necessary changes. Some others were so helpful that we cannot let them remain anonymous. They are Daniel Chestnut, James Claus, Steven Hadley, Terri Hagler, Kory Hoggan, Sheldon Holsinger, Melanie Hunter, Susan Jensen, and Colin Low.

PART 1

Background for International Business

East Asia has become a leading global competitor in the manufacture of products using a wide range of technologies. Here you see a technician assembling circuit boards for computers in Japan. The photo is set against a background showing part of a Japanese 19th century Furisdoe kimono from the late Edo period.

Chapter 1

International Business: An Overview

The world is a chain,
one link in another.
—Maltese Proverb

Objectives

- To define international business and describe how it differs from domestic business

- To define and discuss basic terms relating to international business

- To explain the major motives of companies for engaging in international business and why its growth has accelerated

- To introduce different means a company can use to accomplish its global objectives

- To illustrate the role social science disciplines play in understanding the environment of international business

- To describe the major countervailing forces that affect the performance of international business

Case
Euro Disney[1]

Prior to the 1992 debut of Euro Disney, a French writer expressed the hope that a fire would destroy the 4800-acre theme park. Another wrote, "If we do not resist it, the kingdom of profit will create a world that will have all the appearance of civilization and all the savage reality of barbarism." Critics referred to the park, which lies twenty miles east of and is about one fifth the size of Paris, as a "cultural Chernobyl"; Disney's chairman was pelted by eggs in Paris; and *le Nouvel Observateur* magazine showed a giant Mickey Mouse stepping on the rooftops of Parisian buildings. Disney sought to head off the criticism by explaining in the French press that Walt Disney was of French descent and his ancestors' name was originally D'Isigny. The company also agreed to make French the first language in the park (see Fig. 1.1) (although it would rely heavily on visual symbols).

Despite opposition to the park, Disney's management was optimistic about its success. Management projected 11 million visitors in the first year of operations, and some Disney executives wondered if the park's 50,000-person capacity would accommodate opening-day crowds. This optimism was partially based on the belief that criticism of the project emanated from only a small vocal minority. The late actor Yves Montand summarized the apparent majority French viewpoint when he said, "T-shirts, jeans, hamburgers—nobody imposes these things on us. We like them."

High expectations also were based on the success of Tokyo Disneyland, which exceeded attendance projections its first year, 1984. By 1990, more than 14 million people were visiting that park annually, a figure slightly larger than the attendance at Disneyland in California and about half that at Walt Disney World in Florida. (The four Disney theme parks are shown on Map 1.1.)

Disney announced in 1985 that it would open a park in either Spain or France. Because the park was estimated to provide about 40,000 permanent jobs and attract large numbers of tourists, the two countries courted Disney. The company, in turn, was likened to Scrooge McDuck as it played one country against the other in an attempt to get more incentives. The Spanish government offered to pay 25 percent of the construction costs and claimed that a park in Spain could attract 40 million tourists a year. The French government,

Figure 1.1

Source: The New Yorker, Vol. LXIII, No. 7, April 6, 1987, p. 34.

Map 1.1
Disney's Four Theme
Parks
All four parks are easily
reached from highly popu-
lated areas within higher-
income countries. The
Japanese and French loca-
tions are less suitable for
year-long outside activities
than the U.S. locations are.

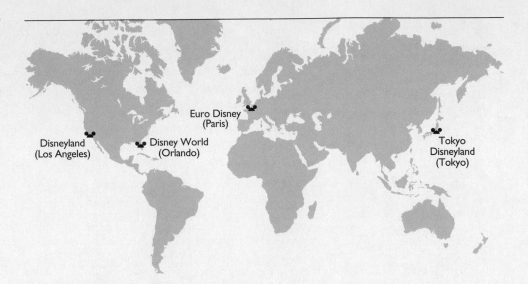

although it estimated only 12 million visitors a year to a French park, offered even greater concessions: to extend the Paris railway to the park (thus linking the park to the rest of Europe) at a cost of almost $350 million, to make available cheaply land on which to build the park, and to lend Disney 22 percent of the funds needed to build it. Other factors also influenced Disney's decision in favor of France:

- Its central location, as shown on Map 1.2. With the opening in 1994 of the tunnel under the English Channel between France and the United Kingdom, 109 million people live within a six-hour drive of the park.
- The number of tourists. The 26 million tourists in Paris each year make it Europe's most visited city.
- The popularity of Disney characters. The French are Europe's primary consumers of Disney products. For example, 10 million French children out of a total French population of about 56 million read the comic book le Journal de Mickey every week.

In addition, although the Spanish climate was more suited for winter attendance, Disney reasoned from its Tokyo experience that visitors would attend the park even in cold weather.

Disney's negotiations with the French government regarding who would own the park were heavily influenced by its experience with Tokyo Disneyland. On entering the Japanese market, the company, to avoid any risk of loss, made an agreement with the Oriental Land Company whereby Disney provided no financing and took no ownership in the park or the property on which it was built. Instead, Disney was paid to provide master planning, design, manufacturing, and training services during construction and consulting services after the park's completion. It also was to receive a 10-percent royalty from admissions and a 5-percent royalty from merchandise and food sales.

Because of the profitability of Tokyo Disneyland, Disney wanted an ownership stake in Euro Disney. The resulting agreement between the French government and Disney gave

Map 1.2
Euro Disney's Central Location
Disney's park near Paris is located such that 109 million people can reach it in six hours or less by car.

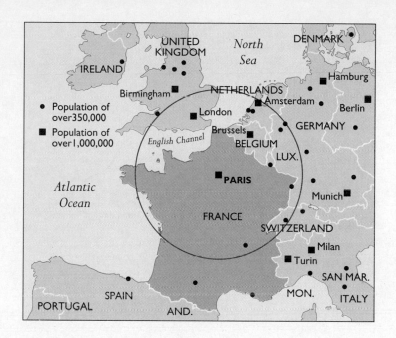

the company the option of owning between 16.7 and 49.9 percent of the French operation, which included investments in various satellite operations—hotels, shopping centers, campgrounds, and other facilities. Based on research that showed that 2.5 million Europeans visited Disney's U.S. parks in 1990, the company opted for a 49-percent stake. The remaining shares were sold to other investors, mainly in France and the United Kingdom, through an international syndicate of banks and securities dealers. In addition to equity, Disney agreed to accept a management fee of between 3 and 6 percent of gross revenue, a 10-percent royalty on admissions proceeds, and a 5-percent royalty on food sales.

The $3.6-billion Euro Disney looks very much like Disney's parks in the United States. For instance, it includes Adventureland, Frontierland, Fantasyland, Mainstreet-USA, and *Le Chateau de la Belle au Bois Dormant* (Sleeping Beauty's Castle), plus six theme hotels outside the park. However, a number of changes were made to cater to European tastes, especially those of the French. Disney built a new attraction, Discoveryland, based on the science fiction stories of Jules Verne and the science fiction art of Leonardo da Vinci, as well as a movie theater featuring European history and French culture. The park emphasizes that Pinocchio was Italian, Cinderella was French, and Peter Pan flew over London. Sleeping Beauty's Castle is cartoon-like so as not to copy nearby authentic castles. There is more architectural detail because of the French penchant for depth and sophistication. For example, Mainstreet-USA is more ornate and Victorian than at the U.S. parks. Because of the Parisian climate, which is colder than that of Florida or southern California, the company included fireplaces, protected waiting lines, more indoor shows, plus a glass dome over the teacup ride. Also, Euro Disney at first sold alcohol only in its hotels and restaurants outside the main gates in order to uphold what Disney's U.S. management saw as the park's family image. However, about a year after opening, alcohol was added to menus of restaurants *inside* the park because visitors from Germany and the United Kingdom feel wine is part of the French experience. The large number of adaptations for Euro Disney contrasts sharply with the few that were made for Tokyo Disneyland. The latter is nearly a replica of the two U.S. parks. Signs are in English and most food is American-style because Japanese youth have embraced American-style culture. In Japan, there has been no criticism about the invasion of a foreign culture.

Euro Disney hired 12,000 employees as early as eight months prior to the park's opening in order to train them for 1200 jobs. All employees must speak French plus at least one other European language; they wear flag lapel pins to indicate which languages they speak. Except for a handful of top managers, all employees are required by French law to have European Union (EU) passports or permits to work in France. To attract applicants, Disney advertised and/or held recruitment meetings with chambers of commerce in France, Ireland, the Netherlands, Germany, the United Kingdom, Canada, and the United States. Because of French individualism, Disney had to relax some of its U.S. grooming codes to entice French applicants to accept positions.

Certain European customs and attitudes make operating Euro Disney easier than operating the two U.S. parks. For example, in the United States, Disney plans events at different times in order to stagger the hours when people use the restaurant facilities. At Euro Disney, the British are usually finished with lunch before 1 p.m., when the French begin theirs; and the Italians and Spaniards arrive at about the time the French leave.

Euro Disney spent $220 million on a marketing blitz for its opening. Despite this massive effort, the first year's attendance was 20 percent below projections, which was caused in part by the lukewarm attendance of the French (only 29 percent of total attendance, rather than the forecast 50 percent) and which resulted in the 1100-room Newport Hotel closing for the winter because of low bookings. The dismal performance was intensified by lower-than-expected spending by the average visitor for food and souvenirs. Further, a slump in the French property market prompted Euro Disney to delay development of property around the park, including the planned MGM Studio tour park. Within five months of the opening, the price of Euro Disney stock fell from 164 to 68 French francs, prompting some securities analysts to compare the ups and downs of the stock prices to a ride on the roller coaster–like Space Mountain Railroad. The subsequent Euro Disney loss was over $900 million for the first full fiscal year of operations, and the park became the butt of jokes in the press, which called it "Mousechwitz" and "Eurodismal." Euro Disney responded to the loss by dismissing 950 people, mainly from management positions.

Euro Disney's early problems were caused by several factors:

* The leisure habits of Europeans
* Competition
* The cost of visiting the park
* U.S.-French agricultural trade animosity
* Slow-moving and chaotic lines at the park

Typically, Europeans are not very enthusiastic about amusement parks; the adults find it trying to act like children for an entire day. They prefer other types of leisure outings, especially in the winter. (No European amusement park has made money by staying open year-round.) For example, although an estimated 88 percent of people in the United States and Canada visited an amusement park in 1991, only 18 percent in Western Europe did. As a result, several European theme parks—the Mirapolis, Zygofolies, and Magic Planet—failed within the five years preceding Euro Disney's opening. And whereas Disney's U.S. and Tokyo parks opened when visitors to them were seeking ways to fill newly available leisure time, European leisure habits were already well formed.

Many potential Euro Disney customers instead visited the 1992 Olympics and World's Fair in Spain or other European amusement parks that recently sprang up or were refurbished. For example, Walibi, the world's fifth largest amusement-park operator, with headquarters in Belgium, built parks in locations from Amsterdam to Bordeaux. Parc Astérix, a theme park north of Paris modeled after a favorite European comic strip, was renovated and expanded just prior to Euro Disney's opening.

The cost of visiting Euro Disney also was a significant factor for potential visitors. European gasoline prices run as much as five times those in the United States, making family automobile vacations expensive. In addition, Euro Disney's entry and restaurant prices were set well above those in Disney's U.S. parks because the company had to offset the high wages necessary to attract workers to the area, which was plagued by insufficient and high-priced housing. A Paris newspaper estimated that a family of four would spend $280 a day for entry and food. European families, caught in a recession, were leery of spending so much on a day's outing.

Foreign visitors faced additional barriers. Because prices at Euro Disney were set in French francs, the exchange rate of other currencies into francs was an important factor affecting the cost. For example, in 1992, the year Euro Disney opened, European currencies were generally strong relative to the U.S. dollar. Consequently, it cost British tourists, for example, less to visit Disney World in Florida than to visit Euro Disney. They could fly to Disney World on packages that included transportation, hotel, and park entry for $115 a day compared to a similar $200-a-day package to Euro Disney. Further, because European currencies can fluctuate substantially in value relative to each other, potential foreign visitors were wary of unexpectedly higher prices. In late 1993, in response to these pricing problems, Euro Disney substantially cut winter prices on admission, meals, and hotel rooms.

Another problem that affected Euro Disney's profitability was animosity in France over trade with the United States. In the fall of 1992, many French farmers went on strike to protest agricultural trade agreements that were being negotiated between the two countries and that they felt would unfavorably affect them. They seized the opportunity to treat Euro Disney as a symbol of the United States by partially blocking transportation to and entry into the park. They were joined by beet farmers whose land had been taken by the French government as the site for Euro Disney.

To complicate matters, if tourists managed to get past the striking farmers, they then faced slow-moving lines for security checks at the park's entry because of political unrest in several European countries. Finally, although Europeans, in accordance with U.S. custom, line up in orderly queues when visiting Disney's U.S. parks, they typically don't do the same in their home countries (such as at ski resorts). Whoever can best shove into a line wins. Hence, the complaint heard most often regarding Euro Disney concerned chaotic lines throughout the park.

Disney executives admitted that Euro Disney was the one thorn in the company's recent performance. Nevertheless, the company remains openly optimistic about its future in Europe as well as in Japan. Disney's master plan, which extends far into the twenty-first century, calls for another park in each of those regions. And whatever Disney does will be noticed by competitors who have theme parks either in planning stages or under way all over Europe and Japan.

Introduction

The Field of International Business

International business is all business transactions—private and governmental— that involve two or more countries. Private companies undertake such transactions for profit; governments may or may not do the same in their transactions.

Why should you study international business? A simple answer is that international business comprises a large and growing portion of the world's total business. Today, you would be hard-pressed to find a company—large or small—that is not affected by global events and competition because most companies sell output to and/or secure supplies from foreign countries and/or compete against products and services that come from abroad.

A more complex answer is that a company that enters the international business field probably will engage in forms of business, such as exporting and importing, that differ from those it is accustomed to on a domestic level. To operate effectively, managers must understand these different forms. In addition, international business usually takes place within a more diverse external environment (the environment outside the company as opposed to its internal one) than is found domestically. The conditions within this external environment—physical, societal, and competitive—affect the way business functions such as marketing are carried out. These relationships are illustrated in Fig. 1.2.

Even if you never have direct international business responsibilities, you may find it useful to understand some of the complexities involved. Companies' international operations and governmental regulation of international business affect company profits, employment security and wages, consumer prices, and national security. A better understanding of international business may help you to make more informed decisions, such as where you want to work and what governmental policies you want to support.

The goal of private business is to increase or to stabilize profits. Success is influenced by
- *Foreign sales*
- *Foreign resources*

Government business may or may not be profit-motivated.

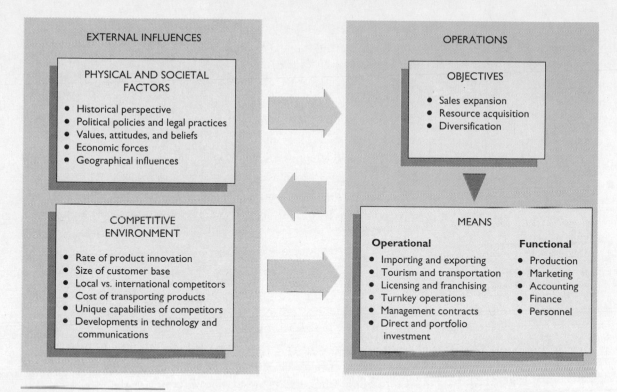

Figure 1.2
International Business: Operations and Influences

The conduct of international operations depends on companies' objectives and the means with which they choose to carry them out. The operations affect, and are affected by, the physical and societal factors and competitive environment encountered. The sizes of the arrows reflect that companies usually affect the external environment less than they are affected by it.

Why Companies Engage in International Business

As shown in the objectives section of Fig. 1.2, companies engage in international business for three primary reasons:

- To expand their sales
- To acquire resources
- To diversify their sources of sales and supplies

Expand sales   Companies' sales are dependent on two factors: the consumers' interest in their products or services and the consumers' willingness and ability to buy them. The number of people and the amount of their purchasing power are higher for the world as a whole than for a single country, so companies may increase their sales by defining certain markets in international terms.

Ordinarily, higher sales mean higher profits, assuming each unit sold has the same markup. For example, Disney promotes its U.S. theme parks in Latin America in order to increase the number of park visitors, and Disney's revenues increase with each additional admission or hotel space that is sold to Latin American tourists. Profits per unit of sales may even increase as sales increase. For example, Disney films such as *Aladdin* and *Beauty and the Beast* cost millions of dollars to produce; but as more people see the films, the average production cost per viewer decreases.

Increased sales are thus a major motive for a company's expansion into international business. Many of the world's largest companies derive over half of their sales from outside their home country. These companies (with their home country in parentheses) include BASF (Germany), Electrolux (Sweden), Gillette (the United States), Michelin (France), Nestlé (Switzerland), Philips (the Netherlands), and Sony (Japan). However, smaller companies also may depend on foreign sales. The National Association of Manufacturers classifies about 150,000 U.S. companies as small, that is, having 400 or fewer employees and total annual sales of less than $70 million. Together, these small companies account for over 20 percent of U.S.-manufactured exports.[2] Many small companies also depend on sales of components to large companies, which in turn sell finished products abroad.

Acquire resources   Manufacturers and distributors seek out products, services, and components produced in foreign countries. They also look for foreign capital and technologies they can use at home. Sometimes they do this to reduce their costs; for example, Disney relies on cheap manufacturing bases in China and Taiwan to supply clothing to its souvenir outlets.[3] The potential benefits of this practice are obvious: Either the profit margin may be increased or the cost savings may be passed on to consumers, who will in turn buy more products, thus producing increased profits through greater sales volume. Sometimes a company buys abroad in order to acquire a service not readily available within the company's home country. For example, Starbuck Coffee, a small but growing chain of Seattle-based coffee houses, contracts to have its decaffeinated coffee processed in Germany because of special decaffeinating technology and equipment located there. Such a strategy may enable a company to improve its product quality and/or to differentiate itself from its competitors—in either case potentially increasing its market share and profits. By using the German decaffeinating process, Starbuck may seek not only to improve the quality of its decaffeinated coffee but also to distinguish itself from its competitors, which do not use the same process.

Diversify sources of sales and supplies   To help avoid wild swings in sales and profits, companies may seek out foreign markets and sources of supplies. Many companies take advantage of the fact that the timing of business cycles—recessions and expansions—differs among countries; that is, sales decrease in a country that is in a recession and increase in one that is expanding economically. In addition, by obtaining supplies of the same product or component from different countries, companies may be able to avoid the full impact of price swings or shortages in any one country.

Reasons for Recent International Business Growth
The amount of international business conducted over time is difficult to determine on a long-term historical basis because early records comparing like data are not available. Even in recent times, gathering like data that can be used to make accurate

comparisons can be difficult. For example, the *reported* value of world trade will drop by about one third once border controls on trade within the European Community (EC) are completely eliminated because accurate trade records among the twelve member countries will no longer be kept.[4] Further, whether business is transacted across or within national boundaries determines whether business is international or domestic; shifting boundaries may cause what were domestic transactions to become international transactions, or vice versa. For example, when the Soviet Union disbanded in 1991, business transactions between Russia and Ukraine changed from domestic to international.

Regardless of these and other problems that impede accurate comparisons, it is generally believed that international business has been growing recently at a faster pace than it did in earlier years and also at a faster pace than domestic business has been recently. For instance, in the early 1970s, less than 5 percent of U.S. production was sold abroad and approximately the same amount of U.S. total purchases were of imported goods and services. Two decades later, these figures had more than doubled, to a little more than 10 percent each.

It seems the reasons companies pursue international business—to expand sales, to acquire resources, and to diversify sources of sales and supplies—would have applied in earlier periods as well. So what has happened in recent years to bring about the increased growth in international business? The answer can be found by examining the following four, sometimes interrelated, factors:

1. Rapid increase in and expansion of technology
2. Liberalization of governmental policies regarding cross-border movement of trade and resources
3. Development of the institutions needed to support and facilitate international trade
4. Increased global competition

Business is becoming more global because
• **Transportation is quicker**
• **Communications enable control from afar**

Expansion of technology Much of what we take for granted today results from technology that has been developed only within the last century. Before then, change occurred slowly. In 1620, the Mayflower trip from Plymouth, England, to Massachusetts took over three months. Another two and a half centuries passed before Jules Verne fantasized that people might go around the world in only eighty days. In recent years, however, the pace of technological advances has accelerated at a dizzying rate, while knowledge of products and services is available more widely and quickly because of tremendous strides in communications and transportation technology. As recently as 1970, there was no commercial transatlantic supersonic travel, faxing, or overseas direct-dial telephone service. Today, the situation is radically different. A traveler can fly from New York to London by Concorde in only three and a half hours (although most people take the customary six-and-a-half-hour flights), and fax and telephone transmissions are almost instantaneous.

By increasing the demand for new products and services, technology has tremendous impact on international business. As the demand increases, so do the number of international business transactions. But conducting business on an international level usually involves greater distances than does conducting domestic business, and greater distances increase operating costs and make control of a company's foreign operations more difficult. Improved communications, such as telephone transmission via satellites, speed up interactions and improve managers' ability to control foreign operations. Disney, for example, probably would be less willing to commit resources to its foreign operations without this ease of communicating.

Lower governmental barriers to the movement of goods, services, and resources enable companies to take better advantage of international opportunities.

Liberalization of cross-border movements   Every country restricts the movement across its borders of goods and services and the resources, such as workers and capital, to produce both. To build Euro Disney, Disney had to negotiate with the French government, and the final agreement between the two parties prevented the company from owning a majority stake in the park as well as restricted the number of employees with experience at the company's U.S. parks who could work at Euro Disney. Disney also must contend with import restrictions, such as taxes, when its Chinese-produced souvenirs cross a border to be sold in its shops in other countries. Such restrictions make international business more expensive to undertake. Because the regulations may change at any time, international business also is riskier.

Generally, governments today impose fewer restrictions on cross-border movements than they did a decade or two ago. Although the decrease in restrictions has been erratic, governments have lowered them for the following reasons:

1. Their citizens have expressed the desire for better access to a greater variety of goods and services at lower prices.
2. They reason that their domestic producers will become more efficient as a result of foreign competition.
3. They hope to induce other countries to reduce their barriers to international movements.

Fewer restrictions enable companies to take better advantage of international opportunities.

Institutional arrangements
• **Are made by business and government**
• **Ease flow of goods**
• **Reduce risk**

Development of supporting institutional arrangements   Much of what we now take for granted has resulted not only from expanding technology but also from the development by businesses and governments of institutions that enable us to effectively apply that technology. Disney can easily distribute films in foreign countries because of advances in transportation facilities as well as the evolution of various institutional arrangements that facilitate trade. For example, as soon as the films arrive in French customs, a bank in Paris can collect the distribution fee, in francs, from the French distributor and then make payment to Disney, in U.S. dollars, at a bank in the United States. In contrast, if business were still being conducted as in the era of early caravan traders, Disney probably would have to accept payment in the form of French merchandise, such as perfume or wine. The merchandise then would need to be shipped back to the United States and sold before Disney could receive a usable income.

Although barter still occurs, it is less common because it can be cumbersome, time-consuming, risky, and expensive. Increasingly, business relies on the institutions that facilitate international trade, among them banks, postal services, and insurance companies. Today, most producers can be paid relatively easily for goods and services sold abroad because of, for example, bank credit agreements, clearing arrangements that convert one country's currency into another's, and insurance that covers damage en route and nonpayment by the buyer.

Consider, for example, the transport of mail internationally. Until the sixteenth century, when the first international postal agreement was enacted (between France and part of what is now Germany), there was no postal system as we know it today; separate arrangements had to be made for payment and shipment of each piece for each country through which it would pass. Today you can mail a letter to any place in the world using only stamps from the country where you mail it, regardless of how many countries the letter must pass through to get to its destination and regardless of the nationality of the company carrying it. For example, Disney can use U.S. postage stamps for a letter sent to its French distributors, even though the letter might be carried on an Indian airline that en route makes a stop in the United Kingdom.

More companies operate internationally because
- **New products quickly become global**
- **Companies can produce in different countries**
- **Domestic companies' competitors, suppliers, and customers become international**

Increase in global competition The pressures of increased foreign competition can persuade a company to expand its business into international markets. It can do this more easily because of the technological, governmental, and institutional developments just discussed. Today, companies can respond rapidly to many foreign sales opportunities. They can shift production quickly among countries because of their experience in foreign markets and because goods can be transported efficiently from most places. Companies also can distribute component and/or product manufacturing among countries to take advantage of cost differences. For example, Kenner carries out some of the more automated parts of its toy production in the United States, with the more labor-intensive production done in Mexico. Also, some Japanese and South Korean companies produce part of their product lines at home and part of their product lines in the United States and then export from each production location.

Once a few companies respond to foreign market and production opportunities, others may see that there are foreign opportunities for them as well. For example, Lego Systems, a Danish theme park operator, saw that its revenues did not suffer from competition with Euro Disney and decided it could compete by opening a U.S. facility. Many other firms have to become more global to maintain competitiveness; failure to do so could be catastrophic for them. For example, consider

Mesta Machine, one of a handful of U.S. companies that supplied equipment to the U.S. steel industry when the United States dominated steel output worldwide. The company overlooked technical advances by foreign equipment manufacturers and ignored the rapid growth of foreign markets. Suddenly it found itself in competition with overseas rivals that could offer lower prices, faster delivery, and the technology demanded by the foreign and U.S. steel industries. Mesta responded too late and went bankrupt.[5]

Means of Engaging in International Business

When a company conducts international business, it must choose from among different operational forms, or means of conducting the business (see Fig. 1.3). In making its choice, a company should consider its objectives and resources as well as the environments in which it will operate. The following discussion introduces the major means by which a company may engage in international business. The first three categories (merchandise exports and imports, service exports and imports, and investments) correspond closely to the categories in which countries keep records in balance of payments accounts, which show their aggregate international transactions. The last two categories (strategic alliance and multinational enterprise) cover other commonly used terms for international business activities that may involve using any of the means in the first three categories.

Merchandise Exports and Imports

Merchandise exports and imports usually are
- **A country's key international economic transaction**
- **A company's first international operation**
- **Continued even after a company diversifies its methods of operating**

Merchandise exports are tangible goods sent out of a country; **merchandise imports** are tangible goods brought in. Because these goods can be seen to leave and enter, they sometimes are referred to as *visible* exports and imports. The terms *exports* and *imports* frequently are used to refer only to *merchandise,* not *service,* exports and imports. In Disney's case, souvenirs are merchandise exports for China or Taiwan when they are sent to the United States or France and merchandise imports for the United States or France when they arrive. For most countries, exporting and importing of goods are the major sources of international revenue and expenditures.

More companies that engage in some form of international business are involved in exporting and importing than in any other type of business transaction. This is especially true of smaller companies, even though they are less likely than large companies to engage in exporting. (Large companies are also more apt to engage in other forms of foreign operations in addition to exporting and importing.) Nevertheless, many small companies are highly successful exporters, especially in growing export sectors.[6]

Importing or exporting is usually (but not always) the first type of foreign operation a company undertakes. This is because at an early stage of international involvement, importing or exporting requires the least commitment of and the least risk to the company's resources, such as capital, personnel, equipment, and pro-

**Figure 1.3
Means of Carrying Out
International
Operations**

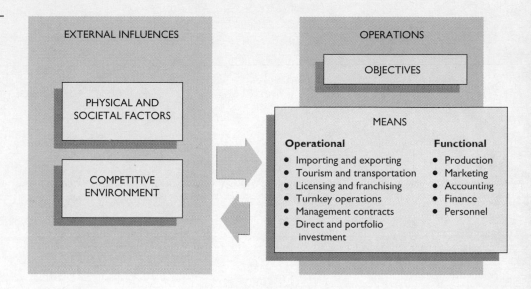

EXTERNAL INFLUENCES

PHYSICAL AND
SOCIETAL FACTORS

COMPETITIVE
ENVIRONMENT

OPERATIONS

OBJECTIVES

MEANS

Operational
• Importing and exporting
• Tourism and transportation
• Licensing and franchising
• Turnkey operations
• Management contracts
• Direct and portfolio
  investment

Functional
• Production
• Marketing
• Accounting
• Finance
• Personnel

duction facilities. For example, a company could engage in exporting by using excess production capacity to produce more goods, which then would be exported. By doing this, it would limit its need to invest more capital in additional production facilities such as plants and machinery. A company also could use trade intermediaries that, for a fee, will take on the company's export-import functions, thus eliminating the need for it to hire additional trained personnel and to maintain a department to carry out foreign sales or purchases.

A company typically does not abandon exporting and importing activities when it adopts other means of operating internationally. Rather, it usually either continues them by expanding its trade to new markets or complements them with new types of business activities.

Service Exports and Imports

Service exports and imports are international earnings other than those derived from the exporting and importing of tangible goods. Earnings received are **service exports**; earnings paid are **service imports.** Because services are not goods that can be seen, they also are referred to as *invisibles.* Service exports and imports take many forms. In this section, we discuss the following sources of such earnings:

• Travel, tourism, and transportation
• Performance of services
• Use of assets

Travel, tourism, and transportation   When Disney exports films from the United States, the films travel internationally, as do Disney executives when they visit Euro Disney on business. International travel, tourism, and transportation are important sources of revenue for airlines, shipping companies, travel agencies, and

Services are earnings other than those derived from goods.
• Examples are travel, transportation, fees, royalties, dividends, and interest.
• They are very important for some countries.
• They involve many special international business operating forms.
• The company often enters licensing and franchising agreements after experience with merchandise trade.

hotels. Some countries' economies, too, depend heavily on revenue from these economic sectors; for example, in Greece and Norway, a significant amount of employment, profits, and foreign exchange earnings comes from foreign cargo that is carried on ships owned by citizens of those countries. Earnings from foreign tourism are more important for the Bahamian economy than are earnings from the export of merchandise. Similarly, the United States has in recent years earned more from foreign tourism than from its exports of agricultural goods.[7]

Performance of services   Some services—such as banking, insurance, rentals (such as of Disney films), engineering, and management services—net companies earnings in the form of **fees,** that is, payments for the performance of those services. On an international level, for example, fees are paid for engineering services that often are handled through **turnkey operations**—construction, performed under contract, of facilities that are transferred to the owner when they are ready to begin operating. Fees also are paid for management services that often result from **management contracts**—arrangements whereby one company provides personnel to perform general or specialized management functions for another company; for example, part of Disney's revenues from Euro Disney comes from management fees.

Use of assets   The use of assets such as trademarks, patents, copyrights, or expertise under contracts, also known as **licensing agreements,** generates earnings called **royalties.** On an international level, for example, Disney has licensed Vigor International, a Taiwanese trading company, to use Disney trademarks for a chain of twenty Mic-Kids retail outlets.[8] Royalties also are paid for franchise contracts. **Franchising** is a way of doing business in which one party (the franchisor) sells another party (the franchisee) the use of a trademark that is an essential asset for the franchisee's business. The franchisor also assists on a continuing basis in the operation of the business, such as by providing components, management services, and/or technology.

Companies often move into foreign licensing or franchising in a market after successfully building exports to that market. This operational form usually involves a greater international commitment of the company's resources than does exporting or importing. The greater commitment results primarily because the company has to send qualified technicians to the foreign country to assist the licensee or franchisee in establishing operations or adapting its current facilities to handle the new product or service.

Dividends and interest paid on foreign investments are also treated as service exports and imports because they represent the use of assets (capital). However, the investments themselves are treated separately in countries' balance of payments accounts.

Investments

Foreign investment involves ownership of foreign property in exchange for financial return. Disney's ownership in Euro Disney is an example of foreign investment. Foreign investment takes two forms: direct and portfolio.

Key features of direct investment are
- **Control**
- **High commitment of capital, personnel, and technology**
- **Access to foreign markets**
- **Access to foreign resources**
- **Higher foreign sales than exporting (often)**
- **Partial ownership (sometimes)**

Direct investment   A **direct investment** is one that gives the investor a controlling interest in a foreign company. Such a direct investment also is called a foreign direct investment (FDI), a term frequently used in this text. Control need not be a 100-percent or even a 50-percent interest. For example, Disney can control Euro Disney with only a 49-percent stake because the remaining ownership is too widely dispersed to counter the company effectively. When two or more companies share ownership of an FDI, the operation is called a **joint venture.** When a government joins a company in an FDI, the operation is called a **mixed venture,** which is a type of joint venture.

FDI is the highest commitment a domestic company can make in international business because it usually involves not only the infusion of capital but also the transfer of personnel and technology. Hence, such investment usually comes after a company has acquired experience in exporting or importing. FDI can provide the controlling company with access to certain resources or to a market. For example, through Disney's direct investment in China, the company can access that country's cheap labor to make clothing, for example, for its Mic-Kids outlets. In addition, its direct investment in Euro Disney enables Disney to service a market it could not otherwise tap: European customers who are unlikely to visit the company's U.S. parks.

Today, more than 37,000 companies worldwide have FDIs that encompass every type of business function—extracting raw materials from the earth, growing crops, manufacturing products or components, selling output, providing various services, and so on. The 1992 value of these investments was about $2 trillion. The sales from the investments were about $5.5 trillion, which was considerably greater than the $4-trillion value of the world's exports of goods and services.[9] For U.S. companies as a whole, sales from output produced abroad through FDIs are many times greater than sales from U.S. production sent abroad as merchandise exports.[10]

FDI is not the domain of large companies only; about 28 percent of U.S. companies engaging in this type of international business are small.[11] For example, many small companies maintain sales offices abroad to complement their export efforts. However, because such companies tend to have smaller foreign facilities and operate in fewer countries, they own only about 3 percent of the value of U.S. FDI. Globally, roughly 1 percent of companies with FDI own about half of the worldwide value of such investment.[12]

This type of investment may take place even though most or all of the capital is raised abroad. For example, the small U.S. computer manufacturer Momenta raised foreign capital within only six months of its founding. This capital funded the company's expansion into Japan, Taiwan, and Singapore.[13]

Key components of portfolio investment are
- Noncontrol of foreign operation
- Financial benefit (for example, loans)

Portfolio investment   A **portfolio investment** is an investment that gives the investor a noncontrolling interest in a company or ownership of a loan to another party. Usually a portfolio investment takes one of two forms: stock in a company or loans to a company or country in the form of bonds, bills, or notes that the investor purchases.

Foreign portfolio investments are important for most companies that have extensive international operations. They are used primarily for short-term financial gain, that is, as a means for a company to earn more money on its money with relative safety. For example, company treasurers routinely move funds among countries to get higher yields on short-term investments.

Strategic Alliance

A **strategic alliance** is an agreement between companies that is of strategic importance to the competitive viability of one or both. The alliance may involve a variety of operational forms, such as joint ventures, licensing, management contracts, minority ownership in each other's company, or long-term contractual arrangements.

Multinational Enterprise

The **multinational enterprise (MNE)** is a company that takes a global approach to foreign markets and production; thus, it is willing to consider market and production locations anywhere in the world. The true MNE usually utilizes most of the operating forms discussed so far. However, it can be difficult to determine whether a company takes this global approach, so narrower definitions of the term *multinational enterprise* have emerged. For example, some say a company, to qualify as an MNE, must have production facilities in some minimum number of countries or be of a certain size. Under this definition, an MNE usually would have to be a giant company. However, this is not always the case; a small company also can take a global approach within its resource capabilities and might use most of the operating forms we have discussed.

A company that has a worldwide approach to markets and production is known as an MNE or TNC. It usually is involved in nearly every type of international business practice.

The term **multinational corporation (MNC)** also is commonly used in the international business arena and often is a synonym for MNE. We prefer the MNE designation because there are many internationally involved companies, such as accounting partnerships, that are not organized as corporations. Another term sometimes used interchangeably with MNE, especially by the United Nations, is **transnational corporation (TNC).** However, this term also is used in a different context—to refer to a company owned and managed by nationals in different countries. For example, Royal Dutch Shell is a company that is jointly owned in the United Kingdom and the Netherlands, and its corporate management is split between the two countries.

MNEs as well as any companies with international operations can be separated into two categories: global companies and multidomestic companies. A **global company,** sometimes called a **globally integrated company,** integrates its operations that are located in different countries. For example, it might design a product or service with a global market segment in mind. Or it might depend on its operations in different countries to produce the components used in its products and services. A **multidomestic company,** sometimes called a **locally responsive company,** allows each of its foreign-country operations to act fairly independently, such as by designing and producing a product or service in France for the French market and in Japan for the Japanese market. These categories also can be combined; for example, production may be global, whereas marketing is multidomestic.

External Influences on International Business

A company's external environment is the aggregate of conditions outside the company that influence its success. A company also influences its external environment, but usually to a lesser degree. As shown in Fig. 1.4, the external environment includes physical factors, such as a country's geography, and societal factors, such as a country's politics, economy, law, and culture; it also includes competitive factors, such as the number and strength of suppliers, customers, and rival companies.

Understanding a Company's Physical and Societal Environments

Managers in the worldwide environment must understand
- **Social science disciplines**
- **All functional business fields**

To operate within a company's external environment, its managers must have, in addition to knowledge of business operations, a working knowledge of the basic social sciences: history, political science, law, anthropology, sociology, psychology, economics, and geography.

Studying *history,* particularly the past relationships among countries and people's attitudes toward business and government, can help businesspeople better understand how international business functions in the present. This understanding also can enable them to plan more effectively for the future.

**Figure 1.4
Physical and Societal Influences on International Business**

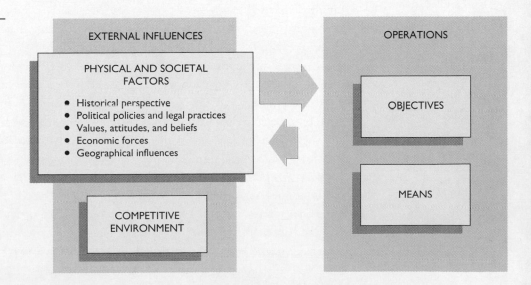

Politics has played and will continue to play an important role in shaping business worldwide. *Political science,* in part, describes the relationships between business and government and explains how the two interact with each other and react when their interests conflict. The political leadership in each country controls whether and how international business will occur in that country. For example, the French government's decision to court Disney enabled the company to buy cheap land, which the government had taken by eminent domain. Political disputes, particularly those that result in military conflicts, can disrupt trade and investment; even localized conflicts can have far-reaching effects. For example, political unrest elsewhere in Europe, along with anti-U.S. feelings in France, caused lower than projected attendance at Euro Disney. In addition, U.S. theme park attendance fell as a result of uncertainty and gas-price increases caused by the Persian Gulf War to liberate Kuwait from Iraq.[14]

Each country has its own laws regulating business. Agreements among countries set international law.

Domestic and international *law* determines largely what a manager of a company operating internationally can do. Domestic law includes regulations in both the home and host countries on such matters as taxation, employment, and foreign-exchange transactions. For example, French law determines how Euro Disney revenues are taxed and how they can be exchanged from francs to U.S. dollars. U.S. law, in turn, determines how and when the losses or earnings from France are treated for tax purposes in the United States. International law in the form of legal agreements between the two countries tempers how the earnings are taxed by both. Only by understanding the treaties among countries and the laws of each country in which a company may want to operate can that company determine where it might profitably operate abroad.

The related sciences of *anthropology, sociology,* and *psychology* describe, in part, people's social and mental development, behavior, and interpersonal activities. By studying these sciences, managers can better understand societal values, attitudes, and beliefs concerning themselves and others. This understanding can help them function better in different countries. Recall that Disney had to counter adverse opinion that held that its new park in France would undermine the integrity of French culture. It also tailored certain aspects of Euro Disney to accommodate the tastes of French visitors.

Economics explains, among other concepts, why countries exchange goods and services with each other, why capital and people travel among countries in the course of business, and why one country's currency has a certain price relative to another's. By studying economics, managers can better understand why, where, and when one country can produce goods or services less expensively than another can. In addition, managers can obtain the analytical tools needed to determine the impact of an MNE on the economies of the host and home countries and the effect of a country's economic policies and conditions on the company. For example, Disney's decision to establish a theme park in France rather than, say, Haiti was based on the belief that the French population and that of other nearby countries could better afford the cost of visiting such a park. The decision also was based on the expectation that the French francs earned from visitors would buy enough U.S. dollars to make Euro Disney profitable.

Managers who know *geography* can better determine the location, quantity, quality, and availability of the world's resources, as well as the best means to exploit them. The uneven distribution of resources results in different products and services being produced or offered in different parts of the world. In the case of Euro Disney, France's colder climate prompted changes in the park's design that weren't needed in the warmer climates in which Disney's U.S. parks are located. Geographical differences also caused problems when Euro Disney imported reindeer from Finland for its first winter holiday season: The reindeer refused to drink the local water, and the wetter weather of France caused some to shed their antlers.[15] Geographical barriers such as high mountains, vast deserts, and inhospitable jungles affect communications and distribution channels for companies in many countries. For certain types of business, climatic conditions such as hurricanes, floods, or freezing weather make it riskier to invest in some areas than in others. These factors also affect the availability of supplies and the prices of agricultural products. In addition, human population distribution around the world and the impact of human activity on the environment exert a strong influence on international business relationships. For example, concern about destroying the world's rain forests may lead to regulations or other pressures that may prompt companies to change the place or method of conducting business activities.

Physical and societal environments affect how a company operates and the amount of adjustment it must make to its operations in a particular country, for example, how it produces and markets its products, staffs its operations, and maintains its accounts. In fact, as shown in Fig. 1.4, each functional area may be influenced by the local external environment. The amount of adjustment is influenced by how much the environments of home and host countries resemble each other and the number of different environments in which the company is operating. In the case of Euro Disney, the company had to alter some of the attractions and require that employees be bilingual. It also undoubtedly must deal with French labor and accounting regulations that differ from those in the United States. These factors and the adjustments companies must make are examined in greater detail later in this text.

The Competitive Environment
In addition to its physical and societal environments, each company operates within the competitive environment for its industry. The competitive environment differs for each company. For example, a large supplier of semiconductors, such as Intel, can exert more influence over computer manufacturers than can either a small semiconductor supplier or a company that supplies the paint for computers. The environment also differs for each industry. For example, the recent rate of product innovations, and hence the change in competition, has been greater for telecommunications than for light bulbs.

The competitive environment also varies among countries. For example, a large domestic market exists in the United States but not in Sweden. One result is that Swedish producers have had to become more highly dependent than U.S. producers are on foreign sales in order to spread fixed costs of product development and production. The Swedish company Electrolux, for instance, had to promote exports very early in its history and depends much more on foreign sales of household appliances than do its main U.S. competitors, GE and Whirlpool. Another result of the larger U.S. market is that foreign companies have to invest much more to gain national distribution in the United States than they do in Sweden. A further competitive factor that differs by country is the speed of product change. For example, as a whole, industry in Japan has recently produced more product innovations than industry in Afghanistan has. Thus a foreign company operating in Japan usually must be more concerned about introducing product innovations than one operating in Afghanistan. Still another competitive difference is whether companies face international or local competitors. On the one hand, Boeing and Airbus compete with each other everywhere they try to sell commercial aircraft; therefore, what they learn about each other in one country is useful in predicting competitive behaviors in all the other countries in which they operate. On the other hand, Kmart faces different retailers as competitors in each of the foreign countries where it operates; thus, it must adjust to multiple competitive reactions differing by country.

These and other competitive differences enable some companies to take better advantage of foreign opportunities. Competitive factors prompt companies to differentiate practices among countries in which they operate. They also can cause companies to choose different means of operating, depending on the country or the product. For example, a company may elect to serve one country by exporting to it and another country with output from a direct investment there. Or, because of the nature of the product, one company may focus on franchising in a country, and another company may choose some other means of marketing there. Some of the most important competitive factors are shown in Fig. 1.5 and will be discussed in later chapters.

**Figure 1.5
The Competitive
Environment and
International Business**

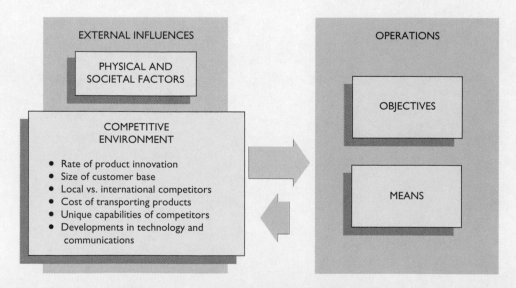

W

e all have our own beliefs as to what is right and wrong based on family and religious teachings, the laws and social pressures of the societies in which we live, our observations and experiences, and our own economic circumstances. Our ethical beliefs tend to be deep-seated; thus our debates with people of opposing views tend to be emotional. Even within a country, vastly opposing viewpoints frequently exist. This is demonstrated in the United States by the recent controversies on abortion, women's roles, gay rights, flag burning, capital punishment, gun control, euthanasia, organ transplants, marijuana usage, and welfare payments. Our own values on given issues may differ from the policies or practices of the companies for which we work, and any of these may differ from the prevalent societal norms or laws.

ETHICAL DILEMMAS

An MNE can encounter situations that give it either narrower or greater latitude in making decisions than it may have in its home country. Normal practices in a given foreign country will be based on that country's ethics; these host-country practices may conflict with the company's domestic practices or with the beliefs of its domestic constituencies. For example, U.S. companies must contend with child labor laws at home that they probably wouldn't encounter in Indonesia.

On the one hand, a company can face pressures to comply with the norms in the foreign country. These pressures may include laws that permit or even require certain practices, competitive advantages for rivals who adapt to local norms, or accusations of meddling if a company tries to impose its home-country practices in the foreign country. On the other hand, companies can face pressures not to comply. These pressures can come from a company's own ethical values, its home-country government, or constituencies that threaten to boycott its products or to spread adverse publicity regarding it or its products.

Despite MNEs' efforts to comply with foreign laws and adhere to foreign customs, they continue to be targets of criticism. Many individuals and organizations have laid out various minimum levels of business ethics that they say a company must follow regardless of the legal requirements or ethical norms prevalent in a location in which it operates.[16] They argue that *legal* permission for some action may be given by uneducated or corrupt leaders who either do not understand or do not care about the consequences. They argue further that ethical norms are based on a long history of learned behavior and MNEs are obligated to affect that learning process by setting good examples.

In practice, governments may be forced into trade-offs among the objectives of their societies, and their actions can lull companies into thinking that society at large will not blame them for governmental decisions. This is not always the case. For example, the French government willingly allowed the incursion of U.S. culture into France and provided Disney with agricultural land at below market prices in order to gain what seemed to be overriding economic benefits for France. In return, however, Disney has suffered heavy criticism for undermining French culture and displacing French farmers.

Within lower-income countries, both societies and companies often must choose between the lesser of two evils. For example, higher-income countries banned the use of the pesticide DDT in order to protect the environment. Companies from those countries subsequently have been criticized for selling DDT to lower-income countries, whose leaders say that without it they cannot feed their populations. As another example, some critics contend that the hiring of children by MNEs in lower-income countries is unethical because the practice denies children access to education needed for their future development. One critic said:

> Whether child labor is practiced in a host country or not, the obligation of a multinational corporation not to hire children as full-time, permanent laborers is transnational. This duty cannot be waived by appealing to cultural practices, traditions, or even shared beliefs.[17]

But what if the choice isn't between working and education? For many of the poor in these countries, there is no opportunity for education, whether or not they work. Without the opportunity for work, many may join the legions of abandoned street children, such as those in Guatemala City who sniff glue to kill hunger pains and steal just enough to subsist. Further, does it make any ethical difference where the output from child labor is sold? Bangladesh criticized a proposed U.S. law that would restrict importation of child-made products, arguing that such a law could force thousands of children into begging or prostitution.[18] Some supporters of using child labor contend it is justified by local poverty, provided the goods are sold locally. However, these same supporters sometimes object if workers in higher-income countries lose their jobs to foreign child laborers, who typically receive only subsistence wages.

Another dilemma is whether MNEs should abandon markets in which they are not allowed to operate according to their own minimum level of ethics. Some people argue that MNEs are so powerful and important that, if they cease operations in such a market, change in the country's policies will result. Others argue that MNEs are better able to bring about change by working within the system.[19] For example, apartheid policies in South Africa, such as that disallowing equal pay for equal work, prompted some companies to cease their South African operations (usually by selling them to white South Africans), while some others elected to stay and work at improving conditions.

Ethics requires judgment, which makes it relative and subjective. However, many multilateral agreements exist that can help a company understand the evolving global ethic and make ethical decisions. These agreements deal primarily with employment practices, consumer protection, environmental protection, political activity, and human rights in the workplace.[20] Despite this growing body of agreements, no set of workable corporate guidelines is universally accepted and observed.

Clearly, many aspects of doing business internationally involve ethical questions. Thus ethical dilemmas related to that chapter's subject matter will be discussed in each chapter of this text.

C O U N T E R V A I L I N G

F O R C E S

In addition to the effect of external and competitive environmental factors, countervailing forces complicate decision making in international business. The strength of one force versus the strength of another influences the choices available to and the decisions taken by companies that compete internationally. For each chapter in this book, these forces are discussed in the section entitled Countervailing Forces. The following discussion highlights this contextual framework.

Global versus Multidomestic Practices

Global practices tend to lower costs and enable companies to deal with global competitors, customers, and suppliers.

Multidomestic practices enable companies to adjust to unique local conditions.

Although companies with international operations often are classified as either global or multidomestic, most companies are mixed: They handle some of their operations with considerable global integration while leaving their country-level managers fairly free to make independent decisions about other business decisions and practices. Any company operating internationally must make trade-offs between the advantages of global practices and those of multidomestic practices. These advantages may vary by product, function, and/or country of operation.[21]

The trends that have influenced the recent worldwide growth in international business—rapid expansion of technology, liberalization of governmental trade policies, development of the institutions needed to support and facilitate international trade, and increased global competition—also usually favor a global approach. One advantage of a global approach is that the company can reduce costs by standardizing as much as possible among the countries in which it operates. For example, by designing a product or service to suit multiple countries, a company can avoid duplicating developmental expenses. It also may reduce manufacturing costs by serving multiple markets from a single production unit. In either case, the company gains from **economies of scale,** that is, a situation in which the cost per unit is lowered as output increases because fixed costs are allocated over more units of production.

A second advantage of a global approach relates to the growing number of companies that operate internationally. Such companies increasingly are dealing with the same competitors, customers, and suppliers in more than one country. Thus, what a company does in one market may affect its other markets. For example, a company's poor relationship with an industrial customer in Brazil could jeopardize its relationship with the same customer in Japan. By integrating its dealings with such competitors, customers, and suppliers, the company may be able to gain global advantages.

However, when a company goes abroad, it faces conditions very different from those it encounters at home—as was amply demonstrated in the Euro Disney case. The company may need to engage in **national responsiveness,** that is, make operating adjustments in order to reach a satisfactory level of performance. In such situations, a multidomestic approach often works better because the company managers abroad are best able to assess and deal with the environments of the foreign countries in which the company operates. As a result, they are given a great deal of independence in running facilities in those countries.

Country versus Company Competitiveness

So far we have addressed competition from the viewpoint of companies. Companies, at least those that are not government-owned, may compete by seeking maximum production efficiency on a global scale. To accomplish this goal, production would be done using the best inputs for the price, even if the production location moved abroad. The output would then be sold wherever it would fetch the best price. Such practices should lead to maximum performance for the company.

But countries also compete with each other. They do so in terms of fulfilling economic, political, and social objectives. Countries are concerned not only with the absolute achievement of these objectives but also with how well they do relative to other countries. In fact, relative performance might be the overriding concern. For example, groups of students and business executives in the United States were asked to choose between the following two growth scenarios: (1) Over ten years, the U.S. economy would grow at 20 percent, while the Japanese economy would grow at 90 percent. (2) Over the same ten years, the U.S. economy would grow at 8 percent, while the Japanese economy would grow at 8.2 percent. Most chose the latter alternative, even though the absolute U.S. performance would be less than half what it would be with the first alternative.[22]

At one time, the performance of a country and that of companies headquartered in that country were considered to be mutually dependent and beneficial; that is, they rose and fell together. For example, consider the once-popular expression "What's good for General Motors is good for the country." The idea was that if General Motors (GM) increased its global share of automobile production, the United States would benefit also—from more automobile sales, tax collections, and jobs, both production and managerial. This benefit was considered possible because almost all of the company's production and sales at the time were in the United States. But today, the relationship between country performance and company performance is not as clear-cut. GM could elect to improve its global or even its domestic market share by producing more cars in its foreign manufacturing units and fewer in the United States. What would this mean for the U.S. competitive performance?

Keep in mind that competition among countries is the means to an end—the end being the well-being of a country's citizens. However, there is no consensus on how to measure well-being. Further, accepted indicators of current prosperity actually may foretell longer-term problems; for example, high current consumption may occur at the expense of investment for future production and consumption.[23]

These measurement problems are at the heart of the controversy regarding how the performance of companies affects the national competitiveness of the countries in which they are headquartered. Consider the hypothetical GM example. Some people would argue that the important indicator is the location of **high-value activities,** that is, activities that either produce high profits or are done by high-salaried employees such as managers. So GM's move to produce more cars abroad could improve the U.S. competitive position by increasing high-value activity at headquarters, in the form of more jobs for managers and executives, while reducing low-value activity in production, in the form of fewer jobs for U.S. assembly-line workers. However, other people would argue that U.S. competitiveness would deteriorate because of a net loss in U.S. jobs and production.[24]

Closely related to this controversy is another regarding whether the nationality of a company's ownership makes any difference. For example, should it matter whether U.S. auto production is owned by Honda in Japan instead of GM in the United States? Some would argue that it would make no difference because the United States gains the jobs and production either way; others would argue that the high-value activity jobs would more likely be in Japan if Honda were the owner.[25] In actuality, there is little hard evidence to support any conclusion regarding the relationship between company and country performance.

Regardless of these unresolved controversies, countries continue to entice companies to locate company headquarters and production facilities within their borders. They do this through regulations and persuasion and by addressing the underlying factors that companies consider when they choose operating locations. In the hypothetical GM example, the U.S. government might enact regulations to prevent GM from expanding abroad, such as by limiting the capital it could send out of the country. Or the government could restrict imports of foreign-produced automobiles. It might try to persuade GM by holding out the possibility of future defense contracts (for companies acting in the "national interest") or simply by appealing to nationalism. To improve the country's investment-worthiness, the U.S. government might seek to address underlying factors of concern to companies in general. It could do so by improving the availability and quality of education, building roads and port facilities, or enacting measures to lower taxes. Any of these incentives could apply only to U.S.-based companies or to any auto company, regardless of nationality.

Business managers need to understand these complexities so they can argue logically and effectively regarding legislation that may affect their operations and so they can adjust to changing governmental regulations and incentives that can affect whether and how companies enter a foreign market. At the same time, they must balance dual roles: In one, they are managers with global efficiency objectives; in the second, they are members of a given society that has national rather than global objectives.

Sovereign versus Cross-National Relationships

Countries compete; they also cooperate. We live in a world of countries that exist primarily because groups of people share a common sense of national identity that sets them apart from and causes them to prefer independence from other people. Countries sometimes cede sovereignty reluctantly because of coercion and international conflicts. However, countries willingly cede sovereignty through treaties and agreements with other countries for the following reasons:

1. To gain reciprocal advantages
2. To attack problems that cannot be solved by one country acting alone
3. To deal with areas of concern that lie outside the territory of all countries

Countries want to ensure that companies headquartered within their borders are not disadvantaged by foreign-country policies, so they enter into reciprocal treaties and agreements with other countries on a variety of commercially related activities, such as transportation and trade. Treaties and agreements may be bilateral (involving only two

Countries reluctantly cede some sovereignty because of
- **Coercion**
- **Military conflicts**

Countries willingly cede some sovereignty to
- **Gain reciprocity**
- **Attack problems jointly**
- **Deal with extraterritorial concerns**

countries) or multilateral (involving a few or many). For example, countries commonly enter into treaties whereby each allows the other's commercial ships and planes to use certain of its seaports and airports in exchange for reciprocal port usage. They may enact treaties that cover commercial aircraft safety standards and fly-over rights or treaties to protect property such as direct investments, patents, trademarks, and copyrights in each other's territory. And they may enact treaties for reciprocal reductions of import restrictions (and then retaliate when others raise barriers by, for example, raising barriers of their own or cutting diplomatic ties).

Countries enact treaties or agreements to coordinate activities along their shared borders, such as building connecting highways and railroads or hydroelectric dams that serve all parties. They also enact treaties to solve problems they either can not or will not solve alone because of one or both of two reasons:

1. The problem is too big or widespread.
2. The problem results from conditions that spill over from another country.

In the first case, the resources needed to solve the problem may be too large, or one country does not want to pay all the costs for a project that also will benefit its competitor country. For example, countries may enact a treaty whereby they share the costs of joint technology development, such as Europe's Esprit program in electronics. In the second case, conditions that involve spill-over effects can occur because one country's economic and environmental policies affect another country or countries. For example, high real interest rates in one country can attract funds from countries in which interest rates are lower, which can disrupt economic conditions in the latter countries. This is why the seven largest industrialized countries (known as the G-7 countries)—Canada, France, Germany, Italy, Japan, the United Kingdom, and the United States—meet regularly to coordinate economic policies. In addition, most environmental experts agree that cooperation among most countries will be needed to achieve meaningful environmental policies that will protect our planet. So far, agreements have been made among some countries on such issues as restricting harmful emissions, keeping waterways unpolluted, preserving endangered species, and banning the use of certain pesticides. Despite these agreements, however, discussions among countries continue on these, and other, issues.

Three areas remain outside the territories of countries—the noncoastal areas of the oceans, outer space, and Antarctica. Until their commercial viability was demonstrated, these areas excited little interest in multinational cooperation. The oceans contain food and mineral resources. They also are the surface over which much international commerce passes. Today, treaties on ocean use set out the amounts and methods of fishing allowed, international discussion attempts to resolve who owns oceanic minerals,[26] and agreements detail how to deal with pirates (yes, pirates are still a problem).[27] In space, radio and television signals are transmitted. Also, specialized manufacturing may soon be feasible in space stations that have germ-free conditions. But much disagreement still exists on who should reap commercial benefits from space. Antarctica has minerals and abundant sea life along its coast and attracts thousands of tourists each year. Consequently, a series of recent agreements have been made that limit its commercial exploitation.

LOOKING TO THE FUTURE

Companies must make decisions today about an uncertain future. If a company waits to see what happens on political and economic fronts, it may already be too late because investments in research, equipment, plants, and personnel training can take many years to complete. The company that correctly guesses now where future opportunities lie will be the one that produces and sells the goods and services consumers want at a price they are willing to pay—and does so in conformity with the rules of the societies in which it operates.

Guessing correctly is not always possible. However, by envisioning different ways in which the future may evolve, a company's management may better avoid unpleasant surprises. Accordingly, each chapter of this text ends with a section that discusses foreseeable ways in which topics covered in the chapter may develop.

Summary

- Companies engage in international business to expand sales, acquire resources, and diversify their sources of sales and supplies.

- International business has been growing rapidly in recent decades because of technological expansion, liberalization of governmental policies on trade and resource movements, development of institutions needed to support and facilitate international transactions, and increased global competition. Because of these factors, foreign countries increasingly are a source of both production and sales for domestic companies.

- When operating abroad, companies may have to adjust their usual methods of carrying on business. This is because foreign conditions often dictate a more appropriate method and because the operating forms used for international business differ somewhat from those used on a domestic level.

- A company can engage in international business through various means, including exporting and/or importing of merchandise and services, direct and portfolio investments, and strategic alliances with other companies.

- Multinational enterprises (MNEs) take a global approach to markets and production. They sometimes are referred to as multinational corporations (MNCs) or transnational corporations (TNCs).

- To operate within a company's external environment, its managers must have not only knowledge of business operations but also a working knowledge of the basic social sciences: history, political science, law, anthropology, sociology, psychology, economics, and geography.

- Countervailing forces influence the conditions in which companies operate and their options for operating internationally. A company's quest for maximum global profits is inhibited by different conditions in foreign countries, rivalry among countries, cross-national treaties and agreements, and ethical dilemmas.

Case
Blockbuster Video[28]

Blockbuster Video is by far the biggest video rental chain in the United States. Its next largest rival, West Coast Video, earns only about 10 percent as much in revenues. Most of Blockbuster's growth occurred between 1987 and 1992; during that time the number of its stores increased from 238 to 2989. This increase was partially due to growth in the video rental market as more people rented tapes for home entertainment on their newly acquired VCRs. Much of it came at the expense of thousands of mom-and-pop-type stores that stocked a small supply of tapes along with their other merchandise.

Blockbuster's primary growth strategy has been to attract customers by offering a large selection of tapes. It rents these videos in very large stores that can accommodate 7000–13,000 tapes representing 5000–8500 different titles. By expanding rapidly, Blockbuster has been able to gain economies of scale to offset the more than $100 million it spends per year on advertising. It buys vast numbers of tapes, which gives it buying clout with the film studios that sell tapes.

To finance its growth in the United States, Blockbuster has relied on acquisitions in exchange for Blockbuster stock, has franchised about half of its stores rather than obtaining ownership, and has raised equity capital for company-owned stores. Philips Electronics of the Netherlands became one of Blockbuster's largest equity sources when it invested $149 million in two stages for a 7.9-percent ownership in the company. Although this amount falls far short of giving Philips a controlling interest, Philips still owns enough shares to have a say in some of Blockbuster's practices; for example, the stores are used to test-market Philips' compact disc interactive (CDI) technology.

Despite its impressive growth, by 1992 Blockbuster had acquired only a 13-percent share of the $11 billion U.S. home video market. Although there was room to grow in the United States, the company announced plans to focus on expanding abroad during the 1990s, with the goal of upping total sales from foreign operations to 25 percent by 1995. In addition to its plans for foreign expansion, Blockbuster announced it would diversify by setting up separate divisions for the retail sale of music, the development of new technologies, and the development and sale of other entertainment.

The shift in market emphasis from domestic to foreign resulted for three reasons: the maturing of the U.S. market for sales of VCRs, the threat of competition from pay-per-view movies, and the growth in retail sales of videotapes for home use—the sell-through market—as opposed to rentals. In the last case, Blockbuster was slow to enter the sell-through market, hence retailers such as Kmart got a head start on gaining market share. Further, because film distributors typically sell rental tapes for about $65 and sell-through tapes for about $14, many more retailers can afford to compete against Blockbuster for tape sales than for tape rentals.

To date, Blockbuster's major foreign expansion has been in the world's higher-income, industrial areas—Canada, Europe, and Japan. This was a logical move, since the market for video rentals is limited by the number of VCRs owned by consumers, a number that varies widely among countries (see Map 1.3). Among countries with a similar percentage of households having televisions (for example, Italy and Sweden, with 92 percent and 93 percent, respectively), the percentage also having VCRs varies substantially (for example, 31 percent for Italy versus 63 percent for Sweden). Within lower-income countries, most households with VCRs use them to record television shows rather than to view rented

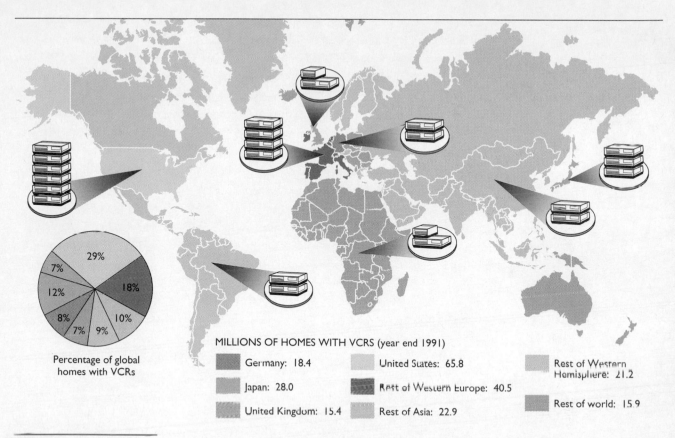

MILLIONS OF HOMES WITH VCRS (year end 1991)

Germany: 18.4   United States: 65.8   Rest of Western Homisphere: 21.2

Japan: 28.0   Rest of Western Europe: 40.5   Rest of world: 15.9

United Kingdom: 15.4   Rest of Asia: 22.9

Percentage of global homes with VCRs

Map 1.3
Numbers of Homes with VCRs Worldwide, 1992
Note that four countries—Germany, Japan, the United Kingdom, and the United States—have 55 percent of the world's homes with VCRs but only about 9 percent of the world's population.

Source: Data from *Screen Digest*, June 1992, pp. 129–146.

videotapes. Two other factors limit the market in lower-income countries: the low cost of movie tickets, which makes videotapes a higher-cost rather than a lower-cost alternative, and competition from stores that rent cheap and unauthorized videotapes, which are sometimes copied directly from television-movie channels in the United States.

Blockbuster entered the British market in 1990 and by the end of 1991 had built fifteen stores. All were company-owned because of difficulty in selling franchises. This difficulty arose for two reasons. First, franchising was not yet developed in the United Kingdom video store market. Second, with only fifteen stores, Blockbuster could not justify large advertising outlays; such advertising is an incentive for investors to buy into franchises. To increase its presence in that country, Blockbuster in 1992 bid on Cityvision, the largest video store chain in the United Kingdom with 775 stores in the United Kingdom and 23 in Austria. To finance this purchase, Blockbuster induced Philips to back its bid in exchange for an option either to buy more Blockbuster stock or to become a joint-venture partner in the U.K. operation. Philips opted for the former. Cityvision's stockholders were offered, in exchange for one share of Cityvision stock, the choice of either 48 pence cash or a share of Blockbuster stock, valued then at 50 pence. The acquisition's total cost was $135 million—about $81 million in cash and the rest in the exchange of stock. The stores initially were operated under the Cityvision name for its stores, Ritz. The stores later were to be converted to Blockbuster stores as a springboard for the company's expansion into France, Germany, and Italy via joint ventures.

In 1991, Blockbuster bought a chain of twenty-five Major Video stores in Canada for conversion into Blockbuster stores. This move brought the company additional economies of scale because much of the Canadian population lives within reception range of TV broadcasts from the United States and hence within range of Blockbuster's advertising. Blockbuster also set up franchise operations in Chile, Mexico, Australia, Spain, Venezuela, and Ireland. The move into Ireland was largely in response to a move into the U.S. market by Xtra-vision, Ireland's largest video chain. By 1990, Xtra-vision had fifty U.S. stores under the Videosmith and Video Library names.

In 1991, Blockbuster decided to enter Japan. It decided on a 50/50 joint venture in order to gain know-how about the market from a knowledgeable Japanese partner, Fujita Shoten. (Fujita Shoten's chairman had established an earlier 50/50 joint venture with McDonald's, which now has about 800 restaurants in Japan. Fujita Shoten also has a stake in Toys 'R Us Japan.) Blockbuster planned to expand through franchising its outlets and expected to have a thousand Japanese stores by the year 2000. In deciding to move into Japan, company executives saw the following conditions that afforded opportunities for Blockbuster:

- There were no major video rental chains in Japan. The largest rental chain, the Culture Convenience Club, had only small-scale outlets.
- There were only 1800 movie theaters in Japan, fewer than one tenth the number in the United States. They were controlled by Japanese film studios that limited distribution of foreign films to about 100 theaters. Despite distribution problems, however, U.S. films had 60 percent of the Japanese film market.
- Existing video stores catered mainly to Japanese males under 25 years of age by renting tapes of pornographic and violent films. Blockbuster would target an older and more family-oriented market and would rent no adult videos.

Blockbuster's management reasoned that there was a big, unfulfilled demand for U.S. videos and that it could introduce these more rapidly into the Japanese market than Japanese competitors could (at the time, the wait for U.S. releases was about a year).

When Blockbuster entered Japan, it planned to earn 12–15 percent of its income from game rentals, as it does in the United States. However, it was unable to meet this goal. Japanese law requires permission from the author of copyrighted material before anyone can sell or rent the material. Of the two giants in the video game industry, Sega Enterprises gave its permission but Nintendo refused.

Because space is so limited and expensive in Japan, Blockbuster had to reduce the size of its stores. However, redesigning the stores' interiors allowed them to carry about 8000 titles and 10,000 tapes. Aside from its ban on adult videos, Blockbuster allows each country's managers to decide which tapes to buy for their stores. All tape purchases are made locally through distributors representing film studios. This arrangement is necessary because the local distributors can perform certain tasks more easily, such as arranging for subtitles or dubbing, dealing with local censorship issues, converting films to the tape format (for example, VHS, Beta, or Secam) preferred in that country, and acquiring local films to meet local demand. On this last point, Hollywood productions dominate markets worldwide; however, where there is a strong local film industry, such as in the United Kingdom and France, there is market demand for more tapes made from local films.

Blockbuster also used its foreign experience to help it grow in the United States. For example, in 1992, the company acquired a 50-percent interest in the Virgin Retail Group, whose stores sell recorded music. This U.K. company owns megastores in the United Kingdom, France, Germany, Italy, Austria, the Netherlands, and Australia. The operations continued to be managed by Virgin, and there were plans for major expansion into the U.S. market. The first store, in Los Angeles, was to be modeled after Virgin's megastores, which offer 200 listening booths, a stage for live performances, and specialty rooms so classical music lovers needn't mix with heavy metal fans.

Questions

1. Why do you think Blockbuster has used various operating forms (company-owned operations, joint ventures, and franchises) for the different foreign markets it has entered?
2. What are the advantages and disadvantages of Blockbuster's expanding abroad rather than concentrating its efforts on the U.S. market?
3. Blockbuster's earliest and primary foreign thrust was into the British market. Do you agree with this expansion priority?
4. Blockbuster bought video store chains abroad that already had well-known names. Why should the company change these stores to Blockbuster stores?
5. What factors other than those presented in the case might inhibit Blockbuster's expansion into lower-income countries?
6. Why would many Cityvision stockholders sell for cash rather than Blockbuster stock?

Chapter Notes

1. Data for the case were taken from Michael Dobbs, "Mickey Mouse Storms the Bastille," *Across the Board,* Vol. 23, No. 4, April 1986, pp. 9–11; Robert Neff, "In Japan, They're Goofy About Disney," *Business Week,* March 12, 1990, p. 64; Yumiko Ono, "Theme Parks Boom in Japan as Investors and Consumers Rush to Get on the Ride," *Wall Street Journal,* August 8, 1990, p. B1; Stewart Toy, Mark Maremont, and Ronald Grover, "An American in Paris," *Business Week,* March 12, 1990, pp. 60–64; Robert Wrubel and Phyllis Feinberg, "Breaking Out of the Mousetrap," *Financial World,* Vol. 157, No. 3, January 26, 1988, pp. 20–22; Steven Greenhouse, "Playing Disney in the Parisian Fields," *New York Times,* February 17, 1991, p. F1; David J. Jefferson and Brian Coleman, "American Quits Chairman Post At Euro Disney," *Wall Street Journal,* January 18, 1993, p. B1; "Trouble at Euro Disney: The Not-So-Magic Kingdom," *Business Week,* September 26,

1992, p. 87; William E. Schmidt, "Visiting Disney's French Kingdom," *New York Times,* May 24, 1992, p. 8; Richard Turner, "Disney Hits Bad Patch After Eisner's Six Years of Giddy Expansion," *Wall Street Journal,* November 12, 1991, p. A1; Martin du Bois, "Meeus Goes After the Mouse for Theme Park Visitors," *Wall Street Journal,* December 3, 1992, p. B4; Roger Cohen, "Resisting Disney: Unmitigated Gaul," *New York Times,* April 9, 1992, p. C1; Peter Gumbel and David J. Jefferson, "Disney Continues Drive to Expand World-Wide," *Wall Street Journal,* November 20, 1992, p. B4; Judson Gooding, "Of Mice and Men," *Across the Board,* March 1992, pp. 40–44; Alan Riding, "Only the French Elite Scorn Mickey's Debut," *New York Times,* April 13, 1992, p. A1; "The Mouse Isn't Roaring," *Business Week,* August 24, 1992, p. 38; Andrew Marton, "Le Monde According to Mickey," *New York Times,* April 12, 1992, p. H33; Shawn Tully, "The Real Estate

Coup at Euro Disneyland," *Fortune,* April 28, 1986, p. 172; "Euro Disney Adding Alcohol," *New York Times,* June 12, 1993, p. 24; Richard Turner, "Disney Posts Solid 3rd-Period Results Despite a Big Drag," *Wall Street Journal,* July 30, 1993, p. B2; Thomas R. King, "Euro Disney's Fiscal Third Quarter Loss," *Wall Street Journal,* July 9, 1993, p. A3; Martin Fletcher, "The Mouse That Snored," *Travel & Leisure,* September 1993, p. 34; William Echikson, "Winter Is Putting Chill in France's Magic Kingdom," *Boston Globe,* January 1, 1993, p. 71; Roger Cohen, "Euro Disney Posts Loss of $900 Million in First Year," *Herald Tribune* (Frankfurt), November 11, 1993, p. 1+; and Roger Cohen, "Euro Disney Trying to Warm Up Winter," *New York Times,* December 12, 1993, Sec. 5, p. 3.
2. "The Stateless World of Manufacturing," *Business Week,* May 1, 1990, p. 103; Jeffrey A. Tannenbaum, "Small Companies Are Finding It Pays To Think Global,"

Wall Street Journal, November 19, 1992, p. B2; Michael Selz, "Small Firms Hit Foreign Obstacles in Billing Overseas," *Wall Street Journal,* December 8, 1992, p. B2; Udayan Gupta, "Small Firms Aren't Waiting to Grow Up to Go Global," *Wall Street Journal,* December 5, 1989, p. B2; and Louis Uchitelle, "Small Companies Going Global," *New York Times,* November 27, 1989, p. 25+.

3. Michael Duckworth, "Disney Plans to Re-Enter China Market As Beijing Promises Copyright Reforms," *Wall Street Journal,* March 24, 1992, p. C19.

4. "Nobody Asked Me, But," *The Exporter,* April 1993, p. 2, using estimates by the General Agreement on Tariffs and Trade.

5. Thomas F. O'Boyle, "Rise and Fall," *Wall Street Journal,* January 4, 1984, p. 1.

6. Andrea Bonaccorsi, "On the Relationship Between Firm Size and Export Intensity," *Journal of International Business Studies,* Vol. 23, No. 4, Fourth Quarter, 1992, pp. 605–635.

7. Antonio N. Fins, Paul Magnusson, and Andrea Rothman, "Suddenly, the U.S. Is Everybody's Oyster," *Business Week,* July 15, 1991, pp. 34–35.

8. Duckworth, loc. cit.

9. United Nations Conference on Trade and Development Programme on Transnational Corporations, *World Investment Report, 1993: An Executive Summary* (New York: United Nations, 1993), pp. 1–4.

10. Jeffrey H. Lowe and Raymond J. Mataloni, Jr., "U.S. Direct Investment Abroad: 1989 Benchmark Survey Results," *Survey of Current Business,* Vol. 71, No. 10, October 1991, pp. 29–46.

11. Figures are for 1990 and taken from Fred R. Bleakly, "Smaller U.S. Firms Trail in Setting Up Operations Abroad," *Wall Street Journal,* August 24, 1993, p. A14, citing a report by Masataka Fujita at a UN conference on small and medium-sized firms.

12. United Nations Conference on Trade and Development Programme on Transnational Corporations. op. cit., p. 4.

13. Gupta, loc. cit.

14. Richard Turner, "Disney Says Net Fell in Quarter and Fiscal 1991," *Wall Street Journal,* October 1, 1991, p. B6.

15. "The Horns of a Dilemma," *The Economist,* Vol. 325, No. 7787, November 28, 1992, p. 80.

16. See, for example, Thomas Donaldson, "Can Multinationals Stage a Universal Morality Play?" *Business & Society Review,* Spring 1992, pp. 51–55; and Richard T. DeGeorge, *Business Ethics* (New York: Macmillan, 1990), Chapters 19 and 20.

17. Donaldson, loc. cit.

18. "Child-Labor Proposal Assailed," *Wall Street Journal,* August 17, 1993, p. A10.

19. John Delaney and Donna Sockell, "Ethics in the Trenches," *Across the Board,* October 1990, pp. 15–21.

20. The agreements are outlined in William C. Frederick, "Moral Authority of Transnational Corporate Codes," *Journal of Business Ethics,* March 1991, pp. 165–176.

21. For a coverage of the various countervailing forces affecting global versus multidomestic practices, see Christopher A. Bartlett and Sumantra Ghoshal, *Transnational Management* (Homewood, Ill.: Irwin, 1992), Chapter 2.

22. Robert B. Reich, "Who Is Them?" *Harvard Business Review,* March-April 1991, pp. 77–88.

23. John D. Daniels, "The Elusive Concept of National Competitiveness," *Business Horizons,* November-December 1991, pp. 3–6.

24. For examples of different views on the relationship of location of headquarters and production with national well-being, see Kenichi Ohmae, *Triad Power: The Coming Shape of Global Competition* (New York: Free Press, 1985); Michael E. Porter, *The Competitive Advantage of Nations* (New York: Free Press, 1990); and Robert B. Reich, *The Work of Nations: Preparing Ourselves for 21st Century Capitalism* (New York: Alfred A. Knopf, 1991).

25. Paul Magnusson, "Why Corporate Nationality Matters," *Business Week,* July 12, 1993, pp. 142–143.

26. David E. Pitt, "U.S. Seeks to 'Fix' Mining Provisions of Sea Treaty," *New York Times,* August 28, 1993, p. 3; "Sea-Law

Treaty Is Ratified," *Wall Street Journal,* December 7, 1993, p. A10.

27. See, for example, G. Pierre Goad, "Strait of Malacca Spill Raises Safety Issue," *Wall Street Journal,* January 25, 1993, p. A10.

28. We wish to acknowledge the cooperation of Mr. Joseph R. Baczko, President and Chief Operating Officer of Blockbuster Entertainment Corporation, for granting information in an interview. Supplementary data were taken from Ken Stewart, "Turf Battle Looms in Emerald Isle; Blockbuster Opening Threatens Xtra-vision," *Billboard,* September 29, 1990, p. 49; Terry Ilott, "Blockbuster Clinches Cityvision Brit Vid Bid," *Variety,* January 27, 1992, p. 69; "Blockbuster Acquires 25 Stores in Canada," *Supermarket News,* Vol. 41, No. 27, July 1, 1991, p. 24; Jeff Clark-Meads, "Philips Elects to Purchase 6 Million Blockbuster Shares," *Billboard,* April 18, 1992, p. 6; Steve McClure, "Blockbuster Hits Japan With Hopes for 1,000 Stores," *Billboard,* April 6, 1991, p. 89; Garth Alexander, "Blockbuster Bends Japan's Video Rules," *Variety,* Vol. 345, No. 2, October 21, 1991, p. 57; Terry Ilott, "Blockbuster's Bid Could Boost U.K. Vid Biz," *Variety,* Vol. 345, No. 8, December 2, 1991, p. 66; Leslie Helm, "Selling Hollywood in Japan," *Los Angeles Times,* September 21, 1992, p. D1; Eleena de Lisser, "Blockbuster's Baczko Quits Two Posts Amid Reorganization and Expansion," *Wall Street Journal,* January 5, 1993, p. B7; Richard Turner, "Disney Leads Shift From Rentals to Sales in Videocassettes," *Wall Street Journal,* December 24, 1991, p. A1; Helene Cooper, "Blockbuster Entertainment, U.K. Firm Plan a Chain of 'Megastores' in the U.S.," *Wall Street Journal,* November 17, 1992, p. B7; Gail DeGeorge, Jonathan B. Levine, and Robert Neff, "They Don't Call It Blockbuster For Nothing," *Business Week,* October 19, 1992, pp. 113–114; and Johnnie L. Roberts, "Blockbuster Officials Envision Superstores For Music Business," *Wall Street Journal,* October 28, 1992, p. B7.

International
Business
Environment

An Atlas

Satellite television transmission now makes it commonplace for us to watch events as they unfold in other countries. Transportation and communication advances and government-to-government accords have contributed to our increasing dependence on foreign products and markets. As this dependence grows, updated maps are a valuable tool. They can show the locations of population, economic wealth, production, and markets; portray certain commonalities and differences among areas; and illustrate barriers that might inhibit trade. In spite of the usefulness of maps, a substantial number of people worldwide have a poor knowledge of how to interpret information on maps and even of how to find the locations of events that affect their lives.

We urge you to use the following maps to locate areas you study in order to build your geographic awareness. Such an awareness will help you identify viable international alternatives when you are a business decision maker.

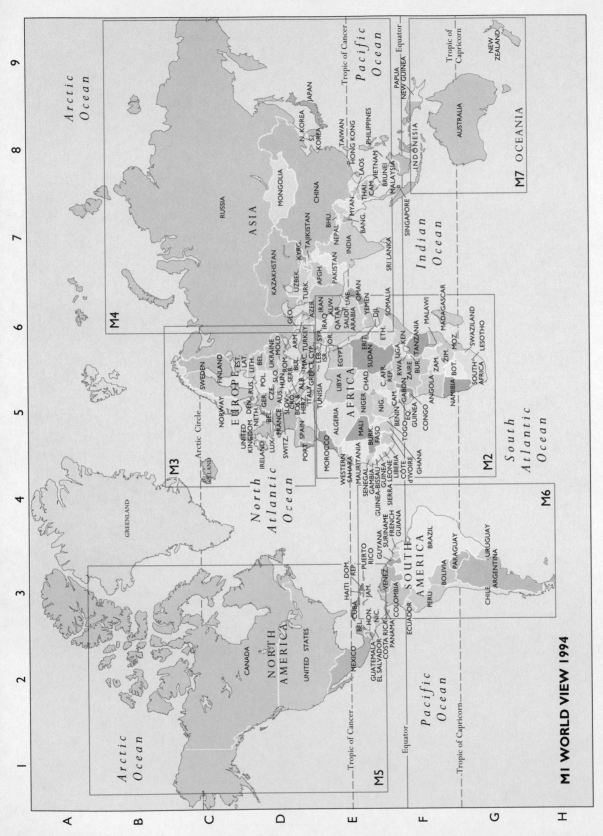

M1 WORLD VIEW 1994

This global view, which forms the main reference for subsequent maps in the Atlas, covers the Earth continent by continent. Rectangles indicate enlarged views of the following areas: M2 Africa, M3 Europe, M4 Asia, M5 North America, M6 South America and M7 Oceania.

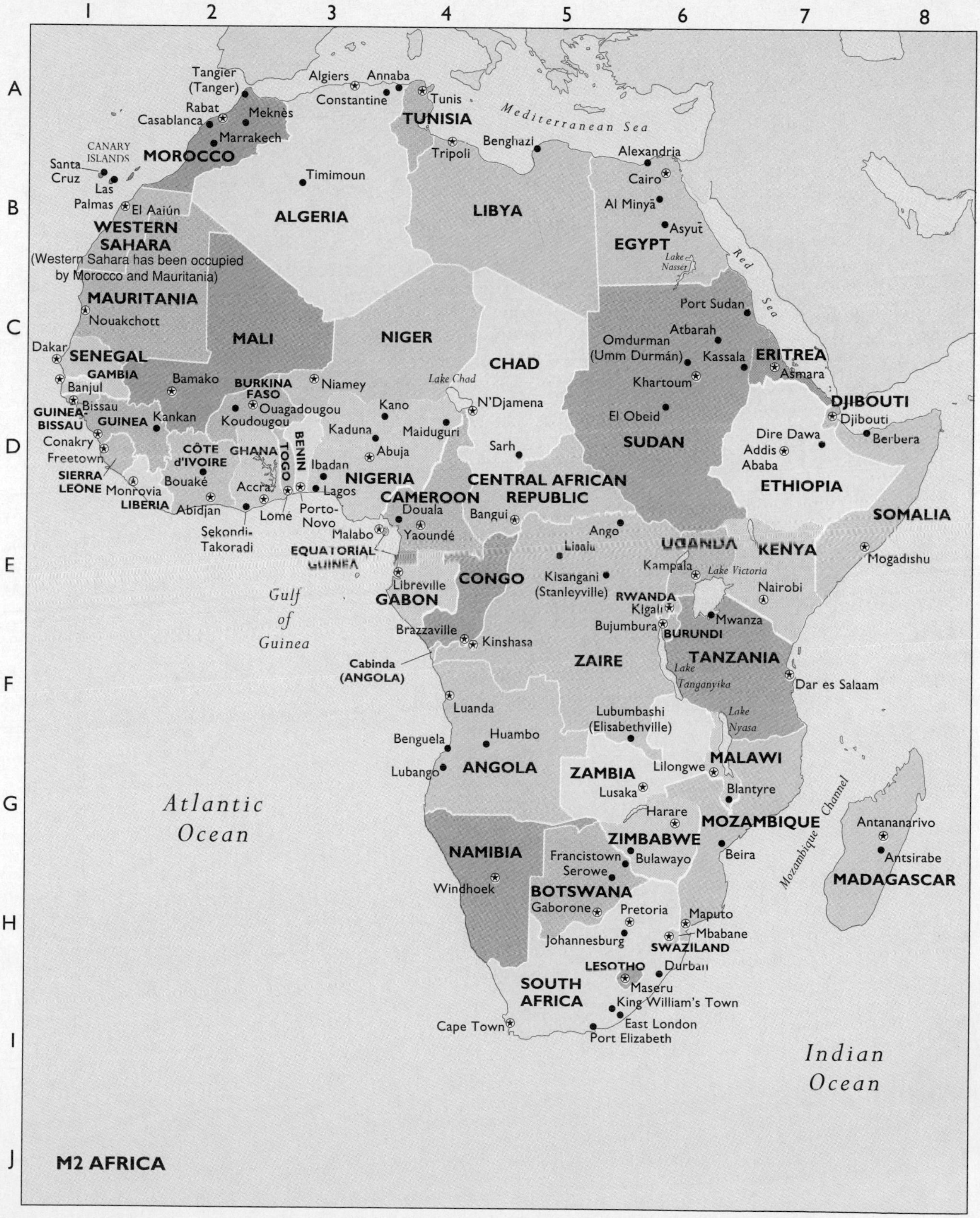

M2 AFRICA
Mediterranean Sea
Red Sea
Atlantic Ocean
Indian Ocean
Gulf of Guinea
Mozambique Channel
Lake Chad
Lake Nasser
Lake Victoria
Lake Tanganyika
Lake Nyasa
CANARY ISLANDS
Santa Cruz
Las Palmas
MOROCCO
Tangier (Tanger)
Rabat
Casablanca
Meknès
Marrakech
ALGERIA
Algiers
Annaba
Constantine
Timimoun
TUNISIA
Tunis
LIBYA
Tripoli
Benghazi
EGYPT
Alexandria
Cairo
Al Minyā
Asyūt
WESTERN SAHARA
(Western Sahara has been occupied by Morocco and Mauritania)
El Aaiún
MAURITANIA
Nouakchott
MALI
Bamako
NIGER
Niamey
CHAD
N'Djamena
Sarh
SUDAN
Port Sudan
Atbarah
Omdurman (Umm Durmán)
Kassala
Khartoum
El Obeid
ERITREA
Asmara
DJIBOUTI
Djibouti
Berbera
ETHIOPIA
Dire Dawa
Addis Ababa
SOMALIA
Mogadishu
SENEGAL
Dakar
GAMBIA
Banjul
GUINEA-BISSAU
Bissau
GUINEA
Conakry
Kankan
SIERRA LEONE
Freetown
LIBERIA
Monrovia
CÔTE d'IVOIRE
Bouaké
Abidjan
BURKINA FASO
Ouagadougou
Koudougou
GHANA
Accra
Sekondi-Takoradi
TOGO
Lomé
BENIN
Porto-Novo
NIGERIA
Kano
Kaduna
Maiduguri
Abuja
Ibadan
Lagos
CAMEROON
Douala
Yaoundé
EQUATORIAL GUINEA
Malabo
GABON
Libreville
CONGO
Brazzaville
CENTRAL AFRICAN REPUBLIC
Bangui
ZAIRE
Kinshasa
Kisangani (Stanleyville)
Lisala
Ango
Lubumbashi (Elisabethville)
UGANDA
Kampala
KENYA
Nairobi
RWANDA
Kigali
BURUNDI
Bujumbura
TANZANIA
Mwanza
Dar es Salaam
Cabinda (ANGOLA)
ANGOLA
Luanda
Huambo
Benguela
Lubango
ZAMBIA
Lusaka
MALAWI
Lilongwe
Blantyre
MOZAMBIQUE
Beira
Maputo
ZIMBABWE
Harare
Bulawayo
NAMIBIA
Windhoek
BOTSWANA
Francistown
Serowe
Gaborone
SOUTH AFRICA
Pretoria
Johannesburg
Durban
King William's Town
East London
Port Elizabeth
Cape Town
SWAZILAND
Mbabane
LESOTHO
Maseru
MADAGASCAR
Antananarivo
Antsirabe
1
2
3
4
5
6
7
8
A
B
C
D
E
F
G
H
I
J

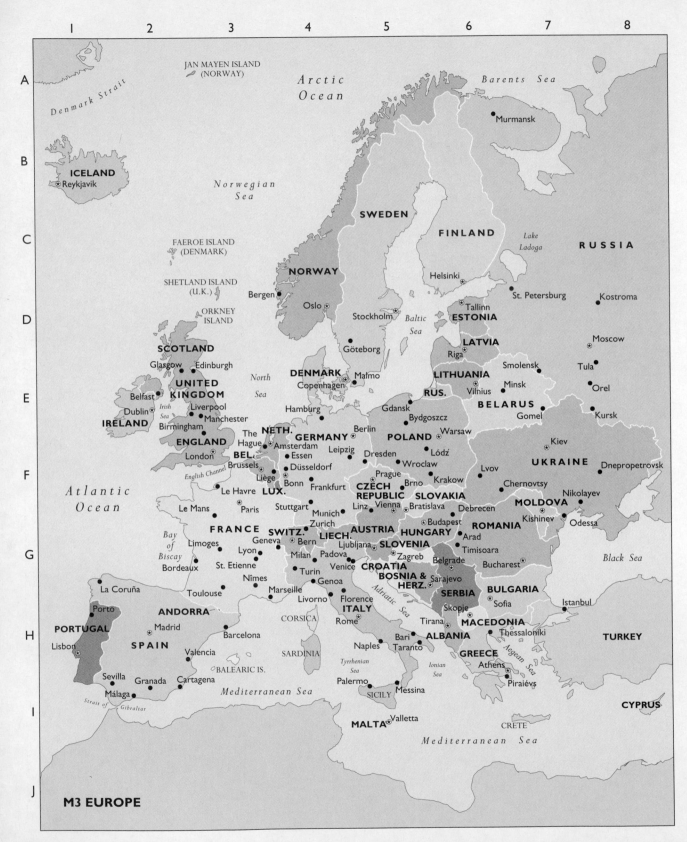

1   2   3   4   5   6   7   8

A   JAN MAYEN ISLAND
(NORWAY)   *Arctic Ocean*   *Barents Sea*

Denmark Strait

Murmansk

B   *Norwegian Sea*

ICELAND
Reykjavik   SWEDEN

C   FAEROE ISLAND
(DENMARK)   FINLAND   Lake
Ladoga   RUSSIA

SHETLAND ISLAND
(U.K.)   NORWAY   Helsinki

D   ORKNEY
ISLAND   Bergen   St. Petersburg   Kostroma

Oslo   Tallinn
Stockholm   Baltic   ESTONIA   Moscow
SCOTLAND   Sea

Glasgow   Edinburgh   Göteborg   Riga   LATVIA   Smolensk
E   UNITED   *North*   Malmo   LITHUANIA   Tula
Belfast   KINGDOM   *Sea*   DENMARK   Copenhagen   RUS.   Vilnius   Minsk   Orel
Dublin   Liverpool   BELARUS   Kursk
IRELAND   *Irish*   Manchester   Hamburg   Gdansk   Gomel
                Sea   Birmingham   NETH.   Berlin   Bydgoszcz   Warsaw   Kiev
            The   GERMANY   UKRAINE
ENGLAND   Hague   Amsterdam   Leipzig   POLAND   Dnepropetrovsk
London   BEL.   Essen   Dresden   Łódź   Lvov
F   Brussels   Düsseldorf   Prague   Wrocław   Krakow   Chernovtsy
English Channel   Liège   Bonn   Frankfurt   CZECH   Brno   Nikolayev
Le Havre   LUX.   REPUBLIC   SLOVAKIA   MOLDOVA
Atlantic   Le Mans   Paris   Stuttgart   Munich   Linz   Vienna   Bratislava   Debrecen   Kishinev   Odessa
Ocean   Zurich   ROMANIA
FRANCE   SWITZ.   LIECH.   AUSTRIA   HUNGARY   Arad
G   Limoges   Geneva   Bern   SLOVENIA   Budapest   Timisoara   Black Sea
Bay   Lyon   Milan   Ljubljana   Zagreb   Belgrade   Bucharest
of   St. Etienne   Padova   Venice   CROATIA
Biscay   Bordeaux   Nîmes   Turin   Genoa   BOSNIA &   Sarajevo   SERBIA   BULGARIA
La Coruña   Marseille   Livorno   HERZ.   Skopje   Sofia   Istanbul
H   Porto   Toulouse   Florence   Tirana   MACEDONIA
PORTUGAL   Madrid   Barcelona   CORSICA   ITALY   Rome   ALBANIA   Thessaloníki   TURKEY
Lisbon   SPAIN   Valéncia   SARDINIA   Naples   Bari   GREECE
Sevilla   Granada   Cartagena   BALEARIC IS.   *Tyrrhenian*   Taranto   *Ionian*   Athens   *Aegean*
Málaga   *Sea*   Palermo   SICILY   Messina   *Sea*   Piraiévs   *Sea*   CYPRUS
I   *Strait of Gibraltar*   *Mediterranean Sea*   MALTA   Valletta   CRETE
                                                Mediterranean Sea

J   M3 EUROPE

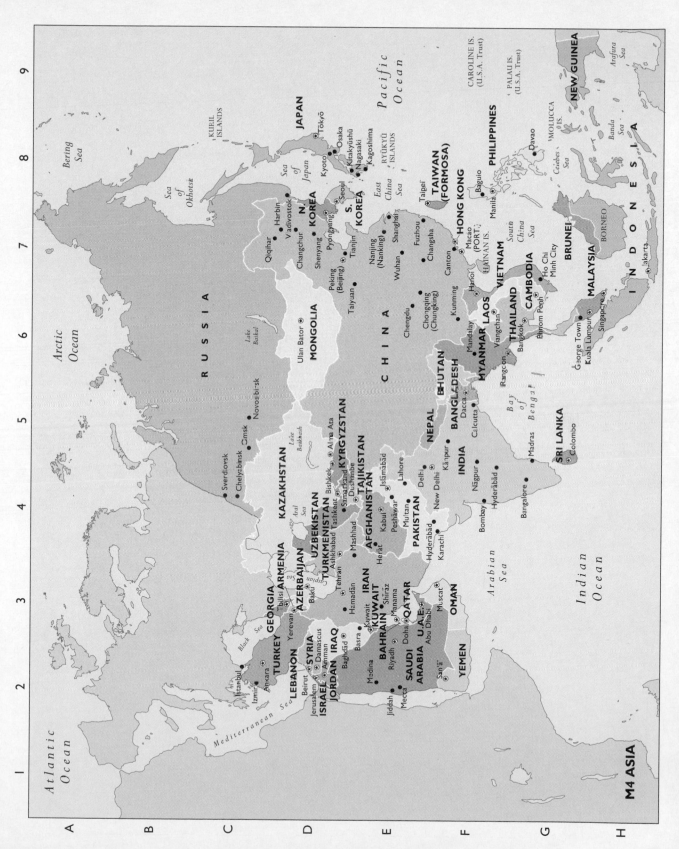

M4 ASIA

Atlantic Ocean

Arctic Ocean

Bering Sea

Sea of Okhotsk

RUSSIA

KURIL ISLANDS

JAPAN

Tōkyō
Osaka
Kyoto
Kitakyūshū
Nagasaki
Kagoshima

Sea of Japan

Vladivostok
Harbin
Qiqihar
Changchun
Shenyang
N. KOREA
Pyongyang
Seoul
S. KOREA

RYŪKYŪ ISLANDS

Pacific Ocean

CAROLINE IS. (U.S.A. Trust)

PALAU IS. (U.S.A. Trust)

NEW GUINEA

Arafura Sea

East China Sea

Taipei
TAIWAN (FORMOSA)

HONG KONG

Fuzhou
Changsha
Canton
Macao (PORT.)
HAINAN IS.

South China Sea

Baguio
Manila
Davao
PHILIPPINES

'MOLUCCA IS.

Celebes Sea

Banda Sea

I N D O N E S I A

BORNEO

Sverdlovsk
Chelyabinsk
Omsk
Novosibirsk

Lake Baikal

MONGOLIA
Ulan Bator

Peking (Beijing)
Tianjin
Taiyuan
Nanjing (Nanking)
Wuhan
Shanghai
Chengdu
Chongqing (Chungking)
Kunming

C H I N A

KAZAKHSTAN

Aral Sea

Lake Balkhash

Alma Ata
Bishkek
KYRGYZSTAN
UZBEKISTAN
Samarkand
Tashkent
TAJIKISTAN
Dushanbe
TURKMENISTAN
Ashkhabad
Mashhad
AFGHANISTAN
Kabul
Herāt
GEORGIA
Tbilisi
ARMENIA
Yerevan
AZERBAIJAN
Baku
Caspian Sea
Tehran
Hamadan
IRAN
Shīrāz

NEPAL
Kāthmāndu
BHUTAN
BANGLADESH
Dacca
Islamabad
Lahore
Delhi
New Delhi
Kānpur
Calcutta
PAKISTAN
Peshāwar
Multan
Hyderābād
Karachi
INDIA
Nāgpur
Bombay
Hyderābād
Bangalore
Madras

Bay of Bengal

SRI LANKA
Colombo

Arabian Sea

Indian Ocean

TURKEY
Istanbul
Izmir
Ankara
Black Sea
LEBANON
Beirut
SYRIA
Damascus
ISRAEL
Jerusalem
JORDAN
Amman
IRAQ
Baghdād
Basra
Kuwait
KUWAIT
Medina
Riyadh
Mecca
Jiddah
SAUDI ARABIA
BAHRAIN
Manama
QATAR
Doha
U.A.E.
Abu Dhabi
Muscat
OMAN
San'ā
YEMEN

Mediterranean Sea

MYANMAR
Mandalay
Rangoon
LAOS
Viangchan
THAILAND
Bangkok
VIETNAM
Hanoi
Ho Chi Minh City
CAMBODIA
Phnom Penh
MALAYSIA
George Town
Kuala Lumpur
Singapore
BRUNEI
Jakarta

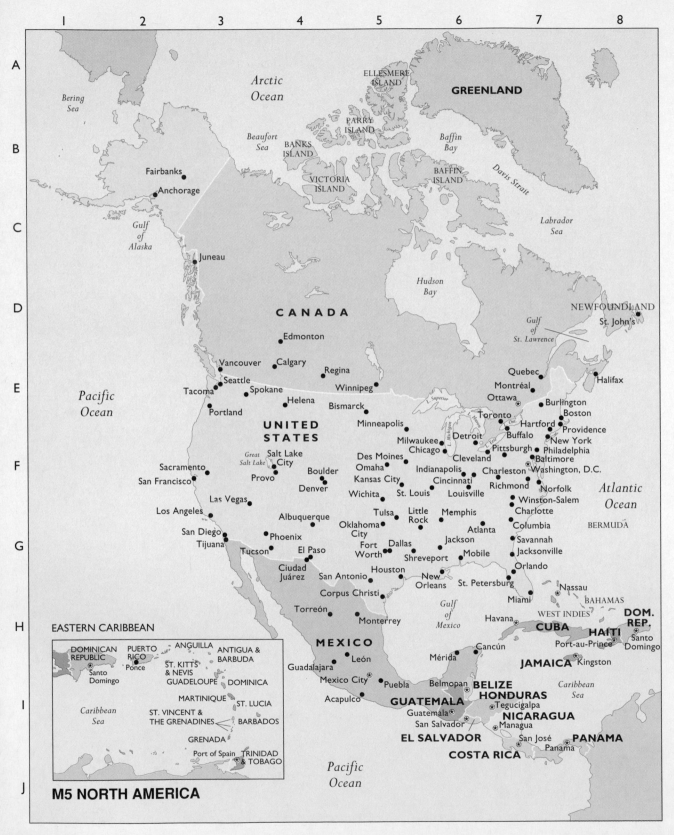

Map grid columns: 1 2 3 4 5 6 7 8
Map grid rows: A B C D E F G H I J

GREENLAND

Arctic Ocean

Bering Sea

ELLESMERE ISLAND

Beaufort Sea

BANKS ISLAND

PARRY ISLAND

Baffin Bay

VICTORIA ISLAND

BAFFIN ISLAND

Davis Strait

Fairbanks

Anchorage

Gulf of Alaska

Labrador Sea

Juneau

Hudson Bay

C A N A D A

NEWFOUNDLAND

St. John's

Edmonton

Gulf of St. Lawrence

Vancouver Calgary

Regina

Quebec

Halifax

Seattle

Winnipeg

Montréal

Tacoma Spokane

Ottawa

Burlington

Pacific Ocean

Helena

Bismarck

L. Superior

Toronto

Boston

Portland

Minneapolis

L. Huron

Buffalo

Hartford

Providence

UNITED STATES

Milwaukee

Detroit

L. Michigan

Pittsburgh

New York

Chicago

Ont.

Cleveland

Philadelphia

Great Salt Lake Salt Lake City

Des Moines

Indianapolis

Cincinnati

Erie

Charleston

Baltimore

Washington, D.C.

Provo

Omaha

Sacramento

Boulder

Kansas City

St. Louis

Louisville

Richmond

Norfolk

San Francisco

Denver

Wichita

Winston-Salem

Atlantic Ocean

Las Vegas

Tulsa

Memphis

Charlotte

BERMUDA

Los Angeles

Albuquerque

Oklahoma City

Little Rock

Atlanta

Columbia

San Diego

Phoenix

Dallas

Jackson

Savannah

Tijuana

Fort Worth

Shreveport

Mobile

Jacksonville

Tucson

El Paso

Houston

New Orleans

Orlando

Ciudad Juárez

San Antonio

St. Petersburg

Nassau

Corpus Christi

Gulf of Mexico

Miami

BAHAMAS

WEST INDIES

DOM. REP.

Torreón

Havana

CUBA

HAITI

Monterrey

Cancún

Port-au-Prince

Santo Domingo

MEXICO

Mérida

JAMAICA Kingston

Guadalajara León

EASTERN CARIBBEAN

DOMINICAN REPUBLIC

Santo Domingo

PUERTO RICO

Ponce

ANGUILLA

ANTIGUA & BARBUDA

ST. KITTS & NEVIS

GUADELOUPE DOMINICA

MARTINIQUE

ST. LUCIA

Caribbean Sea

ST. VINCENT & THE GRENADINES

BARBADOS

GRENADA

Port of Spain TRINIDAD & TOBAGO

Mexico City Puebla

Belmopan

BELIZE

HONDURAS

Caribbean Sea

Acapulco

GUATEMALA

Guatemala

Tegucigalpa

NICARAGUA

San Salvador

Managua

EL SALVADOR

San José

PANAMA

San José

Panama

COSTA RICA

Pacific Ocean

M5 NORTH AMERICA

40

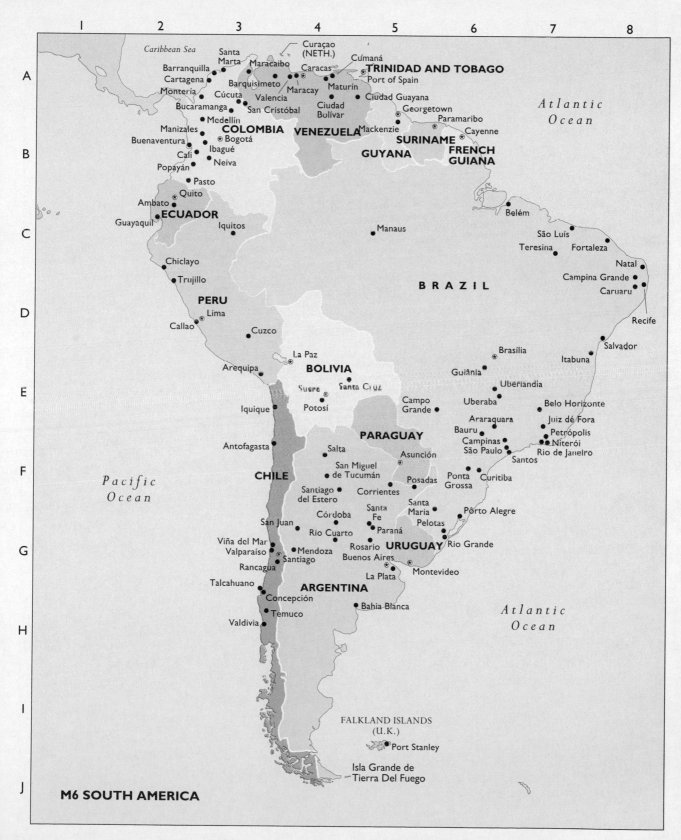

A
Caribbean Sea

Santa Marta
Barranquilla
Cartagena
Maracaibo
Monteria
Barquisimeto
Cúcuta
Valencia
Bucaramanga
San Cristóbal
Manizales
Medellín
COLOMBIA
Buenaventura
Bogotá
Cali
Ibagué
Popayán
Neiva

Curaçao (NETH.)
Caracas
Maracay
Maturín
Ciudad Bolívar
VENEZUELA

Cumaná
TRINIDAD AND TOBAGO
Port of Spain
Ciudad Guayana
Georgetown
Mackenzie
Paramaribo
Cayenne
SURINAME
GUYANA
FRENCH GUIANA

B

Pasto
Quito
Ambato
ECUADOR
Guayaquil
Iquitos

Belém

C
Manaus
São Luís
Teresina
Fortaleza
Natal
Campina Grande
Caruaru

Chiclayo
Trujillo
PERU
BRAZIL

Recife

Callao
Lima
Cuzco

Salvador

D

La Paz
BOLIVIA
Arequipa
Sucre
Santa Cruz
Potosí

Brasília
Goiânia
Itabuna
Uberlândia
Uberaba
Belo Horizonte
Campo Grande
Araraquara
Juiz de Fora
Bauru
Petrópolis
Campinas
Niterói
São Paulo
Rio de Janeiro
Santos

E

Iquique

Antofagasta
PARAGUAY
Salta
Asunción
CHILE
San Miguel de Tucumán
Santiago del Estero
Corrientes
Posadas
Ponta Grossa
Curitiba

F

Córdoba
Santa Fe
Santa Maria
San Juan
Paraná
Pelotas
Viña del Mar
Mendoza
Rosario
URUGUAY
Porto Alegre
Valparaíso
Santiago
Buenos Aires
Rio Grande
Rancagua
La Plata
Montevideo
Talcahuano
ARGENTINA
Bahía Blanca
Concepción
Temuco
Valdivia

G

Pacific Ocean

Atlantic Ocean

Atlantic Ocean

H

I
FALKLAND ISLANDS (U.K.)
Port Stanley

Isla Grande de Tierra Del Fuego

J
M6 SOUTH AMERICA

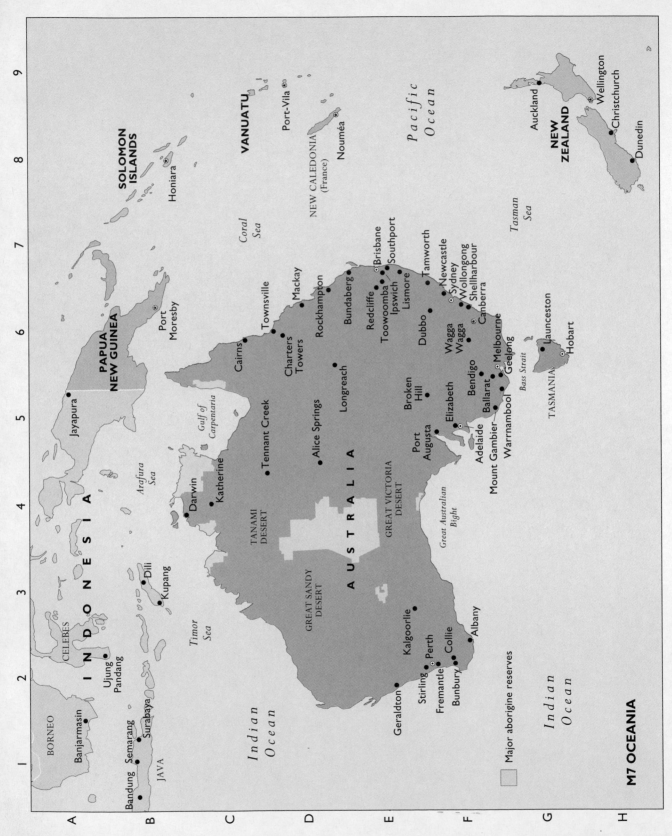

A B C D E F G H

1 2 3 4 5 6 7 8 9

BORNEO

Banjarmasin

C E L E B E S

I N D O N E S I A

Ujung
Pandang

Bandung
Semarang
Surabaya

JAVA

Dili

Kupang

Timor
Sea

PAPUA
NEW GUINEA

Jayapura

Port
Moresby

Arafura
Sea

Gulf of
Carpentaria

Darwin

Katherine

TANAMI
DESERT

GREAT SANDY
DESERT

Tennant Creek

Alice Springs

A U S T R A L I A

GREAT VICTORIA
DESERT

Cairns

Charters
Towers

Townsville

Mackay

Rockhampton

Longreach

Bundaberg

Brisbane
Southport
Toowoomba
Ipswich
Redcliffe
Lismore

Tamworth

Newcastle
Sydney
Wollongong
Shellharbour
Canberra

Dubbo

Wagga
Wagga

Broken
Hill

Elizabeth

Bendigo

Ballarat

Melbourne

Geelong

Warrnambool

Port
Augusta

Adelaide

Mount Gambier

Great Australian
Bight

Bass Strait

TASMANIA

Launceston

Hobart

Tasman
Sea

Coral
Sea

SOLOMON
ISLANDS

Honiara

VANUATU

Port-Vila

NEW CALEDONIA
(France)

Nouméa

Pacific
Ocean

NEW
ZEALAND

Auckland

Wellington

Christchurch

Dunedin

Indian
Ocean

Geraldton

Kalgoorlie

Stirling
Perth
Fremantle
Bunbury
Collie

Albany

Indian
Ocean

Major aborigine reserves

M7 OCEANIA

PART 2

2 Comparative Environmental Frameworks

Africa is a major global supplier of commodities, including minerals and agricultural products. Here you see a worker marking hardwood logs for export in Côte d'Ivoire (Ivory Coast). The photo is set against a background showing part of a mid–20th century Moroccan rug handmade by the Oulad Bou Shaa people from the plains of Marrakech.

Chapter 2

The Human and Cultural Environments Facing Business

*To change customs is
a difficult thing.*
—Lebanese Proverb

Objectives

- To demonstrate problems and methods of examining cultural environments

- To highlight human physical characteristics that may vary among countries and introduce ways in which these characteristics affect business practices worldwide

- To explain the major causes of cultural difference and change

- To examine major customs that differentiate business practices among countries

- To present guidelines for companies that operate internationally

Case
Parris-Rogers
International (PRI)[1]

Many women were among the troops sent by the United States to Saudi Arabia during the 1991 Persian Gulf War to liberate Kuwait from Iraq. In deference to Saudi culture, the Army did not permit them to jog, drive, or show their legs outside the military base. In deference to U.S. sensitivities, Saudi Arabia suspended beheadings in central squares during the Gulf crisis.

A few years earlier, Parris-Rogers International (PRI), a British publishing house, sold its floundering Bahraini operations. This branch had been set up to edit the first telephone and business directories for five Arab states on or near the Arabian peninsula, plus the seven autonomous divisions making up the United Arab Emirates (the region is shown in Map 2.1). Although the U.S. Army had protocol officers to advise it on accepted behavior, PRI had no such guidance. Further, although the Saudis were willing to make some accommodations to assure the defense of their country, PRI's directories were less important to them. The ensuing lack of understanding between the Saudis and PRI and PRI's failure to adapt to a different culture contributed directly to the company's failure.

Most Middle Eastern oil-producing countries have an acute shortage of local personnel, so many foreign workers have been hired. They now make up a large portion of the workforces in those countries. In Saudi Arabia in 1993, for example, 90 percent of the private-sector workforce was foreign-born. Thus when PRI could not find sufficient qualified

Map 2.1
The Scope of PRI's
Business Contract in
the Middle East

PRI's contract included Bahrain, Kuwait, Oman, Qatar, Saudi Arabia, and the United Arab Emirates (Abu Dhabi, Ajman, Dubai, Fuzaira, Ras al-Khaimah, Sharjah, and Umm al-Qaiwain).

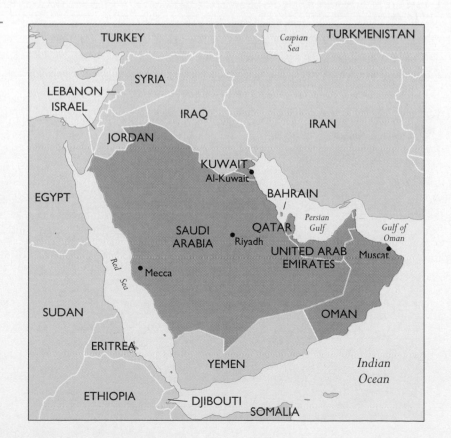

people locally, it filled four key positions through advertisements in London newspapers. Angela Clarke, an Englishwoman, was hired as editor and researcher, and three young Englishmen were hired as salesmen. The four new hires left immediately for Bahrain. None had visited the Middle East before; all expected to carry out business as usual.

The salesmen, hired on a commission basis, expected that by moving aggressively they could make the same number of calls as they normally could in the United Kingdom. They were used to working about eight hours a day, to having the undivided attention of potential clients, and to restricting most conversation to the specifics of the business transaction.

The salesmen found instead an entirely different situation. There was less time to sell, first, because the Muslims were required to pray five times a day and, second, because the workday was reduced even further during Ramadan, the ninth month of the Muslim year. This month is observed as sacred, with fasting from sunrise to sunset. The salesmen also felt that the Arabs placed little importance on appointments. Appointments seldom began at the scheduled time. When the salesmen finally got in to see Arab businessmen, they were often expected to go to a café where the Arabs would engage in idle chitchat. Whether in a café or in the office, drinking coffee or tea seemed to take precedence over business matters. The Arabs also frequently diverted their attention to friends who joined them at the café or in the office.

Angela Clarke, too, encountered considerable resistance as she sought to do her job. And, since she was paid a salary instead of a commission, PRI had to bear all of the expense resulting from her work being thwarted in unexpected ways. PRI had based its government-contract prices for preparing the directories on its English experience. In Bahrain, however, preparing such books turned out to be more time-consuming and costly. For example, in the traditional Middle Eastern city, there are no street names or building numbers. Thus, before getting to the expected directory work, Clarke had to take a census of Bahraini establishments, identifying the location of each with such prepositions as "below," "above," or "in front of" some meaningful landmark.

Clarke encountered other problems because she was a single woman. She was in charge of the research in all thirteen states and had planned to hire free-lance assistants in most of them. But her advertisements to hire such assistants were answered by personal harassment and obscene telephone calls. In addition, Saudi authorities denied her entry to Saudi Arabia, while her visa for Oman took six weeks to process *each time she went there*. These experiences were particularly frustrating for her because both Saudi Arabia and Oman sometimes eased the entry of a single woman when her business was of high local priority. In the states she could enter, Clarke sometimes was required to stay only in hotels that government officials had approved for foreign women, and even there, she was prohibited from eating in the dining room unless accompanied by the hotel manager.

PRI's salesmen never adjusted to working in the new environment. Instead of pushing PRI to review its commission scheme, they tried to change the way the Arab businessmen dealt with them. For example, after a few months they refused to join their potential clients for refreshments and began showing their irritation at "irrelevant" conversations, delays, and interruptions from outsiders. The Arab businessmen responded negatively. In fact, PRI received so many complaints from them that the salesmen had to be replaced. By then, however, irrevocable damage had been done to PRI's sales.

Clarke fared better, thanks to her compromises with Arab customs. She began wearing a wedding ring and registering at hotels as a married woman. When traveling, she ate meals in her room, conducted meetings in conference rooms, and had all incoming calls screened by the hotel operators. To avoid arrest by decency patrols, she wore long-sleeved blouses and below-the-knee skirts in plain blue or beige. Still, in spite of her compromises, her inability to enter Saudi Arabia caused PRI to send in her place a salesman, who was not trained to do the research.

The rapidly growing number of foreigners in the Middle East has created adjustment problems for both the foreigners and the local societies. On the one hand, foreign workers provide needed skills to fuel the increasingly complex economy. On the other hand, many Middle Easterners fear that their presence will erode deep-seated values and traditions. In many cases, foreigners are expected to conform; in others, they are allowed to pursue their own customs in isolation from the local populace. For example, according to traditional Islamic standards, most Western television programming is immoral. However, in some places foreigners are permitted to acquire unscramblers to view Western programs; local people may not.

The Saudi government also has had second thoughts about some of its culture's double standards. For example, at one time, male and female hotel guests were allowed to swim in the same pools in Saudi Arabia. This permission was rescinded, however, because Saudis frequent the hotels. It was feared they might be corrupted by viewing "decadent" behavior. Also, when Angela Clarke and the salesmen first arrived in Bahrain, there were prohibitions on the sale of pork products, including imported canned foods. This prohibition was later modified, but grocers had to stock pork products in separate rooms in which only non-Muslims could work or shop.

These dual and changing standards for foreigners and citizens hamper foreign efforts to adapt. This situation has been further complicated because the Middle East is going through a period of substantial, but uneven, economic and social transformation, well described in the following:

> Changes that in other countries have been spread out over several generations are being accomplished in a few short years. Diesel trucks and jet airplanes are replacing camel caravans, but the camel has not yet been discarded. Modern architecture and broad, tree-lined avenues are replacing mudbrick houses on twisting streets, but mudbrick buildings are still evident. Nomads (Bedouins) are beginning to drive from place to place; but it is common to see a pickup truck or a Mercedes parked beside a traditional tent.[2]

As contact increases between Arabs and Westerners, cultural borrowing and meshing of certain aspects of traditional and modern behavior will increase. These changes are apt to come slowly, perhaps more so than many think. A noted anthropologist summarized the misconception of Saudis that is prevalent in the United States:

> We tend to think of them as underdeveloped Americans—Americans with sheets on. We look at them as undereducated and rather poor at anything technological. All we have to do is to make believers out of them, get them the proper education, teach them English, and they will turn into Americans.[3]

In fact, when Saudi students who have spent time abroad return home, they revert to their traditional behaviors. Foreigners do the same after completing an assignment in Saudi Arabia. While U.S. troops were deployed in Saudi Arabia, an American female soldier said, "I'm thankful I'm not a Saudi woman. I just don't know how they do it." At the same time, a female Saudi doctor said, "It is so strange. I am glad not to be an American woman. Women are not made for violence and guns." These behaviors and attitudes indicate how deeply rooted both Saudi and Western traditions are.

Introduction

The PRI case illustrates how human differences give rise to different business practices in various parts of the world. Understanding the cultures and physical characteristics of groups of people is useful because business employs, sells to, buys from, is regulated by, and is owned by people. An international company must consider these differences in order to predict and control its relationships and operations. When doing business abroad, a company first should determine whether the usual business practices in a foreign country differ from its home-country experience or from what its management ideally would like to see exist. If practices differ, international management then must decide what, if any, adjustments are necessary to operate efficiently in the foreign country. When individuals come in contact with groups whose cultures differ from their own—abroad or within their own countries—they must decide if and how they can cope.

Some differences, such as those regarding acceptable attire, are discerned easily; others may be more difficult to perceive. For example, people in all cultures have culturally ingrained responses to given situations. They expect that people from other cultures will respond the same ways as people in their own culture do and that people in similar stations or positions will assume similar duties and privileges. All of these expectations may be disproved in practice. In the PRI case, the British salesmen budgeted their time and so regarded drinking coffee and chatting about nonbusiness activities in a café as "doing nothing," especially if there was "work to be done." The Arab businessmen, on the other hand, had no compulsion to finish at a given time, viewed time spent in a café as "doing something," and considered "small talk" a necessary prerequisite for evaluating whether they could interact satisfactorily with potential business partners. The Englishmen, because of their belief that "you shouldn't mix business and pleasure," became nervous when friends of the Arab businessmen intruded. In contrast, the Arabs felt "people are more important than business" and saw nothing private about business transactions.

After a company successfully identifies the differences in the foreign country in which it intends to do business, must it alter its customary or preferred practices in order to be successful there? There is no easy answer. Although the PRI case illustrates the folly of not adjusting, international companies nevertheless sometimes have been very successful in introducing new products, technologies, and operating procedures to foreign countries. At times, these introductions have not run counter to deep-seated attitudes. At others, the host society is willing to accept unwanted change as a trade-off for other advantages. In addition, in some cases the local society is willing to accept behavior from foreigners that it would not accept from its own citizens. For example, an American female executive said, "I do business comfortably in Japan. I don't find myself subjected to the same kind of sexism that, they tell me, is prevalent in other areas of Japanese life. I am treated as an American businessperson. . . . Most people overseas are well aware of the differences between Americans and themselves."[4] Members of the host society may even feel they are being stereotyped in an uncomplimentary way when foreigners adjust too much.[5] For example, Angela Clarke might have been even less effective for PRI if she had worn the traditional Arab woman's dress with veil.

The Nation as a Definition of a Society

The nation is a useful definition of society because
- **Similarity among people is a cause and an effect of national boundaries**
- **Laws apply primarily along national lines**

There is no universally satisfactory definition of a society, but in international business the concept of the nation provides a workable one, since basic similarity among people is both a cause and an effect of national boundaries. The laws governing business operations apply primarily along national lines. Within the bounds of a nation are people who share essential attributes perpetuated through rites and symbols of nationhood—flags, parades, rallies—and a subjective common perception of and maintenance of their history, through the preservation of national sites, documents, monuments, and museums. These shared attributes do not mean that everyone in a country is alike. Neither do they suggest that each country is unique in all respects; in fact, nations may include various subcultures, ethnic groups, races, and classes. However, the nation is legitimized by being the mediator of the different interests.[6] Failure to serve adequately in this mediating role may cause dissolution of the nation, as occurred recently in the former Soviet Union and the former Yugoslavia. In 1993, there was ethnic unrest in the form of violence in forty-eight nations; thus the boundaries of countries as we know them are far from secure.[7] Nevertheless, each country possesses certain characteristic physical, demographic, and behavioral norms that constitute its national identity and that may affect a company's methods of conducting business in that country.

Differences in dominant characteristics can influence how business is conducted.

Although each nation comprises people whose physical attributes vary widely, usually some characteristics dominate. The variations are due largely to genetics and become less noticeable as people migrate and intermarry. Even in the absence of mixing among groups, gene frequency (and thus physical characteristics) may change over time because of natural selection as humans adapt to the changing physical environment. There is also some evidence that the cultural environment, including the social norms and responses, may affect physical attributes. For example, infant stress can affect adult height, and dietary habits among some groups can influence resistance to malaria and thus natural selection in malaria-prone regions.[8]

Country-by-country analysis
has limitations because
• Not everyone in a country
   is alike
• Variations within some
   countries are great
• Similarities link groups
   from different countries

In using the nation as a point of reference, remember that some countries have much greater internal variation than do others. Geographical and economic barriers in some countries can inhibit people's movements from one region to another, thus limiting their personal interactions. Decentralized laws and government programs may increase regional separation, and linguistic, religious, and ethnic differences within a country usually preclude the fusing of the population into a homogeneous state. For example, for all the reasons just given, India is much more diverse than Denmark.

Of course, nationality is not the only basis on which to group people. Everyone belongs to various other groups—for example, those based on profession, age, religion, and place of residence. Many similarities exist that in some ways can link groups from different countries more closely than groups within a country. For instance, regardless of the country examined, people in urban areas differ in certain attitudes from people in rural areas, and managers have different work-related attitudes than production workers do.[9] When you compare countries, therefore, you must be careful to examine relevant groups.

There are thousands of possible relationships between human variables and business functions—too many to discuss exhaustively in one chapter.[10] This chapter first concentrates on just a few of the variables that have been found to influence business practices substantially. It then highlights alternative approaches for determining and dealing with differences in foreign countries as well as the changes that may occur in international companies as they come in contact with new human environments.

Physical Attributes

International businesspeople must grasp the sometimes subtle physical differences among societies and determine how they may influence the conduct of business. For example, a given population's susceptibility to certain diseases may affect the market for pharmaceutical products but not the market for automobiles or the accounting practices of pharmaceutical firms. Physical differences can also affect business decisions such as whether and how to change a product, how high to place production machinery, and which advertising message to use.

Appearance is among the most noticeable of human variations. Although most differences in appearance are readily apparent, many subtle variations may be overlooked by nondiscriminating outsiders. For example, Asians complain that Western films and advertisements frequently depict their national backgrounds incorrectly, perhaps by identifying a Chinese as a Japanese or a Korean as a Thai.

An individual's size would seem to be an obvious difference. However, one U.S. company unsuccessfully attempted to sell in Japan men's slacks produced according to U.S. tailoring patterns. Before the company discovered the sizing error, a competitor that cut clothing to fit the slimmer Japanese customer had preempted the market.

Businesspeople must consider societies' self-stereotypes.

Idealized traits have an impact as well. People often adopt culture-wide self-stereotypes that largely reflect wishful thinking. For example, U.S. advertisements typically depict individuals who are younger and thinner than the majority of the target audience. In Germany, the tall Nordic type is the ideal.

Age distribution varies widely among countries because of life expectancies and shifting birthrates. Life expectancy is largely a function of economic factors. Thus it tends to be lower in poor countries, because so many people in those countries lack adequate nutrition and access to medical attention. For example, Bhutan, Sierra Leone, and Niger—all lower-income countries—have life expectancies of 45 years or less, whereas Canada, Japan, and Switzerland—all higher-income countries—have life expectancies exceeding 75 years. Birthrate variations result from attitudes, such as religious prohibitions on birth control, and from economic conditions, such as the cost of educating children. These rates vary among countries and also within countries over time, leading to so-called baby booms and baby busts. Italy offers an example of such shifts. In the early 1980s, it experienced a high birthrate, followed a few years later by the lowest birthrate in the world. Companies must take age distribution into account with respect to product demand. For example, Honda redesigned its Accord to suit the needs of an aging population in the United States.[11]

The Concept of Culture

Businesspeople agree that cultural differences exist but disagree on what they are.

Culture consists of specific learned norms based on attitudes, values, and beliefs, all of which exist in every society. Visitors remark on differences; experts write about them; and people managing affairs across countries find that they affect operating results.[12] Great controversy surrounds these differences because there is an acknowledged problem with measuring variances.[13] Culture cannot easily be isolated from such factors as economic and political conditions and institutions. For example, an opinion survey may reflect a short-term response to temporary economic conditions rather than basic values and beliefs that will have longer-term effects on managing business.

Despite these problems, considerable research indicates that some aspects of culture differ significantly across national borders and have a substantial impact on how business is normally conducted in different countries. Two techniques are commonly used by businesses and academicians to determine national cultural characteristics and differences.[14] One relies on qualitative techniques, such as interviews and observations, to uncover people's ideas, attitudes, and relationships to other people in the society. This technique enables observers to interpret processes and events and to describe national character. Another method relies on comparing the opinions of carefully paired samples of people in more than one country. For example, questionnaires may be used to determine attitudes toward specific business practices, such as an advertising message or shared decision making in the workplace.

Causes of Cultural Difference and Change

Culture is transmitted by various patterns, such as from parent to child, from teacher to pupil, from social leader to follower, and from one age peer to another. Studies among diverse societies indicate that the parent-to-child route is especially important in the transmission of religious and political affiliations.[15] Developmental psychologists believe that by age 10 most children have their basic value systems firmly in place, after which changes are difficult to make. These basic values include such concepts as evil versus good, dirty versus clean, ugly versus beautiful, unnatural versus natural, abnormal versus normal, paradoxical versus logical, and irrational versus rational. The relative inflexibility of values helps explain the deeply rooted opinions of the American female soldier and Saudi female doctor in the PRI case.[16]

However, because of multiple influences, individual and societal values and customs may evolve over time. Change may come about through choice or imposition.[17] Change by choice may take place as a by-product of social and economic change or because of new contacts that present reasonable alternatives. For example, the choice of rural people in many places to accept factory jobs changed their previous customs by requiring them to work regular hours and to forgo social activities with their families during work hours. A person's choice to embrace a different religion requires acceptance of a new set of values and beliefs. Change by imposition has occurred, for example, when colonial powers introduced their legal systems abroad by prohibiting established practices and defining them as being criminal.[18] The process of introducing elements of an outside culture often is referred to as *creolization* or *indigenization*.

Isolation tends to stabilize a culture, whereas contact tends to create cultural borrowing. In addition to national boundaries and geographical obstacles, language is a major factor that affects cultural stability. Map 2.2 shows the world's major language groups. When people from different areas speak the same language, culture is transmitted from one area to another much more easily. Thus more cultural similarity exists among English-speaking countries or among Spanish-speaking ones than between English-speaking and Spanish-speaking countries. This is due partially to heritage and partially to the ease of communicating. Map 2.2 does not include the hundreds of languages that are spoken in limited areas. When people speak only one of those languages, they tend to adhere to their culture because meaningful contact with others is difficult. For example, in Guatemala, the official language is Spanish; however, there are twenty-two ethnic groups, three main ethnic languages, and derivations of those three. These groups have cultures that are much the same as those of their ancestors hundreds of years ago. The Guatemalan Nobel Peace Prize winner Rigoberta Menchú is from the Quiché group. She recounted that parents in that group do not permit their children to go to school, because all public schools use Spanish; by learning Spanish, the children will lose their values and customs. She broke out of this linguistic isolation when she learned Spanish as an adult in order to fight governmental policies.[19]

Map 2.2   Major Languages of the World

Hundreds of languages are spoken globally, but a few dominate. This map shows the eleven major ones. Note that English, French, or Spanish is the primary language in over half of the world's countries. Some other languages, such as Mandarin and Russian, are prevalent in only one country but are important because of the number of native speakers.

Source: From The Economist World Atlas and Almanac, *The Economist Books/Henry Holt & Co., Inc., pp. 116–117. Reprinted with permission.*

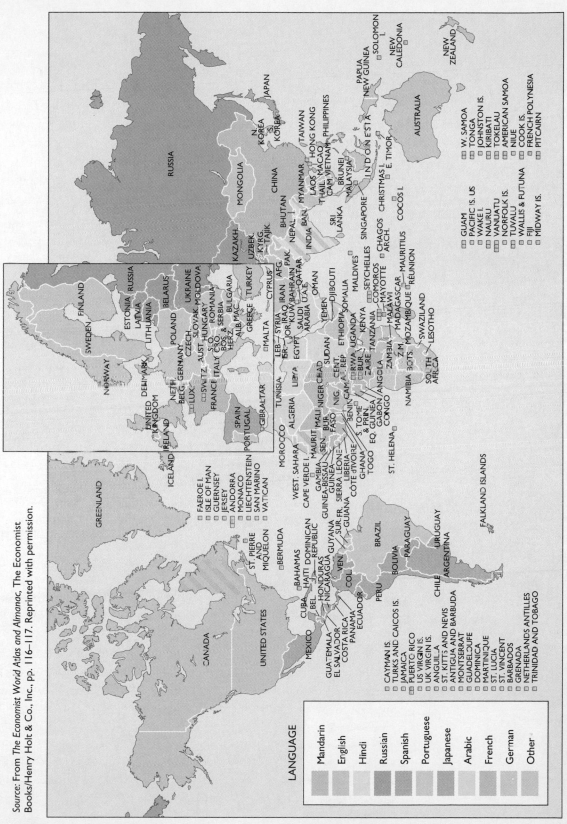

LANGUAGE

Mandarin
English
Hindi
Russian
Spanish
Portuguese
Japanese
Arabic
French
German
Other

Religion is a strong molder of values. Map 2.3 shows the distribution of the world's major religions. Within the major religions—Buddhism, Christianity, Hinduism, Islam, and Judaism—are many factions whose specific beliefs may affect business. For example, some Christian groups forgo alcohol but others do not. Differences among nations that practice the same religion also can affect business. For example, Friday is normally not a workday in predominantly Muslim countries because it is a day of worship; however, Tunisia adheres to the Christian work calendar in order to be more productive in business dealings with Europe.[20] When a religion is dominant in an area, it is apt to have great influence on laws and governmental policies. It also is apt to limit acceptance of products or business practices that are considered unorthodox (recall the Bahraini prohibition of pork in the PRI case). Consequently, foreign companies may have to alter their usual business practices. For example, because of criticism from fervent Hindus, McDonald's agreed not to serve beef in its restaurants in India.[21] In countries in which rival religions vie for political control, the resulting strife can cause so much unrest that business is disrupted. In recent years, violence among religious groups has erupted in India, Lebanon, Northern Ireland, and the former Yugoslavia.

The following discussion provides a framework for understanding how cultural differences affect business.

Behavioral Practices Affecting Business

Group Affiliations

Group affiliations can be
- **Ascribed or aquired**
- **A reflection of resources and position**

The populations of all countries are commonly subdivided into groups, and individuals belong to more than one group. Affiliations determined by birth—known as **ascribed group memberships**—include those based on gender, family, age, caste, and ethnic, racial, or national origin. Affiliations not determined by birth are called **acquired group memberships** and include those based on religion, political affiliation, and professional and other associations. A person's affiliations often reflect that person's class or status in a country's social-stratification system. And every society uses group membership for social stratification, such as by valuing members of managerial groups more highly than members of production groups.

Competence is rewarded highly in some societies.

Role of competence   In some societies, such as that of the United States, a person's acceptability for jobs and promotions is based primarily on competence. This does not mean, of course, that U.S. society has no discrimination against people on the basis of group affiliation. However, the belief that competence should prevail is valued highly enough in the United States that legislative and judicial actions have aimed at preventing discrimination on the basis of sex, race, age, and religion. This value is far from universal. In many cultures, competence is of secondary importance, and the belief that it is right to place some other criterion ahead of competence is just as strong in those cultures as the belief in competence is in the United

Map 2.3   Major Religions of the World

Almost all areas have people of various religious beliefs, but the culture of a region is most influenced by the dominant religion. Note that some countries have different dominant religions in different areas and that religions' areas of dominance transcend national boundaries.

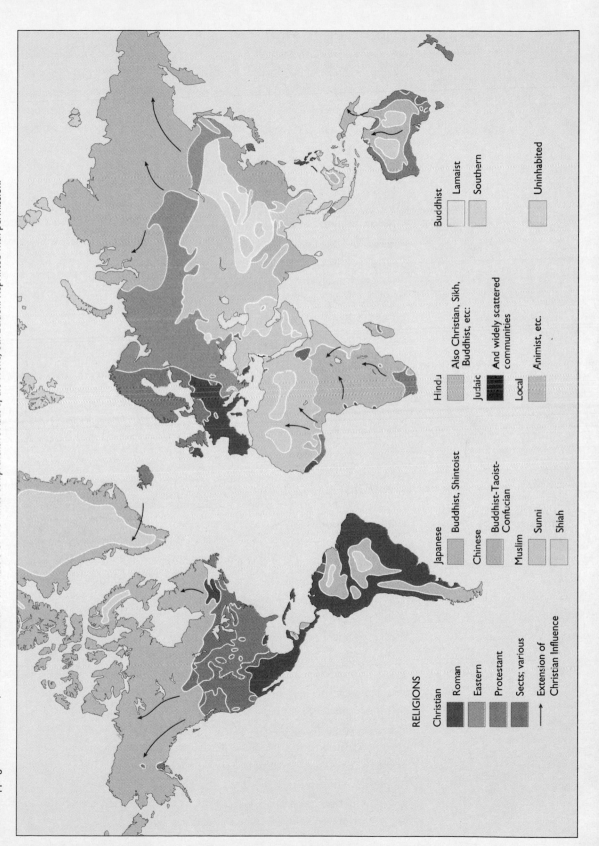

Source: Mapping © Bartholomew, 1990. Extract taken from Plate 5 of *The Times Comprehensive Atlas of the World*, 8th Edition. Reprinted with permission.

RELIGIONS

Christian
- Roman
- Eastern
- Protestant
- Sects; various

→ Extension of Christian Influence

Japanese
- Buddhist, Shintoist

Chinese
- Buddhist-Taoist-Confucian

Muslim
- Sunni
- Shiah

Hindu

Judaic

Local
- Also Christian, Sikh, Buddhist, etc:
- And widely scattered communities
- Animist, etc.

Buddhist
- Lamaist
- Southern

Uninhabited

States. Whatever factor is given primary importance—whether seniority, as in Japan, or some other quality—will largely influence a person's eligibility for certain positions and compensation.[22]

Egalitarian societies place less importance on ascribed group memberships.

The more egalitarian, or open, a society is, the less difference ascribed group membership makes for access to rewards; however, in less open societies, legal proscriptions sometimes enforce distinctions on the basis of ascribed group memberships. In other cases, group memberships prevent large numbers of people from getting the preparation that would equally qualify them. For example, in countries with poor public education systems, elite groups send their children to private schools but other children receive inferior schooling.

Local attitudes may force hiring according to local norms or opinions.

Even when individuals qualify for certain positions and there are no legal barriers to hiring them, social obstacles may make companies wary of employing them. Other workers, customers, local stockholders, or governmental officials may oppose certain groups, making it even more difficult for their members to succeed.

Country-by-country attitudes vary toward
- **Male and female roles**
- **Respect for age**
- **Family ties**

Importance of different group memberships   Although there are countless ways of defining group memberships, three of the most significant are in terms of gender, age, and family. An international comparison reveals the wide differences in attitudes concerning these memberships and how important they are to business considerations.

Gender-Based Groups

There are strong country-specific differences in attitudes toward males and females. The Chinese and Indians show an extreme degree of male preference. Because of governmental and economic restrictions on family size and the desire to have a son to carry on the family name, the practices of aborting female fetuses and killing female babies are widespread.[23]

Recall that in the PRI case the female editor could not get permission to enter Saudi Arabia, a country that exhibits an extreme degree of behavioral rigidity related to gender. Schools are separate, as is most social life, such as wedding parties and zoo outings. A toothpaste commercial for Colgate had to be reshot because censors found the woman's lipstick to be "too sexy."[24] Women are legally prohibited from driving cars and socially restricted from riding in a taxi without a male relative. Only about 10 percent of women work outside the home, and those who do remain separate from men. Most jobs for women are in professions that entail little or no contact with males, such as teaching or providing medical treatment to other women. When women do work in integrated organizations, the Saudis place partitions between them and male employees.

Even among countries in which women constitute a large portion of the working population, vast differences exist in the types of jobs regarded as "male" or "female." For example, in Australia and Canada, more than 40 percent of administrative and managerial positions are filled by women; in Japan and South Korea, that figure is less than 5 percent.[25]

Culturally mandated male and female behaviors may carry over to other aspects of the work situation. For example, Molex, a U.S. manufacturer of connectors, which has a manufacturing facility in Japan, invited its Japanese workers and their spouses to a company dinner one evening. Neither wives nor female employees appeared. To comply with Japanese standards, the company now has a "family day," which the women feel comfortable attending.[26]

Age-Based Groups

Attitudes toward age involve some curious variations. Many cultures assume that age and wisdom are correlated. These cultures usually have a seniority-based system of advancement. In the United States, retirement at age 60 or 65 was mandatory in most companies until the 1980s, and relative youthfulness has been a professional advantage. However, this esteem for youthfulness has not carried over into the U.S. political realm, where there are relatively high minimum-age requirements for many offices and no mandatory retirement age.

Barriers to employment based on age or gender are changing substantially in many parts of the world. Thus statistical and attitudinal studies that are even a few years old may be unreliable. One change has involved the growing numbers of women and men in the United States employed in occupations previously dominated by the other gender. For example, during the 1980s, the proportion of male secretaries, telephone operators, and nurses rose substantially, as did the proportion of female architects, bartenders, and bus drivers. During the same period in Japan, the percentage of females who were employed increased about 10 percent, and the percentage of women in management positions more than doubled.[27]

Family-Based Groups

In some societies, especially those in Mediterranean and Latin American countries, the family constitutes the most important group membership. An individual's acceptance in society is largely based on the family's social status or respectability rather than on the individual's achievement. Because family ties are so strong, there also may be a compulsion to cooperate closely within the family unit while distrusting links involving others. Among Greek businesses, for example, workers in family restaurants cooperate and mobilize their efforts to attain success much more effectively than do workers in large organizations, where people are from many different families.[28]

Importance of Work

In industrial countries, most people work more than they would need to simply to satisfy basic needs.

People work for a number of reasons. Many, especially in industrial societies, could satisfy their basic needs for food, clothing, and shelter by working fewer hours than they do. What motivates them to work more? The reasons for working and the relative importance of work among human activities may largely be explained by the interrelationship of the cultural and economic environments of the particular country. The differences in motivation help to explain management styles, product demand, and levels of economic development.

The motives for working are different in different places.

Protestant ethic   Max Weber, a German sociologist, observed near the beginning of the twentieth century that the predominantly Protestant countries were the most economically developed. Weber attributed this fact to the attitude toward work held by most of those countries, an attitude he labeled the *Protestant ethic*. According to Weber, the Protestant ethic was an outgrowth of the Reformation, when work was viewed as a means of salvation. Adhering to this belief, people preferred to transform productivity gains into additional output rather than into additional leisure.[29]

Although few societies today retain this strict concept of work for work's sake, leisure is valued more highly in some societies than in others. On average, the Japanese take less leisure than do people in any other industrial country, largely because of their high commitment to their employers. In fact, it is estimated that 10,000 Japanese die each year from heart attacks or strokes triggered by overwork.[30] In the United States, another country where incomes probably allow for considerably more leisure time than most people use, there is still much disdain, on the one hand, for the millionaire socialite who contributes nothing to society and, on the other hand, for the person who lives on welfare. People who are forced to give up work, such as retirees, complain strongly of their inability to do anything "useful." This view contrasts with those that predominate in some other societies. In much of Europe, the highest place in the social structure is held by the aristocracy, which historically has been associated with leisure. Therefore, upward mobility is associated with more leisure activities, but only those that are broadening, such as trips, reading, or sports endeavors, and not household-related activities, such as gardening and taking care of children.[31] In rural India, living a simple life with minimum material achievements still is considered a desirable end in itself.

Attitudes toward work may change as economic gains are achieved.

Today, personal economic achievement is considered commendable not only in industrial countries but also in most rapidly developing ones. Some observers note that many economies, in contrast, are characterized by limited economic needs that are an outgrowth of the culture. If incomes start to rise, workers in these economies tend to reduce their efforts, and thus personal income remains unchanged. This cultural trait has been noted as an essential difference that underpins national self-identity in many lower-income countries. Rather than rejecting the labels of "traditional" for themselves and "progressive" for the higher-income nations, leaders of these countries have stressed the need for a superior culture—one that combines material comforts with spirituality.[32] Other observers, however, have argued that limited economic needs may be a very short-lived phenomenon because expectations rise slowly as a result of past economic achievement. Most of us believe we would be happy with just "a little bit more," until we have that "little bit more," which then turns out to be not quite enough.

People are more eager to work if
- **Rewards for success are high**
- **There is some uncertainty of success**

Belief in success and reward   One factor that influences a person's attitude toward working is the perceived likelihood of success and reward. The concepts of success and reward are closely related. Generally people have little enthusiasm for efforts that seem too easy or too difficult, that is, where the probability of either success or failure seems almost certain. For instance, few of us would be eager to run a foot race against either a snail or a racehorse because the outcome in either case is too certain. Our highest enthusiasm occurs when the uncertainty is high—in this example, probably when racing another human of roughly equal ability. The reward for successfully completing an effort, such as winning a race, may be high or low as well. People usually will work harder at any task when the reward for success is high compared with the reward for failure.

The same tasks performed in different countries will have different probabilities of success and different rewards associated with success and failure. In cultures where the probability of failure is almost certain *and* the perceived rewards of success are low, there is a tendency to view work as necessary but ungratifying. This attitude may exist in harsh climates, in very poor areas, or in subcultures that are the objects of discrimination. At the other extreme, in areas such as Scandinavia, where the tax structures and public policies redistribute income from higher earners to low earners, there also is little enthusiasm for work itself. In this case, the probability of success is high and rewards tend to be high, but the rewards are similar regardless of how hard one works. The greatest enthusiasm for work exists when high uncertainty of success is combined with the likelihood of a very positive reward for success and little or no reward for failure. [33]

The work ethic is related to habit.

Work as a habit Another factor in the trade-off between work and leisure is that the pursuit of leisure activities may itself have to be learned. After a long period of sustained work, a person may have problems deciding what to do with free time. This insight helps to explain the continued drive for greater achievement seen in some societies in which most people already have considerable material comforts. One study that attempted to determine why some areas of Latin America developed a higher economic level and greater desire for material achievement than others attributed differences to the fact that some Spanish settlers worked themselves rather than using slave or near-slave labor. In such areas as Antioquia in Colombia, the Spanish settlers who labored themselves developed a work ethic and became the industrial leaders of the country. [34] Clearly, when comparing the importance of work from one country to another, the effects of habit cannot be overlooked. An international company thus may find it easier in some societies than in others to motivate its workforce with shorter hours or longer vacation periods.

High-need achievers want
- **Personal responsibility**
- **To take calculated risks in order to achieve reasonable goals**
- **Performance feedback**

Lower-need achievers often prefer smooth social relationships.

High-need achievement The **high-need achiever** is a person who will work very hard to achieve material or career success, sometimes to the detriment of social relationships or spiritual achievements. [35] Three attributes distinguish high-need achievers:

1. They like situations that involve personal responsibility for finding solutions to problems.
2. They set moderate achievement goals and take calculated risks.
3. They want concrete feedback on performance.

Figure 2.1
Maslow's Hierarchy of Needs and Need-Hierarchy Comparisons
The lower hierarchy on the right has a wider social bar (3) and a narrower self-actualization bar (5) than the upper one. People represented by the lower hierarchy require more affiliation needs to be fulfilled before a self-esteem need (4) will be triggered as a motivator. These people would be less motivated by self-actualization than would those represented by the upper hierarchy.

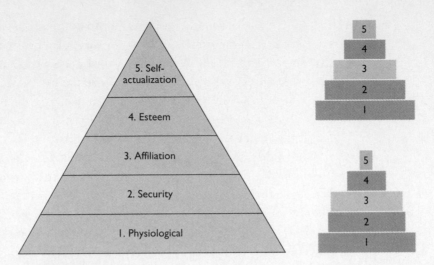

The average manager's interest in material or career success varies substantially among countries, which explains situations in which the local manager reacts in ways that the international management may neither expect nor wish. For instance, a purchasing manager with a high need for smooth social relationships may be much more concerned with developing an amiable and continuing relationship with suppliers than with reducing costs and speeding delivery. Or local managers in some countries may place such organizational goals as employee and social welfare ahead of the foreign company's priorities for growth and efficiency.

Need hierarchy   Abraham Maslow's **hierarchy of needs** is a well-known motivation theory, which is shown schematically in Fig. 2.1. According to Maslow, people try to fulfill lower-order needs sufficiently before moving on to higher ones.[36] People will work to satisfy a need, but once it is fulfilled, it is no longer a motivator. This fulfillment is not an all-or-nothing situation. However, because lower-order needs are more important than higher-order ones, they must be nearly fulfilled before any higher-order need becomes an effective motivator. For instance, the most basic needs are physiological, including the needs for food, water, and sex. Physiological needs may have to be nearly satisfied (say, 85-percent satisfied), before a security need becomes a powerful motivator. The security need, centering around a safe physical and emotional environment, may have to be only 70-percent satisfied before triggering the influence of the need for affiliation, or social belongingness (acceptance by peers and friends). After the affiliation need is sufficiently satisfied, a person may be motivated by an esteem need, the need to bolster one's self-image through receipt of recognition, attention, and appreciation for one's contributions. The highest-order need is that for self-actualization, which refers to self-fulfillment, or becoming all that it is possible for one to become. The relative fulfillment requirements are shown by the horizontal bars in Fig. 2.1.

The ranking of needs differs among countries.

Maslow's theory is helpful for differentiating the reward preferences of employees in different countries. In very poor countries, most workers may be so deprived that a company can motivate them simply by providing enough food and shelter. Elsewhere, other needs have to be addressed to motivate workers. Studies have noted that people from different countries attach different degrees of importance to various needs and even rank some of the higher-order needs differently. For example, in a collectivist culture (one that puts a higher value on equality than on individual freedom), self-actualization will be a less effective motivator than it will be in an individualistic society (one that puts a higher value on individual freedom than on equality). It also has been noted that per capita income tends to be related positively to social attitudes favoring individualism.[37] However, differences exist among higher-income countries as well. For example, in Japan and Spain, group-centered motivational methods may have a more positive impact on employees than do individual job-enrichment methods, which are strong motivators in the United States and the United Kingdom.

Importance of Occupation

The perception of what jobs are "best" varies somewhat among countries.

In every society, certain occupations are perceived to bring greater economic, social, or prestige rewards than others do. This perception to a great extent determines the numbers and qualifications of people who will seek employment in a given occupation. Although overall patterns are universal (for example, professionals are ranked ahead of street cleaners), there are some national differences. For instance, physicians tend to be ranked higher than university professors in the United States, probably because of the importance Americans attach to financial rewards. That ranking is reversed in Japan, probably because of the importance the Japanese attach to education and the disdain they feel for smelly and contagious situations.[38] Similarly, the reluctance of educated people to dirty their hands or associate directly with operative workers sometimes has made it difficult to find lower-level managers in Latin America. To generalize, in the Latin American culture there are three classes, composed of people of leisure, people who work with their minds, and people who work with their hands.[39] The importance of business as a profession also is predictive of how difficult it may be for an international company to hire qualified managers. If jobs in business are not held in high esteem, a company may have to spend more to attract and train local managers, or it may have to rely more on managers transferred from abroad.

Another international difference involves the desire to work for an organization rather than to be one's own boss. For example, the Belgians and the French, more than most other nationalities, prefer, if possible, to go into business for themselves. Thus Belgium and France have more retail establishments per capita than most other countries do. One reason for this is that owning a small or medium-sized enterprise, rather than earning more income, is a means for Belgian and French people to get out of the working class and to move up socially. Further, psychological studies show that Belgian and French workers place a greater importance on personal independence from the organizations employing them than do workers in many other countries.[40]

Jobs with low prestige usually go to people whose skills are in low demand. In the United States, for example, such occupations as babysitting, delivering newspapers, and carrying groceries traditionally have been largely filled by teenagers, who leave these jobs as they age and gain additional training. In most less-developed countries, these are not transient occupations; rather, they are filled by adults who have very little opportunity to move on to more rewarding positions. (In the United States, there is rising concern that many low-paying menial jobs are becoming more permanent, thus perpetuating income disparities.)

Self-Reliance

Superior-subordinate relationships   In some countries, an autocratic style of management is preferred; in others, a consultative style prevails. Studies on what is known as *power distance* show that in Austria, Israel, New Zealand, and the Scandinavian countries, the consultative style is strongly preferred, but in Malaysia, Mexico, Panama, Guatemala, and Venezuela, the autocratic style is favored. There is a significant correlation between national preference for the autocratic style and the incidence of autocratic political leadership.[41] Clearly, it may be easier for organizations to initiate worker-participation methods in some countries than in others.

Trust   Although trust is difficult to measure, various studies indicate that nationalities differ in the degree to which their members trust other people.[42] The greater the degree of trust, the greater are people's eagerness and ability to establish rapport with others. Where trust is high, both managers and subordinates prefer participative to authoritative decision making; they actually tend to function this way. Certainly, one factor leading to acceptance of new products in the United States is the individuals' trust that they will not be cheated by the manufacturer and that they will be protected by the legal system. Acceptance when dealing with a new company may be similar. People of some nationalities have high levels of trust and get right to the point in a business discussion. Conversely, people of other nationalities may spend more time in preliminary discussion before getting down to business. (Recall the PRI case and how the British salesmen felt their Arab clients were engaging in "idle chit-chat.") This difference, although partially a consequence of cultural formalities, also arises in part from the need members of some societies have to seek more cues before deciding whether to trust others in a business relationship.

Degree of fatalism   If people believe strongly in self-determination, they may be willing to work hard to achieve goals and take responsibility for performance. A belief in fatalism, on the other hand, may prevent people from accepting a basic cause-effect relationship. In this regard, religious differences play a part: Conserva-

There are national variations in
• Preference for autocratic versus consultative management
• Degree of trust among people
• Attitudes of self-determination versus fatalism

tive or fundamentalist Christian, Buddhist, Hindu, and Muslim societies tend to view occurrences as "the will of God." In Pakistan, chemistry texts must read, "H_2 + O, by the grace of God, = water."[43] In such an atmosphere, people plan less for contingencies; for example, they may be reluctant to buy insurance. Studies have shown national differences in degree of fatalism even among managers in fairly developed societies.[44]

Individual versus group   Japan has a much more collectivist culture than the United States does. For example, a U.S. scientist was invited to work in a Japanese laboratory; however, he was treated as an outsider until he realized he had to demonstrate his willingness to subordinate his personal interests to those of the group. He did so by mopping the lab floor for several weeks, after which he was invited to join the experiment.[45]

The importance of the family unit varies among societies. There also are differences in what is conceived to constitute a family. In some countries, the typical household includes only a nuclear family (a husband, wife, and minor children). In most countries in the world, however, the typical household may contain a vertically extended family (several generations) and/or a horizontally extended one (aunts, uncles, and cousins). This difference affects business in several ways. First, material rewards from an individual's work may be less motivating in such societies because these rewards are divided among more people. Second, geographical mobility is reduced because relocation means other members of a family also have to find new jobs. Even where extended families do not live together, mobility may be reduced because people prefer to remain near relatives. Third, purchasing decisions may be more complicated because of the interrelated roles of family members. Fourth, security and social needs may be met more extensively at home than in the workplace.

Communications

Language   Linguists have found that even very primitive societies have complex languages that reflect the environment in which their people live. Because of varying environments, translating one language directly into another can be difficult. For example, people living in the temperate zone of the Northern Hemisphere customarily use the word *summer* to refer to the months of June, July, and August. People in tropical zones may use that term to denote the dry season, which occurs at different times in different countries. Some concepts simply do not translate. For instance, in Spanish there is no word to refer to everyone who works in a business organization. Instead, there is one word, *empleados,* that refers to white-collar workers, and another, *obreros,* that refers to laborers. This distinction reflects the substantial class difference between the groups.

English, French, and Spanish have such widespread acceptance (they are spoken prevalently in forty-four, twenty-seven, and twenty countries, respectively) that native speakers of these languages generally are not very motivated to learn others. Commerce and other cross-border associations can be conducted easily with other

All languages are complex and reflective of environment.

A common language within countries is a unifying force.

nations that share the same language. When a second language is studied, it usually is chosen because of its usefulness in dealing with other countries. English and French traditionally have been chosen because of commercial links developed during colonial periods. France recently has begun subsidizing French language training in Eastern Europe and the former Soviet Union because of the possible advantage to its commerce.[46] In countries that do not share a common language with other countries (for example, Finland and Greece), there is a much greater need for citizens to study other languages in order to function internationally.

English, especially American English, words are being added to languages worldwide, partly because of U.S. technology that develops new products and services for which new words must be coined. When a new product or service enters another language area, it may take on an Anglicized name. For example, Russians call tight denim pants *dzhinsi* (pronounced "jeansy"); the French call a self-service restaurant *le self;* and Lithuanians go to the theater to see *moving pikceris.*[47] An estimated 20,000 English words have entered the Japanese language. However, some countries, such as Finland, have largely developed their own new words rather than using Anglicized versions.

Translating one language into another does not always work as intended. The following are examples of signs in English observed in hotels around the world:

France: "Please leave your values at the desk."
Mexico (to assure guests about the safety of drinking water): "The manager has personally passed all the water served here."
Japan: "You are invited to take advantage of the chambermaid."
Norway: "Ladies are requested not to have children in the bar."
Switzerland: "Because of the impropriety of entertaining guests of the opposite sex in the bedroom, it is suggested that the lobby be used for this purpose."
Greece (at check-in line): "We will execute customers in strict rotation."

Even within the same language there often are differences in usage or meaning. *Corn, maize,* and *graduate studies* in the United Kingdom correspond to *wheat, corn,* and *undergraduate studies,* respectively, in the United States. These are among the approximately 4000 words used differently in these two countries. Although the wrong choice of words usually is just a source of brief embarrassment, a poor translation may have tragic consequences. For example, inaccurate translations have been blamed for structural collapses at construction sites in the Middle East.[48] In contracts, correspondence, negotiations, advertisements, and conversations, words must be chosen carefully.

Silent language includes such things as color associations, sense of appropriate distance, time and status cues, and body language.

Silent language   Of course, formal language is not our only means of communicating. We all exchange messages by a host of nonverbal cues that form a *silent language.*[49] Colors, for example, conjure up meanings that are based on cultural experience. In most Western countries, black is associated with death; white has the same connotation in parts of Asia and purple in Latin America. For products to be successful, their colors and their advertisements must match the consumers' frame of reference.

Another aspect of silent language is the distance between people during conversations. People's sense of appropriate distance is learned and differs among societies. In the United States, for example, the customary distance for a business discussion is five to eight feet; for personal business, it is eighteen inches to three feet.[50] When the distance is closer or farther than is customary, people tend to feel very uneasy. For example, a U.S. manager conducting business discussions in Latin America may be constantly moving backward to avoid the closer conversational distance to which the Latin American official is accustomed. Consequently at the end of the discussion, each party may inexplicably distrust the other.

Perception of time, which influences punctuality, is another unspoken cue that may differ across cultures and create confusion. In the United States, participants usually arrive early for a business appointment. For a dinner at someone's home, guests arrive on time or a few minutes late, and for a cocktail party, they may arrive a bit later. In another country, the concept of punctuality may be radically different. For example, a U.S. businessperson in Latin America may consider it discourteous if a Latin American manager does not keep to the appointed time. Latin Americans may find it equally discourteous if a U.S. businessperson arrives for dinner at the exact time given in the invitation.

Cues concerning a person's relative position may be particularly difficult to perceive. A U.S. businessperson, who tends to place a greater reliance on objects as prestige cues, may underestimate the importance of a foreign counterpart who does not have a large private office with a wood desk and carpeting. A foreigner may react similarly if U.S. counterparts open their own entry doors and mix their own drinks.

Body language (the way in which people walk, touch, and move their bodies) also differs among countries. Few gestures are universal in meaning. For example, the "yes" of a Greek, Turk, or Bulgarian is indicated by a sideways movement of the head that resembles the negative headshake used in the United States and elsewhere in Europe. In some cases, one gesture may have several meanings: The joining of the index finger and thumb to form an O means "okay" in the United States, money in Japan, and "I will kill you" in Tunisia.[51] Former U.S. President George Bush once inadvertently caused a diplomatic uproar in Australia by making an obscene gesture; the sign he made is a victory sign in the United States.

Cues—especially those concerning time and status—are perceived selectively and differ among societies.

Perception and processing   We perceive cues selectively. We may identify what things are by means of any of our senses (sight, smell, touch, sound, or taste) and in various ways within each sense. For example, through vision we can sense color, depth, and shape. The cues people use to perceive things differ among societies. The reason for this is partly physiological; for example, genetic differences in eye pigmentation enable some groups to differentiate colors more finely than others can. It also is partly cultural; for example, a relative richness of vocabulary can allow people to notice and express very subtle differences in color.[52] Differences in vocabulary reflect cultural differences. For example, Arabic has more than 6000 different words for camels, their body parts, and the equipment associated with them.[53]

Regardless of societal differences, once people perceive cues, they process them. Information processing is universal in that all societies categorize, plan, and quantify. In terms of categorization, people bring objects together according to their major shared function: A piece of furniture to sit on is called a chair in English, whether it is large or small, wood or plastic, upholstered or not. The languages of all societies have future and conditional tenses; thus all societies plan. All societies have numbering systems as well. But the specific ways in which societies go about grouping things, dealing with the future, and counting differ substantially.[54] For example, in U.S. telephone directories, the entries are organized by last (family) names; in Iceland, they are organized by first (given) names. Icelandic last names are derived from the father's first name: Jon, the son of Thor, is Jon Thorsson, and his sister's last name is Thorsdottir (daughter of Thor).[55]

Idealists determine principles first. Pragmatists settle small issues first and want specific measurable achievements.

Evaluation of information   In spite of vast differences within countries, there are national norms that govern the degree to which people will try to determine principles before they try to resolve small issues, or vice versa. In other words, people will tend toward either **idealism** or **pragmatism.** From a business standpoint, the differences manifest themselves in a number of ways. The idealist sees the pragmatist as being too interested in trivial details, whereas the pragmatist considers the idealist to be too theoretical. In a society of pragmatists, labor tends to focus on very specific issues, such as a pay increase of a dollar per hour. In a society of idealists, labor tends to make less precise demands and to depend instead on mass action, such as general strikes or support of a particular political party, to publicize its principles.[56]

Reconciliation of International Differences

Cultural Awareness

Problem areas that can hinder cultural awareness are
- Things learned subconsciously
- Stereotypes
- Societal subgroups

Where cultural differences exist, businesspeople must decide whether and to what extent they should adapt home-country practices to the foreign environment. But before making that decision, managers must be aware of what the differences are. As discussed earlier in this chapter, there is much disagreement about such differences. Thus building cultural awareness is not an easy task, and no foolproof method exists for doing so.

In any situation, some people are prone to say the right thing at the right time and others to offend unintentionally. Most people are more aware of differences in things they have learned consciously, such as table manners, than of differences in things they have learned subconsciously, such as methods of problem solving. Nevertheless, there is general agreement that awareness and sensitivity can be improved. This chapter has presented a framework of some of the human cultural factors that require special business adjustments on a country-to-country basis. By paying special attention to these factors, businesspeople can start building cultural awareness.

Reading about and discussing other countries and researching how people regard a specific culture can be very instructive. The opinions presented must be measured carefully. Very often they represent unwarranted stereotypes, an accurate assessment of only a subsegment of the particular country, or a situation that has since undergone change. By getting varied viewpoints, businesspeople can better judge assessments of different cultures. In a given society, managers can also observe the behavior of those people who are well accepted or those with whom they would like to be associated in order to become aware of and learn to emulate acceptable behavior. Samsung, Korea's largest company, is experimenting with a cultural awareness program that involves sending 400 junior employees abroad for a year. In the United States, for example, they don't work; rather, they idle at malls, watch people, and try to develop international tastes. The company is convinced this program will pay off in more astute judgments about what customers want.[57]

There are so many behavioral rules that businesspeople cannot expect to memorize all of them for every country in which business relations might be attempted. Wide variations exist even in form of address; for example, it may be difficult to know whether to use a given name or surname, which of several surnames to use, and whether a wife takes the husband's name.[58] Fortunately, there are up-to-date guidebooks that have been compiled for particular geographical areas, based on the experiences of many successful international managers.[59] A manager also may consult with knowledgeable people at home and abroad, from governmental offices or in the private sector.

A person who moves to a foreign country or who returns home after an extended stay abroad frequently encounters **culture shock.** "This is a generalized trauma one experiences in a new and different culture because of having to learn and cope with a vast array of new cultural cues and expectations, while discovering that your old ones probably do not fit or work."[60] People working in a very different culture may pass through stages. First, like tourists, they are elated with "quaint" differences. Later, they may feel frustrated, depressed, and confused—the culture shock phase—and their usefulness in a foreign assignment may be greatly impaired. Fortunately for most people, culture shock begins to ebb after a month or two as optimism and satisfaction improve.[61]

Grouping Countries

Some countries are relatively similar to one another, usually because they share many attributes that help mold their cultures, such as language, religion, geographical location, ethnicity, and level of economic development. In Map 2.4, countries are grouped by attitudes and values based on data obtained from a large number of

Map 2.4
A Synthesis of Country Clusters

Not all countries have been studied extensively in terms of attitudinal variables that may have different effects on the efficient conduct of business. However, it has been noted that, of the countries that have been studied, some can be grouped together as having similar attitudes and values.

Source: Groupings taken from Simcha Ronen and Oded Shenkar, "Clustering Countries on Attitudinal Dimensions: A Review and Synthesis," *Academy of Management Review*, Vol. 10, No. 3, 1985, p. 449.

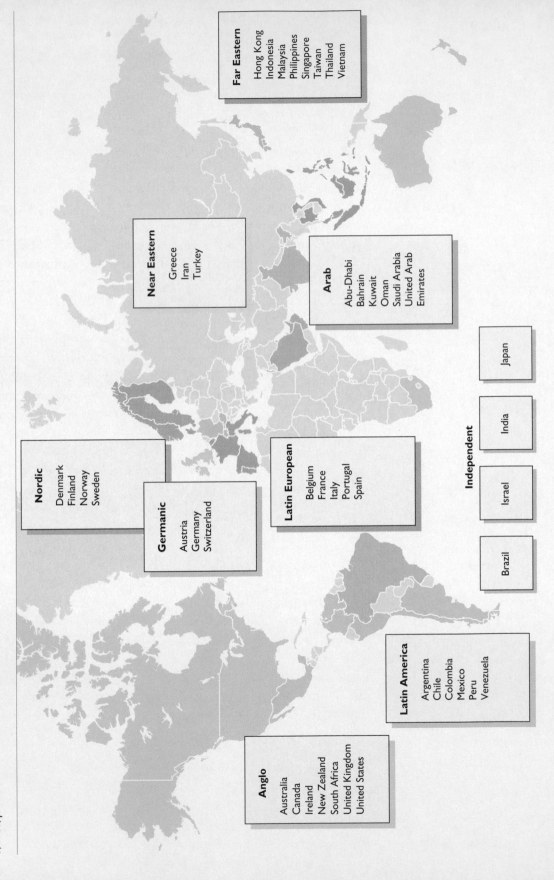

Far Eastern
Hong Kong
Indonesia
Malaysia
Philippines
Singapore
Taiwan
Thailand
Vietnam

Near Eastern
Greece
Iran
Turkey

Arab
Abu-Dhabi
Bahrain
Kuwait
Oman
Saudi Arabia
United Arab
Emirates

Nordic
Denmark
Finland
Norway
Sweden

Germanic
Austria
Germany
Switzerland

Latin European
Belgium
France
Italy
Portugal
Spain

Latin America
Argentina
Chile
Colombia
Mexico
Peru
Venezuela

Anglo
Australia
Canada
Ireland
New Zealand
South Africa
United Kingdom
United States

Independent
Brazil
Israel
India
Japan

cross-cultural studies. A company should expect fewer differences when moving within a cluster (a Peruvian company doing business in Colombia) than when moving from one cluster to another (a Peruvian company doing business in Thailand).[62] Such relationships must be used with caution, however. They deal only with overall similarities and differences among countries, and managers may easily be misled when considering specific business practices to use abroad.

Fitting Needs to the Company Position

Not all companies need to have the same degree of cultural awareness. Nor must a particular company have a consistent degree of awareness during the course of its operations. Since companies usually increase foreign operations over time, they may expand their knowledge of cultural factors in tandem with their expansion of foreign operations. Figure 2.2 illustrates relative degrees of need for cultural awareness. The farther a company moves from domestic business along any of the four axes shown in the figure, the more effort it needs to put into building awareness of cultural differences. Ordinarily, a company will not tackle multiple new functions in many dissimilar countries simultaneously. Thus, for example, a small company that is new to international business may have to gain only a minimal level of cultural awareness, but a highly involved company needs a high level.

On axis A in Fig. 2.2, near the center, a company's foreign operations are focused on achieving a limited functional objective. For example, in a purely market-

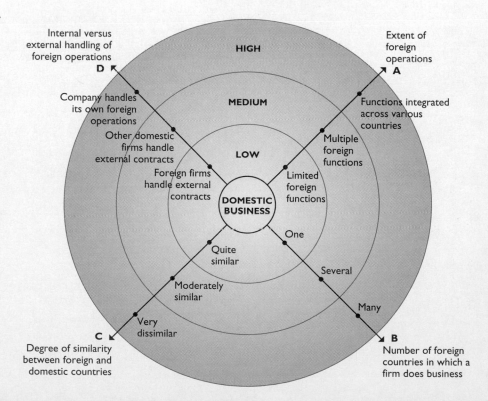

**Figure 2.2
Need for Cultural
Awareness and Extent
of International
Involvement**
The farther out a company moves from the center of the diagram along any of the axes (A, B, C, or D), the more it needs to understand cultural differences. Moving outward on more than one axis at once makes the need for cultural awareness even more pronounced.

seeking operation, such as exporting from the home country, a company must be aware of cultural factors that may influence the marketing program. Consider advertising, which may be affected by the real and ideal physical norms of the target market, the roles of group membership in terms of status and buying decisions, and the perception of different words and images. A company undertaking a purely resource-seeking foreign activity can ignore the effects of cultural variables on advertising but must consider factors that may influence supply, such as methods of managing a foreign workforce. For multifunctional activities, such as producing *and* selling a product in a foreign country, a company must be concerned with a wider array of cultural relationships. At the far extreme of axis A are functions that are integrated across various countries. In these situations, a company must consider the cultural differences between its home country and a foreign country as well as the distinctions among the various foreign countries involved.

Axis B shows that the more countries in which a company is doing business, the more cultural nuances it must consider. For a company at the far extreme of this axis, think of the adjustments a manager from corporate headquarters who visits the company's foreign distributors would undergo. The more countries visited, the more cultural differences would be encountered on the trip and the more predeparture training time would be needed.

Axis C shows the relationship of the similarity between countries and the relative need for cultural awareness. For example, a U.S. firm starting a new business in Australia will find greater cultural similarity and less need for building awareness than if it were starting a new business in Japan.

Axis D indicates that a company may handle foreign operations on its own or contract with another company to handle them. The risk of making operating mistakes because of misunderstanding may effectively be reduced if foreign operations are turned over to another company at home or abroad that is experienced in the foreign country. If the operations are contracted to a company abroad, then some cultural awareness is necessary because of nuances that may influence the relationship between the two companies, such as the means of negotiating an agreement or the ordering of objectives for the operation. As a company gains experience in the foreign country, its managers normally learn to operate efficiently there and may then consider internalizing activities that had previously been contracted to another company.

Polycentrism

Polycentrists are overwhelmed by national differences and risk not introducing workable changes.

In organizations characterized by **polycentrism,** control is decentralized so that "our man in Rio" is free to conduct business in what he thinks is "the Brazilian way." When the concept is taken to extremes, a polycentric individual or organization is "overwhelmed by the differences, real and imaginary, great and small, between its many operating environments."[63] Since most discussions of international business focus on uniquenesses encountered abroad and the attendant problems that companies have experienced, it is understandable that many managers develop a polycentric view. Polycentrism may be, however, an overly cautious response. In reality, it is uncertain how much companies adjust when operating abroad and whether their practices abroad are any more prone to failure than those at home.

A company that is too polycentric may shy away from certain countries or may avoid transferring home-country practices or resources that may, in fact, work well abroad. For example, American Express assembled its worldwide personnel managers for an exchange of views. The complaints from the overseas managers centered on certain corporate directives that they claimed did not fit "their" countries. The impression was created that foreign operations were so unique that each overseas office should develop its own procedures. Further talks, however, revealed that the complaints really focused on only one particular personnel evaluation form. If the company had delegated procedural control, as these overseas managers were suggesting, it would have risked not introducing abroad some of its other standard forms and procedures that would work reasonably well. Furthermore, it would have risked duplicating efforts, which might have been more costly than trying to administer the ill-suited form. The additional discussions also generated for the first time comments from personnel managers in U.S. offices who had received the same corporate instructions. They indicated that they had had just as many problems with the form as their foreign counterparts had. Thus the problem, originally attributed to environmental differences, was seen to be universal.

To compete effectively with local companies, an international company usually must perform some functions in a distinct way. Polycentrism, however, may lead to such extensive delegation or such extensive imitation of proven host-country practices that innovative superiority is lost. Furthermore, control may be diminished as managers within each country foster local rather than worldwide objectives.

Ethnocentrism

Ethnocentrists overlook national differences and
- **Ignore important factors**
- **Believe home-country objectives should prevail**
- **Think change is easily introduced**

Ethnocentrism is the belief that one's own group is superior to others. The term is used in international business to describe a company or individual so imbued with the belief that what worked at home should work abroad that environmental differences are ignored. Ethnocentrism can be categorized into three types:

1. Important factors are overlooked because management has become so accustomed to certain cause-effect relationships in the home country that differences abroad are ignored. To combat this type of ethnocentrism, managers can refer to checklists of human variables in order to assure themselves that all the major factors are at least considered.
2. Management recognizes both the environmental differences and the problems associated with change but is focused on achieving home-country rather than foreign or worldwide objectives. The result may be diminished long-term competitive viability because the company does not perform as well as its competitors and because opposition to its practices develops abroad.

3. Management recognizes differences but assumes that the introduction of change is both necessary and easily achieved. (The problems accompanying this type of ethnocentrism are discussed in the next subsection, "Change Agent or Changed Agent?")

Change Agent or Changed Agent?

Between the extremes of polycentrism and ethnocentrism are hybrid business practices that are neither exactly like the international company's home operations nor exactly like those of the typical host-country company. When the host-country environment is substantially different, the international company must decide whether to persuade people in that country to accept something new (in which case, the company would be acting as a change agent) or to make changes in the company itself.

International companies often use practices that are hybrids of home and foreign norms.

Value system   It is much easier to adapt to things that do not challenge our value systems than to things that do. We usually can be flexible about whether we eat the salad before or after the main course, but we would probably think twice before exposing more of our bodies in public or paying bribes to government officials, actions that would require some moral adjustment if we do not do them in our country. For example, a Spanish textile factory opened in a community of Guatemala, and management tried to install training methods, work hours, and a host of other production "improvements" that were commonplace in more developed areas. Not only did people refuse to work, but soldiers had to protect the factory from the wrath of the community. The management retracted and gave in on those things that were most important to the potential workers. These included a four-hour period between shifts so that males could attend to agricultural duties and females could do household chores and nurse their infants. The workers were willing to work Saturday afternoons in order to compensate for production lost during shift breaks.[64] The important lesson here is that the more a change disrupts basic values, the more the people affected will resist it. When changes do not interfere with deep-seated customs, accommodation is much more likely. In this example, the foreign company, by giving in on matters that were most important to the workers, was able to secure an effective and committed workforce.

The more a change upsets important values, the more resistance it will engender.

Cost-benefit of change   Some adjustments to foreign cultures are costly to undertake; others are inexpensive. Some result in greatly improved performance, such as higher productivity or sales; others may improve performance only marginally. A company must consider the expected cost-benefit relationship of any adjustments it makes abroad. For example, Cummins Engine shuts down its plant in Mexico each December 12 so workers may honor the Virgin of Guadalupe. It throws a celebration in the company cafeteria for employees and their families that includes a priest who offers prayers to the Virgin at an altar.[65] The cost is small in relation to the resultant employee commitment to the company.

The cost of change may exceed the benefit gained.

How companies and businesspeople should react to cultural practices that run counter to their own values is itself a value judgment. On the one hand, *relativism* affirms that ethical truths are relative to the groups holding them; thus intervention would be unethical. On the other hand, *normativism* holds that there are universal standards of behavior that should be upheld; thus nonintervention would be unethical. Respect for other cultures is itself a Western cultural phenomenon that goes back at least as far as St. Ambrose's fourth-century advice: "When in Rome, do as the Romans do."

ETHICAL DILEMMAS

Neither international companies nor their representatives are expected always to adhere to the national norms of a host society. At first glance, lack of any expectation of behavior change would seem to remove ethical questions. However, exposure to certain practices may be so traumatic to foreigners that they cannot perform their duties efficiently. For example, many practices that are considered "wrong" in Western culture are elsewhere either customary or only recently abolished and liable to be reinstated; these practices include slavery, polygamy, concubinage, child marriage, and the burning of widows.[66] Some companies have avoided operating in locales in which such practices occur. Sometimes an MNE pressures a host country to change the "wrong" behaviors. For example, complaints from international business leaders induced Papua New Guinea, which depends on foreign investment, to abandon policies of payback killings.[67]

Although the preceding examples are extreme and rarely, if ever, encountered by most international managers, many other behavioral differences may violate a manager's own ethical code to a lesser degree. It is easier to adjust in these cases, although dilemmas still exist. For example, using gifts and flattery to gain business advantages may seem unethical to some people. But in many countries, particularly in Asia, failure to bring a small gift may not only be considered a breach of etiquette but also be interpreted as indicating a lack of interest in the business relationship. The difference may be explained by the fact that most Westerners are conditioned to express gratitude verbally, and most Asians, particularly Chinese, are conditioned to express appreciation tangibly, such as with gifts.[68] Giving gifts or payments to government officials may be particularly perplexing to Westerners. In many places such gifts or payments are customary to obtain governmental services or contracts. Although this practice is not part of coded regulations and may even be condemned officially, it is so well embedded in local custom and precedent that it has nearly the prescribed enforcement of common law. In Mexico, for example, companies commonly give tips once a month to the mail carrier; otherwise, their mail simply gets lost.[69] The going rate of payment is rather easily ascertained and is usually graduated on the basis of ability to pay. The practice of making payments to government officials is, in effect, a fairly efficient means of taxation in countries that pay civil servants poorly and do not have the means for collecting income taxes. Still, these payments are considered bribes by many Westerners, and the practice frequently is viewed by home-country constituents as so unethical that home-country laws against it are enforced in foreign operations.

In situations such as that of making payments to government officials, companies may incur operational inefficiencies or loss of business if they do not comply with local custom. This brings up the question of whether operational performance should be considered along with potential violation of ethical standards. For example, many people feel it is more acceptable to give payments to government officials when a large, rather than a small, amount of business is at stake and when small, rather than large, payments are expected.

Another thorny ethical question concerns practices by international businesses that do not clash with foreign values directly but that nevertheless may undermine the long-term cultural identity of the host country. Examples of such practices are the use of a company's home-country language and the introduction of products and work methods that effect changes in social relationships. Companies may face unexpected criticism for such practices. They should give consideration to this criticism because of sensitivity to other values and the impact on their own performance. For example, in Finland a strong national identity is expressed through the architecture, and many Finns worry that the inflow of foreign businesses may weaken this identity.[70] In Poland, McDonald's met such unexpected opposition to its architectural plans in Krakow's market square that income was lost because of delays in starting operations.[71]

The Society for Applied Anthropology, whose members advise agencies on instituting change in different cultures, has adopted a code of ethics to protect foreign cultures with which such agencies come into contact. Among the considerations covered by the code is whether a project or planned change actually will benefit the target population. Because the definition of what constitutes a benefit depends on cultural value systems, implementing this code is a challenge. Further, there may be trade-offs to inducing changes. For example, courts in Singapore sentence about 1000 people a year to caning, a punishment that causes permanent scars and is so painful that the recipients typically go into shock. The *New York Times* protested a caning sentence for a U.S. teenager in 1994 on grounds of normativist ethics and of suspicion that his confession was coerced. A Singaporean newspaper countered that this protest was unethical because it might incite harm against Chinese-looking people in the United States.

Companies often lack complete information to guide them in advance of taking action abroad. There are many anecdotes about companies unwittingly violating a foreign country's values, even when they had sought advice from local managers or consultants. For example, consider the area of human rights. In 1948, before most of today's nations were in existence, the United Nations adopted the Universal Declaration of Human Rights. The Declaration has been criticized for having too Western an orientation, which does not consider distinctive values of specific countries or religions. Some provisions that lack universal acceptance include the right to individual ownership of property, the right to governance through universal secret elections, and the implicit statement that the nuclear family is the fundamental unit of society. In fact, not all countries have explicitly declared their concept of human rights. Without such an explicit delineation, there is uncertainty about the accuracy of descriptions of the human rights sentiments of many countries.[72]

Resistance to change may be lower if the number of changes is not too great.

Resistance to too much change   When Sears, Roebuck decided to open its first retail store in Spain, it encountered a major problem with suppliers. Sears tried to deal with its Spanish suppliers in much the same way as it deals with its U.S. ones. Among the many new policies Sears tried to introduce immediately were payments by check, firm delivery dates, standard sizes, no manufacturer's labels, and larger orders. Suppliers either balked or continued to do things their old way and blamed the lapse on forgetfulness.[73] Acceptance by suppliers might have been easier to obtain if Sears had made fewer demands at one time and had phased in other policies more slowly.

People are more willing to implement change when they are involved in the decision to change.

Participation   One way to avoid undue problems that could result from change is to invite the prior participation of stakeholders, such as employees, who might otherwise feel they have no say in their own destinies. By discussing a proposed change with stakeholders in advance, the company may ascertain how strong resistance to the change is, stimulate in the stakeholders a recognition of the need for improvement, and allay their fears of adverse consequences resulting from the change. Managers sometimes think that delegation and participation are unique to highly developed countries, in which people have educational backgrounds that enable them to make substantial contributions. Experience with economic development programs, however, indicates that participation may be extremely important even in the most underdeveloped countries of the world. For example, two of the most successful development programs on record are the Vicos project in Peru and the Etawah project in India.[74] Unlike some other development programs, these projects relied heavily on participation by the people of the communities. This was done despite preferences in both countries for authoritarian leadership.

People are more apt to support change when they expect personal or group rewards.

Reward sharing   Sometimes a proposed change may have no foreseeable benefit for the people whose support is needed to ensure its success. For example, production workers have little incentive to shift to new work practices unless they see some benefits for themselves. In one case, a U.S. company manufacturing electrical appliances in Mexico moved workers easily from radio to black-and-white television production. However, when the company began color television production, the number of product defects inexplicably increased. The company learned that the workers were eager to turn out high-quality black-and-white sets because they or their friends might be consumers. The expensive color sets, however, were so far beyond their means that they had no incentive to be careful in production. The company's solution was to develop a bonus system for quality.

Managers seeking to introduce change should first convince those who can influence others.

Opinion leaders   By discovering the local channels of influence, an international company may locate opinion leaders who can help speed up the acceptance of change. For example, in Ghana, government health workers frequently ask permission from and seek the help of village witch doctors before inoculating people or spraying huts to fight malaria. Doing this achieves the desired result without destroying important social structures. Opinion leaders may emerge in unexpected places, such as among youth in a rapidly changing society. An interesting use of opinion leaders involved a company in Mexico sending low-level workers rather than supervisors to its parent plant in the United States. These workers returned as heros among their peers and were emulated when they demonstrated new work habits.

Companies should time change to occur when resistance is likely to be lower.

Timing   Many good ideas are never applied effectively because they are ill timed. Change brings uncertainty and insecurity. For example, a labor-saving production method will create resistance because people fear losing their jobs, regardless of what management says will happen to employment. However, less resistance will occur if the labor-saving method is introduced when there is a labor shortage rather than a surplus. Attitudes and needs may change slowly or rapidly, so keeping abreast of these changes helps in determining timing.

International companies
• **Change some things abroad**
• **Change themselves when encountering foreign environments**
• **Learn things abroad that they can apply at home**

Learning abroad   The discussion so far has centered on the interaction between an international company and the host society. This interaction is a two-way street. The company not only affects the relationship but is affected by it. The company may change things abroad or alter its activities to fit the foreign environment; it also may learn things that will be useful in its home country or in other operations.

The national practices most likely to be scrutinized for possible use in other countries are those found in the countries that are doing best economically.[75] For example, in the nineteenth century, when Britain was the world economic leader, interest focused on the British cultural character. At the turn of the century, such attention was diverted to Germany and the United States. More recently, it has shifted toward Japan and the newly industrialized countries of Asia. Whether a company is importing or exporting business practices, managers must consider the same factors when questioning whether and how change can be introduced.

C O U N T E R V A I L I N G

F O R C E S

Cultures are becoming more similar in some respects but not in others.

Contact across cultures is becoming more widespread than ever. This should lead to a leveling of cultures, which, on the surface, is occurring. People around the world wear similar clothes and listen to the same recording stars. Similarly, competitors from all over the world often buy the same production equipment, the use of which imposes more uniform operating methods on their workers. This globalization of culture is illustrated by Sweden's entering a calypso (Caribbean) tune in a televised international song contest or the fact that Japanese tourists may hear a Philippine group sing a U.S. song in a hotel in Thailand.[76]

However, below the surface people continue to hold fast to their national differences.[77] In other words, although some tangibles have become more universal, the ways in which people cooperate, attempt to solve problems, and are motivated have tended to remain the same. Religious differences are as strong as ever. And language differences continue to bolster separate ethnic identities. These differences fragment the globe into regions and stymie global standardization of products and operating methods.

One factor that inhibits the leveling of cultures is nationalism. Without perceived cultural differences, people would not see themselves so apart from other nationalities; thus cultural identities are used to mobilize national identity and separateness. This is done by regulating and encouraging the so-called national culture.

Language is regulated in many ways, such as by designating an official language, preventing bilingual education, or requiring "Made in _____" labels printed in the language of the importing country. A religion may be designated a country's official one or made a requisite to holding certain governmental posts or to voting.

Those things that are part of the essential national heritage are perpetuated by marketing them to visitors at home and abroad, as the image of Britain is used in promotions to foreign tourists. They also may be off-limits to foreign ownership. For example, the French government has prevented foreign acquisition of vineyards for reasons based on heritage. Canada prevents foreign ownership in culturally sensitive industries. And, although the game of baseball has spread in popularity from the United States to Japan, when a Japanese group bought the Seattle Mariners team, there was an uproar in the United States—not on economic or national security grounds but on the basis of heritage. Maintaining a national identity may extend beyond heritage. For example, most countries have a national airline that is government subsidized so that there is a national identity associated with the flag painted on the aircraft.

As long as nations seek to perpetuate themselves through the promotion of separate cultural or national identities, companies will be constrained in their global competitive moves.

 **LOOKING TO THE FUTURE**

International companies are likely to continue to face diverse cultural trends in different parts of the world and for different parts of their operations. In some areas, diversity will decrease as small cultural groups are absorbed into more dominant national ones. For example, in recent years such absorption has led to the extinction of many regional languages. Some observers predict that if there is to be rapid educational and technological advancement, cultural change is inevitable.[78] At the same time, there is evidence of emerging subcultures *within* countries because of the influx of people from other countries. Some religious and ethnic groups retain traditional ways rather than assimilate completely. There also is evidence that some groups accept new ideas, products, and technologies more readily than others do.

Three scenarios for future international cultures:
- **Smaller cultures will be absorbed by national and global ones.**
- **Subcultures will transcend national boundaries.**
- **Cultural similarity will be used to mobilize a sense of national identity.**

All of these factors might lead to future problems in defining culture along national lines. Subcultures may transcend borders, and the distinct subcultures within a country may have less in common with each other than they do with subcultures in other countries. Examples of transnational subcultures are the Inuits in Arctic lands and the Kurds of the Middle East. Simultaneously, cultural similarity will continue to be used to mobilize a sense of national identity, for example, religious separatism in Iran, the independence movement among the Croatians, or even "Buy British" campaigns in the United Kingdom. Such activities may retard or even prevent the homogenization of cultures.[79]

An interesting potential scenario is that cultural competition—the promotion of ideas, attitudes, norms, and values—among nations will become more important.[80] With the termination of the Cold War, cultural competition may become a more important means to bring about economic growth as nations try to harness their distinctive human resource capabilities as a means of outperforming other countries.

Summary

- International companies must evaluate their business practices to ensure that national norms in physical and behavioral characteristics are taken into account.

- A given country may encompass very distinct societies. People also may have more in common with similar groups in foreign countries than with different groups in their own country.

- Notable group differences exist in physical traits. Businesspeople must consider the effects that these variables and idealized stereotypes may have on their practices.

- Culture includes norms of behavior based on attitudes, values, and beliefs. Businesspeople agree that there are cross-country differences in these but disagree as to what the differences are.

- Cultural change may take place as a result of choice or imposition; however, isolation from other groups tends to stabilize cultures.

- Group affiliations based on gender, family, age, caste, religion, political preference, professional associations, and ethnic, racial, or national origin often affect a person's degree of access to economic resources, prestige, social relations, and power. An individual's affiliations may determine his or her qualifications and availability for given jobs.

- Some people work far more than is necessary to satisfy their basic needs for food, clothing, and shelter. The relative importance of work is determined largely by the interrelationship of the cultural and economic environments. People are motivated to work for various reasons, including the Protestant ethic, the belief that work will bring success and reward, habit, the need for achievement, and the fulfillment of higher-order needs.

- Different occupations bring different economic, social, and prestige rewards in different countries. People gravitate to jobs for which they perceive they will receive high rewards. The many differences among societies result in varied attitudes toward working for government, business organizations, or oneself.

- National groups differ as to whether they prefer an autocratic or a consultative working relationship, in the degree to which individuals trust others, in attitudes toward self-determination and fate, and in the importance placed on group memberships, especially family-based ones.

- People communicate through both formal language and silent language based on culturally determined cues. Information processing is greatly affected by cultural background. **The failure to perceive subtle distinctions can result in misunderstandings in international dealings.**

- **Companies can build awareness about other cultures. The amount of effort needed to do this depends on the similarity between countries and the type of business operation undertaken.**

- **People working in a foreign environment should be sensitive to the dangers of either excessive polycentrism or excessive ethnocentrism.**

- **In deciding whether to act as a change agent in a host country or to develop new practices to fit the foreign conditions, an international company should consider several factors, including how important the change is to both parties, the cost and benefit to the company of each alternative, the possibility of local participation in decision making, the need to share the rewards of change, the use of opinion leaders, and the timing of change.**

- **There usually is more interest in studying and possibly adopting business practices from countries that are showing the greatest economic success. Cultural factors may determine whether the practices can work successfully in another society.**

- **Although increased contact among people is evoking more widespread cultural similarity among nations, people nevertheless tend to hold onto their basic values. These values are bolstered by efforts to protect cultural separateness and national identity.**

Case
John Higgins[81]

Leonard Prescott, vice president and general manager of Weaver-Yamazaki Pharmaceutical of Japan, believed that John Higgins, his executive assistant, was losing effectiveness in representing the U.S. parent company because of an extraordinary identification with the Japanese culture. (Japan is shown in Map 2.5.)

The parent company, Weaver Pharmaceutical, had extensive international operations and was one of the largest U.S. drug firms. Its competitive position depended heavily on research and development (R&D). Sales activity in Japan started in the early 1930s when Yamazaki Pharmaceutical, a major producer of drugs and chemicals in Japan, began distributing Weaver's products. World War II disrupted sales, but Weaver resumed exporting to Japan in 1948 and subsequently captured a substantial market share. To prepare for increasingly keen competition from Japanese producers, Weaver and Yamazaki established in 1954 a jointly owned and operated manufacturing subsidiary to produce part of Weaver's product line.

Through the combined effort of both parent companies, the subsidiary soon began manufacturing sufficiently broad lines of products to fill the general demands of the Japa-

Map 2.5
Japan

As a nation consisting of islands, Japan's relative historical isolation has led to less cultural borrowing than one finds in most other countries.

Japanese Work Customs

- Low employee turnover
- Advancement based primarily on longevity with the company
- Considerable after-work socializing among employees
- Group work assignments and rewards
- Bottom-up consensus building for decisions

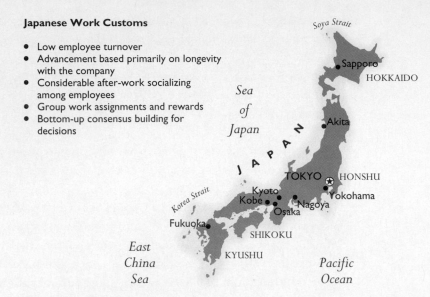

nese market. Imports from the United States were limited to highly specialized items. The company conducted substantial R&D on its own, coordinated through a joint committee representing both Weaver and Yamazaki to avoid unnecessary duplication of efforts. The subsidiary turned out many new products, some of which were marketed successfully in the United States and elsewhere. Weaver's management considered the Japanese operation to be one of its most successful international ventures and felt that the company's future prospects were promising, especially given the steady improvement in Japan's standard of living.

The subsidiary was headed by Shozo Suzuki who, as executive vice president of Yamazaki and president of several other subsidiaries, limited his participation in Weaver-Yamazaki to determining basic policies. Daily operations were managed by Prescott, assisted by Higgins and several Japanese directors. Although several other Americans were assigned to the venture, they were concerned with R&D and held no overall management responsibilities.

Weaver Pharmaceutical had a policy of moving U.S. personnel from one foreign post to another with occasional tours in the home-office international division. Each such assignment generally lasted for three to five years. There were a limited number of expatriates, so company personnel policy was flexible enough to allow an employee to stay in a country for an indefinite time if desired. A few expatriates had stayed in one foreign post for over ten years.

Prescott replaced the former general manager, who had been in Japan for six years. An experienced international businessman who had spent most of his 25-year career at Weaver abroad, he had served in India, the Philippines, and Mexico, with several years in the home-office international division. He was delighted to be challenged with expanding Japanese operations. Two years later, he was pleased with the company's progress and felt a sense of accomplishment in having developed a smoothly functioning organization.

Born in a small Midwestern town, Higgins entered his state university after high school. Midway through college, however, he joined the army. Because he had shown an interest in languages in college, he was able to attend the Army Language School for intensive train-ing in Japanese. Fifteen months later, he was assigned as an interpreter and translator in Tokyo and subsequently took more courses in Japanese language, literature, and history. He made many Japanese friends, fell in love with Japan, and vowed to return there. After five years in the army, Higgins returned to college. Because he wanted to use Japanese as a means rather than an end in itself, he finished his college work in management, graduating with honors, and then joined Weaver. After a year in the company training program, he was assigned to Japan, a year before Prescott's arrival.

Higgins was pleased to return to Japan, not only because of his love for the country but also because of the opportunity to improve the "ugly American" image held abroad. His language ability and interest in Japan enabled him to intermingle with broad segments of the Japanese population. He noted with disdain that U.S. managers tended to impose their value systems, ideals, and thinking patterns on the Japanese, believing that anything from the United States was universally right and applicable.

Under both Prescott and his predecessor, Higgins's responsibilities included trou-bleshooting with major Japanese customers, attending trade meetings, negotiating with government officials, conducting marketing research, and helping with day-to-day adminis-tration. Both general managers sought his advice on many difficult and complex administra-tive problems and found him capable. Prescott became concerned, however, with the notable changes in Higgins's attitude and thinking. He felt that Higgins had absorbed and in-ternalized the Japanese culture to such a degree that he had lost the U.S. point of view. He had "gone native," resulting in a substantial loss of administrative effectiveness.

Prescott mentally listed a few examples to describe what he meant by Higgins's "com-plete emotional involvement" with Japanese culture. The year before, Higgins had married a Japanese woman who had studied in the United States and graduated from a prestigious Japanese university. At that time, Higgins had asked for and received permission to extend his stay in Japan indefinitely. This seemed to Prescott to mark a turning point in Higgins's behavior. Higgins moved to a strictly Japanese neighborhood, relaxed in a kimono at home, used the public bath, and was invited to weddings, neighborhood parties, and even Bud-dhist funerals. Although Weaver had a policy of granting two months' home leave every two years, with paid transportation for the employee and his family, Higgins declined to take trips, preferring instead to visit remote parts of Japan with his wife.

At work, Higgins also had taken on many characteristics of a typical Japanese executive. He spent considerable time listening to the personal problems of his subordinates, main-tained close social ties with many of the men in the company, and had even arranged mar-riages for some of the young employees. Consequently, many employees sought out Higgins in order to register their complaints and demands with management. These includ-ed requests for more liberal fringe benefits, such as more recreational activities and the ac-quisition of rest houses at resort areas. Many employees also complained to Higgins about a new personnel policy, installed by Prescott, that involved a move away from basing pro-motions on seniority and toward basing them on superiors' evaluations of subordinates. The employees asked Higgins to intercede on their behalf. He did so, insisting their de-mands were justified.

Although Prescott believed it was helpful to learn the feelings of middle managers from Higgins, he disliked having to deal with Higgins as an adversary rather than an ally. Prescott became hesitant to ask his assistant's opinion because Higgins invariably raised objections to changes that were contrary to the Japanese norm. Prescott believed that there were dynamic changes occurring in traditional Japanese customs and culture, and he was confident that many Japanese were not tied to existing cultural patterns as rigidly as Higgins seemed to think. This opinion was bolstered by the fact that many Japanese subordinates were more willing than Higgins was to try out new ideas. Prescott also thought that there was no point in a progressive U.S. company's merely copying the local customs. He felt that the company's real contribution to Japanese society was in introducing new ideas and innovations.

Recent incidents had raised some doubts in Prescott's mind as to the soundness of Higgins's judgment, which Prescott had never questioned before. One example involved the dismissal of a manager who in Prescott's opinion lacked initiative, leadership, and general competency. After two years of continued prodding by his superiors, including Prescott, the manager still showed little interest in self-improvement. Both Higgins and the personnel manager objected vigorously to the dismissal because the company had never fired anyone before. They also argued that the employee was loyal and honest and that the company was partially at fault for having kept him on for the last ten years without spotting the incompetency. A few weeks after the dismissal, Prescott accidentally learned that Higgins had interceded on behalf of the fired employee, with the result that Yamazaki Pharmaceutical had taken him on. When confronted with this action, Higgins simply said that he had done what was expected of a superior in any Japanese company.

Prescott believed these incidents suggested a serious problem. Higgins had been an effective and efficient manager whose knowledge of the language and the people had proved invaluable. Prescott knew that Higgins had received several outstanding offers to go with other companies in Japan. And on numerous occasions, Prescott's friends in U.S. companies said they envied him for having a man of Higgins's qualifications as an assistant. However, Prescott felt Higgins would be far more effective if he took a more emotionally detached attitude toward Japan. In Prescott's view, the best international executive was one who retained a belief in the fundamentals of the home point of view while also understanding foreign attitudes. This understanding, of course, should be thorough or even instinctive, but it also should be objective, characterized neither by disdain nor by strong emotional attachment.

Questions

1. How would you contrast Higgins's and Prescott's attitudes toward the implementation of U.S. personnel policies in the Japanese operations?
2. What are the major reasons for the differences in attitude?
3. If you were the Weaver corporate manager responsible for the Japanese operations and the conflict between Higgins and Prescott came to your attention, what would you do? Be sure to first identify some alternatives and then make your recommendations.

Chapter Notes

1. Most data were taken from an interview with Angela Clarke, a protagonist in the case. Additional background information came from Kenneth Friedman, "Learning the Arabs' Silent Language: Interview with Edward T. Hall" [the noted anthropologist quoted in the case], *Bridge,* Spring 1980, pp. 5–6; Samira Harfoush, "Non-Traditional Training for Women in the Arab World," *Bridge,* Winter 1980, pp. 6–7; "British Premier Visits Saudi Arabia," *New York Times,* April 20, 1981, p. A2; Karen Elliott House, "Modern Arabia," *Wall Street Journal,* June 4, 1981, p. 1; James Le Moyne, "Army Women and the Saudis Shock One Another," *New York Times,* September 25, 1990, p. A1; Geraldine Brooks, "Mixed Blessing," *Wall Street Journal,* September 11, 1990, p. A1; Tony Horwitz, "Thought Police," *Wall Street Journal,* May 2, 1991, p. A1+; and Tony Horwitz, "Arabian Backlash," *Wall Street Journal,* January 13, 1993, p. A1.

2. Eve Lee, "Saudis as We, Americans as They," *Bridge,* Winter 1980, pp. 6–7.

3. Hall in Friedman, loc. cit.

4. Lorna V. Williams, "Women in International Business," *American Way,* February 18, 1986, p. 51.

5. June N. P. Francis, "When in Rome? The Effects of Cultural Adaptation on Intercultural Business Negotiations," *Journal of International Business Studies,* Vol. 22, No. 3, 1991, pp. 421–422.

6. Robert J. Foster, "Making National Cultures in the National Ecumene," *Annual Review of Anthropology,* Vol. 20, 1991, pp. 235–260, discusses the concept and ingredients of a national culture.

7. David Binder and Barbara Crossette, "As Ethnic Wars Multiply, U.S. Strives for a Policy," *New York Times,* February 7, 1993, p. A1+.

8. S. Gunders and J. W. M. Whiting, "Mother-Infant Separation and Physical Growth," *Ethnology,* Vol. 7, No. 2, April 1968, pp. 196–206; Thomas K. Landauer and J. W. M. Whiting, "Infantile Stimulation and Adult Stature of Human Males," *American Anthropologist,* Vol. 66, 1964, p. 1008; and R. Boyd and P. J. Richardson, *Culture and the Evolutionary Process* (Chicago: University of Chicago Press, 1985), p. 178.

9. Marshall H. Segall, *Cross-Cultural Psychology: Human Behavior in Global Perspective* (Monterey, Calif.: Brooks/Cole, 1979), p. 143; and Luis R. Gomez-Mejia, "Effect of Occupation on Task Related, Contextual, and Job Involvement Orientation: A Cross-Cultural Perspective," *Academy of Management Journal,* Vol. 27, No. 4, 1984, pp. 706–720.

10. Richard N. Farmer and Barry M. Richman, *Comparative Management and Economic Progress,* rev. ed. (Bloomington, Ind.: Cedarwood, 1970), pp. 20–21, for example, list 15 behavioral variables relating to each of 36 business functions. George P. Murdock listed 72 cultural variables in "The Common Denominator of Culture," in *The Science of Man in the World Crises,* Ralph Linton, ed. (New York: Columbia University Press, 1945), pp. 123–142.

11. Larry Armstrong, "Power, Handling, Comfort—A Solid Sedan," *Business Week,* September 13, 1993, p. 72.

12. Ian Jamieson, *Capitalism and Culture: A Comparative Analysis of British and American Manufacturing Organizations* (Farnborough, England: Gower Press, 1980), Chapter 1.

13. Nancy J. Adler and Jill de Villafranca, "Epistemological Foundations of a Symposium Process: A Framework for Understanding Culturally Diverse Organizations," *International Studies of Management and Organization,* Winter 1982 1983, pp. 7–22.

14. Maureen J. Giovannini and Lynne M. H. Rosansky, *Anthropology and Management Consulting: Forging a New Alliance* (N.P.: National Association for the Practice of Anthropology, Bulletin 9, 1990), pp. 19–27.

15. L. L. Cavalli-Sforza, M. W. Feldman, K. H. Chen, and S. M. Dornbusch, "Theory and Observation in Cultural Transmission," *Science,* Vol. 218, 1982, pp. 19–27.

16. Geert Hofstede, *Cultures and Organizations* (London: McGraw-Hill, 1991), p. 8.

17. William H. Durham, "Applications of Evolutionary Culture Theory," *Annual Review of Anthropology,* Vol. 21, 1992, pp. 331–355.

18. Sally Engle Merry, "Anthropology, Law, and Transnational Processes," *Annual Review of Anthropology,* Vol. 21, 1992, p. 364.

19. Rigoberta Menchú, *I, Rigoberta Menchú: An Indian Woman in Guatemala* (London: Verso, 1984).

20. Vern Terpstra and Kenneth David, *The Cultural Environment of International Business,* 3rd ed. (Cincinnati: South-Western, 1991), p. 93.

21. "Big Mac vs. Sacred Cows," *Business Week,* March 1, 1993, p. 58.

22. Harry C. Triandis, "Dimensions of Cultural Variation as Parameters of Organizational Theories," *International Studies of Management and Organization,* Winter 1982–1983, pp. 143–144.

23. "China's Gender Imbalance," *Wall Street Journal,* June 7, 1990, p. A12.

24. Horwitz, "Arabian Backlash," loc. cit.

25. "U.N. Report: 1,000 Years Needed for Sex Equality," *Herald Times* (Bloomington, Ind.), February 5, 1993, p. A3, reporting on a study by the ILO.

26. Kenneth Dreyfack, "You Don't Have to Be a Giant to Score Big Overseas," *Business Week,* April 13, 1987, p. 63.

27. "The Job Market Opens Up for the 68-Cent Woman," *New York Times,* July 26, 1987, p. E6; Christine L. Williams, *Gender Differences at Work* (Berkeley: University of California Press, 1989); and Urban Lehner and Kathryn Graven, "Quiet Revolution," *Wall Street Journal,* September 6, 1989, p. A1.

28. Triandis, op. cit., p. 146.

29. Max Weber, "The Protestant Ethic and the Spirit of Capitalism," and Kember Fullerton, "Calvinism and Capitalism," both in *Culture and Management,* Ross A. Webber, ed. (Homewood, Ill.: Richard D. Irwin, 1969), pp. 91–112.

30. "Work and Play," *Wall Street Journal,* April 13, 1990, p. A6; James R. Lincoln, "Employee Work Attitudes and Management Practice in the U.S. and Japan: Evidence from a Large Corporate Survey," *California Management Review,* Vol. 32, No. 1, Fall 1989, p. 92; Karen Lowry Miller, "Now Japan Is Admitting It: Work Kills Executives," *Business Week,* August 3, 1992, p. 35; and Yumiko Ono and Jacob M. Schlesinger, "Land of Rising Fun," *Wall Street Journal,* October 2, 1992, p. A1+.

31. Jean J. Boddewyn, "Fitting Socially in Fortress Europe: Understanding, Reaching, and Impressing Europeans," *Business Horizons,* November–December 1992, pp. 35–43.

32. R. Inden, "Tradition Against Itself," *American Ethnologist,* Vol. 13, No. 4, 1986, pp. 762–775; and P. Chatterjee, *Nationalist Thoughts and the Colonial World: A Derivative Discourse* (London: Zed Books, 1986).

33. Triandis, op. cit., pp. 159–160.

34. Everett E. Hagen, *The Theory of Social Change: How Economic Growth Begins* (Homewood, Ill.: Richard D. Irwin, 1962), p. 378.

35. David C. McClelland, *The Achieving Society* (Princeton, N.J.: Van Nostrand, 1961); David C. McClelland, "Business Drives and National Achievement," *Harvard Business Review,* July–August 1962, pp. 92–112; and M. L. Maehr and J. G. Nicholls, "Culture and Achievement Motivations: A Second Look," in *Studies in Cross Cultural Psychology,* Neil Warren, ed. (London: Academic Press, 1980), Vol. 2, Chapter 6.

36. Abraham Maslow, *Motivation and Personality* (New York: Harper, 1954).

37. Hofstede, op. cit., pp. 72–78; and for an earlier comparison among countries, see Mason Haire, Edwin Ghiselli, and Lyman Porter, *Managerial Thinking* (New York: Wiley, 1966), pp. 90–103.

38. Donald Treiman, *Occupational Prestige in Comparative Perspective* (New York: Academic, 1977), especially Appendix C.

39. Robert R. Rehder, *Latin American Management Development and Performance* (Reading, Mass.: Addison-Wesley, 1968), p. 16.

40. Geert Hofstede, "National Cultures in Four Dimensions," *International Studies of Management and Organization,* Spring-Summer 1983, pp. 54–55; Boddewyn, op. cit., p. 36.

41. Hofstede, op. cit., pp. 50–57.

42. See, for example, Geza Peter Lauter, "Sociological-Cultural and Legal Factors Impeding Decentralization of Authority in Developing Countries," *Academy of Management Journal,* September 1969, Vol. 12, No. 3, pp. 367–378; Richard B. Peterson, "Chief Executives' Attitudes: A Cross-Cultural Analysis," *Industrial Relations,* May 1971, Vol. 10, No. 2, pp. 194–210; and G. Katona, B. Strumpel, and E. Zahn, "The Sociocultural Environment," in *International Marketing Strategy,* H. B. Thorelli, ed. (Middlesex, England: Penguin, 1973).

43. Mary Williams Walsh, "Heaven Only Knows What Comes Next in Pakistani Science," *Wall Street Journal,* September 13, 1988, p. 1.

44. L. L. Cummings, D. L. Harnett, and D. J. Stevens, "Risk, Fate, Conciliation and Trust: An International Study of Attitudinal Differences among Executives," *Academy of Management Journal,* September 1971, p. 294, found differences among the United States, Greece, Spain, Central Europe, and Scandinavia.

45. Book review of Patricia Gercik, *On the Track with the Japanese* (Kodansha, 1992), by James B. Treece, *Business Week,* December 28, 1992, p. 20.

46. "Language Lessons," *Wall Street Journal,* August 9, 1990, p. A6.

47. Vivian Ducat, "American Spoken Here—and Everywhere," *Travel & Leisure,* Vol. 16, No. 10, October 1986, pp. 168–169; Bill Bryson, *The Mother Tongue: English and How It Got That Way* (New York: Morrow, 1990).

48. Christian Hill, "Language for Profit," *Wall Street Journal,* January 13, 1977, p. 34.

49. This term was first used by Edward T. Hall, "The Silent Language in Overseas Business," *Harvard Business Review,* May–June 1960, and included five variables (time, space, things, friendships, and agreements).

50. Ibid.

51. Emmanuelle Ferrieux, "Hidden Messages," *World Press Review,* July 1989, p. 39.

52. For a survey of major research contributions, see Harry C. Triandis, "Reflections on Trends in Cross-Cultural Research," *Journal of Cross-Cultural Psychology,* March 1980, pp. 46–48.

53. Benjamin Lee Whorf, *Language, Thought and Reality* (New York: Wiley, 1956), p. 13.

54. Segall, op. cit., pp. 96–99.

55. Tony Horwitz, "Iceland Pushes Back English Invasion in War of the Words," *Wall Street Journal,* July 25, 1990, p. A8.

56. E. Glenn, *Man and Mankind: Conflict and Communication Between Cultures* (Norwood, N.J.: Ablex, 1981).

57. "Sensitivity Kick," *Wall Street Journal,* December 30, 1992, p. A1.

58. Peter Gosling, "Culture and Commerce: What's in a Name?" *Southeast Asia Business,* No. 6, Summer 1985, pp. 30–38.

59. A list of books appears in Katherine Glover, "Do's & Taboos," *Business America,* August 13, 1990, p. 5. See also Roger Axtell, *Do's and Taboos Around the World* (New York: John Wiley, 1992).

60. Philip R. Harris and Robert T. Moran, *Managing Cultural Differences* (Houston: Gulf, 1979), p. 88, quoting Kalervo Oberg.

61. Adrian Furnham and Stephen Bochner, *Culture Shock* (London: Methuen, 1986), p. 234.

62. Ben L. Kedia and Rabi S. Bhagat, "Cultural Constraints on Transfer of Technology Across Nations: Implications for Research in International and Comparative Management," *Academy of Management Review,* Vol. 13, No. 4, October 1988, pp. 559–571.

63. Hans B. Thorelli, "The Multi-National Corporation as a Change Agent," *The Southern Journal of Business,* July 1966, p. 5.

64. Manning Nash, "The Interplay of Culture and Management in a Guatemalan Textile Plant," *Culture and Management,* Ross A. Webber, ed., pp. 317–324.

65. Marjorie Miller, "A Clash of Corporate Cultures," *Los Angeles Times,* August 15, 1992, p. A1.

66. Bernard Lewis, "Western Culture Must Go," *Wall Street Journal,* May 2, 1988, p. 18.

67. Merry, op. cit., pp. 366–367.

68. Boye de Mente, *Chinese Etiquette and Ethics in Business* (Lincolnwood, Ill.: NTC, 1989).

69. William Stockton, "Bribes Are Called a Way of Life in Mexico," *New York Times,* October 25, 1986, p. 3.

70. Pirkko Lammi, "My Vision of Business in Europe," in *Business Ethics in a New Europe,* Jack Mahoney and Elizabeth Vallance, eds. (Dordrecht, the Netherlands: Kluwer Academic, 1992), pp. 11–12.

71. "Golden Arches Raise Eyebrows in Poland," *The State* (Columbia, S.C.), September 10, 1993, p. 5A.

72. Alison Dundes Renteln, "The Concept of Human Rights," *Anthropos,* Vol. 83, 1988, pp. 343–364.

73. "Problems of Opening a Retail Store in Spain," *Wall Street Journal,* March 27, 1967, p. 1.

74. Conrad M. Arensberg and Arthur H. Niehoff, *Introducing Social Change: A Manual for Americans Overseas* (Chicago: Aldine, 1964), pp. 123–125.

75. Ian Jamieson, "The Concept of Culture and Its Relevance for an Analysis of Business Enterprise in Different Societies," *International Study of Management and Organization,* Winter 1982, pp. 71–72.

76. Foster, op. cit., p. 236.

77. J. D. Child, "Culture, Contingency and Capitalism in the Cross-National Study of Organizations," in *Research in Organizational Behavior,* L. L. Cummings and B. M. Staw, eds. (Greenwich, Conn.: JAI, 1981), Vol. III, pp. 303–356; Andre Laurent, "The Cross-Cultural Puzzle of International Human Resource Management," *Human Resource Management,* Vol. 25, No. 1, pp. 91–102.

78. Peter Blunt, "Cultural Consequences for Organization Change in a Southeast Asian State: Brunei," *Academy of Management Executive,* Vol. 2, No. 3, Fall 1988, p. 239.

79. Lourdes Arizpe, "On Cultural and Social Sustainability," *Development,* Vol. 1, 1989, pp. 5–10.

80. J. Ørstrøm Møller, "The Competitiveness of U.S. Industry: A View from the Outside," *Business Horizons,* November–December 1991, pp. 27–34.

81. The case is a condensed version of the original by M. Y. Yoshino. Reprinted with permission of Stanford University Graduate School of Business, ©1963 by the Board of Trustees of the Leland Stanford Junior University.

Chapter 3

The Political and Legal Environments Facing Business

Half the world knows not how the other half lives.

—English Proverb

Objectives

- To discuss the different functions that political systems perform

- To compare democratic and totalitarian political regimes and discuss how they can influence managerial decisions

- To describe how management can formulate and implement strategies to deal with the political environment

- To study the different types of legal systems and the legal relationships that exist between countries

- To examine the major legal issues in international business

Case
The Taipan's
Dilemma[1]

Peter Such, the chairman, or *taipan,* of Swire Pacific Ltd. is faced with important and pressing strategic decisions. As taipan of one of the three major *hongs,* or family-controlled foreign trading houses, that figure prominently in Hong Kong business circles, Such must decide what to do when Hong Kong reverts to China's control in 1997.

The three hongs began as British-owned, nineteenth-century traders to China. Although all have begun diversifying out of Hong Kong, they, and Swire in particular, still will depend greatly on the economy of Hong Kong and thus will need to reach some sort of accommodation with China.

As shown in Map 3.1, Hong Kong is a British Crown Colony that comprises Hong Kong Island, Kowloon Peninsula, and the New Territories. It is one of the world's major seaports. Why will Hong Kong's revised status be a problem to the hongs? The answer lies partly in the history of the region and partly in what it is today. Until the mid-seventeenth century, China sought to minimize its contact with foreigners by restricting foreign trade to the port at Macao, 75 miles south of Canton. These restrictions resulted from a long history of mutual distrust and misunderstanding between the Chinese and foreigners. In the late eighteenth century, the Chinese were persuaded to open up more of their ports, a decision they soon regretted. By the middle of the nineteenth century, they again sought to restrict foreign trade to Canton. Under one of the new regulations, Western traders had to deal exclusively with a group of Chinese merchants called "officially authorised merchants," who were charged with fixing prices, regulating trade volume, and policing the behavior of the Westerners.

Despite the history of restrictions, trade between China and the West flourished. And trade between Britain and China became particularly important: The British wanted Chinese tea; the Chinese wanted the opium British traders shipped in from India. Although opium was officially illegal in China, its use was widespread: By the 1830s an estimated 4–12 million Chinese were addicted to the drug. The Chinese government sought to halt its importation; not surprisingly, the British protested. The eventual results were three Opium Wars between the two countries within a period of twenty-one years (1839–1860). In all three, China emerged the loser. The First Opium War netted for the British permanent ownership of the island of Hong Kong and its harbor (among other concessions). From the Third Opium War, they gained Kowloon. The New Territories, which comprise 90 percent of the land area of Hong Kong, came under British control in 1898 under the terms of a 99-year lease that will expire in 1997.

In the middle of the nineteenth century, Hong Kong was barren, virtually uninhabited, and disease-ridden. Also one of the best harbors in the world, it served two purposes for the British: It was a secure base from which traders could manage their operations and a good deep-water port that could serve as a naval base. Its acquisition was largely due to the lobbying efforts of Jardine, Matheson and Company, the oldest of the Hong Kong hongs, whose owner, William Jardine, persuaded the British government that a permanent base on the China coast was needed.

Until recently, the issue of the expiration of the 99-year lease obtained in 1898 was largely ignored. However, real estate in Hong Kong tends to be leased on a 15-year basis.

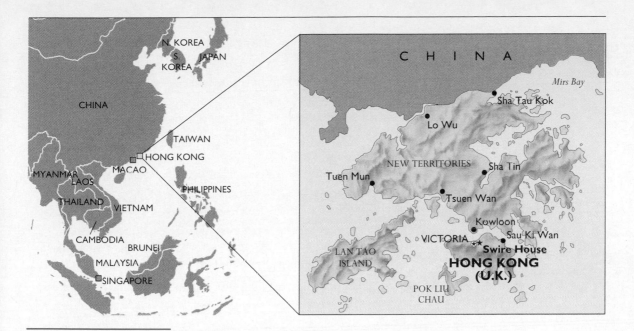

Map 3.1
Hong Kong
Hong Kong, situated at the mouth of the Pearl River, is a free-market economy surrounded by (and becoming more closely integrated with) China.

In 1982, therefore, nervousness on the part of the Hong Kong business community led then British Prime Minister Margaret Thatcher to initiate talks with the Chinese government to determine the island's status beginning in 1997. Currently, Hong Kong, as a British colony, is presided over by a governor who is appointed by the Queen of England typically for a term of five years. The governor holds all final executive and administrative powers, is advised by the Executive Council, which is appointed by the governor, and legislates through the Legislative Council, which is largely appointed by the governor. The British Parliament acts as the democratic check against potential autocratic rule by the governor and local bureaucracy.

After prolonged negotiations, in 1984 the British and Chinese signed the Sino-British Joint Declaration on the future of Hong Kong. Under the agreement, China will assume control over Hong Kong on July 1, 1997, at which time Hong Kong will become a Special Administrative Region of China. The agreement also calls for "one country, two systems." This provision provides that Hong Kong and China—together, "one country"—will have two governmental systems. China will continue its current economic structure, which involves heavy governmental control (a system that is, however, undergoing significant transition, as will be discussed in Chapter 4); Hong Kong will retain its separate political and economic status for fifty years and continue to enjoy the free-wheeling, free-market economy that historically has flourished so successfully there. The Joint Declaration along with the Basic Law, the post-1997 Hong Kong constitution developed by China, provides a sense of direction for economic and political change. Together, they call for Hong Kong's courts to have a judicial system separate from China's. This is a vital concern if Hong Kong is to remain an important international financial and commercial center; it means law will be based on British law, which, unlike China's, supports a free-market system.

Although Hong Kong's political and economic future after 1997 seemed settled by the 1984 declaration, instability and uncertainty once again arose in 1989 when Chinese citizens demonstrated for more democratic freedoms at Tiananmen Square in Beijing. Because of those demonstrations and the resultant killing of Chinese citizens, the extent to which China would allow Hong Kong to continue with its relatively democratic system became questionable. This uncertainty was enhanced in 1991 when Hong Kong's first free elections were held. The Basic Law provides for the direct election of eighteen of the sixty members of the Legislative Council. The 1991 election produced some surprising results. In that election, sixteen of the eighteen winners were directly or indirectly supported by the United Democratic party, a fiercely pro-democracy Hong Kong party, and no candidate backed by China was voted in. Then, in 1992, the new, and possibly last, governor of Hong Kong, Chris Patten, proposed that further steps be taken to strengthen democracy in Hong Kong. Although his proposals were within the bounds of the Basic Law, the Chinese felt they went too far and would not consider them.

Given the political instability in Hong Kong, why don't companies just leave? What is the attraction? One reason is an economic incentive. Hong Kong, along with other Asian countries such as Singapore, Taiwan, and South Korea, is a newly industrializing country (NIC) and has experienced significant growth in the last several decades. Today it is one of Asia's financial and manufacturing centers and has one of the world's largest ports. It serves as the **entrepôt,** or export/import intermediary, for China. As the largest trader with and investor in China, it is that country's window on the world. It basically has no agricultural industry or raw materials and so must import most of its food, water, and materials; it therefore has developed a strong export strategy. An estimated 75 percent of Hong Kong's manufactured goods are made for export. Key exports include textiles, plastics, electronics, watches, and clocks. Hong Kong's major market for finished goods is the United States, and its major market for parts and semimanufactured goods is China. Because of low wages in China, Hong Kong companies have most of their labor-intensive work done there rather than in Hong Kong. Hong Kong managers are ideally qualified to work with the Chinese because they understand the Chinese culture better than Westerners do.

Another important reason for companies to stay in Hong Kong is the role of its government. Hong Kong's governmental policy has been termed "positive noninterventionist." For example, wages are set by the market rather than by the government, and taxes and subsidies play no part in Hong Kong business. Governmental ownership of goods and services is limited to the police, the postal services, the water supply, and the airport. (The government does own the land in Hong Kong, which it sells through public auction. Its conservative land policies have kept the price of land in Hong Kong very high.)

Political and economic uncertainty may leave local residents uncomfortable, but foreigners—led by the Japanese—continue to invest huge sums in Hong Kong. Foreign investors, too, are nervous about the region's future. However, they are betting that the Chinese government will not do anything to interfere with the important role Hong Kong plays in China's economy: An estimated 75 percent of foreign investment in China and 40 percent of China's foreign-exchange earnings are generated by Hong Kong.

In addition to political uncertainty, Hong Kong faces other threats that could influence a company's decision to remain there, including increasing trade restrictions in foreign markets and increasing competition from other Asian countries. Given these challenges, Hong Kong is likely to undergo a political and economic transformation in the coming decades.

What does all of this mean for the hongs? All are faced with deciding how much they should diversify out of Hong Kong by 1997. Jardine Matheson made the first major outward move when it shifted its registered office to Bermuda in 1984, even though its operating divisions still are located primarily in Hong Kong.

Another of the three major hongs, Hutchison Whampoa, appears to be holding firm in Hong Kong while looking for investment opportunities in other countries, such as the United States and Canada. As a former chairman of the company noted, "My own view is that economic pluses outweigh political minuses. One tended to assume [in the early 1980s] that politics always came before economics in Communist countries, and maybe they still do. However, there's a great deal of evidence to show that Communism at the end of the day has also to produce an economic result."

For Swire, it's a different story. The hong, started in 1816 in Liverpool, England, began business in China under the name *Taikoo,* which means "great and ancient." Many of its products still carry the Taikoo name. Although Swire has operations worldwide, its major ones are in Hong Kong. Further, 80 percent of its assets are in Hong Kong, making it the colony's largest public company. Of Swire's 1991 revenues of HK$ 33.6 billion, 67.6 percent were from aviation, primarily Cathay Pacific Airways, which is 51 percent owned by Swire; 15.2 percent were from a segment Swire calls Industries, which includes Coca-Cola beverages, Taikoo Sugar, and Swire Engineering; 13.9 percent were from trading activities; and the remainder were from various activities, including insurance, offshore oil and shipping services, and property trading and investment. Because a large portion of its earnings come from Cathay Pacific and from properties located in Hong Kong, leaving would be difficult for Swire. Clearly, it is in the taipan's best interests to work with rather than to avoid China.

Introduction

As noted in the opening case, MNEs must operate in countries that are characterized by different political, legal, and economic frameworks, diverse levels of economic development, and a variety of economic conditions. To each of an infinite number of situations, the MNE brings a frame of reference based on its domestic experience as well as its lessons from foreign settings. For the company to be successful, its management must carefully analyze the interaction between corporate policies and the political, legal, and economic environments in order to maximize efficiency. This chapter discusses the political and legal systems that managers are likely to encounter and the factors they need to consider as they make strategic decisions about operations in different countries.

**Figure 3.1
Market and Nonmarket Environments for Business**
Managers need to develop strategies to cope with both market and nonmarket environments. The market environment involves the interaction between households (or individuals) and companies to allocate resources. The nonmarket, or political, environment involves public institutions, such as government agencies, and nonpublic institutions, such as environmental interest groups.

Source: From David P. Baron, *Business and Its Environment,* ©1993, Englewood Cliffs, N.J.: Prentice-Hall, p. 7. Reprinted with permission.

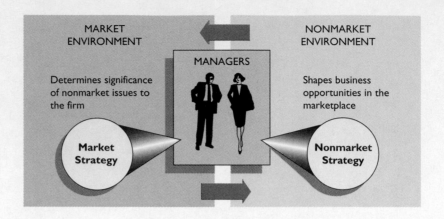

Public institutions: the government, governmental agencies, and government-owned businesses

Nonpublic institutions: special interest groups, such as environmentalists

The Political Environment

Figure 1.2 identified the environments that influence managerial decisions. The political environments in a company's home country and the countries in which it does business are important external influences on management.

More specifically, Fig. 3.1 illustrates the interaction between the market and nonmarket environments in a country. The market environment involves the interactions between households (or individuals) and companies to allocate resources, free from governmental ownership or control. The nonmarket, or political, environment refers to public institutions (such as the government, government agencies, and government-owned businesses) and nonpublic institutions (such as environmental and other special interest groups that represent specific individuals or groups).[2] Managers must establish corporate strategies for both the market and nonmarket environments, individually and combined. For example, the British-Chinese negotiations over the future of Hong Kong—a political issue—caused Jardine Matheson to move its corporate headquarters to Bermuda—a market strategy.

The Political System and Its Functions

The role of the political system is to integrate the society.

The political system is influenced by forces from within and outside a country.

The political system is designed to integrate the parts of a society into a viable, functioning unit. A country's political system has an enormous impact on how business is conducted domestically and/or internationally. It influences and is influenced by various factors. In Hong Kong, for example, political change is influenced by China because it takes control of Hong Kong in 1997; by Britain because the British government still appoints Hong Kong's governor and has a strong vested interest in its future; and by the United States because of the strong trading relationship between it and Hong Kong. The political system also is influenced by a variety

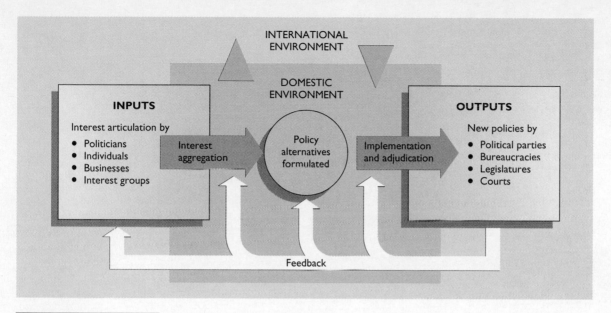

Figure 3.2
The Political System and Its Functions
Policy alternatives are formulated from the inputs of different foreign and domestic entities, and then implemented. Once implemented, the outputs of these policies are tested in the marketplace and revised as necessary.

Source: From *Comparative Politics Today: A World View,* 3rd Ed., by Gabriel A. Almond and G. Bingham Powell, Jr. Copyright ©1984 Gabriel A. Almond and G. Bingham Powell, Jr. Reprinted by permission of Harper Collins College Publishers.

Political process functions are
• Interest articulation
• Interest aggregation
• Policy making
• Policy implementation and adjudication

Interest aggregation is the collection of interests in the political system.

of internal factors, such as the nature of the population, the size and influence of corporations and governmental bureaucracies, and the strength of the politicians. For example, important factors influencing the political process in Hong Kong are the general population, the large companies that are investing and doing business there, and emerging politicians, including those who are members of the pro-democracy United Democratic Party.

Figure 3.2 illustrates the interaction of the process functions, inputs, and outputs in any political environment. The process functions in the figure are interest articulation and aggregation, formulation of policy alternatives, and implementation and adjudication of policies. Politicians, individuals, businesses, and interest groups provide inputs through the process of interest articulation, that is, making their desires known. These inputs then are aggregated through a process called interest aggregation so that policy alternatives can be formulated that stand a chance of making it through the political process. The alternatives are debated, and policies are made, usually by political structures such as political parties, governmental bureaucracies, state and federal legislatures, and courts. Next the policies are implemented, and any controversial features of them are adjudicated through the court process to determine if they are legal.[3]

These process functions occur regardless of whether a country is democratic. This is true, for example, of the United Kingdom and North Korea, which differ in this regard only in degree. There is much wider interest articulation in the United Kingdom than in North Korea, and the steps of interest aggregation, policy making, and implementation and adjudication involve more checks and balances in the former country than in the latter.

Basic Political Ideologies

An ideology is the systematic and integrated body of constructs, theories, and aims that constitutes a sociopolitical program.

Pluralistic societies are those in which a variety of ideologies coexist.

Ethnic differences are tearing apart many countries in Eastern Europe and the former Soviet Union.

A political ideology is the systematic and integrated body of constructs (complex ideas), theories, and aims that constitutes a sociopolitical program. Most modern societies are pluralistic from a political point of view; that is, different ideologies coexist within the society because there is no official ideology accepted by everyone. Pluralism is an outgrowth of the fact that groups within countries often differ significantly from each other in language (for example, the former Yugoslavia, with its many different languages and alphabets), ethnic background (for example, South Africa), or religion (for example, Northern Ireland). As noted in Chapter 2, these and other cultural dimensions strongly influence the political system.

The ultimate test of any political system is its ability to hold a society together despite pressures from different ideologies tending to split it apart. The more widely different and strongly held the articulated ideas are, the more difficult it is to aggregate them and formulate policies. Ideologies already have broken apart many countries in the 1990s, including the former Yugoslavia, the former Czechoslovakia, and the former Soviet Union.

The other side of the coin is the role ideologies, language, religion, and ethnic background play in bringing countries together. In one example involving violence, Serbs in the former Yugoslavia initiated conflict in that region and brought together Serbs from different countries in an attempt to form a new country, a "Greater Serbia." Also, one reason China wants Hong Kong back is because of ethnic Chinese ties.

An example of how such pressures affect national boundaries over time can be seen in Maps 3.2 through 3.5. The Austro-Hungarian Empire (see Map 3.2) was broken up (somewhat arbitrarily) after World War I, into Austria, Czechoslovakia, Hungary, Romania, and Yugoslavia (Map 3.3). With the advent of communist rule after World War II countries often were formed from different ethnic groups held together by totalitarian rule rather than by any particular logic. Yugoslavia, for example, comprised peoples that were ethnically and religiously very different from each other (Roman Catholic Croats, Greek Orthodox Serbs, and Muslim Bosnians). Further, the Croats and Serbs were on opposite sides during World War II, and Croats were accused of murdering thousands of Serbs. (Some have termed the bloodshed by Serbs in recent years "a thousand years of payback" for earlier Croat atrocities.) As shown in Map 3.5, the recent break-up of the communist bloc resulted in the disintegration of countries due to the loss of totalitarian control and to ethnic and other differences. Understanding historical roots is essential to understanding the political environment.

A Political Spectrum

The two extremes on the political spectrum are democracy and totalitarianism.

Political ideologies are many and varied, so it is difficult to fit them neatly into a continuum that represents degrees of citizen participation in decision making. Figure 3.3 presents a general schematic of the various forms of government. The two extremes in a theoretical sense are democracy and totalitarianism. From these two,

Map 3.2
Europe on the Eve of World War I
The German, Russian, Ottoman, and Austro-Hungarian empires dominate the continent.

Source: From *The Boston Globe Magazine*, 2/21/93. Reprinted courtesy of The Boston Globe.

various degrees of participation have evolved. Change continues to occur rapidly around the world, and many authoritarian regimes are being replaced by different types of democracies.

Democracy

Democratic systems involve wide participation by citizens in the decision-making process.

In representative democracy, majority rule is achieved through periodic elections.

The ideology of pure democracy derives from the ancient Greeks, who believed that citizens should be directly involved in the decision-making process. According to the ideal, *all* citizens should be equal politically and legally, should enjoy widespread freedoms, and should actively participate in the political process. In reality, the complexity of society increases as the population increases, and so full participation becomes impossible. Consequently, most modern democratic countries actually practice various forms of representative democracy, in which citizens elect representatives to make decisions rather than voting on every specific issue.

Contemporary democratic political systems share the following features:

1. Freedom of opinion, expression, and press, and freedom to organize
2. Elections in which voters decide who is to represent them
3. Limited terms for elected officials
4. An independent and fair court system with high regard for individual rights and property
5. A relatively nonpolitical bureaucracy and defense infrastructure
6. A relative accessibility to the decision-making process[4]

Map 3.3
Europe after World War I

The empires have been broken up. Finland, Ukraine, and the Baltics are freed; Romania is enlarged; Poland, Czechoslovakia, Yugoslavia, and Turkey are created.

Source: From *The Boston Globe Magazine,* 2/21/93. Reprinted courtesy of The Boston Globe.

Factors for evaluating freedom are
- **Political rights**
- **Civil liberties**

Political rights include
- **Fair and competitive elections**
- **Power for elected representatives**
- **Ability to organize**
- **Safeguards on rights of minorities**

Civil liberties include
- **Freedom of the press**
- **Equal rights under the law**
- **Personal social freedoms**
- **Freedom from governmental indifference and corruption**

A key element of democracy is freedom in the areas of political rights and civil liberties. Each year, a list is published of countries ranked according to the degree to which these freedoms exist. The major indicators for political rights are

- The degree to which fair and competitive elections occur
- The ability of voters to endow their elected representatives with real power
- The ability of people to organize into political parties or other competitive political groupings of their choice
- The existence of safeguards on the rights of minorities

The major indicators for civil liberties are

- The existence of freedom of the press
- Equality under the law for all individuals
- The extent of personal social freedoms
- The degree of freedom from extreme governmental indifference or corruption

As noted in Table 3.1, countries are classified as "free" (76 countries), "partly free" (65 countries), and "not free" (42 countries). "Not free" countries include both communist and noncommunist totalitarian states. Since 1980, the trend has been away from "not free" countries toward "free" countries.[5]

Map 3.4
Europe after World War II
Germany is divided. Eastern European nations come under Soviet control.

Source: From *The Boston Globe Magazine,* 2/21/93. Reprinted courtesy of The Boston Globe.

Although pure democracy does not exist in modern countries, various forms of representative government exist in which citizens vote for individuals to represent them and to make collective decisions. Voting eligibility may be based on gender, as in Switzerland until recently; religious affiliation, as in Israel; the attainment of a certain minimum age, as in the United States; or racial classifications, as in South Africa until recently. In some democracies, such as the United States, voting is optional; in others, such as Peru, it is mandatory.

In a parliamentary system, the majority party forms the government.

One form of democracy is parliamentary government, an excellent example of which is found in the United Kingdom. The United Kingdom is divided into geographical districts, and a representative is elected to represent each district in the House of Commons. General elections must be held at least every five years. After a general election, the monarch asks the leader of the party that has the majority of seats in the House of Commons to form a government. The party with the second-largest number of seats becomes the opposition. Other parties can align with either the majority party or the opposition party. The members of each party select the person who leads that party. The leader of the majority party becomes the prime minister and selects a cabinet.[6]

France has a presidential form of government with a separately elected parliament.

The French form of parliamentary government involves the direct election of a president who is in power for seven years and selects a premier and, upon the recommendation of the premier, a Council of Ministers. A parliament composed of a

**Map 3.5
Europe after
Communism**
Germany reunites, and the
Soviet Union, Yugoslavia,
and Czechoslovakia break
up, creating twenty-two
countries.

Source: From *The Boston Globe
Magazine*, 2/21/93. Reprinted
courtesy of The Boston Globe.

In a coalition parliamentary
government, minority par-
ties form a coalition to gain
majority control and the
power to form the
government.

Mexico has a single-domi-
nant-party democracy.

National Assembly elected by the people and a Senate selected by the National Assembly is responsible for legislation.[7] Despite having a parliament, France has a system of government more like that of the United States than that of the United Kingdom. For example, like the U.S. system, the French system separates the executive and legislative branches.

In most democratic countries, multiple political parties may participate in the election process. Many democracies have only a few dominant parties, so it usually is not difficult for them to form a government. The exceptions to this are Italy and Israel, in which there are so many political parties that the government in power is usually a minority government formed from a coalition of several minority parties. In these countries, whenever a vote of no confidence is taken, a new coalition must be formed before a new government can be formed. In some democracies, a single dominant party controls political power, for example, in Mexico. That country has been ruled by one political party, the Institutional Revolutionary Party (PRI), since it acquired its independence from Spain. Its members are Mexico's elite, who are the most educated and the most experienced in government. The PRI does not have a particularly ideological thrust; it is mainly interested in keeping the country together.

Figure 3.3
The Political Spectrum
Although democratic and totalitarian governments are extremes, there are variations to each approach. For example, democratic governments range from radical on one side (advocates of political reform) to reactionary (advocates of a return to past conditions). The majority of democratic governments, however, lie somewhere in between.

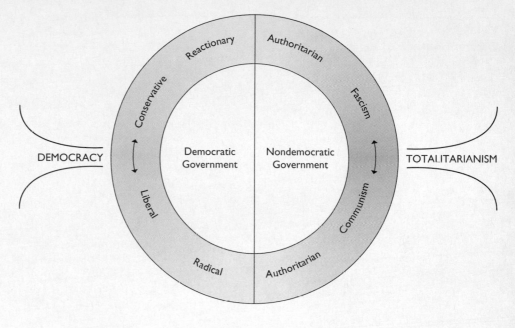

Hong Kong is a quasi-democracy that is classified as a partly free, related territory.

Hong Kong is an interesting example of a quasi-democracy. Freedom House classifies Hong Kong as a partly free, related territory rather than as a free country. The British Parliament has served as the democratic check against any governor, who is selected by the Queen, having absolute power. However, the Chinese residents of Hong Kong have little real democratic power because although freedom of expression is guaranteed, freedom to select the government doesn't exist. As mentioned in the opening case, Hong Kong's governor, the Legislative Council, and the totalitarian government of China are debating what Hong Kong's government will be like beginning in 1997.

Democracies differ not only in the amount of citizen participation in decision making but also in the degree of centralized control. Canada, for example, gives significant political power to the provinces at the expense of its federal government. Thus a major difficulty in negotiating the Canada-U.S. Free Trade Agreement (FTA) was that many provinces had their own trade barriers that had to be considered. The United States, in contrast, has always considered states' rights important as a counterweight to encroaching intervention and control by the central government, yet it has a stronger federal government than Canada does. Companies may have difficulty determining how to act in decentralized democratic systems because they face many sometimes conflicting laws. For example, because of different state tax systems in the United States, foreign companies need to locate their U.S. headquarters carefully. The states even differ in their approach to taxing income from different states. In contrast, the political and legal systems of France and Japan are more highly centralized. Companies consequently find it easier to deal with those countries' systems, since there is less variation from one part of the country to another.

Table 3.1
List of Countries by Level of Freedom, 1992*

Free

Argentina	Ireland	Switzerland	French Southern and Antarctic
Australia	Israel	Trinidad and Tobago	Territories (France)
Austria	Italy	Tuvalu	Gibraltar (U.K.)
Bahamas	Jamaica	United Kingdom	Greenland (Den.)
Bangladesh	Japan	United States	Guadeloupe (France)
Barbados	Kiribati	Uruguay	Guam (U.S.)
Belgium	Latvia	Vanuatu	Isle of Man (U.K.)
Belize	Lithuania	Venezuela	Liechtenstein (Switz.)
Benin	Luxembourg	Western Samoa	Madeira (Port.)
Bolivia	Malta	Zambia	Mahore (France)
Botswana	Marshall Islands		Martinique (France)
Brazil	Mauritius		Melilla (Spain)
Bulgaria	Micronesia	**Related territories**	Monaco (France)
Canada	Mongolia	American Samoa (U.S.)	Montserrat (U.K.)
Cape Verde Islands	Namibia	Andorra (France, Spain)	Netherlands Antilles (Neth.)
Chile	Nauru	Anguilla (U.K.)	New Caledonia (France)
Costa Rica	Nepal	Aruba (Neth.)	Niue (N.Z.)
Cyprus	Netherlands	Azores (Port.)	Norfolk Islands (Aust.)
Czechoslovakia	New Zealand	Belau (Palau) (U.S.)	North Marianas (U.S.)
Denmark	Norway	Bermuda (U.K.)	Pitcairn Islands (U.K.)
Dominica	Papua New Guinea	British Virgin Islands (U.K.)	Puerto Rico (U.S.)
Dominican Republic	Poland	Canary Islands (Spain)	Reunion (France)
Ecuador	Portugal	Cayman Islands (U.K.)	St. Helena and Dependencies,
Estonia	St. Christopher-Nevis	Ceuta (Spain)	Ascension and Tristan da
Finland	St. Lucia	Channel Islands (U.K.)	Cunha (U.K.)
France	St. Vincent and the	Christmas Islands (Aust.)	St. Pierre-Miquelon (France)
Gambia	Grenadines	Cocos (Keeling Islands) (Aust.)	San Marino (Italy)
Germany	Sao Tome and Principe	Cook Islands (N.Z.)	Tokelau (N.Z.)
Greece	Slovenia	Easter Island/Rapanui (Chile)	Turks and Caicos (U.K.)
Grenada	Solomon Islands	Falkland Islands (U.K.)	U.S. Virgin Islands (U.S.)
Honduras	South Korea	Faeroe Islands (Den.)	Wallis and Futuna
Hungary	Spain	French Guiana (France)	Islands (France)
Iceland	Sweden	French Polynesia (France)	

Totalitarianism

In a totalitarian system, decision making is restricted to a few individuals.

Democracy is at one end of the political spectrum, and totalitarianism is at the other. In a totalitarian state, a single party, individual, or group of individuals monopolizes political power and neither recognizes nor permits opposition. Participation in decision making is restricted to a few individuals. In Table 3.1, totalitarian regimes are in the "partly free" and "not free" categories.

Theocratic totalitarianism is the form prevalent in Muslim countries. With secular totalitarianism, control is often enforced through military power.

Totalitarian governments typically take one of two forms: theocratic or secular. In theocratic totalitarianism, religious leaders are also the political leaders. This form is best exemplified in Middle Eastern Islamic countries such as Iran. In secular totalitarianism, the government often imposes order through military power and is based on worldly rather than religious concepts. Examples of this form are found in Cambodia, Haiti, and Iraq.

Table 3.1 (cont.)

Partly free			Not free	
Albania	Kyrgystan	Thailand	Afghanistan	Rwanda
Algeria	Lebanon	Tonga	Brunei	Saudi Arabia
Angola	Lesotho	Tunisia	Burkina Faso	Seychelles
Antigua and	Madagascar	Turkey	Burma/Myanmar	Somalia
Barbuda	Malaysia	Turkmenistan	Burundi	Sudan
Armenia	Mali	Ukraine	Cambodia	Syria
Azerbaijan	Mexico	Uzbekistan	Cameroon	Tanzania
Bahrain	Moldova	Yemen	Chad	Togo
Belarus	Morocco	Zimbabwe	China (PRC)	Uganda
Bhutan	Mozambique		Cuba	United Arab Emirates
Central African	Nicaragua	**Related territories**	Djibouti	Vietnam
Republic	Niger	Hong Kong (U.K.)	Equatorial Guinea	Yugoslavia
Colombia	Nigeria	Northern Ireland	Georgia	Zaire
Comoros	Pakistan	(U.K.)	Ghana	
Congo	Panama	Macao (Port.)	Guinea	**Related territories**
Croatia	Paraguay	Western Sahara	Haiti	Bophuthatswana (S.A.)
Egypt	Peru	(Mor.)	Iran	Ciskei (S.A.)
El Salvador	Philippines		Iraq	East Timor (Indo.)
Ethiopia	Romania		Kenya	Eritrea (Sudan)
Fiji	Russia		Kuwait	Irian Jaya (Indo.)
Gabon	Senegal		Laos	Kashmir (India)
Guatemala	Sierra Leone		Liberia	Occupied Territories (Israel)
Guinea-Bissau	Singapore		Libya	Tibet (China)
Guyana	South Africa		Malawi	Transkel (S.A.)
India	Sri Lanka		Maldives	Venda (S.A.)
Indonesia	Suriname		Mauritania	
Ivory Coast	Swaziland		North Korea	
Jordan	Taiwan		Oman	
Kazakhstan	Tajikistan		Qatar	

*This list is based on data developed by Freedom House's *Comparative Survey of Freedom*. The *Survey* analyzes factors such as the degree to which fair and competitive elections occur, individual and group freedoms are guaranteed in practice, and press freedom exists. In some countries, the category reflects active citizen opposition rather than political rights granted by a government. More detailed and up-to-date *Survey* information may be obtained from Freedom House.

Source: R. Bruce McColm, *Freedom in the World: Political Rights and Civil Liberties 1992–1993*, New York: Freedom House, 1993. Reprinted with permission.

Communism is a form of secular totalitarianism that relates political and economic systems.

Communism is a form of secular totalitarianism. Under communism, the political and economic systems are virtually inseparable. According to Karl Marx, the nineteenth-century German philosopher and political economist who founded world communism, economic forces determine the course taken by a society. He predicted that the capitalist societies eventually would be overcome by two types of revolution—political and social. The political revolution would precede and ignite the social revolution, which would be a long-term transformation based largely on eliminating economic inequities. This social revolution would be guided by what Marx called a dictatorship of the proletariat, that is, the working class. In theory, the proletariat dictatorship would remain in power only long enough to smooth the transition to communism. The government would be responsible for organizing society into groups in order to obtain as much input as possible for the decision-making process. Then, as the social revolution neared completion, the dictatorship would disappear and full communism would take its place.

Even casual observation reveals that real-world communism has differed markedly from theoretical communism. Marx's concept of democratic centralism gave way to totalitarian or autocratic centralism, with no general participation in decision making, especially from those with opposing viewpoints. In recent years communism has been discredited in most parts of the world. The Eastern European countries and the former Soviet Union have moved away from communism to various degrees. And, as communism moves toward democracy, the link between economics and politics in communist countries has been weakened, making "free" communist countries such as Lithuania possible. China, North Korea, and Vietnam, however, are still communist countries with strong centralized authoritarian control over the political process.

The Impact of the Political System on Management Decisions

There is a dichotomy between governmental control and consumer control of the political system and the economy.

Every political system struggles with the balance between decentralized decision making by individuals and centralized regulation and control of decisions by governments. Even democratic governments are faced with this dichotomy, but it is creating great conflict in the former totalitarian states of Eastern Europe and the former Soviet Union as their political systems evolve toward democracy and their economic systems toward free-market economies.

Managers need to understand the critical functions that a government performs in the economy.

Managers must deal with varying degrees of governmental intervention and, as was brought out in the Hong Kong case, varying degrees of political stability. To do so, they must understand the critical functions that a democratic government performs in the economy, for example:

1. Protect the liberty of its citizens
2. Promote the common welfare of its citizens
3. Provide for public goods such as national defense and transportation and communications systems
4. Handle market defects such as entry barriers and insufficient consumer knowledge and power
5. Deal with spillover effects and externalities[8]

One type of public good whose development currently is under debate in many industrial countries is an information highway—a mechanism for the rapid, widespread transmittal of electronic data. Market defects are barriers to the efficient and effective running of a market economy. They interfere with the supply and demand of products and with the ability of consumers to make rational choices. Examples of spillover effects are the many developments and applications that have commercial purposes the private sector can exploit. Externalities refer to by-products of the manufacturing process, such as pollution. Some governments largely ignore polluting externalities in the name of economic development, whereas others control pollution very carefully.

In the United States, governmental functions derive from the Declaration of Independence and the Constitution. The founders of the United States had to come to grips with the lack of liberties that had forced the Revolution and the need to decide what government should actually do for the people. Today, these issues are being considered in newly emerging democracies worldwide. The major collective interests that the framers of the Constitution recognized were perfecting the union, promoting justice and order, and providing for the common defense and welfare. Beyond that, the debate between those who desire minimal governmental interference and those who desire a strong central government heavily involved in economic activities has continued without resolution.[9] Thus the legal environment flows from the political environment and has a strong impact on the way companies operate around the world.

The political process affects international business through regulation of cross-border transactions.

The political process also affects international business through laws that regulate business activity at both the domestic and international levels. Governments may deal with international transactions on a unilateral basis or through treaties and conventions. An MNE must be concerned with the laws in its home country that regulate cross-border transactions and must understand legal requirements in each country in which it operates.

Various U.S. government agencies deal with international issues.

In addition to understanding governmental functions, managers also must realize that governmental action is not always consistent. In the United States, for example, significant conflict exists within government regarding how and to what extent international business activities should be regulated. No specific government agency deals with international issues, so conflicting policies can be expected. For example, at least three different U.S. government agencies share responsibility for regulating exports: the State Department, the Department of Defense, and the Department of Commerce. State is responsible for the overall political relationships between the United States and other countries, Defense is responsible for national defense, and Commerce is responsible for facilitating commercial—including export—activities. These agencies also have three different viewpoints on how to regulate exports. For example, the Clinton administration announced in 1993 that it intended to remove most restrictions on the sale of high-technology products—especially computers—that have possible defense uses. Commerce and State had always favored liberalizing such restrictions, whereas Defense had always supported them.[10]

Formulating political strategies is complicated by the range of participants in the decision-making process, differences in logic, and institutional power.

Formulating and Implementing Political Strategies

Formulating political strategies often is more complicated than formulating competitive marketplace strategies. Nonmarket issues attract different participants than do market issues. In addition, important components of political strategies are implemented in public view; such exposure can constrain the actions of companies. Further, the logic of collective and political action is different from that of market action. Unlike market issues, which are resolved by voluntary agreements, political issues are resolved by institutions that have the power to compel action, regulate activities, and structure the conditions under which market participants operate.[11]

Political action always is a sensitive area. However, there are certain steps that a company must follow if it wants to establish an appropriate political strategy:

1. Identify the issue. What is the specific issue facing a firm—protectionism, environmental standards, worker rights?
2. Define the nature of the politics of the issue.
3. Assess the potential political action of other companies and of special interest groups. Who are the parties that are affected and able to generate political pressure? What are their strategies likely to be?
4. Identify important institutions and key individuals—legislatures, regulatory agencies, courts, important personalities.
5. Formulate strategies. What are the key objectives, the major alternatives, and the likely effectiveness of alternative strategies?
6. Determine the impact of implementation. What will be the public relations fallout in the home and host countries if the action taken is unpopular?
7. Select the most appropriate strategy and implement.[12]

Implementing a strategy involves marshaling whatever resources are necessary to accomplish the company's political objectives. In the United States, lobbyists are hired by a company, whether domestic or foreign, to educate and persuade decision makers about the merits of the company's position. However, there has been heavy criticism of the practice of hiring lobbyists who have departed recently from the government agency that is likely to take action against the company. As the ethical dimensions of government-business relationships have gained prominence even in relatively totalitarian countries, companies have greater reason to examine carefully their policy formulation and implementation strategies.

A company also can attempt to influence governmental action from the bottom up by using a grass-roots campaign or by building coalitions of different groups that share the company's interests. For example, to fight U.S. trade protectionism in the form of tariffs or quotas on imported automobiles, foreign automobile manufacturers might try to convince consumers that, as a result of such actions, they would be worse off because of higher prices or reduced availability. Further, Honda pointed out to U.S. consumers in 1992 that many of its cars were made in the United States by U.S. workers and thus should not be discriminated against.

Part of the problem with establishing a political strategy is that democracies deal with companies differently than do totalitarian regimes. In general, democracies

Establishing a political strategy involves identifying and defining the political situation, important institutions, and key individuals.

Lobbyists educate and persuade decision makers.

Foreign companies often enlist the support of consumers to combat government restrictions on sales.

The laws of democratic countries often are more flexible than those of totalitarian countries.

can be influenced through lobbying. However, companies sometimes abuse their power by engaging in bribery and other illicit activities. In a totalitarian regime, companies usually operate in a more stable environment. However, when such a regime is overthrown, the changes for business tend to be larger and more rapid than change typically is within a democracy. For example, when the Soviet Union broke up, companies that had entered into contracts with the former central government found that these contracts were not binding on the governments of the individual republics.

The Legal Environment

Closely related to the political system, the legal system is another dimension of the external environment that influences business. Managers must be aware of the legal systems in the countries in which they operate, the nature of the legal profession, both domestic and international, and the legal relationships that exist between countries. Both totalitarian and democratic countries have legal systems, but the independence of the law from political control may differ markedly from one to the other. In addition, some totalitarian systems, notably those of China and the former Soviet Union, are not well equipped to deal with market economies in a legal sense, primarily because their legal systems do not provide for issues that arise in such an economic environment.

Kinds of Legal Systems

A common law system is based on tradition, precedent, custom and usage, and interpretation by courts.

Legal systems usually fall into one of three categories: common law, civil law, and theocratic law. The United States and the United Kingdom are examples of countries with a common law system, although the United States also has the properties of a civil law system, as evidenced by its Uniform Commercial Code, which regulates business. Common law is based on tradition, precedent, and custom and usage, and the courts fulfill an important role in interpreting the law according to those characteristics. Because the United Kingdom originated common law in the modern setting, its former and current colonies, such as Hong Kong, also have common law systems.

A civil law system is based on a very detailed set of laws organized into a code.

The civil law system, also called a codified legal system, is based on a very detailed set of laws that are organized into a code. This code is the foundation for doing business. Over seventy countries, including Germany, France, Japan, and the former Soviet Union, operate on a civil law basis.

The two legal systems differ primarily in that common law is based on the courts' interpretations of events, whereas civil law is based on how the law is applied to the facts. An example of an area in which the two systems differ in practice is contracts. In a common law country, contracts tend to be very detailed, with all contingencies spelled out. In a civil law country, contracts tend to be shorter and less specific because many of the issues that a common law contract would cover already are included in the civil code. Also civil law tends to be less adversarial than common law, since judges rely on detailed legal codes rather than on precedent. This is one reason why British and U.S. law firms encounter so much resistance when they enter civil law countries. They are used to the competitive, adversarial approach that the common law system engenders, an approach that tends to shake up the more orderly systems.

A theocratic law system is one based on religious precepts, such as Islamic law.

The third type of legal system is the theocratic law system, which is based on religious precepts. The best example of this system is the Islamic one, which is found in Saudi Arabia and is followed to some degree in other principally Muslim countries. Islamic law, known as *Shair'a,* is based on the following sources:

- The Koran, the sacred text
- The Sunnah, or decisions and sayings of the Prophet Muhammad
- The writings of Islamic scholars, who derive rules by analogy from the principles established in the Koran and the Sunnah
- The consensus of Muslim countries' legal communities[13]

Since the tenth century A.D., Islamic law has been frozen; that is, it cannot be changed, modified, or extended, even though conditions have changed significantly. Islamic law is a moral rather than a commercial law and was intended to govern all aspects of life. Many Muslim countries have legal systems that are a unique blend of the Islamic law system and a common or civil law system derived from previous colonial ties.

Islamic law does not permit banks to pay or benefit from interest, so they share profits with depositors.

An example of how Islamic law influences business can be found in banking. According to Islamic law, banks cannot charge interest or benefit from interest, which is viewed as usury, and investments in commodities such as alcohol or tobacco are forbidden.[14] There are approximately a hundred banks worldwide that offer Islamic banking, including the multinationals Citibank and Barclays. The Malaysian government, in an attempt to bring more Muslim Malays into the economic system, announced in 1993 that all commercial banks should offer Islamic banking services. Because of Islamic law's prohibitions against interest, those Muslims who save in these banks are paid a share of the profits made by the bank that uses the funds. The profit share is roughly the same as the current interest rate.[15]

Of U.S. civil law cases,
- **One quarter involve torts and contracts**
- **Three quarters involve small claims, divorces, or wills**

Regardless of the legal system, the practice of law can be divided into criminal and civil. Although business practices can be found to violate criminal law, business issues more commonly are considered in the context of civil law. A study of civil law cases in the United States found that most involved small claims, divorces, and wills; only 14 percent involved contracts and 10 percent involved torts. Torts are wrongful acts; many tort cases are product-liability ones, in which an injured person tries to recover money for damages that are economic (such as medical expenses and lost wages) or noneconomic (such as pain and suffering). The number of suits involving torts has increased dramatically in the United States for a variety of reasons. Almost unique characteristics of the U.S. legal system are that lawyers take contingency fees (fees determined by a percentage of the final judgment if the case is won), groups can file class action lawsuits, pretrial "discovery" requires the submission of volumes of information by both sides, and juries, rather than judges, decide cases and set damages.[16] The cost of torts in the United States has reached 2.4 percent of GNP, compared with between 0.4 and 0.8 percent of GNP for most other industrial countries.

Different legal systems provide different safeguards for consumers. For example, it appears that consumers have less access to and assistance from the legal community in Japan than in the United States. The United States has 312 lawyers per 100,000 of population compared with only 101.6 lawyers per 100,000 in Japan. Also, the Japanese legal system differs from the U.S. system in that legal prices are set by the Japanese Federation of Bar Associations, foreign lawyers are prohibited from advising on local law or hiring domestic lawyers to do so, and consumer information about legal services is limited by advertising restrictions. In addition, in Japan consumers are discouraged from filing civil suits because of the high cost of legal services and the long delays in the legal process. A survey of 194 big Japanese manufacturers found that only 24 had ever faced a product-liability suit at home and, of those, only 7 had lost. Further, one auto company had been hit with 250 product-liability suits a year in the United States and only 2 in Japan.[17] Thus it appears that in Japan consumers have less legal protection and corporations have fewer legal problems than is the case in the United States.

The Legal Profession

A lawyer has been defined as a "specialist in the normative ordering of human relations."[18] Recently, increased discussion has focused on the expanding number of lawyers and their impact on the world economy. MNEs must use lawyers for a variety of services, such as negotiating contracts and protecting intellectual property. Lawyers and their firms vary among countries in terms of how they practice law and service clients.

Law firms that service international clients have changed over the years. In general, most law firms are quite small. In the United Kingdom and the United States, for example, 60 percent of lawyers are in firms of five persons or fewer.[19] Although the business expansion in the 1960s and 1970s, especially in the area of mergers and acquisitions, led to larger law firms, the 1980s slowdown in the world's economy resulted in a subsequent shrinking in firm size. There are still large firms servicing multinational clients, but many MNEs, concerned about upward-spiraling legal fees, have established their own in-house legal staffs and have begun to rely on out-

The United States has the most lawyers of any country in the world and is one of the highest in the number of lawyers per capita.

Most legal firms are small.

Large firms have surfaced in response to worldwide merger and acquisition activity.

side firms primarily for specialized work. However, smaller companies involved in international business still rely on outside legal counsel for help with a wide variety of issues, such as agent/distributor relationships and the protection of intellectual property.

Just as MNEs have invested abroad to take advantage of expanding business opportunities, law firms have expanded abroad to service their clients. Laws vary from country to country, and legal staffs need to understand local practices. There definitely has been an expansion of legal services across national boundaries, even though law firms have had to overcome significant barriers as they have expanded abroad. Those barriers include restrictions on foreign firms from hiring local lawyers, from forming partnerships with local law firms, or even from entering the country to practice law. However, changes have been taking place in the international legal environment recently. For example, the single European market (discussed in Chapter 7) has resulted in an upsurge in merger and acquisition activity and the reduction of national barriers to legal services. In addition, Japan lifted its ban on foreign lawyers in 1987, and several British and U.S. law firms have since established a presence there. On the other hand, the aggressiveness of U.S. and British law firms in markets that were run as cozy clubs has resulted in additional protectionism. For example, a 1992 French law requires all foreign lawyers not already practicing in France to pass a French law exam if they want to practice there, even if the area in which they intend to offer services involves foreign practices. In addition, the law prohibits new U.S. firms from opening offices in France.[20] This prohibition hampers U.S. law firms in efforts to expand abroad to service their clients. It also can prevent U.S. investors in France from gaining access to legal service from a firm of their choice.

Foreign firms are barred from practicing law in some countries.

Legal Issues in International Business

National laws affect how critical elements of the management process are performed. They can relate to business within the country or business among countries. Some national laws on local business activity influence both domestic and foreign companies, for example, in the areas of health and safety standards, employment practices, antitrust prohibitions, contractual relationships, environmental practices, and patents and trademarks. Laws also exist that govern cross-border activities, such as the investment of capital, the repatriation of earnings, and customs duties on imports. Business activity also is governed by international laws, such as treaties governing the cross-border transfer of hazardous waste.

Several subsequent chapters discuss legal issues in international business, for example, different laws for the regulation of trade and investments, taxes, intellectual-property protection, regulation of financial flows and of ownership, reporting requirements, contractual relationships, extraterritoriality, international treaties, and dispute resolution.

Impact of laws on business:
- **National laws affect all local business activities.**
- **National laws affect cross-border activities.**
- **International treaties and conventions govern cross-border transactions.**

Key legal issues in international business:
- **Trade and investment regulation**
- **Intellectual property protection**
- **Financial flows regulation**
- **Taxation**
- **Reporting requirements**
- **Ownership regulation**
- **Contractual relationships**
- **International treaties**
- **Dispute resolution**

Ethical dilemmas involve a balancing of means and ends. *Means* refers to the actions that are taken, which may be right or wrong; *ends* refers to the results of the actions, which may also be right or wrong. Ethics teaches that "people have a responsibility to do what is right and to avoid doing what is wrong."[21] Questions of right and wrong refer to intentions, which are a function of the various cultural issues that were discussed in Chapter 2. Some people argue that cultural relativism, or the belief that behavior has meaning only in its specific cultural or ethical context, implies that no specific method exists for deciding whether behavior is appropriate. However, we contend that individuals must seek justification for their behavior, and that justification is a function of cultural values (many of which are universal), legal principles, and economic practices.

ETHICAL DILEMMAS

Some people also argue that the legal justification for ethical behavior is the only important one. By this standard, a person or company can do anything that is not illegal. However, there are five reasons why the legal argument is insufficient:

1. The law is not appropriate for regulating all business activity because not everything that is unethical is illegal. This would be true of many dimensions of interpersonal behavior, for example.

2. The law is slow to develop in emerging areas of concern. Laws take time to be legislated and tested in courts. Further, they cannot anticipate all future ethical dilemmas; basically they are a reaction to issues that have already surfaced. Countries with civil law systems rely on specificity in the law, and there may not be enough laws actually passed that deal with ethical issues.

3. The law often is based on moral concepts that are not precisely defined and that cannot be separated from legal concepts. Thus moral concepts must be considered along with legal ones.

4. The law is often in need of testing by the courts. This is especially true of case law, in which the courts establish precedent.

5. The law is not very efficient. A reliance on legal rulings on every area of ethical behavior would not be in anyone's best interests.[22]

In spite of the pitfalls of using the law as the major basis for deciding ethical disputes, there also are good reasons for at least complying with it:

1. The law embodies many of a country's moral beliefs and is thus an adequate guide for proper conduct.

2. The law provides a clearly defined set of rules. Following those rules at least establishes a good precedent. Some are afraid to go beyond the law because of the potential legal liability that could result if they did.

3. The law contains enforceable rules that all must follow; thus it puts everyone on an equal footing. For example, everyone working for a company established in the United States must comply with the Foreign Corrupt Practices Act, which prohibits bribery of foreign governmental officials for business benefit. As long as everyone complies with the law, no one will have an edge due to bribery. However, laws are still subject to interpretation and often contain loopholes.
4. The law represents a consensus derived from significant experience and deliberation. It should reflect careful and wide-ranging discussions.[23]

The problem for companies that use a legal basis for ethical behavior is that laws vary among countries. For example, a major area of contention between industrial and developing countries during the GATT Uruguay Round was the protection of intellectual property, such as computer software. The industrial countries, which have strong laws concerning intellectual-property rights, argued that developing countries need to strengthen such laws and their enforcement. U.S. software manufacturers have noted that in some Asian countries it is possible to buy a heavily discounted pirated version of new software in one store and then go next door and purchase a photocopy of the documentation for the legal version. Using a legal basis for ethical behavior would mean that such purchases are ethical because they occur in countries that either do not have laws on intellectual-property rights or do not enforce the laws.

One could argue that the moral values that cross cultures will be embodied in legal systems, but, as the software example demonstrates, that is too simplistic. Not all moral values are common to every culture. In addition, strong home-country governments may try to extend their legal and ethical practices to the foreign subsidiaries of domestically headquartered companies—an action known as extraterritoriality. For example, a subsidiary of a U.S. company operating in China might be forced to follow some U.S. laws, even though China has no comparable laws and other companies operating there are not subject to the U.S. laws. In some cases, such as with health and safety standards, extraterritoriality should not cause problems. In other cases, such as with restrictions on trade with enemies of the United States, extraterritoriality may cause tension between the foreign subsidiary and the host-country government.

As noted above, the law provides a clearly defined set of rules, which companies often follow strictly because of concerns about potential legal liability. However, a company may seek a loophole in order to accomplish some important objective. Evaluating potential liability and legality of actions varies between countries with civil law systems and those with common law ones. Civil law countries tend to have a large body of laws that specify the legality of various behaviors; common law countries tend to rely more on cases and precedents than on statutory regulations. A company must pay attention to laws to ensure the minimum level of compliance in each country in which it operates. When faced with conflicting laws, however, management must decide which applies. The forces of national sovereignty may encourage managers to follow the adage "When in Rome, do as the Romans do."

Differences in legal and political systems drive companies to adopt multidomestic strategies.

COUNTERVAILING FORCES

Politics clearly affects corporate strategies through national policies and governmental influence on cross-border transactions. Because of differences in national laws, legal practices are multidomestic. Acquiring good legal counsel in the countries in which a company does business is essential. Global legal firms provide legal assistance for MNEs doing business in different parts of the world, but their value is in having good lawyers in different countries rather than a few lawyers that understand all laws in all countries.

Some legal issues, however, are cross-border in nature. A good example is protecting intellectual property. Although each country has its own intellectual-property laws, most countries are part of cross-national treaties and conventions that allow firms to acquire widespread protection for intellectual property. Thus a company can establish a global strategy for the protection of intellectual property by using a legal expert who is familiar with applicable treaties and conventions.

Differences in legal and political systems drive companies toward multidomestic rather than global strategies. Local differences require managers to make adjustments in virtually all areas of business—including marketing, finance, and human resources.

Both political and legal dimensions are at the heart of sovereignty. Smaller countries are very concerned that they could be dominated politically by larger countries. In many international trade agreements, such as the European Union (EU) and the North American Free Trade Agreement (NAFTA), smaller countries have attempted to protect their interests against the larger countries. This has been true, for example, of Denmark within the EU and of Mexico within NAFTA. In fact, Denmark nearly left the EU because it feared too many decisions affecting Danish individuals and companies would be made by EU bureaucrats.

Countries prefer to have their own laws enforced on their own soil. This is problematic for foreign companies, whose managers and workers might not understand local laws. Whether or not they have such understanding they usually must use local courts to resolve local disputes. A country that tries to enforce its laws in another country through extraterritoriality threatens that other country's national sovereignty. Such action is usually met with significant resistance.

As a counterforce to sovereignty, treaties and conventions can modify or set aside national laws. The very purpose of treaties is to subjugate national law to the greater good of the group of countries that sign a treaty. If no national laws were to be changed, treaties would not be needed. However, because treaties moderate sovereignty, they are difficult to implement. For example, U.S. environmentalists have been concerned that NAFTA could result in U.S. environmental legislation being changed in such a way that could harm the environment. Despite these kinds of problems, treaties can be very useful in promoting better interaction between countries and a better operating environment for companies operating internationally.

LOOKING TO THE FUTURE Tomorrow's political environment promises many important developments. Although it is clear from events of the early 1990s that totalitarianism is being challenged, it is fighting back in many parts of the world. In spite of the euphoria that accompanied the liberalization of Eastern Europe and the former Soviet Union, democracy is very fragile in many emerging nations. Reactionary forces seeking a return to nondemocratic rule are still very strong. And ethnic factionalism will continue to threaten the future of many countries and may spill over into surrounding ones.

The legal environment will see an increase in the number of treaties and conventions. The forces of national sovereignty are very much alive, but the closer cooperation among the countries of Europe is forcing countries in other parts of the world to join together in cross-national cooperation. In addition, countries will continue to work through organizations such as the United Nations to solve international problems, especially those involving damage to the environment.

Summary

- To be successful, managers must learn to deal with public institutions (such as the government, government agencies, and government-owned businesses) and nonpublic institutions (such as environmental and other special interest groups) in addition to market forces.

- The political process involves inputs from various interest groups, articulation of issues that affect policy formulation, aggregation of those issues into key alternatives, development of policies, and implementation and adjudication of the policies.

- Most complex societies are pluralistic; that is, they encompass a variety of ideologies.

- The ultimate test of any political system is its ability to hold a society together despite pressures from different ideologies.

- In democracies, there is wide participation in the decision-making process; in totalitarian regimes, only a relative few may participate, although some are beginning to allow greater participation in the decision-making process. Totalitarian regimes can be either secular or theocratic.

- Factors considered in measuring freedom include the degree to which fair and competitive elections occur, the extent to which individual and group freedoms are guaranteed, and the existence of freedom of the press.

- Managers of MNEs must learn to cope with varying degrees of governmental intervention in economic decisions, depending on the countries in which a company is doing business.

- As governments become more democratic, they influence their citizens and institutions by protecting liberty, promoting the common welfare of citizens, providing for public goods, handling market defects, and dealing with spillover effects and externalities.

- The political impact on international business activities is relatively complex because the domestic political process is subject to various influences and managers must deal with different political processes in different countries.

- In formulating political strategies, managers must consider the possible political actions that could affect the company, the different constituencies that might influence those political actions, the political strategies that would be in the best interests of the company, and the costs of implementing those strategies.

- Common law systems are based on tradition, precedent, and custom and usage. Civil law systems are based on a detailed set of laws organized into a code. Theocratic legal systems are based on religious precepts, as exemplified by Islamic law.

- Many law firms have increased their size in order to better service corporate clients in domestic and international mergers and acquisitions.

- There are national laws that govern local business activity of both domestic and foreign firms, national laws that govern cross-border activities, and international laws that govern cross-border activities.

- The legal environment can influence international companies in various ways, for example, by regulating trade and investment and protecting intellectual property.

- Although there is legal justification for some ethical behavior, the law is not an adequate guide for all such behavior. The legality of an action is one element that should be considered, but not the only one.

Case
Bata, Ltd.[24]

In 1990, the management of Bata, Ltd. had a critical decision to make concerning the possibility of reinvesting in Czechoslovakia, or what is now the Czech Republic and Slovakia. This decision was greatly complicated by the long and significant history between Bata and Czechoslovakia.

As war swept across Europe in 1939, Tom Bata, Sr., was faced with a difficult situation. His father, the ninth generation of a family of Czechoslovakian shoemakers, had built a worldwide shoe network in twenty-eight countries, using machinery and the mass-production technology of the 1920s. On his father's death, Tom Bata, Sr., was left with the responsibility of expanding that empire during a period of great political uncertainty worldwide. Because of the Nazi invasion of Czechoslovakia and the uncertain future engendered by the resulting occupation, Tom Bata, Sr., sought to preserve his father's business by abandoning his Czechoslovakian operations and emigrating to Canada with a hundred of his managers and their families. His Czech operations were subsequently taken over by the communists after World War II.

Since that time, Bata's decision has been ratified through strong growth worldwide. The company is a family-owned business that produces approximately 1 million pairs of shoes daily, generating an estimated $3 billion in revenues annually through sales in 6200 company-owned retail outlets and 125 independent retailers in 115 nations. Its 66,000 employees work in factories and engineering facilities in sixty-eight countries, as well as the retail outlets. Bata's influence is so pervasive that the word for shoe in many parts of Africa is "bata."

Bata is run as a decentralized operation in which its managers are free to adjust operating procedures to local environments, within certain parameters. It is a multidomestic company. Tom Bata, Jr., who has taken over from his father, travels extensively to check on quality control and to ensure good relations with the governments of the countries in which Bata operates.

Although Bata has factories and operations of various forms in many countries, it does not own all of those facilities. Where possible, it owns 100 percent of them. The governments of some countries, however, require less-than-majority ownership. In some cases, Bata provides licensing, consulting, and technical assistance to companies in which it has no equity interest.

The company's strategy for serving world markets is instructive. Some MNEs try to lower costs by achieving economies of scale in production, which means they produce as much as possible in the most optimally sized factory and then serve markets worldwide from that single production facility. Bata serves its different national markets by producing in a given market nearly everything it sells in that market. It does this in part because substantial sales volume in the countries in which it produces enable it to achieve economies of scale very quickly. It may seem difficult to believe that Bata can always achieve economies of scale, especially since the company has production facilities in some small African nations. However, Bata's management believes that the company can achieve scale economies very easily because its shoe production is a labor-intensive operation. It also tries to buy all its raw materials locally, although this is not always possible, especially in some poorer countries.

Bata also prefers not to export production; when possible, it chooses local production to serve the local market rather than imports. However, sometimes Bata becomes entangled with local governments when it imports some raw materials but does not export. In such cases, it must adjust to local laws and requirements for operation.

Bata avoids excessive reliance on exports partly to reduce its risks. For example, if an importing country were to restrict trade, Bata could possibly lose market opportunity and market share. In addition, Tom Bata, Sr., noted the benefit to a developing country of not exposing itself to possible protectionism:

> We know very well what kind of a social shock it is when a plant closes in Canada. Yet in Canada we have unemployment insurance and all kinds of welfare operations, and there are many alternative jobs that people can usually go to. In most of the developing countries, on the other hand, it's a question of life and death for these people. They have uprooted themselves from an agricultural society. They've come to a town to work in an industry. They've brought their relatives with them because working in industry, their earnings are so much higher. Thus a large group of their relatives have become dependent on them and have changed their lifestyle and standard of living. For these people it is a terrible thing to lose a job. And so we are very sensitive to that particular problem.

Bata operates in many different types of economies. It has extensive operations in both industrial democratic countries and developing countries. However, it was soundly criticized for operating in South Africa and thus tacitly supporting the white minority political regime. It also has been censured for operating in totalitarian regimes, such as that in Chile. In the latter case, Tom Bata, Sr., countered by pointing out that the company had been operating in Chile for over forty years, during which time various political regimes were in power.

Although Bata's local operations have not been nationalized often, the company has had some fascinating experiences with such actions. For example, in Uganda, Bata's local operations were nationalized by Milton Obote, denationalized by Idi Amin, renationalized by Amin, and finally denationalized by Amin. During that time, the factory continued to operate as if nothing had happened. As Tom Bata, Sr., explained, "Shoes had to be bought and wages paid. Life went on. In most cases, the governments concluded it really wasn't in their interest to run businesses, so they canceled the nationalization arrangements."

Despite Bata's ability to operate in any type of political environment, Tom Bata, Sr., prefers a democratic system. He feels that both democratic and totalitarian regimes are bureaucratic, but a democracy offers the potential to discuss and change procedures, whereas under totalitarianism it sometimes is wisest to remain silent.

Bata has a multifaceted impact on a country. Its product is a necessity, not a luxury. The company's basic strategy is to provide footwear at affordable prices for the largest possible segment of the population. The production of shoes is labor-intensive, so jobs are created, which increases consumers' purchasing power. Although top management may come from outside the country, local management is trained to assume responsibility as quickly as possible. Because the company tries to get most of its raw materials locally, sources of supplies usually are developed. Further, it likes to diversify its purchases, so it usually uses more than one supplier for a given product, which leads to competition and efficiencies.

South Africa presented unique challenges for Bata management. The size of the country's population is just under that of Nigeria, Egypt, or Ethiopia. Thus South Africa had long been considered a good place in which to invest because of its large market size. Further, South Africa's per capita GNP was the largest in Africa. However, the country's main attraction was the incredibly high rate of return that companies could earn, which was largely the result of low labor costs and extensive mineral wealth. The large market allowed companies to achieve economies of scale in production while exploiting the low labor costs.

But the situation deteriorated rapidly in the early 1980s. A relatively stagnant economy, political strife resulting from apartheid, including the policy of not granting political freedom and civil liberties to blacks, prompted foreign companies and governments to pressure the government for political reforms. The Canadian attitude toward South Africa was very negative. Canada's government issued very conservative voluntary guidelines on new investments in South Africa. As a result, Bata sold its holdings in South Africa in 1986. It did not identify the buyer or the sales price, and it denied that apartheid was the reason for its pulling out. Company personnel stated, "It really was a business decision that took into account all of the factors with respect to investment in South Africa at the present time." Under the terms of the sale, the Bata company name and trademark could no longer be used in South Africa, and all ties with Canadian headquarters were broken. In addition, the new buyer apparently assured that the jobs of the workers, most of whom are black, would be preserved.

Bata's possible reinvestment in Czechoslovakia posed different problems. Sometimes investment decisions are an affair of the heart. Although the communists had taken over Bata's operations in 1945, Tom Bata, Sr., was interested in restarting operations in Czechoslovakia. The problem was, who owned the plants? The Czech government wanted some kind of compensation for the factories, but Tom Bata, Sr., felt the factories were still his. Some experts believed the company would eventually receive an equity investment in the huge facilities in exchange for its managerial expertise, marketing help, and capital. It was estimated that it would take as much as $100 million to modernize the plants, which currently employ 85,000 people and turn out 100 million pairs of shoes annually. The acquisition of such a huge operation would perpetuate Bata's multidomestic, decentralized structure that is built around manufacturing centers.

Questions

1. Evaluate the different ways in which Bata has interacted with foreign political systems in its investments and operations abroad.
2. What are the advantages and disadvantages to both Bata and the Czech Republic of having Bata take over the manufacturing operations?
3. Do you think Bata made the correct decision to pull out of South Africa? Why? Under what conditions should it return?

Chapter Notes

1. The major sources for the case are as follows: William H. Overholt, "Hong Kong: A Look at the Coming Decade," *Pacific Rim Business Digest,* October 1990, pp. 5–10; David E. Sanger, "As Hong Kong's Elite Leave, Investors from Japan Arrive," *New York Times,* May 29, 1990, p. A1; Pete Engardino, "In Asia, the Sweet Taste of Success," *Business Week,* November 26, 1990, p. 96; *CulturGram: Hong Kong* (Provo, Utah: Brigham Young University, January 1988); "The Dragon's Embrace," *The Economist,* August 26, 1989, pp. 51–52; David Lethbridge, ed., *The Business Environment in Hong Kong,* 2nd ed. (Oxford, England: Oxford University Press, 1984); Swire Pacific Limited *Annual Report, 1991; The Swire Group* (Hong Kong: Swire Group Public Relations Hong Kong, November 1991); John Newhouse, "Tweaking the Dragon's Tail," *The New Yorker,* March 15, 1993, pp. 89–103; Richard Meyer, "Hostage," *Fortune,* September 18, 1990, pp. 22–27; Jagannath Dubashi, "Changing the Guard," *Fortune,* April 2, 1991, pp. 56–59; "A Rebuke for Mother," *The Economist,* September 21, 1991, p. 46; "A Not-So-Little Rebellion," *The Economist,* December 7, 1991, p. 39; "Patten Sets the Path," *The Economist,* October 10, 1992, pp. 35–36; and "New Medicine for Hong Kong," *The Economist,* February 20, 1993, pp. 31–32.

2. David P. Baron, *Business and Its Environment* (Englewood Cliffs, N.J.: Prentice-Hall, 1993), pp. 7–9.

3. Gabriel A. Almond and G. Bingham Powell, Jr., general editors, *Comparative Politics Today: A World View* (Boston: Little, Brown, 1984), pp. 1–9.

4. Robert Wesson, *Modern Government—Democracy and Authoritarianism,* 2nd ed. (Englewood Cliffs, N.J.: Prentice-Hall, 1985), pp. 41–42.

5. R. Bruce McColm, *Freedom in the World: Political Rights & Civil Liberties 1991–1992* (New York: Freedom House, 1992), p. 61.

6. *Europa Yearbook,* 1989, pp. 2679–2692.

7. Ibid., pp. 1013–1018.

8. Alfred A. Marcus, *Business & Society: Ethics, Government, and the World Economy* (Homewood, Ill.: Richard D. Irwin, 1993), p. 216.

9. Ibid., p. 241.

10. Andy Pasztor and John J. Fialka, "Export Controls to be Relaxed," *Wall Street Journal,* September 20, 1993, p. 2.

11. Baron, op. cit., p. 162.

12. Baron, op. cit., pp. 177–179.

13. Ray August, *International Business Law Text, Cases, and Readings* (Englewood Cliffs, N.J.: Prentice-Hall, 1993), p. 51.

14. Aline Sullivan, "Westerners Look at Risks and Rewards of Islamic Banking," *International Herald Tribune,* January 30, 1993, p. 1.

15. "For God and GDP," *The Economist,* August 7, 1993, pp. 34–35.

16. "Survey: The Legal Profession," *The Economist,* July 18, 1992, p. 11.

17. Ibid., p. 14.

18. Ibid., p. 3.

19. Ibid., p. 5.

20. Ibid., p. 7.

21. Marcus, op. cit., pp. 49–52.

22. John R. Boatright, *Ethics and the Conduct of Business* (Englewood Cliffs, N.J.: Prentice-Hall, 1993), pp. 13–16.

23. Ibid., pp. 16–18.

24. The material for the case was taken from the following sources: Dean Walker, "Shoemaker to the World," *Executive,* January 1981, pp. 63–69; Gary Vineberg, "Bata Favors Free Trade but Tempers Asia Stance," *Footwear News,* Vol. 39, No. 24, June 13, 1983, p. 2+; Ira Breskin and Gary Vinesbert, "Parent Bata Looks After Far Flung Footwear Family," *Footwear News,* Vol. 39, No. 23, June 6, 1983, p. 1+; "After Sullivan," *The Economist,* June 13, 1987, p. 71; Robert Collison, "How Bata Rules Its World," *Canadian Business,* September 1990, pp. 28–34; Peter C. Newman, "The Return of the Native Capitalist," *Macleans,* March 12, 1990, p. 53; Tammi Gutner, "Bringing Back Bata," *International Management,* November 1990, pp. 41–43; and "Faded Euphoria," *Fortune,* July 1, 1991.

Chapter 4

The Economic Environment

*Poverty does not destroy virtue,
nor does wealth bestow it.*
—Spanish Proverb

Objectives

- To discuss different economic systems

- To divide countries into different economic categories

- To discuss key economic issues that influence international business

- To assess the transformation process from central planning to market economy and how it affects international firms

Case
McDonald's
Corporation[1]

Some historians trace the origin of the hamburger to Russia. Supposedly, sailors took a dish made of raw ground beef and hot spices from Russia to the port of Hamburg, where the recipe was altered, popularized, and given its name. Hamburgers eventually showed up in England and then North America. If this historical account is accurate, then when McDonald's Corporation opened its first Moscow restaurant in 1990, the hamburger's round-trip journey was complete.

McDonald's entry into Russia capped a long and involved negotiation process. During the 1976 Olympics in Montreal, George A. Cohon, president of McDonald's Canadian subsidiary, made the first contact with Soviet officials. This began lengthy negotiations that culminated in the signing of a protocol agreement in 1987, shortly after the Soviets enacted legislation permitting joint ventures with Western companies. After that, the pace of negotiations quickened, until in 1988 a formal agreement was signed. In the meantime, McDonald's had opened restaurants in Hungary and Yugoslavia, thus providing the company with valuable experience in operating in communist countries.

These moves were highly compatible with McDonald's growth strategy. By the mid-1980s, the company was expanding more rapidly outside the United States than inside, and company executives reasoned that if they were to meet the company's rapid growth objectives, that trend must continue. It did. By the end of 1992, McDonald's had over 13,000 restaurants in sixty-four countries. Its foreign sales had reached 44 percent of total company sales—up from 37.2 percent in 1991 and 19 percent in 1981—reflecting an increase of 18 percent compounded annually between 1981 and 1991, compared to only an 8-percent increase for domestic sales during the same period. This rapid expansion is expected to continue. The company forecasts that between 1992 and 1997, it will add 400–600 foreign stores each year and increase sales at 20 percent annually.

The McDonald's-Russian joint venture is between McDonald's Canadian subsidiary and the Moscow City Council. McDonald's has a 49-percent interest, the maximum allowed by Soviet law when the formal agreement was signed in 1988. (Since 1990, foreigners may own a 99-percent interest in a joint venture.) The minority ownership has not proved to be a problem, however, because Russian law requires at least a three-quarters majority vote to approve important decisions. Therefore, the representatives of McDonald's and the City Council must agree on all major decisions.

On the other hand, supply procurement has proved to be a major hurdle, as it has for all foreign companies operating in Russia. The problem has several causes:

* The rigid bureaucratic system
* Supply shortages caused by distribution and production problems
* Available supplies not meeting McDonald's quality standards

Even with the Moscow City Council being majority owner in the venture, not to mention having the backing of the Kremlin, the company repeatedly ran into negative responses, such as "Sorry, you're not in my five-year plan," when it attempted to obtain such materials as sand or gravel to build the restaurant. The company had to negotiate to ensure it would be allocated, in the Soviet central plan, sufficient sugar and flour, which were (and still are) in chronically short supply. Even for some products in sufficient supply, such as mustard, government regulations prevented Soviet manufacturers from deviating from standard recipes in order to comply with McDonald's needs. In other cases, strict allocation regulations dictated that Soviet plants sell all output to existing Soviet companies, thus leaving them no chance to produce products for McDonald's. Yet another problem was that some supplies simply were not produced or consumed in the Soviet Union, including iceberg lettuce, pickling cucumbers, and the Russet Burbank potatoes that are the secret behind McDonald's french fries.

To handle these problems, McDonald's scoured the country for supplies, contracting for such items as milk, cheddar cheese, and beef. To help ensure ample supplies of the quality products it needed, it undertook to educate Soviet farmers and cattle ranchers on how to grow and raise those products. In addition, it built a $40-million food-processing center about 45 minutes from its first Moscow restaurant. And because distribution was (and still is) as much a cause of shortages as production was, McDonald's carried supplies on its own trucks. Some other needed supplies the company had to import. (Today, 98 percent of supplies come from the Commonwealth of Independent States, which comprises most of the former republics of the Soviet Union.)

The company placed one small help-wanted ad and received about 27,000 Russian applicants for its 605 positions. It sent 6 Russian managers to its hamburger university outside Chicago for six months' training and another 30 managers for several months' training in Canada or Europe. The company translated training and operations manuals and videotapes into Russian so that trainees could learn everything from how to wash windows and mop floors to how to assemble a Big Mac.

In order to establish a Western image, McDonald's used its name and familiar golden arches in Moscow. However, in 1993 a law was passed in that city requiring all stores to have Russian names, or at least names transliterated into the Cyrillic alphabet. Just as PepsiCo chose Cyrillic letters to convey the sound of "Pepsi" in Russian, McDonald's used the following Cyrillic letters that retain the sound of its name: **МАКДОНАЛДС**.

One problem McDonald's did not encounter was attracting customers. When the company opened its restaurant in Hungary, it quickly had to eliminate its advertising because of unexpectedly heavy consumer response. On the basis of this experience, McDonald's did no advertising prior to its Moscow opening. However, Russian television covered the upcoming event extensively. When the restaurant's doors opened for the first time in January 1990, it was almost impossible to accommodate the crowd, even though the restaurant's 700 indoor seats made it the largest McDonald's anywhere in the world. (An additional 200 seats outside could not be used because of cold weather.) An estimated 30,000 people were served the first day, eclipsing the previous daily record of 9100 set in Budapest. The crowds continued to arrive, even though the price of a Big Mac, french fries, and soft drink equaled a Russian worker's average pay for four hours of work. In contrast, lunch at a state-run or private sector cafe cost 15–25 percent as much as a meal at McDonald's. Presently, the Moscow McDonald's is serving an estimated 50,000 customers a day.

Shortly after its Moscow success, McDonald's turned its attention to China. Pizza Hut, another major U.S. fast-food chain, already had opened its first restaurant in that country. McDonald's management knew that the cost of a Big Mac meal in China, in relation to a typical Chinese consumer's income, would be even higher than it was in Moscow. However, a Pizza Hut pizza costs about two weeks' wages for the average Chinese worker; yet that restaurant consistently served to capacity. Spurred by Pizza Hut's success, McDonald's opened a 500-seat restaurant in Shenzhen, China, near Hong Kong.

What is the future of McDonald's in places such as the former Soviet Union, Eastern Europe, and China? Since opening its first restaurants in China and Russia, the company has opened more restaurants in those countries. It also is studying the feasibility of opening restaurants in Ukraine, St. Petersburg, and the Balkan states. The managing director of McDonald's Development Corporation said, "We'll do one store, one country at a time, and plans will be made as we grow and develop."

Several factors control McDonald's expansion abroad. Key among these are the size and growth rate of different economies. Most of the company's foreign restaurants are in high-income countries (those with per capita incomes of $7911 or more in 1991). For example, Japan has the greatest number, at 865 restaurants. Seventy-four percent of company-operated foreign restaurants are in England, Canada, and Germany; 72 percent of franchised foreign restaurants are in Canada, Germany, Australia, Japan, and France. Sales were slow in Canada and England in 1991 because of weak local economies, whereas they were strong in France, Japan, Germany, and Australia because of the success of new restaurants as well as higher sales in existing ones.

Although the main thrust of McDonald's expansion has been in the industrial countries, the developing countries have significant expansion potential. The following developing countries (those with per capita incomes of less than $7911 in 1991) already have restaurants: Brazil, Hong Kong, Taiwan, Philippines, Singapore, Puerto Rico, and Mexico. Working with these countries involves challenges very different from those connected with doing business in high-income countries, as you will see later in this chapter.

Introduction

As a company considers where in the world to build factories and sell products, it must analyze the countries in which it may do business. Understanding the economic and political environments of these countries can help the company predict how trends and events in those environments might affect its future performance there.

In this chapter, we discuss the economic environments of the countries in which a U.S. company may want to operate. This **country analysis** "examines the economic strategy of the nation state. It takes the holistic approach to understanding how a country, and in particular its government, has behaved, is behaving, and may behave."[2] Country analysis requires, in part, understanding national goals, priorities, and policies; we discussed these in Chapter 3. It also involves understanding economic performance as indicated by economic growth, inflation, and budget and trade deficits. We discuss these in the next several chapters as we lay the economic foundation for an analysis of international business. This chapter focuses on the various types of world economies and how differences in them affect managerial decisions. The economic issues addressed include those that are apparent in the McDonald's case:

- Differences in size and economic growth rate for various countries and how those differences influence investment decisions
- The impact of central planning on the availability of supplies
- The availability of disposable income in spite of low per capita income
- The existence of appropriate infrastructure, such as transportation

Classifying Economic Systems

In a market economy, resources are allocated and controlled by consumers, who "vote" by buying or not buying goods.

In a command economy, resources are allocated and controlled by governmental decision.

Economic systems usually are classified as capitalist, socialist, or mixed. However, it also is possible to classify them according to two other criteria:

- Type of property ownership—private or public
- Method of resource allocation and control—a market economy or a command economy (in which resources are allocated and controlled by the government)

These two criteria can be expanded to include mixed ownership and control. Figure 4.1 shows these classifications. Note that Hong Kong probably fits in block A, whereas China is best located in the upper left-hand corner of block I but may soon be in block E or F. The United States probably lies in the upper part of block D.

With private ownership, individuals own the resources.

With public ownership, the government owns the resources.

Ownership of the means of production in theory ranges from complete private ownership to complete public ownership. In reality, these extremes do not exist.

**Figure 4.1
Interrelationships between Control of Economic Activity and Ownership of Production Factors**
Although the most logical combinations of ownership and control are sectors A and I, most countries in the world have mixed economies with a variety of combinations of ownership and control.

CONTROL \ OWNERSHIP	Private	Mixed	Public
Market	A	B	C
Mixed	D	E	F
Command	G	H	I

Control/Ownership	Control/Ownership	Control/Ownership
A. Market/Private	D. Mixed/Private	G. Command/Private
B. Market/Mixed	E. Mixed/Mixed	H. Command/Mixed
C. Market/Public	F. Mixed/Public	I. Command/Public

Most countries lie somewhere in the mixed ownership range. For example, the United States is considered to be the prime example of a private enterprise system, yet the government owns some means of production and actively produces in such sectors of the economy as education, the military, the postal service (which is in the quasi-public sector), and certain utilities. Similarly, the control of economic activity in theory ranges from market to command.

The next several sections examine more closely market, centrally planned, and mixed economies.

Market Economy

The market mechanism involves an interrelationship of price, quantity, supply, and demand.

In a market economy, two societal units play important roles: the individual and the company. Individuals own resources and consumer products; companies use resources and produce products. The market mechanism involves an interaction of price, quantity, supply, and demand for resources and products, as follows:

- Labor is supplied by the individual if the company offers an adequate wage.
- Products are consumed if the price is within a certain acceptable range.
- A company sets its wages on the basis of quantity of labor available to do a job.
- Resources are allocated as a result of constant interplay between individuals and companies, between individuals, and between companies (for example, when the output of one company is the input of another)

Consumer sovereignty is the freedom of consumers to influence production by exercising their power of choice regarding purchases.

The key factors that make the market economy work are consumer sovereignty—that is, the right of the consumer to decide what to buy—and freedom of the enterprise to operate in the market. As long as both the individual and the company are free to make economic decisions, the interplay of supply and demand should ensure proper allocation of resources.

Market economies have been very successful in most industrial countries. However, a perfect market economy doesn't exist because of the influence of three factors: large corporations, labor unions, and government policies.

Large corporations, labor unions, and government policies limit consumer and business freedom in any market economy.

A large corporation can reduce market pressures somewhat by exerting control over the purchase of resources or the sale of products. Because of the relative largeness of the corporation and the relative smallness of the individual shareholder, a wide gap exists between ownership and control of decision making. Thus, decisions may not be motivated strictly by market conditions. However, the rising importance of small entrepreneurial companies in industrial countries, creating jobs and thus impacting on individuals, has demonstrated that a company does not need to be large in order to be successful.

Labor unions evolved in response to the power exerted by the owners and managers of business over the labor market. Unions have won tremendous benefits for their members in terms of higher salaries, fringe benefits, work conditions, and bargaining power. As a result, however, market forces have been seriously disrupted; many unions control entry into the workforce and restrict the freedom of workers to change occupations in response to supply and demand.

Government policies, including fiscal and monetary policies, continue to shape world economies, directly affecting employment, production, consumption of goods and services, and the growth of the money supply. As will be pointed out in Chapter 6, the government also intervenes in the free flow of goods internationally through protectionist measures.

Centrally Planned Economy

In a centrally planned economy, the government sets goals and determines the price and quantity of what is produced.

In a centrally planned economy, the government coordinates the activities of the different economic sectors. Goals are set for every enterprise in the country; the government determines how much is produced, by whom, and for whom. In this type of economy, the government is assumed to be a better judge of how resources should be allocated than are businesses or consumers. As a result of the recent political and economic changes in Eastern Europe and the former Soviet Union, however, few countries use strict central planning today. Most countries in this category have been moved into a new one called historically planned economies (HPEs), which comprises countries that previously used central planning as their primary economic system but may no longer do so.

Mixed Economy

Mixed economies are characterized by different mixtures of market and central-planning control and public and private ownership of resources.

In actuality, no economy is either purely market determined or completely centrally planned. Hong Kong and China represent opposite ends of the spectrum of mixed economies. In practice, however, what we call mixed economies generally have a higher degree of government intervention than is found in Hong Kong and a greater degree of reliance on market forces than is found in China. Government intervention can be regarded in two ways: government ownership of the means of production and government influence in economic decision making. Ownership is easy to quantify statistically; influence, however, is a matter of policy and custom and therefore is more difficult to measure precisely.

Many industrial (high-income) countries such as Germany and Sweden have relatively low levels of government ownership but a strong tradition of social welfare supported by taxes. The United Kingdom has a similar system, although the government is more heavily involved in corporate ownership.

Japan's MITI has given strategic direction to that country's investment and production priorities.

Japan offers an illustration of government intervention in the form of influence. At the close of World War II, Japan, unlike other countries involved in the war, such as France and Italy, decided to leave ownership of the means of production in the private sector rather than nationalizing key industries. Japanese policymakers focused on setting targets and using fiscal incentives to direct the flow of investment. The Ministry of International Trade and Industry (MITI) was organized to guide industrial development through "strategic planning and authority (both formal and informal) over investment and production priorities."[3] MITI was more concerned with developing a vision for the economy than with setting up a blueprint for it.

Measuring Productivity

Government's role in capitalistic societies is represented by several indicators, including central government expenditures and revenues as a percentage of gross national product. The **gross national product (GNP)** is the broadest measure of economic activity and is defined as "the market value of final goods and services newly produced by domestic factors of production."[4] Note that the production by domestic factors could take place at home or abroad.

Another measure often used is gross domestic product. The **gross domestic product (GDP)** measures the value of production that occurs within a country's borders without regard to whether the production is done by domestic or foreign factors of production. For most countries, the GNP and the GDP are very similar. However, the GDP more accurately reflects economic activity within a country's borders.

Figure 4.2 compares data on central government expenditures and revenues as a percentage of GNP in several countries. Note the wide divergence among countries, with Japan showing the lowest percentages and the Netherlands the highest.

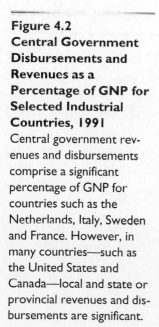

Countries differ greatly in terms of size of government revenues and expenditures relative to GNP.

**Figure 4.2
Central Government
Disbursements and
Revenues as a
Percentage of GNP for
Selected Industrial
Countries, 1991**
Central government revenues and disbursements comprise a significant percentage of GNP for countries such as the Netherlands, Italy, Sweden and France. However, in many countries—such as the United States and Canada—local and state or provincial revenues and disbursements are significant.

Source: World Bank, *World Development Report* (New York: Oxford University Press, 1993), pp. 258–261.

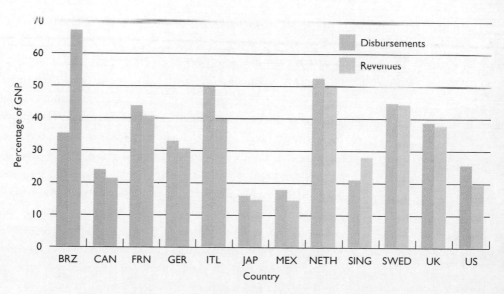

Country	Abbreviation	Disbursements	Revenues
Brazil	BRZ	35.1	67.9
Canada	CAN	23.9	21.3
France	FRN	43.7	40.9
Germany	GER	32.5	30.6
Italy	ITL	49.6	39.9
Japan	JAP	15.8	14.5
Mexico	MEX	18.1	14.7
Netherlands	NETH	52.5	49.7
Singapore	SING	22.1	27.7
Sweden	SWED	44.2	44.4
United Kingdom	UK	38.2	37.4
United States	US	25.3	19.8

As we commented earlier, however, the Japanese government's influence in the economy extends beyond actual expenditures. Also, the figure does not reflect *total* government revenues and expenditures, only those for the central government. In countries such as the United States, where the costs of many services such as education are borne by the states, total government expenditures and revenues vary significantly from those of the central government alone. For example, total tax revenues in the United States are 30.1 percent of GNP, but central government revenues are only 19.8 percent of GNP. Total tax revenues as a percentage of GNP for some of the other countries listed in Figure 4.2 are 35.3 percent for Canada, 43.8 percent for France, 38.1 percent for Germany, and 30.6 percent for Japan.[5] Note the big difference between these numbers and those in the figure for Canada and Japan and the smaller differences for France and Germany. These differences reflect the relative importance of the central government versus local governments for these countries.

Models of Successful Market Economies

Countries currently transforming their economies from centrally planned to free market obviously aspire to become economic successes, not failures. Several models of successful free-market economies are available for emulation, and considerable debate continues within HPEs regarding which to choose. The social-welfare market economies of Northern Europe are characterized by heavy government spending and high taxation to pay for such social services as health care, education, subsidized housing for the poor, and unemployment benefits. The consumer-directed market economies, such as that of the United States, involve minimal governmental participation and the promotion of growth through mobility of production factors, including high labor turnover. Administratively guided market economies, such as Japan's, require considerable cooperation among government, management, and workers to achieve growth and full employment with low labor turnover on a nonmandated basis. Regardless of model differences, however, several factors are common to all the successful market economies:

1. Typically, more means of production are privately owned than government owned.
2. Markets are very competitive. In larger economies such as those of Japan and the United States, the competition is primarily among companies producing domestically. In smaller economies, which are less able to support multiple producers, international competition is important for encouraging producers to become more efficient and more responsive to market needs.
3. Currencies are sound in terms of low inflation rates and convertibility. Thus, residents have enough confidence to make savings and investments that fuel the economy.
4. Private institutions amass financial resources through the savings of the country's citizens. These resources are then made available for public and private projects that promote economic growth and support social welfare.

Three models of market economies are
- **Social welfare**
- **Consumer-directed**
- **Administratively guided**

Characteristics of market economies:
- **Predominance of privately owned production factors**
- **Competitive markets**
- **Strong currencies**
- **Institutional support**
- **Well-functioning infrastructure**
- **Investment opportunities for individuals**

5. Well-functioning infrastructures (such as telecommunications, schools, and transportation facilities) are in place, and efforts are made to protect the environment.
6. Investment opportunities are available for individuals.

No centrally planned economy began the process of transforming to a free-market economy with any of these conditions in place to the extent seen today in successful market economies. For example, although some Eastern European HPEs could boast high educational development for their citizens, development of other infrastructure, such as roads and telephone systems, was inadequate. In addition, few people in the West could imagine how despoiled the Eastern European physical environment had become under communist rule. Years of insufficient investment in clean air and water, along with ill conceived industrial policies, left a legacy that still threatens to become a full-blown environmental disaster.[6]

Political-Economic Synthesis

Democratic governments usually mix best with private ownership and control of resources.

Except for central planning and communism, we have made no attempt to link an economic philosophy or system with a particular political philosophy or regime. A logical linkage is a democratic form of government with a market economy and private ownership of the means of production. The assumption is that voters, like consumers, are rational, understand their own self-interest, and prefer to make their own decisions. Japan, the United States, Switzerland, Germany, Canada, Colombia, Ecuador, and Argentina have this combination of political and economic systems.

Democratic socialists believe that elected governments should own resources and control the economic system.

Democratic socialists, however, have a different viewpoint. They believe that because economics and politics are so closely connected, voters should rely on their elected government to control the economic system; that is, the part of the economy not owned by the government should be regulated by the government. Democratic socialists reason that in order to have an economy that is democratically controlled and that provides the security necessary for liberty, resources and production factors must be owned or regulated by a welfare-oriented government. France, when controlled by the Socialists, was a good example of democratic socialism. Radical democratic socialists support a mix of government-owned companies, cooperatives, small-scale private companies, and "freelancers" (for example, journalists and artists).[7]

The extremes of political-economic combinations are converging in mixed economies.

Clearly, numerous combinations of political and economic systems are possible. Generally, the more a country leans toward political totalitarianism, the greater is its reliance on government intervention in the economy. However, most democratic countries have experimented with different degrees of government intervention in the economy, and many totalitarian countries have not resorted to ownership of the factors of production as a method of control. The extremes tend to converge to a mix of public and private interaction in matters of ownership and control. In the case of the industrial countries, the emphasis seems to be on control rather than on ownership.

Privatization is occurring in most countries that have had significant government ownership of enterprises.

Most countries that have significant central planning and government control and ownership of resources and production factors are **privatizing,** that is, selling government-owned enterprises to private companies and individuals. These governments are finding it increasingly difficult to manage the economy as well as provide adequate support for public enterprises. Those enterprises often are operated under political rather than business guidelines, and resources are not used as efficiently as they might be in the private sector. Governments with huge budget deficits frequently point to the drag on the economy induced by inefficient public enterprises.

Classifying Countries

The First World consists of the high-income industrial countries.

The Second World comprises those countries that formerly had centrally planned economies, now considered developing countries.

Developing countries are located primarily in Africa, Asia, and Latin America.

Table 4.1 classifies countries into economic categories based on per capita GNP, a common approach for grouping countries. This classification, provided by the World Bank, has changed in recent years because of rapid changes in political and economic systems. Historically, countries have been classified by the World Bank as First World, Second World, or Third World, depending on their per capita income. The First World countries are the industrial countries categorized as high-income economies in the table. The Second World countries are those that formerly had been centrally planned economies and now are called HPEs. These countries are undergoing rapid change and are found in both the upper-middle-income and the lower-middle-income categories. The Third World countries, also known as developing countries or less developed countries (LDCs), are the lower-middle-income and low-income economies. These countries are found in Asia, Africa, and Latin America. Most of Latin America's population lives in middle-income countries. African countries are concentrated more in the low-income and lower-middle-income categories.

Key Economic Indicators
Key economic indicators are

- Per capita income
- Quality of life
- Purchasing power
- Percentage of GDP generated from agriculture versus that generated from industry

Most of the world's wealth is in the industrial countries.

Per capita income Countries traditionally are compared on the basis of per capita income. As shown in Fig. 4.3 and Map 4.1, the world's wealth is located primarily in the high-income countries. The low- and middle-income countries, where the vast majority of the world's population lives, do not have a proportional share of per capita income. It is interesting to note from the map that the industrial countries are north of the equator (except for Australia and New Zealand). Thus, the so-called North-South dialogue consists of discussions on economic development between the rich Northern Hemisphere countries and the poorer Southern Hemisphere countries.

Table 4.1
World Bank Categories for Economies

The industrial countries are in the high-income category, and the developing countries are in the middle- and low-income categories.

High-income economies (22 countries with 1991 per capita GNP of $7911 or more)	Upper-middle-income economies (22 countries with 1991 per capita GNP between $2555 and $7911)	Lower-middle-income economies (43 countries with 1991 per capita income between $635 and $2555)	Low-income economies (40 countries with 1991 per capita income of $635 or less)
Ireland	Botswana	Bolivia	Mozambique
Israel	South Africa	Côte d'Ivoire	Tanzania
New Zealand	Lithuania	Senegal	Ethiopia
Spain	Hungary	Philippines	Uganda
Hong Kong	Venezuela	Papua New Guinea	Bhutan
Singapore	Argentina	Cameroon	Guinea-Bissau
United Kingdom	Uruguay	Guatemala	Nepal
Australia	Brazil	Dominican Republic	Burundi
Italy	Mexico	Ecuador	Chad
the Netherlands	Belarus	Morocco	Madagascar
Belgium	Russian Federation	Jordan	Sierra Leone
Austria	Latvia	Tajikistan	Bangladesh
France	Trinidad and Tobago	Peru	Lao People's Democratic Republic
Canada	Gabon	El Salvador	Malawi
United States	Estonia	Congo	Rwanda
Germany	Portugal	Syrian Arab Republic	Mali
Denmark	Oman	Colombia	Burkina Faso
Finland	Puerto Rico	Paraguay	Niger
Norway	Korea, Republic of	Uzbekistan	India
Sweden	Greece	Jamaica	Kenya
Japan	Saudi Arabia	Romania	Nigeria
Switzerland	Yugoslavia	Namibia	China
		Tunisia	Haiti
		Kyrgyzstan	Benin
		Thailand	Central African Republic
		Georgia	Ghana
		Azerbaijan	Pakistan
		Turkmenistan	Togo
		Turkey	Guinea
		Poland	Nicaragua
		Bulgaria	Sri Lanka
		Costa Rica	Mauritania
		Algeria	Yemen, Republic of
		Panama	Honduras
		Armenia	Lesotho
		Chile	Indonesia
		Iran, Islamic Republic of	Egypt, Arab Republic of
		Moldova	Zimbabwe
		Ukraine	Sudan
		Mauritius	Zambia
		Czechoslovakia	
		Kazakhstan	
		Malaysia	

Source: World Bank, *World Development Report* (New York: Oxford University Press, 1993), pp. 238–239.

Map 4.1   The World's Wealth Measured in Per Capita Income, 1991

Except for Australia and New Zealand, the world's richest nations are in the Northern Hemisphere. The map shows economies classified by income group: Low-income means a per capita GNP of $635 or less; middle-income means a per capita GNP of $636–$7910; high-income means $7911 or more.

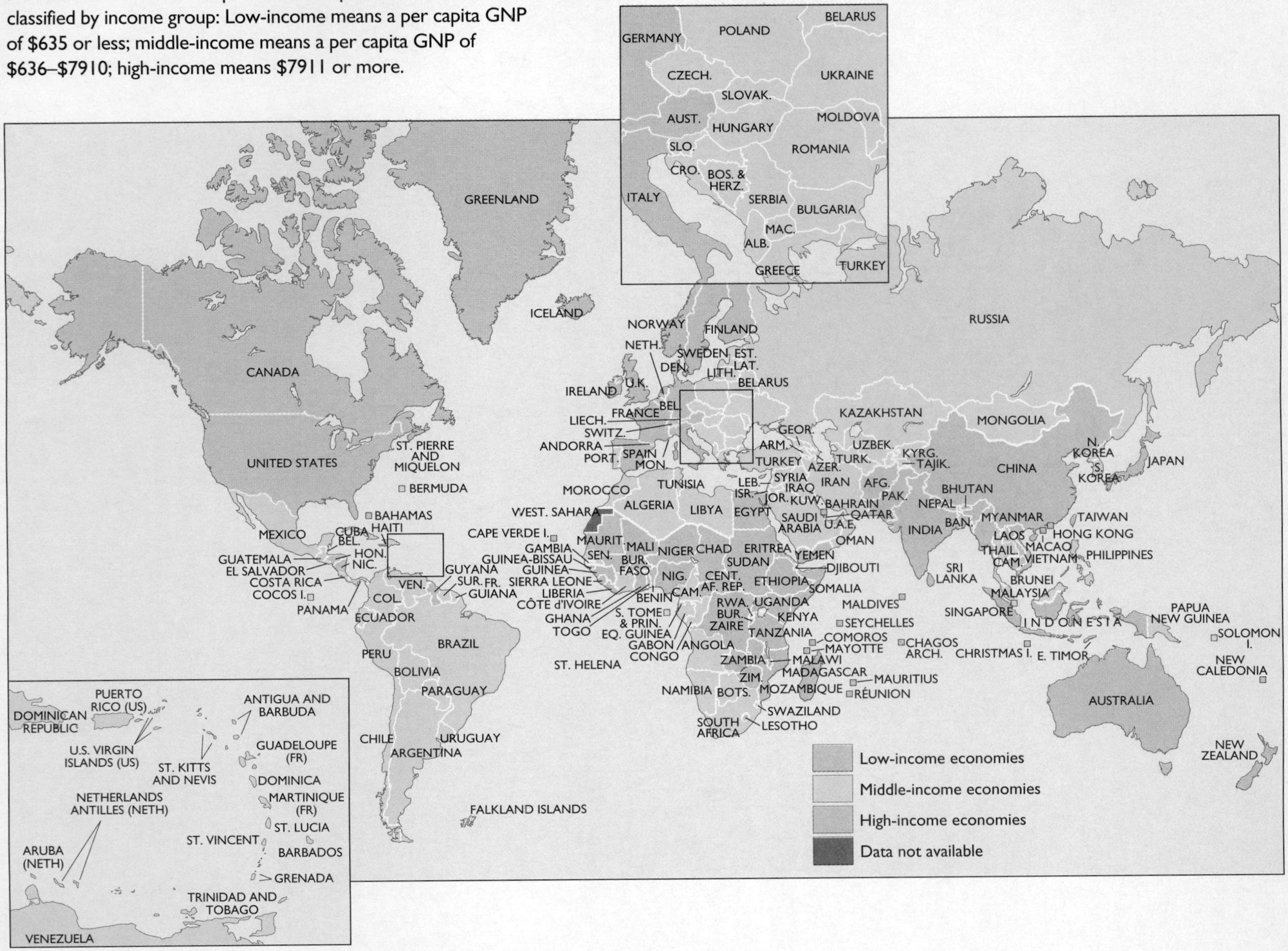

Legend:
- Low-income economies
- Middle-income economies
- High-income economies
- Data not available

Figure 4.3
Per Capita GNP by
Income Category, 1991
The world's wealth is located primarily in the high-income countries. The majority of the world's population is underrepresented in per capita income.

Source: World Bank, *World Development Report* (New York: Oxford University Press, 1993), pp. 238–239.

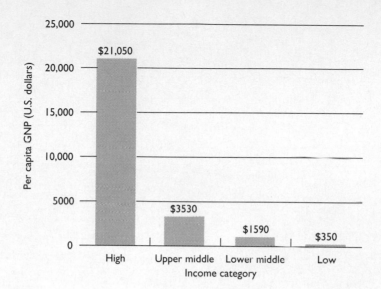

However, per capita income figures can hide potential market opportunities. A good example of this involves McDonald's in China. With that country reporting per capita income of just barely over $300 per year, you could assume that few people there can afford a McDonald's hamburger. Yet, there is strong demand for McDonald's products in China, just as in Eastern Europe and Russia.

Measurements of the quality of life are life expectancy, educational standards, and individual purchasing power.

Quality of life Per capita income does not represent the quality of life. The United Nations publishes an annual human development report in which it ranks countries according to various measures of human happiness, such as life expectancy, educational standards, and individual purchasing power. Table 4.2 provides recent human development rankings for a sample of industrial and developing countries. Note that the human development ranking does not mirror the GNP per capita ranking; for example, Canada ranks eleventh in GNP per capita, whereas it ranks second in human development.[8]

Wide disparities in literacy and life expectancy rates are particularly noticeable among the developing countries. For example, Vietnam's literacy rate is 88 percent, and Gambia's is only 27 percent. And a baby born in Martinique can expect to live 76 years, whereas one born in Guinea-Bissau probably will die before age 40.[9]

Purchasing power Per capita income also does not represent **purchasing power,** that is, what a sum of money actually can buy. For example, when purchasing power was factored in, Japan's per capita income of $24,420 fell to an adjusted level of only $14,311. Compare these figures with those for the United States: The per capita income and adjusted per capita income are almost the same at approximately $21,000.[10]

Percentage of GDP generated from agriculture The differences between the richest and poorest countries also can be demonstrated by looking at the percent-

Table 4.2
Economic Wealth versus Well-Being

This is a sampling of countries' ratings in "human development" as computed by the United Nations Human Development Program.

Country	"Human development" score	"Human development" ranking	GNP per capita ranking	Mean number of years of schooling
Industrial nations				
Japan	0.983	1	3	10.7
Canada	0.982	2	11	12.1
Norway	0.978	3	6	11.6
Switzerland	0.978	4	1	11.1
Sweden	0.977	5	5	11.1
United States	0.976	6	10	12.3
Australia	0.972	7	20	11.5
France	0.971	8	13	11.6
the Netherlands	0.970	9	17	10.6
United Kingdom	0.964	10	21	11.5
Iceland	0.960	11	9	8.9
Germany	0.957	12	8	11.1
Developing nations				
Barbados	0.928	20	34	8.9
Hong Kong	0.913	24	24	7.0
Trinidad	0.877	31	46	8.0
South Korea	0.872	33	37	8.8
Costa Rica	0.852	42	76	5.7
Kuwait	0.815	52	15	5.4
Mexico	0.805	53	60	4.7
Brazil	0.730	70	53	3.9
Cuba	0.711	75	101	7.6
Saudi Arabia	0.688	84	31	3.7
South Africa	0.673	85	57	3.9
China	0.566	101	142	4.8
Iran	0.557	103	59	3.9
El Salvador	0.503	110	102	4.1
Kenya	0.369	127	144	2.3
India	0.309	134	146	2.4
Haiti	0.275	137	143	1.7
Cambodia	0.186	148	168	2.0
Angola	0.143	160	126	1.5
Somalia	0.087	166	171	0.2
Afghanistan	0.066	171	169	0.8

Source: From Paul Lewis, "New U.N. Index Measures Wealth as Quality of Life," May 23, 1993, p. A6. Copyright ©1993 by The New York Times Company. Reprinted with permission.

As countries shift from low-income to high-income economies, they also shift from agriculture to manufacturing to services.

age of GDP generated from agriculture rather than from services or industry. Note from Map 4.2 that the amount of GDP derived from agriculture is less than 6 percent in the industrial countries; in the poorer, developing countries, that amount is more than 20 percent.

The difficulty for managers is that they cannot lump all developing countries into one category and assume that conditions are the same in all countries in that

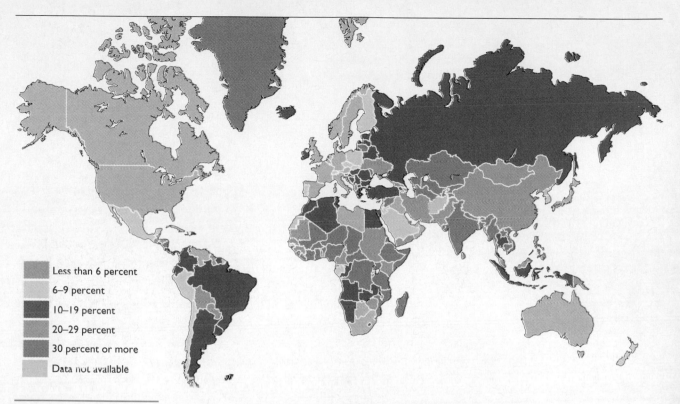

Less than 6 percent

6–9 percent

10–19 percent

20–29 percent

30 percent or more

Data not available

Map 4.2
Percentage of GDP Derived from Agriculture
The industrial countries have a smaller percentage of their GDP tied up in agriculture than is the case with the developing countries.

category. There may be some common problems, which we discuss below, but there are wide differences between countries—even within a category. Managers need to understand and adapt to those differences.

Key Economic Issues

What are some of the issues that companies must confront and handle as they develop a competitive strategy, and how do these factors influence management decisions? Clearly, a variety of cultural, legal, political, and economic factors influence the management of global companies. The impact of these factors varies considerably from country to country. Obviously, the environment in a developing HPE such as China differs greatly from that in an industrial country such as Germany.

Even though there is great disparity among the developing countries, they share many problems and characteristics. Some of the most frequently mentioned problems are inflation, heavy external debt, weak currencies, shortage of skilled workers, political and economic instability, overreliance on the public sector for economic development, war and insurrection, mass poverty, rapid population growth, weak commodity prices, and environmental degradation.

We cannot discuss all of these problems in this chapter. We will, however, cover five important economic factors that influence management decisions:

Five key economic factors that influence international business:
• **Economic growth**
• **Privatization**
• **Inflation**
• **Payments imbalances**
• **External debt**

- Economic growth
- Privatization
- Inflation and its impact on currency stability
- Payments imbalances
- External debt

Other factors are discussed in subsequent chapters.

Economic Growth

Companies would like every country to have political stability, a low inflation rate, and a high real growth rate. If this were the case, even if a company did not expand its share in each market, it would still be able to increase revenues at the same pace as the general economy grew. However, although developing countries provide large market potential and exhibit strong economic growth overall, investing in them can be riskier than investing in industrial countries.

Figure 4.4 illustrates real growth in GDP for industrial and developing countries during the periods 1970–1980 and 1980–1991. In recent years, growth has been especially strong in East and South Asia, where it is boosted by the region's tremendous market size; Asia's population is ten times North America's and six times Europe's. In contrast, the industrial countries have experienced relatively slower growth, a troublesome sign because they historically have tended to fuel growth in the rest of the world. Further, although the countries that comprise the Organization for Economic Cooperation and Development (OECD) accounted for 74 percent of the world's GNP in 1990, compared with only 9 percent for Asia (excluding Japan), the *growth rates* in Asia today are averaging 8 percent annually, compared with barely 2 percent in OECD countries. (The OECD includes the industrial countries of Western Europe plus Canada, the United States, Japan, Australia, and New Zealand.) The combination of large populations and faster growth rates could, by 2050, result in 57 percent of the world's GNP being accounted for by Asia (excluding Japan), compared with only 12 percent by the OECD countries.[11] Thus, companies looking for greater sales and earnings will increasingly look toward the faster-growing economies of Asia rather than the slower-growing economies of the industrial world or of the poorer, developing countries.

This disparity in growth rates creates a major problem: Industrial countries tend to invest in the fastest-growing economies, and such investment heightens the disparity. For example, of the total foreign investments in the developing world between 1986 and 1991, 55 percent went to six countries: Mexico, China, Malaysia, Argentina, Brazil, and Thailand. The poorest of the poor received very little.[12]

The McDonald's case illustrates the impact that the disparity in growth rates can have on corporate strategy. Just as growth rates are high in developing countries, so are McDonald's sales. In contrast, weak economic growth, such as that in Canada and England in 1991, results in weak sales. As McDonald's seeks to expand its sales base, it probably will target the rapidly growing markets of Latin America and Asia.

Developing countries have exhibited strong growth but investment in them remains risky.

Economic growth has been especially strong in East and South Asia.

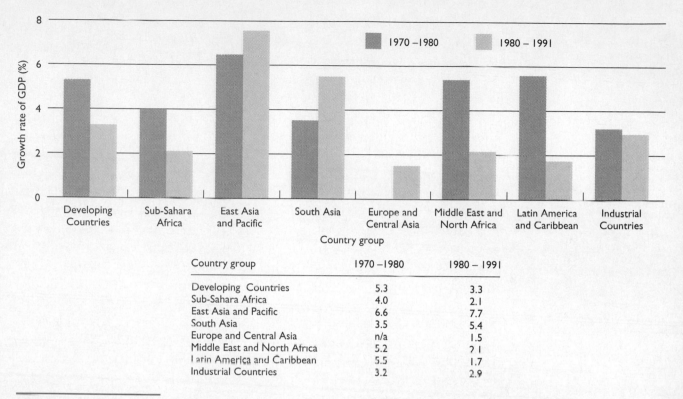

Country group	1970 –1980	1980 – 1991
Developing Countries	5.3	3.3
Sub-Sahara Africa	4.0	2.1
East Asia and Pacific	6.6	7.7
South Asia	3.5	5.4
Europe and Central Asia	n/a	1.5
Middle East and North Africa	5.2	2.1
Latin America and Caribbean	5.5	1.7
Industrial Countries	3.2	2.9

Figure 4.4
Real Rate of Growth of GDP
Economic growth in recent years has been especially strong in East Asia and South Asia. Developing countries provide large market potential and exhibit strong economic growth overall, but investing there tends to be riskier than in the industrial countries.

Source: World Bank, *World Development Report* (New York: Oxford University Press, 1993), pp. 240–241.

Privatization

An interesting trend that began in the 1980s was privatization of business. Initiatives taken by many industrial as well as developing countries during the 1960s and 1970s to absorb industry into the public sector had not been very successful. However, significant strides were made between 1988 and 1992 toward reversing those trends. For example, most privatization in industrial countries during this period occurred in the United Kingdom, although the process took on increased importance in Germany in 1992 because of privatization of former East German enterprises. As for the developing countries, in 1988, they raised only $2.5 billion from privatization; in 1992, they raised $23.3 billion. Most efforts during this period occurred in Mexico and Argentina.[13] The next several sections take a closer look at some privatization efforts.

Privatization in France France has been only marginally active in terms of privatization. The privatization program of the former socialist government was called "ni-ni"—neither privatization nor nationalization. Most efforts involved selling only minority interests in government-owned enterprises, with little involvement by foreign investors. When the conservatives came into power in 1993, they vowed to privatize all banks, insurance companies, and competitive enterprises such as Renault, Elf Aquitaine, and Pechiney. In line with this policy, the announced merger in 1993 of Renault and Volvo, the Swedish auto company, included the possibility of the French government's selling of its interest in Renault. To help fund the country's privatization effort, the conservatives have sought to attract significant foreign capital by encouraging increased foreign involvement and by allowing foreigners to hold a larger percentage of French companies.[14]

Privatization in Russia   Privatization in the Russian economy—as in Eastern Europe and China—differs significantly from that in the industrial or developing market economies. The Russian approach calls for decentralizing enterprises in order to remove them from the control of the old branch ministries, which are rooted in central planning. However, Russian privatization also favors keeping insiders in control of enterprises. Each Russian citizen receives a voucher that can be used to purchase stock in formerly state-owned enterprises or investment funds that in turn invest in companies. Insiders may buy up to 51 percent of their enterprise at 1.7 times its book value unadjusted for inflation—almost a giveaway. In addition, investment funds may not own more than 10 percent of the shares of any one company. These practices effectively leave former managers in charge of their old enterprises. Further, because workers usually end up with more power as a result of decentralization, there is more incentive to put earnings into wages and bonuses rather than into dividends, a practice that discourages investment.[15]

Russia also does not implement its privatization program uniformly. Internal conflicts have encouraged conservatives in some regions of the country to stop privatization; others, however, continue to support it and are making good progress.[16] Thus, we see that in Russia privatization means basically decentralization of decision making, a definition that differs from that used in industrial and other developing countries.

Privatization in Eastern Europe   In Eastern Europe, privatization has taken various forms. Selling shares to outsiders has not been very successful, however, for several reasons: "the unattractiveness of investment in Eastern Europe state enterprises, the slowness of the process, the problems of valuation, the shortage of domestic capital and the unwillingness of foreign investors to enter at a large enough scale."[17]

The Czech Republic offers the best example of mass privatization. In a program similar to Russia's, all citizens received vouchers to use for investing in enterprises or investment funds. Enterprises could offer one of several different privatization projects in which potential investors could place their vouchers. However, over 70 percent of the vouchers went into investment funds, many of which were controlled by banks. The result was a concentration of ownership. Although the approach resembles Russia's, Russians are not allowed to use their vouchers as freely as the Czechs. The Hungarians and Poles, too, have found it difficult to privatize at the same level as the Czechs.

The five most likely candidates to gain ownership of Eastern Europe's enterprises are the national governments, foreigners, existing managers, banks and other fi-

Russian privatization involves decentralization of enterprises but with managerial control by former managers.

Potential buyers for Eastern European state-owned enterprises are
- **The national governments**
- **Foreign investors**
- **Existing managers**
- **Banks and other financial intermediaries**
- **New owner-managers**

nancial intermediaries, and new owner-managers. Although the Russians seem to favor existing managers, Eastern Europeans are having the best success with new owner-managers. In this case, as state-owned enterprises auction off their assets, new owner-managers are picking them up at bargain prices. However, it is difficult to transform the giant state-owned enterprises. They are so big and inefficient that they make poor targets for acquisition. In addition, democracies in Eastern European countries are still so fragile that there is great political risk inherent in the breakup or dissolution of large employers.

Privatization in Argentina   In some cases, severe internal and external national debt has been an incentive to speed the privatization effort. For example, the Argentine government sold four state-owned enterprises in 1990. These included the national telephone company, in which the government sold 60 percent of its ownership interest to private investors, and the national airline, Aerolineas Argentinas.

Many of Argentina's privatization efforts have been very successful.[18] Some, however, have gone awry. For example, when selling Aerolineas Argentinas, the government initially retained a 5-percent interest, sold 10 percent to the Argentine airline's employees, and sold 30 percent to Iberia—the state-owned Spanish airline. Other investors held the rest of the shares. Initially, the government expected that through the sale it could rid itself of fiscal responsibility for the airline as well as eliminate $2.01 billion in foreign debt. However, huge losses and other problems made a mockery of the privatization process. The Argentine government had to buy back most of the privately held shares and thus became the largest single stockholder.

In all countries, the problem with privatization is selling the inefficient, unproductive enterprises, not those that have a chance to survive. Where permitted, the privatization process enables foreign companies to pick up assets and gain access to markets through acquisition. In addition, international businesspeople accustomed to dealing with government-owned enterprises are finding a new breed of managers in the newly privatized enterprises with which they do business.

Inflation

Inflation affects interest rates, exchange rates, the cost of living, and consumer and investor confidence.

Hyperinflation is a rate of inflation that is extremely high (at least 1 percent per day) for a sustained period of time.

Inflation is a dimension of the economic environment that affects interest rates, exchange rates, the cost of living, and the general confidence in a country's political and economic system. For example, fear of inflation in Germany prompts the government's unwillingness to stimulate the economy in order to achieve more rapid economic growth. A comparison of annual increases in the consumer price index for selected countries is shown in Table 4.3. In 1992, compared with the previous three years, inflation began to slow for the world in general and the industrial countries in particular. This improvement primarily occurred in former hyperinflationary economies such as that of Argentina, where prices had been rising in excess of 1 percent per day.

Table 4.3
Percentage Change in Consumer Price Index over Previous Year

In 1992, compared with the previous three years, inflation began to slow in the world in general and the industrial countries in particular. Improvement was especially noteworthy in countries such as Argentina that formerly experienced hyperinflation.

Country or category	Year			
	1989	1990	1991	1992
World	17.0%	21.3%	12.7%	11.9%
Industrial countries	4.5	5.0	4.3	3.0
Canada	5.0	4.8	5.6	1.5
France	3.5	3.4	3.2	2.4
Germany	2.8	2.7	3.5	4.0
Japan	2.3	3.1	3.3	1.7
United Kingdom	7.8	9.5	5.9	3.7
United States	4.8	5.4	4.2	3.0
Developing countries	74.8	103.7	49.1	51.8
Argentina	3079.8	2314.0	171.7	24.9
Brazil	1287.0	2937.8	440.9	1008.7
Hong Kong	9.7	9.7	11.0	9.6
Korea	5.7	8.6	9.7	6.2
Mexico	3.9	3.7	4.0	1.4
Peru	3398.7	7481.7	409.5	73.5

Source: International Monetary Fund, *International Financial Statistics* (Washington, D.C.: IMF, September 1993), pp. 59, 61.

However, inflation was still out of control in some Latin American countries, such as Brazil, and in Russia. Companies with dealings in those countries have difficulty planning for the future and running profitable operations. They must change prices almost daily in order to maintain sufficient cash flow to replace inventory and keep operating. Accurate inflation forecasting also is difficult, and so companies end up underpricing or overpricing products. This practice results in a cash-flow shortage or a price that is too high to allow the company to maintain market share.

Inflation of the magnitude seen in Brazil and Russia also creates problems for companies that deal in imports and exports. If the exchange rate depreciates at the same pace as inflation rises, then the prices foreigners pay for the exports of the inflationary country will not change. However, an exchange rate that depreciates slower than inflation rises causes prices to increase in importing countries. The local companies soon find they cannot compete in world markets. A depreciating currency also causes the cost of inputs to rise, thus further fueling inflation. To keep its costs from being affected much by exchange-rate changes, the Moscow McDonald's developed a strategy of purchasing as many inputs as possible in Russia. However, inflation in Moscow is pushing up local costs and forcing McDonald's to raise prices as well.

Inflation causes political destabilization. If the government tries to control inflation by controlling wages, the real income of the population declines and frustration

Inflation is a major source of political destabilization.

sets in. If the government decides to do nothing, the economy may deteriorate to the point that real incomes fall anyway. Instituting tighter fiscal controls when the government is already in a fragile position is very difficult. This is clearly the problem that faces both Brazil and Russia and strikes fear in the Chinese government. As mentioned earlier in this chapter, China has been experiencing rapid economic growth that began in the early 1990s. However, this growth, if allowed to get out of hand, could reignite inflation, thus devaluing the Chinese currency and forcing the government to slow down economic growth. Such instability concerns foreign investors, who hesitate to invest significant amounts of money in the country.[19]

Payments Imbalances

The balance of payments summarizes all international transactions between domestic residents and foreign residents.

A country's **balance of payments** summarizes all international transactions between domestic and foreign residents. Table 4.4 identifies the major components of the U.S. balance of payments for 1992.

The concept of double-entry accounting is used for the balance of payments; that is, each transaction is represented by two entries of equal value. In Table 4.4, debit entries have a negative (minus) sign and credit entries have a positive (plus) sign. Debit entries reflect payments by domestic residents to foreign residents. Al-

---

Table 4.4
Balance-of-Payments Accounts of the United States (in billions of dollars), 1992

The balance of payments consists of the current account and the capital account. The former showed a deficit in 1992.

Current account		
Exports of goods, services, and income		726.9
Merchandise	439.3	
Services	178.5	
Income receipts from assets	109.2	
Imports of goods, services, and income		−758.0
Merchandise	−535.5	
Services	−118.3	
Income payments on assets	−108.9	
Net unilateral transfers		−31.4
Current account balance		−62.5
Capital account		
Increase in U.S.-owned assets abroad (capital outflow)		−44.9
U.S. official reserve assets	3.9	
Other U.S. assets	−48.8	
Increase in foreign-owned assets in United States (capital inflow)		120.4
Foreign official reserve assets	40.3	
Other foreign assets	80.1	
Capital account balance		75.5
Statistical discrepancy		−13.0

Source: Survey of Current Business, March 1993, p. 66. Data are preliminary.

though this concept appears simple, transactions are not recorded as they are in elementary accounting. In balance-of-payments accounts, import data come from customs records, and export data come from a different source. In addition, errors may occur in recording transactions, and many items, such as expenditures by tourists, must be estimated. Thus, the balance-of-payments accounts include an item called "Statistical discrepancy," which is used to balance the total debits and credits.

Two main categories in the balance of payments are the current account and capital account.

Current account   The current account summarizes a country's real transactions involving currently produced goods and services. These transactions are grouped in the following categories:

- Merchandise trade account
- Services account
- Income receipts and payments on assets accounts
- Unilateral transfers account

A trade surplus occurs when a country exports more goods than it imports.

The **merchandise trade account** measures the trade deficit or surplus. Its balance is derived by subtracting merchandise imports from merchandise exports. A negative result indicates a balance-of-trade deficit; a positive result, a balance-of-trade surplus. An export is considered positive because it results in a payment received from abroad—an inflow of cash. An import is considered negative because it results in a payment made to a seller abroad—an outflow of cash. For example, in 1992, the United States incurred a balance-of-trade deficit of $96.2 billion, of which $49.2 billion was with Japan alone. However, the United States no longer specifically publishes this balance.

The **services account** measures the following transactions: travel and transportation, tourism, and fees and royalties. For example, when a German tourist vacations in the United States, that person's total expenditures are considered to be a service *export*—that is, a cash inflow from Germany. When a U.S. tourist vacations in Germany, that person's total expenditures are considered to be a service *import*—that is, a cash outflow to Germany.

Income receipts and payments on assets accounts measure foreign investment in the United States and U.S. investment abroad. For example, a dividend received by a U.S. company from one of its subsidiaries in Brazil is considered to be an income *receipt;* the dividend creates a positive, or credit, entry in these accounts. A dividend sent by, for example, BMW of America to its parent company in Munich is considered to be an income *payment;* this dividend creates a negative, or debit, entry in the accounts.

Unilateral transfers are payments made to a country for which no goods or services are received. For example, to help defray the cost of the Gulf War in 1991, many countries made payments to the United States. These payments were represented by a positive entry under unilateral transfers in the U.S. balance-of-payments accounts.

In summary, the current account balance is the arithmetic sum of the exports and imports of goods, services, and income, and net unilateral transfers.

The capital account measures transactions involving previously existing rather than currently produced assets.

Capital account   The capital account measures transactions that involve existing assets. For example, when the British firm Grand Metropolitan Plc purchased Häagen-Dazs, the U.S. ice cream company, that purchase was recorded in the United States as a capital inflow—a credit in the capital account. Table 4.4 identifies two major categories in the capital account: U.S. and foreign official reserve assets and other U.S. and foreign assets. Official reserve assets are transactions involving central banks, that is, the official government institutions such as the Federal Reserve Bank in the United States that establish national monetary policy. Other U.S. and foreign assets refer to direct investments such as the British firm's purchase of Häagen-Dazs as well as investments in government treasury bills and stocks of private companies.

Balance-of-payments surpluses and deficits can influence trade policy and the value of currencies.

Impact of different balances on business   What difference does it make whether a country has a surplus or deficit in one of its balance-of-payments accounts? There probably is no direct effect; however, the events that comprise the balance-of-payments data influence exchange rates (as discussed in Chapter 10) and government policy (as discussed in Chapter 6), which, in turn, influence corporate strategy. For example, as mentioned earlier in this section, the United States has experienced a balance-of-trade deficit with Japan in recent years, a situation that has turned into a major political issue. Consequently, the U.S. government has been pressuring the Japanese government to reduce that deficit by expanding Japan's economy in order to attract more exports from the United States. In addition, Japanese auto companies are being encouraged to buy more auto parts from U.S. parts manufacturers. Thus, the balance-of-trade deficit has resulted in new business opportunities for U.S. companies.

Similar analogies can be drawn for other countries. Although world exports must equal world imports, some countries will have surpluses and others deficits. It is not just the existence of a surplus or deficit that concerns global managers but the reasons behind the surplus or deficit and the possible responses of foreign-exchange markets and governments.

External Debt

The regions in which external debts are largest are Latin America and Africa.

One consequence of the rapid increase in oil costs during the 1970s was the equally rapid increase in many countries' external debt. This burgeoning debt resulted as developing countries sought help from foreign private or government institutions to finance oil imports and other products necessary for development. At the time, the two regions where the largest borrowing occurred were Latin America and Africa.

Figure 4.5 identifies the major debtors among the developing countries in 1991. Note the tremendous debt of Brazil and Mexico. It is interesting to observe that in 1986, South Korea was third; in 1991, it ranked tenth. A major problem with large debt is that countries find it difficult to pay even the interest, let alone the principal. The **debt-service ratio**—the ratio of interest payments plus principal amortization to exports—is quite high in some countries, especially in the Western Hemisphere. An increasing share of such a country's export earnings is going to service its debt; thus, less is available for economic development. For example, in the poorest developing countries that are severely indebted, one quarter of export earnings are allocated to debt servicing, yet this allocation pays only half the scheduled amount.[20]

Foreign debt as a percentage of GDP also is a good indicator of the huge burden that debt can be. Map 4.3 shows the distribution of severe debt in Latin America, Africa, Eastern Europe, and some parts of Southeast Asia.

As debts rise, crises are inevitable. The first occurred in Poland in the 1970s. At that time, it appeared that Poland would have to default (refuse to pay back its loans), and many experts were unsure of the impact this would have on the international financial community. The next, and most serious, crisis occurred in August 1982, when Mexico, with nearly four times the debt of Poland, could not fulfill its debt-service obligations. As a result, it was forced to reschedule principal and interest payments. When a country reschedules debt, it changes the interest rate of the loan and/or the timing of the payments of principal and interest. In the early 1980s, most other large debtors, especially Brazil and Argentina, were in the same position as Mexico and had to go through rescheduling.

In 1987, the crisis reached critical proportions, especially among Latin American debtors. Brazil declared a moratorium on interest and principal payments to commercial creditors—basically, it suspended payments—arguing that it could not

Figure 4.5
External Debt of Selected Developing Countries, 1991

The two largest borrowing regions of the world were Latin America and Africa, led by Brazil and Mexico. The large amount of debt creates cash-flow problems for developing countries as they must use an increasing share of their export earnings to pay principal and interest.

Source: World Bank, *World Development Report* (New York: Oxford University Press, 1993), pp. 278–279.

Country	Abbreviation	Total debt, 1991 (in billions)
Brazil	BRZ	$116.514
Mexico	MEX	101.737
Indonesia	INDO	73.629
India	IND	71.557
Argentina	ARG	63.707
China	CHI	60.802
Poland	POL	52.481
Turkey	TUR	50.252
Egypt	EGY	40.571
South Korea	SK	40.518
Venezuela	VEN	34.372

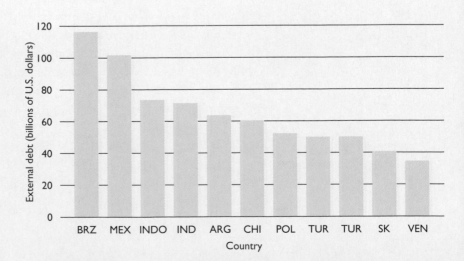

Map 4.3   Foreign Debt as a Percentage of GDP

Countries are classified according to what they owe abroad as a percentage of GDP. The largest amounts of total debt outstanding are held by Brazil, Mexico, and Argentina. Of the seventeen most highly indebted countries, measured by interest payments as a percentage of exports, nine are in Latin America, including eight of the top ten.

Source: *The Economist World Atlas and Almanac,* The Economist Books/Prentice-Hall Press, pp. 84–85. Reprinted by permission.

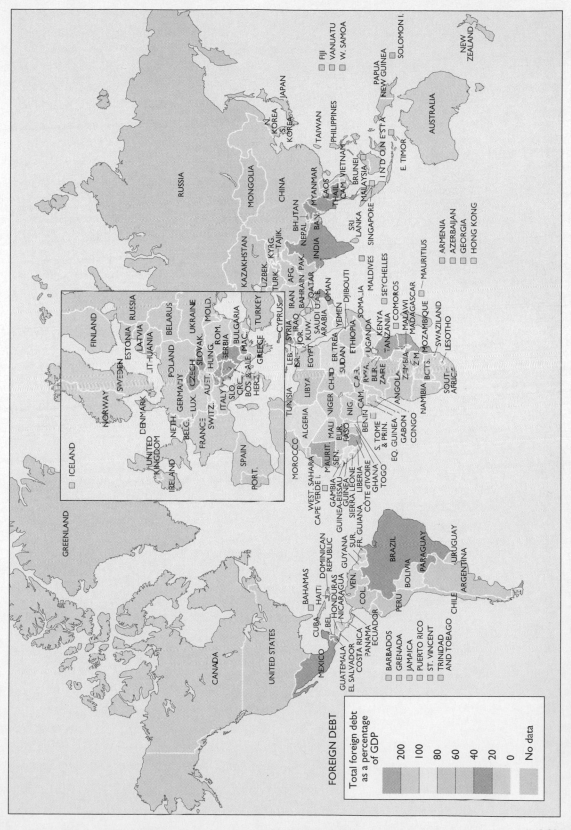

FOREIGN DEBT

Total foreign debt
as a percentage
of GDP

200
100
80
60
40
20
0
No data

The debt crises of the 1980s resulted in several defaults and reschedulings of loans.

afford the $5 billion in annual interest payments, which represented 12 percent of its budget.[21] In response to the increasing uncertainty regarding repayment of Latin American loans, many banks began setting aside large reserves in case those debtors defaulted. A bank establishes reserves by funneling some of its earnings into a reserve account. Doing this allows it to reduce earnings a little each year, especially profitable years, rather than being surprised by a major default and having to reduce earnings all at once. However, the practice of setting aside large reserves is problematic because it weakens the bank's lending ability and financial strength.

The IMF provides economic advice to help countries solve debt problems and get new loans; it also has created controversy.

The International Monetary Fund (IMF), which will be discussed in greater detail in Chapter 10, has played a crucial role in helping debtor nations restructure their economies. In country after country, the IMF has recommended strong economic restrictions as a precondition to granting a loan. These restrictions typically have involved a combination of export expansion, import substitution, and drastic reductions in public spending. In many developing countries, IMF restrictions have touched off heated debate and sorely tested the political stability of the government. Strict IMF controls sparked riots in several countries, including Egypt and Venezuela. And when the IMF attempted to establish such controls in Russia, the Russian government simply ignored them.

In many cases, an IMF loan is a prerequisite for persuading international commercial banks to reschedule a country's debts. Usually, the IMF periodically monitors the targets it sets as a precondition to releasing funds. Private international banks often use the results of this monitoring to determine their lending policies regarding the monitored country.

Managers of MNEs are concerned about high debt because of the difficulty of operating in an environment that is politically and economically unstable. In such an environment, imports often are curtailed and hard currency is difficult to obtain. In addition, governments may institute a variety of macroeconomic measures to control debt, including slowing down economic growth, which could have a negative impact on companies' sales opportunities.

Transformation to a Market Economy

The demolition of the Berlin Wall and the overthrow of Eastern European communist dictatorships in 1989 renewed Western interest in doing business in countries that previously had been considered off limits. These countries were those that had had nonmarket economies (NMEs), or centrally planned economies (CPEs), or that had been commonly called the Second World or the Eastern Bloc. (The latter term was political rather than geographic. East-West trade referred to business between communist and noncommunist countries rather than to trade between the Eastern and Western Hemispheres.)

A major ethical dilemma implied in this chapter concerns the obligations of industrial countries to assist developing ones. Some of the areas in which the industrial countries might be seen as having an ethical obligation to provide support are access to markets for developing countries' exports, foreign aid, and repayment of loans.

First, developing countries must have access to markets in industrial countries in order to sell products. Many developing countries have domestic markets of limited size, and their trade with each other is not significant. For example, Latin American countries on average export only about 10 percent of their products to other Latin American countries but almost 20 percent of them to the United States. However, during the recent period of relatively high unemployment in industrial countries protectionism has threatened to cut off developing countries' access to industrial markets. If industrial countries discriminate against exports from developing countries, they are hurting those countries' prospects for further development.

ETHICAL DILEMMAS

As for foreign aid, there has been increasing pressure in the United States to cut down the amount of such aid in order to put the funds to use in improving the domestic economy. However, the United States and other industrial countries benefit from trade with developing countries not only through gaining access to their markets but also through utilizing their resources. Some industrial countries view foreign aid as a means of putting resources back into developing countries. For example, the Scandinavian countries contribute a larger percentage of their GDPs to foreign aid than do the United States and Japan. And other rich European countries, such as Germany and the Netherlands, provide funding to their developing neighbors Spain and Portugal to help them improve their infrastructure. In contrast, when the United States and Mexico were debating NAFTA in 1993, much of the opposition to the agreement came from people who wondered how it was going to be funded rather than how the United States could provide more resources to Mexico to help develop the economy.

A third ethical issue concerns the repayment of loans. Because of the overwhelming size of the external debt of many developing countries, one possible solution (discussed earlier in this chapter) is forgiveness of some or all of such debt. Another possibility is to restructure it so that repayment is less burdensome to a developing country's economic growth. Forgiveness might be more appropriate for loans made by governments of industrial countries than for those made by private-sector banks. But, in any case, some feel the industrial countries need to make an effort to be part of the solution to the debt crisis rather than just part of the problem.

The process of transformation to a market economy differs from country to country; no single formula can be applied to all. In addition, the various historically planned economies (HPEs) differ greatly in their commitment to and progress toward transformation of their centrally planned economies into market economies. At one end of the spectrum is the former German Democratic Republic (East Germany), which has been reunited with and absorbed into the German Federal Republic (West Germany), although with great difficulty. At the other end of the spectrum is Cuba, which has committed to neither reforms nor market transformation. It is unlikely Cuba will embark on transformation any time soon. Fidel Castro, Cuba's leader, said in 1989, in reference to the political liberalization and other changes within Eastern Europe, "We are witnessing sad things in other socialist countries, very sad things. We are astonished at the phenomena that we see."[22]

In the middle of the spectrum of economic transformation are the other HPEs. For example, Hungary and the Czech Republic are in the process of transformation, but Bulgaria and Romania continue to maintain that a combination of central planning and market economy is possible.[23] Poland is committed but has not had time to complete the change, and Algeria already has moved far from its earlier central planning doctrines and policies. China, like Bulgaria and Romania, is committed to a combination of central planning and market economy; thus, it has embarked on some reforms but still adheres to communistic and central planning principles. Table 4.5 classifies the HPEs according to geographical location and provides population and per capita GDP data, where available.

Western interest in doing business with HPEs has been renewed because of
• **Improved political relationships**
• **Prospects of economic growth**

Why do these changes bring renewed Western interest in doing business with HPEs? The answer is partly political, partly economic. Most HPEs experienced slow economic growth during the 1970s and 1980s; consequently, the outlook for expanded commercial activities seemed bleak. However, along with reforms and transformation has come a thawing of Cold War tensions. With that comes the hope that governments of these countries will eliminate their trade barriers, thereby encouraging rejuvenated economic growth and increased business opportunities.

There is significant interest among MNEs in Eastern European HPEs and China.

Much of the recent optimism has centered around business possibilities in the Eastern European HPEs and China. Interest in the former is due to their level of economic development, and the latter has been the focus of attention because of its huge population and rapid economic growth. These conditions help explain why McDonald's has entered Hungary, Russia, and China but not Mongolia. Although Eastern European HPEs have per capita incomes that are only about one tenth as large as those of Western industrial countries, these incomes are still about ten times larger than those in such African HPEs as Somalia and Mozambique. Further, although the per capita incomes of the Eastern European HPEs are close to those of some Latin American developing countries, the former share certain characteristics favorable to rapid economic development that most of the latter don't have, including more highly educated populations and more equality of income and social status.

China has a high growth rate.

China is a special case. Although its per capita income is only about one quarter of that of Eastern European HPEs, its recent economic growth rate is much higher,

Table 4.5
Estimated Population and Per Capita GDP for Historically Planned Economies (HPEs), 1992

The HPEs have wide differences in population and per capita GDP, but the highest per capita GDPs among them are found in Eastern Europe and the former Soviet Union.

Region	Country	Population (millions)	Per capita GDP (U.S. dollars)
Asia	Afghanistan	16.1	200[*]
	Cambodia	7.3	130[†]
	China, People's Republic of	1169.6	n/a
	Korea, Democratic Republic of	22.2	1100[†]
	Lao People's Democratic Republic	4.4	200[‡]
	Mongolia	2.3	900[†]
	Myanmar (formerly Burma)	42.6	530[‡]
	Vietnam	70.0	220[†]
	Yemen, Democratic Republic of	10.4	545[§]
Africa	Algeria	26.7	2130[†]
	Angola	8.9	950[†]
	Benin	5.0	410[‡]
	Congo	2.4	1070[§]
	Ethiopia	54.3	130[§]
	Guinea	7.8	410[§]
	Madagascar	12.6	200[†]
	Mozambique	15.5	120[†]
	Somalia	7.2	210[**]
	Tanzania	27.8	290[*]
North and South America	Chile	13.5	2300[†]
	Cuba	10.8	1580[†]
	Nicaragua	3.9	425[†]
Eastern Europe	Albania	3.25	n/a
	Bulgaria	8.47	815
	Croatia	—	—
	Czech Republic	10.40	2550
	Hungary	10.30	3446
	Poland	38.30	1895
	Romania	23.20	610
	Slovakia	5.26	1820
	Slovenia	—	—
Former Soviet Union	Armenia[††]	3.5	2955
	Azerbaijan	7.2	2870
	Belarus[††]	10.3	5729
	Estonia	1.6	5390
	Georgia	5.5	3065
	Kazakhstan[††]	17.0	3803
	Kyrgystan[††]	4.5	2436
	Latvia	2.7	5689
	Lithuania	3.7	4034
	Moldova[††]	4.4	3600
	Russia[††]	148.8	5396
	Tajikistan[††]	5.5	1613
	Turkmenistan[††]	3.8	2682
	Ukraine[††]	51.9	4397
	Uzbekistan[††]	21.1	2321

[*]1989 estimate
[†]1991 estimate
[‡]1991
[§]1990 estimate
[**]1998
[††]Member of the Commonwealth of Independent States

Source: "The Winter of Discontent," *Time*, December 7, 1992, pp. 38–39; and "Survey: Eastern Europe," *The Economist*, March 13, 1993, p. 18.

rivaling those of its East Asian neighbors. Even the World Bank concedes that its low per capita income figures may not accurately describe the dynamic Chinese economy. Because of China's large economy and understated per capita income, there is greater market potential in that country than might seem apparent.

In spite of perceived greater opportunities in HPEs, entry into them is not without costs and risks. For example, the success of McDonald's Russian venture required many deviations from the company's usual procedures; some of these deviations were as follows:

- Participating in long and complex negotiations
- Taking ownership (as opposed to franchising) to compensate for the lack of entrepreneurs with investment capital
- Selecting partners who have political clout rather than food or distribution experience
- Creating sources of supplies that did not previously exist
- Training employees to be customer-oriented in the face of overwhelming consumer demand for the products
- Accepting that it will take much longer to repatriate, or return profits to the parent company

Very likely, for the foreseeable future, HPEs will continue to be spread out across the economic spectrum. The closer a country is to central planning, the more Western managers will encounter situations traditionally associated with doing business with CPEs rather than with HPEs.

Political and Economic Volatility

Western business with HPEs has been compared to a light switch: it turns on and then turns off.[24] The McDonald's case illustrates how business volatility is created by changing political attitudes. McDonald's negotiations with the Soviets began in 1976 and continued without significant progress until the Soviets enacted joint venture legislation in 1987. From that point, negotiations concluded swiftly and start-up followed soon afterward.

Volatility of East-West trade has occurred when
- **HPE actions change**
- **Different leaders come into power in the East or the West**

Sometimes volatility has resulted from unpopular actions by HPEs (such as the Soviet invasion of Afghanistan) or cooperation against a common enemy (such as the alliance against Germany in World War II). In some cases, it may result from the ascendancy either of new political decision makers in the East or of leaders in the West who hold differing philosophies about business interactions with dictatorships and/or countries with central planning (for example, U.S. trade sanctions against Nicaragua).

Although relations between most HPEs and the Western industrialized countries have been more congenial since 1989, the risk of future sanctions by the West still exists. In 1991, the Russian military opened fire against protestors in Lithuania. That same year, the Chinese government convicted human rights advocates who had participated in the Tiananmen Square riots of "counterrevolutionary propaganda." In 1994, China's continued human rights violations, along with trade-related issues, prompted the United States to consider revoking China's most-favored-nation (MFN) status.

Political volatility makes managers reluctant to expend resources.

Most companies prefer to invest their capital and human resources in endeavors that can be expected to continue for a long time. For this reason, persistent uncertainty about political relations with some HPEs causes some companies to hesitate to commit resources to business development in those countries. On the one hand, Western businesses have witnessed increased political interactions. On the other, they also realize that past experience shows how rapidly business can change because of politics and how it can continue to fluctuate over time.

It also is important to realize that a country's attaining a market economy does not guarantee its economic success; in fact, most of the world's developing countries currently qualify as market economies. But economic development is a very complex process; there have been very few successes in the twentieth century. The HPEs vary widely in terms of factors that may affect their growth, with or without a high degree of transformation. These factors include the following:

- Educational level of the population
- Quantity and distribution of natural resources
- Degree of national cohesiveness
- Access to investment capital
- Extent of existing industrial structure
- Entrepreneurial experience among the population
- Development of infrastructure

Some HPEs want to
- **Become market economies**
- **Make reforms within a central planning system**
- **Stay as they are**

Companies contemplating commercial activities in HPEs should examine development potential as well as prospects for economic transformation. The key to successfully transforming any HPE to a market economy is achieving certain changes in the general economic environment, including monetary stabilization, currency convertibility, and price and trade liberalization.[25] Once a private sector appears, these economic changes are the ones that will keep the transformation process working.

Russia's Transformation

Russian transformation is being hindered by political turmoil.

For Russia, transformation to a market economy has been difficult because the government has been trying simultaneously to change the country's economy and its political system while coming to grips with the end of an empire whose parts were politically and economically interdependent. The resulting political turmoil is exacerbated by the battle between conservatives who are afraid of moving too fast and

Russia is trying to move to a market economy, instill democracy, and recover from the breakup of the Soviet Empire.

reformers who want to install capitalism quickly through privatization and price decontrol.

The Soviet economy was cumbersome, inefficient, and corrupt, but somehow it seemed to function. However, the breakup of the central Soviet government and the loss of the relationship Russia had with the other fourteen Soviet republics and the former Eastern Bloc countries resulted in the implosion of the economy. For example, in 1992, Russia's GDP fell by about 23 percent and unemployment rose from 59,000 in January to 905,000 in November. Also in 1992, prices were decontrolled. Prior to that, prices were controlled by the government and goods were distributed by means of consumers waiting in long lines, because of shortages. Price decontrol resulted in more products being brought to market, but at the cost of significantly higher prices and inflation that soared to over 1000 percent annually. Fully two thirds of the Russian people live below the poverty line. The ruble, valued at 120 per U.S. dollar in early 1992, had plummeted to a shocking 1787 per U.S. dollar by April 1994.

Eastern Europe's Transformation

GDP is beginning to grow again in Eastern European countries.

In the three years following the overthrow of communism in 1989 and 1990, economic growth in Eastern Europe ground to a halt. From 1990 to 1992, GNP fell by 40 percent in Czechoslovakia, 32 percent in Hungary, and 32 percent in Poland. However, by 1992, the worst appeared to be over. Poland's GDP grew slightly, while Czechoslovakia's stabilized and began to rise by the end of the year, a trend that continued through 1993.[26]

Eastern Europe's macroeconomic problems are shortages and inflation.

Its microeconomic problems arise from having invested in the wrong industries.

The process of transforming HPEs to market economies attempts to solve two types of problems that are universal in Eastern Europe: macroeconomic problems that involve shortages and inflation and microeconomic problems that involve investments in the wrong industries. As price controls ended and markets opened up all over Eastern Europe, shortages began to disappear fairly quickly. However, central planning had resulted in highly inefficient industries and the transformation of state-owned enterprises resulted in a sharp drop in production, much of which was unwanted and unnecessary anyway. Today, the output of the private sector is growing much more rapidly than that of the remaining public sector.[27]

As Eastern European countries transform, they are finding their budget deficits rising, not because of higher government expenditures, but because of weak revenue collections. Failing enterprises are not paying taxes, resulting in continuing revenue shortfalls.

China's Transformation

The Chinese economy is growing rapidly, but the political system is not moving toward democracy.

In 1978, China's government launched reforms designed to transform the Chinese economy on the basis of a new vision—a turning away from central planning, government ownership, and import substitution and a movement toward greater decentralization and opening up of the Chinese economy. Since then, the Chinese economy has grown to four times its size in 1978; by 2002, it is estimated to be eight times as large as in 1978.[28]

The Chinese economy is being rapidly decentralized but not necessarily privatized.

The Chinese approach to transformation differs significantly from those taken in Russia and Eastern Europe. The Chinese leadership is not at all interested in democratic reform. It continues to hold tight to totalitarian political control, while trying to pacify citizens with economic growth. Recently, most of such growth has been along the coast and near the special economic zones, but current reforms are rapidly moving economic changes into the much poorer interior. Privatization is not an issue, but economic activity has been decentralized swiftly. Centralized state-owned enterprises now control only half of GNP, and their share is rapidly dwindling as economic power is pushed down to the regional and local levels, resulting in what looks like a loose federation of regional economies.[29]

Overseas Chinese are major investors in China.

One major advantage China enjoys is a high rate of investment by overseas Chinese. "Today, at least 75 percent of the mainland's roughly 28,000 enterprises with significant foreign equity are financed by ethnic Chinese who live outside China. Hong Kong and Taiwan account for two-thirds [Hong Kong is the largest source of foreign investment in China]."[30] In contrast to Russia and Eastern Europe, significant foreign investment is moving into China.[31]

Stumbling Blocks to Transformation

Many factors can impede the orderly progress toward a successful market economy, as described for Russia, Eastern Europe, and China. The major hurdles are as follows:

- Economic shocks resulting from the transformation
- Continued existence of soft budgets
- Problems with existing management
- Concentration of production in one facility
- Limited availability of investment funds
- Consequences of environmental damage

Economic shocks   As part of bringing about a market transformation, some negative economic consequences are inevitable, at least in the short term. The basic problem is that the costs are up front, but the benefits come much later. For example, increasing efficiency through allowing foreign competition brings with it unemployment. But HPEs are not accustomed to unemployment and do not have the safety nets of fall-back compensation, retraining facilities, and job-relocation assistance that have been developed over a long period in industrial countries. In addition, price decontrol brings rapid inflation because the old prices were below the true market values. When Poland deregulated most of its prices, a standard joke among its citizens was, "We used to have long lines and empty shelves. Now we have no lines, full shelves, but no money to buy what's on the shelves."

Statistics may understate the degree of hardship arising from economic shocks. The full-employment rates HPEs enjoyed earlier masked the fact that many employees were simply performing "make work" assignments. And although official prices were lower prior to deregulation, before-and-after price comparisons do not take into account shortages and quality differences. For example, some goods in short supply sold at official prices even though they may have been resold in the black market at higher prices. Further, many goods with prices that were lower before deregulation could not be sold afterward at any price; their quality and safety records were so poor that no one wanted them. Where central planning overstates employment and understates prices, there is a familiar joke: "We pretend to work, and they pretend to pay us."[32]

A backlash due to short-term economic hardships may impede economic transformation.

Economic shocks are politically dangerous. Workers and consumers have high expectations for economic transformation—perhaps too high. To the extent that they are adversely affected by unemployment and higher prices (a lowering of real income), even in the short term, they may lose confidence in the elected political leadership and in the transformation process itself, thus slowing or preventing change.

Soft budgets allow government-owned enterprises to get subsidies to cover losses.

Soft budgets   A **soft budget** is a financial condition in which an enterprise spends more than it earns and the difference is met by some other institution, typically the government or a government-controlled financial institution. The HPEs all have legacies of soft budgets from the period when it was unthinkable that an enterprise would not survive. Even within an environment of transformation, pressures remain to continue soft-budget practices. This happens for several reasons.

First, new managers may claim that their operating inefficiencies are due to excesses created before they took their posts; therefore, they argue, their enterprises must continue to receive subsidies until they can effect operating reversals. (Even within market economies, companies have successfully used this argument to receive indirect subsidies via import restrictions. A good example of this is the U.S. steel industry.)

Second, some economists argue that soft budgets encourage enterprises to limit profits. This practice decreases funds available as wages to workers and dividend payments to stockholders, which in turn reduces consumption and frees funds for growth-generating investment.

Third, HPEs are burdened with many large and inefficient enterprises that for economic and political reasons they can ill afford to let die in the short term. Fearing economic disruptions if new facilities displace old ones, HPEs have gone so far as to require ventures by foreign automobile firms to be carried out in existing (inefficient) facilities.

When profits don't have to be made, there are few incentives for improving efficiency.

Cushioned by a soft budget, a company's management has an incentive to make deals with authorities instead of effecting efficiencies that could help the company survive. For example, during the 1980s, many Chinese enterprises switched from measuring performance on the basis of gross output to measuring it on the basis of profit. But this change occurred without eliminating soft budgets within the banking system and some productive sectors. Because the banking system faced no real budget constraints, it continued to lend to enterprises regardless of their inefficiencies. In addition, continuing the soft budgets in some sectors enabled even some of the enterprises that were evaluated on the basis of profits to raise those profits, largely by gaining access to subsidized credit and subsidized inputs rather than by raising sales or cutting real production costs.[33]

HPEs lack sufficient people who understand how to manage in a market economy.

Existing managers   Many government-owned enterprises are plagued by mammoth bureaucracies that are difficult to replace. As a government eliminates central planning without also substituting knowledgeable owners to whom enterprise managers can report, there is little control over these managers' actions. Another problem, more acute in countries in which people have no memory of market operations, is that most managers have no experience in operating without a central plan that tells them what to produce and to whom to sell. They also may lack experience in controlling subordinates by hiring and firing them or by finding means of compensation as a way of motivating them. Very few of these managers understand how to read or compile financial statements, how to respond to market signals (such as changes in demand), or how to market products when there is competition and no pent-up demand, especially in Western export markets. They also may lack a strong work ethic because of their experiences with low pay and high job security. Further, egalitarian attitudes, especially in Russia and China, result in successful entrepreneurs sometimes being seen as speculators— a contemptuous label.[34]

Large single-site monopolies are hard to break up.

Production concentration   Russia has enterprises that are not only state-owned but also monopolies that produce in only one facility. These enterprises tend to be highly integrated vertically; that is, they produce most of the components they need in the one location because they cannot be assured of obtaining supplies elsewhere. These facilities tend to operate inefficiently. But breaking them up and privatizing is made more difficult because their sheer size can make selling them problematic.

   For potential new competitive producers, the existence of these enterprises creates many problems. New producers must compete with these mammoth state-owned monopolies. They will probably encounter problems in obtaining supplies that could necessitate their having to build their own vertically integrated operations (recall that McDonald's had to develop many of its own sources of supplies). And they face difficulties selling to industrial customers that already have long associations with existing government-owned enterprises.

Funds availability[35]   There is a consensus that transformation to a successful market economy is very expensive. Huge capital investments are needed to develop infrastructure, improve the environment, modernize factories, and educate managers to operate within a market system. Simultaneously, there is substantial consumer pressure on enterprises to produce goods and services that historically were in short supply. These pressures limit government efforts to continue diverting funds from consumer spending to capital spending as had been done in the past.

The high external debt of some countries hampers their ability to receive large infusions of foreign capital. Most banks have become cautious as a result of past debt crises; they are unwilling to lend more money to countries already heavily indebted.

It is uncertain whether HPEs can get the vast funds they need for development.

Many suggest that Western banks and governments should simply write off the debts so that HPEs can start with a clean slate. Those arguments are offered on the basis of humanitarian concerns (the populations suffered long enough under repressive regimes) and precedence (German debts were forgiven a few years after the end of World War II). However, a massive write-off is unlikely for two reasons. First, benefits would accrue primarily to those countries that have not repaid their debts; a country such as Romania, which has no large debt, would receive no benefits after having endured a harsh austerity program. Second, singling out HPEs would seem unfair to the large, debt-ridden developing countries of Latin America, Asia, and Africa. In any case, a write-off could more easily be accomplished for debt to government than for debt to private banks. Poland, for example, owed most of its external debt to other governments; thus a partial write-off for Poland in 1990 was easier than a write-off would be for Hungary, which owes most of its external debt to foreign private banks.

Others propose a program like the Marshall Plan for Eastern Europe. Realistically, such a program seems unlikely. The largest Western economy, the United States, has substantial balance-of-payments problems of its own and so is unlikely to finance massive assistance to other countries. In addition, such a program's effectiveness is questionable. The great success of the Marshall Plan in Western Europe after World War II resulted not only from the huge infusions of capital, but also because the goal was simply to bring the war-devastated economies back to their relatively high levels of five or six years earlier. However, some HPEs never have been at a high developmental level. Further, in some countries central-planning regimes have been in power for so long that few people can recall successful earlier situations that must be emulated if rapid development is to take place.

Environmental problems will be difficult for HPEs to resolve.

Environmental damage   Environmental damage is another major concern for HPEs. Since harm to human health is the most important consequence of such damage, the two most important problems are air and water pollution. The former results from suspended metal dusts and particulate materials. The latter is exacerbated by careless disposal of toxic or nuclear waste that threatens the quality of surface and ground water in some areas.[36] The major causes of environmental pollution are heavy coal use; old technology, especially in the metallurgy industry; and low energy prices, which serve as a disincentive to save energy and raw materials.

Some argue that air pollution in the main towns and cities of Eastern Europe is no worse than in Western European cities, such as Athens, Madrid, and Milan, that have similar income levels and industrial structures. These analysts claim that environmental problems in Eastern Europe today are at the level they were in Western

Europe and North America twenty to thirty years ago. In actuality, water pollution and environmental damage from inadequate nuclear waste management are far more serious in Eastern Europe today than they were in the industrial countries thirty years ago. The cost of environmental cleanup will be significant and will reduce the amount of investment capital available to transform HPEs to market economies.

Adapting to Foreign Economic Environments

A company based in the United States is accustomed to and has devised ways to survive in the U.S. economic system. However, when such a company wants to do business in another country for the first time, it needs to find answers to questions such as the following:

1. Under what type of economic system does the country operate?
2. Is the company's industry in that country's public or private sector?
3. If it is in the public sector, does the government also allow private competition in that sector?
4. If the company's industry is in the private sector, is it moving toward public ownership?
5. Does the government view foreign capital as being in competition with or in partnership with public or local private enterprises?
6. In what ways does the government control the nature and extent of private enterprise?
7. How much of a contribution is the private sector expected to make in helping the government formulate overall economic objectives?

These questions appear simple; however, because of the dynamic nature of political and economic events, the answers are complex. Many foreign companies are still investing in Hong Kong even though the conditions that will exist after 1997, when Hong Kong reverts to China, are very uncertain. Hong Kong companies such as Swire are investing outside of that country because of the same uncertainty. Companies attempting to invest in Eastern Europe and the former Soviet Union are experiencing enormous difficulties because the economic environment in those countries is very different from any other in the world, and the changes taking place there are so rapid and unpredictable.

Companies intending to do business in foreign markets must be aware of their own experiences and how those have helped shape their managerial philosophies and practices. In addition, they must determine how the new environment differs from their more familiar domestic environment and decide how managerial philosophy and practice must be changed to adapt to the new conditions.

C O U N T E R V A I L I N G

F O R C E S

Small companies that do business with developing countries and HPEs potentially face the problems of inadequate financial resources, managerial expertise, and/or patience required to succeed. The resource commitment is significant, as illustrated by the McDonald's case. However, many small companies successfully trade with or invest in developing countries by exploiting a product niche. For example, before McDonald's opened its first restaurant in Moscow, a U.S. entrepreneur with limited financial resources operated a Nathan's Famous Hot Dogs mobile unit in that city. From one pushcart, he served about 1000 customers a day, and the venture was very profitable. To ensure he could always obtain needed supplies, he bought meat each day from the Central Market, where farmers sell from their private production at a significant premium over the prices offered by the state stores.[37]

Another major issue is national sovereignty. As HPEs go through the transition to market economies, they are getting a lot of advice from Western countries that are providing financial aid as well as from international organizations such as the IMF. Although the HPEs need the aid and the advice, they are trying to develop strategies that fit their unique situations and so don't always follow all the advice offered. This is especially a problem when their actions are contrary to the advice offered by aid-granting countries and organizations.

LOOKING TO THE FUTURE

The OECD countries are in serious economic difficulties, and it will be a few years before they begin to experience solid economic growth. Most of the current growth is in the developing countries, especially those in South and Southeast Asia. The growth rates in those regions are creating a large and relatively wealthy market that a company's management must take into account when setting a global strategy. In particular, China is rapidly becoming the economic powerhouse of Asia. Not only will it continue to be a competitor in light manufacturing and textiles, but its industrial base will improve over the next few years. When President Clinton agreed in 1993 to continue MFN status for China, he basically gave U.S. companies the green light to increase their trade with that country. However, this trade could be curtailed in the future if China does not make progress in correcting human-rights abuses, controlling its proliferation of weapons, and opening its markets in order to reduce its trade surplus with the United States.

The area of real concern is Eastern Europe and the former Soviet Union. Eastern European countries are farther along in the economic transformation process than Russia is. Now that their growth rates are improving, these countries should find it easier to attract foreign capital to take advantage of cheap labor, close proximity to Western European markets, and rising standards of living. Although the current political environment in that part of the world is still too unstable for significant near-term foreign investment, it is definitely an area that companies will be watching.

Summary

- The economic system determines who owns and controls resources. In a market economy, individuals allocate and control resources; in a centrally planned economy, the government allocates and controls resources.

- Two important societal units for a market economy are the individual and the company.

- Consumer sovereignty is somewhat curtailed by large corporations, labor unions, and government policies.

- Governments having centrally planned economies coordinate the activities of the different economic sectors.

- Countries are classified according to three income levels: high (primarily the industrial countries that are members of the OECD), middle, and low. The middle- and low-income countries are often called developing countries.

- Historically planned economies (HPLs) are those that once were (and in some cases still are) heavily involved in central planning.

- As countries become more prosperous and their economies shift from low-income to high-income categories, the percentage of gross domestic product (GDP) derived from agriculture decreases and that derived from industry and services increases.

- The greatest economic growth is in the developing countries, especially those in Asia.

- Industrial and developing countries are trying to privatize government-owned enterprises in order to help eliminate their budget deficits.

- So far in the 1990s, hyperinflation (an annual inflation rate of 1000 percent or more) has subsided somewhat, but it is still found in Brazil. Argentina and Peru as well as some of the Eastern European countries and Russia continue to have high inflation rates.

- Significant deficits in the current account balances of countries cause trade friction, a possible renewal of inflation, pressure on currencies, and loss of investor confidence.

- Severely indebted countries, especially the poorest of the developing countries, must use a significant percentage of their export earnings to service their debt, leaving too little for development.

- Political and economic changes within the former communist countries have led to optimism in the West about doing business in those countries because political barriers may be lessened and economic growth will enhance market potential.

- In this century, political relationships between Western countries and HPEs have varied significantly, resulting in business relationships that also have fluctuated substantially. This has been especially true of trade between the United States and the former Soviet Union.

- Not all HPEs plan to transform themselves into market economies. Further, transformation to a market economy will not necessarily make an HPE economically successful.

- Russia's transformation has been complicated by its transition to democracy, the breakup of the Soviet empire, and the political problems of balancing conservative efforts to retain central control over the economy and reformist efforts to move quickly to a market economy.

- Eastern European countries have approached transformation of their economies differently, and their private sectors are creating significantly more economic growth than their public sectors are.

- China's transformation has involved large infusions of capital from overseas Chinese and decentralization of economic decision making.

- The major barriers to economic transformation in HPEs are economic shocks, continued use of soft budgets to bail out some government-owned enterprises, incompetent management, concentration of production in huge enterprises, limited funds availability, and environmental damage.

- Managers need to analyze countries to determine how a particular government has behaved, is behaving, and will behave.

Case
Motorola in China[38]

In the spring of 1993, one year after Motorola announced that it would build a $120-million factory in Tianjin, China, the company's top managers were faced with the decision as to whether or not they should lobby U.S. government officials to extend MFN status to China. They had to decide how important China was to Motorola's future expansion in Asia and what the ramifications would be of lobbying in behalf of the Chinese.

Motorola in Asia

To understand Motorola's position in China, it is important to see how the Chinese operations fit in the company's overall Asian strategy. Approximately half of Motorola's sales come from outside the United States, and Europe generates about 25 percent of total sales. Asia, which accounts for slightly over 20 percent of total sales, is where sales are growing the fastest. Motorola's head of international business predicts that in the next decade Asian sales will grow two or three times faster than European and U.S. sales.

About 85 percent of Motorola's revenues come from mobile communications and semiconductors, and those businesses are growing rapidly. Although Motorola has operated in Japan, Singapore, Hong Kong, and Taiwan for years, it is only recently pushing ahead in China. Up to this point, Japanese and Hong Kong operations have generated most of Motorola's success. C. D. Tam, the corporate vice president and general manager of Motorola Asia Pacific Semiconductor Products Divisions, believed that Asia should be considered as an important market as well as a processing location. Tam was the first Chinese employee to be promoted by Motorola in Asia, and he worked hard to bring more Asians into the business. His goal has been to train outstanding Chinese technical people to become managers. Although Motorola was using Asia as a place to manufacture semiconductors, Tam had to convince top management that electronics would flourish in the region as well.

Further, Motorola management believes that a company can never be a total supplier to a geographical region without having the ability to design and create new products. Thus the establishment of design centers in Hong Kong and Taiwan helped Motorola to develop a stronger identification with the Asian market. However, China seems to be the future; its large, rapidly growing market is too significant for Motorola to ignore.

Motorola's Chinese Venture

On March 27, 1992, Motorola announced that it would build a $120-million factory in northern China to manufacture semiconductors, cellular phones, radio paging systems, and computer software. The move was interesting, because Motorola had announced in 1988 that it would invest $300 million in a plant in China, but the tragedy in Tiananmen Square changed that. The facility, which was due to be completed in 1993, was expected to employ several hundred people initially, with employment rising to nearly a thousand by the late 1990s. Motorola's decision was influenced by improved conditions in China and by the fact that its major competitors—NEC of Japan, Philips of the Netherlands, and BTM of Belgium—also announced that they would be building plants in China.

When the Tianjin plant was announced, it was the largest totally U.S.-funded enterprise in China. The plant, which is wholly owned by Motorola rather than being a joint venture with a government agency, initially was designed to export 70 percent of its total output and sell the remainder, especially semiconductors, in the Chinese market. Motorola had intended to recoup its investment in the plant through the export sales.

By the end of 1992, even though the plant was not finished, it already was producing radio pagers. However, it was selling its entire weekly output of 10,000 pagers in the Chinese market. Then, in early 1993, Motorola announced that it would more than double its initial investment and most of the new funds would be targeted for the production of silicon chips and semiconductors.

A major part of Motorola's expansion plans is the recruitment of engineers. It anticipates that it will have to hire 250 engineers in the next few years. Although there are many technically qualified engineers in China, they have a difficult time applying their knowledge developing innovative new products. In order to recruit the best and the brightest, Motorola is providing student scholarships, donating computer equipment, and providing internships for students. Motorola also has a program called "Cadres 2000," through which it places up to twenty top recruits in leadership training programs and rotates them through Motorola operations worldwide.

Tianjin

Why did Motorola select Tianjin rather than somewhere else in China as the location of its production facilities? Tianjin, China's third largest city, is less than 100 miles from Beijing. Not only is it the largest of China's northern ports, but it has the largest container terminal in the country. Citizens of Tianjin are very conscious of trailing behind Beijing and Shanghai in terms of economic development, and so the local government is very eager to attract foreign developers. Because Tianjin's standard of living has lagged behind that in other rapidly developing parts of China, it is difficult for people to afford to move elsewhere. However, the explosion of growth in Tianjin has provided wide-ranging financial opportunities for entrepreneurs, with potential earnings far surpassing what they could get as managers of government-owned enterprises.

From the beginning of 1992 to early 1993, thirteen land development projects involving foreigners had been approved by Tianjin's local government. Most of the interest in development has come from the Taiwanese and Hong Kong Chinese—as is the case in most of China—but large MNEs such as Coca-Cola, NEC, and Motorola have invested in Tianjin. Further, Chase Manhattan applied to the government in April 1993 to open a branch office in Tianjin. Although Chase originally had tried to serve the Chinese market from Beijing or Hong Kong, it decided to expand because of the acceleration in economic growth in China and the decentralization of economic planning. In addition, the Tianjin Economic Development Council offered a variety of tax incentives.

Because Tianjin has been designated by the Chinese government as an Economic and Technology Development Zone, the incentives it can offer foreign investors have created an unprecedented demand for quality commercial and residential accommodations. Within the special zone, simplified approval processes help foreign investors begin operations more quickly. Also, once a project is approved, the scope of business activity is not restricted to the export market, allowing companies to sell to the domestic market.

Tianjin has always had the reputation of being a conservative business center. One reason is that the city's officials have always watched Beijing to make sure that Tianjin did not grow faster than the capital. In addition, Tianjin is the oldest industrial city in China, and investors in heavy industry tend to take a cautious and long-term view. On the other hand, a strong selling point for Tianjin is its close proximity to the central government. As one official stated, "We can get documents approved within 90 days. Can Xiamen or other southern cities do that? Motorola decided to set up its operations here rather than Xiamen because, the company told us, we have permission to visit Zhongnanhai (where the top Beijing leaders live) anytime we want." In addition, Tianjin is the gateway to Beijing. Thus investors have access not only to Beijing but also to the rest of the country.

China's MFN Status

Given Motorola's strategy in Asia in general and in China in particular, the debate over MFN status was an important one. If China were to lose its MFN status, significantly higher tariffs would be levied on its products as they entered the United States, putting it at a competitive disadvantage. Although China held MFN status in 1993, it was up for renewal that June by President Clinton. In the spring of 1993, pollsters found that the U.S. public was relatively ambivalent about the renewal of MFN status for China, but that TV images of the Chinese government's crackdown on students and other demonstrators in Tiananmen Square on June 4, 1989 were still on people's minds. Motorola was being pressured by the Chinese government to lobby the U.S. government in favor of MFN status so that the company could maintain continued access to the Chinese market, but U.S. government policy was strongly influenced by President Clinton's campaign promises to make MFN status contingent on China's improvement of civil rights, its opening of markets to foreign (especially U.S.) products, and the reduction or elimination of its arms shipments to other countries in the region.

However, the China lobby, a group of influential companies that includes Boeing, General Electric, Weyerhauser, and the trucking, aerospace, and apparel industries, directed a campaign that included letters and visits to the White House and Congress to explain the importance of China to the U.S. economy. Although China itself did not lobby heavily in its own behalf, it has received strong support from the China lobby and other sources over the years. In 1990, the Chinese commercial counselor to the United States wrote letters to important businesses and said, "Display your impact in the U.S. government, the Congress, as well as news mediums, do some promotion work to maintain the MFN status with an aim to . . . avoid the [loss] of bilateral interests." In addition, Chinese officials visited the United States in 1993 and placed orders totaling more than $1 billion for airplanes, cars, telecommunications and oil equipment, fertilizer and other products. The hidden message is that China would love to buy lots of U.S. products, as long as the MFN status is renewed. What position should Motorola take?

Questions

1. How would you recommend that Motorola try to influence the U.S. government in terms of trade policy toward China? What are the risks of this strategy?
2. What are the advantages and disadvantages to Motorola of investing in Tianjin relative to other locations in China or Asia?
3. What are the advantages to the United States and to China of Motorola's foreign investment in Tianjin?
4. What are some of the problems with the Chinese economic environment that could affect Motorola's success in China?

Chapter Notes

1. Jeffrey A. Tannenbaum, "Franchisers See a Future in East Bloc," *Wall Street Journal,* June 5, 1990, p. B1+; Erich E. Toll, "Hasabburgonya, Tejturmix and Big Mac to Go," *Journal of Commerce,* August 24, 1988, p. 1A; Tricia A. Dreyfuss, "Negotiating the Kremlin Maze," *Business Month,* Vol. 132, November 1988, pp. 55–63; Vincent J. Schodolski, "Moscovites Stand in Line for a 'Beeg Mek' Attack," *Chicago Tribune,* February 1, 1990, Sec. 1, pp. 1–2; Bill Keller, "Of Famous Arches, Beeg Meks, and Rubles," *New York Times,* January 28, 1990, p. A1+; "McDonald's," *The Economist,* Vol. 313, No. 7629, November 18, 1989, p. 34; Peter Gumbel, "Muscovites Queue Up at American Icon," *Wall Street Journal,* February 1, 1990, p. A12; "Big Mac in China," *Wall Street Journal,* September 10, 1990, p. A12; Don Jeffrey, "Overseas Sales Get McD Off to a Strong Start in '87," *Nation's Restaurant News,* May 11, 1987, p. 172; John F. Love, "McDonald's Behind the Arches," *Restaurant Business Magazine,* Vol. 86, No. 1, January 1, 1987, pp. 101–106; "Fast Food," *Time,* October 2, 1989, p. 83; Ann Blackman, "Moscow's Big Mak Attack," *Time,* February 5, 1990, p. 51; Jeffrey M. Hertzfeld, "Joint Ventures: Saving the Soviets from Perestroika," *Harvard Business Review,* Vol. 69, No. 1, January–February 1991, pp. 80–91; "McDonald's Sees 20% Annual Growth in Foreign Income," *New York Times,* May 7, 1993, p. C3; McDonald's *Annual Report,* 1991; Celestine Bohlen, "How Do You Spell Big Mac in Russian?" *New York Times,* May 25, 1993, p. B1; Bill Essig, "Russia's Economy Shows an Appetite for U.S. Fast Food," *Wall Street Journal,* February 26, 1993, p. B2; and Oleg Vikhanski and Sheila Puffer, "Management Education and Employee Training at Moscow McDonald's," *European Management Journal,* March 1993, pp. 102–107.

2. Bruce R. Scott, "Country Analysis," Harvard Business School, #382–105, March 1984.

3. *World Development Report, 1984* (Washington, D.C.: World Bank, 1984), p. 67.

4. Andrew B. Abel and Ben S. Bernanke, *Macroeconomics* (Reading, Mass.: Addison-Wesley, 1992), p. 30.

5. Steven Greenhouse, "A Foreign Notion for Washington: U.S. Needs Higher Taxes," *The New York Times,* November 20, 1992, p. E2.

6. Ibid.; and Peter Kraljic, "The Economic Gap Separating East and West," *McKinsey Quarterly,* Spring 1990, pp. 62–74.

7. John R. Freeman, *Democracy and Markets: The Politics of Mixed Economies* (Ithaca, N.Y.: Cornell University Press, 1989), p. 7.

8. Paul Lewis, "New U.N. Index Measures Wealth as Quality of Life," *The New York Times,* May 23, 1993, p. A6.

9. Tim Carrington, "Economic Disparities Vex Developing World," *Wall Street Journal,* September 27, 1993, p. A1.

10. John Labate, "The World Economy in Charts," *Fortune,* July 27, 1992, p. 66.

11. Urban C. Lehner, "Indicators Point to Coming Asian Century," *Wall Street Journal,* May 17, 1993, p. A12.

12. Carrington, loc. cit.

13. Gerd Schwartz and Paulo Silva Lopes, "Privatization: Expectations, Trade-offs, and Results," *Finance & Development,* June 1993, p. 15.

14. Barbara Casassus, "How French Privatization Could Go into Fast-Forward," *Global Finance,* March 1993, p. 59.

15. Roman Frydman and Andrzej Rapaczynski, "Privatization in Eastern Europe: Is the State Withering Away?" *Finance & Development,* June 1993, p. 12.

16. Rose Brady and Deborah Stead, "Now, Fault Lines Split Russia Itself," *Business Week,* May 3, 1993, pp. 48–49.

17. Frydman and Rapaczynski, op. cit., p. 11.

18. Thomas Kamm, "Bungled Buyout," *Wall Street Journal,* May 20, 1993, p. A1.

19. Joyce Barnathan and Lynne Curry, "Inflation Has China Running Scared," *Business Week,* June 14, 1993, pp. 48–49.

20. Masood Ahmed and Lawrence Summers, "A Tenth Anniversary Report on the Debt Crisis," *Finance & Development,* September 1992, p. 5.

21. Jeffrey Ryser, Stephen Baker, and Elizabeth Weiner, "The Debtors' Revolt Is Spreading in Latin America," *Business Week,* December 28, 1987, pp. 88–89.

22. "Castro Laments 'Sad Events' in Other Communist Nations," *New York Times,* November 9, 1989, p. A6; and Howard W. French, "Dreary Havana Flirts with Capitalism," *New York Times,* December 6, 1990, p. A4.

23. Paul Marer, "Roadblocs to Economic Transformation in Central and Eastern Europe and Some Lessons of Market Economies," in *United States–Soviet and East European Relations: Building a Congressional Cadre,* Dick Clark, ed. (Queenstown, Md.: Aspen Institute, 1990), pp. 17–27.

24. This term was used by R. D. Schmidt, vice chairman of Control Data, in "U.S.-USSR Trade: An American Businessman's Viewpoint," *Columbia Journal of World Business,* Vol. 18, No. 4, Winter 1983, p. 36.

25. Frydman and Rapaczynski, op. cit., p. 10.

26. "East Europe Survey: More Than Half-Way There," *The Economist,* March 13, 1993, p. 9.

27. Ibid.

28. "China Survey: The Titan Stirs," *The Economist,* November 28, 1992, pp. 3–4.

29. Barnathan and Curry, op. cit., pp. 55–57.

30. Andrew Brick, in George Melloan, "China's Miracle Workers Mostly Live Elsewhere," *Wall Street Journal,* March 8, 1993, p. A11.

31. "The Overseas Chinese: A Driving Force," *The Economist,* July 18, 1992, p. 21.

32. Charles Wolf, Jr., "Less Pain, More Gain for the East Bloc," *Wall Street Journal,* November 19, 1990, p. A14; and Robert Pear, "Jobless to Soar in East, C.I.A. Says," *New York Times,* May 17, 1990, p. A6.

33. Sadao Nagaoka and Izak Atiyas, "Tightening the Soft Budget Constraint in Reforming Socialist Economies" (Washington, D.C.: The World Bank, Industry Development Division, May 1990), pp. 3–16; and Dwight H. Perkins, "China's Industrial and Foreign Trade Reforms," in *Foreign Economic Liberalization: Transformations in Socialist and Market Economies,* András Köves and Paul Marer, eds. (Boulder, Colo.: Westview, 1991), p. 279.

34. Jeffrey Sachs, "Poland and Eastern Europe: What Is to Be Done?" in Köves and Marer, op. cit., pp. 238–239; Kraljic, loc. cit.; and "Now for the Acid Test," *Euromoney,* November 1990, pp. 40–47.

35. Most of the concepts and information in this section were taken from Steven Greenhouse, "Evolution In Europe," *New York Times,* August 6, 1990, p. A4; Paul Marer, "East Europe's Debt Situation in Global Perspective: Utopian Versus Realistic Solutions," in *Growth and External Debt Management,* H. W. Singer and Soumitra Sharma, eds. (London: Macmil-

lan, 1989), pp. 237–245; Igor Reichlin, Rose Brady, David Greising, and Amy Borrus, "Brother, Would You Lend Moscow a Dime?" *Business Week,* December 10, 1990, pp. 44–45; Bill Keller, "Soviet Economy: A Shattered Dream," *New York Times,* May 13, 1990, p. A1+; Sheryl W. Dunn, "Debt Is Squeezing Hotels in China," *New York Times,* May 28, 1990, p. 23; Peter Gumbel and Laurie Hays, "Western Suppliers Halt Deliveries to Soviets; Payment Delays Cited," *Wall Street Journal,* March 12, 1990, p. A5; and Richard A. Melcher and Rose Brady, "Is the Soviet Union Becoming a Deadbeat?" *Business Week,* February 26, 1990, p. 44.

36. Gordon Hughes, "Cleaning Up Eastern Europe," *Finance & Development,* September 1992, pp. 17–18.

37. Richard Poe, "Guerrilla Entrepreneurs," *Success,* September 1990, pp. 34–36.

38. Leon Hadar, "U.S. Public in Two Minds about Move to Extend China's MFN Status," *Business Times,* June 15, 1993; Michael Weisskopf, "Backbone of the New China Lobby: U.S. Firms," *Washington Post,* June 14, 1993, p. A1; Calvin Sims, "China Steps Up Spending To Keep U.S. Trade Status," *New York Times,* May 7, 1993, p. A1; James McGregor, "Talks on China's Trade Status Begin, Made Trickier by Human-Rights Issues," *Wall Street*

Journal, May 12, 1993, p. A4; Pete Engardio, "Motorola in China: A Great Leap Forward," *Business Week,* May 17, 1993, pp. 58–59; "Motorola Expanding Investment in China," *San Francisco Chronicle,* February 22, 1993, p. C2; "Motorola Electronics Ltd. Begins Construction in Tianjin," *Xinhua General News Service,* June 9, 1992; Michiyo Nakamoto, "Motorola Builds Semiconductor Plant in China," *Financial Times,* May 19, 1992, p. 4; "China Plant for Motorola," *New York Times,* March 28, 1992, Sec. 1, p. 49; "Tianjin Stakes Bid for Third Exchange," *South China Morning Post,* January 31, 1993, p. 4; "Tianjin Development Zone Makes Great Achievements," *Xinhua General News Service,* December 7, 1992; "Firms Clamour for Tianjin Building," *South China Morning Post,* September 30, 1992, Supplement, p. 6; Mark Stevens, "Chase in Move to Widen China Base," *South China Morning Post,* April 8, 1993, Business Section, p. 6; Sarah Shaw, "Firm Signs Historic Deal," *South China Morning Post,* February 17, 1993, Supplement, p. 6; "Asia Beckons," *The Economist,* May 30, 1992, p. 63; and Brenton Schlender, "China Really Is on the Move," *Fortune,* October 5, 1992, pp. 114–128.

3 Theories and Institutions: Trade and Investment

South America is a major global supplier of commodities, including minerals and agricultural products. Here you see Brazilian workers sorting cashew nuts, which are native to Brazil, for export. The photo is set against a background showing part of a fabric from the Ica valley of Peru, the location of one of the many South American civilizations "discovered" after Columbus's voyages.

Chapter 5

International Trade Theory

*A market is not held
for the sake of one person.*

—African (Fulani) Proverb

Objectives

- To explain theories of trade patterns that exist in the absence of governmental trade restrictions

- To discuss how global efficiency can be increased through free trade

- To point out the underlying assumptions of trade theories

- To introduce prescriptions for altering trade patterns

- To explore how business decisions determine whether international trade takes place

nkan Trade[1]

Sri Lanka, which means "resplendent land," is an island country of more than 16 million people off the southeast coast of India. Lying just above the equator, it is 270 miles long and 140 miles across at its widest point (see Map 5.1). It has a hot tropical climate with two monsoon periods, yet the central mountain region is cool enough to experience frost. Known as Ceylon from the early sixteenth century until 1972, Sri Lanka is in many ways typical of most developing countries. It has a low per capita income (about $500 per year), high dependence on a few primary products for its foreign-exchange earnings, insufficient foreign-exchange earnings to purchase all desired consumer and industrial imports, and a high unemployment rate. In many other ways, however, Sri Lanka is atypical of developing countries. On various measurements comparing the quality of life among countries, Sri Lanka ranks fairly high. Its 87-percent literacy rate is one of the highest in Asia, and its standards of nutrition, health care, and income distribution are among the highest in the Third World. Its life expectancy of 70 years is one of the highest in the developing world, and its recent population growth rate of 1.4 percent per year is one of the lowest.

Although Sri Lanka did not achieve independence from the United Kingdom until 1948, it has a long recorded history of international trade. By the middle of the third century B.C., special quarters of its capital had been set apart for "Ionian merchants." King Solomon sent his galleys to Sri Lanka to purchase gems, elephants, and peacocks with which to woo the Queen of Sheba. Sinbad and Marco Polo sailed there. Sri Lanka sent ambassadors to Claudius Caesar during the Roman Empire and later established trade links with China. One by one, the European powers came to dominate the island in order to acquire products unavailable at home. The Portuguese, for example, sought such products as cinnamon, cloves, and cardamom, and the English developed the island's economy with tea, rubber, and coconuts, which replaced rice as the major agricultural crops.

Since its independence, Sri Lanka has looked to international trade policy as a means of helping to solve such problems as (1) shortage of foreign exchange, (2) overdependence on one product and one market, and (3) insufficient growth of output and employment. For-

Map 5.1
Sri Lanka
The island nation of Sri Lanka lies off the southeast coast of India.

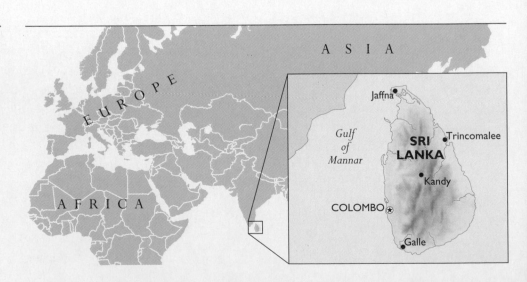

eign exchange is needed to buy imports. Advances in international communications and transportation have contributed to rising economic expectations among Sri Lankans, which in turn have translated into preferences for foreign products or foreign machinery to produce them. These desires have grown more rapidly than have foreign-exchange earnings.

Sri Lanka also has been concerned about its overdependence on a single export product and market. Until 1975, more than half of the country's export earnings were from tea. This made Sri Lanka vulnerable in two ways. First, world demand for tea has not grown as rapidly as that for many other products, particularly manufactured ones. Therefore tea has not been as viable a means of increasing economic growth, employment, or foreign-exchange earnings as have some other products. Second, tea prices can fluctuate substantially because of a bumper crop or natural disaster in any tea-exporting country. In fact, the wholesale price of tea has changed by as much as 90 percent from one year to the next. This makes planning for long-term business or governmental projects very difficult. Because Sri Lanka is a former British colony, many Sri Lankans also have been concerned that the country cannot be politically and economically independent as long as trade centers on the British market. At the time of independence, for example, one third of Sri Lankan exports went to the United Kingdom. Sri Lanka was thus potentially vulnerable to British political demands and economic downturns.

Because of these varied but interrelated problems, Sri Lanka has attempted since independence to earn more foreign exchange by exporting more of its traditional commodities—tea, rubber, and coconuts. In addition, from 1960 until 1977, Sri Lanka sought to diversify its production by restricting imports in order to encourage local production, which would thus save foreign exchange. In 1977, with a change of government, the focus shifted to the development of new industries that could export a part of their production and thus earn more foreign exchange. After another change in political leadership in 1988, Sri Lanka greatly reduced import restrictions. Whether the diversification has occurred through import substitution or export development, the intended outcome has been to create growth and jobs by using unemployed people and other unemployed resources. By moving to new products, the country has become less dependent on the tea market and on sales to any single market.

The decision to develop exports of nontraditional products raises the questions of what those products should be and how to get companies to produce them for foreign markets. The government has taken numerous steps to ease restrictions on imports in order to judge where competitive advantages lie and then to assist those industries that could survive import competition. However, governmental authorities were not satisfied to sit back and wait for imports to determine the country's whole future industrial thrust. They felt that some entirely new industries might need assistance. The export development division of the Ministry of Industries was instrumental in creating a methodology to identify appropriate products for development and promotion.

An obvious way of selecting product groups was to identify nontraditional products that were already being exported in small amounts, since such ability to export indicated the potential for growth. The export development division also sought other products that could offer Sri Lanka a potential advantage in foreign competition. They first identified products that would call for the use of semiskilled and skilled labor because labor costs in Sri Lanka were low, the labor force was fairly well educated, and unemployment and underemployment were high. The division then narrowed that group of products to include only those for which Sri Lanka had indigenous raw materials for production and packaging. This was deemed to be an important competitive indicator because it would be costly to import materials that would then have to be processed before being reexported. Finally, the division examined markets in which Sri Lanka was probably most able to sell. This examination was based on an analysis of demand in two types of markets: those in which Sri Lanka had special market concessions and therefore would experience minimal trade barriers, and those that were geographically close to Sri Lanka and could be served with minimum transport costs.

Seventeen products emerged and were ranked by export potential and expected benefits for the country. The leading items were as follows:

- Processed tea (packaged teabags and instant tea)
- Ready-made garments (shirts, pajamas, and dresses)
- Chemical derivatives of coconut oil
- Edible fats
- Bicycle tires and tubes
- Other rubber products such as automobile tires and tubes

Other items included canvas footwear, passionfruit juice, canned pineapple, ceramicware, seafood (lobster and shrimp), handicrafts, and gems.

Identifying the most likely competitive industries encouraged some businesspeople to consider investments in new areas. In addition, the government established industrial development zones. Companies that produced in and exported their production from these zones could qualify for up to a 10-year tax holiday plus another 15 years of tax concessions, depending on the size of the investment and the number of employees. They also could defer taxes on imported goods and components until the resulting products were sold domestically. If the products were exported, there were no import taxes.

The first producers to take advantage of the incentives were textile and footwear companies that had special access to the U.S. and European markets. Since then the company base has become more diverse and includes companies making PVC film and carpets and companies entering information into computerized data banks.

Sri Lanka also has encouraged the export of services, particularly earnings from its workers abroad and from foreign tourists visiting the country. For example, several hundred thousand Sri Lankans work in foreign countries and send remittances to their families. The government has encouraged visits by foreign tourists, and in 1992, about 400,000 went to Sri Lanka. And yet the country continues to have a foreign-exchange shortage. As imports have entered Sri Lanka more easily and as incomes have risen, consumers have demanded even more foreign products.

The move to establish new export industries is accomplishing many of its objectives. Manufacturing has grown as a portion of total exports, and tea has fallen by more than half.

By 1992, garments accounted for 38.1 percent of total exports; tea, although still a top export, accounted for only 23.5 percent. In addition, Sri Lanka's export markets have become more dispersed, with such countries as the United States, Saudi Arabia, Germany, and India gaining in importance. Nevertheless, the country is still vulnerable to economic and political conditions abroad. When UN trade sanctions were placed on Iraq after its 1991 invasion of Kuwait, Sri Lanka not only lost the Iraqi market, which accounted for 24 percent of its tea exports, but about 100,000 workers returned from the Middle East. Sri Lanka also has recently suffered from ethnic violence. Many potential customers have been reluctant to depend too heavily on Sri Lankan exports for fear that the violence will disrupt delivery. This violence also has caused governmental funds to shift toward defense and away from infrastructure development, and more infrastructure development is necessary to attract investment needed for export capacity.

Introduction

Trade theory focuses on these questions:
- **What products to import and export?**
- **How much to trade?**
- **With whom to trade?**

Why study trade theory? Authorities in all countries wrestle with the problems of what, how much, and with whom their country should import and export. Once they make decisions, officials enact trade policies to achieve the desired end results. These policies, in turn, affect business. They influence which products companies might be able to sell in those countries from both domestic and foreign sources. They also affect what companies can produce in given countries and where they can produce in order to serve given markets. This was demonstrated in the Sri Lanka case: Government officials in that country have created activist policies to try to achieve trade objectives. Some other countries take a more laissez-faire approach, allowing market forces to determine trading relations, on the premise that governmental policies and actions lead in practice to less optimum results for economies. Whether taking activist or laissez-faire approaches, countries rely on a shared body of trade theory.

Although some theories precede events (for example, Einstein's theory of relativity was a necessary antecedent to the atomic experiments that followed several decades later), international trade was practiced long before any trade theories had evolved. Sri Lankan trade, for example, predated recorded trade theories by more than 1500 years.

Some theories explain trade patterns that exist in the absence of governmental interference.

Two types of theories about trade are relevant to international business (see Table 5.1). The first type deals with the natural order of trade; that is, it examines and explains trade patterns under laissez-faire conditions. Theories of this type pose questions of how much, which products, and with whom a country will trade in the absence of restrictions among countries. The second type of theory prescribes governmental interference with the free movement of goods and services among countries in order to alter the amount, composition, and direction of trade. These theories have "Yes" under the question "Should government control trade?" in the table.

Table 5.1
Emphases of Major Theories

	Description of natural trade			Prescriptions of trade relationships			
Theory	How much is traded?	What products are traded?	With whom does trade take place?	Should government control trade?	How much should be traded?	What products should be traded?	With whom should trade take place?
Mercantilism	—	—	—	Yes	✔	✔	✔
Neomercantilism	—	—	—	Yes	✔	—	—
Absolute advantage	—	✔	—	No	—	✔	—
Country size	✔	✔	—	—	—	—	—
Comparative advantage	—	✔	—	No	—	✔	—
Factor-proportions	—	✔	✔	—	—	—	—
Product life cycle (PLC)	—	✔	✔	—	—	—	—
Country similarity	—	✔	✔	—	—	—	—
Dependence	—	—	—	Yes	—	✔	✔

Some theories explain what governmental actions should strive for in trade.

Because no single theory explains all natural trade patterns and because all prescriptions are relevant to some of the actions taken by governmental policymakers, this chapter examines a variety of approaches. However, the subject of governmental interference in trade is so broad that an entire chapter is devoted to discussion of many of the specific arguments and methods (see Chapter 6). Both the descriptive and prescriptive theories have considerable impact on international business. They provide insights about favorable market locales as well as potentially successful products. The theories also increase understanding about the kinds of governmental trade policies that might be enacted and predict how those policies might affect competitiveness.

Mercantilism

According to mercantilism, countries should export more than they import.

Why has Sri Lanka been so dependent on raw materials rather than manufactured products? Perhaps the answer lies in **mercantilism,** the trade theory that formed the foundation of economic thought from about 1500 to 1800.[2] That theory held that a country's wealth was measured by its holdings of treasure, usually in the form of gold. According to mercantilist theory, countries should export more than they import and, if successful, would receive the value of their trade surpluses in the form of gold from the country or countries that ran deficits. Nation-states were emerging during the period 1500–1800, and gold served to consolidate the power of central governments. The gold was invested in armies and national institutions that served to solidify the people's primary allegiances to the new nation with a lessening of bonds to such traditional units as city-states, religions, and guilds.

In order to export more than they imported, governments established monopolies over their countries' trade. Restrictions were imposed on most imports, and many exports received subsidies. Colonial possessions, such as Sri Lanka under

British rule, were used to support this trade objective. First, they supplied many commodities that the mother country might otherwise have had to purchase from a nonassociated country. Second, the colonial powers sought to run trade surpluses with their own colonies as a further means of obtaining revenue. They did this not only by monopolizing colonial trade but also by preventing the colonies from engaging in manufacturing. Thus the colonies had to export less highly valued raw materials and import more highly valued manufactured products. Mercantilist theory was intended to benefit the colonial powers, and the imposition of regulations based on this theory caused much discontent in the British colonies and was a background cause of the American Revolution.

As the influence of the mercantilist philosophy weakened after 1800, the colonial powers seldom acted to limit the development of industrial capabilities within their colonies. However, institutional and legal arrangements continued to make colonies dependent on raw material production and to tie their trade to their industrialized mother countries. Sri Lanka, like the many other countries that have attained independence since World War II, began with such a production structure and trade pattern. Efforts to alter this pattern are discussed later in this chapter in the section on independence, interdependence, and dependence.

Running a favorable balance of trade is not necessarily a beneficial situation.

Some terminology of the mercantilist era has endured. The **favorable balance of trade,** for example, still indicates that a country is exporting more than it is importing. An **unfavorable balance of trade** indicates a trading deficit. Many of these terms are misnomers: For example, the word *favorable* implies benefit, and *unfavorable* suggests disadvantage. In fact, it is not necessarily beneficial to run a trade surplus; nor is it necessarily disadvantageous to run a trade deficit. A country that is running a surplus, or favorable balance of trade, is, for the time being, importing goods and services of less value than those it is exporting.[3] In the mercantilist period, the difference was made up by a transfer of gold, but today it is made up by holding the deficit country's currency or investments denominated in that currency. In effect, the surplus country is granting credit to the deficit country. If that credit cannot eventually buy sufficient goods and services, the so-called favorable trade balance actually may turn out to be disadvantageous for the country with the surplus.

A country that practices neomercantilism attempts to run an export surplus to achieve some social or political objective.

Recently, the term **neomercantilism** has been used to describe the approach of countries that apparently try to run favorable balances of trade in an attempt to achieve some social or political objective. For instance, a country may try to achieve full employment by producing in excess of the demand at home and sending the surplus abroad. Or a country may attempt to maintain political influence in an area by sending more merchandise to the area than it receives from it.

Absolute Advantage

So far we have ignored the question of why countries need to trade at all. Why can't Sri Lanka (or any other country) be content with the goods and services produced within its territorial confines? In fact, many countries, practicing mercantilist policy, did try to become as self-sufficient as possible through local production of goods and services.

In his 1776 book, *The Wealth of Nations,* Adam Smith questioned the mercantilists' assumption that a country's wealth depends on its holdings of treasure.[4] He said instead that the real wealth of a country consists of the goods and services available to its citizens. Smith developed the theory of absolute advantage, which holds that different countries can produce some goods more efficiently than others; thus global efficiency can be increased through free trade. Based on this theory, he questioned why the citizens of any country should have to buy domestically produced goods when those goods could be purchased more cheaply from abroad.

Smith reasoned that if trade were unrestricted, each country would specialize in those products that resulted in a competitive advantage for it. Each country's resources would shift to the efficient industries because the country could not compete in the inefficient ones. Through specialization, countries could increase their efficiency because of three reasons:

- Labor could become more skilled by repeating the same tasks.
- Labor would not lose time in switching from the production of one kind of product to another.
- Long production runs would provide incentives for the development of more effective working methods.

A country then could use its specialized production excess to buy more imports than it could have otherwise produced. But in what products should a country specialize? Although Smith believed the marketplace would make the determination, he thought that a country's advantage would be either natural or acquired.

Natural Advantage

A country may have a **natural advantage** in producing a product because of climatic conditions, access to certain natural resources, or availability of an abundant labor force. The climate may dictate, for example, which agricultural products can be produced efficiently. For example, Sri Lanka's climate supports production of tea, rubber, and coconuts, and its ample labor force enables this production to be harvested and processed. Climate also is a factor in Sri Lanka's export of services because foreign tourists visit its beaches. Sri Lanka imports wheat and dairy products. If it were to increase its production of wheat and dairy products, for which its climate is less suited, it would have to use land now devoted to the cultivation of tea, rubber, or coconuts, thus decreasing the output of those products. Conversely, the United States could produce tea (perhaps in hothouses) but at the cost of diverting resources away from products such as wheat, for which its climate is naturally suited. These two countries can trade tea for wheat and vice versa more cheaply than each could become self-sufficient in the production of both. Moreover, the more diverse the climates of two countries, the more likely it will be for them to have natural advantages that favor trade with one another.

Most countries must import ores, metals, and fuels from other countries whose natural resources are plentiful. No one country is large enough or sufficiently rich in physical resources to be independent of the rest of the world except for short periods. Sri Lanka, for example, exports natural graphite but must import natural nitrates. Another natural resource is soil, which, when coupled with topography, is an important determinant of the types of products that can be produced most efficiently in different areas.

Variations in natural advantages also help to explain where certain manufactured or processed products might be best produced, particularly if transport costs can be reduced by processing an agricultural commodity or natural resource prior to exporting it. Recall that Sri Lankan authorities sought to identify industries that could use the country's primary commodities such as tea. Processing into instant tea decreases bulk and thus is likely to reduce transport costs on tea exports. Producing canned liquid tea could add weight, however, thus lessening the internationally competitive edge.

Acquired Advantage

Most of the world's trade today involves manufactured goods and services rather than agricultural goods and natural resources. The production location of such goods is determined largely by an **acquired advantage,** commonly in either product or process technology. An advantage in product technology refers to an ability to produce a different or differentiated product. For example, Denmark exports silver tableware, not because there are rich Danish silver mines but because Danish companies have developed distinctive products. An advantage in process technology refers to an ability to produce a homogeneous product more efficiently. For example, Japan has exported steel in spite of having to import iron and coal, the two main ingredients necessary for steel production. A primary reason for Japan's success is that its steel mills encompass new labor-saving and material-saving processes.

Rapid technological changes have created new products, displaced old ones, and altered the relative positions of countries in world trade. The most obvious examples of change are new products, such as jets and computers, which make up a large portion of international business. Products that existed in earlier periods have increased their share of world trade because of technological changes in the production process, as with automobiles, or because new uses have been found for them, as with soybeans and fish meal. Other products have been at least partially displaced by substitutes, such as artificial fibers for cotton, wool, and silk and synthetic rubber and synthetic nitrate for the natural products. Some products that were once major exports, such as natural ice, have been displaced by mechanically made products.[5] Still other products have experienced reduced growth in demand because of newly developed conservation methods. For example, thinner tin cans and finer copper wire that can carry more telephone messages simultaneously have resulted

Acquired advantage refers to technology and skill development.

ASSUMPTIONS

Sri Lanka

1. 100 units of resources available
2. 10 units to produce a ton of wheat
3. 4 units to produce a ton of tea
4. Uses half of total resources per product
   when there is no foreign trade

United States

1. 100 units of resources available
2. 5 units to produce a ton of wheat
3. 20 units to produce a ton of tea
4. Uses half of total resources per product
   when there is no foreign trade

PRODUCTION

	Tea (tons)	Wheat (tons)
Without Trade:		
Sri Lanka (point A)	12½	5
United States (point B)	2½	10
Total	15	15
With Trade:		
Sri Lanka (point C)	25	0
United States (point D)	0	20
Total	25	20

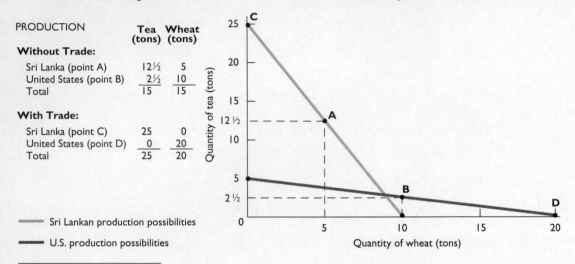

········ Sri Lankan production possibilities

━━━━ U.S. production possibilities

**Figure 5.1
Production Possibilities
with Absolute
Advantage**

in less demand for these metals. Because most technological advances have emanated from the most industrialized (richer) countries, companies from these countries control a greater share of the trade and investment in the manufacturing sector, which has been the major growth area. Consequently, many poorer countries have had a proportionately smaller share of international business.

Resource Efficiency Example

The idea of absolute advantage in international or domestic trade can be demonstrated using two countries (or regions within one country) and two commodities. In this example, the countries are Sri Lanka and the United States, and the commodities are tea and wheat. Since we are not yet considering the concepts of money and exchange rates, we shall treat the cost of production in terms of the resources needed to produce either tea or wheat. This is a realistic treatment in that real income depends on the output of goods associated with the resources used to produce them.

Start with the assumption that Sri Lanka and the United States are the only countries and each has the same amount of resources (land, labor, and capital) that can be used to produce either tea or wheat. Let's say that 100 units of resources are available in each country (shown in Fig. 5.1). In Sri Lanka, assume that it takes 4 units to produce a ton of tea and 10 units per ton of wheat. In the United States, it takes 20 units per ton of tea and 5 units per ton of wheat. Sri Lanka is thus more efficient (that is, takes fewer resources to produce a ton) than the United States in tea production, and the United States is more efficient than Sri Lanka in wheat production.

Consider a situation in which the two countries have no foreign trade. If Sri Lanka and the United States each were to devote half of its resources to producing tea and half to producing wheat, Sri Lanka would be able to produce 12½ tons of tea and 5 tons of wheat (point A in Fig. 5.1), and the United States could produce 2½ tons of tea and 10 tons of wheat (point B in the figure). Since each country has only 100 units of resources, neither can increase wheat production without decreasing tea production, or vice versa. Without trade between the two countries, the combined production would be 15 tons of tea (12½ plus 2½) and 15 tons of wheat (5 plus 10). If each country specialized in the commodity for which it had an absolute advantage, Sri Lanka then could produce 25 tons of tea and the United States 20 tons of wheat (points C and D in the figure). You can see that through specialization the production of both products can be increased (from 15 to 25 tons of tea and from 15 to 20 tons of wheat). By trading, global efficiency is increased, and the two countries can have more tea and more wheat than they would without trade.

Theory of Country Size

The theory of absolute advantage does not deal with country-by-country differences in specialization; however, some recent research based on country size helps to explain how much and what types of products will be traded.

Bigger countries differ in several ways from smaller countries. They
- **Tend to export a smaller portion of output and import a smaller part of consumption**
- **Have higher transport costs for foreign trade**
- **Can handle large-scale production**

Variety of resources The **theory of country size** holds that countries with large land areas are more apt to have varied climates and natural resources, and therefore they generally are more nearly self-sufficient than are smaller countries. Most of the very large countries, such as Brazil, China, India, the United States, and Russia, import much less of their consumption and export much less of their production than do small countries, such as Uruguay, the Netherlands, and Iceland.[6]

Transport costs Although the theory of absolute advantage ignored transport costs, these costs affect large and small countries differently. Normally, the farther the distance, the higher the transport costs. The average distance between the production location and markets is higher for the international trade of large countries. Assume, for example, that the normal maximum distance for transporting a given product is 100 miles because, beyond that distance, prices increase too much. Most U.S. production locations and markets are more than 100 miles from the Canadian or Mexican border. In the Netherlands, however, almost all production locations and markets are within 100 miles of its borders. Transport costs thus make it more likely that small countries will trade internationally.

Scale economies Although land area is the most obvious way of measuring a country's size, countries also can be compared on the basis of economic size. Countries with large economies and high per capita incomes are more likely to produce goods that use technologies requiring long production runs. This is because these countries develop industries to serve their large domestic markets, and those industries tend to be competitive in export markets as well.[7] In addition, high expenditures on R&D create high fixed costs. Thus the technologically intensive company from a small nation may have a more compelling need to sell abroad than would a company with a large domestic market. In turn, this pulls resources from other industries and companies within the company's domestic market, causing more national specialization than in a larger nation.[8]

Comparative Advantage

Gains from trade will occur even in a country that has absolute advantage in all products because the country must give up less efficient output to produce more efficient output.

What happens when one country can produce all products at an absolute advantage? In 1817, David Ricardo examined this question and expanded on Adam Smith's theory of absolute advantage to develop the theory of **comparative advantage.** Ricardo reasoned that there may still be global efficiency gains from trade if a country specializes in those products that it can produce more efficiently than other products, without regard to absolute advantage.[9] Although initially this theory may seem incongruous, a simple analogy should clarify its logic. Imagine that the best physician in a particular town also happens to be the best medical secretary. Would it make economic sense for the physician to handle all the administrative duties of the office? Definitely not. The physician can earn more money by devoting all of his or her professional energies to working as a physician, even though that means having to employ a less skillful medical secretary to manage the office. In the same manner, a country will gain if it concentrates its resources on producing the commodities it can produce most efficiently. It then will buy from countries with fewer natural or acquired resources those commodities it has relinquished.

Production Possibility Example

In this example, assume that the United States is more efficient in producing both tea and wheat than Sri Lanka is. The United States thus has an absolute advantage in the production of both products. As in the earlier example of absolute advantage, again assume that there are only two countries and each country has a total of 100 units of resources available. In this example, it takes Sri Lanka 10 units of resources to produce either a ton of tea or a ton of wheat, whereas it takes the United States only 5 units of resources to produce a ton of tea and 4 units to produce a ton of wheat (see Fig. 5.2). If each country uses half of its resources in the production of each product, Sri Lanka can produce 5 tons of tea and 5 tons of wheat (point A in the figure), and the United States can produce 10 tons of tea and 12½ tons of wheat (point B in the figure). Without trade, neither country can increase its production of tea without sacrificing some production of wheat, or vice versa.

Although the United States has an absolute advantage in the production of both tea and wheat, it has a comparative advantage only in the production of wheat. This is because its advantage in wheat production is comparatively greater than its advantage in tea production. So, by using the same amounts of resources, the United

**Figure 5.2
Production Possibilities
with Comparative
Advantage**

ASSUMPTIONS

Sri Lanka

1. 100 units of resources available
2. 10 units to produce a ton of wheat
3. 10 units to produce a ton of tea
4. Uses half of total resources per product
   when there is no foreign trade

United States

1. 100 units of resources available
2. 4 units to produce a ton of wheat
3. 5 units to produce a ton of tea
4. Uses half of total resources per product
   when there is no foreign trade

PRODUCTION	Tea (tons)	Wheat (tons)
Without Trade:		
Sri Lanka (point A)	5	5
United States (point B)	10	12½
Total	15	17½
With Trade (increasing tea production):		
Sri Lanka (point C)	10	0
United States (point D)	6	17½
Total	16	17½
With Trade (increasing wheat production):		
Sri Lanka (point C)	10	0
United States (point E)	5	18¾
Total	15	18¾

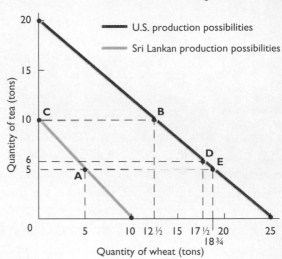

States can produce 2½ times as much wheat as Sri Lanka but only twice as much tea. Although Sri Lanka has an absolute disadvantage in the production of both products, it has a comparative advantage (or less of a comparative disadvantage) in the production of tea. This is because Sri Lanka is half as efficient as the United States in tea production and only 40 percent as efficient in wheat production.

Without trade, the combined production would be 15 tons of tea (5 in Sri Lanka plus 10 in the United States) and 17½ tons of wheat (5 in Sri Lanka plus 12½ in the United States). By trading, the combined production of tea and wheat within the two countries can be increased. For example, if the combined production of wheat is unchanged from when there was no trade, the United States could produce all 17½ tons of wheat by using 70 units of resources (17½ tons times 4 units per ton). The remaining 30 U.S. units could be used for producing 6 tons of tea (30 units divided by 5 units per ton). This production possibility is shown as point D in Fig. 5.2. Sri Lanka would use all its resources to produce 10 tons of tea (point C in the figure). The combined wheat production has stayed at 17½ tons, but the tea production has increased from 15 to 16 tons.

If the combined tea production is unchanged from the time before trade, Sri Lanka could use all its resources on producing tea, yielding 10 tons (point C in Fig. 5.2). The United States could produce the remaining 5 tons of tea by using 25 units of resources. The remaining 75 U.S. units could be used to produce 18¾ tons of wheat (75 divided by 4). This production possibility is shown as point E in the figure. Without sacrificing any of the tea available before trade, wheat production has increased from 17½ to 18¾ tons.

If the United States were to produce somewhere between points D and E in Fig. 5.2, both tea and wheat production would increase over what was possible before trade took place. Whether the production target is an increase of tea or wheat or a combination of the two, both countries can gain by having Sri Lanka trade some of its tea production to the United States for some of that country's wheat output.

Some Assumptions of the Theories of Specialization

Full employment is not a valid assumption.

Full employment   The physician/secretary analogy we used earlier assumed that the physician could stay busy full-time practicing medicine. If we relax this assumption, then the advantages of specialization are less compelling. The physician might, if unable to stay busy full-time with medical duties, perform secretarial work without having to forgo a physician's higher income. The theories of absolute and comparative advantage both assume that resources are fully employed. When countries have many unemployed resources, they may seek to restrict imports in order to employ idle resources even though those will not be employed efficiently.

Countries' goals may not be limited to economic efficiency.

Economic efficiency objective   The physician/secretary analogy also assumed that the individual who can do both medical and office work is interested primarily in maximization of profit, or maximum economic efficiency. Yet, there are a number of reasons why physicians might choose not to work full-time at medical tasks. They might find administrative work relaxing and self-fulfilling. They might fear that a hired secretary would be unreliable. They might wish to maintain secretarial skills in the somewhat unlikely event that administration, rather than medicine, commands higher wages in the future. Countries also often pursue objectives other than output efficiency. They may avoid overspecialization because of the vulnerability created by changes in technology and by price fluctuations.

Division of gains   Although specialization brings global efficiency gains, the earlier discussion did not indicate how the increased output of tea and wheat will be divided between Sri Lanka and the United States. If both nations receive some share of the increased output, both will be better off economically through specialization and trade. However, many people, including governmental policymakers, are concerned with relative as well as absolute economic growth. If they perceive a trading partner is gaining too large a share of benefits, they may prefer to forgo absolute gains for themselves in order to prevent relative losses.[10]

Two countries, two commodities   For the sake of simplicity, Ricardo originally assumed a very simple world composed of only two countries and two commodities. Our example made the same assumption. Although unrealistic, this assumption does not diminish the theory's usefulness. Economists have applied the same reasoning to demonstrate efficiency advantages in multiproduct and multicountry situations.

Transport costs   Neither the theory of absolute advantage nor that of comparative advantage considered the cost of moving products from one country to another. However, this is not a serious limitation. Although specialization might reduce the amounts of resources necessary for producing goods, resources also are needed to move the goods internationally. If it costs more units of resources to transport the goods than are saved through specialization, then the advantages of trade are negated.

Mobility   The theories of absolute and comparative advantage assume that resources can move freely from the production of one good to another domestically but that they are not free to move internationally. Neither assumption is completely valid. For example, a displaced textile worker in New England might not move easily into an aerospace job in California. That worker probably would have difficulty working in such a different industry and might have trouble moving to a new area. However, contrary to the theories, there is some international mobility of resources—consider the Sri Lankan workers who have gone to the Middle East.

Resources are neither as mobile nor as immobile as the theories of absolute and comparative advantage assume.

Services   The theories of absolute and comparative advantage deal with commodities rather than services; however, an increasing portion of world trade is in services. This fact does not render the theories obsolete, however, because resources must go into producing services as well as commodities. For instance, the United States trades services for commodities and services for services. Some services that the United States sells extensively to foreign countries are education (many foreign students attend U.S. universities) and credit card systems and collections. However, the United States is a net importer of shipping services. To become more self-sufficient in international shipping, the United States might have to divert resources from their more efficient use in higher education or the production of competitive products.

Factor-Proportions Theory

According to the factor-proportions theory, factors in relative abundance are cheaper than factors in relative scarcity.

Smith's and Ricardo's theories did not help to identify the types of products that would most likely give a country an advantage. Those theories assumed that the workings of the free market would lead producers to the goods they could produce more efficiently and away from those they could not produce efficiently. About a century and a quarter later, two Swedish economists, Eli Heckscher and Bertil Ohlin, developed the **factor-proportions theory,** which held that differences in countries' endowments of labor relative to their endowments of land or capital explained differences in factor costs. These economists proposed that if labor were abundant in relation to land and capital, labor costs would be low and land and capital costs high. If labor were scarce, labor costs would be high in relation to land and capital costs. These relative factor costs would lead countries to excel in the production and export of products that used their abundant, and therefore cheaper, production factors.[11]

Land-Labor Relationship

On the basis of the factor-proportions theory, Sri Lankan authorities reasoned that their country had a competitive advantage in products that used large numbers of abundant semiskilled workers. The factor-proportions theory appears logical on the basis of casual observation of worldwide production and exports. In countries in which there are many people relative to the amount of land—for example, Hong Kong and the Netherlands—land prices are very high. Regardless of climate and soil conditions, neither Hong Kong nor the Netherlands excels in the production of goods requiring large amounts of land, such as sheep or wheat. These goods are produced in countries such as Australia and Canada, where land is abundant relative to the number of people. Casual observation of manufacturing proportions also seems to substantiate the theory. For example, in Hong Kong the most successful industries are those in which technology permits the use of a minimum amount of land relative to the number of people employed: Clothing production is housed in multistory factories in which workers share minimal space. Hong Kong does not compete in the production of automobiles, however, which requires much more space per worker.

Labor-Capital Relationship

Where labor is abundant in relation to capital, you might expect cheap labor rates and export competitiveness in products requiring large amounts of labor relative to capital. The opposite can be anticipated when labor is scarce. For example, Iran and Tunisia excel in the production of handmade carpets that differ in appearance as well as in production method from the carpets produced in industrial countries by machines purchased with cheap capital.

U.S. imports show a high intensity of less skilled labor. U.S. exports are labor-intensive compared with U.S. imports.

However, the labor-to-capital relationship in foreign trade is sometimes surprising. For example, Wassily Leontief found that the more successful U.S. exporting industries had a higher labor intensity than those that faced the most import competition.[12] Because of the presumption that the United States has abundant capital relative to labor, this surprising finding is known as the **Leontief paradox.** Several possible explanations for it have been proposed.

Production factors are not homogeneous, especially labor.

One of the most plausible is that the factor-proportions theory assumes production factors to be homogeneous. Labor skills are, in fact, very different within and among countries, since different people have different amounts and types of training and education. Training and education require capital expenditures that do not show up in traditional capital measurements, which include only plant and equipment values. If the factor-proportions theory is modified to account for different labor groups and the capital invested to train these groups, it seems to hold. If labor is viewed not as a homogeneous commodity but rather by categories, the industrial countries actually have a more abundant supply of highly educated labor (on which a high capital expenditure has been made) than of other types. Industrial country exports embody a higher proportion of professionals such as scientists and engineers; thus those countries are using their abundant production factors. Exports of less developed countries (LDCs), on the other hand, show a high intensity of less skilled labor.[13]

Technological Complexities

The factor-proportions analysis becomes more complicated when the same product might be produced by different methods, such as with either high inputs of labor or high inputs of capital. Canada produces wheat in a capital-intensive way (high level of machinery per worker) because of its abundance of low-cost capital relative to labor; in contrast, India produces wheat by using a much smaller number of machines and more of its abundant and cheap labor. When there is more than one way to produce the same output, it is the relative input cost that determines which country can produce the product more cheaply. The fact that products can be produced in different ways is another possible explanation of the Leontief paradox in that the U.S. industries facing the most competition because of cheap foreign labor are the ones that have responded most intensively by substituting machines for labor.

Technological advancements have resulted in transport cost reductions that in turn have permitted greater economies of scale. This has led to more international specialization, not only in type of product but also in type of task to produce a given product.[14] For example, a company may locate its research activities and management functions primarily in countries with a highly educated population and its production work where less skilled, and less expensive, workers can be employed.

The Product Life Cycle

Another theory attempts to explain world trade in manufactured products on the basis of stages in a product's life.[15] Briefly, the theory of **product life cycle (PLC)** states that certain kinds of products go through a continuum, or cycle, that consists of roughly four stages—introduction, growth, maturity, and decline—and that the location of production will shift internationally depending on the stage of the cycle. The stages are highlighted in Table 5.2.

Stage 1: Introduction

Innovation, production, and sales in same country New products usually are developed because there is a nearby observed need and a market for them. This means that a U.S. company is most apt to develop a new product for the U.S. market, a French company for the French market, and so on. To illustrate how this works, producers in both the United States and France observed the need for longer-term food preservation as more women worked outside the home and had less time for food shopping. In the United States, the prevalence of large kitchens and cheap electricity encouraged U.S. innovators to develop and become leaders in the production of frozen food, which could be stored in large freezer compartments. In France, however, large freezer compartments were impractical, so French innovators led in the development of food packaging (such as boxed milk) that would eliminate the need for refrigeration. Once an R&D group has created a

According to the PLC theory, the production location for many products moves from one country to another depending on the stage in the product's life cycle.

The introduction stage is marked by
- *Innovation in response to observed need*
- *Exporting by the innovative country*
- *Evolving product*

Table 5.2
International Changes during a Product's Life Cycle
Overall, production and sales in LDCs grow in relative importance during a product's life cycle.

	Life cycle stage			
	Introduction	Growth	Maturity	Decline
Production location	• In innovating (usually industrial) country	• In innovating and other industrial countries	• Multiple countries	• Mainly in LDCs
Market location	• Mainly in innovating country, with some exports	• Mainly in industrial countries • Shift in export markets as foreign production replaces exports in some markets	• Growth in LDCs • Some decrease in industrial countries	• Mainly in LDCs • Some LDC exports
Competitive factors	• Near-monopoly position • Sales based on uniqueness rather than price • Evolving product characteristics	• Fast-growing demand • Number of competitors increases • Some competitors begin price-cutting • Product becoming more standardized	• Overall stabilized demand • Number of competitors decreases • Price is very important, especially in LDCs	• Overall declining demand • Price is key weapon • Number of producers continues to decrease
Production technology	• Short production runs • Evolving methods to coincide with product evolution • High labor and labor skills relative to capital input	• Capital input increases • Methods more standardized	• Long production runs using high capital inputs • Highly standardized • Less labor skill needed	• Unskilled labor on mechanized long production runs

new product, that product theoretically can be manufactured anywhere in the world, even though its sales are intended primarily for the market in which consumers' needs were first observed. In practice, however, the early production generally occurs in a domestic location because the company wishes to use its excess capacity and because it is useful for the company to locate near the intended consumers in order to obtain rapid market feedback and to save transport costs.

Location of innovation   It is useful to know where new products are developed. Indications are that nearly all the world's technology emanates from the industrial countries; thus the early manufacturing and sales of new products primarily occur in industrial countries. Many reasons account for the dominant position of industrial countries, including competition, demanding consumers, the availability of scientists and engineers, and high incomes, which permit risking expenditures on research that may or may not yield gainful results.

wo of the issues discussed in this chapter are laissez-faire versus activist trade policies and independence versus dependence of countries. Debate over either of these issues typically is emotional because different values underlie the various positions.

For example, the argument in favor of laissez-faire (free-trade) policy is based on the achievement of global economic efficiency. However, this chapter showed that countries' goals may not be limited to economic efficiency. Further, some argue that free trade, although leading to lower costs, will not result in production locations that are optimal with respect to factor endowments. This is because production costs are partly dependent on standards imposed by individual countries—such as requirements for worker safety or the disposal of wastes. These standards reflect the social and environmental values of the

ETHICAL DILEMMAS

countries' citizens. Because standards vary among countries, the costs incurred by producers vary as well. Some industries affected by import competition—for example, the U.S. electronics and steel industries—reason that their home-country governments should protect them because foreign producers do not have to adhere to the stringent requirements that raise production costs.[16] For example, one of the biggest differences in standards exists between the United States, which has enacted clean air legislation, and Eastern Europe, which has few laws regulating pollution.[17]

Some argue that cost differences reflect not differences in efficiency but rather differences in social and environmental values. Other questions have been raised in recent years about labor conditions, such as low wages in Mexico, anti union directives in Malaysia, apartheid policies in South Africa, and the use of jailed workers in China. Ethical questions are raised as to whether it is reasonable to assume that all countries should have similar standards, whether countries should limit imports of competing products because of differences in standards, and whether companies should locate production to capitalize on less stringent standards that allow them to lower their costs.

In the opening case, Sri Lanka embarked on an activist trade policy to reduce its dependence on a single trading partner and a single product for its export earnings. A country also may be concerned about its overall trade dependence. In this context, relativists hold that it would be unethical for outsiders to interfere in a country's trade policy. In contrast, normativists argue that other countries have a duty to put pressure on a country when its trade policies cause hardship to its own citizens. For example, Bhutan, a country nestled between China and India, pursues maximum independence in its trade policies and travel laws in order to preserve its culture and environment. Further, all its citizens must wear traditional dress and buildings must conform with traditional architecture. Bhutan's foreign minister said that with more trade and contact, "within a year or two our value system would change."[18] But its isolation contributes to Bhutan's ranking as one of the poorest countries in the world. Because it depends on foreign aid for about 65 percent of its budget, many argue that donors should use the aid as leverage to force Bhutan to liberalize its trade policies in order to help its citizens.

During recent decades, the United States has held a leading position in product innovations; however, there is evidence that the U.S. share of new product development has been declining and that Japan may now be the world's leading innovator.[19] There also is evidence that innovation is the main source of competitive strength. But because innovations can be imitated, companies in the leading countries must continually develop innovations in order to stay in the forefront.[20] The innovations or improvements may come in the product itself or in the method of manufacturing or distributing the product.[21]

Exports and labor   At the introduction stage of a product life cycle, a small part of the production may be sold to customers in foreign markets who have heard about the new product and actively seek it. These foreign customers are most likely to be found in countries with similar market segments—in the case of U.S. companies, in other industrial countries.

The production process is apt to be more labor-intensive in this stage than in later stages. Because the product is not yet standardized, it must be produced by a process that permits rapid changes in product characteristics, as dictated by market feedback. This implies high labor input as opposed to automated production, which is more capital-intensive. Furthermore, the capital machinery necessary to produce a product on a large scale usually develops later than product technology, only when sales begin to expand rapidly enough (Stage 2) to warrant the high development costs of the machines for the new process.

The fact that the United States excels in the development of new products, which usually are made in labor-intensive ways, helps to explain the Leontief paradox, which showed that the United States generally exports labor-intensive products. Because U.S. wage rates are known to be among the highest in the world, how can the United States compete? According to one view, this ability stems from the monopoly position of original producers, which allows them to pass on costs to consumers who are unwilling to wait for possible price reductions later. Much evidence of this behavior is based on eventual price decreases of products such as calculators and VCRs. Another explanation is that although U.S. labor is paid a high hourly wage, its education and skill levels make it adept and efficient when production is not yet standardized. When production becomes highly automated, U.S. labor becomes less competitive because unskilled labor may be quickly trained to perform highly repetitive tasks efficiently.

Stage 2: Growth

Growth is characterized by
- **Increases in exports by the innovating country**
- **More competition**
- **Increased capital intensity**
- **Some foreign production**

As sales of the new product grow, competitors enter the market. At the same time, demand is likely to grow substantially in foreign markets, particularly in other industrial countries. In fact, demand may be sufficient to justify producing in some foreign markets in order to reduce or eliminate transport charges and tariffs.

Either the innovator or a competitor may begin producing abroad, but the output at this stage is likely to stay almost entirely in the foreign country with the new manufacturing unit. Let's say, for example, that the new manufacturing unit is in Japan. The output will be sold mainly in Japan for several reasons:

1. There is growth in the Japanese market.
2. Unique product variations are being introduced for Japanese consumers.
3. Japanese costs may still be high because of production start-up problems.

Because sales are growing rapidly in many markets, there are greater incentives at this level for the development of process technology. However, product technology may not yet be well developed because of the number of product variations introduced by competitors that are trying to take a leadership position by gaining market share. Thus the production process may still be characterized as labor-intensive during this stage, although it is becoming less so. The original producing country will increase its exports in this stage but face the loss of certain key export markets in which local production has commenced.

Stage 3: Maturity

Maturity is characterized by
- **Decline in exports from the innovating country**
- **More product standardization**
- **More capital intensity**
- **Increased competitiveness of price**
- **Production startups in LDCs**

In Stage 3, maturity, worldwide demand begins to level off, although it may be growing in some countries and declining in others. There often is a shake-out of producers such that product models become highly standardized, making cost a more important competitive weapon. Longer production runs become possible for foreign plants, which in turn reduce per unit cost. The lower per unit cost enables sales to increase more in LDCs.

Because markets and technologies are widespread, the innovating country no longer has a production advantage. In fact, there are incentives to begin moving plants to LDCs where unskilled but inexpensive labor can be used effectively for standardized (capital-intensive) processes.

Stage 4: Decline

Decline is characterized by
- **Concentration of production in LDCs**
- **Innovating country becoming net importer**

As a product moves to the declining stage, those factors occurring during the mature stage continue to evolve. The markets in industrial countries decline more rapidly than those in LDCs as affluent customers demand ever-newer products. By this time, market and cost factors have dictated that almost all production is situated in LDCs, which export to the declining or small-niche markets in industrial countries.

Verification and Limitations of PLC Theory

Studies have found behavior to be consistent with the predictions of the PLC model for certain consumer durables, synthetic materials, and electronics.[22] However, there are many other types of products for which production movements do not take place:[23]

1. Products that, because of very rapid innovation, have extremely short life cycles, which make it impossible to achieve cost reductions by moving production

from one country to another. For example, product obsolescence occurs so rapidly for many electronic products that there is little international diffusion of production.

2. Luxury products for which cost is of little concern to the consumer.

3. Products for which international transport costs are so high that there is little opportunity for export sales, regardless of the stage within the product life cycle.

4. Products for which a company can use a differentiation strategy, such as advertising, in order to maintain consumer demand without competing on the basis of price.[24]

5. Products that result when specialized knowledge is important for linking present output with the training of technical labor and the development of the next generation of technology. This seems to explain the long-term U.S. dominance of medical equipment production and German dominance in rotary printing presses.[25]

In addition, changes in technology and demand conditions might lead to all kinds of permutations. For example, microchip production began in the United States and moved largely abroad, as would be predicted by PLC theory; but then most production returned to the United States in response to further product innovations and changing market conditions.

Regardless of the type of product, there has been an increased tendency on the part of MNEs to introduce new products at home and abroad almost simultaneously as they move from multidomestic to global strategies. In other words, instead of merely observing needs within their domestic markets, companies develop products and services to serve observable market segments that transcend national borders. In so doing, they eliminate the leads and lags that are assumed to exist as a product is diffused from one country to another. Further, companies sometimes produce abroad simply to take advantage of production economies rather than in response to growing foreign markets. Singer, for example, produces certain sewing machine models in Brazil to sell in export markets, not to supply the Brazilian market.

Trade Patterns

Country Differences

So far in this chapter, the theories explaining why trade takes place have focused on the differences among countries. These theories tend to explain most of the trade among dissimilar countries, such as trade between an industrial country and an LDC or trade between a temperate country and a tropical one. On the basis of these theories, you would expect that the greater the dissimilarity among countries, the greater the potential for trade. For example, great differences in climatic conditions will lead to highly differentiated agricultural products. Countries that

Most trade theories emphasize differences among countries in
• Climate
• Factor endowment
• Innovative capability

**Figure 5.3
Value of World Trade
between Developed
and Less Developed
Countries, for Selected
Years**
Between 1948 and 1972,
LDCs' export share de-
clined substantially; however, since then, their
position has improved
somewhat.

Source: Statistical Yearbook, 1968
(New York: United Nations,
1969), pp. 398–399; *Statistical
Yearbook, 1973* (New York: United Nations, 1974), pp. 402–409;
Direction of Trade Statistics, De-
cember 1992, pp. 2–6; and *Direc-*
tion of Trade Statistics Annual
1970–74 (Washington, D.C.: International Monetary Fund, n.d.),
pp. 8–35.

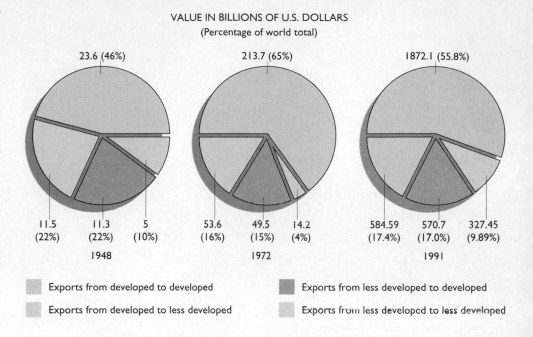

VALUE IN BILLIONS OF U.S. DOLLARS
(Percentage of world total)

23.6 (46%)   213.7 (65%)   1872.1 (55.8%)

11.5 (22%)   11.3 (22%)   5 (10%)   53.6 (16%)   49.5 (15%)   14.2 (4%)   584.59 (17.4%)   570.7 (17.0%)   327.45 (9.89%)

1948   1972   1991

Exports from developed to developed   Exports from less developed to developed

Exports from developed to less developed   Exports from less developed to less developed

differ in labor or capital intensities will differ in the types of products they can produce efficiently. And national differences in innovative abilities will affect how pro
duction of a product will move from one country to another during the product's
life cycle. A number of other factors help explain global trade patterns.[26] The most
important factors are described in this section.

Country-Similarity Theory

Observations of actual trade patterns reveal that most of the world's trade occurs
among countries that have similar characteristics, specifically among industrial, or developed, countries, which have highly educated populations and are located in temperate areas of the globe (see Fig. 5.3). Thus overall trade patterns seem to be at
variance with the traditional theories that emphasize country-by-country differences.

    The fact that so much trade takes place among industrial countries is due to the
growing importance of acquired advantage (product technology) as opposed to natural advantage (agricultural products and raw materials) in world trade (see Fig.
5.4). The **country-similarity theory** holds that once a producer has developed a
new product in response to observed market conditions in the home market, it will
turn to markets that are perceived to be the most similar to those at home. In other
words, consumers in industrial countries will have a high propensity to buy high-
quality and luxury products, whereas consumers in lower-income countries will
buy few of these products.[27]

    Although the markets within the industrial countries might have similar demand
characteristics, differences exist in how these countries specialize in order to gain
acquired advantages. Countries do this through the apportionment of their research

**Most trade today occurs
among apparently similar
countries.**

**Figure 5.4
World Trade by Major
Product Category as
Percentage of Total
World Trade, for
Selected Years**
Manufactures account for
the largest portion of
world trade.

*Includes products not classified
by reporting countries.
†Includes raw materials, fuels,
minerals, and chemicals.

Source: S. Woytinski and E.S.
Woytinski, *World Commerce and
Governments* (New York: Twenti-
eth Century Fund, 1955); *United
Nations Statistical Yearbook,* 1973
(New York: United Nations,
1974), p. 56; *International Trade
Statistics Yearbook,* 1990, Vol. I
(New York: United Nations,
1992), p. 590.

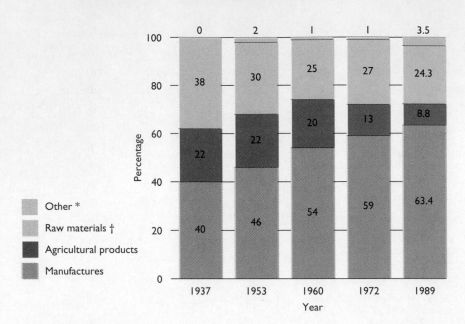

efforts. For example, the technical efforts of the United States are strongest in mining, Japan's are in information and instruments, France's in nuclear physics, and
Switzerland's in textiles.[28] Countries also do this by apportioning spending among
physical items (plant and equipment), human skills, and technological development.[29] Further, those domestic industries in which there is intense competitive rivalry will probably innovate faster and develop international advantages.[30]

Wars and Insurrection

Military conflicts disrupt traditional international business patterns as participants
divert their transportation systems and much of their productive capacity to the war
effort. In addition, political animosity and transport difficulties may interfere with
trading channels. For example, Iraq's international trade fell sharply after its 1990
invasion of Kuwait as other countries either severed trade relations or disrupted supply lines. The composition of trade changes because of a shift from consumer goods
to industrial goods that can be used in meeting military objectives. Increased global
interrelationships lend far-reaching impact to today's military conflicts. A particularly notable example was the worldwide oil price increase resulting from Iraq's
invasion of Kuwait. Even national disturbances may have widespread international
implications. The Chilean disruptions in the early 1970s, for example, had a substantial effect on world copper production and usage. The civil war within Lebanon resulted in a shift in international banking from Beirut to Bahrain and Cyprus.

Pairs of Trading Relationships

Although the theories regarding country differences and similarities help to explain
broad world trade patterns, such as between industrial countries and LDCs, they do

Military conflicts
• **Change what is produced**
• **Increase risks of interna-
tional business**
• **Have a growing global ef-
fect on business**

**Trading partners are affect-
ed by**
• **Distance**
• **Competitive capabilities**
• **Cultural similarity**
• **Relations between
countries**
• **Business cycles**

little to explain specific pairs of trading relationships. Why, for example, will a particular industrial country buy more from one LDC than another? Why will it buy from one industrial country rather than another? Although there is no single answer to these questions that will explain all product flows, the distance between two countries accounts for many of these world trade relationships. This is especially true for products for which the transport cost is high relative to the production cost.

But transport cost is not the only factor; nor is it an insurmountable one. For example, New Zealand has favorable climatic and soil conditions for growing apples. It also has an opportunity to compete out of season in the Northern Hemisphere. However, these advantages are not unique; Chile, Argentina, and South Africa have them as well. Furthermore, these three countries have cost advantages in land, labor, and freight. Nevertheless, New Zealand was able to increase its share of global apple exports during the 1980s by increasing yields, developing new premium varieties, bypassing intermediaries to sell directly to supermarkets abroad, and consolidating efforts through a national marketing board.

Cultural similarity, as expressed through language and religion, also helps explain much of the direction of trade. Apparently importers and exporters find it easier to do business in a country they perceive as being similar. Likewise, much of the trade between specific industrial countries and LDCs is explained by historic colonial relationships; and much of the lack of trade among nations in the Southern Hemisphere is due to the absence of historic ties. Importers and exporters find it easier to continue business ties than to develop new distribution arrangements in countries in which they are less experienced.

Political relationships and economic agreements among countries may discourage or encourage trade between certain pairs of countries. For example, political animosities between the United States and Cuba have caused mutual trade to be almost nonexistent for about four decades and have replaced U.S. sugar imports from Cuba with imports from such countries as Mexico and the Dominican Republic. Aid shipments, such as from the United States to Israel, also occur because of close political ties. The agreement by the European Union (EU) to remove all trade barriers among member countries has caused a greater share of those countries' total trade to be conducted within the group.

During economic booms, trade tends to grow more rapidly than production does. The opposite occurs during periods of slow economic growth. The reason for this cyclical relationship is that consumers and governmental policymakers consider many foreign goods marginal and thus curtail imports as the economy slackens. Producers also may attempt to export only when they have surpluses and will add capacity to serve foreign markets only if demand there is sustained for a long period. This relationship not only affects total world trade, but also affects particular markets as growth rates differ among countries. For example, during most of the 1980s, Latin American economies performed very poorly, and they took a smaller share of U.S. exports. In the 1990s, the share of U.S. exports going to Latin America increased sharply as those economies grew faster than European ones did.[31]

Independence, Interdependence, and Dependence

The concepts of independence, interdependence, and dependence help to explain world trade patterns and countries' trade policies. They form a continuum, with independence at one extreme, dependence on the other, and interdependence somewhere in the middle. No countries are located at either extreme of this continuum; however, some tend to be closer to one extreme than the other.

Independence

In a situation of independence, a country would have no reliance on others for any goods, services, or technologies. However, because all countries engage in trade, no country has complete economic independence from other countries. The most recent instances of economic near-independence were seen in the Liawep tribe, found in Papua New Guinea in 1993, and in Albania from the end of World War II until the death of dictator Enver Hoxha in 1985.[32] Isolation from other societies brought certain advantages to the Liaweps and Albanians: They did not have to be concerned, for example, that another society might cut off their supply of essential foods or tools. Of course, for both societies the price of independence was having to do without goods they could not produce themselves. A further disadvantage of independence is that it hinders a country's ability to borrow and adapt technologies already in existence; such borrowing and adaptation can add significantly to a country's economic growth rate.[33] In most countries, governmental policy has focused on achieving the advantages of independence without paying too high a price in terms of consumer deprivation. This is done by trying to forge trade patterns that are minimally vulnerable to foreign control of supply and demand.

Interdependence

One way to limit a country's vulnerability to foreign changes is through interdependence, or the development of trade relationships on the basis of mutual need. France and Germany, for example, have highly interdependent economies. Each depends about equally on the other as a trading partner; thus neither is likely to cut off supplies or markets, because the other could retaliate effectively. Such interdependence sometimes results in pressures by international companies on their governments to sustain trade relations. For example, much of world trade is intracompany trade—that is, companies export components and finished products between their home country and foreign facilities—therefore, any trade cessation would adversely affect these companies. Similarly, when the U.S. government proposed trade sanctions against Chinese imports because of China's human rights record, U.S. companies protested because of the export sales they would lose.

Dependence

Recently, many developing countries have decried their dependence, realizing that they rely too heavily on the sale of one primary commodity and/or on one country as

---

No country is completely dependent or independent, although some are closer to one extreme or the other.

Too much economic independence means doing without certain goods, services, and technologies.

Interdependence is mutual dependence.

Too much dependence causes a country to be vulnerable to events in other countries.

Table 5.3
Dependence of Selected LDCs on
One Commodity for Export Earnings

LDC	Commodity	Percentage of exports
Cuba	Sugar	73.4
El Salvador	Coffee	61.0
Gabon	Petroleum	79.5
Ghana	Cacao	58.3
Jamaica	Aluminum ores	58.0
Liberia	Raw materials (nonpetroleum)	90.3
Macao	Clothing	64.0
Mali	Cotton	57.5
Mauritania	Iron ore	49.1
Niger	Uranium and thorium ores	83.2
Rwanda	Coffee	81.2
Somalia	Live animals	97.5

Source: 1987 Yearbook of International Statistics, Vol. 1 (New York: United Nations Department of International Economic and Social Affairs, 1990).

a customer and supplier. Whereas most LDCs depend on one commodity for more than 25 percent of their export earnings, Iceland is the only industrialized country with this high a dependence (on fish). And whereas about one quarter of LDCs depend on one country (almost always an industrial one) for more than half of their export earnings, Canada is the only industrialized country with this high a dependence (on the United States). Tables 5.3 and 5.4 show dependencies on one commodity or partner for selected LDCs. Because the economies of LDCs are small, these countries tend to be much more dependent on a given industrial country than the industrial country is dependent on them. Mexico, for example, depends on the United States for over 60 percent of its imports and exports, whereas the United States depends on Mexico for less than 5 percent of its imports and exports. Thus Mexico can be much more adversely affected by U.S. policies than the United States can be affected by Mexican policies. Furthermore, LDCs primarily depend on production that competes on the basis of low-wage inputs.[34] This sort of dependence has led to a widespread belief that dependence will retard LDCs' development.[35]

Although theorists and policymakers wishing to lower dependency have proposed a number of different approaches, they all suggest that LDCs intervene in the foreign trade markets. As shown in the opening case, Sri Lanka has attempted to diversify its exports by developing nontraditional products that its policymakers believe can ultimately compete in world markets. But some LDCs see that they have little opportunity to diversify production away from a basic commodity for which there is global oversupply. For them, the best economic assurance is continued dependence on an industrial country that preferentially imports their products.[36]

Trade strategies among developing countries As was emphasized earlier in this chapter, most LDCs depend on the export of primary products. The manufactured goods they export are usually mature products requiring high inputs of unskilled or

Table 5.4
Dependence of Selected LDCs on
One Trading Partner

LDC	Export market	Percentage of exports
Central African Republic	Belgium	50.9
Indonesia	Japan	42.7
Libya	Italy	41.9
Mexico	United States	70.5
Réunion	France	83.1
Saint Lucia	United Kingdom	67.4
Somalia	Saudi Arabia	86.5

Source: International Trade Statistics Yearbook (New York: United Nations Department of International Economic and Social Affairs, 1990).

semiskilled labor. Although these distinctions are true in an overall sense, they nevertheless obscure some differences among groups of developing countries. Those countries that do export manufactured goods can be placed into one of three categories based on type of good and country. Countries in the first group—Hong Kong, Singapore, Taiwan, South Korea, Israel, Portugal, and Greece—lack natural resources and have concentrated on exporting mature labor-intensive products. All of these countries have emphasized marketing, design, and information about foreign markets as a means of becoming competitive. Countries in the second group—Argentina, Brazil, Mexico, and Turkey—have natural resources, which they can use for further processing into manufactured goods, and domestic markets large enough to support economies of scale. These countries have had success in exporting capital goods and chemicals and other intermediate goods. Countries in the third group—India, Pakistan, Egypt, and Indonesia (large poor nations)—have developed exports of standardized intermediate goods such as textiles, plywood, and cement that are not typical labor-intensive commodities.[37]

Why Companies Trade Internationally

Most trade theories are based on a national perspective, but decisions to trade are usually made by companies.

Most trade theories approach trade from a national perspective; that is, they begin with a question such as "Why should Sri Lanka trade?" Regardless of the advantages that a country may gain by trading, international trade ordinarily will not begin unless companies within the country have competitive advantages that will enable them to be viable traders. Further, these companies must perceive that there are opportunities for exporting and importing. Because companies have limited resources, they must decide whether to exploit those resources domestically or internationally. Only if they perceive that the international opportunities might be greater than the domestic ones will they divert their resources to the foreign sector. To understand why trade takes place, it is therefore useful to understand the competitive advantages and trade opportunities accruing to individual businesses.

Competitive Advantages

A recent study of a hundred industries in ten major trading nations focused on how the competitive advantage of a country is related to the companies operating within it. The purpose of the study was to determine why specialized competitive advantages differ among countries; for example, Italian companies have an advantage in the ceramic tile industry and Swiss companies have one in the watch industry. A conclusion of the study was that four conditions have been important for competitive superiority: demand; factor endowment; related and suporting industries; and firm strategy, structure, and rivalry. These are shown in Fig. 5.5 in what is called the *Porter diamond*. All four of these conditions have already been discussed in the context of other trade theories, but how they combine affects the development and continued existence of competitive advantages. Usually, but not always, all four conditions need to be favorable for an industry within a country to attain global supremacy.

Both PLC theory and country-similarity theory show that new products (industries) usually arise from observation of nearby need or demand. Further, start-up production usually is located near the observed market. This was the case for the modern ceramic tile industry in Italy after World War II: there was a postwar housing boom, and consumers of new housing wanted cool floors because of the hot Italian climate. The second condition of the Porter diamond—factor endowment—influenced both the choice of tile to meet consumer demand and the choice of Italy as the production location. Wood, for example, was less available and more expensive than tile, and most production factors (skilled labor, capital, technology,

**Figure 5.5
Determinants of Global Competitive Advantage**
The Porter diamond shows the interaction of four conditions that usually need to be favorable if an industry in a country is to gain a global competitive advantage.

Source: Michael E. Porter, *The Competitive Advantage of Nations* (New York: Free Press, 1990), p. 72.

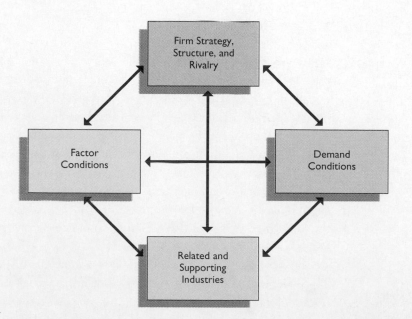

and equipment) were available within Italy on favorable terms. Although white clays had to be imported, the lack of availability of a natural resource (natural advantage) is not necessarily an insurmountable obstacle, as the earlier discussion of acquired advantage pointed out. The third condition—the existence of nearby related and supporting industries (enamels and glazes)—was also favorable. Thus, the combination of three conditions—demand, factor endowment, and related and supporting industries—influenced companies' decisions to initiate production of ceramic tiles in postwar Italy. The ability of these companies to develop and sustain a competitive advantage required favorable circumstances for the fourth condition—firm strategy, structure, and rivalry. Barriers to market entry were low in the tile industry (some companies started up with as few as three employees), and hundreds of companies initiated production. Rivalry became intense as companies tried to serve increasingly sophisticated Italian consumers. These circumstances forced breakthroughs in both product and process technologies, which gave the Italian producers advantages over foreign producers.

Although the Italian tile industry illustrates the usual conditions necessary for the development of a global advantage, the existence of favorable conditions is not sufficient to guarantee that an industry will start up and develop in a given locale. Entrepreneurs may face favorable conditions for many different lines of business. In fact, comparative advantage theory holds that resource limitations may cause companies in a country not to try to compete in some industries, even though an absolute advantage may exist. For example, conditions in Switzerland would seem to have favored success if companies in that country had become players in the personal computer industry; however, Swiss companies preferred instead to protect the global positions they had already attained in such product lines as watches and scientific instruments.

Export Opportunities

Incentives to export include
- **Use of excess capacity**
- **Reduced production costs per unit**
- **Increased markup**
- **Spread of risk**

Incentives to import include
- **Cheaper supplies**
- **Additions to product line**
- **Reduction of risk of non-supply**

Use of excess capacity   Companies frequently have immediate or long-term output capabilities for which there is inadequate domestic demand. This excess capacity may be in the form of known reserves of natural resources or in the form of product-specific capabilities that cannot be easily diverted to producing other goods for which there might be an adequate domestic demand.

As shown earlier in this chapter, small countries tend to trade more than large countries. One reason is that process technology may allow a company to produce efficiently only on a large scale, larger than the demand in the domestic market. Consider automobile production, for example: Volvo has a much greater need to export from the small Swedish market than General Motors does from the large U.S. market.

Cost reduction   Studies have shown that a company can generally reduce its costs by 20–30 percent each time its output is doubled, a phenomenon known as the **experience curve**.[38] For instance, with a 20-percent cost reduction and an initial cost of $100 per unit, the second unit produced will cost $80, the fourth $64, and so on.

The reduction may come about because of several factors: covering fixed costs over a larger output, increasing efficiency because of the experience gained through producing large quantities of units, and making quantity purchases of materials and transportation. Therefore it is obvious that the market leader may garner cost advantages over its competitors. One way a company can increase output is by defining its market in global rather than domestic terms. In fact, this may give a company a **first-mover advantage** that discourages the entry of other companies in the industry. However, the gains from the experience curve must be weighed against additional costs arising from exporting, such as those for product adaptation, management time, inventory increases, and more credit extension. These costs may outweigh the advantages of developing foreign markets.[39]

Greater profitability   A producer might be able to sell the same product at a greater profit abroad than at home. This may happen because the competitive environment in the foreign market is different, possibly because the product is in a different stage of its life cycle there. Thus a mature stage at home may force domestic price cutting, while a growth stage abroad may make foreign price reductions unnecessary. Greater profitability also may come about because of different governmental actions at home and abroad that affect profitability—for example, differences in the taxation of earnings or the regulation of prices. If, however, companies must divert efforts from domestic sales in order to service foreign markets, they may lack the resources to sustain their overall growth objectives.[40]

Risk spreading   By spreading sales over more than one foreign market, a producer might be able to minimize fluctuations in demand. This may come about because business cycles vary among countries and because products might be in different stages of their life cycles in different countries. For example, Donaldson Co., a U.S. manufacturer of filters, air cleaners, and mufflers, achieved record earnings in 1991 despite the fact that its two major U.S. customers, Caterpillar and Deere, were facing a recession.[41] Another factor in spreading risk through exportation is that a producer might be able to develop more customers, thereby reducing its vulnerability to the loss of a single customer or a few.

Import Opportunities
The impetus for trade involvement may come from either the exporter or the importer. In either case, there must be both a seller and a buyer. Impetus may come from an importer because that company is seeking out cheaper or better-quality supplies, components, or products to be used in its production facilities. Or a company may be actively seeking new foreign products that complement its existing lines. These would give the importer more to sell, which also might enable it to use excess capacity in its distribution sales force.

If international procurement of supplies and components lowers costs or improves the quality of finished products, the procuring company may then be better able to combat import competition for the finished products. Or it may be able to compete more effectively in export markets. The automobile industry exemplifies global competition that depends on subcontractors, including foreign ones, to reduce production costs.[42]

An importer, like an exporter, might be able to spread its operating risks. By developing alternative suppliers, a company is less vulnerable to the dictates or fortunes of any single supplier. For example, many large U.S. steel customers, such as the automobile industry, have diversified their steel purchases to include European and Japanese suppliers. This strategy has reduced the risk of supply shortages for the U.S. automobile industry in case of a strike among steelworkers in the United States; at the same time, however, it has contributed to the problems of the U.S. steel industry.

COUNTERVAILING FORCES

When countries have few restrictions on foreign trade, companies have greater opportunities to gain economies of scale by servicing markets in more than one country from a single base of production. They also can pursue global, as opposed to multidomestic, strategies more easily. But governmental trade restrictions are very mixed from one country to another, from one point in time to another, and from one product or service to others within the same economies. Companies are further constrained when transport costs are high relative to cost savings from long production runs.

Overall, it is probably safe to say that trade restrictions have been diminishing; however, other governmental actions often counter the effects of reduced restrictions. Given the importance of acquired advantage in world trade, it is understandable that governments take active roles in promoting the production of goods and services that will result in a high income for their domestic constituency. In other words, they try to alter their absolute and comparative advantages. There are two basic approaches. The first is to alter the conditions shown on the Porter diamond in Fig 5.5. For example, a country may upgrade production factors, such as by improving human skills through education, providing infrastructure (for example, transportation, communications, capital markets, and utilities), promoting a highly competitive environment so that companies are forced to make improvements, and inducing consumers to demand an ever higher quality of products and services.[43] This approach is general; that is, it creates conditions that may affect a wide variety of industries. A very different approach is to target specific production sectors. This approach usually has resulted in no more than small payoffs;[44] however, there are a few successes. South Korea, for example, has been transformed in a fairly short time from a poor agricultural country to a net exporter of key manufactured products. To achieve this transformation, the South Korean government took an active role in targeting key sectors (especially steel, automobiles, and consumer electronics) to ensure that they obtained needed capital. In the case of steel, the government created a state-owned company. The government gave incentives for companies to acquire foreign technology and improve on it and to train workers in quality control procedures. In addition, the government invested heavily in education in order to improve the input quality of employees. Not only did South Korea increase the educational attendance rate, it also increased the proportion of people studying to be scientists and engineers in institutions of higher education.[45] Regardless of whether a government takes a general or targeted approach, the relative competitive position of specific companies and production locations may be altered.

LOOKING TO THE FUTURE

If present trends continue, relationships among factor endowments (land, labor, and capital) will continue to evolve. The population growth rate is much higher in LDCs, especially those of sub-Saharan Africa, than in developed countries. Two possible consequences of this growth are continued shifts of labor-intensive production to LDCs and of agricultural production away from densely populated areas. At the same time, the finite supply of natural resources may lead to price increases for these resources (except for short respites). This may work to the advantage of LDCs because supplies in industrial countries have been more fully exploited.

Given the success of some Asian countries, the future is likely to bring greater efforts on the part of governments worldwide to improve trade advantages. There will be further discussions on the appropriateness of transferring successful trade policies from one country to another. For example, the collectivist approach that works so well in Japan, Taiwan, and South Korea may not be appropriate for the individualistic societies of the United Kingdom and the United States.[46]

Four factors are worth monitoring because they could cause product trade to become relatively less significant in the future:

1. There are some indications that protectionist sentiment is growing. This could prevent competitively produced goods from entering foreign countries.
2. As economies grow, efficiencies of multiple production locations also grow; thus country-by-country production may replace trade in many cases.
3. Flexible, small-scale production methods using robotics may enable even small countries to produce many goods efficiently for their own consumption, thus eliminating the need to import those goods.
4. Services are growing more rapidly than products as a portion of production and consumption within industrial countries; consequently, product trade may become a less important part of countries' total trade. Further, many of the rapid-growth service areas, such as home building and dining out, are not easily tradeable; thus trade in goods plus services could become a smaller part of total output and consumption.

Summary

- **Trade theory is useful because it helps to explain what might be produced competitively in a given locale, where a company might go to produce a given product efficiently, and whether governmental practices might interfere with the free flow of trade among countries.**

- **Some trade theories deal with the question of what will happen to international trade in the absence of governmental interference; others prescribe how** governments should interfere with trade flows in order to achieve certain national objectives.

- Mercantilist theory proposed that a country should try to achieve a favorable balance of trade (export more than it imports) in order to receive an influx of gold. Neomercantilist policy also seeks a favorable balance of trade, but its purpose is to achieve some social or political objective.

- Adam Smith developed the theory of absolute advantage, which holds that consumers will be better off if they can buy foreign-made products that are priced more cheaply than domestic ones.

- According to the theory of absolute advantage, a country may produce goods more efficiently because of a natural advantage (for example, raw materials or climate) or because of an acquired advantage (for example, technology or skills).

- The theory of country size holds that because countries with large land areas are more apt to have varied climates and natural resources, they are generally more nearly self-sufficient than smaller countries are. A second reason for this greater self-sufficiency is that large countries' production centers are more likely to be located at a greater distance from other countries, thus raising the transport costs of foreign trade.

- David Ricardo's comparative advantage theory holds that total output can be increased through foreign trade, even though one country may have an absolute advantage in the production of all products.

- Some of the assumptions of the trade theories of absolute and comparative advantage have been questioned by policymakers. These are that full employment exists, that output efficiency is always a country's major objective, that there are no transport costs among countries, that countries are satisfied with their relative gains, and that resources move freely within countries but are immobile internationally.

- The factor-proportions theory holds that a country's relative endowments of land, labor, and capital will determine the relative costs of these factors. These factor costs, in turn, will determine which goods the country can produce most efficiently.

- The product life cycle (PLC) theory states that many manufactured products will be produced first in the countries in which they were researched and developed. These are almost always industrialized countries. Over the product's life cycle, production will tend to become more capital-intensive and will be shifted to foreign locations.

- According to the country-similarity theory, most trade today occurs among industrial countries because they share very similar market segments.

- LDCs have been increasingly concerned that they are overly vulnerable to events in other countries because of their high dependence on one export product and/or one trading partner. As LDCs try to become more independent of the external environment, however, they face the risk that their own consumers may have to pay higher prices or do without some goods.

- Although most trade theories deal with cross-country benefits and costs, trading decisions usually are made at the company level. Companies must have competitive advantages to be viable exporters. They may seek trading opportunities in order to use excess capacity, lower production costs, or spread risks.

Case
The Cashew[47]

The cashew tree today is best known for its nuts, which account for about 20 percent of the value of nuts produced worldwide—about equal to the value of almonds or hazelnuts. U.S. imports of cashew nuts in 1992 totaled about $250 million.

The fruit of the tree (known as the cashew apple), however, drew the earliest attention. The Tupi Indians of Brazil first harvested the cashew apple in the wild. They later introduced it to early Portuguese traders, who in turn propagated the plant in other tropical countries. (See Map 5.2 for major production locations.) But attempts to grow the tree on plantations proved unsuccessful because the cashew was vulnerable to insects in the close quarters of plantations. Instead, some of the abandoned plantation trees propagated new trees in the wild where they thrived in the forests of India, East Africa, Indonesia, and Southeast Asia.

Several factors inhibited early use of the cashew nut. First, cashew fruit matures before the nut, so the fruit is spoiled by the time the nut can be harvested usefully. Second, the processing of cashew nuts is tedious and time-consuming. In the 1920s, however, a processing industry developed in India, and the nuts became more valuable than the fruit because they became so popular among Indian consumers. India maintained a virtual monopoly on cashew processing until the mid-1970s. This monopoly was due to three factors.

1. India was the largest producer of wild cashews.
2. Early demand occurred in India, meaning that any other country would have to incur added transport charges in order to reach the Indian market.
3. Most importantly, the Indian workers were particularly adept at the process technology.

Cashew nut processing was very labor-intensive and required manual dexterity and low wage rates. The nut is contained beneath layers of shell and thin skin. To remove the shell, the nut must be placed in an open fire for a few minutes and then tapped (while still hot) with a wooden hammer. If the nut is broken in the tapping, its value decreases considerably. Once the shell is removed, the nut is placed in an oven for up to ten hours, after which the skin is removed by hand while the nut is still warm. Removal is done without the

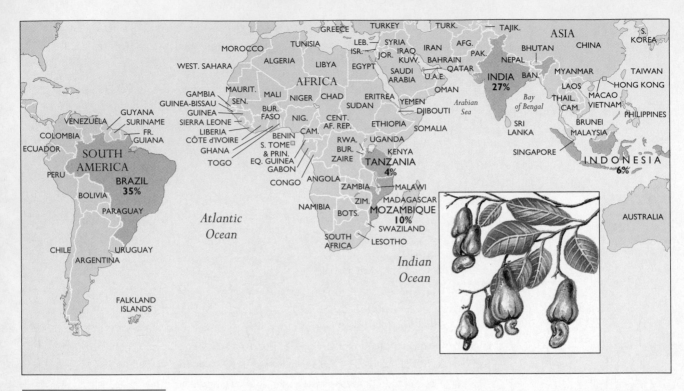

Map 5.2
Locations of World's Cashew Nut Production

The major cashew-producing areas are all in the tropics. This map shows the locations of the five largest producers. The inset shows the cashew fruit and nuts.

Source: Percentages refer to share of world cashew nut production as shown in *FAO Production Yearbook,* Vol. 44, 1990.

use of fingernails or any sharp objects that can mark or break the surface. The nuts are then sorted and graded into twenty-four different categories by the size of the pieces. The highest grade typically sells at about four times the price of the lowest grade, which is sold almost entirely to the confectionery industry.

Through the years, several factors began to threaten India's prominence as a cashew producer. As demand for the nuts grew in the United States and the United Kingdom, a shortage developed. Because the nuts were unsuited to plantation growth, India turned to East Africa, especially Mozambique, Tanzania, and Kenya, for supplies. Those countries were experiencing high unemployment and at first were eager to sell the raw nuts.

By the 1950s, India was no longer the world's major consumer, and the East African countries began to realize that they might be able to bypass India by processing the raw nuts themselves. Cashew-processing methods were well known, so there was no technological obstacle. There was another barrier, however, that blocked early competition from East Africa. The Indian labor force worked on making handicrafts at home as children and, as a result, by the time they were employed in cashew processing, could perform delicate hand operations efficiently. Without this training, the East Africans were at a fatal disadvantage.

Although the Africans' inability to compete granted a reprieve to the Indian industry, it put them on notice that they were vulnerable to supply cutoffs. The Indian Council for Agricultural Research, the International Society for Horticultural Sciences, and the Indian Society for Plantation Crops expanded their efforts to increase India's production of raw nuts. Concomitantly, three different companies developed mechanical equipment to replace hand processing. The Sturtevant Tropical Products Institute developed a method now used by a London equipment manufacturer, Fletcher and Stewart, which cracks the shells with a steel plate. Oltremare Industria of Italy and Widmer and Ernst of Switzerland both developed shell-cutting machines. Equipment was sold to East African countries and to Brazil in the 1970s. These countries decreased their exports of raw nuts to India in order to maintain supplies for their own processing.

Two factors have kept India's hand-processing industry afloat. First, the machinery breaks many cashew nuts, so Indian processors still face little competition in the sale of higher-grade nuts. At any time, however, newer machinery might solve the breakage problem, again threatening the approximately 200 Indian processors and their 300,000 employees. Furthermore, there is increased competition for the lower-grade output. Second, Indian processors have been able to obtain increased supplies of raw nuts as Indian production of these has increased. Pesticide technology now makes cashew tree plantations feasible, thus increasing the number of trees per acre. Furthermore, Indian experimentation in hybridization, vegetative propagation, and grafting and budding techniques promises to increase the output per tree to five times what it was in the wild. Nevertheless, Brazil, with abundant land and plantation technology, bypassed India in 1990 to become the world's largest producer.

The Indian processors were adversely affected by the thawing of the Cold War. Because India could no longer compete as well in its traditional North American and European markets for lower-grade nuts, a larger proportion of those nuts was sold during the 1980s to the Soviet Union, which became India's largest cashew nut customer in terms of tonnage. The Soviets bought the nuts at a price above world market levels, and their buying habits were believed to have a political motive. These sales decreased substantially when the Soviet Union broke up.

There is potential for an excess supply of cashew nuts, which might result from plantation techniques and improved technology in India and elsewhere. To find outlets for a possible nut glut, the All-India Coordinated Spices and Cashew Nut Improvement Project has centered on finding new markets for products from the cashew tree. The cashew apple, for example, is available in far greater tonnage than is the cashew nut. It has been discarded in the past because processors could get either fruit or nut but not both, and the nuts have been considered more valuable. Experimentation is going on to harvest both the fruit and the nut. The fruit also is being studied for commercial use in candy, jams, chutney, juice, carbonated beverages, syrup, wine, and vinegar. A second area of research is in the use of cashew nutshell liquid (oil), which was once discarded as a waste product. It is now used extensively in industrial production of friction dusts for formulation in brake linings and clutch facings. So far, however, the extraction of cashew nutshell liquid has been too costly to make the product fully competitive with some other types of oils.

Questions

1. What trade theories help to explain where cashew tree products have been produced historically?
2. What factors threaten India's future competitive position in cashew nut production?
3. If you were an Indian cashew processor, what alternatives might you consider to maintain future competitiveness?

Chapter Notes

1. Mike Levin, "Sri Lanka: Getting the Numbers Right," *Asian Business,* April 1992, pp. 40–44; "No Sri Lankan Tea for Iraq," *Wall Street Journal,* August 31, 1990, p. A8; Ramesh Venkataraman, "Sri Lanka: Bad Old Politics and Great New Economics," *Wall Street Journal,* April 4, 1991, p. A14; "Sri Lanka Investment: Inside or Outside the Free Trade Zone?" *Business Asia,* April 24, 1981, pp. 134–135; P. Murugasu, "Selecting Products for Export Development," *International Trade Forum,* October–December 1979, pp. 4–7; "United States Congress Speaks on Sri Lanka," bulletin issued by the Embassy of the Democratic Socialist Republic of Sri Lanka, Washington, April 1979; Lucien Rajakarunanayake, "Sri Lanka: Patterns of Serendipity" (Washington, D.C.: Embassy of Sri Lanka, May 1975); Colin de Silva, "Sri Lanka, the 'Resplendent Isle,' " *New York Times,* February 14, 1984, Sec. xx, p. 9; *World Development Atlas, 1989* (Washington, D.C.: International Bank of Reconstruction and Development, 1989), p. 9; Sarath Rajapatirana, "Foreign Trade and Economic Development: Sri Lanka's Experience," *World Development,* Vol. 16, No. 10, October 1988, pp. 1143–1158; and Vinita Piyaratna, "A Year of Living Optimistically," *Asian Business,* April 1993, pp. 37–38.

2. The mercantilist period is not associated with any single writer. A good coverage of the philosophy of the era may be found in Eli Heckscher, *Mercantilism* (London: George Allen & Unwin, 1935).

3. For a discussion of the problems with running a trade surplus, see Maria Shao, William J. Holstein, and Steven J. Dryden, "Taiwan's Wealth Crisis," *Business Week,* No. 2993, April 13, 1987, pp. 46–47.

4. The book has been reprinted by various publishers. For the specific references in this chapter, the edition used was Adam Smith, *The Wealth of Nations* (New York: The Modern Library, n.d.).

5. "The Ice Trade," *The Economist,* December 21, 1991–January 3, 1992, pp. 47–48.

6. Stephen P. Magee, *International Trade* (Reading, Mass: Addison-Wesley, 1980), pp. 10–12.

7. G. C. Hufbauer, "The Impact of National Characteristics and Technology on the Commodity Composition of Trade in Manufactured Goods," in *The Technology Factor in International Trade,* Raymond Vernon, ed. (New York: Columbia University Press, 1970), pp. 145–231; Paul Krugman, "Scale Economies, Product Differentiation, and the Patterns of Trade," *American Economic Review,* December 1980, Vol. 70, pp. 950–959.

8. For a discussion of scale efficiencies, see James R. Tybout, "Internal Returns to Scale as a Source of Comparative Advantage: The Evidence," *AEA Papers and Proceedings,* May 1993, pp. 440–444; for a discussion specific to R&D, see Rachel McCulloch, "The Optimality of Free Trade: Science or Religion?" *AEA Papers and Proceedings,* May 1993, pp. 367–371.

9. David Ricardo, *On the Principles of Political Economy and Taxation,* originally published in London in 1817, has since been reprinted by a number of publishers.

10. For a good discussion of this paradoxical thinking, see Paul R. Krugman, "What Do Undergraduates Need to Know about Trade?" *American Economic Review Papers and Proceedings,* May 1993, pp. 23–26.

11. Bertil Ohlin, *Interregional and International Trade* (Cambridge, Mass.: Harvard University Press, 1933).

12. W. W. Leontief, "Domestic Production and Foreign Trade: The American Capital Position Re-examined," *Economia Internationale,* February 1954, pp. 3–32.

13. See, for example, Anne O. Krueger, "Trade Policies in Developing Countries," in *Handbook of International Economics,* Vol. 3, Ronald W. Jones and Peter Kenen, eds. (Amsterdam: North-Holland, 1984), pp. 519–569; and Bela Balassa, *The Newly Industrialized Countries in the World Economy* (New York: Pergamon, 1981), Chapter 7.

14. Mark Casson, "Multinationals and Intermediate Product Trade," in *The Economic Analysis of the Multinational Enterprise: Selected Papers,* Peter J. Buckley and Mark Casson, eds. (London: Macmillan, 1985).

15. Raymond Vernon, "International Investment and International Trade in the Product Life Cycle," *Quarterly Journal of Economics,* May 1966, pp. 190–207; Paul Krugman, "A Model of Innovation, Technology Transfer, and the World Distribution of Income," *Journal of Political Economy,* Vol. 87, April 1979, pp. 253–266; and David Dollar, "Technological Innovation, Capital Mobility, and the Product Cycle in North-South Trade," *American Economic Review,* Vol. 76, No. 1, pp. 177–190.

16. John M. Culbertson, "The Folly of Free Trade," *Harvard Business Review,* No. 5, September–October 1986, pp. 122–128.

17. Barbara Rosewig and Richard Koenig, "Sweeping Change," *Wall Street Journal,* May 25, 1990, p. A1+.

18. John Ward Anderson and Molly Moore, " 'Ethnic Cleansing' Charges Echo in Himalayan Bhutan," *Washington Post,* April 8, 1994, p. 1994, p. A1+.

19. Barnaby J. Feder, "Europe's Technology Revival," *New York Times,* May 21, 1984, p. D1+; William J. Broad, "Novel Technique Shows Japanese Outpace Americans in Innovation," *New York Times,* March 7, 1988, p. 1+; and National Science Foundation, *International Science and Technology Data Update,* NSF 91-309 (Washington: 1991), pp. 7–17.

20. Michael E. Porter, *The Competitive Advantage of Nations* (New York: Free Press, 1990).

21. Robert B. Reich, "The Real Economy," *The Atlantic Monthly,* Vol. 267, No. 2, February 1991, pp. 35–52.

22. For good summaries of the studies testing the theory as well as recent tests, see James M. Lutz and Robert T. Green, "The Product Life Cycle and the Export Position of the United States," *Journal of International Business Studies,* Winter 1983, pp. 77–93; and Alicia Mullor-Sebastian, "The Product Life Cycle Theory: Empirical Evidence," *Journal of International Business Studies,* Winter 1983, pp. 95–105.

23. Ian H. Giddy, "The Demise of the Product Life Cycle in International Business Theory," *Columbia Journal of World Business,* Spring 1978, pp. 90–97.

24. This has been argued as a factor enabling industrial countries to charge high prices to LDCs while purchasing LDC manufactured products at the lowest possible prices. See Frances Stewart, "Recent Theories of International Trade: Some Implications for the South," in *Monopolistic Competition and International Trade,* Henry Kierzowski, ed. (Oxford, England: Oxford University Press, 1984).

25. David Dollar and Edward N. Wolff, *Competitiveness, Convergence, and International Specialization* (Cambridge, Mass.: MIT Press, 1993).

26. For a good overview of studies on this subject as well as an empirical analysis, see Rajendra K. Srivastava and Robert T. Green, "Determinants of Bilateral Trade Flows," *Journal of Business,* Vol. 59, No. 4, October 1986, pp. 623–639.

27. Stefan B. Linder, *An Essay on Trade Transformation* (New York: Wiley, 1961).

28. Daniele Archibugi and Mario Planta, *The Technological Specialization of Advanced Countries* (Dordrecht, the Netherlands: Kluwer Academic Publishers, 1992), pp. 46–57.

29. Dollar and Wolff, loc. cit.

30. Michael E. Porter, "The Competitive Advantage of Nations," *Harvard Business Review,* Vol. 90, No. 2, March–April 1990, p. 78.

31. Keith Bradsher, "American Exports to Poor Countries Are Rapidly Rising," *New York Times,* May 10, 1992, p. A1+; Kevin Kelly and Michael J. Mandel, "Exports Go Pffft," *Business Week,* August 3, 1992, pp. 20–21; Lucinda Harper, "Slowdown in Mexico Is Felt in the U.S.," *Wall Street Journal,* September 29, 1992, p. A2; and Al Ehrbar, "Trading Up," *Wall Street Journal,* January 18, 1993, p. A1+.

32. "New Tribe Found in New Guinea," *Herald Times* (Bloomington, Ind.), June 28, 1993, p. 1; Robin Knight, "Albania Peeks Out, Never Forgetting 'Life Is Earnest,'" *U.S. News & World Report,* Vol. 102, No. 18, May 11, 1987, p. 36.

33. David Dollar, "What Do We Know about the Long-Term Sources of Comparative Advantage?" *AEA Papers and Proceedings,* May 1993, pp. 431–435.

34. Refik Erzan and Alexander J. Yeats, "Implications of Current Factor Proportions Indices for the Competitive Position of the U.S. Manufacturing and Service Industries in the Year 2000," *Journal of Business,* Vol. 64, No. 2, 1991, pp. 229–253.

35. For a very good survey of the literature (pro and con) on this point, see Jose Antonio Ocampo, "New Developments in Trade Theory and LDCs," *Journal of Developing Economies,* Vol. 22, No. 1, 1986, pp. 129–170.

36. "Farm Trade: Gone Bananas," *The Economist,* March 28, 1992, pp. 76–77.

37. Hollis Chenery and Donald Keesing, "The Changing Composition of Developing Country Exports," in *The World Economic Order: Past and Prospects,* Sven Grassman and Erik Lundberg, eds. (London: Macmillan, 1981), pp. 82–116.

38. See, for example, Boston Consulting Group, *Perspective in Experience* (Boston:

Boston Consulting Group, 1970); and Robert D. Buzzell, Bradley T. Buzzell, Gale Sultaw, and Ralph G. M. Sultaw, "Market Share: A Key to Profitability," *Harvard Business Review,* Vol. 58, No. 1, 1975.

39. For discussion of the first-mover advantage, see E. Helpman and P. Krugman, *Market Structure and Foreign Trade: Increasing Returns, Imperfect Competition, and the International Economy* (Cambridge, Mass.: MIT Press, 1985). For problems of small companies, see Jacques Liouville, "Under What Conditions Can Exports Exert a Positive Influence on Profitability?" *Management International Review,* Vol. 32, No. 1, 1992, pp. 41–54.

40. Will Mitchell, J. Myles Shaver, and Bernard Yeung, "Getting There in a Global Industry: Impacts on Performance of Changing International Presence," *Strategic Management Journal,* Vol. 13, 1992, pp. 419–432.

41. Richard C. Marais and Michael Schuman, "Hong Kong Is Just Around the Corner," *Forbes,* October 12, 1992, pp. 50–58.

42. Ulli Arnold, "Global Sourcing—An Indispensable Element in Worldwide Competition," *Management International Review,* Vol. 29, No. 4, 1989, p. 22.

43. Porter, loc. cit.

44. Paul Krugman and Alasdair M. Smith, eds., *Empirical Studies of Strategic Trade Policies*

(Chicago: University of Chicago Press, 1993).

45. Alice H. Amsden, "Asia's Next Giant," *Technology Review,* May–June 1989, pp. 47–53.

46. G. C. Lodge and E. F. Vogel, *Ideology and National Competitiveness* (Boston: Harvard Business School Press, 1987).

47. Data for this case were taken from "L'anacarde ou noix de cajou," *Marches Tropicaux,* June 13, 1980, pp. 1403–1405; R. J. Wilson, *The Market for Cashew Nut Kernels and Cashew Nutshell Liquid* (London: Tropical Products Institute, 1975); J. H. P. Tyman, "Cultivation, Processing and Utilization of the Cashew," *Chemistry and Industry,* January 19, 1980, pp. 59–62; Jean-Pierre Jeannet, "Indian Cashew Processors, Ltd.," ICH Case 9-378-832 (Boston: Harvard Business School, 1977); Jean-Pierre Jeannet, "Note on the World Cashew Nut Industry," ICH Case 9-378-834 (Boston: Harvard Business School, 1977); "Meanwhile, Back in Mozambique," *Forbes,* Vol. 11, No. 16, November 16, 1987, p. 110; and U.S. Department of Commerce, Bureau of the Census, U.S. Imports of Merchandise International Harmonized System Commodity Classification, 1992, on CD-ROM.

Chapter 6

Governmental Influence on Trade

A little help does a great deal.
—French Proverb

Objectives
- To evaluate the rationale for governmental policies to enhance and/or restrict trade

- To examine the effects of pressure groups on trade policies

- To compare the protectionist arguments used in developed countries with those used in developing ones

- To study the potential and actual effects of governmental intervention on the free flow of trade

- To give an overview of the major means by which trade is restricted, regulated, and liberalized

- To show that governmental trade policies create business uncertainties

Case
Automobile Imports[1]

In late 1993, 117 countries agreed through the General Agreement on Tariffs and Trade (GATT) to the removal of many trade restrictions. This agreement is set to take effect on July 1, 1995. Known as the Uruguay Round, it includes a stipulation that each country will be allowed to negotiate a voluntary export restriction (VER) for only one industry. A VER is not completely voluntary, however. It is negotiated between countries, one of which "voluntarily" limits exports of a product to another because it reasons that otherwise the other government might set even more stringent import restrictions.

At the time of the Uruguay Round, the United States had 47 VERs, and the agreement called for phasing out almost all of these. The U.S. automobile industry has worried that it may not be the one industry the federal government will continue to protect through a VER. The industry has been partially protected since 1981 by a series of VERs with Japan. The most recent of these, which began in April 1993, limits Japanese automobile exports to the United States to 1.65 million units a year. Still, even with these trade constraints, the U.S. automobile industry has had problems.

General Motors (GM) and Ford posted 1992 losses of $23.5 billion and $7.4 billion, respectively—the two largest yearly losses ever incurred by U.S. companies. U.S. automakers blamed most of their problems on Japanese imports. Ford's CEO called for Japan to eliminate its huge trade surplus with the United States, of which about three quarters was for automobiles and parts.

Different groups have disagreed on whether Japanese automobile imports should have been limited, whether the agreements have served the objectives for which they were intended, and whether new controls should continue to be placed on such imports.

The first spurt of Japanese imports was of small cars as a result of the 1973 oil shortage; however, soon after the shortage ended, U.S. consumers largely returned to Detroit's major product—large cars with rear-wheel drive. Then, in 1979 and 1980, a second oil shortage hit. The foreign share of the U.S. new-car market subsequently increased from 17 percent to 25.3 percent, most of which was held by Japan. Managers of the U.S. automakers and officials of the United Auto Workers (UAW) spoke out favoring import restrictions. This was a milestone because the automobile industry and its union had long been supporters of free trade and had in the past publicly opposed import restrictions on such products as steel. The first ceiling under the resultant VER was for 1.68 million cars, a figure that climbed as high as 2.3 million for 1990.

At the time of the first VER, the U.S. automakers were not holding their own in sales of the small cars that they had been producing for several years. Japanese automakers, the primary automobile exporters to the United States, were evidently as surprised as Detroit was by the sudden shift in demand. They lacked capacity to fill U.S. orders quickly, yet many buyers were willing to wait six months for delivery of a Honda rather than purchase a U.S.-manufactured model. The reasons for this preference among U.S. consumers for Japanese automobiles were debatable. Some observers cited price differences created by labor-cost differences. Those who accepted this view largely favored the taxing of imports in order to raise their prices. Yet, on the basis of a canvass of 10,000 U.S. households, the Motor and Equipment Manufacturers Association found that imports strongly outranked domestic small cars in perceived fuel economy, engineering, and durability. People who accepted these results were opposed to limiting imports.

The initial arguments for protecting or aiding the U.S. automobile industry were based on two premises:

1. The costs of unemployment are higher than the increased costs to consumers of limiting imports.
2. U.S. production could become fully competitive with imports if actions were taken to help it overcome its temporary problems.

The first premise takes into account such factors as personal hardship for people displaced in the labor market; diminished purchasing power, which adversely affects demand in other industries; and the high taxes that would be needed to support unemployment insurance and food stamps. A *New York Times* poll showed that 71 percent of Americans felt it was more important to protect jobs than to have access to cheaper foreign products. The second premise reflects such factors as the historical competitive capability of U.S. automakers, the possibility of scale economies for U.S. production, and the much higher productivity possible with new plants.

Some protectionists have argued that the restraints worked. By 1984, the U.S. automobile industry had recovered, announcing record profits. However, the turnaround also was due in part to the economy's recovery from a recession. In any case, GM, Ford, and Chrysler (the Big Three) were able to invest heavily in more automated plants and to trim inventory costs. The Economic Strategy Institute, a private research group, reported that Ford had become more cost-efficient than Toyota or Honda at making small four-cylinder cars. In 1992, the Ford Taurus passed the Honda Accord as the top-selling automobile in the United States. Further, GM and Ford losses for 1992 were heavily influenced by one-time charges for future medical benefits and by operations in Europe rather than U.S. performance.

Other protectionists have argued that the allocations under the VER have been too high, thus contributing to a fall in North American employment at GM, Ford, and Chrysler. In addition, the Big Three have claimed that Japanese companies sell automobiles in the United States at artificially low prices.

Antiprotectionists have blamed the problems of U.S. automakers on poor management decisions and maintained that consumers and taxpayers should not be expected to reward the companies by footing the bill to see them through what has been a crisis of their own making. Antiprotectionists assert that any assistance, even short-term, results in at least one of the following consequences: higher taxes because of subsidies to companies, higher prices for foreign cars (which are preferred by many consumers), or the need to buy domestic cars (which many perceive as inferior). Some antiprotectionists also have held that governmental assistance in limiting imports might result in foreign retaliation against U.S. industries that are more competitive with foreign production—Japan, for example, might curtail purchases of U.S.-made aircraft.

Antiprotectionists have argued further that U.S. consumers have had little choice except to buy more expensive cars. Because Japanese producers were not able to increase their U.S. profits by selling more cars, they did so instead by selling more luxurious models and raising prices. During the three years of the original export restraints, the price of the average Japanese import increased by $2600; a Wharton Econometrics study attributed $1000 of this increase to import restraints. Meanwhile, the prices of U.S.-made cars increased by 40 percent. These price increases made both U.S. and Japanese automakers more profitable.

Although most people agree that U.S. automakers have used profits to become more efficient, critics argue that they have spent too little on product development, concentrating on acquisitions instead. Some of these acquisitions were of interests in small foreign automakers, such as GM's interest in Lotus and Saab, Chrysler's in Lamborghini and Maserati, and Ford's in Aston Martin and Jaguar. None have been particularly profitable. In addition, the companies made large acquisitions outside the automobile industry. For example, GM bought Hughes Aerospace and EDS; Ford invested in a savings bank and consumer finance company; and Chrysler bought four rental car companies, Gulfstream Aerospace, and Electrospace Systems.

Since the first restrictions were placed on Japanese automobile imports, the question of which companies and which production to protect has become more complicated. Clearly, the UAW has been primarily interested in maintaining jobs. UAW representatives were instrumental in helping to convince Japanese companies to set up U.S. operations, primarily to assemble vehicles. (Some of these operations are listed in Table 6.1.) The UAW wants much more, though; it is pushing to have more parts for those cars made in the United States. It estimated that only 38 percent of the parts were made in North America and that Japanese companies were keeping the higher-skilled and higher-paid production jobs in Japan. The UAW also has proposed legislation to force U.S.-owned companies to "invest at home and produce vehicles covering the full range of market segments." This push for "local content" runs counter to some of the policies being pursued by some U.S. automakers. These companies are trying to produce "global" cars in order to obtain maximum economies of scale and are buying parts from countries where they can be produced more cheaply (such as die-cast aluminum parts from Italy). For example, the Ford Escort, which was assembled in the United States, the United Kingdom, and Germany, contained parts from many countries. Further, many automobiles sold under Big Three brand names have been made abroad by other companies. These include the Ford Festiva, made by Kia Motors in South Korea; GM's Pontiac LeMans, made by Daewoo Motors in South Korea; and Chrysler's Dodge and Plymouth Colt and Vista, made by Mitsubishi Motors in Japan (see Fig. 6.1). The competitive situation is complicated by the fact that GM owns 36.7 percent of Isuzu Motors, Ford owns 25 percent of Mazda, and Chrysler, until recently, owned 24 percent of Mitsubishi. In addition, Japanese-owned operations in the United States, such as Honda and Mazda, are now exporting parts and finished vehicles to Japan.

Meanwhile, the UAW has been concerned that automobile import restrictions largely affect only Japan and only assembled vehicles. Therefore the VER does not affect Ford's investment of $500 million in Mexico to produce 130,000 Mazda cars per year for sale in the United States.

Table 6.1
Japanese Automakers' Investments in the United States

Year	Company
1982	Honda
1983	Nissan
1984	Toyota*
1987	Toyo Kogyo (Mazda)
1988	Mitsubishi†
1988	Toyota
1989	Subaru-Isuzu‡
1989	Honda
1992	Nissan
1993	Toyota

*Joint venture with GM for New United Motors Manufacturing
†Joint venture with Chrysler
‡Joint venture between the two companies

Figure 6.1

Source: By permission of Chip Bok and Creators Syndicate.

Introduction

Why study about governmental influence on trade? At some point, you may work for or own stock in a company whose performance, or even survival, may depend on governmental protectionist measures. You also are affected as consumers and taxpayers in the amounts you pay for goods and taxes.

All countries seek to influence trade, and each has
- Economic, social, and political objectives
- Conflicting objectives
- Interest groups

The automobile imports case is not atypical. No country in the world permits an unregulated flow of goods and services across its borders. Restrictions commonly are placed on imports and occasionally on exports. Direct or indirect subsidies frequently are given to industries to enable them to compete with foreign production either at home or abroad. In general, governmental influence is exerted in an attempt to satisfy economic, social, or political objectives. Often these objectives conflict (for example, increased employment versus lower automobile prices). There also is much disagreement regarding the likely employment effects of trade policies—for example, employment increases for autoworkers versus possible decreases for workers in other industries if foreign countries retaliate against U.S. trade policies by restricting their imports of some U.S.-made products.

Not surprisingly, any proposal for reform of trade regulations results in heated debate among interest groups that believe they will be affected. Of course, those that are most directly affected (stakeholders) are most apt to speak up. Stakeholders whose livelihood depends on U.S. automobile production (workers, owners, suppliers, and local politicians) perceive the losses from import competition to be considerable. Workers see themselves as being forced to take new jobs in new industries, perhaps in new locales. They may experience prolonged periods of unemployment, reduced incomes, insecure work conditions, and unstable social surroundings. People threatened in this way are liable to constitute a very strong pressure group. In contrast, workers in an industry that is affected only indirectly, through retaliation, such as the aircraft industry, do not readily perceive the same threat and so are less vocal. Neither do consumers usually understand how much prices rise because of import restrictions. For example, in the United States in 1992, import restrictions resulted in the average consumer paying $360 extra for food and the average family between $200 and $420 extra for clothing. And most countries restrict trade even more than the United States does.[2] However, consumers have not been active in uniting to protest import limitations vigorously.

The Rationale for Governmental Intervention

Unemployment

The unemployed can form an effective pressure group for import restrictions.

Pressure groups pose a real challenge to governmental policymakers and businesspeople. There is probably no more effective pressure group than the unemployed because no other group has the time and incentive to picket or to write letters in volume to governmental representatives.

One problem with restricting imports in order to create jobs is that other countries might retaliate. The most frequently cited example occurred in 1930 when the United States raised import restrictions to their highest levels ever. In a matter of months, other countries countered with their own restrictions, and the United States lost rather than gained jobs as its exports diminished.[3] In recent years, new import restrictions by a major country have almost always brought quick retaliation. For example, when the United States restricted automobile imports from Japan, Japanese pressure groups forced import restrictions on U.S. orange juice.

Import restrictions to create domestic employment
• May lead to retaliation by other countries
• Are less likely to be met with retaliation if implemented by small economies
• May decrease export jobs because of price increases for components
• May decrease export jobs because of lower incomes abroad

Two factors may mitigate the effects of retaliation. First, there may be less tendency to retaliate against a small country (in terms of economic power) that restricts imports. For example, Peruvian automobile import restrictions have caused no Japanese retaliation because the loss of sales by Japanese producers is too low. Second, if redistribution because of retaliation decreases employment in a capital-intensive industry but increases it in a labor-intensive industry, employment objectives may be achieved. For example, the United States limits imports of apparel, a labor-intensive good. Any resultant foreign retaliation against, say, U.S.-produced soybeans, a capital-intensive good, would probably threaten fewer U.S. jobs than would be gained from maintaining apparel production. Even if there is no retaliation, the net number of jobs gained for the economy as a whole is bound to be smaller than the number of jobs in the newly protected industry. That is because import-handling jobs would be lost.

Imports also may help create jobs in other industries, and these industries may form pressure groups against protectionism. Consider the apparel industry in the United States. Such companies as Warnaco and Liz Claiborne joined retailers to protest textile import restrictions because they needed the variety and quality of foreign-made cloth to compete against global companies. Or consider Caterpillar Tractor, one of the largest U.S. exporters. It buys crankshafts from Germany and Japan to cut costs enough to be competitive in foreign markets.[4] Imports also stimulate exports, although less directly, by increasing foreign income and foreign-exchange earnings, which are then spent on new imports by foreign consumers.

If import restrictions do result in a net increase in domestic employment, there still will be costs to some people in the domestic society in the form of higher prices or higher taxes. For example, the first three years of Japan's VER are estimated to have cost the United States $160,000 per job saved.[5] If protection seems permanent, the domestic industry may lag behind in technological and product development as well.

Higher prices or higher taxes must be compared with the costs of unemployment resulting from freer trade. It may be preferable to find some means by which individuals are compensated for their losses and/or can be moved to new employment. These tasks are challenging. First, it is hard to put a price on the distress suffered by people who must either be out of work, change jobs, or move. Second, it is difficult for working people to understand that they may be better off financially if part of their taxes go to help support people whose positions were lost because of imports. Finally, it may be equally difficult to convince people to accept handouts in lieu of their old jobs.

A complicating factor is that potentially displaced workers are frequently the ones who would be least able to find alternative work. In the garment industry, for example, sewing and cutting jobs are being transferred in great numbers from industrial to developing countries. Canada is an industrial country that has been losing these jobs. Forty-one percent of its sewing and cutting workers speak English as a second language, and the record of retraining these immigrants has not been very successful because their educational level is too low compared to the needs of expanding industries.[6]

Many countries assist workers who are affected adversely by imports by supplementing their unemployment benefits. Workers often spend the funds on living expenses in the hope they will be recalled to their old jobs. Some observers argue that too little is done to retrain and relocate displaced workers. However, the reality is that these workers, especially many older ones, lack much of the educational background necessary for them to be trained in any reasonable period of time. Further, predictions of future employment needs have been far from accurate; consequently, jobs may not materialize in the industries for which training is provided.

Infant-Industry Argument

One of the oldest arguments for protectionism was presented as early as 1792 by Alexander Hamilton. The **infant-industry argument** holds that an emerging industry should be guaranteed a large share of the domestic market until it becomes efficient enough to compete against imports. The infant-industry argument is based on the logic that although the initial output costs for an industry in a given country may be so high as to make it noncompetitive in world markets, over time the costs will decrease to a level sufficient to achieve efficient production. The cost reductions may occur for two reasons: As companies gain economies of scale, total unit costs are reduced to the levels of the competition, and as employees gain experience, they become more efficient.

Although it is reasonable to expect costs to decrease over time, they may not go down enough. Therefore two problems exist in using trade protection as a means of obtaining international competitiveness for a domestic industry. First, identifying those industries that have a high probability of reaching adulthood is difficult. Examples of industries that grew to be competitive because of governmental protection are certainly available—automobile production in Brazil and South Korea are good examples. However, in many other cases—such as automobile production in Argentina and Australia—the industries remain in an infantile state even after many years of operation. If infant-industry protection is given to an industry that does not reduce costs sufficiently, chances are its owners, workers, and suppliers will constitute a formidable pressure group that may effectively prevent the importation of a cheaper competitive product.

Second, even if policymakers can ascertain which industries are likely to reach productive adulthood, it does not necessarily follow that those industries should receive governmental assistance. There are, of course, many examples of entrepreneurs who endured early losses to gain future benefits, and policymakers may argue that assistance should be given only if the entry barriers to new companies are very high. Some segment of the economy must absorb the higher cost of local production during infancy. Most likely, it will be the consumer, who will pay higher prices. However, a government may subsidize an industry so that consumer prices are not increased; in this case, it is the taxpayer who will absorb the burden. For the infant-industry argument to be fully viable, future benefits should exceed early costs.

Industrialization Argument

In recent years, many countries have sought protection to increase their level of industrialization, for several reasons:

1. Emphasizing industrialization will increase output more than would emphasizing agriculture.
2. Inflows of foreign investment in the industrial area will promote growth.
3. Diversification away from traditional agricultural products or raw materials is necessary to stabilize trade fluctuation.
4. The prices of manufactured goods tend to rise more rapidly than the prices of primary products do.

Countries with a large manufacturing base generally have higher per capita incomes than do countries without such a base. Since the Industrial Revolution in England in the late eighteenth century, a number of countries, such as the United

---

Countries seek protection to promote industrialization because that type of production
- **Brings faster growth than agriculture**
- **Brings in investment funds**
- **Diversifies the economy**
- **Brings more price increases than primary products do**

States and Japan, have developed an industrial base while largely preventing competition from foreign-based production. Like the infant-industry argument, the argument favoring industrialization holds that importing cheaper products from abroad will prevent the establishment of domestic industry if free-market conditions are allowed to prevail. The industrialization argument differs from the infant-industry argument in that proponents say objectives will be achieved even if domestic prices do not become globally competitive.

Marginal agricultural returns   In many LDCs, too much of the population is engaged in agriculture. This is particularly true in economies such as those of India or Egypt, where little additional arable land is available. Consequently, many people may be able to leave the agricultural sector without greatly affecting such a country's agricultural output. If these surplus workers can be employed in the manufacturing sector, their output is likely to contribute a net gain to the economy because so little agricultural production is sacrificed in the process. If the cost of the domestically manufactured product is higher than that of an imported one, sales of the imported product must be restricted to ensure survival of the domestic industry. Doing this will result in either higher prices or higher taxes; nevertheless, real output should rise in the economy.

Shifting people out of agriculture is not without risk. Several problems can result:

When a country shifts from agriculture to industry:
• Output increases if the marginal productivity of agricultural workers is very low.
• Demands on social and political services in cities may increase.
• Development possibilities in the agricultural sector may be overlooked.

1. Individuals' expectations may be raised and left unfulfilled, leading to excessive demands on social and political services. Indeed, a major problem facing LDCs today is the massive migration to urban areas of people who cannot be easily absorbed. There is no work for them either because the industrialization process has proceeded too slowly or because they lack the rudimentary skills and work habits necessary for employment in manufacturing.

2. Agriculture may in fact be a better means of effecting additional output than industry is. Not all LDCs are utilizing their land fully, nor is industrial development the only means of economic growth. The United States, Canada, and Argentina grew rapidly during the nineteenth century, in large part through agricultural exports, and they continue to profit from such exports. Australia, New Zealand, and Denmark maintain high incomes along with substantial agricultural specialization.

3. If protection is to be given to manufacturing companies, policymakers must decide on which type of industry to protect so that consumer price and tax increases are minimized.

4. Too much of a shift from rural to urban areas may reduce agricultural output in LDCs, further endangering their self-sufficiency. Interestingly, most of the world's agricultural production and exports come from the so-called industrial countries because they have highly efficient and capital-intensive agricultural sectors, which have permitted resources to move efficiently to the manufacturing sector without decreasing agricultural output.

Promoting investment inflows   Import restrictions also may increase direct investment. When the purchase of foreign-made products is restricted, foreign companies may shift production to avoid the loss of a lucrative or established market. The influx of foreign companies may hasten a country's move from agriculture to industry as well as contribute to growth by adding to the stock of capital and technology per worker employed. For example, Mexico's automobile import restrictions influenced foreign automakers to invest there. Investment inflows also may add to employment, which is an especially attractive benefit from the standpoint of most policymakers.

Diversification   Export prices of most primary products fluctuate widely. Price variations due to such uncontrollable factors as weather affecting supply or business cycles abroad affecting demand can wreak havoc on economies that depend on the export of primary products. This is particularly true when an economy depends very heavily on a few commodities for employment of its population and for its export earnings. For example, the Côte d'Ivoire's exports fell by one quarter over two years when cocoa and coffee prices plummeted.[7] Because a large number of LDCs heavily depend on just one primary commodity, they frequently can afford foreign luxuries one year but are unable to afford replacement parts for essential equipment the next.

However, a greater dependence on manufacturing does not guarantee diversification or stable export earnings. Most GNPs of LDCs are small; consequently, a change may simply shift dependence from one or two agricultural products to one or two manufactured ones.

Terms of trade for LDCs may deteriorate because
• Demand for primary products grows more slowly
• Production cost savings for primary products will be passed on to consumers

Terms of trade   The **terms of trade** constitute the quantity of imports that a given quantity of a country's exports can buy. The prices of raw materials and agricultural commodities have not risen as fast as the prices of finished products have. As a result, over time it takes more primary products to buy the same amount of manufactured goods. Further, the demand for primary products does not rise as rapidly, so most LDCs have become increasingly poorer in relation to developed countries. This condition supposedly warrants the protection of emerging manufacturing companies that produce nontraditional raw materials and agricultural commodities.[8] The declining terms of trade for LDCs have been explained in part by lagging demand for agricultural products and by changes in technology that have saved on utilization of raw materials. A further explanation sometimes offered is that because of competitive conditions, savings due to technical changes that lower production costs of primary products are largely passed on to consumers, whereas cost savings for manufactured products go to higher profits and wages.[9]

Industrialization emphasizes either
• Products to sell domestically or
• Products to export

Import substitution versus export promotion   By restricting imports, a country may produce for local consumption goods it formerly imported. This is known as **import substitution.** In recent years, many countries have questioned whether import substitution is the best way to develop new industries through protection. If the protected industries do not become efficient, consumers may have to pay higher prices or higher taxes for an indefinite period of time to support them. In addition, because capital equipment and other supplies usually must be imported, foreign-exchange savings are minimal. These countries have witnessed the rapid growth of other countries, such as Taiwan and South Korea, which have achieved a favorable balance of payments and rapid economic growth by promoting export industries, an approach known as **export-led development.** Thus some countries are now trying to develop industries for which export markets should logically exist, such as the processing of raw materials that they currently are exporting. This change affects MNEs' operations in these countries because such companies may have to develop export markets for their foreign production rather than being able to sell it in each country of production.

In reality, it is not easy to distinguish between the two types of industrialization, nor is it always possible to develop exports. Industrialization may result initially in import substitution, yet export development of the same products may be feasible later. The fact that a country concentrates its industrialization activities on products for which it would seem to have a comparative advantage does not guarantee that exports can be generated. There are various trade barriers, discussed later in this chapter, that are particularly problematic to the development of manufacturing exports from nonindustrialized countries. In addition, economic conditions in other countries, such as a recession, can hinder their consumers' ability to buy the exported products.

Economic Relationships with Other Countries
Countries also restrict trade because they are concerned about their economic or political positions relative to other countries.

Balance-of-payments adjustments   Because the trade account is a major component of the balance of payments for most countries, governments make many attempts to modify what would have been an import or export movement in a free-market situation.

Trade restrictions may have an uneven effect on industries, but a country can choose to restrict the least essential imports.

Direct influence on trade differs from the other means of balance-of-payments adjustment (deflation of the economy or currency devaluation) primarily because of its greater selectivity. This may be either an advantage or a disadvantage compared to other adjustment mechanisms. For example, if a country is running a deficit, either a devaluation or a domestic deflation can make domestically produced goods and services less expensive than foreign ones, resulting in a widespread effect on both imports and exports as well as on such service accounts as tourism. Because of the breadth of industries affected, fairly small changes relative to other countries' prices may substantially affect payments balances, which in turn minimizes the burden of adjustment on any single industry. Direct influence on trade may, however, allow a country to choose the types of products or services to be affected. For example, the importation of luxury items may be curtailed, but rules governing imports of needed foodstuffs may be left unchanged.

Price-control objectives   A few countries hold monopoly or near-monopoly control of certain resources. To maintain control and the resulting high prices, they enforce strict export regulations. However, this type of policy encourages smuggling and requires high prevention costs. For example, South Africa and Colombia pay high prices to prevent diamonds and emeralds, respectively, from flooding world markets. Further, export controls may be ineffective. For example, Brazil lost its world monopoly in natural rubber after a contrabandist brought rubber plants into Malaysia; it now has practically no world sales. Also, if prices are kept too high, substitutes may be developed. For example, the high price of Chilean natural nitrate led to the development of a synthetic, and high sugar prices in the mid-1970s led to the development of a corn-derivative substitute.

A country also may limit exports of a product that is in short supply so that domestic consumers may buy it at a lower price than if foreign purchasers were allowed to bid the price up. In recent years, Argentina did this with wheat and the United States with hides and soybeans. The primary danger of these policies is that the lower prices at home will not entice producers to expand domestic output, whereas foreign output is expanded. This may lead to long-term market loss.

Countries also fear that foreign producers will price their exports so artificially low that they drive domestic producers out of business, resulting in a costly dislocation for workers and industries. If entry barriers are high, it is argued that the surviving foreign producers may even be able to extract monopoly profits or limit exports so that industries in their own countries will have preferential supplies. There have been allegations that Hitachi, the only producer of a key computer chip, delayed deliveries to Cray Research, the leading U.S. supercomputer producer, to give Japanese computer companies an advantage.[10] However, no evidence supports the contention that foreign producers charge monopoly prices after domestic producers are displaced. For example, low import prices have eliminated most U.S. consumer electronics production, yet U.S. prices for consumer electronics are among the world's lowest.[11] The ability to price artificially low abroad may result from high domestic prices due to a monopoly position at home or from subsidies or sponsorship policies of the home-country government.

The underpricing of exports (usually below cost or below the home-country price) is often referred to as **dumping.** Most countries prohibit imports of dumped products, but enforcement usually occurs only if the imported product disrupts domestic production. If there is no domestic production, then the only host-country effect is a subsidy to consumers there. Home-country consumers or taxpayers seldom realize that they are in effect subsidizing foreign sales. The U.S. antidumping legislation is extremely controversial. Under it, a foreign company can be fined if it makes less than an 8-percent profit on its export price or if its export price is as little as 0.5 percent below its domestic price, even though currency-value fluctua-

Export restrictions may
- **Keep up world prices in a monopoly situation**
- **Make it extremely costly to prevent smuggling**
- **Lead to substitution**
- **Keep domestic prices down by increasing domestic supply**
- **Give producers less incentive to increase output**
- **Shift foreign production and sales**

Import restrictions may
- **Prevent dumping from being used to put domestic producers out of business**
- **Get other countries to bargain away restrictions**
- **Get foreign producers to lower their prices**

tions may account for a much greater difference.[12] Further, the means of comparing prices is often arbitrary. For example, the U.S. government compared the prices of new Mazda minivans in Japan with those of used ones in the United States and the prices of small New Zealand kiwis in the United States with those of large ones in New Zealand as the basis to convict companies of dumping.[13]

Trade restrictions are used to reduce prices in foreign countries by forcing other countries to bargain away their import restrictions. For example, the United States passed the Super 301 clause in its 1988 trade act. This clause permits a threat of trade retaliation to be included in negotiations in order to get other countries to reduce import barriers for U.S. exports. Within two years, the United States used the clause successfully against Brazil and Japan and unsuccessfully against India.[14] The danger in this mechanism is that each country may escalate restrictions rather than bargain them away.

A final price argument for governmental influence on trade is the **optimum-tariff theory,** which holds that a foreign producer will lower its prices if a tax is placed on its products. If this occurs, benefits shift to the importing country. For example, assume that an exporter has costs of $500 per unit and is selling to a foreign market for $700 per unit. With the imposition of a 10-percent tax on the imported price, the exporter may choose to lower its price to $636.36 per unit, which, with a 10-percent tax of $63.64, would keep the price at $700 for the importer. The exporter may feel that a price higher than $700 would result in lost sales and that a profit of $136.36 per unit instead of the previous $200 per unit is better than no profit at all. An amount of $63.64 per unit has thus shifted to the importing country. As long as the foreign producer lowers its price by any amount, some shift in revenue goes to the importing country and the tariff is considered to be an optimum one. There are many examples of products whose prices did not rise as much as the amount of the imposed tariff; however, it is very difficult to predict whether exporters will in fact reduce their profit margins.

Political Objectives

Much governmental action on trade is based not on economic reasoning but rather on political imperatives such as the following:

- Maintenance of essential industries (especially defense)
- Prevention of shipments to enemy countries
- Maintenance or extension of spheres of influence
- Conservation of activities that help preserve a national identity

In protecting essential industries, countries must
- Determine which ones are essential
- Consider costs and alternatives
- Consider political consequences

Maintaining essential industries   A major consideration behind governmental action on trade is the protection of essential domestic industries during peacetime so that a country is not dependent on foreign sources of supply during war. This is called the **essential-industry argument.** On the basis of this argument, the U.S. government subsidizes domestic production of silicon so that domestic computer chip producers will not have to depend entirely on foreign suppliers.[15] This argument for protection has much appeal in rallying support for import barriers. However, in times of real crisis or military emergency, almost any product could be considered essential. Because of the high cost of protecting an inefficient industry or a higher-cost domestic substitute, the essential-industry argument should not be (but frequently is) accepted without a careful evaluation of costs, real needs, and alternatives. Once an industry is afforded protection, the protection is difficult to terminate. For example, the United States continued subsidies to mohair producers for many years after mohair was no longer essential for military uniforms.[16]

Dealing with enemy countries   Defense arguments often are used to prevent exports, even to friendly countries, of strategic goods that might fall into the hands of potential enemies or that might be in short supply domestically.[17] This policy may be valid if the exporting country assumes there will be no retaliation that prevents it from securing even more essential goods. Even then, it is possible that the importing country simply may find alternative supply sources or develop a production capability of its own.

Trade controls on nonstrategic goods also may be used as a weapon of foreign policy to try to prevent another country from easily meeting its economic and political objectives. For example, China tried to keep Taiwan from buying French fighter jets by announcing that French companies would be banned from bidding on a Chinese subway contract if the sale were made.[18] Another example was the international cessation of trade with Iraq after its 1990 invasion of Kuwait. Iraq's loss of oil exports was a severe economic blow, amounting to 43 percent of the combined GNPs of Iraq and Kuwait. But there were also costs to the countries imposing the sanctions. Oil prices rose, hurting LDCs especially. The United States, formerly the largest exporter to Iraq, lost sales of $1.29 billion a year; the losses were concentrated within those companies doing business in Iraq. For example, NRM-Steel had already produced equipment for an export order; the trade freeze reduced its 1990 earnings by about 20 percent.[19]

Maintaining spheres of influence   There are many examples of governmental actions on trade to support spheres of influence. Aid, credits, and purchases are frequently tied into a political alliance or even to votes within international bodies. For example, under the Caribbean Basin Initiative, the United States places practically no import restrictions on most products from Caribbean countries; in exchange, however, those countries must sign extradition treaties with the United States and cooperate in preventing controlled substances from entering the United States.[20] Most major powers buy at higher than world prices from certain LDCs in order to maintain their influence over those countries. The United States has done so with sugar-producing countries and France with citrus-producing ones. In country-to-country negotiations, governmental officials may even trade off some of the economic advantages of companies headquartered in their own countries in order to gain political advantages.

Preserving national identity   Countries are held together partially through a common sense of identity that sets their citizens apart from other nationalities. To protect this separateness, countries limit foreign products and services in certain sectors. For example, most restrict foreign airlines from carrying passengers within their domestic markets. One reason for this is the national identity associated with the flags on these carriers. Also, France has protected its movie industry out of fear that the English language and Anglo-Saxon culture will weaken its cultural identity. This protection has taken the form of government subsidies for film making and limits on the percentage of foreign films that can be shown on French television.[21]

Forms of Trade Control

The previous section focused on the end objectives sought by governments when they attempt to influence exports or imports. Attaining any of the objectives depends in great part on groups at home that pressure for actions their members believe will have the most positive (or least negative) influence on them. Because the actions taken on foreign trade by one country will have repercussions abroad, retaliation from foreign governments looms as a potential obstacle to achieving the desired objectives. The choice of instruments to achieve trade goals is therefore important, since domestic and foreign groups may respond differently to them. One way to understand the types of instruments is to distinguish between those that affect quantity movements indirectly by directly influencing prices and those that affect quantity movements directly.

Another common distinction is between tariff barriers and nontariff barriers: Tariff barriers affect prices; nontariff barriers may affect either price or quantity directly. A **tariff,** or **duty,** is a governmental tax levied on a good shipped internationally. Figure 6.2 illustrates how either type of barrier affects both the price and the quantity sold, although in a different order and with a different impact on producers. Parts (a) and (b) both have downward-sloping demand curves (D) and upward-sloping supply curves (S). In other words, the lower the price, the higher the quantity demanded; the higher the price, the larger the supply made available for sale. The intersection of the S and D curves illustrates the price (P_1) and quantity sold (Q_1) without governmental interference. When a tax (tariff) raises the price from P_1 to P_2 in (a), the amount consumers are willing to buy will fall from Q_1 to Q_2. Producers don't benefit because the price increase goes to taxes rather than to them. Part (b) shows a restriction in available supply; therefore a new supply curve (S_1) is imposed. The quantity sold now falls from Q_1 to Q_2. At the lower supply, the price rises from P_1 to P_2, which reflects the intersection of the D and S_1 curves. The major difference in the two approaches is that producers raise the price in (b), which helps compensate them for the decrease in quantity sold. In (a), producers sell less *and* are unable to raise their price because the tax has already done this.

M any critics argue that trade policy should be used to pressure other countries to change certain of their policies. For example, some pressure groups in the United States have sought to restrict U.S. trade with China unless China alters its human-rights and arms-export practices. Others argue that such trade restrictions result in high costs that are borne largely by people who have no control over the unpopular policies. For example, U.S. restrictions on exports to China would jeopardize many U.S. jobs because China is one of the largest and fastest-growing export markets for the United States.[22] Further, the restrictions would have the greatest effect on those workers in China whom the United States would least like to see harmed—workers in Guandong, the province that has moved most rapidly to free-market conditions. Similarly, embargos on Cuba and Iraq were intended to weaken and change their political leadership and practices; however, the general population in those countries, rather than the political leaders, has borne the burden of deprivation. Further, the embargos have not caused a change of leadership in either country.

The United States also has considered trade sanctions in an effort to force Taiwan to curtail trade in parts of endangered animals—rhino horns and tiger bones for example—which have been valued for centuries in that country's traditional medicine. Groups in Taiwan have argued against the sanctions on grounds of fairness. They have pointed out that political solidarity has caused the United States not to consider similar sanctions against China and South Korea, even though both of those countries engage heavily in the trade of endangered animals' parts.

Whether to use trade as a means of affecting conditions in other countries is not the only dilemma; there is disagreement on how to evaluate another country's practices. For example, some critics have suggested that trade policies be used as a means of pressuring Brazil to change its environmental practices—specifically to restrict the cutting of Amazon forests. Others have argued that any undesirable situation should be examined in relation to a country's overall record. They maintain that Brazil's overall environmental record—in particular, its limiting of adverse exhaust emissions by converting automobile engines to use methanol instead of gasoline—is too good to justify trade pressures.

A dilemma also arises when a product that could be dangerous is nevertheless permitted entry by an importing country. For example, some LDCs accept toxic wastes (for a fee) on the grounds that doing this generates income that would otherwise be forgone. However, it is the workers in these LDCs who will have to bear any adverse health consequences due to the toxic wastes.

Figure 6.2
Comparison of Trade Restrictions

In (a), the tax on imports raises the price, which decreases the quantity demanded. In (b), the quantity limit on imports decreases the supply available and raises prices. The price rise in (b) is charged by producers.

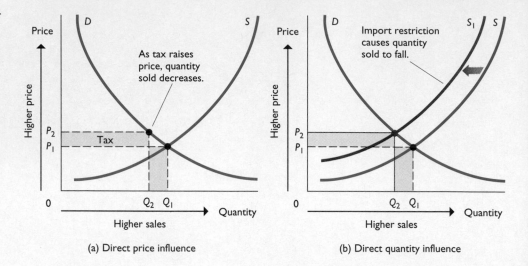

(a) Direct price influence   (b) Direct quantity influence

Tariffs may be levied
- **On goods entering, leaving, or passing through a country**
- **For protection or revenue**
- **On a per unit or a value basis**

Tariffs

The most common type of trade control is the tariff. If collected by the exporting country, it is known as an *export tariff*; if collected by a country through which the goods have passed, it is a *transit tariff*; if collected by the importing country, it is an *import tariff*. The import tariff is by far the most common.

Import tariffs primarily serve as a means of raising the price of imported goods so that competitively produced domestic goods will gain a relative price advantage. A tariff may be classified as protective in nature even though there is no domestic production in direct competition. For example, a country that wants to reduce the foreign expenditures of its citizens because of balance-of-payments problems may choose to raise the price of some foreign products, even though there are no close domestic substitutes, in order to curtail import consumption.

Tariffs also serve as a source of governmental revenue. Import tariffs are of little importance to large industrial countries, but are a major source of revenue in many LDCs. This is because governmental authorities in LDCs may have more control over ascertaining the amounts and types of goods passing across their frontiers and collecting a tax on them than they do over determining and collecting individual and corporate income taxes. Although revenue tariffs are most commonly collected on imports, many countries that export raw materials use export tariffs extensively. New Caledonia, for example, has such a tariff on nickel. Transit tariffs were once a major source of revenue for countries, but they have been nearly abolished through governmental treaties.

A tariff may be assessed on a per unit basis, in which case it is known as a *specific duty*. It also may be assessed as a percentage of the value of the item, in which case it is known as an *ad valorem duty*. If both a specific duty and an ad valorem duty are charged on the same product, the combination is known as a *compound duty*. A specific duty is easier to assess because customs officials do not need to determine a value on which to calculate a percentage. During periods of normal inflation, the specific duty will, unless changed, become a smaller percentage of the value and therefore be less restrictive to imports.

A major tariff controversy concerns industrial countries' treatment of manufactured exports from LDCs that are seeking to diversify and increase earnings by adding manufactured value to their exports of raw materials. Raw materials frequently can enter industrial countries' markets free of duty; however, if processed, those same materials usually have a tariff assigned to them. Because an ad valorem tariff is based on the total value of the product, nonindustrial countries have argued that the *effective tariff* on the manufactured portion is higher than would be indicated by the published tariff rate. For example, a country may charge no duty on coffee beans but may assess a 10-percent ad valorem tariff on instant coffee. If $5 for a jar of instant coffee covers $2.50 in coffee beans and $2.50 in processing costs, the $0.50 duty is effectively 20 percent on the manufactured portion, since the beans could have entered free of duty. This situation has made it more difficult for LDCs to find markets for their manufactured products. In addition, many of the products they are best able to produce are the ones that in industrial countries are produced by workers who are ill equipped to move easily to new employment. The result is the formation of pressure groups to keep these products out. A further problem is that when LDCs' products have preferential import restrictions, the most successful exporting LDCs reach thresholds at which they lose preferential status. For example, Taiwan, Singapore, Hong Kong, and South Korea no longer have preferential treatment in the United States. The preferential treatment originally resulted from pressures by LDCs in the United Nations Conference on Trade and Development (UNCTAD) and is known as the Generalized System of Preferences (GSP).

Another controversy concerns who bears the brunt of paying tariff costs. Some critics have claimed that in the United States, the burden falls mainly on the poor. This claim is illustrated by the following examples:

- Mink furs are duty-free. With the money a mother saves on her mink, perhaps she can afford to buy her child a polyester sweater, which carries a 34.6-percent tariff.
- Lobster is duty-free. With the savings, struggling parents may be able to afford infant-food preparations, which carry a 17.2-percent tariff.
- Orange juice carries a 36-percent tariff, but Perrier bottled water is assessed only 0.4 cent per liter.
- Fresh broccoli carries a 25-percent tariff, but, happily, truffles are duty-free.
- Footwear valued at not more than $3 a pair and having rubber or plastic outer soles and uppers is tariffed at 48 percent. If the footwear is valued at more than $12, the tariff is only 20 percent.[23]

Unfortunately, we do not know whether these examples are selective or typical. Further, price is only one type of burden on the poor. For example, the tariff on broccoli is imposed to ensure employment of migrant workers who plant and harvest the crops. A similar tariff on truffles would not help their employment because the United States lacks sufficient quantities of truffles to make their harvesting commercially viable.

Nontariff Barriers: Direct Price Influences

Governmental subsidies may help companies be competitive.
- **Subsidies to overcome market imperfections are least controversial.**
- **There is little agreement on what a subsidy is.**
- **There has been a recent increase in export-credit assistance.**

Subsidies   Although countries sometimes make direct payments to producers to compensate them for losses incurred from selling abroad, they most commonly provide other types of assistance to make it cheaper or more profitable for companies to sell overseas. For example, most countries offer their potential exporters an array of services—for example, providing information, sponsoring trade expositions, and establishing foreign contacts.[24] From an economic standpoint, service subsidies frequently are more justifiable than tariffs because they usually are designed to overcome, rather than create, market imperfections. There also are economies to be gained by disseminating information widely. Further, other countries are not likely to complain about such types of assistance. However, some observers may contend that users should be the only ones to share the costs. At any rate, export assistance is apt to result in less opposition than would import restrictions.

Other types of subsidies are more controversial, and companies frequently assert that they face unfair competition from subsidized production. There is little agreement on what a subsidy is. Did Canada subsidize exports of fish because it gave grants to fishermen to buy trawlers? Did the United Kingdom subsidize steel when the government-owned steel company had severe losses? Did the United States block some automobile imports because states made numerous concessions to convince foreign automakers to locate plants there?[25] Recently, questions also have been raised about various governments' support of R&D and about tax programs that directly or indirectly affect export profitability. One interesting subsidy case involves commercial aircraft. The United States subsidizes Boeing and McDonnell Douglas indirectly through payments for developments in military aircraft that have commercial applications; the EC subsidizes Airbus Industrie directly. The United States and the EC have set up a bilateral agreement to allow subsidies on commercial aircraft production but to limit the amount.[26]

Other forms of governmental export assistance are foreign aid and loans. These forms are nearly always "tied"—that is, the recipient must spend the funds in the donor country, making some products competitive abroad that might otherwise be noncompetitive. Tied aid is especially important in winning contracts to supply telecommunications and build railways and electric-power projects. About one third of capital goods traded worldwide are financed through tied-aid packages.[27] Most industrial countries also provide repayment insurance for their exporters, thus reducing the risk of nonpayment for overseas sales. Another scheme has been to combine aid with loans so that the interest rate on paper does not look as low to competitor countries as it really is.

Because it is difficult for customs officials to determine if invoice prices are honest:
- **They may arbitrarily increase value.**
- **Valuation procedures have been developed.**

Customs valuation   Customs officials used to have fairly wide discretion in determining the value of an imported product for affixing an ad valorem duty. For example, if the invoice value of a shipment was $100, customs officials might use instead the domestic wholesale or retail price or even an estimation of what the product would cost if it were produced domestically. This meant that they might charge a duty on a value much higher than $100. This discretion was permitted to prevent exporters and importers from declaring an arbitrarily low price on invoices in order to avoid incurring as high a tariff as would otherwise be imposed.[28] In practice, however, the discretionary powers sometimes were used as an arbitrary means of preventing the importation of foreign-made products by assessing the value too high.

Most countries now have agreed on a procedure for assessing values. First, customs officials must use the invoice price. If there is none or if its authenticity is doubtful, they then must assess on the basis of the value of identical goods. If this isn't possible, they must assess on the basis of similar goods coming in at about the same time. If this basis cannot be used, officials may compute a value based on final sales value or on reasonable cost.

The fact that so many different products are traded creates another valuation problem. It is easy (by accident or on purpose) to classify a product so that it will require a higher duty. With over 13,000 categories of products, a customs agent must use discretion to determine if silicon chips should be considered "integrated circuits for computers" or "a form of chemical silicon." A few examples should illustrate the possible problems. The U.S. Customs Service had to determine whether sport utility vehicles, such as the Suzuki Samurai and the Land Rover, were cars or trucks. They assessed the 25-percent duty on trucks instead of the 2.5-percent duty on cars, but doing this excluded the vehicles from the VER quota. Later, a federal trade court ruled them to be cars. Procter & Gamble's Duncan Hines Muffin Mix operation had to suspend production for seven weeks while awaiting a favorable ruling that the topping brought in from its Canadian plant should not be classified as sugar. Nike had to pay almost $9 million in back fees when the U.S. Customs Service ruled that its Air Jordan shoes should be assessed a duty as a synthetic rather than a leather shoe.[29]

Other direct price influences   Countries frequently use other means to affect prices, including special fees (for example, for consular and customs clearance and documentation), requirements that customs deposits be placed in advance of shipment, and minimum price levels at which goods can be sold after they have customs clearance.

Nontariff Barriers: Quantity Controls

A quota may
- **Set the total amount to be traded**
- **Allocate amounts by country**

Quotas   The most common type of import or export restriction based on quantity is the **quota.** From the standpoint of imports, a quota most frequently limits the quantitative amount of a product allowed to be imported in a given year. The amount frequently reflects a guarantee that domestic producers will have access to a certain percentage of the domestic market in that year. For many years, the sugar import quota of the United States was set so that U.S. producers would have about half of the home market. In this case, the total quota was further allocated by country on the basis of political considerations rather than price. The consumer price of imported sugar equaled that of more expensive domestically produced sugar, since lowering the consumer price on imports could not increase the quantity of imports sold. This sort of restriction of supply usually will increase the consumer price because there is little incentive to use price as a means of increasing sales. In the case of import tariffs, the gains from price increases to consumers are received in the form of governmental revenue in the importing country. In the case of quotas, however, the gains are most likely to accrue to producers or exporters in the producing country as added per-unit profits.[30] Windfall gains could accrue to intermediaries in the importing country if they bought at a lower, world-market price and then sold at the higher, protected domestic price.

Problems arise when quotas are allocated among countries because officials must ensure that goods from one country are not transshipped to take advantage of another country's quota. This has been a problem with Chinese- and Vietnamese-made garments that are transshipped through various countries.[31] Similarly, the product may be transformed into one for which there is no quota. For example, until completion of the GATT negotiations under the Uruguay Round, Japan did not allow rice imports but did permit imports of processed food containing rice; thus Sushi Boy, a restaurant chain in Japan, was able to import frozen sushi (which was 80-percent rice) from the United States.[32] Or a product may be transshipped as components that are not subject to the same import restrictions.[33]

Import quotas are not necessarily intended to protect domestic producers. For example, Japan maintains quotas on many agricultural products not produced in Japan. Imports are allocated as a means of bargaining for sales of Japanese exports as well as to avoid excess dependence on any one country for essential food needs, since supplies could be cut off by adverse climatic or political conditions.

Export quotas may be established to assure domestic consumers of a sufficient supply of goods at a low price, to prevent depletion of natural resources, or to attempt to raise an export price by restricting supply in foreign markets. To restrict supply, some countries have banded together in various commodity agreements that have restricted and allocated exports by producing countries of such commodities as coffee and oil; the result is that prices are raised to importing countries.

A specific type of quota that prohibits all trade is known as an **embargo.** Like quotas, embargos may be placed on either imports or exports, on whole categories of products regardless of destination, on specific products to specific countries, or on all products to given countries. Although embargos are generally imposed for political purposes, the effects may be economic in nature. For example, the United States imposed an embargo on Nicaragua between 1984 and 1990 because of political animosity toward the Sandinista party in power. But the effects on Nicaragua were economic: The country had difficulty getting supplies, particularly replacement parts for machinery that had been made in the United States, and it could not easily sell its banana crop, most of which previously went to the United States.

"Buy local" legislation   If government purchases are a large part of total expenditures within a country, the determination of where governmental agencies will make their purchases is of added importance in international competitiveness. Most governments give preference to domestic producers in their purchases of goods, sometimes in the form of content restriction (that is, a certain percentage of the product being purchased must be of local origin) and sometimes through price mechanisms (for example, a governmental agency may be able to buy a foreign-made product only if the price is at some predetermined margin below that of a domestic competitor).

There is abundant legislation worldwide that simply prescribes a minimum percentage of domestic value that a given product must have for it to be sold legally within the country. In the opening case, the local content proposed for cars sold in the United States would be, if implemented, a type of such legislated protection. Among similar legislation implemented in other countries have been Mexico's requirement for automobile components and Brazil's for electronics.

Standards   Countries commonly have set classification, labeling, and testing standards in a manner that allows the sale of domestic products but inhibits that of foreign-made ones. The ostensible purpose of these standards is protecting the safety or health of the domestic population. However, thwarted exporters have argued that such restrictions sometimes are imposed just to protect domestic producers. This has been argued, for example, by U.S. producers that fatten beef with hormones and are disallowed sales in the EC.

Specific permission requirements   Many countries require that potential importers or exporters secure permission from governmental authorities before conducting trade transactions, a procedure known as a **licensing arrangement.** To gain a license, a company may have to send samples abroad in advance. Requiring licenses may not only restrict imports or exports directly by denial of permission but also result in further deterrence of trade because of the cost, time, and uncertainty involved in the process. Similar to a licensing arrangement is a **foreign-exchange control,** which is a requirement that an importer of a given product must apply to its governmental authorities to secure foreign exchange to pay for the product. As with licensing agreements, failure to grant the exchange, not to mention the time and expense involved in completing forms and awaiting replies, constitutes an obstacle to the conduct of foreign trade.

Administrative delays   Closely akin to specific permission requirements are intentional administrative delays on entry, which create uncertainty and raise the cost of carrying inventory. For example, France required that all imported VCRs arrive through a small customs entry point that was both remote and inadequately staffed. The resultant delays effectively kept Japanese recorders out of the market until Japan limited its penetration of the French market through a negotiated VER.[34] Also, Peruvian customs officials routinely have taken months to clear merchandise and then charged customs storage fees that amounted to a high portion of the product's value.

Reciprocal requirements   In recent years, an upsurge has occurred in requirements that exporters take merchandise in lieu of money, generally because the importer is short of foreign exchange to purchase what it wants. For example, Colombia paid for buses from Spain's ENESA with coffee, and China purchased railroad engineering services from Italy's Tecnotrade with coal.[35] However, these barter transactions, referred to as **countertrade,** or **offsets,** often require exporters to find markets for goods outside their lines of expertise; thus many companies avoid this type of business.

Restrictions on services   Trade restrictions usually are associated with governmental interference in the international movement of goods. In addition to depending on earnings from the sale of goods abroad, many countries depend substantially on revenue from the foreign sale of such services as transportation, insurance, consulting, and banking. These services account for about 30 percent of the value of all international trade.[36] Countries engage in widespread discrimination that favors their own companies. For example, the United States restricts foreign-owned ships from carrying cargo between its domestic ports. Japan is the world's largest market for life insurance but effectively holds foreign insurers to about 2 percent of that market.[37] In the case of international airline traffic, countries engage in complex negotiations to assure that their home-based airlines gain an acceptable market share. For example, to protect Air France the French government forced U.S. carriers to cut capacity between the United States and France. The United States allows Japan Air Lines to carry passengers between Los Angeles and Brazil in exchange for Japan's allowing United Airlines to carry passengers between Tokyo and Australia.[38] More subtle practices of which countries have been accused include Japanese airlines' getting cargo cleared more quickly in Tokyo than foreign carriers can, Germany's requiring models for advertisements in German magazines to be hired through a German agency (even if the advertisement is made abroad), Spain's restriction of the dubbing of foreign films, which forces people to read subtitles, and Germany's prohibition against its insurance brokers helping German clients arrange insurance abroad.[39]

Extent of restrictions   Countries tend to point fingers at others in terms of restrictions, yet it is difficult to calculate which country is most restrictive. Table 6.2 shows some of the U.S. restrictions that the Canadian government has complained about.

Table 6.2
Selected U.S. Nontariff Barriers

Type	Examples
Subsidies	• Preferential procurement, overhead payments, and capital assistance to U.S. defense and NASA contractors • Agricultural export subsidies and promotional programs, particularly in grains and oilseeds • Low-interest loans and payment guarantees on agricultural exports
Quotas	• Sugar and dairy products import quotas
Domestic preferences	• Buy American Act and other acts favoring U.S.-produced goods in purchases by U.S. government • Set-aside programs for small, disadvantaged, minority, labor surplus, and female-owned businesses, which favor U.S. producers in government contracts • Requirements that cargo transported by water domestically must be on U.S.-built, -owned, and -manned ships
Customs and administrative procedures	• Country of origin markings that raise costs and render some products (for example, bricks) unfit for sale • Lengthy inspections and testing and limited ports of entry that cause some perishable goods to spoil
Technical and regulatory barriers	• Limited quarantine facilities for live animals • Holding of copyrighted or trademarked materials in customs 30 days to determine if there is any infringement • About 44,000 standards jurisdictions that often overlap and require testing • License requirements for milk imports and interstate milk shipments that do not permit imports • Grading, sizing, and quality and maturity standards that are different for imported horticultural products • Different distribution requirements for imported wine and beer

Source: Selected examples were taken from "Register of United States Barriers to Trade, 1992," *External Affairs and International al Trade Canada,* April 1992.

The Role of GATT

GATT is the world's major trade-liberalization organization. It
• Sets rules for negotiations
• Monitors enforcement

The most important trade-liberalization activity in the post—World War II period has been through the General Agreement on Tariffs and Trade (GATT), which began in 1947 with 23 members and by 1993 had 117 members. GATT has given the world a basic set of rules under which trade negotiations take place and a mechanism for ensuring these rules are implemented. The most recent negotiations, the Uruguay Round, began in 1986 and reached agreement in 1993. Although each signatory country needs to ratify the agreement, this ratification is expected. If ratified, the provisions of this round will take effect July 1, 1995; however, in many cases signatory countries have a lengthy period in which to comply. For example, LDCs such as Brazil and India will have ten years before they must honor foreign patent registrations, and industrial countries will have ten years to phase out quotas on fabrics and clothing imports.

Most-Favored-Nation Clause

To belong to GATT, countries must adhere to the **most-favored-nation (MFN) clause.** This clause requires that if a country, such as the United States, grants a tariff reduction to one country, for example, a cut from 20 percent to 10 percent on wool sweaters from Australia, it must grant the same concession to all other countries. The MFN clause also applies to quotas and licenses. Although the clause initially was intended to be unconditional, countries have always made exceptions.[40] The most important exceptions are as follows:

1. LDCs' manufactured products have been given preferential treatment over those from industrial countries. For example, most industrial countries grant tariff preferences to LDCs under the Generalized System of Preferences (GSP).
2. Concessions granted to members within a trading alliance, such as the EU or the North American Free Trade Association (NAFTA), have not been extended to countries outside the alliance.
3. Countries that arbitrarily discriminate against products from a given country are not necessarily given MFN treatment by the country whose products are discriminated against. For example, the United States does not give MFN treatment to a number of countries in the former communist bloc.
4. Nonsignatory countries are not always treated in the same way as those that grant concessions. For example, only countries signing GATT's Government Procurement Code, which calls for nondiscrimination against imports in government procurement, are granted automatic permission to bid on public works contracts open to foreign bids.
5. Countries sometimes stipulate exceptions based on their existing laws at the time of signing a GATT agreement, such as Switzerland's exclusion of agricultural trade.
6. Exceptions are made in times of war or international tension. For example, the United Kingdom suspended MFN treatment of Argentina when the two countries went to war in 1982 over ownership of islands in the South Atlantic, known as The Falklands in the United Kingdom and as Islas Malvinas in Argentina.

GATT-Sponsored Rounds

GATT's most important activity has been sponsoring rounds, or sessions, named for the place in which each begins. These have led to a number of multilateral reductions in tariffs and nontariff barriers for its members. The process of granting reductions is across the board; that is, countries may agree to lower all tariffs by a given percentage, not necessarily the same percentage for all countries, over some specified time period. Given the thousands of products traded, it would be nearly impossible to negotiate each product separately and even more difficult to negotiate each product separately with each country separately. Nevertheless, each country brings to the negotiations certain products and services and certain protective devices it considers exceptions to its own across-the-board reductions. These exceptions sometimes lead to no reductions by the countries making them. For example, in the Uruguay Round, France did not eliminate protection of its film industry, nor did the United States eliminate its restrictions on shipping trade. Exceptions sometimes lead to negotiated reductions in order to gain concessions from other countries. In the Uruguay Round, for example, the United States first said that its antidumping laws would not be negotiated. But because these laws are so unpopular in LDCs, the United States finally agreed to cede antidumping disputes to an international tribunal in exchange for LDCs' agreement to protect patents, trademarks, and copyrights, the nonprotection of which had been very unpopular in the United States. Such negotiations have resulted in vast tariff reductions (see Fig. 6.3)—an indication not only that countries are committed to work jointly toward freer trade but also that tariffs are the easiest trade barrier to tackle.

Tokyo Round   The Tokyo Round, signed in 1979, resulted in an overall reduction in tariffs, including a 35-percent reduction each way between the United States and the EC and a 40-percent reduction by Japan on U.S. imports into that country. Despite these reductions, the primary thrust of the negotiations involved grappling with the increasingly important and complex nontariff barriers, especially in five specific areas: industrial standards, government procurement, subsidies and countervailing duties, licensing, and customs valuation. In each of these areas, conference members agreed on a code of conduct for GATT countries, as follows:[41]

- The Agreement on Industrial Standards provides for treating imports on the same basis as domestically produced goods.

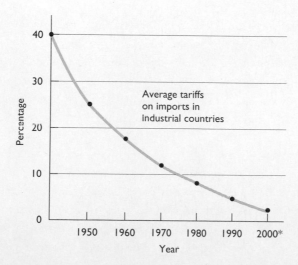

Figure 6.3
Progress on Tariffs
The eight GATT rounds since 1947 have reduced tariffs significantly.

*Estimated

Source: Herring in *The Christian Science Monitor* © 1993 The Christian Science Publishing Society.

- The Agreement on Government Procurement calls for treating bids by foreign companies on a nondiscriminatory basis for most large contracts.
- The Agreement or Code of Conduct on Subsidies and Countervailing Duties recognizes domestic subsidies as appropriate policy tools whose implementation, however, should avoid any adverse impact on other countries. With the exception of agricultural products, export subsidies are prohibited. This agreement also spells out procedures regarding the possible use of countervailing duties against a second country if the first country believes its domestic companies are being harmed by the second country's subsidy.
- The Licensing Code commits members to simplifying their licensing procedures significantly and to treating both foreign and domestic companies in a nondiscriminatory manner.
- The Customs Valuation Code calls for either c.i.f. or f.o.b. valuation (either invoice value with or invoice value without transportation and insurance included) and bans certain types of valuation methods, such as basing value on the selling price of the product in the importing country. (Specific customs valuation procedures were discussed in an earlier section of this chapter.)

Uruguay Round   These negotiations, which began in 1986, took more than seven years and achieved less than had been originally envisioned. The experience exemplifies the growing difficulty of reducing trade restrictions through globally oriented trade agreements. A primary problem is that less sensitive concessions have already been made and attention has moved toward services and away from products—both areas are of such high domestic sensitivity that politicians are very reluctant to yield to international pressures during negotiations. Further, trade in many services, such as construction and the professions, involves the potential movement of people internationally. One immediately encounters immigration issues, difficult licensing requirements, and conflicting opinions over qualifications.[42] Other problems include:

- The fact that talks become more cumbersome as more countries become GATT signatories
- The expectation on the part of industrial countries that LDCs also should make trade concessions
- The demands by LDCs that industrial countries should import products that affect marginal workers in those countries.[43]

Nevertheless, some tangible changes were made at the Uruguay Round. Virtually every participating country made concessions that politically were unpopular with its domestic pressure groups. For example, import restrictions were reduced by the United States and India on textiles, by Japan and South Korea on rice and dairy products, and by the EU on grains. Other changes concerned tariffs, quotas, subsidies, services, and settlement of disputes.[44]

Overall, the 117 nations agreed to reduce tariffs by about one third: 36 percent by industrial countries and 24 percent by LDCs. Most of the reductions by industrial countries will be on products primarily traded with each other. Quotas on textiles, finished apparel, and many agricultural products are to be eliminated; however, those on agricultural products will be replaced by tariffs of as much as several hundred percent. The ability to use VERs is greatly curtailed, to one industry per country. Subsidy reductions were agreed on for a number of agricultural products, such as grains, and for research in such goods as computer chips. LDCs agreed to open their markets for legal, accounting, and other services. They also agreed to protect patents, trademarks, and copyrights for a twenty-year period.

In some areas in which no agreement was reached, such as import restrictions on audiovisual materials and the protection of domestic shipping companies, the pact contains broad free-trade principles, which may ease the process of future negotiations. In other areas, the fact that sectors such as financial services, insurance, and telecommunications were discussed at all is a "first" and may presage future agreements.

Perhaps the biggest change resulting from the Uruguay Round is the agreement to replace the GATT secretariat with the Multilateral Trading Organization (MTO). The MTO will have more authority to oversee trade. It also will be able to assess trade penalties against a country when two thirds of the members find it in violation of trade agreements. Previously, GATT rules necessitated unanimity for trade penalties, and no country was apt to vote against itself when there were complaints against it. Instead, the GATT Council would investigate a complaint to determine whether allegations were valid. If so, GATT had to depend on a mutual commitment to cooperate in order to make countries alter their trade practices. This approach usually worked. For example, the United States eliminated custom-user fees after the GATT Council investigated complaints from Canada and the EC, and Japan lifted quotas on eight processed-food products after complaints from the United States. The MTO should be important in resolving antidumping disputes.

Meshing Protection and International Business Strategy

Governmental actions concerning trade are usually examined in terms of their effects on such broad objectives as balance of payments, income distribution, employment, and tax receipts or on such narrow objectives as decreasing steel imports versus increasing citrus exports as a trade-balancing measure. The fact that changes in governmental actions may substantially alter the competitiveness of facilities in given countries creates uncertainties about which businesses must make decisions. These decisions affect companies that are facing import competition as well as those whose exports are facing protectionist sentiment.

Foreign Competition and U.S. Automakers

When facing import competition, companies can
- **Try to get protection**
- **Make domestic output competitive**
- **Move abroad**
- **Seek other market niches**

A U.S. automaker facing foreign competition in the United States has a number of options:

- Pushing for import restrictions or other forms of governmental assistance
- Effecting internal adjustments, such as cost efficiencies, product innovations, or improved marketing
- Moving production to a lower-cost country and exporting to the United States
- Concentrating on market niches in which there is less import competition.

Clearly, there are substantial costs, as well as considerable uncertainty as to outcome, associated with any one of these options.

As you saw in the opening case, the U.S. automobile industry was successful in lobbying for the first option, a success attributable in part to unanimous U.S. automakers' support for import protection. It also pursued the second option by instituting various cost-saving measures. Cost breakthroughs are not always feasible, however, and when they do occur, the innovations may be short-lived as foreign competitors respond with like improvements. The benefit of moving production abroad (the third option), such as Ford's sourcing in Mexico, could be negated if the United States afterward prohibited importation from the foreign plant. The likelihood of import restrictions in such a situation would be inversely related to the number of producers following this option. In other words, because Ford, Chrysler, and GM all went to foreign sourcing, there has been no strong coalition to push for import controls on foreign-produced components, except within labor. The Big Three also have pursued the fourth option in that all have arranged for foreign companies to supply their small cars, thus enabling them to concentrate more of their production efforts on larger cars, for which there is less foreign competition. A company should attempt to assess the costs and probabilities of each alternative before embarking on a program.

The potential protection of the U.S. automobile industry also created problems for companies that were planning to export to the U.S. market. They could lobby against the protection, try to devise process or product technologies that would overcome the restrictive measures, or locate their production in the United States. As was the case for domestic automakers, each option involved costs and risks. And like the U.S. companies, Japanese automakers attempted each to some extent. They lobbied with the Japanese government to take steps to counter U.S. actions. They developed allies, such as associations of foreign-car importers and distributors, either to lobby on their behalf or not to take sides with the Big Three in the United States. They continued efforts to reduce costs in case tariffs were imposed. They developed capabilities for adding more luxury items so that profits might not diminish if quotas were imposed. They also negotiated arrangements to produce outside Japan, such as in Mexico and the United States, in case sanctions would be taken only against Japanese output.

Approaches to the International Environment

From the preceding discussion, it is clear not only that companies may take different approaches to counter changes in the international competitive environment but also that their attitudes toward protectionism are influenced by the investments they have already made to develop their international strategies.[45] Companies most apt to lose with increased protectionism are those that depend primarily on trade (whether market seekers or resource acquirers) and those that have integrated their production among different countries. Those most apt to gain are companies with single or multidomestic production facilities, such as production in the United States to serve the U.S. market and production in Mexico to serve the Mexican market. There also are differences among companies in their perceived abilities to compete against imports. In nearly half of the situations over the last sixty years in which protection has been proposed for a U.S. industry, one or more companies in the industry have been against protection. This is because they enjoy competitive advantages through such means as scale economies, relationships with suppliers, or differentiated products. They believe not only that they can compete but also that they will gain more power by having imports compete primarily against their weak domestic competitors, thus fragmenting that competition.[46]

COUNTERVAILING

FORCES

Because of difficulties in coming to a global agreement through GATT, countries are turning more to regional approaches for trade liberalization. If they can do this successfully, companies' responses may be much more of a hybrid of global and multidomestic practices as they find opportunities to coordinate their practices on a more regional basis. For example, many automakers have pushed for longer production runs, but these runs are limited by trade restrictions. They have been better able to increase runs for the European region than they have for the world as a whole because trade barriers have been eliminated within the EU. But regional trading arrangements, discussed in the next chapter, have a history of starts and stops as countries seek to protect their own economic interests; therefore, there are uncertainties.

The discussion in Chapter 5 showed that countries attempt to become more competitive by, for example, upgrading production factors such as human skills. However, countries have objectives other than economic competitiveness that, when pursued, may harm their domestic production and economic efficiency. Several of these have been alluded to in this chapter. For example, the cessation of trade for political reasons may hurt a country's exporters, sometimes abruptly, and may cause other domestic companies to encounter supply problems. The maintenance of certain industries for strategic reasons also may cause resource utilization to be distorted, for example, by shifting production from efficient to inefficient facilities. Countries also negotiate agreements that may place their domestic companies or production at a competitive disadvantage because it is the price to pay for some other concession or expected outcome. All these actions greatly alter how companies can compete globally.

Countries prefer to act independently; however, they cede authority on trade when they perceive cooperation to be in their overall best interest. For example, the United States barred imports of tuna from Mexico, Venezuela, and Vanuatu because they permit the use of nets that can trap dolphins; however, the United States rescinded its ban after GATT ruled this violated the trade accord.[47] Further, there are other trade agreements besides GATT. For instance, multilateral treaties, such as restrictions on ivory trade to save elephants, protect endangered species. Export control agreements prevent LDCs from acquiring technology and goods needed to produce advanced weapons. An example is the Nuclear Suppliers Group and the Coordinating Committee on Multilateral Export Controls (Cocom), which was first established to prevent such exports to communist bloc countries, some of which are now parties to the agreement.[48] However, countries are free to withdraw from agreements. For example, Iceland withdrew from the International Whaling Commission in 1992.[49]

LOOKING TO THE FUTURE

New arguments for protectionism may gain importance in the foreseeable future and give rise to more bilateral agreements. One such agreement involves countries' equal access to one another's markets on a product-by-product basis and is sometimes called a **strategic-trade policy**.[50] The basis for this policy is the argument that in industries in which increased production will greatly decrease cost, either from scale economies or learning effects, producers that lack equal access to a competitor's market will have a disadvantage in gaining enough sales to be cost-competitive. This has been noted, for example, in the semiconductor, aircraft, and telecommunications industries, especially in relation to government procurement policies, production and export subsidies, and import restrictions. But the argument for equal access also is presented as one of fairness. For example, under the Uruguay Round, the U.S. government will permit foreign financial-services companies to operate in the United States; however, it also announced that this permission will be rescinded if the companies' home countries do not open their financial markets to U.S. companies. One may envision the increased use of bilateral agreements and retaliation to bring about a so-called level playing field, or a quid pro quo arrangement.

The Uruguay Round largely skirted the issue of environmental standards for products and their production. Countries with strict environmental regulations will undoubtedly consider imposing "green countervailing duties" to compensate for the cost advantages of operating where regulations are lax. Producers facing these import restrictions undoubtedly will claim that environmental standards are really a ruse to protect domestic producers. In fact, the EU has already challenged U.S. fuel efficiency standards for automobiles on these grounds.[51]

A number of issues were unresolved in the Uruguay Round. Countries effectively agreed to continue disagreeing; therefore talks will continue among small groups of GATT members. The most important of these concern trade in services—especially financial, shipping, audiovisual, and telecommunications—and subsidies for agriculture, steel, and aircraft.

Although the above examples seem to indicate a growing difficulty in bringing about freer trade, there are other more optimistic indications regarding trade growth. Global trade has been growing rapidly and should continue to do so, in part because of the movement in many countries to privatize formerly government-owned companies and to open up import markets so that domestic companies will be forced to operate more efficiently by having to compete. These movements have been especially important in Eastern Europe and in the newly industrialized countries of Asia. Even such highly protected countries as Mexico, Brazil, and Argentina have begun liberalizing imports.

Summary

- **Despite the potential resource benefit of free trade, no country permits an unregulated flow of goods and services.**

- **Given the possibility of retaliation and the fact that imports as well as exports create jobs, it is difficult to determine the effect on employment of protecting an industry.**

- **Policymakers have not yet solved the problem of income redistribution due to changes in trade policy.**

- **The infant-industry argument for protection holds that without governmental prevention of import competition, certain industries would be unable to move from high-cost to low-cost production.**

- **Because industrial countries are generally more advanced economically than nonindustrial ones are, governmental interference is often argued to be beneficial if it promotes industrialization.**

- **Direct influence on trade is a more selective means of solving balance-of-payments disequilibrium than either changes in currency values or internal price adjustments.**

- **Trade controls are used to regulate prices of goods traded internationally. Their objectives include protection of monopoly positions, prevention of foreign monopoly prices, greater assurance that domestic consumers get low prices, and lower profit margins for foreign producers.**

- **Much of the governmental interference in international trade is motivated by political rather than economic concerns, including maintaining domestic supplies of essential goods and preventing potential enemies from gaining goods that would help them achieve their objectives.**

- **Many nonindustrial countries are seeking export markets within the industrialized world for their manufactured products but argue that the effective tariffs on their products are too high.**

- **Trade controls that directly affect price and indirectly affect quantity include tariffs, subsidies, arbitrary customs-valuations methods, and special fees.**

- **Trade controls that directly affect quantity and indirectly affect price include quotas, "buy-local" legislation, arbitrary standards, licensing arrangements, foreign-exchange controls, administrative delays, and requirements to take goods in exchange.**

- **The General Agreement on Tariffs and Trade (GATT) is the main negotiating body through which countries have multilaterally reduced trade barriers and agreed on simplified mechanisms for the conduct of international trade. However, recent experience indicates that further trade liberalization on a global basis will be harder to achieve.**

- **A company's development of an international strategy will greatly determine whether it will benefit more from protectionism or from some other means for countering international competition.**

Case
Oilseed Trade
Negotiations[52]

The EU must use ten times the fertilizer on the same area as is used in Argentina, Australia, and Thailand, which have a greater natural advantage in agriculture. The EU's ability to remain competitive in many agricultural products has been due to protection from imports and high subsidies to farmers, especially in France. For example, the French government pays its farmers almost twice the world market price for wheat.

The high European agricultural subsidies have come about for two reasons. First, like most areas of the world, the EU has sought more self-sufficiency in food in order to be less vulnerable to conditions abroad. Second, the so-called green revolution (the rapid and high increase in food output) has proceeded faster than people can be absorbed in the urban areas within the EU; so agricultural subsidies have been used to keep more workers employed on farms. For example, in 1960, 25 percent of all French people lived or worked on farms, but by 1993, despite subsidies, only 6 percent remained. In contrast, the move from rural to urban areas occurred earlier and much more gradually in the United States, where the percentage of people on farms fell from 8.5 percent in 1960 to a bit below 3 percent in 1993.

The result of subsidies in the EU, the United States, and elsewhere has been an overproduction of many agricultural products. The effect of EU subsidies on U.S. exports has been substantial. Once the dominant agricultural exporter, the U.S. fell to second place behind the EU in 1992 as EU-subsidized output competed in world markets. U.S. farmers were particularly concerned about the drop in oilseed exports (oilseeds are soybeans, sunflower seeds, and other seeds). In the early 1980s, the U.S. shipped about $3.5 billion a year in oilseeds to Europe, but by 1991 the amount had fallen to about $1.8 billion. GATT dispute panels twice found European subsidies of oilseeds to be improper; however, the United States held off from retaliating for fear of triggering a trade war. Studies indicated that the United States was losing about $1 billion a year in oilseed exports to the EU because of the impasse.

In late 1992, the United States decided it would threaten sanctions against EU imports in an attempt to negotiate away the EU restrictions on oilseeds. To make such a strategy work, the United States had to choose product(s) very carefully. It did so using the following criteria:

- The product(s) had to be believable; that is, the threat could be carried out without incurring too much of a hardship for U.S. consumers or the U.S. economy. For example, certain chemicals and pharmaceuticals could not be bought easily elsewhere and so would not qualify as believable.
- The United States felt France was the major culprit; therefore it wanted to find product(s) that primarily would hurt French exporters rather than exporters from other EC countries. Further, because each member country has a vote, this tactic would limit the ability of France to line up support for further retaliation against the United States. This criterion eliminated such products as olive oil and gin.
- The United States wanted to threaten to place import restrictions on French agricultural products so that the French farm lobby would be divided; that is, oilseed interests would be pitted against other agricultural interests.

The United States announced that if the oilseed controversy were not resolved within a month, it would impose 200-percent tariffs on $300 million worth of EU exports to the United States (see Map 6.1). The major targets were 240 varieties of white wine, which ac-

**Map 6.1
Proposed U.S. Trade
Restrictions on EU
Members during
Oilseed Negotiations**

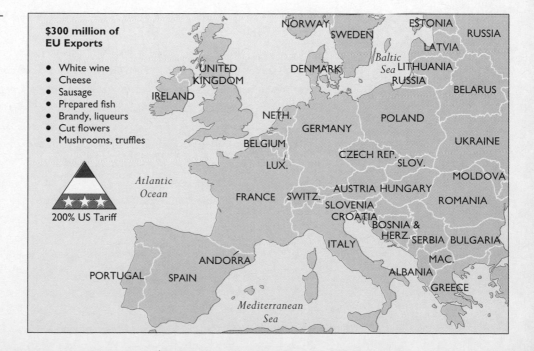

counted for $270 million, or 90 percent, of the targeted imports. Other products included certain cheeses, sausage, prepared fish, brandy and liqueurs, cut flowers, and mushrooms and truffles. Although France was the largest exporter to the United States of both white and red wines, white wines were targeted because U.S. consumers think more highly of and drink more domestic white wines than red ones. However, because Germany is also a major white wine exporter, the United States was not able to limit its sanctions to France. Thus Germany allied itself with France in the negotiations. As soon as the United States made its announcement, U.S. wine merchants cut back on French orders so as not to be caught a month later with high-priced inventories they could not sell. (It was estimated that a bottle of French wine that previously had retailed for $18.83 would jump in price to $56.23.) The cutback caused temporary price increases of wine in the United States and decreases in France.

Before the one-month deadline, the EU offered to negotiate, and the United States took a more conciliatory position in the trade talks. The United States wanted the EU to cut oilseed production from 13 million metric tons to between 7.5 and 8 million metric tons, or to about the level produced in 1986 when U.S. farmers first began protesting the EU subsidies. The two sides finally agreed that the EU would idle 15 percent of the land used to produce subsidized oilseeds in the first year and another 10 percent in subsequent years. However, this agreement would not control production, and so U.S. agricultural interests were concerned that the least productive farmland would be idled, reducing output only to about 10.5 million tons.

Questions

1. If the EU had decided to counter U.S. threats with further retaliation against U.S. products, what products might it have picked for maximum effectiveness?
2. The United States subsidizes its agricultural production and exports in various ways. Is there an ethical dilemma involved in its trying to get other countries to dismantle their subsidy programs?
3. At the time of the oilseed trade negotiations, France had an unemployment rate of about 10 percent and mounting racial tensions in working-class neighborhoods. What constraints did these conditions put on French politicians negotiating an agreement?
4. Shortly after the oilseed agreement with the EU, U.S. rice growers began pressuring the U.S. government to threaten import restrictions against Japan in order to open up the protected Japanese rice market. If the United States were to do this, what product(s) would be (a) likely candidate(s)? Would the possibility of reaching an agreement with Japan be as high as with the EU?
5. What risks were apparent in the U.S. announcement to limit EU imports?

Chapter Notes

1. The data for the case were taken from "U.S. Autos Losing a Big Segment of the Market—Forever?" *Business Week*, March 24, 1980, pp. 78–85; "7 of 10 Americans Agree," *New York Times*, November 6, 1980, p. A23; Leslie Wayne, "The Irony and Impact of Auto Quotas," *New York Times*, April 8, 1984, p. F1+; "Brock Vows to End Import Quotas on Japanese Cars," *Wall Street Journal*, May 3, 1984, p. 29; Rachel Dardis and Jia-Yeong Lin, "Automobile Quotas Revisited: The Costs of

Continued Protection," *The Journal of Consumer Affairs,* Vol. 19, No. 2, Winter 1985, pp. 277–292; Owen Bieber, "Are Japan's U.S. Auto Plants Unfair?" *New York Times,* May 13, 1990, p. F13; United States General Accounting Office, *Foreign Investment: Growing Japanese Presence in the U.S. Auto Industry* (Washington: GAO/NSIAD-88-111, 1988); Doran P. Levin, "Honda Blurs Line Between American and Foreign," *New York Times,* March 14, 1990, p. A1+; "Mazda Motor Corp.," *Wall Street Journal,* July 26, 1989, p. 23; Melinda Grenier Guiles, "GM Puts 'Captive Imports' to New Test," *Wall Street Journal,* September 16, 1988; "Loss Leaders," *Business Week,* March 1, 1993, p. 46; Joseph B. White, "Big Three Auto Makers Put on Display of Unity in Trade, Regulatory Matters," *Wall Street Journal,* January 11, 1993, p. A3; Neal Templin, "Ford, Chrysler Back Cap on Japan Cars; GM Balks," *Wall Street Journal,* May 15, 1992, p. A2; David Woodruff, "Why Detroit Doesn't Need the Protection It Wants," *Business Week,* February 8, 1993, p. 32; Paul Magnusson and David Woodruff, "Why Detroit Hit the Brakes," *Business Week,* February 22, 1993, p. 36; Andrew Pollack, "Japan Takes a Pre-emptive Step on Auto Exports," *New York Times,* January 9, 1993, p. 17; Alex Taylor III, "U.S. Cars Come Back," *Fortune,* November 16, 1992, pp. 52+; "Free Trade's Fading Champion," *The Economist,* April 11, 1992, pp. 65–66; and Lee Smith, "A Dangerous Fix for Trade Deficits," *Forbes,* May 4, 1992, pp. 96–97.

2. "Guilty on All Counts," *The Economist,* August 21, 1993, quoting a GATT pamphlet, "Trade, the Uruguay Round and the Consumer."

3. James J. Kilpatrick, "How Not to Create Jobs," *Nation's Business,* March 1983, Vol. 77, No. 1, p. 5.

4. John Andrew, John Helyar, and Bill Johnson, "Silver Lining," *Wall Street Journal,* February 29, 1984, p. 19; Peter Truell, "Textile Makers Demanding More Protection Threaten Hopes for Seamless U.S. Trade Policy," *Wall Street Journal,* May 16, 1990, p. A20; and Eduardo Lachica, "Alliance of Textile and Apparel Makers Splits as Senate Mulls Import-Quota Bill," *Wall Street Journal,* July 13, 1990, p. A10.

5. Robert W. Crandell, "Import Quotas and the Automobile Industry: The Costs of Protectionism," *Brookings Review,* Summer 1984, pp. 8–16.

6. Alexander Dagg, "Keeping the Jobs at Home," *Globe and Mail* [Toronto], July 3, 1990, p. 18.

7. Roger Thurow, "Ivory Coast's Reliance on Commodities Topples It from Its Role-Model Pedestal," *Wall Street Journal,* May 9, 1989, p. A16.

8. Peter F. Drucker, "The Changed World Economy," *Foreign Affairs,* Vol. 64, No. 4, Spring 1986; and Lloyd G. Reynolds, "Economic Development in Historical Perspective," *American Economic Review,* May 1980, p. 92.

9. Supportive of the premises are Raul Prebisch, *The Economic Development of Latin America and Its Principal Problems* (New York: United Nations Department of Economic Affairs, 1950); Charles P. Kindleberger, *The Terms of Trade: A European Case Study* (New York: Wiley, 1956); and W. Arthur Lewis, *Aspects of Tropical Trade, 1883–1965* (Stockholm: Almquist and Wiksells, 1969). Nonsupportive are M. June Flanders, "Prebisch on Protectionism: An Evaluation," *Economic Journal,* June 1964; Theodore Morgan, "The Long-Run Terms of Trade Between Agriculture and Manufacturing," *Economic Development and Cultural Change,* October 1959; and Gottfried Haberler, "Terms of Trade and Economic Development," in *Economic Development of Latin America,* H. Ellis, ed. (New York: St. Martin's, 1961).

10. John Diebold, "Beyond Subsidies and Trade Quotas," *New York Times,* November 2, 1986, p. F3.

11. Mark M. Nelson, "U.S. Is Wary of EC Import Regulations," *Wall Street Journal,* June 29, 1989, p. B1.

12. James Bovard, "No Justice in Anti-Dumping," *New York Times,* January 28, 1990, p. F13.

13. James Bovard, "Clinton's Dumping Could Sink GATT," *Wall Street Journal,* December 9, 1993, p. A14.

14. Peter Truell, "U.S. Won't Seek Trade Retaliation Against India," *Wall Street Journal,* June 13, 1990, p. A6; and Clyde H. Farnsworth, "U.S. Likely to Forgo Sanctions Against India," *New York Times,* June 14, 1990, p. D2.

15. Hazel Bradford and Evert Clark, "When the Pentagon Wants Something America Doesn't Have," *Business Week,* No. 2970, October 27, 1986, p. 46.

16. "Honey, Wool and Mohair Subsidies Are Cut," *New York Times,* October 3, 1993, p. A12.

17. Eduardo Lachica, "U.S., South Korea Reach Agreement on Sale of Aircraft," *Wall Street Journal,* September 10, 1990, p. C17; John Maroff, "U.S. Export Ban Hurting Makers of New Devices to Code Messages," *New York Times,* November 19, 1990, p. A1+; Arvind Parkhe, "U.S. National Security Export Controls: Implications for Global Competitiveness of U.S. High-Tech Firms," *Strategic Management Journal,* Vol. 13, 1992, pp. 47–66; Eduardo Lachica, "U.S., 26 Other Nations to Control Exports That Could Be Used in Nuclear Bombs," *Wall Street Journal,* April 3, 1992, p. A4; and Gerald F. Seib, "Transfer of Russian Missile Technology to India Leads to U.S. Trade Sanctions," *Wall Street Journal,* May 12, 1992, p. A6.

18. "France Confirms Sale of Fighter Jets to Taiwan," *Wall Street Journal,* January 8, 1993, p. A6.

19. Karen Pennar, "Will the Embargo Work? A Look at the Record," *Business Week,* September 17, 1990; and Eugene Carlson, "Enterprise," *Wall Street Journal,* August 29, 1990, p. B2.

20. William P. Corbett, Jr., "A Wasted Opportunity: Shortcomings of the Caribbean Basin Initiative Approach to Development in the West Indies and Central America," *Law and Policy in International Business,* Vol. 23, No. 4, 1992, p. 959.

21. Alan Riding, "French Cinema Circling the Wagons," *New York Times,* September 18, 1993, p. 12.

22. Amy Borrus and Pete Engardio, "Will Congress Shanghai China Policy?" *Business Week,* February 22, 1993, p. 59; and Robert Keatley, "Trade Rights as Well as Civil Rights Will Factor into China's MFN Status," *Wall Street Journal,* June 4, 1993, p. A10.

23. James Bovard, "Our Taxing Tariff Code—Let Them Eat Lobster!" *Wall Street Journal,* March 28, 1990, p. A12.

24. F. H. Rolf Seringhaus, "The Impact of Government Export Marketing Assistance," *International Marketing Review,* Vol. 3, No. 2, Summer 1986, offers a detailed discussion of the effects. Masaaki Kotabe and Michael R. Czinkota, "State Government Promotion of Manufacturing Exports: A Gap Analysis," *Journal of International Business Studies,* 4th quarter, 1992, pp. 637–657, shows activities at the state level within the United States.

25. Robert B. Reich, "Beyond Free Trade," *Foreign Affairs,* Vol. 61, No. 4, Spring 1983, p. 786.

26. "Subsidise, Apologise," *The Economist,* April 4, 1992, pp. 80–82; and Asra Q. Nomani and Bushan Bahree, "Aircraft Firms Move to Delay Issue at GATT," *Wall Street Journal,* December 10, 1993, p. A3+.

27. Clyde H. Farnsworth, "U.S. Will Tie Aid to Exports in Bid to Curb the Practice," *New York Times,* May 16, 1990, p. C1, referring to a study by the National Foreign Trade Council; Robert Letovsky, "The Export Finance Wars," *Columbia Journal of World Business,* Vol. 25, Nos. 1 & 2, Spring/Summer 1990, pp. 25–35; and Gerald F. Seib, "Export-Credit Programs, Useful Tool Abroad, Can Leave Taxpayers at Home Holding the Bag," *Wall Street Journal,* June 5, 1992, p. A12.

28. Amy Borrus, Bruce Einhorn, and Pete Engardio, "Will a Customs Dragnet Snag Big U.S. Retailers?" *Business Week,* May 25, 1992, p. 46.

29. Shoba Purushothaman, "Customs Classification Codes Confuse Importers, Who Cry 'Trivial Pursuit,'" *Wall Street Journal,* September 27, 1988, p. 38; Eduardo Lachica, "U.S. Designates Suzuki Samurai

as Truck Import," *Wall Street Journal,* January 5, 1989, p. A3; David Rogers, "Customs Service Puts Its Foot Down on Nike," *Wall Street Journal,* April 18, 1990, p. B6; and Douglas Harbrecht and James B. Treece, "Tread Marks on Detroit," *Business Week,* May 31, 1993, p. 30.

30. Joan Berger, "Tariffs Aren't Great, but Quotas Are Worse," *Business Week,* No. 2989, March 16, 1987, p. 64.

31. Borrus et al., loc. cit.; Eduardo Lachica, "Evasion of Duties on Chinese Imports Costs U.S. Up to $300 Million a Year," *Wall Street Journal,* May 8, 1992, p. A3; and Jonathan M. Moses, "Chinese Agency Indicted by U.S. in Customs Case," *Wall Street Journal,* October 10, 1992, p. A15.

32. Andrew Pollack, "U.S. Sushi? Tokyo Frets. Sushi Boy Says Yes," *New York Times,* September 21, 1992, p. A5; Andrew Pollack, "Japan, Relenting, Plans to Allow Import of U.S.-Made Sushi," *New York Times,* October 4, 1992, p. 4; and "Sushi Boy Went Bankrupt, Japanese Sushi Importer Fails," *Wall Street Journal,* December 15, 1993, p. A10.

33. Eduardo Lachica, "Legal Swamp," *Wall Street Journal,* June 18, 1992, p. A1+; John P. Simpson, "Rules of Origin in Transition: A Changing Environment and Prospects for Reform," *Law and Policy in International Business,* Vol. 22, No. 4, 1991, pp. 665–672; and Janet Novack, "It's Like a Big Balloon," *Forbes,* July 20, 1992, p. 48.

34. "Japan to Curb VCR Exports," *New York Times,* November 21, 1983, p. D5.

35. "New Restrictions on World Trade," *Business Week,* July 19, 1982, p. 119.

36. John Templeman, Bill Javetski, Jeffrey Reyser, and Barbara Buell, "The New Trade Talks Look Jinxed," *Business Week,* No. 2965, September 22, 1986, p. 47; and Phedon Nicolaides, "Economic Aspects of Services: Implications for a GATT Agreement," *Journal of World Trade,* Vol. 23, No. 1, February 1989, pp. 125–236.

37. Laurie McGinley, "Bush Plan Seeks to Stem Decline of U.S. Ship Lines," *Wall Street Journal,* June 18, 1992, p. A4; and Robert Neff and Douglas Harbrecht, "U.S. Insurers Start Making Noise in Japan," *Business Week,* March 1, 1993, p. 56.

38. Seth Payne, Andrea Rothman, and Stewart Toy, "France Wants to Give American Planes the Gate," *Business Week,* April 6, 1992; and Bruce Ingersoll, "U.S. Rules Japan Violated Agreement on Avia-

tion, Threatens Retaliation," *Wall Street Journal,* February 5, 1993, p. C19.

39. Laura Wallace, "Rising Barriers," *Wall Street Journal,* October 5, 1981, p. 1; Nina Darnton, "Spain Restricting the Dubbing of Foreign Movies," *New York Times,* June 4, 1984, p. C11; Chris Best, "Free Trade in the International Insurance Industry," *Risk Management,* August 1986, p. 12; J. J. Boddewyn and Iris Mohr, "International Advertisers Face Government Hurdles," *Marketing News,* May 8, 1987, p. 20; and Joan M. Feldman, "The Dilemma of 'Open Skies,'" *New York Times Magazine,* April 2, 1989, p. 31+.

40. Gary C. Hufbauer, "Should Unconditional MFN Be Revised, Retired, or Recast?" in *Issues in World Trade Policy,* R. H. Snape, ed. (New York: St. Martin's, 1986), pp. 32–55; and Frieder Roessler, "The Scope, Limits and Function of the GATT Legal System," *The World Economy,* Vol. 8, No. 4, September 1985, pp. 287–298.

41. Ann V. Morrison, "Tokyo Round Agreements Set Rules for Nontariff Measures," *Business America,* Vol. 9, No. 14, July 7, 1986, pp. 11–13.

42. Bhushan Bahree, "New Chief Confronts a Changing GATT," *Wall Street Journal,* June 11, 1993, p. A6.

43. Clyde H. Farnsworth, "U.S., Despite Dispute, Will Go to Trade Talks," *New York Times,* November 14, 1990, p. C1+; and Paul Magnusson, "The GATT Talks: Forget the Darn Deadline," *Business Week,* November 19, 1990, p. 51.

44. The following discussion is taken from "The Shape of the Accord," *New York Times,* December 15, 1993, p. C18; and "The Uruguay Round's Key Result," *Wall Street Journal,* December 15, 1993, p. A6.

45. For a discussion of changes in MNEs' lobbying efforts for protectionism, see Giles Merrill, "Coping with the 'New Protectionism': How Companies Are Learning to Love It," *International Management,* Vol. 41, No. 9, September 1986, pp. 20–26.

46. Eugene Salorio, "Trade Barriers and Corporate Strategies: Why Some Firms Oppose Import Protection for Their Own Industry," unpublished DBA dissertation, Harvard University, 1991.

47. Bob Davis, "GATT Report Says Trade Liberalization Will Aid Global Environment Protection," *Wall Street Journal,* February 12, 1992, p. A2.

48. Eduardo Lachica, "U.S., 26 Other Nations to Control Exports That Could Be Used

in Nuclear Bombs," *Wall Street Journal,* April 3, 1992, p. 4; and Karen Elliott House, "We Need a Foreign Policy President," *Wall Street Journal,* November 3, 1992, p. A14.

49. Keith Schneider, "Balancing Nature's Claims and International Free Trade," *New York Times,* January 19, 1992, p. E5.

50. Ravi Sarathy, "The Interplay of Industrial Policy and International Strategy: Japan's Machine Tool Industry," *California Management Review,* Vol. 31, No. 3, Spring 1989, pp. 132–160; David B. Yoffie and Helen V. Milner, "An Alternative to Free Trade or Protectionism: Why Corporations Seek Strategic Trade Policy," *California Management Review,* Vol. 31, No. 4, Summer 1989, pp. 111–131; and Laura D'Andrea Tyson, *Who's Bashing Whom?* (Washington: Institute for International Economics, 1993).

51. Timothy Noah, "Environmental Groups Say Deal Poses Threats," *Wall Street Journal,* December 16, 1993, p. A12.

52. Data for the case were taken from John Schwartz, Scott Sullivan, Rich Thomas, and Jane Whitmore, "Break Out the Chardonnay," *Newsweek,* November 30, 1992, p. 60; Bill Javetski, Patrick Oster, and John Templeman, "Bush's First Shot May Avert a Trade War," *Business Week,* November 23, 1992, p. 34; "The GATT Trade Talks: Bushwhacked," *The Economist,* October 24, 1992, pp. 74–75; Bob Davis, "U.S., EC Impasse May Lead to Trade War," *Wall Street Journal,* November 5, 1992, p. A2; Keith Bradsher, "Progress in Trade Talks with Europe," *New York Times,* November 3, 1992, p. C1; E. S. Browning, "As France's Farm Population Dwindles, A Practical Rescue Plan Proves Elusive," *Wall Street Journal,* December 1, 1992, p. A18; Bob Davis, "Tough Trade Issues Remain as EC, U.S. Agree on Agriculture," *Wall Street Journal,* November 23, 1992, p. A1; Bob Davis, "U.S., EC Extend Talks Over Dispute on Farm Trade," *Wall Street Journal,* November 3, 1992, p. B4; Martin Crutsinger, "Wine War Questions Addressed," *Herald-Times* (Bloomington, Ind.), November 7, 1992, p. C7; Paul Magnusson, Bill Javetski, and Patrick Oster, "Is Washington Getting Ready to Give Up on GATT?" *Business Week,* November 9, 1992, p. 42; and Scott Kilman, "U.S. Is Steadily Losing Share of World Trade in Grain and Soybeans," *Wall Street Journal,* December 3, 1992, p. A1.

Chapter 7

Economic Integration and Cooperative Agreements

*Marrying is easy, but
housekeeping is hard.*
—German Proverb

Objectives

- To define different forms of economic cooperation on a regional and global basis

- To describe the static and dynamic effects and the trade creation and diversion dimensions of economic integration

- To compare different types of regional economic integration, such as the European Union (EU) and the North American Free Trade Agreement (NAFTA)

- To describe the rationale for, and current trends in, commodity agreements

- To discuss other bilateral and multilateral treaties affecting international business

Case
Ford in Europe[1]

In 1992, Ford Motor Company was the world's second largest automaker (5.76 million units), below GM (7.15 million units) and above Toyota Motor Corporation (4.70 million units). In Europe, it was in fifth place with an 11.3-percent market share (see Table 7.1). Yet Ford was losing money—$7.4 billion worldwide and $1.3 billion in Europe in 1992, following 1991 losses of $2.3 billion worldwide and $1.1 billion in Europe.

Despite Ford's long history and its market prominence in Europe, the company was clearly having some problems. After the EEC [the European Economic Community, later known as the European Community (EC) and, since the fall of 1993, the European Union (EU)] was organized in 1957, many U.S. MNEs had to change their method of serving European markets. For example, some companies began producing in Europe rather than serving that market through exports, either because they feared new tariff barriers would preclude continued sales or because they thought the enlarged market would enable them to achieve the economies of scale needed for efficient production there. Some companies that were already producing in Europe began to consolidate their operations rather than continuing to separate them on a multidomestic basis.

Ford was in the latter situation. The company first began operating in Europe through its British subsidiary in 1913 and acquired its German subsidiary in 1926. During the next several decades, Ford's European operations operated as separate subsidiaries that reported to U.S. headquarters but did not coordinate their policies in any meaningful way. This occurred because individual countries had different environments and unique tariff and nontariff barriers to trade. Ford noted in its 1960 *Annual Report,*

> The historical patterns of trade and commerce among nations are undergoing significant changes. Trade groupings, such as the European Economic Community and the European Free Trade Association, are being established. Similar groupings are being considered in Latin America and by some of the African countries. Further changes in trade patterns have been brought about in a number of countries by government regulations that make it advantageous to manufacture locally.
>
> The Company and its subsidiaries are responding to these trends, which bear promise of increasing competition for world automobile markets, by exploring opportunities to strengthen and to expand their international operations.

The changing environment prompted Ford to realize it could consider Europe to be one common market rather than a collection of individual markets. Shortly after the establishment of the EEC, Ford changed its management structure to include its European operations under one umbrella organization. Its two large U.K. and German manufacturing centers remained an important dimension of the new strategy, but they were no longer considered separate, independently operating companies. Despite nationalistic tendencies on the part of host-country management, Ford decided that, from the company's perspective, it was best to obliterate national boundaries. As the German managing director noted,

> The pooling of the two companies cut the engineering bill in half for each company, provided economies of scale, with double the volume in terms of purchase—commonization of pur-

Table 7.1
Western European Automobile Market Share
(as a percentage), by Company, 1989–1992

Although Volkswagen is the leader of the European
automobile market in terms of market share, two
U.S. companies—GM and Ford—have nearly a quarter
of the market.

Company	Year			
	1989	1990	1991	1992
Volkswagen	17.6%	17.7%	19.3%	17.3%
Peugeot	14.8	17.4	14.6	12.2
General Motors	11.6	12.3	12.6	12.2
Fiat	14.8	13.8	12.9	11.5
Ford	12.5	11.8	12.7	11.3
Renault	12.7	11.6	12.2	10.6

Source: "1993 Market Data Book," *Automotive News*, p. 3.

chase, common components—and provided the financial resources for a good product program at a really good price that we could still make money on.

Ford began designing and assembling similar automobiles throughout Europe, rather than engineering separate cars in each market, a strategy that resulted in such models as the Escort, the Capri, and the Fiesta. It also designed common components to be used in Ford automobiles. Acknowledging the importance of market size in developing this plan, one Ford executive commented, "Neither the British nor the German company could have come up with the Capri separately, tooled it separately. Only with the whole volume of Europe in prospect did the Capri become a viable product development program."

In the mid-1980s, Ford continued its European expansion. It explored the possibility of merging its European unit with Fiat in order to allow Ford's strength in northern Europe to combine with Fiat's strength in southern Europe. However, each company was so strong and so convinced of its need to control the merged operation that the proposed merger never occurred. Ford wanted to maintain control over its global strategy, which was being developed in the United States. Fiat was controlled by the Agnelli family in Italy, and loss of control to a foreign company, especially from a country not in the EC, would have been explosive politically. Also, Fiat's management objected to being subordinate to Ford's management.

As part of Ford's evolving European strategy, its management decided to design automobiles in Germany and the United Kingdom (Ford's largest European market) and manufacture them in Belgium, Germany, Spain, and the United Kingdom. The company also entered into production and product-development agreements with other automakers such as Nissan and Volkswagen to serve the European market.

Ford's European strategy for the 1990s is being significantly influenced by two factors: Euro-recession and Japanese competition. As this chapter will discuss, a major advantage of economic integration is market expansion. However, even the large market of the EC suffered economically in the early 1990s. In the fall of 1992, Europe's slowdown turned into a full-fledged recession, and in 1993, the Western European market was expected to contract by 3.5 percent of its size in 1992. Ford not only saw sales and profits fall; it also lost market share. Further, the economic slowdown forced automakers such as Ford to lay off workers and cut back capital expenditures.

The second major influence is Japanese competition. European automakers are significantly less efficient than their American and Japanese counterparts. For example, German automakers require about 40 hours of labor to assemble a car, compared with about 30 hours for other European manufacturers and about 20 hours in Japan. Ford has upgraded its quality and lowered the amount of time it takes to manufacture a car. An MIT study determined that a Ford plant in Germany is one of the most efficient non-Japanese plants in the world; workers need just under 19 hours to build a new car, compared with 15 hours for a similar Japanese car.

The Europeans have effectively kept the Japanese out of their market. However, the drive to a more unified European market is opening up Europe to the Japanese. They will be allowed by the EU to capture up to 16 percent of the market by 1999 and will have unlimited access to the market thereafter. To jump European trade barriers, the Japanese have established a number of plants in Europe—primarily in the United Kingdom—to serve that market. These are expected to produce at least 600,000 units per year by 1997. Ford and other European automakers fear the increased access to the European market during the rest of this decade will give the Japanese an estimated 36 percent of market growth. The Europeans are already negotiating with the Japanese to cut back on exports to Europe, and many companies want to count Japanese transplant automobiles (Japanese automobiles manufactured in Europe) as part of the allowable Japanese market share.

Ford is trying to improve its European prospects in three ways: cutting costs, developing a new product line, and pushing exports of European products. The first method—cutting costs—has already been discussed. As for the second method, Ford introduced a new product, the Mondeo, in 1993. This automobile is expected to be the new "world car" for Ford, replacing the former "world car"—the Escort—which never actually attained that status. The U.S. and European versions of the Mondeo will have 75–80 percent of their parts in common, allowing Ford to gain economies of scale in development and production. Third, Ford is trying to increase exports of European-produced automobiles, which currently are sold in thirty-eight countries. Ford of Europe exported 40,000 vehicles in 1992 and was expected to increase worldwide exports by 50 percent in 1993, primarily because of the new Mondeo. Its exports to Eastern Europe are projected to grow to 50,000 units by 1998, up from 13,500 in 1992 and just 1000 in 1990. The unified European market clearly provides many challenges and opportunities for Ford.

Introduction

The Great Depression plunged the world into a period of isolation, trade protectionism, and economic chaos. In the mid- to late-1940s, countries decided greater cooperation was needed to help them emerge from the wreckage of World War II. The spirit of cooperation was designed to promote economic growth and stability. This chapter discusses some of the important forms of such cooperation, such as regional economic integration and commodity agreements.

Why do you need to understand the nature of these arrangements? Regional trading groups are an important influence on MNEs' strategy, as Ford learned. They can define the size of the regional market and the rules under which companies must operate. Companies in the initial stages of foreign expansion must be aware of the regional groups that encompass countries targeted for manufacturing locations or market opportunities. As companies proceed toward greater multinationalism, they find they must change their organizational structure and operating strategies to take advantage of regional trading groups. For example, as noted in the opening case, Ford altered its European organization soon after the formation of the EEC. This chapter explains how such regional groups affect structure and strategy.

Regional Economic Integration

Economic integration abolishes cross-national economic discrimination.

In the 1950s and 1960s, regional economic integration gained significant momentum. Economic integration involves the organizing of individual countries into groups that then abolish restrictions on the trade of goods and services with member countries and also may engage in other activities that promote their citizens' welfare. As noted in Chapter 6, the General Agreement on Tariffs and Trade (GATT) is a multinational approach to economic integration intended to get the world to move toward becoming a free-trade area. However, this movement is far too slow and not comprehensive enough to be considered a substitute for economic integration by smaller groups of countries.

Geographical proximity is an important reason for economic integration.

When we consider some of the major examples of economic integration, such as the European Union (EU), the European Free Trade Association (EFTA), the North American Free Trade Agreement (NAFTA), and the Latin American Integration Association (ALADI), the concept of geographical proximity stands out. Neighboring countries tend to become involved in integrative activities for several reasons:

- The distances to be traversed between such countries are shorter.
- Consumers' tastes are more likely to be similar, and distribution channels can be more easily established in adjacent economies.
- Neighboring countries may have a common history, awareness of common interests, and so forth and may be more willing to coordinate their policies.[2]

Figure 7.1
Levels of Economic Integration
The extent of economic cooperation is greater for a customs union than for a free-trade area, and greater for a common market than for a customs union. The highest level of cooperation is attained through complete economic integration.

	1	2	3	4
Free-trade area				
Customs union				
Common market				
Complete economic integration				

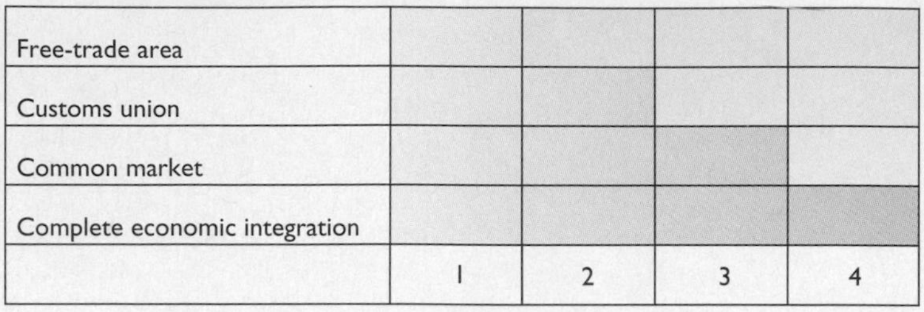

1. Abolish tariffs among member countries
2. Establish common external tariff
3. Abolish restrictions on factor mobility
4. Establish common fiscal and monetary policies

Also important are ideological and historical similarities. For example, Cuba, because of its communist political and economic philosophy, was a member of the former COMECON (the Council for Mutual Economic Assistance), an association of communist countries that was disbanded when the former Soviet Union broke up.

There are four basic types of economic integration (see Fig. 7.1):

Major types of economic integration:
• **Free-trade area—no internal tariff**
• **Customs union—common external tariffs**
• **Common market—factor mobility**
• **Complete economic integration**

1. *Free-trade area (FTA).* Tariffs are abolished among FTA members, but each member maintains its own external tariff against non-FTA countries. Examples of this level of economic integration are NAFTA, EFTA, and ALADI.

2. *Customs union.* Levying a common external tariff is combined with the abolition of all internal tariffs. When the EEC was established, member countries decided to establish a customs union as an intermediate step toward more complete integration. When the EU negotiates at the GATT rounds, it does so as a regional bloc, not as individual countries. In contrast, Canada, the United States, and Mexico negotiate separately at GATT, since they are part of a free-trade area rather than a customs union.

3. *Common market.* All the characteristics of a customs union are combined with the abolition of restrictions on mobility of production factors such as labor and capital.

4. *Complete economic integration.* Fiscal and monetary policies are unified to create even greater economic harmonization.[3] This level also implies a degree of political integration. Complete economic integration is clearly the direction in which the EU is moving, especially since recent discussions have centered on the creation of a European central bank and a common currency.

The Effects of Integration

Regional integration has political, social, and economic effects.

Regional integration has social, political, and economic effects. For example, in the social sense Canadians did not want to include liberalization of trade and investment in the film, television, and print media in the U.S.-Canada FTA because some feared Canadian culture would be undermined by U.S. culture as transmitted through movies, TV programs, and magazines. The Europeans, too, have fought hard to preserve their national culture identities by controlling foreign films' access to television. The EU and its predecessors have worked diligently to improve the social conditions of individuals within member countries. Laws relative to the environment and relationships between workers and employers are part of the more complete unification of Europe.

From a political standpoint, integration results in a partial loss of sovereignty. This concept is discussed in the Countervailing Forces section of this chapter.

With trade creation, resources shift from the least- to the most-efficient producers.

The economic aspects of integration dominate the concerns of MNEs. As noted in Chapter 6, the imposition of tariff and nontariff barriers disrupts the free flow of goods and therefore affects resource allocation. Economic integration is designed to reduce or eliminate those barriers. It produces both static and dynamic effects. Static effects result when trade barriers are reduced, giving consumers access to more new goods. As consumers purchase goods having the best quality and lowest prices, resources shift from the least efficient to the most efficient producers. This is the trade-creation aspect of integration. Production shifts from one country to another for reasons of comparative advantage, allowing consumers access to more goods at a lower price than would have been possible without integration. Companies that are protected in their domestic markets face real problems when the barriers are eliminated and they attempt to compete with more efficient producers.

With trade diversion, discrimination against outside producers diverts trade to less-efficient producers within the country or group.

Integration also may lead to trade diversion because it results in discrimination against outside producers. For example, assume U.S. companies are importing the same product from Mexico and Taiwan. If the United States enters into an FTA with Mexico but not with Taiwan, some trade will be diverted from Taiwan to Mexico to take advantage of the elimination of tariffs between that country and the United States. This does not mean, however, that Mexican products are any better or cheaper (in the absence of integration) than the Taiwanese goods are.

One dynamic effect of integration is that as markets grow, companies achieve economies of scale.

Dynamic effects of integration are changes in total consumption and in internal and external efficiencies that result from market growth. Reduction of trade barriers automatically increases total demand. As resources shift to the more efficient producers, these companies are able to expand output to take advantage of the larger market, which results in trade creation. This dynamic change in market size allows companies to produce goods more cheaply, since the fixed costs of production can be spread out over more units.

Efficiency increases because of competition.

Another important dynamic effect is the increase in efficiency due to increased competition. Many MNEs in Europe have attempted to grow through mergers and acquisitions in order to achieve the size necessary to compete in the larger market. For example, Ford entered into design and production agreements with other manufacturers in order to be more competitive in the European environment.

It is important to understand the specific situations of a few examples of regional integration, especially the EU. By understanding the goals and objectives of different regional groups, it is easier to understand their influence on corporate strategy.

The European Union

European Evolution to Integration

World War II left in its wake economic as well as human destruction throughout Europe. To help rebuild Europe, the U.S. Congress passed the Marshall Plan, a $13-billion aid package. The sixteen-country Organization for European Economic Cooperation (OEEC) was established to facilitate utilization of the aid as well as to improve currency stability, combine economic strengths, and improve trade relations. As early as 1943, it had been noted that "European countries are too small to give their peoples the prosperity made attainable by modern conditions. They need wider markets."[4] However, the OEEC did not appear strong enough to provide the necessary economic growth. Thus further efforts at cooperation were initiated. One major school of thought held that a common market should be developed to:

- Result in the elimination of all restrictions to the free flow of goods, capital, and persons
- Allow for the harmonization of economic policies
- Create a common external tariff

Consequently, in March 1957, the European Economic Community (EEC) was established via the Treaty of Rome. Its members were Belgium, France, Italy, Luxembourg, the Netherlands, and West Germany (now Germany since the reunification with East Germany) (see Map 7.1). It expanded its membership to include Denmark, Ireland, and the United Kingdom (in 1973), Greece (in 1981), and Portugal and Spain (in 1986). It is considering other countries as members. The name of the EEC has changed over time to reflect even closer integration. During the 1980s, the EEC gave way to the European Community (EC), reflecting a broader sense of cooperation than merely economic. In the fall of 1993, the EC gave way to the European Union to reflect the closer cooperation resulting from the adoption of the Maastricht Treaty, which will be discussed later in this section.

European Free Trade Association

A second major school of thought rejected the notion of total European integration and favored instead a free-trade area, which would eliminate all restrictions on the free flow of industrial goods among member countries, while permitting each country to retain its own external tariff structure. This approach provides the benefits of free trade among members but allows each member to pursue its own economic objectives with nonmember countries. It was especially beneficial for the United Kingdom, which had favorable trade relationships with Commonwealth countries and considered a common external tariff too restrictive of national sovereignty.

Following this line of thought, the Stockholm Convention of May 1960 created the European Free Trade Association (EFTA), which comprised seven OEEC coun-

Map 7.1
European Trade and Economic Integration
The two major groups involved in European integration are the European Union (EU) and the European Free Trade Association (EFTA). These groups are likely to merge in the near future.

1957 Treaty of Rome establishes the EEC; members are Belgium, France, Italy, Luxembourg, The Netherlands, and West Germany.

1960 Stockolm Convention creates EFTA; members are Austria, Denmark, Norway, Portugal, Sweden, Switzerland, and the United Kindom.

1967 EEC is consolidated with the European Coal and Steel Community and Euratom, forming the European Community(EC).

1973 The United Kingdom, Ireland, and Denmark join the EC.

1981 Greece becomes an EC member.

1986 Finland becomes a full member of EFTA; Spain and Portugal join the EC.

1991 Liechtenstein becomes an EFTA member.

1993 Single European Act is adopted. Treaty of Maastricht is signed, and EC changes its name to EU.

tries that were not in the EEC: Austria, Denmark, Norway, Portugal, Sweden, Switzerland, and the United Kingdom (see Map 7.1). Iceland joined in 1970; Finland, an associate member since 1961, became a full member in 1986; and Liechtenstein joined as a full member in 1991. Denmark, Portugal, and the United Kingdom left EFTA in 1986 to become full members of the EC. As of the end of 1993, EFTA was composed of Austria, Finland, Iceland, Liechtenstein, Norway, Sweden, and Switzerland. By 1991, tariffs or import duties had been removed on all imports from member countries except agricultural products.

EFTA countries trade more extensively with the EU than with each other.

The growing strength of the EU and its widening scope of integration are making it difficult for EFTA members to maintain their separate status outside the EU. In 1990, the EC accounted for 60 percent of EFTA's imports and 58 percent of EFTA's exports, making it EFTA's major trading partner.[5]

Major EU Programs

The EEC was initially interested in the following broad categories of activity:

The EEC was intended to lead to a free flow of resources, a harmonization of policies, and a common external tariff.

- The free movement of goods through the elimination of tariff barriers
- The free movement of people, services, and capital
- The establishment of a common transportation policy

As noted in Table 7.2, the first reduction in internal tariffs occurred in 1959, and all internal tariffs had been eliminated by 1968.

CAP was established to stabilize earnings to producers and provide food for consumers.

In 1962, the EEC established the Common Agricultural Policy (CAP) as an important element of its overall economic policy. CAP's objectives were to increase

Table 7.2
European Union Milestones
From its inception in 1957, the EU has been moving toward complete economic integration.

1957	Treaty of Rome establishing the European Economic Community (EEC), or Common Market, signed. Original members were Belgium, France, Italy, Luxembourg, the Netherlands, and West Germany.
1959	First reduction in EEC internal tariffs.
1962	Common Agricultural Policy (CAP) established.
1967	Agreement reached on value-added tax (VAT) system; EEC changes name to European Community (EC).
1968	All internal tariffs eliminated and a common external tariff imposed.
1973	Denmark, Ireland, and the United Kingdom become members.
1979	European Parliament directly elected for the first time.
1979	European Monetary System comes into effect.
1981	Greece becomes a member.
1985	Lord Cockfield presents a white paper to the European Commission outlining 300 steps to eliminate all remaining barriers to internal trade in goods and services. This is endorsed by the member countries and becomes EC policy.
1986	Spain and Portugal become members.
1987	Single European Act (SEA) comes into effect, improving decision-making procedures and increasing the role of the European Parliament.
1992	Target date (December 31) for eliminating all trade barriers within the European Community.
1993	Treaty of Maastricht adopted by member countries; EC becomes the European Union (EU).
1999	Target year for monetary union.

Source: Ernst & Whinney, Europe 1992: The Single Market, p. 6; updated.

farm productivity, establish a fair standard of living for farmers, stabilize markets, ensure food security, and set reasonable consumer prices.[6] A series of tariffs and price supports were set up to achieve these objectives and to protect agricultural goods from foreign competition. The protection was intended to avoid excessive price (and therefore income) fluctuations; also the EEC believed world market prices reflected intervention by other governments. Thus a threshold price was established as the lowest internal price for imports, and a variable levy was imposed to raise import prices to the threshold level.[7]

CAP has affected both member and nonmember consumers and producers. Much of the EU's current budget is used to pay price supports (subsidies) to farmers. These subsidies are a significant tax burden to consumers. They also have al-

CAP has created trade tensions between the EU countries and others, especially the United States.

lowed EU farmers to be competitive in world markets. Nonmember countries have found it difficult to sell to EU consumers products for which subsidies make EU farmers more competitive. Nonmembers also have had trouble competing with subsidized EU exports.[8] These subsidies have been a major source of contention in GATT negotiations, especially in the Uruguay Round (discussed in Chapter 6).

The EU's Organizational Structure

Complexity usually breeds bureaucracy. The simpler types of integration, such as free-trade areas, usually can be managed fairly simply. The more complex types of integration, however, such as that pursued by the EU, usually require a very extensive bureaucracy to protect the goals of member countries and administer according to the agreed-upon rules.

The key to the EU's success is the balance between common and national interests that is monitored and refereed through the following major institutions:

- The European Council
- The European Commission
- The Parliament
- The Council of Ministers
- The Court of Justice

The European Council is composed of the heads of state of all EU members.

The European Council is made up of the heads of state of all EU members. It meets twice a year in the capital of the member country whose head of state is currently the president of the Council of Ministers to discuss issues relating to the EU, especially foreign affairs.

The European Commission draws up and implements policies.

The European Commission, headquartered in Brussels, is the EU's watchdog. Its members, appointed by the governments of the EU countries, consist of a president, six vice presidents, and ten other members; their allegiance is to the EU rather than to an individual government. The Commission drafts and implements policies (subject to approval by the Council of Ministers) and ensures that member countries adhere to treaties and laws. It resembles the executive branch of a democratic government but is weaker.[9]

The Parliament consults on all EU legislation.

The Parliament, headquartered in Luxembourg, is elected directly by the populaces of the member countries. Its representatives adhere to particular political and economic views rather than to the wishes of the individual governments, and they are seated in Parliament by political party, not nationality. Different countries' representatives who have similar political leanings often form coalitions. The Parliament is not as powerful as a legislative body in a democracy, but it has veto power over the EU's budget. In addition, the Parliament consults on all EU legislation. The Parliament has been likened to the U.S. House of Representatives if it were on wheels (because the Parliament travels to so many different locations) and if its views could be safely ignored.

The Council of Ministers makes major policy decisions for the EU.

The Council of Ministers, also headquartered in Brussels, is the real power behind the bureaucracy. Composed of one representative from the government of each member country, it is entrusted with deciding major policy issues for the EU, which includes approving the Commission's proposed policies. It also makes the final decision on all EU legislation. The actual membership of the Council depends on the agenda. If environmental issues are being discussed, for example, the environmental ministers of all member countries attend.

The Court of Justice is the appeals court for EU law.

The Court of Justice, also headquartered in Luxembourg, is customarily composed of one representative from each member country. It serves as the supreme appeals court for EU law. The Commission or a member country can bring other members to the Court for failing to meet treaty obligations. Likewise, member countries, companies, or institutions can bring the Commission or the Council to the Court for failure to act properly under the treaty.

Europe 1992

As Table 7.3 shows, in 1991 the EC had 345.9 million people and the world's second largest combined GDP, making it a formidable economic bloc. However, the early part of the 1980s was a difficult time for the EC. From 1970 to 1975, the

Table 7.3
Comparative Data on Five Major Trade Groups, 1991
The EC (now the EU) and NAFTA are the dominant trade groups in terms of total GDP and per capita GDP.

Group*	Population (in millions)	GDP (in billions of U.S. dollars)	Per capita GDP (in U.S. dollars)
ALADI (Latin American Integration Association)	380.9	1,018.1	2,673.0
ASEAN (Association of South East Asian Nations)	322.7	345.7	1,071.0
EC (European Community)	345.9	6,101.955	17,642.0
EFTA (European Free Trade Association)	32.8	824.3	25,164.0
NAFTA (North American Free Trade Agreement)	363.3	6,404.161	17,628.0

*The countries that form the above groups are as follows.
ALADI: Argentina, Bolivia, Brazil, Chile, Colombia, Ecuador, Mexico, Paraguay, Peru, Uruguay, and Venezuela
ASEAN: Brunei, Indonesia, Malaysia, Philippines, Singapore, and Thailand
EC: Belgium, Denmark, France, Greece, Ireland, Italy, Luxembourg, the Netherlands, Portugal, Spain, United Kingdom, and West Germany
EFTA: Austria, Finland, Iceland, Liechtenstein, Norway, Sweden, and Switzerland
NAFTA: Canada, Mexico, and the United States

Source: World Development Report, 1993 (Washington, D.C.: The World Bank, 1993).

EC's GDP averaged 2.7 percent growth per year, but this figure dropped to approximately 1.4 percent annually from 1980 through 1985. In contrast, the United States recorded 2.2 percent and 2.5 percent growth rates for those periods, respectively, and Japan experienced rates of 7.6 percent and 3.8 percent, respectively.[10] It was evident the EC needed more than the elimination of tariffs to achieve economic growth. A variety of nontariff barriers was keeping it from being a true common market and from enjoying the benefits of expanded market size.

As a result of these and other issues, the president of the European Commission decided to pursue a strategy of eliminating the remaining barriers to a free and open Europe. Consequently, a white paper issued in 1985 identified 282 proposals that needed to be enacted to complete an internal market. The target date for implementation of the proposals was December 31, 1992, giving rise to the use of the phrase "Europe 1992" to refer to the elimination of the remaining barriers to trade and investment among EC members. The proposals included in the 1985 white paper to the European Commission can be divided into the following general areas:

1. Frontier controls and rules and procedures for the cross-border shipment of goods
2. Freedom of movement and right of people to settle in member countries
3. Technical and standards harmonization
4. Opening up of governmental procurement markets
5. Liberalization of financial services
6. Gradual opening up of the information-services market
7. Liberalization of transportation services
8. Creation of suitable conditions for industrial cooperation without fear of antitrust violation in the fields of company law and intellectual and industrial property
9. Removal of fiscal barriers[11]

Once the proposals, called directives, were approved by the EC bureaucracy, they were turned over to the members' governments for passage into each country's national law. By the time the single market came into effect on January 1, 1993, most of the directives were ready for national approval. However, not all directives have been implemented by *all* twelve members. The ranking of member countries from most to least effective in implementing the directives into national law is Denmark, Italy, the United Kingdom, Belgium, France, Portugal, the Netherlands, Spain, Germany, Luxembourg, Ireland, and Greece.[12]

To make the Europe 1992 program more understandable to both members and nonmembers, the EC established the Directorate-General 15 (DG 15) of the European Commission to oversee enforcement and application. An advisory committee of the DG 15 has established contact points in the ministries in each member's government charged with enforcing various directives. A hearing committee hears complaints from companies on the enforcement of directives. Ultimately, the European Commission can take a dispute to the Court of Justice for resolution.[13]

Europe 1992 was aimed at the elimination of the remaining barriers to the free transfer of goods, services, and capital.

The white paper of 1985 identified 282 proposals that needed to be adopted to eliminate barriers to European integration.

Few of the Europe 1992 directives have been adopted by all countries, but most have been adopted by a majority.

Internal and External Impact of the Single European Market

It is important to understand that Europe 1992, also known as the Single European Market, is a process, not just a date. The initiatives targeted for December 31, 1992 will take years to adopt and implement.

There are several major internal concerns about the single market, especially in the United Kingdom and Denmark. The first, expressed by the free-market side of the EU membership, is the spread of bureaucracy, centralization, overregulation, and socialism. As former U.K. Prime Minister Margaret Thatcher said, "We haven't worked all these years to free Britain from the paralysis of socialism only to see it creep through the back door of central control and bureaucracy from Brussels."[14]

A second concern is the acceptance of key changes, such as the harmonization of the **value-added tax (VAT),** a tax that is a percentage of the value added to a product at each stage of the business process. Although consumers in high-tax countries might welcome the lowering of the average VAT, consumers in low-tax countries would not appreciate the increase of the average VAT.

A third worry is the potential effect on unemployment. Although most experts believe the Single European Market will bring faster economic growth and the creation of jobs, local unions are not convinced. In northern Europe, in particular, unions are concerned that the free movement of capital will cause companies to seek lower costs in southern Europe. Because of the significant recession in Europe in 1992 and 1993, the unemployment rate for the EU as a whole had risen to nearly 12 percent in 1993. Two reasons often mentioned for the high unemployment level, especially among the British, are the relatively rigid labor markets in Europe and the high nonwage social costs built into the total labor cost. The slippage of European competitiveness relative to that of Japan and the United States has many Europeans worried about the future labor picture.[15]

A fourth concern is the possible elimination of small and medium-sized companies. This could occur for two reasons:

1. Competition due to the absence of trade barriers, which will expand the reach of large, efficient companies as they take advantage of better distribution systems
2. The wave of mergers and acquisitions taking place as companies attempt to grow in order to compete with U.S. and Japanese rivals in Europe

Although the European Commission is supposed to regulate mergers, only 1 out of 137 mergers referred to it from September 1990 to March 1993 was blocked; 113 mergers were approved within one month.[16]

The major external concern regarding the Single European Market is often referred to as "Fortress Europe." Many people fear European regulations will favor European companies and exclude foreign, especially U.S. and Japanese, companies. Although that does not seem to be the case so far, foreign MNEs are adopting a variety of strategies to reserve a place in Europe. Some large MNEs—such as Ford, Coca-Cola, and IBM—are more European in terms of their geographical spread than many European companies are, as the opening case demonstrated. The medium-sized companies currently operating in Europe are taking part in the merger-and-acquisition wave to expand their sizes and market shares. And those that serve Europe merely through exports are establishing offices there in order to have a physical presence within the market.[17]

MNEs are uncertain about just how to act in the EU. EU law supersedes national law. Thus, if a directive has been approved by the EU bureaucracy, MNEs can operate in member countries under the conditions of the directive, even if it has not been approved locally. In some cases, however, companies attempting to adhere to directives have been hampered by national laws. For example, a U.S. university shipped to its branch campus in Spain fifty personal computers that adhered to EU directives on voltage and other characteristics. However, the Spanish authorities delayed the shipment because the keyboards did not have the Spanish letter ñ. The EU eventually ruled that this requirement constituted a trade barrier, and the Spanish agreed to discontinue the practice.[18]

> **Foreign MNEs need to assess the impact of national differences in developing global or regional marketing strategies.**

Despite the appearance of a unified common market, there are still significant national differences. One study of the European strategies of twenty-two Fortune 500 corporations with European central offices concluded:

> Although Europe is becoming more open, differences in culture, language, and feelings of nationalism make it imperative that it not be approached as a completely homogeneous market which can be treated like any other global market. Management of American multinationals must, therefore, assess the impact of these differences on customers and consumers in determining the proper balance between global, Pan-European, and national or regional marketing strategies as they consider the European Community market integration process.[19]

The Treaty of Maastricht

> **The Treaty of Maastricht calls for establishing European economic, monetary, and political union.**

Not content with the economic integration envisaged in the Europe 1992 program, EC leaders met in Maastricht, the Netherlands, in December 1991 and approved the Treaty of Maastricht. This treaty was designed to take the EC to a higher level. It is divided into two parts: economic and monetary union (EMU) and political union. EMU, which is discussed in greater detail in Chapter 10, is designed to result in a common European currency by 1999. In order to get to a common currency, members would have to bring their monetary and fiscal policies closer together so that inflation rates, interest rates, budget deficits as a percentage of GDP, and public debt as a percentage of GDP would be reasonably similar.

> **Political union involves**
> - **Common European citizenship**
> - **Joint foreign, defense, immigration, and policing policies**
> - **Harmonization of social policy on workers' issues**

The prospect of political union brings up a number of issues, such as a common European citizenship; joint foreign, defense, immigration, and policing policies; and the harmonization of social policy concerning working conditions and employees' rights. In addition, the Parliament would be strengthened significantly by giving it veto power over new national laws.[20]

> **Some countries (such as France and Germany) want closer European integration. Others (such as the United Kingdom and Denmark) want less centralized control.**

The Treaty of Maastricht was not easy to design because there are strong federalist tendencies in countries such as France and Germany and an abhorrence of centralized control from Brussels on the part of countries such as the United Kingdom and Denmark. Those opposing federalist tendencies included in the treaty the principle of **subsidiarity,** which implies that EU interference should occur only in areas of common concern and that most policies should be set at the national level. Further, not all countries accepted all points in the treaty. For example, regarding monetary union, the United Kingdom and Denmark opted out of the agreement; regarding social policy relating to employees, eleven states opted in (only the United Kingdom chose not to become involved).[21]

After the euphoria that followed the signing of the treaty died down, the real work began—each country had to approve it by national referendum or parliamentary vote. The Danes initially rejected the treaty in a 1992 national referendum because of concerns over the potential loss of sovereignty to the EU. By 1993, however, all member countries had approved the treaty.

EU Expansion

The Treaty of Maastricht provides for a meeting to be held in 1996 to revise the original Treaty of Rome, primarily because the EU might expand by several more countries by the year 2000. In 1991, the member countries of EFTA and the EC signed a pact establishing a European Economic Area for the purpose of bringing EFTA members in compliance with the EC's single-market plan and abolishing the remaining barriers to the flow of goods, services, and people throughout Western Europe.[22]

The EU is likely to expand by accepting EFTA members.

However, in 1993, Austria, Finland, Norway, and Sweden officially applied to join the EC as full members. It was anticipated that referendums would be held in each country in 1994, and full membership would take effect in 1995. These new member countries would be welcome additions to the EU because their per capita incomes are high relative to those of other members. This added wealth would improve the flow of transfer payments to the EU's poorer southern countries.[23]

Full EU membership is expected to affect EFTA countries primarily in the following ways:

1. The countries will have to adopt CAP, which will benefit consumers more than farmers, since farm subsidies are higher in EFTA than in the EU.
2. EU competition policy will extend to a wide range of domestic activities such as state subsidies and restrictive business practices that are more prevalent in EFTA countries.
3. A large transfer of wealth from EFTA countries to EU countries will occur because per capita GDP is 40 percent higher in the former than it is in the latter.[24]

The next area of EU expansion could be in Eastern Europe and countries such as Turkey. The Eastern European countries most likely to be considered would be Bulgaria, the Czech Republic, Hungary, Poland, Romania, and Slovakia. Their combined population is slightly larger than that of the EFTA countries, but their average per capita GDP is about half as large. There is disagreement on when these countries might join the EU, with some predicting entrance by the year 2000 and others saying no sooner than 2010.[25]

North American Integration

The Canada-U.S. Free Trade Agreement

The United States and Canada historically have engaged in various forms of mutual economic cooperation. One is the Automotive Products Trade Agreement, effective in 1965, which provides for qualified duty-free trade in specified automotive products. In the early 1980s, the two countries discussed developing free trade in specific sectors, such as steel and textiles. This discussion then was expanded to include a broader discussion of free trade, and by 1987 negotiations were being held to open up trade even more between them.

There already was significant trade between the two countries. The United States and Canada have a combined GDP that exceeds that of the EU. They are each other's largest trading partner, and their two-way trade—$219 billion in 1992—is the world's largest. The United States accounts for about 75 percent of Canada's exports and imports, and Canada accounts for 20 percent of U.S. imports and 25 percent of its exports. In addition to automobile trade, U.S. exports to Canada consist primarily of manufactured end-products, such as machinery, computers, and telecommunications equipment. Canada exports to the United States mainly raw materials and semiprocessed goods, including paper, oil, natural gas, minerals, and electric power.[26] However, Canada's major exports to the United States also include automobiles and auto parts. This is of major importance to Ford, which has established a North American strategy to go along with its European strategy.

The United States was concerned about the amount of governmental subsidies Canada gave its domestic businesses. Nevertheless, it was eager to gain greater access to investment opportunities in Canada. Meanwhile, Canada sought exemption from U.S. laws that protected U.S. producers from Canadian competition. Canadians also preferred dealing with an international tribunal to resolve trade disputes rather than having to deal with U.S. antidumping and countervailing duty legislation. Further, Canadian manufacturers estimated they would be able to cut costs by an estimated 20 percent as a result of the economies of scale that would follow from freer access to U.S. markets.

The U.S.-Canada FTA created the largest trading bloc in the world in terms of GDP.

The FTA will eliminate tariffs on bilateral trade by 1998.

The negotiations that began in 1987 resulted in the Canada-U.S. Free Trade Agreement (FTA), which became effective January 1, 1989. The FTA will eliminate all tariffs on bilateral trade by January 1, 1998, although more than 85 percent of the bilateral trade was subject to tariffs of 5 percent or less even before the FTA took effect. As a result of the FTA, Canada liberalized its investment rules, which will make it easier for U.S. companies to invest in Canada. Despite this liberalization, the U.S. share of total FDI in Canada fell to less than 70 percent in the early

1990s compared with 80 percent in 1978, primarily because of increased FDI from other countries. In contrast, Canada has increased its FDI in the United States to become the fourth largest foreign investor in the United States, following the United Kingdom, Japan, and the Netherlands.

Trade disputes between the United States and Canada are resolved by a five-member binational panel of experts.

The FTA also resulted in the creation of a new mechanism to resolve trade disputes between the United States and Canada. A five-member binational panel of trade experts has the power to overrule decisions of tribunals in either country on disputes involving companies or individuals from either country. This mechanism has been very successful: The panel rarely votes along country lines or merely rubber stamps the decisions of national bodies. Consequently, it has overturned several national decisions.[27]

Economic recession in Canada and concerns over the loss of sovereignty have made the FTA unpopular in Canada.

However, implementation of the FTA has been neither easy nor popular, especially in Canada. At the time the agreement was signed, Canadians were concerned about several possible effects on Canada:

- Losing cultural identity
- Becoming too closely integrated with a more violent society (that of the United States)
- Aligning with a declining economic power
- Forfeiting independence in foreign policy
- Being overwhelmed by the United States

Clearly, the FTA has resulted in some changes in both countries, but its long-range impact remains unclear. In the early 1990s, Canada was in a severe recession and also lost more than 400,000 manufacturing jobs. It was difficult to determine, however, whether the job loss was due to the FTA or the recession. Companies have regarded the FTA as an opportunity to set up single rather than multiple plants to serve the combined markets, but there has been no clear shift of production to one country or the other. Canadian business, however, has changed its market emphasis. Rather than cultivating east-west business relationships within Canada, it has been focusing on north-south relationships between Canadian provinces and contiguous U.S. states. This could weaken the federal alliance in Canada and strengthen Canadian-U.S. ties.[28]

Products flow between the U.S. and Canada duty-free. The rules of origin require that they be certified as originating in either the U.S. or Canada.

An important part of the FTA is the concept of local content and rules of origin. Because the FTA is a free-trade agreement and not a customs union, each country has its own tariff schedule with respect to the rest of the world. Thus a product entering the United States from Canada must be accompanied by a commercial or customs invoice that identifies the origin of the product. Otherwise an exporter from a third country would always ship the product to the country with the cheaper tariff and then re-export it to the second country duty-free.

To qualify for duty-free provisions of the FTA, a product's local content must be at least 50 percent of the value.

Local content for the FTA is 50 percent of value. This means that for a product shipped from the United States to Canada or vice versa to qualify for the FTA's duty-free provisions, at least 50 percent of the value added to the product must originate in North America. A good example of the problems that can arise with local content rules involves Honda, which builds in North America two thirds of the cars it sells there. In 1991, the U.S. Customs Service determined that less than 50 percent of the value of each Honda Civic being shipped into the United States from Canada originated in North America. It argued that the Civic was simply a collection of parts shipped from Japan to Canada and assembled there, and that most of the local content of the automobile was depreciation on machinery shipped to Canada from Japan.[29] Obviously, this situation created serious tension between Canada and the United States, as well as between Japan and the United States.

North American Free Trade Agreement

In February 1991, Mexico approached the United States to establish a free-trade agreement. The formal negotiations that began in June 1991 included Canada. The resulting North American Free Trade Agreement (NAFTA) was announced by the Canadian Prime Minister and the U.S. and Mexican Presidents in August 1992 and became effective on January 1, 1994.

Like the Canada-U.S. FTA, NAFTA has a logical rationale. Although Canada-Mexico trade is not significant, U.S.-Mexico trade is. The United States is Mexico's largest trading partner, accounting for 70 percent of its exports and imports in 1991, compared with 61.6 percent and 61.4 percent, respectively, in 1971. Mexico is the third-largest trading partner of the United States and on track to surpass Japan as the second-largest market for U.S. products. Studies relating U.S. exports to growth in Mexican GNP have shown a strong positive correlation; that is, U.S. exports to Mexico increase at a rate as great as or greater than the growth rate of the Mexican economy.[30]

NAFTA is the largest trading bloc in the world in terms of population and GDP.

As shown in Table 7.3, NAFTA is a powerful trading bloc with a combined population and total GDP greater than those of the EU. When EFTA members join the EU, NAFTA will drop to second place. However, it could be just the beginning of a much larger free-trade agreement involving the countries of North, Central, and South America.

NAFTA deals with the following areas:

NAFTA calls for the elimination of tariff and nontariff barriers, the harmonization of trade rules, and the liberalization of restrictions on services and foreign investment.

- Market access—tariff and nontariff barriers, rules of origin, governmental procurement
- Trade rules—safeguards, subsidies, countervailing and antidumping duties, health and safety standards
- Services
- Investment
- Intellectual property
- Dispute settlement[31]

Mexico has made significant strides in tariff reduction since it joined GATT in 1986. At that time, its tariffs averaged 100 percent. Since then, it has reduced tariffs to less than 20 percent in most cases. Under NAFTA, Mexico will lower tariffs to zero for most trade with the United States and Canada.

NAFTA should provide the static and dynamic effects of economic integration.

NAFTA is expected to provide the static and dynamic effects of economic integration discussed earlier in this chapter. For example, Canadian and U.S. consumers are expected to benefit from lower-cost agricultural products, a static effect of economic liberalization. They also are expected to benefit from the large and growing Mexican market, which has a huge appetite for U.S. products; this benefit is a dynamic effect.

In addition, NAFTA is a good example of trade diversion. Many U.S. companies have established manufacturing facilities in Asia to take advantage of cheap labor and ship products from those facilities to the United States. It is anticipated that NAFTA members will be able to use each other rather than Asian countries as locations for trade and investment. This movement has already begun in the automobile industry: U.S. automakers such as Ford have established manufacturing facilities in Mexico to serve the U.S. market.

However, there also are some problems with NAFTA concerning the following issues:

- Rules of origin
- Job loss
- The environment
- Extension of the agreement

Local content for NAFTA is 62.5 percent of value for automobiles.

Rules of origin   As mentioned earlier in this section, local content for the Canada-U.S. FTA is 50 percent. However, U.S. labor argued for a much higher local content for automobiles because it worried that outside countries, especially Japan, would use Mexico as an assembly location for the automobile industry and as a springboard to the United States. The final decision was that local content must be 62.5 percent for passenger vehicles and 60 percent for other vehicles and auto parts based on net cost.[32]

The major U.S. and Canadian concern over NAFTA is the possible loss of jobs.

Job loss   Clearly, the number one concern of U.S. and Canadian citizens regarding NAFTA is job loss. In Canada, more than 400,000 manufacturing jobs were lost in the first three years of the 1990s. One expert estimated that the flood of manufacturing jobs to low-wage Mexico could result in Canadian manufacturing jobs falling from 20 percent of the workforce in 1992 to only 8 percent by 2000.[33] Although this view may be too pessimistic, it is indicative of the emotions stirred up by NAFTA.

Mexicans also are worried about losing jobs. U.S. companies are already investing in Mexico to take advantage of cheap labor and to jump tariff barriers. In the NAFTA environment, however, the barriers will disappear, and Mexicans fear that U.S. and Canadian companies may supply the Mexican market from large manufacturing facilities in their own countries.

Table 7.4
Hourly Wages in Manufacturing for Selected Countries, 1991
Hourly wages of manufacturing workers are significantly higher in Canada and the United States than in Mexico, where wages are also lower than in the newly industrialized Asian countries.

Country	Wage
Canada	$17.31
United States	15.45
Taiwan	4.42
Singapore	4.38
Korea	4.32
Hong Kong	3.58
Mexico	2.17

Source: U.S. Department of Labor, Bureau of Labor Statistics, *International Comparisons of Hourly Compensation Costs for Production Workers in Manufacturing,* 1991, Report 825; and Stephen Baker, Geri Smith, and Elizabeth Weiner, "The Mexican Worker," *Business Week,* April 19, 1993, p. 84.

Hourly manufacturing wages in Mexico are $2.17 per hour, compared with $15.45 in the United States and $17.31 in Canada.

The number of U.S. jobs probably will increase as a result of NAFTA because of three factors: the reduction in trade barriers, the expansion of FDI in Mexico, and the growth in Mexican income.

Some U.S. environmentalists are worried that NAFTA will lead to a worsening of the Mexican environment and a relaxation of U.S. environmental regulations.

Although in recent years wages have been rising more rapidly in Mexico than in Canada or the United States, hourly manufacturing costs remain significantly lower in Mexico than in the other two countries (see Table 7.4). For example, hourly wages for Mexican workers in the automobile industry are higher than $2.17, but those in the maquiladora industry along the U.S.-Mexican border are lower than $2.17. In addition, Mexican wages are lower than those in the newly industrialized countries of Asia. However, the fears of job loss in Canada and the United States are not unfounded. Between 1977 and 1989, employment by U.S. nonbank affiliates in Mexico grew by 39.4 percent, compared with a decline of 11.2 percent for employment by U.S. nonbank affiliates in Canada.[34]

The exact impact on jobs depends on who is making the guess and the assumptions used. A pessimistic study often quoted by U.S. NAFTA opponents predicted 5.9 million U.S. jobs would be lost because of NAFTA. This figure was determined by counting all the jobs in U.S. industries in which labor costs accounted for at least 20 percent of total expenses and the average hourly wage exceeded $7. The assumption was that companies would be tempted to move production to Mexico under these conditions to take advantage of low labor costs.[35] It is possible that some jobs may move because of this reason, but U.S. NAFTA supporters argued that companies that wanted to take advantage of low Mexican wages could have done so before NAFTA. In addition, companies could choose to seek lower wages in Asia without having to wait for NAFTA, and it would simply allow those jobs to move closer to home. In any case, the liberalization of investment laws under NAFTA will make FDI in Mexico even more attractive.

Most other studies concluded there would be a slight gain in U.S. manufacturing jobs as a result of NAFTA. However, the numbers are not staggering because the Mexican economy is not yet big enough. For example, one study suggested that NAFTA would create 242,000 new jobs and displace about 112,000 existing jobs, resulting in a net gain of 130,000 jobs, only slightly over 0.1 percent of total U.S. employment in 1991.[36]

The rationale behind expectations of improved U.S. employment possibilities is threefold:

1. Lowering Mexican trade barriers is expected to have a larger impact than lowering U.S. trade barriers because Mexican tariffs averaged just over 10 percent in 1990, compared with only 4 percent for U.S. tariffs.
2. Increases in U.S. and Canadian FDI in Mexico are expected to result in the importation of U.S. and Canadian capital and intermediate goods.
3. Increases in wealth in Mexico are expected to boost Mexican demand for imports (the dynamic effect of economic integration).[37]

The environment Some U.S. environmentalists are convinced NAFTA will result in destruction of Mexico's environment and relaxation of U.S. environmental standards, as well as cause U.S. and Canadian companies to invest in Mexico because of its lax environmental standards and enforcement. The environmentalists' major concerns are air and water pollution and the use of pesticides and other chemicals in Mexican agriculture. There is a strong positive correlation between pollution and economic growth, so it may be true that pollution could worsen in Mexico if NAFTA stimulates economic growth. However, Mexican environmental standards are getting tougher and enforcement of those standards is improving. There is no evidence to support the idea that environmental standards and enforcement would lag behind as the economy grows. One could argue that NAFTA actually could force Mexico to strengthen its standards and enforcement. In addition, studies show that countries with low income levels cannot spend much money to clean up the environment, and that cleanup begins when income levels rise.

There also is some concern that if the United States and Canada were to exclude Mexican products on the grounds that they resulted from environmentally unsound production processes, Mexico could take both countries to court and charge that environmental concerns are a nontariff trade barrier. Clearly, U.S. and Canadian environmental standards must not be weakened, so a process is needed to protect them.

Finally, it is possible but highly unlikely that lax environmental standards will cause a mass migration of production facilities to Mexico. Other factors, such as market access and transport and labor costs, have greater impact on where investment flows. In addition, the cooperation that will occur through NAFTA should eliminate future environmental regulatory differences.

Nevertheless, a coalition of environmental groups convinced a U.S. Federal District Court judge to rule that an agreement could not be signed until an environmental impact study was carried out. Although the ruling was eventually overturned, it was a serious challenge to the ability of President Clinton to enter into the treaty.[38]

NAFTA probably will be extended to other Latin American countries.

NAFTA extension   When the United States began its discussions with Mexico and Canada, it perceived any resultant agreement would be part of a larger effort to pull together North, Central, and South America into an "Enterprise of the Americas." The idea was to have the United States enter into a series of bilateral trade relationships with Latin American countries that would result in a "hub and spokes" arrangement, with the United States as the hub and other countries as the spokes. Eventually, these bilateral relationships would result in one huge multilateral relationship involving the Americas. Chile was being courted as the next addition to NAFTA after the original three countries completed their negotiations and began implementation in 1994. Preliminary steps needed to prepare Chile and other Latin American countries involved lowering trade barriers and reducing or eliminating restrictions to FDI.[39]

Much of the criticism of NAFTA in the United States centered on three major ethical dilemmas. The first of these concerned the closing of U.S. plants in order to move production to Mexico to take advantage of low wages. If such moves are made to increase profits rather than to preserve market share, the criticism will mount—especially since the U.S. economy is not creating significant numbers of new jobs for domestic workers. Even though the economy began to recover in late 1993 and early 1994, job creation was weaker than it had been during previous recoveries from recessions. Total U.S. employment may rise as a result of NAFTA, but there could be job losses in certain industrial sectors and some geographical areas. On the one hand, it can be argued that a company should preserve U.S. jobs in order to sustain the country's industrial base. This is the argument of organized labor. On the other hand, it can be argued that a company must do whatever is necessary to remain competitive; otherwise, it will go out of business and stockholders will lose their investment. If moving production (and therefore jobs) to Mexico to take advantage of low wages is the best way to preserve a continuous stream of earnings, a company has an ethical obligation to its stockholders to make the move. Thus the ethical dilemma involves a choice between two different groups—employees and stockholders—and it may not be possible to pick an alternative that will bring a positive outcome for both.

ETHICAL DILEMMAS

The second ethical dilemma involves companies' treatment of union organizers in Mexico. In early 1994, for example, Honeywell Inc. was accused of firing employees who were trying to organize a union at a Mexican manufacturing facility where workers' average pay was $1.00 per hour. Is it ethical for Honeywell or other U.S. companies to discourage union-organizing activities in a country where labor unions are not as well established or as independent as they are in the United States?

The third dilemma concerns the environmental impact of NAFTA. Some environmental interest groups charge that U.S. companies that move production to Mexico may be contributing to environmental degradation in that country or trying to take advantage of weaker environmental legislation and lax enforcement there. If the home country's environmental laws are stricter than a host country's, which laws should an MNE follow? Would it be considered imperialistic to ignore the host-country laws and apply more stringent environmental standards? Many U.S. companies with foreign investments have chosen to do that. Mattel, for example, requires a higher workplace standard for its subcontractors in China than the Chinese government does. A related question is whether one sovereign country (such as the United States) is justified in telling another (Mexico) how much and how fast to clean up its environment. This question goes beyond the ethical aspects of companies' decision making and encompasses the ethical behavior of governments and pressure groups in trying to force their standards on other countries.

Latin American Integration

Latin America needs economic cooperation to enlarge its market size.

Economic integration in Latin America has changed over the years. Two of the original examples of regional economic integration in Latin America, the Latin American Free Trade Association (LAFTA) and the Caribbean Free Trade Association (CARIFTA), changed their names to the Latin American Integration Association (ALADI) and the Caribbean Community and Common Market (CARICOM). They also changed the focus of their activities. In spite of this evolution, the initial rationale for integration remains. The post–World War II strategy of import substitution to resolve balance-of-payments problems was doomed because of Latin America's small national markets. Therefore it was felt that some form of economic cooperation was needed to enlarge the potential market size so that Latin American companies could achieve economies of scale and be more competitive worldwide.

Three types of economic integration are found in Latin America:
• Free-trade areas
• Common markets
• Partial economic preferences

A study by the Inter-American Development Bank (IDB) identified three types of integration in Latin America: free-trade areas, common markets, and partial economic preferences.[40] The following subsections discuss examples of these three approaches found in Central America and the Caribbean and in the rest of Latin America.

Regional Integration in Central America and the Caribbean

CACM and CARICOM are common markets in Central America and the Caribbean, respectively.

Map 7.2 identifies the two major trading groups in the Central American/Caribbean region: the **Caribbean Community and Common Market (CARICOM)** and the **Central American Common Market (CACM).** The Caribbean Free Trade Association was formed in 1965 and was replaced in 1973 by CARICOM in order to bring the Caribbean countries closer together economically. Most CARICOM members have established a common external tariff. They also are trying to eliminate all barriers to intraregional trade and to establish a common currency, CARICOM investment fund, hassle-free tourist travel within the region, and free movement of skilled workers and professionals between member countries.[41]

CACM was originally established in 1961; it fell apart because of hostilities between El Salvador and Honduras. Subsequently, in 1991, the governments of Costa Rica, El Salvador, Guatemala, and Honduras decided to establish a new common market that would involve the elimination of intrazonal trade barriers and the establishment of a common external tariff. CACM and CARICOM members also are trying to establish a free-trade area that would include all countries in both groups.

Integration in the Rest of Latin America

Free-trade area   In 1960, Mexico and the South American countries formed a free-trade area called the **Latin American Free Trade Association (LAFTA).** One of LAFTA's major goals was to eliminate all tariff and nontariff barriers among member countries and to gradually move Latin America toward a common market. However, that program proved to be too rigid and ambitious. By 1980, it became clear LAFTA was not working, primarily because its members traded more with the United States

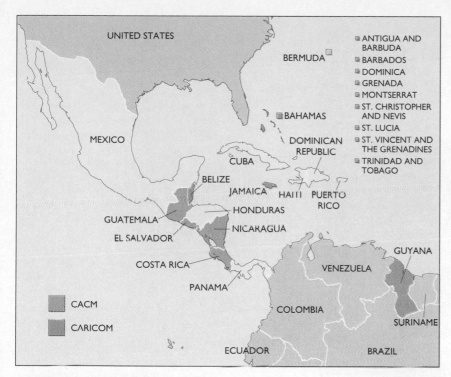

Central American
Common Market (CACM)

Members	Date of entry	
Costa Rica	Sept.	1963
El Salvador	May	1961
Guatemala	May	1961
Honduras	April	1962
(withdrew	Jan.	1971)
Nicaragua	May	1961

Caribbean Community and
Common Market (CARICOM)

Participating Members	Date of entry	
Antigua and Barbuda	May	1974
Bahamas*	July	1983
Barbados	Aug.	1973
Belize	May	1974
Dominica	May	1974
Grenada	May	1974
Guyana	Aug.	1973
Jamaica	Aug.	1973
Montserrat	May	1974
St. Christopher and Nevis	May	1974
St. Lucia	May	1974
St. Vincent and the Grenadines	May	1974
Trinidad and Tobago	Aug.	1973

*The Bahamas is a member state of the community but is not a participant in the common market.

Map 7.2
Economic Integration in Central America and the Caribbean
Countries in Central America and the Caribbean have shifted their forms of integration from free-trade areas to common markets: the Central American Common Market (CACM) and the Caribbean Community and Common Market (CARICOM).

than with each other. In addition, most of the benefits of membership accrued to Argentina, Brazil, and Mexico. Thus there was little incentive to reduce the barriers to intrazonal trade as among EU members. After LAFTA's failure, member countries formed two other groups: the Andean Group and ALADI (see Map 7.3).

Common market   The **Andean Group** (see Map 7.3) was formed by several members of LAFTA that were close to each other geographically and that felt it necessary to have more than just free trade among themselves. Thus they included provisions for a common external tariff, restrictions on the inflow of FDI, and the integration of economic and social policies. The Andean Group decided to develop subregional industries and allocate these industries among group members, which would enable more evenly distributed development. However, political and economic problems of the region have kept it from achieving the full benefits of integration: Only 5.8 percent of its total 1990 trade was intrazonal.[42] In hopes of attracting more outside capital, the Andean Group relaxed its restrictions on FDI by allowing foreign investors to be treated the same under the law as domestic investors and by removing limits on the repatriation of profits back to the home country of the investor. In addition, the original goal of establishing regional industries has given way to assisting small and medium-sized industries in the region.

Map 7.3
Latin American Economic Integration

The Latin American Integration Association (ALADI) evolved from the Latin American Free Trade Association (LAFTA). The Andean Group and MERCOSUR are subgroups of ALADI designed to address special needs of member countries.

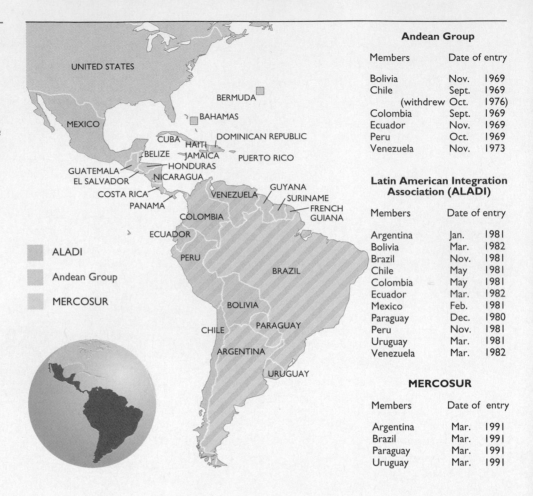

Andean Group

Members	Date of entry	
Bolivia	Nov.	1969
Chile	Sept.	1969
(withdrew	Oct.	1976)
Colombia	Sept.	1969
Ecuador	Nov.	1969
Peru	Oct.	1969
Venezuela	Nov.	1973

Latin American Integration Association (ALADI)

Members	Date of entry	
Argentina	Jan.	1981
Bolivia	Mar.	1982
Brazil	Nov.	1981
Chile	May	1981
Colombia	May	1981
Ecuador	Mar.	1982
Mexico	Feb.	1981
Paraguay	Dec.	1980
Peru	Nov.	1981
Uruguay	Mar.	1981
Venezuela	Mar.	1982

MERCOSUR

Members	Date of entry	
Argentina	Mar.	1991
Brazil	Mar.	1991
Paraguay	Mar.	1991
Uruguay	Mar.	1991

ALADI

Andean Group

MERCOSUR

The Andean Group wants to establish a common market by 1996.

Until 1990, the Andean Group experienced little progress in guiding its members' commercial policies. At the 1990 group meeting, members decided to form an Andean Common Market by 1996. Internal tariffs were phased out by 1993, and a common external tariff was tentatively approved. Subsidy programs for intrazonal trade also were to be phased out.[43]

Partial economic preferences   The **Latin American Integration Association (ALADI),** which consists of most of the countries originally in LAFTA (see Map 7.3) is an example of partial economic preferences. By 1980, it had become clear LAFTA was not working: Intrazonal trade among members was only 14 percent of their total annual trade. One of LAFTA's major goals was to eliminate all tariff and nontariff barriers among member countries and gradually move Latin America toward a common market. However, that program proved to be too rigid and ambitious.

ALADI is at the partial economic preferences level of integration, which allows member countries to establish flexible forms of economic integration.

ALADI, established in 1980, is much more flexible and less ambitious than LAFTA was. It gives members an opportunity to establish a series of bilateral agreements that may be extended to other countries if desired. This arrangement allows countries with common interests to progress faster than often occurs when dis-

Only 10.7 percent of ALADI trade is intrazonal.

parate members have to compromise and thereby possibly dilute an agreement's effectiveness. Instead of across-the-board tariff cuts, ALADI set up a more flexible regional tariff preference and other forms of economic cooperation. By 1989, only 10.7 percent of the trade of ALADI countries was intrazonal.[44]

Some argue that ALADI's modest achievements are due to its limited mandate. However, ALADI has established a system of preferential tariffs linked to the level of development of each member country. It also has set up a system of reciprocal trade credits in order to reduce the use of foreign exchange in regional trade. Further, ALADI conducts studies and keeps record of trade among its member countries.[45]

> **MERCOSUR is a subregional group consisting of Argentina, Brazil, Paraguay, and Uruguay.**

A major subregional group that has spun off from ALADI is **MERCOSUR** (shown in Map 7.3), which is composed of Argentina, Brazil, Paraguay, and Uruguay. MERCOSUR, established in 1991, hopes by the end of 1995 to set up a customs union and common market that would result in a market twice the size of Canada's. It also hopes to reduce internal tariffs to zero by the end of 1994 for Argentina and Brazil and by the end of 1995 for Paraguay and Uruguay. In addition, MERCOSUR is working on a common external tariff set at 35 percent initially and the coordination of members' exchange rate and economic policies.[46] However, disparities and disputes among members will make MERCOSUR's goals difficult to attain within the announced time frames.

What do all of these efforts mean to outside investors? Most Latin American countries demonstrate a high degree of protectionism; therefore, most foreign investors—primarily, but not exclusively, U.S. MNEs—have looked at Latin America as a series of individual national markets. However, the combination of strong economic growth and closer economic cooperation is causing many companies to rethink their strategies. In the very near future, foreign investors will be able to view Latin America as one large market that can be served by single large facilities that can achieve economies of scale. That move would help eliminate many of the inefficiencies currently existing in Latin American plants.[47]

Asian Integration Efforts

> **The member countries of ASEAN—Brunei, Indonesia, Malaysia, the Philippines, Singapore, and Thailand—have wide disparities in population and economic strength.**

The major type of economic integration in Asia is a free-trade area, the **Association of South East Asian Nations (ASEAN).** Organized in 1967, ASEAN comprises Brunei, Indonesia, Malaysia, the Philippines, Singapore, and Thailand (see Map 7.4). It is promoting cooperation in many areas, including industry and trade. Member countries are very protected in terms of tariff and nontariff barriers. Yet they hold promise for market and investment opportunities because of their large market size (322.7 million people) and rapid economic growth (7.8 percent in 1991). However, the countries differ in several ways, especially population and GDP. For example, Indonesia, with 200 million people, is the world's fourth most populous country, whereas Singapore has only 2.8 million people and Brunei only 450,000. However, Indonesia has a per capita income of only $489 compared to Singapore's $11,656.

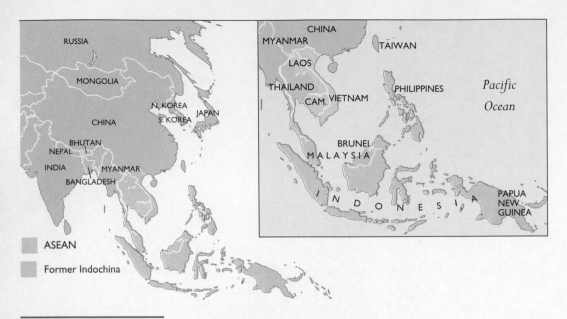

Map 7.4
The Association of South East Asian Nations
ASEAN is a regional group whose member countries have a total population that is approximately the same size as that of the EU countries or the NAFTA countries, but their per capita GDP is smaller. However, economic growth rates of ASEAN members are among the highest in the world.

Japan uses the raw materials of ASEAN countries, processing them into finished goods for export back to those countries.

On January 1, 1993, ASEAN officially formed the ASEAN Free Trade Area (AFTA). AFTA's goal is to cut tariffs on all intrazonal trade to a maximum of 5 percent by January 1, 2008. The weaker ASEAN countries would be allowed to phase in their tariff reductions over a longer period. However, it is unclear how the tariff reduction will affect intrazonal trade, which was about 18 percent of the area's total 1990 trade. The feeling is that there are other impediments to trade, such as exchange rates, transportation costs, and nontariff barriers.[48]

The Japanese, who are not members of ASEAN, have been very successful in investing in and exploiting raw materials in ASEAN countries and using those materials to manufacture finished goods in Japan, which are then re-exported to ASEAN countries. The result has been serious tensions within ASEAN, as some members have claimed that Japan is doing economically what it was not able to do militarily in World War II.[49]

A major factor in ASEAN's future success is the opening of the former Indochina (Cambodia, Laos, and Vietnam), which is a resource-rich area of over 400 million people. Toward that end, in 1992 ASEAN signed a treaty of amity and cooperation with Laos and Vietnam, countries that will need strong trade and investment linkages to bring them up to ASEAN's level.[50]

African Cooperation

Several forms of African integration exist, and they are not necessarily mutually exclusive. The Ivory Coast, for example, is a member of several different organizations in Africa that promote political and/or economic development. The major African groups are shown on Map 7.5:

**Map 7.5
African Unity**
Although there are several regional economic groups in Africa, trade among their member countries is still quite small. African countries rely heavily on trading relationships with industrial countries to absorb regional exports.

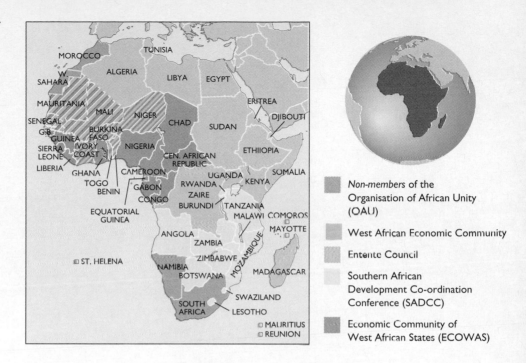

Non-members of the Organisation of African Unity (OAU)

West African Economic Community

Entente Council

Southern African Development Co-ordination Conference (SADCC)

Economic Community of West African States (ECOWAS)

- **West African Economic Community** (Benin, Burkina Faso, Ivory Coast, Mali, Mauritania, Niger, and Senegal)
- **Entente Council** (Benin, Burkina Faso, Ivory Coast, Niger, and Togo)
- **Economic Community of West African States (ECOWAS)**
- **Organisation of African Unity (OAU)** (nearly every country in Africa)
- **Southern African Development Co-ordination Conference (SADCC)** (Angola, Botswana, Lesotho, Malawi, Mozambique, Swaziland, Tanzania, Zambia, and Zimbabwe)

African integration is difficult because markets are small, resource endowments are similar, and intrazonal trade is low.

Although several groups are involved in African political and economic integration, intrazonal trade is only 5 percent of Africa's total. Also, two thirds of its external trade is with industrial countries, primarily but not exclusively former colonial powers. As a result of the worldwide recession and drop in commodity prices, Africa has had serious economic problems in recent years. In addition, African countries are concerned about growing regionalization in Europe and North America. They fear they will be locked out of those markets as different "fortresses" are established.

Africa, primarily through the OAU, has established two primary objectives for the 1990s: realizing economic integration and establishing a mechanism for a settlement of internal conflicts. In 1991, the OAU ministerial council signed an agreement to establish an African Economic Community. As of mid-1993, twenty-nine OAU members had ratified the agreement, still six short of the two-thirds majority needed to bring it into force.[51]

To accomplish the goals envisaged by OAU, several regional economic groups are attempting to improve the flow of goods and capital in their regions. ECOWAS is the premier group, and it is changing its treaty to strengthen the relationships in Africa. Because it has been mired in the Liberian conflict, however, much of its activity has been political in nature.[52]

Clearly, there is considerable overlap among the African groups. Most try to cooperate in some form of economic integration, although the level of integration tends to be fairly low. In general, the countries are so poor and their economic activity so low that there is an insufficient basis for cooperation. Most African countries rely heavily on agriculture or natural resources as a major source of export revenues, so there is not much reason to lower the barriers to the primary products. Major industrial effort is fairly rare, and industries still need protection before the doors to competition are opened. However, such protection retards the development of a free-trade area. African groups also are seeking regional cooperation in other areas, such as transportation, other forms of infrastructure, small industrial projects, and so forth. There is a strong feeling that political and economic integration must occur if African countries are to survive.

Commodity Agreements

So far this chapter has focused on how countries cooperate to reduce trade barriers, but this section deals with how countries use commodity agreements to stabilize the price and supply of selected commodities.

A **commodity agreement** is a form of economic cooperation designed to stabilize and raise prices. As of 1992, there were forty-nine commodity agreements in force worldwide, with the majority involving food and agricultural raw materials.[53] Commodity agreements are of two basic types: producers' alliances and international commodity control agreements (ICCAs). Producers' alliances are exclusive memberships of producing and exporting countries. Examples are the Organization of Petroleum Exporting Countries (OPEC) and the Union of Banana Exporting Countries. ICCAs are based on cooperation between producing and consuming countries and provide for equal voting rights for both groups. Examples of ICCAs are the International Cocoa Organization and the International Sugar Organization.[54]

Most developing countries traditionally have relied on the export of one or two commodities to supply the foreign currencies from industrial countries they need for economic development. This is especially true of the African developing countries. However, commodity prices are not stable. For example, as illustrated in Fig. 7.2, prices dropped significantly between 1980 and 1986 before finally recovering; beverage prices, however, continued to fall through 1992. In the past decade, the prices of Africa's major exports—coffee, tea, and cocoa—have fallen 10 percent on average, causing a significant shortfall in foreign-exchange earnings. Since one third of African countries' export earnings are used to service debt, this is a significant problem.[55]

A commodity agreement is designed to stabilize the price and supply of a good; it takes the form of a producers' alliance or an ICCA.

Commodity prices fluctuate significantly due to natural forces as well as supply and demand factors.

**Figure 7.2
Commodity Price
Trends, 1976–1992**
Commodity prices have
fluctuated widely in the last
two decades, creating wide
variations in the earnings
of exporting countries.

Source: Data from International
Monetary Fund, *International Financial Statistics Yearbook,* August
1993, p. 7.

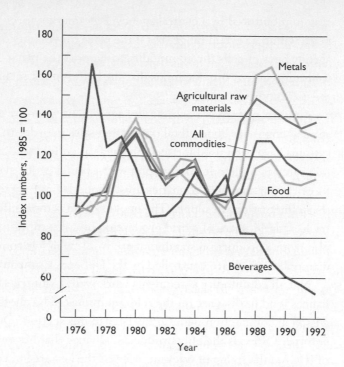

Both consumers and producers often prefer a stabilized pricing system that allows
for predictions of future costs and earnings and thus facilitates planning. Unfortunately, many short-term factors cause price instability, leading to fluctuations in export
earnings. The most important of these factors are

- Natural forces such as inclement weather and its results
- Relatively price-insensitive demand
- Relatively price-insensitive supply (in the short run)
- Business cycles in industrial countries that can cause sudden changes in demand

**Changes in a commodity's
price cause changes in an exporting country's total revenue as a result of shifts in
demand, shifts in supply, and
price elasticity of
demand.**

**Buffer-stock systems and
quota systems attempt to
keep commodity prices relatively high.**

**A buffer-stock system is a
commodity agreement by
which reserve stocks of the
good are bought and sold to
regulate the price.**

The impact price changes have on an exporting country's total revenue depends on
several variables. If a price change results from a shift in demand, total revenue will
move in the same direction as the change. That is, if the price rises because of an increase in demand for the commodity, total revenue also will rise. This is especially
true for mineral products that are sensitive to economic activity in industrial markets.
If the price change results from a shift in supply, then price and demand will move in
opposite directions. That is, if the price falls because of an increase in the commodity's supply on the market, the demand will rise. Whether total revenue rises depends
on the elasticity of demand, that is, the responsiveness of demand to price changes. If
demand is insensitive to price changes, as is often the case with commodities, then a
price rise probably will not increase total revenue, even though demand rises.

The types of commodity agreements most frequently adopted are the buffer-
stock system and the quota system. A **buffer-stock system** is a partially managed

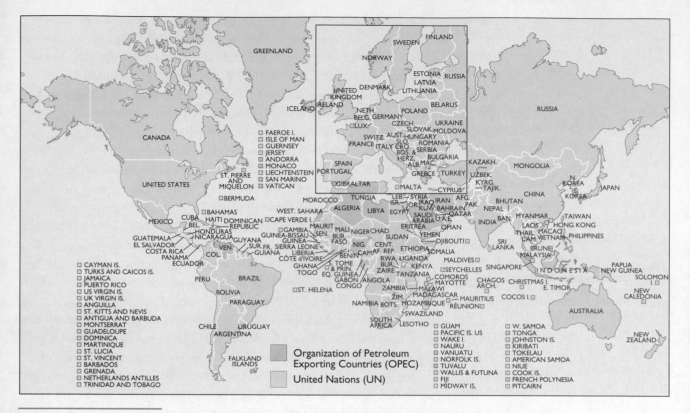

Map 7.6
OPEC and the UN
The Organization of Petroleum Exporting Countries (OPEC) primarily consists of oil-producing countries in the Middle East, but Algeria, Gabon, Indonesia, Libya, Nigeria, and Venezuela also are members. The United Nations (UN) encompasses most of the countries of the world.

OPEC's control over prices began to erode because of reduced demand and increased production by non-OPEC countries.

3. Consuming countries were not able to supply their own needs.

4. Substitutes were not readily available.

World oil prices dropped slightly between 1975 and 1978, but they rebounded in 1979 and 1980, peaking at about $35 per barrel.

In the early 1980s, however, OPEC's resolve began to weaken. Although oil consumption increased steadily over most of the 1970s, the 1979–1980 rebound resulted in a drop in demand for oil in the industrial countries. The major reasons for the decline in consumption were the worldwide recession, the increase in crude-oil prices, the substitution of other fuels for oil, the effectiveness of national energy policies aimed at conservation, the changing structure of industry, and the decreasing importance of energy-intensive industries.[61]

Some interesting trends subsequently developed in the oil industry. First, oil consumption as a percentage of total worldwide energy consumption declined from 48 percent to 40 percent by 1983; use of natural gas, coal, hydroelectric power, and nuclear energy increased at the expense of oil. However, OPEC oil supplies met 54 percent of the growth in primary-energy consumption in 1992 compared with 40 percent in 1985, and many experts suggest that dependence on OPEC is growing. Many experts also predict that oil's share of total worldwide energy consumption, which decreased from 45.7 percent in 1980 to 39.6 percent in 1990, will equal that of natural gas. And the Persian Gulf countries have less than 20 percent of the world's gas reserves, compared with more than 40 percent of the world's oil reserves. The former Soviet Union has 45 percent of the world's gas reserves. Further, the percentage of worldwide oil consumption accounted for by North America and Western Europe decreased, whereas it increased for the rest of the world, especially the booming economies of Asia.

Finally, OPEC's output decreased by 50 percent over the past decade. Part of the decrease was due to the fall in oil demand in general, but part of it was traced to the increase in oil supplied by non-OPEC members, primarily the former Soviet Union, Mexico, and the United Kingdom.[62] OPEC's share of worldwide oil production was 40.7 percent in 1992, compared with a high of 55.5 percent in the 1970s and a low of 29.9 percent in 1985. Although OPEC's control over world oil supplies had been slipping, especially at the 1985 production low, its grip began to loosen even more in 1987 and early 1988. Prices fell to $15 per barrel in 1988, and producer countries could not agree to slow down production in order to stabilize prices. Low prices continued to devastate the U.S. oil industry, and oil exploration in the United States nearly ceased.

However, in the late 1980s a major problem began to develop between Iraq and both Kuwait and Saudi Arabia. Prices had fallen so far in 1988 that the non-OPEC countries agreed to cut production if the OPEC countries would do the same. However, Saudi Arabia would not agree. The Saudis felt existing quotas should be enforced and did not want to lower production further. In late 1988, Iran and Iraq finally agreed to the same quota, and in 1989, prices rose to about $18 per barrel. OPEC ministers agreed to increase production levels a little, but Kuwait did not want to be bound by those limits. Although oil prices had risen by mid-1990 to slightly over $20 per barrel, Iraq's President Saddam Hussein attributed low world oil prices to Kuwait's quota-busting production. This was part of his motivation for invading Kuwait in August 1990. Prices quickly rose to over $41 per barrel, but oil-producing countries increased output to take up the slack. By the end of 1990, prices had fallen to around $25 per barrel.[63]

As the Persian Gulf conflict concluded and production resumed in Kuwait and Saudi Arabia, yet another major problem was brewing in the region. The breakup of the former Soviet Union caused oil production to slacken somewhat, but the global recession caused demand to remain flat in 1991 and 1992. As Kuwait sought to increase its production quota to generate the funds it needed to restructure and rebuild its economy, it ran into the problems of the recession and the lack of interest on the part of other OPEC members in reducing their quotas to maintain a stable price.[64]

> The invasion of Kuwait was caused largely by that country's desire to increase oil production rather than hold to its quota.

The United Nations

This chapter has discussed several examples of regional cooperation to demonstrate the successes and failures among the various types of integration. Obviously, when countries join together, they can accomplish a great deal. Of the numerous bilateral and multilateral organizations, treaties, and agreements, the **United Nations (UN)** is one of the most visible and extensive (see Map 7.6 for members). Its major purposes are the following:

- To maintain international peace and security
- To develop friendly relations among countries
- To achieve international cooperation in solving international problems of an economic, social, cultural, or humanitarian nature
- To be a center for harmonizing national efforts in these areas

Although most UN efforts appear to be political, some activities influence MNEs.

The UN has established several organizations that can influence MNEs.

The UN Economic and Social Council is responsible for economic, social, cultural, and humanitarian facets of UN policy. This group organized a Commission on Transnational Corporations to secure effective international arrangements for the operations of MNEs and to further global understanding of the nature and effects of MNEs' activities. The commission has studied a variety of topics, such as transfer pricing, taxation, and international standards for accounting and reporting. The UN also has established several regional economic commissions to study economic and technological problems of different regions and to recommend ways to solve those problems.

A number of other bodies have been set up by the UN, some dealing with issues relating to MNEs. One such group is the United Nations Conference on Trade and Development (UNCTAD). UNCTAD has been especially active in dealing with relationships between developing and industrial countries regarding commodities, manufacturing, shipping, invisibles, and trade-related financing.

UNCTAD is promoting a cooperative approach between industrial and developing countries to solve economic problems.

When UNCTAD was established in 1964, the Cold War was in full swing. Basically, members of the body divided themselves into four groups: Central and Eastern European countries that had centrally planned economies, the former Soviet Union, plus a few other similar economies; the OECD countries; the Group of 77 (developing countries); and China. UNCTAD conferences were held every four years beginning in 1964, and the first seven tended to be very confrontational. The last meeting before the end of the Cold War was held in 1987. Initial concerns focused on commodity prices and efforts to stabilize and expand export earnings of the developing countries. Despite the polemics, debates, and disagreements, UNCTAD played a key role in the emergence of the Generalized System of Preferences, a maritime shipping code, special international programs to help the poorest countries, and international aid targets.[65]

UNCTAD VIII, held in Cartagena during February 1992, took place in an entirely different political environment. By then, the Soviet Union no longer existed, and many developing countries realized they needed to establish economic policies based on market forces in order to create employment and increase income. The old alliances disappeared, and shifting coalitions were created to form a consensus. The session reflected a broad consensus on market-oriented economic policies and political pluralism. UNCTAD will focus on important issues by establishing:

- Standing committees on commodities, poverty alleviation, economic cooperation among developing countries, and services
- Special Committee on Preferences and Intergovernmental Group of Experts on Restrictive Business Practices
- Ad hoc groups to deal with investment and financial flows, nondebt-creating financing for development, new mechanisms for increasing investment and financial flows, trade efficiency, comparative experiences with privatization, expansion of trading opportunities for developing countries, and the interrelationship between investment and technology transfers.[66]

The Environment

Governments, companies, and individuals are cooperating to solve serious environmental problems.

Pollution of the air, land, and sea clearly poses a threat to the future of the planet, and governments, companies, and individuals are concerned about the present and future state of the environment. Although many environmental problems are national in nature, they have cross-national ramifications and require cross-national agreements.

Major types of environmental degradation mentioned most often are ozone depletion, air pollution, acid rain, water pollution, waste disposal, and deforestation. Ozone depletion results from the burning of fossil fuels and the emission of ozone-depleting chemicals, such as chlorofluorocarbons (CFCs). Ozone depletion may lead to global warming and the destruction of life as a result of excessive exposure to ultraviolet radiation. In 1987, the EC countries and twenty-four others signed a protocol that called for halving CFC usage by 1998. In 1990, seventy-five countries signed an accord to strengthen provisions of the protocol, calling for all countries to eliminate CFC usage by 2000. A $200-billion fund was set up to help subsidize developing countries' usage of CFC substitutes.[67] These are good examples of multinational efforts to attack a global problem.

A major source of water pollution is leakage of chemicals from underground storage tanks, landfills, waste dumps, and industrial storage lagoons. For example, one concern is that ground leaks in Mexico could contaminate water sources in the United States.

The Rio Earth Summit culminated in a series of initiatives designed to solve environmental problems.

The Rio Earth Summit, held in June 1992, brought together people from around the world to discuss key environmental issues. The resulting Rio Declaration sets out fundamental principles for environmentally responsive behavior.[68] The problem with international environmental agreements is that each country is headed in its own direction, and countries differ significantly in how they deal with environmental issues. This problem is especially acute in developing countries, where some of the worst environmental damage is taking place and laws tend to be the most lax. Thus, some MNEs might be tempted to save costs by locating production facilities in countries in which environmental laws are weak.

However, many MNEs are among the world's most environmentally responsible companies; they seek to reduce costs by redesigning manufacturing processes to more efficiently use inputs. For example, DuPont, the U.S.-based chemical company, voluntarily spends approximately $50 million a year more on environmental projects than is required by law. Its goal is zero pollution in all its activities.[69] Its management found that costs actually were reduced when production processes were designed to be more environmentally sound.

COUNTERVAILING FORCES

An underlying theme of this chapter's discussion is the loss of national sovereignty in the pursuit of economic and political integration. When Europeans began moving toward the Single European Market, during a time of economic expansion in Europe, loss of sovereignty was not a major issue. The one exception was the view of British Prime Minister Margaret Thatcher that the United Kingdom could not allow the European bureaucracy to grow to the point that British sovereignty would be undermined too much. And when the Danes first rejected the Treaty of Maastricht, it was clear they did not want to lose their sovereignty to Europe's larger countries.

Germany presents another example of the conflict between self-interest and the common good. When reunification with East Germany began, all other programs—including the Single European Market—took a back seat. Clearly, Germany has been pouring billions into the former East Germany and is concerned about the impact of this fiscal stimulus on its inflation rate. Even though the rest of Europe needed lower interest rates to stimulate economic growth, Germany has maintained high interest rates to solve its own problems.

In contrast, the application of several EFTA countries to become members of the EU is an indication that maintaining national sovereignty is not as important to them as being involved in EU policy deliberations. National sovereignty versus the common good is a major issue for NAFTA as well. For example, the side agreements on labor and the environment that were developed in the United States can be seen as efforts to subordinate Mexico's sovereignty to the United States, while maintaining U.S. sovereignty over employee and environmental policies.

Economic integration can stir up a conflict between national sovereignty and the common good of member countries.

LOOKING TO THE FUTURE

It has been argued that the 1990s is the decade of the Triad Strategy, which takes into consideration three important areas: Asia (especially Japan), North America, and Europe (the EU, especially). Because the combined GDP of these three is so vast, companies need to develop a Triad Strategy that includes trade and investment with all of them. The liberalization of Eastern Europe probably will cause the EU's economic power to expand considerably in the 1990s. As noted in Chapter 4, the countries that formed the republics of the former Soviet Union (with the possible exception of the Baltic states) may form a regional trading bloc to take advantage of their former economic ties. However, the Commonwealth of Independent States is not as likely to join the EU as are its former Eastern European satellites that were members of COMECON. In addition, the realization of the

The Triad Strategy argues for a presence in Europe, North America, and Asia (primarily Japan).

"Enterprise of the Americas" could considerably expand the trade and investment bases of North, Central, and South America.

Although nationalism will keep the EU from becoming a United States of Europe, significant economic harmonization will occur in the near future. However, a number of issues important to a Single European Market were not solved by December 31, 1992. Thus, Europe 1992 must be regarded as a process, not a specific date. Other key developments will be the EU's acceptance of the EFTA countries and the place of the former Soviet Union in the "European House."

With NAFTA having taken effect in 1994, some very exciting areas of cooperation will continue to come out of the Americas. The rest of Latin America will find that economic cooperation will be essential to continued peace and prosperity. The ability of the democratically elected governments to remain in power and to develop the democratic tradition within their countries should enhance regional cooperation. A series of bilateral agreements eventually will result in a large multilateral agreement spanning the Americas.

An important issue will be the stability of commodity prices. Low commodity prices will make it difficult for exporting countries to earn enough foreign exchange to service foreign debt and to modernize. Conversely, even though most major oil-consuming countries have cut consumption as a percentage of GDP, high oil prices can have a devastating impact on their economic growth. Although the recession of the early 1990s reduced oil demand and helped hold down prices, there was fear that any significant price increase would touch off an inflationary spiral that would damage economic recovery. In 1990 it was estimated that each $1 drop in the price of a barrel of crude oil would cut the cost of gasoline in the United States by more than $2 billion per year and cut the U.S. trade deficit by $3 billion.[70] Obviously, a price increase would cause the opposite effect in the short term.

How will these trends affect management decisions? Corporate strategy must take market size into consideration, and regional integration certainly affects the size of markets. Further, as integration proceeds in Europe and in North America, companies can make production-location decisions based on economies of scale because they don't have to worry about tariff barriers. Also, as technical standards become more harmonized, companies will not have to make so many adjustments to product categories.

Summary

- **Efforts at regional economic integration began to emerge after World War II as countries saw benefits of cooperation and larger market sizes. The major types of economic integration are the free-trade area, the customs union, the common market, and complete economic integration.**

- **In its most limited form, economic integration allows countries to trade goods without tariff discrimination (a free-trade area). In its most extensive form, all factors of production are allowed to move across borders, and some degree of social, political, and economic harmonization is undertaken (complete economic integration).**

- The static effects of economic integration improve the efficiency of resource allocation and affect both production and consumption. The dynamic effects involve internal and external efficiencies that arise because of changes in market size.

- Trade diversion occurs when the supply of products shifts from countries that are not members of an economic bloc to those that are.

- Once protection is eliminated among member countries, trade creation allows MNEs to specialize and trade based on comparative advantage.

- Regional, as opposed to global, economic integration occurs because of the greater ease of promoting cooperation on a smaller scale.

- The European Union (EU) is an effective common market that has abolished most restrictions on factor mobility and is harmonizing national political, economic, and social policies. As of 1993, it comprised Belgium, Denmark, France, Germany, Greece, Ireland, Italy, Luxembourg, the Netherlands, Portugal, Spain, and the United Kingdom.

- Some of the EU's major goals are to abolish intrazonal restrictions on the movement of goods, capital, services, and labor; to establish a common external tariff; to achieve a common agricultural policy; to harmonize tax and legal systems; to devise a uniform policy concerning antitrust; and to supersede national currencies.

- By December 31, 1992, the EU had removed most of its remaining barriers to the free flow of goods and services.

- Several EFTA members have applied for membership in the EU. Their acceptance will make the EU the world's largest and richest trading bloc. The next countries that may be considered for EU membership are some of the former communist countries of Eastern Europe.

- The Canada-U.S. Free Trade Agreement (FTA) was expanded in 1993 to include Mexico, becoming the North American Free Trade Agreement (NAFTA). It is designed to eliminate tariff barriers and liberalize investment opportunities. The inclusion of other Latin American countries would make this an even more powerful economic bloc.

- Economic integration in Latin America has not been as successful as that in Europe and North America, but it has been more successful than that in Africa. Many Latin American efforts are bilateral and subregional in nature.

- **Many developing countries rely on commodity exports to supply the hard currency they need for economic development. Instability in commodity prices has resulted in fluctuations in export earnings. Commodity agreements, utilizing buffer stocks or quotas or combinations of the two, are established in the hope of stabilizing prices.**

- **The Multifibre Arrangement (MFA) was established to protect textile and garment manufacturers in industrial countries from competition from manufacturers in developing countries. It allows importing countries to set up quotas to protect domestic producers.**

- **The Organization of Petroleum Exporting Countries (OPEC) was successful as a producers' alliance in the 1970s and effectively forced historic increases in crude-oil prices. However, the drop in worldwide demand and the increase in supplies from non-OPEC producers have reduced its influence.**

Case
Snider Mold Co. and NAFTA[71]

In 1993, James Meinert, president of Snider Mold Co., was trying to decide whether to continue supplying the Mexican market with products manufactured in the company's plant in Mequon, Wisconsin, or to establish manufacturing operations in Mexico.

In the 1960s, Snider Mold Co., a $10-million Wisconsin company that manufactures precision steel molds used by plastics manufacturers, got started in the Mexican market by making some molds that produced seats for the four stadiums being built in Mexico City for the 1966 Olympics. Since it began exporting to Mexico, Snider has tripled its sales and the size of its workforce, and its exports now account for 25 percent of sales.

When Snider first began penetrating the Mexican market, Meinert had a hard time getting information about the competitors. So he went to Mexico and found some retail stores that carried plastic chairs of the type that were manufactured using molds like Snider sells. Then he tipped the chairs upside down to find out who the manufacturers were.

The molds Snider manufactures, which cost an average $100,000 each, are made for specific products and must be precision-designed for those products by the company's engineers. Using computer-aided design, the engineers develop a three-dimensional design of the mold. Then a skilled machinist uses a computerized milling machine to carve the mold from a rectangular hunk of steel. Snider has sold to Mexico molds for a school chair, a seat for a soccer stadium, and a two-passenger seat for Mexico City's new metro system. Probably half of the company's molds are for the automotive industry. For example, Nissan-Mexico used Japanese companies to produce its molds but shifted to Snider when it became evident that the local content of its Mexican-assembled automobiles would have to increase in order to qualify for NAFTA's tariff-free provisions.

Meinert is pretty happy with the skilled workers he can find in the Mequon area, which has five technical schools. Snider employs about forty workers, who start at $8 per hour and can double their hourly wage within a few years. Meinert knows there are highly skilled workers in Mexico, too, but the demand also is very high. In fact, wages in Mexico for skilled labor—especially bilingual skilled labor—are approaching those at the Wisconsin plant.

One of Meinert's major concerns is Mexico's tariff structure. Currently, a 20-percent duty applies to molds that are imported from the United States to Mexico. This is actually an improvement compared to the duty when Snider first started selling in Mexico. As the duty has come down, business has really increased. He also is concerned about protection of patents and trademarks. He feels many small companies fear exporting, especially to countries in which patent enforcement is inadequate, because they fear their buyers in foreign countries will eventually copy the products and take away business.

Another area of concern is customer service. Meinert feels that the ideal supplier is close to the customer and that Snider therefore must continue servicing, repairing, maintaining, changing, and upgrading the molds it sells to Mexican companies. However, it is difficult to ship a mold from Mexico City to Mequon for servicing when the mold weighs two to three tons. Thus, Snider sends tools to Mexican buyers so that they can perform their own maintenance, even though these tools also are subject to a duty at the border.

Questions

1. What are the major factors influencing Meinert's decision whether to keep manufacturing in the United States or to move production facilities to Mexico?
2. How will NAFTA influence that decision?
3. What do you recommend Meinert should do, and why?

Chapter Notes

1. The information in this case is from the following sources: various issues of the Ford Motor Company's *Annual Report;* "1993 Market Data Book," *Automotive News;* Kathy Jackson, "Ford of Europe Doubles Exports," *Automotive News,* March 15, 1993, p. 2; "Tough at the Top," *The Economist,* March 13, 1993, p. 76; Richard Johnson, "Ford, Mazda Go Separate Ways in Europe," *Automotive News,* March 8, 1993; Robert L. Simison, "European Auto Makers, Bracing for Downturn, Plan Big Job Cuts," *Wall Street Journal,* March 5, 1993, p. A8; Joseph B. White, "GM, Ford, Coming Out of U.S. Slump, Face Pressure from European Recession," *Wall Street Journal,* March 3, 1993, p. A3; Richard A. Melcher and John Templeman, "Ford of Europe: Slimmer, But Maybe Not Luckier," *Business Week,* January 18, 1993, pp. 44, 46; "Ford, VW Cleared by EC Commission to Manufacture Vans," *Wall Street Journal,* December 24, 1992, p. 10; Neal Templin, "Ford to Post Loss for Year, Plans Layoffs," *Wall Street Journal,* December 17, 1992, p. A3; Diana T. Kurylko, "Automakers Brace for Tough Times," *Automotive News,* December 14, 1992, p. 1;

Timothy Aeppel, "Ford Reaches Fork in Road in Its European Operations," *Wall Street Journal,* October 6, 1992, p. 88; Diana T. Kurylko, "Ford Ready to Give Europe 2 New Cars a Year," *Automotive News,* June 15, 1992, pp. 3, 18; *Forbes,* July 1, 1972, pp. 22–26; *Forbes,* April 2, 1979, pp. 44–48; Roger Cohen, "Ford-Fiat: How Their Contest of Wills Prevented a 'Perfect Marriage' in Europe," *Wall Street Journal,* November 21, 1985, p. 34; James B. Treece et al., "Can Ford Stay on Top?" *Business Week,* September 28, 1987, pp. 78–86; and Richard A. Melcher, "Ford Is Ready to Roll in the New Europe," *Business Week,* December 12, 1988, p. 60.

2. Ibid., p. 40.
3. Ibid., p. 4.
4. Michel-Pierre Montet, "Europe's Spiritual Origins," *International Management,* January 1989, p. 39.
5. "European Free Trade Association," *Europa World Yearbook,* 1993, p. 149.
6. Sanjeev Gupta, Leslie Lipschitz, and Thomas Meyer, "The Common Agricultural Policy of the EC," *Finance & Development,* June 1989, p. 37.
7. Ibid.

8. Ibid., pp. 38–39.
9. Philip Revzin, "United We Stand . . .," *Wall Street Journal,* September 22, 1989, p. R5.
10. Ernst & Whinney, *Europe 1992: The Single Market,* September 1988, pp. 5–6.
11. Price Waterhouse, *EC Bulletin,* December 1987/January 1988, p. 1.
12. "The Single Market: Not Yet," *The Economist,* April 10, 1993, pp. 72, 74; and Bob Straetz, "A Top Priority for the EC in 1993: Implementing the Single Internal Market," *Business America,* March 8, 1993, p. 11.
13. Straetz, op. cit., pp. 14–15.
14. Frank Comes and Jonathan Kapstein, "Reshaping Europe: 1992 and Beyond," *Business Week,* December 12, 1988, p. 50.
15. Charles Goldsmith and Peter Gumbel, "EC, Its Competitiveness Waning, Argues Over Trimming Safety Net," *Wall Street Journal,* June 22, 1993, p. A10; and "The Economics of European Disintegration," *The Economist,* May 22, 1993, p. 56.
16. "Getting Away With Merger," *The Economist,* June 12, 1993, p. 92.
17. John F. Magee, "1992: Moves Americans Must Make," *Harvard Business Review,* May–June 1989, pp. 78–84.

18. Straetz, loc. cit.
19. James R. Krum and Pradeep A. Rau, "Organizational Responses of U.S. Multinationals to EC-1992," *Journal of International Marketing,* Vol. 1, No. 2, 1993, p. 67.
20. "The Maastricht Treaty: Where's the Beef?" *The Economist,* May 1, 1993, p. 54.
21. "The Deal is Done," *The Economist,* December 14, 1991, pp. 51–54.
22. Mark M. Nelson and Martin du Bois, "Pact Expands Europe's Common Market," *Wall Street Journal,* October 23, 1991, p. A12.
23. "A Strange New Pattern of Stars," *The Economist,* February 6, 1993, p. 56.
24. "Will More Be the Merrier?" *The Economist,* October 17, 1992, p. 75.
25. Lori Cooper and Marie Treinen, "European Integration—The EC and Beyond," *Business America,* March 8, 1993, pp. 16–18.
26. "North America," *Business International IL&T,* August 1992, p. 1.
27. Ibid., p. 3.
28. Michael S. Serrill, "Back on Track," *Time,* December 21, 1992, pp. 48–49.
29. Paul Magnusson, James B. Treece, and William J. Symonds, "Honda: Is It an American Car?" *Business Week,* November 18, 1991, pp. 105–112.
30. Linda M. Aguilar, "NAFTA: A Review of the Issues," *Economic Perspectives* (Federal Reserve Bank of Chicago, 1992), p. 12.
31. Ibid., p. 14.
32. Linda M. Aguilar, "The North American Free Trade Agreement: The Ties That Bind," *Chicago Fed Letter,* September 1992, p. 3.
33. Sherrill, op. cit., pp. 48–49.
34. Aguilar, loc. cit.
35. Don E. Newquist, "Perot Is Dead Wrong on NAFTA," *New York Times,* May 10, 1993, p. A15; and Ramon Moreno, "NAFTA and U.S. Jobs," *Federal Reserve Board of San Francisco Weekly Letter,* Number 93–24, June 24, 1993, p. 1.
36. Moreno, loc. cit., quoted from G. Hufbauer and J. Schott, *North American Free Trade. Issues and Recommendations* (Washington, D.C.: Institute for International Economics, 1992).
37. Moreno, loc. cit.
38. Bob Davis and Asra Q. Nomani, "Federal Judge's Ruling Could be Death Blow to Free-Trade Accord," *Wall Street Journal,* July 1, 1993, p. A1; and Steven Greenhouse, "Judge in a Ruling That Could Delay Trade Pact," *New York Times,* July 1, 1993, p. C1.
39. "Wilson Foresees Chile in NAFTA Next Year," *Newsletter,* Canadian Consulate General, Los Angeles, April 30, 1993, p. 2.
40. "Inter-American Development Bank Predicts Renewed Push for Economic Integration in Latin America," *IMF Survey,* December 10, 1984, p. 369+.
41. Jay Dowling, "Caribbean Common Market Has Broad Economic Agenda," *Business America,* March 23, 1992, p. 7.
42. "Andean Group," *Europa World Yearbook,* 1993, p. 93.
43. Laurie MacNamara, "Andean Region Makes Integration Effort," *Business America,* March 23, 1992, p. 5.
44. *Europa World Yearbook, 1990,* p. 173.
45. Preston Brown and Carolyn Karr, "Trade Accords Flourish; U.S. Policy Shifts; Barriers Lowered," *New York Law Journal,* June 1, 1993.
46. "The Mercosur Countries Are Potentially a Huge Market," *Business America,* March 23, 1993, p. 8.
47. Geri Smith, Gail DeGeorge, and John Pearson, "Multinationals Step Lively to the Free-Trade Bossa Nova," *Business Week,* June 15, 1992, pp. 56–57, 60.
48. Raphael Pura, "ASEAN Nations Agree on AFTA Details, but Analysts See Little Immediate Impact," *Asian Wall Street Journal,* December 21, 1992, p. 2.
49. Donald J. Lecraw, "Trading Blocs and Trade Cooperation Among Pacific Rim Countries," paper delivered at the Academy of International Business annual meeting, October 1990.
50. "Dreams of Gold," *The Economist,* March 20, 1993, p. 21.
51. Huang Pengnian and Zhu Yunlong, "Africa Works Hard for Economic Integration," *Xinhua General News Service,* June 25, 1993.
52. Remi Oyo, "West Africa: ECOWAS Stresses Benefits of Regional Integration," *Inter Press Service,* May 26, 1993.
53. "Commodities," *Europa World Yearbook 1993,* 34th Edition, Vol. 1 (London: Europa Publications, 1993), pp. 212–215.
54. *Encyclopedia of Public International Law,* Vol. 1 (Amsterdam: North-Holland, 1992), p. 687.
55. Pengnian and Yunlong, op. cit.
56. *Encyclopedia of Public International Law,* p. 688.
57. "Textiles: Experts Paint Bleak Picture of European Industry," *European Information Service European Report,* May 8, 1993.
58. Jim Ostroff, "Textiles-Import Tide Ebbing," *HFD—The Weekly Home Furnishings Newspaper,* Vol. 67, No. 9, p. 30.
59. Ying-Pik Choi, Hwa Soo Chung, and Nicolas Marian, *The Multi-Fibre Arrangement in Theory and Practice* (London: Frances Pinter, 1985).
60. "The Middle East Squeeze on Oil Giants," *Business Week,* July 29, 1972, p. 56.
61. "International Oil Market Prospects," *Currency Profiles* (New York: Henley Centre for Economic Forecasting and Manufacturers Hanover Trust Company, December 1984), p. 6.
62. Ibid., pp. 6–7.
63. James Tanner, "Looming Shock," *Wall Street Journal,* December 10, 1990, p. A1; James Tanner, "OPEC Ministers See Price Collapse If Oil Glut Occurs," *Wall Street Journal,* December 12, 1990, p. A2; and *Chicago Fed Letter* (Chicago: The Federal Reserve Bank of Chicago, November 1990).
64. Bhushan Bahree and James Tanner, "OPEC Members Agree to Freeze Output Quotas," *Wall Street Journal,* June 11, 1993, p. A2.
65. Grant B. Taplin, "Revitalizing UNCTAD," *Finance & Development,* June 1992, p. 36.
66. Ibid., p. 37.
67. Buchholz, op. cit., p. 138.
68. Andrew Steer, "The Road from Rio," *Finance & Development,* September 1992, p. 20.
69. Kirkpatrick, op. cit., p. 48.
70. James Tanner, "Looming Shock."
71. Matt Moffett, "Southern Strategies," *The Wall Street Journal,* 10/29/92, p. 1. Reprinted by permission of *The Wall Street Journal,* ©1994 Dow Jones & Company, Inc. All Rights Reserved Worldwide. Also based on an interview with James Meinert, President of Snider Mold Co.

Chapter 8

Foreign Direct Investment

Who moves picks up,
who stands still dries up.
—Italian Proverb

Objectives

- To explain why direct investments and portfolio investments are viewed differently by investors and governments

- To demonstrate how foreign direct investments may be acquired

- To evaluate the relationship between foreign trade and international factor mobility, especially direct investment

- To classify the major types of motivations for direct investment

- To illustrate the circumstances that lead companies to seek foreign supplies through their foreign direct investments

- To introduce the advantages of foreign direct investments

- To show the major global patterns of direct investment

Case
Bridgestone Tire Company[1]

In 1992, Bridgestone Tire Company became the world's largest manufacturer of rubber products. Between 1978 and 1987, its tire sales grew from the fifth largest to third largest in the world, a position the company still holds. Almost all the company's sales efforts until the mid-1980s were geared toward its home market in Japan, yet its foreign sales grew, mainly through indirect exports. Indirect exports occurred because Bridgestone was a major supplier to Japanese automobile companies. Bridgestone tires were part of the original equipment on exported Japanese automobiles, so they arrived in foreign markets in which the company made little or no export effort. Direct exports also began to grow as foreign consumers wanted Bridgestone replacements on the Japanese cars they had purchased. In the mid-1980s, Bridgestone's top management believed that it was essential to grow outside of Japan, a belief based on the assumption that by 1990 or 1995 there would be only a few major tire companies in the world. The prediction of industry consolidation proved correct, as shown in Map 8.1. Management also believed it would be difficult to sustain growth in Japan because exceeding the 50 percent market share Bridgestone held would be hard.

But even earlier, in 1980, Bridgestone's president had announced that the company's first priority would be to establish a manufacturing presence in the United States. Accordingly, it bought a truck-tire plant from Firestone in 1982. Probably the major factor underlying this priority was the company's high direct and indirect export sales to the United States. Firestone approached Bridgestone in 1984 and again in 1986 to discuss some type of U.S. partnership or sales arrangement, but Bridgestone was not ready for such a big step. By 1987 one out of every ten new cars sold in the United States carried Bridgestone tires. Some dealers also carried Bridgestone tires as replacements; however, Bridgestone had only 2 percent of this larger market. Bridgestone gradually became more confident about its ability to manage and control an automobile-tire manufacturing investment in the highly competitive U.S. market. Part of this confidence derived from the company's success in three areas: with foreign manufacturing facilities in four developing countries, in Australia after buying out Uniroyal there, and with U.S. truck-tire manufacturing after 1982.

Then, in 1988, Bridgestone surprised analysts by buying Firestone's tire operations for $2.6 billion. This purchase gave Bridgestone five North American plants, which supplied about 40 percent of the tires for North American vehicles built by Ford and 21 percent of those built by GM, as well as plants in Portugal, Spain, France, Italy, Argentina, Brazil, and Venezuela. Although Bridgestone remained the world's third-largest tire company, this acquisition put it very close to the two largest companies, Goodyear and Michelin. However, Michelin's purchase of Uniroyal Goodrich in 1989 pushed it clearly into the number one position and was further evidence of tire-industry consolidation.

But why should Bridgestone manufacture automobile tires in the United States? Why not continue exporting, since sales had grown by this means? Several factors had a potential negative impact on Bridgestone's export activities to the United States. First was government-imposed restrictions on tire imports. Although imports of replacement tires comprised a very small part of the U.S. market, these imports could be restricted if sales of U.S.-made tires went down. Second, and more probable, was action taken against imports of Japanese automobiles, which would jeopardize the sale of original-equipment tires. The

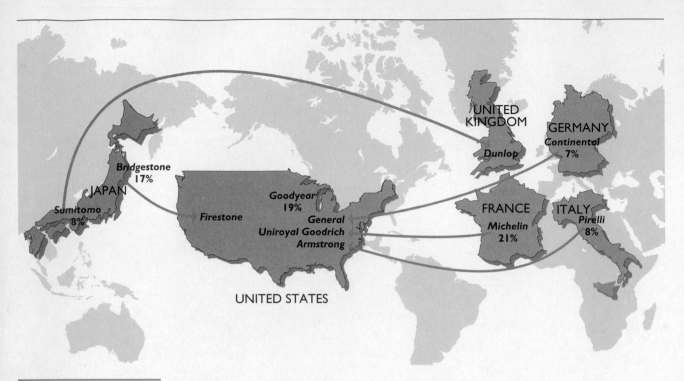

Map 8.1
Major Global Tire Producers and Their Recent Foreign Acquisitions
The percentages give the companies' 1990 global market share of tire sales. The arrows indicate the direction of recent acquisitions.

possibility of import restrictions already had led four major Japanese automakers to begin some U.S. production, and all opted for U.S.-made tires once their plants were operating. Further, in late 1987, Germany's Continental Tire, which recently had bought General Tire, announced a joint venture in the United States with two Japanese companies, Toyo and Yokohama, aimed at gaining business from the Japanese automakers' U.S. plants. If this venture proved successful, even Bridgestone's sales in Japan might be jeopardized because the automakers might prefer to buy from one global supplier. This risk was especially important with Toyota, which bought 40 percent of Bridgestone's original-equipment tires. Third, exports also might be imperiled if Japanese costs went up in relation to U.S. costs. Because of high transport costs for tires, which are bulky relative to their value, shipping them over large distances, except as part of vehicles' original equipment, usually is difficult. U.S. producers even depended on multiple U.S. plant locations in order to minimize transport costs.

Bridgestone's ability to overcome the high costs of transportation for exports (between $3 and $12 per tire, depending on size) was due largely to the low value of the yen relative to the U.S. dollar. Most of Bridgestone's costs were in yen, so a fall in the yen's value resulted in lower costs in terms of U.S. dollars; thus Bridgestone could absorb the costs of international transportation. When the yen strengthened, Bridgestone's dollar costs went up. By mid-1986, the strong yen put the competitive sales price below Bridgestone's break-even point. The yen strengthened even more in 1987 and 1988, making it even more difficult for the company to serve the U.S. market by exporting to it. However, the strong yen meant that Bridgestone probably would pay less in yen for an investment in the United States.

But why buy Firestone rather than starting up a new automobile-tire facility? Probably the major factor was an expectation of overcapacity in the industry brought on largely by the increased use of radial tires, which last longer than nonradials. Because Firestone already had secured a significant market share, an acquisition would add less capacity to a glutted market than a start-up operation would, and most of the output could be sold to Firestone's existing customers. Nevertheless, by the early 1990s U.S. overcapacity kept U.S. tire prices low. Further, Bridgestone found that the Firestone operations were less efficient than it had anticipated. On top of that, Firestone lost the GM account. Although Bridgestone reorganized U.S. operations and invested heavily to modernize Firestone facilities, the company's U.S. losses in the early 1990s about equaled its profits in Japan.

Introduction

Studying foreign direct investment (FDI) is important because production facilities abroad comprise a large and increasingly important part of international companies' activities and thus are an integral part of their strategic thrusts. No one explanation or theory encompasses all the reasons for such investment.[2]

The Bridgestone case illustrates the numerous factors that influenced one Japanese company's decision to produce in a foreign country. Before deciding to invest in U.S. production facilities, Bridgestone faced a sequence of decisions. One of the first decisions was whether to serve foreign markets. The company was content with the Japanese market as long as it could expand rapidly within that market. However, once it had acquired a large and fairly stable share of a maturing market, in order to sustain growth, it had to consider either product diversification or geographical diversification—either of which would involve new risks.[3] Bridgestone chose to diversify geographically because its managers believed its competitive advantage was more specific to the production of tires than to knowledge of the Japanese market. For example, Bridgestone spends heavily on R&D and has made notable breakthroughs in both product and process technologies.[4] It first entered foreign markets through exporting and was successful at that. Nevertheless, its management felt it could not sustain an export market in the United States because of the high transport costs for tires, the possibility that the U.S. government might impose import restrictions, preferences of final or industrial consumers for a U.S.-made product, and an uncertain cost structure created by the changing yen/dollar relationship.

Bridgestone still might have chosen to license its technologies and/or its name to producers already active in the U.S. market, which would have generated revenues without the risk of operating in an alien environment. It elected not to do this for several reasons. First, by this time, the perceived risk of operating in the United States was minimal because of Bridgestone's growing foreign experience and the likelihood that it could sell output to Japanese automakers with whom it had experience. In fact, there was risk in not operating in the United States because Toyo and Yokohama could use their U.S. presence as a means of undermining Bridgestone's Toyota connection in Japan. Second, the company felt it must be located in growth markets if it were to survive the expected consolidation in the industry. Transferring technology to other tire producers eventually might undermine Bridgestone's ability to compete in other markets.

The Bridgestone case also illustrates that FDI may be acquired in alternative ways. Neither the motives nor the methods for acquiring such investment illustrated in the case are conclusive. This chapter further examines those various motives and methods.

The growth of FDI has resulted in a heightened interest in three other questions:

1. What is, or should be, a company's pattern of investment in terms of where to operate abroad?
2. What effect does foreign direct investment have on national economic, political, and social objectives?
3. Should a company choose to operate abroad through some form other than direct investment, such as licensing?

These questions are discussed from an introductory standpoint in this chapter and explored more thoroughly in subsequent chapters: question 1 in Chapter 10, question 2 in Chapter 11, and question 3 in Chapter 16.

The Meaning of Foreign Direct Investment

The Concept of Control

Direct investment usually implies an ownership share of at least 10 or 25 percent.

You saw in Chapter 1 that for direct investment to take place, control must follow the investment; otherwise, it is known as portfolio investment. The share of ownership necessary for control is not clear-cut. If stock ownership is widely dispersed, then a small percentage of the holdings may be sufficient to establish control of managerial decision making. However, even a 100-percent share does not guarantee control. If a government dictates whom a company can hire, what the company must sell at a specified price, and how earnings will be distributed, then it could be said that control has passed to the government. Governments frequently do impose these decisions on companies. But it is not only governments that may jeopardize the stockholders' control. If some resource the company needs in order to operate is not regulated by the company's owners, then those who control that resource may exert substantial influence on the company. Because direct investments can be difficult to identify, governments have had to establish arbitrary definitions. Usually, they stipulate that ownership of a minimum of 10 or 25 percent of the voting stock in a foreign enterprise allows the investment to be considered direct.

The Concern about Control

When foreign investors control a company, decisions of national importance may be made abroad.

Governmental concern   Why should anyone care whether an investment is controlled from abroad? Many critics of the practice are concerned that the national interest of the host country will not be best served if a multinational company makes decisions from afar on the basis of its own global or national objectives. For example, on the one hand, GM, a U.S. company, owns a 100-percent interest in Vauxhall Motors in the United Kingdom. GM's control of Vauxhall through this direct investment means that GM's corporate management in the United States is concerned directly with and makes decisions about personnel staffing, export prices, and the retention versus payout of Vauxhall's profits. This level of control concerns the British public because decisions that directly affect the British economy are being made, or at least can be made, in the United States. The British government, on the other hand, owns slightly less than 1 percent of GM. Because this is not enough for control, the British government expends no time or effort in making management decisions for GM. Nor is the U.S. populace concerned that vital GM decisions will be made in the United Kingdom. This does not mean that noncontrolled investments are unimportant, however. They may substantially affect a country's balance of payments, and they may play an important part in a company's financial management and strategy.

Investors who control an organization
• Are more willing to transfer technology and other competitive assets
• Usually use cheaper and faster means of transferring assets

Investor concern   Control also is very important to many investors who are reluctant to transfer certain vital resources to another domestic or foreign organization that can make all its operating decisions independently. These resources may include patents, trademarks, and management know-how, which when transferred can be used to undermine the competitive position of the original holders. This desire to deny rivals access to competitive resources is referred to as the **appropriability theory.**[5] For example, Bridgestone was hesitant to transfer either product technology, such as its SuperFiller radials, or process technology, such as its mold changeover methods, to other companies. Its management was well aware of how acquired technology can be used to competitive advantage: Between the end of World War II and 1979, much of Bridgestone's technology came from Goodyear, which held a noncontrolling interest in Bridgestone. Even if the acquirer does not use the technology to compete directly, it may prevent the original holders from using that technology to further global objectives.

In addition, operating costs may decrease when control is retained, for several reasons:

1. The parent and subsidiary are likely to share a common corporate culture.
2. The company can use its own managers, who understand its objectives.
3. The company can avoid protracted negotiations with another company.
4. The company can avoid possible problems of enforcing an agreement.

This control through self-handling of operations (internal to the organization), rather than through contracts with other companies, is often called **internalization.**[6]

Despite the advantages of control, many circumstances exist in which assets are transferred to noncontrolled entities, such as transferring trademarks and technology through licensing agreements. In addition, companies lack resources to control all aspects of their production, supplies, and sales, so they funnel their resources to those activities that are most important to their strategies and their performance.

Methods of Acquisition

Direct investments usually, but not always, involve some capital movement.

Foreign direct investment traditionally has been considered an international capital movement that crosses borders when the anticipated return (accounting for the risk factor and the cost of transfer) is higher overseas than at home. Although most FDIs involve some type of international capital movement, an investor may transfer many other types of assets. For example, Westin Hotels has transferred very little capital to foreign countries. Instead, it has transferred managers, cost control systems, and reservations capabilities in exchange for equity in foreign hotels. An example of a direct investment made completely by transferring nonfinancial resources instead of capital was the Plessey (British) acquisition of Airborne Accessories Corporation in the United States. Plessey had two assets that were vital to Airborne Accessories: technology and established sales capabilities outside the United States. Plessey offered the owners notes in exchange for the ownership. Although the interest and principal on these notes was to be paid strictly out of the earnings of the acquired company, the owners reasoned that this interest was a higher return than they could get by continuing to own and manage Airborne themselves.

Aside from committing nonfinancial resources, there are two other means of acquiring assets that do not involve international capital movements in a normal sense. First, funds a company earns in a foreign country may be used to establish an investment. For example, a company that exports merchandise but holds payment for those goods abroad can use settlement to acquire an investment. In this case, the company merely has exchanged goods for equity. Although this method is not used extensively for initial investment, it is a major means of expanding abroad. Initially a company may transfer assets abroad in order to establish a sales or production facility. If the earnings from the facility are used to increase the value of the foreign holdings, FDI has increased without a new international capital movement. Second, companies in different countries can trade equity. For example, Naarden Company in the Netherlands acquired a share of Flavorex in the United States by giving Flavorex owners stock in Naarden, a move that helped integrate the competitive strategies of the two companies.

The Relationship of Trade and Factor Mobility

Whether capital or some other asset is transferred abroad initially to acquire a direct investment, the asset is a type of production factor. Eventually, the direct investment usually involves the movement of various types of production factors as investors infuse capital, technology, personnel, raw materials, or components into their operating facilities abroad. Therefore it is useful to examine the relationship of trade theory to the movement of production factors.

The Trade and Factor Mobility Theory

Both finished goods and production factors are partially mobile internationally.

We explained in Chapter 5 that trade often occurs because of differences in factor endowments among countries. But contrary to historical treatises on trade, production factors themselves also may move internationally. Factor movement is an alternative to trade that may or may not be a more efficient allocation of resources. If neither trade nor the production factors could move internationally, a country would have to either forgo consuming certain goods or produce them differently, which in either case would usually result in decreased worldwide output and higher prices. In some cases, however, the inability to utilize foreign production factors may stimulate efficient methods of substitution, such as the development of new materials as alternatives for traditional ones or of machines to do hand work. For example, the production of synthetic rubber and rayon was undoubtedly accelerated because wartime conditions made it impractical to move silk and natural rubber, not to mention silkworms and rubber plants.

Substitution

There are pressures for the most abundant factors to move to an area of scarcity.

When the factor proportions vary widely among countries, pressures exist for the most abundant factors to move to countries with greater scarcity, where they can command a better return. Thus in countries with an abundance of labor relative to land and capital, laborers tend to be unemployed or poorly paid; if permitted, these workers will gravitate to countries that have relatively full employment and higher wages. Similarly, capital will tend to move away from countries in which it is abundant to those in which it is scarce. For example, Mexico is a net recipient of capital from the United States, and the United States is a net recipient of labor from Mexico. If finished goods and production factors were both completely free to move internationally, the comparative costs of transferring goods and factors would determine the location of production.

A hypothetical example, shown in Fig. 8.1, should illustrate the substitutability of trade and factor movements under different scenarios. Assume the following:

- The United States and Mexico have equally productive land available at the same cost for growing tomatoes.
- The cost of transporting tomatoes between the United States and Mexico is $0.75 per bushel.
- Workers from either country pick an average of two bushels per hour during a 30-day picking season.

The only differences in price between the two countries are due to variations in labor and capital cost. The labor rate is $20.00 per day, or $1.25 per bushel, in the

**Figure 8.1
Comparative Costs
Based on Trade and
Factor Mobility
Assumptions:
Tomatoes in the
United States and
Mexico**
The lowest costs occur
when trade and production
factors are both mobile.

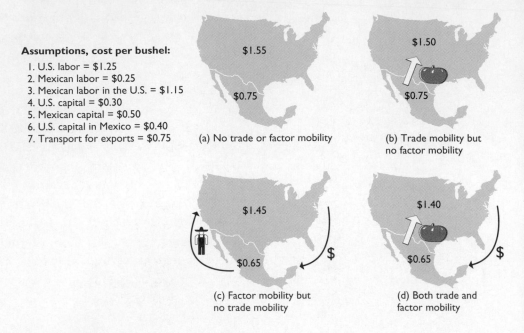

Assumptions, cost per bushel:
 1. U.S. labor = $1.25
 2. Mexican labor = $0.25
 3. Mexican labor in the U.S. = $1.15
 4. U.S. capital = $0.30
 5. Mexican capital = $0.50
 6. U.S. capital in Mexico = $0.40
 7. Transport for exports = $0.75

(a) No trade or factor mobility

(b) Trade mobility but
no factor mobility

(c) Factor mobility but
no trade mobility

(d) Both trade and
factor mobility

United States and $4.00 per day, or $0.25 per bushel, in Mexico. The capital needed to buy seeds, fertilizers, and equipment costs the equivalent of $0.30 per bushel
in the United States and $0.50 per bushel in Mexico.

If neither tomatoes nor production factors can move between the two countries (see Fig. 8.1a), the cost of tomatoes produced in Mexico for the Mexican
market is $0.75 per bushel ($0.25 of labor plus $0.50 of capital), whereas those
produced in the United States for the U.S. market cost $1.55 per bushel ($1.25 of
labor plus $0.30 of capital). If trade restrictions on tomatoes are eliminated be-
tween the two countries (Fig. 8.1b), the United States will import from Mexico
because the Mexican cost of $0.75 per bushel plus $0.75 for transporting the
tomatoes to the United States will be less than the $1.55 per bushel cost of grow-
ing them in the United States.

Consider another scenario in which neither country allows the importation of
tomatoes but both allow certain movements of labor and capital (Fig. 8.1c). Mexican workers can enter the United States on temporary work permits for an incremental travel and living expense of $14.40 per day per worker, or $0.90 per
bushel. At the same time, U.S. capital can be enticed to invest in Mexican tomato
production, provided the capital earns the equivalent of $0.40 per bushel, less than
the Mexican going rate but more than the capital would earn in the United States.
In this situation, Mexican production costs per bushel will be $0.65 ($0.25 of Mexican labor plus $0.40 of U.S. capital) and U.S. production costs will be $1.45
($0.25 of Mexican labor plus $0.90 of travel and incremental costs plus $0.30 of
U.S. capital). Note that each country could reduce its production costs—from
$0.75 to $0.65 in Mexico and from $1.55 to $1.45 in the United States—by bringing in abundant production factors from abroad.

With free trade and the free movement of production factors (Fig. 8.1d), Mexico will produce for both markets by importing capital from the United States. According to the above three assumptions, doing this will be cheaper than sending labor to the United States. In reality, neither production factors nor the finished goods they produce are completely free to move internationally. Slight increases or reductions in the extent of restrictions can greatly alter how and where goods may be produced most cheaply.

In the United States recently, for legal reasons, capital has flowed out more freely than labor has flowed in. The result has been an increase in U.S.-controlled direct investment to produce goods that are then imported back into the United States. In fact, capital moves globally more easily than does labor. Furthermore, technology, particularly in the form of more efficient machinery, generally is more mobile internationally than labor is. Thus differences in labor productivity and costs explain much of the movement of trade and direct investment.

Complementarity of Trade and Direct Investment

Factor mobility via direct investment often stimulates trade because of the need for
• **Components**
• **Complementary products**
• **Equipment for subsidiaries**

Despite the increase in direct investment to produce goods for re-importing, companies usually send substantial exports to their foreign facilities; thus FDI usually is not a substitute for exporting.[7] Many of these exports would not occur if overseas investments did not exist. In these cases, factor movements stimulate trade rather than substituting for it. One reason for this phenomenon is that domestic operating units may ship materials and components to their foreign facilities for use in a finished product. For example, most automobiles sold in Mexico are assembled there, and automakers such as Chrysler ship parts to Mexico for assembly.[8] Foreign subsidiaries or affiliates also may buy capital equipment or supplies from home-country companies because of confidence in their performance and delivery or to achieve maximum worldwide uniformity. A foreign facility may produce part of the product line while serving as sales agent for exports of its parent's other products. Bridgestone, for example, continued to export its automobile tires from Japan for several years while using the sales force of its U.S. truck-tire manufacturing operations to handle those imports.

Motivations for Direct Investment

Businesses and governments are motivated to engage in FDI in order to
• **Expand markets**
• **Acquire resources**
Governments may additionally be motivated by some desired political advantage.

Companies engage in direct investment abroad for the same reasons they pursue international trade:

1. To expand markets by selling abroad
2. To acquire foreign resources (for example, raw materials, production efficiency, and knowledge)

When governments are involved in direct investment, an additional motive may be to attain some political advantage. Any of these three objectives may be pursued by engaging in any one of three forms of foreign involvement. One of these forms, the sale of services (for example, licensing or management contracts) often is avoided either because the company fears it will lose control of key competitive assets or because greater economies exist with self-ownership of production. The following discussion concentrates on the remaining two forms, trade and direct investment, and emphasizes why direct investment is chosen despite most firms considering it riskier to operate a facility abroad than at home.

Market-Expansion Investments

Transportation

Early trade theorists usually ignored the cost of transporting goods. More recently, location theorists have considered total landed cost (cost of production plus shipping) to be a more meaningful way of determining where production should be situated. When the cost of transportation is added to production costs, some products become impractical to ship over great distances. For example, one factor that influenced Bridgestone's decision to invest in the United States was the high cost of transporting tires relative to their production price. Many other products are impractical to ship great distances without a very large escalation in the price; a few of these products and their investing companies are newspapers (Thompson Newspapers, Canadian), margarine (Unilever, British-Dutch), dynamite (Nobel, Swedish), and soft drinks (PepsiCo, U.S.). For these companies, it is necessary to produce abroad if they are to sell abroad. When companies move abroad to produce basically the same products that they produce at home, their direct investments are known as **horizontal expansions.**

Lack of domestic capacity   As long as a company has excess capacity at its home-country plant(s), it may be able to compete effectively in limited export markets despite high transport costs. This might occur because fixed operating expenses are covered through domestic sales, thus enabling foreign prices to be set on the basis of variable rather than full costs. Such a pricing strategy may erode as foreign sales become more important or as output nears full plant-capacity utilization. This helps to explain why companies, even those with products for which shipping charges are a high portion of total landed costs, typically export before producing abroad. Another major factor is that companies want a better indication that they can sell a sufficient amount in the foreign country before committing resources for production there. Finally, companies may want to learn more about the foreign operating environment by exporting to it before investing in production facilities within it. Once they have experience in foreign production, they are more apt to shorten the export-experience time before they produce abroad in a new location.

Transportation increases costs so much that it becomes impractical to ship some products.

Excess domestic capacity
- *Usually leads to exporting rather than direct investment*
- *May be competitive because of variable cost pricing*

This reluctance to expand total capacity while there is still substantial excess capacity is similar to the basis for a domestic-expansion decision. Internationally as well as domestically, growth is incremental. This process can be more readily understood by drawing a parallel of how growth may take place domestically. Most likely, a company will begin operations near the city in which its founders reside and will begin selling only locally or regionally. Eventually, sales may be expanded to a larger geographic market. As capacity is reached, the company may build a second plant in another part of the country to serve that region and to save on transport costs. Warehouses and sales offices may be located in various cities in order to assure closer contact with customers. Purchasing offices may be located near suppliers in order to increase the probability of low-cost delivery. In fact, the company may even acquire some of its customers or suppliers in order to reduce inventories and gain economies in distribution. Certain functions may be further decentralized geographically, such as by locating financial offices near a financial center. As the product line evolves and expands, operations continue to disperse. In the pursuit of foreign business, not surprisingly, growing companies eventually find it necessary to acquire assets abroad.

In large-scale process technology, large-scale production and exportation usually reduce unit landed costs by spreading fixed costs over more units of output.

In small-scale process technology, country-by-country production usually reduces unit landed costs, since transportation is minimized.

Scale economies   Costs of transportation must be examined in relation to the type of technology used to produce a good. The manufacturing of some products necessitates plant and equipment that use a high fixed-capital input. In such a situation, especially if the product is highly standardized or undifferentiated from those of competitors, the cost per unit is apt to drop significantly as output increases. Products such as ball bearings, alumina, and semiconductor wafers fall into this category. Large amounts of such products are exported because the cost savings from scale economies overcome added costs of transportation.

The required scale of production must be considered in relation to the size of the foreign market being served. For example, many European companies have production facilities in both the United States and Canada. These companies are likely to sell the U.S. output only in the United States because of the large market there, whereas much of the Canadian output is sold in their home countries to gain large-scale production.[9]

Products that are more differentiated and labor-intensive, such as pharmaceuticals and certain prepared foods, are not as sensitive to scale economies. For these types of products, transport costs may dictate smaller plants to serve national rather than international markets.[10] David's Cookies, for example, first entered the Japanese market with ingredients mixed in the United States. However, because there was little cost reduction obtained by mixing bigger batches of batter, the company switched to preparing ingredients in Japan to overcome the cost of transportation incurred when exporting.[11]

If imports are highly restricted, companies
- **Often produce locally to serve the local market**
- **Are more likely to produce locally if market potential is high relative to scale economies**

Trade Restrictions

We have shown that for various reasons, a government can make it impractical in many ways for companies to reach their market potential through exportation alone. Companies may find they *must* produce in a foreign country if they are to sell there. For example, Mexico made it impractical for microcomputer companies to continue exporting into the Mexican market by requiring that within five years locally produced microcomputers would have to comprise 70 percent of the microcomputer market. Although many producers questioned whether they could maintain the same prices and quality by producing in Mexico as they could by exporting to Mexico, these producers nevertheless made Mexican investments because they were reluctant to abandon a growing market.[12] Such governmental decrees are not unusual. They undoubtedly favor large companies that can afford to commit large amounts of resources abroad, while making foreign competitiveness more difficult for very small companies, which can only afford exportation as a means of serving foreign markets. This does not mean that smaller companies have no FDI. Many do, such as Amsco International, a producer of sterilization equipment, and Interlake, a manufacturer of fluid-handling products.[13] However, such companies must serve the world from a handful of manufacturing bases rather than building plants in nearly all places in which they have sales.

How prevalent are trade restrictions as an enticement for making direct investments? There is substantial anecdotal evidence of decisions by companies to locate within protected markets, yet studies of aggregate movements of direct investment are inconclusive regarding the importance of trade barriers.[14] Some studies have not found import barriers to be an important enticement, perhaps because the studies have had to rely on actual tariff barriers as the measure of restrictions. This reliance overlooks the effects of nontariff constraints, indirect entry barriers, and potential trade restrictions. For example, Bridgestone reacted to potential trade restrictions rather than to the actual existence of tariffs on tires. Further, companies sometimes will make a limited foreign investment as a means of defusing protectionist sentiments, thus prolonging their export capabilities.[15]

Import barriers almost certainly are a major enticement to direct investment, but they must be viewed along with other factors, such as the market size of the country imposing the barriers. For example, import trade restrictions have been highly influential in enticing automobile producers to locate in Mexico. Similar restrictions by Central American countries have been ineffective because of their small markets. However, Central American import barriers on products requiring lower amounts of capital investment and therefore smaller markets (for example, pharmaceuticals) have been highly effective at enticing direct investment.

Removing trade restrictions among a regional group of countries also may attract direct investment, possibly because the expanded market may justify scale economies. Or the removal of trade restrictions may result in **trade diversion,** a situation in which exports shift to a less efficient producing country because of preferential trade barriers. In turn, companies may invest to take advantage of the trade diversion. For example, the Taiwanese textile industry could export substantial clothing products into the United States as long as it faced the same duties as producers from other countries did. The reduction of duties through NAFTA offers tariff-saving advantages for Mexican production to serve the U.S. market that Taiwanese production does not have; so there has been some trade diversion from the more efficient output in Taiwan to less efficient output in Mexico. Many Taiwanese companies have reacted to NAFTA's passage in 1993 by setting up factories in Mexico, and many U.S.-owned firms have shifted factories from Taiwan to Mexico.[16]

Consumer-Imposed Restrictions

Government-imposed legal measures are not the only trade barriers to otherwise competitive goods; consumer desires also may dictate limitations. For example, consumers may demand that merchandise be altered so substantially that scale economies from exporting are infeasible. They also may prefer to buy domestically produced goods even when they are more expensive, perhaps because of nationalism, a belief that foreign-made goods are inferior, or the fear that service and replacement parts for imported products will be difficult to obtain.

Product change   A company often must alter a product to suit local tastes or requirements. This may compel the use of local raw materials and market testing. Test marketing and altering a product at a great distance from production is most difficult and expensive. For example, Coca-Cola sells some drinks (made from local fruits) abroad that are not available in the United States. It is definitely much cheaper to make those drinks overseas.

Product alteration affects company production in two other ways. Initially, it means an additional investment; as long as an investment is needed to serve the foreign market anyway, management might consider locating facilities abroad. Next, it may mean that certain economies from large-scale production will be lost, which may shift the least-cost location from one country to another. The more the product has to be altered for the foreign market, the more likely it is that production will be shifted abroad.

Nationalism   The impact of nationalistic sentiments on investment movements is not easily assessed; however, some evidence does exist. In many countries, promotional campaigns have been instituted to persuade people to buy locally produced goods. For example, in the United States, some manufacturers have promoted "Made in the USA" to appeal to consumers of products that have been hit with import competition; a specific example is the campaign by the American Fiber, Textiles, and Apparel Coalitions to push "Crafted with Pride in the U.S.A."[17] In addition, some Japanese companies, fearing that adverse public opinion might lead to curbs on television imports, announced they would establish U.S. production plants.[18]

Product image   The link between product image and direct investment is clearer than that between nationalism and direct investment. A product's image may stem from the merchandise itself or from beliefs concerning after-sales servicing. In

Consumers sometimes prefer domestically produced goods because of
- **Compatibility between these products and local preferences**
- **Nationalism**
- **A belief that these products are better**
- **A fear that foreign-made goods may not be delivered on time**

tests using commodities that were identical except for the label indicating country of origin, consumers were found to view products differently on the basis of their source.[19] There are examples of eventual image changes, such as the general improvement in the image of Japanese products that occurred concomitantly with the decline in image for U.S. products. However, it may take a long time and be very costly for a company to try to overcome image problems caused by manufacturing in a country that has a lower-status image for a particular product. Consequently, there may be advantages to producing in a country that has an existing high image.

Delivery risk   Many consumers fear that service and/or replacement parts for foreign-made goods may be difficult to obtain from abroad. Industrial consumers often prefer to pay a higher price to a nearby producer in order to minimize the risk of nondelivery due to distance and strikes. For example, Hoechst Chemical of Germany located one of its dye factories in North Carolina because the textile industry in that region feared that delivery problems would plague the cheaper German imports. Related to this potential problem is the global rise in **just-in-time (JIT) manufacturing systems,** which decrease inventory costs by having components and parts delivered as they are needed in production. These systems favor nearby suppliers who can deliver quickly.

Following Customers

Many companies sell abroad indirectly; that is, they sell products, components, or services domestically, which then become embodied in a product or service that their domestic customer exports. For example, Bridgestone sold tires to Toyota and Honda, which in turn exported fully assembled cars (including the tires) to foreign markets. In such situations, the indirect exporters commonly follow their customers when those customers make direct investments. Bridgestone's decision to make automobile tires in the United States was based partially on its desire to continue selling to Honda and Toyota once those companies initiated U.S. production. Its truck-tire investment was in turn instrumental in Yasuda Fire & Marine Insurance Co.'s decision to establish a U.S. investment in order to provide worker's compensation insurance to Bridgestone's U.S. operations.[20]

Companies can keep customers by following them abroad.

Following Competitors

Within oligopolistic industries (those with few sellers), several investors often establish facilities in a given country within a fairly short time.[21] Much of this concentration may be explained by internal or external changes, which affect most oligopolists within an industry at about the same time. For example, in many industries, most companies experience capacity-expansion cycles at about the same time. Thus they would logically consider a foreign investment at approximately the same time. Externally, they might all be faced with changes in import restrictions or market conditions that indicate a move to direct investment in order to serve

In oligopolistic industries, competitors tend to make direct investments in a given country at about the same time.

consumers in a given country. In spite of the prevalence of these motivators, many movements by oligopolists seem better explained by defensive motives.

Much of the research in game theory shows that people often make decisions based on the "least-damaging alternative." The question for many companies is, "Do I lose less by moving abroad or by staying at home?" Assume that some foreign market may be served effectively only by an investment in the market, but the market is large enough to support only one producer. To solve this problem, competitors could set up a joint operation and divide the profits among themselves; however, antitrust laws might discourage or prevent this. If only one company establishes facilities, it will have an advantage over its competitors by garnering a larger market, spreading its R&D costs, and making a profit that can be reinvested elsewhere. Once one company decides to produce in the market, competitors are prone to follow quickly rather than let that company gain advantages. Thus the decision is based not so much on the benefits to be gained but rather on the greater losses sustained by not entering the field. In most oligopolistic industries (for example, automobiles, tires, and petroleum), this pattern helps to explain the large number of producers relative to the size of the market in some countries. Closely related to this pattern is the decision to invest in a foreign competitor's home market to prevent that competitor from using high profits obtained in that market to invest and compete elsewhere.[22]

Changes in Comparative Costs

The least-cost production location changes because of inflation, regulations, and productivity.

A company may export successfully because its home country has a cost advantage. The home-country cost advantage depends on the prices of the individual factors of production, the size of the company's operations, the cost of transporting finished goods, any regulations on how to produce, and the productivity of the combined production factors. None of these conditions is static; consequently, the least-cost location may change over time. Recall that Bridgestone's decision to locate in the United States was based partly on the fact that Japanese costs (measured in dollars) grew much faster than U.S. costs did, largely because of a rise in the value of the yen relative to the dollar.

The concept of shifts in comparative production costs is closely related to that of resource-seeking investments. A company may establish a direct investment to serve a foreign market but eventually import into the home country from the country to which it was once exporting. Production costs are discussed in the following section on resource-seeking investments.

Resource-Seeking Investments

The cartoon in Fig. 8.2 is consistent with the popular image that FDI is motivated by the availability of cheap labor abroad. Although this is true to some extent, that image overlooks some of the costs of producing abroad. For example, Quality

Figure 8.2

Source: From *The Wall Street Journal,* 12/15/83. Reprinted by permission of Cartoon Features Syndicate.

"I'm sorry to report that after the first, I'll be moving operations to Taiwan."

Coils, a small maker of electromagnetic coils, moved from the United States to Mexico but had so many problems with absenteeism, low productivity, and long-distance management that it moved back home after a few years.[23] Further, there are cost advantages from direct investment that are not fully encompassed in the popular labor-oriented image.

Vertical Integration

In international vertical integration, raw materials, production, and marketing are often located in different countries.

Most vertical integration is supply-oriented.

Vertical integration is control of the different stages (sometimes collectively called a value chain) as a product moves from raw materials through production to its final distribution. As products and their marketing become more complicated, there is a greater need to combine resources that are located in more than one country. If one country has the iron, a second has the coal, a third has the technology and capital for making steel and steel products, and a fourth has the demand for steel products, there is great interdependence among the four and a strong need to establish tight relationships in order to ensure that production and marketing continue to flow. One way to help assure this flow is to gain a voice in the management of one of the foreign operations by investing in it. Most of the world's direct investment in petroleum may be explained by this concept of interdependence. Since much of the petroleum supply is located in countries other than the countries having a heavy petroleum demand, the oil industry has become integrated vertically on an international basis.

Certain economies also may be gained through vertical integration. Because supply and/or markets are more assured, a company may be able to carry smaller inventories and spend less on promotion. This greater assurance also may permit considerably greater flexibility in shifting funds, taxes, and profits among countries.

Advantages of vertical integration may accrue to a company through either market-oriented or supply-oriented investments in other countries. Of the two, there have been in recent years more examples of supply-oriented investments designed to obtain raw materials in other countries. This is because of the growing dependence on LDCs for raw materials and the lack of resources among firms in LDCs to invest substantially abroad. This movement of capital and technology to LDCs is consistent with a theory that holds that factor mobility is most efficient when the more mobile factors, such as capital, move so as to combine with the less mobile ones, such as natural resources. Without the capital movement, the natural resources might not be exploited efficiently.[24]

Rationalized Production

In rationalized production, different components or portions of a product line are made in different parts of the world. The advantages are
- Factor-cost differences
- Long production runs
The challenges are
- Satisfying governments that local production takes place
- Higher risk of work stoppages
- Record keeping

Companies increasingly produce different components or different portions of their product line in different parts of the world to take advantage of varying costs of labor, capital, and raw materials. Doing this is called **rationalized production.** For example, rationalized production resulted in approximately 2000 plants in Mexico, known as *maquiladoras,* that are integrated with operations in the United States. Semifinished goods can be exported from the United States to Mexico duty-free, provided they will be re-exported from Mexico. Once the labor-intensive portion of the production is accomplished in Mexico—such as sewing car seats for GM or building TV cabinets for Panasonic—duties on the finished goods re-entering the United States are charged only on the amount of value added in Mexico.[25] As NAFTA is phased in, the maquiladora program will disappear because there no longer will be a requirement to re-export from Mexico; nevertheless, rationalized production will undoubtedly continue between the United States and Mexico.

Many companies shrug off the possibility of rationalized production of parts. They fear work stoppages in many countries because of strikes or a change in import regulations in just one country. As an alternative to parts rationalization, a complete product can be produced in a given country; however, only part of a company's product range is produced in that country. For example, a U.S. subsidiary in France may produce only product A, another subsidiary in Brazil only product B, and the home plant in the United States only product C. Each plant sells worldwide so that each can gain scale economies and take advantage of differences in input costs that may result in differences in total production cost. Each may get concessions to import because it can demonstrate that jobs and incomes are developed locally.

Another possible advantage of this type of rationalization is smoother earnings when exchange rates fluctuate. Consider the value of the Japanese yen relative to the U.S. dollar. Honda produces some of its line in Japan and then exports this production to the United States. Honda also produces some of its line in the United States and then exports this production to Japan. If the yen strengthens, Honda may have to cut its profit margin to stay competitive on its exports to the United States. But this cut may be offset by a higher profit margin on the exports to Japan.[26]

Access to Production Factors

A company may establish a presence in a country in order to improve its access to knowledge and other resources.

The practice of seeking abroad some input not easily or inexpensively available in the home country closely resembles vertical integration. Many foreign companies have offices in New York City in order to gain better access to what is happening within the U.S. capital market or at least to what is happening within that market that can affect other worldwide capital occurrences. The search for knowledge may take other forms as well. For example, a U.S. pharmaceutical firm may conduct in Peru research not allowed in the United States. Real examples are C.F.P. (French), which bought a share in Leonard Petroleum in order to learn U.S. marketing so as to compete better with other U.S. oil firms outside the United States, and McGraw-Hill, which has an office in Europe to allow it to uncover European technical developments.

The Product Life Cycle Theory

The product life cycle theory explains why
- **New products are produced mainly in industrial countries**
- **Mature products are more likely to be produced in LDCs**

In Chapter 5, we explained the product life cycle (PLC) theory in relation to trade and production location.[27] This theory shows how, for market and cost reasons, production often moves from one country to another as a product moves through its life cycle. During the introductory stage, production occurs in only one (usually industrial) country. During the growth stage, production moves to other industrial countries, and the original producer may decide to invest in production facilities in those foreign countries to earn profits there. In the mature stage, production shifts largely to developing countries, and the same company may decide to control operations there as well.

Governmental Investment Incentives

Governmental incentives may shift the least-cost production location.

In addition to restricting imports, countries frequently encourage direct investment inflows by offering tax concessions or a wide variety of other subsidies. Such incentives affect the comparative cost of production among countries and entice companies to invest in a particular country to serve national or international markets. Many central and local governments offer direct-assistance incentives, including tax holidays, accelerated depreciation, low-interest loans, loan guarantees, subsidized energy or transport, and the construction of rail spurs and roads to serve a plant facility. For example, South Carolina offered BMW $150 million in tax breaks and other incentives.[28]

Political Motives

Governments take ownership of FDI or give incentives to direct investors in order to
- **Gain supplies of strategic resources**
- **Develop spheres of influence**

Trade sometimes is driven by political motives. For example, as we discussed in Chapter 5, during the mercantilist period, European powers sought colonies in order to control those colonies' foreign trade and extend their own spheres of influence. Since the passing of colonialism, some countries continue to pursue many of the old colonial aims by encouraging their domestically based companies to control vital sectors in the economies of LDCs.[29] For example, a U.S. company that controls the production of a vital raw material in an LDC can effectively prevent unfriendly countries from gaining access to the production. It also may be able to prevent local processing, dictate its own operating terms, and hold down prices on production sent to the home country. Similarly, the United Kingdom, France, Italy, and Japan established national oil companies with governmental participation (B.P., C.F.P., E.N.I., and J.P.D.C., respectively) in order to lessen their reliance on U.S. multinational petroleum firms, which might give preference to the United States in the allocation of supplies.[30] In the process of gaining control of resources, industrial nations also acquire much political control.

Sometimes one country may encourage MNE expansion into other countries so that it can gain greater control over vital resources. Japan, for example, depends heavily on foreign sources for certain foodstuffs, lumber, and raw materials; therefore Japanese governmental agencies have assisted Japanese MNEs that undertake foreign investments in those sectors in order to protect Japan's supply sources.[31]

Control of resources is not necessarily the political reason for encouraging direct investment. For example, during the early 1980s, the U.S. government instituted various incentives designed to increase the profitability of U.S. investment in Caribbean countries that were unfriendly to Cuba's Castro regime. The incentives were designed to lure more investment to the area, thus strengthening the economies of those friendly nations and making it difficult for unfriendly leftist governments to gain control.

When governments own and control companies that operate internationally, the investments have not always been politically motivated.[32] Countries simply may be acting in terms of any of the rational economic motives discussed earlier in this chapter.

Buy-versus-Build Decision

There are advantages and disadvantages to either acquiring an interest in an existing operation or constructing new facilities. A company must consider both alternatives carefully.

Reasons for Buying

The advantages of acquisition of an existing operation include
- **Avoiding start-up problems**
- **Easier financing**
- **Adding no further capacity in the market**

Whether a direct investment is made by acquisition or start-up depends, of course, on which companies are available for purchase. The large privatization programs occurring in many parts of the world have put hundreds of companies on the market, and MNEs have exploited this new opportunity to invest abroad. There are many reasons for seeking acquisitions. One concerns the difficulty of transferring some resource to a foreign operation or acquiring that resource locally for a new facility. One resource that is particularly difficult to acquire is personnel, especially if the local labor market is tight. Instead of paying higher compensation than competitors do to entice employees away from their old jobs, a company can buy an existing company, which gives the buyer not only labor and management but also a whole organizational structure through which these personnel may interact. Through acquisitions, a company also may gain the good will and brand identification important to the marketing of mass consumer products, especially if the cost and risk of breaking in a new brand are high. Further, a company that depends substantially on local financing rather than on the transfer of capital may find it easier to gain access to local capital through an acquisition. Local capital suppliers may be more familiar with an ongoing operation than with the foreign enterprise. In addition, an existing company sometimes may be acquired through an exchange of stock, thus circumventing home-country exchange controls.

In other ways, acquisitions may reduce costs and risks as well as provide quicker results. A company may be able to buy facilities, particularly those of a bankrupt operation, for less than it would cost to build them at current construction costs. If an investor fears that a market does not justify added capacity, as in the Bridgestone case, acquisition enables it to avoid the risk of depressed prices and lower unit sales per producer, which might result from new facilities. Finally, by buying a company, an investor avoids the high expenses caused by inefficiencies during the start-up period and gets an immediate cash flow rather than tying up funds during construction.[33]

Reasons for Building

Companies may choose to build if
- **No desired company is available for acquisition**
- **Acquisition will carry over problems**
- **Acquisition is harder to finance**

Although acquisitions offer advantages, a potential investor will not necessarily be able to realize them. Foreign investments frequently are made where there is little or no competition, so finding a company to buy may be difficult. In addition, local governments may prevent acquisitions because they fear lessening competition or market dominance by foreign enterprises. Those companies that can be acquired might embody substantial problems for the investor: Personnel and labor relations may be both poor and difficult to change, ill will rather than good will may have accrued to existing brands, or facilities may be inefficient and poorly located in relation to future potential markets. For example, Bridgestone has had a hard time turning around the poor performance of its U.S. Firestone operations, caused in part by the company's uncertainty regarding whether to emphasize the Firestone or the Bridgestone name. Many other Japanese investors have faced problems with their U.S. acquisitions.[34] Finally, local financing may be easier rather than harder to obtain if the investing company builds facilities, particularly if it plans to tap development banks for part of its financial requirements.

Advantages of Foreign Direct Investment

Most successful domestic companies, especially those with unique advantages, invest abroad.

Direct investment makes companies more successful domestically.

Are companies profitable because they are multinational or multinational because they are profitable? Such a "chicken-or-egg" type of question has hounded direct investment theorists. On the one hand, evidence indicates that very successful domestic companies (both large and small) are most likely to commit resources to FDI; on the other hand, ownership of FDI appears to make companies more successful domestically.[35]

E thical questions concerning direct investment activities have been widely debated. On the one hand, direct investment may lead to better global use of resources. On the other, a disproportionate share of the costs may have to be borne by only a few people. For example, transferring production from a domestic to a foreign location will cause some employees to lose their jobs, and many of them may not easily find new positions. For these employees, there is little solace in the economic gains that go to previously unemployed workers abroad or the lower consumer prices resulting from the foreign production. Some people argue that the plight of these newly unemployed workers is no different from the results of technological change—for example, the replacement of workers in clothes pin factories when electric clothes dryers were adopted. Thus, they should be handled no differently. Others argue that displacement due to a move abroad is different because the workers cannot move abroad to take advantage of the new opportunities there and because the change occurs within the same company. They argue that the company has an ethical obligation to ease employees' adversity by giving advance notice of the move and providing assistance, such as through training and help with job searches.

ETHICAL DILEMMAS

Companies say that such moves are motivated by changes in external conditions over which they have no control, such as costs, taxes, market location, or regulations. For example, Acme Boots announced in 1993 that it was moving out of the United States to gain tax advantages in Puerto Rico; this move stranded its U.S. employees, some of whom had up to thirty years' service. Many critics argue that it is unethical for governments to lure companies away from existing locations by offering lucrative incentives and that it is unethical for companies to move. Do home-country governments have any ethical obligations, especially if their policies, such as environmental regulations or high tax rates, burden domestic producers disproportionately compared to foreign ones?

Rationalized production also may lead to global efficiencies through coordinated utilization of the cheap inputs of unskilled labor from LDCs and the expensive inputs of high-skilled labor and technology from industrial countries. Critics of MNEs contend that this is unethical because the process perpetuates economic distinctions between the "have" and "have not" countries. Others argue that the LDC labor would otherwise be unemployed. Do companies or governments have any ethical obligation to the unskilled laborers in their domestic markets who can find little in the way of employment?

Privatization programs recently have been stimulated by sales of enterprises to foreign investors. Is it ethical to transfer to foreign investors assets that belong to the country as a whole? Does it make any difference whether the state enterprises were profitable? In some cases, such as Argentina's sale of its national airline to Iberia of Spain, the ownership changes from domestic state ownership to foreign state ownership. Do such situations have the same ethical implications as sales to foreign private companies do?

Monopoly Advantages before Direct Investment

One explanation for why companies engage in FDI is that they perceive they hold some supremacy over similar companies in the countries into which they go. This edge often is called a **monopoly advantage.** The advantage results from a foreign company's ownership of some resource that is unavailable at the same price or terms to the local company. The resource may be patents, product differentiation, management skills, access to markets, or the like. Because of the increased cost of transferring resources abroad and the perceived greater risk of operating in a different environment, the company will not move unless it expects a higher return than it can get at home and a higher return than the local firm abroad makes.[36]

Large groups of companies may enjoy certain monopoly advantages, which may explain their relative ability and willingness to move abroad. For example, when capital is an integral part of a new investment, the company that can borrow in a country with a low interest rate has an advantage over the company that cannot. Prior to World War I, Great Britain was the largest source of direct investment because of the strength of the pound sterling and the resulting lower interest rates on borrowing sterling funds. From World War II until the mid-1980s, the strength of the U.S. dollar gave an advantage to U.S. firms. After that, this advantage shifted to Japanese companies.[37]

A related advantage is the relative buying power of different currencies in terms of the plant and equipment they will purchase. During the two and a half decades following World War II, the U.S. dollar was very strong, and it was perhaps overvalued in later years. As a result, by converting dollars to other currencies, U.S. companies could purchase a greater output capacity in foreign countries than they could after the dollar began to slide downward in 1971. The reverse was true for companies from such countries as Japan and Germany, which invested more heavily in the United States during the late 1970s and mid-1980s, when the yen and mark increased their purchasing power.

Currency values do not, however, provide a strong explanation for direct investment patterns. There was a two-way investment flow between the United States and Germany and between the United States and Japan when the dollar was weak as well as when the dollar was strong. Then, in the first half of the 1980s, U.S. companies did not significantly increase investment abroad, but foreign companies invested heavily in the United States despite the strong dollar. The major reasons were high real interest rates in the United States and a relatively strong U.S. economy. In the late 1980s, when the dollar was weak again, direct investment flowed both to and from the United States in record amounts.[38] Therefore the currency-strength scenario only partially explains direct investment flows and must be viewed along with other motives for direct investment.

Companies with foreign investments tend to
- **Be more profitable**
- **Have more stable sales and earnings**

Advantages after Direct Investment

In order to support the large-scale expenditures (such as spending for R&D) that are necessary to maintain domestic competitive viability, companies frequently must sell on a global basis. To do this, they often must establish direct investments abroad. The advantage accruing to more internationally oriented companies from spreading out some of the costs of product differentiation, R&D, and advertising is apparent in a comparison of their profitability with that of other companies. Among industry groups and groups of companies of similar size that spent comparable amounts on advertising and R&D and had similar capital intensity, the more internationally oriented companies in almost every case earned more than the other companies.[39]

Economies in various countries are in different stages of the business cycle at different times. Companies that operate in different economies can reduce fluctuations in year-to-year sales and earnings more than can those that operate only in a domestic environment.[40] Thus MNEs effectively reduce their operating risks.

Direct Investment Patterns

Although foreign direct investment began centuries ago, its biggest growth has occurred in recent years. During the 1980s, for example, world trade grew slightly faster than the world's gross product; however, flows of FDI grew at about three times the rate of world exports.[41] This growth resulted from several factors, particularly the more receptive attitude of governments to investment inflows, the process of privatization, and the growing interdependence of the world economy. By the early 1990s, the global stock of FDI had reached about $2 trillion and included about 170,000 investments by about 37,000 companies.[42]

Country of Origin

For worldwide FDI,
- Almost all ownership is by companies from industrial countries
- LDC ownership is increasing

The developed countries account for a little over 90 percent of all direct investment outflows. This is understandable, since more companies from those countries are likely to have the resources in the forms of capital, technology, and managerial skills that enable them to invest abroad. Nevertheless, considerable recent growth has occurred in direct investment from the developing countries; their share of global outflows grew from less than 2 percent in the 1970s and early 1980s to more than 5 percent in the late 1980s and early 1990s. Today, hundreds of LDC firms, primarily from the newly industrialized countries, have FDIs.[43]

During much of the post–World War II period, the United States was the dominant investor. However, its share has been falling as the share from other industrial countries, especially Japan, has increased. (See Table 8.1.) Recently, FDI has been flowing more rapidly into the United States than from the United States; at the beginning of 1993, the book value (based on the costs when the investments were made) of direct investment within the United States was about 86 percent of the book value of U.S.-owned direct investment abroad.[44] The largest investors in the

Table 8.1
Outward Flow of Foreign Direct Investment by Industrial Country (as percentage)
Note the decline in share for the United States and the gains for Japan and France.

Country	Period			
	1961–1970	1971–1980	1981–1988	1990–1991
United States	66.3%	44.4%	21.6%	15.9%
United Kingdom	10.5	18.2	21.4	10.0
Japan	2.0	6.0	16.7	21.2
Germany	5.8	7.7	8.5	15.0
France	3.7	4.6	7.2	15.6
Netherlands	3.8	9.2	6.6	7.0
Canada	2.1	3.7	5.2	1.0
Other*	5.8	6.2	12.8	14.3
Total	100.0%	100.0%	100.0%	100.0%

*Refers to other OECD (industrial) countries.

Source: OECD, *International Direct Investment and the New Economic Environment*, The Tokyo Round Table (Paris: OECD, 1989), p. 60; and *The Economist*, September 19, 1992, p. 17.

United States were the United Kingdom and Japan, accounting for about 26 and 21 percent, respectively, of FDI in the United States.

Location of Investment

Most FDI occurs in industrial countries because they have the
- **Biggest markets**
- **Lowest perceived risk**
- **Least discrimination toward foreign companies**

The major recipients of FDI are industrial countries, which received about 83 percent of the world's total from 1986 to 1990, about 74 percent in 1991, and about 68 percent in 1992.[45] The small share going to LDCs has caused concern about how they will meet their capital needs. This pattern parallels the outward flow of U.S.-owned direct investments, as shown in Fig. 8.3. At the beginning of 1993, about a quarter of such investments were in LDCs.

The interest in developed countries has resulted for three main reasons:

1. More investments have been market-seeking, and the developed countries have more income to spend.
2. Political turmoil in many LDCs has discouraged investors.
3. The industrial nations, through the OECD, are committed to liberalizing direct investment among their members, and they are parties to the Declaration on International Investment and Multinational Enterprises.[46]

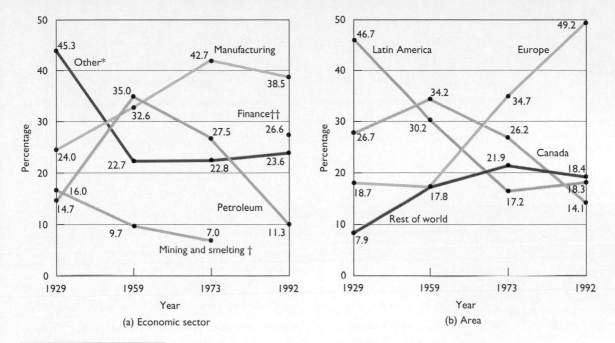

(a) Economic sector

(b) Area

**Figure 8.3
Changing Pattern of
U.S. Direct Investment
Abroad by Economic
Sector and Geographic
Area (as percentage of
value)**
The largest portion of U.S.
FDI is in manufacturing
and in Europe.

*Includes transportation, trade,
utilities, and other service
industries.
†Included in "Other" after 1973.
††Finance (except banking), insurance, and real estate included
in "Other" before 1992.

Source: Survey of Current Business,
various issues.

The highest recent growth
in FDI has been in services.

The OECD operates (with exceptions) under a principle that foreign-controlled
companies should be treated no less favorably than domestic ones in such areas as
taxes, access to local capital, and government procurement. The OECD member
countries also have agreed on procedures through which direct investors can resolve situations that may result from conflicting laws between their home and host
countries.

Economic Sector of Investment

Trends in the distribution of FDI generally conform to long-term economic
changes in the home and host countries. Over time, the portion of FDI accounted
for in the raw materials sector that includes mining, smelting, and petroleum has
declined. The portion in manufacturing, especially resource-based production,
grew steadily from the 1920s to the early 1970s but has since stabilized. In the
1980s, FDI in the service sector (especially banking and finance) grew rapidly, as
did FDI in technology-intensive manufacturing. By 1990, services accounted for
about 50 percent of the world stock of FDI, followed by manufacturing and the primary sector.[47] Figure 8.3 shows that the U.S. sectoral distribution historically is
similar to the global one.

COUNTERVAILING

FORCES

Direct investment is an integral means of carrying out either global or multidomestic practices. Market-seeking direct investments—those that take place because companies must produce within the markets they serve (because of high costs of transportation or trade restrictions)—generally favor multidomestic practices. Direct investments that are motivated by consumer or competitor moves are more likely to parallel global practices. Resource-seeking investments to bring about vertical integration or rationalized production usually entail global practices as well.

Direct investment, because of its implied control, permits companies to make decisions to maximize global performance. When they depend instead on licensing or foreign production contracts, the interests of their partner companies may constrain their ability to implement global practices.

Direct investments help to serve global efficiency by transferring resources to where they can be used more effectively; however, countries distort movements by restricting the inward or outward flow of direct investments and by giving incentives for companies to locate within their boundaries. Although these distortions are less important in motivating investments and their locations than political conditions and natural economic forces are, they are additional variables that managers must consider. To the extent that countries give preferential treatment to domestically headquartered or state-owned firms, the environment in which companies compete internationally is further complicated.

LOOKING TO THE FUTURE

In the near future, as in the recent past, FDI should continue to grow more rapidly than international trade or gross national products. The reasons for this growth should remain as described in this chapter. However, resource-seeking investments might grow more rapidly than market-seeking investments for two reasons: Trade restrictions on products continue to be reduced, making the use of least-cost production facilities more practical, and companies have more experience in manufacturing abroad and thus perceive less risk in integrating global production.

FDI in services also may continue to grow in relative importance for several reasons:

- The difficulty of removing protectionist barriers on service trade
- The need of service providers (such as investment bankers, advertising agencies, and insurance companies) to react quickly to the overseas needs of their clients
- The need of service companies to provide a full geographic range of activities to clients that are global

Western Europe, North America, and Japan should continue to be the major sources and recipients of FDI because of the wealth of the companies based there and the outlook for economic growth within those regions. The special trading relationship being developed in North America and in the EU should further stimulate this growth. The former communist nations should get much more attention now that regulatory changes permit some foreign ownership and as potential investors become more optimistic about risk and opportunities there. Among LDCs also, regulatory changes should be a factor. Such countries as Argentina, Brazil, and Mexico are privatizing many state companies and allowing levels of foreign investment that have until very recently been prohibited. These moves should stimulate those countries' receipt of FDI.

Summary

- Direct investment is the control of a company in one country by a company based in another country. Because control is difficult to define, some arbitrary minimum share of voting stock owned is used to define direct investment.

- Countries are concerned about who controls operations within their borders because they fear decisions will be made contrary to the national interest.

- Companies often prefer to control foreign production facilities because the transfer of certain assets to a noncontrolled entity might undermine their competitive position and they can realize economies of buying and selling with a controlled entity.

- Although a direct investment abroad generally is acquired by transferring capital from one country to another, capital usually is not the only contribution made by the investor or the only means of gaining equity. The investing company may supply technology, personnel, and markets in exchange for an interest in a foreign company.

- Production factors and finished goods are only partially mobile internationally. Moving either is one means of compensating for differences in factor endowments among countries. The cost and feasibility of transferring production factors rather than finished goods internationally will determine which alternative results in cheaper costs.

- Although FDI may be a substitute for trade, it also may stimulate trade through sales of components, equipment, and complementary products. Foreign direct investment may be undertaken to expand foreign markets or to gain access to supplies of resources or finished products. In addition, governments may encourage such investment for political purposes.

- The price of some products increases too much if they are transported internationally; therefore foreign production often is necessary to tap foreign markets.

- As long as companies have excess domestic capacity, they usually try to delay establishing foreign production.

- The extent to which scale economies lower production costs influences whether production is centralized in one or a few countries or dispersed among many countries.

- Because most FDIs are undertaken for the purpose of selling the output in the country in which the investments are located, governmental restrictions that prevent the effective importation of goods are a compelling force that cause companies to establish such investments.

- Consumers may feel compelled to buy domestically produced goods even though these products are more expensive. They also may demand that products be altered to fit their needs. Both of these considerations may dictate the need for a company to establish foreign operations to serve its foreign markets.

- FDI sometimes has chain effects: When one company makes an investment, some of its suppliers follow with investments of their own, followed by investments by their suppliers, and so on.

- Within oligopolistic industries, companies often invest in a foreign country at about the same time. This sometimes occurs because they are responding to similar market conditions and sometimes takes place because they wish to negate competitors' advantages in that market.

- Vertical integration is needed to control the flow of goods from basic production to final consumption in an increasingly interdependent and complex world distribution system. It may result in lower operating costs and enable companies to transfer funds among countries.

- Rationalized production involves producing different components or different products in different countries to take advantage of different factor costs.

- The least-cost production location may shift over time, especially in relation to stages of a product's life cycle. It also may change because of governmental incentives that effectively subsidize production.

- Countries may encourage domestically headquartered companies to invest abroad in order to gain advantages over other countries.

- There are advantages and disadvantages to FDI by either acquisition or start-up.

- Monopolistic advantages help to explain why companies are willing to take what they perceive to be higher risks of operating abroad. Certain countries

and currencies have had such advantages, which helps to explain the dominance of companies from certain countries at certain times.

- FDI may enable MNEs to spread certain fixed costs more than domestic companies can. It also may enable them to gain access to needed resources, to prevent competitors from gaining control of needed resources, and to smooth
sales and earnings on a year-to-year basis.

- Most FDI originates from and goes to developed countries. The fastest recent
growth of FDI has been in the service sector.

Case
Electrolux
Acquisitions[48]

The Swedish company Electrolux, the world's largest manufacturer of electrical household
appliances, once pioneered the marketing of vacuum cleaners. However, not all products
bearing the Electrolux name have been controlled by the Swedish firm. For example, Electrolux vacuum cleaners were independently manufactured and sold in the United States
from the 1960s until 1987. The company also manufactures Eureka vacuum cleaners.

Electrolux pursued its early international expansion largely to gain scale economies
through additional sales. Unlike competitors from larger countries, Electrolux had too
small a domestic market to absorb fixed costs. When additional sales were not possible
through exporting, Electrolux still was able to gain certain scale economies by establishing
foreign production. R&D expenditures and certain administrative costs thus could be
spread out over the additional sales made possible by foreign operations. Additionally,
Electrolux concentrated on standardized production to achieve further scale economies
and rationalized production of parts.

Until the late 1960s, Electrolux concentrated primarily on manufacturing vacuum cleaners and building its own facilities in order to effect expansion. Throughout the 1970s, however, it expanded largely by acquiring existing companies whose product lines differed from
its own. The compelling goal was to add appliance lines to complement those developed internally. Profits enabled the company to go on an acquisitions binge. It acquired two
Swedish companies that made home appliances and washing machines because its management felt that it could use its existing foreign-sales networks to increase the sales of those
companies. In 1973, it acquired another Swedish company, Facit, which already had extensive foreign sales and facilities. Electrolux also acquired vacuum-cleaner producers in the
United States and in France; then, to gain captive sales for vacuum cleaners, it bought commercial cleaning services in Sweden and the United States. The company went on to purchase a French kitchen-equipment producer (Arthur Martin), a Swiss home appliance
company (Therma), and a U.S. cooking-equipment manufacturer (Tappan).

Except for the Facit purchase, these acquisitions involved companies that had complementary lines that would enable the new parent to gain certain scale economies. However,
not all of the products of the acquired companies were related, and so Electrolux sought
to sell off unrelated businesses. In 1978, for example, Electrolux bought a diverse Swedish
firm, Husqvarna, because of its kitchen-equipment lines. Electrolux was able to sell Husq-

varna's motorcycle line but could not get a good price for the chain-saw line. Reconciled to being in the chain-saw business, Electrolux then acquired chain-saw manufacturers in Canada and Norway, thus becoming one of the world's largest chain-saw producers. The company made approximately fifty acquisitions during the 1970s.

In 1980, Electrolux announced a takeover different from those of the 1970s—the acquisition of Granges, Sweden's leading metal producer and fabricator. Granges was itself an MNE (1979 sales of $1.2 billion) with about 50 percent of its sales outside Sweden. The managing directors of the two companies indicated that the major advantage of the takeover would be the integration of Granges' aluminum, copper, plastics, and other materials into Electrolux's appliance production. Many analysts felt that the timing of Electrolux's bid was based on indications that Beijerinvest, a large Swedish conglomerate, wanted to acquire a nonferrous-metals mining company. Other observers thought Electrolux would have been better off continuing international horizontal expansion, as in the 1970s.

Since the Granges takeover, Electrolux has resumed its acquisition of appliance companies. It bought Italy's Zanussi to become Europe's top appliance maker with 23 percent of that market. In 1986, it acquired White Consolidated Industries, the U.S. manufacturer of such appliance brands as Frigidaire, White-Westinghouse, Kelvinator, and Gibson. This made Electrolux the largest appliance maker in the world; however, this lead was short-lived, as Whirlpool acquired a controlling interest in the appliance business of Philips, a Dutch giant. Whirlpool added its name (Philips/Whirlpool) to appliances sold in Europe through its acquired operations there. Its plan is to drop the Philips part of the brand name once European consumers have accepted the Whirlpool name. Electrolux countered Whirlpool's move by acquiring a 10-percent holding, with an option to buy another 10 percent, in the German appliance maker AEG.

Meanwhile, other producers were growing through consolidation as well. Maytag, for example, acquired such brands as Magic Chef, Admiral, and Norge and then combined European operations with Hoover. The Electrolux president, Anders Scharp, said that industry consolidation would not allow for much more growth through acquisition of household-appliance companies. Further Electrolux acquisitions would concentrate on outdoor products and commercial appliances. A key question is whether Electrolux can continue making so many acquisitions, because its profits as a percentage of sales have been declining. The company has had a penchant for buying poorly performing companies cheaply and then spending heavily to turn them around.

Electrolux and its competitors were becoming global appliance producers even though the appliance industry traditionally had been one in which companies sold little outside their home countries. Although the varying sizes of kitchens among countries has complicated international standardization of models, Electrolux is betting that life-styles in the industrialized nations will be increasingly similar. If the company is right, it could take advantage of economies of scale in technical breakthroughs and designs. However, Electrolux admitted its difficulty in streamlining operations. Within Europe alone, it has 40 different brands of refrigerators selling 120 basic designs with 1500 variants, and the company is adding models to hit specialty niches.

Questions

1. How do Electrolux's reasons for direct investment differ from Bridgestone's?
2. How has Electrolux's strategy changed over time? How have these changes affected its direct investment activities?
3. What are the main advantages and possible problems of expanding internationally primarily through acquisitions as opposed to building new facilities?
4. Should Electrolux have taken over Granges?
5. What will be the future global competitive environment in household appliances and how does that fit in with Electrolux's strategy?

Chapter Notes

1. Data for the case were taken from Edward Noga, "Bridgestone," *Automotive News*, April 20, 1981, p. E10; David Pauly, "Bridgestone Tire: Made in Japan," *Newsweek*, August 11, 1980, pp. 62–64; Mike Tharp, "Bridgestone, Japan's Tire Giant, Now Seeking International Role," *New York Times*, November 21, 1980, p. D4; "Japan: Why a Tiremaker Wants a U.S. Base," *Business Week*, January 14, 1980, p. 40; Bernard Krisher, "A Different Kind of Tiremaker Rolls into Nashville," *Fortune*, Vol. 105, No. 6, March 22, 1982, pp. 136–145; Zachary Schiller and James B. Treece, "Bridgestone May Try an End Run around the Yen," *Business Week*, February 2, 1987, p. 31; Jonathan P. Hicks, "A Global Fight in the Tire Industry," *New York Times*, March 10, 1988, p. 29; Jonathan P. Hicks, "Decreasing Demand and Global Competition Propel Consolidation," *New York Times*, February 11, 1990, p. F8; Zachary Schiller and Roger Schreffler, "So Far, America Is a Blowout for Bridgestone," *Business Week*, August 6, 1990, pp. 82–83; Zachary Schiller and Roger Schreffler, "Why Tiremakers Are Still Spinning Their Wheels," *Business Week*, February 26, 1990, pp. 62–63; "When the Bridge Caught Fire," *Economist*, September 7, 1991, pp. 72–73; Bridgestone advertisement in *Wall Street Journal*, October 1, 1992, p. A13; and "1991 Tire Industry Facts," *Modern Tire Dealer*, January 1992.
2. Some surveys of the considerable number of explanations may be found in Jean J. Boddewyn, "Foreign and Domestic Divestment and Investment Decisions," *Journal of International Business Studies*, Vol. XIV, No. 3, Winter 1983, pp. 23–35; A. L. Calvet, "A Synthesis of Foreign Direct Investment Theories and Theories of the Multinational Firm," *Journal of International Business Studies*, Spring–Summer 1981, pp. 43–60; John H. Dunning, "Toward an Eclectic Theory of International Production," *Journal of International Business Studies*, Spring–Summer 1980, pp. 9–31; Robert Grosse, "The Theory of Foreign Direct Investment," *Essays in International Business*, No. 3, December 1981, pp. 1–51; M. Z. Rahman, "Maximisation of Global Interests: Ultimate Motivation for Foreign Investments by Transnational Corporations," *Management International Review*, Vol. 23, No. 4, 1983, pp. 4–13; Alan M. Rugman, "New Theories of the Multinational Enterprise: An Assessment of Internalization Theory," *Bulletin of Economic Research*, Vol. 38, No. 2, 1986, pp. 101–118; and T. A. Corley, "Progress in Multinational Studies at Reading and Elsewhere, 1981–86" (Reading, England: University of Reading Department of Economics, Discussion Papers in International Investment and Business Studies, No. 120, 1989).
3. For a discussion of the effect of growth change on growth alternatives, see Briance Mascarenhas, "Strategic Group Dynamics," *Academy of Management Journal*, Vol. 32, No. 2, June 1989, pp. 333–352.
4. Krisher, op. cit., p. 141; and Roger Schreffler, "Bridgestone's New Rolling Thunderbolt," *Automotive Industries*, Vol. 165, No. 12, December 1985, p. 55.
5. Internalization theory, or holding a monopoly control over certain information or other proprietary assets, builds on earlier market-imperfections work by Ronald H. Coase, "The Nature of the Firm," *Economica*, Vol. 4, 1937, pp. 386–405. It has been applied by such writers as M. Casson, "The Theory of Foreign Direct Investment," Discussion Paper No. 50 (Reading, England: University of Reading International Investment and Business Studies, November 1980); and Stephen Magee, "Information and the MNC: An Appropriability Theory of Direct Foreign Investment," in *The New International Economic Order*, Jagdish N. Bhagwati, ed. (Cambridge, Mass.: MIT Press, 1977), pp. 317–340.
6. Alan M. Rugman, *Inside the Multinationals: The Economics of Internal Markets* (New York: Columbia University Press, 1981); and David J. Teece, "Transactions Cost Economics and the Multinational Enterprise," *Berkeley Business School International Business Working Paper Series*, No. IB–3, 1985.
7. Masaaki Kotabe, "Assessing the Shift in Global Market Share of U.S. Multinationals," *International Marketing Review*, Vol. 6, No. 5, 1989, pp. 20–35.
8. Stephen Baker, "A Free-for-All for Carmakers South of the Border," *Business Week*, October 16, 1989, p. 32.
9. Masaaki Kotabe and Glenn Omura, "Sourcing Strategies of European and Japanese Multinationals: A Comparison," *Journal of International Business Studies*, Spring 1989, pp. 113–133.
10. Yves Doz, "Managing Manufacturing Rationalization within Multinational Companies," *Columbia Journal of World Business*, Fall 1978.
11. Clyde Haberman, "Made in Japan: U.S. Cookie," *New York Times*, February 17, 1984, p. B6.
12. Lawrence Rout, "Mexico Limits U.S. Makers of Computers," *Wall Street Journal*, February 1, 1982, p. 31.
13. Stephen Baker, Kevin Kelly, Robert D. Hof, and William J. Holstein, "Mini-Nationals Are Making Maximum Impact," *Business Week*, September 6, 1993, pp. 66–69.
14. Studies that found import barriers to be an important enticement include Sanjaya Lall and N. S. Siddharthan, "The Monopolistic Advantages of Multinationals: Lessons from Foreign Investment in the U.S," *The Economic Journal*, Vol. 92, No. 367, September 1982, pp. 668–683; T. Horst, "Firm and Industry Determinants of the Decision to Invest Abroad," *Review of Economics and Statistics*, August 1972, pp. 258–266; John H. Dunning, *American Investment in British Manufacturing Industry* (London: Allen and Unwin, 1958); and D.

Orr, "The Determinants of Entry: A Study of the Canadian Manufacturing Industries," *Review of Economics and Statistics,* Vol. 57, 1975, pp. 58–66. Those not finding import barriers to be important include R. E. Caves, M. E. Porter, A. M. Spence, and J. T. Scott, *Competition in the Open Economy: A Model Applied to Canada* (Cambridge, Mass.: Harvard University Press, 1980); and B. Balassa, "Effects of Commercial Policy on International Trade, the Location of Production and Factor Movements," in *The International Allocation of Economic Activity,* Bertil Ohlin, ed. (New York: Holmes & Meier, 1977).

15. Jagdish N. Bhagwati, Elias Dinopoulos, and Kar-yiu Wong, "Quid Pro Quo Foreign Investment," *American Economic Review,* May 1992, pp. 186–190.

16. Diana Solis, "Mexico's Garment Industry Is Pivotal to Plans to Boost Economy Via Exports," *Wall Street Journal,* January 19, 1993, p. A8; and James P. Miller, "Zenith Is Shifting Taiwan Jobs to Mexico, Signaling Trend in Other Manufacturers," *Wall Street Journal,* November 12, 1991, p. A4.

17. Kenneth Dreyfack, "Draping Old Glory Around Just about Everything," *Business Week,* October 27, 1986, pp. 66–67; Sherri McLain and Brenda Sternquist, "Ethnocentric Consumers: Do They 'Buy American'?" *Journal of International Consumer Marketing,* Vol. 4, Nos. 1/2, 1992, pp. 39–58.

18. "Toshiba Plans to Build Color-TV Plant in U.S.," *Wall Street Journal,* April 5, 1977, p. 43, and "Mitsubishi U.S. Unit to Assemble TV Sets in Irvine, California, Plant," *Wall Street Journal,* April 14, 1977, p. 7, show two examples of responses to nationalistic advertisements by Zenith.

19. Philippe Cattin, Alain Jolibert, and Coleen Lohnes, "A Cross-Cultural Study of 'Made in' Concepts," *Journal of International Business Studies,* Vol. XIII, No. 3, Winter 1982, pp. 131–141; Robert D. Schooler, "Bias Phenomena Attendant to the Marketing of Foreign Goods in the U.S.," *Journal of International Business Studies,* Spring 1971, pp. 71–80; and A. Nagashima, "A Comparison of Japanese and U.S. Attitudes toward Foreign Products," *Journal of Marketing,* January 1970, pp. 68–74.

20. Steven P. Galante, "Japanese Have Another Trade Barrier: Limiting Business to Compatriot Firms," *Wall Street Journal,* April 12, 1984, p. 36.

21. Edward B. Flowers, "Oligopolistic Reactions in European and Canadian Direct Investment in the United States," *Journal of International Business Studies,* Fall–Winter 1976, pp. 43–55; Frederick Knickerbocker, *Oligopolistic Reaction and Multinational Enterprise* (Cambridge, Mass.: Harvard University, Graduate School of Business, Division of Research, 1973). For

opposing findings, see Lall and Siddharthan, loc. cit.

22. E. M. Graham, "Exchange of Threat Between Multinational Firms as an Infinitely Repeated Noncooperative Game," *The International Trade Journal,* Vol. IV, No. 3, pp. 259–277.

23. Bob Davis, "Illusory Bargain," *Wall Street Journal,* September 15, 1993, p. A1+.

24. K. Kojima, *Direct Foreign Investment: A Japanese Model of Multinational Business Operations* (London: Croom Helm, 1978).

25. Stephen Baker, David Woodruff, and Bill Javetski, "Along the Border, Free Trade Is Becoming a Fact of Life," *Business Week,* June 18, 1990, pp. 41–42; and Lisa R. Van Wagner, "Putting Together the Pieces," *Export Today,* April 1992, pp. 10–11.

26. Sarkis Khoury, David Nickerson, and Venkatraman Sadanad, "Exchange Rate Uncertainty and Precommitment in Symmetric Duopoly: A New Theory of Multinational Production," *Recent Developments in International Banking and Finance,* Vols. IV and V, 1991; Jan Karl Karlsen and Michael H. Moffett, "On the Appropriateness of Economic or Strategic Exposure Management," Danish Summer Research Institute Paper, Copenhagen Business School, Copenhagen, Denmark, 1992; and "Who's Afraid of the Big, Bad Yen? Not Japanese Exporters," *Business Week,* October 12, 1992, pp. 49–50.

27. Raymond Vernon, "International Investment and International Trade in the Product Cycle," *Quarterly Journal of Economics,* May 1966, pp. 191–207.

28. Robert Weigand, "International Investments: Weighing the Incentives," *Harvard Business Review,* Vol. 61, No. 4, July–August 1983, pp. 146–152; and Krystal Miller, "BMW to Build Factory in U.S., Employ 2000," *Wall Street Journal,* June 23, 1992, p. A2.

29. Among the many treatises on this subject is Carlos F. Diaz Alejandro, "International Markets for Exhaustible Resources, Less Developed Countries and Transnational Corporations," in *Economic Issues of Multinational Firms,* Robert G. Hawkins, ed. (New York: JAI Press, 1977).

30. M. Y. Yoshino, *Japan's Multinational Enterprises* (Cambridge, Mass.: Harvard University Press, 1976), pp. 53–57.

31. Terutomio Ozawa, "Japan's Resource Dependency and Overseas Investment," *Journal of World Trade Law,* January–February 1977, pp. 52–73.

32. For a good discussion of differences in European government-owned enterprises, see Renato Mazzolini, *Government Controlled Enterprises* (New York: Wiley, 1979).

33. Joann S. Lublin, "Japanese Increasingly View Takeovers as Faster, Cheaper Way

to Enter Europe," *Wall Street Journal,* July 21, 1989, p. A12.

34. Erle Norton, "Last of the U.S. Tire Makers Ride Out Foreign Invasion," *Wall Street Journal,* February 4, 1993, p. B4; and Emily Thornton, "How Japan Got Burned In the USA," *Fortune,* June 15, 1992, pp. 114–116.

35. Mascarenhas, loc. cit.; Yui Kimura, "Firm-Specific Strategic Advantages and Foreign Direct Investment Behavior of Firms: The Case of Japanese Semiconductor Firms" (Niigata, Japan: International Management Research Institute, International University of Japan, 1988).

36. Stephen H. Hymer, *A Study of Direct Foreign Investment* (Cambridge, Mass.: MIT Press, 1976); Alan M. Rugman, "Internationalization as a General Theory of Foreign Direct Investment: A Re-Appraisal of the Literature," *Weltwirtschaftliches Archiv,* Band 116, Heft 2, 1980, pp. 365–379; and Yojin Jung, "Multinationality and Profitability," *Journal of Business Research,* Vol. 23, 1991, pp. 179–187.

37. Robert Z. Aliber, "A Theory of Direct Foreign Investment," in *The International Corporation,* Charles P. Kindleberger, ed. (Cambridge, Mass.: MIT Press, 1970), pp. 28–33; and Robert Johnson, "Distance Deals," *Wall Street Journal,* February 24, 1988, p. 1.

38. Louis Uchitelle, "Overseas Spending by U.S. Companies Sets Record Pace," *New York Times,* May 20, 1988, p. 1+; and "Investing Abroad Is Paying Off Big for U.S. Companies," *Business Week,* November 6, 1989, p. 34.

39. John D. Daniels and Jeffrey Bracker, "Profit Performance: Do Foreign Operations Make a Difference?" *Management International Review,* Vol. 29, No. 1, 1989, pp. 46–56.

40. Joseph C. Miller and Bernard Pras, "The Effects of Multinational and Export Diversification on the Profit Stability of U.S. Corporations," *Southern Economic Journal,* Vol. 46, No. 3, 1980, pp. 792–802; Alan M. Rugman, "Foreign Operations and the Stability of U.S. Corporate Earnings: Risk Reduction by International Diversification" (Vancouver: Simon Fraser University, 1974); and A. Servern, "Investor Evaluation of Foreign and Domestic Risk," *Journal of Finance,* May 1974, pp. 545–550.

41. United Nations Centre on Transnational Corporations, *World Investment Report 1991: The Triad in Foreign Direct Investment* (New York: United Nations, August 1991), p. 4.

42. United Nations Conference on Trade and Development, *World Investment Report 1993: An Executive Summary* (New York: United Nations, 1993), pp. 1–4.

43. Ibid.; and R. Van Hoesel, "Multinational Enterprises from Developing Countries

with Investments in Developed Economies: Some Theoretical Considerations," University of Antwerp Centre for International Management and Development, Discussion Paper #1992/E16.

44. Russell B. Scholl, Jeffrey H. Lowe, and Sylvia E. Bargas, "The International Investment Position of the United States in 1992," *Survey of Current Business,* June 1993, pp. 42–54.

45. United Nations Conference on Trade and Development, op. cit., p. 8.

46. Enery Quinones Lellouche, "How OECD Governments Co-Operate on Investment Issues," *OECD Observer,* June/July 1992, p. 10; and Marie-France Houde, "Foreign Direct Investment," *OECD Observer,* June/July 1992, pp. 9–13.

47. Ibid., p. 15.

48. Background data for this case may be found in "Why Electrolux Wants a Materials Supplier," *Business Week,* February 18, 1980, pp. 78–79; Alan L. Otten, "Electrolux, a Big Success in Appliances, Is Helped by Decentralized Operations," *Wall Street Journal,* June 4, 1980, p. 16; "Electrolux to Proceed with Granges Offer, Providing Sweden Acts," *Wall Street Journal,* June 18, 1980, p. 29; Sharon Tully, "Electrolux Wants a Clean Sweep," *Fortune,* Vol. 114, No. 4, August 18, 1986, pp. 60–62; "On a Verge of a World War in White Goods," *Business Week,* November 2, 1987, pp. 91–94; "Electrolux Shifts the Focus of Its Acquisition Program," *Wall Street Journal,* March 22, 1988, p. 27; James P. Miller, "Whirlpool Plans Brand Recognition Effort in Europe," *Wall Street Journal,* January 1, 1990, p. A12; "Have Europe's Top Acquirers Added Shareholder Value?" *Mergers & Acquisitions,* March–April 1989, pp. 60–68; William Echikson, "Electrolux, in Bid for European Unity, Seeks Common Refrigerator for Continent," *Wall Street Journal,* August 21, 1990, p. C13; Christopher Lorenz, "The Birth of a 'Transnational,'" *The McKinsey Quarterly,* Autumn 1989, pp. 72–93; Norman C. Remich, Jr., "State-of-the-Industry in Europe," *Appliance Manufacturer,* April 1991, pp. 60–62; and Stephen D. Moore, "Electrolux, Daimler-Benz's AEG Reach Pact on Appliance Lines," *Wall Street Journal,* June 24, 1992, p. A14.

PART 4

World Financial Environment

North America has become a major global supplier of services, such as management, marketing, and financial services. Here you see traders at a stock exchange in the United States, which accounts for about 43 percent of the world's stock market capitalization. The photo is set against a background showing part of a mid–19th century American quilt in the variable star pattern.

Chapter 9

Foreign Exchange

*All things are
obedient to money.*
—English Proverb

Objectives

- To discuss the terms and definitions of foreign exchange

- To describe how the foreign-exchange market works for immediate and long-term transactions

- To explain the role of convertibility in foreign-exchange transactions

- To illustrate how countries control foreign exchange through licensing, multiple rates, import deposit requirements, and quantity controls

- To describe how the foreign-exchange market is used in commercial and financial transactions

Now we were really flush with francs, and I had a sudden insight into the truth of monetarism. The idea is that individual behavior is significantly governed by the possession of a certain kind of asset, called "money." Here I was with dollar currency, traveler's checks, credit cards, and checks on an account in an internationally known bank. With a call to my broker, I could get a telegraphic transfer of a large amount of money from a money-market fund. Compared to my total liquid assets, the amounts of French currency I ever held were minute. But the difference between feeling that I had little French currency and feeling that I had much was significant. When I felt that I had little, I tried to hold onto it, fearing to find myself in a place or time when it would be indispensable to me. When I felt that I had much, I was quite prepared to get rid of it, lest I have it "left over" at some point, or have to trade it in at a great loss. I had demonstrated that money matters. How much it matters I leave to econometrics.

Dishes or Riches?

Feeling flush with francs, we presented ourselves on the day before we were to leave Paris at a very expensive restaurant for lunch. As soon as I looked at the menu, my franc anxiety returned. I had never seen such prices. I began a hasty and not reassuring estimate of how many francs were in my wallet and my wife's pocketbook. There was nothing on the menu to indicate that credit cards were accepted. I couldn't see any money passing at other tables or even anyone signing checks. Presumably the waiter knew without being told whose lunch was to be charged to the duc de Guermantes. But he would know that I wasn't the *duc* of anything. For one thing, I had had to borrow a coat and tie from the checkroom to get admitted in the first place. I wondered how many hours of dishwashing it would take to work off 500 francs. When the check came I inquired, appearing as confident as I could, whether they took credit cards. The answer was affirmative, and I was rich again.

That left us with an unexpectedly large amount of francs. Even after some splurging, I had some to turn in at the bank at the airport, where I sold at 5.77 to the dollar francs that I had bought at an average price of 4.9787. I was glad to get rid of them. Now I could stop thinking about centimes and resume thinking about trillions of dollars in the budget or the GNP.

Introduction

To be effective, both MNEs and small import and export companies must understand exchange rates. The exchange rate can influence where a wholesaler or a retailer buys and sells products. It also can influence where a manufacturer acquires raw materials or components and produces products. Further, it can affect the location of capital that a company needs in order to expand. For example, in 1993 and 1994, the Japanese yen was so strong against the U.S. dollar that sales of Japanese automobiles fell significantly in comparison with those of U.S. automobiles. This occurred because the importers had to convert too many dollars into the stronger yen to pay for the imports. As the importers passed on the higher cost to the consumers, their sales began to drop. Thus many Japanese automakers shifted more of their production to the United States so that they could escape the problem of the rising yen.

For most of us on a personal level, the experiences Herbert Stein relates in the opening case ring true. However, the exchange of money has become easier in many countries since 1990, as the following demonstrates:

> Say I'm in Paris, it's late evening, and I need money [as the Steins did]. The bank I go to is closed, of course, but outside sits an ATM, an automated teller machine—and look what can be made to happen, thanks to computers and high-speed telecommunications. I insert my ATM card from my bank in Washington, D.C., and punch in my identification number and the amount of 1500 francs, roughly equivalent to $300. The French bank's computers detect that it's not their card, so my request goes to the CIRRUS system's inter-European switching center in Belgium, which detects that it's not a European card. The electronic message is then transmitted to the global switching center in Detroit, which recognizes that it's from my bank in Washington. The request goes there, and my bank verifies that there's more than $300 in my account and deducts $300 plus a fee of $1.50. Then it's back to Detroit, to Belgium, and to the Paris bank and its ATM—and out comes $300 in French francs. Total elapsed time: 16 seconds.[2]

Like this traveler, most students who study abroad quickly learn the value of the ATM.

In a business setting, there is a fundamental difference between making payment in the domestic market and making payment abroad. In a domestic transaction, only one currency is used; in a foreign transaction, two or more currencies may be used. For example, a U.S. company that exports $100,000 worth of skis to a French distributor will ask the French buyer to remit payment in dollars, unless the U.S. company has some specific use for French francs—say that it imports parts from France and can use the francs to pay the French exporter.

Assume you are a U.S. importer who has agreed to purchase a certain quantity of French perfume and to pay the French exporter 20,000 francs for it. How would you go about paying? First, you would go to the international department of your local bank to buy 20,000 francs at the going market rate. Let's assume the franc/dollar exchange rate is 5.8855 francs per dollar. Your bank then would debit your demand deposit account by $3398.18 plus transaction costs and give you a special check payable in francs made out to the exporter. The exporter would deposit it in a Paris bank, which then would credit the exporter's account with 20,000 francs. The transaction would be complete.

Foreign exchange includes currencies and other instruments of payment denominated in currencies.

The special checks and other instruments for making payments abroad are referred to collectively as **foreign exchange.** It is sometimes difficult to understand and relate to different currencies as you saw in the opening case. A complete understanding of foreign exchange includes knowing the global and national context in which exchange rates are set and how foreign exchange is used in international transactions. This chapter discusses foreign exchange, the nature of risk, and the risk aversion strategies adopted by companies involved in international business. The first step in comprehending foreign exchange is understanding certain key markets and the definitions of basic terms as they apply to those markets.

Terms and Definitions

An exchange rate is the number of units of one currency needed to acquire one unit of another currency.

An **exchange rate** is the number of units of one currency that must be given to acquire one unit of another currency. For example, on January 27, 1994, it took $0.16991 to purchase one French franc. The exchange rate, then, is the link between different national currencies that makes international price and cost comparisons possible.

The spot rate is the exchange rate quoted for transactions that require either immediate delivery or delivery within two days.

The interbank market is the foreign-exchange market among commercial banks.

The forward rate is the rate quoted for transactions that call for delivery after two business days.

The **spot rate** is the rate quoted for current foreign-currency transactions. It applies to interbank transactions that require delivery of the purchased currency within two business days in exchange for immediate cash payment for that currency. This exchange process is called **settlement. Interbank transactions** are exchanges between commercial banks that collectively make up the **interbank market,** which is the market for trades that take place between such banks. The spot rate also applies to over-the-counter (OTC) transactions, which usually involve nonbank customers and require same-day settlement. The **forward rate** is a contractual rate between a foreign-exchange trader and the trader's client for delivery of foreign currency sometime in the future, after at least two business days but usually after at least one month.

The Spot Market

Most foreign-currency transactions take place between foreign-exchange traders, so the rates are quoted by the traders, who work for foreign-exchange brokerage houses or commercial banks. This is one of the confusions identified in the opening case. The rates are quoted by traders, not the buying or selling party. The traders always quote a bid (buy) and offer (sell) rate. The bid is the price at which the trader is willing to buy foreign currency, and the offer is the price at which the trader is willing to sell foreign currency. In the spot market, the **spread** is the difference between the bid and offer rates and is the margin on which the trader earns a profit on the transaction. Thus the rate quoted by a trader for the British pound might be $1.5067/77. This means the trader is willing to buy pounds at $1.5067 each and sell them for $1.5077. Obviously, a trader wants to buy low and sell high.

The spread in the spot market is the difference between the bid (buy) and offer (sell) rate quoted by the foreign-exchange trader.

A direct quote is the number of units of the domestic currency needed to acquire one unit of the foreign currency.

An indirect quote is the number of units of the foreign currency needed to acquire one unit of the domestic currency.

In this example, the foreign currency is quoted by the trader at the number of U.S. dollars for one unit of that currency. This method of quoting exchange rates is called in the United States the **direct quote,** or **normal quote.** A rate quoted in terms of the number of units of the foreign currency for one unit of the domestic currency is called the **reciprocal quote,** or **indirect quote,** because it is the inverse of the direct quote. For example,

$$\frac{£1}{\$1.5077} = 0.6633 \text{ British pounds (£) per U.S. dollar (\$)}$$

The direct quote is often called U.S. terms.

In the United States, the direct quote is commonly used for domestic business. This practice often is referred to as **U.S. terms** (or the **American system**). For interna-

The indirect quote is often called European terms.

tional business, banks often use the indirect quote. This practice is called **European terms** (or **Continental terms**). The U.S. dollar customarily is used as the base currency for international transactions; the other currency in the transaction is the quoted currency. The base currency is in the denominator in the quote; the quoted currency is in the numerator. The quote is given as the number of units of the quoted currency for one unit of the base currency.

Most large newspapers, especially those devoted to business or those having business sections, quote exchange rates daily. For example, the *Wall Street Journal* provided the direct and indirect quotes given in Table 9.1. The spot rates shown are the selling rates for interbank transactions of $1 million and more. In addition to the spot rates for each currency, the forward rates are provided for the British pound, Canadian dollar, French franc, German mark, Japanese yen, and Swiss franc.

The cross rate is an exchange rate computed from two other exchange rates.

A final important definition that applies to the spot market is the **cross rate.** This rate is computed from two other exchange rates. Because most foreign-currency transactions are denominated in terms of U.S. dollars, it is common to see two nondollar currencies related to each other by a cross rate. As an example, let's use the indirect quotes for the Swiss franc and German mark and figure the cross rate with the franc as the quoted currency and the mark as the base currency. In Table 9.1, the spot rates for these currencies are 1.4598 francs per U.S. dollar and 1.7305 marks per U.S. dollar. The cross rate is calculated as follows:

$$\frac{1.4598 \text{ francs}}{1.7305 \text{ marks}} = 0.8436 \text{ francs per mark}$$

This means 1 mark equals 0.8436 francs. This cross rate commonly would be quoted as 84.36.

The *Wall Street Journal* publishes a cross-rate table along with the dollar-exchange rates. Table 9.2 identifies the cross rates for several key currencies. In the rows are the direct quotes for each currency. For example, starting in the Swiss franc row and going across it to the German mark column, we find that the cross rate is 0.84487 francs per mark, which is the direct quote for Swiss francs (the number of francs for one unit of the foreign currency). In the columns are the indirect quotes for each currency. Using the same example, 0.84487 francs per mark is the indirect quote in terms of German marks (the number of units of the foreign currency for one mark). (The cross rate of 0.84487 francs per mark is slightly different from the cross rate computed above because different sources are used to compute the exchange rates.)

German and Swiss managers keep track of the cross rate because they trade extensively with each other and any material shifts in the cross rate could signal a change in the prices of goods. For example, assume a German exporter sold a product worth 100 marks to a Swiss importer for 84.49 francs. If the cross rate were to change to 0.900 francs per mark, the German exporter and the Swiss importer would have to make some interesting decisions. If the exporter kept the price to the importer at 100 marks, the importer would have to come up with 90

Table 9.1
Exchange Rates, Thursday, January 27, 1994[*]

	U.S. $ equiv.		Currency per U.S. $	
Country	Thurs.	Wed.	Thurs.	Wed.
Argentina (peso)	1.01	1.01	.99	.99
Australia (dollar)	.7090	.7084	1.4104	1.4116
Austria (schilling)	.08220	.08155	12.17	12.26
Bahrain (dinar)	2.6518	2.6518	.3771	.3771
Belgium (franc)	.02800	.02769	35.71	36.11
Brazil (cruzeiro real)	.0022599	.0023175	442.50	431.50
Britain (pound)	1.5077	1.4950	.6633	.6689
30-day forward	1.5050	1.4919	.6645	.6703
90-day forward	1.4997	1.4868	.6668	.6726
180-day forward	1.4934	1.4807	.6696	.6754
Canada (dollar)	.7609	.7612	1.3143	1.3138
30-day forward	.7605	.7607	1.3150	1.3145
90-day forward	.7599	.7602	1.3159	1.3155
180-day forward	.7594	.7596	1.3169	1.3165
Czech. Rep. (koruna)				
Commercial rate	.0331741	.0330841	30.1440	30.2260
Chile (peso)	.002382	.002382	419.80	419.80
China (renminbi)	.114873	.114873	8.7053	8.7053
Colombia (peso)	.001226	.001226	815.65	815.65
Denmark (krone)	.1487	.1475	6.7256	6.7783
Ecuador (sucre)				
Floating rate	.000489	.000489	2044.03	2044.03
Finland (markka)	.18002	.17835	5.5549	5.6068
France (franc)	.16991	.16876	5.8855	5.9255
30-day forward	.16945	.16827	5.9015	5.9429
90-day forward	.16861	.16748	5.9307	5.9710
180-day forward	.16766	.16655	5.9645	6.0042
Germany (mark)	.5779	.5732	1.7305	1.7445
30-day forward	.5764	.5717	1.7348	1.7492
90-day forward	.5740	.5693	1.7422	1.7564
180-day forward	.5713	.5666	1.7504	1.7648
Greece (drachma)	.004023	.003994	248.55	250.35
Hong Kong (dollar)	.12946	.12948	7.7243	7.7230
Hungary (forint)	.0098030	.0097943	102.0100	102.1000
India (rupee)	.03212	.03212	31.13	31.13
Indonesia (rupiah)	.0004725	.0004725	2116.54	2116.54
Ireland (punt)	1.4490	1.4379	.6901	.6955
Israel (shekel)	.3350	.3350	2.9850	2.9850
Italy (lira)	.0005912	.0005887	1691.59	1698.54
Japan (yen)	.009204	.009095	108.65	109.95
30-day forward	.009210	.009101	108.58	109.87
90-day forward	.009227	.009119	108.37	109.66
180-day forward	.009262	.009155	107.97	109.23
Jordan (dinar)	1.4453	1.4453	.6919	.6919
Kuwait (dinar)	3.3504	3.3504	.2985	.2985
Lebanon (pound)	.000586	.000586	1707.00	1707.00
Malaysia (ringgit)	.3629	.3636	2.7555	2.7500
Malta (lira)	2.5284	2.5284	.3955	.3955
Mexico (peso)				
Floating rate	.3221649	.3221649	3.1040	3.1040
Netherland (guilder)	.5157	.5118	1.9389	1.9540
New Zealand (dollar)	.5684	.5684	1.7593	1.7593
Norway (krone)	.1344	.1333	7.4429	7.5007
Pakistan (rupee)	.0332	.0332	30.09	30.09
Peru (new sol)	.4781	.4781	2.09	2.09
Philippines (peso)	.03656	.03656	27.35	27.35
Poland (zloty)	.00004599	.00004595	21746.00	21761.00

Table 9.1 (*cont.*)

Country	U.S. $ equiv.		Currency per U.S. $	
	Thurs.	Wed.	Thurs.	Wed.
Portugal (escudo)	.005755	.005710	173.76	175.13
Saudi Arabia (riyal)	.26669	.26669	3.7497	3.7497
Singapore (dollar)	.6259	.6258	1.5978	1.5980
Slovak Rep. (koruna)	.0299581	.0298686	33.3800	33.4800
South Africa (rand)				
Commercial rate	.2925	.2926	3.4193	3.4173
Financial rate	.2273	.2270	4.4000	4.4050
South Korea (won)	.0012366	.0012353	808.70	809.50
Spain (peseta)	.007161	.007073	139.65	141.39
Sweden (krona)	.1264	.1257	7.9084	7.9584
Switzerland (franc)	.6850	.6805	1.4598	1.4695
30-day forward	.6844	.6798	1.4612	1.4710
90-day forward	.6835	.6791	1.4631	1.4726
180-day forward	.6832	.6786	1.4638	1.4736
Taiwan (dollar)	.037771	.037771	26.48	26.48
Thailand (baht)	.03915	.03915	25.54	25.54
Turkey (lira)	z.0000587	.0000659	z17025.04	15170.63
United Arab (dirham)	.2723	.2723	3.6725	3.6725
Uruguay (new peso)				
Financial	.223713	.223713	4.47	4.47
Venezuela (bolivar)				
Floating rate	.00939	.00939	106.50	106.50
SDR	1.37817	1.37528	.72560	.72712
ECU	1.12270	1.11400	—	—

*The New York foreign exchange selling rates apply to trading among banks in amounts of $1 million and more, as quoted at 3 p.m. Eastern time by Bankers Trust Co., Telerate and other sources. Retail transactions provide fewer units of foreign currency per dollar.

Special Drawing Rights (SDR) are based on exchange rates for the U.S., German, British, French and Japanese currencies. Source: International Monetary Fund.

European Currency Unit (ECU) is based on a basket of community currencies.

z—currency devalued.

Source: From *The Wall Street Journal,* 1/28/94, p. C10. Reprinted by permission of *The Wall Street Journal,* © 1994 Dow Jones & Company Inc. All Rights Reserved Worldwide.

francs to buy the product. On the other hand, the exporter could lower the price to 93.88 marks so that the product would still cost the importer 84.49 francs. Further, if the exporter decided to keep the price at 100 marks, the importer would have two options:

1. Increase the price to reflect the higher cost of the product and thus keep the profit margin the same as before
2. Keep the price the same and end up with a smaller profit margin due to the higher cost of the product

If the product were especially price-sensitive, neither the exporter nor the importer would want to see the price rise in Switzerland.

Table 9.2
Key Currency Cross Rates, Late New York Trading, January 27, 1994

	Dollar	Pound	SFranc	Guilder	Peso	Yen	Lira	D-Mark	FFranc	CdnDlr
Canada	1.3158	1.9855	.90049	.67877	.42390	.01212	.00078	.76080	.22354	—
France	5.8863	8.882	4.0284	3.0365	1.89636	.05423	.00348	3.4035	—	4.4736
Germany	1.7295	2.6098	1.1836	.89218	.55718	.01593	.00102	—	.29382	1.3144
Italy	1690.0	2550.1	1156.55	871.78	544.44	15.568	—	977.13	287.10	1284.4
Japan	108.55	163.80	74.288	55.997	34.971	—	.06423	62.764	18.441	82.50
Mexico	3.1040	4.6839	2.1243	1.6012	—	.02860	.00184	1.7947	.5273	2.3590
Netherlands	1.9385	2.9252	1.3266	—	.62452	.01786	.00115	1.1208	.32932	1.4732
Switzerland	1.4612	2.2050	—	.75378	.47075	.01346	.00086	.84487	.24824	1.1105
U.K.	.66269	—	.45352	.34186	.21350	.00610	.00039	.38317	.11258	.50364
U.S.	—	1.5090	.68437	.51586	.32216	.00921	.00059	.57820	.16989	.75999

Source: From *The Wall Street Journal*, 1/28/94, p. C10. Reprinted by permission of *The Wall Street Journal*, © 1994 Dow Jones & Company, Inc. All Rights Reserved Worldwide.

The Forward Market

The spot market is for foreign-exchange transactions within two business days. However, some transactions may be entered into on one day but not completed until after two business days. For example, a French exporter of perfume might sell perfume to a U.S. importer with immediate delivery but payment not required for thirty days. The U.S. importer is obligated to pay in francs in thirty days and may enter into a contract with a trader to deliver francs in thirty days at a forward rate, the rate today for future delivery.

> **A discount exists when the forward rate is less than the spot rate.**
>
> **A premium exists when the forward rate exceeds the spot rate.**

Thus the forward rate is the rate quoted by foreign-exchange traders for the purchase or sale of foreign exchange in the future. The difference between the spot and forward rates is known as either the **forward discount** or the **forward premium** on the contract. If the domestic currency is quoted on a direct basis and the forward rate is less than the spot rate, the foreign currency is selling at a discount. If the forward rate is greater than the spot rate, the foreign currency is selling at a premium.

As an example, let's compute the spread, or the difference between the spot and forward rates for ninety-day contracts, for Canadian dollars and Japanese yen. Direct quotes for these currencies and the resulting points for each are given in Table 9.3. The spread in Canadian dollars is 10 points; because the forward rate is less than the spot rate, the Canadian dollar is at a discount in the ninety-day forward market.

Table 9.3
Hypothetical Direct Quotes for Canadian Dollars and Japanese Yen

Rate	Canadian dollars	Japanese yen
Spot	0.7609	0.009204
Forward (90-day)	0.7599	0.009227
Points	−10	+23

The spread in Japanese yen is 23 points; because the forward rate is greater than the spot rate, the yen is at a premium in the ninety-day forward market.

The discount or premium also can be quoted in terms of an annualized percentage using the following formula:

$$\text{Premium (discount)} = \frac{F_0 - S_0}{S_0} \times \frac{12}{N} \times 100$$

where

F_0 = the forward rate on the day the contract is entered into
S_0 = the spot rate on that day
N = the number of months forward
100 is used to convert the decimal figure to a percentage (for example,
 $0.05 \times 100 = 5\%$)

Using Canadian dollars in the formula yields

$$\text{Discount} = \frac{0.7599 - 0.7609}{0.7609} \times \frac{12}{3} \times 100 = -0.5257$$

That is, the Canadian dollar is selling at a discount of 0.5257 percent under the spot rate.

Forward markets do not exist for all currencies in all countries. For example, as Table 9.1 indicates, there is no forward market in the United States for the Brazilian cruzeiro real. This is because a forward contract in cruzeiros generally is not available in the interbank market. Given Brazil's high inflation rate, there is an excess supply of cruzeiros; thus it would be practically impossible for the interbank market to balance purchases of cruzeiro contracts with sales of cruzeiro contracts. The interbank market is too thin (that is, it does not have enough transactions) to warrant forward contracts. When this is the case, buyers and sellers must account for potential foreign-currency risk in some other way, such as by adjusting the selling price.

How the Foreign-Exchange Market Works

Basic Spot and Forward Markets

Brokers are specialists who facilitate transactions in the interbank market.

Having defined the various exchange rates and explained how they are quoted, we can examine how foreign currencies are traded. Most foreign-exchange transactions are conducted by commercial banks. Significant trades take place between foreign-exchange brokers, specialists who facilitate interbank transactions. In addition, investment banks such as Goldman Sachs and Morgan Stanley are heavily involved in foreign-currency trading.

Figure 9.1
Average Daily Volume in World and U.S. Foreign-Exchange Markets, 1989 and 1992
The average daily volume of foreign-exchange transactions was $880 billion worldwide in April 1992. Estimates in 1993 pushed that volume to over $1 trillion.

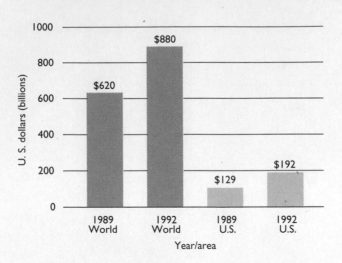

A swap is an exchange of currencies in the spot market accompanied by an agreement to reverse the transaction in the future.

An option is the right but not the obligation to trade a foreign currency at a specific exchange rate.

The foreign-exchange market is massive (see Fig. 9.1). For example, worldwide foreign-exchange trading in April 1992 was nearly $900 billion daily. It was estimated that by the end of the year, this volume had risen to $1 trillion daily.[3]

Of total worldwide volume, 48 percent is conducted in the spot market, primarily the interbank market (see Fig. 9.2). The next-largest category is the swap market. A **swap** is a simultaneous spot and forward transaction. For example, a U.S. company might need British pounds for thirty days; it enters into a spot contract to exchange dollars for pounds and enters into a simultaneous forward contract to exchange the pounds for dollars in thirty days when the pounds are no longer needed. The forward contract of this swap transaction enables the company to know exactly how many dollars it will receive for the pounds in thirty days rather than waiting to convert at the spot rate in thirty days. The forward contract thus eliminates the foreign-exchange risk.

The other major foreign-exchange transactions are outright forwards, options, and futures contracts. All nonspot foreign-exchange instruments are collectively called **derivatives.** The **outright forward** is a forward contract that is not connected to a spot transaction. For example, an MNE might be receiving British pounds in ninety days and thus may enter into a forward contract to trade pounds for dollars in ninety days. The advantage of the outright forward is that it sets the amount of dollars that will be paid or received and establishes the cost up-front. The size of the contract is relatively flexible, and there is no brokerage cost attached to the contract since a broker is not used.

An **option** is the right but not the obligation to buy or sell a foreign currency within a certain time period (an American option) or on a specific date (European option) at a specific exchange rate (the strike price). For example, assume a company purchases an option to buy Japanese yen at 105 yen per dollar (0.00952 dollars per yen). If at the time the company wants to buy yen, the rate is 115 yen per dollar

**Figure 9.2
Average Daily
Worldwide Foreign-
Exchange Transactions
by Type, April 1992**
On a worldwide basis, spot transactions were the most common type of foreign-exchange transaction, and forward transactions—whether outright or as part of a swap—were close behind. In the United States, options traded over-the-counter comprise 1.4 percent of the market volume, and other derivatives account for 3.5 percent. Swaps and outright forwards comprise 32.4 percent and 5.3 percent, respectively, and the spot market accounts for 50.4 percent.

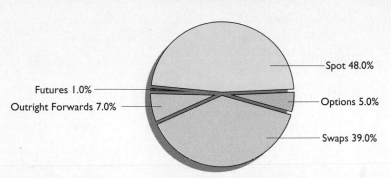

TYPES OF FOREIGN EXCHANGE
TRANSACTIONS

Spot 48.0%
Futures 1.0%
Outright Forwards 7.0%
Options 5.0%
Swaps 39.0%

A futures contract specifies in advance the exchange rate to be used, but it is not as flexible as a forward contract.

(0.00870 dollars per yen), it would not exercise the option because buying yen at the market rate would cost less than buying them at the option rate. However, if the market rate at that time is 100 yen per dollar (0.01 dollars per yen), the company would exercise the option because buying at the option rate would cost less than buying at the market rate. The option provides the company more flexibility than a forward contract would; however, the company must pay the brokerage fee and the premium regardless of whether it exercises the option.

The **futures contract** resembles the forward contract in that it specifies an exchange rate sometime in advance of the actual exchange of currency. However, it is less flexible than a forward contract because it is for a specific currency amount and a specific maturity date; a forward contract, in contrast, can be tailor-made to fit the size of the transaction and the maturity date. Forward contracts depend on a client's relationship with a bank's foreign-exchange trader, but a futures contract can be entered into by anyone through a securities broker.

International Transactions

The foreign-exchange market is based on the economic law of supply and demand. Governments often intervene to control the flow of currency by buying or selling currency in the open market. However, most of the action in the foreign-exchange market revolves around the commercial banks in the world's major money centers. Trading between such banks is called the interbank market. This market exists to protect the banks against foreign-exchange risk. It also provides them with an expanded market in which they can earn a profit. For example, assume Citibank enters into a forward contract to deliver U.S. dollars for British pounds in thirty days. It then has an exposure in British pounds. To eliminate the exposure, Citibank may go to the interbank market to find another bank that will enter into a contract to deliver dollars for pounds in thirty days. The difference between Citibank's buy and sell rates in the interbank market determines its profit.

Foreign-exchange trades occur twenty-four hours a day worldwide.

Foreign-exchange trading occurs worldwide in an increasingly integrated way. The foreign-exchange market operates twenty-four hours a day during the business week; the only time it is silent is after the New York market closes on Friday afternoon and before the Sydney market opens on Monday morning (which would be Sunday evening New York time). Most large money-center banks have added night shifts of traders so they can trade twenty-four hours a day. Most foreign-currency transactions take place in markets as they become fully operative; thus traders must be aware of international time zones (see Map 9.1). The following explains:

> The world's communication networks are now so good, and so many countries have fairly unrestricted markets that we can talk of a single world market. It starts in a small way in New Zealand around 9:00 a.m. New Zealand time, just in time to catch the tail end of the previous night's New York market. Two or three hours later, Tokyo opens, followed an hour later by Hong Kong and Manila and then half an hour later by Singapore. By now, with the Far East market in full swing, the focus moves to the Near and Middle East. Bombay opens two hours after Singapore, followed after an hour and a half by Abu Dhabi, with Jeddah an hour behind, and Athens and Beirut an hour behind still. By this stage, trading in the Far and Middle East is usually thin and perhaps nervous as dealers wait to see how Europe will trade. Paris and Frankfurt open an hour ahead of London, and by this time Tokyo is starting to close down, so the European market can judge how the Japanese market has been trading by the way they deal to close out positions. By lunch-time in London, New York is starting to open up, and as Europe closes down, positions can be passed westward. During the afternoon in New York, trading tends to be quiet. The problem is that there is nowhere to pass a position to. The San Francisco market, three hours behind, is effectively a satellite of the New York market. Very small positions can be passed on to New Zealand banks, but the market there is extremely limited.[4]

The largest markets for foreign exchange are in the United Kingdom, the United States, and Japan.

The largest foreign-exchange markets in 1992 were in the United Kingdom, the United States, and Japan (see Fig. 9.3). The U.K. market was important historically because it was the financial center of the former British empire. Today its importance comes from its close proximity to continental Europe and the fact that it is the center of all U.S. dollar transactions that occur outside of the United States.

**Figure 9.3
Average Daily Worldwide Foreign-Exchange Volume by Country, April 1992**
The largest volume of foreign-exchange transactions occurs in the United Kingdom (London). The United States and Japan are in second and third place.

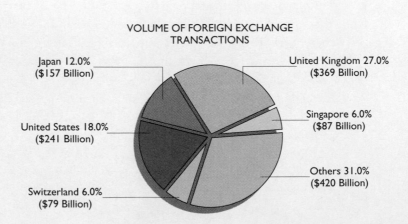

VOLUME OF FOREIGN EXCHANGE
TRANSACTIONS

Japan 12.0%
($157 Billion)

United Kingdom 27.0%
($369 Billion)

Singapore 6.0%
($87 Billion)

United States 18.0%
($241 Billion)

Others 31.0%
($420 Billion)

Switzerland 6.0%
($79 Billion)

Map 9.1
International Time Zones
Note that in the former Soviet Union standard time zones are advanced one hour.

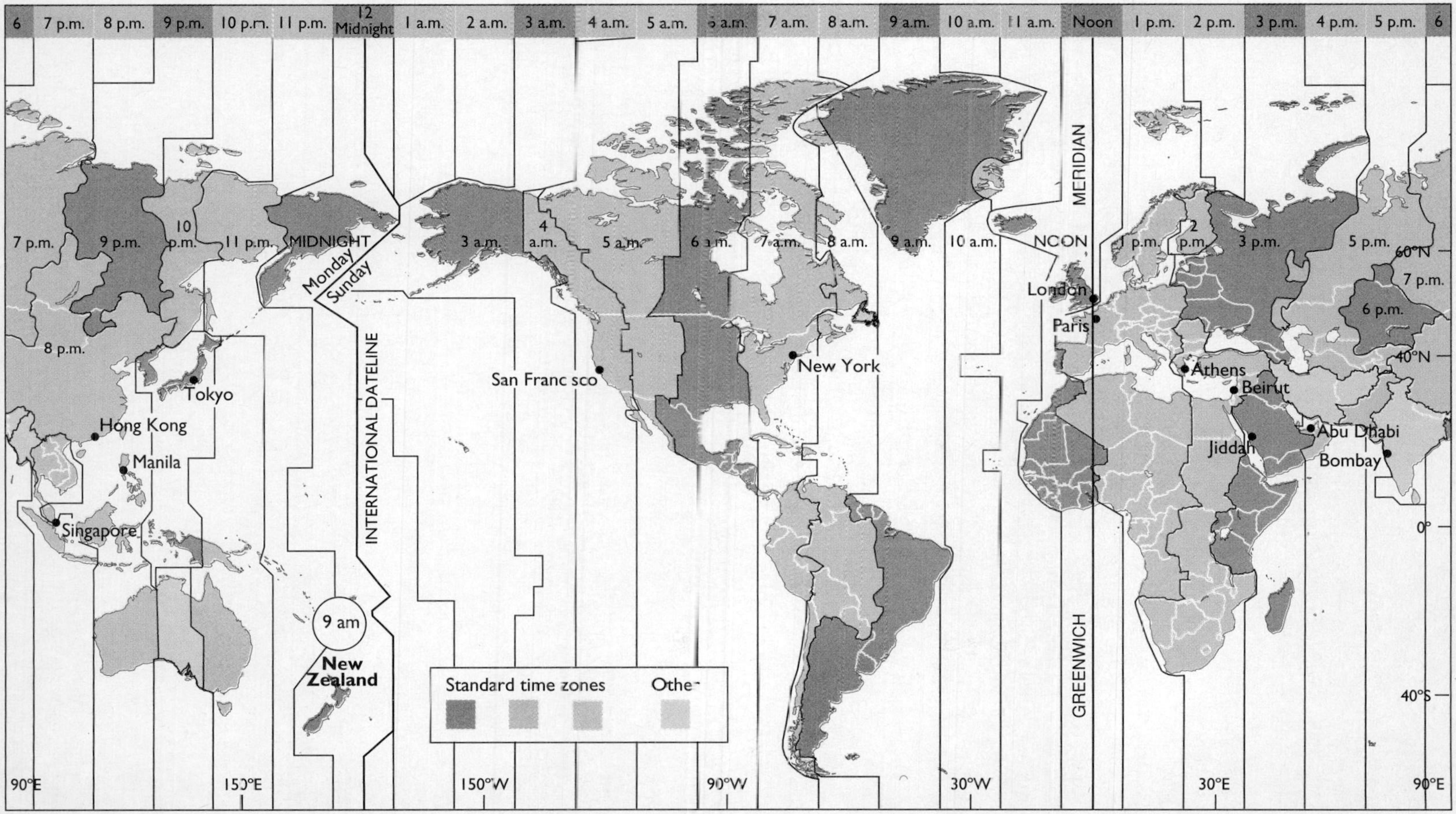

Figure 9.4
Average Daily Worldwide Foreign-Exchange Transactions by Currency, April 1992
The most actively traded currencies are the U.S. dollar, the German mark, the Japanese yen, and the British pound. The largest two-way flow of currencies involves the U.S. dollar and the German mark. Because all foreign-exchange transactions involve two currencies, the total volume shown here is 200 percent.

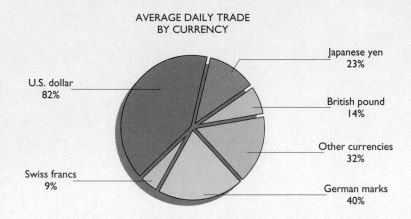

AVERAGE DAILY TRADE
BY CURRENCY

Japanese yen
23%

British pound
14%

Other currencies
32%

German marks
40%

Swiss francs
9%

U.S. dollar
82%

The world's most actively traded currencies in 1992 were the U.S. dollar, the German mark, the Japanese yen, and the British pound (see Fig. 9.4). The composition of currency trades in the United States mirrors that in the world as a whole, with the U.S. dollar involved in 89 percent of the trades, the German mark in 39 percent, the Japanese yen in 25 percent, and the British pound in 11 percent. From a trade point of view, the three largest markets for U.S. products are Canada, Japan, and Mexico, yet of the three, only the Japanese yen shows up as a major traded currency in the United States. Foreign exchange occurs for many reasons other than in conjunction with exporting and importing; some of these reasons are speculation, interbank trades, and foreign investment.

The Role of Banks in Foreign Exchange

Foreign currencies are traded in various markets (see Fig. 9.5). The most important ones are the interbank market and specialized markets such as the Chicago Mercantile Exchange (CME), the London International Financial Futures Exchange (LIFFE), the Philadelphia Stock Exchange (PSE), and the over-the-counter (OTC) market.

Seven of the world's ten largest banks in 1993 were Japanese banks (see Table 9.4); however, they were not the most profitable. Further, when it comes to foreign-exchange trading, these Japanese banks are not as significant, compared with banks from other countries, as they are for other banking transactions. When managers look for a bank, they consider its ability to get clients the lowest price and to transact large deals quickly, in the widest possible range of currencies, in maturities up to one year, and, if possible, outside regular London hours.[5]

Each year, *Euromoney* surveys banks and corporations to identify their customers' favorite banks and the leading traders in the interbank market (see Tables 9.5 and 9.6). Criteria considered in selecting the top foreign-exchange traders include

- Ranking in specific locations, such as London, Zurich, and New York
- Capability to handle major currencies, such as the U.S. dollar and German mark

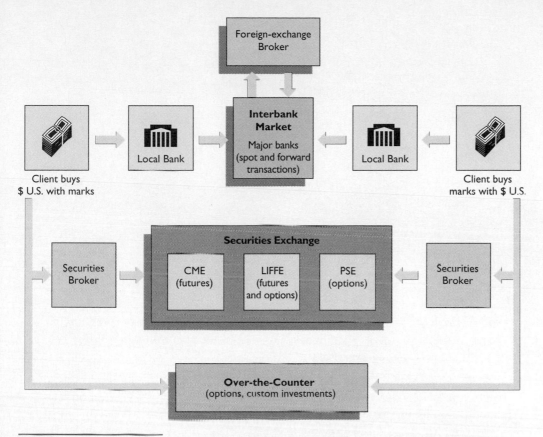

Figure 9.5
Structure of Foreign-Exchange Markets
A company interested in exchanging currency can work with a bank, a stock broker on a securities exchange, or an investment banker in the OTC market. Banks deal with each other in the interbank market, primarily through foreign-exchange brokers.

Citibank's foreign-exchange success results from its customer focus, size, and currency coverage.

- Capability to handle major cross trades, for example, those involving the dollar and German mark, whose number has grown to 40 percent of foreign-exchange trades in the spot market
- Capability to handle specific currencies
- Capability to handle derivatives such as options, swaps, and forward contracts
- Research capabilities

For each of the fifteen years the survey has been conducted, Citibank has been ranked the favorite bank of customers.[6] Citibank leads in this category for three main reasons: its customer focus, size, and currency coverage. In terms of customer focus, its foreign-exchange salespeople emphasize client relations through corporate hospitality (cocktail receptions, dinners, extravagant ski weekends, and trips to the Olympic games for the big customers), product development, and close relationships with clients.[7]

Citibank is the world's biggest multinational bank. It has six hundred employees in foreign-exchange operations and maintains foreign-exchange dealing rooms in ninety of its branches worldwide. Its currency coverage also is impressive. It trades

Table 9.4
Largest Banks in the World

Rank	Bank	Country	Capital (billions of U.S. dollars)
1	Sumitomo Bank	Japan	19.542
2	Dai-Ichi Kangyo Bank	Japan	17.377
3	Sanwa Bank	Japan	17.155
4	Fuji Bank	Japan	17.045
5	Mitsubishi Bank	Japan	15.982
6	Sakura Bank	Japan	15.608
7	Credit Agricole	France	15.606
8	Union Bank of Switzerland	Switzerland	12.802
9	Industrial Bank of Japan	Japan	12.053
10	HSBC Holdings	Britain	11.798

Source: Banker, 1993.

in 140 currency pairs (such as the dollar and the mark) and also deals effectively in **exotic currencies,** also called **exotics,** which are those of developing countries, such as the Russian ruble and the Malaysian ringgit.

Exotics are difficult for corporations to work with because start-up costs are high, regulations change daily, realignments of exchange rates are common, and volatility and liquidity are very unpredictable.[8] Banks such as Citibank help their clients with exotics by cutting through the regulations on buying and selling, using local networks to manage foreign-exchange positions, dealing with difficult exchange-rate systems, dealing with exchange controls on investments and subsequent repatriation of capital, and getting information on potential changes in rates. The banks also help their clients manage positions and move funds. The specific financial instruments that are used, such as bills of exchange and letters of credit, are discussed in Chapter 14.

Clearing Mechanisms

Prior to 1992, foreign-exchange trades occurred primarily through the Reuters Dealing 2000 Phase 1 computer system, via telephone conversations between traders, or through foreign-exchange brokers. The Dealing 2000 Phase 1 system, introduced in 1981, enabled foreign-exchange traders to deal with another trader or bank via computer. In an average week, 16,000 traders, engaged in 1 million conversations, used this system to execute 40–50 percent of foreign-exchange trades. However, these trades represent 96 percent of foreign-exchange trades that take place by computer.[9] About 10 percent of foreign-exchange trades are conducted between traders over the telephone, with the remaining 30–40 percent executed anonymously through foreign-exchange brokers.[10] In 1992, Reuters introduced the Dealing 2000 Phase II system. This new system enables users to execute trades

Foreign-exchange trading occurs through Reuters' computerized system, through telephone calls between traders, and through foreign-exchange brokers.

Table 9.5
Customers' Favorite Banks

	Rank	
Bank	1993	1992
Citibank	1	1
Chemical	2	2
Deutsche Bank	3	13
JP Morgan	4	6
HSBC/Midland*	5	†
Swiss Bank Corporation	6	15
Barclays	7	3
Chase Manhattan	8	12
Union Bank of Switzerland	9	7
Royal Bank of Canada	10	16
ABN Amro	11	—
BankAmerica	12	4=
NatWest	13	8
Goldman Sachs	14	17=
Bankers Trust	15	9
First Chicago	16	14
Bank of Montreal	17	20
Standard Chartered	18	19
Banque Nationale de Paris	19	—
Morgan Stanley	20	—

*Includes Hongkong Bank and Midland.
†Midland ranked joint fourth, Hongkong Bank ranked tenth.

Source: Euromoney Supplement, May 1993.

Table 9.6
Top Interbank Traders

	Rank	
Bank	1993	1992
Chemical	1	1
Bankers Trust	2	3
Union Bank of Switzerland	3	5
Citibank	4	2
HSBC/Midland	5	—
Barclays	6	4
Chase Manhattan	7=	8=
First Chicago	7=	7
Lloyds	9	—
BankAmerica	10=	—
JP Morgan	10=	6
NatWest	10=	8=

Source: Euromoney Supplement, May 1993.

against the best bid-offer prices of traders that participate in the system anonymously. Bankers fear, however, that Reuters is poised to take over global foreign-exchange trading. Consequently, competing trading systems have surfaced since the Dealing 2000 Phase 1 system was introduced in 1981, and some of these are sponsored by banks.

The Chicago Mercantile Exchange

The CME is the world's second-largest futures exchange and deals primarily in futures contracts for British pounds, Canadian dollars, German marks, Swiss francs, Japanese yen, and Australian dollars.

The Chicago Mercantile Exchange (CME) is the world's second-largest futures exchange, led only by the Chicago Board of Trade. It opened the International Monetary Market (IMM) in 1972 to deal primarily in futures contracts for the British pound, the Canadian dollar, the German mark, the Swiss franc, the Japanese yen, and the Australian dollar. These contracts are for specific amounts and have a specific maturity date. For example, a futures contract in Japanese yen is set by the IMM at 12.5 million yen. If you wanted to buy futures for 100 million yen, you would have to buy eight yen contracts from a broker. The contract sizes for the other currencies are 125,000 German marks, 100,000 Canadian dollars, 62,500 British pounds, 125,000 Swiss francs, and 100,000 Australian dollars. The "Futures Prices" section of the *Wall Street Journal* provides daily quotes on these contracts.

Even though these futures contracts have fixed maturity dates, they have a ready market. Brokers make deals on the exchange floor rather than over the telephone, as in the forward markets for banks. Futures contracts at the CME also tend to be for small amounts relative to the transactions normally encountered in the interbank market. Further, the Commodity Futures Trading Commission limits how much the futures prices may vary each day, whereas there are no such restrictions in the banking market. Finally, the CME requires a margin, or deposit.

The CME has been losing business to both the Philadelphia Stock Exchange and the over-the-counter market because of their more creative financial offerings and their ability to tailor offerings to clients. It has been estimated that CME activity in foreign-exchange futures and options is only 1 percent of the global foreign-exchange market, compared with 5 percent as recently as 1990.[11] As a result, the CME is struggling to find its niche in the currency markets. Its major users are the managed-money funds that speculate in currency markets and smaller companies that lack the lines of credit needed to trade in the interbank market with larger companies.[12] In June 1993, the CME introduced a new type of futures contract that allows it to compete more effectively with the banks.[13] It also joined with Reuters and the Chicago Board of Trade in 1987 to establish Globex, a 24-hour trading system that allows traders to continue trading after the exchanges close. However, most trades—even in the liquid currency market—take place in the time zones of the traders involved, so the volume of activity has been disappointing.[14]

The London International Financial Futures Exchange

LIFFE deals in futures contracts and is the world's third-largest futures market.

The London International Financial Futures Exchange (LIFFE), which opened in September 1982, deals in futures contracts of fixed sizes in British pounds, German marks, Swiss francs, Japanese yen, and **Eurodollars,** which are dollars banked outside of the United States. This market should provide an alternative to the interbank market for avoiding foreign-exchange risk in Europe. In 1992, LIFFE surpassed the Chicago Board of Trade as the largest trader of futures and futures options in a single session. However, overall, LIFFE is the third-largest futures market behind the Chicago Board of Trade and the CME. It has become the leading overseas exchange used by speculators and money managers and investors for **hedging** their foreign-currency holdings, that is, protecting them against a loss in value.[15]

The Philadelphia Stock Exchange

The PSE trades currency options.

The Philadelphia Stock Exchange (PSE) is the only exchange in the United States that trades foreign-currency options. The CME trades options on futures contracts rather than spot contracts. Each option is for a specific amount of currency. For example, each British pound option is for 31,250 pounds. Options also are provided for Australian dollars, Canadian dollars, German marks, Japanese yen, and Swiss francs.

The PSE has been growing relative to the CME and Chicago Board of Trade, for several reasons. Much of the growth has come from MNEs. Although options cost more, big companies prefer them to futures (the CME instrument) because of their greater flexibility. PSE options are settled in cash, whereas CME options turn into futures contracts at maturity; corporate users therefore consider PSE options to be more convenient.[16]

Over-the-Counter Market

The OTC market involves nonbank financial institutions such as Goldman Sachs that deal in foreign-exchange contracts.

The over-the-counter (OTC) market has exploded in growth in recent years. Its major players are nonbank financial institutions such as Goldman Sachs (the market leader among investment banks), Merrill Lynch, and Credit Suisse First Boston (CSFB). The strength of the OTC market is the understanding these investment bankers have of investors and people who move capital. They are constantly developing new products that are individually tailored for companies and not found elsewhere. Also, the OTC market can set contracts of any size rather than in the fixed contract sizes required in the other exchanges.[17]

The strategies of the different institutions are interesting. Merrill Lynch's is "to build up a core of sophisticated customers to whom we could offer tailor-made, usually structured, products. In fact, one of [our] most important aims was to market our foreign-exchange services to other parts of Merrill Lynch—the securities business, the M&A [merger and acquisition] teams, and the asset managers." Goldman Sachs, which tends to work with the largest, most sophisticated asset managers and those corporations that run their treasury operations as profit centers, is "in the business of providing innovative product ideas and trading strategies for more sophisticated users who, in general, are looking at currencies as an asset class."[18] This market is increasingly specializing, forcing the generalists out.

Convertibility

Residents and nonresidents of a country can exchange a convertible currency for other currencies.

A key aspect of exchanging one currency for others is its convertibility. For example, although it is easy to convert U.S. dollars into Russian rubles, it has not always been easy to convert rubles into dollars. Therefore the U.S. dollar is considered freely convertible, but until recently, the Russian ruble was not.

Most countries today have nonresident, or external, convertibility. For example, all nonresidents with deposits in French banks in francs may at any time exchange all of those deposits for the currency of any other country. In other words, a U.S. exporter to France can be paid in francs and be assured that those francs can be converted to dollars or some other currency. However, not all countries permit nonresident convertibility. Lack of currency convertibility is a major problem for MNEs attempting to invest in many developing countries. For example, with limited exceptions, Peruvian enterprises are not allowed to hold foreign-exchange balances abroad and must sell foreign currency to a Peruvian bank within ten working days of receipt.[19]

Fully convertible currencies are those that the government allows both residents and nonresidents to purchase unlimited amounts of any foreign currency with. Between 20 and 25 percent of countries do not have payments restrictions, which are defined as official actions directly affecting the availability or cost of exchange or involving undue delay. All other countries have a combination of restrictions on payments for current transactions and restrictions on payments for capital transactions.[20]

A hard currency is a currency that is usually fully convertible and strong or relatively stable in value in comparison with other currencies.

Hard currencies, such as the U.S. dollar and Japanese yen, are currencies that are usually fully convertible. They also are relatively stable in value or tend to be strong in comparison with other currencies. They are desirable assets to hold. Currencies that are not fully convertible are often called **soft currencies,** or **weak currencies.**

Exchange Restrictions

Some governments impose exchange restrictions to control access to foreign exchange. The devices they use include import licensing, multiple exchange rates, import deposit requirements, and quantity controls.

Licensing

Licensing occurs when a government requires that all foreign-exchange transactions be regulated and controlled by it.

Governmental licenses fix the exchange rate by requiring all recipients, exporters, and others who receive foreign currency to sell it to the central bank at the official buying rate. A country's central bank is the institution usually empowered to establish monetary policy (these banks are discussed in greater detail in Chapter 10). It, or some other governmental agency, rations the foreign currency it acquires by selling it at fixed rates to those needing to make payment abroad for goods considered essential. An importer may purchase foreign exchange only if that importer has obtained an import license for the goods in question. In Kenya, for example, products being considered for importation are grouped into three schedules. Import licenses are valid for three or six months, depending on the schedule in which the product fits. For example, Schedule 1 imports comprise mainly high-priority capital goods, raw materials, and intermediate inputs, and the license for these goods is relatively automatic. This is not true of Schedule IIIC, which consists of products that are domestically produced or for which domestic substitutes are available.[21] Also, in the African nation of Rwanda, all imports valued over RF100,000 require licenses, as do those valued at less than RF100,000 if payment is required in foreign exchange.[22]

Multiple Exchange Rates

In a multiple exchange-rate system, a government sets different exchange rates for different types of transactions.

Another way to control foreign exchange is to establish more than one exchange rate. This is called a **multiple exchange-rate system.** A 1991 survey of exchange-rate arrangements found that thirty countries used multiple rates for imports and twenty-eight used them for exports.[23] There are several ways to determine multiple exchange rates. Some countries require a premium or discount on foreign-exchange transactions in specific industries or with specific countries. Further, if a government wants to discourage imports, it can establish a very high exchange rate for the transactions it does not favor, thereby making those imports very expensive.

A good example of multiple exchange rates involves the South African rand. South Africa has a commercial rate and a financial rate for the rand; both are government-sanctioned, but the rates can be very different, as Table 9.1 illustrates. The commercial rate is used for such transactions as exporting merchandise. The financial rate is used for such transactions as the remission of dividends. For example, at a financial rate of 4.4000 rands, a U.S. MNE with a subsidiary in South Africa would get fewer dollars for its rands than it would at a commercial rate of 3.1493 rands. Thus South Africa would save hard-currency reserves.

Import Deposit Requirement

Some governments require an import deposit, that is, a deposit prior to the release of foreign exchange.

Another form of foreign-exchange control are advance import deposits. In 1989, Colombia had an 85-percent advance exchange license deposit for import payments. Although that requirement was abolished in 1991, the 1991 survey on exchange arrangements also revealed that twenty-one countries used some form of advance import deposits.[24]

Quantity Controls

With quantity controls, the government limits the amount of foreign currency that can be used in a specific transaction.

Governments also may limit the amount of exchange for specific purposes. These types of control, called **quantity controls,** often are used in conjunction with tourism. For example, in 1991 Brazilian residents temporarily staying abroad for educational or health purposes could purchase up to the equivalent of US$1000 per month, and those engaged in business travel and presentations abroad were allowed a special daily allowance that ranged from US$250 to US$400.[25]

The Uses of the Foreign-Exchange Market

Commercial banks collect foreign exchange, lend foreign exchange, and buy and sell foreign exchange.

The major facilitators of foreign-exchange transactions are the international departments of the commercial banks, which perform three essential financial functions: collections, lending, and buying and selling of foreign currency. In performing collections, the bank serves as a vehicle by which payments are made between its domestic customers and foreign nationals. Lending usually takes place in the currency of the country where the bank is established, but the bank might be able to provide loans in a foreign currency if it has a branch in that country.

The purchase or sale of foreign currency is undertaken by a commercial bank for many purposes. For instance, travelers going abroad or returning from a foreign country will want to purchase or sell foreign currency. Residents of one country wanting to invest abroad also need to purchase foreign currency from a commercial bank. For example, suppose a Canadian exporter is to receive payment from a U.S. importer in U.S. dollars and wants to use the funds to make payment for raw materials purchased in Norway. The bank in this case simultaneously serves as a collector and acts as a dealer in a foreign-exchange transaction.

There are a number of reasons why companies use the foreign-exchange market. The most obvious is for transactions involving imports and exports. For example, a U.S. company importing products from an overseas supplier might have to convert U.S. dollars into a foreign currency to pay that supplier.

Companies also use the foreign-exchange market for financial transactions, such as those relating to FDI. For example, if a U.S. company decided to establish a manufacturing plant in Mexico, it would have to convert dollars into pesos to make the investment. After the Mexican subsidiary generated a profit, it would have to convert pesos to dollars to send a dividend back to the U.S. parent.

Arbitrage is the buying and selling of foreign currencies at a profit due to price discrepancies.

Sometimes companies deal in foreign exchange to make a profit, even though the transaction is not connected to any other business purpose, such as trade flows or investment flows. Usually, however, this type of foreign-exchange activity is more likely to be pursued by foreign-exchange traders and investors. One type of profit-seeking activity is **arbitrage,** which is the purchase of foreign currency on one market for immediate resale on another market (in a different country) in order to profit from a price discrepancy. For example, a trader might sell U.S. dollars for Swiss francs, the Swiss francs for German marks, and then the German marks for U.S. dollars, the goal being to end up with more dollars at the end of the process. Assume the trader converts 100 dollars into 150 Swiss francs when the exchange rate is 1.5 francs per dollar. The trader then converts the francs into 225 German marks at an exchange rate of 1.5 marks per franc and finally converts the marks into 125 dollars at an exchange rate of 1.8 marks per dollar. In this case, arbitrage yields $125 from the initial sale of $100.

Interest arbitrage involves investing in interest-bearing instruments in foreign exchange in an effort to earn a profit due to interest-rate and exchange-rate differentials.

Interest arbitrage is the investing in debt instruments in different countries. For example, a trader might invest $1000 in the United States for ninety days or convert $1000 into British pounds, invest the money in the United Kingdom for ninety days, and then convert the pounds back into dollars. The investor would try to pick the alternative that would be the highest-yielding at the end of ninety days.

Speculators take positions in foreign-exchange markets with the major objective of earning a profit.

Foreign-exchange transactions also can be used to speculate for profit or to protect against risk. **Speculation** is the buying or selling of a commodity, in this case foreign currency, where the activity contains both an element of risk and the chance of great profit. For example, an investor could buy German marks in anticipation of the mark's strengthening against other currencies. If it does, the investor earns a profit; if it weakens, the investor incurs a loss. Speculators are important in the foreign-exchange market because they spot trends and try to take advantage of them. Thus they can be a valuable source of both supply of and demand for a currency.

As protection against risk, foreign-exchange transactions can be used to hedge against a potential loss due to an exchange-rate change. For example, a U.S. parent company expecting a dividend in British pounds in ninety days could enter into a forward contract to hedge the dividend flow. It could go to the bank and agree to deliver pounds for dollars in ninety days at the forward rate. Doing this would eliminate the risk of an unfavorable shift in the exchange rate by locking in a specific forward rate for the dividend flow.

Are speculators destabilizing the world monetary system? When the British pound was under pressure in the fall of 1992, speculator George Soros was rumored to have made over $1 billion betting against the pound. Although the British government had publicly stated that it would support the pound, Soros didn't believe it. His feeling was that the European Monetary System (EMS), the system linking together the currencies of Europe (see the discussion in Chapter 10), was not working as intended, thereby creating a bias against the weak currencies. As a result of his analysis, he began selling pounds to the Bank of England at an artificially supported price. When it was clear the government could not continue its support, the bottom fell out of the market. Soros bought back his pounds at a significantly cheaper price. Later, in 1993, he wrote an article for the *Times* of London stating that he expected the mark to fall against all major currencies. As soon as the article hit the streets, the dollar rose against the mark, from 1.6250 marks to 1.6368 marks.[26]

Is it ethical to speculate, especially against your own country's currency? If governments and central banks are infuriated by the actions of speculators, is speculation therefore wrong? Just because a government states that it will support a currency doesn't mean it has the fiscal and monetary policies and the foreign-exchange reserves to do so or that its actions are in the long-term best interests of the country. Governments support the value of their currencies for many reasons, and speculators test the strength of their resolve. When Ronald Reagan was shot during his presidency, speculators bet against the dollar. However, the Fed intervened to support the dollar's value and take the steam out of the speculatory action. When government support of the currency is designed to hide a fundamental weakness in the country's economy, speculators are more aggressive in determining how serious the government's intervention effort is. In early 1994, for example, the dollar was subject to serious speculative pressure, and the Fed intervened on Friday, April 29, to support its value. There was talk that the Fed would raise short-term interest rates to accomplish its goal. When that did not happen, speculators sold dollars and pushed the value down further; then they waited to see what the government's next action would be.

Thus, speculators may push the market in the direction it needs to go. That is certainly what Soros feels. He does a careful economic analysis of major currencies to see if their values are supported by economic fundamentals, such as inflation and interest rates. If their prices are out of line with their values, he will trade in order to make a profit. His actions and those of other speculators force governments to decide how much they will support their currencies' values, given the underlying fundamentals. That is, speculators force governments to confront market realities.

Foreign-exchange trading generates a higher volume of transactions at a lower cost, favoring large companies over small ones.

COUNTERVAILING FORCES Size and scale are important dimensions of foreign-exchange trading. The larger the foreign-exchange transaction, the lower the cost. Trades are quoted not only in terms of the specific currencies involved but also in terms of the size of the transaction. Although any bank can deal in foreign exchange, it is the size, geographical spread, and range of available currencies that cause a bank to rank above others. Time and again, corporate treasurers select specific banks because of their range of services. This is no market for the small player.

If this is the case, how do the small players survive? How can the exporter who is going to receive $50,000 in foreign currency for a sale going to make money? Must the exporter use one of the top commercial banks to be successful? Fortunately, the foreign-exchange market is available to anyone at spot. The relatively high transactions cost for small transactions will cut into the exporter's profitability, but not significantly. However, for the small exporter in a regional market, finding a local bank that understands the foreign-exchange market and can deliver the service may be difficult. The local bank will likely work through a larger money-center bank for trades, especially those involving derivatives.

LOOKING TO THE FUTURE Significant strides have been made and will continue to be made in the development of foreign-exchange markets. The speed at which transactions are processed and information is transmitted globally will certainly lead to greater efficiencies and more opportunities for foreign-exchange trading. For example, ten years ago, options were seldom discussed, but since 1989, the number of options transactions has jumped 124 percent. The options market will continue to grow in importance because of the flexibility of this type of contract, the range of products available in the OTC market, and the instability in the foreign-exchange markets—especially in Europe. Further, transactions costs will come down and companies will learn how to use options more effectively.

In addition, exchange restrictions that hamper the free flow of goods and services should diminish as governments gain greater control over their economies. A common European currency will allow cross-border transactions in Europe to progress more smoothly. Further, under NAFTA, the Mexican government will be forced to slow inflation and stabilize the Mexican currency in order to allow trade to flow more smoothly.

Finally, technological developments may not cause the foreign-exchange broker to disappear entirely, but they will certainly cause foreign-exchange trades to be executed more quickly and cheaply. The real issue in the future is whether banks can mount a challenge to Reuters before Reuters locks up the world of foreign-exchange trade.

Summary

- **A major distinction between domestic and international transactions for goods and services is that one currency is used for domestic transactions but more than one currency is used for international transactions.**

- An exchange rate is the value of one currency in terms of another. The spot rate is the rate quoted by a foreign-exchange trader for current transactions; the forward rate is that quoted for a contract to receive or deliver the foreign currency in the future.

- The difference between the spot and forward rates is the discount or premium. The foreign currency is selling at a discount if the forward rate is less than the spot rate and at a premium if the forward rate is greater than the spot rate.

- Most foreign-exchange transactions occur through traders at commercial banks, with nearly half of the transactions occurring in the spot market rather than the forward market.

- Most foreign-exchange transactions take place in the interbank market rather than between banks and nonbanking institutions.

- Derivatives are swaps, outright forwards, options, and futures contracts. Swaps and forwards are the most popular, but options are growing in importance. An option is the right but not the obligation to buy or sell foreign currency.

- The world's largest foreign-exchange markets are in the United Kingdom, the United States, and Japan.

- The average daily trading volume in foreign exchange exceeds $1 trillion, and the most actively traded currencies are the U.S. dollar, the German mark, the Japanese yen, and the British pound.

- Nonbank foreign-exchange trading takes place in the over-the-counter market through institutions such as Goldman Sachs and at the Chicago Board of Trade and CME (futures contracts), LIFFE, and the PSE (options).

- Although the Japanese banks are the world's largest, they are not the preferred players in terms of foreign-exchange transactions.

- The most important characteristics of the banks that provide foreign-exchange services are their size, geographical spread, ability to deal in derivatives (especially options), and currency coverage.

- Foreign-exchange trades are handled through Reuters' computerized system, telephone communications, and foreign-currency brokers.

- A convertible currency can be freely traded for other currencies. Some countries' currencies are partially convertible in that residents are not allowed to convert them into other currencies but nonresidents are.

• **Some governments control foreign exchange through import licensing, multiple exchange rates, import deposit requirements, or quantity controls.**

Case
The Mexican Peso[27]

On August 31, 1976, the Mexican peso was cut loose from its exchange rate of 12.5 pesos to the dollar, which had been established in 1955. From 1955 to 1976, the exchange rate had been maintained artificially through various mechanisms. Import controls and market intervention were used extensively to allow the peso to appear more stable than it was, thereby frustrating MNEs operating in Mexico. Many companies established manufacturing operations in Mexico only to find that the government eventually phased out their ability to import needed raw materials and components. During the 1970s, pressure began to build for a change in the peso's value. Tourism, a major source of foreign exchange, began to taper off because of rising prices resulting directly from general inflation in the economy.

Mexico began importing more than it was exporting, which resulted in an outflow of pesos. Further, exporters to Mexico preferred to convert their pesos into dollars. Governmental use of Mexico's existing dollar reserves to buy back the pesos would have depleted those reserves severely. So, instead Mexico chose to maintain its level of reserves by increasing its short-term external borrowing of dollars. However, this move would eventually have resulted in principal and interest payments that could rob Mexico of what little foreign-exchange reserves it could gather.

Because of these and other pressures, Mexican officials agreed to devalue the peso to 20.5 pesos per dollar on August 31, 1976. They hoped this devaluation would absorb some of the excess supply of pesos in the market and allow the economy to stabilize. The government also considered establishing more elaborate foreign-exchange controls so that spot transactions could be allocated according to governmental priorities. In the end, Mexico decided on devaluation rather than foreign-exchange controls because the latter would require establishing an elaborate bureaucracy to administer them.

Unfortunately, the solution to the problem was short-lived. From 1976 to mid-1981, the peso held its postdevaluation level, but inflation and other forces that had created the problems leading up to the 1976 devaluation reemerged. Imports again exceeded exports, tourism fell steadily, foreign credit became tight and expensive, and world oil prices and demand softened considerably. However, the Central Bank of Mexico steadfastly maintained that a relatively modest 15–20-percent devaluation would correct the imbalances in the economy, and officials appeared to be in no hurry to make any changes.

The situation continued to worsen. In the absence of capital controls, wealthy Mexicans spent their money abroad on consumer durables and investments that would shelter them against another devaluation. With the government's continuing to exude confidence up to the last hour, a devaluation of over 40 percent was announced on February 17, 1982, bringing the new rate to 38.50 pesos per dollar. At the same time, the government announced that it hoped to keep the exchange rate to a level of 38–43 pesos for the rest of 1982. Yet scarcely a week later, on February 26, it announced another devaluation, this time to 47.25 pesos.

The two devaluations were not successful. In August 1982, after still another devaluation, the government decided to establish two exchange rates: an official rate and a free-market rate. Unfortunately, the official rate was only 49 pesos, and the free-market rate shot up to 105 pesos. In September 1982, the government nationalized all private banks and instituted currency controls. It also established a fixed priority list for determining who would get foreign exchange.

During the 1980s, the peso continued to weaken. Its fall was fueled by inflation that averaged a low of 59.2 percent in 1984 and a high of 159.2 percent in 1987. The peso dropped to a 1983 year-end rate of 143.9 pesos per dollar. By the end of 1988, it had plummeted to 2281 pesos per dollar.

In 1988, there were two exchange markets in Mexico: the controlled market and the free market. There also were import controls and controls on access to foreign exchange. In the controlled market, importers could acquire foreign exchange for the full value of merchandise already imported for which payment had not yet been made. Full advance payment for all imports was also allowed, provided the value of the goods did not exceed US\$10,000 or the payment was made through a letter of credit. For purchases that exceeded US\$10,000, only 20-percent advance payment was allowed.

After newly elected President Carlos Salinas de Gortari took office December 1, 1988, he speeded up the process of economic liberalization by lifting restrictions on trade and foreign investment and by embarking on an ambitious privatization program. It soon became obvious that the kingpin of his economic program was inflation control. As Fig. 9.6 shows, the rate of increase in the consumer price index has slowed since 1988 in Mexico. Using a value of 100 in 1985 as the base year, the Mexican consumer price index reached 2010.9 in 1992. This compares to a 1992 index of 130.9 in the United States and 166,879,000 in Brazil.

As inflation has come down, the peso/dollar exchange rate has stabilized. Figure 9.7 illustrates how the slope of the curve has flattened out in recent years. The exchange rate at the end of 1992 was 3115.4 pesos per dollar (the government changed the decimal placement in 1993 so that the exchange rate became 3.1154 pesos per dollar). As noted in Table 9.1, the value of the peso was 3.1040 per dollar on January 27, 1994, but the peso had weakened to 3.3000 per dollar by April 26, 1994.

**Figure 9.6
Quarterly Changes in the Consumer Price Index for the United States and Mexico, 1986–1992**

A major problem for the stability of the Mexican peso is the decline in the CPI in Mexico relative to that in the United States. As the inflation gap widens, there will be increased pressure on Mexico to devalue its currency.

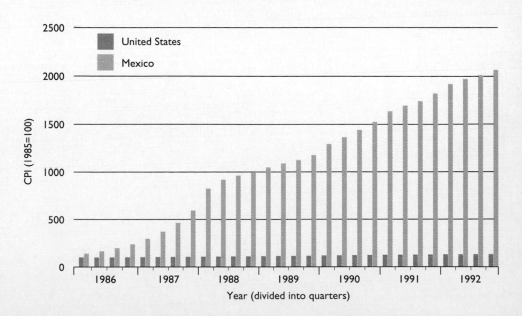

Figure 9.7
The Peso/Dollar
Exchange Rate,
1988–1992
The Mexican peso lost significant value against the U.S. dollar after 1988 but has stabilized in recent years. In 1993, Mexico dropped the last three zeros from the peso's face value so that it was quoted at 3.1050 per dollar by the end of that year and 3.3995 by September 29, 1994.

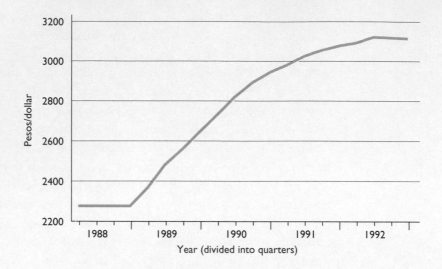

NAFTA is causing corporate treasurers to pay more attention to the peso. Previously, the peso was perceived as being tightly managed—spreads were too wide and liquidity too low. Because of the two-way trade between the United States and Mexico, the only exchange rate that really mattered was the peso/dollar rate. However, Mexico has been reaching out to Europe to diversify its trading relationships, and significant European investment should generate cross trades.

The real issue is the future of the peso. Three possible scenarios are a gradual downward drift, a mini-devaluation, and a sudden and drastic nosedive. It is clear from Figs. 9.6 and 9.7 that the peso is overvalued. Inflation is rising much faster than the peso is devaluing against the dollar. Mexico cannot continue along this course forever. Even though the annual inflation rate in Mexico is below 20 percent, it is still higher than that in the United States. Also at the root of Mexico's instability is the trade deficit. Mexico's first-quarter 1987 trade surplus turned into a trade deficit that is continuing to grow (see Fig. 9.8). As

Figure 9.8
Mexico's Balance of
Trade, 1987–1992
Beginning in 1987, the Mexican trade surplus rapidly turned to a deficit. If this deficit does not improve, there will be increased pressure to devalue the peso.

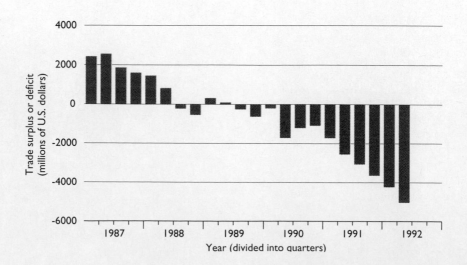

the demand for foreign products increases over that for Mexican products, pressure will come to bear on the peso. If this pressure continues, Mexico might be forced to implement currency controls to keep the peso from free-falling.

Questions

1. In 1993, there were no forward contracts available on foreign-exchange markets for the Mexican peso and no futures or options. Why? Under what conditions might there be an OTC market?
2. Why did the Mexican government establish a controlled foreign-exchange market, and how did that market differ from the free market?
3. What problems do you think you would face as a businessperson operating in a country in which there are multiple exchange rates and controls on currency trading?
4. Why do you think the Mexican government has tried to eliminate foreign-exchange controls? What are the keys to success for those efforts?

Chapter Notes

1. Herbert Stein, "Foreign Travels, Foreign Exchange Travails," *The Wall Street Journal,* 8/27/90, p. A10. Reprinted by permission of *The Wall Street Journal,* © 1994 Dow Jones & Company, Inc. All Rights Reserved Worldwide.
2. Peter T. White, "The Power of Money," *National Geographic,* January 1993, p. 82.
3. Steve Lohr, "Profiting from Turmoil in Currencies," *New York Times,* October 13, 1992, p. C1; Bank for International Settlements Monetary and Economic Department, *Central Bank Survey of Foreign Exchange Market Activity in April 1992* (Basel: BIS, March 1993); and Federal Reserve Bank of New York, "Summary of Results of the U.S. Foreign Exchange Market Turnover Survey Conducted in April 1992."
4. Julian Walmsley, *The Foreign Exchange Handbook* (New York: Wiley, 1983), pp. 7–8.
5. "How Investors Choose a Bank," *Euromoney,* January 1993, p. 52.
6. "Foreign Exchange: Citibank," *Euromoney,* July 1992, p. 59.
7. "Citi Finds the Way to Forex Clients' Hearts," *Euromoney,* May 1993, p. 83.
8. Euan Hagger, "Handle Exotics with Care," *Euromoney,* October 1992, p. 71.
9. "Banks Retaliate in Dealing-Room War," *Euromoney,* May 1993, p. 87.
10. Peter Lee, "Foreign Exchange: Bye-Bye Brokers," *Euromoney,* April 1992, p. 14.
11. Laurie Morse, "Risk and Reward: Chicago Looks to Rolling Contracts to Gather Investors," *Financial Times,* June 7, 1993, p. 19.
12. Jeffrey Taylor, "Foreign Currency Trades Slow at Merc as Firms Back Away," *Wall Street Journal,* October 20, 1992, p. C1.
13. Alice Ratcliffe, "CME Launches Novel Currency Contract on Sterling," Reuters, June 15, 1993.
14. Tracy Corrigan and Laurie Morse, "Trouble After Hours—Since Its Launch, the Globex Trading System Has Provoked Much Criticism," *Financial Times,* June 3, 1993, p. 17.
15. William B. Crawford Jr., "In Historic Session, London Outtrades Chicago Markets," *Chicago Tribune,* September 18, 1992, p. 3.
16. Taylor, loc. cit.
17. Ibid.
18. "The Banks' Golden Egg," *Euromoney,* May 1992, p. 78.
19. International Monetary Fund, *Exchange Arrangements and Exchange Restrictions: Annual Report 1991* (Washington, D.C.: IMF, 1991), p. 385.
20. Ibid., p. 585.
21. Ibid., p. 273.
22. Ibid., p. 419.
23. Ibid., pp. 580–585.
24. Ibid., p. 110.
25. Ibid., p. 62.
26. Allen R. Myerson, "When Soros Speaks, World Markets Listen," *The New York Times,* June 10, 1993, p. C1.
27. "Hedging in Mexico," *Finance & Treasury,* May 17, 1993, p. 5; Richard Moxon, "The Mexican Peso," in *International Finance Cases and Simulation,* Robert S. Carlson, H. Lee Remmers, Christine Hekman, David K. Eiteman, and Arthur I. Stonehill, eds. (Reading, Mass.: Addison-Wesley, 1980), pp. 22–23; "Acme Do Mexico, S.A.," a case by Ingo Walter, Graduate School of Business, New York University, 1983; Lawrence Rout, "Mexican Firms May Be Able to Get Dollars...," *Wall Street Journal,* September 3, 1982, p. 3; Lawrence Rout, "Mexicans Start Picking Up the Pieces after Last Week's 30% Devaluation," *Wall Street Journal,* February 23, 1982, p. 30; Lawrence Rout, "Mexico Seeking to Hold Peso at 38 to Dollar," *Wall Street Journal,* February 22, 1982; Lawrence Rout, "Mexico Ponders the Peso's Problems," *Wall Street Journal,* January 28, 1982, p. 27; and "Mexico Eases Down the Peso," *Business Week,* August 31, 1981, p. 79.

Chapter 10

The Determination of Exchange Rates

*A fair exchange
brings no quarrel.*

—Danish Proverb

Objectives

- To describe the International Monetary Fund and its role in the determination of exchange rates

- To discuss the major exchange-rate arrangements used by countries for their currencies

- To identify the major determinants of exchange rates in the spot and forward markets

- To show how to forecast exchange-rate movements using factors such as balance-of-payments statistics

- To explain how exchange-rate movements influence business decisions

Case
The Chinese
Renminbi[1]

China's currency is the renminbi, and its unit of account is the yuan. At the end of 1993, China announced it would adjust its exchange-rate system beginning January 1, 1994. After that date, rather than continuing to manage the system as a dual-track foreign-exchange system, it would allow the renminbi to float according to market forces.

The concept of a managed exchange rate as represented by the dual-track system was part of the centrally planned economy under which China has operated for decades. The People's Bank of China (PBC) is the country's central bank. The State Administration of Exchange Control (SAEC), operating under the PBC's control, is responsible for implementing exchange-rate regulations and controlling foreign-exchange transactions in accord with state policy.

The dual-track system provided for two government-approved exchange rates: the official exchange rate and the swap-market rate. Under that system, the SAEC published official exchange rates for the U.S. dollar and twenty other currencies daily. The SAEC set the official exchange rate for the renminbi based on China's balance-of-payments situation and the exchange rates of its major competitor countries, such as South Korea and Taiwan. For example, when the official rates were first set in 1986, the rate was set at 3.72 yuan per dollar; by the end of 1993, the official rate was 5.8145 yuan per dollar.

The official exchange rate was used primarily by government-owned companies. It also was used to purchase Foreign Exchange Certificates (FECs). FECs were a separate form of currency developed in 1980 for use by foreigners and foreign companies when paying for their expenses in China. However, the PBC decided to stop issuing FECs in 1994 and gradually withdraw them from circulation.

The other half of the dual-market system is the swap market, which was created in Shenzhen in 1985 for foreign and local businesses that had received official approval to exchange yuan and hard currency. The currency values in the swap market were based on supply and demand. Gradually, other swap centers opened up; the next three were located in the Special Economic Zones of Shantou, Xiamen, and Zhehai (see Map 10.1). In 1988, $6.2 billion in transactions occurred in the swap market, and in 1992, the volume exploded to $26 billion. By the end of 1993, there were around a hundred swap centers, one in most major cities in China. The largest was in Shanghai, which had brokers representing twenty-one Chinese financial institutions and twenty-two foreign institutions and reported 1993 trading of $5.29 billion, up 49 percent from the previous year. By the end of 1993, it was estimated that 80 percent of the hard-currency transactions in China were occurring in the swap market. At that time, the swap rate was 8.7 yuan per U.S. dollar, a significant discount over the official rate of 5.8 yuan per dollar.

In addition to the two government-approved markets—the official market and the swap market—a black market also existed. The black-market rate was at an even deeper discount than the swap rate was.

In announcing the new floating-rate system, the PBC made it clear that governmental authorities were going to continue to intervene in foreign-exchange markets and to use monetary and interest-rate policy to stabilize exchange rates. The new, floating-rate system was expected to benefit foreign MNEs that previously had had to record transactions at a variety of different exchange rates, for example, registering their foreign-currency-based capital at the official exchange rate and remitting their yuan profits at the much higher swap rate.

Map 10.1
Major Trade and Economic Centers in China

Much of the rapid economic growth in China has taken place in the Special Economic Zones, especially along the coast. For example, the initial foreign-currency swap center was in Shenzen, followed by centers in Shantou, Xiamen, and Zhehai. Recently, economic development is spreading inland.

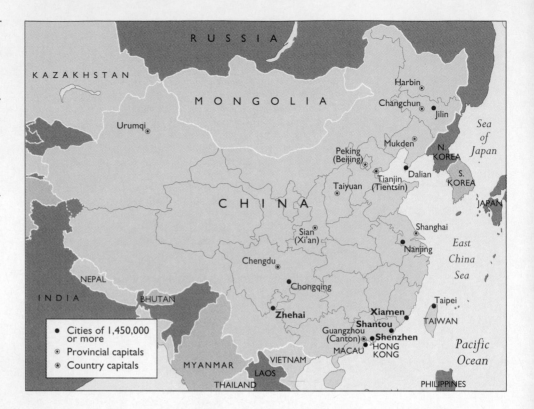

A problem with the new system is financial instability within the entire Chinese system. The state banks hold more than 85 percent of the country's financial assets, which are used to fund government-owned industrial enterprises, two thirds of which lose money. Less than 20 percent of bank lending goes to the private sector. Although the official budget deficit is only 3–4 percent of GNP, the unofficial estimate—which includes the hidden cost of bank-financed subsidies to government-owned enterprises—is closer to 10 percent. As a result of these problems and rapid economic growth, China may soon run the risk of exorbitant inflation levels similar to Russia's. Such inflation would destroy the foreign-exchange market and make it even more difficult for companies to gain access to hard currency in order to import supplies and capital goods.

After the PBC governor resigned in 1993, First Vice Minister Zhu Rongji was given responsibility for monetary policy in China. This appointment brought a little order into the foreign-exchange system and somewhat stabilized both the swap and the black market. However, Zhu faced a difficult task in stabilizing the renminbi for the long term and creating a positive climate for foreign-exchange trading in China.

As part of the move to the new exchange-rate system, the Chinese government closed the swap centers in early 1994. The swap center in Shanghai was replaced by the National Foreign Exchange Center, which is a national interbank center at which appointed banks can trade and settle foreign currencies. The remaining swap centers either became branches of the interbank system or economic information centers.

The change in the exchange-rate system is intended to help the renminbi become a fully convertible currency so that China can more easily join GATT, which considers multiple exchange-rate systems to be trade barriers. The renminbi initially was classified as partially convertible; however, it is expected to become fully convertible. This is likely to take place by the time Hong Kong is absorbed into China in 1997, if not sooner. However, the move to a single currency will not be easy—nor will companies find the new monetary environment in China risk-free.

Introduction

As discussed in Chapter 9, an exchange rate represents the number of units of one currency needed to acquire one unit of another currency. Although this definition seems simple, it is important that managers understand how an exchange rate initially is set and why it changes. Such understanding can help them anticipate and respond to exchange-rate changes and make decisions about situations that are influenced by those changes, such as the sourcing of raw materials and components, the location of manufacturing and assembly, and the location of final markets.

The International Monetary System

The International Monetary Fund

The IMF was organized to promote exchange-rate stability and facilitate the international flow of currencies.

The Great Depression, economic isolation, and trade wars of the 1930s were followed by the global conflict of World War II. Toward the close of World War II in 1944, the major Western governments met in Bretton Woods, New Hampshire, to determine the international institutions that were needed to bring relative economic stability and growth to the free world. As a result of the meetings, the **International Monetary Fund (IMF)** and World Bank were organized in 1945.

The agreement establishing the IMF initially was signed by 29 countries; by 1993, it had been signed by 167. The IMF's major objectives are

- To promote exchange-rate stability
- To maintain orderly exchange-rate arrangements
- To avoid competitive currency devaluations
- To establish a multilateral system of payments
- To eliminate exchange restrictions
- To create standby reserves

Par value is the benchmark value of a currency, initially quoted in terms of gold and the U.S. dollar.

The **Bretton Woods Agreement,** named after the location of the 1944 conference, established a system of fixed exchange rates under which each IMF member country established a par value for its currency based on gold and the U.S. dollar. This par value became a benchmark by which the country related its currency to the other currencies of the world. Currencies were allowed to vary within 1 per-cent of par value (extended to 2.25 percent in December 1971), depending on sup-ply and demand. Further moves from par value and formal changes in par value are made with the IMF's approval.

Because the U.S. dollar was strong during the 1940s and 1950s, currencies of IMF member countries were denominated in terms of gold and U.S. dollars. By 1947, the United States held 70 percent of the world's official gold reserves. Therefore, governments bought and sold dollars rather than gold. It was under-stood, although not formalized, that the United States would redeem gold for dol-lars, and the relative values of these two standards became fixed. The dollar thus became the world benchmark for trading currency.

When a country joins the IMF, it is assigned a quota related to its national in-come, monetary reserves, trade balance, and other economic indicators. The quota determines a country's voting power and other issues and is paid when the country joins the IMF.

The Board of Governors is the IMF's highest authority. It is composed of one representative from each member country. The number of votes a country has de-pends on the size of its quota. Although the Board of Governors is the ultimate au-thority on key matters, it delegates day-to-day authority to a 24-person Board of Executive Directors.

Problems with Liquidity

One serious problem with the Bretton Woods system was that, in practice, rigidity replaced stability. Countries did not allow an exchange-rate change to occur until a crisis developed with their currency. It became increasingly evident that the value of the dollar, as the world's reserve currency, had to remain fixed against gold. All other countries expected the dollar's value to remain stable. As other countries' economies began to strengthen, it appeared that gold and internationally acceptable currencies—initially part of a country's official reserves—could not fulfill many countries' reserve requirements. There was a greater demand for reserve assets to fund international transactions than there were assets available. Also, the growing accumulation of dollars outside the United States during the 1960s threatened to wreck the stability of the system of fixed exchange rates. The excess supply of dol-lars threatened to push down the value of the dollar, which would have hurt the of-ficial reserves of countries using dollars as their primary reserve asset. Thus many countries wanted to replace their reserves with gold. As trade increased, the ratio of reserves to trade decreased sharply.[2]

The SDR is
- **A unit of account devel-oped by the IMF**
- **Designed to increase inter-national reserves**

To help increase international reserves, the IMF created the **Special Drawing Right (SDR)** in 1970. The SDR is a unit of account that was distributed to countries to expand their official reserves bases. For example, Brazil could trade some of its SDRs to the United States for dollars. The SDR initially was denominated in gold and later determined by a basket of sixteen currencies. On January 1, 1981, the IMF began to use a simplified basket of five currencies for determining valuation: The

U.S. dollar made up 40 percent of the value of the SDR; the German mark, 19 percent; and the Japanese yen, the French franc, and the British pound, 13 percent each. That is, the value of the basket is the sum of the values of the five currencies, but each one has a specific weight. These weights were chosen because they broadly reflected the relative importance of the currencies in international trade and payments.

Although the SDR was intended to serve as a substitute for gold, it has not taken over the role of gold or the dollar as a primary reserve asset. The SDR is intended eventually to become the principal reserve asset in the international monetary system.[3] The IMF uses the SDR rather than a specific national currency in most of its official reports. In addition, several countries base the value of their currency on the value of the SDR or that of a combination of the SDR and another currency.

Evolution to Floating Exchange Rate

The IMF's initial system was one of fixed exchange rates. Because the U.S. dollar was the cornerstone of the international monetary system, its value remained constant with respect to the value of gold. Countries could change the value of their currency against gold and the dollar, but the value of the dollar remained fixed.

Partly because of inflationary pressures that began to build in the United States in the mid-1960s, the U.S. trade surplus began to shrink. Continued outflow of private and government long-term capital, coupled with the diminishing trade surplus, caused an increasing deficit in the balance of trade. As it became apparent that the first U.S. balance-of-trade deficit in the twentieth century would occur in 1971, it was clear something had to be done.

On August 15, 1971, President Richard Nixon announced a new economic policy that included suspending the exchange of gold for dollars and instituting an import surcharge. These moves were an attempt to force the other industrial countries to the bargaining table in the hope of restructuring the world monetary order. The resulting Smithsonian Agreement of December 1971 had several important aspects:

- An 8-percent devaluation of the dollar (an official drop in the value of the dollar against gold)
- A revaluation of some other currencies (an official increase in the value of each currency against gold)
- A widening of exchange-rate flexibility (from 1 percent to 2.25 percent on either side of par value)
- A commitment on the part of all countries to reduce trade restrictions in order to allow goods and services to flow according to supply and demand

This restructuring of the international monetary system did not last. World currency markets remained unsteady during 1972, and the dollar was devalued again by 10 percent in early 1973. Major currencies began to float against each other instead of relying on the Smithsonian Agreement. The year-end trade-weighted value of the U.S. dollar against the world's major currencies for 1970–1992 is shown in Fig. 10.1.

Currencies making up the SDR basket are the U.S. dollar, the German mark, the Japanese yen, the French franc, and the British pound.

The SDR is used by the IMF in its official reports.

Exchange-rate flexibility was widened in 1971 from 1 percent to 2.25 percent on either side of par value.

Figure 10.1
Trade-Weighted Value of the U.S. Dollar, 1970–1992
In 1971, the U.S. dollar was devalued for the first time since the IMF was established. In 1973, the dollar began to float against other major currencies. From 1980 to 1985, the dollar's value rose substantially but then fell again.

Source: Data from *Economic Report of the President, 1992* (Washington, D.C.: U.S. Government Printing Office, 1993), p. 4.

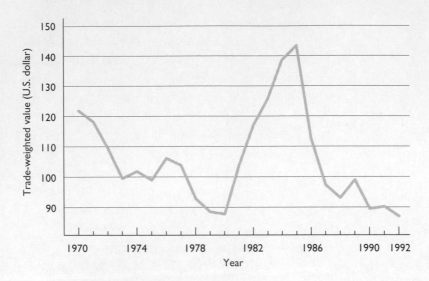

The Jamaica Agreement of 1976 resulted in greater exchange-rate flexibility.

Because the Bretton Woods Agreement was based on a system of fixed exchange rates and par values, the IMF had to change its rules in order to permit floating exchange rates. The Jamaica Agreement of 1976 amended the original rules to permit greater exchange-rate flexibility. However, there was some concern that the international monetary system would collapse under the freedom of flexible exchange rates; thus the agreement reiterated the importance of pursuing exchange stability.

The move toward greater flexibility can occur on an individual-country basis as well as an overall system basis. As noted in the opening case, China adopted an official exchange rate that was significantly overvalued compared to the rates in the swap and black markets. However, the Chinese government also realized it needed to free up the currency in order to join the international community and facilitate currency trades.

Exchange-Rate Arrangements

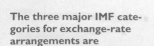

The three major IMF categories for exchange-rate arrangements are
• **Pegged exchange rates**
• **Limited-flexibility arrangements**
• **More flexible arrangements**

The Jamaica Agreement formalized the break from fixed exchange rates. As part of this move, the IMF began to permit countries to select and maintain an exchange-rate arrangement of their choice, provided they communicate their decision to the IMF. Each year the countries notify the IMF of the exchange-rate arrangement they will use, and the IMF classifies each country into one of three broad categories:

1. *Pegged exchange rates.* These countries' currencies are pegged to a single currency or to a composite of currencies.
2. *Limited-flexibility arrangements.* These countries' exchange rates have displayed limited flexibility compared with either a single currency or group of currencies.
3. *More flexible arrangements.* These countries' exchange rates are fairly flexible (this category includes floating currencies such as the Chinese renminbi).[4]

Map 10.2 identifies the countries that fit in each category. Each category is subject to change each year. For example, in 1986, currencies of thirty-two countries were pegged to the U.S. dollar (21.2 percent of the total), compared with only twenty-three in 1993 (13.8 percent of the total). Further, there were forty-six countries in the more flexible category in 1986 (30.5 percent of the total), compared with seventy-three in 1993 (43.7 percent of the total).

It is important for MNEs to understand the exchange-rate arrangements for the currencies of countries in which they are doing business so that they can more accurately forecast trends. It is much easier to forecast a future exchange rate for a relatively stable currency that is pegged to the U.S. dollar than for a currency that is freely floating and relatively unstable.

Pegged Exchange Rates

> With a pegged exchange rate, a country fixes the value of its currency to another currency or basket of currencies.

Countries using this category of exchange-rate arrangements **peg,** or fix, the value of their currency to that of another currency or basket of currencies, with very narrow margins of 1 percent or less. Some countries in the latter subcategory have selected a basket of currencies that differs from that of the SDR. For example, in 1990 the Mozambique metical was "pegged to a weighted basket consisting of ten major currencies, with the weights reflecting the relative importance of these currencies in Mozambique's external transactions in goods and services."[5] (By 1993, however, Mozambique had switched to the "independently floating" subcategory.)

Limited-Flexibility Arrangements

The limited-flexibility category of exchange-rate arrangements is divided into two subcategories. In the first, "flexibility limited in terms of a single currency," exchange rates fluctuate within a 2.25-percent margin. For all four countries shown on Map 10.2, the U.S. dollar is the benchmark for the currencies. The 2.25-percent margin is consistent with the Smithsonian Agreement.

> The EMS is a limited-flexibility arrangement in which EU countries agree to limit the values of their currencies by means of a parity grid.

The second subcategory, "flexibility limited through cooperative arrangement," refers to the **European Monetary System (EMS).** The EMS was created in 1979 as a means of creating exchange-rate stability within the European Community (EC), now the European Union (EU). This system was intended primarily to facilitate trade among EC members by minimizing exchange-rate fluctuations. Currently, a series of exchange relationships link the currencies of most EU members through a parity grid. A central exchange rate is determined for the currency of each country participating in the EMS based on the **European Currency Unit (ECU).** The ECU resembles the SDR in concept, except its basket includes the currencies of all EU countries, including those not part of the EMS. The EU is considering using the ECU as its common currency. In addition, MNEs can use the ECU for accounting purposes. There also are ECU bonds and ECU traveler's checks available.

Once the central exchange rate is determined for the currency of each EMS country, a parity exchange rate is determined for each pair of countries. For exam-

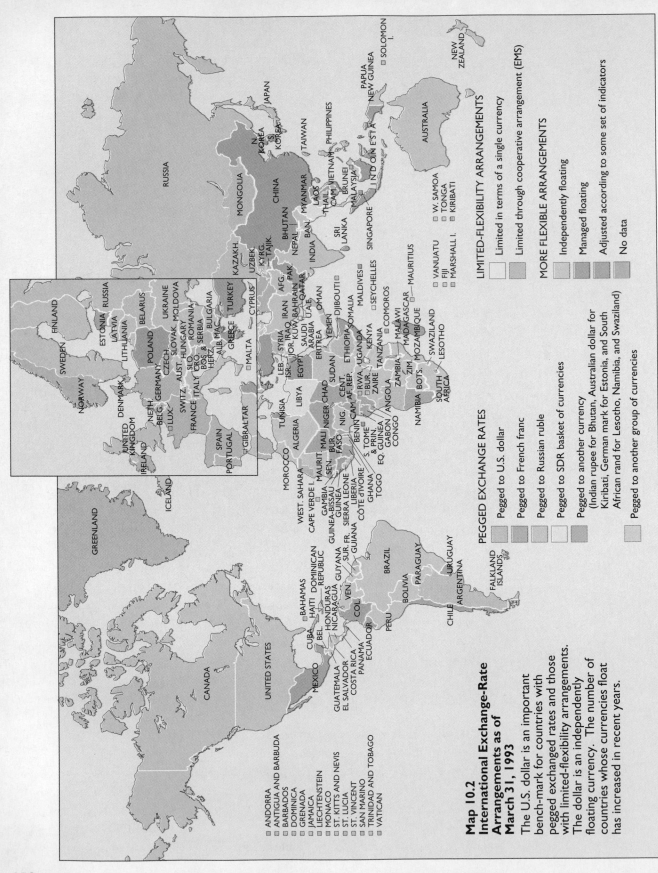

Map 10.2
International Exchange-Rate Arrangements as of March 31, 1993

The U.S. dollar is an important bench-mark for countries with pegged exchanged rates and those with limited-flexibility arrangements. The dollar is an independently floating currency. The number of countries whose currencies float has increased in recent years.

PEGGED EXCHANGE RATES

Pegged to U.S. dollar

Pegged to French franc

Pegged to Russian ruble

Pegged to SDR basket of currencies

Pegged to another currency
(Indian rupee for Bhutan, Australian dollar for Kiribati, German mark for Estonia, and South African rand for Lesotho, Namibia, and Swaziland)

Pegged to another group of currencies

LIMITED-FLEXIBILITY ARRANGEMENTS

Limited in terms of a single currency

Limited through cooperative arrangement (EMS)

MORE FLEXIBLE ARRANGEMENTS

Independently floating

Managed floating

Adjusted according to some set of indicators

No data

ANDORRA
ANTIGUA AND BARBUDA
BARBADOS
DOMINICA
GRENADA
JAMAICA
LIECHTENSTEIN
MONACO
ST. KITTS AND NEVIS
ST. LUCIA
ST. VINCENT
SAN MARINO
TRINIDAD AND TOBAGO
VATICAN

ple, there is a parity rate for the French franc and the German mark, for the French franc and the Italian lira, and so on. Until 1993, bilateral exchange rates were allowed to deviate from the EMS parity rate by only 2.25 percent before the central banks of the countries involved were to intervene to protect the integrity of the central rate. The exceptions to this were the Spanish peseta and the British pound, which were permitted to fluctuate by 6 percent. However, the EMS went through several changes in 1992 and 1993: Italy and Great Britain dropped out of the system in 1992, and the allowed deviation from the parity rates increased from 2.25 percent to 15 percent in 1993.

More Flexible Arrangements

Currencies of the countries with more flexible arrangements float independently, with governmental intervention to influence but not neutralize the speed of exchange-rate change. The leaders of the major industrial countries in this category meet periodically to discuss common economic issues; exchange-rate values are often on the agenda. For example, at the 1985 Plaza meeting of the G-7 (which was held at the Plaza Hotel in New York City), the governments of Canada, France, Germany, Italy, Japan, the United Kingdom, and the United States announced that the dollar had been strong too long. This declaration caused the dollar to begin to slide. (However, there also were strong economic fundamentals that contributed to the dollar's fall, such as a widening U.S. balance-of-trade deficit.)

It is interesting to note how this category of exchange-rate arrangements has changed in the last several years. In 1986, nineteen currencies were independently floating (12.6 percent of the total); in 1993, forty-eight were (28.7 percent of the total). Russia is an example of a country that recently joined the IMF and declared its currency to be independently floating. Because of hyperinflation, the ruble dropped from a value of less than 10 rubles per U.S. dollar as recently as 1991 to over 1700 rubles per dollar in March 1994. As Russia tries to implement the transition from a centrally planned to a market economy, its foreign-exchange market is working less than perfectly, even though the ruble is freely floating. For example, in 1993 exchange rates differed significantly from one part of the country to another. At one point, the buy/sell rate for the ruble in terms of the dollar was 1190/1270 in Moscow, 1250/1350 in Nizhiey Novgorod, and 1500/1600 in Khabarovsk. Arbitrageurs were able to convert rubles to dollars in Moscow at one rate, take the dollars to another city and convert them into rubles at a higher rate, and bring the rubles back to Moscow to convert into dollars at an even higher rate, resulting in profits of 20–40 percent, after bribes to customs officials.[6]

For countries in the "managed floating" subcategory, their governments usually set exchange rates for short intervals, such as a week at a time, and buy and sell the currency at that rate for that period. The Chinese renminbi now fits in this category, as does the Mexican peso, which was discussed in Chapter 9.

The final subcategory of more flexible arrangements, "adjusted according to some set of indicators," includes Chile. The Chilean peso is "pegged to the U.S.

dollar, at a rate adjusted at daily intervals according to a schedule established on the basis of the domestic rate of inflation during the previous month, less the estimated world rate of inflation."[7]

Black Markets

Of the 167 IMF member countries, 48 have currencies that are independently floating. Many of the others control their currencies fairly rigidly. Some license foreign exchange, as noted in Chapter 9, so that neither residents nor nonresidents enjoy full convertibility. In many of these countries, a black market parallels the official market and is aligned more closely with the forces of supply and demand than the official market is. The less flexible a country's exchange-rate arrangement is, the more likely there is to be a black market. The black market exists because the government buys dollars for less than people think they are worth. According to economic theory, if the government's official rate for the currency is overvalued, the black market tends to undervalue the same currency. The true economic value is probably somewhere in between.

The black market is problematic for companies because it provides a more accurate measure of a currency's value than does the official market. This is especially important in financial reporting. For example, a U.S. company operating in China prior to elimination of the swap market in 1993 and keeping its books in renminbi would have recorded its balance sheet as well as its results at the official rate of 5.8 yuan per dollar rather than the swap-market rate of 8.7 or the black-market rate, which may have been even higher than 8.7. Thus the company's balance sheet would have been overvalued in dollar terms. However, if the same company were to declare a dividend, it would have had to convert renminbi into dollars at the swap rate, not the official rate; the company would get about 33 percent fewer dollars at that rate. Thus the elimination of the dual-market system in China should eventually eliminate the need for a black market.

A black market will closely approximate real supply and demand for a currency.

The Role of Central Banks

Each country has a central bank that is responsible for the policies that affect the value of its currency on world markets. The central bank in the United States is the Federal Reserve System (the Fed), a system of twelve regional banks. The New York Federal Reserve Bank handles the Fed's intervention in foreign-exchange markets. Intervention policies are determined by the Federal Open Market Committee. However, the Fed does not act independently of the rest of the U.S. government; in particular, the Secretary of the Treasury is legally responsible for stabilizing the dollar's value.[8] Further, as mentioned earlier in this chapter, the EU is considering establishing a single European currency that would replace individual national currencies; that move would require a central bank of Europe to help establish monetary policy and intervene in currency markets.

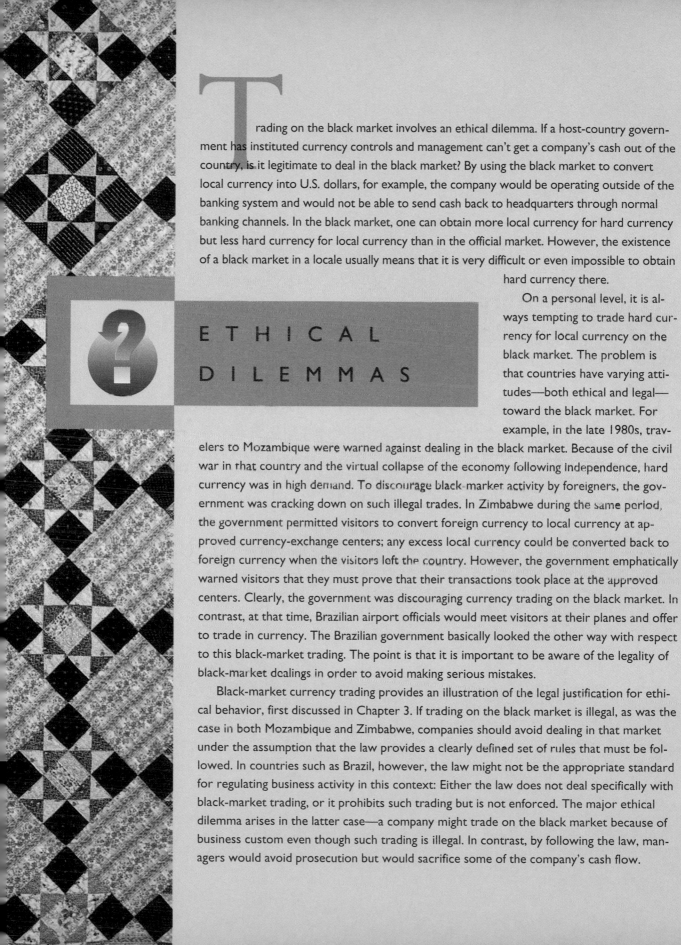

T rading on the black market involves an ethical dilemma. If a host-country government has instituted currency controls and management can't get a company's cash out of the country, is it legitimate to deal in the black market? By using the black market to convert local currency into U.S. dollars, for example, the company would be operating outside of the banking system and would not be able to send cash back to headquarters through normal banking channels. In the black market, one can obtain more local currency for hard currency but less hard currency for local currency than in the official market. However, the existence of a black market in a locale usually means that it is very difficult or even impossible to obtain hard currency there.

ETHICAL DILEMMAS

On a personal level, it is always tempting to trade hard currency for local currency on the black market. The problem is that countries have varying attitudes—both ethical and legal—toward the black market. For example, in the late 1980s, travelers to Mozambique were warned against dealing in the black market. Because of the civil war in that country and the virtual collapse of the economy following Independence, hard currency was in high demand. To discourage black-market activity by foreigners, the government was cracking down on such illegal trades. In Zimbabwe during the same period, the government permitted visitors to convert foreign currency to local currency at approved currency-exchange centers; any excess local currency could be converted back to foreign currency when the visitors left the country. However, the government emphatically warned visitors that they must prove that their transactions took place at the approved centers. Clearly, the government was discouraging currency trading on the black market. In contrast, at that time, Brazilian airport officials would meet visitors at their planes and offer to trade in currency. The Brazilian government basically looked the other way with respect to this black-market trading. The point is that it is important to be aware of the legality of black-market dealings in order to avoid making serious mistakes.

Black-market currency trading provides an illustration of the legal justification for ethical behavior, first discussed in Chapter 3. If trading on the black market is illegal, as was the case in both Mozambique and Zimbabwe, companies should avoid dealing in that market under the assumption that the law provides a clearly defined set of rules that must be followed. In countries such as Brazil, however, the law might not be the appropriate standard for regulating business activity in this context: Either the law does not deal specifically with black-market trading, or it prohibits such trading but is not enforced. The major ethical dilemma arises in the latter case—a company might trade on the black market because of business custom even though such trading is illegal. In contrast, by following the law, managers would avoid prosecution but would sacrifice some of the company's cash flow.

In spite of the unique nature of each country's central bank system, there is some semblance of international cooperation in the form of the **Bank for International Settlement (BIS)** in Basel, Switzerland. The BIS acts as a central banker's bank. It gets involved in swaps and other currency transactions between central banks in the major industrial countries. It also is a gathering place where central bankers discuss monetary cooperation.

Central bank assets are kept in two major forms—gold and foreign-exchange reserves. The ratio of one to the other varies by country. For example, the central bank's asset ratio in Denmark is 10 percent gold and 90 percent foreign-exchange reserves; in France, the split is fairly even. In 1991, global monetary reserves for IMF members were primarily in foreign exchange, in part because the IMF values gold reserves at 10 percent of their market value. Many countries value their gold reserves at their cost when acquired rather than at market value. Of all foreign-exchange reserves in 1992, 55.8 percent were in U.S. dollars, 18.5 percent in German marks, and 10.6 percent in Japanese yen.[9]

Because most central banks consider gold to be the major reserve asset, their holdings remain fairly constant. Central banks are concerned primarily with liquidity to ensure they have the cash and flexibility needed to protect their countries' currencies. The mix of currencies in a country's reserves is based on its major **intervention currencies,** that is, the currencies in which the country trades the most. The degree to which a central bank actively manages its reserves to earn a profit varies by country. Generally, Asian banks, especially the Central Bank of Malaysia, are more aggressive than are European central banks or the Fed in generating reserve profits.[10]

European central banks played a role in the July–August 1993, currency crisis when, to prop up their currencies, many purchased or borrowed German marks from the Bundesbank (Germany's central bank) and then used the marks in currency markets to buy their own currencies, creating a demand and increasing the price. The Bundesbank sold $35 billion in marks in one day to help support other European currencies. Unfortunately, its efforts failed, and other European currencies fell in value against the mark.

The Determination of Exchange Rates

Exchange rates are determined under one of three major types of exchange-rate systems: freely fluctuating, managed fixed, and automatic fixed. Other factors that affect exchange rates are inflation, interest-rate differentials, and technical factors.

Freely Fluctuating Currencies

Currencies that freely fluctuate respond to supply and demand conditions relatively free from government intervention. This concept can be illustrated using a two-country model involving the United States and Japan. Figure 10.2 shows the equilibrium exchange rate in the market and then a movement to a new equilibrium

Figure 10.2
Equilibrium Exchange Rate

Comparatively high inflation in the United States compared with Japan raises the demand for yen but lowers the supply of yen, increasing the value of the yen in terms of U.S. dollars. If the Japanese government wants to keep the dollar/yen exchange rate at e_0, it needs to sell yen for dollars in order to increase the supply of yen in the market and therefore decrease the exchange rate.

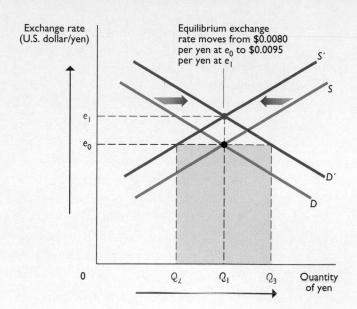

level as the situation changes. The demand for yen in this example is a function of U.S. demand for Japanese goods and services, such as automobiles, and yen-denominated financial assets, such as securities. The supply of yen, which in this illustration is tied to the demand for dollars, is a function of Japanese demand for U.S. goods and services and dollar-denominated financial assets. Initially, the supply of and demand for yen in Fig. 10.2 meet at the equilibrium exchange rate e_0 (for example, 0.008 dollars per yen, or 125 yen per dollar) and the quantity of yen Q_1.

Assume demand for U.S. goods and services by Japanese consumers drops because of, say, relatively high U.S. inflation. This would result in reduced supply of yen in the foreign-exchange market, causing the supply curve to shift to S'. Simultaneously, the increasing prices of U.S. goods might lead to an increase in demand for Japanese goods and services by U.S. consumers. This in turn would lead to an increase in demand for yen in the market, causing the demand curve to shift to D' and finally leading to an increase in the quantity of yen and an increase in the exchange rate. Thus the new equilibrium exchange rate would be at e_1 (for example, 0.0095 dollars per yen, or 105 yen per dollar). From a dollar standpoint, the increased demand for Japanese goods would lead to an increase in supply of dollars as more consumers tried to trade their dollars for yen, and the reduced demand for U.S. goods would result in a drop in demand for dollars. This would result in a reduction in the dollar's price, indicating a devaluation of the dollar.

Managed Fixed Exchange-Rate Systems

In the preceding example, Japanese and U.S. authorities allowed changes in the exchange rates between their two currencies to occur in order for currencies to reach a new exchange-rate equilibrium. In fact, however, one or both countries might not want exchange rates to change. For example, assume the United States and Japan decide to manage their exchange rates. The U.S. government might not want its currency to weaken because its companies and consumers would have to pay more for Japanese products, which would lead to more inflationary pressure in the United States. The Japanese government might not want the yen to strengthen because it would mean unemployment in its export industries. But how can the governments keep the values from changing when the United States is earning too few yen? Somehow the difference between yen supply and demand must be neutralized.

In a managed fixed exchange-rate system, the New York Federal Reserve Bank would hold foreign-exchange reserves, which it would have built up through the years for this type of contingency. It could sell enough of its yen reserves (make up the difference between Q_1 and Q_3 in Fig. 10.2) at the fixed exchange rate to maintain that rate. Or the Japanese central bank might be willing to accept dollars so that U.S. consumers can continue to buy Japanese goods. These dollars would then become part of Japan's foreign-exchange reserves.

The fixed rate could continue as long as the United States had reserves and/or as long as the Japanese were willing to add dollars to their holdings. Unless something changed the basic imbalance in the currency supply and demand, however, the New York Federal Reserve Bank would run out of yen and the Japanese central bank would stop accepting dollars because it would fear holding too many. At this point, it would be necessary to change the exchange rate so as to lessen the demand for yen.

Once a country determines that intervention will not work, it must adjust its currency's value. If the currency is freely fluctuating, the exchange rate will seek the correct level according to the laws of supply and demand. However, a currency that is pegged to another currency or to a basket of currencies usually is changed on a formal basis with respect to its reference currency or currencies. This formal change is more accurately termed a devaluation or revaluation, depending on the direction of the change. As noted earlier, if the foreign-currency equivalent of the domestic currency falls (or the domestic-currency equivalent of the foreign currency rises), then the domestic currency has been devalued in relation to the foreign currency. The opposite happens in the case of a revaluation.

Automatic Fixed Exchange-Rate System

As with the managed fixed exchange-rate system, assume that Japan and the United States agreed to maintain fixed exchange rates by setting their domestic money supplies on the basis of the amount of reserves held by their central banks and by denominating their currency values in terms of their reserve assets. Now suppose the United States has a shortage of yen. Under an automatic fixed exchange-rate system, the United States hypothetically would sell gold to get the needed yen. However, unlike with the managed system, there would be automatic adjustments to prevent the United States from running out of gold. As the United States sold off some of its gold, its money supply, which is tied to the amount of gold it holds, would fall. This would lead to higher interest rates and lower investment in the United States, followed by increased unemployment and lower prices. Meanwhile,

---

A government buys and sells its currency in the open market as a means of influencing the currency's price.

Devaluation occurs when a government reduces the value of its currency relative to that of a foreign currency.

Revaluation occurs when a government increases the value of its currency relative to that of a foreign currency.

the increase in gold in Japan would have the opposite effect. The higher U.S. interest rates and the decrease in U.S. prices relative to the Japanese rate and prices would cause an increase in the supply of yen in the United States as funds flowed in for investment and to purchase U.S. goods and services. This would result in a strengthening of the dollar and a weakening of the yen.

This system differs from the others in that the adjustment of exchange rates does not depend on government intervention but rather on changes in the domestic money supply. A change in exchange rate for a freely fluctuating currency is more a function of the supply and demand of the currency in the foreign-exchange market than in the domestic money market. Thus, although the law of supply and demand can determine exchange rates in an open market, many governments intervene in the market to influence exchange-rate movements. Although the automatic fixed exchange-rate system is possible, it is not as widely used as freely fluctuating currencies and managed fixed exchange-rate systems.

Purchasing-Power Parity

If the domestic inflation rate is lower than that in a foreign country, the domestic currency should be stronger than that of the foreign country.

Purchasing-power parity (PPP) is the key theory that explains the relationships between currencies. In essence, it claims that a change in relative inflation must result in a change in exchange rates in order to keep the prices of goods in two countries fairly similar. According to the PPP theory, if for example, Japanese inflation were 2 percent and U.S. inflation were 3.5 percent, the dollar's value would be expected to fall by the difference in inflation rates. Then the dollar would be worth fewer yen than before the adjustment, and the yen would be worth more dollars than before the adjustment.

The following formula can be used to relate inflation to exchange-rate changes:

$$\frac{e_t - e_0}{e_0} = \frac{i_{h,t} - i_{f,t}}{1 + i_{f,t}}$$

where

$e =$ the exchange rate quoted in terms of the number of units of the domestic (home) currency for one unit of the foreign currency
$i =$ the inflation rate
h indicates the home country (in these examples, the United States)
f indicates the foreign country (in these examples, Japan)
0 indicates the beginning of a period
t indicates the end of the period

The anticipated future exchange rate is given by

$$e_t = e_0 \left(\frac{1 + i_{h,t}}{1 + i_{f,t}} \right)$$

For example, assume the consumer price index (CPI) went from 100 to 103.5 in the United States and from 100 to 102 in Japan during a period when the exchange rate at the beginning of the period was 125 yen to the dollar, or 0.008 dollars per yen. The inflation rates are

$$i_{h,t} = \frac{103.5 - 100}{100} = 0.035$$

$$i_{f,t} = \frac{102 - 100}{100} = 0.02$$

Now the formula above gives

$$e_t = 0.008 \left(\frac{1 + 0.035}{1 + 0.02} \right) = 0.00812$$

The exchange rate at the end of the period is 0.00812 dollars per yen, or 123.2 yen per dollar. Thus the yen is worth more dollars, and the dollar is worth fewer yen when inflation is higher in the United States than in Japan.

As explained in the opening case, inflation is a major concern for the Chinese government. If it cannot control China's economy and lower its inflation rate, stabilizing the currency's value will be very difficult. The fear is that the renminbi will lose significant value against the U.S. dollar.

The PPP theory is very useful in explaining the relationship between inflation and exchange rates, but it is not perfect. It requires making assumptions about the equilibrium exchange rate at a starting point. Further, currencies are rarely related accurately in a two-country world. When several currencies are involved, it is difficult to use prices to determine an equilibrium rate. Also, exchange rates are essentially a function of internationally traded goods, whereas inflation rates relate to all goods, traded or not. Since 1973, the world essentially has shifted to a floating-rate regime, and so exchange rates have not conformed very closely to the PPP theory. In 1986, for example, the market exchange rate for the Japanese yen was 168 yen per dollar. However, the exchange rate equalized according to the PPP theory should have been 223, a difference of 24.2 percent. Also, the German mark was 12.5 percent weaker against the U.S. dollar than it should have been in 1986, and the British pound was 19.3 percent stronger than it should have been.[12] A more recent example involves the Japanese yen. In January 1993, the yen/dollar exchange rate was 124.6 yen per dollar; by the end of June, it was 107.10 yen per dollar. With the annual U.S. inflation rate at approximately 3.5 percent, the annual inflation rate in Japan would have had to be a negative 11 percent for the PPP theory alone to predict exchange rates.

Another good illustration of the fallibility of the PPP theory for estimating exchange rates is the Big Mac index of currencies used by The Economist each year. The price of a Big Mac can be used to estimate the exchange rate between the dollar and another currency (see Table 10.1). For example, in 1994, a Big Mac cost an average of $2.30 in the United States and ¥391 in Japan. Dividing the yen price by the dollar price yields an exchange rate of 170 yen per dollar, according to the PPP theory. However, the actual exchange rate was 104 yen per dollar, so the yen was overvalued compared to the dollar. In other words, it would take more dollars to buy a Big Mac in Japan than it would in the United States. Based on the actual exchange rate, a Big Mac would cost $3.77 in Japan rather than $2.30. The overvalued yen would

Table 10.1
Big Mac Currencies: The Hamburger Standard

	Big Mac prices		Actual dollar exchange rate, 5/4/94	implied PPP[†] of the dollar	Local currency undervaluation (−) or overvaluation (+) (%)[**]
	Price in local currency[*]	Price in dollars			
United States[‡]	$2.30	2.30	—	—	—
Argentina	Peso3.60	3.60	1.00	1.57	+57
Australia	A$2.45	1.72	1.42	1.07	−25
Austria	Sch34.00	2.84	12.0	14.8	+23
Belgium	BFr109	3.10	35.2	47.39	+35
Brazil	Cr1,500	1.58	949	652	−31
Britain	£1.81	2.65	1.46[‡‡]	1.27[‡‡]	+15
Canada	C$2.86	2.06	1.39	1.24	−10
Chile	Peso948	2.28	414	412	−1
China	Yuan9.00	1.03	8.70	3.91	−55
Czech Republic	CKr50	1.71	29.7	21.7	−27
Denmark	DKr25.75	3.85	6.69	11.2	+67
France	FFr18.5	3.17	5.83	8.04	+38
Germany	DM4.60	2.69	1.71	2.00	+17
Greece	Dr620	2.47	251	270	+8
Holland	Fl5.45	2.85	1.91	2.37	+24
Hong Kong	HK$9.20	1.19	7.73	4.00	−48
Hungary	Forint169	1.66	103	73.48	−29
Italy	Lire4,550	2.77	1,641	1,978	+21
Japan	¥391	3.77	104	170	+64
Malaysia	M$3.77	1.40	2.69	1.64	−39
Mexico	Peso8.10	2.41	3.36	3.52	+5
Poland	Zloty31,000	1.40	22,433	13,478	−40
Portugal	Esc440	2.53	174	191	+10
Russia	Rouble2,900	1.66	1,775	1,261	−29
Singapore	$2.98	1.90	1.57	1.30	−17
South Korea	Won2,300	2.84	810	1,000	+24
Spain	Ptas345	2.50	138	150	+9
Sweden	Skr25.5	3.20	7.97	11.1	+39
Switzerland	SFr5.70	3.96	1.44	2.48	+72
Taiwan	NT$62	2.35	26.4	26.96	+2
Thailand	Baht48	1.90	25.3	20.87	−17

[*]Prices vary locally
[†]Purchasing-power parity: local price divided by price in United States
[**]Against the dollar

[‡]Average of New York, Chicago, San Francisco, and Atlanta
[‡‡]Dollars per pound

Source: From *The Economist,* 4/9/94, p. 88. © 1994 The Economist Newspaper Group, Inc. Reprinted with permission.

make it expensive for American tourists to shop in Japan, but would make the United States a bargain for Japanese tourists.

Interest Rates

To relate interest rates to exchange rates, we first must relate interest rates to inflation. This is accomplished using the **Fisher Effect,** the theory that the nominal interest rate r in a country is determined by the real interest rate R and the inflation rate i as follows:

$$(1 + r) = (1 + R)(1 + i)$$

According to this theory, if the real interest rate is 5 percent, the U.S. inflation rate is 2.9 percent, and the Japanese inflation rate is 1.5 percent, then the nominal interest rates for the United States and Japan are computed as follows:

$$r_{US} = (1.05)(1.029) - 1 = 0.08045, \text{ or } 8.045 \text{ percent}$$

$$r_{J} = (1.05)(1.015) - 1 = 0.06575, \text{ or } 6.575 \text{ percent}$$

Thus the difference between U.S. and Japanese interest rates is a function of the difference between their inflation rates. If their inflation rates were the same (zero differential) but interest rate was 10 percent in the United States and 6.575 percent in Japan, investors would place their money in the United States, where they could get the higher real return.

The bridge from interest rates to exchange rates can be explained by the **International Fisher Effect (IFE),** the theory that the interest-rate differential is an unbiased predictor of future changes in the spot exchange rate. An unbiased predictor is one that is neither consistently above nor consistently below the actual future spot exchange rate. This does not mean the interest-rate differential is an accurate predictor, just that it is unbiased.

For example, the IFE predicts that if nominal interest rates in the United States are higher than those in Japan, the dollar's value should fall in the future by that interest-rate differential, which would be an indication of a weakening, or depreciation, of the dollar. Remember from the example of the Fisher Effect that nominal interest rates were higher in the United States than in Japan because inflation was higher in the United States. Thus, if inflation is lower in Japan than in the United States, the dollar is expected to be weaker against the yen. This prediction flows from the example used earlier in the discussion of freely fluctuating currencies, in which consumers would demand Japanese goods rather than U.S. goods, causing an increase in demand for yen and a contraction in supply of yen (see Fig. 10.2). These events in turn would lead to a strengthening of the yen or a weakening of the dollar.

The interest-rate differential also is the most important factor in determining the forward exchange rate. For example, if exchange rates between the United

If the nominal interest rate in one country is lower than that in another, the first country's inflation rate is expected to be lower so that real interest rates are equal.

The IFE implies that the currency of the country with the lower interest rate will strengthen in the future.

Forward exchange rates are determined primarily by interest-rate differentials.

States and Japan remained constant but the U.S. interest rate was significantly greater than the Japanese interest rate, investors would always invest in the United States. In theory, the forward rate would be the rate that exactly neutralized the difference between U.S. and Japanese interest rates. If the U.S. interest rate was higher than the Japanese interest rate, the forward exchange rate for the U.S. dollar would be lower than that for the Japanese yen by the interest-rate differential. Thus the yield in dollars from the U.S. investment would equal the yield in dollars from the yen investment converted at the forward rate. That is, the forward rate allows investors to trade currencies freely for future delivery at no exchange risk and without any difference in interest income. If a difference were to exist, traders would take advantage of it and earn income until it was eliminated.

Although the interest-rate differential is the critical factor for a few of the most widely traded currencies, the expectation of the future spot rate also is very important. Normally, a trader will automatically compute the forward rate using the interest-rate differential and then adjust it for the expected future spot rate where necessary. Some quoted forward rates are based strictly on such expected spot rates rather than on interest-rate differentials. This is especially true for currencies that are not traded very widely and not totally convertible.

Other Factors

Various other factors can cause exchange-rate changes. One important determinant in a world of political and economic uncertainty is confidence. During times of turmoil, people prefer to hold currencies that are considered safe-haven ones. For example, during the early 1980s, the U.S. dollar was considered a safe-haven currency, and this perception was an important source of its strength. For example, when the value of Mexican peso began to slide during that period, local investors transferred large amounts of pesos out of Mexico via dollar transfers until the Mexican government clamped down. The investors had no confidence in the peso and preferred to hold dollar balances outside of Mexico. In 1990, after Iraq invaded Kuwait, the dollar strengthened a little because of the safe-haven perception, but more negative economic fundamentals, such as the U.S. trade deficit, eventually forced it back down. Again, during the first few days of the 1993 European monetary crisis, the dollar rose in value as a safe haven. When the markets quieted down, however, it fell back.

In addition to basic economic forces and confidence in leadership, exchange rates are also influenced by a number of technical factors, such as the release of national economic statistics, seasonal demands for a currency, and a slight strengthening of a currency following a prolonged weakness, or vice versa. An example of the effect of a technical factor occurred in August 1993 when the exchange-rate mechanism of the EMS changed from permitting a 2.25-percent deviation from parity rates to allowing a 15-percent deviation. Traders felt that the dollar would tend to soften as central banks in Europe repurchased the marks they borrowed from the Bundesbank to prop up their currencies.[13]

Other key factors affecting exchange-rate movements are confidence and technical factors, such as the release of economic statistics.

Forecasting Exchange-Rate Movements

The preceding section looked at the effect of the law of supply and demand on exchange rates, showed how governments intervene to manage exchange-rate movements, and explained how inflation and interest rates can be important determinants of exchange rates. This section identifies factors that can be monitored in order to get an idea of what will happen to exchange rates.

Managers need to be concerned with the timing, magnitude, and direction of an exchange-rate movement.

Because various factors influence exchange-rate movements, managers must be able to analyze those factors in order to formulate a general idea of the timing, magnitude, and direction of an exchange-rate movement. However, prediction is not a precise science, and many things can cause the best of predictions to differ significantly from reality.

For freely fluctuating currencies, the law of supply and demand determines market value. However, very few currencies in the world float freely without any government intervention; most are managed to a certain extent, which implies that governments need to make political decisions regarding the value of their currencies. Assuming governments use a rational basis for managing these values (an assumption that may not always be realistic), managers can monitor the same factors the governments follow in order to try to predict values. These factors are

- Capital controls
- Exchange-rate spreads
- Balance-of-payments statistics
- Foreign-exchange reserves
- GNP or GDP growth
- Government spending
- Relative inflation rates
- Money-supply growth
- Interest-rate differentials
- Trends in exchange-rate movements[14]

The Balance of Payments and Forecasting

Major factors to consider in predicting exchange-rate movements include balance-of-payments statistics.

A country's balance of payments (discussed in Chapter 4) is important to forecasting exchange rates. For example, the yen's climb toward its post–World War II highs against the dollar in mid-1993 seemed strange given the relatively low inflation in the United States and the political instability in Japan. However, traders were reacting to Japan's current-account surplus of $10.71 billion in June 1993, which was up 14 percent from the preceding year. As one trader said, "The foreign-exchange markets don't look at [economic] growth or politics. They look at trade."[15] Another example of the impact of the balance of payments involves the Mexican peso. In mid-1993, some experts predicted a fall in the peso because of

Mexico's growing current-account deficit, which by the end of 1992 had been $22.5 billion, nearly 7 percent of Mexico's GDP. However, other experts felt Mexico's reserves of $24 billion and its rumored standby letter of credit of $20 billion with the New York Federal Reserve Bank were enough to bolster the currency.[16]

It is important to monitor the current-account balance, which includes merchandise trade, services, and unilateral transfers, because of the sheer volume of transactions that balance reflects and because that balance summarizes the real transactions that occur in a country. More specifically, the balance of merchandise trade is the most basic measure of a country's transactions with the rest of the world. For some countries, however, the balance of services is just as important. This is especially true for countries that generate significant amounts of foreign exchange through tourism or that have significant amounts of inflows or outflows of FDI.

Capital flows also must be monitored when forecasting exchange-rate movements. For example, although relatively high U.S. interest rates have slowed the U.S. economy, they also have made the United States relatively more attractive to investors, particularly from Japan. Thus the United States has been able to finance its balance-of-trade deficit in part with an inflow of long-term foreign capital.

Using balance-of-payments statistics to forecast exchange rates requires looking at several balances, such as the balance-of-merchandise trade, the current-account balance, and the basic balance (the current-account balance plus the balance on long term capital). For example, in mid-1990, Japan had the world's biggest current-account surplus, a growth rate of 5 percent, and an inflation rate half that of the industrial countries, yet it also had a weak yen and a declining stock market. The problem was that Japan's basic balance was in trouble. The current-account surplus was more than offset by an outflow of capital, and the yen's PPP value was closer to 170–200 yen per dollar than to 135–140 yen per dollar. At the same time, Germany also had a large current-account surplus. However, unlike Japan, it had a low capital outflow, and so the German mark was strong rather than weak.[17]

Fundamental and Technical Forecasting

Fundamental forecasting uses trends in economic variables to predict future exchange rates.

Technical forecasting uses past trends in exchange rate movements to spot future trends.

Forecasting exchange rates can be done using either of two approaches: fundamental or technical. Fundamental forecasting involves using trends in economic variables to predict future rates. The data can be plugged into an econometric model or evaluated on a more subjective basis. Technical forecasting involves using past trends to spot future trends. Technical forecasters, or chartists, assume that if current exchange rates reflect all facts in the market, then under similar circumstances future rates will follow the same patterns.[18]

However, all forecasting is imprecise. A corporate treasurer who wants to forecast an exchange rate, say, the relationship between the British pound and the U.S. dollar, might use a variety of sources, both internal and external to the company. Many treasurers and bankers use outside forecasters to obtain input for their own forecasts. Forecasters need to provide ranges or point estimates with subjective probabilities based on available data and subjective interpretation. Biases that can skew forecasts include the following:

- Overreaction to unexpected and dramatic news events
- Illusory correlation, that is, the tendency to see correlations or associations in data that are not statistically present but that are expected to occur on the basis of prior beliefs
- Focusing on a particular subset of information at the expense of the overall set of information
- Insufficient adjustment for subjective matters, such as market volatility
- Inability to learn from one's past mistakes
- Overconfidence in one's ability[19]

Good treasurers and bankers develop their own forecasts of what will happen to a particular currency and use fundamental or technical forecasts of outside forecasters to corroborate these. Doing this helps them determine whether they are considering important factors and whether they need to revise their forecasts in light of outside analyses. However, it is important to understand that no matter how carefully prepared a forecast is, it is still a guess. Forecasting includes predicting the timing, direction, and magnitude of an exchange-rate change. The timing is often a political decision, and therefore not necessarily rational or predictable. And although the direction of a change probably can be predicted, the magnitude is difficult to forecast.

For example, currency forecasting is important for Chrysler because of its foreign investments, foreign market opportunities, and foreign sourcing of components. The company uses three forecasting models. Realizing that exchange rates are difficult to forecast, it bases its short-term forecasts—one week to one month—largely on qualitative information provided by local managers. It also uses outside currency traders who specialize in short-term forecasts. Over the medium term—one to three years—Chrysler focuses more on macroeconomic indicators, especially fiscal and monetary policy. The company's long-term forecasting is more imprecise but utilizes the same indicators as for the medium-term forecasts along with structural shifts occurring in the economy.[20]

Business Implications of Exchange-Rate Changes

Marketing Decisions

A devaluation of a currency could help the country's imports become more expensive and its exports less expensive.

On the marketing side, exchange rates can affect demand for a company's products at home and abroad. For example, if Mexico's exports became too expensive because of its relatively high inflation, it might force down the value of its currency. Although inflation would cause the peso value of Mexican products to rise, the devaluation would mean that less foreign currency would be required to buy pesos.

Thus Mexican products would remain competitive. An interesting ramification of such a peso devaluation would be the impact the cheaper Mexican goods would have on exporters from other countries. For example, the cheaper Mexican goods flooding the market in Argentina might take away market share from Italian exporters, thus affecting the Italian economy.

When the U.S. dollar fell in value in 1992, foreign shoppers flocked to the United States to buy cheaper merchandise. For example, Swatch watches that cost $350–$400 overseas were selling for $80; Timberland moccasins that sold for $235 in Japan could be purchased for $120; and Sony Walkmans, which cost $100 in Italy, could be purchased for $50.[21] A related problem confronted the German electrical equipment manufacturer, Siemens AG. In the mid-1980s, when the U.S. economy was strong and the mark was rising against the dollar, Siemens simply increased its prices and passed on the exchange-rate difference to consumers. In 1992, however, when the U.S. economy was very weak, Siemens, fearing it might lose market share, hesitated to burden consumers with price increases.[22]

Production Decisions

Exchange-rate changes also can affect production decisions. For example, a manufacturer in a country where wages and operating expenses are high might be tempted to locate production in a country such as Brazil, whose currency is rapidly losing value. A foreign currency would buy lots of Brazilian currency, thus making the company's initial investment relatively cheap. Further, goods manufactured in Brazil would be relatively cheap in world markets. However, the company could accomplish the same purpose by going to any country whose currency is expected to remain weak in relation to that of the company's home country. For example, BMW made the decision to invest in production facilities in South Carolina because of the unfavorable exchange rate between the mark and the dollar. However, the company announced plans to use the facilities not only to serve the U.S. market, but also to export to Europe and other markets.[23]

Financial Decisions

Finally, exchange rates can affect financial decisions, primarily in the areas of sourcing of financial resources, remittance of funds across national borders, and reporting of financial results. In the first area, a company might be tempted to borrow money where interest rates are lowest. However, recall that interest-rate differentials often are compensated for in money markets through exchange-rate changes.

In deciding about cross-border financial flows, a company would want to convert local currency into its home-country currency when exchange rates are most favorable so that it can maximize its return. However, countries with weak currencies often have currency controls, making it difficult for MNEs to manage the flow of funds optimally.

Finally, exchange-rate changes can influence the reporting of financial results. A simple example illustrates the impact exchange rates can have on income. If a U.S.

When a currency changes in value, exporters and importers need to decide whether to change prices.

Companies might locate production in weak-currency countries because
• Initial investment there is relatively cheap
• Such a country is a good base for inexpensive exportation

Exchange rates can influence the sourcing of financial resources, the cross-border remittance of funds, and the reporting of financial results.

company's Mexican subsidiary earns 1 million pesos when the exchange rate is 3.12 pesos per dollar, the dollar equivalent of its income is $320,513. If the peso depreciates to 4 pesos per dollar, the dollar equivalent of that income falls to $250,000. The opposite will occur if the local currency appreciates against that of the company's home country.

COUNTERVAILING
F O R C E S

A country may give up some control over its currency to gain greater access to global markets.

Both MNEs and small companies involved in exporting and importing must consider the full range of implications of exchange-rate changes on marketing, production, and financial decisions. From a marketing standpoint, it might seem that small companies would be more likely to invoice sales in their home-country's currency in order to avoid foreign-exchange risk. However, this strategy is pursued by both large and small companies that are inexperienced in foreign sales. As companies move along the learning curve, they are more likely to consider invoicing sales in the foreign currency as a marketing strategy.

Small companies view production decisions differently than do MNEs. They are more likely to manufacture in the home-country market rather than rely on FDI in weak-currency countries as a means for manufacturing products for worldwide sale. The latter strategy is more common of large MNEs. However, small companies may subcontract production to independent manufacturers abroad in order to take advantage of lower-cost production in weak-currency countries.

The use of cross-border cash flows in the financial area is more complex for MNEs than for smaller companies. The financial flows of smaller companies are usually limited to purchases and sales, whereas those of MNEs involve the full range of activities—receivables and payables, dividends, royalties, management fees, and loans.

Another major issue surrounding foreign exchange is the potential for some loss of sovereignty. As noted in the opening case, China was forced to change its exchange-rate system in order to join GATT. By creating a more open foreign-exchange system, China was admitting it needs to bring its entire economy into harmony with the world economy. In the long run, this economic openness also may affect China's political system. Another example involving partial loss of sovereignty concerns the EMS. As discussed in Chapter 7, the Treaty of Maastricht includes a significant monetary component. A major goal of the treaty is to establish a common currency called the ECU by 1999. To accomplish this, the EU wants to set up a European central bank and to coordinate economic policies. A member country, to participate in the common currency, will have to bring its economic performance into conformity with the other members in such areas as inflation, interest rates, budget deficits, total public debt, and currency stability. For example, a successful candidate will have to have an inflation rate no more than 1.5 percent above the average of the three EU countries with the lowest rates of inflation.[24]

Unfortunately, the EMS suffered a crisis in 1992 and 1993. Germany, which was experiencing inflation in excess of 4 percent, had put over $250 billion into the reunification with the former East Germany. Thus the Bundesbank was forced to adopt a tight monetary policy that included keeping interest rates high as an anti-inflation measure. Because the EMS exchange-rate mechanism requires that currencies stay closely linked together, other EU member countries were forced to keep their interest rates high. However, Italy, Spain, and the United Kingdom were very concerned about high unemployment. Speculators bet that these countries would not want to keep their interest rates and, therefore, their exchange rates at artificially high levels. In September 1992, market forces against the pound and lira were so strong that Italy and the United Kingdom dropped out of the EMS and allowed their currencies to float, and Ireland, Portugal, and Spain were forced to devalue their currencies. Both Italy and the United Kingdom said they were interested in rejoining the EMS, but not until they could correct fundamental economic problems.[25]

During 1993, member countries worked hard to overcome their differences in order to salvage the EMS. France, with one of Europe's lowest inflation rates, was attempting to maintain the parity of the franc with the mark to keep it one of the strongest European currencies, leading some to predict that Europe might disintegrate into a two-tiered market: the strong-currency countries of Belgium, France, Germany, and the Netherlands versus everyone else. However, the fragile peace depended on German interest rates. In July 1993, the pressure finally became too great. On Friday, July 30, Germany decided to keep interest rates high. The EMS was pushed to the brink of collapse. Speculators immediately began selling the currencies of Belgium, Denmark, France, Portugal, and Spain. Finally, finance ministers decided to increase the allowed deviation from parity rates from 2.25 percent to 15 percent rather than end the EMS completely.[26] Clearly, a price of EU membership is loss of sovereignty over fiscal and monetary policy and thus over exchange rates.

LOOKING TO THE FUTURE

The international monetary system has undergone significant reform in the past two decades. As HPEs undergo transition to market economies, they will experience significant pressure on their exchange rates. High inflation rates and weak demand for their currencies will lead to major devaluations. These certainly are key factors affecting the Russian ruble. In addition, former Soviet republics will need to decide whether to maintain a close relationship with the ruble or to establish a tie with a Western European currency.

The exchange-rate mechanism will continue to be an indicator of success for the EU. If EU member countries cannot better harmonize their monetary and fiscal policies, there will be no common currency by 1999. The key is whether members such as Germany can agree to control inflation and interest rates for the good of other members. In addition, for a common currency to become a reality, the EMS must return to a 2.25-percent allowed deviation from parity rates and both Italy and the United Kingdom must rejoin the system.

Among countries with more flexible exchange-rate arrangements, those whose rates are adjusted according to some set of indicators or managed floating will need to gain greater control over their economies in order to move to the "independently floating" subcategory. Countries whose currencies independently float are under constant pressure to control inflation and to keep from being tempted to intervene in the markets. The greater the instability, the more likely central banks are to try intervention.

Companies will continue to face constant pressure to understand the factors influencing particular exchange rates and to adjust corporate strategy in anticipation of exchange-rate movements. This will become easier only if exchange-rate volatility diminishes, which does not appear likely to occur in the near future.

Summary

- The International Monetary Fund (IMF) was organized in 1944 to promote exchange-rate stability, maintain orderly exchange-rate arrangements, avoid competitive currency devaluations, establish a multilateral system of payments, eliminate exchange restrictions, and create standby reserves.

- The Special Drawing Right (SDR) was instituted by the IMF to increase international reserves.

- The exchange-rate arrangements of countries that are members of the IMF are divided into three categories: pegged exchange rates, limited-flexibility arrangements, and more flexible arrangements.

- The European Monetary System (EMS) had a major crisis in 1993, jeopardizing the EU goal of establishing a common currency by 1999.

- Many countries that strictly control and regulate the convertibility of their currency have a black market that maintains an exchange rate that is more indicative of supply and demand than is the official rate.

- The Bank for International Settlements (BIS) in Switzerland acts as a central banker's bank. It facilitates communication and transactions among the world's central banks.

- Central banks use foreign-exchange reserves to support their countries' currencies and to earn a profit.

- The demand for a country's currency is a function of the demand for its goods and services and the demand for financial assets denominated in its currency.

- A central bank intervenes in money markets by creating a supply of its country's currency when it wants to push the value of the currency down or by creating a demand for the currency when it wants to strengthen its value.

- Devaluation of a currency occurs when formal governmental action causes the foreign-currency equivalent of that currency to fall (or that currency's equivalent for the foreign currency to rise). A depreciation occurs when a change in the same direction is permitted by the government but not formally acted on as such.

- Some factors that determine exchange rates are purchasing-power parity (relative rates of inflation), differences in real interest rates (nominal interest rates reduced by the amount of inflation), confidence in the government's ability to manage the political and economic situation, and certain technical factors that result from trading.

- The major determinant of the forward exchange rate is the interest-rate differential between currencies.

- Major factors managers should monitor when trying to predict the direction, magnitude, and timing of an exchange-rate change include balance-of-payments statistics, foreign-exchange reserves, relative inflation rates, interest-rate differentials, and trends in exchange-rate movements. Also, they must look at the political situation.

- Exchange rates can affect business decisions in three major areas: marketing, production, and finance.

Case
The Japanese Yen[27]

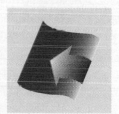

In 1993, Nissan, the large Japanese automaker, was trying to determine what to do about prices. As the yen/dollar exchange rate moved from its 1992 year-end level of 124.75 yen per dollar toward parity between yen and dollar, Nissan management was exploring several options: increase prices, keep prices the same and absorb the difference in profit margins, or move more production out of Japan to the United States or other low-cost countries.

To appreciate Nissan's dilemma, it is important to gain an historical perspective on the yen and its value against the dollar (see Map 10.3). As noted earlier in this chapter, the Japanese yen is classified as an "independently floating" currency by the IMF. As recently as 1985, the yen was trading at 251 yen per dollar. By 1985, the dollar began its long slide against the yen, and by the end of 1988, a dollar was worth only 125.85 yen (see Table 10.2). However, in 1989 and early 1990, there was a period of weakening of the yen against the dollar. The dollar rose to 132.05 yen at the end of the first quarter of 1989 and was at 144.1, 139.3, and 143.45 at the end of the second, third, and fourth quarters, respectively.

These moves in 1989 went against conventional wisdom. Most economists felt the rate would move to 100 yen per dollar by the end of 1989, but a number of domestic and international problems subsequently tempered their enthusiasm and led to a weakening of the yen: a stock scandal that included many of Japan's top political and business leaders (the Recruit Scandal), the Tiananmen Square incident in China, and the reunification of East and West Germany. In addition, there was a great deal of confidence in the U.S. government's ability to manage the U.S. economy. However, there was a huge gap between dollar-denominated and yen-denominated securities that drove up the demand for dollars. Part of the difference in interest rates was explained by the difference in consumer prices, but investors still could get a relatively higher real return on investments in securities in the United States.

- **Some factors that determine exchange rates are purchasing-power parity (relative rates of inflation), differences in real interest rates (nominal interest rates reduced by the amount of inflation), confidence in the government's ability to manage the political and economic situation, and certain technical factors that result from trading.**

- **The major determinant of the forward exchange rate is the interest-rate differential between currencies.**

- **Major factors managers should monitor when trying to predict the direction, magnitude, and timing of an exchange-rate change include balance-of-payments statistics, foreign-exchange reserves, relative inflation rates, interest-rate differentials, and trends in exchange-rate movements. Also, they must look at the political situation.**

- **Exchange rates can affect business decisions in three major areas: marketing, production, and finance.**

Case
The Japanese Yen[27]

In 1993, Nissan, the large Japanese automaker, was trying to determine what to do about prices. As the yen/dollar exchange rate moved from its 1992 year-end level of 124.75 yen per dollar toward parity between yen and dollar, Nissan management was exploring several options: increase prices, keep prices the same and absorb the difference in profit margins, or move more production out of Japan to the United States or other low-cost countries.

To appreciate Nissan's dilemma, it is important to gain an historical perspective on the yen and its value against the dollar (see Map 10.3). As noted earlier in this chapter, the Japanese yen is classified as an "independently floating" currency by the IMF. As recently as 1985, the yen was trading at 251 yen per dollar. By 1985, the dollar began its long slide against the yen, and by the end of 1988, a dollar was worth only 125.85 yen (see Table 10.2). However, in 1989 and early 1990, there was a period of weakening of the yen against the dollar. The dollar rose to 132.05 yen at the end of the first quarter of 1989 and was at 144.1, 139.3, and 143.45 at the end of the second, third, and fourth quarters, respectively.

These moves in 1989 went against conventional wisdom. Most economists felt the rate would move to 100 yen per dollar by the end of 1989, but a number of domestic and international problems subsequently tempered their enthusiasm and led to a weakening of the yen: a stock scandal that included many of Japan's top political and business leaders (the Recruit Scandal), the Tiananmen Square incident in China, and the reunification of East and West Germany. In addition, there was a great deal of confidence in the U.S. government's ability to manage the U.S. economy. However, there was a huge gap between dollar-denominated and yen-denominated securities that drove up the demand for dollars. Part of the difference in interest rates was explained by the difference in consumer prices, but investors still could get a relatively higher real return on investments in securities in the United States.

Map 10.3
Japan and the Yen
The Japanese yen has strengthened significantly against the U.S. dollar since World War II. Although the yen fluctuates against the dollar daily, the year-end yen/dollar exchange rate is indicative of the movement of the yen's value over time.

Year	Exchange rate yen/dollar at year's end
1970	357.65
1975	305.15
1980	203.0
1981	219.9
1982	235.0
1983	232.2
1984	251.1
1985	200.5
1986	159.1
1987	123.5
1988	125.85
1989	143.45
1990	134.4
1991	125.2
1992	124.75
1993	111.85

There were clearly some trouble spots in the Japanese economy. In late 1989, the stock market began to decline and inflationary pressures began to rise. In early 1990, there was open debate between the Ministry of Finance and the Bank of Tokyo over what the interest-rate policy should be. That debate drove the stock market down even further and shook investors' confidence in the Japanese government's ability to manage the economy and, therefore, the exchange rate.

Japan had once enjoyed the world's largest current-account surplus (that is, an excess of exports over imports), but since 1987 that surplus fell by one third because of a huge outflow of Japanese capital. Prices on Japanese assets, especially land and buildings, had risen dramatically, and Japanese investors found they could get a better yield on their money outside Japan. Thus the Japanese invested $26 billion overseas in 1989, up 21 percent from 1988. Japan's export of capital actually exceeded its current-account surplus.

As inflation fears began to rise in Japan, the natural response would have been to increase interest rates. The governor of the Bank of Japan decided to increase interest rates in December 1989, but the furor that ensued caused him to delay any further increases. Given that interest rates in the United States also were high at the time as a result of inflationary concerns, the demand for yen fell and the demand for dollars rose, increasing the price of the dollar in terms of yen. Although the yen was falling, the Japanese government couldn't figure out how to stop it. In the first three months of 1990, the Bank of Japan used 17 percent of its foreign-exchange reserves to sell dollars for yen, hoping to prop up the yen. The United States contributed to this effort by selling dollars for yen, but it didn't want to push the dollar down too much for fear of losing its battle against inflation. Both Japan and the United States tried to convince the governments of other countries, such as Germany and the United Kingdom, to go along with efforts to support the yen, but the

Table 10.2
Selected Economic Data for Japan, Other Countries, and the World, 1985–1992

Consumer prices and government bond rates tend to be lower in Japan than in the industrial countries in general and the United States in particular.

	1985	1986	1987	1988	1989	1990	1991	1992
Yen/dollar year-end exchange rate	200.50	159.10	123.50	125.85	143.45	134.4	125.2	124.75
Consumer prices*								
World	10.1	7.2	9.2	13.1	17.0	21.3	12.4	11.8
Industrialized countries	4.1	2.4	3.0	3.4	4.5	5.0	4.3	3.0
Developing countries	35.3	27.0	35.3	57.0	80.0	104.8	48.1	51.7
Germany	2.2	−0.1	0.2	1.3	2.8	2.7	3.5	4.0
Japan	2.0	0.6	0.0	0.7	2.3	3.1	3.3	1.7
United Kingdom	6.1	3.4	4.1	4.9	7.8	9.5	5.9	3.7
United States	3.6	1.9	3.7	4.0	4.8	5.4	4.2	3.0
Government bond rates								
Germany	6.87	5.92	5.84	6.10	7.09	8.88	8.63	7.96
Japan	6.34	4.94	4.21	4.27	5.05	7.36	6.53	4.94
United Kingdom	10.62	9.87	9.48	9.36	9.58	11.08	9.92	9.15
United States	10.62	7.68	8.38	8.85	8.50	8.55	7.86	7.01
Current account balance	49.17	85.83	87.02	79.61	56.99	35.87	72.91	—
Merchandise-trade balance	55.99	92.82	96.42	95.0	76.89	63.58	103.09	—

*Consumer prices reflect the change in the consumer price index over the prior year.

Source: Various issues of *International Financial Statistics* (Washington, D.C.: IMF).

U.S. government wanted those countries to use their own currencies rather than U.S. dollars. However, speculators realized that intervention would not solve the problems and that the solution lay in interest-rate policy.

By the end of the summer of 1990, many analysts were predicting that the exchange rate would be at 160 yen to the dollar by the end of the year. However, the U.S. economy began to weaken, and, as the U.S. government tried to avoid a recession, interest rates came down. The Persian Gulf War momentarily strengthened the dollar against the yen, but the economic fundamentals were more important. As Japanese interest rates rose and U.S. interest rates fell, the demand for the dollar fell, and so did the price. By the end of 1990, the exchange rate was hovering at 130 yen per dollar, after experiencing a high of 124.33 in the previous 12 months and a low of 159.79.

Relative calm reigned in 1991 and 1992 in terms of the yen/dollar exchange rate. In 1991, the rate fell gradually from 141 yen per dollar at the end of the first quarter to 125.2 yen per dollar by the end of the fourth quarter. As noted in Fig. 10.2, the yen continued its gradual climb against the dollar. The relationship between the yen and the dollar was actually more stable than that between the dollar and most European currencies.

In early 1993, the yen/dollar relationship began to change. The major catalyst was the G-7 meeting in February 1993, whose agenda was expected to include a forced appreciation of the yen. On February 24, however, U.S. Treasury Secretary Lloyd Bentsen stated there would be no communique at the end of the meeting. A massive sell-off of the dollar against the yen resulted. It was felt U.S. President Clinton was using a strong yen as one way to eliminate the huge trade deficit between the United States and Japan, which had reached $49.4 billion in 1992. As Fig. 10.3 shows, the dollar's plunge continued past the end of 1993's first quarter.

By spring, several yen/dollar scenarios were being discussed, with no real consensus emerging. For example, *The Economist* Intelligence Unit expected the exchange rate to be back to 125 yen per dollar within three months. Others, however, were forecasting that the yen would move to parity against the dollar and could plunge to double-digit levels.

This uncertainty created serious problems for firms. Nissan, for example, had based its financial plans for 1993 on a dollar trading at 120 yen, but the rise to 105 yen by mid-June meant a $600-million drop in profits. In 1985, after the Plaza Accord, when the yen doubled in value against the dollar, the Japanese economy was in strong shape, corporate profits were high, and U.S. automakers were in disarray. However, 1993 was a very different year. There was a difference of opinion as to the impact of exchange rates on competitiveness. Some experts argued that Japanese exporters could not be profitable at an exchange rate of 115 yen per dollar or higher, and one expert concluded that only 80 percent of Japan's exporters could be profitable at a rate of 120 yen. Given the 1993 political crisis in Japan and the relatively weak Japanese economy, most experts did not believe the yen would rise as much as it did. However, an economically weaker Europe and a large Japanese trade surplus caused the yen to continue to strengthen against the dollar. Corporate profits had declined three years in a row as of the fiscal year ending March 31, 1993, and the stronger yen was expected to cause profits to decline for a fourth year. For consumer electronics and automobiles, for example, profits were about 6 percent of sales in 1985 but only 1 percent of sales in 1993. One economist estimated that an average exchange rate of

**Figure 10.3
The Value of the U.S. Dollar in Terms of Yen, January 1991–April 1993**
The dollar steadily lost value against the yen in the early 1980s. By early 1994, its value had fallen to less than 100 yen per dollar.

Source: Data from various editions of *International Financial Statistics* (Washington, D.C.: IMF).

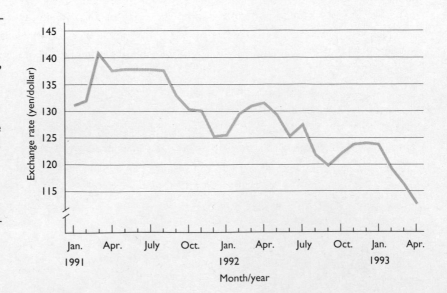

105 yen per dollar would cause real GNP growth to decline to 1 percent in the 1993 fiscal year and profits to fall by 33 percent.

As the Japanese economy continued to be weak, consumers became more price conscious and decided to make room for relatively cheap imports, thus creating more pressure on Japanese companies and taking away domestic cash flow that could have been used to subsidize export business.

In response to the yen's rise, Honda added $100 to $450 to the sticker prices of its various models, most of them assembled in the United States using Japanese parts. However, Matsushita Electric Corporation hesitated to raise prices, fearing sales would decline. Further, many Japanese producers of color TV sets did not plan to raise prices because most of their sets were made in countries in which labor is cheaper than in either Japan or the United States.

Thus Nissan was caught in a major dilemma: It did not know how U.S. competitors would respond to a price increase or what consumers would do if those U.S. companies did not increase prices, since they were becoming more competitive with the Japanese companies in terms of quality. One clear way Nissan could avoid the foreign-exchange penalty was to increase its U.S. production, as BMW did. However, it was concerned about how that might appear to its workers in Japan who might have to be laid off in the midst of a slowdown there. In addition, Nissan still would have to import many of its components.

Questions

1. What are some of the major factors that have influenced the yen/dollar exchange rate in the past decade? Have different factors become more important at different times? *(yes)*

   What are the major options available to Nissan in the strong yen environment? Which approach would you recommend, and why?

   the yen strengthens from 125 to 105 yen per dollar and Nissan imports an auto valued at ¥1,875,000 into the United States. What would be the impact of the rate change on the dollar cost of the auto? If the same car were manufactured in the United States at a cost of $15,000 and 40 percent of the parts were imported from Japan, what impact would the exchange-rate change have on the dollar ... percent of the parts were imported from Japan?

Evaluation of the IMF,"
...ent, September 1984,

pp. 72–73.
...und, *International
...gton, D.C.:* IMF,

*Exchange
...trictions An-
...D.C.:* IMF,

...assed
...e 28,

1993, p. 1 (appeared originally in the *Boston Globe*).

7. International Monetary Fund, op.cit., p. 97.
8. Julian Walmsley, *The Foreign Exchange Handbook* (New York: Wiley, 1983), pp. 84–90.
9. Simon Brady, "How Central Banks Play the Market," *Euromoney,* September 1992, p. 57.
10. Ibid., pp. 49–57.
11. Michael R. Sesit, "For Now, Central Bankers Regain Reins," *Wall Street Journal,* August 4, 1993, p. C1.

12. *International Economic Conditions* (Federal Reserve Bank of St. Louis, August 1987), p. 1.

13. Sesit, op. cit., p. C13.

14. David K. Eiteman, Arthur I. Stonehill, and Michael H. Moffett, *Multinational Business Finance,* 6th ed. (Reading, Mass.: Addison-Wesley, 1992), p. 162.

15. Quentin Hardy and Yumiko Ono, "Yen's Run-Up, Despite Political Crisis, Underscores Japan's Trading Strength," *Wall Street Journal,* August 5, 1993, p. A9.

16. "Mexico's Peso: Gone Tomorrow?" *The Economist,* May 29, 1993, pp. 87–88.

17. "The Japanese Paradox," *The Economist,* 7 April 1990, p. 77.

18. "Forecasting Currencies: Technical or Fundamental?" *Business International Money Report,* October 15, 1990, pp. 401–402.

19. Andrew C. Pollock and Mary E. Wilkie, "Briefing," *Euromoney,* June 1991, pp. 123–124.

20. "Forecasting at Chrysler," *F&T Risk Advisor,* April 1993, p. 7.

21. Julia Lawlor, "Weak Dollar Draws Foreign Shoppers," *USA Today,* November 18, 1992, p. B1.

22. Lindley H. Clark, Jr., and Alfred L. Malabre, "Foreign Firms' Units in U.S. Feel Pinch But Resist Raising Prices as Dollar Falls," *Wall Street Journal,* September 9, 1992, p. A2.

23. Oscar Suris, "BMW Expects U.S.-Made Cars to Have 80% Level of North American Content," *Wall Street Journal,* August 5, 1993, p. A2.

24. "How To Get Good Marks, or ECUs," *The Economist,* December 14, 1991, p. 52.

25. For background, see the following articles: "A Rough Year," *The Economist,* December 19, 1992, pp. 19–20; Michael R. Sesit, Stephen D. Moore, and Glenn Whitney, "The Financial Tension in Europe Is Spreading After Move by Sweden," *Wall Street Journal,* September 10, 1992, p. A1; Bill Javetski, John Templeman, Richard A. Melcher, and Mike McNamee, "Europe's Money Mess," *Business Week,* September 28, 1992, pp. 30–31; and Bill Javetski, William Glasgall, Richard A. Melcher, Patrick Oster, and Sabrina Kiefer, "Continental Drift: Now, A Two-Tiered Economy May Evolve," *Business Week,* October 5, 1992, pp. 34–36.

26. For background, see the following articles: Michael Sesit, Glenn Whitney, and Terence Roth, "German Stance on Rates Sends ERM to Brink," *Wall Street Journal,* July 30, 1993, p. C1; Craig R. Whitney, "Europeans Agree To Let Currencies Fluctuate Widely," *New York Times,* August 2, 1993, p. A1; Alan Riding, "Europe Is Picking Up the Pieces of a Hobbled Monetary System," *New York Times,* August 3, 1993, p. A1; and "Warm Hands,

Cold Heart," *The Economist* p. 65.

27. Most information for the cas the following sources: "Ecor rencies," *Euromoney,* May 19 Mike McNamee, "Only High Half the Yen's Big Slide," *Bus* 82; "The Japanese Paradox," 7 April 1990, p. 77; Steven H "Yen for Trouble," *Barron's,* 1990; *International Financial S* issues; Alexei Bayer, "Watch *Finance & Treasury,* April 26, Michael Williams, "Japan's C Surplus Eases, But Some Sa Won't Continue," *Wall S* 16, 1993, p. A9; Fred R. Firms Act to Lift U.S. P Weakness Against Ye June 28, 1993, p. A2: Yumiko Ono, "Yer litical Crisis, Unde Strength," *Wall S* 1993, p. A9; "Ba *The Economist,* J Uchitelle, "No Yen," *New Y* p. C1; Doug Vehicles R Steady R 16, 199 Look *Trea*

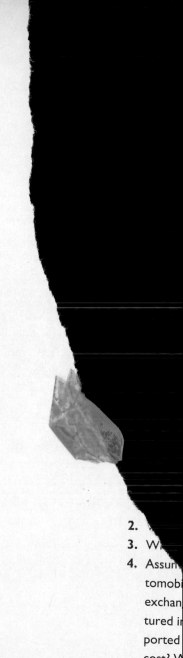

2.

3. W

4. Assur
   tomobi
   exchan
   tured i
   ported

uly 31, 1993,

came from
omies on Cur-
0, p. 145;
r Rates Can
ness Week, p.
The Economist,
Nagourney,
6 March
atistics, various
ing the Yen,"
1993, p. 6;
Global Trade
y May's Fall
treet Journal, June
Bleakley, "Japanese
rices, Citing Dollar's
n," Wall Street Journal,
Quentin Hardy and
's Run-Up, Despite Po-
rscores Japan's Trading
treet Journal, August 5,
shed by the Mighty Yen,"
une 5, 1993, p. 81; Louis
Quick Gain from Stronger
rk Times, April 26, 1993,
las Lavin, "Sales of Domestic
ose 15.5% in Early June Amid
ecovery," Wall Street Journal, June
, p. A2; and Joseph Neu, "Time to
t Yen/Dollar Positions," Finance &
sury, March 1, 1993, p. 7.

The Middle East has about two thirds of the world's known oil reserves. Here you see a manager in Saudi Arabia viewing an oil storage facility of Aramco, the world's largest petroleum company. The photo is set against a background showing part of a double saddlebag from Shiraz (Qashqai), Iran.

Chapter 11

Country Evaluation and Selection

*If the profits are great,
the risks are great.*

—Chinese Proverb

Objectives

- To discuss company strategies for sequencing the penetration of countries and committing resources

- To explain how clues from the environmental climate can help managers limit geographic alternatives

- To examine the major variables a company should consider when deciding whether and where to expand abroad

- To overview methods and problems of collecting and comparing information internationally

- To describe some simplifying tools for determining a global geographic strategy

- To introduce how final investment, reinvestment, and divestment decisions are made

Case
Ford Motor
Company[1]

Ford is a large company by any standard—the world's fourth largest industrial company and the second largest automaker. But when it became highly involved internationally, it was still a small company. Ford began operations in 1903 and exported the sixth car it built. By 1911, the company boasted that a man could drive around the world and stop every night at a garage handling Ford parts. By 1930, Ford was manufacturing or assembling automobiles in twenty foreign countries and had sales branches in another ten. Today, Ford cars and trucks are distributed through more than 10,500 dealers in more than 200 countries and territories. Yet as large and internationally involved as Ford is, it must allocate its limited financial and human resources to maintain emphasis on those markets and production locations that are most compatible with corporate expectations and objectives.

Although foreign expansion was a stated objective at Ford's first annual meeting, the company initially was passive about where the emphasis would be. Ford's first foreign sales branches and assembly operations, in Canada, England, and France, were established because people in those countries made proposals to Ford. Ford also made international expansion decisions on a highly decentralized basis. Much of its European expansion was handled through the British operation, and its British Commonwealth expansion was implemented through the Canadian company. Where sales grew most rapidly, for example, in Argentina, Uruguay, and Brazil, Ford established assembly operations in order to save on costs of transportation by limiting the bulk of shipments. Much of Ford's early expansion, therefore, was based not on scanning the globe to choose the best locations, but rather on taking advantage of opportunities as they came along.

Ford's pattern of international activities also has been influenced by policies that the company's management considered essential. One of these stated that Ford would manufacture or assemble only at production facilities in which it had a controlling interest. The concept of control in Ford's case went beyond that of voting shares. For example, in 1930, a Ford group inspected potential production sites in China and reported to Henry Ford that the title for any Ford land purchase in China would have to be made in the name of a Chinese citizen because a foreigner couldn't own land in China. Henry Ford's response was simply, "No." In the 1950s and 1960s, Ford extended this concept of control to the point where nothing short of 100-percent ownership was acceptable. This policy further influenced Ford's geographic emphasis, causing Ford to expend resources to buy out a minority interest in its British company. It also meant abandoning production in India and Spain in 1954 because their governments insisted on sharing ownership. (Ford recommended Spanish production in 1976. It also no longer adheres to the 100-percent ownership policy.)

Political conditions also have helped to forge Ford's foreign-investment pattern. For example, during World War II its French facility was bombed and subsequently not replaced. Its Hungarian and Romanian assembly facilities were seized by communist governments in 1946. Not until 1977 did Ford establish a separate department to evaluate the external political environment. Changes in government regulations often have caused Ford to commit a high proportion of its resources to a given area during a given period. This occurred, for example, when Mexico required a higher portion of local content (costs incurred locally, usually as a percentage of total costs) in vehicles sold in Mexico, thus forcing Ford to increase its Mexican investment or risk losing sales there.

Despite its extended and heavy commitment to foreign operations, Ford's production and sales are highly concentrated in a few countries. Ford sells in over 200 countries and territories and has production in 30, yet Fig. 11.1 shows that nearly 80 percent of its unit car and truck sales and over 90 percent of its car and truck production are in only 5 countries. Because of Ford's heavier commitments in some countries than in others, its competitive position is much stronger in some markets than in others. In the United Kingdom and Taiwan, its market shares in 1992 were about 22 and 23 percent, respectively. But in France and Japan, they were less than 9 and 1 percent, respectively.

Ford's dependence on multiple markets and facilities has minimized year-to-year sales and profit fluctuations. This has occurred because demand and price levels move differently in various countries. For example, from 1981 to 1982, Ford's U.S. vehicle production fell by 91,600 units; however, its EC output increased by 64,900 units. In 1980, Ford lost over $2 billion in the United States, earned $775 million in the United Kingdom, and lost $200 million elsewhere in the world. Between 1988 and 1989, its North American net income fell by $1.4 billion, but its net income elsewhere was almost steady. These data illustrate not only the positive effect of geographic diversification on the smoothing of earnings, but also the importance of shifting resources in order to exploit areas of greatest profit potential.

With huge amounts of fixed assets already in place, Ford cannot easily abandon countries and then pick them up again. It can, however, compare the attractiveness of each country with actual and potential Ford operations and move toward greater emphasis on those countries that have the most promising outlooks. For example, in the late 1980s, Ford put more emphasis on the Taiwanese automobile market because that market grew faster than any of the company's more established ones. Ford examines each country separately for each of its major product groups because different market conditions may have varying effects on different product groups.

Ford uses a country-comparison matrix to aid decision makers in choosing where to make strong marketing efforts. Ford ranks countries on one axis in terms of how attractive each one appears in terms of potential sales of a specific product being considered, for example, tractors, trucks, or automobiles. On the other axis, the company ranks the countries in terms of Ford's competitive capabilities for the specific markets. The resultant

**Figure 11.1
Ford's 1992 Unit Vehicle Sales and Production (as percentage of total)**
Ford's global production is more concentrated than its sales.

Source: Ford Around the World, Ford International Public Affairs News Release, August 1993; and *Ford Annual Report 1991.*

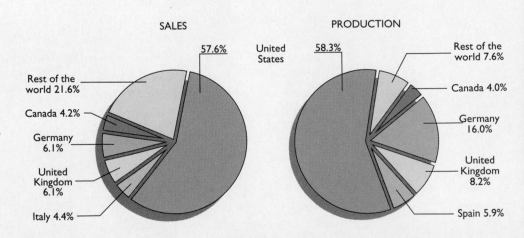

plotting helps narrow the focus to areas that both look attractive and seem to offer the best fit with Ford's unique capabilities. This is by no means the end of the evaluation process. The exercise does, however, enable the decision makers at Ford to concentrate on more detailed analyses of a manageable list of alternatives and to progress to interrelated decisions, such as where to locate production facilities for the chosen markets.

Introduction

In its early stages, international expansion tends to be passive.

Later expansion cannot take advantage of all opportunities.

Examining international geographic strategies is important because companies seldom have enough resources to take advantage of all opportunities. Committing human, technical, and financial resources to one locale may mean forgoing projects in other areas. Consequently, geographic alternatives are an integral part of a company's decisions on allocating resources. Ford's pattern of international expansion is typical of many companies. In the early stages, companies may lack the experience and expertise to devise strategies for sequencing countries in the most advantageous way. Instead, they respond to opportunities that become apparent to them, and many of these turn out to be highly advantageous. As they gain more international experience, however, they actively decide which locations to emphasize for sales and production.

Choosing Sites for Marketing and Production

In choosing geographic sites, a company must decide
- **Where to sell**
- **Where to produce**

Companies must determine where to market and where to produce. For example, a U.S. company may decide to sell in Canada either by producing in Canada or by exporting to Canada from the United States or another country. Companies also must ascertain where to locate such specialized units as R&D departments and regional headquarters. The answers to two questions— "Which markets should be served?" and "Where should production be located to serve these markets?" are frequently the same, particularly if transport costs or government regulations mean that local production is necessary for serving the chosen market. For example, many service industries, such as hotels, construction, and retailing, must locate facilities near their foreign customers. In other cases, sales and production may be in different countries; for example, Ford serves the Italian market with vehicles produced primarily in its German facilities. Nevertheless, market-location and production-location decisions are connected because to sustain a long-term competitive advantage, early product innovations usually must be linked with later cost advantages.[2]

Decisions on market and production locations may be highly interdependent for other reasons. For example, a company may have excess production capacity already in place that will influence its relative capabilities to serve markets in different countries. Or it may find a given market very attractive but forgo sales there because it is unwilling to invest in needed production locations.

Overall Geographic Strategy

The determination of an overall geographic strategy must be dynamic because conditions change and results do not always conform to expectations. A plan must be flexible enough to let a company both respond to new opportunities and withdraw from less profitable activities. Unfortunately, there is little agreement on a comprehensive theory or technique for optimizing resource allocation among countries. Further, companies need to make assumptions about such widely varying factors as future costs and prices, competitors' reactions, and technology. Nevertheless, several approaches frequently are used.

A company may expand its international sales by marketing more of its existing product line, by adding products to its line, or by some combination of these two. Most companies begin by asking "Where can we sell more of our products?" instead of "What new product can we make in order to maximize sales in a given market?"[3] Therefore, in this chapter we assume that for the most part, the company has decided on its product line or product portfolio.

Scanning for Alternatives

Without scanning, a company
- **May overlook opportunities**
- **May examine too many possibilities**

Recall that Ford used scanning techniques in comparing countries on the basis of broad variables. It did this so that decision makers could perform a much more detailed analysis of a manageable number of geographic alternatives that looked most promising. Scanning is useful because otherwise a company might consider too few or too many possibilities.

Risk of Overlooking Opportunities

As a company tries to optimize its sales or minimize its costs, it can easily overlook or disregard some promising options. Some locations may not be rejected; instead they may be skipped simply because managers either never think of them or decide to go where "everyone else is going." For example, recently many U.S. companies have forgone the world's fastest-growing markets in the developing countries while expanding in the more stable markets of Europe.[4]

Further, certain locales sometimes are lumped together and rejected before being sufficiently examined for expansion possibilities. Zambia, for instance, might not be considered because "Africa is too risky."[5] Or a country may be eliminated because of conditions in a nearby country, as occurred for many Latin American countries because of apprehension concerning investment there after the Cuban revolution.[6]

Risk of Examining Too Many Opportunities

A detailed analysis of every alternative might result in maximized sales or the pinpointing of a least-cost production location; however, the cost of so many studies would erode profits. For a company with 1000 products that might locate in any of 150 countries, there are 150,000 different situations to be analyzed. For each, other alternatives must be considered as well, such as whether to export or to set up a foreign production unit. Any conditions that would greatly enhance the probability of making an investment should be examined before a more detailed feasibility study is completed.

The Environmental Climate

Ford rejected certain potential investments because of its inability to gain sufficient control of the proposed operation. In any company, decision makers' perceptions of the **environmental climate** (those external conditions in host countries that could significantly affect the success or failure of a foreign business enterprise) will determine whether a detailed feasibility study will be undertaken and the terms under which a project will be initiated. The environmental analysis is key in limiting alternatives to a manageable number.

Influential Variables

The factors that have the most influence on the placement of sales and production emphasis are market size, ease and compatibility of operations, costs, and resource availability. Some of these variables are more important for the sales-allocation decision; others are more important for the production-location decision; others affect both.

The ranking, or prioritizing, of countries is useful for aiding decision makers in determining the order of entry into potential markets and setting the allocation of resources and rate of expansion among the different markets. The former determination assumes a company cannot or does not want to go everywhere at once; consequently, it chooses to allocate its resources first to more desirable locations. The latter assumes a company already is selling or producing in many locales, perhaps even in all that are feasible, but wants to decide how much of its effort should be expended in one country rather than another.

Market Size

Sales potential is probably the most important variable in ascertaining which locations will be considered and whether an investment will be made.[7] The assumption, of course, is that sales will be made at a price above cost; consequently, where there are sales, there will be profits.

As in the Ford case, many companies begin selling in an area very passively. A company may appoint an intermediary to promote sales for it or a licensee to produce on its behalf. If there is a demonstrated increase in sales, the company may consider investing more of its own resources. The generation of exports to a given country is an indication that sales may be made from production located in that country. As long as no threat to export sales exists, however, there is little to motivate a company to shift to production abroad.

In some cases, a company may be able to obtain past and current sales figures on a country-to-country basis for the type of product it wants to sell; in many cases,

Examining key variables helps companies
• Determine the order of entry
• Set the rates of resource allocation among countries

Expectation of sales growth is probably a potential location's major attraction.

however, such figures are unavailable. Either way, management must make projections about what will happen to future sales. Such data as GNP, per capita income, growth rates, size of the middle class, and level of industrialization often are used as broad indicators of market size and opportunity.[8] Then, groups of countries may be further broken down according to such variables as dependence on private versus government spending or inflation rate.[9]

The triad market of the United States, Japan, and Western Europe accounts for about half of the world's total consumption and an even higher proportion of purchases of such products as computers, consumer electronics, and machine tools.[10] It is not surprising therefore that most MNEs expend a major part of their efforts on these areas.

Ease and Compatibility of Operations

Companies are highly attracted to countries
- **That are located nearby**
- **That share the same language**
- **That have large populations and high per capita incomes**

Geographic, language, and market similarities   Recall in the Ford case that earnings and vehicle sales were smoothed because of Ford's operations in various parts of the world. Investors generally prefer such smoother performance patterns.[11] Therefore, it might seem that companies would go first to those countries whose economies are least correlated with that of the home country. For example, U.S. economic cycles differ markedly from those in major Latin American countries, so you might expect U.S. companies to be motivated to smooth earnings by investing heavily in Latin America.[12] However, evidence suggests the contrary for U.S. companies, whether they go abroad in related or unrelated operations in terms of marketing systems, production technologies, or vertical or horizontal products.[13]

Regardless of the industry involved, U.S. companies usually make their first direct investment in Canada; the United Kingdom and Mexico alternate in the second and third positions; and Germany, France, and Australia generally rotate among the fourth, fifth, and sixth spots.[14] This remarkable similarity in pattern among dissimilar industries seems to occur because decision makers prefer to go where they perceive it's easier to operate. For U.S. companies, Canada and Mexico rank high because of geographic proximity, which makes it easier and cheaper for the companies to control their foreign subsidiaries. Also, at the early stages of international expansion, managers feel more comfortable doing business in their own language and in a similar legal system; this explains the appeal of Canada, the United Kingdom, and Australia to U.S. companies. Language and cultural similarities also may lower operating costs and risks. Finally, market similarity tends to exert considerable influence on the locations of initial foreign operations. All six of the countries preferred by U.S. companies except Mexico have high per capita incomes, and all except Canada and Australia have large populations. Once companies have sequenced their market entries, they may grow at different rates within those markets.

The degree of red tape is not directly measurable.

Red tape   Companies frequently compare the degrees of red tape necessary to operate in given countries. Red tape includes such things as how difficult it is to get permission to operate, to bring in expatriate personnel, to obtain licenses to produce and sell certain goods, and to satisfy government agencies on such matters as taxes, labor conditions, and environmental compliance. Red tape is probably the major factor contributing to the low amount of foreign investment in India.[15] The degree of red tape is not directly measurable; therefore, companies commonly have people familiar with operating conditions in a group of countries rate the countries as high, medium, or low on this factor.

There is the best chance for a proposal to be accepted when a location
- **Offers size, technology, and other factors familiar to company personnel**
- **Allows a high percentage of ownership**
- **Permits profits to be easily remitted**

Fit with company capabilities and policies After the alternatives are pared to a reasonable number, companies must prepare much more detailed feasibility studies. These studies can be expensive. Companies very often commit to locations that are far from optimal because the more time and money they invest in examining an alternative, the more likely they are to accept that project regardless of its merits.[16] From the start, a feasibility study should have a series of clear-cut decision points so that sufficient information is gathered at each stage and so that, if a study is unlikely to result in an investment, it may be terminated before it becomes too costly.

One way to make the number of alternatives more manageable is to ensure that proposals fit the organization's general framework. Such proposals, if presented to management decision makers, will have a higher probability of acceptance.[17] For example, consideration may be limited to locales in which variables such as product type and plant size will be within the experience of present managers. From a policy standpoint, management may find it useful to ensure its proposal group includes personnel with backgrounds in each functional area—marketing, finance, personnel, engineering, and production. Although various factors might cause ultimate decision makers to reject a proposal once a feasibility study is completed, two stand out as sufficiently important to sway many organizations: restrictions on the percentage of ownership that can be held and the maximum allowed remittance of profits.[18]

Local availability of resources in relation to the company's needs is another consideration. Many foreign operations require that imported resources be combined with local inputs; this requirement may severely restrict the feasibility of given locales. For example, the international company may need to find local personnel who are sufficiently knowledgeable about the type of technology being brought in. Or it may need to add local capital to what it is willing to bring in. If local equity markets are poorly developed and local borrowing is very expensive, the company may consider locating in a different country.

The fit for a particular country is important. Consider marketing capabilities, and assume that a company has developed a product in one country and successfully marketed it through mass advertising methods. Normally it is far easier and less costly to move that product into a country for which product alterations are minimal or unnecessary and where there are few advertising restrictions. Increasingly, however, companies are using a **lead country strategy,** which involves introducing a product on a test basis in a small-country market that is considered representative of a region before investing to serve larger-country markets. For example, Colgate-Palmolive used the strategy for its Optims shampoo.[19]

Costs and Resource Availability

So far, the discussion has centered on market-seeking operations. However, international companies also engage in the pursuit of foreign resources. The analysis is somewhat simpler for a resource that is to be transferred, such as a raw material or technology, than for a resource that will be used to make a product or component abroad for export into other markets. A company eventually must examine the costs of labor, raw material inputs, capital, taxes, and transfer costs in relation to productivity in order to determine a least-cost location. Before all this information is collected in a final feasibility study, certain indicators help decision makers narrow the alternatives to be considered.

Employee compensation is the most important cost of manufacturing abroad for most companies, accounting for over 60 percent of costs, not including taxes.[20] In most cases, current labor costs, trends in those costs, and unemployment rates are useful for approximating cost differences among countries. Labor, however, is not a homogeneous commodity. If a country's labor force lacks the specific skill levels required, a company may have to implement an expensive alternative in order to use the labor, such as training, redesigning production, or adding supervision. In the case of specialized units, such as an R&D lab, the existing availability of specific skills is almost essential. And for regional headquarters, it is important to be near specialized private and public institutions such as banks, factoring firms, insurance groups, public accountants, freight forwarders, customs brokers, and consular offices, all of which handle certain international functions.

Any other important costs should be added into the analysis. If precise data are unavailable, useful proxies on operating conditions may be used. For example, if a country's infrastructure is well developed and components can be easily imported, operating costs are more likely to be relatively low. If the country already turns out competitive products embodying inputs similar to those required for the production being considered, labor costs of the planned operation probably will be sufficiently low.

The continual development of new production technologies makes cost comparisons among countries more difficult. As the number of ways in which the same product can be made increases, a company must compare, for example, the cost of producing with a large labor input in Thailand and that of producing with robotics in the United States. Or it might have to compare large-scale production to reduce fixed costs per unit by serving multi-country markets and multiple smaller-scale production units to reduce transport and inventory costs.

Because of other considerations, a company may not necessarily opt for the least-cost location. For example, BMW calculated that Mexico would be the least-cost location for North American production; however, the company chose a U.S. location because it feared that a Mexican-made vehicle would lack the same luxury image.[21] And the Japanese firm Sharp Manufacturing moved its microwave assembly from Malaysia to the United States in order to gain access to better transportation facilities for export sales to Europe.[22]

Costs—especially labor costs—are an important factor in the production-location decision.

Companies should consider different ways to produce the same product.

Return on Investment: Country-Comparison Considerations

Is a projected rate of return of 9 percent in Nigeria the same as a projected rate of 9 percent in France? Should return on investment be calculated on the basis of the entire earnings of a foreign subsidiary or just on the earnings that can be remitted to the parent? Does it make sense to accept a low return in one country if doing so will help the company's competitive position elsewhere? Is it ever rational to invest in a country that has an uncertain political and economic future? These are but a few of the unresolved questions that companies must consider when making international capital-investment decisions.

Risk and Uncertainty

Most investors prefer certainty to uncertainty.

Given the same expected return, most decision makers prefer a more certain to a less certain outcome. An estimated rate of **return on investment (ROI)** is calculated by averaging the various returns deemed possible for investments. Table 11.1 shows that two identical projected ROIs may have very different certainties of achievement as well as different probabilities. In the table, the certainty of a 10-percent projected ROI is higher for investment B than for investment A (40 percent versus 30 percent). Further, the probability of earning at least 10 percent is also higher for B than for A (70 percent versus 65 percent). Experience shows that most, but not all, investors will choose alternative B over alternative A. In fact, as uncertainty increases, investors may require a higher estimated ROI.

Often it is possible to reduce risk or uncertainty, such as by insuring against the possibility of nonconvertibility of funds. However, such actions are apt to be costly for a company. In the initial process of scanning to develop a manageable number of alternatives, the company should give some weight to the elements of risk and uncertainty. At the later and more detailed stage of the feasibility study, management

Table 11.1
Comparison of ROI Certainty
To determine the estimated ROI, (1) multiply each ROI as a percentage by its probability to derive a weighted value and (2) add the weighted values.

ROI as percentage	Investment A Probability	Investment A Weighted value	Investment B Probability	Investment B Weighted value
0	.15	0	0	0
5	.20	1.0	.30	1.5
10	.30	3.0	.40	4.0
15	.20	3.0	.30	4.5
20	.15	3.0	0	0.0
Estimated ROI		10.0%		10.0%

should determine whether the degree of risk is acceptable without incurring additional costs. If it is not, management needs to calculate an ROI that includes expenditures, such as for insurance, to increase the outcome certainty of the operation.[23]

National boundaries play a role in the degree of certainty of return that investors perceive for alternative investments. As long as a company is conducting business entirely within one country, alternative investment projects fall within similar political and economic environments. Further, experience in operating within that country, as well as in operating abroad in similar countries, increases the probability that the company will make accurate assessments of consumer, competitor, and government actions.[24] This is consistent with the description earlier in this chapter of how companies generally invest first in those foreign countries that they perceive to be similar to the home country. It also helps to explain why reinvestments or expanded investments within a country in which a company has extensive operations often are evaluated very differently than are proposed moves into a new country. (The reinvestment decision will be discussed later in this chapter.)

Competitive Risk

A company's innovative advantage may be short-lived. Even when the company has a substantial competitive lead time, the time may vary among markets. One strategy for exploiting temporary monopoly advantages is known as the **imitation lag;** to pursue this strategy, a company moves first to those countries most likely to develop local production themselves and later to other countries.[25] Local availability of technology and high international freight costs generally result in a more rapid development of local production. If technology is available in a country, local producers may start manufacturing well before foreign companies are willing to sell the technology. If freight costs are high for exports to the country, a local producer may, despite inefficiencies, be able to gain a cost advantage over imported goods.

Companies also may develop strategies to find countries in which there is least likely to be significant competition. For example, Kao, Japan's top maker of toiletries and home-cleaning products, has concentrated its international expansion in Southeast Asia because that market has been growing and because U.S. and European competitors are less entrenched there.[26] L. M. Ericsson, the Swedish telephone-equipment producer, has developed technology aimed at the needs of small countries, partially because this technology fits its home market and partially because its competitors have concentrated their efforts more on the larger markets.[27] Ericsson has taken this strategy a step further: It puts most of its investments in those developing countries that lack colonial ties to Europe because its major competitors have longstanding distributional advantages and the support of the government in many former colonies.

Monetary Risk

If a company's expansion occurs through direct investment abroad, access to the invested capital and the exchange rate on its earnings are key considerations. The concept of liquidity preference is a common theory that helps explain capital-budgeting decisions in general and can be applied to the international expansion decision.

Liquidity preference is the theory that investors usually want some of their holdings to be in highly liquid assets, on which they are willing to take a lower return. Liquidity is needed in part to make near-term payments, such as paying out dividends; in part to cover unexpected contingencies, such as stockpiling materials if a strike threatens supply; and in part to be able to shift funds to even more profitable opportunities, such as purchasing materials at a discount during a temporary price depression.

Sometimes companies want to sell all or part of their equity in a foreign facility so that the funds may be used for other types of expansion endeavors. However, the ability to find local buyers varies substantially among countries, depending largely on the existence of a local capital market.

Assuming a company does find a local purchaser for its foreign facility, chances are that it intends to use the funds in another country. If the funds are not convertible, the selling company will be forced to spend them in the host country. Of more pressing concern for most investors is the ability to convert earnings from operations abroad and the cost of doing so. It is not surprising that most investors are willing to accept a lower projected ROI for projects in countries with strong currencies than for those in countries with weak currencies.[28]

Political Risk

Political risk may come from wars and insurrections, takeover of property, and/or changes in rules.

A major concern of international companies is that the political climate will change in such a way that their operating position will deteriorate. Political actions that may affect company operations adversely are governmental takeovers of property, either with or without compensation; operational restrictions that impede the company's ability to take certain actions; and damage to property or personnel. The Ford case illustrates these risks: Ford's operation in Hungary was taken over by the government; the one in Mexico was given different operating requirements; and the one in France was bombed. Three approaches to predicting political risk will be discussed next: analyzing past patterns, using expert opinion, and the building of models based on instability measurements.

Management can make predictions based on past patterns.

Analysis of past patterns Companies cannot help but be influenced by what has happened in a country. However, predicting political risk on the basis of past patterns holds many dangers. Political situations may change rapidly for better or worse as far as foreign companies are concerned. For example, the perceived political risk of doing business in Vietnam improved rapidly during the early 1990s as its government sought foreign investment and trade.[29] However, the historical record of violence, expropriations, and regulation of international business is indicative of the broad climate for operations in that country.

Substantial variations in political risk frequently exist within countries as well. For example, except in a few countries, government takeovers of companies have been highly selective. For example, in Peru, Cerro's mining interests and ITT's telephone company were nationalized, but Cerro's manufacturing companies and ITT's hotel were not. Operations most likely to be nationalized are those that may have a considerable and visible widespread effect on a given country because of their size, monopoly position, importance to national defense, or dependence of other industries on them.

Similarly, unrest that leads to property damage and/or disruption of supplies or sales may not endanger the operations of all foreign companies. This may be because of the limited geographic focus of the unrest. For example, there was no property damage or business disruption in Slovenia after the breakup of Yugoslavia; however, other areas in the former Yugoslavia were severely hit. In the United States, race riots have resulted in high property damage but only in limited sections of large cities. In other cases, protestors may target only the most visible foreign companies. For example, French protests at Euro Disney did not carry over to most other U.S.-owned facilities in France.

Asset takeover or property damage does not necessarily mean a full loss to investors. Most takeovers have been preceded by a formal declaration of intent by the government and a subsequent legal process to determine compensation to the foreign investor. In addition to the asset's book value, other factors must be considered in determining the adequacy of compensation. First, the compensation may earn a different ROI elsewhere. Second, other agreements (such as purchase and management contracts) may create additional benefits for the former investor.

Companies should
- **Examine views of governmental decision makers**
- **Get a cross-section of opinions**
- **Use expert analysts**

Opinion analysis   A second approach for political-risk analysis is to analyze the opinions of knowledgeable people about the situation in a country.[30] In this approach, management attempts to ascertain the evolving opinions of people who may influence future political events affecting business. The first step involves reading statements made by political leaders both in and out of office to determine their philosophies on business in general, foreign input to business, the means of effecting economic changes, and their feelings toward given foreign countries. Although published statements are readily available, they may appear too late for a company to react.

Management should analyze the context of statements to determine whether they express true intentions or were made merely to appease particular interest groups or social classes. It is not uncommon, for example, for political leaders to make emotional appeals to the poor based on allegations that foreign business is draining wealth from the country while, at the same time, quietly negotiating entry and giving incentives to new foreign companies. Examination of the country's investment plans offers further insights into the political climate.

The second step in determining opinions and attitudes involves visits to the country in order to "listen." Embassy officials and foreign and local businesspeople are useful sources of opinions about the probability and direction of change. Journalists, academicians, middle-level local governmental authorities, and labor leaders usually reveal their own attitudes, which often reflect changing political conditions that may affect the business sector.

A more systematic method of determining opinions is to use a panel of analysts with experience in a country and have them rate categories of political conditions over different time frames. For example, these analysts might rate a country in terms of the fractionalization of political parties that could lead to disruptive changes in government in the near future or beyond. A company also may rely on commercial risk-assessment services, such as those published by *Business International, Economist Intelligence Unit, Euromoney,* and *International Business Communications.*

Instability assessment A third method for predicting political risk is to build models based on instability measurements. The greater the political instability, the greater is the possibility of change in the political climate. Although political instability has been found to be a major concern of businesspeople, there is no general consensus as to what constitutes dangerous instability or how such instability can be predicted. The lack of consensus is illustrated by the diverse reactions of companies to the same political situations. For example, in the early 1990s Peru had high inflation, guerrilla warfare, political assassinations, and a fall in industrial output; yet many foreign companies perceived the time to be opportune to invest in Peru.[31] Other uncertainties include the time lag between a political event and an investor's ability to react. Further, similar symptoms of social unrest may result in different political consequences in different countries. For example, an antiregime demonstration in Iran may have different political consequences for investors than one in Mexico would.[32] At times, political parties may change rapidly with little effect on business; at other times, sweeping changes for business may occur without a change in government. Rather than political stability itself, the direction of change in government seems to be very important.

One theory holds that when there is a high and growing level of frustration within a country, that country's political leaders may try to blame foreign investors for the problems causing frustration. They may place more operational restrictions on foreign investors or take over their property. Frustration occurs when there is a difference between the level of aspirations and the level of welfare and expectations—the higher the difference, the higher the level of frustration.[33] Because frustration, aspirations, welfare, and expectations cannot be measured directly, substitutes must be used. For example, growth in urbanization, literacy, radios per capita, and labor unionization are all measurable indicators of growth in aspirations. Variables such as infant survival rate, caloric consumption, hospital beds per capita, piped water supply per capita, and income per capita are measurable indicators of welfare. Variables such as the changes in per capita income and in gross investment rates are indicators of expectations. This approach to predicting actions toward foreign investors has considerable potential, since it predicts future trends rather than looking to the past and is based on a lead time that might be sufficient for management to adjust operations in order to minimize losses.

Political instability does not always affect all foreign businesses in a country.

Business Research

Information is needed at all levels of control.

Business research is undertaken to reduce uncertainties in the decision process, to expand or narrow the alternatives under consideration, and to assess the merits of existing programs. Efforts to reduce uncertainties include attempts to answer such

questions as these: "Can qualified personnel be hired?" "Will the economic and political climate allow for a reasonable certainty of operations?" Alternatives may be
expanded by asking "Where are possible new sources of funds or sales?" or they
may be narrowed by querying "Where among the alternatives would operating
costs be lowest?" Evaluation and control are improved by assessing present and past
performance: "Is the distributor servicing sufficient accounts?" "What is our market
share?" Clearly, there are numerous details that, if ascertained, can be useful in
meeting the company's objectives.

How Much Research?

**Companies should compare
the cost of information with
its value.**

A company can seldom, if ever, gain all the information its managers would like.
This is partially due to time constraints, since markets or raw materials may need to
be secured before competitors gain control of them. Further, contracts that call for
bids or proposals usually have deadlines. The cost of information is another factor.
The larger area to be considered for international decisions compounds the number
of alternatives and complexities; thus, it is useful to limit the extent of information
gathering. This can be done by estimating the costs of data collection as well as the
probable payoff from the data in terms of revenue gains or cost savings. In this way,
a company can rank research projects on the basis of expected return from the costs
of data collection.

Problems with the Data

The lack, obsolescence, and inaccuracy of data on many countries make much research difficult and expensive to undertake. In most industrial countries, such as
the United States, governments collect very detailed demographic and purchasing
data, which are available cheaply to any company or individual. (But even in the
United States, GNP figures are estimated to be understated by as much as 15 percent, and the 1990 census may have missed between 4 and 6 million people.[34])
Using samples based on available information, a company can draw fairly accurate
inferences concerning market-segment sizes and locations, at least within broad
categories. In the United States, the fact that so many companies are publicly
owned and are required to disclose much operating information enables a company
to learn competitors' strengths and weaknesses. Further, companies may rely on a
multitude of behavioral studies dealing with U.S. consumer preferences and experience. With this available information, a company can devise questionnaires or test-
market with a selected sample so that responses should reflect the behavior of the
larger target group to whom the company plans to sell. Contrast this situation to
that in a country whose basic census, national income accounts, and foreign trade
figures are suspect and where no data are collected on consumer expenditures. In
such countries, business is conducted under a veil of secrecy, consumers' buying
behavior is speculated on, market intermediaries are reluctant to answer questions,
and expensive primary research may be required before meaningful samples and
questions can be developed.

Reasons for Inaccuracies

Inaccuracies result from
• Inability to collect data
• Purposeful misleading

For the most part, incomplete or inaccurate published data result from the inability of many governments to collect the needed information. Poor countries may have such limited resources that other projects necessarily receive priority in the national budget. Why collect precise figures on the literacy rate, the leaders of a poor country might reason, when the same outlay can be used to build schools to improve that rate?

Education affects the competence of governmental officials to maintain and analyze accurate records. Economic factors also hamper record retrieval and analysis, since hand calculations may be used instead of costly electronic data-processing systems. The result may be information that is years old before it is made public. Finally, cultural factors affect responses. Mistrust of how the data will be used may lead respondents to answer incorrectly, particularly if questions probe financial details.

Of equal concern to the researcher is the publication of information designed to persuade businesspeople to follow a certain course of action. Even if governmental and private organizations do not purposely publish false statements, many may be so selective in the data they include that false impressions are created. Therefore, it is useful for companies to consider carefully the source of such material in light of possible motives or biases.

However, not all inaccuracies are due to governmental collection and dissemination procedures. A large proportion of the studies by academicians that purport to describe international business practices are based on broad generalizations that may be drawn from too few observations, nonrepresentative samples, and/or poorly designed questionnaires.

People's desire and ability to cover up data on themselves—such as unrecorded criminal activity—may distort published figures substantially. For example, economic data on Colombia do not include cocaine revenue, yet that revenue is estimated to exceed that from all other Colombian exports combined.[35] In the United States, illegal income from such activities as drug trade, bribery, and prostitution is not included in GNP figures. About a quarter of the GNP in Italy goes unreported because of tax evasion.[36] And the following illustrates a similar problem in Argentina:

> . . . only 130,000 out of 3 million people who were supposed to pay the three main taxes actually did. When tax agents hit the streets in search of evaders, they found that 40 percent of the people registered had declared false addresses, including one who claimed to live in the middle of the River Plate, another in a church, and a third in a soccer stadium.[37]

Comparability problems arise from
• Differences in collection methods, definitions, and base years
• Distortions in currency conversions

Comparability problems   One important variable businesspeople need to consider when contrasting data from different countries is the year in which collection was done. Censuses, output figures, trade statistics, and base-year calculations are published for different periods in different countries. Thus it may be necessary for the researcher to make estimates of current figures based on projected growth rates.

There also are numerous definitional differences among countries; for example, a category as seemingly basic as "family income" may mean something different depending on the country. For one thing, such relatives as grandparents, uncles, and cousins may be included in the definition of "family." Similarly, some countries define literacy as some minimum level of formal schooling, others as attainment of certain specified standards, and still others as simply the ability to read and write one's name. Further, percentages may be published in terms of either adult population (with different ages used for adulthood) or total population. The definitions of accounting rules such as depreciation also can differ and so result in substantially altered comparability of net national product figures among countries. Accounting differences also have led to debates on whether Japan has a higher savings rate than the United States does.[38]

Countries differ in how they measure investment inflows. Some governments record the number of foreign investment projects. Some record the value of investments in the local currency, and others value them in U.S. dollars or another major international currency. Where value of investments is used, another question is how much of the total value is recorded as "foreign investment." Some governments record the total value of the project, regardless of what portion may be locally owned or financed; some record the value of foreign capital invested; and others record the percentage of the project owned by foreign interests.[39]

Figures on national income and per capita income are particularly difficult to compare because of differences in income dispersion. A country with a large middle class will have consumption patterns quite distinct from those in a country in which large portions of the population are excluded from the money economy. For instance, in Benin, at least half the population effectively earns nothing, which means that the per capita income of the remaining half is actually at least double what the published figure shows for the country as a whole. Those outside the money economy obviously have consumption levels that are greater than zero, since they may grow agricultural products and produce other goods, which they consume or barter. The extent to which people in one country produce for their own consumption (for example, grow vegetables, bake bread, sew clothes, or cut hair) will distort comparisons with other countries that follow different patterns.

A further problem concerns exchange rates, which must be used to convert countries' financial data to some common currency. A 10-percent appreciation of the Japanese yen in relation to the U.S. dollar will result in a 10-percent increase in the per capita income of Japanese residents when figures are reported in dollars. Does this mean that the Japanese are suddenly 10 percent richer? Obviously not, since their yen income, which they use for about 85 percent of their purchases in the Japanese economy, is unchanged and buys no more. Even if changes in exchange rates are ignored, purchasing power and living standards are difficult to compare, since costs are so affected by climate and habit. Exchange rates constitute a very imperfect means of comparing national data.[40]

External Sources of Information

The organizations and publications that deal wholly or in part with information on international business are too numerous to explore in depth in this book. Generally, however, the main sources of such information are governmental agencies, international organizations, and companies that make a living from supplying it or would like to supply services connected with the conduct of international business.

Individualized reports   In most countries, there are market-research and business-consulting companies that will conduct studies for a fee. Naturally, the quality and the cost of these studies vary widely. They generally are the most costly information source because the individualized nature restricts proration among a number of companies. However, the fact that the client can specify the information wanted often makes the expense worthwhile.

Specialized studies   Some research organizations prepare fairly specific studies that they sell to any interested company at costs much lower than for individualized studies. These specialized studies sometimes are printed as directories of companies that operate in a given locale, perhaps with financial or other information about the companies. They also may be about business in certain locales, forms of business, or specific products. They may combine any of these elements as well; for example, a study could deal with the market for imported auto parts in Germany.

Service companies   Most companies that provide services to international clients— for example, banks, transportation agencies, and accounting firms—publish reports that are available to potential clients. These reports usually are geared toward either the conduct of business in a given area or some specific subject of general interest, such as tax or trademark legislation. Since they are intended to reach a wide market of companies, these reports usually lack the specificity a company may want for making a final decision. However, much of the data give useful background information. Some service companies also offer informal opinions about such things as the reputations of possible business associates and the names of people to contact in a company.

Governmental agencies   Governments and their agencies are another source of information. Statistical reports vary in subject matter, quantity, and quality among countries. When a government or governmental agency wants to stimulate foreign business activity, the amount and type of information it makes available may be substantial. For example, the U.S. Department of Commerce not only compiles such basic data as news about and regulations in individual foreign countries but also will help set up appointments with businesspeople abroad.

International organizations and agencies   Numerous organizations and agencies are supported by more than one country. These include the United Nations (UN), the International Monetary Fund (IMF), the Organization for Economic Cooperation and Development (OECD), and the European Union (EU). All of these organizations have large research staffs that compile basic statistics as well as prepare reports and recommendations concerning common trends and problems. Many of the international development banks even help finance investment-feasibility studies.

Trade associations   Trade associations associated with various product lines collect, evaluate, and disseminate a wide variety of data dealing with technical and competitive factors in their industries. Much of these data are available in the trade journals published by such associations; others may or may not be available to nonmembers.

Information service companies   A number of companies have information-retrieval services that maintain databases from hundreds of different sources, including many of those already described. For a fee, or sometimes for free at public libraries, a company can obtain access to such computerized data and arrange for an immediate printout of studies of interest.

Internal Generation

MNEs may have to conduct many studies abroad themselves. Sometimes the research process may consist of no more than observing keenly and asking many questions. Investigators can see what kind of merchandise is available, can see who is buying and where, and can uncover the hidden distribution points and competition. In some countries, for example, the competition for ready-made clothes may be from seamstresses working in private homes rather than from retailers. The competition for vacuum cleaners may be from servants who clean with mops rather than from other electrical-appliance manufacturers. Surreptitiously sold contraband may compete with locally produced goods. Traditional analysis methods would not reveal such facts. In many countries, even bankers have to rely more on clients' reputations than on their financial statements. Shrewd questioning may yield very interesting results.

Companies frequently set certain minimum criteria on which to base a decision. If a company regards a total market of 35 million as satisfactory, it is fruitless to spend the time and money on determining where within the range from 90 to 100 million the market actually lies.

Often a company must be extremely imaginative, extremely observant, or both. For example, one soft-drink manufacturer wanted to determine the market share it held relative to its competitors in the Mexican market. Management's attempts to make estimates from the points of distribution were futile because of the extremely widespread distribution. The company hit on two alternatives, both of which turned out to be feasible: The manufacturer of bottle caps was willing to reveal how many caps it sold to each of its clients, and customs would supply data on the import volume of soft-drink concentrate used by each competitor.

Tools for Comparing Countries

Environmental Scanning

International companies have become much more sophisticated in their **environmental scanning,** which is the systematic assessment of external conditions that might affect a company's operations. For example, a company might assess societal attitudes that might foreshadow legal changes. Most MNEs employ at least one executive to conduct environmental scanning continuously. The most sophisticated of these companies tie the scanning to the planning process and integrate information on a worldwide basis. Companies are most likely to seek economic and competitive information in their scanning process, and they depend heavily on managers based abroad to supply them with information.[41]

Grids

A grid may be used to compare countries on whatever factors are deemed important. Table 11.2 is an example of a grid with information placed into three categories. Certain countries may be eliminated immediately from consideration because of characteristics decision makers find unacceptable. These factors are in the first category of variables, where country I is eliminated. Values and weights are assigned to other variables so that a country may be ranked according to attributes that are important to the decision makers. In the table, for example, country II is graphically pinpointed as high return–low risk, country III as low return–low risk, country IV as high return–high risk, and country V as low return–high risk.[42]

Both the variables and the weights will vary by product and company, depending on the company's internal situation and its objectives. The grid technique is useful even when a comparative analysis is not being done; a company may be able to set a minimum score necessary for either investing additional resources or committing further funds to a more detailed feasibility study. Grids do tend to get cumbersome, however, as the number of variables increases. Further, though they are useful in ranking, they often obscure interrelationships among countries.

Opportunity-Risk Matrix

To show more clearly the summary of data that can be illustrated on a grid, we can plot risk on one axis and opportunity on the other, a technique used by many companies, such as Borg-Warner.[43] Figure 11.2 is an example that is simplified to include only six countries. The grid shows that the company has current operations in four of the countries (all except countries A and E). Of the two nonexploited countries, country A has low risk but low opportunity and country E has low risk and high opportunity. If resources are to be spent in a new area, country E appears to be a better bet than country A. Of the other four countries, there are large commitments in country F, medium ones in countries C and D, and a small one in country B. In the future time horizon being examined, it appears that coun-

Grids are tools that
- May depict acceptable or unacceptable conditions
- Rank countries by important variables

With an opportunity-risk matrix, a company can
- Decide on indicators and weight them
- Evaluate each country on the weighted indicators
- Plot to see relative placements

Table 11.2
Simplified Grid to Compare Countries for Market Penetration

Decision makers may choose which variables to include in the grid; this table is merely an example. Note also that decision makers may weight some variables as more important than others. Here country I is immediately eliminated because the company will go only where 100-percent ownership is permitted. Countries II and IV are estimated to have the highest return; and countries II and III are estimated to have the lowest risk.

Variable	Weight	Country				
		I	II	III	IV	V
1. Acceptable (A), Unacceptable (U) factors						
a. Allows 100-percent ownership	—	U	A	A	A	A
b. Allows licensing to majority-owned subsidiary	—	A	A	A	A	A
2. Return (higher number = preferred rating)						
a. Size of investment needed	0–5	—	4	3	3	3
b. Direct costs	0–3	—	3	1	2	2
c. Tax rate	0–2	—	2	1	2	2
d. Market size, present	0–4	—	3	2	4	1
e. Market size, 3–10 years	0–3	—	2	1	3	1
f. Market share, immediate potential, 0–2 years	0–2	—	2	1	2	1
g. Market share, 3–10 years	0–2	—	2	1	2	0
Total			18	10	18	10
3. Risk (lower number = preferred rating)						
a. Market loss, 3–10 years (if no present penetration)	0–4	—	2	1	3	2
b. Exchange problems	0–3	—	0	0	3	3
c. Political-unrest potential	0–3	—	0	1	2	3
d. Business laws, present	0–4	—	1	0	4	3
e. Business laws, 3–10 years	0–2	—	0	1	2	2
Total			3	3	14	13

try F will have low risk and high opportunity. Country D's situation is expected to improve during the studied period; country C's situation is deteriorating; and country B's appears mixed (it will have better opportunity but more risk). Note that the world averages being used for comparison also shift during the period under consideration. The matrix is important as a reflection of the placement of a country *relative* to other countries.

But how are values plotted on such a matrix? It is up to the company to determine which factors are good indicators of risk and opportunity; the factors chosen then must be weighted to reflect their importance. For instance, on the risk axis a company might give 40 percent (0.4) of the weight to expropriation risk, 25 percent (0.25) to foreign-exchange controls, 20 percent (0.2) to civil disturbances and terrorism, and 15 percent (0.15) to exchange-rate change, for a total allocation of 100 percent. Each country then would be rated on a scale of 1 to 10 for each variable, with 10 indicating the best score and 1 the worst. The score on each variable

**Figure 11.2
Opportunity-Risk
Matrix**
Countries above the hori-
zontal dashed line have less
risk and those to the right
of the vertical dashed line
have greater opportunity
than the current world
average. The dotted lines
represent a projection of
the world average for
these variables in the future. Country D currently
has greater than average
risk; in the future it will
have less risk than the projected world average.

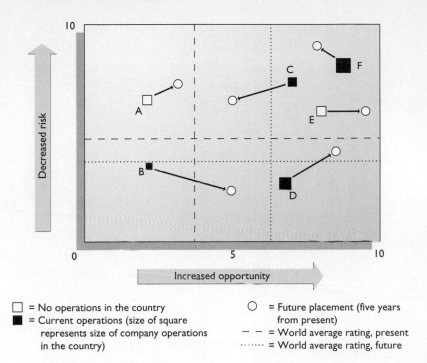

is multiplied by the weight allocated to it. For instance, if country A were given a
rating of 8 on the expropriation-risk variable, the 8 would be multiplied by 0.4 for
a score of 3.2. All of country A's risk-variable scores would then be summed to
give the placement of that country on the risk axis. A similar procedure would find
the plot location of country A on the opportunity axis. Once the scores are determined for each country, management can determine the average scores for risk and
for opportunity, thereby dividing the matrix into quadrants.

A key element of this kind of matrix, and one that is not always included in
practice, is the projection of the future country location. Such a placement's usefulness is obvious if the projections are realistic. Therefore, it is helpful to have forecasts made by people who are knowledgeable not only about the countries but also
about forecasting methods.

Country Attractiveness–Company Strength Matrix

The country attractive-
ness–company strength ma-
trix highlights the fit of a
company's product to the
country.

Another commonly used matrix approach highlights a company's specific product
advantage on a country-by-country basis. This approach was briefly explained in the
Ford case. Ford uses it for its tractor operations, for example. On the country-
attractiveness scale, Ford ranks countries from highest to lowest attractiveness for
tractors specifically; on the company-strength scale, it ranks its competitive strength
in tractors by country. The method of performing the ranking is the same as for the
opportunity-risk matrix. Ford's weighted scale for country attractiveness includes
such variables as market size, market growth, price controls, red tape, requirements

for local content and exports, inflation, trade balance, and political stability. Ford's weighted scale for company strength includes market share, market-share position, product fit to the country's needs, absolute profit per unit, percentage profit on cost, quality of the company's distribution in comparison with that of competitors, and the fit of the company's promotion program to the country in comparison with its competitors'.[44]

Figure 11.3 illustrates this type of matrix for market expansion before countries are plotted. The company should attempt to concentrate its activities in the countries that appear in the top left-hand corner of the matrix and to take as much equity as possible in investments there. In this position, country attractiveness is the highest, *and* the company has the best competitive capabilities to exploit the opportunities. In the top right-hand corner, the country attractiveness is also high, but the company has a weak competitive strength for those markets, perhaps because it lacks the right product. If the cost is not too high, the company might attempt to gain greater domination in those markets by remedying its competitive weakness. Otherwise, it might consider either **divestment** (reducing its investment) or strengthening its position through joint-venture operations with another company whose assets are complementary. Divestment instead of investment ordinarily should be attempted in countries in the bottom right-hand corner. Income may be "harvested" by pulling out all possible cash that can be generated while at the same time not replacing depreciated facilities. Licensing still offers potential because it may generate some income without the company's having to make investment outlays. In other areas, the company must analyze situations individually in order to decide which approach to take. These are marginal areas that require specific judgment.

**Figure 11.3
Country
Attractiveness—
Company Strength
Matrix**
Although countries are not plotted on this matrix, those that would appear closest to the top left-hand corner are the most desirable for operations and those that would be closest to the bottom right-hand corner are the least desirable.

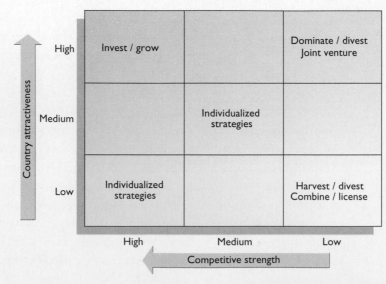

Markets shift among countries not only because of product life cycles but also because of changing conditions that may affect demand unevenly. Companies enhance their competitive capabilities by emphasizing the markets with higher growth prospects. When growth in sales prospects is due to product life cycle conditions or overall economic conditions, companies have few, if any, ethical qualms. However, some companies have been criticized for promoting potentially dangerous products more heavily abroad when domestic demand decreases. For example, the use of the pesticide DDT has been banned in the United States for environmental reasons, but U.S. companies export DDT. Also, until recently, U.S. tobacco sales were declining because of health scares and restrictions on advertising; tobacco companies have countered with heavy cigarette promotion in developing countries in which markets are growing. At the end of the Cold War, U.S. defense contractors turned more attention to foreign countries, many of which had either repressive regimes or conflicts that might escalate substantially. Relativists maintain it would be unethical to prohibit such sales. A complicating factor is that conditions abroad sometimes vary enough that product restrictions should differ.

ETHICAL DILEMMAS

MNEs sometimes have been criticized for doing *any* business in countries with repressive regimes on the grounds that their presence strengthens those regimes. In fact, MNEs favor locations in which there is an unbelligerent workforce, and such regimes often foster this characteristic; thus, FDI often increases when a dictatorship, especially a military one, is in power. Once again, relativist versus normativist viewpoints come into play.

MNEs have justified their foreign investments largely on the grounds that those investments promote global efficiencies through low-cost production and high sales. But some moves into foreign markets are made to counteract what would otherwise be a competitor's advantage. For example, Caterpillar established operations in Japan, the home market of Komatsu, its major global competitor. This move lowered Komatsu's Japanese profits, which had been accounting for 80 percent of its worldwide cash flow, and made it more difficult for the company to expand abroad.[45] Such a move can be justified on competitive grounds but not on global efficiency grounds. Is it ethical? Would it make any difference whether Caterpillar makes a profit in Japan? What if such an action led to reduced competition in the United States?

Similarly, MNEs often respond to countries' trade restrictions by locating behind these tariff walls. In fact, they sometimes negotiate a monopoly position behind such walls in LDCs. The MNEs argue that such moves are necessary because markets would otherwise be lost; however, it is hard to justify these moves on global efficiency grounds. This brings up the dilemma of whether countries should work toward regulating FDI with global efficiency as their objective or whether each country should continue to be allowed to serve its own interests by competing for FDI.

Diversification versus Concentration Strategies

Strategies for ultimately reaching a high level of commitment in many countries are
• Diversification—go to many fast and then build up slowly in each
• Concentration—go to one or a few and build up fast before going to others
• A hybrid of the two

Ultimately, a company may gain a sizable presence and commitment in most countries; however, there are different paths to that position. At one extreme, with a **diversification strategy,** the company will move rapidly into most foreign markets, gradually increasing its commitments within each of them. This can be done, for example, through a liberal licensing policy for a given product to ensure there will be sufficient resources for the initial widespread expansion. The company eventually will increase its involvement by internalizing activities that it initially contracted to other companies. At the other extreme, with a **concentration strategy,** the company will move to only one or a few foreign countries until it develops a very strong involvement and competitive position there. There are, of course, hybrids of these two strategies, for example, moving rapidly to most markets but increasing the commitment in only a few. The following subsections discuss major variables a company should consider when deciding which strategy to use.[46] (See Table 11.3.)

Sales Response Function

An increasing sales response rate favors concentration; a decreasing sales response rate favors diversification.

The **sales response function** is the amount of sales created at different levels of marketing expenditure. For example, if the first $100,000 of marketing expenditure in a given country yields $1 million of sales, the next $100,000 yields

Table 11.3
Product and Market Factors Affecting Choice between Diversification and Concentration Strategies

If the conditions under "prefer diversification" exist, a company is likely to benefit by moving rapidly into many countries simultaneously; otherwise, the company might move to just one or a few foreign countries until a substantial presence is developed there.

Product or market factor	Prefer diversification if:	Prefer concentration if:
1. Sales response function*	Decreasing	Increasing
2. Growth rate of each market	Low	High
3. Sales stability in each market	Low	High
4. Competitive lead time	Short	Long
5. Spillover effects	High	Low
6. Need for product adaptation	Low	High
7. Need for communication adaptation	Low	High
8. Economies of scale in distribution	Low	High
9. Program control requirements	Low	High
10. Extent of constraints	Low	High

*The terms used in the original article for "decreasing" and "increasing" were "concave" and "S curve," respectively.

Source: Igal Ayal and Jehiel Zif, "Marketing Expansion Strategies in Multinational Marketing," *Journal of Marketing,* Vol. 43, Spring 1979, p. 89. Reprinted by permission of the American Marketing Association.

$800,000, and the third $100,000 yields $600,000, the response is decreasing. On the other hand, if the first $100,000 yields $600,000, the second $800,000, and the third $1 million, the response is increasing. There are products that follow each pattern over similar expenditure levels. A company that had $300,000 to spend on a marketing program for which there is the same decreasing response in each country would create more sales by spreading entry over three countries. Doing this would yield $3 million ($1M + $1M + $1M), whereas a concentration in one country would yield only $2.4 million ($1M + $0.8M + $0.6M). If the same $300,000 were spent on a product with an increasing response, however, a concentration strategy would yield better results: $2.4 million ($0.6M + $0.8M + $1M) as opposed to $1.8 million ($0.6M + $0.6M + $0.6M).

Growth Rate in Each Market

Fast growth favors concentration because companies must use resources to maintain market share.

When the growth rate in each market is high, a company usually should concentrate on a few markets because it will cost a great deal to maintain market share and costs per unit are typically lower for the market-share leader. Slower growth in each market may result in the company's having enough resources to build and maintain a market share in several different countries.

Sales Stability in Each Market

International diversification has been shown to have an even stronger relationship to profit stability than product diversification does.[47] Recall the Ford case and the earlier description of how earnings and sales are smoothed because of operations in various parts of the world. This smoothing results from the leads and lags in the business cycles. In addition, a company whose assets and earnings base are in a variety of countries will be less affected by occurrences within a single one; for example, a strike or expropriation will affect earnings from only a small portion of total corporate assets. Further, currency appreciation in some countries may offset depreciation in others.

The more stable that sales and profits are within a single market, the less need there is for a diversification strategy. Similarly, the more interrelated markets are, the less smoothing is achieved by selling in each. For example, Ford seemingly would get less of a smoothing effect between France and Germany, because their economies are so interrelated through the EU, than between either of those two countries and the United States.[48]

Competitive Lead Time

The longer the lead time, the more likely the company is to use a concentration strategy.

The first company to enter a market often gains advantages in terms of brand recognition and because it can line up the best suppliers, distributors, and local partners. This is called **first-in advantage** and may be difficult for followers to counteract.[49] However, so many resources may be necessary to capitalize on the first-in advantage that companies may be unable to move quickly into many markets. Thus, sequential entry is more common than simultaneous entry into multiple markets. If a company determines that it has a long lead time before competitors are likely to be able to copy or supersede its advantages, then it may be able to maintain control of the expansion by following a concentration strategy and still beat competitors into other markets.

It has been argued that being first into Eastern Europe, before the process of economic transformation, may have been a disadvantage in some cases. For example, before transformation, PepsiCo had to sign cumbersome agreements with communist governments, but after the fall of those governments Coca-Cola was able to move very quickly and flexibly.[50]

Spillover Effects

Spillover effects are situations in which the marketing program in one country results in awareness of the product in other countries. This can happen, for example, if the product is advertised through media viewed cross-nationally. In such situations, a diversification strategy has advantages because additional customers may be reached with little additional incremental cost.

Need for Product, Communications, and Distribution Adaptation

Adaptation means additional costs for the company because it
- **May not have the resources to spread to many markets**
- **Cannot readily gain economies of scale through diversification**

Products and their marketing may have to be altered for sale in foreign markets. The adaptation process is often costly and may lead to two factors that favor a concentration strategy. First, the additional costs may limit the resources the company has for expansion in many different markets. Second, the fixed costs incurred for adaptation cannot be as easily spread over sales in other countries as a means of reducing total unit costs.

Program Control Requirements

Diversification often implies external arrangements that may cause control to be lost.

The more a company needs to control its operations in a foreign country, the more likely it is that it should develop a concentration strategy. This is because the company will need to use more of its resources to maintain that control. Its need for more control could result for various reasons, including fear that an external arrangement will create a competitor or the need for highly technical assistance for customers.

Extent of Constraints

Constraints limit resources from going to many locations simultaneously.

Constraints on what a company can do may be internal or external. For resource availability, for example, the higher the constraints, the more likely a concentration strategy is. If certain specialized technical personnel is the key resource needed to introduce a new product into foreign markets, a shortage of those personnel both within and outside the company will limit the number of countries into which the company can expand rapidly. Or if there are constraints on where the personnel can be moved, the company may find it difficult to expand into many different markets rapidly.

Evaluation of Investment Proposals

Internal and accounting rates of return are the most popular measurements for precise projections.

So far we have examined comparative opportunities on a very broad basis. At some point, a company must do a much more detailed analysis of specific projects and proposals in order to make allocation decisions. Companies use a variety of financial criteria to evaluate foreign investments, with internal rate of return and accounting rate of return being the measurements most frequently used.[51]

Measurement Problems

The derivation of meaningful rate-of-return figures is not easy when foreign operations are concerned. Profit figures from individual operations may obscure the real impact those operations have on overall company activities. For example, if a U.S. company were to establish an assembly operation in Australia, the operation could either increase or decrease exports from the United States. Alternatively, the same company might build a plant in Malaysia to produce with cheaper labor; however, doing that would necessitate more coordination costs at headquarters.[52] Or perhaps by building a plant in Brazil to supply components to Volkswagen of Brazil, the company may increase the possibility of selling to Volkswagen in other countries. As a result of the Australian, Malaysian, or Brazilian projects, management would have to make assumptions about the changed profits in the United States and elsewhere.

The preceding discussion assumes that although overall company returns are difficult to calculate, those for the operating subsidiary are fairly easily ascertained. However, this is not the case. Much of the sales and purchases of foreign subsidiaries may be made from and to units of the same parent company. The prices charged on these transactions will affect the relative profitability of one unit compared to another. Further, the basis on which to estimate the net value of the foreign investment may not be realistically stated, particularly if part of the net value is based on exported capital equipment that is obsolete at home and useless except in the country where it is being shipped. By stating a high value, the company may be permitted to repatriate a larger portion of its earnings.

Noncomparative Decision Making

Most proposals are decided on a go–no-go basis if they meet minimum-threshold criteria.

Because companies have limited resources at their disposal, it might seem that they maintain a storehouse of foreign investment proposals that may be ranked on the basis of some predetermined criteria. If this were so, management could simply start allocating resources to the top-ranked proposal and continue down the list until no further investments were possible. This is seldom the case, however. About three quarters of final investment proposals are evaluated separately, and the decision that is made on each is commonly known as a **go–no-go decision.**[53] This decision is usually based on a requirement that the project meet some minimum-threshold criteria. Of course, before a go–no-go decision is made, a good deal of weeding out of possible projects at various scanning and decision points has occurred.

Two major factors restricting companies from comparing investment opportunities are cost and time. Clearly, most companies cannot afford to conduct very many investigations simultaneously. Comparisons also can be restricted because feasibility studies are apt to be in various stages of completion at a given time. For example, suppose the investigation process is complete for a possible project in Australia but ongoing research is being conducted for projects in New Zealand, Japan, and Indonesia. Can the company afford to wait for the results from all the surveys before deciding on a location? The answer is, probably not. The time interval between completions probably would invalidate much of the earlier results and necessitate updating, added expense, and further delays. Another time-inhibiting problem is governmental regulations that require a decision within a given period. External time limits also may be imposed by other companies that have made partnership proposals. If no answer is forthcoming within a short period, a proposal may be made to a different potential partner.

Finally, companies must answer to both stockholders and employees. Few can afford to let resources lie idle or be employed for a low rate of return during a waiting period. This applies not only to financial resources but also to such resources as technical competence, since the lead time over competitors is reduced when a company delays a decision.

Reinvestment Decisions

A company may have to make new commitments to maintain competitiveness abroad.

Most of the net value of foreign investment has come from reinvesting earnings abroad rather than from transferring new capital abroad. Decisions to replace depreciated assets or to add to the existing stock of capital from retained earnings in a foreign country differ somewhat from original investment decisions. Once committed to a given locale, a company may find it doesn't have the option of moving a substantial portion of the earnings elsewhere—to do so would endanger the continued successful operation of the given foreign facility. For example, the failure to expand might result in a falling market share and a higher unit cost than that of competitors.

Aside from competitive factors, a company may need several years of almost total reinvestment and allocation of new funds to one area in order to meet its objectives. Over time, the earnings may be used to expand the product line further, integrate production, and expand the market served from present output. Another reason for treating reinvestment decisions differently is that once there are experienced personnel within a given country, they may be the best judges of what is needed for that country; therefore, certain investment decisions may be delegated to them.

Divestment Decisions

Companies must decide how to get out of operations if
- **They no longer fit the overall strategy**
- **There are better alternative opportunities**

Companies commonly reduce commitments in some countries because those countries have poorer performance prospects than do others. For example, although Woolworth depended on its German stores for about a quarter of its operating profits, the company reasoned it should divest itself of more than 500 of those stores because of forecasted lower earnings in Germany, growth prospects in Latin America, and the need to expand its Foot Locker operations elsewhere in Western Europe.[54] In addition, Chevron announced a $2-billion downsizing of its U.S. home operation in order to increase its business abroad.[55]

Some indications suggest that companies might fare better by planning divestments better and by developing divestment specialists. Companies have tended to wait too long before divesting, trying instead expensive means of improving performance. Local managers, who fear losing their positions if the company abandons an operation, propose additional capital expenditures. In fact, this question of who has something to gain or lose is a factor that sets decisions to invest apart from decisions to divest. Both types of decisions should be highly interrelated and geared to the company's strategic thrust. Ideas for investment projects typically originate with middle managers or with managers in foreign subsidiaries who are enthusiastic about collecting information to accompany a proposal as it moves upward in the organization. After all, the evaluation and employment of these people depend on growth. They have no such incentive to propose divestments. These proposals typically originate at the top of the organization after upper management has tried most remedies for saving the operation.[56]

Divestments may occur by selling or closing facilities. The option of selling usually is preferred because the divesting company receives some compensation. However, a company that considers divesting because the outlook for the country's political and economic future is poor may find few potential buyers except at very low prices. In such situations, the company may try to delay divestment, hoping the situation will improve. If it does, the firm that waits out the situation generally is in a better position to regain markets and profits than one that forsakes its operation. For example, many MNEs divested their South African operations during the late 1980s primarily because of internal political unrest caused by South Africa's policy of apartheid, trade embargoes by foreign investors' home-country governments, and consumer pressure from outside South Africa. As more companies attempted to divest, there were fewer buyers that were able to buy facilities even at lower prices. By the early 1990s, the dissolution of apartheid laws brought a renewed positive outlook on South Africa's future. Companies that had remained (such as Hoechst, Crown Cork & Seal, and Johnson Matthey) were able to move much faster in the early 1990s to increase their South African business than were companies that had abandoned the market.[57]

A company cannot always simply abandon an investment either. Governments frequently require performance contracts, such as substantial severance packages to employees, that make a loss from divestment greater than the direct investment's net value. Further, many large MNEs fear adverse international publicity and difficulty in reentering a market if they do not sever relations with a foreign government on amicable terms. During the early 1990s, several foreign investors, including Occidental Petroleum and Email and Elders, decided to take losses and leave the Chinese market, but the Chinese government made their departures slow and expensive.[58]

Managers are less likely to propose divestments than investments.

C O U N T E R V A I L I N G

F O R C E S

In the quest for competitiveness, companies with global strategies often seek least-cost production locations by moving into developing countries because of labor-cost differences. However, advantages may be short-lived for several reasons:

- Competitors follow leaders into low-wage areas.
- There is little first-in advantage for this type of production migration.
- Foreign costs rise quickly because of pressure on wage or exchange rates.

As a result, some companies, especially those with rapidly evolving technologies, seek to locate production close to product-development activities. Doing this allows for a tight linkage between product and process technologies (for example, making smaller disk drives is as much a manufacturing problem as it is a technical one), a faster market entry with new products, and unique production technologies that cannot be easily copied by competitors.[59] These factors tend to push more of a company's production into industrial countries, in which most R&D occurs. Market-seeking location decisions, whether in pursuit of global or of multidomestic strategies, also favor industrial countries for both production and sales locations. Evidence indicates that new products diffuse to developing countries slowly and incompletely.[60]

Trade barriers give companies impetus to expand sequentially by starting in those countries with the largest markets. As these barriers are removed, particularly on a regional basis, companies may more easily commence sales strategies almost simultaneously in various countries. Large markets in which there is protectionism have a greater advantage in attracting production than do large markets that can be effectively served from production locations in smaller countries with trade access to the larger markets.

LOOKING TO
THE FUTURE

International geographic expansion is a two-tiered consideration: How much of a company's sales and production should be outside its home country? And how should outside sales and production be allocated among countries? As yet, no comprehensive model exists to answer these questions, and perhaps differences among companies and dynamic environmental conditions make such a model impractical. Meanwhile, companies are apt simply to place more emphasis on certain locales than on others as they see opportunities evolving. Typical of this tendency was a prediction by Procter & Gamble's CEO that more than half of that company's sales would come from abroad within the next few years, which would nearly double its foreign dependence, with sales growing more rapidly in the Far East than elsewhere.[61]

For large companies, an intriguing question is whether they are approaching an optimum ratio between domestic and foreign operations. Some data suggest they are.[62] An emphasis on more foreign business is perhaps inevitable when a company starts from a low base of international dependence. Yet the advantage of "more is better" should hold only until the company reaches some optimum combination of domestic and foreign operations. Otherwise, it would continue to improve its performance until it had no domestic operations at all—not a logical situation. If some companies are approaching their optimum positions, they can be expected to grow domestically and internationally at about the same rate in the future.

The need to allocate among opportunities because of insufficient resources is liable to play an even more important role in the near future. The opening up of Eastern Bloc economies, the global move toward privatization, and the more liberal allowance of majority ownership have combined to create more opportunities from which to choose. At the same time, companies have not increased their resource bases concomitantly to enable them to take advantage of all these new opportunities. Further, many companies in the late 1980s and early 1990s overextended their debt positions, particularly with leveraged buyouts; these debt positions might inhibit unrestricted international expansion.

Because data availability should continue to improve, global environmental scanning will assume greater importance. Companies will continue to need information because of global strategies of competitors and economic and political volatility. However, the information explosion will present new challenges as timely analyses may necessitate even greater reliance on tools that reduce the number of alternatives under consideration.

Summary

- Because companies do not have sufficient resources to exploit all opportunities apparent to them, two major considerations facing companies are which markets to serve and where to locate the production to serve those markets.

- Market- and production-location decisions are often highly interdependent because markets often need to be served from local production, because firms seek nearby outlets for excess capacity, and because firms may be unwilling to invest in those production locations necessary to serve a desired market.

- Scanning techniques aid decision makers in considering alternatives that might otherwise be overlooked. They also help limit the final detailed feasibility studies to a manageable number of those that appear most promising.

- The ranking of countries is useful for determining the order of entry into potential markets and for setting the allocation of resources and rate of expansion to different markets.

- Because each company has unique competitive capabilities and objectives, the factors affecting the geographic expansion pattern will be slightly different for each. Nevertheless, certain variables that have been shown to influence most companies are the relative size of country markets, the ease of operating in the specific countries, the availability and cost of resources, and the perceived relative risk and uncertainty of operations in one country versus another.

- The amount, accuracy, and timeliness of published data vary substantially among countries. A researcher should be particularly aware of different definitions of terms, different collection methods, and different base years for reports, as well as misleading responses.

- Sources of published data on international business include consulting firms, governmental agencies, international agencies, and organizations that serve international businesses. The cost and specificity of these publications vary widely.

- Some tools frequently used to compare opportunities in various countries are grids that rate country projects according to a number of separate dimensions and matrices on which companies may plot one attribute on a vertical axis and another on the horizontal axis, such as risk and opportunity or country attractiveness and company strength.

- Using a similar amount of internal resources, a company may choose initially to move rapidly into many foreign markets with only a small commitment in each (a diversification strategy) or to pursue a strong involvement and commitment in one or a few locations (a concentration strategy).

- The major variables a company should consider when deciding whether to diversify or concentrate are the sales response to incremental increases in marketing expenditure, the growth rate and sales stability in each market, the expected lead time over competitors, the degree of need for product and marketing adaptation in different countries, the need to maintain control of the expansion program, and the internal and external constraints the company faces.

- ROI figures alone do not reveal the full impact of a specific foreign investment on total corporate performance. Companies must assess such factors as effects on earnings in other countries.

- Once a feasibility study is complete, most companies do not rank investment alternatives but rather set some minimum-threshold criteria and either accept or reject a foreign project based on those criteria. This type of decision results because multiple feasibility studies seldom are finished simultaneously and there are pressures to act quickly.

- Reinvestment decisions normally are treated separately from new investment decisions because a reinvestment may be necessary to protect existing resources' viability and because there are people on location who can better judge the worthiness of proposals.

- Companies must develop locational strategies for new investments and devise means of deemphasizing certain areas and divesting if necessary.

Case
Mitsui in Iran[63]

In 1989 Mitsui and the Iran National Petrochemical Industries Company (IRNA) announced the dissolution of a joint venture, the Iran-Japan Petrochemical Company (IJPC), at Bandar Khomeini, Iran (see Map 11.1). The joint venture agreement was signed in 1971. Planning for the project began in 1973 and construction in 1976. As implied by the name of the joint venture, the project's purpose was to make petrochemicals using petroleum-based supplies from Iran. A Mitsui-led group of five Japanese companies owned 50 percent of the venture, with the remainder held by IRNA, an Iranian government-owned company. At the time of the dissolution, estimates of the two companies' investment were between $4 billion and $5 billion. The agreed-on abandonment of the project allowed Mitsui to claim about $1.25 billion in risk insurance from the Japanese government; however, Mitsui had to pay IRNA $952 million to withdraw from the project.

Work on the project had been suspended several times. First, the Iranian revolution brought work to a halt in 1979, when completion was estimated to occur within six months. Construction resumed in 1980 but was halted again a few months later because of Iraqi attacks. Although the project escaped extensive damage from the attacks, the facilities were to have depended on naphtha supplies from a refinery in Abadan that was almost totally destroyed. During these early years of construction, Mitsui was called on several times to add as much as $60 million to the project. In 1981, Mitsui finally stopped work because it feared the plant would become a "bottomless pit." This led to two years of exhaustive negotiations and sharp exchanges between Mitsui and the Iranian government. By the end of 1983, the Iranian government agreed to put up some additional funds, provided the future ownership share would be adjusted to reflect the capital contribution and Mitsui would send a survey team of a hundred engineers and experts to the site to get the project rolling again. Work did resume but stopped again in 1984 after further Iraqi attacks. Late in that same year, construction began anew, and completion was estimated to occur in three

Map 11.1
Southern Iran and
Neighboring Areas
Note the nearness to Iraq of Bandar Khomeini, the site of the joint venture, and Abadan, the source of naphtha supplies.

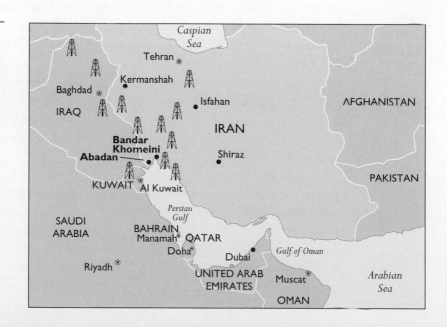

and a half years at a project cost in excess of $4 billion, compared with the original $500-million budget. Then in 1987, Iraq attacked again, and the Iranian government put the site off-limits to representatives of Mitsui or the Japanese government.

The scope of the project was significant for Mitsui, Iran, and Japan. If completed, it would be the largest foreign investment anywhere in the world by Japanese interests. For Mitsui, the venture was a substantial portion of its total investment and even more significant in terms of its foreign assets. At the time it became involved in Iran, Mitsui was at an early stage of developing foreign production. It had only smaller projects for Chinese coal development and for natural gas in Southeast Asia and Canada.

Meanwhile, Iran put a very high priority on completing the facility. Of the Shah's dozen or so billion-dollar projects, it was the only one that continued under the Khomeini regime. Iranian government officials indicated that Mitsui's decisions on its future participation would affect Iran's overall economic relations with Japan. The Iranian prime minister told a Japanese government survey team that the Iranian government would ensure stable supplies of crude oil to Japan if the project was completed. The question of oil supplies was a very sensitive issue because of Japan's dependence on foreign sources for over 99 percent of its petroleum needs. Japan depended more on Iran than on any other single oil source; but it also depended on Iraq. An official of Japan's Ministry of International Trade and Industry (MITI) said, "The project will decide the destiny of the fiduciary relations between Japan and the Middle East and eventually, the destiny of Japan's energy security."

Mitsui insured against war damage with the Japanese government's export insurance program. This insurance covered the cost of equipment that originated in Japan as well as losses caused by discontinuation of work, but it was originally due to expire in 1987. Prior to the expiration, Mitsui could apply for the war loss; however, if the Japanese government was unable to inspect the site, settlement could be much less than the damage. Doing this also would mean abandoning ownership in the project. Alternatively, Mitsui could apply for discontinuation of work for six months at an even lower settlement, while keeping its asset ownership. Finally, Mitsui could stall for settlement; however, if the site were to be attacked after the insurance expired but before inspection, the insurance might not cover the damage. In the meantime, the Japanese government wanted Mitsui to withhold claims because of its relationship with Iran and because the claims could wipe out Japan's export insurance program. Furthermore, a payment to Mitsui for withdrawal required an agreement between the governments of Iran and Japan, and Iran still wanted to see the project completed. Given the interest of Iran and Japan, Mitsui was able to negotiate an insurance extension until the end of 1989.

In 1988, Iran and Iraq agreed to a cease-fire. After inspecting the facility, Mitsui refused to invest any more money. It claimed that the damage from bombing and corrosion would require at least the same amount of investment expenditure as had been incurred up until that time. These costs would make the plant uneconomical. Iran claimed that the project could be completed for only 35 percent of the original cost. This disagreement led to nearly two years of negotiations on the terms of cancellation and on how to divide the losses incurred on the project. The Iranian government stalled settlement in an attempt to obtain Japanese economic assistance to reconstruct the nation's war-ravaged economy. Mitsui wanted an amicable settlement in order to pave the way for new ventures in Iran.

After agreement was reached between Mitsui and Iran, the Iranian government negotiated with Hyundai and Daewoo from Korea to put $2 billion into the Bandar Khomeini project. This was part of a larger deal in which the two companies would build tankers for Iran, to be paid for with crude oil.

Meanwhile, a Mitsui publication said, "The experience that we have gained through this project (IJPC) will be put to full use in our future business activities." The same report indicated that the plan is "to make Mitsui a truly global enterprise" with Europe and Asia the current "major focuses of our globalization policy."

Questions

1. What might Mitsui have done to prevent the Iranian losses?
2. Should Mitsui have sought an insurance settlement in 1987 rather than getting an extension of coverage?
3. Where should companies such as Mitsui put their geographic emphasis now? What tools could help them decide?
4. Evaluate the risks and opportunities for Hyundai and Daewoo from participation in the Bandar Khomeini project.

Chapter Notes

1. Data for the case were taken from "Ford in Britain," *Economist*, February 28, 1981, pp. 66–67; Gilbert D. Harrell and Richard O. Kiefer, *MSU Business Topics*, Winter 1981, pp. 5–15; Mira Wilkins and Frank Ernest Hill, *American Business Abroad: Ford on Six Continents* (Detroit: Wayne State University Press, 1964); Alan Nevins, *Ford: Expansion and Challenge: 1915–33*, Vol. II (New York: Charles Scribner's Sons, 1957); "Ford Annual Report," various years; "How Safe Is It to Invest Abroad?" *International Management*, October 1979, pp. 67–70; Steven Prokesch, "Can Europe Save Ford's Future: Again?" *New York Times*, October 28, 1990, p. F1+; and "Ford Around the World," *Ford International Public Affairs*, Dearborn, Michigan, various issues.
2. Masaaki Kotabe, "Patterns and Technological Implications of Global Sourcing Strategies," *Journal of International Marketing*, Vol. 1, No. 1, 1993, pp. 26–43.
3. Karen B. Hisey and Richard E. Caves, "Diversification Strategy and Choice of Country: Diversifying Acquisitions Abroad by U.S. Multinationals, 1978–1980," *Journal of International Business Studies*, Summer 1985, p. 52, show that between 70 and 85 percent of foreign acquisitions have been in related businesses.
4. Gene Koretz, "Where America's Bottom Line May Be Squeezed Overseas," *Business Week*, September 20, 1993, p. 22, refers to a study by Rosanne M. Cahn of First Boston Corp.
5. Yair Aharoni, *The Foreign Investment Decision Process* (Boston: Harvard University Graduate School of Business, 1966), pp. 52–53.
6. K. Fatehi-Sedeh and M. H. Safizadeh, "The Association Between Political Instability and Flow of Foreign Direct Investment," *Management International Review*, Vol. 29, No. 4, 1989, pp. 4–13.
7. John T. Harvey, "The Determinants of Direct Foreign Investment," *Journal of Post Keynesian Economics*, Vol. 12, No. 2, Winter 1989–90, pp. 260–272.
8. For overall export indicators, see Robert T. Green and Ajay K. Kohli, "Export Market Identification: The Role of Economic Size and Socioeconomic Development," *Management International Review*, Vol. 31, No. 1, 1991, pp. 37–50.
9. For a good discussion, see Ellen Day, Richard J. Fox, and Sandra M. Huszagh, "Segmenting the Global Market for Industrial Goods: Issues and Implications," *International Marketing Review*, Vol. 5, No. 3, Autumn 1988, pp. 14–27.
10. Kenichi Ohmae, "Becoming a Triad Power: The New Global Corporation," *International Marketing Review*, Autumn 1986, pp. 36–49; and "Foreign Investment and the Triad," *The Economist*, August 24, 1991, p. 57.
11. Raj Aggarwal, "Investment Performance of U.S.-Based Companies: Comments and a Perspective on International Diversification of Real Assets," *Journal of International Business Studies*, Spring–Summer 1980, pp. 98–104; and Rolf Buhner, "Assessing International Diversification of West German Corporations," *Strategic Management Journal*, Vol. 8, January–February, 1987, pp. 25–37.
12. Y. M. Geyikdagi and N. V. Geyikdagi, "International Diversification in Latin America and the Industrialized Countries," *Management International Review*, Vol. 29, No. 3, 1989, pp. 62–71.
13. Hisey and Caves, op. cit., pp. 58–62.

14. Irving B. Kravis and Robert E. Lipsey, "The Location of Overseas Production and Production for Export by U.S. Multinational Firms," *Journal of International Economics,* Vol. 12, May 1982, pp. 201–223.
15. Robert Steiner, "India Investors Overcome Bombs and Riots, But Not Bureaucracy," *Wall Street Journal,* May 28, 1993, p. C1.
16. Rodman L. Drake and Allan J. Prager, "Floundering with Foreign Investment Planning," *Columbia Journal of World Business,* Summer 1977, pp. 66–77.
17. Aharoni, op. cit., pp. 54–56.
18. These were found in studies of reactions to the Ancom investment code by Robert E. Grosse, *Foreign Investment Codes and the Location of Direct Investment* (New York: Praeger, 1980), pp. 122–123.
19. Christopher Power, "Will It Sell In Podunk? Hard to Say," *Business Week,* August 10, 1992, pp. 46–47.
20. Kravis and Lipsey, op. cit., p. 212.
21. Robert Keatley, "Luxury-Auto Makers Consider Mexico: Its Low-Cost Labor vs. Image Perception," *Wall Street Journal,* November 27, 1992, p. A4.
22. Karen E. Thuermer, "Selecting a New Location Is a Matter of Meeting Criteria," *Export Today,* April 1993, pp. 20–23.
23. See, for example, Briance Mascarenhas, "Coping With Uncertainty in International Business," *Journal of International Business Studies,* Vol. 13, No. 2, Fall 1982, pp. 87–98; Philip J. Stein, "Should Your Firm Invest in Political Risk Insurance?" *Financial Executive,* March 1983, pp. 18–22; and Pravin Banker, "You're the Best Judge of Foreign Risks," *Harvard Business Review,* Vol. 61, No. 2, March–April, 1983, pp. 157–165.
24. For an analysis of the importance of these variables in the decision-making process, see Joseph La Palombara and Stephen Blank, *Multinational Corporations in Comparative Perspective* (New York: The Conference Board, 1977), pp. x–xii.
25. Robert B. Stobaugh, Jr., "Where in the World Should We Put That Plant?" *Harvard Business Review,* January–February 1969, pp. 132–134.
26. Masayoshi Kanabayashi, "Japan's Top Soap Firm, Kao, Hopes to Clean Up Abroad," *Wall Street Journal,* December 17, 1992, p. B5.
27. For more information on the Ericsson strategy, see Thomas Hout, Michael E. Porter, and Eileen Rudden, "How Global Companies Win Out," *Harvard Business Review,* September–October 1982, p. 102.
28. Marie E. Wicks Kelly and George C. Philippatos, "Comparative Analysis of the Foreign Investment Evaluation Practices by U.S. Based Manufacturing Multinational

Companies," *Journal of International Business Studies,* Vol. 13, No. 3, Winter 1982, p. 39.
29. Robert Greenberger, "Heading for Hanoi," *Wall Street Journal,* February 9, 1993, p. A1.
30. Lee C. Nehrt, "The Political Climate for Private Investment: Analysis Will Reduce Uncertainty," *Business Horizons,* June 1972, pp. 52–55; Herbert Cahn, "The Political Exposure Problem: An Often Overlooked Investment Decision," *Worldwide P & I Planning,* May–June 1972, pp. 20–22.
31. Sally Bowen, "Foreign Money Pours Back," *Euromoney,* April 1993, pp. 120–121.
32. Douglas Nigh, "The Effect of Political Events on United States Direct Foreign Investment: A Pooled Time-Series Cross Sectional Analysis," *Journal of International Business Studies,* Vol. 16, No. 1, 1985, pp. 1–17; S. Desta, "Assessing Political Risk in Less Developed Countries," *The Journal of Business Strategies,* Vol. 5, No. 5, 1985, pp. 40–53; Thomas L. Brewer, "Instability in Developing and Industrial Countries: Methodological and Theoretical Issues," *Journal of Comparative Economics,* Vol. 11, 1987, pp. 120–123; and Fatehi-Sedeh and Safizadeh, loc. cit.
33. Harold Knudsen, "Explaining the National Propensity to Expropriate: An Ecological Approach," *Journal of International Business Studies,* Spring 1974, pp. 51–69.
34. Karen Pennar and Christopher Farrell, "Notes from the Underground Economy," *Business Week,* February 15, 1993, pp. 98–101; and Felicity Barringer, "Federal Survey Finds Census Missed 4 Million to 6 Million People," *New York Times,* April 19, 1991, p. A8.
35. Peter Nares, "Getting a Fix on Colombia's Largest Export," *Wall Street Journal,* November 25, 1983, p. 13.
36. Maureen Kline, "Italy Goes After Tax Cheats (Again), With a Big Plan to Get Small Business," *Wall Street Journal,* November 9, 1992, p. A7.
37. Maria E. Estenssoro, "When an Economy Goes Underground," *New York Times,* July 26, 1987, p. F3.
38. Kenichi Ohmae, "Americans and Japanese Save About the Same," *Wall Street Journal,* June 14, 1988, p. 30.
39. William A. Stoever, "Methodological Problems in Assessing Developing Country Policy toward Foreign Manufacturing Investment," *Management International Review,* Vol. 29, No. 4, 1989, p. 71.
40. Steven Greenhouse, "Comparing Wealth as Money Fluctuates," *New York Times,* August 23, 1987, p. E3, discusses the problem of comparing purchasing power.

41. John F. Preble, Pradeep A. Rau, and Arie Reichel, "The Environmental Scanning Practices of U.S. Multinationals in the Late 1980's," *Management International Review,* Vol. 28, No. 4, 1988, pp. 4–14.
42. This classification scheme is adapted from Carl Noble and Virgil Thornhill, "Institutionalization of Management Science in the Multinational Firm," *Columbia Journal of World Business,* Fall 1977, pp. 13–15.
43. Risk and opportunity are considered essential elements for incorporation in any portfolio analysis. See, for example, Yoram Wind and Susan Douglas, "International Portfolio Analysis and Strategy: The Challenge of the 80s," *Journal of International Business Studies,* Vol. 12, No. 2, Fall 1981, pp. 72–73; and "How Borg-Warner Uses Country-Risk Assessment as a Planning Element," *Business International,* November 9, 1979, pp. 353–356.
44. Harrell and Kiefer, loc. cit.
45. Craig M. Watson, "Counter-Competition Abroad to Protect Home Markets," *Harvard Business Review,* January–February 1982, p. 40.
46. Igal Ayal and Jehiel Zif, "Market Expansion Strategies in Multinational Marketing," *Journal of Marketing,* Vol. 43, Spring 1979, pp. 84–94.
47. Joseph C. Miller and Bernard Pras, "The Effects of Multinational and Export Diversification on the Profit Stability of U.S. Corporations," *Southern Economic Journal,* Vol. 46, No. 3, 1980, pp. 792–805.
48. Ibid., p. 804.
49. Briance Mascarenhas, "Order of Entry and Performance in International Markets," *Strategic Management Journal,* October 1992, pp. 499–510.
50. Janet Guyon and Michael J. McCarthy, "Coke Wins Early Skirmishes in Its Drive to Take Over Eastern Europe From Pepsi," *Wall Street Journal,* November 11, 1992, p. B1+.
51. Kelly and Philippatos, op. cit., p. 32.
52. Andrew Bartmess and Keith Cerny, "Building Competitive Advantage Through a Global Network of Capabilities," *California Management Review,* Winter 1993, pp. 78–103.
53. Kelly and Philippatos, loc. cit.
54. Jeffrey A. Trachtenberg, "Woolworth Explores Sale of German Unit," *Wall Street Journal,* November 10, 1992, p. A16.
55. Frederick Rose, "Chevron to Sell Nearly a Third of U.S. Refining," *Wall Street Journal,* September 28, 1993, p. A3.
56. Jean J. Boddewyn, "Foreign and Domestic Divestment and Investment Decisions: Like or Unlike?" *Journal of International Business Studies,* Vol. 14, No. 3, Winter 1983, p. 28.

57. Elizabeth Weiner and Mark Maremont, "Business Gets Ready to March Back to Pretoria," *Business Week,* February 25, 1991, p. 53.

58. Julia Leung, "For China's Foreign Investors, the Door Marked 'Exit' Can Be a Tight Squeeze," *Wall Street Journal,* March 12, 1991, p. A14.

59. Bartmess and Cerny, loc. cit.

60. Mascarenhas, loc. cit.

61. Keith H. Hammonds, citing John G. Smale, "P&G's Worldly New Boss Wants a More Worldly Company," *Business Week,* October 30, 1989, pp. 40–42.

62. John D. Daniels and Jeffrey Bracker, "Profit Performance: Do Foreign Operations Make a Difference?" *Management International Review,* Vol. 29, No. 1, 1989, pp. 46–56.

63. Atsuko Chiba, "Mitsui Led Group Must Pay More Money or Pull Out of Iran Petrochemical Project," *Wall Street Journal,* November 25, 1980, p. 30; "Mitsui Halts Iran Plant's Start-up," *New York Times,* April 24, 1981, p. D1; Youssef M. Ibrahim, "Japan Threatened by Iran-Iraq War," *Wall Street Journal,* November 8, 1983; Suleiman K. Kassicieh and Jamal R. Nassar, "Revolution and War in the Persian Gulf: The Effect on MNCs," *California Management Review,* Vol. 26, No. 1, Fall 1983, pp. 88–99; "Construction to Resume on War-Damaged Plant," *Journal of Commerce,* July 11, 1984, p. 22B; and "Japan Foreign Minister to Visit Iran to Query on Gulf Safety, Mitsui's Complex," *Oilgram News,* June 5, 1987, p. 2; "Mitsui in Fiscal 1990," *Mitsui Trade News,* September–October 1990, pp. 2–3; Roger Vielvoye, "Bandar Khomeini Project," *Oil & Gas Journal,* August 28, 1989, p. 31; "Iran Said to Seek Replacement for Mitsui to Rebuild Bandar Khomeini Plant," *Platt's Oilgram News,* June 14, 1989, p. 2; A. E. Cullison, "Mitsui Scraps Iran Complex," *Journal of Commerce and Commercial,* March 15, 1989, p. 1A+; and "Petrochemicals," *Oil and Gas Journal,* August 19, 1991, p. 31.

Chapter 12

The Impact of the Multinational Enterprise

If a little money does not go out,
great money will not come in.
—Chinese Proverb

Objectives

- To examine the conflicting objectives of MNE stakeholders

- To discuss problems in evaluating MNE activities

- To evaluate the major economic impacts—balance of payments and growth—of MNEs on home (donor) and host (recipient) countries

- To introduce the major criticisms about MNEs

- To give an overview of the major political controversies surrounding MNE activities

Case
MNEs in Canada[1]

Canadians long have had a love-hate relationship with foreign-owned companies in their country. For example, they have wanted the jobs foreign investment creates, but they worry that the country's economic independence and cultural identity may be lost. These conflicts also underlie the mixed feelings among Canadians about the U.S.-Canada Free Trade Agreement (FTA) and that agreement's expansion into the North American Free Trade Agreement (NAFTA). On the one hand, a Royal Bank of Canada study estimated that by 2000 Canada will need $1.4 trillion for energy investment alone, of which $300 billion will have to come from foreign sources. On the other hand, Canada's population is less than 10 percent of that of the United States, and more than two thirds of Canadians live within 100 miles of the 4000-mile U.S.-Canadian border (see Map 12.1). Their smaller population has led many Canadians to fear that their own companies will be unable to survive in an FTA market eleven times bigger than the Canadian market; U.S. companies, on the other hand, will have to adapt to an only slightly larger market. Further, the proximity of most Canadians to the border has meant they watch primarily U.S.-made television programs and movies. On this issue, the president of the government agency Investment Canada, Paul Labbe, said, "More non-Canadian control in cultural industries is not welcome." Overall, because of this love-hate attitude, Canada's policies toward FDI have varied over time and among provinces.

Map 12.1
Population Distribution in Canada

More than two thirds of Canada's people live within 100 miles of the U.S. border. This map shows Canada's provinces and largest cities.

Source: This map is based on information taken from map sheet number MCR 4046, copyright 1985, Her Majesty the Queen in Right of Canada, with permission of Energy, Mines and Resources Canada.

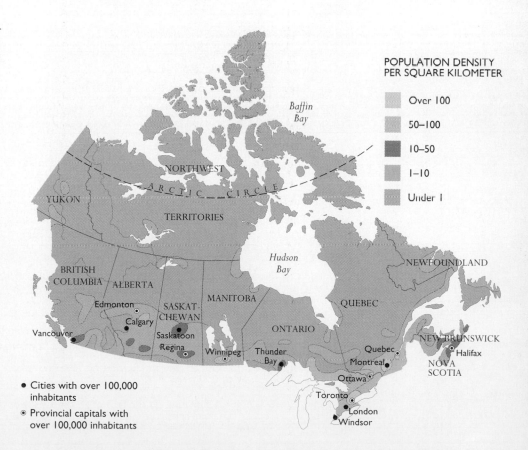

In 1972, after decades of Canada's luring foreign capital, an estimated 74 percent of the total corporate assets in Canada were foreign-owned. Of those total corporate assets, the U.S. ownership share was about 60 percent. No other advanced economy was so dominated by foreign ownership. Such a degree of foreign control was unusual even among developing countries. At that time, foreign ownership in Canada was restricted in industries considered to be particularly important to national sovereignty, including banks and other financial institutions, newspapers, magazines, broadcasting, and the uranium industry. Evolving public opinion favored increased restrictions. However, given the existing ones, what difference did it make that other companies were controlled outside Canada? Would operations, decisions, or benefits be any different under Canadian ownership? Obviously, many Canadians thought so.

One concern was the type of production taking place in Canada. Another was the level of job positions available for Canadians within Canadian subsidiaries of foreign companies. The Science Council, a governmental advisory board, contended that Canadian subsidiaries performed very little R&D, even in high-technology industries. Further, very little production of newer sophisticated products was being done in Canada. Instead, Canadian subsidiaries depended primarily on manufacturing mature products and components, which generally had a lower profit margin and employed a higher proportion of less-skilled people than did the more innovative output occurring in the MNEs' home countries. In addition, since the corporate headquarters of the MNEs were located abroad, Canadians in subsidiary operations could reach upper-level management positions only by leaving Canada. Given the high educational level of the Canadian population and the shrinking opportunities for advancement in Canada, a net flow abroad of highly skilled technical and managerial people was occurring—a so-called *brain drain*. Many of these workers joined the parent companies' operations, meaning that Canada then had to import the costly technical advancements that its own citizens helped to develop abroad. Thus many Canadians expected that greater Canadian control over company ownership would increase opportunities in Canada for Canadian workers and would make the country less dependent on foreign technology.

Critics of foreign ownership also largely agreed that in conflict situations, foreign investors would do what was best for home-country, rather than Canadian, interests. Many observers believed that if given a choice of exporting from Canada or the home country, the MNEs would choose the latter. Some critics were particularly upset when the U.S. government prevented Canadian subsidiaries of U.S. companies from exporting to China when the United States had no trade relations with that country. These export limitations reduced Canadian foreign-exchange earnings, and this reduction proved significant because dividend remittances to parent companies exceeded the flow of foreign capital into Canada.

Responding to these concerns, the Canadian government passed the Foreign Investment Review Act (FIRA) in late 1973. FIRA provided that the Foreign Investment Review Agency would screen any proposed foreign acquisition of 5 percent or more of an existing Canadian company and recommend to Parliament whether the investment was of "significant benefit" to Canada. The act applied to Canadian companies with assets of at least C$250,000 or annual sales exceeding C$3 million. By the end of 1974, the law had been extended to cover new investments and expansion of foreign-controlled companies into new areas of business.

The term *significant benefit* was not defined specifically. Some factors considered when determining significant benefit were the effects on employment, exports, competition, productivity, and industrial efficiency. Approval also depended on the degree of Canadian participation in a venture, although no quota of Canadian representation in a company's management was specified.

After the 1980 elections, a ten-year National Energy Program was announced to reduce foreign ownership in the energy industry to 50 percent. This program led to the "benefit" of an 8-percent drop in foreign control of oil and gas but sparked a two-year outflow of direct and portfolio investment as many foreign investors feared a political environment that would not allow them to operate profitably. This outflow in turn led to downward pressure on the Canadian dollar and upward pressure on Canadian interest rates.

While FIRA was in effect, some people favored greater control, contending that the act had a positive impact but did not go far enough. These critics showed that although foreign companies increased their R&D activity in Canada, the amount they undertook comprised a smaller share of total Canadian R&D than those companies' share of Canadian assets. The critics asserted that Canadian control would produce increases in R&D and gave as examples the Canadian takeover of de Havilland from the Hawker Siddeley Group of the United Kingdom and of Canadair from General Dynamics of the United States. Under Canadian ownership and management, these companies greatly increased R&D, developed new products, increased employment, and began competing internationally.

Those who wanted fewer controls questioned whether Canada could fulfill its technological and capital needs if controls resulted in reduced FDI inflow. First, they questioned whether indigenously controlled companies would undertake in Canada the kind of R&D that foreign companies were criticized for not undertaking. As an example, these analysts cited Northern Telecom, Canada's telecommunications giant, which maintains R&D facilities in the United States. Second, they showed that technology flows more quickly, more cheaply, and with fewer restrictions between a parent and a subsidiary than by license among independent companies. Among controlled operations, however, a number of investors transferred technology or depended on Canadian R&D so that Canada served as the production base for worldwide sales (for example, Westinghouse, steam turbines; Motorola, mobile radios; Honeywell, hydronic valves; and Garrett Manufacturing, control systems).

After the 1984 elections, FIRA was replaced by a new act and implementing agency called Investment Canada. Whereas FIRA's purpose had been to limit foreign control of the Canadian economy, the new act has sought to encourage FDI. Investment Canada reduced substantially the number of investment applications subject to scrutiny. Under it, direct takeovers of Canadian companies with assets of less than C$5 million and indirect takeovers of those with assets under C$50 million need not be examined. The old criterion that an investment be of "significant benefit" to Canada was replaced with a loosely defined "net benefit" to Canada.

But how liberal has Canada become toward foreign investors? There is no definitive answer. On the one hand, Canada has permitted some very large foreign takeovers, such as the purchase of 51 percent of Hiram Walker by the British company Allied-Lyons. On the other hand, Canadians remain worried about foreign domination, especially from the United States. Four of Canada's ten largest companies are U.S. direct investments; and U.S. majority-owned nonbank investments employ about 10 percent of the total private workforce in Canada. Further, FDI accounts for about 40 percent of Canadian manufacturing employment. Recently, Canadians have questioned the value of the inflow of Japanese investment, especially since the provinces have competed with each other in the incentives they offer to attract that investment. However, Canadians have welcomed the influx of capital that has accompanied the immigration of thousands of Hong Kong's wealthy residents who have left that territory in anticipation of its 1997 takeover by China. Some Canadians also worry that both Canadian-controlled and foreign-controlled companies will choose to locate more of their production within the United States to be nearer to population centers within the FTA and NAFTA and to avoid paying Canada's higher social-benefit taxes.

Introduction

As MNE managers and as national citizens, we need to understand the impact of MNEs. Chapter 11 discussed how companies allocate resources among countries to optimize their performance; however, this allocation is constrained and altered by governmental perceptions of the impact of MNEs. Managers must be aware of these perceptions and attempt at times to change them. As citizens, we need to argue for governmental policies that will enhance important national interests.

Pressure groups push to restrict MNEs' activities at home and abroad.

The opening case illustrates the ambivalence of Canadians toward FDI. In other countries as well, the rapid growth of MNEs has been controversial. In fact, powerful pressure groups in both home and host countries have pushed their governments to implement policies either restricting or enhancing the movement of MNEs. These groups are sure to play an even greater role in the future expansion of international business. This chapter examines the major contentions regarding MNEs' practices and the main evidence supporting or refuting those contentions.

The sheer size of MNEs is an issue.
- **Some have sales larger than many countries' GNPs.**
- **Some MNE executives deal directly with heads of state.**

The primary criticism is that MNEs are inadequately concerned about national societal interests because of their global bases of operations. Further, the sheer size of many of these companies concerns the countries in which they do business. For example, the sales of GM, Exxon, and Mitsubishi exceed the GNP of such medium-sized economies as Argentina, Indonesia, Poland, and South Africa. Large MNEs such as these have considerable power in negotiating business arrangements with governments; outcomes are sometimes of greater consequence than are many treaties among countries. In fact, the executives of MNEs frequently deal directly with heads of state when negotiating the terms under which their companies may operate. But not all MNEs are large. The number of smaller firms engaging in foreign operations has grown. Their entry often is preferred by LDC governments because they may be more willing to yield to host-country wishes, increase competition because of their numbers, and supply smaller-scale technology more suited to LDC needs.[2]

Evaluating the Impact of the MNE

Trade-offs among Constituencies

To survive, a company must satisfy different groups, often referred to collectively as **stakeholders.** These include stockholders, employees, customers, and society at large. In the short term, the aims of these groups conflict. Stockholders want additional sales and increased productivity, which result in higher profits and larger returns going to them. Employees want additional compensation. Customers want lower prices. And society at large would like to see increased corporate taxes or corporate involvement in social functions. In the long term, all of these aims must be achieved adequately or none will be attained at all because each stakeholder group is powerful enough to cause the company's demise.

Management must be aware of these various interests but serve them unevenly at any given period. At one time, most gains may go to consumers; at another, to stockholders. Making necessary trade-offs is difficult in the domestic environment. However, abroad, where corporate managers are relatively unfamiliar with customs and power groups, the problem of choosing the best alternative is compounded; this is particularly true since dominant interests differ among countries. For example, in the early 1990s, GM faced different priorities in different parts of the world. In South Korea, much higher wage-rate increases than the global average caused it to increase emphasis on labor savings in production in its Daewoo joint venture, while profits suffered. In much of Western Europe, society as a whole (consumers and nonconsumers alike) demanded more pollution-abatement equipment on automobiles, while wages increased only moderately. In Mexico, new legislation tied GM's growth to employment growth in its maquiladoras there, putting the emphasis on hiring more people in labor-intensive activities. Simultaneously, GM announced it would transfer a surplus two-liter-engine production line to China, where issues regarding employment, compensation, and environmental cleanup gave way to increasing stockholder profits and reducing consumer prices.[3]

The most cumbersome problem in overseas relationships is not so much one of trying to serve conflicting interests within countries but rather of handling cross-national controversies in a manner that will achieve global business objectives. Constituencies in any given country seek to fulfill their own, rather than global, objectives. For example, labor in the United States has been little concerned about the number of global jobs created by their employers, such as those created in Mexico. Instead, it has lobbied only for legislation to increase the number of jobs within the United States. Thus management's task is complicated, since decisions made in one country may have repercussions in another.

Among the many decisions managers must make are those concerning:

• Locations of production, decision making, and R&D
• Methods of acquisition and operation

- Markets to be served from production
- Prices to charge
- Use of profits

In the opening case, for example, many Canadians were concerned about such issues. Assume a U.S. investor has production facilities in both the United States and Canada. Which facility will export to Venezuela? Clearly, this decision will determine where profits, taxes, employment, and capital flows will be located. Interests in either country, as well as in Venezuela, may claim that they should have jurisdiction over the sales.

Trade-offs among Objectives

An MNE's actions may affect a wide range of economic, social, and political objectives of a given country. A positive effect on one objective, such as full employment, may be concomitant with a negative effect on another objective, such as domestic control over economic matters. In other words, there must be trade-offs. A country finds it difficult to rank its objectives, since it naturally wants only benefits without costs, which is seldom possible to achieve. Despite the widespread effects of MNEs on various parts of the social system, much of the literature analyzing these companies attempts to isolate effects to a single given objective. This sometimes occurs because a solution is needed for a given problem, such as a country's balance-of-payments deficit, and sometimes because pressure groups want to win support for their positions.

In international transactions involving MNEs, people sometimes erroneously assume that if one party gains, the other must lose. That may happen, but it also is possible that both parties will either gain or lose. No party would participate willingly in a cross-national transaction in the belief that the deal would harm its priorities. Controversies develop because things do not work out as anticipated, the precedence given to the objectives changes, and disagreements arise over the distribution of gains when it is acknowledged that both parties have benefited overall. The last problem is at the heart of most controversies. As described in the opening case, Canada has tried to encourage foreign investment while also securing more benefits from it. This was done with FIRA and later with Investment Canada.

Cause-Effect Relationships

The observation that two factors move in relation to each other does not prove an interconnection between them. Yet a number of recent events have been attributed to the growth in the number of MNEs and the portion of global business for which they account. Opponents of MNEs have linked them to inequitable income and power distribution, environmental debasement, and societal deprivation. Their proponents have linked them to increased tax revenues, employment, and exports. These linkages are particularly prone to arise when governments consider either restricting or encouraging FDI. Although the data presented by opponents or propo-

The effects of an MNE's activities may be simultaneously positive for one national objective and negative for another.

In an international transaction,
- *Both parties may gain*
- *Both parties may lose*
- *One party may gain and the other lose*
- *Even when both parties gain, they may disagree over the distribution of the benefits*

Countries want a greater share of benefits from MNEs' activities.

It is extremely hard to determine whether societal conditions are caused by MNEs' actions.

nents of MNEs often are accurate and convincing, it is not certain what would have happened had MNEs not operated or not followed certain practices. Technological developments, competitors' actions, and governmental policies are just three of the variables that encumber cause-effect analysis.

Individual and Aggregate Effects

The philosophy and actions of each MNE are unique.

One astute observer has said, "Like animals in a zoo, multinationals (and their affiliates) come in various shapes and sizes, perform distinctive functions, behave differently, and make their individual impacts on the environment."[4] Thus it is difficult to make general statements about MNEs' effects. Much of the literature on the subject, from the viewpoints of both protagonists and antagonists, takes isolated examples and presents them as typical. The examples chosen usually make interesting reading because of their spectacular or extreme nature, but it is dangerous to make policies based on the exceptional rather than the usual.

Some countries have tried to evaluate MNEs and their activities individually. Although this might lead to greater fairness and better control, it is a cumbersome and costly process. Therefore, many countries apply policies and control mechanisms to all MNEs. Although doing this eliminates some of the bureaucracy, it carries with it the risk of throwing out some "good apples" along with the bad. Further, when examining foreign investments on either an individual or an aggregate basis, governments have been far from perfect in predicting future impacts. Given these caveats, this chapter will examine the major impacts of MNEs.

Economic Impact of the MNE

Balance-of-Payments Effects

One country's surplus is another's deficit, but long- and short-term economic goals differ.

Place in the economic system   The discussion of the effect that trade and investment transactions have on the balance of payments often leads to incentives, prohibitions, and other types of governmental intervention as countries try to regulate the capital flows that parallel trade and investment movements.[5] The distinction between balance-of-payments effects and other cross-national effects is that gains are a zero sum; that is, one country's surplus shows up as another's deficit. If both countries were looking only at a limited time period and if both were interested only in the balance-of-payments effects of international transactions, then one country might justifiably be described as a winner at the expense of the other. In fact, objectives are not this limited. A country may be willing to endure balance-of-payments deficits in order to achieve other aims, such as price stability or economic growth, or it may be willing to forgo short-term surpluses in favor of long-term ones, or vice versa.

The effect of an individual FDI may be positive or negative.

Effect of individual FDI   Two extreme hypothetical examples of the effects of FDI illustrate the need to evaluate each investment activity separately in order to determine its effect on the balance of payments. In the first example, a foreign company purchases a Haitian-owned company by depositing dollars in a Swiss bank for the former owners. No changes are made in management or operations, so profitability remains the same. However, dividends now are remitted to the foreign owners rather than remaining in Haiti, and so there is a net drain on foreign exchange for Haiti and a subsequent inflow to another country. In the second example, a foreign company purchases unemployed resources (land, labor, materials, and equipment) in Haiti and converts them to the production of formerly imported goods. Because of rising demand, all earnings are reinvested in Haiti; thus the entire import substitution results in a gain in foreign exchange.

The formula to determine effects is simple, but the data to use must be estimated and are subject to assumptions.

Most investments or nonequity arrangements (such as licensing or management contracts) fall somewhere between these two simplistic and extreme examples and are not evaluated so easily, particularly when policy makers attempt to apply regulations to aggregate investment movements. There are numerous measurement difficulties, but guidelines are gradually emerging. A basic equation for making an analysis is

$$B = (m - m_1) + (x - x_1) + (c - c_1)$$

where

$$B = \text{balance-of-payments effect}$$
$$m = \text{import displacement}$$
$$m_1 = \text{import stimulus}$$
$$x = \text{export stimulus}$$
$$x_1 = \text{export reduction}$$
$$c = \text{capital inflow for other than import and export payment}$$
$$c_1 = \text{capital outflow for other than import and export payment}$$

Although the equation is simple, the problem of choosing the proper values to assign to the variables is formidable. For instance, let's try to evaluate the effect of a Honda automobile plant in the United States. To calculate the **net import change** $(m - m_1)$, we would need to know how much would be imported in the absence of the plant. Clearly, the amount that Honda produces and sells in the United States is only an indication because the selling price, product characteristics, and quality of those automobiles may be different from what would otherwise be imported. Further, some of the sales may have been at the expense of other automobile plants in the United States. The value of m_1 should include equipment, components, and materials brought in for manufacturing the product locally. For example, Honda buys many parts from suppliers who import them. The value of m_1 also should include estimates of import increases due to upward movements in national income caused by the capital inflow. For instance, if U.S. national income is assumed to rise $2 million as a result of the investment, the recipients of that income will spend some portion on imports, which is known as the **marginal propensity to import.** If this proportion is calculated to be 10 percent, imports should rise by $200,000.

The **net export effect** $(x - x_1)$ is particularly controversial because conclusions vary widely depending on the assumptions made. For the Honda example, it can be argued that a U.S. plant merely substitutes for Japanese exports and production. However, MNEs, regardless of nationality, argue that moves abroad are defensive; that is, restrictions of governments and shifts in cost advantages, such as a strong yen relative to the dollar, make foreign production inevitable. By moving abroad, MNEs pick up business that would otherwise go to foreign companies. MNEs have argued further that the investments stimulate exports of complementary products that can be sold through foreign-owned facilities. Data show, in fact, that U.S. companies investing the most abroad are the ones whose exports are also growing most rapidly.[6] Again, we must make assumptions about the amount of these exports that could have materialized had the subsidiaries not been established.

The **net capital flow** $(c - c_1)$ is the easiest figure to calculate because of controls at most central banks. The problem with using a given year for evaluation purposes is the time lag between the outward flow of investment funds and the inward flow of remitted earnings from the investment. Thus what appears at a given time to be a favorable or unfavorable capital flow may in fact prove over a longer period to be the opposite. For example, the time it would take Honda to recoup the capital outflow is affected by its need to reinvest funds in the United States, its ability to borrow locally, and its perception of the future dollar/yen exchange rate. Given the number of variables, the capital flows will vary widely among companies and projects. A further complication arises because MNEs may transfer funds in disguised forms, such as through transactions between parent and subsidiary operations at arbitrary rather than market prices, thus misstating the real returns on the investments.

Although the equation presented above is useful for broadly evaluating the balance-of-payments effects of investments, it should be used with caution. As mentioned earlier, there are data problems. In addition, an investment movement might have some indirect effects on a country's balance of payments that are not readily quantifiable. For example, an investor might bring new technological or managerial efficiencies that are then emulated by other companies. What these other companies do may affect the country's external economic relations.

The balance-of-payments effects of FDI usually are
- **Positive for the host country and negative for the home country initially**
- **Positive for the home country and negative for the host country later**

Aggregate assumptions and responses   Fairly widespread consensus exists that MNEs' investments are initially favorable to the host country and unfavorable to the home country but that the situation reverses after some time. This occurs because nearly all investors plan eventually to remit to the parent company more than they send abroad. If the net value of the FDI continues to grow through retained earnings, dividend payments for a given year ultimately may exceed the total capital transfers required for the initial investment. The time period before reversal may vary substantially, and there is much disagreement as to the aggregate time span required.

In the case of U.S. companies' FDI, for example, more than half of the net increase in value in recent years typically has come from the reinvestment of funds earned abroad. This means that the increase in claims on foreign assets has not been coming primarily from a flow of capital to the foreign operations. It also means that the FDI's net value has become so large that the return flow of funds to the United States from foreign earnings exceeds the outward flow for increasing investment abroad.

From the standpoint of home countries, restrictions on capital outflow improve short-term balance-of-payments deficits, since there should be an immediate improvement in the capital account. But restrictions on capital outflows reduce future earnings inflows from foreign investments. Consequently, the restrictions are useful only in buying the time needed to institute other means for solving balance-of-payments difficulties.

Governments also have sought to attract inflows of long-term capital as a means of developing production that will either displace imports or generate exports. The problem for investment recipients, then, is how to take advantage of the benefits of foreign capital while also minimizing the long-term adverse effects on their balance of payments. Many host countries have approached this problem by valuing new FDI only on the basis of contributions of freely convertible currencies, industrial equipment, and other physical assets, not contributions of good will, technology, patents, trademarks, and other intangibles. This valuation is then tied into regulations on the maximum repatriation of earnings. The maximum is stated as a percentage of the investment's value; by holding down the stated value, the host-country government can minimize eventual repatriation of earnings. In this respect, governments often exert strict control over the prices of equipment brought in, especially when the investor is also the equipment supplier, so that the investment value is not overstated. Governments also often are interested in receiving part of the capital contribution in the form of loans and in local holdings of equity so that the future outward capital flow is reduced and has an upward limit.

Home and host countries make policies to try to improve short- or long-term effects:
- **Home countries establish outflow restrictions.**
- **Host countries impose repatriation restrictions, asset-valuation controls, and conversion to debt as opposed to equity.**

Growth and Employment Effects

Unlike balance-of-payments effects, the effects of MNEs on growth and employment are not necessarily a zero-sum game among countries. Classical economists assumed production factors were at full employment; consequently, a movement of any of these factors abroad would result in an increase in output abroad and a decrease at home. Even if this assumption were true, the gains in the host country might be greater or less than the losses in the home country.

The argument that both the home and the host countries may gain from FDI rests partly on the assumption that resources are not necessarily fully employed and partly on the industry-specific and complementary nature of capital and technology. For example, a brewer, such as Anheuser-Busch, may be producing maximally for its domestic market and be limited in developing export sales because of high transportation costs. Anheuser-Busch may not easily move into other product lines

Growth and employment effects are not a zero-sum game because MNEs may use resources that were unemployed or underemployed.

or readily use its financial resources to effect domestic productivity increases. By establishing a foreign production facility, the company may be able to develop foreign sales without decreasing resource employment in the United States. In fact, it may hire additional domestic personnel to manage the international operations and receive dividends and royalties from the foreign use of its capital and technology, thus further increasing domestic income.

Home-country labor claims that jobs are exported through FDI.

Home-country losses   The United States is the home country for the largest amounts of foreign licensing and direct investment. Therefore, its policies understandably arouse some of the major critics of such outward movements. One of these critics is organized labor, which argues that foreign production often displaces what would otherwise be U.S. production. For example, a criticism of Stanley Works' movement of some tool production abroad was that it took place at the expense of domestic factory improvement, which might have made U.S. output more competitive.[7] Critics also cite many examples of highly advanced technology that has been at least partially developed through governmental contracts and then transferred abroad. In fact, some U.S. MNEs are moving their most advanced technologies abroad and are even, in some cases, producing abroad before they do so in the United States. An example is General Dynamics' transfer of aerospace technology to Japan to produce fighter planes. According to critics, if General Dynamics did not transfer the technology, Japan would purchase the products in the United States, thus increasing U.S. employment and output. These critics further argue that the technology transfer (mainly to Mitsubishi) will speed the process of Japan's seizing control of future global aircraft and electronics sales. However, Japan might have developed the technology itself had General Dynamics not made the sale, even though this would have delayed Japan's acquisition of aircraft.[8]

Host countries may gain through
- **More optimal use of production factors**
- **Utilization of idle resources**
- **Upgrading of resource quality**

Host-country gains   Most observers agree that an inflow of investment by MNEs can initiate increased local development through a more optimum combination of production factors and the utilization or upgrading of idle resources. A company is motivated to move resources such as capital and technology abroad because the potential return is higher in an area where they are in shortage than in an area of abundance.

The mere existence of resources in a country is no guarantee they will contribute to output. MNEs may enable idle resources to be used. Oil production, for instance, requires not only the presence of underground deposits but also the knowledge of how to find them and the capital equipment to bring the oil to the surface. Production is useless without markets and transportation facilities, which an international investor may be able to supply. Access to foreign markets, particularly the investor's home market, may be particularly important to developing countries that lack the knowledge and resources necessary to sell there. An example is the sale of Mexican asparagus in the United States under the recognized Green Giant label. U.S. consumers associate the brand name with known quality;

it might be prohibitively expensive for Mexican producers to gain the same brand recognition on their own.[9] Another less tangible aspect of FDI is greater resource utilization: Through exposure to new consumer products, the local labor force may develop new wants, which could encourage them to work longer and harder to acquire the additional goods and services.

MNEs' upgrading of resources may be brought about through educating local personnel to utilize equipment, technology, and modern production methods. Even such seemingly minor programs as those promoting on-the-job safety may result in a reduction of lost worker time and machine downtime. The transference of work skills increases efficiency, thereby freeing time for other activities. Further, additional competition may force existing companies to become more efficient.[10]

Host countries may lose if investments by MNEs
- **Replace local companies**
- **Take the best resources**
- **Destroy local entrepreneurship**

Host-country losses   Some critics have claimed that there are examples of MNEs making investments that domestic companies otherwise would have undertaken. The result may be the displacement of local entrepreneurs and entrepreneurial drive or the bidding up of prices without additional output. Such critics argue, for example, that by their ability to raise funds in various countries, MNEs can reduce their capital cost relative to that of local companies and apply the savings either to attracting the best personnel or to enticing customers from competitors through greater promotional efforts. However, evidence for these arguments is inconclusive. MNEs frequently do pay higher salaries and spend more on promotion than local companies do, but it is uncertain whether these differences result from external advantages or represent required added costs of attracting workers and customers when entering new markets. Added compensation and promotion costs may negate any external cost advantages obtained from access to cheaper foreign capital. Additionally, in many instances, the local competition also has access to that cheaper capital.

Critics also contend that FDI destroys local entrepreneurial drive, which has an important effect on development. Since the expectation of success is necessary for the inauguration of entrepreneurial activity, the collapse of small cottage industries in the face of MNEs' consolidation efforts may make the local population feel incapable of competing. However, the presence of MNEs sometimes may increase the number of local companies in host-country markets since MNEs serve as role models that local talent can emulate.[11] Further, an MNE often buys many services, goods, and supplies locally and thus may stimulate local entrepreneurship. For example, Bougainville Copper Limited (BCL) established a development foundation in Papua New Guinea to help set up new businesses. BCL has used local sources of goods and services and has contracted out many activities that formerly had been done by company personnel.[12] In fact, true entrepreneurs will find areas in which to compete; consequently, in any country there are success stories that can be emulated.

Another argument is that investors have access to high technology abroad that they may use in their home countries. This access may prevent original developers from maintaining proprietary advantages. It may also prevent production from remaining in the country where the innovation originated as the product moves through the life cycle. For example, foreign investment, especially from Japan, has increased rapidly in high-tech industries in California's Silicon Valley. This may allow non-U.S. companies to develop competitive capacities in their home countries that are based on U.S. scientific and technical investments.[13] The ability of MNEs to make these investments may be due to a reluctance of U.S. capital suppliers to wait for potential long-term returns. As a result, there have been U.S. legislative proposals to limit foreign ownership and establish funding to assist start-up of high-tech enterprises.

Finally, critics frequently contend that MNEs absorb local capital, either by borrowing locally or by receiving investment incentives. This raises the local cost of funds and/or makes insufficient funds available to local companies. Although subsidiaries have borrowed heavily in local markets and have exploited investment incentives, the link to the ability of local companies to finance expansion is unclear. For MNEs to have a noticeable effect on capital availability in a country, the amount of funds diverted to those investors would have to be larger in relation to the size of the capital market than is probably the case. Further, few MNEs acquire all resources locally; the additional resources brought in usually should yield a gain for the economy.

Host countries at times have not only prohibited the entry of MNEs believed to inhibit local companies, but also restricted local borrowing by MNEs and provided incentives for them to locate in depressed areas in which resources are idle rather than scarce.

Of particular concern to many countries is the foreign purchase of local companies. The employment effects continue to be debated because of assumptions about what would have happened had the acquisition not taken place, particularly when it involves a company that is not doing well. Consider Bridgestone's acquisition of Firestone. Firestone was already laying off workers, and Bridgestone further reduced employment through its restructuring. However, Bridgestone invested heavily to make Firestone more competitive. It is impossible to say for certain whether there was more or less employment because of the acquisition. For this reason, the employment effects of recent FDIs in the United States have been evaluated as both negative and positive.[14] Canada's FIRA and Investment Canada typify the policies of many countries in that they treat acquisitions more favorably than foreign investments started from scratch.

General conclusions   Clearly, not all MNE activities will have the same effect on growth in either the home or the host country; nor are the effects of MNEs' activities easily determined. Although there are dangers in attempting to categorize, the following generalizations are helpful in understanding the circumstances under which foreign investment is most likely to have a positive impact on the host country:[15]

FDI is more likely to generate growth
• When the product or
  process is highly
  differentiated.
• When the foreign in-
  vestors have access to
  scarce resources
• In the more advanced
  LDCs

1. *LDCs versus developed countries.* LDCs are less likely than developed countries to have domestic companies capable of undertaking investments similar to those in which foreign investors engage. Foreign investment in developing countries is therefore less likely to be simply a substitute for domestic investment; thus it yields more growth than if it were located in developed countries.

2. *Degree of product sophistication.* When the foreign investor undertakes to produce highly differentiated products or to introduce process technologies, it is less likely that local companies could undertake similar production on their own. The differentiation may derive from product style, quality, or brand name as well as from technology.

3. *Access to resources.* A foreign investor that has access to resources local companies cannot easily acquire is more likely to generate growth than merely to substitute for what local companies would otherwise do. Some of these resources are capital, management skills, and access to external markets.

4. *Degree of development of the LDC.* Foreign investors are more likely to transfer technology and serve as role models for growth in the more economically advanced of the LDCs. In the least developed of these countries, the investment may have a negative impact on growth if it merely exploits cheap labor that otherwise would be subsisting.[16]

Political and Legal Impact of the MNE

Countries are concerned
that MNEs are
• Foreign-policy instruments
  of their home-country
  government
• Independent of any
  government
• Pawns of their host-country government

Because of the size of many MNEs, there is much concern that they will undermine through political means the sovereignty of nation-states. The foremost concern is that an MNE will be used as a foreign-policy instrument of its home-country government.[17] Because the home countries of most MNEs are industrial countries, it is understandable that this concern is taken most seriously in LDCs. It is not restricted to them, however, as was demonstrated in the opening case.

Two other sovereignty issues are raised less frequently. One is that the MNE may become independent of both the home and the host countries, making it difficult for either country to take actions considered to be in its best interests. The second is that the MNE might become so dependent on foreign operations that the host country can use it as a foreign-policy instrument against its home country or another country.

Extraterritoriality

Extraterritoriality occurs
when governments apply
their laws to companies' foreign operations.

Chapter 3 discussed extraterritoriality. Host countries generally abhor any weakening of their sovereignty over local business practices. MNEs fear situations in which home-country and host-country laws conflict, since settlement inevitably must be between governmental offices, with companies caught in the middle. Laws need not be in complete conflict for extraterritoriality to come into play. Those requiring companies to remit earnings or to pay taxes at home on foreign earnings certainly have affected foreign expansion and local governments' control over such expansion. For example, French companies such as Moet-Hennessy, Piper-Heidsieck, Tattinger, and Mouton-Rothschild are prevented by French law from using the name *champagne* for the sparkling wine they produce in California.[18] Although extraterritoriality may result from legal differences between any two countries, the United States has been criticized the most for attempting to control U.S. companies abroad. The criticism has resulted from U.S. companies' dominance in FDI and from the extent of the U.S. government's efforts to control the companies' actions, such as through enforcement of trade restrictions and antitrust laws.

Trade restrictions   The primary focus of criticism has been the U.S. government's attempt to apply its Trading with the Enemy Act to foreign subsidiaries of U.S. companies to keep them from selling to certain unfriendly countries. Through a series of presidential orders, foreign subsidiaries have been prevented from making sales to such countries as Libya, Nicaragua, South Africa, and Vietnam, even though the orders violated the laws of some of the countries in which the subsidiaries were operating, such as France and Canada, which require that the sales be made.[19] The Cuban situation has been a particularly thorny issue between Canada and the United States. Throughout most of the 1980s, the United States permitted foreign subsidiaries of U.S. companies to sell to Cuba; however, the Cuban Democracy Act of 1992 changed that. The result was adverse foreign opinion, especially in Canada, which led to discussions there on whether FDI from the United States should be limited and whether the Canada-U.S. FTA should be reconsidered. And Canada was not alone in its concern. The UN General Assembly voted on a non binding resolution calling for an end to the thirty-year U.S. embargo of Cuba; only Israel and Romania voted with the United States.[20] Subsidiaries of U.S. companies also have been restricted from participating in the Arab boycott of Israel, even though the boycott is a foreign-policy instrument of the countries in which the subsidiaries are located.[21]

Antitrust laws   A second focus of criticism has been the U.S. government's antitrust actions. The United States has acted against domestic firms' foreign investments when there has been concern about possible harm to U.S. consumers.[22] At various times, the U.S. government has

- Delayed U.S. companies from acquiring facilities in foreign countries—for example, Gillette's purchase of Braun in Germany was held up
- Prevented U.S. companies from acquiring facilities in the United States that were owned by a company they were taking over abroad—for example, Gillette's purchase of a division of Sweden's Stora Kopparbergs Bergslags could not include that division's subsidiary, U.S. Wilkinson Sword
- Forced U.S. companies to sell their interests in foreign operations—for example, Alcoa's spin-off of Alcan

- Restricted entry of goods produced by foreign combines in which U.S. companies participated—for example, Swiss watches and parts[23]

The actions the companies were restrained from taking were legal in the countries in which they would have occurred. The Canadian cabinet, the British House of Lords, and the Australian parliament even enacted laws that forbade Gulf Oil, Rio Tinto Zinc, and Westinghouse from supplying information to the U.S. Justice Department about their participation in a uranium cartel outside the United States. The Canadian government, one of the principal organizers of the cartel, was particularly outraged that the U.S. Justice Department wanted information on U.S. companies' activities in Canada.[24] From a reverse standpoint, the United States objected to the EU's antitrust prosecution of IBM because it felt the EU did not have jurisdiction.

One cumbersome problem for U.S. companies has been the U.S. Justice Department's ambiguity regarding their relationships to other companies abroad. This ambiguity has been partially mitigated by the publication of foreign merger guidelines, including case situations illustrating how antitrust enforcement principles would be applied.[25] Relationships that might be subject to challenge include participation in cartels to set prices or production quotas, granting of exclusive distributorships abroad, and formation of joint R&D and/or manufacturing operations in foreign countries. The United States also has signed a number of bilateral treaties with other industrialized countries that call for mutual consultation on restrictive business practices.

Key Sector Control

Political concerns include fear of
- **Influence over or disruption of local politics**
- **Foreign control of sensitive sectors of the local economy**

Closely related to the extraterritoriality issue is the fear that if foreign ownership dominates key industries, then decisions made outside of the country may have extremely adverse effects on the local economy or may exert an influence on local politics. This suggests two questions: Are the important decisions actually made outside the host countries? If so, are these decisions any different from those that would be made by local companies?

Many business decisions can and have been made centrally; examples are what, where, and how much to produce and sell and at what prices. These decisions might cause different rates of expansion in different countries and possible plant closings with subsequent employment disruption. Further, by withholding resources or allowing strikes, the MNE also may affect other local industries adversely.

Some observers argue that governments generally have more control over companies headquartered in their countries than over foreign companies' subsidiaries. Even MNEs with substantial operations abroad may have primary loyalty to their home countries. This loyalty arises because most MNEs have a majority of their assets, sales, employees, managers, and stockholders in their home countries. They depend on their home countries for most of their R&D and other innovations that enable them to compete globally. Their home-country governments have access to their global financial records and can tax them on their global earnings, which host-country governments cannot do. Further, MNEs can ask their home-country government for assistance in resolving conflicts of interest but cannot expect a foreign government to intercede on their behalf with the home-country government.[26] Given these factors, it is not surprising that in conflict situations companies tend to favor their home country's objectives over a host country's.

Political fears include the beliefs that international companies may serve as instruments of foreign policy for their home-country governments and that they also may be powerful enough to disrupt or influence local politics. The former fear is largely a carryover from colonial periods, when such companies as Levant and the British East India Company very often acted as a political arm of their home-country government. This fear has resurfaced in the case of Japanese investment in the United States. Critics have pointed out that the Japanese government and Japanese companies lobby strongly to affect U.S. government policy. Together they spend more than all political parties do for House and Senate elections, and more than the five most influential U.S. business organizations combined.[27]

There also is a fear that powerful foreign companies, by withholding resources at the request of their home-country government, might influence the political process. For example, in the mid-1970s the U.S. State Department requested that Gulf Oil suspend its operations in Angola in an effort to weaken Soviet-backed factions that were taking control of the Angolan government. Several months later, Gulf received State Department permission to deal directly with the leftist government in order to resume operations. In the mid-1980s, the story was repeated for other U.S. companies operating in Libya and Nicaragua. In 1988, the U.S. government urged U.S. companies not to pay taxes or debts to the Panamanian government because of its alleged drug dealings.[28] Not only LDCs are concerned by such actions. France and the United Kingdom, for example, are anxious because if U.S. computer companies were to withhold output, they could create havoc in French and British companies, research laboratories, and governmental offices that depend on them.

Aside from establishing policies that generally restrict the entry of foreign investment, countries have selectively prevented foreign domination of so-called **key industries**, those that might affect a very large segment of the economy or population by virtue of their size or influence. Different countries view key industries differently. For example, NAFTA specifies that foreign investors from the three member countries generally are to be treated no less favorably than domestic investors are. But foreign ownership has been limited by Canada in cultural industries (recall the Canadian concerns in the opening case), by the United States in the airline and communications industries, and by Mexico in the energy and rail industries.[29] Many countries have nationalized foreign-owned mining, utility, and transportation companies. In other cases, governments have required management by local personnel in order to ensure that the industries can survive, if necessary, without foreign domination. In the United States since 1989, the President can halt any foreign investment that endangers national security, and although national security is not defined in the enabling legislation, enforcement has been extended to include economic security. The first use of the legislation prevented a Japanese firm, Tokuyama Soda Company, from acquiring General Ceramics.[30] In a few cases, governments have supported the development of competitive local companies to ward off foreign domination. These include consortia of computer manufacturers (for example, ICL in the United Kingdom, Telefunken and Nixdorf in Germany, and Siemens, CII, and Philips in Germany and the Netherlands) and consortia of aircraft producers (for example, Messerschmitt-Boelkow-Blohm in Germany, British Aerospace in the United Kingdom, Aeritalia in Italy, and Construcciones Aeronauticas in Spain).[31]

State-owned enterprises   When an MNE is a state-owned enterprise, the political concern about home-country control of the MNE is different only in degree. Although any MNE may in time of conflict favor home-country interests, the government-owned enterprise may be more prone to do so and do so more quickly. Government officials in the home country may be able to influence such a company more readily. Renault, for example, did not hesitate to transfer production from Spain to France in order to avoid employment reductions in the latter, its home country; a private French MNE may not have come to this decision as easily.[32]

MNE Independence

The discussion so far has centered on the fear that MNEs are unduly influenced by their home-country governments. Many observers also fear that these companies can, by playing one country against another, avoid coming under almost any unfavorable restriction. For instance, if they do not like the wage rates, union laws, fair-employment requirements, or pollution and safety codes in one country, they can move elsewhere or at least threaten to do so. In addition, they can develop structures to minimize their payment of taxes anywhere.

This ability to play one country off against another, especially if the countries are within a regional trade agreement, is more likely to be evident when an MNE is negotiating initial permission to operate in a country. For example, France has become less bureaucratic in approving FDI, a change that was implemented after an experience in which GM opened a plant in Spain to export to France after France had refused GM entry.[33] However, the fact that companies, once operating, are generally reluctant to abandon fixed assets in one country to move abroad indicates that these charges are probably exaggerated. Further, the country from which a company moves can usually restrict importation of the goods it produces abroad under more favorable conditions.

Host-Country Captives

Critics have alleged that MNEs may become so dependent on foreign operations that they begin attempting to influence their home-country government to adopt

MNEs can play one country against another but are reluctant to abandon fixed resources.

policies favorable to the foreign countries, even when those policies may not be in the best interests of the home country. Such assertions are difficult to support because there is always disagreement on what policy actually will be in a country's "best interests." However, there certainly are many examples of lobbying efforts by MNEs seeking the adoption of policies that are more palatable to the foreign countries where they are doing business. For instance, MNEs have lobbied for different U.S. treatment of governments in Angola, Nicaragua, and South Africa.

Political Involvement

Historically, foreign companies exerted a great influence on local politics.

There is concern that foreign companies will meddle in local politics to foster their own objectives rather than local ones. As recently as 1949, an association of six European companies handled 66 percent of Nigeria's imports and 70 percent of its exports; other European companies had a virtual monopoly on shipping and banking in that country. Because of this economic power, the foreign companies, through forced regulations, forbade Nigerian competition and employment except in the more menial and lower-paying activities. Despite the examples that make headlines, such as the discovery in 1972 of offers by ITT to support a group that planned to overthrow the Chilean government, most evidence shows that MNEs have avoided local political involvement in recent years. Even in the ITT situation, the argument could be made that the action did not differ from that taken by many locally controlled companies facing nationalization. Nevertheless, such instances kindle fears of a return to earlier periods when some foreign investors did manage to pick local leadership supportive of their activities, with no concern for the effect on the local population.

Bribery

Payments to government officials have been widespread and have been intended to
- **Secure business from competitors**
- **Facilitate services**
- **Ensure safety of employees and facilities**

No discussion of the impact of MNEs would be complete without mentioning payments to government officials. Investigations of U.S. MNEs in the 1970s and of Italian companies in the 1990s, along with much anecdotal information from various years, indicate that the practice has been widespread. MNEs as well as local companies have made payments to officials in industrial as well as developing countries and in communist as well as noncommunist countries.[34]

The situation is complicated by the fact that there are cross-national differences in the rules governing payments. For example, the United States prohibits corporate payments to political parties, but most other countries do not. Also, even if two countries have similar laws on payments, one may enforce them and the other may not.

An important motive for bribery is to secure government contracts that otherwise might not be forthcoming at all or to obtain them at the expense of competitors. For example, Foote, Cone & Belding Communications made payments to the Italian Health Ministry to obtain portions of an AIDS awareness ad campaign.[35] Another important motive is to facilitate governmental services that companies are entitled to receive but that officials otherwise might delay, such as product registrations, construction permits, and import clearances. Other reported payments have been to reduce tax liabilities, to keep a competitor from operating in a specific country (by General Tire in Morocco), and to gain governmental approval for price increases (by a group of rubber companies in Mexico). Some companies have made payments because of extortion. For example, Mobil made payments to forestall the closing of its Italian refinery, and Boise Cascade, IBM, and Gillette made payments to protect the safety of their employees.

Most reported payments have been in cash, but in some cases they have included products made by the company, such as ITT's gift of a color TV set to a Belgian official. Some payments have been made directly to governmental officials by the companies; most, however, have been made via intermediaries and by diverse methods. For example, the relative of a person having influence over a purchasing decision sometimes has been put on the payroll as a consultant. In other cases, the person having influence has been paid as a middleman at a fee exceeding normal commissions. Another common practice has been to overcharge a government agency and rebate the overcharge to an individual, usually in a foreign country. One company (Pullman) even used its auditor to effect payment to a governmental official.

Bribery scandals have resulted in the replacement of chiefs of state in Honduras, Italy, and Japan. Prince Bernhard of the Netherlands resigned all his public functions after charges that he had accepted a $1.1-million payoff. Officials have been jailed in a number of countries, including Pakistan, Iran, and Venezuela. Officials in a number of companies have resigned, been fined, or gone to jail.

In 1977, the United States passed the Foreign Corrupt Practices Act (FCPA), which makes certain payments to foreign officials illegal. One of the seeming inconsistencies in the act is that payments to officials to expedite their compliance with the law are legal, but payments to other officials who are not directly responsible for carrying out the law are not. For example, a $10,000 payment to a customs official to clear legally permissible merchandise is legal, but even a small payment to a government minister to influence the customs official is illegal.[36] The former payment is allowed because in many countries, governmental officials delay compliance of laws indefinitely until they do receive payments, even though such payments may be illegal in those countries.

> The U.S. legislation on bribery is controversial because
> - Some payments to expedite compliance with law are legal, but others are not
> - Extraterritoriality issues emerge
> - Business may be lost

National Differences in Attitudes toward MNEs

In theory, host countries may take completely restrictive or laissez-faire positions toward MNEs. In actuality, their policies fluctuate over time but are seldom completely restrictive or completely laissez-faire. Currently, countries such as Bhutan and Cuba are close to the restrictive end, and countries such as the United States and the Netherlands are near the laissez-faire end of the continuum. However, countries between these extremes have policies with varying degrees of restrictions as they attempt to attract investment and receive the most benefit from it. In general, countries have become less restrictive in recent years because those economies more open to the entry of FDI have fared better.

Many argue that there are ethical inconsistencies due to the double standard for regulating payments by business versus those by governments. For example, U.S. governmental aid is frequently given as a bribe, with the understanding that the host country will grant political concessions in return. There is little effort to blame the donor when it is discovered that officials in host countries have siphoned off aid funds for themselves. A second inconsistency is that some bribes are allowed, but others are not. Further, some argue that judging the morality of bribery should be accompanied by consideration of the morality of interference with a custom that may be legally and culturally acceptable in a given country. In addition, it is sometimes argued that unethical "means" are justified to arrive at a desirable "end." For example, IBM and other U.S. companies claimed that the FCPA caused them to lose a contract for air traffic control systems in Mexico.

ETHICAL DILEMMAS

They also alleged that their inability to make payments to Mexican authorities led to Mexico's installation of inferior technology.[37] Is this outcome a justification for bribery?

In addition to extraterritoriality, there are a number of pressures on MNEs to follow certain practices abroad. In many cases, MNEs are criticized regardless of whether they give in to these pressures. For example, the U.S. State Department criticized Eli Lilly's refusal to sell its herbicide tebuthiuron to the U.S. government for the eradication of coca plants in Peru. Some argue it is unethical to withhold products useful in the war on drugs. But Lilly was concerned because the product was considered too potent to use on U.S. cropland, had not been tested in Peruvian soil conditions, and was still being tested for adverse health effects.[38] Similarly, the U.S. Defense Department criticized the German firm, Bayer, for refusing to let its U.S. subsidiary sell the U.S. Army chemicals that could be used to make poison gas.[39] Some maintain it is unethical for headquarters to dictate that a foreign subsidiary cannot sell something to its host-country government. But had these companies given in to pressures from the U.S. governmental agencies, they most certainly would have been faced with other criticism, or even boycotts.

To illustrate further, Coca-Cola's Guatemalan bottling franchisee was involved in a violent labor dispute. The Guatemalan government supported the bottler and was rumored to be implicated in the kidnapping or murder of more than a dozen workers involved in the unionization effort. Union groups outside Guatemala asked Coca-Cola to use its influence to persuade the bottler and government to cease thwarting the unionization process. Coca-Cola refused on the grounds that it did not own the bottler and had a policy of nonintervention with independent bottlers and governments on labor matters. But then, the International Union of Food and Allied Workers mounted an international boycott against Coca-Cola; the company subsequently stepped in and managed to restore peace.[40] From an ethical standpoint, what should Coca-Cola have done?

Operational Impact of International Business Activities

The relationship between MNEs and societies has generated so many allegations and controversies that it is impossible to examine all of them in this chapter. A number of them deal not so much with whether international business should take place but rather with certain practices. In these cases, the targets are specific operational areas of management that, fortunately, can be examined in later chapters of this book. They are no less important than the overall areas discussed in this chapter and are listed here to illustrate the wide range of criticisms:

- In transferring technology to LDCs, MNEs set prices too high and restrict sales too stringently (Chapter 15).
- MNEs' centralization and control of key functions in their home countries perpetuate the neocolonial dependence of LDCs (Chapter 16).
- Sensitive information about countries is disseminated internationally by MNEs' global intelligence networks (Chapter 16).
- MNEs introduce superfluous products that do not contribute to social needs and that perpetuate class distinctions (Chapter 17).
- MNEs avoid paying taxes (Chapter 19).
- Through artificial transfer pricing, MNEs undermine attempts by governments to manage their countries' economic affairs (Chapter 20).
- The best jobs are given to citizens of the country in which an MNE has its headquarters (Chapter 21).
- Inappropriate technology is introduced into LDCs by MNEs (Chapter 21).
- National labor interests are undermined because of MNEs' global activities (Chapter 21).

C O U N T E R V A I L I N G

F O R C E S

This entire chapter is essentially about countervailing forces. How do they affect a company's ability to choose a global versus a multidomestic strategy? Stakeholders, at home and abroad, seldom look specifically at the strategies MNEs follow; rather, they look at whether MNEs satisfy their interests. Fortunately for MNEs, satisfying stakeholders' interests is seldom a zero-sum situation; therefore MNEs—whether following global or multidomestic practices—usually can demonstrate positive impacts from their operations on the objectives of both home and host countries. For example, employment effects may be positive on both home and host countries, whether or not domestic and foreign operations are highly independent of each other. An MNE thus may have considerable, but not complete, latitude in deciding to produce separately for each market or to integrate its production substantially among the markets. This is because either option, if successful, will lead to employment in both the home and host countries. Furthermore, an MNE may be able to centralize production and export into other markets because importing countries are willing to forgo local production in order to satisfy pressures from consumers.

In spite of the rivalry among countries and their desire to influence MNEs to serve their interests, countries frequently have acted cooperatively in dealing with MNEs. These dealings will be discussed extensively in Chapter 13.

LOOKING TO THE FUTURE

As long as there is nationalism, governments will try to garner a larger share of the benefits from the activities of MNEs. In the short term, most countries will probably welcome FDI. Debt problems limit the ability of LDCs and HPEs to access sufficient capital, except through investment inflows. Budget-deficit problems are likely to make the United States take a positive stance toward receiving FDI. The EU probably will welcome investment inflows to attain the growth its unification is aimed at. However, in the longer term, FDI may be less welcome. Historically, the attitudes toward FDI have tended to vary, leaning toward more restrictions when economies are thriving. Yet, it is possible that if rapid growth does not occur in some LDCs and HPEs after they receive substantial FDI, they may learn to regard as models such countries as Japan and South Korea, which have grown rapidly without much FDI.

Where MNEs are controlled will continue to be an issue. Some MNEs (such as Nestlé, SKF, ABB, ICI, CPC, Coca-Cola, and Heinz) now have so many nationalities represented in their top management ranks, it is difficult to accuse them of favoring home-country interests. However, their internationalization leaves them open to the criticism of acting in their own, rather than national, interests. On the other hand, some MNEs (including Sandoz, Volvo, Michelin, Matsushita, and United Technologies) have few shares held outside their home countries and practically no foreigners in high-level corporate positions.[41]

Summary

- **Management must understand the need to compromise and to satisfy the conflicting interests of stockholders, employees, customers, and society at large. Internationally, the problem is more complex because the relative strengths of competing groups vary among countries. Further, satisfying interests in one country may cause dissatisfaction in another.**

- **The effects of MNEs are difficult to evaluate because of conflicting influences on different countries' objectives, intervening variables that obscure cause-effect relationships, and differences among MNEs' practices. Countries are interested not only in their absolute gains or losses but also in their performance relative to other countries.**

- **Since a balance-of-payments surplus in one country must result in a deficit else-where, trade and investment transactions have been scrutinized closely for their effects. However, countries often are willing to accept short-term deficits in order to achieve a long-term surplus or other economic gains.**

- **The basic effects of FDI on a country's balance of payments theoretically can be determined, but disagreements exist about many assumptions that must be made concerning the relationship between such investment and trade. Projects differ so much that it is difficult to generalize and to make effective policies that apply to large groups of investors.**

- **Governments have attempted to use FDI to improve their balance-of-payments positions through regulating capital flows, requiring partial local owner-ship, limiting local borrowing by foreign investors, and stipulating that a part of capital inflows must be in the form of loans rather than equity.**

- **The growth and employment effects of MNEs do not necessarily benefit one country at the expense of another. Much of these effects are due to the relative employment of resources with and/or without the MNEs' activities.**

- **MNEs may contribute to growth and employment by enabling idle resources to be used, using resources more efficiently, and upgrading resources' quality.**

- **The factors affecting growth and employment include the location in which MNEs operate, product sophistication, competitiveness of local companies, governmental policies, and degree of product differentiation.**

- **Political concerns about MNEs center around the fear that they may be used as foreign-policy instruments of home-country or host-country governments or that they may avoid the control of any government.**

- **Extraterritoriality is the application of home-country laws to the operations of companies abroad. This sometimes leads to conflicts between home and host countries and may put an MNE in the untenable position of having to violate the laws of one country or the other.**

- **Countries most fear foreign control of key sectors in their economies because decisions made abroad may disrupt local economic and political stability. Fur-ther, the foreign investors then may have enough power to adversely affect local sovereignty. Thus foreign ownership in key sectors of countries' economies often is restricted.**

Case
Foreign Real-Estate
Holdings in the
United States[42]

Compared to other countries, the United States has relatively few restrictions on foreign investors. Foreign control is prohibited in only a handful of industries, primarily in the areas of transportation and communication. These prohibitions have resulted because of the importance of these areas in moving essential commodities and informing the public in time of crisis. Historically, the only period in which there was a widespread concern in the United States about foreign ownership was in the late nineteenth century, when temporary prohibitions were placed on foreign ownership of agricultural land. This history does not mean that direct investment cannot be prohibited. In 1989, the United States passed legislation to prevent takeovers that, based on a case-by-case examination, would adversely affect national security.

The United States also has been a relatively safe place for investments. The only confiscations have been of properties held by interests from enemy countries during the two world wars and of Iranian assets when U.S. embassy personnel were held as hostages in Iran. More recently, Libyan and Kuwaiti assets were frozen but not expropriated. (The Revolutionary War could be seen as a confiscation of thirteen English investments.) No wars have been fought on U.S. land for over a hundred years; thus the loss of property through political unrest has been negligible.

After World War II, direct investment flows went out of the United States as U.S. companies took advantage of ample resources, a strong dollar, and a welcome from foreign governments to establish facilities. In the late 1960s, the U.S. Department of Commerce established offices to lure investors to the United States, and several states began including foreign companies in their industrial promotion efforts. Although direct investment into the United States accelerated, the movement went largely unnoticed by the general public, in part because no approval by U.S. authorities was necessary before making such an investment. It was not even necessary to register anywhere that a foreign investment had been made. Many of the investors maintained a low profile and were not known, even by governmental officials, to be foreigners.

The 1973 oil embargo and the publicity about the substantial influx of direct investment to the United States during the next few years led to Congress's adopting legislation to survey the extent of FDI and practices of foreign investors in the United States. Subsequent legislation requiring foreign investors to report the establishment of a new U.S. business or acquisition of an interest in an existing U.S. business became effective in 1979. However, this has not been enough to assure people who are concerned about the foreign influx. The purchase of Rockefeller Center by Mitsubishi bolstered U.S. nationalistic feelings. A 1988 poll showed that 78 percent of people in the United States favor "a law to limit the extent of foreign investment in American business and real estate."

Some criticism of foreign investment in the United States is in response to the more stringent control of such investment in other countries. The attitude is summed up as "Why don't we treat them as harshly as they treat us?" Much of the concern, however, has focused on specific key sectors deemed vital to national interests, including banking, food, computers, high technology, oil, and coal. One area that has been singled out is real estate, especially agricultural and residential land.

Figure 12.1
U.S. Real Estate: Who Invests?

Ownership of commercial real estate in the United States in 1989, including property owned by government or religious organizations and by private individuals.

Source: Data from The Roulac Group of Deloitte & Touche, "Real Estate Capital Flows," San Francisco, 1990.

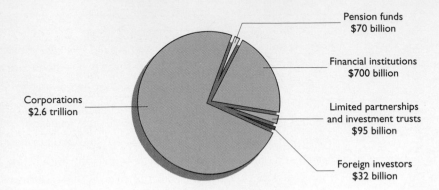

Pension funds
$70 billion

Financial institutions
$700 billion

Limited partnerships
and investment trusts
$95 billion

Foreign investors
$32 billion

Corporations
$2.6 trillion

The Agricultural Foreign Investment Disclosure Act of 1978 requires that agriculture land transfers to foreigners be reported. The interest in real estate has evolved primarily because it is a sector with an historical emotional tie for Americans. The country was largely settled by landless persons who were able to better themselves economically because of the availability of free or cheap land; thus any threat of foreign control of real estate has been viewed negatively. Even after the disappearance of the western frontier, land has been valued because of the high priority placed on relatively cheap agricultural products and on housing. Numerous reports have alleged that large foreign real-estate purchases tended to inflate prices, especially in Hawaii where there has been much Japanese investment. Many in the United States fear that rising prices will put land out of reach of the average American. Some also fear that agricultural output will be exported abroad rather than being sold to Americans.

But how widespread is foreign ownership? Figure 12.1 shows that only about 1 percent of U.S. real estate is foreign-owned. The U.S. Department of Agriculture estimates that less than 0.5 percent of U.S. farmland is owned by foreign investors, and much of this has been acquired by foreign paper companies such as Bowater of the United Kingdom and Abitibi of Canada. Considerable publicity also has been given to foreign purchases of housing and office buildings, particularly by Japanese investors in the early 1980s and especially in Miami, Honolulu, and Los Angeles (three areas in which foreign purchasers have been very active). But the biggest foreign real estate buyers in the early 1990s were state-owned Chinese companies, which kept low profiles by buying smaller income-generating commercial buildings and hotels. The movement of funds (capital flight) from LDCs, particularly those with corrupt dictatorships, has been massive as people have perceived a risk in keeping their money there.

Although no federal restrictions have been enacted in the United States, twenty of the fifty states have restrictions on ownership of property by foreigners. Only three states (Iowa, Missouri, and Minnesota) have singled out agricultural property for special treatment. They did this in the late 1970s because of fear that foreign purchases would cause farmland prices to jump. In fact, the prices plummeted in the late 1980s, as did Japanese investment in U.S. property. By the 1990s, U.S. landowners, real-estate brokers, and investment bankers were seeking out foreign buyers, especially from China, Hong Kong, and Taiwan.

Questions

1. In the interests of the United States, should federal restrictions be placed on the foreign acquisition of real estate?
2. If restrictions were implemented, what should they cover (for example, type of land, nationality of purchaser, use of land, or size of holdings)?
3. Should foreign ownership be restricted in economic sectors other than real estate?
4. What are the likely consequences if the United States does or does not place new limitations on foreign real estate investments?

Chapter Notes

1. Data for the case were taken from "Limits Proposed to Canada Operations," *Wall Street Journal*, February 4, 1972, p. 8; "Canadian Brain Drain," *Wall Street Journal*, May 22, 1973, p. 1; "Canada Passes Law to Screen Investments Made There by Foreigners Starting in '74," *Wall Street Journal*, December 14, 1973, p. 21; Mitchell C. Lynch, "Canada to Tighten Foreign Ownership Rein Further as Economic, Job Pictures Improve," *Wall Street Journal*, May 4, 1973, p. 24; Edward Carrigan, "Canada Must Control Own Industry If It's to Progress," *Citizen* (Ottawa), June 27, 1980, p. 6; John Urquhart, "Canada Drive," *Wall Street Journal*, February 18, 1981, p. 1+; Herbert E. Meyer, "Trudeau's War on U.S. Business," *Fortune*, April 6, 1981, pp. 74–82; Harold Crookell, "The Future of U.S. Direct Investment in Canada," *Business Quarterly*, Vol. 48, No. 2, Summer 1983, pp. 22–28; "Canada Takes 'Positive' Step to Attract Foreign Investment," *American Banker*, January 2, 1985, p. 2; "Investment Canada: Invitation to Foreign Capital," *Mergers & Acquisitions*, Vol. 20, No. 4, March–April 1986, pp. 84–85; "America's Half-Open Door," *Economist*, Vol. 302, No. 7481, January 17, 1987, p. 66; John Urquhart and Peggy Berkowitz, "Northern Angst," *Wall Street Journal*, September 22, 1987, p. 1 1; D. J. Daly and D. C. MacCharles, *Canadian Manufactured Exports: Constraints and Opportunities* (Montreal: The Institute on Research on Public Policy, 1986); Brian Milner and Elizabeth Moore, "Auto Makers Masterful at Game of Incentives," *Globe & Mail* (Toronto), August 26, 1989, p. B16; United Nations Centre on Transnational Corporations, *Transnational Corporations in World Development* (New York: United Nations, 1988), pp. 213, 257; Raymond J. Mataloni, Jr., "U.S. Multinational Companies' Operations in 1990," *Survey of Current Business*, August 1992, pp. 62–63; Lyne Smith and Jon Arnold, "Doing Business in Canada: A Current Appraisal," *Export Today*, January–February 1993, pp. 54–56; Lindsay N. Meredith and Dennis R. Maki, "The United States Export and Foreign Direct Investment Linkage in Canadian Manufacturing Industries," *Journal of Business Research*, Vol. 24, 1992, pp. 73–88.

2. Shujaat Islam, "Producing Prosperity: Multinationals in the Developing World," *Harvard International Review*, Spring 1993, pp. 42–44+.

3. Most of the examples were taken from *General Motors Public Interest Report 1990* (Detroit: General Motors Corp., May 15, 1990).

4. John H. Dunning, "The Future of Multinational Enterprise," *Lloyds Bank Review*, July 1974, p. 16.

5. The following discussion draws on problems reported in several studies that attempted to assess the balance-of-payments effects of foreign direct investments. For a good example of opposing arguments and conclusions, see Richard Bernal, "Foreign Investment and Development in Jamaica," *Inter-American Economic Affairs*, Vol. 38, No. 2, Autumn 1984, pp. 3–21; and Ciaran O'Faircheallaigh, "Foreign Investment and Development in Less Developed Countries," *Inter-American Economic Affairs*, Vol. 39, No. 2, Autumn 1985, pp. 27–35.

6. Masaaki Kotabe, "Assessing the Shift in Global Market Share of U.S. Multinationals," *International Marketing Review*, Vol. 6, No. 5, 1989, pp. 54–69.

7. Louis Uchitelle, "The Stanley Works Goes Global," *New York Times*, July 23, 1983, p. F1+.

8. Stephen Kreider Yoder, "U.S. Defense Chief Approves an Accord with Japan for Joint Production of Jet," *Wall Street Journal*, June 6, 1988, p. 10; and Eduardo Lachica, "Politics & Policy," *Wall Street Journal*, April 10, 1989, p. A14.

9. David M. Henneberry, "U.S. Foreign Direct Investment in the Developing Nations: A Taxonomy of Host-Country Policy Issues," *Agribusiness*, Vol. 2, No. 1, 1986, p. 97.

10. Ignatius J. Horstmann and James R. Markusen, "Firm Specific Assets and the Gains from Direct Foreign Investment," *Economica*, February 1989, pp. 41–48.

11. Emilio Paguolatos, "Foreign Direct Investment in U.S. Food and Tobacco Manufacturing and Domestic Economic Performance," *American Journal of Agricultural Economics*, Vol. 65, No. 2, May 1983, pp. 405–412.

12. O'Faircheallaigh, op. cit., p. 31.

13. David J. Teece, "Foreign Investment and Technological Development in Silicon Valley," *California Management Review*, Vol. 34, No. 2, Winter 1992, pp. 88–106.

14. See, for example, Thomas Omestad, "Selling Off America," *Foreign Policy*, No. 76, Fall 1989, pp. 119–140; "Foreign Investment in the United States," Hearing before the Subcommittee on Economic Stabilization of the Committee on Banking, Finance and Urban Affairs, House of Representatives, Serial No. 101-65 (Washington, D.C.: U.S. Government Printing Office, 1989), pp. 21–23; and Edward M. Graham and Paul R. Krugman, *Foreign Direct Investment in the United States* (Washington, D.C.: Institute for International Economics, 1990).

15. U.S. Department of Commerce, *The Multinational Corporation: Studies on U.S. Foreign Investment*, Vol. 1 (Washington, D.C.: 1972), p. 61.

16. Jonghoe Yang and Russell A. Stone, "Investment Dependence, Economic Growth, and Status in the World System: A Test of 'Dependent Development,'" *Studies in Comparative International Development*, Vol. 20, No. 1, Spring 1985, pp. 98–120.

17. For a good discussion of various means of gaining political objectives through economic dependency, see Adrienne Armstrong, "The Political Consequences of Economic Dependence," *Journal of Conflict*

Resolution, Vol. 25, No. 3, September 1981, pp. 401–428.

18. Frank J. Prial, "Wines of America: A Rich Harvest for Foreign Investors," *New York Times,* June 8, 1988, p. 15+.

19. "Review & Outlook: Exporting Leadership," *Wall Street Journal,* April 9, 1984, p. 28, gives recent examples of disagreements.

20. Frank J. Prial, "U.N. Votes to Urge U.S. to Dismantle Embargo on Cuba," *New York Times,* November 25, 1992, p. A1.

21. See, for example, "Anti-Boycott Charges Are Settled by Fines for Nine Companies," *Wall Street Journal,* October 13, 1983, p. 16; and Elizabeth Weiner and Laurence J. Tell, "Out of South Africa: Divestment Hits a Snag," *Business Week,* July 6, 1987, p. 53.

22. Eduardo Lachica, "U.S. Decides to Enforce Antitrust Laws Against Collusion by Foreign Concerns," *Wall Street Journal,* April 7, 1992, p. C9.

23. These are but a few of the types of antitrust actions. See J. Townsend, "Extraterritorial Antitrust Revisited—Half a Century of Change," paper presented at the Academy of International Business, San Francisco, December 1983; and "U.S. Seeks to Block Gillette's Purchase of Wilkinson Assets," *Wall Street Journal,* January 11, 1990, p. B6.

24. "Extraterritorial Trouble," *Wall Street Journal,* December 20, 1979, p. 7; and "Down under with the U.S. Courts," *Wall Street Journal,* May 1, 1981, p. 24.

25. Eleanor M. Fox, "Updating the Antitrust Guide on International Operations—A Greener Light for Export and Investment Abroad," *Vanderbilt Journal of Transnational Law,* Vol. 15, Fall 1982, pp. 713–766.

26. Yao-Su Hu, "Global or Stateless Corporations Are National Firms with International Operations," *California Management Review,* Vol. 34, No. 2, Winter 1992, pp. 107–126.

27. Pat Choate, "Political Advantage: Japan's Campaign for America," *Harvard Business Review,* Vol. 68, No. 5, September–October 1990, pp. 87–103.

28. "Gulf Oil Seeks Talks to Resume Operations under Angola Regime," *Wall Street Journal,* February 24, 1976, p. 17; and Rose Gutfeld, "U.S. Urges Firms Not to Pay Taxes, Debts to Noriega," *Wall Street Journal,* April 1, 1988, p. 30.

29. "What Is NAFTA?" *Wall Street Journal,* September 15, 1993, p. A16.

30. Clyde H. Farnsworth, "U.S. Stops Japanese Acquisition," *New York Times,* April 18, 1989, p. D1+.

31. Tim Carrington, "Europe's Plan to Build New Fighter Plane Puts Western Firms on Cutthroat Course," *Wall Street Journal,* May 23, 1988, p. 10.

32. Renato Mazzolini, "Government Policies and Government Controlled Enterprises," *Columbia Journal of World Business,* Fall 1980, pp. 47–54.

33. E. S. Browning, "France Now Tries to Offer Welcome to Japanese Firms," *Wall Street Journal,* April 20, 1989, p. C15.

34. See, for example, Richard H. Heindel, "America Business Bribery Shakes the World—Can America Remake It? *Intellect,* April 1977, p. 313.

35. Maureen Kline, "Three U.S.-Related Companies Dragged into Italian Investigation," *Wall Street Journal,* June 25, 1993, p. A7.

36. John S. Estey and David W. Marston, "Pitfalls (and Loopholes) in the Foreign Bribery Law," *Fortune,* October 9, 1978, pp. 182–188.

37. "Mexico Asks IBM for Proof of Alleged Bribe Request," *Wall Street Journal,* February 8, 1993. For the means-versus-end discussion, see Kent Hodgson, "Adapting Ethical Decisions to a Global Marketplace," *Management Review,* May 1992, pp. 53–57.

38. "Lilly Won't Sell Herbicide to U.S. for Anti-Coca Use," *Wall Street Journal,* May 25, 1988, p. 36.

39. "Bayer Refuses to Sell U.S. a Chemical for Poison Gas," *Wall Street Journal,* March 29, 1990, p. A11.

40. Islam, loc. cit.

41. William J. Holstein, Stanley Reed, Jonathan Kapstein, Todd Vogel, and Joseph Weber, "The Stateless Corporation," *Business Week,* May 14, 1990, p. 103.

42. Data for the case were taken primarily from "Foreign Share of Farms, 0.5%," *New York Times,* January 28, 1980, p. D1; *International Report,* July 25, 1979, p. 3; "Overview of Restrictions on Foreign Ownership of Agricultural Land in the United States," unpublished report of the law offices of Dechert Price & Rhoads, submitted to the International Business Forum of Pennsylvania Briefing Courses, 1980; Cindy Skrzycki and Maureen Walsh, "America on the Auction Block," *U.S. News & World Report,* March 30, 1987, pp. 56–58; Pat Houston, "Buy Your North 40 While It's Dirt-Cheap," *Business Week,* April 20, 1987, p. 92; Walter S. Mossberg, "Most Americans Favor Laws to Limit Foreign Investment in U.S., Poll Finds," *Wall Street Journal,* March 8, 1988, p. 28; Cynthia F. Mitchell, "Buying America," *Wall Street Journal,* April 28, 1988, p. 1; Elisabeth Rubinfien, "The Price Is Right," *Wall Street Journal,* June 15, 1988, p. 1+; Joan Lebow, "The Flow of Money into Real Estate," *Wall Street Journal,* July 24, 1989, p. B1; "Is U.S. Real Estate Leaving the Japanese Cold?" *Business Week,* July 23, 1990, p. 20; David Bailey, George Harte, and Roger Sugden, "U.S. Policy Debate Towards Inward Investment," *Journal of World Trade,* No. 26, 1992, pp. 65–90; Rick Wartzman, "Keep Out," *Wall Street Journal,* November 2, 1992, p. A1+; and Joyce Barnathan, Bruce Einhorn, and Gail DeGeorge, "The Chinese Are Coming, The Chinese Are Coming," *Business Week,* April 26, 1993, p. 83.

Chapter 13

International Business Diplomacy

Without trouble
there is no profit.
—African (Hausa) Proverb

Objectives

- To show the complementarity of interests between countries and MNEs

- To illustrate negotiations between business and government in an international context

- To trace the changing involvements of home-country governments in the settlement of MNEs' disputes with host governments

- To highlight the collective means by which companies and/or governments may seek to strengthen their positions with respect to each other

- To clarify the role of public relations in international business-government conflicts

- To explain the position of companies and governments in the uneven global enforcement of intellectual property rights

Case
Aramco[1]

Saudi Arabia has one quarter of the world's known oil reserves. Between 1985 and 1992, the country jumped from seventh place to first among oil exporters to the United States. One company, Aramco, accounts for over 90 percent of the Saudi production and has more than double the output of the two next-largest oil companies in the world, Royal Dutch Shell and Exxon. Aramco's ownership, policies, and division of earnings from the outset have depended on interactions among the private oil companies participating in Aramco, the U.S. government, and the Saudi Arabian government. As the objectives and power of these three parties have evolved, so have the operations of Aramco. Reviewing some events that preceded and followed Aramco's first oil output in 1939 will help you understand these changing relationships.

U.S. policy toward U.S. oil companies historically has seemed contradictory because governmental objectives have been subject to trade-offs as well as changing priorities. U.S. objectives have included preventing domestic monopolistic practices by oil companies, ensuring sufficient and cheap oil supplies for U.S. needs, and strengthening the U.S. political position in strategic areas worldwide. On the one hand, the U.S. government dismembered the Standard Oil Trust in order to stimulate domestic competition; on the other hand, it allowed, even encouraged, joint actions abroad by oil companies when those actions would help achieve the second and third objectives just mentioned.

At least as far back as 1920, the United States realized that in the long term its domestic oil supplies would be insufficient. In the short term, however, worldwide oil supplies could not easily be sold as rapidly as they could be produced. In this environment, U.S. oil companies were in a position to serve both U.S. and Middle Eastern interests. In the 1920s and 1930s, the U.S. government wanted U.S. oil companies to gain concessions in the Middle East to help assure a long-term U.S. supply and to weaken the relative positions of the British and the French. The U.S. companies were welcomed in the Middle East as competitors to Shell Oil Company, British Petroleum (BP), and France's Compagnie Française des Petroles (CFP). They also were welcomed because they offered some sales in the United States that would otherwise be impossible.

During the 1920s and 1930s, some of the U.S. oil companies also made secret arrangements abroad that proved unpopular with the U.S. public. For example, Exxon (formerly called Esso, or Standard Oil of New Jersey) agreed with BP and Shell to a system of world prices based on U.S. oil prices. Exxon's chief executive was forced to resign in 1942 after exposure of his restrictive agreements with the I. G. Farben Company, a major participant in Hitler's World War II efforts. In situations such as these, the oil companies were not acting as instruments of U.S. foreign policy as they were originally conceived to do; instead, they were acting independently of any government. Later they were accused of becoming captive to Middle Eastern Arab policies.

The first two companies to participate in Saudi Arabian oil production were Socal (Standard Oil of California) and Texaco, which formed a joint venture and negotiated large concessions in the 1930s. They built Saudi Arabia's first schools and compiled its first historical records. The U.S. government had no representatives there at that time, so the two companies conducted some quasi-official diplomacy that continued throughout World War II. They organized construction of a pipeline to the Mediterranean in 1945 and received permission from the U.S. government to use steel, which was very scarce. In 1948, Exxon and Mobil joined the original companies, Socal and Texaco, in what became known as Aramco. Mobil owned 10 percent, and each of the others held a 30-percent interest.

These four companies, along with three others (Gulf, Shell, and BP), were known as the Seven Sisters. Before the 1970s, they collectively controlled such a large share of the world's oil from multiple sources that they were nearly invulnerable to the actions of any single country. By 1950, the United States was entrenched in the Cold War, and although it held military supremacy over the former Soviet Union, the Truman Administration wanted to maintain cordial relationships with strategic countries. When King ibn-Saud demanded substantial revenue increases from Aramco, the U.S. government became directly involved in the negotiations. A plan was devised in 1951 that allowed the oil companies to maintain their ownership but pay 50 percent of Aramco's profits as taxes to Saudi Arabia. The companies then could deduct those taxes from their U.S. tax obligations so that, in effect, the increase in revenue to Saudi Arabia was entirely at the expense of the U.S. Treasury.

In 1952, Saudi Arabia learned from Iran's experience what might happen if demands on Aramco were pushed further. Iran expelled Shah Reza Pahlevi and nationalized British oil holdings. All major oil companies boycotted Iranian oil and brought the Mossadegh government to the brink of economic collapse. With CIA support, the Shah returned, and a new oil company replaced the nationalized holdings. The Seven Sisters shared 95-percent ownership of this new Iranian oil company.

Both Presidents Eisenhower and Kennedy proclaimed the importance to U.S. foreign policy of the oil companies' Middle Eastern activities and intervened to prevent antitrust action against them in their joint dealings abroad. (Map 13.1 shows the dominance of the Middle East in percentage of proven oil reserves.) In addition to preventing Soviet entry into the Middle East, the United States was able to sidestep certain Arab-Israeli conflicts by being publicly pro-Israel and having the Aramco partners perform most of the direct interactions with Saudi Arabia. Saudi Arabia was unhappy with U.S. policies toward Israel but could not influence them.

When the Seven Sisters gained 95 percent of the Iranian oil holdings, the other 5 percent went to smaller, independent U.S. companies that previously had depended on the Seven Sisters for supplies. This marked the beginning of greater competition among distributors. It also meant producing countries could make agreements with the independents to gain a greater portion of the spoils. Yet as late as 1960, the producing countries were still unable to prevent the major companies from unilaterally abrogating concessions by reducing the price they paid for oil. This price decrease, which reduced the governmental revenues of petroleum-exporting countries, led to a meeting in Caracas of representatives from five oil-producing countries and the formation of the Organization of Petroleum Exporting Countries (OPEC). OPEC's purposes were to prevent oil companies from unilaterally lowering prices, to gain a greater share of oil revenues, and to move toward domestic rather than foreign ownership of the assets. At the time, however, in the early 1960s, OPEC lacked the power to flex its muscles.

Three new trends during the 1960s weakened the Seven Sisters and strengthened Saudi Arabia's position in Aramco:

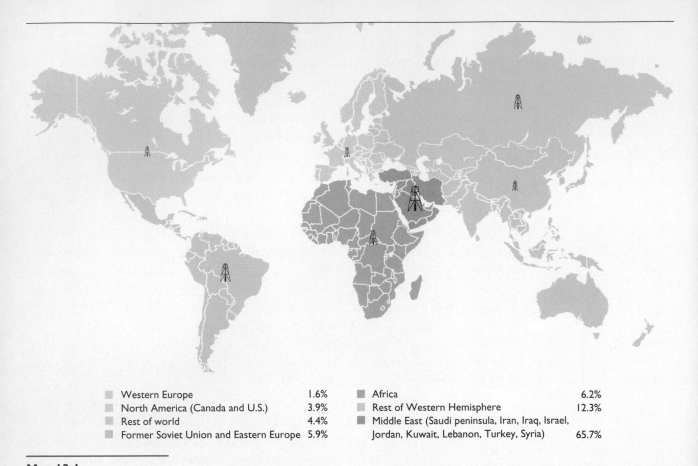

Western Europe	1.6%	Africa	6.2%
North America (Canada and U.S.)	3.9%	Rest of Western Hemisphere	12.3%
Rest of world	4.4%	Middle East (Saudi peninsula, Iran, Iraq, Israel,	
Former Soviet Union and Eastern Europe	5.9%	Jordan, Kuwait, Lebanon, Turkey, Syria)	65.7%

Map 13.1
Regional Shares of Proved Oil Reserves
Note that nearly two thirds of the world's known oil reserves are in the Middle East.

1. Other oil companies were continually emerging, and they made concessions in countries previously not among the major suppliers, such as Occidental in Libya, ENI in the former Soviet Union, and CFP in Algeria. These smaller companies lacked the Seven Sisters' diversification of supplies and thus were less able to move to other supply sources if a country tried to change the terms of an agreement unilaterally.

2. Because of rapidly expanding industrial economies, oil demand was growing faster than supply; the earlier oil glut was quickly becoming an oil squeeze. No longer could even the Seven Sisters afford to boycott major supplier countries as they had earlier boycotted Iran.

3. The threat of military intervention to protect oil investors was lessening. The failure of the United States to support the abortive efforts of the British and the French to prevent the Egyptian takeover of the Suez Canal demonstrated that the major Western powers were unlikely to unify their efforts. Although the United States had invaded Lebanon successfully in 1958, it was less prone to intervene again in the Middle East. The Soviet Union's growing strength meant there was a greater risk of a major war resulting from such intervention. The United States also was increasing its military involvement in an unpopular war in Vietnam and so was less able to lend military support to U.S. oil companies in the Middle East.

In 1970, Muammar el-Qaddafi of Libya demanded increased prices from Occidental. Since Occidental was almost completely dependent on Libya for crude oil, the company relented. Qaddafi then confronted other oil companies that no longer had sufficient alternative supplies and gained concessions from them as well. Libya's success was noted by other countries, which used OPEC to further strengthen their negotiating positions by dealing collectively with the oil companies. OPEC's Teheran Agreement of 1971 immediately increased prices. The embargo by Arab OPEC members in 1973 demonstrated that they had sufficient power to impose further economic demands and to cause Western powers to modify their political positions, particularly in relation to Israel. OPEC then had eleven members and controlled about 93 percent of the world's oil exports.

As the largest OPEC producer, Saudi Arabia has been able to utilize its strengths in several ways. Between 1972 and 1980, its government bought a 100-percent ownership share in Aramco operations. As smaller companies gained a larger share of the world oil sales and as national governments in Sweden, Germany, Japan, and France began buying directly from oil-producing countries, Saudi Arabia has increased the number of customers for its crude from the original four Aramco partners.

How has Aramco's government-owned status affected the operations of Exxon, Texaco, Socal, and Mobil in Saudi Arabia? The companies have been able to exploit their many assets successfully in order to maintain a profitable presence in Saudi Arabia. They have realized that Saudi Arabia's increased oil revenues enable the Saudis to be a lucrative customer; they also know that Saudi Arabia is closely allied to the West, particularly the United States, on whom it depends for technical and defense assistance.

The four oil companies continue to help manage the Saudi oil industry because they can make contributions that the Saudis cannot acquire easily from other sources. As the major employers before the Saudis' purchase of Aramco, they had demonstrated they could train Saudis, attract qualified personnel from abroad, and run an efficient operation. As Aramco has expanded and moved into new activities, they have continued these efforts through lucrative contract arrangements. For example, Mobil is a joint-venture partner with the Saudi government in a refinery and a petrochemical complex. About 12,000 (one quarter) of Aramco's employees are non-Saudi. Although foreigners have been replaced in nearly all top managerial positions, there is a near consensus that foreigners will be needed increasingly in technical positions, such as in finding and extracting oil. However, engineering companies, such as Bechtel and Fluor, now compete with the oil companies for major contracts in these areas.

The oil companies' contributions to Aramco's success have continued after they sold their assets to the Saudi government between 1972 and 1980. Their contributions include some continued day-to-day management, the contracting of foreign workers, the infusion of technology, the training of Saudi personnel, and the marketing of crude oil exports when sales are not made directly to a foreign government. The marketing contribution took on more importance in the late 1980s, when there was a glut due to new supplies (for example, from Mexico) and decreased demand. To ensure future sales, Aramco entered into a joint venture with Texaco in 1988, buying a 50-percent interest in Texaco's refining assets and marketing system in twenty-three U.S. states.

In 1990 Saudi Arabia's future ability to supply petroleum became uncertain when Iraq occupied Kuwait and amassed its armed forces on the Saudi Arabian border. The threat to Saudi oil supplies was an important factor in the U.S. decision to push for the UN-sanctioned 1991 liberation of Kuwait. The oil companies also have been important in molding U.S. foreign policy through lobbying and advertising campaigns that proclaim, "We would like to suggest that there is only one realistic possibility: that the United States adopt a neutral position on the Arab-Israeli dispute and a pro-American rather than a pro-Israel policy in the Middle East." Given their potential and actual contributions to Saudi Arabia, the oil companies were able to sell their Aramco interest at prices above the net book value of assets. They have successfully secured a continued source of crude oil, although sometimes at a contract price above the world spot price, and have profited from management and technical contracts.

Introduction

The operating terms of international companies
- **Are influenced by governments of home and host countries**
- **Shift as priorities shift and as strengths of parties change**

Chapters 11 and 12 discussed how MNEs and host countries evaluate each other. Discord during such evaluation, if carried to the extreme, may result in the particular business-government relationship ending as either companies refuse to operate in the locale or governments refuse to grant original or continued operating permission. Short of the extremes are practices that, although not deemed ideal by either party, are sufficiently satisfactory to permit an evolving relationship. Thus it is useful to examine international business diplomacy because terms of operations are highly influenced by attempts of international companies and governments to improve their own positions relative to one another. As the Aramco case illustrates, the terms under which companies operate abroad are greatly influenced by both home- and host-country policies, and those terms change over time as governmental priorities shift and the relative strengths of the parties evolve. These strengths are affected by such factors as competitive changes, the resources the parties have at their disposal, validation by public opinion, and joint efforts with other parties.

Bargaining Factors

Nature of Assets

MNEs and host countries have mutually useful assets.

As discussed in Chapters 11 and 12, the host country and the MNE may each control assets that are useful to the other. Thus they have incentives to agree on the establishment of operations and to ensure that the operations continue functioning. For example, countries control access to their own markets and to unique resources such as land for agricultural production, raw materials, port facilities, cheap or specialized labor, technologies, and reasonable interest rates on funds. A company may need to acquire some of these resources in order to maintain a viable competitive position elsewhere in the world. Companies control assets that are both scarce and needed by host countries. Figure 13.1 shows assets that may be used to foster host-country growth, employment, balance-of-payments, and environmental objectives. The MNE also may have access to or control of foreign markets because it owns the

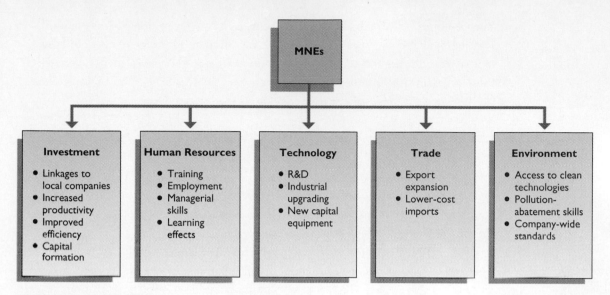

Figure 13.1
Resources and
Contributions of MNEs
By contributing directly to
investment, human re-
sources, technology, trade,
and the environment, the
MNE contributes to host-
country objectives con-
cerning the items listed.

Source: Adapted from Transnational Corporations and Management Division, *World Investment
Report 1992: Transnational Corporations: Engines of Growth, An Executive Summary* (New York:
United Nations, 1992), p. 13.

Alternative sources for acquiring resources affect
company and country bar-
gaining strengths.

The biggest bargaining
strengths for countries are
• Large markets
• Political stability

companies that make import purchases. It further may be able to affect home-
country sentiments on limiting importation of the foreign-made production.

Strengths of the Parties

Bargaining school theory holds that the negotiated terms for a foreign investor's operations depend on how much the investor and host country need each other's assets.[2]
If either a company or a country has assets that the other strongly desires and if there
are few (or no) alternatives for acquiring them, negotiated concessions may be very
one-sided. For example, the Aramco case illustrated that when a few large companies
dominated the extraction, processing, shipment, and final sale of an oversupply of oil,
developing countries with petroleum deposits could do little but accept the terms
they were offered. If a government refused the terms, a company easily could find another country that would accept a similar proposal. As the supply of oil diminished
and petroleum-producing countries found alternative means for exploiting their resources, the terms of the concessions gradually evolved more in favor of those producing countries. But such shifts have not always favored countries. For example,
Mexico's economic growth during the 1970s was so great that it could require foreign
companies to accept minority ownership when establishing operations. However, oil
prices plummeted in the 1980s, and capital left Mexico because of fear of its slipping
economy. Consequently, Mexico loosened its regulations to allow majority and even
100-percent foreign ownership. Clearly, there are vast differences in bargaining
strength among countries, among industries, and among companies.

Country bargaining strength   Generally, companies prefer to establish investments in highly developed countries because those countries offer large markets
and a high degree of stability. Countries such as the United States, Canada, and
Germany are large recipients of foreign investment without making many conces-

sions to the investors. In all of these countries, however, regional areas vie for investments by offering incentives. In addition, companies prefer to avoid the red tape involved in ad hoc negotiations to gain permission for investment. Although there are a few exceptions, developed countries are less likely than LDCs to examine and negotiate investment proposals on a case-by-case basis.

Company bargaining assets include
- **Technology**
- **Product differentiation**
- **Ability to export output**
- **Local product diversity**

Company bargaining strength   Although companies have a variety of assets they can contribute to their foreign operations, some industries have traditionally enjoyed better bargaining positions than have others. For example, foreign ownership in such areas as agriculture and extractive industries is not very welcome in many countries because of historical foreign domination of these sectors and belief that the land and subsoil are public resources.

The bargain struck between the foreign investor and the host country also is influenced by the number of companies offering similar resources.[3] Foreign investors are more likely to gain a high percentage of ownership in foreign operations when they have few competitors and when they control certain types of assets. These assets include the following:

- Technology. For example, IBM has been allowed 100-percent ownership of operations in a number of countries because of the local need for its unique technology. Other companies, however, have been refused the same. The French government also approved IBM's minority stake in state-owned Groupe Bull because of the company's specialized technology related to reduced instruction set computing (RISC).[4]
- Control of a well-known branded product. For example, Coca-Cola apparently has been able to gain local consumer allies who believe its differentiated products are superior.
- Ability to export output from the foreign investment, especially when exports go to other entities controlled by the parent company. These investments gain foreign exchange that might otherwise not be forthcoming. For example, GM was allowed 100-percent ownership of its Mexican maquiladora operations but had to share ownership in its other manufacturing facilities serving Mexican consumers.

A larger extent of foreign ownership also is allowed when there is greater product diversity, probably because a variety of products offers wider future opportunities to save foreign exchange through import substitution.

Surprisingly, the amount of capital needed to set up operations has not usually affected investors' bargaining power. At least two factors play a role here:

1. A large investment may be examined much more closely than a small one because of the potential impact (positive or negative) it might have on the economy (that is, the host country wants the benefits of the capital inflow but is leery of being so dependent on foreign ownership).

2. The host-country government may be more likely to borrow funds externally to invest in large enterprises.

However, the ability to contribute large amounts of capital may improve future bargaining strengths of companies. Many LDCs have encountered debt-servicing problems since the mid-1980s, so they must depend more on FDI for their future capital needs. And the size of the potential investor may be a factor in that governments may not want to commit resources to negotiating with companies that are too small to make a substantial impact. For example, Nigeria will negotiate the barter of oil for imports but only with companies whose annual sales are at least $100 million.[5]

Home-Country Needs

The home-country
government
• Has economic objectives
of its own
• Has direct political relations with the host country

The interplay between the needs of the MNE and those of the host country is not the only bargaining factor. The home country government seldom takes a neutral position in the relationship. Like the host-country government, the home-country government is interested in achieving certain economic objectives, such as increased tax revenues and full employment. It may give incentives to or place constraints on the foreign expansion of home-based companies in order to gain what it sees as its due share of the rewards from their transactions. Recall in the Aramco case that the U.S. government gave tax concessions to oil companies to induce them to exploit foreign opportunities. However, the ability of either the home or host government to influence MNEs is tempered by the political interests and relations of the two governments.[6]

The influence of home-country governments is illustrated by the example of France's selling off interest in its government-owned switchmaker, CGCT. The U.S. government pressured the French government to accept AT&T's bid by threatening to bar U.S. government purchases of French equipment. Germany's Chancellor personally lobbied the French Prime Minister on behalf of Siemens's bid. Caught between two foreign powers, the French government accepted the bid of a Swedish company, Ericsson.[7]

Other External Pressures

Decision makers in business
and government must consider opinions of other affected groups.

The complementary nature of the assets that MNEs and countries control would seem, at first, to dictate a mutual interest in finding means to ensure that mutual benefits are pursued. Although there are pressures to do this, there also are constraints, particularly on governmental decision makers. Pressure may come from local companies with which the foreign investor is presently or potentially competing, from political opponents who seize the "external" issue as a means of inciting an unsophisticated population against present political leadership, or from critics who reason that more benefits may accrue to the country through alternative means. Companies also may face pressures from stockholders, workers, consumers, governmental officials, suppliers, and foreign groups that are concerned with their own interests rather than the achievement of worldwide corporate objectives. These pressures may result in a relationship between company and host country quite different from what might be expected on a purely economic basis. Each party should understand the types and strengths of these external groups, since they affect the extent to which either side may be able to give in on issues under discussion.

Negotiations in International Business

Increasingly, negotiations are used as a means of deciding the terms by which a company may initiate, carry on, or terminate operations in a foreign country. At one time, negotiations prevailed only for direct investments; more recently, however, they sometimes have been extended to other operating arrangements, such as licensing agreements, debt repayment, and large-scale export sales. The following discussion highlights investment negotiations, but most of the points apply to other forms of operations as well. The negotiation process often leads to two-tiered bargaining: An MNE first must reach an agreement with a local company in order to purchase an interest in it, sell technology or products to it, or loan money to it. Once that agreement is set, a governmental agency may approve or disapprove the terms or propose entirely different ones. Even when the government is not directly involved in the negotiations, the participants may take its needs into consideration.

Bargaining Process

Acceptance zones   Before becoming involved in overseas negotiations, a manager usually will have some experience with a domestic bargaining process that is somewhat similar to that in the foreign sphere. For example, collective bargaining with labor as well as agreements to acquire or merge facilities with another company usually start with an array of proposals from both sides, just like negotiations with a foreign country. The total package of proposals undoubtedly includes provisions that one side or the other is willing either to give up entirely or to compromise on. These are used as bargaining tokens, permitting each side to claim that it is reluctantly giving in on some point in exchange for compromise on some other point. They also serve as face-saving devices, allowing either side to report to interested parties that it managed to extract concessions. On some points, however, it is unlikely that any compromise can be reached.

As in domestic negotiations, the outcome of foreign negotiations will depend partly on other recent negotiations or events, which serve as models. The relevant domestic model when deciding, for example, whether to give workers an additional holiday may be the economy as a whole, the industry, the local area, or recent company experience elsewhere. Abroad, what has transpired recently either between other companies and a host-country government or between similar types of companies or the same company in similar countries may serve as a common reference. Negotiations are unlikely to stray too far from that established precedent.

Finally, there are zones of acceptance and nonacceptance for the proposals presented. If the acceptance zones overlap, an agreement is possible. If zones have no overlap, positive negotiations are not possible. For example, if GM insisted on 100-percent ownership of a Japanese facility and the Japanese government insisted on 51-percent local ownership, there would be no overlap of acceptance zones in which to negotiate. However, if Chrysler insisted on a "controlling" interest in a Mexican facility (say, 25 percent) but would take as much as it could get and the Mexican government required "substantial" local ownership (say, 10 percent) and wanted to maximize it, there would be a wide zone that would be acceptable to both parties (for instance, 25–90 percent for Chrysler's ownership). The final agreement would be based on each party's negotiating ability and strengths and on the other concessions that each made in the process. Because each side could only speculate on how far the other was willing to go, the exact amount of ownership allowed might fall anywhere within the overlapping acceptance zones. Even after an agreement is reached, whether the maximum concessions have been extracted from the parties remains uncertain.

Range of provisions   The major difference between domestic and foreign negotiations is a matter of degree. International negotiations may take much longer and may involve many provisions unheard of in the home country, such as a negotiated tax rate. Further, governments vary widely in their attitudes toward foreign investors; therefore their negotiating agendas also vary widely.

Most countries in recent years have used incentives to attract foreign investors. Although these incentives usually are also available to local companies, those companies may lack the resources to be in a strong bargaining position. For example, when Chrysler announced it would build a factory to manufacture minivans in Europe, the company was wooed by representatives of various European governments. The company finally decided on Austria, whose government agreed to contribute about $145 million, or about one third of the plant's cost. Other direct incentives countries have offered foreign investors include tax holidays, employee training, R&D grants, accelerated depreciation, low-interest loans, loan guarantees, subsidized energy and transportation, and the construction of rail spurs and roads.[8] Countries also provide indirect incentives, such as a trained labor force that is likely to accept employers' work conditions tranquilly.

When companies negotiate to gain concessions from a foreign government, they should understand some of the problems the provisions might bring:

- Companies may face more domestic labor problems because of claims that they are exporting jobs in order to gain access to cheap labor.
- The output from the foreign facility may be subject to claims of dumping because of the subsidies given by the host government. For example, Toyota forwent British governmental assistance for fear other EC countries would not as readily allow its sales.
- It may be more difficult to evaluate management performance in the subsidized operation.[9]

Finally, it should be noted that there is always a risk that promises will be broken as situations change.

Negotiations are seldom a one-way street. Companies agree to many different performance requirements, including

- Foreign-exchange deposits to cover the cost of imports and capital repatriation
- Limits on payments for services
- Requirements to create a certain number of jobs or amount of exports
- Provisions to reduce the amount of equity held in subsidiaries
- Price controls
- Minimum levels of local input into products manufactured
- Limits on the use of expatriate personnel and on old or reconditioned equipment
- Control of prices for goods imported or exported to the parent company's controlled entities
- Demands to enter into joint ventures[10]

Renegotiations

Agreements evolve after operations begin; the company position is usually, but not always, stronger before entry.

For early foreign investments in LDCs, it was common to obtain concessions on fixed terms for long periods or to expect that the original terms would not change. (These early investments were largely made in the commodity and utility sectors.) This situation has almost ceased to exist. Not only may the terms of operations be bargained before any operations are set up, but the same terms may be rebargained any time after operations are underway.

Generally, a company's best bargaining position exists before it begins the specific operations in a foreign country. Once the capital and technology have been imported and local nationals have been trained to direct operations, the foreign company is needed much less than before.[11] Further, the company now has assets that are not easily moved to more favorable locales. The result is that the host country may be in a better position to extract additional concessions from the company. For instance, after Peru received loans from Britain's Midland Bank, it was in a much stronger position to renegotiate their repayment with copper and other raw materials rather than with cash.[12] However, a company that is aware of and responsive to the changing needs and desires of the local economy can maintain or even improve its bargaining position by offering the infusion of additional resources the host country needs. One tactic is to promise to bring in (or withhold) the latest technology developed abroad. Another is to use plant expansion or export markets as bargaining weapons. A host government also may restrain from pushing too hard on established companies for fear this will make the country less attractive to other companies with which the government would like to do business.

A specific type of renegotiation involves the valuation of company properties that have come under governmental ownership. The shift in ownership may be gradual, as for Saudi Arabia's increased ownership in Aramco, or immediate, as with Libya's nationalization of Exxon and Mobil holdings. The Chilean nationalization of ITT holdings illustrates some of the valuation issues that can arise.[13] The

Chilean government offered about one third the properties' book value, arguing that the equipment was run-down and customers were complaining about service. ITT countered that the book value understated the properties' true value because a high return on assets had been earned and could be expected to continue in the future. The government responded by saying that the return on assets was due to the rates charged to customers by a monopolistic industry rather than to the equipment value. Each party proposed outside appraisal of the value, but each wanted to select appraisers and valuation criteria favorable to its position.

Behavioral Characteristics Affecting Outcome

In international negotiations, misunderstandings are a strong possibility because of cross-country cultural differences as well as possible language differences. Further, the background and expertise of governmental officials may be quite distinct from those of businesspeople; thus they face each other from different occupational cultures. In addition, the individuals involved may react on the basis of how they think their own performances are being evaluated. Therefore the direction of negotiations involving company managers on one side and governmental officials on the other may be uncertain from the start. Finally, it is always possible that one side or the other wants to terminate bargaining but is hesitant to do so for fear of alienating future relationships with the other party.

Cultural factors In the 1930s, the humorist Will Rogers quipped, "America has never lost a war and never won a conference." Many participants and observers agree with this assessment of U.S. performance in business negotiations abroad. Much of the problem stems from cultural differences that lead to misunderstandings and mistrust across the conference table. Although this discussion cannot delineate all the possible cultural differences, Table 13.1 illustrates some that exist among negotiators from Japan, North America, and Latin America.

The following cultural factors are especially important to U.S. negotiators:

- Individual U.S. negotiators are more likely to have the power to make decisions than their counterparts from some other countries; U.S. negotiators may lose confidence when those counterparts must reach a group decision or keep checking with their head office.
- U.S. negotiators want to get to the heart of the matter quickly; negotiators from some other cultures want to spend time developing rapport and trust before addressing business details.
- U.S. negotiators attempt to separate the issues into pragmatic categories (getting closure on items in a linear fashion), whereas some negotiators with other cultural backgrounds view negotiations more holistically.
- U.S. negotiators typically expect a broader range of bargaining on issues such as price than do many of their foreign counterparts. For example, U.S. negotiators often see Asians as stubborn and are seen by them as inconsistent.
- U.S. negotiators are more prone to set deadlines and then make concessions at the last minute to meet the schedule.[14]

Misunderstandings may result from differences in
- **Nationalities**
- **Professions**
- **Languages**

Some cultural differences among negotiators are evident:
- Some negotiators are decision makers; some are not.
- Some take a pragmatic view; others take a holistic view.
- Some use gifts and flattery.
- Some expressions do not translate well.

Table 13.1

Negotiation Styles from a Cross-Cultural Perspective

Negotiators from Japan, North America (Canada and the United States), and Latin America are all influenced by their own backgrounds and cultures; consequently, some misinterpretations may develop in international negotiations.

Japanese	North American	Latin American
Emotional sensitivity highly valued	Emotional sensitivity not highly valued	Emotional sensitivity valued
Hiding of emotions	Dealing straightforwardly or impersonally	Emotionally passionate
Subtle power plays; conciliation	Litigation; not as much conciliation	Great power plays; use of weakness
Loyalty to employer; employer taking care of employees	Lack of commitment to employer; breaking of ties by either employee or employer if necessary	Loyalty to employer (who is often family)
Group decision making by consensus	Teamwork provides input to a decision maker	Decisions come down from one individual
Face saving crucial; decisions often made on basis of saving someone from embarrassment	Decisions made on a cost-benefit basis; face saving does not always matter	Face-saving crucial in decision making to preserve honor, dignity
Decision makers openly influenced by special interests	Decision makers influenced by special interests but often this is not considered ethical	Execution of special interests of decision maker expected, condoned
Not argumentative; quiet when right	Argumentative when right or wrong, but impersonal	Argumentative when right or wrong; passionate
What is down in writing must be accurate, valid	Great importance given to documentation as evidential proof	Impatient with documentation, seen as obstacle to understanding of general principles
Step-by-step approach to decision making	Methodically organized decision making	Impulsive, spontaneous decision making
Good of group is the ultimate aim	Ultimate aim is profit motive or good of the individual	What is good for group is good for the individual
Cultivation of a good emotional social setting for decision making; getting to know decision makers	Decision making impersonal; avoidance of involvements, conflict of interest	Personalism necessary for good decision making

Source: Reprinted from Pierre Casse, *Training for the Multicultural Manager: A Practical and Cross-Cultural Approach to the Management of People.* Copyright 1982, Washington, D.C.: Society for Intercultural Education, Training and Research (SIETAR International). Reprinted with permission.

- U.S. negotiators often find it very difficult to establish rapport with foreign negotiators, for example, through culturally and legally acceptable gifts, through asking their advice and opinion, or through purposely losing at golf.

However, even negotiators who understand a foreign culture's subtleties may be thrown off because their foreign counterparts are adjusting their behavior based on their understanding of the cultural differences.[15]

It may be difficult for negotiators to find words to express their exact meaning in another language, which may result in occasional pauses while translators resort to dictionaries. Further, facial expressions differ by culture and, even if understood, are difficult to judge because of the time lag between the original spoken statement and its receipt in a second language. Since English is so widely understood worldwide, people with a different native language may understand quite well most of what is said in English, giving them the opportunity to eavesdrop on confidential comments and to reflect on possible responses while remarks are being translated into their language. The degree of precision in language desired by either side also may be complicated by cultural factors.

Evidence also exists that cultural factors influence whether interpreters are acceptable. For example, Saudi managers generally prefer to negotiate in English, even if their English is not very good. When interpreters are used, it is usually preferable for each side to have its own. Good interpreters help to brief their teams on cultural factors affecting the negotiation process. But even with interpreters, negotiators cannot be certain that their statements are fully understood, especially if they use slang or attempt humor that is culture-specific. This is illustrated by the experience of a U.S. politician who spoke through an interpreter in China:

> With typical American forthrightness, he said, "I'm going to tell you where I'm coming from." The interpreter said, "He'll now give you the name of his home town." Then he said, "I'm going to lay all my cards on the table." The interpreter said, "He'll play cards now." Then, making a joke, he said, "I'm not a member of any organized political party; I'm a Democrat." The interpreter said, "I think he just made a joke. Please laugh." The audience laughed and the politician knew he had their rapt attention.[16]

The importance of cultural factors may change during renegotiations because the parties already know each other. If the relationship was amicable in the original negotiations, that quality is likely to be carried over. However, if the past relationship has been hostile, the renegotiations may be suffused by even more suspicion and obstruction than existed during the original process.[17]

Professional conflict Governmental and business negotiators may start with mutual mistrust due to historic animosity or to differences in the status of their professional positions. The businesspeople may come armed with business and economic data that are not well understood by governmental officials, who may counter with sovereignty considerations that are nearly incomprehensible to the businesspeople. Thus it may take considerable time before each side understands and empathizes with the other's point of view. Even then, it is possible neither will attempt to develop a relationship designed to assure the achievement of long-term objectives. Negotiators may see their rewards as dependent on immediate results and perhaps not expect to be closely connected with longer-term problems.

The viewpoint discrepancy has been particularly evident as many LDCs have attempted to sell state-owned enterprises to foreign investors. The managers within these enterprises are suspicious of MNEs, fearful of foreign domination, and worried about their jobs after privatization.[18]

Business and governmental officials may mistrust each other and may not understand each other's objectives.

Negotiators should find some means to reinstitute future contacts.

Termination of negotiations   When one or both parties want to end serious consideration of proposals, the method of cessation can be extremely important. It may affect the negotiators' positions with their superiors. Also affected may be future transactions between the country and company, the company's operations elsewhere in the world, and the country's dealings with other foreign companies. Because termination is an admission of failure to achieve the original objectives, negotiators are prone to publicly blame others in order to save face. Such accusations may complicate future dealings the country or the company may have with other parties. Fearing adverse consequences from termination, negotiators sometimes drag out the process until a proposal eventually dies unnoticed. Although termination is stressful, when it is necessary, the parties should attempt to find means that allow each to save face and that avoid publicity as much as possible.

Simulation can be used to anticipate others' approach, but it is hard to simulate stress situations.

Preparation for negotiations   Role-playing is a valuable technique for training negotiators for projects requiring a foreign government's approval. By practicing their own roles and those of the government's negotiators and by researching the country's culture and history to determine attitudes toward foreign companies, a company's negotiators may be much better able to anticipate responses and plan their own actions.[19]

Choice of negotiators depends on
• **The importance of the deal**
• **The functions involved**

Using simulation presupposes that the company knows who will be negotiating for the other side. The choice of negotiators will depend on the project's importance, the functional areas being considered, and the level of government involved. Commonly, MNEs use a team approach so that appropriate people with the necessary range of functional responsibilities are involved in the decision making. It also is common to use people at different organizational levels at different points in the negotiations. One factor not easily simulated is the possible stress from being away from family and co-workers for an extended period. Because of this factor, the location of negotiations may give one side or the other an advantage in bargaining.

Home-Country Involvement in Asset Protection

Historical Background

In the nineteenth century, the home countries ensured through military force and coercion that prompt, adequate, and effective compensation would be received by investors in cases of expropriation, a concept known as the **international standard of fair dealing.**[20] The host countries had little to say about this standard. As late as the period between the two world wars, the United States on several occasions sent troops into Latin America to protect investors' property. However, the 1917 Soviet confiscations of foreign private investment without compensation led to policies of noncoercive interference by home countries in cases of expropriation. In conferences attended by developing countries at The Hague in 1930 and at Montevideo in 1933, participants established a treaty stating that "foreigners may not claim rights other or more extensive than nationals."[21] On the basis of this doctrine, Mexico used its own courts in 1938 to settle disputes arising from expropriation of foreign agricultural properties in 1915.[22] This same doctrine formed the precedent for later set- tlements and, in the absence of specific treaties, still remains largely in effect.

Except for the abortive attempt by British, French, and Israeli forces to prevent Egypt's takeover of the Suez Canal, there has been no major attempt since World War II at direct military intervention to protect property of home-country citizens. (There have been, however, threatened or actual troop movements by large powers to LDCs during this period. Property protection possibly was a motive for these movements.) The concept of nonintervention has been strengthened by a series of UN resolutions and by the fact that most expropriations have been selective rather than general, that is, involving a few rather than all foreign companies. In these cases, it is thought that intervention might lead to further takeovers and jeopardize settlements for the affected companies.

Nevertheless, **dependencia theory** holds that LDCs have practically no power as host countries when dealing with MNEs. Their assets are of little importance in bargaining. Further, MNEs can enlist the loyalties of their home governments as well as of local elites in order to maintain their power.[23] Although home-country governments no longer are as likely to resort to military intervention, they some- times use other means to support MNEs, such as trade pressures, aid, and influence with international lending agencies.[24]

The Use of Bilateral Agreements

Bilateral agreements im- prove climates for invest- ments abroad, but they
• Usually lack settlement mechanisms
• Do not protect against gradual changes

To improve foreign-investment climates for their investors, many industrial coun- tries have established bilateral treaties with other countries, often after long and difficult negotiations.[25] Although these agreements differ in detail, they generally provide for home-country insurance to investors to cover losses from expropria- tion, political violence, governmental contract abrogation, and currency control and to exporters to cover losses from nonpayment in a convertible currency. For example, the United States offers policies for small companies through the Small Business Administration and for companies in general through the Overseas Private Investment Corporation (OPIC) and Eximbank. Coverage also is available through private insurers, international agencies such as the World Bank's Multilateral In- vestment Guarantee Agency, and some host-country governments. The home country, by approving an insurance contract, agrees to settle investors' losses on a government-to-government basis. For example, Texaco acquired OPIC insurance to invest in restoring production at idle Russian oil wells.[26] If Texaco suffered losses as a result of political risk, OPIC would pay Texaco and then the U.S. government would seek settlement from Russia. Other types of bilateral agreements include treaties of friendship, commerce, and navigation as well as prevention of double taxation. All these efforts help promote factor mobility by MNEs.

A major problem with these agreements is they do not normally provide a mech- anism for settlement. For example, a host government simply may lack the financial resources to settle in an appropriate currency. Even if it has the resources, whether the amount of payment should be settled in local courts, in external courts, or through negotiations remains unclear. Many host countries resist bilateral treaties because they imply an abrogation of sovereignty over business activities conducted within their borders and provide more protection for foreign-owned property than for that owned by their own citizens.[27] Bilateral agreements also do not protect against gradual changes in operating rules, which can reduce substantially the profits of foreign operations. For example, Jamaica forced Revere Copper and Brass to make payments greater than those provided by the original investment agreement. The result was an operating loss that the investment insurance did not cover.[28]

Home-Country Assistance as a Negotiating Weapon

Home countries may improve terms for their investors by
- **Suspending aid to countries that nationalize property**
- **Offering aid in exchange for better investor treatment**

Home countries have used the promise of aid or loans or the threat to withhold them as a means of effectively extracting from host governments terms that are more acceptable to home-country investors. For example, in response to Brazilian nationalizations, the Hickenlooper Amendment of 1961 provided for the suspension of aid to any country that nationalizes properties of U.S. citizens or that has moved to nullify existing contracts and fails within a "reasonable" period of time to take appropriate steps for settlement. This amendment has been used officially only once—after Ceylon (now Sri Lanka) nationalized certain Esso and Caltex properties in 1962. Ceylon countered by expropriating additional assets of the same companies. However, in Ceylon's 1965 elections, the opposition party, which promised to settle the dispute, was elected. One day after the new government took office, a settlement was worked out. The effectiveness of the amendment in the Ceylon situation, as well as in other instances, is difficult to assess. In several cases, aid has been reduced after takeovers, and the consequences have varied.

Instead of withholding aid or loans, home governments sometimes have promised that one or both would be made available if conflict is either avoided or resolved on terms more acceptable to the home-country investors. For example, France agreed to give Algeria economic aid over five years in exchange for continued operations by French enterprises in Algeria.[29]

A home country's use of aid or loans, either as a means of averting property takeovers or as a factor in settling valuation disputes, certainly may be an effective weapon at times, especially since a host country may depend heavily on funds from foreign governments and international agencies as either a supplement or an alternative to foreign private investment. However, the problems with this technique are numerous. Threats or promises from a foreign country may make host-country leaders appear to be manipulated by foreign powers; thus they may become even more adamant. Further, a home-country government may apply its financial weapons inconsistently, since its concern is primarily with political alliances and concessions rather than with the properties of a few of its citizens. On the one hand, a home country may be willing to give aid in exchange for favorable votes on a UN resolution or for permission to locate a military base in the host country. On the other hand, it may be unwilling to give aid because it fears public opinion would shift against it for trying to "buy" favorable treatment for its companies. A further problem may occur when home-country taxpayers object to their payments going abroad in order to assure the safety and continued profitability of the investments of a few of their fellow citizens.

There is a long tradition of governmental help for home-country companies engaged in international business. This chapter discusses many of these efforts, which include treaties to ease the flow of resources among countries, as well as pressures on other countries to protect MNEs' tangible and intangible assets. In addition, governments establish commercial offices at home and abroad. Among other things, these offices supply trade and business information on foreign countries. What constitutes an appropriate amount of governmental assistance is argued largely in economic terms, such as whether export financing programs constitute subsidies that warrant retaliation. But there also are ethical questions about such assistance.

ETHICAL DILEMMAS

Consider data collection and dissemination. The U.S. government collects and publishes a wide variety of data on business activities and performance in foreign countries. It then makes these data available at low cost. As long as the information is collected openly and is available at low cost to anyone (U.S. citizens as well as foreign citizens), there seems to be no ethical question. However, there may be some point at which the method of collection, the type of information collected, or the restrictions on dissemination overstep ethical boundaries. For example, with the end of the Cold War, the U.S. Central Intelligence Agency (CIA) indicated that it was considering the collection and analysis of more business-economic data that would be shared with U.S. companies.[30] With a yearly budget of about $30 billion and substantial high technology for information gathering, the CIA might be able to gain more competitively useful information than companies or other government agencies could. From an ethical standpoint, the following questions about such information might raise issues:

- Is it acquired by the CIA or another U.S. government agency?

- Is it collected openly or clandestinely?

- Is it in the public domain or proprietarily owned by companies?

- Is it made available to anyone or only U.S. companies?

In 1993, the CIA uncovered a French-government spying scheme to collect engineering data and sales strategies on forty-nine U.S. aerospace and defense companies. Does the French scheme justify CIA data collection "because others are doing it"?

Multilateral Settlements

Multilateral settlements of disputes may be handled by a neutral country or group or courts in countries that are not involved.

When MNEs or home-country governments are unable to reach agreement with a host country, they may agree to have a third party settle the dispute. For trade disputes, the International Chamber of Commerce in Paris, the Swedish Chamber of Commerce, and specialized commodity associations in London frequently are enlisted. Because the trade transactions are generally between private groups, these disputes do not create the type of widespread emotional environment often attendant on foreign-investment disputes.

Examples of active third-party involvement in settling investment disputes are extremely rare because such involvement requires a relinquishment by host countries of sovereignty over activities within their own borders. The International Center for Settlement of Investment Disputes operates under the auspices of the World Bank and provides a formal organization to which parties can submit their disputes. However, both parties must agree to its use, and countries have been reluctant to do so. As a result of the center's failure to offer potential investors sufficient risk protection in LDCs, the World Bank established the Multilateral Investment Guarantee Agency in 1988. This agency offers insurance against losses from expropriations, war, civil disturbances, currency convertibility, and breach of contract.[31]

A notable example of a multilateral settlement involved claims between the United States and Iran. This situation differed from many other attempted settlements because each country had large amounts of investments in the other's territory. In fact, when the two governments froze each other's assets, Iran had substantially more invested in the United States than the United States had in Iran. The two countries agreed to appoint three arbitrators each to an international tribunal at The Hague, and those six selected three more. Part of the assets the United States had held were set aside for the payment of arbitrated claims, and small amounts have been relinquished as Iran has settled with U.S. investors on a case-by-case basis.[32]

In a few cases, courts in countries uninvolved in a dispute may be used. For example, Kennecott Copper, whose investments in Chile were nationalized in 1972, successfully contested in French courts payment from French importers to the Chilean government on the grounds that Kennecott still owned the operations.[33] In 1987, Britain's High Court ruled that the Libyan government could withdraw $292 million from the London facility of Bankers Trust, even though $161 million of this was on deposit in New York and the U.S. government had frozen Libyan assets in U.S. banks at home and abroad.[34]

After expropriation of their Libyan facilities, California Standard, Texaco, and Arco placed notices in the leading newspapers and periodicals of the major oil-consuming countries warning that they might file lawsuits against purchasers of Libyan oil, which the oil companies claimed for themselves. They also had arbitrators appointed by the International Court of Justice (the World Court) in The Hague, who ruled in the companies' favor and set an amount of compensation.[35]

Unfortunately, there have been many examples of countries failing to consent to that court's judgments; thus it handles few cases.[36]

Consortium Approaches

In a consortium, companies or countries join together to strengthen their bargaining positions.

As mentioned in Chapter 12, a company may at times be able to play one country against another, or a government may be able to do the same with MNEs. When in a relatively weak position, companies or countries may be able to join together in a consortium to present a united front when dealing with a powerful entity.

Petroleum
The Aramco case offers a good example of companies banding together on one side and countries joining forces on the other. The unity has strengthened both sides and at different points has helped to give advantages to one over the other.

ANCOM
The Andean Group (ANCOM) sought a common policy toward foreign capital, trademarks, patents, licenses, and royalties. The aims of this common policy were to limit the role of MNEs and to prevent them from serving all the member countries by locating in a country with less stringent regulations. This attempt to get ANCOM members to adhere to a common stance has been less than successful. Nevertheless the attempt contrasts with the approach of the EU, which has not had a common policy. When France sought to restrict MNE penetration within its market by withholding ownership permission, its efforts were ineffective because MNEs could serve the French market through production in Belgium, Ireland, or Spain, where they were welcome.

Arab Boycott
The Arab boycott is a loose arrangement whereby Arab countries may cease business with companies doing business with Israel.

As part of their boycott of Israel, Arabs have sought to weaken that country by not purchasing Israeli goods and by refusing to do business with companies that sell strategic tools and certain resources to Israel.[37] The arrangement is a loose one, permitting countries to participate only when they feel it is in their best interests to do so. The prevention of trade between Israel and Arab states is not an unusual type of practice, nor does it have much impact on most MNEs. However, it often does force MNEs headquartered in other countries to sell either in the Arab countries or in Israel, but not in both. (China at times also has retaliated by disallowing certain business with a given country whose companies do business with Taiwan in sensitive areas.) By banding together, the Arab countries represent a very formidable market, causing many MNEs to think twice about doing business with Israel.

A distinguishing feature of the Arab boycott is that it involves a so-called secondary boycott, which means that business is restricted with companies that do business with a boycotted company. For example, Ford is boycotted by the Arab

League. The company was negotiating a joint venture in the United States with Toyota; however, Saudi Arabia threatened retaliation against any company that concluded a joint venture or production-licensing agreement with Ford. Because Saudi Arabia was the world's second-largest importer of Japanese cars, Toyota broke off negotiations with Ford.[38]

A second distinguishing feature of the Arab boycott for U.S. companies is that the U.S. Export Administration Act prohibits their providing information on their directors when registering operations in Arab countries. Both Sara Lee and Safeway Stores broke this law and were fined, even though the information provided was available from public sources.[39]

U.S. companies also are prohibited from terminating Israeli business in order to do business in Arab countries. This prohibition brings up questions of motives. For example, Baxter International, a company blacklisted by the Arab League, divested from Israel and signed a joint-venture agreement in Syria a year later. Baxter officials claimed the Israeli move was made simply because of inadequate financial performance; however, the company was convicted after it was learned that it began discussions with Syrian authorities before selling its Israeli plant and submitted applications to Syrian authorities only three days after the plant's closing.[40]

Codes of Conduct

Collective attitudes toward MNE activities
- **Are clarified by a number of organizations**
- **Are usually fairly vague**
- **Involve voluntary compliance**
- **May make it easier for countries to legislate**

The first widespread attempt to regulate FDI on a multilateral basis was made in 1929 by the League of Nations. Then, the attention was on foreign exploitation of the tropical commodities industry. Proposals were discarded quickly, however, with the onset of the Great Depression. Since World War II, several attempts have been made to deal with the relationship between MNEs and governments. Among these were the International Trade Organization (ITO) of 1948, which never became operative, the attempts in 1951 by the UN Economic and Social Council (ECOSOC) to regulate antitrust, and the 1961 Code for Liberalization of Capital Movements established by the Organization for Economic Cooperation and Development (OECD).[41] It appears that none of these attempts has had much effect on MNEs' operations.

In 1975, the Center on Transnational Corporations was created at the United Nations as a result of complaints from many LDCs (the so-called Group of 77, which now comprises more than 100 LDCs). The Center collects information on MNE activities, is a forum for publicizing common complaints, and has considered the adoption of several codes of conduct for MNE activities. The OECD, which is composed of industrial countries, approved its own code in 1976. Both the codes considered by the Group of 77 and that adopted by the OECD are necessarily vague so that consensus may be reached among various countries as well as among groups within them. The codes also are voluntary; thus adoption does not guarantee enforcement. However, they may clarify a collective attitude toward specific MNE practices that could make it easier to pass restrictive legislation at the national level without fear that the legislation will be greatly out of step with external public opinion.[42]

Joint Company Activities

To counter production dominance by foreign companies, countries have encouraged their own manufacturers to consolidate. They have given governmental assistance for R&D and preference to their own companies in awarding governmental contracts. Two of the most notable efforts have been the development of Airbus Industrie, a consortium in Europe to compete against Boeing in aircraft production, and the development of various cooperative arrangements in Europe to counter IBM's dominance.[43] Other European cross-national efforts have occurred in such fields as consumer appliances, medical electronics, telecommunications, and television. For example, the EC's Esprit program provided $5 billion to fund electronics research, and the Eureka program, involving about 1600 companies, 99 percent of them European, was established to develop a wide range of technologies.[44]

In another approach, two or more companies from different countries band together, not so much to strengthen the initial negotiating terms but rather to improve their positions in possible later negotiations. By investing a smaller amount in a given locality, each company can invest in more countries, thus reducing the impact of loss in one. Further, in conflict situations a host government may be more hesitant to deal simultaneously with more than one home government.

Companies also may band together to pressure a government to take action against a competitor. For example, when IBM proposed an exemption from shared ownership for a new Mexican venture, forty-three computer-related companies, including Hewlett-Packard and Apple, successfully joined to advertise and lobby so that IBM would not be treated preferentially.[45]

External Relations Approaches

The Need by Countries

Countries that want to attract more FDI sometimes have found either that they are inadequately known to investors or that investors have false impressions of the business possibilities within their borders. To overcome either bad publicity or no publicity at all, many countries have implemented public-relations programs to deal with publicizing themselves overseas. These programs are extremely varied and include participating in world fairs and exhibits to promote a country's image, advertising to provide data on its economy, and organizing conferences abroad to explain its attractiveness. For example, Vietnam, Laos, and Cambodia have held conferences to explain their changed attitudes toward foreign investors. Also, it is common to see full-page advertisements in publications aimed at business managers with such titles as "Reasons to Invest in the Dominican Republic" and "Invest in Morocco. It may never have crossed your mind."

Company Approaches

Many companies strongly believe that by acting as a good corporate citizen abroad, they will reduce local animosities and remove concerns that might affect their short- or long-term competitive ability. Some have even gone so far as to set their own published codes of conduct. These actions may not be sufficient, however, since employees, governmental officials, consumers, and other groups may not know or understand what the company is doing. W. R. Grace's chairman, J. Peter Grace, said, "No matter how responsibly a corporation behaves, it will be viewed with skepticism unless it effectively communicates its activities, its plans,and its goals to its many publics."[46]

Because of conflicting pressures from different groups, an MNE can almost always be accused of bad behavior by someone. For instance, if it offers higher wages, it may be accused of monopolistic practices and of stimulating inflation by attracting workers from competitors. If it pays only the going wage, it may be accused of exploiting the workers. By understanding the relative power of competing groups it serves, the MNE at least may be able to emphasize practices that benefit most of the groups that are in a position to help or hurt it substantially. A good rule for serving a given group is to try to maximize benefits without excessively disrupting the local situation. Within any given economy, there usually is a range of prices, wages, and returns on investment. The MNE thus may be able to be among the leaders (for example, by offering wage rates or investment returns that are among those of the top quarter of companies) without being accused of disruptive practices, and still satisfy the groups directly involved.

The theologian Saint Augustine recounted in the fifth century that in his youth he used to pray, "Give me chastity and continence, but not yet." Like Saint Augustine, many companies try to put off public-relations efforts as long as possible. Often a company's public-relations efforts are defensive; that is, they occur in response to public criticism. Once a company is on the defensive, however, these efforts may be too little, too late. For example, Gulf & Western reacted to adverse criticism, primarily in the United States, about its labor-relations practices in the Dominican Republic by committing $100 million over a ten-year period to improve worker welfare through such initiatives as housing construction and education programs. Several years later, however, the criticism had not subsided measurably, and Gulf & Western announced it would cease operations in that country.[47]

Companies should work to increase the number of local supporters and dampen potential criticism. Opinion surveys of such interested parties as customers and workers can be conducted to allay misconceptions and anticipate criticism, thereby heading off potentially more damaging accusations. Many MNEs use advocacy publicity at home and abroad in an aggressive effort to win support for their international activities.[48] Such publicity may take the form of newspaper and magazine ads, reports, and films showing the positive effects a company's activities have had on home- and host-country societies. MNEs also have developed systematic means of identifying and reacting to external conditions that may adversely affect their operations abroad.[49]

Although it may not always be possible to dispel criticism from abroad, the MNE can do several things to mitigate it. One is to consider what is important to people in the host country. Another may be as fundamental as having the parent company managers continue an existing policy. On the question of what to centralize and what to decentralize, there is much to be said for permitting local managers to determine policies concerning local customs and social matters. On such sensitive issues as employment and worker output, changes should be made only after consultation with interested parties. Headquarters personnel also may serve a useful public-relations function locally; they have higher status than local managers do and so may sometimes be better received by higher governmental authorities.

Allies through Participation

An MNE also may foster local participation designed both to reduce the image of foreignness and to develop local proponents whose personal objectives may be fulfilled by the company's continued operations. The parent company can follow policies that involve assisting the development of local suppliers from whom it purchases, establishing stock-option plans, and gradually replacing home-country personnel with local nationals. If management directly informs local union officials about possible company actions, the officials may cooperate with management rather than confront it. Carried to extremes, however, local participation can result in the host country's becoming less dependent on the foreign company. Thus the company's strategy might be to hold out some resources so that it remains needed. For instance, a centralized R&D laboratory could be in charge of new product development, whereas the local R&D facility could handle adaptations for local market and production conditions.

Some companies have taken on additional social functions to build local support. For example, Dow Chemical financed a kindergarten in Chile, Citibank participated in a reforestation program in the Philippines, and McDonald's sponsored a telethon in Australia to raise funds for disabled children. Johnson & Johnson sends Kenyans abroad to study nursing. Merck gives away millions of doses of a drug to fight river blindness in Africa. GM publishes a public-interest report to highlight its involvement in a wide array of activities, such as environmental clean-up programs in Mexico and Eastern Europe, cancer research, AIDS education, and global celebration of Earth Day.[50]

Companies sometimes have been permitted greater latitude in their operations when they have agreed to invest in priority operations outside their normal line of business. These benefits have been gained through negotiated accords, such as a mining company's agreement to lay out two plantations in Nigeria in exchange for relative freedom in operating its mining venture.[51]

Good corporate citizenship and the attendant publicity may not be enough to guarantee that business activity can continue. If public opinion is against foreign private ownership in general, all foreign companies lose out. For a company doing business as a key company in a key sector, criticisms may come simultaneously from so many directions that the company defense gradually loses strength. Even in these exceptional situations, a company's external affairs department may identify the worst

The MNE might increase the number of local proponents through
- Ownership sharing
- Avoiding direct confrontation
- Local management
- Local R&D

problem areas. If this is done sufficiently in advance, the company may forestall adverse actions and establish policies to prevent or minimize losses. These policies may include decreasing new-parent obligations, selling ownership to local governments or private investors, and shifting into less visible types of local enterprises.

Occasionally, an MNE may find it advantageous to be uncompromising in its dealings with a government, even when the adversarial positions are reported publicly. It may do this because it determines it has a sufficiently strong bargaining position or because it perceives compromises will weaken its position in other countries. Even in these instances, however, the MNE should attempt to keep the government from losing face. For example, Gulf & Western negotiated for five years with the Thai government for a zinc mine and refinery without coming to an agreement. Then the company closed its office in Bangkok, an action widely reported as an effort to bully the Thai government into accepting the company's terms. Within a week, the government did accept an agreement, but Gulf & Western said that the office closing was simply a cost-reduction measure taken during a transition period.[52]

Protection of Intellectual Property Rights

International treaties and agreements help safeguard patents, trademarks, and copyrights.

Most of the discussion in this chapter has centered on foreign direct investment; however, one of the key areas of business-government and government-to-government conflicts recently has involved intellectual property rights (IPRs), sometimes referred to as intangible assets.[53] The poet and essayist Ralph Waldo Emerson said, "If a man can write a better book, preach a better sermon, or make a better mousetrap than his neighbor, though he builds his house in the woods, the world will make a beaten path to his door." But if someone else gets hold of the design for the better book, sermon, or mousetrap, the number of people beating the way will be divided.

IPRs are associated with both industrial property, such as inventions and distinctive identifications of companies and products, and artistic property, such as books, recordings, films, and computer programs. Companies with substantial intangible assets want protection through enforceable patents, trademarks, and copyrights so that they may gain all the sales and profits as returns on the investments they made to create the property. They argue that the social benefit of protection is positive because there otherwise would be less incentive to develop new industrial and artistic property. However, critics argue that protection creates a social cost through high monopoly prices. This argument has been used, for example, to restrict the patentability of pharmaceuticals in many countries so that medicines are more affordable.

Countries differ substantially in their protection of IPRs, through laws and their enforcement. Generally, LDCs offer less protection because few of their companies create substantial intangible assets; therefore they can gain local production and low prices without making payments to companies in industrial countries. Even when two countries have similar levels of protection, their approaches differ. For example, U.S. patent applications are secret, are usually granted within two years, and are valid for seventeen years; in contrast, Japanese applications are public, are granted in four to six years, and are valid for twenty years.[54] Because of different national approaches to IPRs, both companies and countries have stakes in any international agreements that are reached.

Patents

The first major attempt to achieve cross-national cooperation in the protection of patents, trademarks, and other property rights was the Paris Convention, initiated in 1883 and periodically revised. This convention gave rise to the International Bureau for the Protection of Industrial Property Rights (BIRPI). Its main thrust is to grant foreigners whose countries are Convention members the same status accorded a country's own citizens in the protection of property rights. A second major provision is that a registration in one country has a grace period of protection before registration must be made in other member countries. The Inter-American Conference of 1910 on Inventions, Patents, Designs, and Models was initiated among the United States and Latin American countries to accomplish the same objectives as the Paris Convention.

The three most important contemporary cross-national patent agreements are the Patent Cooperation Treaty (PCT) of the World Intellectual Property Organization (WIPO), the European Patent Convention (EPC), and the EEC Patent Convention.[55] The PCT and EPC allow companies to make a uniform patent search and application, which is then passed on to all signatory countries.

Patent-infringement battles are both costly and complex and may take years to settle. On the international level, the rapid development of technology and the different patent rules and regulations in different countries make keeping up with patents difficult.[56] Companies are forced to change their patents from country to country to meet local needs, and patent infringement is often hard to prove. For example, a company in Italy, where there is no patent protection on pharmaceuticals, could manufacture a drug patented by a company in the United States and sell it anywhere in the world. If the U.S. company were to bring suit, it would have to prove patent infringement; however, it would have difficulty getting the proof in Italy.

Another problem is that the duration of patent protection varies among countries. For example, Canada has a shorter protection period on drugs than does the United States. A result is that generic production of a drug may begin in Canada while the same drug is sold only by prescription in the United States, and Canadian producers may export the generic product to compete against U.S. firms elsewhere in the world.

Trademarks

Companies may spend millions of dollars to develop brand names. If a brand name is not protected by a trademark, then other companies may produce under the same brand name. For example, New Zealand growers began marketing gooseberries as kiwifruit in the 1960s but neglected to register a trademark; now kiwifruit are marketed from many places.[57] Even if a brand name has a trademark, it may become generic and thus enter the public domain. "Yo-yo" is actually a foreign trademark that has become a generic word in the United States. Because the Japanese have no name for vulcanized rubber, they call it "goodyear." One development in cross-national cooperation for trademark protection is the Trademark Registration Treaty, commonly known as the Vienna Convention. The United States, the United Kingdom, Germany, and Italy were among the industrialized countries that signed it initially.

Common-law countries require that a trademark be used before an application for its registration can be filed. Codified-law countries (those using statutory rather than common law) traditionally have not required use as a precondition to registration or recognized it as a valid protection against infringement. According to the Vienna Convention, a country may not require the use of a trademark as a prerequisite to obtain or maintain registration until three years after its international registration. Once the trademark has been registered internationally, each country must accept it or provide grounds for refusal within fifteen months after its registration so that the company will have sufficient time to act before the three-year period is completed.

Copyrights

Most large publishing and recording companies have extensive foreign interests and can be influenced easily by foreign competition. Without international copyright laws, a foreign producer could feasibly copy a book or tape and then distribute it at cut-rate prices in the country in which it was first produced. The Universal Copyright Convention (UCC), the major cross-national agreement, honors the copyright laws of its signatory countries.

Piracy

Not all countries are members of the various conventions to protect IPRs. Of those that are, some enforce the agreements haphazardly. The terms *piracy* and *counterfeiting* are used to describe production without the consent of the company holding the patent, trademark, or copyright. Reports of lost sales due to piracy vary substantially; but all estimates are significant. One study measured the loss in worldwide sales for U.S. companies as between 2.8 and 14.3 percent, depending on the industry.[58] Piracy has occurred for several reasons:

- Cashing in on massive advertising by placing well-known trademarked labels on copies of products is tempting and has happened with almost every type of goods. Fake labels even go on merchandise that the copied companies do not make; an example is the Jordache label on disco bags and caps.
- Technology allows copyrighted material such as tapes to be duplicated cheaply without loss of quality.[59]

- Some countries offer little protection for certain products. For example, when the drug company Pfizer introduced Feldene, an antiarthritic drug, to Argentina, five Argentine companies were already selling generic copies in the market.[60]
- Many people see nothing morally wrong in buying counterfeit goods. For example, the Software Publishers Association estimates the software industry loses $10 to $12 billion a year, and its executive director said, "It's ironic that people who would never think about stealing a candy bar from a drugstore seem to have no qualms about copying a $500 software package."[61]

What about gains or losses for consumers? Sometimes they get good-quality merchandise with a prestige label for a fraction of what the legitimate product would have cost. Some companies have even contracted counterfeiters to be legitimate suppliers. Often, however, shoddy or even dangerous merchandise is substituted for the original goods. For example, a hundred Nigerian children died from a cough medicine, and talcum powder was found in anti-ulcer drugs sold in Europe.[62]

Various manufacturers' associations have sprung up worldwide to deal collectively with piracy. Among the deterrents that have been proposed are greater border surveillance, stiffer penalties for dealing in counterfeit goods, and cessation of aid to countries that do not join and adhere to international agreements. The United States has threatened Super 301 trade sanctions against countries that do not adequately protect intellectual property. Companies such as Apple Computer and Union Carbide also are successfully tracking down infringers on their own and bringing cases against them, but it is difficult to prove infringement when slight changes are made to trademarks or product models. Other companies are using high technology, such as holographic images and magnetic or microchip tags, to identify the genuine products. This has cost them millions of dollars for detecting devices.[63] Vuitton, a French luggage manufacturer, is using a withdrawal strategy—it sells registered and numbered goods only in company-owned retail outlets. Still other companies are warning the public of imitations and advising consumers on how to discern the genuine product.[64]

COUNTERVAILING FORCES

The relationships of MNEs, home governments, and host governments involve constantly shifting coalitions. These three parties would like maximum independence; however, each is limited by resources and actions taken by the others. For example, MNEs usually prefer independence in order to follow global strategies that lead them to the least-cost production locations and biggest markets. But their ability to invoke these strategies is tempered by governmental regulations on factor flows and foreign-ownership limitations. To overcome these impediments, MNEs temporarily coalesce on specific issues. For instance, a group of companies might lobby their home-country government to pressure another government to open its market and protect foreign assets there.

Gaining this governmental support may require the MNEs to make concessions that limit their global strategies in other ways. To overcome those new limitations may require additional coalitions, and the results almost always necessitate new trade-offs.

Similarly, countries want independence in the form of sovereignty. But as this chapter illustrated, they sign treaties with other countries and reach agreements with MNEs in order to gain needed resources at the expense of losing some control over their domestic activities.

 **LOOKING TO THE FUTURE** Probably the most significant factor influencing possible change in business-government diplomacy is the end of the Cold War, which pitted the communist and noncommunist blocs against each other for nearly half a century. During that period, governments tended to influence business activities because of political-military objectives, sometimes protecting their home-based companies in order to gain or maintain spheres of influence abroad and sometimes withholding support for fear it might lead an otherwise neutral country to support the other bloc. But political schisms are not yet a thing of the past, and thus managers must continue to contend with cross-national animosities when planning international expansion strategies.

New alignments of countries based on economic factors may well replace some of the political-military rivalries of the recent past. For example, a new economic rivalry between Europe and North America may become as intense as the old political rivalry between the communist and noncommunist blocs. Companies thus may still have to satisfy national interests in their operations to the same degree as before. In the short term, it appears most countries will welcome foreign companies' operations or at least take a laissez-faire attitude toward them because of a belief that, on balance, they serve the countries' national economic interests. But there are likely to be many exceptions, for example, India and South Korea, which traditionally have not welcomed wholly owned foreign operations. Another exception centers on the privatization of state-owned enterprises, for which prospective buyers must negotiate on much more than the price. Still another exception involves negotiations in countries transforming from centrally planned to market economies, which are apt to be very long and complex.

Further, historically there have been broad swings in host-country attitudes toward foreign ownership. The present welcoming of FDI could easily reverse, particularly if governments feel their own constituencies are not receiving a just share of global economic benefits. Regardless of the direction national policies take, companies are likely to face ever more sophisticated governmental officials when they negotiate their operating terms abroad.

It is probably safe to say that companies headquartered in different countries will continue to become more entwined through joint ventures, licensing, contract buying, and other arrangements. Many of these companies also will continue to depend more on sales and production outside their home countries, while simultaneously bringing in more stock-holders and top managers from abroad. These activities may strengthen their positions with respect to all governments but may weaken them relative to their home-country governments, which will no longer see them as representing a national interest.

Government-to-government cooperation to deal with MNEs is apt to develop slowly, at least on a global scale. There are simply too many divergent interests among countries that tend to divide them on issues of economic development, product-specific interests, and regional viewpoints. One such issue is the protection of intangibles—it pits the interests of industrial countries, which create most of the products that can be patented, trade-marked, or copyrighted, against the interests of many LDCs, which do not want to pay for their use. In this area there may be more linkages to other aspects of overall economic policy, such as the cessation of trade preferences for countries that do not protect IPRs. There also may be more attempts by small groups of countries, such as those operating in trading blocs, to band together to unify or coordinate policies toward MNEs.

Summary

- **Although host countries and MNEs may hold resources that, if combined, could achieve objectives for both, conflict may cause one or both parties to withhold those resources, thus preventing the full functioning of international business activities.**

- **Both MNE managers and host-country governmental officials must respond to interest groups that may perceive different advantages or no advantage at all to the business-government relationship. Therefore the relationship's final outcome may not be the one expected from a purely economic viewpoint.**

- **Negotiations increasingly are used to determine the terms under which a company may operate in a foreign country. This negotiating process is similar to the domestic processes of company acquisition and collective bargaining. The major differences in the international sphere are the much larger number of provisions, the general lack of a fixed time duration for an agreement, and the need to agree on valuation of a company's property.**

- **The terms under which an MNE may be permitted to operate in a given country will be determined to a great extent by the relative degree to which the company needs the country, and vice versa. As the relative needs evolve over time, new terms of operation will reflect the shift in bargaining strength.**

- **Generally, a company's best bargaining position is before it begins operation. Once resources are committed to the foreign operation, the company may not be able to move elsewhere easily.**

- Since international negotiations are conducted largely between parties whose cultures, educational backgrounds, and expectations differ, it is very difficult for these negotiators to understand each other's sentiments and present convincing arguments. Role-playing offers negotiators a means of anticipating responses and planning an approach to the actual bargaining.

- Historically, developed countries used military intervention and coercion to ensure that the terms agreed on between their investors and host countries would be carried out. A series of international resolutions have caused the near demise of these methods for settling disputes. Recently, developed countries have used the promise of giving or withholding loans and/or aid and the threat of trade sanctions.

- Several bilateral treaties have been established in which host countries agree to compensate investors for losses from expropriation, civil disturbances, and currency devaluation or control. These agreements often are not clear about the means of settlement for the losses.

- International organizations or groups in countries not involved in a dispute are frequently used to arbitrate trade disputes among individuals from more than one country. This method has been used very rarely to settle investment disputes, however, because governments are reluctant to relinquish sovereignty over what occurs within their borders.

- To prevent companies from playing one country against another or countries from playing one company against another, groups of governments or companies occasionally have banded together to present a unified front in order to improve the terms under which international business is carried out.

- Public relations may be used by both companies and countries to develop a good image, overcome a bad one, and create useful proponents for their positions. If successful, this strategy may result in better terms of operation for either side.

- International agreements have been made to protect important intangible property such as patents, trademarks, and copyrights. Since millions of dollars are often spent in the development of these assets, worldwide protection is important for their owners.

- Recently, a big problem for companies has been the pirating of intangible assets in countries that have not signed international agreements or do not actively enforce their own laws on protection of IPRs.

Case
PepsiCo in India[65]

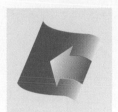

Despite PepsiCo's operations in nearly 150 countries and territories, its chairman, D. Wayne Calloway, said, "We are still basically an American company with offshore interests. As the nineties progress, that's going to change. We'll be a truly global consumer products company." A key part of that strategy was the company's launching of an Indian snack-food and soft-drink joint venture in 1990. At that time, the company announced plans to invest $1 billion in India during the 1990s. Calloway also said, "We see ourselves as partners in India's progress. . . . We look forward to delivering the kinds of products, technologies, and marketing know-how that serve India's priorities."

The Global Competitive Situation

Two companies, Coca-Cola and PepsiCo, have dominated the global market for soft drinks. The United States has been the biggest market, with annual per capita consumption of about thirty-two cases. Analysts agree that this consumption figure is so large that almost all growth must come from building market share rather than getting people to increase consumption. Even so, the companies have promoted the consumption of soft drinks at breakfast and have added new soft-drink varieties to try to increase consumption. The fierce competition between the two companies within the United States has resulted in industry returns on assets and sales that are less than half what they have been abroad. In 1990, within the United States the two companies were close rivals: Coca-Cola held about 40 percent of the market and PepsiCo about 32 percent. But in terms of total global sales, Coca-Cola's 47-percent share was more than double PepsiCo's; consequently, Coca-Cola has been much stronger where profits are higher and where sales growth is expected to be much faster. For example, per capita consumption outside the United States is only about 14 percent of that in the United States; thus there is much more room to grow. In 1989, Coca-Cola earned almost 80 percent of its profits outside the United States, as opposed to only 15 percent for PepsiCo. Globally, players other than Coca-Cola and PepsiCo are small in comparison. However, some have large shares in specific country or regional markets; an example is Cadbury Schweppes in the United Kingdom.

In the soft-drink industry, it is generally conceded that there is a tremendous advantage in being first into a market. Not only is brand loyalty built up fast and difficult to change, but the early entrants gain the best bottlers/distributors. Coca-Cola preceded PepsiCo into Western Europe, Latin America, and Japan, and PepsiCo has had an uphill battle building market share in those areas. For example, it actually lost market share in France during the late 1980s, and when it started doing well in the United Kingdom through a bottler/distributor contract with Cadbury Schweppes, Coca-Cola stole the contract away from PepsiCo. PepsiCo, however, beat Coca-Cola into the former Soviet Union in 1974 and thus dominates that market.

Because of the first-in advantage, PepsiCo has pushed hard in recent years to enter markets in which Coca-Cola is not dominant. For example, PepsiCo entered Myanmar ahead of Coca-Cola in 1990. In the early 1990s, both companies announced large capital investments in emerging markets and in LDCs in which the other held advantages. Some of the notable examples are shown on Map 13.2.

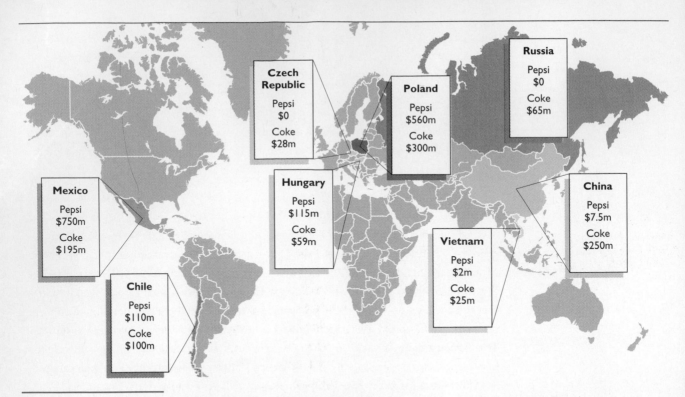

Map 13.2
Selected Capital
Investment
Announcements (Early
1990s): Pepsi and Coke
Note that PepsiCo and
Coca-Cola are investing to
counter each other's
strong position in Russia
and Mexico, respectively.

Source: Data were taken from
company reports and appeared
in Kenneth H. Hammonds, "Just
What They Need," *Business
Week,* August 30, 1993, p. 46.

Indian Market Potential

PepsiCo had been in the Indian market during the mid-1950s but pulled out because of lack
of profitability. Coca-Cola had operated in India since 1950 but left in 1977 because of disagreements with the Indian government. Coca-Cola's departure created an opportunity for
PepsiCo; however, it did not begin its three years of formal negotiations with the Indian
government until 1985. After Coca-Cola's departure, an Indian company, Parle Exports,
became the dominant supplier in India with its soft drink, Thums Up. By 1988, Parle Exports had estimated annual sales of about $150 million, which made up between 60 and 70
percent of the market. It also was exporting a mango pulp drink, Maaza Mango, to various
markets, including the United States.

   The Indian market for soft drinks has been growing rapidly. When Coca-Cola departed,
annual soft-drink sales were a little over a half-billion bottles a year. By 1990, they were
about 3 billion bottles a year and were expected to quadruple during the 1990s. India's
population growth was expected to make it surpass China as the world's most populated
country. Further, India's middle class is much larger than China's; it was estimated at 150
million people when PepsiCo entered formal negotiations with the Indian government.
By 1992, this market was estimated at 300 million. Additionally, many observers have predicted that India will eventually become an economic giant; thus growing incomes should
support more sales. Another indication of market potential was that India's per capita consumption of soft drinks was estimated at only 3 bottles per year in 1989, compared to 13
bottles per year in neighboring Pakistan. Coca-Cola was selling 122 bottles per capita annually in Latin America, also a low-income area.

Indian Attitude toward Foreign Investment

India's attitude was summed up by the president of the Associated Chambers of Commerce and Industry of India, who said, "The basic thing is that most of our people, in all political parties, have no concept of how the world is moving. My political friends think it's the seventeenth century and that every investment, like the East India Company, is going to come into India and take over." His reference was to the long domination of India by British, French, and Portuguese interests, which had extracted great wealth from India without returning noticeable benefit to its economy.

India has approved foreign investment on a case-by-case basis with approval necessary at the highest governmental level. By the time PepsiCo began its negotiations, the maximum equity holding allowed for foreign investors was only 40 percent of an Indian enterprise. Further, foreign companies were required to develop exports to compensate for imported equipment and components and for dividend payments.

Because of this political sensitivity, negotiations tended to be long and usually were public. Little action was apt to take place during election periods because politicians were afraid of adverse reaction if they supported the entry of foreign companies. For example, when PepsiCo began its negotiations Gillette recently had been granted approval on an investment. Gillette wanted to move into India because it has the world's highest unit razor-blade sales. Gillette spent seven years negotiating during two changes of government and finally agreed to settle for a 24-percent equity holding, to export 25 percent of its output, and not to use its name on its products. The name issue has been important to Indian authorities because of a belief that many consumers will think wrongly that a foreign-associated product is better and because a locally associated brand name would provide greater continuity if the foreign investor left the market on its own or by government decree.

Coca-Cola and IBM both left India at about the same time because of the strict operating restrictions that had come about after their initial entry. Coca-Cola objected to three governmental demands: that it reduce its equity holding from 100 to 40 percent, that it divulge its formula, and that it use dual trademarks so that Indian consumers would familiarize themselves with a local logo. Coca-Cola was particularly adamant about the latter two demands. It always had relied on the mystique of a secret formula for its promotion, and it feared an expropriation once the new trademark became accepted.

There also has been a pervading feeling among non-Indian companies that Indian competitors can and do use a great deal of influence to prevent foreign competition. Officially, the foreign company is told that its application has simply run into "political difficulties," but behind the scenes, Indian business leaders align themselves with Indian political leaders. For example, when Coca-Cola was given its directives in 1977, Ramesh Chauhan, the head of Parle Exports, was an ally of Prime Minister Moraji Desai, and Coca-Cola executives were close to Indira Gandhi, the head of the opposition party.

The Negotiations

PepsiCo first negotiated a contingent joint-venture arrangement with two Indian companies it felt could ease the negotiation process. One of these was a division of Tata Industries, perhaps India's most powerful private company. The second was a government-owned company, Punjab Agro Industries, whose involvement gave the appearance that the public interest would be served in the venture.

Although the initial investment was only $15 million, approval had to be given at the cabinet level. There were twenty parliamentary debates, fifteen committee reviews, and 5,000 articles in the press about the proposed investment over a three-year period.

PepsiCo and its partners proposed that the new company be located in the politically volatile state of Punjab, where they enlisted the support of Sikh leaders who lobbied publicly on their behalf. They claimed that Sikh terrorism might be subdued by providing jobs and help to Punjabi farmers. The partners estimated that the investment would create 25,000 jobs in the Punjab and another 25,000 elsewhere. They also pointed out that China and the former Soviet Union had allowed entry of foreign soft-drink producers; thus India was out of step even with other socialist countries. They argued further that new technology and know-how would prevent some of the wastage of Punjabi fruits, estimated to be about 30 percent. Finally, they contended that the lack of competition with foreign companies had kept prices and profit margins artificially high so that there was little incentive for local companies to grow and distribute widely. Competitive soft-drink sales were limited primarily to the largest cities.

Opponents contended that foreign capital and imports should be restricted to those high-technology areas in which India lacked expertise, that the venture's proposed production of processed foods (such as potato chips, corn chips, fruit drinks, and sauces) would simply displace what could be made in the home, and that imported equipment would hurt India's balance of payments. Also, journalists widely reported that PepsiCo had a CIA connection aimed at undermining India's independence.

Meanwhile, in 1987 another U.S.-based company, Double-Cola, successfully terminated a secret six-year negotiation. The agreement called for the company to open three bottling plants immediately and another twenty-seven later. Double-Cola apparently had an advantage in that it was controlled by nonresident Indians in London, and the Indian Prime Minister, Rajiv Gandhi, wanted to lure investment from Indians living overseas. Double-Cola also promised to use Indian raw materials and to reinvest profits in India.

The agreement with the PepsiCo group, signed in 1988, included the following provisions:

1. The company would export five times the value of its imports, about $150 million over the first ten-year period of operations.
2. Soft-drink sales would not exceed 25 percent of the joint venture's sales.
3. PepsiCo would limit its ownership to 39.9 percent.
4. Seventy-five percent of concentrate would be exported.
5. The joint venture would establish an agricultural research center.
6. The company could sell Pepsi Era, 7-Up Era, and Miranda Era.
7. The joint venture would set up fruit and vegetable processing plants.

Aftermath and Renegotiation

Once PepsiCo's venture was approved, Coca-Cola made an application to re-enter the Indian market through production within an export processing zone. Producing in this way would allow 25 percent of output to be sold within India rather than in export markets. This proposal threatened PepsiCo because the Coca-Cola name was still well-remembered in India; cans of Coke were even smuggled in from Nepal. But after sixteen months, Coca-Cola's application was denied, leading a Coca-Cola official to say that India "doesn't follow its own rules."

In late 1989, a new prime minister, V. P. Singh, took power in a minority government. As finance minister in the mid-1980s, he had promoted liberalizing FDI. However, after taking power, he almost immediately made conflicting statements about such investment. In early 1990, the PepsiCo venture began production of snack foods and announced that soft-drink production would start up by summer. Prime Minister Singh announced the government would reexamine the PepsiCo agreement.

Several things then happened in quick succession. Because of India's strict FDI regulations, the U.S. government, without public reference to PepsiCo, threatened to impose trade sanctions against India under its Super 301 legislation. Indian governmental officials and the joint venture's management then met secretly. Subsequently, PepsiCo agreed to place a new logo, Lehar, above the Pepsi insignia. It also lobbied publicly against Super 301 sanctions against India. The U.S. government backed down. And India's Minister of Food Processing Industries announced tax breaks for food processors.

In 1991, P. V. Narasimha Rao was elected Prime Minister and launched broad economic changes, including a more welcome attitude toward FDI. A Foreign Investment Promotion Board was established, and ownership requirements were changed to allow 51-percent foreign ownership of companies. The new policies gave confidence to foreign investors, and both IBM and Coca-Cola re-entered the market. Coca-Cola announced its return in 1993 through a joint venture with Parle Exports and agreed to export three times the value of its imports; it also announced it would export plastic beverage cases to compensate for its imports of concentrate. Nevertheless, when asked if India's hostility toward foreign investors might return, IBM's general manager replied, "Yes, it could."

Questions

1. Did PepsiCo make too many concessions in order to enter the Indian market? Could the company have negotiated better terms?
2. In light of later events, should Coca-Cola have abandoned the Indian market in 1977?
3. From an Indian standpoint, evaluate the government's restrictions on FDI.
4. What behavioral factors might affect negotiations involving managers and government officials from the United States and India?

Chapter Notes

1. Data for the case were taken from Louis Morano, "Multinationals and Nation-States: The Case of Aramco," *Orbis,* Summer, 1979, pp. 447–468; "Oil New Power Structure," *Business Week,* December 24, 1979, pp. 82–88; "Saudi Takeover of Aramco Looms," *Wall Street Journal,* August 6, 1980, p. 21; Ted D'Affisio, "Aramco Long-Term Contract with Saudis May Pressure Oil Company Earnings," *The Oil Daily,* February 9, 1987, p. 3; "Saudis Reportedly Map Changes for Aramco," *New York Times,* May 10, 1988, p. 34; "Arabian Might," *The Economist,* December 24, 1988, p. 79; "Aramco Has Been the Bridge Between Two Nations," *The Oil Daily,* September 18, 1989, p. B-19; Andrew Pollack, "Saudi Stake of U.S. Com-

panies," *New York Times,* August 21, 1990, p. C1+; John J. Fialka, "In a Saudi Oil Colony, Workers Live in Fear—or So They Hear," *Wall Street Journal,* August 31, 1990, p. A8; Gene G. Marcial, "If a Shooting War Breaks Out, Fluor Will Win," *Business Week,* December 10, 1990, p. 209; John Rossant and Robert Buderi, "Aramco Toughs It Out," *Business Week,* February 4, 1991, p. 44; and Gerald F. Seib and Peter Waldman, "Best of Friends," *Wall Street Journal,* October 26, 1992, p. A1+.

2. J. Grieco, "Foreign Investment and Development: Theories and Evidence," in *Investing in Development: New Roles for Private Capital?* T. Moran, ed. (New Brunswick, N.J.: Transaction Books, 1986); and D. Encarnation, *Dislodging Multinationals: India's Strategy in Comparative Perspective* (Ithaca, N.Y.: Cornell University Press, 1989).

3. Nathan Fagre and Louis T. Wells, Jr., "Bargaining Power of Multinationals and Host Governments," *Journal of International Business Studies,* Vol. 8, No. 2, Fall 1982, pp. 9–23, studied ownership percentages of foreign investors in Latin America.

4. Laurence Hooper, "France Chooses IBM to Bolster Groupe Bull," *Wall Street Journal,* January 29, 1992, p. A3.

5. Masaaki Kotabe, "Creating Countertrade Opportunities in Financially Distressed Developing Countries: Framework and Nigerian Example," *International Marketing Review,* Vol. 6, No. 5, 1989, pp. 36–49.

6. Many of these conflicts are discussed in "The Multinationals: An Urgent Need for New Ties to Government," *Business Week,* March 12, 1979, pp. 74–82; and John C. Banks, "Negotiating International Mining Agreements: Win-Win Versus Win-Lose Bargaining," *Columbia Journal of World Business,* Winter 1987, pp. 67–71.

7. Thane Peterson, Frank J. Comes, Jonathan Kapstein, Steven J. Dryden, and John J. Keller, "The Swedes Give AT&T and the U.S. Painful Black Eyes," *Business Week,* No. 2997, May 4, 1987, pp. 44–45. For a discussion of U.S. government efforts to persuade Japan to remove its barriers to direct investment, see Marcus W. Brauchli, "U.S. to Prod Tokyo on Easing Investment," *Wall Street Journal,* November 2, 1989, p. A18.

8. "Global Wrapup," *Business Week,* September 28, 1992, p. 58. For other recent examples see Bernard Wysocki, Jr., "For Sale," *Wall Street Journal,* September 20, 1991, p. R10.

9. Robert Weigand, "International Investments: Weighing the Incentives," *Harvard Business Review,* Vol. 61, No. 4, July–August 1983, pp. 146–152; Stephen E. Guisinger, "Do Performance Requirements and Investment Incentives Work?" *The World Economy,* Vol. 9, No. 1, March

1986, pp. 79–96; and Joann S. Lublin, "Toyota Spurns British Aid for Auto Plant," *Wall Street Journal,* April 18, 1989, p. A22.

10. R. Hal Mason, "Investment Incentives and Performance Requirements: A Case Study of Food Manufacturing," a paper presented to the Academy of International Business, San Francisco, December 29, 1983, which was a summary of a larger report submitted to the World Bank.

11. William A. Stoever, "Renegotiations: The Cutting Edge of Relations between MNCs and LDCs," *Columbia Journal of World Business,* Spring 1979, pp. 6–7; and Dennis J. Encarnation and Suchil Vachani, "Foreign Ownership: When Hosts Change the Rules," *Harvard Business Review,* Vol. 63, No. 5, September–October 1985, pp. 152–160.

12. Eric Berg, "Peru to Pay Part of Debt in Goods," *New York Times,* September 17, 1987, p. 25+.

13. Stoever, op. cit.

14. These and other differences are noted in John L. Graham and Roy A. Herberger, Jr., "Negotiators Abroad—Don't Shoot from the Hip," *Harvard Business Review,* Vol. 61, No. 4, July–August 1983, pp. 160–168; Toshyuki Arai, "Negotiating with Japanese Corporations," *Export Today,* November–December 1992, pp. 32–35; and David L. James, "Don't Think About Winning," *Across the Board,* April 1992, pp. 49–51.

15. Nancy J. Adler, Richard Brahm, and John L. Graham, "Strategy Implementation: A Comparison of Face-to-Face Negotiations in the People's Republic of China and the United States," *Strategic Management Journal,* Vol. 13, No. 6, September 1992, p. 463.

16. James, loc. cit.

17. Stoever, op. cit., pp. 12–13.

18. William A. Stoever, "Why State Corporations in Developing Countries Have Failed to Attract Foreign Investment," *International Marketing Review,* Vol. 6, No. 3, 1989, pp. 62–77.

19. Julian Gresser, "Breaking the Japanese Negotiating Code: What European and American Managers Must Do to Win," *European Management Journal,* Vol. 10, No. 3, September 1992, pp. 286–293.

20. George Schwarzenberger, "The Protection of British Property Abroad," *Current Legal Problems,* Vol. 5, 1952, pp. 295–299; Oliver J. Lissitzyn, *International Law Today and Tomorrow* (Dobbs Ferry, N.Y.: Oceana Publications, 1965), p. 77; and Gillis Wetter, "Diplomatic Assistance to Private Investment," *University of Chicago Law Review,* Vol. 29, 1962, p. 275.

21. Ian Brownlie, *Principles of Public International Law* (Oxford, England: Oxford University Press, 1966), pp. 435–436.

22. Green H. Hackworth, *Digest of International Law* (Washington, D.C.: U.S. Government Printing Office, 1942), pp. 655–661.

23. P. Evans, *Dependent Development: The Alliance of Multinational, State, and Local Capital in Brazil* (Princeton: Princeton University Press, 1979); and Osvaldo Sunkel, "Big Business and 'Dependencia': A Latin American View," *Foreign Affairs,* April 1972, pp. 417–531.

24. C. Lipson, *Standing Guard: Protecting Foreign Capital in the Nineteenth and Twentieth Century* (Berkeley, Calif.: University of California Press, 1985).

25. Paul Jensen, "Political Risk Coverage Eases Entry into Perilous Markets," *Export Today,* November–December 1992, pp. 39–42.

26. Caleb Solomon, "Texaco Receives U.S. Assistance for Russian Project," *Wall Street Journal,* September 3, 1993, p. A3.

27. David R. Mummery, *The Protection of International Private Investment* (New York: Praeger Publishers, 1968), p. 49.

28. "OPEC Contends Levy Against Revere Copper Wasn't Expropriation," *Wall Street Journal,* June 15, 1977, p. 35.

29. Mummery, op. cit., p. 98.

30. Amy Borrus, "Why Pinstripes Don't Suit the Cloak-and-Dagger Crowd," *Business Week,* May 17, 1993, p. 39; and Jeff Cole, "Hughes Aircraft Cancels Paris Display After Warning of a French Spy Scheme," *Wall Street Journal,* April 26, 1993, p. A4.

31. "New World Bank Agency for Investments Sets Debut," *Wall Street Journal,* April 13, 1988, p. 20; "World Bank Agency Reinsures GE Project," *Wall Street Journal,* June 6, 1990, p. A16; Ibrahim F. I. Shihata, "Encouraging International Corporate Investment: The Role of the Multilateral Investment Guarantee Agency," *Columbia Journal of World Business,* Spring 1988, pp. 11–18; and "World Bank Agency Boosts Investment Coverage," *Journal of Commerce,* July 14, 1992, p. 21A.

32. William A. Stoever, "Issues Emerging in Iranian Claims Negotiations," *Wall Street Journal,* May 7, 1981, p. 26; James B. Stewart and Peter Truell, "U.S. Firms Win Some, Lose Some at Tribunal Arbitrating $5 Billion in Claims Against Iran," *Wall Street Journal,* November 15, 1984, p. 38; and Gerald F. Seib, "Administration Rejects Iranian Overture to Link Hostage Talks and Frozen Assets," *Wall Street Journal,* August 9, 1989, p. A5.

33. "Chile Halts Shipments to France of Copper from El Teniente Mines," *Wall Street Journal,* October 17, 1972, p. 12.

34. John Marcom, Jr., "U.K. Court Says U.S. Bank Owes Money to Libya," *Wall Street Journal,* September 3, 1987, p. 12.

35. "Arco Unit Awarded Payment from Libya's Takeover of Assets," *Wall Street*

Journal, April 4, 1977, p. 4; and "California Standard, Texaco Win Ruling Against Libya Takeover of Oil Holdings," *Wall Street Journal,* March 3, 1977, p. 4.

36. Burton Yale Pines, "Hollow Chambers of the World Court," *Wall Street Journal,* April 12, 1984, p. 30; and Bob Hagerty and Jonathan M. Moses, "Libya Dispute With U.S., Britain Unlikely to be Resolved by Court," *Wall Street Journal,* March 31, 1992, p. B12.

37. For further discussions of the subject, see Jack G. Kaikati, "The Challenge of the Arab Boycott," *Sloan Management Review,* Winter 1977, pp. 83–100; and Dan S. Chill, *The Arab Boycott of Israel* (New York: Praeger, 1976).

38. "Saudis Warn Toyota on Ford," *New York Times,* June 24, 1981, p. D5.

39. "Sara Lee Corp. Agrees to $725,000 Payment in Anti-Boycott Case," *Wall Street Journal,* August 8, 1988, p. 4.

40. Sue Shellenbarger, "Off the Blacklist," *Wall Street Journal,* May 1, 1990, p. A1+; Julia Flynn Siler, David Greising, and Tim Smart, "The Case Against Baxter International," *Business Week,* October 7, 1991, pp. 106–114; Thomas M. Burton, "Baxter's Chairman Says Illegal Actions Over Arab Boycott Were Unintentional," *Wall Street Journal,* May 3, 1993, p. A4.

41. Don Wallace, Jr., *International Regulation of Multinational Corporations* (New York: Praeger, 1976), pp. 5–26.

42. For a discussion of how codes may presage national regulations, see Richard L. Rowan and Duncan C. Campbell, "The Attempt to Regulate Industrial Relations through International Codes of Conduct," *Columbia Journal of World Business,* Vol. 18, No. 2, Summer 1983, pp. 64–80.

43. David W. Cravens, H. Kirk Downey, and Paul Lauritano, "Global Competition in the Commercial Aircraft Industry," *Columbia Journal of World Business,* Winter 1992, pp. 47–58.

44. Thane Peterson, "Can Europe Catch Up in the High-Tech Race?" *Business Week,* October 23, 1989, pp. 142+.

45. Charles T. Crespy, "Global Marketing Is the New Public Relations Challenge," *Public Relations Quarterly,* Vol. 31, No. 2, Summer 1986, pp. 5–8.

46. "Corporate Citizenship: Outstanding Examples Worldwide," *Top Management Report,* 1979, p. 2.

47. Belmont F. Haydel, "Case Study of a Social Responsibility Program: Gulf & Western Industries, Inc., in the Dominican Republic in Employee Health, Housing, Education, Sports, and General Welfare, and Other Assistance to the Dominican Republic," paper presented to the Academy of International Business, New York, October 7, 1983;

Pamela G. Hollie, "G. & W. to Sell Dominican Holdings," *New York Times,* June 13, 1984, p. D1.

48. For a discussion of the advertising part of the promotion, see S. Prakash Sethi, "Advocacy Advertising and the Multinational Corporation," *Columbia Journal of World Business,* Fall 1977, pp. 32–46.

49. Douglas Nigh and Philip L. Cochran, "Issues Management and the Multinational Enterprise," *Management International Review,* Vol. 27, No. 1, 1987, pp. 4–12; and Richard E. Wokutch, "Corporate Social Responsibility Japanese Style," *Academy of Management Executive,* Vol. 4, No. 2, 1990, pp. 56–74.

50. "Corporate Citizenship: Outstanding Examples Worldwide," *Top Management Report,* 1979, p. 2; Belmont F. Haydel, "Description and Analysis of Johnson & Johnson's Strategic Management Process of Its Live for Life Program," paper presented at the Academy of International Business Northeast Annual Meeting, Baltimore, Md., June 5, 1989; "1992 General Motors Public Interest Report"; Michael Schroeder and Jonathan Kapstein, "Charity Doesn't Begin at Home Anymore," *Business Week,* February 25, 1991, p. 91; and Elyse Tanouye, "Merck's Drug Giveaway Hits Roadblocks," *Wall Street Journal,* September 23, 1992, p. B1.

51. Frans G. J. Derkinderen, "Transnational Business Latitude in Developing Countries," *Management International Review,* Vol. 22, No. 4, 1982, p. 58.

52. "Thailand Zinc Talks by Gulf and Western Unit Run into Snag," *Wall Street Journal,* February 25, 1977, p. 22; and "Gulf and Western Thailand Unit Accepts Plan for $90 Million Zinc Mine, Refinery," *Wall Street Journal,* March 2, 1977, p. 12.

53. A good overview of the issues can be found in Keith E. Maskers, "Intellectual Property Rights and the Uruguay Round," *Economic Review: Federal Reserve Bank of Kansas City,* First Quarter 1993, pp. 11–26.

54. Eric Schine and Paul Magnusson, "Clay Jacobson Calls It Patently Unfair," *Business Week,* August 19, 1991, p. 48.

55. William T. Ryan and Doria Bonham-Yeaman, "International Patent Cooperation," *Columbia Journal of World Business,* Vol. 17, No. 4, Winter 1982, pp. 63–66.

56. Thomas J. Maronick, "European Patent Laws and Decisions: Implications for Multinational Marketing Strategy," *International Marketing Review,* Vol. 5, No. 2, Summer 1988, pp. 20–30.

57. "Think New Zealand," *Forbes,* June 8, 1992, p. 74.

58. R. Feinberg and D. Rousslang, "The Economic Effects of Intellectual Property Rights Infringements," *Journal of Business,* 1990, pp. 79–90.

59. Steven Erlanger, "Thailand, Where Pirated Tapes Are Everywhere and Profitable," *New York Times,* November 27, 1990, pp. B1–B2.

60. Michael G. Harvey and Ilkka A. Ronkainen, "International Counterfeiters: Marketing Success Without the Cost and the Risk," *Columbia Journal of World Business,* Vol. 20, No. 3, Fall 1985, p. 39.

61. Peter H. Lewis, "As Piracy Grows, the Software Industry Counterattacks," *New York Times,* November 8, 1992, p. 12F.

62. "Fake Drugs," *Economist,* May 2, 1992, pp. 85–86.

63. Louis Kraar, "Fighting the Fakes from Taiwan," *Fortune,* Vol. 107, No. 11, May 30, 1983, pp. 114–116; "Two Who Smuggled Counterfeit Computers Get Prison and Fines," *Wall Street Journal,* May 1, 1984, p. 62; and Todd Mason, "How High Tech Foils the Counterfeiters," *Business Week,* May 20, 1985, p. 119.

64. Harvey and Ronkainen, op. cit., p. 43.

65. Data for the case were taken from Sheila Tefft, Cheryl Debes, and Dean Foust, "The Mouse That Roared at Pepsi," *Business Week,* September 7, 1987, p. 42; Subrata N. Chakravarty, "How Pepsi Broke into India," *Forbes,* November 27, 1989, pp. 43–44; Lincoln Kaye, "Pepping Up the Punjab," *Far Eastern Economic Review,* October 27, 1988, pp. 77–78; Steven R. Weisman, "Pepsi Sets Off a Cola War in India," *New York Times,* March 21, 1988, p. 28; Anthony Spaeth, "India Beckons—and Frustrates," *Wall Street Journal,* September 22, 1989, pp. R23–R25; "A Passage to India," *Panorama,* February 1989, n.p.; Anthony Ramirez, "It's Only Soft Drinks at Coca Cola," *New York Times,* May 21, 1990, p. C1+; Barbara Crossette, "After Long Fight, Pepsi Enters India," *New York Times,* May 24, 1990, p. C2; Michael J. McCarthy, "India Gives Final Approval to Pepsi's Plans," *Wall Street Journal,* May 24, 1990, p. A5; Anthony Spaeth, "Political Turbulence in India Raises Questions About the Country's Economy," *Wall Street Journal,* August 8, 1990, p. A8; Anthony Spaeth and Ajay Singh, "India Rejects Coca-Cola's Bid to Sell Soft Drinks, Giving Pepsi an Advantage," *Wall Street Journal,* March 16, 1990, p. B5; "Losses at PepsiCo Venture in India," *New York Times,* February 16, 1991, p. 33; Rahul Jacob, "India Is Opening for Business," *Fortune,* November 16, 1992, pp. 128–130; Susan Dubey, "India Clears Some Foreign Investments, Sending Bullish Signal on Reform Drive," *Wall Street Journal,* June 24, 1993, p. A8; "India Clears Venture, Includes Coke's Return," *New York Times,* June 24, 1993, p. C3; and "Coke Returns to India," *Herald Times* (Bloomington, Ind.), p. B6.

P A R T 6
Corporate Policy and Strategy

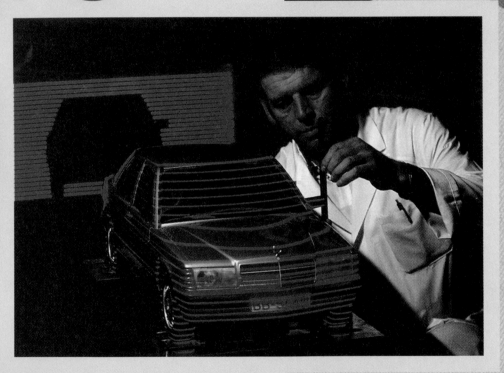

Europe is a global leader in manufactured products, especially those encompassing new designs. Here you see a designer for Daimler-Benz in Germany obtaining microscopically precise measurements with a laser scanner to improve the aerodynamics of new models of automobiles. The photo is set against a background showing part of a German tapestry (circa 1926) by Ruth Hollós.

Chapter 14

Export and Import Strategies

*There may be trade
and none able to do it.*
—Chinese Proverb

Objectives

- To identify the key elements of export and import strategies

- To compare direct and indirect selling of exports

- To discuss the role of several types of trading companies in exporting

- To show how freight forwarders help exporters with the movement of goods and the accompanying documentation

- To identify the methods of receiving payment for exports and the financing of receivables

Case
Grieve Corporation[1]

As noted in the Chinese proverb on the preceding page, it is not always easy to engage in trade, especially for small companies. The top fifty U.S. exporters generate about 30 percent of U.S. merchandise exports, and their shipments are bigger on average than are the shipments of smaller exporters. However, there are an estimated 100,000 U.S. companies engaged in export activity, and most of them are small, as is Grieve Corporation of Round Lake, Illinois, near Chicago.

As recently as 1992, Grieve Corporation manufactured industrial ovens and furnaces for the U.S. market. Whenever a customer moved overseas, the company would continue to supply that customer with product, but eventually this market would begin to erode. After a while, the customer would source locally. The company had not considered exports proactively for three main reasons:

1. *The nature of its product.* Industrial ovens and furnaces are rather large and bulky and also relatively expensive. Top management assumed the product's size would make shipping costs so high that Grieve would price itself out of the market. For example, a recent shipment of a furnace overseas entailed shipping costs of $11,000.
2. *Doubts about its success abroad.* Grieve is a small business, and top management assumed it could not be successful internationally. Managers were so busy doing all that needed to be done in the domestic market with a relatively thin management structure that they just didn't have time to think strategically about the international market.
3. *Concern about competition.* More seasoned exporters from Germany, Japan, and the United Kingdom offered relatively fierce competition. Even within the United States, the company had strong competition from local producers in markets outside the Chicago area.

However, Grieve realized that something had to be done. It was losing customers overseas to local suppliers, and it was beginning to experience competition from abroad. Top management realized it needed to combat the competition or lose the market entirely. In 1992, Patrick J. Calabrese, Grieve's president, attended a one-day seminar featuring the U.S. ambassadors to the ASEAN countries. He left that seminar convinced there might be strong market opportunities in one of the world's fastest-growing regions. However, he was not familiar with the market, and the company had no sales offices or representatives in the ASEAN countries. He also was concerned about the British, German, and Japanese competition already entrenched in that market.

To learn more about the market, Calabrese worked with a representative of the Chicago office of the International Trade Administration of the U.S. Department of Commerce's U.S. & Foreign Commercial Service. This office helped him plan a trip to Asia by arranging for interpreters at each stop on his itinerary and meetings with U.S. embassy personnel. His trip was intended primarily to determine market potential and identify possible agents. Calabrese had received inquiries from some distributors that were familiar with Grieve's product line; however, he had not pursued them. In addition to these distributors, Calabrese used the U.S. Department of Commerce's Agent/Distributor Service to identify several other possible distributors. After researching their product lines, Calabrese narrowed the list to the most likely candidates. He then developed company literature for each country and price lists for the product line. All of this information was forwarded in advance to the potential agents.

The trip was a big success for Grieve. Interviews were held with twenty-eight potential agents over twenty-eight days, and exclusive agents were signed up in each country. Each agent then completed a training session that familiarized the agent with Grieve and its products. The company subsequently placed firm orders through several of these new agents. It also identified several trade shows at which its products could be displayed.

Calabrese quickly learned that he had to cut shipping costs. So Grieve redesigned its packaging to be more compact. In addition, it began shopping among freight forwarders to find the best rates, which varied depending on the forwarder's experience and its relationship with a particular steamship company.

Calabrese also learned how important it was for him to visit potential customers in Asia personally rather than relying on a sales manager. He said:

> The one thing that I found is that almost to an individual [Asian customers] are very keen on a personal association. If I were to give anybody advice, I would never send a second-level individual. Never send a marketing manager or sales manager; I would send a top manager. If your company isn't too large to prohibit it, I would send the president or chairman. On the other end, you are talking to the owner of a small distributer or the president of a small manufacturing company and you've got to meet them on an equal level. My limited experience is they are very cognizant of this; in other words, they are pretty much attuned to a president talking to a president. They also like to feel secure that they are dealing with someone who can make decisions.
>
> Another thing I found is that potential customers want to feel that you are financially secure and that you have sufficient funding to continue to work with them for a period of years, because it takes some time and some money on our end to get these people going.
>
> Follow-up is incredibly important. I heard all kinds of stories about American businessmen who would come over and spend a day and talk to potential customers and leave catalogues. Then the first time the potential customers would send a fax asking for information, they didn't hear from them for two weeks, and that just turns them right off.

Although Grieve faces high transport costs and significant competition from foreign companies as it works to penetrate foreign markets, top management is optimistic. The company has a good product. As Calabrese pointed out, "Our strength is that we are selling engineered products, using our forty-five years of expertise to build something for them."

Introduction

As the Grieve case demonstrates, successful exporting is a complex process. A company either makes what it sells or sells what it makes. Once it has identified the product it wants to sell, it must explore market opportunities, a process that involves a significant amount of market research that may or may not be supported by the home-country government. Next, it must develop a production strategy, prepare the goods for market, determine the best strategy for getting the goods transported to market, sell the product, and receive payment. All of these steps require careful planning and preparation. The Grieve case demonstrated that a company has limited capabilities. Without a separate export staff, it must rely on specialists such as freight forwarders to move goods from one country to another, agents or distributors to sell the products, banks to collect payment, and, often, the U.S. & Foreign Commercial Service to identify market opportunities and potential distributors.

Research conducted on the characteristics of exporters has focused on two basic propositions:

1. The probability of being an exporter increases with company size.
2. Export intensity is positively correlated with company size.

The research has definitely confirmed the first proposition but not the second. The first proposition is based on the idea that small companies can grow in the domestic market and avoid undertaking the risks of exporting, but large companies must export if they are to increase sales.[2] The exceptions are small high-tech or highly specialized companies that operate in market niches with a global demand and small companies that sell expensive capital equipment.[3]

A good example of this idea in operation is found in the United States. As noted in Table 14.1, the largest exporters in the United States in terms of export revenues are also among the elite of the Fortune 500 largest industrial companies. Only nineteen of the top fifty exporters are not among the fifty largest U.S. industrial corporations, and all but four of the fifty largest exporters are among the hundred largest U.S. companies. However, there are some differences among the top U.S. exporters. The number one exporter, Boeing, manufactures all its airplanes in the United States, and exports accounted for 57.5 percent of its total sales in 1992. For second-place GM, exports accounted for only 10.6 percent of total sales. In addition, most of GM's exports were intracompany transfers of components from the United States to manufacturing facilities in foreign locations rather than sales to final consumers. It is estimated that intracompany sales make up one quarter of all U.S. exports.[4] In addition, one fifth of U.S. exports are generated by U.S. affiliates of foreign companies. The top four foreign exporters from the United States in 1992 were Toyota ($2 billion), Matsushita ($1.537 billion), Honda ($1.483 billion), and Siemens ($780 million).[5]

U.S. trade data from 1991 confirm that smaller exporters make smaller shipments (approximately $25,000 per shipment), and bigger exporters make bigger shipments (approximately $40,000 each). As Figure 14.1 shows, shipments worth $100,000 and up accounted for 56 percent of the total dollar value of exports; however, they accounted for only 5 percent of the total number of shipments.[6] Thus 95 percent of export shipments but only 44 percent of export volume comes from approximately 94,000 small U.S. exporters.

The probability of a company's being an exporter increases with the size of the company.

Export intensity is *not* positively correlated with company size.

The largest exporters in the United States also are among the largest industrial corporations.

Smaller exporters make smaller shipments; larger exporters make larger shipments.

Table 14.1

Top Fifty U.S. Exporters

The largest U.S. exporters are primarily aircraft, automobile, computer, and food products companies. Most of these major exporters generate at least 10 percent of total sales from exports.

Rank 1992	Rank 1991	Company (headquarters)	Major exports	U.S. Exports 1992 (millions of dollars)	U.S. Exports Percent change from 1991	U.S. Exports As percentage of total sales %	U.S. Exports Rank	Total Sales 1992 (millions of dollars)	Total Sales Fortune 500 rank
1	1	Boeing (Seattle)	Commercial aircraft	17,486.0	(2.1)	57.5	1	30,414.0	12
2	2	General Motors (Detroit)	Motor vehicles and parts	14,045.1	(6.8)	10.6	35	132,774.9	1
3	3	General Electric (Fairfield, Conn.)	Jet engines, turbines, plastics, medical systems	8,200.0	(4.8)	13.2	27	62,202.0	5
4	4	IBM (Armonk, N.Y.)	Computers and related equipment	7,524.0	(1.9)	11.6	31	65,096.0	4
5	5	Ford Motor (Dearborn, Mich.)	Motor vehicles and parts	7,220.0†	(1.6)	7.2	45	100,785.6	3
6	6	Chrysler (Highland Park, Mich.)	Motor vehicles and parts	7,051.8	14.3	19.1	14	36,897.0	11
7	7	McDonnell Douglas (St. Louis)	Aerospace products, missiles, electronic systems	4,983.0	(19.1)	28.5	6	17,513.0	23
8	12	Philip Morris (New York)	Tobacco, beverages, food products	3,797.0	24.0	7.6	42	50,157.0	7
9	11	Hewlett-Packard (Palo Alto, Calif.)	Measurement and computation products, systems	3,720.0	15.4	22.6	10	16,427.0	24
10	8	E.I. Du Pont de Nemours (Wilmington, Del.)	Specialty chemicals	3,509.0	(7.9)	9.4	38	37,386.0	8
11	14	Motorola (Schaumburg, Ill.)	Communications equipment, semiconductors	3,460.0	18.2	25.9	8	13,341.0	32
12	10	United Technologies (Hartford, Conn.)	Jet engines, helicopters, cooling equipment	3,451.0	(3.8)	15.7	17	22,032.0	16
13	9	Caterpillar (Peoria, Ill.)	Heavy machinery, engines, turbines	3,341.0	(9.9)	32.8	4	10,194.0	44
14	13	Eastman Kodak (Rochester, N.Y.)	Imaging, chemicals, health products	3,220.0	6.6	15.6	18	20,577.0	19
15	15	Archer Daniels Midland (Decatur, Ill.)	Protein meals, vegetable oils, flour, grain	2,700.0	3.8	28.9	5	9,344.1	50
16	17	Intel (Santa Clara, Calif.)	Microcomputer components, modules, and systems	2,339.0	21.3	39.1	3	5,985.4	91
17	16	Digital Equipment (Maynard, Mass.)	Computers and related equipment	1,900.0	(13.6)	13.5	24	14,027.1	27
18	18	Allied-Signal (Morristown, N.J.)	Aircraft and automotive parts, chemicals	1,810.0	4.7	15.0	21	12,089.0	36
19	20	Unisys (Blue Bell, Pa.)	Computers and related equipment	1,795.8	12.4	21.3	11	8,421.9	62
20	19	Sun Microsystems (Mountain View, Calif.)	Computers and related equipment	1,783.6	11.1	49.2	2	3,627.9	139
21	21	Raytheon (Lexington, Mass.)	Electronic systems, engineering and construction projects	1,760.0	13.1	19.3	13	9,118.8	54
22	22	Weyerhaeuser (Tacoma, Wash.)	Pulp, newsprint, paperboard, logs, lumber	1,500.0	(3.2)	16.2	16	9,259.9	51
23	25	Merck (Rahway, N.J.)	Health care products, specialty chemicals	1,489.8	11.0	15.2	20	9,800.8	47
24	26	Minnesota Mining & Manufacturing (St. Paul, Minn.)	Industrial, electronic, and health care products	1,433.0	12.4	10.3	36	13,883.0	28
25	31	Westinghouse Electric (Pittsburgh)	Electrical products and electronic systems	1,360.0	19.2	11.2	32	12,100.0	35
26	*	IBP (Dakota City, Neb.)	Fresh/frozen beef, pork, and related by-products	1,300.0	30.3	11.7	30	11,129.7	42
27	33	Xerox (Stamford, Conn.)	Copiers, printers, document processing services, supplies	1,292.0	24.2	7.1	46	18,089.0	21
28	23	Dow Chemical (Midland, Mich.)	Chemicals, plastics, consumer specialties	1,247.0	(9.4)	6.5	47	19,080.0	20
29	29	Textron (Providence, R.I.)	Aerospace and commercial products	1,244.0	6.2	14.9	22	8,347.5	63
30	27	International Paper (Purchase, N.Y.)	Pulp, paperboard, wood products	1,200.0‡	—	8.8	40	13,600.0	31
31	*	RJR Nabisco Holdings (New York)	Food and tobacco	1,171.0	16.9	7.4	43	15,734.0	26

(cont.)

Table 14.1 (cont.)

Rank 1992	Rank 1991	Company (headquarters)	Major exports	U.S. Exports 1992 (millions of dollars)	Percent change from 1991	As percentage of total sales %	Rank	Total Sales 1992 (millions of dollars)	Fortune 500 rank
32	28	Union Carbide (Danbury, Conn.)	Chemicals, plastics	1,125.0	(6.3)	18.2	15	6,167.0	88
33	37	Compaq Computer (Houston)	Computers and related equipment	1,104.0§	16.2	26.7	7	4,132.2	119
34	30	Hoechst Celanese (Bridgewater, N.J.)	Chemicals, plastics, fibers	1,072.0	(7.4)	15.2	19	7,044.0	77
35	38	FMC (Chicago)	Armored military vehicles, chemicals	997.7	9.3	25.0	9	3,992.4	125
36	35	Abbott Laboratories (Abbott Park, Ill.)	Drugs, diagnostic equipment	996.7	4.1	12.6	29	7,894.2	56
37	39	Miles (Pittsburgh)	Chemicals, health care and imaging products	956.0**	9.0	14.7	23	6,499.0	82
38	*	Apple Computer (Cupertino, Calif.)	Computers, related equipment	934.7	20.8	13.2	26	7,086.5	76
39	32	Monsanto (St. Louis)	Food ingredients, herbicides, chemicals, drugs	927.0	(17.8)	10.9	34	8,485.0	60
40	43	Bristol-Myers Squibb (New York)	Drugs, medical devices, consumer products	915.0†	13.4	7.8	41	11,805.0	40
41	45	Exxon (Irving, Texas)	Petroleum, chemicals	906.0	21.8	0.9	50	103,547.0	2
42	34	Aluminum Co. of America (Pittsburgh)	Aluminum products	886.0	(8.4)	9.2	39	9,588.4	49
43	*	Georgia Pacific (Atlanta)	Pulp, building products, containerboard, paper	859.0	30.0	7.3	44	11,847.0	39
44	44	Lockheed (Calabasas, Calif.)	Aerospace products, electronics, missile systems	831.0	24.8	10.0	37	10,138.0	45
45	42	Honeywell (Minneapolis)	Building, industrial, and aviation control systems	830.0	2.7	13.3	25	6,254.0	86
46	40	Cooper Industries (Houston)	Petroleum and industrial equipment	805.0	(3.6)	13.1	28	6,158.5	89
47	*	Cummins Engine (Columbus, Indiana)	Diesel engines, diesel engine parts	781.0	48.5	20.8	12	3,749.2	132
48	46	Deere (Moline, Ill.)	Farm and industrial equipment	778.0	9.1	11.2	33	6,960.7	79
49	48	Tenneco (Houston)	Farm, construction, and automobile equipment	702.0	1.4	5.2	49	13,606.0	30
50	41	Rockwell Intl. (El Segundo, Calif.)	Electronics, auto parts, high-speed printing presses	701.0	(15.3)	6.4	48	10,995.1	43
Totals				135,440.2				1,055,383.8	

*Not on last year's list
†Fortune estimate
‡Excludes some U.S. exports
§Exports from United States and Canada
**Owned by Bayer AG, Germany

Source: From Fortune, *6/14/93. © Time Inc. All rights reserved.*

494

**Figure 14.1
Export Shipments of
Various Sizes as
Percentages of Total
Dollar Value of Exports**
Out of a total dollar value
of $420 billion, over half is
accounted for by large
shipments valued at
$100,000 or higher.

Source: SED's Bureau of Census,
© Copyright 1992, Trade Data
Reports, Inc.

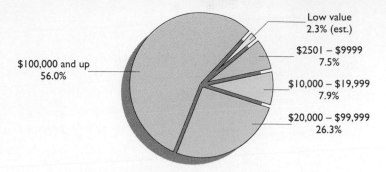

Total value of exports = $420 billion

**For many large exporters,
exports are a small percentage of their total sales.**

However, the data does not support the proposition that export intensity is positively correlated with company size. This proposition is based on the premise that as companies grow, exporting becomes a proportionally larger percentage of their total sales. It assumes small companies have limited resources, lack the scale economies in manufacturing that would allow them to export, and perceive a high risk to exporting. However, many of the larger exporters have a small percentage of exports to total sales (see Table 14.1). Thus, although several studies have shown some correlation between company size and initiation of export activity, they do not support the fact that smaller companies do not export or that larger ones continue to rely more on exports.[7]

Grieve is a perfect example illustrating these concepts. Although considered a small company in terms of total sales, its export revenues are significant and are the key to its survival. It must export in order to maintain its market share abroad and its competitive position in the United States relative to foreign suppliers.

Export Strategy

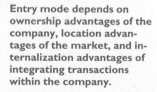

**Entry mode depends on
ownership advantages of the
company, location advan-
tages of the market, and internalization advantages of
integrating transactions
within the company.**

Demand in foreign countries can be serviced in various ways. The choice of entry mode is a function of different factors, such as the ownership advantages of the company, location advantages of the market, and internalization advantages of integrating transactions within the company.[8] Ownership advantages relate to specific assets and are a function of company size, international experience, and ability to develop differentiated products. For example, Boeing trades on its ownership advantage through the development of sophisticated aircraft; doing the same would be difficult for a new entrant to the market to duplicate. Location advantages of the market are a combination of market potential (the size and growth potential of the market) and investment risk. For example, Southeast Asia possesses location advantages due to being one of the world's fastest-growing regions, a major reason why Grieve decided to explore that area as an export market. Internalization advantages refer to the benefits of holding onto specific assets or skills within the company and integrating them into its activities rather than licensing or selling them. For example, Grieve Corporation could have explored licensing its technology to manufacturers in Southeast Asia but preferred to maintain control over its technology and serve Southeast Asia through exports from its own U.S. plants.

In general, companies that have lower levels of ownership advantages either do not enter foreign markets or use low-risk entry modes such as exporting. Exporting also requires a lower level of investment than do other modes, such as foreign investment, but it offers a lower risk/return alternative. Exporting allows significant management operational control but does not provide as much marketing control, since the exporter is farther from the final consumer and often must deal with independent distributors abroad that control many of the marketing functions.[9]

However, the choice of exporting as an entry mode is not just a function of these ownership, location, and internalization advantages. It also is a function of the company's overall strategy. This is illustrated by the following questions, which any company must consider before it decides to enter the export market:

- What does the company want to gain from exporting?
- Is exporting consistent with other company goals?
- What demands will exporting place on its key resources—management and personnel, production capacity, and financing—and how will these demands be met?
- Are the expected benefits worth the costs, or would company resources be better used for developing new domestic business?[10]

These are strategic questions that must take into account global concentration, synergies, and strategic motivations. Global concentration refers to the fact that many global industries have only a few major players, and a company's strategy for penetrating a particular market might be a function of what competitors are doing. Global synergies arise when the company's specific inputs, such as R&D, marketing, or manufacturing, are shared by its subunits worldwide. Global strategic motivations refer to the reasons why a company might want to enter a market. For example, it might enter a market in a specific country as a means of combating a competitor in that market, not just because of specific market or profit potential.[11]

Exporting occurs for several good reasons. Raw materials must be exported to the manufacturer, components to the assembly operation, and finished goods to foreign distributors and consumers. Sometimes this process occurs within the confines of a vertically integrated company, allowing the exporter to sell directly to the next level through an intracompany transaction. In many cases, however, the sale is to an outsider, and the exporter may sell directly to the buyer or indirectly through an intermediary.

Factors Favoring Exportation

The most common means by which companies begin international activity is through exporting. Even those with sizable foreign contractual arrangements and investments usually continue to export to achieve their overall objectives.

Exporting
• **Expands sales**
• **Achieves economies of scale in production**
• **Is less risky than FDI**
• **Allows the company to diversify production locations**

Companies get involved in exporting primarily to increase sales revenues. This is true for service companies as well as manufacturers. Many of the former, such as advertising and public accounting firms, export their services to meet the needs of clients working abroad. Grieve, a manufacturer, exported products to clients that had moved abroad. Companies that are capital- and research-intensive, such as biotechnology and pharmaceutical companies, must export in order to spread their capital base over a larger sales volume.

Export sales also can be a means of alleviating excess capacity in the domestic market. Also, some companies export rather than investing abroad because of the perceived high risk of operating in foreign environments. Finally, many export to a variety of different markets as a diversification strategy. Since economic growth is not the same in every market, broadly based exports allow a company to take advantage of strong growth in one market to offset weak growth in another. For example, Grieve is developing markets in Southeast Asia to expand its sales base and diversify its markets from strictly U.S. sales.

Stages of Export Involvement

Many companies begin exporting by accident rather than by design. Consequently, they tend to encounter a number of unforeseen problems. They also may never get a chance to see how important exports can be. For these reasons, developing a good export strategy is important.

As Figure 14.2 shows, there are five stages of export involvement:

1. Partial interest in exporting
2. Exploring exporting
3. Experimental exporter
4. Experienced exporter with limited scope
5. Experienced exporter

These stages are not based on company size but rather on degree of export involvement—both large and small companies can be at any stage.

Research on these stages has identified a number of interesting points:

As companies move from partial interest in exporting to being experienced exporters, they tend to export to more countries and expect exports as a percentage of total sales to grow.

• Company size (as measured by total employment) generally is larger the higher the stage of export involvement.
• However, the average size of companies in Stage 2 is larger than that of those in Stage 3.
• Some executives of larger companies in Stage 2 are reactively drawn into exporting because of competitive pressures. Clearly, this was the case for Grieve.
• Companies in Stage 2 and above plan to increase the number of countries to which they will export in the future, but this is not true of those in Stage 1.
• As a corollary to the preceding point, companies in Stage 2 and higher expect that exports as a percentage of total sales will continue to grow. This is not true of companies in Stage 1.

- As companies progress from Stage 1 to Stage 5, their managers tend to increase their personal foreign travel experience and interest in foreign culture.[12]

One could assume that Grieve fits somewhere between Stage 4 and Stage 5.

**Figure 14.2
Stages of Export
Development**
As companies gain greater expertise and experience in exporting, they diversify their markets to countries that are farther away or have business environments that differ from that of their home country.

Source: From "State Government Promotion of Manufacturing Exports: A Gap Analysis," Masaaki Kotabe and Michael R. Czinkota, *Journal of International Business Studies,* Vol. 23, No. 4, Fourth Quarter 1992, p. 642. Reprinted with permission.

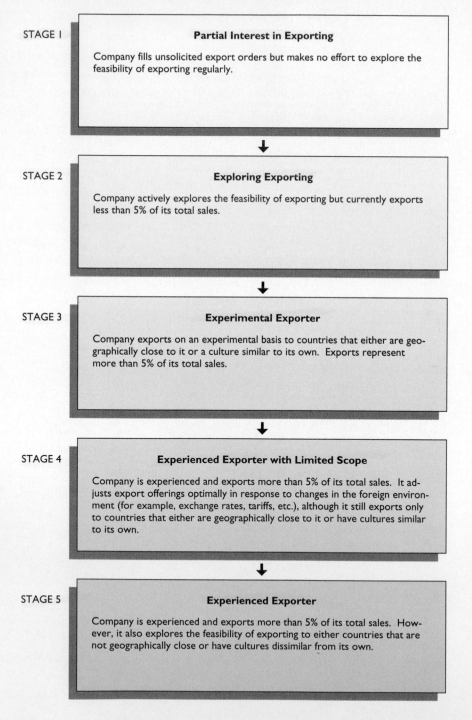

STAGE 1

Partial Interest in Exporting

Company fills unsolicited export orders but makes no effort to explore the feasibility of exporting regularly.

STAGE 2

Exploring Exporting

Company actively explores the feasibility of exporting but currently exports less than 5% of its total sales.

STAGE 3

Experimental Exporter

Company exports on an experimental basis to countries that either are geographically close to it or a culture similar to its own. Exports represent more than 5% of its total sales.

STAGE 4

Experienced Exporter with Limited Scope

Company is experienced and exports more than 5% of its total sales. It adjusts export offerings optimally in response to changes in the foreign environment (for example, exchange rates, tariffs, etc.), although it still exports only to countries that either are geographically close to it or have cultures similar to its own.

STAGE 5

Experienced Exporter

Company is experienced and exports more than 5% of its total sales. However, it also explores the feasibility of exporting to either countries that are not geographically close or have cultures dissimilar from its own.

Potential Pitfalls

To understand the important elements in an export strategy, it is important first to identify the major problems that exporters often face. Aside from problems that are common to international business in general and not unique to exporting, such as language and other culturally related factors, the following mistakes, identified by the U.S. Department of Commerce, are among those most frequently made by companies new to exporting:

1. Failure to obtain qualified export counseling and to develop a master international marketing plan before starting an export business
2. Insufficient commitment by top management to overcome the initial difficulties and financial requirements of exporting
3. Insufficient care in selecting overseas agents or distributors
4. Chasing orders from around the world instead of establishing a base of profitable operations and orderly growth
5. Neglecting export business when the U.S. market booms
6. Failure to treat international distributors on an equal basis with their domestic counterparts
7. Unwillingness to modify products to meet other countries' regulations or cultural preferences
8. Failure to print service, sales, and warranty messages in locally understood languages
9. Failure to consider use of an export management company or other marketing intermediary when the company does not have the personnel to handle specialized export functions
10. Failure to consider licensing or joint-venture agreements (This factor is especially critical in countries that have import restrictions.)[13]

These mistakes do not necessarily reflect the major problems that exporters themselves are concerned about, although there is some overlap. The list of export-related problems given in Figure 14.3 focuses more on the procedural issues that managers face once their companies become involved in exporting.

Designing an Export Strategy

Designing an export strategy involves the following steps:

In designing an export strategy, a company must
- **Assess export potential**
- **Get expert counseling**
- **Select market or markets**
- **Set goals and get the product to market**

- *Assess the company's export potential by examining its opportunities and resources.* It would not be smart to commit to exporting if the company does not have the production capacity to deliver the product.
- *Obtain expert counseling on exporting.* Most governments provide assistance for their domestic companies, although the extent of commitment varies by country. For U.S. companies, the best place to start is with the nearest International Trade Administration (ITA) office. Such assistance is invaluable in helping an ex-

EXPORT-RELATED PROBLEMS

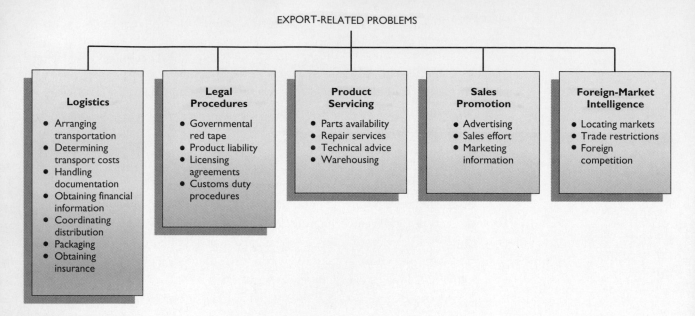

Logistics	Legal Procedures	Product Servicing	Sales Promotion	Foreign-Market Intelligence
• Arranging transportation • Determining transport costs • Handling documentation • Obtaining financial information • Coordinating distribution • Packaging • Obtaining insurance	• Governmental red tape • Product liability • Licensing agreements • Customs duty procedures	• Parts availability • Repair services • Technical advice • Warehousing	• Advertising • Sales effort • Marketing information	• Locating markets • Trade restrictions • Foreign competition

Figure 14.3
Export-Related
Problems
The five major categories of export-related problems are logistics, legal procedures, product servicing, sales promotion, and foreign-market intelligence.

Source: From "State Government Promotion of Manufacturing Exports: A Gap Analysis," Masaaki Kotabe and Michael R. Czinkota, *Journal of International Business Studies,* Vol. 23, No. 4, Fourth Quarter 1992, p. 651. Reprinted with permission.

porter get started. In the Grieve case, for example, Calabrese used a lot of information provided by the U.S. government to learn about Asian markets. Other government agencies also assist exporters. As a company's export plan increases in scope, it probably will want to secure specialized assistance from banks, lawyers, freight forwarders, export management companies, export trading companies, and others.

• *Select a market or markets.* This key part of the export strategy may be done passively or actively. In the former case, the company learns of markets by responding to requests from abroad that result from trade shows, advertisements, or articles in trade publications. A more active approach is that taken by Grieve's Calabrese, who selected Southeast Asia as an area for export development as a result of a seminar he attended featuring the U.S. ambassadors to the ASEAN countries. A company also can determine the markets to which products like its own are currently being exported. For example, *U.S. Census Trade Statistics* identifies the markets for different classifications of exports, and the National Trade Data Bank (NTDB) provides specific industry reports for different countries. The NTDB is updated monthly, so potential exporters can get the most recent studies.

• Regardless of how the company obtains market information, it is important that it pick a market or markets in which to concentrate a push strategy. Because national markets differ, the company should focus on a few key markets rather than try to develop global expertise all at once. Often, the initial markets are geographically close to the company's home country or are in countries that closely resemble the home country culturally. For both of these reasons, Canada and the United Kingdom are important to U.S. exporters. Once the primary, secondary, and tertiary markets have been determined, the company needs to research each to determine their major economic trends.

- *Formulate an export strategy.* This step usually involves considering the following factors: the company's export objectives, both immediate and long term; specific tactics the company will use; a schedule of activities and deadlines that will help the company achieve its objectives; and the allocation of resources to accomplish the different activities.
- *Determine how to get the goods to market.*

It is important that a company organize its exporting efforts. Table 14.2 provides a sample business plan a company can use to establish a specific export strategy. It requires the company to understand its expertise in export procedures as well as to gauge the availability of corporate resources to support exporting.

Export Intermediaries

A company that either exports or is planning to export must decide whether certain essential activities are to be handled by its own staff or through contracts with other companies. The following functions must be carried out:

1. Stimulate sales, obtain orders, and do market research
2. Make credit investigations and perform payment collection activities
3. Handle foreign traffic and shipping
4. Act as support for the company's overall sales, distribution, and advertising staff

Companies use external specialists for exporting before developing internal capabilities.

Performing these functions can be costly and can require expertise a company doesn't have. Thus most companies initially use external specialists and/or intermediary organizations to assume some or all of these functions, although a company later may develop in-house capabilities to perform them. Specialists are useful for such duties as preparing export documents, preparing customs documents in the importing country, and identifying the best means of transportation. And most companies can benefit at some time from using an intermediary organization. Some of these act as agents on behalf of the exporter, and some take title to the goods and sell them abroad. Others are involved in certain specialized aspects of the export process; for example, a freight forwarder is responsible for moving the products from the domestic to foreign markets.

Companies may market their products either directly or indirectly through external specialists or intermediary organizations.

A company that is determining whether to market a product directly using its own staff or indirectly using external specialists and/or intermediary organizations must consider company size, nature of the product, previous export experience and expertise, and business conditions in the selected foreign markets.[14]

Table 14.2
An Export Business Plan
When establishing an export business plan, management needs to assess the company's strengths, determine one or two markets for initial concentration, and commit time and resources to developing personnel and supporting the export activities.

I.   **Executive summary**
   A. Key elements of the plan
   B. Description of business and target markets
   C. Brief description of management team
   D. Summary of financial projections

II. **Business history**
   A. History of company
   B. Products/services offered and their unique advantages
   C. Domestic-market experience
   D. Foreign-market experience
   E. Production facilities
   F. Personnel—international experience and expertise
   G. Industry structure, competition

III. **Market research**
   A. Target countries
      1. Primary
      2. Secondary
      3. Tertiary
   B. Market conditions in target countries
      1. Existing demand
      2. Competition
      3. Strengths and weaknesses of the economy—barriers to entry, etc.

IV. **Marketing decisions**
   A. Distribution strategies
      1. Indirect exporting
      2. Direct exporting
      3. Documentation
      4. Direct investment, strategic alliances
   B. Pricing strategy
   C. Promotion strategy

V.   **Legal decisions**
   A. Agent/distributor agreements
   B. Patent, trademark, copyright protection
   C. Export/import regulations
   D. ISO 9000
   E. Dispute resolution

VI. **Manufacturing and operations**
   A. Location of production facilities for exports
   B. Capacity of existing facilities
   C. Plans for expansion
   D. Product modification necessary to adapt to local environment

VII. **Personnel strategies**
   A. Personnel needed to manage exports
   B. Experience and expertise of existing personnel
   C. Training needs of existing personnel
   D. Hiring needs in the short term and long term

VIII. **Financial decisions**
   A. Pro forma financial statements and projected cash flows assuming export activity
   B. Identification of key assumptions
   C. Current sources of funding—private and bank funding
   D. Financial needs and future sources of funding
   E. Tax consequences of export activity
   F. Potential risk and sources of protection

IX. **Implementation schedule**

Direct Selling

Exporters undertake **direct selling** to give them greater control over the marketing function and to earn higher profits. When selling direct, a manufacturer normally sells to retailers, but it may sell to a sales representative or agent operating on a commission basis or to a foreign distributor who takes title to the product and earns a profit on the final sale to the consumer.

A **sales representative** resembles a manufacturer's representative in the United States. The representative usually operates either exclusively or nonexclusively within an assigned market and on a commission basis, without assuming risk or responsibility. For example, Grieve's agents operated on an exclusive basis in their respective markets. A **distributor** in a foreign country is a merchant that purchases the products from the manufacturer and sells them at a profit. Distributors usually carry a stock of inventory and service the product. They also typically deal with retailers rather than end users in the market.

Companies should consider the following points about each potential foreign sales representative or distributor:

- The size and capabilities of its sales force
- Its sales record
- An analysis of its territory
- Its current product mix
- Its facilities and equipment
- Its marketing policies
- Its customer profile
- The principals it represents and the importance of the inquiring company to its overall business
- Its promotional strategies[15]

Foreign retailers are outlets primarily for consumer goods and can be serviced by traveling salespeople or by catalogs or trade fairs. Sales of products manufactured to specification, however, are made directly to the end user. This practice is more common in industrial marketing than in consumer marketing.

A company that has sufficient financial and managerial resources and decides to export directly rather than working through an intermediary must set up a solid organization. This organization may take any number of forms ranging from a separate international division, to a separate international company, to full integration of international and domestic activities. Whatever the form, there commonly is an international sales force separate from the domestic sales force because of the different types of expertise required in dealing in foreign markets.

Indirect Selling

In **indirect selling,** the exporter deals through an indirect intermediary, which is another domestic company, before entering the international marketplace. That in-

Direct selling involves sales representatives, agents, distributors, or retailers.

A sales representative usually operates on a commission basis.

A distributor is a merchant who purchases the products from the manufacturer and sells them at a profit.

Commission agents work for the buyer.

termediary may act as a **commission agent** for the manufacturer and not take title. The commission agent usually acts on behalf of the foreign buyer and tries to find a specific product at the cheapest price. The agent is paid a commission by the foreign purchasing agent. An indirect intermediary also may purchase a product from the manufacturer and sell it abroad.

EMCs provide export services for a specific exporter or group of exporters.

The two major types of indirect intermediaries are the **export management company (EMC)** and **export trading company (ETC).** EMCs and ETCs sometimes act as agents operating on a commission and sometimes take title to the merchandise and earn income through the margin. The two differ in that an EMC is supply-driven and an ETC is demand-driven.

Export Management Companies

An EMC usually acts as the export arm of a manufacturer, although it also can deal in imports, and often uses the manufacturer's own letterhead in communicating with foreign sales representatives and/or distributors. The EMC's primary function is to obtain orders for its clients' products through the selection of appropriate markets, distribution channels, and promotion campaigns. It collects, analyzes, and furnishes credit information and advice regarding foreign accounts and payment terms. The EMC also may handle documentation, arrange transportation (including the consolidation of shipments to reduce costs), set up patent and trademark protection in foreign countries, and counsel and assist in establishing alternative forms of doing business, such as licensing or joint ventures.[16]

EMCs operate on a contractual basis, usually for two to five years, and provide exclusive representation in a well-defined foreign territory. The contract specifies pricing, credit and financial policies, promotional services, and basis for payment. An EMC might operate on the basis of a commission for sales (unless it takes title to the merchandise) and a retainer for other services. EMCs usually concentrate on complementary and noncompetitive products so that they can present a more complete product line to a limited number of foreign importers.

EMCs in the United States are mostly small, entrepreneurial ventures that tend to specialize by product, function, or market area.

In the United States, most EMCs are small, entrepreneurial ventures that tend to specialize by product, function, or market area. Although EMCs perform an important function for companies that need their expertise, a manufacturer that uses an EMC may lose control over foreign sales. Thus the manufacturer needs to balance the desire for control with the cost of performing the export functions directly.[17]

An example of an EMC is International Trade and Marketing Corp. (ITM), a Washington, D.C.–based EMC that has exclusive agreements with ten U.S. suppliers of orthopedic equipment and supplies. ITM specializes by product line but markets those lines worldwide. It takes title to 90 percent of the merchandise it sells and operates on a commission for the remaining 10 percent.[18]

Export Trading Companies

ETCs tend to operate on the basis of demand rather than supply.

In the fall of 1982, the U.S. government enacted the Export Trading Company Act, which removed some of the antitrust obstacles to the creation of ETCs in the United States. It was hoped that ETCs would lead to greater exports of U.S. goods and services. ETCs resemble EMCs but operate more on the basis of demand than of supply. ETCs are like independent distributors that match up buyers and sellers. ETCs find out what foreign customers want and then identify different domestic suppliers for the products. Rather than representing a manufacturer, an ETC looks for as many manufacturers as it can find to supply overseas customers.

Four major types of ETCs were identified in the U.S. legislation:

1. Newly formed ETCs that receive antitrust certification
2. ETCs organized by state and local governments
3. ETCs created by commercial banks
4. ETCs initially organized by U.S. companies to handle their own exports

The first type consists of business enterprises that would like to cooperate for foreign sales but have difficulty cooperating for domestic sales because of antitrust concerns. The U.S. government set strict guidelines on how companies qualify for exemption from antitrust considerations: Cooperation must not lessen competition in the United States. One example of the second type, ETCs organized by state and local governments, is the Port Authority of New York and New Jersey. This ETC, known as XPORT, courts smaller companies that produce high-technology products that have an export potential. Most large money-center banks have applied for permission to establish the third type of ETC. These applications must be approved by the Federal Reserve Board before the bank can start export operations. Many of the banks concentrate on customers in their geographical market and in parts of the world in which they already have a good banking network.

The fourth type of ETC consists of those initially set up by U.S. companies to handle their own export business. Many of these have expanded to include products produced by other companies. For example, Control Data's ETC was established to handle countertrade agreements for sales of products to Eastern European countries as well as developing countries. Then it began aggressively seeking products of other companies.

However, the ETC concept has not really taken hold in the United States. It has worked well for undifferentiated products such as agricultural products but not for differentiated products that require significant individual attention. In the United States, differentiated products are handled best by EMCs that specialize in those products.

Japanese Trading Companies

As mentioned above, EMCs and ETCs are small ventures in the United States. More than 60 percent of the export intermediaries that responded to a U.S. Department of Commerce survey in 1989 stated that they employ six or fewer persons. Their gross revenues also tend to be small. Because of their size, most EMCs and ETCs specialize by product line and by geographical area.

ETCs can be formed by
• Competitors and be exempt from antitrust laws
• State and local governments
• Money-center banks
• Major corporations

Japanese trading companies are known as *sogo shosha.*

However, this is not true of the European and Asian trading companies, which tend to be quite large. When one thinks of trading companies, the giants such as Mitsui, Marubeni, and Mitsubishi of Japan come to mind. The **sogo shosha,** the Japanese equivalent word for trading company, can trace its roots back to the late nineteenth century, when Japan embarked on an aggressive modernization process. At that time, the trading companies were referred to as *zaibatsu,* large, family-owned businesses composed of financial and manufacturing companies usually held together by a large holding company. These companies were very powerful, so U.S. General Douglas MacArthur broke them up after World War II and made many of their activities illegal.

The *sogo shosha* initially took the primary role of acquiring raw materials for Japan's industrialization process and then finding external markets for its goods. When these trading companies were first organized after World War II, their primary functions were handling paperwork for import and export transactions, financing imports and exports, and providing transportation and storage services. However, their operations expanded significantly to include investing in production and processing facilities, establishing fully integrated sales systems for certain products, expanding marketing activities, and developing large bases for the integrated processing of raw materials.[19]

Japanese trading companies are the world's largest companies in terms of sales.

Japanese trading companies are part of bank-centered *keiretsu* or industrial-group *keiretsu.*

Although there are thousands of trading companies in Japan, the sixteen major ones control a majority of Japan's exports and imports. Table 14.3 illustrates the size of the largest *sogo shosha* relative to other large companies in the world. Of the ten largest companies in the world in terms of sales, six are the Japanese trading companies listed in the table. The *sogo shosha* generate tremendous sales volumes, even though they are not very profitable and their global ranking in terms of market value is not significant. For example, of the world's top one hundred firms in terms of market value, only one Japanese trading company is listed—Mitsubishi Corporation at number ninety-seven. Even in Japan, the trading companies are not significant in terms of market value, but seven of the ten largest companies in Japan measured in terms of revenues are trading companies.[20]

Table 14.3
The World's Top Ten Corporations in Sales Revenues
Japanese trading companies dominate in terms of global sales revenue.

Rank/company	Sales (billions of U.S. dollars)
1. Itochu	180.0
2. Sumitomo Corp.	168.3
3. Mitsubishi Corp.	166.1
4. Marubeni	161.8
5. Mitsui & Co.	160.2
6. Exxon	117.0
7. General Motors	113.0
8. Nissho Iwai	105.6
9. Ford Motor	100.0
10. Toyota Motor	94.9

Source: Business Week, July 12, 1993.

Most *sogo shosha* are part of a larger corporate relationship called a **keiretsu.** Several, such as Mitsubishi, Mitsui, and Sumitomo, are in bank-centered *keiretsu.* Others are in industrial-group *keiretsu.* In a *keiretsu,* one company agrees to become a stockholder in another in order to build a long-term and very close business relationship. Mitsubishi Corporation, the *sogo shosha* of the group of Mitsubishi companies, has the advantage of working with very powerful financial and industrial partners.

The *sogo shosha* have faced various challenges recently, many of which have resulted from changes in both the Japanese and international economies. For example, banks that have become more internationally oriented have begun to dispute the trading companies' role in trade financing, and manufacturers are questioning their role in marketing. Generally, manufacturers turn away from the *sogo shosha* as several factors come into play:

Manufacturers turn away from trading companies if markets are large, technology is complex, or marketing requirements are specific.

- The market grows larger and more significant. An example is the relationship between Marubeni Corporation and Nissan. Marubeni has invested in automobile dealerships in Belgium to import Nissans. It also imports Nissans into Poland and other European countries, but Nissan exports directly to France, Germany, and the United Kingdom, its major European markets.[21]
- Technology becomes more complex. In this case the *sogo shosha* may have difficulty dealing with the product's technical requirements.
- The marketing and service requirements become more specific and involved.[22]

Finally, the *sogo shosha* are beginning to get more involved in foreign investment. The Japanese historically have preferred to sell abroad through exportation rather than through direct investment, the opposite of the strategy of U.S. companies. However, the nature of the international marketplace is causing the trading companies to consider increasing their direct investments because many of their client companies have their own manufacturing niches and have decided to expand these operations abroad.[23] This trend not only illustrates a change in locational strategy but also indicates a diversification of revenue base by the trading companies.

However, not all Japanese trading companies are large. Many of the smaller ones are similar to U.S. trading companies in that they have few employees and specialize in certain product lines. Many of these set up offices in the United States to import products from Japan and are trying to act as intermediaries for U.S. companies that want to export their products to Japan.[24]

Piggyback Exports

Piggyback exports are products exported by a company through another manufacturer's channels of distribution.

Sometimes an exporter can use another exporter as an intermediary. For example, a company may agree to supply products to a foreign distributor even though it does not produce the entire range of products. Then it might look for other manufacturers to fill the gaps in the product line. In this way, the second manufacturer becomes an exporter indirectly by using the first exporter's distribution channels.

Toys 'R' Us uses a variation on this idea. Many of the companies that supply products to Toys 'R' Us are not directly involved in exporting toys to other countries. However, when Toys 'R' Us began establishing stores overseas, it offered many of the same products as in its U.S. stores. Thus some suppliers became exporters through their continued relationship with Toys 'R' Us overseas. In its Japanese stores, for example, Toys 'R' Us initially provided a mixture of roughly two thirds Japanese toys and one third imports, including Huffy bikes, Mattel's Barbie dolls, and Tonka trucks.[25]

Foreign Freight Forwarders

A foreign freight forwarder is an export or import specialist dealing in the movement of goods from producer to consumer.

Dealing in air and ocean transportation involves a number of institutions and documentation with which the typical exporter does not have expertise. This is true even if the manufacturer is exporting components to a foreign subsidiary controlled by a common parent company. Commonly the services of a **foreign freight for-warder** are employed. Even export management companies and other types of trading companies often use the specialized services of foreign freight forwarders.

The typical freight for-warder is the largest export intermediary in terms of value and weight handled.

On average, the foreign freight forwarder is the largest export intermediary in terms of value and weight handled; however, the services offered are more limited than those of an EMC. The freight forwarder manages the movement of cargo from origin to destination. Once a foreign sale has been made, the freight forwarder acts on behalf of the exporter in obtaining the best routing and means of transportation based on space availability, speed, and cost. This process involves getting the products from the manufacturing facility to the air or ocean terminal and then overseas. The forwarder secures space on planes or ships and necessary storage prior to shipment, reviews the letter of credit, obtains export licenses, and prepares necessary shipping documents. It also may advise on packing and labeling, purchase transportation insurance, repack shipments damaged en route, and warehouse products, which saves the exporter the capital investment of warehousing.

The freight forwarder's compensation usually is a percentage of the shipment value, paid by the exporter, with a minimum charge dependent on the number of services provided. The forwarder also receives a brokerage fee from the carrier. Despite these costs, using a freight forwarder still is usually less costly for an exporter than providing the service internally, particularly since most companies find it difficult to utilize a traffic department full-time and to keep up with shipping regulations. The forwarder also provides the advantages of being able to get space more easily because of its close relationship with carriers and to consolidate shipments in order to obtain lower rates.

Air and Ocean Freight

Of total global trade, ninety-nine percent calculated by *weight* moves by ocean, but 34 percent calculated by *value* is shipped by air.[26] Although ocean freight is the cheapest way to move merchandise, it also is the slowest. Thus even though it still dominates global trade, its position is eroding somewhat. As mentioned in the opening case, Grieve's president believes in getting quotes from different freight forwarders when booking space on cargo ships. Ocean freight rates are based on space first, and weight second. Rate schedules also differ depending on the ports involved and the direction the goods travel. For example, different rates apply to shipments from the United States to Germany and to shipments from Germany to the United States. Forwarders help manufacturers get the best contract and help prepare the products for export. Exporters can load merchandise in a container for shipment overseas, or they can rely on a freight forwarder to consolidate their shipment with others in order to fill a container.

Ocean freight is dominant in terms of total weight of products traded, but air freight is significant in terms of value of products shipped.

Three trends favor the air-freight business: more frequent shipments, lighter-weight shipments, and higher-value shipments.[27] As companies attempt to lower carrying costs (inventory storage) and move to just-in-time inventory management, they must rely on quick and timely delivery of merchandise. Air freight is much more effective in accomplishing these objectives than is ocean freight.

Documentation

Freight forwarders also can help exporters fill out documents related to exporting. These documents differ from those used in domestic transportation, and most manufacturers need a freight forwarder to determine which are needed and how to complete them. One of these documents is an **export license.** Each country determines whether domestic products or products transshipped through its borders can be exported to certain countries. In the United States, an exporter needs to check with the U.S. Department of Commerce to determine if its products can be shipped under a general license or if they must be exported under an individually validated license (IVL). For example, exports of certain high-tech products might be restricted for national security reasons, so an exporter must apply for an IVL to determine whether the exportation is permitted.

Of the many documents that must be completed, some of the most important (excluding financial documents, which are discussed in the next section) are as follows:

- A *commercial invoice* is a bill for the goods from the buyer to the seller. It contains a description of the goods, the address of buyer and seller, and delivery and payment terms. Many governments use this form to assess duties.
- A *bill of lading* is a contract between the owner of the goods and the carrier (truck, rail, air, or ocean). The customer needs a copy of the bill of lading in order to take possession of the goods when they arrive in the foreign port.
- A *consular invoice* sometimes is required by countries as a means of controlling imports.
- A *certificate of origin* indicates where the products originate and usually is validated by an external source, such as the chamber of commerce. It helps countries determine the specific tariff schedule for imports.
- A *shipper's export declaration* controls exports and is used to compile trade statistics.
- An *export packing list* itemizes the material in each individual package, indicates the type of package, and is attached to the outside of the package. The list is used by the shipper or freight forwarder and sometimes by customs officials to determine the nature of the cargo and whether the correct cargo is being shipped.[28]

Export Financing

Three major issues relate to the financial aspects of exporting: the price of the product, the methods of payment, and the financing of receivables.

Product Price

Product pricing of exports involves many of the same factors that must be considered in domestic pricing, including the following:

- Quality perception of the product as conveyed through price
- Prices of competitive products

- Different prices for different market segments
- Extent of discounts and allowances

However, there also are some differences. A major consideration is how the price takes exchange rates into consideration. If the exporter bills in the home-country currency, the importer absorbs the foreign-exchange risk and must decide whether to pass on any exchange-rate differences to the consumer. If the exporter bills in the currency of the importer's country, the foreign-exchange risk falls on the exporter. Another difference between domestic and export pricing is that price escalation results because of transportation costs, duties, and multiple wholesale channels in the importing countries.

Finally, the price may depend on dumping laws in the importing country. Recall from Chapter 6 that dumping refers to the sale of exports below cost or below what they are sold for in the domestic market. In 1993, when the Japanese yen rose significantly against the U.S. dollar, U.S. automakers threatened to ask for dumping sanctions from the U.S. government unless Japanese automakers increased their prices to reflect the increased import costs. An exporter must be aware of the dumping laws in each foreign market and the degree to which these laws are enforced.

Methods of Payment

The flow of money across national borders is complex and requires the use of special documents. Foreign trade usually is financed on credit. Exporters rarely get paid right away because of collection and foreign-exchange problems.

In descending order in terms of security, the basic methods of payment for exports are

Methods of payment are
- **Cash in advance**
- **Letter of credit**
- **Documentary collection or draft**
- **Open account**
- **Consignment**
- **Countertrade**

- Cash in advance
- Letter of credit
- Documentary collection or draft
- Open account
- Other payment mechanisms, such as consignment sales or countertrade

If payment is to be made by a documentary collection or draft, also known as a *commercial bill of exchange,* the drawer (exporter) instructs the drawee (importer) to transfer the face amount on the bill of exchange at a given time. The transfer is made to a designated payee, possibly to the exporter's bank at which the drawer has an account, or directly to the exporter. If the exporter requests payment be made immediately, the exchange instrument is called a **sight draft.** If payment is to be made later, for example, thirty, sixty, or ninety days after delivery, the instrument is called a **time draft.** These drafts generally contain a significant amount of information about the shipment, and the terms need to be spelled out clearly. Bankers assist in establishing a commercial bill of exchange and usually charge the exporter a fee that is a small percentage of the amount of payment.

A letter of credit obligates the buyer's bank to pay the exporter.

With a bill of exchange, it is always possible the importer will not be able to make payment to the exporter at the agreed-upon time. A **letter of credit,** however, obligates the buyer's bank in the importing country to accept a draft (a bill of exchange) presented to it, provided the draft is accompanied by the prescribed documents. A documentary letter of credit stipulates that payment will be made by the bank on the basis of the documents, not on the terms of the sale. A letter of credit denominated in the exporter's currency means the exporter incurs no risk of loss as a result of possible exchange-rate fluctuations.

When an exporter requires a letter of credit, the importer is responsible for arranging for it at the importer's bank. An exporter that receives this guarantee from an importer's bank can rely on the credit of the bank in addition to the as yet unverified credit of the importer. This arrangement has the advantage of enabling the seller to draw a bill of exchange on the importer's bank rather than on the importer and therefore to have no difficulty in selling or discounting the draft. Figure 14.4 explains the relationships among the parties to a letter of credit.

A revocable letter of credit may be changed by any of the parties to the agreement.

An irrevocable letter of credit requires all parties to agree to a change in the documents.

A letter of credit can be revocable or irrevocable. A **revocable letter of credit** is one that can be changed by any of the parties involved. However, both exporter and importer may prefer an **irrevocable letter of credit** (see Fig. 14.5), which is a letter that cannot be canceled or changed in any way without the consent of all parties to the transaction. With this type of letter, the importer's bank is obligated to pay and is willing to accept any drafts (bills of exchange) at sight, meaning these drafts will be paid as soon as the correct documents are presented to the bank. It is important to note that all the conditions on the letter of credit— such as the method of transportation and the description of the merchandise—must be adhered to precisely by the exporter; otherwise, the letter of credit is invalid.

Figure 14.4
Letter-of-Credit Relationships
A letter of credit guarantees the exporter that the importer's bank will pay for the imports. The credit relationship exists between the importer and the importer's bank (the opening bank). A confirmed letter of credit has an added guarantee from the exporter's bank: If the importer's bank defaults, the exporter's bank must pay.

Source: Adapted from *Export and Import Financing Procedures* (Chicago: The First National Bank of Chicago), p. 22.

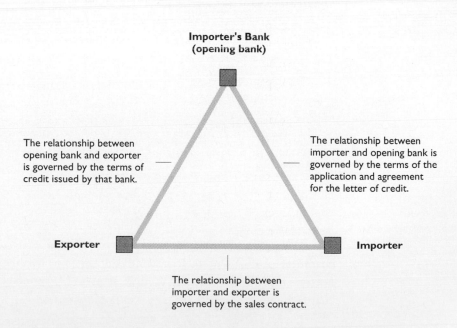

Importer's Bank (opening bank)

The relationship between opening bank and exporter is governed by the terms of credit issued by that bank.

The relationship between importer and opening bank is governed by the terms of the application and agreement for the letter of credit.

Exporter

Importer

The relationship between importer and exporter is governed by the sales contract.

Figure 14.5
An Export Letter of Credit

A letter of credit is a precisely worded document whose terms must be adhered to in order for the exporter to receive payment.

Source: Philadelphia National Bank, A CoreStates Bank

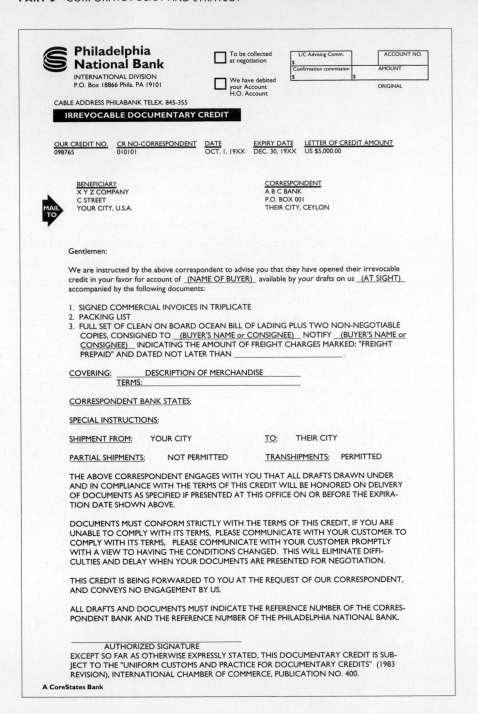

Gentlemen:

We are instructed by the above correspondent to advise you that they have opened their irrevocable credit in your favor for account of __(NAME OF BUYER)__ available by your drafts on us __(AT SIGHT)__ accompanied by the following documents:

1. SIGNED COMMERCIAL INVOICES IN TRIPLICATE
2. PACKING LIST
3. FULL SET OF CLEAN ON BOARD OCEAN BILL OF LADING PLUS TWO NON-NEGOTIABLE COPIES, CONSIGNED TO __(BUYER'S NAME or CONSIGNEE)__ NOTIFY __(BUYER'S NAME or CONSIGNEE)__ INDICATING THE AMOUNT OF FREIGHT CHARGES MARKED: "FREIGHT PREPAID" AND DATED NOT LATER THAN _____.

COVERING: _____ DESCRIPTION OF MERCHANDISE _____
TERMS: _____

CORRESPONDENT BANK STATES:

SPECIAL INSTRUCTIONS:

SHIPMENT FROM: YOUR CITY   TO: THEIR CITY

PARTIAL SHIPMENTS: NOT PERMITTED   TRANSHIPMENTS: PERMITTED

THE ABOVE CORRESPONDENT ENGAGES WITH YOU THAT ALL DRAFTS DRAWN UNDER AND IN COMPLIANCE WITH THE TERMS OF THIS CREDIT WILL BE HONORED ON DELIVERY OF DOCUMENTS AS SPECIFIED IF PRESENTED AT THIS OFFICE ON OR BEFORE THE EXPIRATION DATE SHOWN ABOVE.

DOCUMENTS MUST CONFORM STRICTLY WITH THE TERMS OF THIS CREDIT, IF YOU ARE UNABLE TO COMPLY WITH ITS TERMS, PLEASE COMMUNICATE WITH YOUR CUSTOMER TO COMPLY WITH ITS TERMS, PLEASE COMMUNICATE WITH YOUR CUSTOMER PROMPTLY WITH A VIEW TO HAVING THE CONDITIONS CHANGED. THIS WILL ELIMINATE DIFFICULTIES AND DELAY WHEN YOUR DOCUMENTS ARE PRESENTED FOR NEGOTIATION.

THIS CREDIT IS BEING FORWARDED TO YOU AT THE REQUEST OF OUR CORRESPONDENT, AND CONVEYS NO ENGAGEMENT BY US.

ALL DRAFTS AND DOCUMENTS MUST INDICATE THE REFERENCE NUMBER OF THE CORRESPONDENT BANK AND THE REFERENCE NUMBER OF THE PHILADELPHIA NATIONAL BANK.

_____
AUTHORIZED SIGNATURE
EXCEPT SO FAR AS OTHERWISE EXPRESSLY STATED, THIS DOCUMENTARY CREDIT IS SUBJECT TO THE "UNIFORM CUSTOMS AND PRACTICE FOR DOCUMENTARY CREDITS" (1983 REVISION), INTERNATIONAL CHAMBER OF COMMERCE, PUBLICATION NO. 400.

A CoreStates Bank

A confirmed irrevocable letter of credit adds an obligation to pay for the exporter's bank.

A letter of credit transaction may involve a confirming bank in addition to the parties mentioned above. With a **confirmed letter of credit,** the exporter has the guarantee of a bank in the exporting country as well as the guarantee of the importer's bank. If this letter of credit is irrevocable, none of the conditions can be changed unless all four parties to it agree in advance.

An exporter occasionally may sell on **open account.** This means the necessary shipping documents are mailed to the importer before any payment from or definite obligation on the part of the buyer. Releasing goods in this manner is somewhat unusual because the exporter risks default by the buyer. An exporter ordinarily sells under such conditions only if it successfully conducted business with the importer for an extended time. This is generally the arrangement used when the importer and exporter are related entities.

Financing Receivables

A cash-flow analysis can help an exporter determine if it has sufficient working capital to carry it from production through collection. The increased distances and time involved in exportation can create cash-flow problems for the exporter. This is especially true if the exporter extends payment through a time draft.

Because exporting is risky, banks often are unwilling to provide funding for it. This is a major problem for small exporters that do not have the working capital to sustain themselves over the long timeline between production and payment. They complain that banks will not fund small needs for working capital arising from exporting but provide funding readily to domestic clients that are greater credit risks. Small exporters need to find a way to guarantee their export revenues so that banks will lend them working capital.

One approach for doing this is to apply for governmental guarantees. The U.S. government, for example, provides funding under the programs of the **Export-Import Bank (Eximbank).** Eximbank provides loans directly to public or private buyers abroad, loans to financial intermediaries that make loans to international buyers, and guarantees to banks that lend to foreign buyers. It also provides lines of credit or guarantees to creditworthy exporters for up to 85 percent of the U.S. export value of each covered transaction.[29] Further, it gives U.S. exporters access to export-related loans from financial institutions.

The U.S. Department of Agriculture provides guarantees for U.S. bank financing of foreign purchases of U.S. agricultural products. These guarantees are made in cases in which exports would not be possible without the credit.

Small U.S. exporters also can take advantage of the International Trade Loan Program of the Small Business Administration (SBA), which guarantees long-term financing to help them establish or expand international operations. Loans of up to $1 million for facilities and $250,000 for working capital are available. The major criticism of the SBA guarantees is the huge volume of paperwork necessary to apply for one.

Insurance is provided by two major agencies: Eximbank and the **Overseas Private Investment Corporation (OPIC).** These are the major risks covered by OPIC:

- Inability to convert into dollars the local currency that is received by the investor as profits, earnings, or return on the original investment
- Loss due to expropriation, nationalization, or confiscation by action of a foreign government

- Loss due to political violence such as war, revolution, insurrection, and/or civil strife
- Loss of business income due to interruption of the business caused by political violence or expropriation[30]

These risks relate primarily to foreign investment. However, insurance also can cover exposure to loss on cash flows arising from various contractual arrangements.

Eximbank has many insurance programs. One of the most important is the new-to-export policy, which is short-term (up to 180 days) and available to small businesses as defined by the SBA. Eximbank assumes 95 percent of the commercial risk and 100 percent of the political risk involved in extending credit to the exporter's overseas customers.

In addition to U.S. government guarantees, various state and local guarantees are available. Further, each country has its own approach to export assistance in the financial area. Companies that do not pay attention to working capital needs and potential risks may find themselves out of cash and thus lose interest in the export market.

Countertrade

Countertrade refers to any one of a number of different arrangements by which goods and services are traded for each other.

Countertrade often takes place because of a foreign-exchange shortage.

Sometimes countries have so much difficulty generating enough foreign exchange to pay for imports that they need to devise creative ways to get the products they want. Although this shortage of foreign exchange is associated primarily with HPEs and developing countries, it also can affect industrial countries. For example, Canada and Australia found they had to enter into special agreements with McDonnell-Douglas to pay for military aircraft they wanted to purchase. Thus, both companies and governments often are forced to resort to creative ways of settling payment, many of which involve trading goods for goods as part of the transaction. **Countertrade** refers to any one of several different arrangements by which goods and services are traded for each other, on either a bilateral or a multilateral basis. More specifically, it is defined as "… a practice whereby a supplier commits contractually—as a condition of sale—to reciprocate and undertake certain specified commercial initiatives that compensate and benefit the buyer."[31] Countertrade is significant today because of credit shortages and a lack of hard currency in many countries, especially in the countries of the former Soviet Union.

Barter

Barter occurs when goods are traded for goods.

Barter, the oldest form of countertrade, is a transaction in which goods are traded for goods of equal value without any flow of cash. Many problems attend the negotiating of a barter agreement. Nevertheless, there are recent examples of successful bartering.

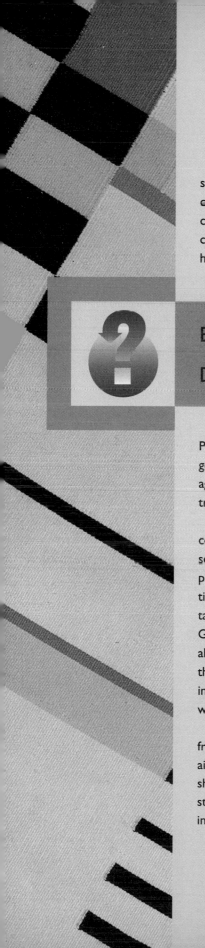

A major area of concern for some companies is the exportation of hazardous substances, especially pesticides and chemicals. Generally, companies should accept the ethical norms of a host country for products that are exported to it; however, regulations concerning pesticides are more lax in many developing countries than they are industrial countries. Thus exporting pesticides or harmful chemicals that are illegal in a company's home country but not in the host country raises an ethical dilemma. There is a major argument over the concept of prior informed consent (PIC), which would require each exporter of a banned or restricted chemical to obtain through its home-country government the express consent of the importing country to receive the banned or restricted substance. Countries favoring the PIC concept argue that many developing countries are not adequately informed of the danger of certain chemicals and therefore need the assistance of industrial countries. Those against PIC argue that this principle infringes on the national sovereignty of importing countries and replaces their ethical norms with those of the exporting country.[32]

ETHICAL DILEMMAS

Governments often control the export of so-called sensitive technology to certain countries. Before the Iron Curtain fell in 1989, Toshiba shipped to the former Soviet Union sensitive technology that could be used in submarine warfare. The company transshipped products through different ports in order to disguise the sale and shield itself from prosecution. However, this illegal activity was eventually uncovered. Another example of the exportation of sensitive technology involves the arming of Saddam Hussein prior to the Persian Gulf War. A British company was found guilty of exporting a large gun, disguised as industrial pipes, that could be used as an offensive weapon. The company lied about the nature of the export but eventually was found out. In addition, German companies were guilty of selling to Libya chemicals that could be used in chemical warfare. In these cases, documents were falsified to keep the authorities from finding out the transactions' true nature.

Sometimes shippers lie to freight forwarders about the nature of their products. One freight forwarder was working with a company that was shipping large drums to Sweden by air. The forwarder asked the shipper if the drums contained hazardous materials, and the shipper said no. In fact, unfortunately, the drums contained a very toxic material. This substance leaked through the drum and ate through the bottom of a 747 just as it was landing in Sweden.

For example, prior to the convertibility of the Russian ruble, PepsiCo agreed to swap Pepsi syrup and bottling equipment for Russian vodka, and Occidental Petroleum arranged sales of fertilizer plants and pipelines to the former Soviet Union in exchange for ammonia. Figure 14.6 illustrates how a barter transaction was structured involving the trading company Marc Rich and the Ukraine government. According to the agreement, Marc Rich provided 300,000 tons of raw sugar to Ukraine, where the sugar was refined. Marc Rich then received as payment 20 percent of the refined sugar and some of Ukraine's sugar harvest.[33]

Offset Trade

> In offset trade, the exporter sells goods for cash but then undertakes to promote exports from the importing country in order to help it earn foreign exchange.

Another type of countertrade, called **offset trade,** is becoming increasingly important. Under an offset agreement, a U.S. company, for example, exports merchandise to a foreign country and receives hard currency for the sale. However, it agrees with the foreign country to offset that outward flow of hard currency by creating export opportunities for businesses in that country so that they can earn hard currency.

A good example of how a company might have to deal with offset trade involves McDonnell-Douglas and the sale of F-18A fighter aircraft to Canada in 1980. This sale was to net McDonnell-Douglas nearly $3 billion, a significant amount of money for one transaction. Over the eight-year period specified for delivery dates, Canada would average imports of several hundred million dollars per year. Given the weakness of the Canadian dollar in relation to the U.S. dollar at the time of the sale, this significant increase in imports concerned the Canadian government. Consequently, the negotiations for the sale of the aircraft involved not only the technical capabilities of the F-18As and their cost but also the industrial benefits that McDonnell-Douglas could promise the Canadian government. The Canadian offset agreement covered fifteen years with a three-year grace period. The total program commitment of $2.9 billion must be covered from the following three areas: aerospace and electronics (minimum 60 percent), advanced technology (minimum 6 percent), and diversified activities (maximum 40 percent). The aerospace and electronics area, the most important of the three, involves designated production, co-production, technology transfer, and joint R&D. The diversified activities portion of the offset agreement involves investment/technology development, export development, and tourism development.

Figure 14.6
A Barter Transaction
The trading company, Marc Rich, provides raw sugar from country A to Ukraine (country B), where it is refined. Parts of the refined sugar and some of Ukraine's sugar harvest are shipped back to Marc Rich to be sold on world markets. The proceeds of these sales will compensate the trading company for the initial shipment of raw sugar.

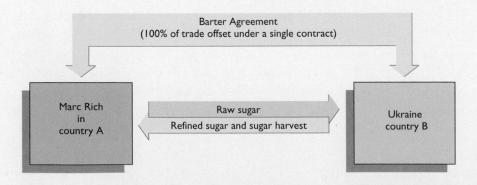

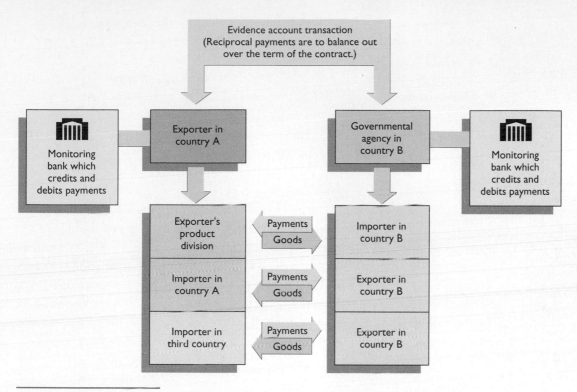

Figure 14.7
An Offset Transaction
In this form of counter-trade, the exporter (in country A) is required to find ways for the importing country (country B) to earn foreign exchange to pay for the exports.

Source: From Pompiliu Verzariu, *Countertrade, Barter, Offsets,* © 1985, New York: McGraw-Hill, p. 32. Reprinted with permission.

Another example of an offset transaction is Caterpillar's satisfaction of a countertrade obligation with the state of Western Australia by selling an Australian-produced high-speed ferry to the Philippines for A$15 million. For its part, Caterpillar is supplying the marine engines for the vessel.[34]

Figure 14.7 shows how a complex transaction such as the F-18A sale to Canada might be structured. As noted in the figure, the transaction involves the primary exporter, the importing government, and other secondary exporters and importers.

Whether companies become involved in the complexities of offset trade depends mainly on the strength of demand for their products, whether they have alternative sources of supply, and the extent of foreign-exchange problems in the buying country. In any case, offset trade results primarily from foreign-exchange shortages and is a good example of how companies and governments can compensate for such a shortage through creative business transactions.

The Import Strategy

Importers need to be concerned with procedural and strategic issues.

There are two different types of considerations for potential importers: procedural and strategic. Procedural considerations relate more to the rules and regulations of the customs agency of a country. Strategic issues refer to the long-term reasons why a company would rather buy products from foreign than domestic sources.

The following procedural steps must be considered by an importer once a foreign source for products has been determined:

- Ship the products to the importing country by air, land, or ocean
- Clear customs
- Pay the exporter
- Store the products until they can be sold
- Sell the products and collect payment

An import broker is an intermediary that helps an importer clear customs.

Importing requires a certain degree of expertise in dealing with institutions and documentation, which a company may not have aquired. Consequently, the company may elect to work through an **import broker.** The import broker is a person who obtains various governmental permissions and other clearances before forwarding necessary paperwork to the carrier that is to deliver the goods from the dock to the importer. Import brokers in the United States are certified as such by the U.S. Customs Service to perform the functions necessary to bring products into the country. In some cases, personnel working for intermediaries such as public accounting firms, freight forwarders, and EMCs are certified as import brokers.

The Role of Customs Agencies

Customs agencies assess and collect duties and ensure import regulations are adhered to.

When importing goods into any country, a company must be totally familiar with the customs operations of the importing country. In this context, "customs" refers to the country's import and export procedures and restrictions, not its cultural aspects. The primary duties of the U.S. Customs Service, for example, are "the assessment and collection of all duties, taxes, and fees on imported merchandise, the enforcement of customs and related laws, and the administration of certain navigation laws and treaties." As a major enforcement organization, it "combats smuggling and frauds on the revenue and enforces the regulations of numerous other Federal agencies at ports of entry and along the land and sea borders of the United States."[35] An importer needs to know how to clear goods, the duties that must be paid, and the special laws that exist.

On the procedural side, when merchandise reaches the port of entry, the importer must file documents with customs officials in which a tentative value and tariff classification are assigned to the merchandise. The U.S. government has over 10,000 tariff classifications, and approximately 60 percent of them are subject to interpretation; that is, a particular product could fit more than one classification. Then customs officials examine the goods to determine whether there are any restrictions on their importation. If there are none, the importer pays the duty and the goods are released. The amount of the duty depends on the product's country of origin, the type of product, and other factors.[36]

A broker or other import consultant can help an importer minimize import duties by doing the following:

- *Valuing products in such a way that they qualify for more favorable duty treatment.* Different product categories have different duties. For example, finished goods typically have a higher duty than do parts and components.

- *Qualifying for duty refunds through drawback provisions.* Some exporters use in their manufacturing process imported parts and components on which they paid a duty. In the United States, the drawback provision allows exporters to apply for a refund of 99 percent of the duty paid on the imported goods, provided the goods are used in the manufacture of goods that are exported.

- *Deferring duties by using bonded warehouses and foreign trade zones.* Companies do not have to pay duties on imports stored in bonded warehouses and foreign trade zones until the goods are removed for sale or used in a manufacturing process.

- *Limiting liability by properly marking an import's country of origin.* Because governments assess duties on imports based in part on the country of origin, a lower duty on an import may be had by ensuring that the import's country of origin is accurate. For example, in the United States, if an article or its container is not properly marked when it enters the country, a marking duty equal to 10 percent of the customs value of the article is assessed.[37]

Drawback provisions are an important part of the U.S. tariff code because they encourage domestic manufacturing by allowing U.S. companies to use foreign components in the manufacturing process without having to include the duty paid on the merchandise in costs and sales prices. A direct identification drawback is permitted on imported merchandise that is actually used to manufacture goods for export, provided the imported goods are not used for final consumption in the United States and are exported within five years of the import date. Sometimes domestic merchandise is substituted for merchandise that was imported for eventual export, in which case substitution drawback is permitted for duties on the imported merchandise.

Documentation

When a shipment arrives at a port, the importer must file specific documents with the port director in order to take title to the shipment. Some of the documents relate directly to customs and determine whether or not the importer has the right to bring the products into the country. These documents are of two different types: those that determine whether customs will release the shipment, and those that contain information for duty assessment and statistical purposes.[38] The specific documents required by customs vary by country but include an entry manifest, a commercial invoice, and a packing list. For example, the commercial invoice, prepared by the exporter, contains information such as the port of entry to which the merchandise is destined, information on the buyer and seller, a detailed description of the merchandise, the purchase price of the item and the currency used for the sale, and the country of origin.

Other documents refer to the transfer of title from the exporter to the importer. One such document is the **bill of lading.** The bill of lading serves as a receipt for goods delivered to the common carrier for transportation, a contract for

---

Margin notes:

Drawback provisions allow U.S. exporters to apply for a refund of 99 percent of the duty paid on imported components, provided they are used in the manufacture of goods that are exported.

Importers must submit to customs documents that determine whether the shipment is released and what duties are assessed.

A bill of lading is a document that determines who has title over the shipment.

the services to be rendered by the carrier, and a document of title.[39] Usually, it requires the transportation company to retain control of the goods until the importer has fulfilled the financial obligations of the sale. As mentioned earlier in this chapter, the exporter might require the importer to obtain a letter of credit with the importer's bank. When the merchandise arrived at the port of entry, the bill of lading would require that the bank be notified of the arrival. The bank would then notify the importer so that the payment process could be put into motion.

Many small companies also are successful exporters.

COUNTERVAILING FORCES

The export strategy outlined in this chapter is based on the perspective of a company's efforts to penetrate foreign markets through goods or services manufactured or developed in the home country. However, many exports are intracompany in nature. For example, Ford might manufacture carburetors in Italy, export them to a Ford assembly plant in Germany, and export the final product—automobiles—to consumers in Belgium. Such intracompany shipments tend to fulfill a global strategy of production, assembly, and sales to the consumer. This strategy is investigated in more detail in Chapter 18. However, when Grieve is determining how to sell its ovens in different world markets, it examines each market separately and tries to ascertain how to adapt its product to consumer's needs in each country.

An article on mini-nationals, that is, companies with average sales of $600 million, pointed out that successful exporters in this size category must keep focused—they must concentrate on being number one or number two in technology niches they have developed.[40] This competitive strategy applies to countries as well. Some of the industrial and newly industrializing countries of Asia—such as Hong Kong, Japan, Korea, Singapore, and Taiwan—have grown rapidly through exporting. They have established fiscal and monetary policies and provided direct governmental assistance in promoting exports, thus creating jobs and significant wealth. Japan's huge trade surplus with the rest of the world—especially with the United States and Europe—has created considerable ill will, which in turn has resulted in pressure on Japan to correct its trade imbalance. In response to this pressure, some companies have voluntarily reduced their exports in order to help the Japanese government improve the country's relations with the rest of the world.

Multilateral trade groups such as the EU and NAFTA are designed to eliminate tariff and nontariff barriers in order to spur exports. However, exporters still find numerous trade barriers that keep them from selling their products in foreign markets. Countries are challenged to continue their cooperation in reducing trade restrictions so that exporters can increase their access to markets and operate in a more stable and predictable environment.

LOOKING TO THE FUTURE

Exporting continues to differ among countries in terms of its importance in generating GDP and, therefore, jobs. When the global economy is growing and barriers come down, exports tend to increase. When the world is in an economic slowdown, as in 1992–1993, nontariff barriers to trade combine with low demand to slow the rate of export growth. Thus any predictions of export activity are directly tied to predictions of economic growth. And future economic growth is tied to efforts to reduce trade barriers. Examples of these efforts are the EU and NAFTA. When barriers to trade rise, exporters from large countries such as the United States pull back their exporting efforts and focus on domestic markets.

Advances in transportation and communications will continue to facilitate export growth and make it easier for companies to get involved in global activity. One example of advances in communication is electronic data interchange, the electronic movement of information. As freight forwarders continue to automate, they become able to transmit documents electronically, which will reduce border delays in getting goods to market. Also, advances in communications will allow shippers to track shipments more accurately so that they can predict when the shipments will arrive in port to be claimed by the importer.

An area in which companies probably will receive little relief in the next few years is governmental assistance, especially in the financial area. Most industrial countries have serious federal budget deficits, a result of economic slowdown and reduced tax receipts, and so have been forced to privatize and cut governmental services. One of those areas affected will be exports. In the United States, for example, cutbacks in funding to the Department of Commerce, the SBA, and Eximbank have made it more difficult for exporters to get assistance, especially access to loan guarantees. This situation will not improve soon; thus pressure will continue on the small exporter to penetrate markets alone.

Summary

- **The probability of a company's becoming an exporter increases with company size, but the extent of exporting does not directly correlate with size.**

- ***Fortune*'s top fifty exporters account for 30 percent of U.S. exports; smaller companies tend to have smaller-sized shipments on average than do larger ones.**

- **Companies new to exporting (and also some experienced exporters) often make many mistakes. One way to avoid those is to develop a comprehensive export strategy that includes an analysis of the company's resources as well as of market opportunities.**

- **Companies get involved in exporting to increase sales revenues, utilize excess capacity, and diversify markets.**

- **As a company establishes its export business plan, it must assess export potential, obtain expert counseling, select a market or markets, formulate its strategy, and determine how to get its goods to market.**

- **Exporters may deal directly with agents or distributors in a foreign country or indirectly through export management companies or other types of trading companies.**

- Trading companies, such as the Japanese *sogo shosha,* can perform many of the functions that manufacturers lack the expertise for. In addition, exporters can use the services of other specialists, such as freight forwarders, to facilitate exporting. These specialists can help an exporter with the complex documentation that accompanies exports.

- There are three major issues that relate to the financial aspects of exporting: the price of the product, the method of payment, and the financing of receivables.

- Export prices are a function of domestic pricing pressures, the impact of exchange rates, and price escalation due to longer channels of distribution, tariffs, and so forth.

- In descending order in terms of security, the basic methods of payment for exports are cash in advance, letter of credit, documentary collection or draft, open account, and other payment mechanisms such as consignment sales or countertrade.

- A letter of credit is a financial document that obligates the importer's bank to pay the exporter.

- Governmental agencies in some countries, such as Eximbank in the United States, provide assistance in terms of direct loans to importers, bank guarantees to fund exporters' working-capital needs, and insurance against commercial and political risk.

Case
Sunset Flowers of
New Zealand, Ltd.[41]

After eighteen months of residing in the United States, John Robertson, a New Zealander, glances frequently at a map of the United States on his wall, wondering when he will get the time and resources to travel into the various metropolitan areas of the central, southern, and eastern states. Through such travel, he believes, he can gain an improved appreciation of the characteristics of the markets for fresh-cut flowers, an item that he began importing into the United States from New Zealand during his summer "vacation" from school.

In August 1981, Robertson and his family left New Zealand for Seattle so he could study for his MBA degree at the University of Washington. A month earlier, he had resigned from his job and leased their house and small farm. On completion of the degree, the Robertsons intended to return to New Zealand, where John would seek employment in a senior management position with a company involved in exporting.

New Zealand is a country the size of Oregon with a population of 3 million. The relatively small size of its population base coupled with its distance from world markets (see Map 14.1) inhibits its ability to establish an industrial base competitive with those of the

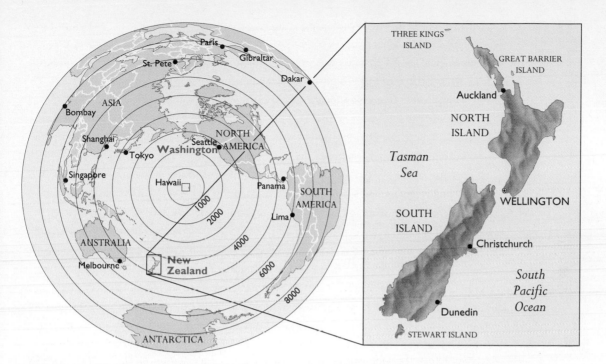

Map 14.1
New Zealanders' View of the World

New Zealand is an industrial country that is one of only two OECD members in the Southern Hemisphere. The great distance from this country to major world markets, such as the United States, is an important barrier that an exporter such as Sunset Flowers of New Zealand needs to overcome.

world's leading industrial countries. Therefore New Zealand depends heavily on world trade, importing fuel and manufacturing products and gaining most of its foreign exchange through exports of agricultural produce. Its f.o.b. exports average around 22 percent of its GDP, compared with the U.S. figure of 8 percent (f.o.b. stands for "free on board," which includes the cost of the product to the city of export but excludes international shipping costs). To hold its place in the world economy, New Zealand lobbies hard to remove the restrictions imposed on imported agricultural products by the EU, Japan, and the United States. Along with this campaign, efforts are being made to diversify into horticultural products such as fresh flowers and fruit.

Immediately prior to leaving New Zealand, Robertson had worked for almost four years as the financial manager of a company involved in growing, wholesaling, and exporting live ornamental trees and shrubs. To sell its products on world markets, the company used agents, including two based in the United States, one in Japan, and one in Europe. The agents were paid retainers and typically provided services for several exporters. The experience gained from working for this company provided Robertson with a background in the procedures necessary for exporting. It also gave him insight into the problems that exporters face when trying to compete in foreign markets, where control over representation is hindered by distance and lack of knowledge of business procedures.

It was while working for this company that Robertson was introduced to cut-flower products. The Robertsons raised enough money to purchase a farm and then became acquainted with their neighbors, the Pratts, who were first-class horticulturalists. The Pratts had developed a new variety of the Leucadendron plant that yielded a beautiful, red leaflike flower, which the Robertsons and Pratts felt could be exported successfully.

During their first year of production, the Robertsons and Pratts formed a new entrepreneurial venture. They exported their yield through an established export company whose principal line of business was exporting fresh fruit and vegetables. The company had a large market share of this business and also had assumed a significant share of the exports of cut flowers from New Zealand. The New Zealand cut-flower export industry was small and, with the exception of trade in orchids, immature. Export companies provided the many part-time cut-flower growers with the marketing infrastructure that they themselves were unable to put together.

As the harvesting season progressed, the returns paid to the venture by the exporter declined until they reached a point at which production levels of 10,000 stems or fewer became only marginally profitable. Gary Pratt and John Robertson met with the exporter to discuss the trends. The exporter explained that price was a function of volume and that the lower prices resulted from the increased volumes of cut flowers being placed on world markets. Export market returns were substantiated by documentation.

Pratt and Robertson were not convinced by the explanation. However, they knew little about world markets for fresh-cut flowers, and they could only speculate as to the reasons for the price movements. As there were no other established cut-flower export companies to turn to, the only way to research the matter seemed to be to do so themselves. Robertson's going to the United States for his MBA studies presented the opportunity to carry out some research there.

During his first semester of school, Robertson had little time to do research. At the end of the winter quarter of 1982, when he picked up a sample cart of Leucadendron flowers consigned by Pratt to him at Sea-Tac Airport, his ideas on how to approach the market were not yet defined. He took the flowers home and, on inspection, found that they had kept well in transit and their quality was good.

In the six days remaining before school began again, Robertson decided to concentrate on researching the production and shipping costs associated with the product, production forecasts, import procedures, the basic structure of the U.S. cut-flower industry, and market reaction to the Leucadendron.

When he had picked up the samples from the airport, Robertson had been told by airline officials that if he was going to undertake imports of invoice value greater than $250, he would have to engage the services of a customs broker. Presuming such brokers to be the experts on import procedures, he made an appointment with one. The broker was most helpful. Imported cut flowers had to be inspected by the U.S. Department of Agriculture (USDA) on arrival. Once given clearance, duty was assessed at the rate of 8 percent on f.o.b. value. The broker would arrange for these clearances through the USDA and the U.S. Customs Service. The broker would charge a fee for such services. Robertson learned that this fee is fixed for shipments regardless of size but varies among brokers; the broker with whom the meeting was held charged $50 per shipment. The broker also volunteered to arrange for freight forwarding companies to handle transportation to foreign markets.

As Robertson prepared his market strategy, he consulted numerous U.S. publications that helped him get a feel for the U.S. market. In addition, he asked Pratt to mail him a copy of a market-research publication funded by the New Zealand Export-Import Corpo-ration that included research on the U.S. flower market. From that publication, he learned that the major agricultural exports from New Zealand in order of importance were kiwi fruit, apples, berryfruit, processed kiwi fruit, flowers and plants, squash, frozen vegetables, onions, and other products.

Robertson finally contacted a Seattle wholesaler who was willing to place a large order for flowers, provided he was given exclusive rights to distribute the flowers in Washington State. Robertson was pleased with the reaction from the wholesaler but was aware that he had made the approach with insufficient preparation. Had he underpriced the product? Was the wholesaler's credit sound? Were exclusive rights typically given in this industry, and should he have conceded them? Was the reaction one that is normal when a new product is shown to a market? Would repeat orders be placed? In addition to these market-related issues, there were administrative and organizational issues to consider. What should be his role in the marketing chain? Should he act as an agent taking a commission or buy from Pratt and resell the product? What form of organization should he establish?

Questions

1. What were the issues that Robertson had to consider in developing his strategy for ex-porting flowers from New Zealand to the United States?
2. What were the intermediaries that Robertson used, and what roles did they play?
3. What did Robertson have to worry about in terms of import procedures?
4. What role should Robertson play in the marketing chain, and why?

Chapter Notes

1. "Exporting Pays Off," *Business America,* May 17, 1993, p. 19; and interview with Mr. Patrick J. Calabrese, president of Grieve Corporation.
2. Andrea Bonaccorsi, "On the Relationship Between Firm Size and Export Intensity," *Journal of International Business Studies,* Vol. 23, No. 4, Fourth Quarter 1992, p. 606.
3. Ibid.
4. Therese Eiben, "U.S. Exporters Keep on Rolling," *Fortune,* June 14, 1993, p. 130.
5. Ibid.
6. Leslie Stroh, "The Fact Sheet: Fishing Where the Trout Are," *Clearinghouse on State International Politics,* Vol. 3, No. 5, July 1993, p. 3.
7. Hans-Georg Gemunden, "Success Factors of Export Marketing: A Meta-Analytic Cri-tique of the Empirical Studies" in *New Per-spectives on International Marketing,* S. J. Paliwoda, ed. (London: Routledge, 1991); S. Tamer Cavusgil, "Organizational Char-acteristics Associated with Export Activi-ty," *Journal of Management Studies,* Vol. 21, No. 1, pp. 3–22; and Michael R. Czinkota and Wesley J. Johnston, "Ex-porting: Does Sales Volume Make a Dif-

ference?" *Journal of International Business Studies,* Vol. 14, Spring–Summer 1983, pp. 147–153.
8. John H. Dunning, "The Eclectic Para-digm of International Production: Some Empirical Tests," *Journal of International Business Studies,* Vol. 19, Spring 1988, pp. 1–31.
9. Sanjeev Agarwal and Sridhar N. Rama-swami, "Choice of Foreign Market Entry Mode: Impact of Ownership, Location and Internalization Factors," *Journal of In-ternational Business Studies,* Vol. 23, No. 1, First Quarter 1992, pp. 2–5.
10. U.S. Department of Commerce, *A Basic Guide to Exporting,* January 1992, p. 1-1.
11. W. Chan Kim and Peter Hwang, "Global Strategy and Multinationals' Entry Mode Choice," *Journal of International Business Studies,* Vol. 23, No. 1, First Quarter 1992, pp. 32–35.
12. Masaaki Kotabe and Michael R. Czinkota, "State Government Promotion of Manu-facturing Exports: A Gap Analysis," *Jour-nal of International Business Studies,* Vol. 23, No. 4, Fourth Quarter 1992, pp. 641–646.

13. "Ten Most Common Mistakes of New-to-Export Ventures," *Business America,* April 16, 1984, p. 9.
14. TransNational, Inc., *A Basic Guide to Export-ing* (Washington, D.C.: U.S. Department of Commerce, September 1986), p. 17.
15. U.S. Department of Commerce, op. cit., pp. 4–6.
16. Philip MacDonald, *Practical Exporting and Importing,* 2nd ed. (New York: Ronald Press, 1959), pp. 30–40; and TransNa-tional, Inc., op. cit., p. 17.
17. "Basic Question: To Export Yourself or To Hire Someone To Do It for You?" *Busi-ness America,* April 27, 1987, pp. 14–17.
18. Richard Barovick and Patricia Anderson, "EMCs/ETCs: What They Are, How They Work," *Business America,* July 13, 1992, p. 2.
19. Marubeni Corporation, *The Unique World of the Sogo Shosha* (Tokyo: Marubeni Cor-poration, 1978), p. 14.
20. *Forbes,* July 19, 1993, p. 142; and Larry Holyoke, Paula Dwyer, Steward Toy, and Christopher Power, "A Topsy-Turvy Year for Giants," *Business Week,* July 12, 1993, p. 53.

21. "Marubeni to Enter Car Dealer Business in Europe," *Agence France Presse*, August 21, 1993.
22. Kichiro Hayashi and Stefan H. Robock, "The Uncertain Future of the Japanese General Trading Companies," *Kajian Ekonomi Malaysia*, December 1982, p. 61.
23. Masaaki Kotabe, "Changing Roles of the Sogo Shoshas, the Manufacturing Firms, and the MITI in the Context of the Japanese 'Trade or Die' Mentality," *Columbia Journal of World Business*, Fall 1984, pp. 33–42.
24. Michael J. McDermott, "Language Limiting Smaller Trading Firms," *Crain's New York Business*, November 11, 1991, p. 29.
25. Robert Neff, "Guess Who's Selling Barbies in Japan Now?" *Business Week*, December 9, 1991, pp. 72–76.
26. E. J. Miller, "Trends Bode Well for Air," *Distribution*, July 1992, p. 36.
27. Ibid.
28. U.S. Department of Commerce, *A Basic Guide to Exporting*, pp. 12-2 and 12-3.

29. William A. Delphos, "Financing," *Business America*, March 25, 1991, p. 18.
30. Ibid., p. 22.
31. Pompiliu Verzariu, "Trends and Developments in International Countertrade," *Business America*, November 2, 1992, p. 2.
32. Tom L. Beauchamp and Norman E. Bowie, *Ethical Theory and Business*, 4th ed. (Englewood Cliffs, N.J.: Prentice-Hall, 1993), pp. 514–515.
33. "Marc Rich to Supply Ukraine with Sugar," *International Trade Finance*, March 21, 1993.
34. "Caterpillar Discharges Australian Trade Obligation," *International Trade Finance*, June 18, 1993.
35. U.S. Department of the Treasury, *Importing into the United States* (Washington, D.C.: Superintendent of Documents, U.S. Government Printing Office, May 1984), p. 28.
36. Robert P. Schaffer, "Maximize Your Import Profits . . . Minimize Your Customs Duties," *Review* (New York: Price Waterhouse).

37. Ibid.; and U.S. Department of the Treasury, U.S. Customs Service, *Importing into The United States* (Washington, D.C.: U.S. Government Printing Office, September 1991), p. 41.
38. U.S. Department of the Treasury, op. cit., p. 7.
39. Philadelphia National Bank, *International Trade Procedures* (Philadelphia, 1977), p. 30.
40. Stephen Baker, Kevin Kelly, Robert D. Hof, and William J. Holstein, "Mini-Nationals Are Making Maximum Impact," *Business Week*, September 6, 1993, pp. 66–69.
41. Adapted from Harry R. Knudson, "Sunset Flowers of New Zealand, Ltd.," *Journal of Management Case Studies*, Winter 1985, Volume 1, No. 4. Reprinted with permission.

Chapter 15

Collaborative Strategies

When one party is willing,
the match is half made.
—American Proverb

Objectives

- To explain the major motives that should guide companies in their choice of operational form for global business activities

- To differentiate the major operational forms by which companies may tap the potential of international business

- To describe the considerations that companies should explore when entering into international contractual arrangements with other companies

- To emphasize that multiple operational forms may exist simultaneously and that companies must develop means by which to coordinate these diverse activities

Case
Grupo Industrial Alfa
S.A. (GIASA)[1]

Mexican-based Grupo Industrial Alfa S.A. (GIASA), usually referred to as Alfa, is a true conglomerate. Its annual sales of over $2 billion make it Latin America's twenty-first largest company and Mexico's seventh largest. But most of the companies ranked ahead of Alfa are either state- or foreign-owned; thus Alfa is the fourth largest company in Latin America that is both privately and domestically owned.

From its founding in 1894 until 1974, Alfa's activities were part of a family enterprise in Monterrey controlled by the Garza and Sada families. During this time, the company had been affected only slightly by foreign competition. Its major lines of business—steel, beer, and banking—included products and services not easily imported into Mexico because steel imports were restricted and the other products and services usually needed to be produced near customers. There also were prohibitions against foreign ownership in these sectors. However, although the company was relatively immune from foreign competition, its outlook was for slow growth.

In 1973, the Mexican government sought to counter foreign control of companies by enacting laws that provided for restrictions on foreign equity in new ventures and on the expansion of existing investments having large foreign ownership. The Garza and Sada families saw these Mexicanization laws as an opportunity to diversify into growth industries that foreigners from that point on would find more difficult to control. They reasoned they might be able to buy some subsidiaries from foreign companies that were unwilling to accept minority ownership. They also reasoned they were in a good position to share in cooperative arrangements with foreign companies that sought business activities involving Mexico. Further, they felt that to capitalize on these possibilities, they would be better off shedding the family image. By extending ownership beyond the family, they could raise capital by selling additional shares. Further, good professional management could be attracted to the company. In 1974, they divided the enterprise into four companies—Alfa, Cydsa, Visa, and Vitro—and went public by issuing shares in each of them. At that time, the assets of the newly formed Alfa were estimated at $315 million, of which 75 percent was in steel (all monetary amounts in this case are in U.S. dollars). Alfa's management, with help from some top international consulting groups, agreed that diversification should be based on the objectives of minimizing cyclical changes in earnings, entering growth industries, and utilizing resources for which Mexico had advantages.

Between 1974 and 1976, Alfa expanded much less than had been anticipated but did manage to acquire the TV production facilities and brands of three U.S. companies: Philco, Magnavox, and Admiral. Through these acquisitions, Alfa captured 35 percent of Mexico's market for TV sets as well as the right to continue using the three trade names for sales in Mexico.

By 1980, Alfa had assets of $1.9 billion, sales representing 1.2 percent of Mexico's GDP, 157 subsidiaries, and 49,000 employees. Two events external to Alfa contributed to its growth. First, huge oil and natural gas reserves were discovered in Mexico. Second, a pro–private-enterprise president, José Lopez Portillo was elected. Lopez Portillo offered many incentives for industry, including nearly free energy. Suddenly foreign companies were rushing to find ways of expanding their business in Mexico. Most expansion had to involve Mexicans. Alfa was large, had good profitability, and possessed management that had

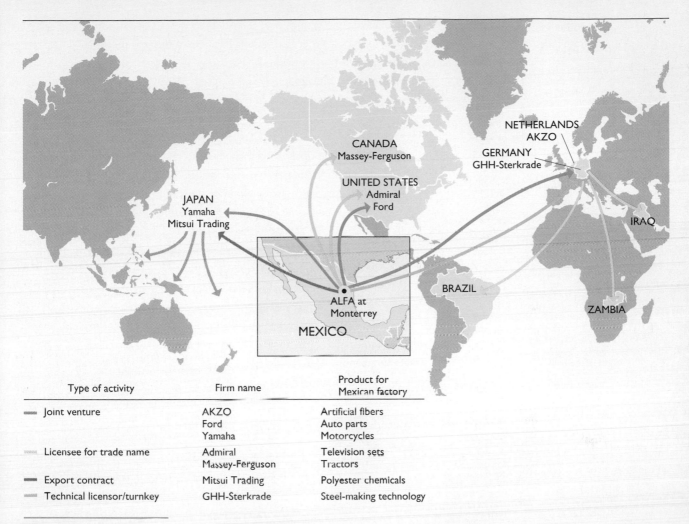

Type of activity	Firm name	Product for Mexican factory
Joint venture	AKZO	Artificial fibers
	Ford	Auto parts
	Yamaha	Motorcycles
Licensee for trade name	Admiral	Television sets
	Massey-Ferguson	Tractors
Export contract	Mitsui Trading	Polyester chemicals
Technical licensor/turnkey	GHH-Sterkrade	Steel-making technology

Map 15.1
Alfa's International Strategic Alliances
This map shows only a sampling of the company's strategic alliances for sales and production within and outside Mexico.

a good reputation; thus it was in an excellent position to acquire the foreign resources it wanted. In fact, its biggest problem was in how to choose among the many opportunities. (Map 15.1 shows some of the alliances Alfa made with foreign companies.)

Alfa established numerous Mexican companies in which it owned a majority interest, with a foreign partner holding a minority interest. The foreign partners came from a number of countries, including Japan (Hitachi, electric motors; Yamaha, motorcycles), Canada (International Nickel, nonferrous metal exploration), the Netherlands (AKZO, artificial fibers), and Germany (BASF, petrochemicals). For two U.S. companies—Ford and Du Pont—the joint-venture operations involved substantial departures from usual policies. Ford's 25-percent interest in a Mexican plant making aluminum cylinder heads for the U.S. and Canadian automobile markets was the first minority interest the company had ever taken in a joint venture. Du Pont had taken minority interests before accepting 49 percent to Alfa's 51 percent in a Mexican synthetic fibers joint venture; however, it had always managed the ventures. In this case, Alfa managed the venture because its policy was to import technology but maintain management control.

In many of these joint-venture operations, the Mexican output has used the trademark developed by the foreign partner. Doing this has helped the product gain Mexican consumer acceptance. For this reason, when Alfa bought 100 percent of Massey-Ferguson's tractor operation in Mexico in 1979, it paid the Canadian company a royalty fee to use the Massey-Ferguson trade name. In the aluminum cylinder head joint venture, Ford was attracted not by a captive Mexican market, but rather by the lower costs of producing components to serve the U.S. and Canadian markets. In addition to cheap energy, Mexico offered an abundance of cheap labor and no taxes on reinvested earnings. Motors built under the Hitachi brand name have been produced in Mexico for 25 percent below the Japanese cost. And Alfa itself became interested in export markets: It established a sales arrangement under which Japan's Mitsui Trading Company would handle exports of Alfa's polyester chemicals abroad.

Alfa developed a method of producing steel by direct reduction, thus bypassing the high capital costs of blast furnaces. To transfer this patented technology to new plants in other countries would have required substantial on-site personnel and construction assistance. Alfa lacked both personnel that could be spared and foreign construction experience, so it transferred the technology to four foreign engineering companies: GHH-Sterkrade (Germany), Kawasaki Heavy Industries (Japan), and Pullman Swindell and Dravo (both from the United States). Those companies have in turn acted as agents on behalf of Alfa and constructed steel plants in such countries as Brazil, Indonesia, Iran, Iraq, Venezuela, and Zambia. Alfa continues to receive fees for the use of the technology in foreign mills, and the engineering companies receive fees for building the plants, in what are known as turnkey projects.

For Alfa to expand and maintain management control between 1976 and 1980, it had to borrow and recruit managers outside of Mexico. Alfa ended up with debt of almost $3 billion owed to over 130 banks; about 75 percent of this was payable in U.S. dollars. Alfa also had to pay highly to attract managers with the backgrounds it wanted. Then oil prices plummeted, and the Mexican peso was devalued. By 1981, Alfa was losing so much money it had to receive Mexican government aid of $680 million to keep afloat. Between 1980 and 1985, Alfa had to shut down forty of its subsidiaries and reduce the number of its employees by almost 19,000. Meanwhile, many of the foreign companies that had made agreements with Alfa in the 1970s found that their expected Mexican expansion (via joint ventures with Alfa) had been put on hold. These included, for example, BASF and Hercules. Alfa simply lacked the resources to carry out so many agreements with so many different foreign companies.

By 1987, foreign banks had converted part of Alfa's debt into a 27-percent stake in the company rather than have Alfa default. By 1989, Mexico's economy and Alfa's financial situation had turned around to such an extent that Alfa was able to buy back the foreign banks' ownership, an event hailed in the Mexican press as the "Mexicanization" of Alfa. Once again, Alfa embarked on expansion through alliances with foreign companies; for example, in 1992 it announced contracts to supply aluminum cylinder heads to Chrysler and to build a joint-venture plant with Bekaert of Belgium to make steel wire.

Introduction

International business may be conducted in various ways. The truly experienced MNE with a fully global orientation usually uses most of the operational forms available, selecting them according to specific product or foreign operating characteristics. Many of these forms involve collaboration with other companies. When this collaboration is of strategic importance to one or more of the companies involved, it is known as a strategic alliance. In reality, the term *strategic alliance* often is used to describe a wide variety of collaborations, whether or not they are of real strategic importance. Collaborations involve different opportunities and problems than do trade or wholly owned direct investment; thus studying them is important.

The Alfa case illustrates the use of several different types of collaborative strategies to exploit international opportunities. Alfa established joint ventures with foreign companies, engaged in acquiring and selling process and product technology through licensing and turnkey contracts, and paid for the use of trademarks through licensing agreements.

This chapter discusses the most common means by which companies commit resources to the foreign sector, prompted either by their own desire or by external pressures that force them to accept certain parameters. The chapter also covers the problems of control when one company enters into an agreement that makes another company responsible for handling its business objectives. For example, BASF and Hercules both lost control of their Mexican expansion plans when Alfa became unable to comply with the agreements.

Some Variables Affecting Companies' Choice of Operational Form

The choice of operational form may necessitate trade-offs among objectives.

Factors influencing companies' choice include legal factors, cost, experience, competition, risk, control, and product complexity.

The forms of foreign operations differ in terms of both the amount of resources a company commits to foreign operations and the proportion of the resources located at home rather than abroad. Exports, for example, may result in a lower additional resource commitment than foreign direct investment will if excess domestic capacity can be used. If a company must increase capacity, then this increase may take place by investing the resources either at home or abroad. The increase in capacity involves a substantial commitment to foreign operations, whether or not the assets are in a foreign location. A company may be able to reduce its total resource commitment by contracting with other companies to conduct activities on its behalf or by sharing ownership in international business endeavors. Before examining these other operational forms, we need to discuss some of the major factors that companies should consider when selecting a form of operation in a given market. We will cover them more intensively when we discuss specific types of collaborative arrangements.

Throughout this discussion, keep in mind that there are trade-offs. For example, a decision to own 100 percent of a foreign subsidiary normally will help the parent company achieve the objective of controlling decisions; however, it may simultaneously reduce the parent's achievement of the objective of minimizing exposure to political risk.[2]

Legal Conditions

Legal factors may be
- **Direct prohibitions against certain operating forms**
- **Indirect (for example, regulations affecting profitability)**

As the Alfa case showed, a company may be constrained in its choice of operating form regardless of its preferences. Some of the foreign companies discussed, such as Ford, may have preferred to wholly own the Mexican operation but were not legally permitted to do so. In addition to the outright prohibition of certain operating forms, other legal factors may influence the company's choice. These include differences in tax rates and in the maximum funds that can be remitted, actual or possible enforcement of antitrust provisions, and stipulations as to the circumstances in which a proprietary asset will be in the public domain and available for others to use.

Cost

Sometimes it is cheaper to get another company to handle work, especially
- **At small volume**
- **When the other company has excess capacity**

To produce or sell abroad, a company must incur certain fixed costs. At a small volume of business, it may be cheaper for it to contract the work to someone else than to handle it internally. A specialist can spread the fixed costs over services to more than one company. If business increases enough, the contracting company then may be able to handle the activities more cheaply itself. Companies therefore should periodically reappraise the question of internal versus external handling of their varied operations.

External contracting of operations also may be lower in cost because another company may have excess production or sales capacity that can be easily utilized. Utilizing this capacity also may reduce start-up time and thus result in an earlier cash flow. Further, the contracted company may have environment-specific knowledge, such as how to deal with Mexican regulations and labor, that would be expensive for the contracting company to gain on its own. Also, contracting companies may lack the resources to "go it alone"; by pooling their efforts, they may be able to undertake activities that otherwise would be beyond their means. This is especially important for small companies.[3]

Cooperative ventures may, however, increase operating costs. There are additional expenses involved in negotiating with another company or in transferring technology to it. Also, there usually are added headquarters costs involved in maintaining ongoing relationships with another company. Further, there may be additional control costs as reports must comply to the needs of more than one company.

Experience

As they gain experience, companies take on more direct involvement abroad.

In their early stages of international development, few companies are willing to expend a large portion of their resources on foreign operations; they may not even have sufficient resources for rapid expansion abroad. Consequently, they usually move through stages of increased levels of international involvement. In the early stages, they attempt to conserve their own scarce resources and to maximize the proportion of the resources that are at home rather than abroad. This leads them to operational forms that transfer the burden of foreign commitment to outsiders. For example, Alfa's need to use resources domestically and its lack of foreign experience influenced its decision to contract with foreign engineering companies in order to transfer steel-making processes abroad. As companies and their foreign activities grow, they tend to view the foreign portions of their businesses differently. They move toward handling more operations internally and locating a larger proportion of resources abroad.[4] However, the cost of switching from one form to another—for example, from licensing to wholly owned facilities—may be very high because of having to gain expertise from and possibly pay termination fees to another company.[5]

Competition

> Companies have a wider choice of operating form when there is less likelihood of competition.

When a company has a desired, unique, difficult-to-duplicate resource, it is in a good position to choose the operating form it would most like to utilize. When there is the possibility of competition, it may have to settle on a form that is lower on its priority list; otherwise, a competitor may preempt the market. The possibility of competition also may lead to a strategy of rapid international expansion, which may be possible only by developing external arrangements with other companies (because of limited resources).

Minimization of competition in given markets also may be achieved through cooperative arrangements that exclude entry, share resources, or divide output. The effectiveness will depend in part on the type of form selected as well as the permissiveness of governmental authorities regarding the specific agreement.

Risk

> The higher the perceived risk, usually the greater is the desire to operate as part of strategic alliances.

There are many types of risk. However, the possibility that political or economic changes will affect the safety of assets and their earnings is often at the forefront of management's concern about foreign operations. One way to minimize loss from foreign political occurrences is to minimize the base of assets located abroad. Doing this may dictate external arrangements so that the asset base is shared by others. This move also might reduce political risk because a government may be less willing to move against a shared operation for fear of encountering opposition from more than one company.

> External operating forms allow for greater spreading of assets among countries.

One way to spread risk is to place operations in a number of different countries. This strategy reduces the chance that all foreign assets will be simultaneously subject to such adversity as political unrest, exchange control, or even a slowing of sales caused by a local recession. Maximum losses as well as year-to-year changes in consolidated earnings may thus be minimized. For companies that have not yet attained widespread international operations, operational forms that minimize their resource expenditures may permit a more rapid dispersion of operations. These forms will be less appealing for companies whose activities are already widely extended or those that have ample resources for such extension.

Control

The more a company deals externally, the more likely it is to lose control over decisions that may affect its global optimization, including those regarding quality, new product directions, and where output will be expanded. External arrangements also imply the sharing of revenues, a serious consideration for undertakings with high potential profits. Such arrangements also risk allowing information to pass more rapidly to potential competitors. Some analysts suggest that the loss of control over flexibility, revenues, and competition has been the most important variable guiding companies' priorities for forms of foreign operation.[6]

Product Complexity

There are costs associated with transferring technology to another entity. Usually it is cheaper to transfer within the existing corporate family, such as from parent to subsidiary, than to transfer to another company (internalization theory, discussed in Chapter 8). The cost difference is especially important when the technology is complex because a subsidiary's personnel are more likely to be familiar with approaches the parent uses. For this reason, it has been noted that the higher the level of technology, the more likely it is that a company will expand abroad with its own facilities rather than contracting with another company to produce abroad on its behalf.[7]

Prior Expansion of the Company

When a company already has operations in place within a foreign country, some of the advantages of contracting with another company to handle production or sales are no longer as prevalent. The company knows how to operate within the foreign country and may have excess capacity that can be used for new production or sales. However, much depends on whether the existing foreign operation is in a line of business or performs a function that is closely related to the product, service, or activity being transferred abroad. When there is similarity, as with production of a new type of office equipment when the company already produces office equipment, there is the highest probability that the new production will be handled internally. In highly diversified companies or where operations are limited (such as when subsidiaries only produce components for the parent), the existing foreign facility may be handling goods or functions so dissimilar to what is being planned that it is easier to deal with an experienced external company.

Similarity of Country

Similarity between home and host countries is a two-edged sword. On the one hand, management is more confident of its ability to operate in those foreign countries whose environments it perceives to be similar to that of its home country. U.S. companies, for example, are much more likely to handle operations internally in other English-speaking countries than in non–English-speaking ones. On the other hand, language and cultural differences impede communications and increase coordination costs among companies, especially if technology is being transferred. In these situations, some level of FDI may be needed so that personnel are more likely to move to the foreign locale to facilitate cross-national information flows.[8]

Licensing

MNEs want returns from their intangible assets.

Under a **licensing agreement,** a company (the licensor) grants rights to intangible property to another company (the licensee) for a specified period, and, in exchange, the licensee ordinarily pays a royalty to the licensor. The rights may be exclusive (monopoly within a given territory) or nonexclusive. The U.S. Internal Revenue Service classifies intangible property into five categories:

Licensing agreements may be
- **Exclusive or nonexclusive**
- **Used for patents, copyrights, trademarks, and so forth**

1. Patents, inventions, formulas, processes, designs, patterns
2. Copyrights for literary, musical, or artistic compositions
3. Trademarks, trade names, brand names
4. Franchises, licenses, contracts
5. Methods, programs, procedures, systems, and so forth

Usually, the licensor is obliged to furnish technical information and assistance, and the licensee is obliged to exploit the rights effectively and to pay compensation to the licensor.

Economic Motives

Licensing often has an economic motive, such as the desire for faster start-up, lower costs, or access to additional resources.

Frequently, a new product or process may affect only part of a company's total output and then only for a limited time. The sales volume may not be large enough to warrant establishing overseas manufacturing and sales facilities. Further, during the period of commencing operations on its own, the company faces the risk that competitors will develop improvements that will negate its advantages. As discussed earlier in this chapter, a company that is already operating abroad may be able to produce and sell at a lower cost and with a shorter start-up time. For the licensor, the risk of operating facilities and holding inventories is reduced. The licensee may find that the cost of the arrangement is less than if the development were accomplished internally.

For industries in which technological changes are frequent and affect many different products, such as chemicals and electrical goods, companies in various countries often exchange technology rather than compete with each other on every product in every market. Such an arrangement is known as **cross-licensing.** Cross-licensing does have its problems, however. It may violate antitrust regulations if it results in restricting one of the parties' entry into a market. The regulations regarding this are extremely complex, and good legal assistance is necessary for any licensing agreement. Also, some of the parties may produce more innovations than others do. For example, American Home Products participated in pharmaceutical arrangements with several foreign drug makers, which later terminated the arrangements because American Home produced few important drugs on its own.[9]

Even without a cross-licensing arrangement, a licensor may learn from a licensee. For example, Black & Decker's Heli-Coil, a fastener technology, was licensed abroad. Subsequent information on the foreign applications and testing was valuable to Black & Decker in marketing Heli-Coil in the United States.[10]

Another economic consideration concerns the resources a company has at its disposal, of particular concern for small companies. But large ones also may be constrained. Chrysler, for example, has insufficient resources to establish its own facilities everywhere that overseas production is necessary for Jeep sales. For some of the largest markets, such as India and Australia, Chrysler has subsidiaries. For some smaller markets, such as Sri Lanka and Pakistan, it uses licensing arrangements.

Strategic Motives

Licensing can yield a return on a product that does not fit the company's strategic priority.

Large diversified companies are constantly reevaluating and altering their product lines to put their efforts where their major strengths best complement their assessment of high profit potential. This may leave them with products or technologies that they do not wish to exploit themselves but that may be profitably transferred to other companies. For example, GE developed a microorganism that destroys spilled oil by digesting it.[11] Because the product does not fit into its major lines of business, the company has marketed the technology to other companies. Companies also may license trademarks. For example, neither Chrysler nor Coca-Cola wants to be in the clothing business, so Murjani Merchandising has licensed the Jeep and Coca-Cola logos, which are valuable for selling a variety of merchandise.[12] However, a licensing arrangement's limited time frame may allow a licensor to move to a different operating form if use of the particular technology or trademark is later deemed to be of strategic importance.[13]

Political and Legal Motives

Licensing hinders nonassociated companies from usurping the asset.

Licensing can also be a means of protecting an asset. This may occur for two reasons. First, many countries provide very little de facto protection for foreign property rights such as trademarks, patents, and copyrights unless authorities are prodded consistently. To prevent pirating of these proprietary assets, companies sometimes have made licensing agreements with local companies, which then monitor to ensure that no one else uses the asset locally. Second, some countries provide protection only if the internationally registered asset is exploited locally within a specified period. If a company does not use the asset within the country during that specified period, then whatever entity first does so gains the right to it. For example, in Mexico City, Gucci, Chemise La Coste, and Cartier shops unrelated to the European houses are in close proximity. The Cartier shop copies a Cartier watch dial, bracelet, presentation box, and storefront to the smallest detail, but it puts cheap movements and poor-quality gold filling in the watches. This has hurt

Cartier's reputation among unsuspecting buyers, who then refuse to buy in the authentic stores in New York and Paris. Had Cartier licensed the use of its name in Mexico early on, it might have preempted the nonassociated use there. Instead, Cartier has opened a real shop close to the bogus one in an attempt to educate and steer clients to its legitimate products.[14]

A company that doesn't license may find that another company can exclude its market entry at a later date or can compete in certain areas by exploiting the asset, as in the situation described in Mexico. Western Electric, for example, has a liberal licensing policy in order to avoid patent litigation.

Problems and Provisions

Hardly any aspect of international business has been as controversial in recent years as licensing. Given that virtually all royalties are paid to organizations in industrial countries, it is perhaps inevitable that groups within LDCs have criticized the amounts and methods of payment. Since MNEs view their technologies and trademarks as integral parts of their asset bases, it is perhaps just as inevitable that they are skeptical about transferring the use of those technologies and trademarks to other organizations. The following discussion highlights major concerns of licensors, licensees, and host-country governments that might be incorporated into a formal agreement.

Control and competition By transferring rights to another company, the licensor undoubtedly loses some control over the asset. A host of potential problems attend this lack of control and should be settled in the original licensing agreement. Provision should be made for the following:

Transferring rights to an asset can create control problems, such as
• Inadequate working of the license
• Poor quality of the product
• Developing a future competitor

• Terminating the agreement if the parties do not adhere to the directives
• Methods of testing for quality
• Each party's obligations concerning expenditures on sales development
• Geographical limitations on the asset's use

Without these provisions, the license may be inadequately worked, the two parties may find themselves in competition with each other, or a poor-quality product in one country may jeopardize product image and sales elsewhere. For example, Oleg Cassini, Inc., licensed the U.S. subsidiary (Jovan) of the Beecham Group from the United Kingdom to promote and extend sales of various Cassini fragrances, cosmetics, and beauty aids worldwide. Jovan subsequently introduced Diane Von Furstenberg products instead and denied Cassini the right to license the Cassini name to other companies. Cassini sued. The case was settled when Jovan agreed to market the Cassini products; however, their sales of the products through discount stores won Cassini an award in a later suit for image injury.[15]

Some companies have well-known trademarked names that they license abroad for the production of some products that they have never produced or had expertise with. For example, the Pierre Cardin label is used by over 800 licensees in ninety-three countries to produce hundreds of different products, from clothing to sheets and clocks to deodorants. Monitoring and maintaining control of so much diversity is very difficult. Two U.S. companies, Saks Fifth Avenue and Eagle Shirt-makers, dropped sales of Pierre Cardin–labeled products because the lack of quality control on some licensees' products adversely affected the image of others.[16]

Depending on the licensed asset, either the licensor or the licensee risks developing a future competitor after the licensing agreement expires (appropriability theory, discussed in Chapter 8). If a brand or trademark is involved, the licensee may develop consumer preferences and have to turn the market over to the licensor. If know-how or patents are involved, the licensee may be able to exploit the assets long after the agreement is terminated. Even before an agreement is terminated, the two parties may come into competition with each other because one has made improvements on the licensed technology that make the original patents obsolete. Thus, companies commonly provide in the original agreement for the possible use and sharing of superseding technology built on knowledge from the original.

Secrecy The value of many technologies would diminish if they were widely known or understood. Agreements historically have included provisions that a licensee will not divulge this information. In addition, some licensors have held onto the ownership and production of specific components so that licensees will not have the full knowledge of the product or the capability to produce an exact copy of it. Secrecy is an issue when companies are negotiating agreements to transfer process technology. Many times, a company wants to sell techniques it has not yet used commercially. A buyer is reluctant to buy "a pig in a poke," but a licensor that shows the process to the potential licensee risks having the process used without payment. It has become common to set up preagreements in order to protect all parties.

In licensing agreements,
• Seller does not want to give information without assurance of payment
• Buyer does not want to pay without evaluating information

Another controversial area is the degree of secrecy surrounding the financial terms of licensing agreements. In some countries, for example, governmental agencies must approve royalty contracts. Sometimes these authorities consult with their counterparts in other countries regarding similar agreements in order to improve their negotiating position with MNEs. Many MNEs object to this procedure because they believe that contract terms are proprietary information with competitive importance and that market conditions usually dictate the need for very different terms in different countries.

Stage of technology development Technology may be old or new, obsolete or still in use at home, when it is transferred to a foreign company.[17] For example, Crown Cork and Seal held onto its three-piece manufacturing technology for cans until it developed two-piece technology; then the older technology was licensed to LDCs. Many other companies transfer technology at an early or even a developmental stage so that products are introduced almost simultaneously in different markets. For example, an alliance between AT&T and Eo licenses "personal communicator" technology to Matsushita so that the product will be available in Japan at about the same time AT&T sells it in the United States.[18] On the one hand, new technology may be worth more to a licensee because it may have a longer useful life. On the other hand, newer technology, particularly that in the development phase, may be worth less because of its more uncertain market value.

Payment   The amount and type of payment under licensing arrangements vary widely. Each contract tends to be negotiated on its own merits. Figure 15.1 shows the major factors that determine the payment amount. In the upper left-hand box, agreement-specific factors underlie negotiated clauses that may affect the value to the licensee. For example, the value will be greater if potential sales are high, such as with long-term exclusive worldwide rights, before the asset becomes obsolete. The upper right-hand box in the figure, environment-specific factors, lists other conditions that may affect the value. For example, the licensee might pay a low amount if its government sets upper limits on payment or if other companies are vying to sell similar technology. Because neither the licensor nor the licensee can be sure of the price the other is willing to accept, the bottom of the figure illustrates how the bargaining range is based on their expectations.

Many governments of LDCs set price controls on what licensees can pay or insist on prohibitions or restrictions.[19] One thorny issue regarding sales restrictions, from the point of view of LDCs, is that licensees usually are prevented by contract from exporting; thus small-scale production spreads fixed costs inadequately, and high prices must be charged to consumers. MNEs have countered that extending sales territories would necessitate high royalties because the companies could not sell exclusive rights to parties in other countries. MNEs also have argued that the development of process technologies for small-scale production often is too costly but is done when economically feasible.

Taxes may be assessed differently depending on how payments are arranged under a licensing agreement—for example, as income or as a capital gain—thus affecting after-tax receipts. Payment also may be deferred in order to delay tax liability. Fees for using an asset may be paid in a lump sum, based either on a percentage of sales value or on a specific rate applied to usage, or on some combination of these methods.

It is common to negotiate a "front-end" payment to cover transfer costs and then follow with another set of fees based on actual or projected usage. This is done because few technologies may be moved abroad simply by transferring publications and reports. The negotiation process is itself expensive and must be followed by engineering, consultation, and adaptation. The early stages of production usually are characterized by low quality and low productivity.[20] The substantial costs of the transfer process increasingly are charged to the licensee so that the licensor is motivated to assure a smooth adaptation.

Sales to controlled entities   Many licenses are given to companies owned in part by the licensor. Nearly 80 percent of licensing fees received in the United States are

Licensing payments vary widely because of
- Fixed fee versus usage arrangements
- Value to the licensee
- Regulatory and competitive factors
- Negotiating ability of parties

Sales of rights to controlled entities are common because
- These entities are separate legally
- Licensing arrangements protect value when ownership is shared

**Figure 15.1
Determinants of
Compensation for
International Licensing
of Technology**
The upper left-hand box
lists factors in the licensing
agreement that can affect
the technology's value to
the licensee. The upper
right-hand box gives fac-
tors external to the negotiations that can affect
pricing. The bottom por-
tion shows how the bar-
gaining range derives from
the licensor's and the licensee's estimates of profits and costs.

Source: Kang Rae Cho, "Issues of
Compensation in International
Technology Licensing," *Manage-
ment International Review,* Vol. 28,
No. 2, 1988, p. 76, as adapted
from Franklin R. Root and Farok
J. Contractor, "Negotiating
Compensation in International
Licensing Agreements," *Sloan
Management Review,* Winter
1981, p. 25.

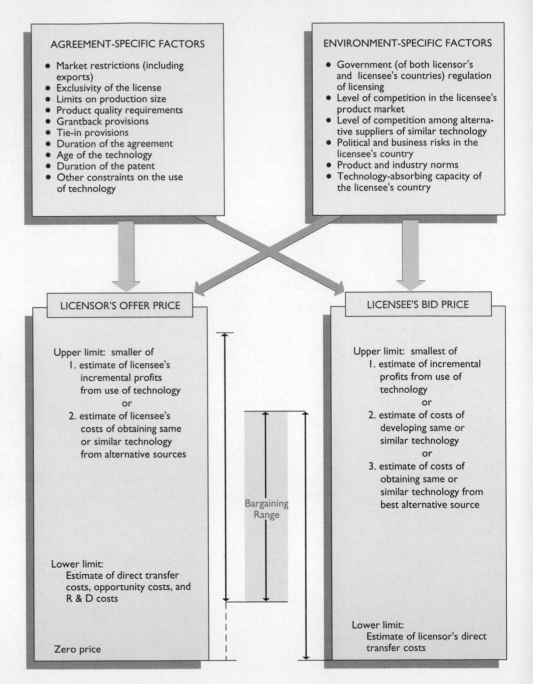

from affiliated companies.[21] A license may be needed to transfer technology abroad
because operations in a foreign country, even if 100 percent owned by the parent,
usually are separate companies from a legal standpoint. When there is present or
potential shared ownership, a separate licensing arrangement also may be a means
of compensating for contributions beyond the mere investment in capital and managerial resources.

Franchising

Franchising involves provision of a trademark and continual infusion of necessary assets.

Franchising is a specialized form of licensing in which the franchisor not only sells an independent franchisee the use of a trademark that is an essential asset for the franchisee's business, but also more than nominally assists on a continuing basis in the operation of the business. In many cases, the franchisor also provides supplies.[22] For example, Holiday Inn grants to franchisees the good will of the Holiday Inn name and support services to get started, such as appraisal of a proposed motel site. As part of the continual relationship, Holiday Inn offers reservations services and training programs to help ensure the venture's success. In a sense, a franchisor and a franchisee act almost like a vertically integrated company because the parties are interdependent and each produces part of the product or service that ultimately reaches the consumer.

Many types of products and many countries are involved in franchising.

Franchising is said to have originated when King John of England granted franchises to tax collectors. In the eighteenth century, German brewers franchised beer halls as distributors.[23] Today, franchising is most associated with the United States and accounts for about one third of U.S. retail sales.[24] About 75 percent of those sales are in car and truck dealerships, gasoline service stations, and soft-drink bottling. The number of foreign franchises by U.S. companies has grown very rapidly since the early 1970s. In 1989, approximately 20 percent of U.S. franchise systems had foreign operations, with four countries—Canada, Japan, the United Kingdom, and Australia—accounting for about two thirds of outlets. A 1992 survey showed that about half of U.S. franchisors without foreign units planned to grow internationally within the next five years.[25] The fastest growth areas of U.S. companies have been food and business services.

Not all franchising is by U.S. companies. Foreign-owned franchise operations are growing rapidly in the United States. Pronuptia, a French bridal wear franchisor, and food franchisors such as Wimpy's and Bake 'N' Take from the United Kingdom and Wienerwald from Germany have been among some of the earliest and most successful. There also has been a surge of foreign acquisition of franchisors based in the United States.[26] Burger King, Hardees, Holiday Inn, Howard Johnson's, Baskin-Robbins, Meineke Discount Mufflers, and Great American Cookie are U.S. franchisors that have been acquired by non-U.S. companies.

Organization

A franchisor most often penetrates a foreign country by setting up a master franchise and giving that organization (usually a local one) the rights for the country or region.[27] The master franchisee then may open outlets on its own or develop subfranchisees. Royalty payments by the subfranchisees are made to the master franchisee, which then remits some predetermined percentage to the franchisor. For example, McDonald's very successful Japanese operations are handled this way.

In about 20 percent of cases, franchisors enter foreign markets by dealing directly with individual franchisees. Doing this is sometimes difficult because the franchisor may be insufficiently known to convince many local people to make investments. It therefore is common for a franchisor to enter with some company-owned outlets that serve as a showcase to attract franchisees.

Operational Modifications

Securing good locations can be a major problem.[28] Finding suppliers can be the source of added difficulties and expense. For example, McDonald's had to build a plant to make hamburger buns in the United Kingdom, and it had to help farmers develop potato production in Thailand.[29] Another concern for foreign franchise expansion has been governmental or legal restrictions that make it difficult to gain satisfactory operating permission.

Many franchise failures abroad result from the franchisor's not developing enough domestic penetration first; thus franchisors may lack sufficient cash and management depth. However, even a franchisor that is well established domestically may have difficulty in attaining foreign penetration, as evidenced by problems of Burger King in the United Kingdom, Wendy's in Australia, and Long John Silver's in Japan.[30] It is simply difficult to persuade people in a host country to invest in a venture that is not yet well known there. A dilemma for successful domestic franchisors is that their success has been largely due to three factors: product and service standardization, high identification through promotion, and effective cost controls. When entering many foreign countries, these companies may encounter various restraints that may make it difficult to conform to home-country methods. Yet the more adjustments that are made to the host-country's different conditions, the less a franchisor has to offer a potential franchisee. Franchisors' success in Japan has been due in large part to that country's enthusiastic assimilation of Western innovations; thus companies such as McDonald's have been able to copy their U.S. outlets almost exactly. Yet such food franchisors as Dunkin' Donuts and Perkits Yogurt fared poorly in the United Kingdom because it was too difficult to change certain British eating habits. However, if the companies had offered menus that were more acceptable to the British, there would have been nothing different about their product to offer a franchisee. Even in countries in which franchises have been successful, some operating adjustments usually have been necessary. For example, Kentucky Fried Chicken had to redesign its equipment and stores in Japan to save space because of higher rents. To cater to Japanese tastes, it eliminated mashed potatoes and put less sugar in its cole slaw. Pizza Hut alters its toppings by country, and in Saudi Arabia it must have two dining rooms—one for single men and one for families (single women are not allowed to go out without their families). McDonald's changed the pronunciation of its name in Japan to "MaKudonaldo" and substituted Donald for Ronald McDonald because of pronunciation difficulties among Japanese.[31]

Contract Problems

Some problems that plague franchising agreements are no different from those with licensing agreements. Contracts must be spelled out in detail, but if courts must rule on disagreements, both parties are apt to lose something in the settlement. A good example occurred with McDonald's in France. The company granted a license for up to 166 French stores to Raymond Dayan at less than its normal fee because of doubts the French would ever take to fast-food restaurants. Dayan, with the help of McDonald's, found very good Paris locations for fourteen stores, which he opened over a period of several years and operated successfully. However, under the franchise agreement McDonald's had the right to revoke the agreement if the company found the stores fell short of its cleanliness standards. McDonald's cancelled the agreement on these grounds. A court case resulted, and Dayan claimed that McDonald's action was simply a ruse to make him pay McDonald's usual licensing fee. He lost out on further expansion with the McDonald's trademark; but McDonald's lost something, too. When Dayan took down the McDonald's signs, he immediately replaced them with signs saying O'Keefe's Hamburgers—and he had the clientele, the know-how, and the best locations in Paris.[32] These stores were later sold to the French firm Quick, the largest fast-food chain in France.

Management Contracts

Management contracts are used primarily when
• The owned operation has been expropriated
• A company needs to manage a new facility
• A company needs to manage an operation in trouble

One of the most important assets a company may have at its disposal is management talent. The transmission of management skills internationally has depended largely on foreign investments that deploy expatriate managers and specialists to foreign countries. Management contracts are a means by which a company may use part of its management personnel to assist a foreign company for a specified period for a fee. Thus the company may gain income with little capital outlay. Contracts usually are drawn to cover three to five years, and fixed fees or fees based on volume rather than profits are most common.

Management contracts are sometimes established when a foreign investment has been nationalized and the former owner is invited to continue supervising the operations until local management is trained. In this case, the management structure may remain substantially the same, although board membership would change. A good example of this was described in the Aramco case in Chapter 13. A contract can be advantageous in this type of situation because it may:

• Facilitate getting resources out of the country in addition to those agreed upon in the divestment negotiations
• Ingratiate the company with local authorities so that future business operations are possible
• Ensure continued access to raw materials or other resources needed from the country

Management contracts also are established when a foreign company is perceived to be able to manage an existing or new operation more efficiently than can the home-country owners. For example, the British Airports Authority (BAA) won a fifteen-year contract to manage the Pittsburgh International Airport.[33]

From the standpoint of the host country, the need to receive direct investment as a means of gaining management assistance is removed. From the standpoint of the management company, contracts help it avoid the risk of losing capital assets when returns on investment are too low and capital outlays are too high. A management contract may also be a means for the supplier to gain foreign experience, thus increasing its capacity to internationalize. For example, Ansett Transport Industries of Australia developed contracts to operate Air Vanuatu for the government of Vanuatu. This led to other management contracts in the South Pacific, which in turn led to Ansett holding equity interests in Transcorp Airways (Hong Kong), Air New Zealand, Air Norway, Ladeco (Chile), and America West (United States).[34]

Management contracts do create potential problems, not the least of which is that they subsidize the training of future competitors. Additionally, bad feelings may result if the management company incurs start-up inefficiencies, does not train local managers quickly, or expresses opinions on policy that differ from those of an organization contracting with it. Although the contractor is responsible for managing, it may frequently be unable to control the employees, particularly in government-owned facilities. For example, in Holiday Inn's ten-year contract in Tibet, the management was precluded from giving incentives to or disciplining its staff; consequently, there was little that could be done when waiters and waitresses took their lunch breaks all together at the same time as guests showed up for lunch.[35]

Turnkey Operations

Turnkey operations
- **Are most commonly performed by construction companies**
- **May develop into future competitors**

Turnkey projects involve a contract for construction of operating facilities that are transferred for a fee to the owner when they are ready to commence operations. Companies performing turnkey operations are frequently industrial-equipment manufacturers that supply some of their own equipment for the project. Most commonly, they are construction companies. They also may be consulting firms or manufacturers that decide that an investment on their own behalf in the country is infeasible.

The customer for a turnkey operation is very often a governmental agency. As with a management contract, a company building a turnkey facility may be developing a future competitor. Yet many companies have chosen to perform design and construction duties, particularly where there are restrictions on foreign ownership. Recently, most large projects have been in NICs or oil-exporting countries, both of which are moving rapidly toward infrastructure development and industrialization. Of course, not all such projects are developing potential competitors. Airports and port facilities, for example, do not lend themselves to competition.

One characteristic that sets this business apart from most other international business operations is the size of the contracts. Most are for hundreds of millions of dollars, and many are for billions, which means that only a few very large companies—such as Bechtel, Fluor, and Kellogg Rust—account for most of the international market. Smaller companies either are largely excluded from direct contracts, such as those awarded as part of the rebuilding of Kuwait, or serve as subcontractors for primary turnkey suppliers. However, even the very large companies are vulnerable because of their dependence on giant projects, which can disappear with economic downturns. For example, Fluor took heavy losses when oil prices fell and oil exporters suspended construction expansion.[36]

Contract size has prompted the companies to hire executives with top-level governmental contacts abroad. These executives can gain entry to the right decision makers to negotiate their proposals in foreign countries. Pullman-Kellogg, for example, secured a large fertilizer-plant contract in Nigeria by sending Andrew Young, a former UN ambassador who enjoys immense personal prestige in Africa, to negotiate the contract. The nature of these contracts also has placed importance on ceremony, such as opening a facility on a country's independence day or getting a head of state to inaugurate a facility in order to build good will for future contracts. Although public relations is important, other factors— such as price, export financing, managerial and technological quality, experience, and reputation—are necessary to sell contracts of such magnitude.[37]

Payment for a turnkey operation usually is made in stages, as a project develops. Commonly, 10–25 percent comprises the down payment, with another 50–65 percent paid as the contract progresses, and the remainder paid once the facility actually is operating in accordance with the contract. Because of the long time frame between conception and completion, the company performing turnkey operations is exposed to possible currency fluctuations and so, if possible, should be covered by escalation clauses or cost-plus contracts. Because the final payment is made only if the facility is operating satisfactorily, it is important to specify very precisely what constitutes "satisfactorily." For this reason, many companies insist on performing a feasibility study as part of the turnkey contract in order not to build something that, although desired by local governmental authorities, nevertheless may be too large or inefficient. Even though a facility may be built exactly as desired, its inefficiency could create legal problems that hold up final payment.

Many turnkey contracts are for construction in remote areas, necessitating massive housing construction and importation of personnel. Projects may involve building an entire infrastructure under the most adverse conditions.

If a company holds a monopoly on certain assets or resources, such as the latest refining technology, other companies find it difficult to be competitive in building facilities. As the production process becomes known, however, the number of competitors for performing turnkey operations increases. U.S. companies have moved largely toward projects involving high technology, whereas companies from such countries as India, Korea, and Turkey can compete better for conventional projects for which low labor costs are important.[38]

Custom Contracts

Companies that at one time would have integrated vertically by making direct investments for the extraction of raw materials in foreign countries now face many foreign-ownership restrictions on the extractive process. Because the local owners frequently continue to need certain resources that the foreign companies control, contracts may be established by which raw materials are traded for those resources. For example, as the Saudi Arabian government increased its ownership share of Aramco, it still needed management and exploration assistance, which the oil companies traded for commitments on preferred status for oil sales. On the basis of this precedent, several other oil-producing countries have made arrangements in which an oil company takes all exploration and development risks in exchange for a share of the oil produced.

One of the fastest growth areas for contract arrangements has been with projects that are too large for any single company to handle, for example, new aircraft and weapons systems. From such a project's inception, companies from different countries agree to take on the high cost and high risk of developmental work for different components needed in the final product; then a lead company buys the components from the companies that did parts of the developmental work.

The major aluminum producers have developed swap contracts that allow them to save transport costs. These companies are all vertically integrated, but not in each country in which they operate. Alcan might give Pechiney semiprocessed alumina in Canada in exchange for the same amount of semiprocessed alumina delivered to Alcan in France. Similarly, Ford's European plants make cars for Mazda to sell in Europe, and Mazda's Japanese factories make vehicles for Ford to sell in Japan.[39]

Improving Access to Foreign Technology

With most of the operational forms we've discussed—licensing, franchising, management contracts, turnkey operations, and other contractual arrangements—an organization in one country may gain access to scientific or managerial technology from an organization in another country. With such assets, a company may be in a much better position to compete domestically and internationally. Therefore, it is not surprising that many companies are establishing mechanisms that increase their chances of gaining advantages before their competitors do. Some of these mechanisms are as follows:

• Establish company units to monitor journals, technical conferences, patent-office publications, and databases sold by companies that clip information from thousands of periodicals in multiple languages.[40] This monitoring helps ensure that the company learns of new developments, thereby enabling decision makers to decide whether to ignore the innovations, try to counteract them through in-house developments, or establish an operational link with the individuals or organizations that are apparently leading the field.

- Develop formal links with academic and other research organizations at home and abroad in order to learn of possible breakthroughs before they are publicized in professional journals.

- Increase visibility by participating in trade fairs, distributing brochures, and nurturing contacts with technical acquisition consultants. This visibility may encourage innovators to think of one particular company rather than another when they seek out clients.

- Establish cooperative research projects with foreign companies, thereby gaining scale economies and the use of personnel from other organizations.

- Set up some R&D activities in foreign countries in order to utilize foreign talent that would not be likely to emigrate to the company's home country.[41]

Shared Ownership

When a company does take an ownership interest in foreign operations, it may or may not share the ownership. There are various types of ownership sharing, as well as several reasons for selecting a particular equity amount.

The Argument for 100-Percent Ownership

Advantages of 100-percent ownership:
- **Easier to control foreign operations**
- **No sharing of profits**

Most businesspeople would prefer to have a 100-percent interest in foreign operations in order to ensure control and to prevent dilution of profits. Without other stockholders, the parent company has greater freedom to enact measures that, although not in the best interest of the particular operation, are in the best interest of the company as a whole. With other stockholders, the parent has much less freedom, since even minority stockholders may be very vocal to their governments about practices that are not in the subsidiary's best interest. In fact, most countries have legislation to protect minority stockholders. For example, Freuhauf-France received export orders that, although in the best interest of that subsidiary, were not considered by its U.S. majority owners to be in the best interest of Freuhauf's worldwide operations. When Freuhauf-France did not fulfill the export orders, the minority stockholders contested the action in French courts. This left the majority stockholders with the option of either filling the export orders or paying damages to the minority stockholders.[42]

Even when the majority stockholders act in what they consider to be the local company's best interest, conflicts with local stockholders may arise because of different opinions as to what businesses should be doing. Some points of possible conflict are dividend pay-out versus earnings retention, degree of public disclosure of activities, and degree of cooperation with various governmental agencies.

The argument for 100-percent ownership is simple: Many companies contend that if they own all the resources necessary for the successful foreign operation and are willing to contribute these resources, they should not have to share ownership.

Reasons for Shared Ownership

In spite of the advantages of owning 100 percent of a foreign facility, ownership sharing is popular.[43] The reasons for this are undoubtedly a combination of outside pressures and internal willingness to take partial ownership.

Some countries require ownership sharing with local stockholders because they feel it enhances their economic or political objectives. In addition, many companies feel that by bringing in local capital they take on a local character that decreases governmental and societal criticism (thus reducing certain types of political risks) and may bring captive sales to the participating stockholders. Sharing ownership is much more common in some industries than in others; it is especially likely in those where a high capital outlay is necessary to develop a new product or build a production unit. This higher capital outlay necessitates additional outside resources. Further, local governments exert greater pressure for ownership sharing on those companies having the most significant impact on the economy.

Internally, there has been a need to bring outside resources into foreign operations. By sharing ownership in some existing foreign operations, many companies have been able to spread faster geographically. This rapid expansion has prevented competitors from gaining dominant market shares and also allowed maximum sales growth, which helps to spread such relatively fixed costs as R&D spending over a larger sales base.

A major reason for sharing ownership of foreign operations is to gain more assured synergy among assets held by two or more organizations in different countries. For example, Whirlpool had appliance technology, and the Mexican firm Vitro had skills to manage a labor force; the two companies combined their assets to make washing machines in Mexico. Companies also may combine certain resources to combat larger and more powerful competitors. For example, Volvo's 20-percent interest in Renault and Renault's 25-percent interest in Volvo's car subsidiary enhanced their joint development and production of technically advanced components at low cost; thus they could better compete against larger auto companies such as GM and Volkswagen.[44] Almost any type of asset can be combined. For instance, one company has manufacturing capabilities, and another has distribution. The two may have research capabilities that complement each other. But why share ownership instead of setting up nonequity contractual arrangements? Simply, shared ownership of even a minority amount increases the likelihood, but gives no assurance, of say-so over the operation.

Equity as a Control Mechanism

The problem of deciding how much equity is necessary for control is cumbersome. With a few exceptions, the larger the percentage of equity held, the more likely it is that the owner of this equity will control the company's decisions and policies. Many companies are willing to share ownership but usually will specify whether the sharing includes control. For example, if a company retains only a minority holding in its foreign operations, ordinarily it still can control policies and decisions if the remaining ownership is widely fragmented. For example, after the 1973 Mexicanization law discussed in the Alfa case, many foreign companies sought to maintain management control in spite of minority equity positions by selling 51 percent of their shares to a broad ownership market through the Mexican stock exchange. BASF maintained management control by transferring a majority interest in its pharmaceutical company to Bancomer, a large Mexican bank. The bank was interested simply in diversifying its investment holdings and had no desire to manage.[45] A company may maintain control by dividing profits on the basis of shares but giving voting rights only to one class of stockholders. Or it may stipulate that board decisions require more than a majority, thus giving veto power to minority stockholders. It also may stipulate that its own directors will appoint management and key officers.[46]

When no single company has control, the operation may lack direction. In discussing the problems of a company that was jointly owned by a U.S. organization and a Japanese one, a Sterling Drug spokesperson said, "You must decide right off the bat whether you'll control it or will put confidence in the Japanese organization."[47] This opinion is supported by studies showing that when two or more partners attempt to share in an operation's management, failure is much more likely than when one partner dominates.[48] However, studies also show that joint ventures with an even split in ownership are more likely to succeed. It is management control rather than financial control that is important; when one partner has both, the dominant company tends to overlook the other company's interests.[49]

Joint Ventures

Joint ventures
- **Need not be 50/50 companies**
- **May involve various combinations of ownership**

A type of ownership sharing very popular among international companies is the joint venture, in which a company is owned by more than one organization. Recall from the opening case that Alfa participates in numerous joint ventures. Although a joint venture usually is formed for the achievement of a limited objective, it may continue to operate indefinitely as the objective is redefined. Joint ventures are sometimes thought of as 50/50 companies, but often more than two organizations participate in the ownership. Further, one organization frequently controls more than 50 percent of the venture. The type of legal organization may be a partnership, corporation, or some other form permitted in the country of operation. When more than two organizations participate, the resultant joint venture is sometimes called a consortium.

Almost every conceivable combination of partners may exist in a joint venture, including the following:

- Two companies from the same country joining together in a foreign market, such as Exxon and Mobil in Russia
- A foreign company joining with a local company, such as Sears Roebuck and Simpsons in Canada
- Companies from two or more countries establishing a joint venture in a third country, such as that of Diamond Shamrock (U.S.) and Sol Petroleo (Argentine) in Bolivia
- A private company and a local government forming a joint venture (sometimes called a mixed venture), such as that of Philips (Dutch) with the Indonesian government.

Even some government-controlled companies have had joint ventures abroad, such as Dutch State Mines with Pittsburgh Plate Glass in the United States. The more companies involved, the more complex the ownership arrangement will be. For example, Australia Aluminum is owned by two U.S companies (American Metal Climax and Anaconda), two Japanese companies (Sumitomo Chemical Company and Showa Denko), one Dutch company (Holland Aluminum), and one German company (Vereinigte Aluminum Werke).

The arguments for and against shared ownership also apply to joint ventures. Certain types of companies tolerate joint ventures more than others do.[50] Companies with a higher tolerance include those that are new at foreign operations and those with decentralized domestic decision making, very often multiproduct companies. Because these companies are accustomed to extending control downward in their organizations, it is easier for them to do the same thing internationally.

Many joint ventures have problems, primarily because the partners evolve different objectives for them. For instance, one partner may want to reinvest earnings for growth and the other may want to receive dividends. In addition, one partner may offer much closer management attention to the venture than the other does. If things go wrong, the more active partner blames the less active partner for its lack of attention, and the less active partner blames the more active one for making poor decisions.[51] Further, one partner may be suspicious that the other is taking more from the venture (particularly technology) than it is. When each partner offers market expansion and technology to the other, both are apt to see substantial gains. For example, Toshiba offered Motorola access to the Japanese market, and Motorola gave Toshiba access to the U.S. market for technologies that were complementary rather than competitive.[52] Therefore the choice of a joint-venture partner is crucial, particularly if a company is forced into a shared-ownership arrangement because of governmental regulations. For this reason, many companies will develop joint ventures only after they have had long-term positive experiences with the other company through distributorship, licensing, or other contractual arrangements. Compatibility of corporate cultures also is important in cementing relationships.[53]

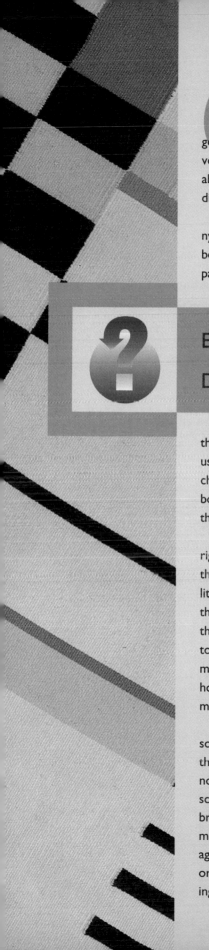

Collaborative arrangements may allow companies to skirt the intent of government regulations; thus deciding whether to take advantage of legal loopholes involves ethical considerations. Further, one partner in a collaborative arrangement may be able to extract benefits in excess of those specified in the agreement; therefore ethical dilemmas also arise concerning partnership relations.

One legal loophole involves payments to government officials. For example, a U.S. company may not be able to sell its own output in a foreign country without paying bribes that would be illegal under the FCPA. By licensing production to a producer in that country, the U.S. company no longer is legally culpable because the necessary bribes are paid by the local company abroad; however, the U.S. company may be ethically implicated because of knowingly fostering the bribes.

There are various means by which companies sometimes are able to control a foreign operation with a minority interest. If the limit on ownership is governmentally imposed to assure domestic control, is it ethical to use these loopholes? For example, British Airways and USAir agreed to the former's purchase of a minority interest in the latter and to British Airways' having veto power over board decisions. American Airlines successfully fought the veto provision on the grounds that it violated the intent of the U.S. law requiring U.S. airlines to be domestically controlled.

Much global licensing is to entities controlled by MNEs. The price charged for licensing rights is very controversial. By varying the price, MNEs effectively may transfer more of their profits from one country to another. Home-country critics have contended that too little is charged, and thus profits are transferred to countries having low tax rates. Many of the countries having low tax rates are LDCs. They have contended the opposite, arguing that MNEs have artificially minimized their profits in LDCs in order to either move funds to countries with stronger currencies or gain certain concessions from host governments.[54] Obviously, MNEs cannot be shifting profits simultaneously to the home and the host country; however, is it ethical for them to try to avoid exchange controls or to minimize taxes through the loophole of licensing to themselves?

All partners put resources into collaborative arrangements; however, proportion of resources contributed and ability to extract benefits may vary among partners. This brings up the question of whether any partner should take resources from the operation that are not specified in the agreement. For example, one partner in a joint venture may transfer a scientist to the operation who, in addition to working on the venture's R&D, learns about breakthroughs that would be useful to that partner. Would it be ethical to pass this information along? Or a highly qualified manager may be hired by a joint venture. After the manager gains experience, would it be ethical for one of the partners in the venture to hire him or her away? Would the ethical issues be any different if one partner felt it was contributing more than the other relative to its income from the venture?

When a joint venture has problems, partners may renegotiate new working relationships that allow it to continue by altering its activities, ownership, or management structure.[55] In about three quarters of situations involving break-ups, one partner buys the other's interest.[56]

Managing Foreign Arrangements

Contracts with Other Companies

Even though a company may find it beneficial to rely on other companies at home or abroad to carry out part or all of its foreign business functions, the company's management is not relieved of responsibility for these functions. Periodically, management must assess whether the functions should be carried out internally. Great care should be taken to ensure that the best companies are involved and that they are performing the job of making, selling, or servicing the product adequately.

If an outside company can perform the same functions (assuming the same quality) more cheaply, a company should give little consideration to taking on the duties itself. If the company can do them more cheaply itself, it should nevertheless consider if its resources can be put to even better use elsewhere. Three subjective factors also enter into the analysis:

1. Management may feel incapable of doing as good a job as an outside company can.
2. Management may feel that the commitment of resources abroad would incur too large a risk for the company.
3. Management may feel that competitive risks increase when activities are not under its own control.

Because situations change, decisions should be reexamined from time to time.

In choosing another company to handle overseas business, management should consider that company's professional qualifications, personnel attributes, and motivation. Unfortunately, there is no way to measure these factors precisely and no magic formula for weighing one factor against another. The proven ability to handle similar business is one key professional qualification. Another is the importance the company places on its reputation.

Many possible conflicts can develop between the companies. Although any contract should provide for its termination and include means to settle disputes, contract termination and formal settlement of disputes are costly and cumbersome. If possible, it is much better for both parties to settle disagreements on a personal basis. The ability to develop a rapport with the management of another company is thus an important consideration in choosing a representative.

Management also should estimate potential sales, determine whether quality standards are being met, and assess servicing requirements in order to check whether the other company is doing an adequate job. Mutual goals should be set so

When contracting another company, a company must
- *Continue to monitor performance*
- *Assess whether to take over operations itself*
- *Work out conflicts and disputes*

that both parties understand what is expected, and the expectations should be spelled out in the contract.

Multiple Forms

A company usually will use various operating forms simultaneously.

Most companies move through stages of increased international involvement. Exporting usually precedes foreign production, and contracting with another company to handle foreign business generally precedes handling it internally. A company may be at different stages for different products and for different markets. It also may feel that differences in countries' characteristics necessitate diverse forms of involvement. Because of the multiproduct nature of most companies, varied products sold in the same country also may necessitate different stages. Further, more than one form may exist within the same operating unit. For example, a company may license technology and export to its joint venture.

Tension may develop internally as a company's international operations change and grow. For example, moving from exporting to foreign production may reduce the size of a domestic product division. Various profit centers all may perceive they have rights to the sales in a country the company is about to penetrate. Legal, technical, and marketing personnel may have entirely different perspectives on contracts. Under these circumstances, a team approach to evaluating decisions and performance may work. A company also must develop means of evaluating performance by separating those things that are controllable and noncontrollable by personnel in different profit centers.

C O U N T E R V A I L I N G

F O R C E S

Over forty years ago, John Kenneth Galbraith wrote that the era of cheap invention was over and "because development is costly, it follows that it can be carried out only by a firm that has the resources associated with considerable size."[57] The statement seems prophetic in terms of the estimated billions of investment dollars needed to bring intercontinental satellite-telephone systems or a new commercial aircraft to market. Such sums are generally out of reach for companies acting alone; but governments continue to limit company size through antitrust constraints and restrictions on foreign takeovers in key sectors. Further, markets must be truly global if high development costs are to be recouped; but governments continue to generate standards, such as for high-definition television, that will fragment markets globally. Thus there is a technological push toward larger investment in product and market that is countered by political constraints. One alternative is to use governmental funds to support large developmental projects; however, such support—especially for competitive prestige—seems to be waning internationally. The only other alternative is to develop strategic alliances among entities in different countries in order to get the needed investment while satisfying multiple governments. Such alliances are already developing, for example, that involving Motorola and Lockheed from the United States with British Aerospace, Deutsche Aerospace, and France's Matra Marconi for a satellite-telephone system. Government research agencies also are allying, such as those of Russia and South Africa for mining technology and those of various governments for space technology.[58]

Although some product developments require huge sums, most are much more modest. Nevertheless, companies lack all the product- and market-specific resources to go it alone everywhere in the world, especially if national differences dictate operating changes on a country-to-country basis. These situations present opportunities for alliances that employ complementary resources from different companies.

LOOKING TO THE FUTURE

As more businesses are becoming international, competition is becoming more global and more interrelated. Thus what happens competitively in one country is more likely to affect competitive viability in other countries. To expand more rapidly to meet this challenge, companies are turning increasingly to alliances with other companies. At one extreme are international mergers and acquisitions. At the other extreme are completely independent operations. The collaborative arrangements discussed in this chapter might be considered half-way houses to full merger and acquisition. These alliances may become larger and more complex. One prediction is that **relationship enterprises,** that is, networks of strategic alliances among big companies, spanning different industries and countries, will develop and be held together by common goals that make them act almost like a single company. Their sales may approach a trillion dollars, larger than the GDPs of all but about a half dozen countries. For example, Boeing, British Airways, TNT (an Australian parcel-delivery company), Siemens, and SNECMA (a French aero-engine manufacturer) might team up to build airports and sell their aircraft, technology, and services.[59]

Regardless of how they evolve, alliances will bring both opportunities and potential problems as companies move simultaneously to new countries and to contractual arrangements with new companies. For example, alliances must overcome differences in a number of areas:

- Societal cultures that may cause partners to perceive and interpret situations differently
- National contexts that lead to assumptions based on familiar governmental policies, institutions, and industry structures
- Corporate cultures that influence ideologies and values underlying company practices
- Strategic directions that result from partners' interests
- Management styles and organizational structures that cause partners to interface ineffectively[60]

Further, the additional operating alternatives may strain the decision-making and control processes.

Summary

- **The forms of foreign operations differ in terms of internal versus external handling of activities and in terms of the proportion of resources committed at home rather than abroad.**

- Although the form employed for foreign operations should be examined in terms of a company's strategic objectives, the choice often will involve a trade-off among objectives.

- Among the factors that will influence the choice of operating form are legal conditions, the company's experience, competitive factors, political and economic risks, and the nature of the assets to be exploited.

- Licensing is granting another company the use of some rights, such as patents, copyrights, or trademarks, usually for a fee. It is a means of establishing foreign production that may minimize capital outlays, prevent the free use of assets by other companies, allow the receipt of assets from other companies in return, and allow for income in some markets in which exportation or investment is not feasible.

- Among the major controversies concerning the terms of licensing agreements are loss of control of use of assets possibly affecting future competitive relationships, secrecy concerning technology and contract terms, and method and amount of payment.

- Franchising differs from licensing in that a trademark is an essential asset for the franchisee's business and the franchisor assists in the operation of the business on a continuing basis.

- Management contracts are a means of securing income with little capital outlay. They usually are used for expropriated properties in LDCs, new operations, and facilities with operating problems.

- Turnkey projects involve a contract for construction of operating facilities owned and run by someone else. Recently, these projects have been large and diverse, necessitating specialized skills and abilities to deal with top-level governmental authorities.

- In the absence of vertical control of operations through ownership, companies increasingly are achieving similar objectives through long-term contractual and output-sharing arrangements.

- Companies usually want to own 100 percent of their foreign operations, if possible, in order to secure control of those operations and prevent the dilution of profits. However, ownership sharing is widespread because host countries want local participation and because rapid foreign expansion requires companies to bring in outside resources.

- **Joint ventures are a special type of ownership sharing in which equity is owned by two or more organizations. There are various combinations of owners, including local governments and private companies and two or more companies from the same or different countries.**

- **A common motive for jointly owned operations is to take advantage of complementary resources that companies have at their disposal.**

- **Contracting for the outside management of a company's foreign business does not negate management's responsibility to ensure company resources are being worked adequately. Doing this involves constantly assessing the other company's work and evaluating new alternatives.**

- **Companies may use different forms for their foreign operations in different countries or for different products. As diversity increases, the task of coordinating and managing the foreign operations becomes more complex.**

Case
International Airline
Alliances[61]

In 1993, four European airlines began discussing the formation of a holding company. KLM, Swissair, and SAS each would own 30 percent of the merged operations, and Austrian Airlines would own 10 percent. This alliance, if implemented, would create the second-largest passenger traffic network in Europe, after that of British Airways, and the world's seventh largest carrier. (Map 15.2 shows the home bases of the world's twenty-five largest airlines.) This announcement came shortly after Air Canada acquired 24 percent of the voting stock in Continental, and British Airways obtained 19.9 percent of the voting stock in USAir. Three years earlier, KLM had secured a substantial but minority equity interest in Northwest. There have been many other partial acquisitions among airlines in different countries. For example, Delta and Swissair own a stake in each other, as do Singapore Airlines and Swissair. Swissair also has an interest in Austrian Airlines. American Airlines has an interest in Air New Zealand, SAS in British Midland, Air France in CSA (Czech Republic), KLM in Air U.K., British Airways in Air Russia, and Iberia in VIASA (Venezuela). In addition to new ownership stakes among airlines, other recent alliances have blurred the competitive distinctions among the major international carriers.

Although airline alliances have increased recently, such alliances have been important almost from the start of international air travel. Airlines have been motivated by a combination of regulatory, cost, and competitive factors, but their alliances have changed over time in response to evolving conditions, such as changes in the type of regulations facing airlines.

Regulatory Factors
Countries have always seen airlines as key industries; thus they have wanted domestic service that is nationally controlled. For example, the United States grants U.S.-based airlines the right to carry all passengers between domestic points, and it limits foreign ownership in U.S.-based airlines to 25 percent of voting stock and 49 percent of total equity. Many coun-

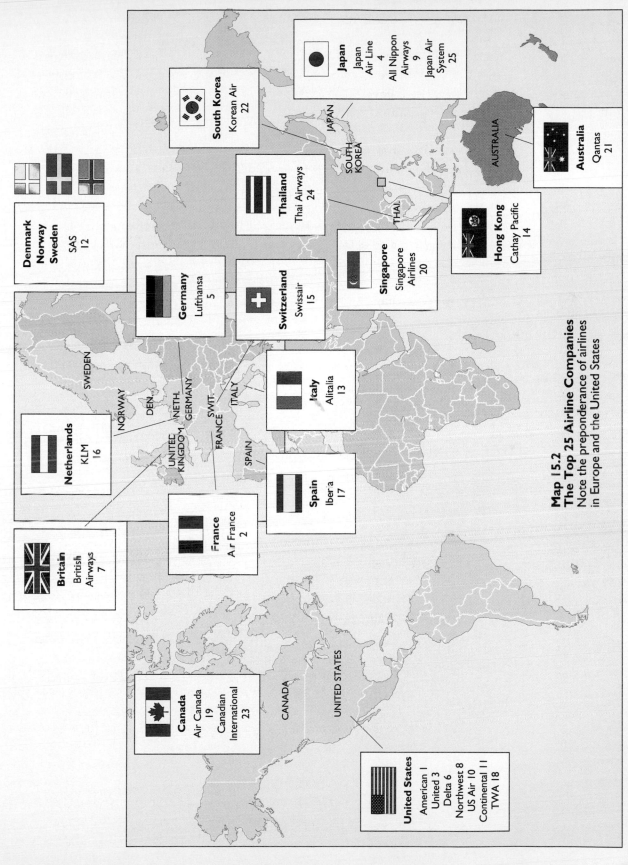

Map 15.2
The Top 25 Airline Companies
Note the preponderance of airlines in Europe and the United States

Japan
Japan Air Line 4
All Nippon Airways 9
Japan Air System 25

South Korea
Korean Air 22

Australia
Qantas 21

Thailand
Thai Airways 24

Hong Kong
Cathay Pacific 14

Denmark
Norway
Sweden
SAS 12

Singapore
Singapore Airlines 20

Germany
Lufthansa 5

Switzerland
Swissair 15

Netherlands
KLM 16

Italy
Alitalia 13

Britain
British Airways 7

France
Air France 2

Spain
Iberia 17

Canada
Air Canada 19
Canadian International 23

United States
American 1
United 3
Delta 6
Northwest 8
US Air 10
Continental 11
TWA 18

Source: The names of the largest airlines are from "The Top 50 Airline Companies," *Fortune,* November 2, 1992, p. 92.

557

tries have ensured national control through whole or partial government ownership of airlines; examples are Iberia, KLM, Lufthansa, and Thai Airlines. Many government-owned airlines are monopolies, and many lose money that is made up through governmental subsidies. Governments further protect their airlines by regulating numerous operational aspects:

- Which foreign carriers have landing rights
- Which airports and aircraft those carriers can use
- Frequency of flights
- Whether foreign carriers can fly beyond the country (For instance, the Japanese government restricted United from flying from the United States beyond Japan to Australia.)
- Overflight privileges
- Fares that may be charged

The restrictions and rights generally are agreed upon through treaties, usually to give more or less reciprocal treatment to each country's carriers but sometimes to protect the system of national ownership. For example, the International Air Transport Association (IATA) comprises nearly all the world's airlines. Given the extent of governmental ownership of airlines, governments effectively comprise the membership. Today, IATA is mainly concerned with global safety standards; however, at times it has restricted competition on routes by requiring uniform fares, meal service, and baggage allowances.

Five factors influence governments' protection of their airlines:

1. Countries believe they can save money by maintaining smaller air forces and relying on domestic airlines in times of unusual air transport needs. For example, the U.S. government used U.S. commercial carriers to help carry troops to Somalia in 1992.
2. In aviation's early days, airlines were heavily subsidized to carry mail, and governments wanted to support their own fledgling companies rather than foreign ones. This consideration has shifted somewhat because mail subsidies no longer are very important internationally. For example, they now account for less than 0.5 percent of revenues for U.S. airlines.
3. Public opinion favors spending "at home," especially for government-paid travel. Thus the maintenance of national airlines and the requirement that government-paid international travel be on those airlines are viewed as foreign-exchange savings.
4. Airlines are a source of national pride, and aircraft with the national flag symbolize a country's sovereignty and technical competence. This national identification has been especially important for LDCs, whose airlines once were largely foreign-owned. For example, the former PanAm controlled airlines in Brazil, Colombia, Mexico, Panama, and Venezuela. As soon as countries were technically and financially capable, they fostered the development of national airlines and prohibited foreign ownership.
5. Countries have worried about protecting their airspace for security reasons. This is less of a concern today because foreign carriers routinely overfly domestic territories

in order to reach inland gateways. For example, many foreign carriers land international flights at Atlanta, Chicago, and Dallas. Further, overflight treaties are quite common, even among unfriendly nations. For example, Cubana overflies the United States en route to Canada, and American Airlines overflies Cuba en route to South America.

National attitudes and regulations not only give rise to separate national airlines, they also limit airlines' expansion internationally. With few exceptions, airlines cannot fly on lucrative domestic routes in foreign countries. For example, Lufthansa cannot compete on the New York–Los Angeles route. They also cannot easily control a flight network abroad that will feed passengers into their international flights. For example, Air France has no flights to feed passengers into Chicago for connections to Paris, but American has scores of such flights; however, the situation is reversed in Paris, where Air France has a monopoly on air travel within France. Further, airlines usually cannot service pairs of foreign countries. For example, United cannot fly between Brazil and Portugal because it is a U.S. carrier. In order to tap into any of these opportunities, airlines must ally themselves via networks with carriers from other countries.

The recent increase in alliances has been due largely to the 1978 deregulation of U.S. domestic flights, allowing U.S. carriers to fly where they want and charge what they want domestically, as well as to ongoing deregulation within the EU. Deregulation in the United States resulted in a shrinking number of U.S. airlines, along with business concentration—domestic and international—among a few of the survivors. Airline analysts expect the same pattern to emerge in Europe and a few mega-carriers eventually to control most of the world's air traffic. Therefore airlines have sought cooperative agreements to complement their route structures and other capabilities. By buying an interest in a foreign airline, even if it is a minority one because of regulations, an airline gains more assurance of a lasting relationship than it might through mere contracts.

Privatization also has been an impetus to forming alliances. For example, privatized airlines, such as British Airways and Air Canada, can no longer look to their governments for support; instead, they must find new means to be competitive internationally. Similarly, privatization in Eastern Europe and Latin America has enabled foreign carriers to take stakes in countries' airlines in those regions.

Cost Factors

Airlines have always contracted activities in locations where one company has amassed a critical mass of fixed capabilities. Costs may be spread by sharing these capabilities with other airlines. For example, KLM has long handled passenger check-in, baggage loading, and maintenance for a number of other airlines in Amsterdam. Other contracts commonly cover the use of airport gates, ground equipment such as generators, and commissary services. Airlines also sometimes sublease aircraft to each other.

When traffic on a route is low, airlines sometimes make market agreements to fly on alternate days. Or they may agree to share service in the same aircraft, which then has a dual flight designation. PanAm and Aeroflot used to do this between New York and Moscow. Air New Zealand and American do so between Honolulu and Auckland, as do Canadian International and SAS between Copenhagen and Toronto.

The high cost of maintenance and reservations systems has led to recent joint ventures. For example, Swissair, Lufthansa, and Guiness Peat Aviation are partners in a maintenance center in Ireland. United, British Airways, USAir, Swissair, Alitalia, and Air Canada share ownership in Covia, which operates and delivers the Apollo reservation system. Another reservation system, Galileo, is owned by United, British Air, Alitalia, Swissair, KLM, Olympic, Austrian Airlines, AerLingus, Sabena, and Air Portugal.

Competitive Factors

A number of airlines have established marketing agreements in order to complement their route structures. For example, USAir and Air France have blocked space on certain flights, set schedules so that flights have good connections between them, automated seat selection on the connections, and advertised the through-service. These two airlines also are partners in USAir's frequent traveler program, along with six of Air France's European competitors. Continental and SAS have gone a step further through Continental's handling of all operations in its Newark facilities. About one third of SAS traffic from Newark to Scandinavia comes from the Continental connections. SAS also has contracted to help Continental improve its in-flight service. The joint use of facilities within alliances may be the wave of the future because it is nearly impossible to add gates at the largest airports and existing airlines own all the gates.

A problem with these marketing agreements is that the connections from one airline to another show up as separate route codes in reservations systems. These come up last on the screens of travel agents, and the agents tend to recommend the first schedules they see. Further, when passengers see that they must change airlines, they worry that they may have to make connections across great distances within ever larger airline terminals. This puts connections between two different airlines at a disadvantage relative to connections on the same airline. When KLM bought an interest in Northwest, the two airlines were able to secure the same route codes on their connecting flights. Northwest's ticket counters show KLM's logo as well. The alliance gives Northwest service to eighty European cities, whereas American serves only twelve. They have come as close as possible to a merger without actually making one. It is anticipated that British Airways and USAir will be able to share route codes. American Airlines and United at first vowed to fight that; however, United later was successful in making a shared route code agreement with Lufthansa.

Management of Alliances

An impending problem in the proliferation of alliances is the vast network of relationships. The relationships are so intertwined among so many airlines that it is difficult to determine what companies are competing, cooperating, or colluding. Management may find it increasingly hard to be cooperative, say, in joint maintenance agreements while trying to compete head-on on some routes.

Preventing full mergers may be a blessing in some ways because corporate and national cultures may be difficult to mesh. There also are structural differences. For example, pilots at Air Canada are unionized, but those at Continental are not. Analysts conclude that the problems of combining unions after PanAm's acquisition of National was a major contribution to PanAm's eventual demise. However, the lack of control is also a problem. Analysts worry that British Airways, with only a minority of voting stock in USAir, will be unable to make needed changes in that airline.

Other things simply may not mesh well in alliances. The USAir–British Airways agreement is considered synergistic because USAir is strong in the eastern United States, where most transatlantic traffic originates, and British Airways is strong in connections from London to Europe and Asia. But USAir's strength in New York is at LaGuardia Airport, which is purely domestic; therefore most connecting passengers must change airports. When Northwest and KLM allied, it was expected that KLM would help Northwest improve its service; however, the organizations could not work well in that effort.

Questions

1. Discuss a question raised by the manager of route strategy of American Airlines: Why should an airline not be able to establish service anywhere in the world simply by demonstrating that it can and will comply with the local labor and business laws of the host country?

2. The president of Japan Air Lines has claimed that U.S. airlines are dumping air services on routes between the United States and Europe because of the money they are losing. Should prices be set so that carriers make money on routes?

3. What will be the consequences if a few large airlines or networks come to dominate global air service?

4. Some airlines, such as Southwest and Alaska Air, have survived as niche players without going international or developing alliances with international airlines. Can they continue this strategy?

Chapter Notes

1. Data for the case were taken from James Flanigan, "The Strategy," *Forbes*, October 29, 1979, pp. 42–52; "Dravo Agrees to Market Type of Plant for Grupo," *Wall Street Journal*, September 23, 1980, p. 38; Hugh O'Shaughnessy, "A Hive of Private Enterprise," *Financial Times*, May 4, 1979, p. 34; Christopher Lorenz, "A Front-Runner in Mexican Industry," *Financial Times*, June 1, 1979, p. 16; "Mexico: Exporting a Cheaper Way of Making Steel," *Business Week*, June 11, 1979, p. 53; Alan M. Field, "After the Fall," *Fortune*, Vol. 135, No. 8, April 22, 1985, pp. 93–95; Keith Bradsher, "Back from the Brink, Mexico's Giant Alfa Slims Down for Hard Times," *International Management*, Vol. 41, No. 9, September 1986, pp. 65–66; Matt Moffett, "Monterrey Sides with Mexican President," *Wall Street Journal*, May 22, 1989, p. A8; Stephen Baker, "Mexico's Giants March North," *Business Week*, November 13, 1989, pp. 63–64; "Los Grandes Grupos Económicos de la Re-

gion," *America Economica*, December 1991, p. 8; Al Wrigley, "Automakers Pick Mexico Aluminum," *American Metal Market*, August 19, 1992, p. 1; and "Bekaert," *Rubber World*, November 1992, p. 8.

2. For a discussion of the many trade-offs, see James D. Goodnow, "Individual Product: Market Transactional Mode of Entry Strategies—Some Eclectic Decision-Making Formats," paper presented at Academy of International Business meeting in New Orleans, October 24, 1980. For a discussion of the many motives for alliances with foreign companies, see Farok J. Contractor and Peter Lorange, "Why Should Firms Cooperate? The Strategy and Economics Basis for Cooperative Ventures," in *Cooperative Strategies in International Business*, Farok J. Contractor and Peter Lorange, eds. (Lexington, Mass.: D.C. Heath, 1988), pp. 3–28.

3. Michael Selz, "Networks Help Small Companies Think and Act Big," *Wall Street Journal*, November 12, 1992, p. B2;

and Joel Bleeke and David Ernst, "Sleeping with the Enemy," *Harvard International Review*, Summer 1993, pp. 12–14+.

4. Seev Hirsch and Avi Meshulach, "Toward a Unified Theory of Internationalization," Working Paper 10-91 (Copenhagen: Institute of International Economics and Management, 1991); and R. T. Carstairs and L. S. Welch, "Licensing and the Internationalization of Smaller Companies: Some Australian Evidence," *Management International Review*, Vol. 22, No. 3, 1982, pp. 33–44.

5. Bent Petersen and Torben Pedersen, "Research on the Entry Mode Choice of the Firm: How Close to a Normative Theory?" Working Paper 20-92 (Copenhagen: Institute of International Economics and Management, 1992).

6. Ian H. Giddy and Alan M. Rugman, "A Model of Trade, Foreign Direct Investment and Licensing," Working Paper, No. 274A (New York: Columbia University Graduate School of Business, December 1979).

7. Leo Sleuwaegen, "Monopolistic Advantages and the International Operations of Firms: Disaggregated Evidence from U.S. Based Multinationals," *Journal of International Business Studies*, Vol. 16, No. 3, Fall 1985, pp. 125–133; and W. H. Davidson and D. G. McFetridge, "Key Characteristics in the Choice of International Technology Transfer Mode," *Journal of International Business Studies*, Vol. 16, No. 2, Summer 1985, pp. 5–21, found evidence for this point as well as those that follow in this discussion.

8. Peter J. Buckley and Mark C. Casson, "Multinational Enterprises in LDCs: Cultural and Economic Interaction," in *Multinational Enterprises in Less Developed Countries*, Peter J. Buckley and Jeremy Clegg, eds. (London: Macmillan, 1990); and Jeremy Clegg, "The Determinants of Aggregate International Licensing Behaviour: Evidence from Five Countries," *Management International Review*, Vol. 30, No. 3, 1990, pp. 231–251.

9. "American Home Plans Drug Venture in U.S. with French Company," *Wall Street Journal*, June 3, 1981, p. 54.

10. Jeffrey A. Tannenbaum, "Licensing May Be Quickest Route to Foreign Markets," *Wall Street Journal*, September 14, 1990, p. B2.

11. David Ford and Chris Ryan, "Taking Technology to Market," *Harvard Business Review*, March–April 1981, p. 118.

12. Gregory A. Patterson, "Chrysler Signs Licensing Pact for Jeep Name," *Wall Street Journal*, August 30, 1988, p. 24.

13. Richard N. Osborn and C. Christopher Baughn, "Forms of Interorganizational Governance for Multinational Alliances," *Academy of Management Journal*, September 1990, pp. 503–519.

14. Alan Riding, "Cartier's Mexican Look-Alike," *New York Times*, October 17, 1980, p. D1+; and Michael G. Harvey and Ilkka A. Ronkainen, "International Counterfeiters: Marketing Success without the Cost and the Risk," *Columbia Journal of World Business*, Vol. 20, No. 3, Fall 1985, pp. 37–45.

15. "Oleg Cassini Inc. Sues Firm Over Licensing," *Wall Street Journal*, March 28, 1984, p. 5; and "Cassini Awarded $16 Million in Fragrance Line Squabble," *Wall Street Journal*, June 2, 1988, p. 28.

16. William H. Meyers, *New York Times Magazine*, May 3, 1987, pp. 33–35+.

17. Robert T. Keller and Ravi R. Chinta, "International Technology Transfer: Strategies for Success," *Academy of Management Executive*, Vol. 4, No. 2, 1990, pp. 33–43.

18. Louise Kehoe, "AT&T Alliances Open New Market," *Financial Times*, November 17, 1992, p. 19+.

19. Kang Rae Cho, "Issues of Compensation in International Technology Licensing," *Management International Review*, Vol. 28, No. 2, 1988, pp. 70–79; and Keller and Chinta, loc. cit.

20. Edwin Mansfield, "International Technology Transfer: Forms, Resource Requirements, and Policies," *American Economic Review*, May 1975, pp. 372–382.

21. "Royalties and License Fees, 1991," *Survey of Current Business*, September 1992, p. 99.

22. Jerry H. Opack, "Likenesses of Licensing, Franchising," *Les Nouvelles*, June 1977, pp. 102–105.

23. John F. Preble, "Global Expansion: The Case of U.S. Fast-Food Franchisors," *Journal of Global Marketing*, Vol. 6, Nos. 1/2, 1992, p. 186, citing D. Ayling, "Franchising in the U.K.," *The Quarterly Review of Marketing*, Summer 1988, pp. 19–24; and "Franchising: A Tool for Growth in the 1980s," *Forbes*, June 9, 1982, pp. 63–72.

24. James W. Wolfe, "Is There An Overseas Franchise in Your Future?" *Export Today*, June 1992, pp. 51–52.

25. A. Kostecka, *Franchising in the Economy 1986–1988* (Washington, D.C.: U.S. Department of Commerce, February 1988), pp. 8–10; and Arthur Andersen & Co., "Franchising in the Economy: 1989–1992," n.d., p. 109.

26. Mike Connelly, "U.S. Franchising Grows Attractive to Foreign Firms," *Wall Street Journal*, December 22, 1988, p. B2; and Jeffrey A. Tannenbaum, "Foreign Franchisers in U.S. on the Rise," *Wall Street Journal*, June 11, 1990, p. B2.

27. Peng S. Chan and Robert T. Justis, "Franchise Management in East Asia," *Academy of Management Executive*, Vol. 4, No. 2, 1990, pp. 75–85.

28. Joann Lublin, "U.S. Franchisers Learn Britain Isn't Easy," *Wall Street Journal*, August 16, 1988, p. 20.

29. Kathleen Deveny, John Pluenneke, Dori Jones Yang, Mark Maremont, and Robert Black, "McWorld," *Business Week*, October 13, 1986, pp. 78–86.

30. Lawrence S. Welch, "Developments in International Franchising," *Journal of Global Marketing*, Vol. 6, Nos. 1/2, 1992, p. 81–96.

31. Chan and Justis, loc. cit. For other changes by McDonald's in Europe, see Heather Ogilvie, "Welcome to McEurope: An Interview with Tom Allin, President of McDonald's Development Co.," *Journal of European Business*, Vol. 2, No. 67, July–August 1991, pp. 5–12+.

32. "Judge Revokes License of Paris McDonald's," *International Herald Tribune* (Zurich), September 12, 1982, p. 14; and Steven Greenhouse, "McDonald's Tries Paris, Again," *New York Times*, June 12, 1988, p. 1F+.

33. "Affordable Airport Shops?" *New York Times*, November 18, 1992, p. F14.

34. Lawrence S. Welch and Anubis Pacifico, "Management Contracts: A Role in Internationalisation?" *International Marketing Review*, Vol. 7, No. 4, 1990, pp. 64–74.

35. Nicholas D. Kristof, "A Not-So-Grand Hotel: A Tibet Horror Story," *New York Times*, September 25, 1990, p. A4.

36. David J. Jefferson, "Biggest Builder, Fluor, Sees Kuwaiti Contracts As a Mixed Blessing," *Wall Street Journal*, April 18, 1991, p. A1+.

37. *A Competitive Assessment of the U.S. International Construction Industry* (Washington, D.C.: U.S. Department of Commerce, International Trade Administration, July 1984).

38. Joan Gray, "International Construction," *Financial Times*, April 12, 1985, pp. 13–17; and Erdener Kaynak, "Internationalization of Turkish Construction Companies," *Columbia Journal of World Business*, Winter 1992, pp. 61–75.

39. Paul Ingrassia, "Ford Nears Pact to Make Cars in Europe for Mazda in a Buy-Sell Arrangement," *Wall Street Journal*, October 28, 1991, p. A3.

40. F. A. Sviridov, ed., *The Role of Patent Information in the Transfer of Technology* (New York: Pergamon, 1981), p. 137; and Shlomo Maital, "Wanted: Technology Detectives," *Across the Board*, Vol. 26, No. 9, September 1989, pp. 7–9.

41. Robert Ronstadt and Robert J. Kramer, "Getting the Most Out of Innovation Abroad," *Harvard Business Review*, Vol. 60, No. 2, March–April 1982, pp. 94–99; and Beth Karlin and George Anders, "Importing Science," *Wall Street Journal*, October 5, 1983, p. 1+.

42. Carl H. Fulda and Warren F. Schwartz, *Regulation of International Trade and Investment* (Mineola, N.Y.: Foundation Press, 1979), pp. 776–782.

43. Stephen J. Kobrin, "Trends in Ownership of American Manufacturing Subsidiaries in Developing Countries: An Inter-industry Analysis," *Management International Review*, Special Issue 1988, pp. 73–84.

44. Louis Uchitelle, "Mexico's Plan for Industrial Might," *New York Times*, September 25, 1990, p. C2; and E. S. Browning, "Renault, Volvo Agree to Enter into Alliance," *Wall Street Journal*, February 26, 1990, p. A3.

45. George Getschow, "Foreign Investment in Mexico Swells," *Wall Street Journal*, May 1981, p. 34.

46. R. Duane Hall, "International Joint Ventures: An Alternative to Foreign Acquisitions," *Journal of Buyout and Acquisitions*, Vol. 4, No. 2, March–April 1986, pp. 39–45.

47. Mike Tharp, "Uneasy Partners," *Wall Street Journal*, November 8, 1976, p. 28.

48. J. Peter Killing, "How to Make a Global Joint Venture Work," *Harvard Business Review*, Vol. 60, No. 3, May–June 1982, pp. 120–127.

49. Joel Bleeke and David Ernst, "The Way to Win in Cross-Border Alliances," *Har-*

vard Business Review, November–December 1991, pp. 127–135.

50. Thomas Horst, "American Multinationals and the U.S. Economy," *American Economic Review,* May 1976, pp. 150–152; Claudio V. Vaitsos, *Intercountry Income Distribution and Transnational Enterprises* (Oxford: Clarendon Press, 1974); P. Streeten, "Theory of Development Policy," in *Economic Analysis and the Multinational Enterprise,* J. H. Dunning, ed. (London: Allen and Unwin, 1974); G. F. Kopits, "Intrafirm Royalties Crossing Frontiers and Transfer Pricing Behavior," *Economic Journal,* December 1976; and Donald R. Lessard, "Transfer Prices, Taxes, and Financial Markets: Implications of Internal Financial Transfers within the Multinational Firm," paper presented at the New York University Conference on Economic Issues of Multinational Firms, November 4, 1976.

51. Lawrence G. Franko, *Joint Venture Survival in Multinational Corporations* (New York: Praeger, 1971); and Richard H. Holton, "Making International Joint Ventures Work," in *The Management of Headquarters-Subsidiary Relationships in Multinational Corporations,* Lars Otterbeck, ed. (London: Cower, Aldershot, 1981), pp. 255–267.

52. Yumiko Ono, "Borden's Messy Split with Firm in Japan Points Up Perils of Partnerships There," *Wall Street Journal,* February 21, 1991, p. B1+; and Henry W. Lane and Paul W. Beamish, "Cross-Cultural Cooperative Behavior in Joint Ventures in LDCs," *Management International Review,* Vol. 30, special issue, 1990, pp. 87–102.

53. Bleeke and Ernst, loc. cit.

54. John D. Daniels and Sharon L. Magill, "The Utilization of International Joint Ventures by United States Firms in High Technology Industries," *Journal of High Technology Management Research,* Vol. 2, No. 1, 1991, pp. 113–131.

55. Linda Longfellow Blodgett, "Factors in the Instability of International Joint Ventures: An Event History Analysis," *Strategic Management Journal,* Vol. 13, No. 6, September 1992, pp. 475–481.

56. Bleeke and Ernst, loc. cit.

57. John Kenneth Galbraith, *American Capitalism* (Boston: Houghton-Mifflin, 1952), pp. 91–92.

58. "Beam Me Up, Scottie," *Economist,* March 28, 1992, pp. 69–70; Neil Behrmann, "Russians, South Africans Join Forces on Mining," *Wall Street Journal,* June 17, 1992, p. C1+; Brian Coleman and Elisabeth Rubinfien, "Space Race Becomes a Joint Venture," *Wall Street Journal,* November 11, 1992, p. A8; and Richard L. Hudson, "European Phone Companies Reach Out for Partners," *Wall Street Journal,* September 30, 1993, p. B4.

59. "The Global Firm: R.I.P.," *The Economist,* February 6, 1993, p. 69, referring to a view of Cyrus Freidman, vice chairman of Booz, Allen & Hamilton, for study to be published, "The Global Corporation—Obsolete So Soon?"

60. Arvind Parkhe, "Interfirm Diversity, Organizational Learning, and Longevity in Global Strategic Alliances," *Journal of International Business Studies,* Vol. 22, No. 4, Fourth Quarter 1991, pp. 579–601.

61. Data for the case were taken from Andrea Rothman, "U.S. to World: Airline Deals Hinge on Open Skies," *Business Week,* January 11, 1992, p. 46; Christopher J. Chipello, "Midsize Air Canada Plots Survival in Industry of Giants," *Wall Street Journal,* November 12, 1992, p. B2; Andrea Rothman, Seth Payne, and Paula Dwyer, "One World, One Giant Airline Market?" *Business Week,* October 5, 1992, p. 56; "All Aboard," *The Economist,* February 29, 1992, p. 78; "Wings Across the Water," *The Economist,* July 25, 1992, p. 62; Brian Coleman, "Four European Carriers Propose Merger into Continent's Second-Largest Airline," *Wall Street Journal,* April 28, 1993, p. A3; "KLM Is Considering Allying with Swissair, SAS and Austrian Air," *Wall Street Journal,* January 28, 1993, p. A10; Agis Salpukas, "Continental Backs Air Canada's Offer to Merge Systems," *New York Times,* November 10, 1992, p. A1; Agis Salpukas, "Europe's Small Airlines Shelter under

Bigger Wings," *New York Times,* November 8, 1992, p. E4; "USAir, Air France Plan Links Between Businesses," *Wall Street Journal,* September 25, 1990, p. C12; "Code Breakers," *The Economist,* November 21, 1992, pp. 78–79; Brett Pulley, "Northwest Airlines to Cut Up to 40% Fares to Europe," *Wall Street Journal,* February 1, 1993, p. C15; Agis Salpukas, "Lufthansa Drops Plan For U.S.," *New York Times,* November 3, 1992, p. C1; Robert L. Rose and Brian Coleman, "British Airways Purchases Stake in USAir Group," *Wall Street Journal,* January 22, 1993, p. A3; Wendy Zellner, William Symonds, and Andrea Rothman, "This Time, Continental May Actually Fly," *Business Week,* May 10, 1993, p. 70; Bridget O'Brian and Laurie McGinley, "Mixing of U.S., Foreign Carriers Alters Market," *Wall Street Journal,* December 21, 1992, p. B1; Bill Poling, "United, American Spar with USAir, BA over Proposed Deal," *Travel Weekly,* November 12, 1992, p. 49; Joan M. Feldman, "The Dilemma of 'Open Skies,' " *The New York Times Magazine,* April 2, 1989, p. 31+; Paula Dwyer, Andrea Rothman, Seth Payne and Stewart Toy, "Air Raid: British Air's Bold Global Push," *Business Week,* August 24, 1992, pp. 54–61; Philippe Gugler, "Strategic Alliances in Services: Some Theoretical Issues and the Case of Air-Transport Services," paper prepared for the Danish Summer Research Institute (DSRI), Denmark, August 1992; Robert Johnson and Laurie McGinley, "Air Canada and U.S. Partner's Offer for Continental Stake Clears Hurdle," *Wall Street Journal,* January 8, 1993, p. A4; Martin Tolchin, "Shift Urged on Foreign Stakes in Airlines," *New York Times,* January 9, 1993, p. 17; Agis Salpukas, "The Big Foreign Push to Buy into U.S. Airlines," *New York Times,* October 11, 1992, p. F11; and Robert L. Rose and Bridget O'Brian, "United, Lufthansa Form Marketing Tie, Dealing a Setback to American Airlines," *Wall Street Journal,* October 4, 1993, p. A4.

Chapter 16

Control

Form your plans before sunrise.
—Indian-Tamil Proverb

Objectives

- To explain the special challenges of controlling foreign operations

- To describe the alternative organizational structures for international operations

- To show the advantages and disadvantages of decision making at headquarters and at foreign subsidiary locations

- To highlight both the importance of and the methods for global planning, reporting, and evaluating

- To give an overview of some specific control considerations affecting MNEs, such as the handling of acquisitions and the shifts in strategies to fulfill international objectives

Case
Nestlé[1]

The former managing director of Nestlé, Pierre Liotard-Vogt, said, "Perhaps we are the only real multinational company existing." Although this may be something of an exaggeration, it is difficult to find other companies with such a high dependence on foreign involvement. The Swiss-based company, one of the world's fifty largest industrials, was international from the start. Nestlé was formed by a 1905 merger between an American-owned company and a German-owned company. About 98 percent of Nestlé's sales are outside of Switzerland, and about half of the top management at the Vevey headquarters is non-Swiss. A Frenchman, an Italian, a German, and a Swiss who took out U.S. citizenship have at various times held the position of chief executive officer. Map 16.1 shows Nestlé's factories by country and percentages of sales by region. The one area in which the company is still primarily Swiss is in ownership. Until 1988, two thirds of the shares were registered in Switzerland and could be bought only by other Swiss; however, this ownership restriction was changed in response to criticism about Swiss companies' takeovers abroad, particularly unfriendly ones. Nestlé expects that eventually Swiss owners will be a minority.

In 1992, Nestlé's sales from 482 factories in sixty-seven countries were 54.5 billion Swiss francs. With such a wide geographic spread of operations, Nestlé maintains clear-cut policies on where decisions will be made and what roles corporate and host-country managers will play.

A major responsibility of Nestlé's corporate management is to give the company strategic direction. To do this, it decides in which geographic areas and to which products it plans to allocate efforts. For example, in the early 1980s, Nestlé became less dependent on chocolate and Third-World markets by placing more emphasis on culinary products and on the North American market. By the early 1990s, it was placing more emphasis on LDCs, especially China. Throughout most of its history, Nestlé has concentrated on manufacturing, marketing, and wholesale distribution and has avoided vertical expansion into plantations or supermarkets. To maintain this control, its corporate management handles all acquisition decisions as well as those regarding which products will be researched at the centralized facilities in Switzerland. This decision making is handled through product groups, such as the chocolate and confectionery products group. To support these functions, each geographic group is expected to provide a positive cash flow to the parent. In fact, Nestlé tries to move almost all cash to Switzerland, where a specialized staff decides in which currencies it will be held and to what countries it will be transferred.

Headquarters also researches conditions affecting commodities and mandates amounts and prices for purchases of supplies, for example, requiring that all overseas companies contract for a supply of green coffee for, say, three to six months at some maximum price. The company is heavily dependent on introducing new products that may take several years to become profitable, so it must ensure that the more established products remain sufficiently profitable to generate needed funds. If a new product does not become profitable within a reasonable time, such as mineral water in Brazil, or if it has run its cycle of profitability, such as Libby's vegetable-canning operations, or if its development potential seems low, such as Beech-Nut's baby food, management in Switzerland decides to divest the business. Other divestments occur because certain activities of acquired companies do

Map 16.1   Locations of Nestlé Factories

Note that Nestlé's manufacturing is located in sixty different countries.

Source: Nestlé *Annual Report, 1989,* pp. 28–29.

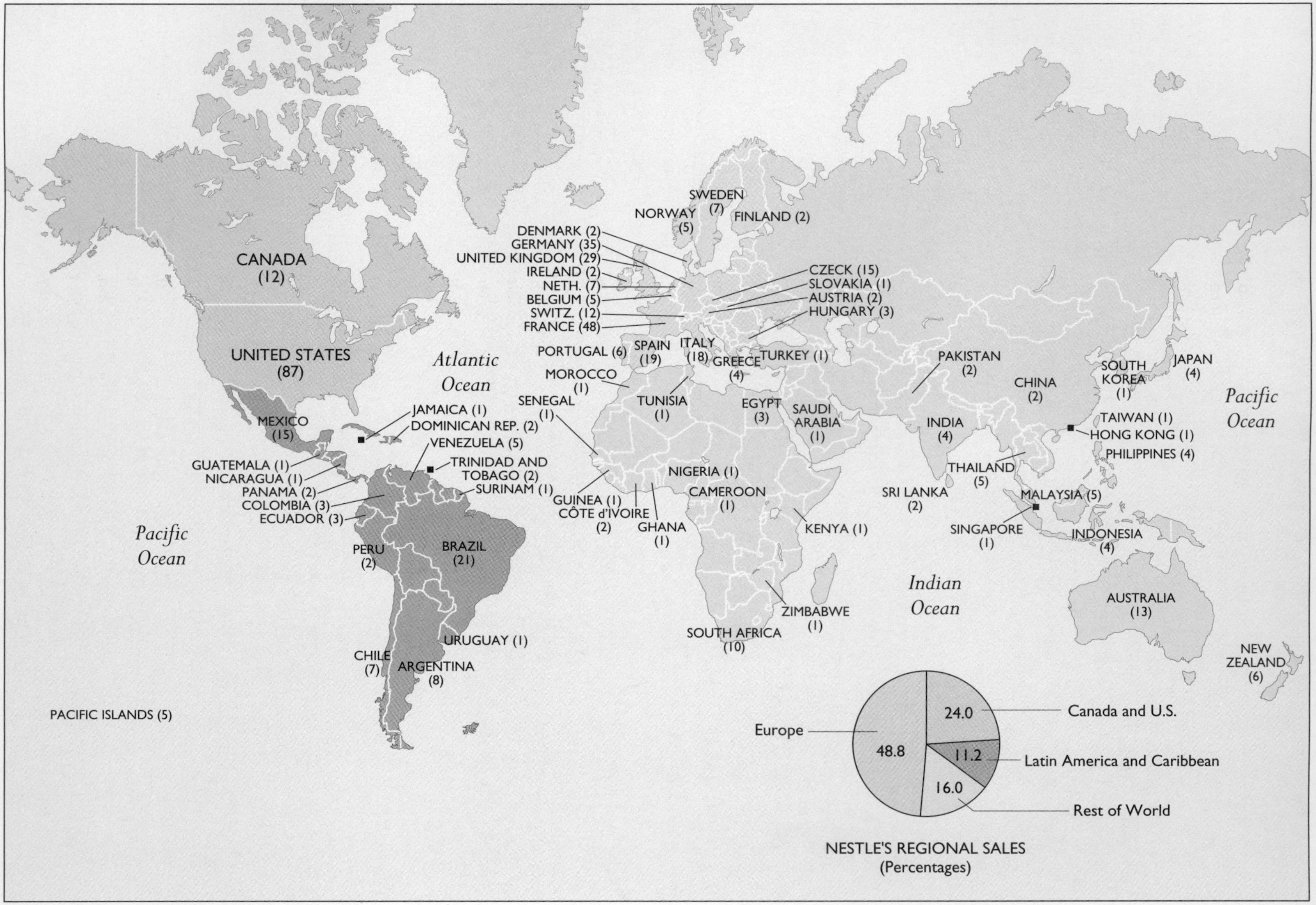

Pacific Ocean

JAPAN (4)

SOUTH KOREA (1)

TAIWAN (1)

HONG KONG (1)

PHILIPPINES (4)

CHINA (2)

MALAYSIA (5)

INDONESIA (4)

AUSTRALIA (13)

NEW ZEALAND (6)

PAKISTAN (2)

INDIA (4)

THAILAND (5)

SINGAPORE (1)

SRI LANKA (2)

Indian Ocean

CZECK (15)

SLOVAKIA (1)

AUSTRIA (2)

HUNGARY (3)

FINLAND (2)

SWEDEN (7)

NORWAY (5)

DENMARK (2)

GERMANY (35)

UNITED KINGDOM (29)

IRELAND (2)

NETH. (7)

BELGIUM (5)

SWITZ. (12)

FRANCE (48)

PORTUGAL (6)

SPAIN (19)

ITALY (18)

GREECE (4)

TURKEY (1)

SAUDI ARABIA (1)

EGYPT (3)

TUNISIA (1)

MOROCCO (1)

SENEGAL (1)

GUINEA (1)

CÔTE d'IVOIRE (2)

GHANA (1)

NIGERIA (1)

CAMEROON (1)

KENYA (1)

ZIMBABWE (1)

SOUTH AFRICA (10)

NESTLE'S REGIONAL SALES
(Percentages)

Europe 48.8

Canada and U.S. 24.0

Latin America and Caribbean 11.2

Rest of World 16.0

Atlantic Ocean

JAMAICA (1)

DOMINICAN REP. (2)

VENEZUELA (5)

TRINIDAD AND TOBAGO (2)

SURINAM (1)

CANADA (12)

UNITED STATES (87)

MEXICO (15)

GUATEMALA (1)

NICARAGUA (1)

PANAMA (2)

COLOMBIA (3)

ECUADOR (3)

PERU (2)

BRAZIL (21)

URUGUAY (1)

ARGENTINA (8)

CHILE (7)

Pacific Ocean

PACIFIC ISLANDS (5)

not fit the corporate development strategy. For example, Nestlé spun off a printing and packaging business that was part of the acquired Buitoni-Perugina operations.

The budget that originates from each country is the main means used to ensure that each area carries its share within the corporation. Budgets are prepared annually, revised quarterly, and subject to approval at corporate headquarters. Actual performance reports are sent to Switzerland monthly, where they are compared with the budget and the previous year's performance. The head of the country and/or area operations must explain any deviations satisfactorily or corporate management will intervene. Corporate headquarters also serves as a source of information. The successes, failures, and general experiences of product programs in one country are passed on to managers in others. For example, information on the success of a white chocolate bar in New Zealand and on a line of Lean Cuisine frozen food in the United States was disseminated this way.

Despite the centralized directives described above, Nestlé's country and/or area managers have a great deal of discretion in certain matters, especially marketing. Product research is centralized so that duplication of efforts is kept to a minimum. When a new product is developed, corporate management offers it to the subsidiaries and may urge initial trials. However, it does not force the subsidiaries to launch a new product if the subsidiary managers do not find it acceptable. If the product is introduced, local managers are fairly free to adapt it as long as corporate management does not find the changes harmful. For example, one of Nestlé's best selling products, Nescafe instant coffee, is blended and colored slightly differently from country to country.

Nestlé relies heavily not only on budgets and reports but also on information-gathering visits to local operations. The company has several policies designed to bring corporate and subsidiary management closer together. One is to alternate people between jobs in the field and jobs at headquarters. For example, the CEO of Nestlé USA spends one week of each month at Vevey. Another is to schedule meetings and training programs to bring large groups of managers together. Still another is to ensure that corporate headquarters management can converse with subsidiary management in at least French and English and preferably in German and Spanish as well. (The executive board conducts business in English.) Further, the compensation system and management style are established purposely to limit turnover among employees.

The policy of making decisions at headquarters changed in the 1980s. During that time, Nestlé became more decentralized, largely because of the management philosophy of Helmut Maucher, who became managing director in 1982. When Maucher took over, three levels of management approval were necessary even to put out a press release. He reduced the corporate staff, pushed more authority down to the operating level, and replaced twenty-five-page monthly reports with a one-page reporting form. In addition, Nestlé at one time sought to balance functional, geographic, and product viewpoints by putting different people in charge of each activity at headquarters. This meant that the heads of all activities had to agree on a decision, sometimes a slow process. To slim down the corporate staff and speed decision making, this structure was replaced under Maucher with a board of general managers that primarily represents the zones into which Nestlé divides the world.

Many company actions require new decisions on where control will be vested. Nestlé's policy of expanding largely through acquisition of existing companies has resulted in situations that do not quite fit the established lines of responsibility. The acquisition policy is founded on the belief that it is more prudent to enter an already highly competitive market by buying an existing company and infusing resources into it than to start up a new operation. Because acquired companies are unlikely to have the exact product and geographic basis to fit Nestlé's structure, these operations must be accommodated. For example, Nestlé acquired Libby, McNeill & Libby, a U.S. company with substantial international operations, including a subsidiary in the United Kingdom. Nestlé had to iron out not only how Libby would relate to Nestlé's existing U.S. operations but also whether the U.K. subsidiary should continue to report to Libby or report to Nestlé's European operations instead. (There was a gradual transition by which the subsidiary eventually reported to the European operations.) Later, the Libby production facilities and distribution center were closed; however, two other Nestlé divisions took on the manufacture and sale of products using the Libby name. In another case, Nestlé's acquisition of Stouffer Foods put it into hotel ownership for the first time. Because Stouffer had been highly profitable and because corporate management at Nestlé's Swiss headquarters lacked hotel experience, initially many more decisions than usual were made at the subsidiary level.

A notable Nestlé acquisition in the United States was of Carnation in 1985. Carnation initially reported directly to Switzerland instead of to North American operations, which had been established in 1981 to consolidate much of the U.S. operations and to allow Swiss headquarters to spend more time on strategic planning rather than supervising day-to-day operations. In 1990, Carnation was consolidated with other U.S. food businesses in a move to save overhead expenses and to gain advantages of scale in combating such U.S. rivals as Kraft General Foods and Con-Agra.

Competitive factors have influenced Nestlé's decisions on what to emphasize. For example, its rapid growth strategy in the United States has been based in part on the realization that the company must maintain a size that is not small relative to its competitors (which have been growing internally and through acquisition). This size helps in dealing with the few large supermarket chains that account for most of Nestlé's sales.

Introduction

Control questions facing all companies:
- **Where are decisions made?**
- **How can the company optimize globally?**
- **How should country units report to headquarters?**

International companies have a wide variety of strategies as well as approaches for implementing those strategies. Nevertheless, many of the problems they face are very similar. The Nestlé case illustrates concerns shared by all international companies: which objectives to pursue, where decisions should be made, how foreign operations should report to headquarters, and how to ensure that global objectives are met. Behind each of these concerns is a more basic one—that of control. The concept of control encompasses much more than just the ownership of sufficient voting shares to direct company policies. **Control** is the planning, implementation, evaluation, and correction of performance to ensure that organizational objectives are achieved. Several factors make control more difficult internationally than it is domestically:

Foreign control is usually more difficult because of
- **Distance—it takes more time and expense to communicate**
- **Diversity—country differences make it hard to compare operations**
- **Uncontrollables—there are more outside stockholders and governmental dictates**
- **Degree of certainty—there often are rapid changes in the environment and data problems**

1. *Distance.* The geographic and cultural distance separating countries increases the time, expense, and possibility of error in cross-national communications. Inquiries and responses between headquarters and subsidiaries' managers may not be fully understood, and the time and expense of gaining verification may hinder the functioning of control systems.

2. *Diversity.* This book has emphasized the need for an MNE to adjust operations to the unique situations encountered in each country in which it operates. When market size, type of competition, nature of the product, labor cost, currency, and a host of other factors differentiate operations among countries, the task of evaluating performance or setting standards to correct or improve business functions is extremely complicated.

3. *Uncontrollables.* Performance evaluation is of little use in maintaining control unless there is some means of taking corrective action. Effective corrective action may be minimal because many foreign operations must contend with the dictates of outside stockholders, whose objectives may differ somewhat from those of the parent, and with government regulations over which the company has no short-term influence.[2]

4. *Degree of certainty.* Control implies setting goals and developing plans to meet those goals. Economic and industry data are much less complete and accurate for some countries than for others. Further, political and economic conditions are subject to rapid change in some locales. These situations impede planning, especially long-range planning, and reduce the certainty of results from plan implementation.

Although these factors make control more difficult in the international context, companies follow procedural and structural practices in an effort to ensure that foreign operations comply with overall corporate goals and philosophies. This chapter discusses five aspects of the international control process:

1. Planning
2. Organizational structure
3. Location of decision making
4. Control mechanisms
5. Special situations

Planning

Companies must mesh objectives with internal and external constraints and set means to implement, monitor, and correct.

Throughout this text, we have emphasized the company's need to adapt its unique resources and objectives to different and changing international competitive situations. This is the essence of planning. Without planning, a company lacks long-range goals and strategies to achieve them. Without planning, it is only by luck that a company picks the best sequence and method of expansion by country.

Without planning, it is also by chance that a company sets policies and practices in a given locale that result in the desired performance. Because planning has been both implicitly and explicitly discussed already, this section presents only an overview of the process.

The Planning Loop

As Fig. 16.1 shows, planning must mesh objectives with the internal and external environments. The details in each planning step include items discussed in the environmental and operational parts of this book. Note that the first step (A) is to develop a long-range **strategic intent** (sometimes called a **mission statement),** an objective that will hold the organization together over a long period while it builds its global competitive viability.[3] Although few companies start with such an intent, most develop one as they progress toward significant international positions. Some, such as Honda and Canon, developed strategic intents long before it seemed they would ever be able to become important competitors.

The next planning step (B) is to analyze internal resources, along with environmental factors in the home country. These resources and factors affect and constrain each company differently. For example, a small company inexperienced in foreign operations may lack financial and human resources, even though it may have unique product capabilities that indicate opportunities abroad. Unlike a larger counterpart, it may have to set a low level of foreign involvement, perhaps by licensing foreign production rather than owning facilities abroad. But it still will need to control its foreign operations through a contract with the licensee that stipulates sales targets, product characteristics, and so on.

Only by making an internal analysis (step B) can a company set the overall rationale for its international activities (step C). For instance, a company faced with rising domestic costs and expanded competition from imports may validly pursue one of several objectives, such as cost reduction, acquisition of resources the competition needs, or diversification into new markets or products. The analysis of internal resources will help to determine which of these objectives is feasible and most important within a foreseeable planning period and will aid in selecting alternatives.

Because each country in which the company is operating or contemplating operating is unique, the local analysis also will have to be made (step D) before the final alternatives can be fully examined (step E). For instance, changes in local stability undoubtedly influenced Nestlé's decision to increase relative emphasis on LDCs. Priorities must be set among alternatives so that programs may be easily added or deleted to implement means of attaining target results (step F) as resource availability or situations change. A parent company may, for example, prefer and plan to remit dividends from one of its foreign subsidiaries back to itself; however, this may not be possible. Management also should consider what it will do with earnings if foreign-exchange controls are put into effect. Further, it must determine the alternatives that will then exist for the parent, which will have to do without the funds. It may be necessary to borrow more at home, remit more from other subsidiaries,

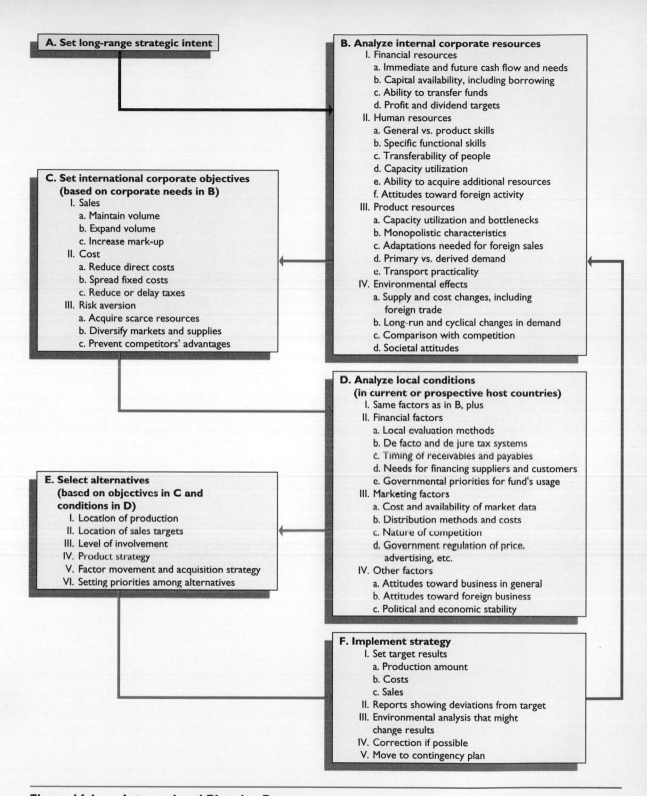

A. Set long-range strategic intent

B. Analyze internal corporate resources
  I. Financial resources
    a. Immediate and future cash flow and needs
    b. Capital availability, including borrowing
    c. Ability to transfer funds
    d. Profit and dividend targets
  II. Human resources
    a. General vs. product skills
    b. Specific functional skills
    c. Transferability of people
    d. Capacity utilization
    e. Ability to acquire additional resources
    f. Attitudes toward foreign activity
  III. Product resources
    a. Capacity utilization and bottlenecks
    b. Monopolistic characteristics
    c. Adaptations needed for foreign sales
    d. Primary vs. derived demand
    e. Transport practicality
  IV. Environmental effects
    a. Supply and cost changes, including
       foreign trade
    b. Long-run and cyclical changes in demand
    c. Comparison with competition
    d. Societal attitudes

C. Set international corporate objectives
  (based on corporate needs in B)
  I. Sales
    a. Maintain volume
    b. Expand volume
    c. Increase mark-up
  II. Cost
    a. Reduce direct costs
    b. Spread fixed costs
    c. Reduce or delay taxes
  III. Risk aversion
    a. Acquire scarce resources
    b. Diversify markets and supplies
    c. Prevent competitors' advantages

D. Analyze local conditions
  (in current or prospective host countries)
  I. Same factors as in B, plus
  II. Financial factors
    a. Local evaluation methods
    b. De facto and de jure tax systems
    c. Timing of receivables and payables
    d. Needs for financing suppliers and customers
    e. Governmental priorities for fund's usage
  III. Marketing factors
    a. Cost and availability of market data
    b. Distribution methods and costs
    c. Nature of competition
    d. Government regulation of price,
       advertising, etc.
  IV. Other factors
    a. Attitudes toward business in general
    b. Attitudes toward foreign business
    c. Political and economic stability

E. Select alternatives
  (based on objectives in C and
  conditions in D)
  I. Location of production
  II. Location of sales targets
  III. Level of involvement
  IV. Product strategy
  V. Factor movement and acquisition strategy
  VI. Setting priorities among alternatives

F. Implement strategy
  I. Set target results
    a. Production amount
    b. Costs
    c. Sales
  II. Reports showing deviations from target
  III. Environmental analysis that might
       change results
  IV. Correction if possible
  V. Move to contingency plan

Figure 16.1   International Planning Process
The initial step is setting the company's long-range strategic intent, followed by a loop in which short- and medium-term steps are taken to achieve the intent.

or forgo domestic expansion or dividends. Without priorities, the company may have to make hurried decisions to accomplish its objectives even partially.

Finally, very specific objectives should be set for each operating unit, along with ways to measure both deviations from the plan and conditions that may cause such deviations. Through timely evaluation, the company can take corrective actions or at least move to contingency means to achieve the objectives. Note that there must be a constant loop from step F to step B to ensure the company is making decisions based on currently relevant situations.[4] Evaluation methods are discussed later in this chapter.

A distinction must be made between operating plans and strategic plans. Strategic plans are longer term and akin to step A, developing the strategic intent. They involve major commitments, such as what businesses the company will be in and where, and are less subject to reevaluation. Operating plans involve short-term objectives and the means to carry them out. The time horizon for operating plans is not clear-cut. For example, the chairman of Unilever pointed out the short-term needs for Unilever's consumer products (three to five years) as compared with much longer-term need for a project such as the Anglo-French Channel Tunnel.[5] Although input for a strategic plan may come from all parts of the organization, only at the corporate level can allocations be made to implement overall planned changes in geographic and product policies. Also, it is usual for members of the corporate staff to be the primary people concerned with making strategic plans, since they have information on the company's worldwide activities, competition, and trends.

Uncertainty and Planning

A company's international operations have more complexity and uncertainty than its domestic ones.

The more uncertainty there is, the harder it is to plan. It is generally agreed that operations in the international sphere involve more uncertainty than do those in the domestic one because of the greater complexity of international operations. Complexity results from the greater number of operating environments (for example, having to evaluate many subsidiaries) and from different requirements for different markets in terms of the tasks performed, because products and how they are made within each subsidiary differ.[6]

Generally, greater complexity and uncertainty are expected to lead to greater need and use for information. However, substantial evidence indicates that the higher the uncertainty, the lower the amount of environmental scanning to collect information.[7] This may be because of the relative inaccessibility of accurate information internationally.

Organizational Structure

No matter how good a plan is, it will achieve little unless there is an appropriate means of implementing it. Organizational structure is a necessary means of implementation that should fit the strategy being pursued. The structure defines how individuals and organizational units are grouped to carry out company activities. The structure that emerges will depend on many factors, including the following:

- Location and type of foreign facilities
- Impact of international operations on total corporate performance
- Nature of assets employed in pursuit of business abroad
- Time horizons for achieving international and overall corporate goals

Companies must establish legal and organizational structures at home and abroad to meet their objectives. These structures may differ among various foreign countries because of the unique nature of activities and different environmental requirements. Layered above the individual country organizations are additional structures that coordinate activities in multiple countries. The form, method, and location of operational units at home and abroad will affect taxes, expenses, and control. Consequently, organizational structure has an important effect on the fulfillment of corporate objectives.

Level of Importance

The more important the specific foreign operations are to total corporate performance, the higher the corporate level to which those units should report. The organizational structure or reporting system therefore should change over time to parallel the company's increased involvement in foreign activities.

At one end of the spectrum is the company that merely exports temporary surpluses through an intermediary who takes title and handles all the export details. This entire operation is apt to be so insignificant to total corporate performance that top-level management is concerned very little with it. In this case, the foreign activities should be handled at a low level in the corporate hierarchy. Anyone in the organization who knows enough about inventories and has time to discern whether orders can be filled could handle the operation.

At the other end of the spectrum is the company that has passed through intermediate stages and now owns and manages foreign manufacturing and sales facilities. Every functional and advisory group within the company undoubtedly will be involved in the facilities' establishment and direction. Because sales, investments, and profits of the foreign operations are now a more significant part of the corporate total, people very high in the corporate hierarchy are involved.

Separate versus Integrated International Activities

A company's international activities may be grouped together (for example, in an international division) or integrated into the product, geographic, or functional structure the company relies on domestically. Figure 16.2 shows simplified examples of different approaches to placing foreign activity within the organizational structure. Most companies basically use one of these approaches.

The more important the foreign operations, the higher in the organizational structure they report.

**Figure 16.2
Placement of
International Activities
within the
Organizational
Structure**
Although most companies
have structures that are
mixed, the five examples
shown here are simplified
versions of the most com-
mon types of structures
for organizations that have
international business
activities.

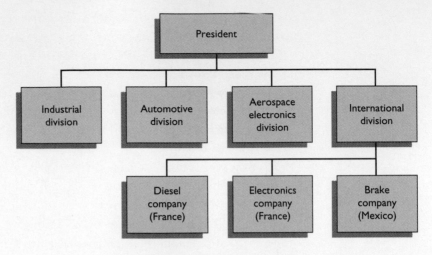

(a) Separation of international operations

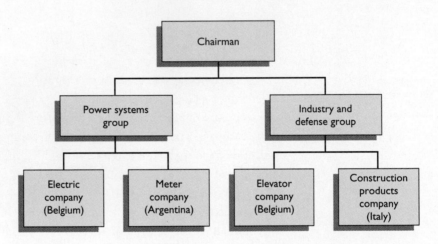

(b) International operations within product group

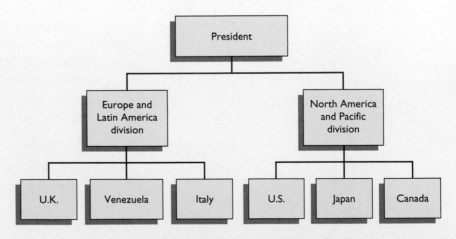

(c) International operations within geographic group

Figure 16.2 (cont.)

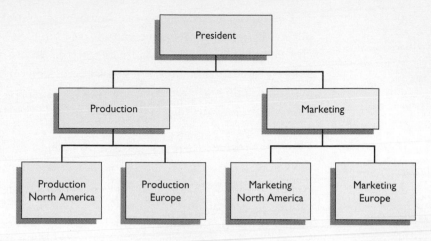

(d) International operations within functional area

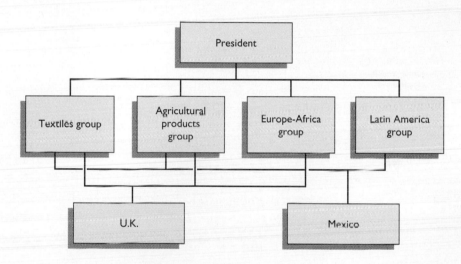

(e) International operations with matrix

An international division
- **Creates a critical mass of international expertise**
- **May have problems getting resources from domestic divisions**

International division   Grouping international activities into their own division allows for specialized personnel to handle such diverse matters as export documentation, foreign-exchange transactions, and relations with foreign governments. It also creates a large enough critical mass that can wield power within the organization. In contrast, international operations integrated with product or functional groups may be so small in comparison to domestic business that the company gives little attention to their development. However, an international division might have to depend on the domestic divisions for product to sell, personnel, technology, and other resources. Further, because domestic division managers are evaluated against domestic performance standards, they may withhold their best resources from the international division in order to improve their own performances.

Part (a) of Fig. 16.2 shows an example of separation of international operations; this structure is used by such companies as Campbell Soup.[8] Although it is not popular among European MNEs, it is among U.S. MNEs.[9] One apparent reason for this difference is that U.S. companies typically depend much more on the domestic market than do European companies. Having a separate international division allows a U.S. company to gain the critical mass discussed above.

Product division   Parts (b), (c), and (d) in Fig. 16.2 show organizational structures in which international operations are integrated rather than handled separately. Product divisions, as illustrated in (b), are particularly popular among companies that have highly diverse product groups, especially those that have become diverse primarily through acquisitions, such as Motorola. Because these groups may have little in common, even domestically, they may be highly independent of each other. Note that different subsidiaries within the same foreign country will report to different groups at headquarters.

Geographic (area) division   Geographic divisions, as shown in part (c) of Fig. 16.2, are used primarily by companies with very large foreign operations that are not dominated by a single country or area. This structure is found more commonly among European MNEs, such as Nestlé, than among U.S. MNEs, because of the dominance of the U.S. domestic market. Recall that Nestlé can use this structure because no one region dominates its operations.

Functional division   Functional divisions, like those shown in part (d) of Fig. 16.2, are popular among extractive companies (such as those involved in oil or bauxite extraction) because they have very homogeneous products for which production and marketing methods are relatively undifferentiated among countries. Exxon uses this structure.

Matrix   Because of the problems inherent in either integrating or separating foreign operations, some companies, such as Dow Chemical, are moving toward matrix organizations, illustrated in part (e) of Fig. 16.2. In this type of organizational structure, a subsidiary reports to more than one group (product, geographic, or functional). This structure is based on the theory that because each group shares responsibility over foreign operations, the groups will become more interdependent, exchange information, and ultimately take strategic global perspectives as they seek to exchange resources with each other. For example, product-group managers must compete among themselves to ensure that R&D personnel responsible to a functional group are assigned to the development of technologies that fall within their product domains. These product-group managers also must compete to ensure that geographic-group managers emphasize their lines sufficiently. And not only do product groups compete; functional and geographic groups also must compete among themselves to obtain resources held by others in the matrix.

Product divisions are popular among international companies with diverse products.

Geographic divisions are popular when foreign operations are large and are not dominated by a single country or region.

Functional divisions are popular among extractive companies.

A matrix organization gives product, geographic, and functional groups a common focus.

Although a matrix organization requires that all major perspectives be represented in strategic decision making, it is not without drawbacks. One is that groups inevitably compete for scarce resources. When lower-level managers fail to agree, management above the group level must decide how to allocate the resources. Such factors as management's faith in a specific executive or group may result in more decisions being made favoring that executive or group.[10] As others in the organization see this occurring, they may perceive that the locus of relative power lies with a certain individual or group. Consequently, managers may divert most of their energies toward the activities that are considered most likely to be accepted, thus perpetuating the difference in relative power. This emphasis may not represent what would be the firm's best strategic direction. Consequently, these interpersonal relationships may diminish some of the advantages of the matrix organization. Any of several alternatives may help to alleviate this problem, such as transferring individuals among groups and developing additional reporting and control systems that reflect on a global basis each of the three groups—product, geographic, and functional. However, these alternatives (discussed in the section titled "Control Mechanisms") are not without costs.

Dynamic Nature of Structures

A company's structure is apt to change as its business evolves. For example, as product lines become more diverse, the overall organization is apt to shift from a functional to a product structure. International business growth also may necessitate structural changes. When a company is only exporting, an export department attached to a product or functional division may suffice. (In most companies, departments are subordinate to divisions.) But if international operations continue to grow and are conducted via overseas production in addition to exporting, a department may no longer be sufficient. Perhaps an international division replaces the department, or perhaps each product division takes on worldwide responsibility for its own products. Most companies prefer their divisions to be of a similar size, so it may be necessary to replace an international division if it becomes too large relative to domestic divisions. For example, in the Nestlé case it would be hard to imagine a single international division handling over 95 percent of the sales.

Because of growth dynamics, companies seldom, if ever, have all their activities corresponding to the simplified organizational structures described here; most have a mixed structure. For example, a recent acquisition might report to headquarters until it can be consolidated efficiently within existing divisions. Or circumstances regarding a particular country, product, or function might necessitate that it be handled separately, apart from the overall structure.

Because of the increase in alliances among companies, control increasingly must come from negotiation and persuasion rather than from authority of superiors over subordinates.

Hetarchies

Companies have traditionally been organized as hierarchies, which are characterized by superior-subordinate relationships. However, many companies now depend heavily on alliances with other companies in which it is not clear-cut that one company is the superior and the other the subordinate; therefore the management of the alliance is shared among so-called equals—a situation known as a **hetarchy** (sometimes spelled heterarchy).[11] Corning is a good example of how a hetarchy works because half of its earnings come from alliances, particularly joint ventures. Formal linkages exist among the alliance partners; however, management at Corning's headquarters serves as a broker, conflict negotiator, and facilitator rather than exerting direct authority over the alliances.[12]

Many Japanese companies are linked similarly in what is known as a **keiretsu,** which is an organization in which each company owns a small percentage of other companies in the group. There are strong personal relationships among high-level managers in the different companies, and there are often interlocking directorships. Sometimes *keiretsus* are vertical, such as that between Toyota and its parts suppliers. However, these differ from vertical arrangements between U.S. auto companies and their suppliers in that continuous and stable business relationships are used much more in Japan to foster the suppliers' cost-cutting and JIT deliveries. Sometimes *keiretsus* are horizontal.[13] For example, the Mitsubishi group consists of twenty-eight core companies in which no single company predominates. The businesses are extremely diverse, including mining, real estate, credit cards, and tuna canning.[14] Typically, the core companies within a *keiretsu* buy and sell with each other only if and to the extent the transactions make business sense. However, long-term interlocking directorships and strong personal relationships among managers in core companies build common interests that do not depend on formal controls. The relationships encourage individual companies to undertake long-term and high-risk investments because they know other members of the *keiretsu* would feel morally obligated to support a core company that developed financial problems. U.S. companies also have substantial interlocking directorships and incidence of personal relationships; however, the specific company-to-company ties tend to be short-term because they terminate when individuals change jobs or retire.[15]

Location of Decision Making

Centralization implies higher-level decision making, usually above the country level.

Although the organizational structure outlines who reports to whom within the MNE, it does not indicate where decisions are made within that framework. Companies must determine where decisions will be made on such diverse questions as product policy, acquisition of funds, and placement of liquid assets. The higher the level within the organization at which decisions are made, the more they are considered to be centralized; the lower the level, the more they are decentralized. Whether decision making should be centralized or decentralized can be addressed from the standpoint of either the company as a whole or some part of it, such as a particular subsidiary operation. This discussion highlights the relationship of country-level operations to other parts of the MNE, such as headquarters, regional offices, or other country-level operations. For purposes of this discussion, decisions made at the foreign-subsidiary level are considered to be decentralized, whereas those made above the foreign-subsidiary level are considered to be centralized. There are opposing pressures for centralization and decentralization; consequently, policies must be adapted to each company's unique situation.

Complete centralization and complete decentralization may be thought of as the extremes. In actuality, companies neither centralize nor decentralize all decisions; instead, they vary policies according to the type of question and the particular circumstances involved. The location of decision making may vary within the same company over time as well as by product, function, and/or country. In addition, actual decision making is seldom as asymmetrical as it may appear on the surface. A manager who has decision-making authority may consult and reach consensus with other managers before exercising the authority. Putting these differences and subtleties aside, this section focuses on the rationale for locating decision control at either the corporate or the subsidiary level. Once this rationale is clear, it is easier to comprehend such elements as organization structure, planning, and evaluation, which parallel the basic centralization or decentralization philosophy.

Corporate Efficiency Factors

Companies must consider how long it takes to get help from headquarters in relation to how rapidly a decision must be made.

Cost and expediency   Although corporate personnel may be more experienced in advising on or making certain decisions, the time and expense involved in centralization may not justify the so-called better advice. Many decisions cannot be put off. Some headquarters' decisions could not be made effectively without face-to-face communication with subsidiary managers or on-the-spot observation. Bringing in corporate personnel may not be warranted.

The distance of foreign operations from headquarters is another crucial factor. For U.S. subsidiaries in either Canada or Mexico, the time and cost of communications with the parent company are low in comparison with those for U.S. subsidiaries located in a more remote country such as the Philippines. The Philippine manager may be forced to decide certain matters on which the Canadian and Mexican managers get corporate assistance.[16] With advances in communications and transportation, however, the distance factor is becoming less important.

Decisions on moving goods or other resources internationally are more likely to be made centrally.

Resource transference   Both product and production factors—capital, personnel, or technology—may be moved from a company's operations in one country to its facilities in another. The movement may be in the best interest of corporate goals, although individual subsidiaries may not do as well if resources are transferred. Decisions involving these relationships usually are made centrally because making them requires information from all operating units and the ability to mesh the various data to achieve overall corporate objectives. Otherwise, reports would have to be disseminated from every unit to every other unit to determine whether a resource from one locale could be used elsewhere, and the dissemination would not guarantee that the resources would get transferred. Similarly, if exports among subsidiaries are needed to maintain a continual production flow (for example, with vertical integration or when interdependent components are needed in the company's final product), centralized control may be required to assure this flow. Another centralized decision may concern jurisdiction over exports. For example, if a company has manufacturing facilities in the United States and Germany, which facility will export to South Africa? By answering that question centrally, the company may avoid price competition among the subsidiaries and at the same time take into consideration comparative production costs, transportation costs, tax rates, foreign-exchange controls, and capacity utilization.

Economies and interrelationships through standardization   Even though world-wide uniformity of products, purchases, methods, and policies may not be best for each individual operation, the overall gain from uniformity may be more than sufficient to overcome individual country losses. For example, standardizing machinery used in the production process may result in savings from quantity discounts on purchases, consolidation of mechanics' training, maintenance of manuals, and carrying of inventories of spare parts. The company may realize economies in almost any corporate activity, such as advertising, R&D, and purchase of group insurance. Product uniformity gives a company greater flexibility in filling orders when supply problems arise because of strikes, disasters, or sudden increases in demand. Production can simply be expanded in one country to meet shortages elsewhere.

Another argument for adhering to uniform policies globally is to ensure that foreign operations do not veer so drastically from the overall line or method of business that control is completely lost. If units in different countries alter products, policies, and methods in different directions, even gradually, the eventual diversity may be so great that economies no longer are possible and personnel, products, and ideas no longer can be interchanged easily.

Increasingly, the people with whom a company must deal (government officials, employees, suppliers, consumers, and the general public) are aware of what that company does in other countries in which it operates. Concessions that have been readily granted in one country may then be demanded in other countries, where they may not be afforded as easily. Suppose that for public-relations purposes, the management in one country decided to give preferential prices to the government and to establish a profit-sharing plan for employees. If the government officials and employees in another country ask for similar treatment, the result may be reduced profits if the company complies or poor public relations if it does not.

Even internal pricing and product decisions can affect demand in other countries. With the growing mobility of consumers, especially industrial consumers, a good or bad experience with a product in one country may eventually affect sales elsewhere. This is especially true if industrial consumers themselves want uniformity in their end products. If prices differ substantially among countries, consumers may even find that they can import more cheaply than they can buy locally.

What is best for the company globally may not be best for the individual country unit.

Global competitive strategies   A company needs to determine whether it is better off emphasizing country-by-country competitive positions or an integrated global position. In addition to the issue of standardized versus differentiated products among countries, it must consider a number of other factors. One is whether large-scale production of components and finished goods can be exported so that costs to buyers in various countries can be reduced. The nature of the production process, transportation costs, and governmental import restrictions all affect the advantages of production integration.

The actual and potential existence of global customers and/or competitors also may dictate a company's decisions to improve global performance at the expense of a particular country's operations. For example, if a supplier gives price concessions to an automaker in Brazil, that supplier may more easily gain business in other countries in which the automaker manufactures. A company also may attack a competitor by producing and selling in the locale that competitor gains its major resources for competing globally.

Competence Arguments

A condition for delegating authority is the belief that those selected will act responsibly; thus the perception of the relative competence of corporate versus local managers will influence the actions that each can pursue. Although there are rational factors affecting this perception, unrealistic attitudes may lead to excessive control being delegated to one or the other set of managers. Unrealistic attitudes include, for example, a belief that only the on-the-spot person knows the situation well enough to make a decision (polycentrism) or that corporate managers are the only individuals capable of making decisions (ethnocentrism).

There are national differences in the degree to which authority is delegated to foreign subsidiaries.[17] For example, Japanese companies tend to delegate more to foreign subsidiaries than U.S. companies do. This difference may reflect Japanese cultural norms of participation and reliance on group decision making, the greater use by Japanese companies of home-country managers who are presumed to think the "headquarters way," or Japanese companies' later expansion abroad, which delayed their movement to global strategies.

The more different the foreign environment is from the home environment, the more delegation occurs. The more confidence there is in foreign managers, the more delegation occurs.

Local conditions   Because local managers are usually in a better position to know what will work locally, they are normally given greater latitude when local conditions are perceived to be significantly different from those in the home country. For example, the corporate managers of a U.S. company will probably feel more competent about dictating practices to a Canadian subsidiary than to a Mexican subsidiary, since the former is presumed to parallel successful U.S. operations more closely. Yet local conditions may be more important for some functions than for others. For example, Nestlé decentralizes most of its marketing decisions because they must be adjusted to local needs; however, foreign-exchange decisions are centralized because of the importance of examining global conditions.

Other factors may seem to dictate altering decision making among operations in different countries. For example, decentralization may seem called for when the local management team is large rather than lean, local managers have worked a long time with the company, and local managers have developed successful track records.[18]

Product factors   The product itself may determine the relative competence of corporate versus local managers. For technically sophisticated products, there usually is little need for local adaptations; consequently, at least for marketing policy, decisions may be made that apply to many countries. A good contrast is between Nestlé's food products, which require geographic differentiation, and GE's power generators and jet engines, which are big-ticket products that require very little local adaptation. The former lend themselves much more to decentralization than do the latter. Also, many products are introduced sequentially, in one market at a time. In such cases, corporate managers often assert control in order to ensure that mistakes made in one market are not repeated in the others. Further, if product technology changes rapidly, there is usually a much greater need for headquarters involvement than if it remains stable for a long period.

> The more uniform the product is globally, the more centralization occurs.

Time and size variables   Small companies, especially those that are fairly new to international operations, may have little if any staff in foreign countries. Further, because they typically have narrow product lines and lean structures, they are able to get key headquarters players in different functions to work closely, both together and with foreign customers or suppliers. For example, such headquarters involvement helped CISCO, a small U.S. manufacturer of networking gear, to gain contracts with Japan's Nippon Telegraph & Telephone, and helped Pall, a small U.S.-based maker of filters, to develop extensive offshore manufacturing.[19] However, as a company's operations grow abroad, it develops a foreign management group that is capable of operating more independently of headquarters in the overseas markets. Simultaneously, corporate managers may no longer be able to deal effectively with international business operations because the company has entered so many different foreign markets; thus foreign operations tend to become more decentralized. But as foreign operations continue to grow, people with foreign experience move into headquarters positions, and headquarters can afford staff specialists to deal with the company's multiple international operations. At that point, recentralization becomes feasible. Nevertheless, if a specific foreign country operation is very large, such as Nestlé's U.S. subsidiary, then it can afford its own specialized personnel and may be treated differently from smaller country operations, like Nestlé's subsidiary in Belize.

> The larger the total foreign operations, the more likely it is that headquarters has specialized staff with international expertise.
> The larger the operations in a given country, the more likely it is that that country unit has specialized staff.

Importance of the decision   Any discussion of location of authority must consider the importance of the particular decisions. This question is sometimes asked: How much can be lost through a bad decision? The greater the potential loss, the higher in the organization the level of control usually is. In the case of marketing decisions,

> More important decisions are made at headquarters.

for example, local autonomy is not nearly as prevalent for product design as for advertising, pricing, and distribution. Product design generally necessitates a considerably larger capital outlay than the other functions do; consequently, the potential loss from a wrong decision is higher. Further, advertising, pricing, and distribution decisions may be more easily reversed if an error in judgment is made. Rather than delineating the decisions that can be made at the subsidiary level, the company can set limits on expenditure amount, thus allowing local autonomy for small outlays while requiring corporate approval on larger ones.

Decentralization Considerations

Subsidiaries' inputs help formulate global strategy through
• **Information**
• **Commitment**

Using subsidiaries effectively The need to develop standardized practices does not suggest that headquarters should generate all the information necessary for decision making. In fact, if the subsidiaries' viewpoints are ignored, the company may not develop the best cross-national or standardized programs. Further, good local managers may gravitate to other companies where they feel they can play a more important role. For example, Procter & Gamble (P&G) at one time allowed its country operations in Europe nearly total autonomy in adapting technology, products, and marketing approaches. To capture Europewide scale economies, P&G put one office in charge of formulating strategy for all of Europe, ignoring local knowledge, underutilizing subsidiaries' strengths, and demotivating subsidiaries' managers. P&G has since moved to greater standardization with other brand-management activities; however, this has been led by teams representing the subsidiary operations. In another case, EMI used feedback only from its home market (the United Kingdom) to decide that its central laboratory would seek to improve its CAT scanners through better image resolution. The company ignored the larger U.S. market, where a different improvement— shorter scan times—was preferred. When GE came out with a scanner that had a shorter scan time, it captured the U.S. market and got bigger scale economies than EMI did. EMI started losing money and had to accept a takeover bid.[20]

By giving groups of overseas employees a great deal of autonomy in certain areas, an MNE may be able to attract a higher caliber of personnel who might not want to work in its home country. For example, European scientists working at IBM's small Zurich laboratory won the Nobel prize for physics in two consecutive years. There are many ways in which subsidiaries can have autonomy over certain activities, such as developing a specific product or technology or conducting certain market testing.

Some companies have even moved the headquarters of certain divisions to foreign countries in response to market or resource conditions. For instance, AT&T moved its corded telephone division from the United States to France; Siemens moved its air-traffic management division from Germany to the United Kingdom; and Hyundai shifted its personal computer division from Korea to the United States. Although these divisional headquarters are still accountable to corporate headquarters, other global operations, including those in the home country, must report to them.[21]

National rather than international strategies   Although a global strategy offers many advantages, there are circumstances in which subsidiaries cannot reasonably be brought into such a scheme. This occurs, for example, with products associated with uniquely national taste preferences.[22] In other situations, subsidiaries may be prevented from being a full part of a global network because governmental protectionism isolates them from competitive threats.[23] In these cases, corporate strategic control may be less appropriate than national control would be.

Local performance considerations   Although some decisions clearly can be made efficiently at the corporate level, this technical efficiency must be weighed against morale problems created when responsibility is taken away from local managers. When local managers are prevented from acting in the best interest of their own operation, they tend to think, "I could have done better, but corporate management would not let me." If local managers cannot participate in developing global strategies, they may lack the positive attitude to "go the extra mile" to implement global strategic decisions.[24] These managers also may lose their commitment to their jobs and thus may not gain the experience needed to advance within the company. The company can help overcome this lack of commitment by developing a reward system that does not penalize managers for decisions that are outside of their control. In fact, a compensation system that rewards local managers partially on the basis of the company's total worldwide performance may enhance the development of global thinking at the country level.

Control Mechanisms

Corporate Culture

Any company has certain common values its employees share. These constitute the **corporate culture** and form a control mechanism that is implicit and helps enforce the company's explicit bureaucratic control mechanisms.[25] MNEs have more difficulty relying on a corporate culture for control because managers from different countries may have different norms pertaining to the management of operations and little or no exposure to the values and attitudes prevalent at corporate headquarters. Nevertheless, many companies encourage a worldwide corporate culture by promoting closer contact among managers from different countries. Also, frequent transfers of managers among operations in different countries develop increased knowledge of and commitment to a common set of values and objectives; thus fewer procedures, less hierarchical communication, and less surveillance are needed.[26] For example, Nestlé moves management trainees around Europe so that they learn to react like Europeans rather than like any specific nationality. Matsushita brings foreign employees to Japan, partly to train them in the company culture but primarily to get Japanese employees to evolve toward a more global culture.[27]

The degree of control corporate headquarters imposes on the selection of top managers for foreign subsidiaries may dictate to a great extent how much formal control over the subsidiaries' operations the corporate personnel feel is necessary. Using home-country nationals in subsidiaries' management or even having headquarters set the standards for local managers' selection and training may be perceived as a means of assuring primary loyalty to the corporate culture rather than the subsidiary culture.[28] Such a procedure may be effective even if the operations are only partially owned or when the parent requires long-range planning assistance from the subsidiaries.[29]

Coordinating Mechanisms

Rather than changing overall structure, many companies are finding mechanisms to pull product, function, and area together.

Because each type of organizational structure has advantages and disadvantages, companies in recent years have developed mechanisms to pull together some of the diverse functional, geographic (including international), and product perspectives without abandoning their existing structures. Some of these mechanisms are as follows:

- Strengthening corporate staffs (adding or creating groups of advisory personnel) so that people with line responsibilities (decision-making authority) are required to listen to different viewpoints (whether or not they take the advice)
- Using more management rotation, such as between line and staff positions or domestic and international ones, in order to break down parochial views
- Placing international and domestic personnel in closer proximity to each other
- Establishing liaisons among subsidiaries within the same country so that different product groups can get combined action on a given issue

Companies also use staff departments (for example, legal or personnel) to centralize functions common to more than one subsidiary. For instance, at Heinz one expatriate-transfer-and-compensation policy is used by all the geographic divisions, thus minimizing duplication of effort.[30]

Reports

Reports must be timely in order to allow companies to respond to their information.

Headquarters needs timely reports in order to allocate resources, correct plans, and reward personnel. The decisions on the use of capital, personnel, and technology are almost continuous; consequently, reports must be frequent and up to date so that these resources are efficiently used. Also, plans need to be updated in order to be realistic and to assure a high probability of meeting desired objectives. Finally, reports are needed to evaluate performance of personnel so as to reward and motivate them.

Written reports are more important in an international setting than in a domestic one because subsidiaries' managers have much less personal and oral contact with line and staff personnel above them. Thus corporate managers miss out on much of the informal communication that could tell them about the performance of the foreign operations.

Types of systems   Most MNEs use reporting systems for foreign operations that resemble those they use domestically.[31] There are several reasons for this:

1. If the systems have been effective domestically, management often believes they also will be effective internationally.
2. There are economies from carrying over the same types of reports. The need to establish new types of reporting mechanisms is eliminated, and corporate management is already familiar with the system.
3. Reports with similar formats presumably allow management to better compare one operation against another.

MNEs' reporting systems are intended primarily to assure adequate profitability by identifying deviations from plans that indicate possible problem areas. The focus may be on short-term performance or on longer-term indicators that match the organization's strategic thrust. The emphasis is on evaluating the subsidiary rather than the subsidiary manager, although the profitability of the foreign unit is an important ingredient in the managerial evaluation.[32]

Not all information exchange occurs via formalized reports. Within many MNEs, certain members of the corporate staff spend much of their time visiting subsidiaries. Although this attention may do much to alleviate misunderstandings, there are some inherent dangers if visits are not conducted properly. On the one hand, if corporate personnel visit the tropical subsidiaries only when there are blizzards at home, the personnel abroad may perceive the trips as mere boondoggles. On the other hand, if a subsidiary's managers offer too many social activities and not enough analysis of operations, corporate personnel may consider the trip a waste of time. Further, if visitors arrive only when the corporate level is upset about foreign operations, local managers may always be overdefensive.

Management versus subsidiary performance   It is generally agreed that subsidiaries should be evaluated separately from their managers so that managers are not penalized for conditions and occurrences outside their control. Beyond this agreement, however, companies differ significantly in what they include in managerial performance evaluations. For example, some hold managers abroad responsible for gains or losses in currency translation. Also, most deduct interest expenses before measuring the profitability of foreign operations.[33] These are examples of environmental factors that some companies consider to be outside the local managers' control.

Another uncontrollable area is when centralized decisions are made that will optimize the entire company's performance. A particular subsidiary may not do as well as it might if left to operate independently. In fact, the normal profit-center records may well obscure the importance the subsidiary has within the total corporate entity.

When evaluating foreign-investment possibilities, most companies set a higher minimum return for investments in high-risk countries. They then logically expect the performance within the high-risk countries to reflect the expected higher return. Most companies agree that including a country-risk factor in performance-evaluation analysis would be useful; however, they also agree that they know of no reasonable way of doing this. They feel that including it would penalize managers in risky countries and make them responsible for events outside their control.[34]

Cost and accounting comparability   Different cost structures among subsidiaries may prevent a meaningful comparison of their operating results. For example, the ratio of direct labor to sales for a subsidiary in one country may reasonably be much higher than that for a subsidiary in another country if the former has low labor and high capital costs in relation to the latter. Different accounting practices also can create problems. Most MNEs keep one set of books that are consistent with home-country principles and another to meet local reporting requirements.

It is hard to compare countries using standard operating ratios.

Evaluative measurement systems   Every evaluative measurement system has shortcomings when applied internationally. Consequently, one that relies on a number of different indicators may be preferable to one that relies too heavily on one indicator. Financial criteria tend to dominate the evaluation of foreign operations and their managers. Although many different criteria are used, the most important for evaluating both the operation and its management are budget compared with profit and budget compared with sales. In addition, operations are evaluated on the basis of return on investment, and management is evaluated on the basis of return on sales. Many nonfinancial criteria also are employed. The only one commonly given much weight in evaluation of operations is market-share increase. However, several are important for evaluating managers, including market-share increase, quality control, and managers' relationship with host governments.[35]

A system that relies on a combination of measurements is more reliable.

One way to overcome the problems of evaluating performance is to look at the budget. Doing this can help the MNE differentiate between a subsidiary's worth and its management's performance. The budget should include the goals for each subsidiary that will help the MNE achieve an overall objective. As long as a subsidiary's managers work toward a budgeted goal rather than a measure such as return on investment, they will experience fewer problems dealing with inflation, exchange-rate changes, and transfer prices.

Companies must evaluate results in relation to budgets.

Planning information acquisitions   This discussion has centered on information needed to evaluate the performance of subsidiaries and their management. Although this information is crucial, corporate management requires additional data, which can be categorized as follows:

Management should reevaluate information needs periodically to keep costs down and should ensure that information is being used.

- Information generated for centralized coordination, such as subsidiary cash balances and needs

- Information relating to external conditions, such as analyses of local political and economic conditions
- Information for feedback from parent to local subsidiaries, such as R&D breakthroughs
- Lateral information between related subsidiaries
- Information for external reporting needs[36]

Because information needs are so broad, companies face two problems: the cost of information relative to its value, and "information glut," that is, redundancy. To cope, some companies use Planned Information Acquisition Analysis (PIAA), which involves periodic reevaluation of each new document or service the company uses.[37] By comparing the number of times sources have been retrieved and found relevant, the company can limit acquisition to the data it considers most valuable.

Another problem is the compatibility of information needed by a subsidiary and by corporate management. Even when different subsidiaries are trying to solve similar problems, their information needs may differ vastly. Consequently, corporate management may be faced with having to compare unlike data or requiring different or additional data, collection of which may be expensive. Some companies allow diversity but send copies and analyses of data to centralized databanks. For many corporate needs, standardization of what data are collected is not necessary, but standardization of coding is so that centralized personnel can compare the performance of subsidiary projects and suggest more refined models for local use.

Local needs for and differences in data processing create problems of compatibility.

Aside from the problem of lack of data or of coding uniformity, a major obstacle to the on-time retrieval of comparable information is the diversity among countries in data processing, especially in terms of equipment and software. Uniformity of approach may be hampered for a company by substantial cost differences in personnel, hardware, and data communications, as well as legislative requirements to buy data-processing equipment, materials, and services locally.[38]

Information centers may permit a choice between centralization or decentralization.

With expanding multinational telecommunications and computer linkages, managers throughout the world can share information almost instantaneously. On the one hand, this may permit more centralization, since truly global implications of policies can be examined. On the other hand, managers in foreign locations may become more autonomous because they have more information at their disposal.

Control in Special Situations

Acquisitions

An acquired company usually does not achieve a complete fit with the existing organization.

As noted in the Nestlé case, a policy of expansion through acquisition can create some specific control problems. For Nestlé, some of its U.S. acquisitions resulted in overlapping geographic responsibilities as well as new lines of business with which corporate management had no experience. Another problem is that existing management in an acquired firm is probably accustomed to considerable autonomy.

The corporate philosophy on ethics is closely related to control issues. If the company takes a normative view of global ethics, it will need to control subsidiary decisions on a host of ethical questions. This location of control may not be the same as for other aspects of operations. An implication of normativism is that if the company decides payments to government officials are unethical, decentralized control over local marketing to governmental agencies would need to be tempered to account for this constraint. Further, the subsidiary and its management would have to be made aware of the corporate ethical view and not be held responsible for performance that suffers through pursuit of the ethical norm.

One ethical dilemma concerns whether a global ethical operating norm should be imposed by headquarters (usually home-country personnel) or developed as a composite of varied global viewpoints. If a company's foreign operations grow as a portion of its total operations or if the location of foreign operations shifts, such a composite of ethics will have to evolve. A company taking a relativistic view will handle ethical questions on a decentralized basis. However, this decentralization may lead to repercussions elsewhere, such as bad publicity in the home country because of the way components were manufactured by a foreign subsidiary.

As companies have expanded operations abroad, host-country societies have become more concerned about how those companies exercise control. One complaint involves the centralization of R&D. Many critics within LDCs have contended that the centralization of decision making by MNEs leads to an ever-increasing movement of management and technical functions to the home country, leaving the menial and low-skilled jobs in the LDCs. The critics recall colonial eras in which people from the colonies were forbidden responsible positions and were dependent on the colonial powers, which controlled their destinies.[39] These critics have been particularly concerned that very little R&D by MNEs is done outside the MNEs' home countries and, of that portion, almost all is done in other industrial countries.[40]

This presents dilemmas for MNEs. There are some potent arguments for centralizing most R&D in home countries. These include the availability of many people to work directly for the company, the proximity to private research organizations and universities doing related work, and the general advantages of centralized authority in reducing duplication of efforts. However, there also are advantages to locating some R&D abroad, for example, to tap into foreign technical resources (especially within the triad of Europe, Japan, and North America) and to work on products for which there is too small a market at home.[41] In the latter case, adaptive R&D may be involved.

Recall that in the Nestlé case, R&D on new products was done in Switzerland to reduce duplication of efforts and to be close to the strategic planners who projected product needs further into the future than could host-country managers, who were more concerned with day-to-day operations. Nestlé did allow country operations the freedom to conduct adaptive R&D but controlled this carefully by requiring headquarters approval of the adaptations. Thus even when a company allows adaptive or new product R&D to be carried out abroad, corporate management may substantially influence it. MNEs with considerable R&D outside their home country seldom allow the foreign operations complete autonomy. Corporate management may allocate budgets, approve plans, and offer suggestions. On the other hand, subsidiaries may offer substantial input for R&D conducted centrally.[42] Because of centralized R&D, even though adaptations may be allowed at the country level, LDCs may be continually at the mercy of interests in industrial countries. Is this centralization ethical? Are there ways in which MNEs can better satisfy their own interests while simultaneously quelling criticism?

Although LDCs complain that MNEs control practices from abroad, they nevertheless assume that a company's headquarters should have enough control to assure that its subsidiaries' operations have no dire effects locally. For example, Union Carbide delegated almost all decision making and day-to-day control to management of its joint venture in Bhopal, India; however, the Indian government blamed headquarters when a chemical leak killed several hundred people. Although an Indian government agency was responsible for making safety inspections at the facility, it was widely known that the agency was inadequately staffed. This brought up ethical questions (as well as legal ones) concerning responsibility. The Indian government, which owned 49.1 percent of the joint venture, denied responsibility because of its lack of a controlling interest and its delegation of management to Union Carbide. Union Carbide, in turn, initially claimed that responsibility rested in the joint venture. The ethical question is whether headquarters should be responsible for actions taken at the subsidiary level and whether minority stockholders should be responsible for what majority stockholders do.

Many countries have passed or are considering legislation that directly or indirectly affects the international data flow. These laws have been enacted for three main reasons:

1. There is concern about individual privacy; in particular, the development and transmission of personnel data might give the company an undue advantage over the individual.
2. Local jobs will be lost if data processing and analysis are done abroad, and resource transmission will occur without payment to the country that created the resource.
3. Corporate networks may be used to pirate military and commercial data to be sent abroad.[43]

Although most MNEs consider data-flow restrictions to be more of a potential than an actual problem, certain regulations already create barriers for them.[44] For example, some regulations require local subsidiaries to maintain copies of and monitor anything they transmit. Consequently, companies are concerned about additional costs and about competitors' acquiring proprietary information. Further, it often is difficult for an MNE to move personnel records in order to maintain centralized records, which assist in making international transfers. For example, Burroughs was unable to transfer its personnel records from Germany to other locations. But, is it ethical for MNEs to transfer the best human resources from abroad to headquarters positions? Would it be ethical to exclude these managers from high-level positions?

Attempts to centralize certain decision-making procedures or to change operating methods may result in distrust, apprehension, and resistance to change. When the acquisition is in a foreign country, resistance may come not only from the personnel but also from governmental authorities. These authorities may use a variety of discretionary means to ensure that decision making remains vested within the country.

Moving from National to Global Strategies

It is difficult to remove control from local operations when their managers are accustomed to much autonomy. This is a particular problem for companies that attempt to move from a multidomestic to a global strategy. Within Europe, for example, many U.S. companies owned very independent operations for decades in the United Kingdom, France, and Germany. These companies often have faced difficult obstacles when integrating these operations because the country managers perceive that integration brings personal and operating disadvantages.

Branch versus Subsidiary

There are tax and liability differences for branches and subsidiaries.

When establishing a foreign operation, a company often must decide between making that operation a branch or a subsidiary. A foreign branch is a foreign operation not legally separate from the parent company; therefore, branch operations are possible only if the parent holds 100-percent ownership. A subsidiary, however, is an FDI that is legally a separate company, even if the parent owns all of the voting stock. Because a subsidiary is legally separate, it is generally concluded that liability is limited to the assets of the subsidiary. Creditors or winners of legal suits therefore do not usually have access to other resources owned by the parent. This concept of limited liability is a major factor in the choice of the subsidiary form; otherwise, claims against a company for its actions in one country could be settled by courts in another. However, there is some evidence that the concept of limited liability will not suffice in future liability disputes. For example, after the Bhopal accident that killed several hundred people through a chemical leak, Union Carbide had to settle with the Indian government for damages of $470 million, an amount far in excess of the value of Union Carbide's 50.9-percent investment in the Indian joint venture.[45]

Because subsidiaries are separate companies, a question arises concerning which decisions the parent may be allowed to make. Generally, this does not present a problem. However, U.S. courts ruled that Timken was conspiring with another company to prevent competition when it dictated which markets its Canadian subsidiary could serve. Another factor related to control is public disclosure. Generally, the greater the control vested by the owners, the greater the secrecy that can be maintained. In this respect, branches are usually subject to less public disclosure because they are not covered by tight local corporate restrictions.

From these examples, it should be clear that there are conflicting control advantages to either the branch or the subsidiary form. Each form also has different tax advantages and implications and may have different initiation and operating costs as well as abilities to raise capital.

Comparison of Legal Forms

A company establishing a subsidiary in a foreign country usually can choose from a number of alternative legal forms. There are too many forms to list in detail in this book; however, some distinctions between them are worth mentioning. In addition to differences in liability, forms vary in terms of the following:

- Ability to transfer ownership
- Number of stockholders required
- Percentage of foreigners who can serve on the board of directors
- Amount of required public disclosure
- Whether equity may be acquired by noncapital contributions
- Types of businesses (products) that are eligible
- Minimum capital required

Before making a decision, an MNE should analyze all of these differences in terms of its corporate objectives.

Shared Ownership

Ownership sharing limits the flexibility of corporate decision making. For example, Nestlé shares ownership with Coca-Cola in a joint venture for the production and sale of canned coffee and tea drinks, and Nestlé has less autonomy for this operation than for those it owns wholly. Nevertheless, Chapter 15 described administrative devices to gain control even with a minority equity interest. A company also can maintain control over some asset needed by the operation abroad, such as a patent, a brand name, or a raw material. In fact, maintaining control is a motive for having separate licensing or franchising agreements or management contracts with a foreign subsidiary.

Nonequity Forms

The use of multiple operating forms, such as exporting, licensing, and joint venture, and the move from one to another may create the need to change areas of responsibility in the organization. Or it may mean that departments in the organization are not equally involved with all forms. For example, the legal department may have little day-to-day responsibility regarding exports but a great deal for licensing to the countries in which the exports are sold. Organizational mechanisms, such as joint committees and the planned sharing of information, are useful to ensure activities complement each other. It also is useful for the company to plan organizational change so as to minimize obstacles when responsibilities shift from one group to another.

A further consideration is how important the nonequity operation is to the company's overall operations. For example, if a company contracts with only one supplier for an essential component, the contract is likely to be controlled more closely and from higher in the organization than would contracts of less strategic importance.

COUNTERVAILING

FORCES

Much of this chapter's material deals with the pressures for global or multidomestic strategies and centralized or decentralized decision making. These pressures affect companies differently, depending on their lines of business. Generally, companies face environments that favor either a strong or a weak need to integrate operations across countries. These environments interface with those that favor either a strong or a weak need to respond to local conditions; thus there are four basic combinations, as illustrated in Fig. 16.3.[46] For example, the food industry (lower right-hand quadrant of the figure) usually has a weak need to integrate operations across countries because scale economies are highly offset by transportation costs. At the same time, it has a high need to adapt to local conditions because tastes, competitors, and distributors differ at the local level. For this industry, there is likely to be a great deal of autonomy at the country level with perhaps a geographic organizational structure.

When decisions are centralized, a company needs mechanisms to ensure that considerable country-specific information flows to headquarters. Industries in the upper left-hand quadrant of the figure, such as engine manufacturers, usually need a lot of centralization. Industries in the upper right-hand quadrant, such as pharmaceuticals, face the biggest challenge because product needs must be balanced with geographic needs. These industries are the most likely candidates to use matrix structures or at least coordinating mechanisms to pull different perspectives together. Industries in the lower left-hand quadrant, such as textiles, have perhaps the greatest flexibility in choosing a workable control system.

**Figure 16.3
Environmental
Influences and Control
of MNEs**
Note how the location of control (and mechanisms to implement control) are influenced by the relative strengths of forces that favor local responsiveness and forces that favor global integration.

Source: Adapted from Figures 2 and 5 and discussion in Sumantra Ghoshal and Nitin Nohria, "Horses for Courses: Organizational Forms for Multinational Corporations," *Sloan Management Review,* Winter 1993, pp. 23–36.

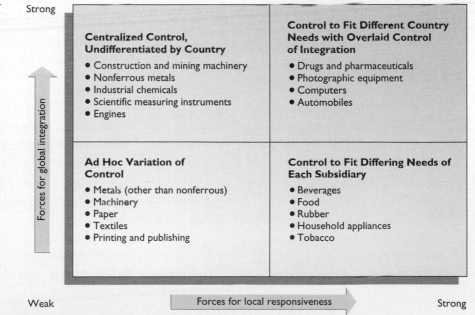

Strong

Forces for global integration

**Centralized Control,
Undifferentiated by Country**
- Construction and mining machinery
- Nonferrous metals
- Industrial chemicals
- Scientific measuring instruments
- Engines

**Control to Fit Different Country
Needs with Overlaid Control
of Integration**
- Drugs and pharmaceuticals
- Photographic equipment
- Computers
- Automobiles

**Ad Hoc Variation of
Control**
- Metals (other than nonferrous)
- Machinery
- Paper
- Textiles
- Printing and publishing

**Control to Fit Differing Needs of
Each Subsidiary**
- Beverages
- Food
- Rubber
- Household appliances
- Tobacco

Weak   Forces for local responsiveness   Strong

LOOKING TO THE FUTURE

As overseas sales and profits as a percentage of total sales and profits increase, there is likely to be more headquarters attention paid to foreign operations. Similarly, there will be pressures to centralize control in order to deal with the growing number of global competitors and the more homogenized needs of global consumers. The need for centralization will present more challenges for MNEs in controlling their global operations.

One challenge involves management's position in foreign facilities, where managers may see the erosion of their autonomy over marketing, production, and financial decisions. To keep those managers motivated, the company may need to include more nationalities on boards of directors and use cross-national management teams to develop practices that are globally rather than nationally oriented. But with such cross-national fertilization comes the risk of clashes between cultural traditions. For example, in work teams at Ericsson Telecom, Americans and Swedes quickly became frustrated with each other over cultural norms the two groups had developed as children. The Swedes had grown up being told that silence is golden and a good job will be recognized, whereas the Americans had learned early that class participation would improve their grades and they needed to promote themselves. The Americans viewed the Swedes as overly detached; whereas the Swedes viewed the Americans as overly aggressive.[47] The lesson is that the human side of the organization may lag behind the need for control from a technical standpoint.

A second challenge for MNEs is a consequence of their size. A number of them already have sales larger than many countries' GDPs. To manage such organizations may require even greater decentralization and more horizontal communication among subsidiaries in different countries that are mutually dependent on parts, products, and resources. This mutual dependence among subsidiaries may in turn require new hetarchical relationships within the organizational structure.

A third challenge concerns information. On the one hand, centralized control may become easier because of faster access to information from abroad. On the other hand, this faster access may be somewhat negated by companies' limited abilities to process greater amounts of information, particularly as they increase their geographic spread of activities, product diversity, and competitive rivalries.

Summary

- **Control is more difficult internationally because of the geographic and cultural distances separating countries, the need to operate differently among countries, the larger number of uncontrollables abroad, and the higher uncertainty resulting from rapid change in the international environment and problems in gathering reliable data in many places.**

- **Good planning should include environmental analysis, a long-range strategy, operating plans, and contingency strategies with inputs from both top-level and subsidiary managers.**

- As a company develops international business activities, the corporate structure must include a means by which foreign operations report. The more important the foreign operations, the higher up in the hierarchy they should report.

- Whether a company separates or integrates international activities, it usually needs to develop some means by which to prevent costly duplication of efforts and to ensure that headquarters managers do not withhold the best resources from the international operations.

- The level at which decisions are made should depend on the relative competence of individuals, the cost of decision making at each level, and the effects the decisions will have on total corporate performance.

- Even though worldwide uniformity of policies and centralization of decision making may not be best for an individual operation, overall company gains may be more than enough to overcome the individual country losses. When top management prevents subsidiaries' managers from doing their best job, however, there may be negative consequences for employee morale.

- Many critics in LDCs argue that centralization of decision making in MNEs continues LDCs' historical dependency on industrial countries. These critics are pressuring for increased decentralization of decision making.

- The corporate culture constitutes an implicit control mechanism. It is more difficult to establish and maintain in MNEs because values differ among countries, but bringing managers together enhances the common culture.

- Timely reports are essential for control so that resources can be allocated properly, plans can be corrected, and personnel can be evaluated and rewarded.

- International reporting systems are similar to those used domestically because home-country management is familiar with them and because uniformity makes it easier to compare different operations.

- The evaluation of subsidiaries and the evaluation of their managers are separate processes; however, some of the same inputs, including financial and nonfinancial criteria, may be used for both.

- Companies are finding it increasingly difficult to get timely and comparable reports from foreign operating units in part because of incompatibility of data-processing systems among countries and restrictions placed on the cross-national flow of data.

• **Special control problems arise for acquired operations, operations that have historical autonomy, and operations that are not wholly owned. The legal status of foreign operations and the organizational forms allowed in the specific country may also raise control problems.**

Case
Westinghouse[48]

In 1980, during a major organizational change at Westinghouse, the company's vice chairman, Douglas Danforth, announced he wanted the company's sales from abroad, which were then 27 percent of total sales, to be increased to 35 percent by 1984. Seventeen countries were identified as having the highest growth potential, and they were given emphasis in implementing this target. In light of Westinghouse's past international growth, the 35-percent figure seemed reachable. However, the company's dependence on foreign sales actually declined during the 1980s; by 1989, foreign sales were only 18 percent of total sales. To understand the relationship between Westinghouse's international goals and its organization of international operations, it is useful to look back at some significant changes over the past two and a half decades.

In 1969, Westinghouse's top management noted with concern that its chief rival, GE, realized 25 percent of its sales from abroad, compared to Westinghouse's 8 percent. Top management was determined to compete more vigorously against GE in foreign markets. Between 1969 and 1971, overseas volume increased to 15 percent of sales, and the chairman, Donald C. Burnham, said, "I've set a goal that 30 percent of our business will be outside the United States. I hope to get there and then set a bigger goal." The spurt in foreign sales largely resulted from the aggressive pursuit of overseas acquisitions. This marked a substantial change in foreign operating practice. Since World War I, when its three European subsidiaries were confiscated, Westinghouse had depended almost entirely on exports and licensing agreements for its foreign sales.

While this growth was taking place, Westinghouse had a separate operation, Westinghouse Electric International Company, located in New York (corporate headquarters are in Pittsburgh). From 1969 to 1971, the International Company operated alongside four other Westinghouse divisions, which were operated as companies; each of these four companies was in charge of a group of diverse products. A major complaint of the International Company was that the four other companies tended to view foreign operations as merely an appendage to which they were unwilling to give sufficient technical or even product assistance. The International Company depended on the product companies for everything it exported, but it had problems obtaining supplies. The product companies were willing to divert output abroad when they had surplus production but were reluctant to do so when they had shortages, largely because the International Company, not the product company, got credit for the sales and profits. Likewise, the product companies were reluctant to lend their best personnel to the International Company to assist in exportation of highly technical products or to support production by foreign licensees and subsidiaries.

Partially as a result of these complaints, Westinghouse eliminated the International Company in 1971. The four product companies were then put in charge of worldwide control of production and sale of their goods. (Westinghouse produces more than 8000 different products in such diverse areas as real-estate finance, nuclear fuel, television production, electronics systems, and soft-drink bottling.) Management reasoned that because of these companies' access to product technology, their personnel would be better able to sell their products and services than the disbanded company was. In addition, because personnel would now be evaluated on their foreign successes, they would be willing to divert resources to international development. Another factor that affected this decision was that GE had made a similar move a few years earlier with apparent success.

When responsibilities were shifted to the product companies, many of the managers from the former International Company did not conceal their belief that "those unsophisticated hicks back in Steeltown couldn't be trusted to find U.S. consulates abroad, let alone customers." Although management in each of the four product companies was free to pursue foreign business or not, each chose to do so, at least for some of their products. Between 1971 and 1976, foreign sales grew to 31 percent of Westinghouse's total sales. During this five-year period, product diversity continued to grow. Product emphasis was accentuated in 1976 when Westinghouse was reorganized into thirty-seven operating groups known as business units. Each unit was given a great deal of autonomy, including a free hand abroad.

From 1976 through 1978, Westinghouse's foreign sales fell to 24 percent of total sales. The extension of responsibility to product units had complicated cooperation among units and created problems with duplication of efforts in foreign markets. For example, a company salesperson called on a Saudi businessman who pulled out business cards from salespeople who had visited him from twenty-four other business units. He asked, "Who speaks for Westinghouse?" In another situation, different units had established subsidiaries in the same country. One had excess cash, and another was borrowing locally at an exorbitant rate. In many cases, large projects required ultimate cooperation among business units to carry out different parts, but units could not agree in time on how to pool resources and lost out to foreign competitors such as Brown Boveri from Switzerland and Hitachi from Japan. In Brazil at one time, three different sales groups were calling on the same customer for the same job.

By 1978, Douglas Danforth was Westinghouse's vice chairman and chief operating officer. He was highly interested in international expansion, not only because he expected greater sales and growth internationally but also because he had previously worked in the Mexican and Canadian subsidiaries. In early 1979, he enlisted a Westinghouse executive to supervise an exhaustive study of the company's international operations and to make a recommendation within ninety days. The study group interviewed Westinghouse personnel in the United States and abroad. It also determined how other companies were handling their international operations. The group recommended a gradual move to a matrix structure by 1983 and the installation of a head of international operations. The international operations were to be organized along geographic lines, including three regions. This plan was adopted, but the number of geographic regions increased to five during the 1980s. To get a consensus among the people in charge of product and geographic operations was a major departure from Westinghouse's product orientation.

Danforth told the company's top 220 managers, "Some of you will adjust and survive, and some of you won't."

To carry out the planned growth, Westinghouse had to mesh geographic group plans with product group plans. For example, if a product group wanted switchgear production in Brazil increased by 40 percent and the Brazilian country manager wanted to increase it by 50 percent, they had either to work out an agreement or to defer the decision to the next-higher level of product and geographic management. Disagreements could effectively go as high as the top-level operating committee, which consisted of the chairman, vice chairman, three presidents of product groups, the top financial officer, and the president of the international group.

During the late 1980s, two major changes occurred at Westinghouse. First, the company continually divested itself of products and services, such as consumer products, that were not currently yielding high returns. This made Westinghouse one of the decade's leaders in earnings-per-share growth but led some analysts to conclude the company was dumping business from which global competitors could profit. For example, its elevator operation had never pushed hard internationally and was earning poorly in the mature North American market. After Westinghouse sold it to the Schindler Group from Switzerland, its sales rose 50 percent in the first half of 1989.

The second big change was a growing dependence on alliances with non–U.S.-based companies. Two alliances involved joint ventures with the Swedish-Swiss company Asea Brown Boveri, one for steam turbines and generators and another for equipment for energy transmission and generation. These joint ventures involved the sell-off to Asea Brown Boveri of 45 percent of Westinghouse's former 100-percent ownership in these businesses, which accounted for a significant part of Westinghouse's total sales. Another alliance involved a start-up venture with Siemens from Germany to produce automation products. In the early 1990s, Westinghouse and Siemens were planning to create other joint ventures to produce industrial circuit breakers and control equipment. In another instance, Westinghouse sold its small and medium motor businesses, which were noncompetitive with cheaper imports, and then formed a joint venture with a Taiwanese manufacturer to produce motors.

Questions

1. What have been the major organizational problems inhibiting Westinghouse's international growth?
2. What organizational characteristics may affect the successful implementation of a matrix organization at Westinghouse?
3. How can a company such as Westinghouse pursue a goal to increase its dependence on foreign operations?
4. How does Westinghouse's increased reliance on alliances relate to its international strategy and structure?
5. Do you believe Westinghouse has a long-term strategic intent? If so, what is it? What do you think it should be?

Chapter Notes

1. Data for the case were taken from "Nestlé Centralizing to Win a Bigger Payoff from the U.S.," *Business Week,* February 2, 1981, pp. 56–58; "Nestlé—At Home Abroad: An Interview with Pierre Liotard-Vogt," *Harvard Business Review,* November 1976, pp. 80–88; Robert Ball, "A Shopkeeper Shakes Up Nestlé," *Fortune,* December 27, 1982, pp. 103–106; Damon Darlin, "Nestlé Hopes to Bring Its Other U.S. Units Up to Level of Its Stouffer Corp. Subsidiary," *Wall Street Journal,* March 15, 1984, p. 33; "Nestlé to Close Libby Units," *New York Times,* September 26, 1985, p. D5; Graham Turner, "Inside Europe's Giant Companies: Nestlé Finds a Better Formula," *Long Range Planning,* Vol. 19, No. 3, June 1986, pp. 12–19; Mark Alpert and Aimety Dunlap Smith, "Nestlé Shows How to Gobble Markets," *Fortune,* January 16, 1989, pp. 74–78; Daniel F. Cuff, "Head of Carnation Gets New U.S. Nestlé Post," *New York Times,* November 12, 1990, p. C4; Zachary Schiller and Lois Therrien, "Nestlé's Crunch in the U.S.," *Business Week,* December 24, 1990, pp. 24–25; John Templeman, Stewart Toy, and Dave Lindorff, "Nestlé: A Giant in a Hurry," *Business Week,* March 22, 1993, pp. 50–54; various company reports; and Sid Astbury, "Food Maker Applies Lessons Learned from Japan," *Asian Business,* Vol. 29, No. 6, June 1993, p. 12.
2. William R. Fannin and Arvin F. Rodrigues, "National or Global?—Control vs. Flexibility," *Long Range Planning,* Vol. 19, No. 5, October 1986, pp. 84–88.
3. Gary Hamel and C. K. Prahalad, "Strategic Intent," *Harvard Business Review,* May–June 1989, pp. 63–76.
4. For two recent discussions of the importance of implementation and the need to revise plans, see William G. Egelhoff, "Great Strategy or Great Strategy Implementation—Two Ways of Competing in Global Markets," *Sloan Management Review,* Winter 1993, pp. 37–50; and Lawrence Hrebeniak, "Implementing Global Strategies," *European Management Journal,* December 1992, pp. 392–403.
5. F. A. Maljers, "Strategic Planning and Intuition in Unilever," *Long Range Planning,* Vol. 23, No. 2, 1990, pp. 63–68.
6. B. Mascarenhas, "Coping with Uncertainty in International Business," *Journal of International Business Studies,* Fall 1982, pp. 87–98; Egelhoff, loc. cit.
7. M. J. Culnan, "Environmental Scanning: The Effects of Task Complexity and Source Accessibility on Information Gathering Behavior," *Decision Sciences,*

No. 14, 1983, pp. 194–206; and N. R. Boulton, W. M. Lindsay, S. G. Franklin, and L. W. Rue, "Strategic Planning: Determining the Impact of Environmental Characteristics and Uncertainty," *Academy of Management Journal,* Vol. 25, No. 3, 1982, pp. 500–509.
8. We wish to acknowledge Allen Morrison for supplying examples of companies he has found in his research that are using the different types of structures. See K. Roth, D. Schweiger, and A. J. Morrison, "Global Strategy Implementation at the Business Unit Level: Operational Capabilities and Administrative Mechanisms," *Journal of International Business Studies,* Vol. 22, No. 3, Third Quarter 1991, pp. 369–402.
9. W. G. Egelhoff, "Strategy and Structure in Multinational Corporations: An Information Processing Approach," *Administrative Science Quarterly,* Vol. 27, 1982, pp. 435–458; John D. Daniels, Robert A. Pitts, and Marietta J. Tretter, "Strategy and Structure of U.S. Multinationals: An Exploratory Study," *Academy of Management Journal,* Vol. 27, No. 2, June 1984, pp. 292–307; and Mohammed M. Habib and Bart Victor, "Strategy, Structure, and Performance of U.S. Manufacturing and Service MNCs: A Comparative Analysis," *Strategic Management Journal,* Vol. 12, 1991, pp. 589–606.
10. C. K. Prahalad, "Strategic Choices in Diversified MNCs," *Harvard Business Review,* July–August 1976, pp. 67–78, explores in depth the problems inherent to the locus of relative power.
11. Ian D. Turner, "Strategy and Organization," *Management Update: Supplement to the Journal of General Management,* Summer 1989, pp. 1–8; and Gunnar Hedlund, "The Hypermodern MNC—A Heterarchy?" *Human Resource Management,* Spring 1986, pp. 9–35.
12. James R. Houghton, "A Chairman Reflects: The Age of the Hierarchy Is Over," *New York Times,* September 24, 1989, p. C2.
13. Vertical versus horizontal *keiretsus* are discussed in Kosaku Yoshida, "New Economic Principles in America—Competition and Cooperation," *Columbia Journal of World Business,* Winter 1992, pp. 31–44.
14. William J. Holstein, James Treece, Stan Crock, and Larry Armstrong, "Mighty Mitsubishi Is on the Move," *Business Week,* September 24, 1990, pp. 98–107.
15. Michael L. Gerlach, "The Japanese Corporate Network: A Blockmodel Analysis," *Administrative Science Quarterly,* March 1992, pp. 105–139.

16. For a discussion of the distance factor, see Jacques Picard, "How European Companies Control Marketing Decisions Abroad," *Columbia Journal of World Business,* Summer 1977, pp. 113–121. Also Robert L. Drake and Lee M. Caudill, "Management of the Large Multinational: Trends and Future Challenges," *Business Horizons,* May–June 1981, p. 84, found that Canadian subsidiaries of U.S. companies did not have the same degree of autonomy as subsidiaries in other countries because of the former's closeness to corporate headquarters.
17. Mark P. Kriger and Esther E. Solomon, "Strategic Mindsets and Decision-Making Autonomy in U.S. and Japanese MNCs," *Management International Review,* Vol. 32, No. 4, 1992, pp. 327–343; and John H. Dunning, "The Governance of Japanese and U.S. Manufacturing Affiliates in the U.K.: Some Country Specific Differences," Working Paper 5–91 (Copenhagen: Institute of International Economies and Management, 1991).
18. Donna G. Goehle, *Decision Making in Multinational Corporations* (Ann Arbor, Mich.: University Research Press, 1980).
19. Stephen Baker, Kevin Kelly, Robert D. Hof, and William J. Holstein, "Mini-Nationals Are Making Maximum Impact," *Business Week,* September 6, 1993, pp. 66–69.
20. Christopher A. Bartlett and Sumantra Ghoshal, "Tap Your Subsidiaries for Global Reach," *Harvard Business Review,* Vol. 64, No. 6, November–December 1986, pp. 87–94.
21. Joann S. Lublin, "Firms Ship Unit Headquarters Abroad," *Wall Street Journal,* December 9, 1992, p. B1; and Pervez Ghauri, "New Structures in MNCs Based in Small Countries: A Network Approach," *European Management Journal,* Vol. 10, No. 3, September 1992, pp. 357–364.
22. James Leontiades, "Going Global—Global Strategies vs. National Strategies," *Long Range Planning,* Vol. 19, No. 6, December 1986, pp. 98–100, discusses how national strategies may be more appropriate in given circumstances.
23. Yves Doz and C. K. Prahalad, "Controlled Variety: A Challenge for Human Resource Management in the MNC," *Human Resource Management,* Vol. 25, No. 1, Spring 1986, p. 57.
24. W. Chan Kim and Renée A. Mauborgne, "Making Global Strategies Work," *Sloan Management Review,* Spring 1993, pp. 11–28.
25. See B. R. Balliga and A. M. Jeager, "Multinational Corporations: Control Systems

and Delegation Issues," *Journal of International Business Studies,* Vol. 15, No. 2, Summer 1984, pp. 25–40; and Vladimir Pucik and Jan Hack Katz, "Information Control, and Human Resource Management in Multinational Firms," *Human Resource Management,* Vol. 25, No. 1, Spring 1986, pp. 121–132.

26. Anders Edström and Jay R. Galbraith, "Transfer of Managers as Coordination and Control Strategy in Multinational Organizations," *Administrative Science Quarterly,* June 1977, p. 251.

27. Templeman et al., loc. cit.; and "The Glamour of Gaijins," *The Economist,* September 21, 1991, p. 80.

28. Samir M. Youssef, "Contextual Factors Influencing Control Strategy of Multinational Corporations," *Academy of Management Journal,* March 1975, pp. 136–145.

29. A. B. Sim, "Decentralized Management of Subsidiaries and Their Performance," *Management International Review,* No. 2, 1977, pp. 47–49.

30. C. A. Bartlett, "MNCs: Get off the Reorganization Merry-Go-Round," *Harvard Business Review,* Vol. 61, No. 2, 1983, pp. 138–146; and Robert A. Pitts and John D. Daniels, "Aftermath of the Matrix Mania," *Columbia Journal of World Business,* Vol. 19, No. 2, Summer 1984, pp. 48–54.

31. David F. Hawkins, "Controlling Foreign Operations," *Financial Executive,* February 1965; V. Mauriel, "Evaluation and Control of Overseas Operations," *Management Accounting,* May 1969; and J. M. McInnes, "Financial Control Systems for Multinational Operations: An Empirical Investigation," *Journal of International Business Studies,* Fall 1971, pp. 11–28.

32. Frederick D. S. Choi and I. James Czechowicz, "Assessing Foreign Subsidiary Performance: A Multinational Comparison," *Management International Review,* Vol. 23, No. 4, 1983, p. 15.

33. Ibid., pp. 18–20.

34. Ibid., p. 22.

35. Ibid., pp. 16–17.

36. George M. Scott, *An Introduction to Financial Control and Reporting in Multinational Enterprises* (Austin: Bureau of Business Research, Graduate School of Business, University of Texas at Austin, 1973), pp. 77–79.

37. J. Alex Murray, "Intelligence Systems of the MNCs," *Columbia Journal of World Business,* September–October 1972, pp. 63–71.

38. Martin D. J. Buss, "Managing International Information Systems," *Harvard Business Review,* Vol. 60, No. 5, September–October 1982, pp. 153–162.

39. Among the many treatments of this subject are Osvaldo Sunkel, "Big Business and 'Dependencia': A Latin American View," *Foreign Affairs,* April 1972, pp. 517–531; Benjamin J. Cohen, *The Question of Imperialism—The Political Economy of Dominance and Dependence* (New York: Basic Books, 1973); and Peter Smith Ring, Stefanie Ann Lenway, and Michelle Govekar, "Management of the Political Imperative in International Business," *Strategic Management Journal,* Vol. 11, 1990, pp. 141–151.

40. Robert D. Pearce and Satwinder Singh, "Internationalisation of Research and Development Among the World's Leading Enterprises," No. 157 (Reading, England: University of Reading Discussion Papers in International Investment and Business Studies, November 1991).

41. Scott D. Julian and Robert T. Keller, "Multinational R&D Siting: Corporate Strategies for Success," *Columbia Journal of World Business,* Fall 1991, pp. 47–57.

42. William A. Fischer and Jack N. Behrman, "The Coordination of Foreign R&D Activities by Transnational Corporations," *Journal of International Business Studies,* Winter 1979, pp. 28–35.

43. The information in this section is taken from Saeed Samiee, "Transnational Data Flow Constraints: A New Challenge for Multinational Corporations," *Journal of International Business Studies,* Vol. 15, No. 1, Spring–Summer 1984, pp. 141–150.

44. M. J. Kane and David A. Ricks, "Is Transnational Data Flow Regulation a Problem?" *Journal of International Business Studies,* Vol. 19, No. 3, 1988, pp. 477–483; and Rakesh B. Sambharya and Arvind Phatak, "The Effect of Transborder Data Flow Restrictions on American Multinational Corporations," *Management International Review,* Vol. 30, No. 3, 1990, pp. 267–289.

45. Sanjoy Hazarika, "Bhopal Payments Set at $470 Million for Union Carbide," *New York Times,* February 15, 1989, p. 1+; and Scott McMurray, "India's High Court Upholds Settlement Paid by Carbide in Bhopal Gas Leak," *Wall Street Journal,* October 4, 1991, p. B12.

46. Sumantra Ghoshal and Nitin Nohria, "Horses for Courses: Organizational Forms for Multinational Corporations," *Sloan Management Review,* Winter 1993, pp. 23–35.

47. Michael Maccoby, *Sweden at the Edge: Lessons for American and Swedish Managers* (Philadelphia: University of Pennsylvania Press, 1991).

48. Data for the case were taken primarily from Hugh D. Menzies, "Westinghouse Takes Aim at the World," *Fortune,* January 14, 1980, pp. 48–53. Other background information may be found in "Westinghouse's Third Big Step Is Overseas," *Business Week,* October 2, 1971, pp. 64–67; in several issues of Westinghouse's *Annual Report;* Thomas H. Naylor, "The International Strategy Matrix," *Columbia Journal of World Business,* Vol. 20, No. 2, Summer 1985, pp. 17–18; Gregory Stricharchuk, "Westinghouse Relies on Ruthlessly Rational Pruning," *Wall Street Journal,* January 24, 1990, p. A6; and "Expansion Through Alliances," *Mergers & Acquisitions,* July–August 1988, p. 15.

7 Functional Management, Operations, and Concerns

Oceania is a global leader in livestock. Here you
see a sheep auction in New Zealand against a
background showing part of a Maori feather
cloak (circa 1930).

Chapter 17

Marketing

*May both seller and buyer
see the benefit.*
—Turkish Proverb

Objectives

- To introduce techniques for assessing market sizes for given countries

- To describe a range of product policies and the circumstances in which they are appropriate

- To contrast practices of standardized versus differentiated marketing programs for each country in which sales are made

- To emphasize how environmental differences complicate the management of marketing worldwide

- To discuss the major international considerations within each of the marketing functions: product, pricing, promotion, branding, and distribution

Case
Marks & Spencer[1]

Britain has often been called a country of shopkeepers, and Marks & Spencer (M & S) is undoubtedly the shopkeeping leader. With nearly 300 stores in the United Kingdom, M & S is that country's largest retailer. Its Marble Arch store in London is in the *Guinness Book of World Records* as the store that takes in more revenue per square foot than any other in the world.

Soft goods (clothes and household textiles) account for about two thirds of the company's sales, and M & S has an estimated 16 percent of the retail clothing sales in the United Kingdom. For some clothing items, it supplies over half the British market. After M & S added food lines to its stores, it became the largest and most profitable of British food retailers.

How has M & S become so dominant in the British market? Since the company's founding in 1884, its philosophy has been to sell durable merchandise at a moderate price. M & S has merchandise made to its specifications. It uses its vast buying power to induce producers to make cost-cutting investments and to compete for its business by offering low prices on merchandise to be sold under its St. Michael trademark. The goods are perceived as having excellent value and quality, so there is little need to discount prices for sales. Because M & S is so well known, it spends little on advertising, decorates its stores austerely, offers very little personal service, and provides no dressing rooms or public bathrooms. Customers receive no sales slips for small purchases, but merchandise is easily returnable.

M & S also has been successful in appealing to the nationalism of its British clientele by promoting heavily the fact that nearly all the clothing it sells originates in the United Kingdom. However, the company admits that the percentage has been falling and will likely fall further as its British suppliers move more of their production abroad. Still, M & S has managed to develop an image that is as British as bed and breakfast or fish and chips. Foreign visitors to Britain usually feel they must visit an M & S store. Consequently, one of the stores has had to post warning signs to shoplifters in five languages.

M & S has experienced foreseeable barriers to continued growth in the United Kingdom. Not the least of its problems has been its high market share. Being already so dominant, M & S would have to add new products or appeal to new market segments to maintain its growth rate. The company has had trouble doing this. For example, it moved into higher-priced clothes by using finer materials for its traditional styles, such as silk blouses and cashmere coats. This initiative was disastrous, however; the Harrods-type customer did not switch to M & S, and many M & S customers traded down to even cheaper retailers. M & S subsequently dropped its higher-priced lines. The company also tried to target a more fashion-conscious market with lines that differed from its traditional styles. Because the merchandise needed for this market changes rapidly, M & S had to get supplies within one week from the time it placed orders instead of allowing up to fourteen weeks, which was customary. Although this move offered hope for domestic growth, an M & S executive said, "Because the company is near saturation in the United Kingdom, its growth must be overseas."

M & S has had mixed success in its foreign operations. It opened its first stores in continental Europe in 1975, in North America in 1976, and in the Far East in 1989. In addition, M & S began exporting its St. Michael–brand merchandise and franchised stores in seventeen countries. Foreign operations and the company's dependence on them are shown on

Map 17.1. Most international growth has taken place since the late 1980s. But the company still depends primarily on the U.K. market.

When the United Kingdom joined the EC, M & S's management saw an opportunity to expand on the continent because clothing from M & S suppliers could enter other EC countries without tariffs. Paris and Brussels were selected as the first locations for stores. Because both cities are French-speaking, management assumed that consumer behavior would be similar in the two. Before opening stores, the company sent a team of observers to Paris for eighteen months so that product differences could be targeted to French-speaking consumers.

The team found substantial differences between French and British consumers. One was in sizes: They noted that "French girls always seem to wear a size smaller than they need with everything obviously relying on the buttons, while we [English] go for a half size too large." French women preferred longer skirts than did British women. French men's preferences, in contrast to those of British men, were for single back vents in jackets, sweaters in a variety of colors (including pastels), and jackets and slacks rather than suits. All of these differences had implications for the merchandise mix and the procurement of supplies.

Despite substantial product research, the company was not well received initially. Many fewer people entered the stores than had been anticipated. M & S management had believed that because the company was so well known in the United Kingdom and so many

**Map 17.1
Geographic Spread of
Marks & Spencer's
Operations**
Although M & S has operations in twenty-four countries, almost 90 percent of its business is in the United Kingdom and Ireland.

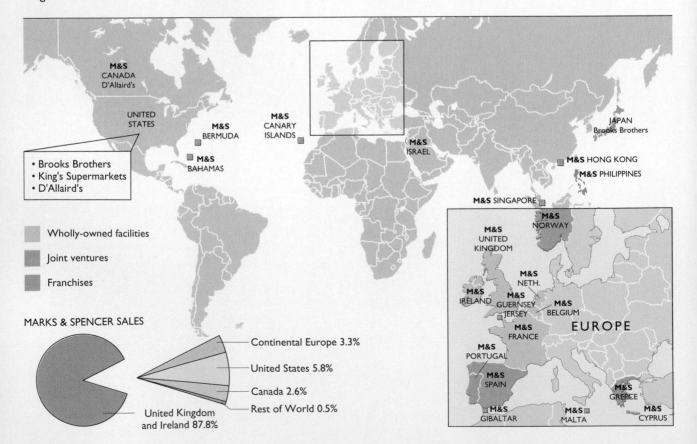

foreign tourists visited its London stores, its reputation had preceded it. Belatedly, management learned that only 3 percent of the French had even heard of M & S or St. Michael before the continental stores were opened. Store locations exacerbated the situation. M & S wanted its first stores to be "flagships" and therefore sought to locate them on the most popular shopping streets. However, store space was at a premium on those streets. Consequently, in Paris the company had to settle for a location where most pedestrian traffic preferred the other side of the street, and in Brussels, it accepted a store with too small a frontage to give an impression of abundant merchandise inside. To entice people into the stores, M & S had to advertise more than it did in the United Kingdom; thus keeping prices low was difficult.

Another factor influencing costs was that M & S's continental stores lacked the buying power enjoyed by its U.K. stores. Initially the company contracted nearly 80 percent of its merchandise from continental sources that were unwilling to treat M & S any more favorably than other retailers already in the market. Most of the remaining merchandise came from the United Kingdom, where M & S had buying clout. Because much of the clothing was made to specifications to meet French and Belgian needs (for example, stronger thread for buttons, single-vent jackets, and pastel sweaters), the British producers had to make these items in short production runs. When initial large sales did not materialize, the British manufacturers were reluctant to keep markups very low. Even when merchandise prices were kept low, M & S found the French highly suspicious of bargains.

Another problem was that French customers were unaccustomed to the M & S stores' interior starkness and lack of service. French women insisted on trying on clothes before they bought them, even if it meant stripping down to their bras on the sales floor. A French fashion writer summed up the customer reaction to the Paris store as "not madly joyful unless of course one is as impervious to English shopping as one is to English cooking."

To attract customers to its Paris store, M & S had to make operating adjustments. The primary change surprisingly was in merchandise, the area in which the company had done so much preliminary research. In trying to copy what the continental retailers were offering in merchandise, M & S simply could not get a more durable product to customers at a sufficiently lower price to attract a mass clientele. However, the company discerned fairly quickly that there was a market segment willing to buy the more English-type merchandise for which it could exert its buying power. M & S now buys only 10 percent of its merchandise from continental sources and has differentiated itself from local competitors by capitalizing on its "Englishness." It concentrates on such items as tan and navy blue sweaters, biscuits (called crackers in the United States), English beer, and even a quiche Lorraine made in the United Kingdom. In deference to French tastes, M & S has carpeted and put dressing rooms in its Paris store.

Not surprisingly, a large portion of the Paris store's early customers were Britishers living in France. This gradually changed as Parisians learned to like wandering through wide aisles with shopping carts and paying for all merchandise at one register. M & S became so successful that it opened additional stores in France. But customers had to be trained. For example, the French did not appreciate Christmas puddings until they learned they had to cook them. One Paris store now sells more merchandise per square meter than any other

tion that can help management decide which markets to analyze more closely and which to emphasize.[3]

Total Market Potential

To determine potential demand, a company's management usually must first estimate the possible sales of the category of products for all companies and then estimate its own market-share potential.

Existing consumption patterns   The **input-output table** is a tool used widely in national economic planning to show the resources utilized by different industries for a given output as well as the interdependence of economic sectors. Tables featuring sectors on both the vertical and horizontal axes show the production (output) of one sector as the demand (input) of another. For instance, steel output becomes an input to the automobile industry, households, government, foreign sector, and even to the steel industry itself. Many countries publish input-output tables. By comparing these with economic projections for an economy as a whole or with plans for production changes in a given industry, management can project the total volume of sales changes for a given type of product as well as the purchases by each sector. There are three major shortcomings of this method, however:

1. For many countries, the data in the input-output tables and in plans or projections of economic changes are too sparse.
2. The assumption that the relationships among sectors and resources are fixed is questionable.
3. The tables may be many years old before they are published and readily available.

Data on other countries   The amount of sales of a product in one country may be based on the same conditions that determine sales in other countries. One such condition is per capita income: As incomes change, the demand for a product may change. For example, Japanese consumption of beef, sugar, hard liquor, and dairy products has grown since 1970 as Japanese per capita income has increased—a trend that closely parallels the U.S. experience in earlier years.[4] Management thus may collect data on the consumption of a given product in countries with different per capita GNPs and then project sales at different income levels by plotting a path through which average demand changes as incomes change (see Fig. 17.1).

Reasonably good fits for many products have been found by using this method. However, so many other variables affect demand, the analysis breaks down for some products in some countries. For example, the number of cars in Switzerland is lower than income would predict because of the public transportation system, difficult terrain, and high import duties. The expenditures on food in Japan are higher than would be predicted by either population or income level because food is expensive and work habits promote eating out.[5] Another problem with this

---

Input-output tables show the relationship among economic sectors.

Sales analysis assumes one country will follow a pattern similar to that of another.

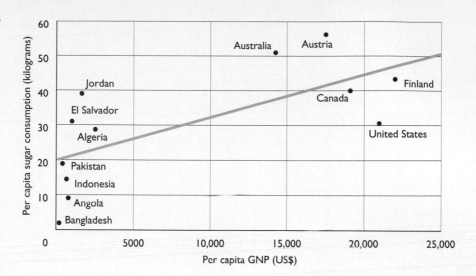

Source: UN Statistical Yearbook, 1988–89.

**Figure 17.1
Per Capita Sugar Consumption and GNP for Selected Countries, 1989**
Plotting data on per capita sugar consumption and GNP for countries for which data are available allows construction of a line that can be used to estimate sugar consumption in countries for which data on GNP are available.

method is that it is static. As technology and prices change, a country may change its consumption pattern much earlier or later than would be indicated by looking at a group of countries in only one time period.

Time-series analysis projects the future by examining past trends.

Time series data   Sometimes sales follow a pattern over time. If this is the case and data are available, a company may be able to make future projections based on past values.[6] Figure 17.2 illustrates sugar consumption in the United States based on time-series data. Note that per capita consumption has fallen since 1970 because of competition from corn and low-calorie sweeteners. This drop contrasts with projections of sugar consumption shown in Fig. 17.1 based on cross-national data. The use of time-series and cross-national data also may be combined. Such analyses within an economy are useful for predicting total demand and for identifying the economic sectors generating this demand.

As income changes, product demand may change by a different percentage.

Income elasticity   A common predictive method is to divide the percentage of change in product demand by the percentage of change in income. An answer greater than 1 means the product demand is **elastic;** that is, sales are likely to increase or decrease by a percentage that is greater than the percentage by which income changes. An answer less than 1 indicates demand is **inelastic;** that is, sales are likely to increase or decrease by a percentage that is less than the percentage change in income. An elasticity of 1.5 would mean that a percentage change in income would result in 1.5 times that percentage change in the demand for the specific product. Demand for necessities, such as food, is relatively less elastic than is demand for discretionary products, such as automobiles. In other words, upward or downward movements in income ordinarily would affect automobile sales more than food sales.

This tool is useful for estimating the expenditures for countries at different income levels. For example, people in the United States spend a lower percentage of

**Figure 17.2
Per Capita Sugar
Consumption in the
United States,
1899–1990**
Plotting per capita sugar
consumption over time al-
lows extrapolation of the
trend to make estimates
for the future.

*Source: Statistical Abstract of the
United States, Supplement 1957,
1972, and 1992.*

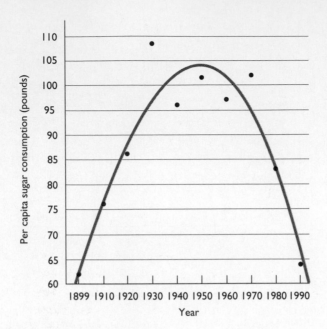

their personal income on food than do South Koreans. The difference is due not to relative appetites but rather to income differences that allow people in the United States to spend more on other types of purchases. Because a large portion of people in South Korea are poor, a change in income level affects food consumption there much more than it would in a higher-income country.[7]

As is true with any method of demand projection, income-elasticity measurements must be approached with caution, especially if a company is making projections in one country based on demand analysis in another. Differences in prices and tastes affect consumers' demand as well. For example, because of price differences, Italy consumes much more fruits and vegetables than Norway does, even though Norway's per capita income is higher. Denmark and Switzerland have very similar per capita incomes, but per capita consumption of frozen food is much higher in Denmark because of the Danes' penchant for convenience.[8]

Demand is related to some economic or other indicator.

Regression Regression is an important means of refining data and making predictions by uncovering relationships among variables. By using data based on the historical relationship between demand for a given product and economic or other indicators or between demand and some indicators in a given time period, a company may construct a regression equation that shows the demand (the dependent variable) based on level of the indicators (the independent variables). This technique allows for consideration of an amount of consumption not directly attributable to changes in the indicators and for the determination of the degree of correlation between the independent and dependent variables. Regression analysis thus can be used to predict demand from changes in related indicators.

Gap Analysis

The tools just described may give an estimation of the market potential in various countries for a given product. Once this rough determination is made, the company must calculate how well it is doing within each market. A useful tool for scanning markets and comparing countries in this respect is **gap analysis,** which is a method for estimating a company's potential sales by identifying market segments that it is not serving adequately.[9] When a company's sales are lower than the estimated market potential for a given type of product, the company has potential for increased sales, which may result from a gap in usage, product line, distribution, or competition.

For example, the two largest Swiss chocolate companies, Nestlé and Interfood, have found very different types of gaps in different countries.[10] Consequently, they have altered their marketing programs among countries. In some markets, they have found substantial usage gaps; that is, less chocolate is being consumed than would be expected on the basis of population and income levels. Industry specialists estimate, for example, that in many countries more than 80 percent of the population has never tasted a chocolate bar. Therefore, they project that if more people in those countries can be persuaded to try chocolate bars, the companies' sales should increase with the market increase. This assumption has led the two companies to promote sales in those areas for chocolate in general.

The U.S. market shows another type of usage gap. Nearly everyone in this market has tried most chocolate products, but per capita consumption has fallen because of growing concern about health. To increase chocolate consumption in general, Nestlé for a short time promoted chocolate as an energy source for the sports-minded. Note, however, that building general consumption is most useful to the market leader; thus Nestlé, with U.S. chocolate sales below those of Mars and Hershey, actually benefited its competitors during the short-lived campaign.

The Swiss chocolate companies also have found that they have product-line gaps in some hot climates in the market for sweetened products. By developing new products, such as chocolate products that melt less easily, they may be able to garner a larger share of that market. These companies also have found chocolate products with which they do not compete directly. Further, in some markets, such as Japan, they have not yet achieved sufficient distribution to reach their sales potentials; therefore Nestlé formed a joint venture with a Japanese cake and candy maker, Fujiya, to make Kit Kat bars and gain more distribution.[11]

Finally, there are competitive gaps—sales by competitors that cannot be explained by differences between one's own product line and distribution and those of the competitors. That is, competitors are making some additional sales because of their prices, advertising campaigns, good will, or any of a host of other factors. For example, in markets such as France and Germany, Nestlé and Interfood feel that most of the potential market demand is being fulfilled but that any increase in sales must come at the expense of competitors.

The difference between total market potential and companies' sales is due to gaps:
- Usage—less product sold by all competitors than potential
- Product line—company lacks some product variations
- Distribution—company misses geographic or intensity coverage
- Competitive—competitors' sales not explained by product and distribution gaps

Product Policy

Most marketing texts categorize companies' product policies, although there is some variation in the categories they use. The treatment of these policies tends to be domestically focused. This section highlights the international application of five commonly used categories of product policies.

Production Orientation

With production orientation, companies focus primarily on production efficiency or the development of the highest-quality product. There is little analysis of consumer needs or of whether consumers will pay for differentiated products or higher quality. Although this approach has largely gone out of vogue, it is used internationally for certain cases:

- Commodity sales, especially those for which there is little need or possibility of product differentiation by country
- Passive exports, particularly those that serve to reduce surpluses within the domestic market
- Foreign-market segments or niches that may resemble the market at which the product is aimed initially

Price is the most important factor in selling many commodities.

Many raw materials and agricultural commodities, such as sugar and tin, are sold primarily on the basis of price because there is universal demand for the undifferentiated product. However, even for commodity sales, there has been a realization that marketing efforts may yield positive international sales results. For example, the promotion of the Chiquita brand on bananas has helped increase global supermarket distribution in a glutted market. In addition, oil producers, such as Petroven and Aramco, have integrated forward by buying branded gasoline-distribution operations abroad. Commodity producers also put efforts into business-to-business marketing in the form of providing innovative financing and assuring timely supplies of high quality.

Passive sales occur when
- **Advertising spills over**
- **Foreign buyers seek new products**

Many companies begin exporting very passively. Sometimes, for unknown reasons, orders or requests for product information simply arrive from abroad. Foreign products are discovered through reports in scientific and trade journals, advertising that spills across borders, buying trips, and observations of products that others have brought into the country. At this point, companies adapt their products very little, if at all, to foreign consumers' preferences. This practice suffices for many companies that view foreign sales as an appendage to domestic sales. This type of company frequently exports only if it has excess inventory for the domestic market. In fact, fixed costs are sometimes covered from domestic sales so that lower prices are offered on exports as a means of liquidating inventories without disrupting the domestic market.[12]

The unaltered domestic product may have appeal abroad.

A company may develop a product aimed at achieving a large share of its domestic market and then find there are market segments abroad willing to buy that product. Sometimes the product may have a universal appeal, such as French champagne. In other situations, a company may be able to target to a mass market at home and a small niche within foreign locations; an example is U.S. bourbon producers.[13] Recall that M & S first tried to sell clothing for the needs of the French mass market but later found a niche of French consumers who would buy what the company was already selling in the United Kingdom. Another situation involves sales to countries that have only a small market potential regardless of whether changes are geared to unique consumer needs. Particularly in small LDCs, MNEs may make few changes because the market size does not justify the expense to them and because competitors are apt to be other MNEs that do not make product alterations. Companies may not even adjust the voltage requirements and plugs of electrical products to local standards, instead leaving the job of conversion to local purchasers.

Sales Orientation

Internationally, sales orientation involves trying to sell abroad what the company is able to sell domestically on the assumption that consumers are sufficiently similar globally. A company may make this assumption because the distance between it and its foreign markets makes information about the foreign markets difficult to obtain. Paradoxically, the more distant a market, the less can be assumed about it.[14] This orientation differs from the production orientation because of its active rather than passive approach to promoting sales. However, there is much anecdotal evidence of foreign failures that have resulted because of assumptions that product acceptance will be the same as at home or that heavy sales efforts abroad can overcome negative foreign attitudes toward the product. Yet, there also are successful examples of transferring products abroad with little or no research on foreign consumers' preferred product characteristics.

Standardization usually reduces costs.

The greatest ability to sell the same product in multiple countries occurs when consumer characteristics are similar and when there is a great deal of spillover in product information, such as between the United States and Canada. Whether a company is exporting or has foreign production facilities, it may cut costs substantially by standardizing its products and spreading developmental costs over a larger volume of output. This usually is done on the basis of the home-country experience, since costs associated with product development, promotional programs, and distributional expertise already have been expended there. Conversely, companies may develop a new product to launch almost simultaneously in multiple countries, as Colgate-Palmolive did with Optims Shampoo.[15] Or, the standardized product may first be developed abroad, for example, Whiskas, a cat food that Mars first developed outside the United States.[16]

Customer Orientation

A customer orientation takes geographic areas as given.

In a company that operates according to sales orientation, management usually is guided by the answers to questions such as these: Should the company send some exports abroad? Where can the company sell some more of product X? That is, the product is held constant and the sales location is varied. In contrast, customer orientation involves asking: What can the company sell in country A? In this case, the country is held constant and the product is varied.

Sometimes a company wants to penetrate markets in a given country because of the country's size, growth potential, proximity to home operations, currency or political stability, or any of a host of other reasons. In the extreme of this approach, a company would move to completely unrelated products. Although an uncommon strategy, some companies have adopted it. For example, Henkel of Germany wanted to diversify into the United States in order to counter an expected sluggish domestic market, but the company's management felt it would be difficult to compete in the United States in its major product lines—detergents and cosmetics. Thus Henkel chose instead to buy the chemical division of General Mills.[17]

As with a production orientation, a company using a customer orientation may do so passively. Increasingly, purchasing agents are setting product specifications and then seeking out contracts for the foreign manufacture of components or finished products. For example, the Hong Kong company S. T. King makes clothing to the specifications of companies such as Calvin Klein. In responding to product requests, a company may make a product that differs markedly from what it sells domestically. In such a situation, the company is less concerned about choosing product characteristics than about pricing and distributing what it is marketing abroad.

Strategic Marketing Orientation

Most companies committed to continual rather than sporadic foreign sales adopt a strategy that combines production, sales, and consumer orientations. Refusal to make changes to accommodate needs of foreign markets means too many sales may be lost, especially if there are aggressive competitors willing to make desired adaptations. Yet expertise concerning a type of product may be very important, and companies want the products they sell abroad to be compatible with their expertise and with their means of dealing with competitors. A company therefore tends to make product variations abroad without deviating very far from its experience. For example, a company accustomed to manufacturing electric typewriters is more apt to move into the production of manual typewriters or personal computers than of tires or detergents. The latter products would probably be too far from management's area of expertise.

An attitude of reacting to consumers' product preferences does not necessarily mean that a company must forgo the economies of standardization. A company may well do market research in a number of countries in order to develop and aim a product at a global market segment, as Canon did in developing a 35-millimeter automatic camera. Instead of merely trying to sell a domestic product abroad, the company designs a product to fit some global market segment, which may mean changing what is sold domestically to correspond to the international standard. Global products may also be possible for industrial users because the purchasers are

The most common strategy is product changes as adaptations, done by degree.

apt to be technically trained decision makers. For example, SKF introduced a line of 20,000 ball bearings to replace 50,000 on a worldwide basis.[18]

Societal Marketing Orientation

Societal marketing orientation implies that successful international marketing requires serious consideration of potential environmental, health, social, and work-related problems that may arise when products are sold abroad.[19] Such groups as consumer associations, political parties, and labor unions are becoming more globally aware and may react negatively and over a long period to adverse effects of products companies sell. Companies must increasingly consider not only how a product is purchased but also how it is disposed of and how it might be changed to be more socially desirable.

Reasons for Product Alteration

Legal factors Explicit legal requirements are the most obvious reason for altering products for foreign markets. The exact requirements vary widely by country but are usually meant to protect consumers. Pharmaceuticals and foods are particularly subject to regulations concerning purity, testing, and labeling. Automobiles sold in the United States must conform to safety and pollution standards not found in many other countries.

When foreign legal requirements are less stringent than domestic ones, a company may not be legally compelled to alter its products for foreign sale. However, the company will have to weigh such decisions as whether following high domestic standards abroad will raise prices and whether domestic or foreign ill will may result if those standards are not met. Some companies have been criticized for selling abroad, especially in LDCs, such products as toys, automobiles, contraceptives, and pharmaceuticals that did not meet home-country safety or quality standards.[20]

One of the more cumbersome adjustments for companies has occurred because of different laws on packaging that are designed to protect the environment. Certain types of containers are prohibited in some countries, aluminum cans in Denmark, for example. Other countries restrict the volume of packaging materials; thus exporters of Scotch whiskey to Germany must remove the bottles from the cardboard boxes. There also are differences in national requirements as to whether containers must be reusable and whether waste materials must be recycled, incinerated, or composted.[21]

A recurring issue is to what extent it is possible to arrive at international product standards to eliminate some of the seemingly wasteful product alterations among countries. Although agreement has been reached on some products (such as for the sprocket dimensions on movie film), other products (such as railroad gauges and electrical socket shapes) continue to vary. In reality, there is both consumer and economic resistance to standardization. For example, the conversion to the metric system on beverage containers meant U.S. consumers had to learn that 236.58 mil-

Legal factors are usually related to safety or health protection.

liliters is the same as 8 fluid ounces for their soft drinks. In an economic sense, the changeover was more costly than simply educating people and relabeling. Containers had to be redesigned and production retooled so that dimensions would be in even numbers. Even for new products or those still under development, such as high-definition television (HDTV), countries seldom reach agreement because they want to protect the investments already made by their domestically based companies.[22] At best, international standards will come very slowly.

Less apparent are the indirect legal requirements that may affect product content or demand. For example, in some countries, importing certain raw materials or components may be difficult or prohibitively expensive, forcing a company to construct an end product with local substitutes that may alter the final result substantially. Legal requirements such as high taxes on heavy automobiles also could shift sales to smaller models, thus indirectly altering demand for tire sales and grades of gasoline.

Examination of cultural differences may pinpoint possible problem areas.

Cultural factors   Consumer buying behavior is complex. It is difficult to determine in advance whether new or different products will be accepted. Some U.S. food franchisors, such as McDonald's, have been highly successful in Japan by duplicating most of their U.S. products and means of distribution—a success attributed to the "enthusiastic assimilation" of Western ways by the Japanese. In contrast, in seemingly more similar Canada (Quebec), McDonald's had to provide cheese curds and hot gravy for french fries to create a dish called *poutine*.[23] However, Western cosmetic companies have been able to garner only small shares of the Japanese cosmetics market because cultural factors render some Western products unsuited to that market: Perfume is seldom used, suntans are considered ugly, and bath oil is impractical in home showers or communal baths.[24] In another case, Armstrong World Industries had heard so much about the so-called world car (one designed to minimize differences in features and components among countries), it reasoned there must be a market for a world gasket. Management found, however, that consumer, and therefore industrial, requirements differed widely. For example, U.S. automobile owners are not bothered by an occasional drop of oil on the garage floor, but Japanese owners will complain to the manufacturer.[25]

Personal incomes and infrastructures affect product demand.

Economic factors   If foreign consumers lack sufficient income, they may be able to buy insufficient quantities of the product the MNE sells domestically. The company therefore may have to design a cheaper model or perhaps sell a product that resembles an older model sold earlier in the home market. For example, NCR has designed crank-operated cash registers to sell in some LDCs. Where incomes are low, consumers may buy many personal items in very small quantities, such as one aspirin, one piece of chewing gum, or one cigarette, a practice that usually necessitates new types of packaging.

Even if a market segment has sufficient income to purchase the same product the company sells at home, the general level of a country's economy may require that products be altered. A country's infrastructure may determine the necessary structural composition and tolerances of products. Further, factory managers have to consider the low educational levels of machine operators when planning equipment purchases. Product simplification may be the result.

Alteration Costs

Cost savings due to uniformity may apply to any part of the marketing program; however, product standardization is where the greatest savings are possible. Some changes are cheap to effect yet have an important influence on demand. One such area is packaging, which is the most common alteration made by exporters.[26] For example, in Panama, Aunt Jemima Pancake Mix and Ritz Crackers are sold in cans rather than in boxes because of the high humidity—a low-cost change with a high potential payoff. Before making a decision, a company should always compare the cost of an alteration with the cost of lost sales if no alteration is made.

One strategy a company can use to compromise between uniformity and diversity is to standardize a great deal while altering some end characteristics. For example, Toyota puts its steering wheels on the left side for the U.S. market, and GM will start putting steering wheels on the right for the Japanese market in the late 1990s.[27] Also, Heinz has found that many nationalities do not like a sweet ketchup, as is preferred in the United States, so it adds spices, curry, or hot pepper, depending on the market.[28] Even when end products appear to be quite different, the standardization of many components is possible. Another strategy is to make product changes less frequently in small markets in order to spread the fixed costs associated with production over a larger amount of sales.

Extent and Mix of the Product Line

Most companies produce multiple products. It is doubtful that all of these products could generate sufficient sales in a given foreign market to justify the cost of penetrating the market. Even if they could, a company may offer only a portion of its product line, such as some products that are not sold at home, or vice versa. For example, GM produces and sells a much more limited variety of models and options in Mexico than it does in the United States. By doing this, GM reduces the amount of capital investment for production and spare parts and allows sales activity to concentrate on fewer products. A company also must decide whether any new products need to be added to the line for sale in certain countries.

In reaching product-line decisions, the company should consider the possible effects on sales and the relative cost of having one product as opposed to a family of products. Sometimes a company finds it must produce and sell some unpopular items if it is to sell the more popular ones, such as sherry glasses to match crystal wine and water glasses. Or a company may be forced into a few short production runs in order to gain the mass market on other products. A company that must set up some foreign production in order to sell in the foreign market may be able to produce locally those products in its line that have longer production runs and import the other products needed to help sell the local production.

If the foreign market is small in relation to the domestic market, selling costs per unit may be high because of the fixed costs associated with selling. In such a situation, the company can broaden the product line to be handled, either by grouping sales of several manufacturers or by developing new products for the local market that the same salesperson can handle.[29] For example, Coca-Cola has added bar mixes in South Africa, a lemonade in Australia, a mango drink in Pakistan, a tomato juice in Belgium, and some mixed juice-based drinks in Mexico and Indonesia.

Product-Life-Cycle Considerations

Product life cycles may differ by country in
• Time of introduction
• Shape of curve

There may be differences among countries in either the shape or length of a product's life cycle. Thus a company that faces declining sales for a product in one country may be able to find a foreign market that will have growing or at least sustained sales for the product. For example, cellular phone producers, such as Ericsson and Motorola, faced a slowing growth in demand in industrial countries during the late 1980s but found that sales in some developing countries were just entering a stage of rapid growth. *Playboy*'s domestic circulation leveled off, but the fall of Eastern European authoritarian regimes created growth opportunities there. Ajax found a much longer growth period for its cleanser in Europe than in the United States because it successfully achieved a product line extension in Europe by promoting additives.[31] Volkswagen relaunched the Beetle in the Brazilian market thirty-four years after its first introduction there and seven years after Brazilian production had stopped.[32] (Safety standards prevented a relaunching in most other markets.)

Pricing

When ranking the importance of marketing-program variables, companies generally place only product above price.[33] A price must be high enough to guarantee the flow of funds required to carry on other activities, such as R & D, production, and distribution. The proper price will not only assure short-term profits but also give the company the resources to build the other elements within its marketing mix that are necessary to achieve long-term competitive viability. Pricing is more complex internationally than domestically because of the following factors:

• Different degrees of governmental intervention
• Greater diversity of markets
• Price escalation for exports
• Changing relative values of currencies
• Differences in fixed versus variable pricing practices
• Strategies to counter international competitors

Governmental Intervention

Every country has laws that affect the prices of goods at the consumer level, but these laws may affect different products in different ways at different times. Restrictions

Governmental price controls may
- **Set minimum or maximum prices**
- **Prohibit certain competitive pricing practices**

may prevent companies from using the strategies they consider optimal in achieving their ends. A governmental price control may set either maximum or minimum price levels. Controls against lowering prices usually are intended to prevent companies from eliminating competitors in order to gain monopoly positions. An example of this type of control is Germany's Unfair Competition Law, which has been interpreted by the German courts to prohibit such items as coupons, boxtops, and giveaway articles unless these will remain a consistent policy of the company throughout the years. A company accustomed to relying on such devices as a means of increasing its sales at home must develop new methods in Germany. Many countries set maximum prices for many products. If costs rise, profit margins contract, sometimes resulting in an unwillingness of producers to continue selling. For example, P&G and some of its suppliers were hit hard by price controls in Venezuela. Although P&G was willing to wait out the situation while negotiating with governmental authorities, its phosphate suppliers could not afford to lower prices on the materials P&G bought for detergents. The company was forced to suspend operations.[34] Price controls also may cause companies to lower the quality of a product; in this case they may consider changing the brand name in order to reintroduce the higher-quality product later.

Another type of control that reduces discretionary pricing specifically targets imports. GATT's Antidumping Code permits countries to establish restrictions against any import that comes in at a price below that charged consumers in the exporting country. This provision makes it more difficult for companies to differentiate markets through pricing. A company might want to export at a lower price than that charged at home for several reasons. One might be to test sales in the foreign market. For example, a company may find it cannot export to a given country because tariffs or transportation costs make the price to foreign consumers prohibitively high. Yet its preliminary calculations show that by establishing foreign production, it may be able to substantially reduce the price to the foreign consumer. Before committing resources to produce overseas, the company may want to test the market by exporting so as to sell the product at the price that would be charged if it was produced locally. Nestlé tested the U.K. market in this way by exporting for a year from Canada to see if enough market would develop to justify completing a $55-million frozen-food plant to make Lean Cuisine products.[35] Shipping such dishes as spaghetti bolognese in refrigerated ships and paying customs duties made the costs of the exported products much higher than their U.K. selling prices; however, the cost of this test was small compared to the value of the information gained and the amount of Nestlé's eventual commitment. A company also may charge different prices in different countries because of competitive and demand factors. For example, it may feel that prices can be kept high in the domestic market by restricting supply to that market. Excess production then can be sold abroad at a lower price, as long as that price covers variable costs and makes some contribution to overhead.

Greater Diversity of Markets
Although there are numerous ways a company can segment the domestic market and charge different prices in each segment, country-to-country variations create

Consumers in some countries simply like certain products more and are willing to pay more for them.

even more natural segments. For example, few sea urchins or tuna eyeballs can be sold in the United States at any price, but they can be exported to Japan, where they are considered delicacies.[36] In some countries, a company may have many competitors and thus little discretion regarding its prices. In others, it may have a near monopoly due either to the stage in the product life cycle or to government-granted manufacturing rights not held by competitors. In near-monopoly situations, a company may exercise considerable pricing discretion, using any of the following:

- A skimming strategy—charging a high price for a new product by aiming first at price-inelastic consumers and progressively lowering the price
- A penetration strategy—introducing a product at a low price to induce a maximum number of consumers to try it
- A cost-plus strategy—pricing at a desired margin over cost

Country-of-origin stereotypes also limit pricing possibilities. For example, exporters in LDCs often must compete primarily on the basis of price because of negative perceptions about their products' quality.[37] But there are dangers in lowering prices in response to adverse stereotypes. For example, in comparisons of consumer perceptions with objective ratings of automobiles, U.S. consumers overrate German automobiles in relation to U.S.-made ones, and Japanese consumers overrate Japanese automobiles in relation to German ones. In effect, German producers may be able to charge a higher margin relative to their U.S. competitors in the United States than they can relative to their Japanese competitors in Japan. Yet any competitor that responds to adverse stereotypes by lowering prices to increase sales actually may reduce the product image even further.[38] This could occur, for example, if German automakers were to lower their prices in the Japanese market, where consumers often equate price with quality.

Cash versus credit buying affects demand.

The total cost of a product to the consumer will be more than the sales price if there are additional charges because of buying on credit. How consumers view these additional charges may affect total demand as well as the sales price they are willing to pay. The tax treatment of interest payments as well as attitudes toward debt affect whether consumers will pay in cash or by credit. For example, the Japanese have been much more reluctant than Americans to rely on consumer credit. Thus in Japan it is less possible than it is in the United States to use credit payments as a means of inducing the sale of goods.

Price Escalation in Exporting

Price generally goes up by more than transport and duty costs.

If standard markups are used within distribution channels, lengthening the channels or adding expenses somewhere within the system will further increase the price to the consumer. For example, assume the markup is 50 percent and the product costs $1.00 to produce. The price to the consumer would be $1.50. However, if production costs were to increase to $1.20, the 50-percent markup would make the price $1.80, not $1.70 as might be expected. In export sales, price escalation occurs for two reasons:

1. Channels of distribution are usually longer because of greater distances and because of the need to contract with organizations that know export procedures and/or how to sell in the foreign market.
2. Tariffs are an additional cost that may be passed on to consumers.

There are several implications of price escalation. Many seemingly exportable products turn out to be noncompetitive abroad. Further, to become competitive in exporting, a company may have to sell its product to intermediaries at a lower price in order to lessen the amount of escalation.

Currency Value and Price Changes

Pricing decisions must consider replacement costs.

For companies accustomed to operating with one relatively stable currency, pricing in highly volatile currencies can be extremely troublesome. Pricing decisions should be made to assure sufficient funds are received so that the company can replenish its inventory and still make a profit. Otherwise, it may be making a "paper profit" while liquidating itself; that is, what shows on paper as a profit may result from the company's failure to adjust for inflation while the merchandise is in stock. The company must consider not only inflation's effect on prices but also the possibility its income taxes will be based on the paper profits rather than on real profits. Table 17.1 illustrates a pricing plan to make a target profit (after taxes) of 30 percent on replacement cost. The company that does not use a similar plan may quickly lack sufficient funds to operate. The longer the collection period, the more important it is for the company to use a graduated pricing model. For example, Peruvian inflation in the late 1980s forced P&G to raise its detergent prices 20–30 percent every two weeks. P&G also eliminated its sixty-day free credit to retailers and began charging interest on fifteen- to thirty-day payments.[39]

Two other pricing problems occur because of inflationary conditions:

1. The receipt of funds in a foreign currency that, when converted, buy less of the company's own currency than had been expected
2. The frequent readjustment of prices necessary to compensate for continual cost increases

In the first case, the company sometimes (depending on competitive factors and governmental regulations) can specify in sales contracts an equivalency in some hard currency. For example, a U.S. manufacturer's sale of equipment to a company in Uruguay may specify that payment be made in dollars or in pesos at an equivalent price, in terms of dollars, at the time payment is made. In the second case, frequent price increases make it more difficult for the company to quote prices in letters or catalogues. Perpetual price rises may even hamper what would otherwise be a preferred distribution method. For example, price increases in vending machine sales are frequently difficult to effect because of the attendant need to change machines and to come up with coins or tokens that correspond to the desired percentage increase in price.

Table 17.1
Effect of Tax and Inflation on Pricing
The pricing structure for sales or collections at the end of the year is calculated as follows: Replacement cost is cost plus inflation until collection, or $1000 + 0.36(1000) = 1360$; income after taxes is profit goal times replacement cost, or $0.30(1360) = 408$. Income after taxes is 60 percent of taxable income; thus taxable income may be calculated as $408 \div 0.6$, or 680; tax is $0.4(680) = 272$; sales price is original cost (1000) plus taxable income (680); markup on replacement is sales price (1680) less replacement cost (1360), or 320.

Assume: Cost at beginning is 1000
36% inflation
40% tax rate
30% profit goal on replacement cost after taxes

If sold and collected at beginning of year		If sold and collected at end of year	
Cost	1000	Replacement cost	1360
Markup	500	Markup on replacement	320
Sales prices	1500	Sales price	1680
− Cost	1000	− Original cost	1000
Taxable income	500	Taxable income	680
Tax @ 40%	200	Tax @ 40%	272
Income after taxes	300	Income after taxes	408

Currency-value changes also affect pricing decisions for any product that has potential foreign competition. For example, when the U.S. dollar is strong, non–U.S.-made goods can be sold more cheaply in the U.S. market. In such a situation, to be competitive U.S. producers may have to accept a lower profit margin. When the dollar is weak, however, foreign producers may have to adjust their margins downward.

When companies sell similar goods in multiple countries, price differences among them must not exceed by much the cost of bringing the goods in from a lower-priced country, or spillover in buying will occur. Soft-drink manufacturers can easily vary their prices by a large percentage from country to country because the transportation costs render large-scale movements across borders impractical. However, with higher-priced items, consumers can feasibly buy abroad and import. For example, at one time importers in the United States and France paid yen to buy Japanese cameras; consequently, the imported price in yen was the same in both countries. But then the franc weakened relative to the dollar, so some U.S. dealers bought French inventories of the Olympus OM-10 for $152 rather than buying them from the official distributor for $224.95. The handling of goods through unofficial distributors is known as the **gray market,** and such handling can undermine the longer-term viability of the distributorship system or upset the balance of capacity utilization among plants. Thus camera manufacturers cut export prices to the United States to prevent such product movements from taking place. However, some companies take advantage of currency swings by switching exports from one location to another. For example, GAF does this with butane diol, a raw material used in plastics.[40]

Fixed versus Variable Pricing

There are country-to-country differences in
- Whether manufacturers set prices
- Whether prices are fixed or bargained in stores
- Where bargaining occurs
- How sale prices can be used

Export prices, particularly to foreign distributors, are often negotiated. Small companies, especially those from LDCs, frequently give price concessions too quickly, thereby limiting their ability to negotiate on a range of marketing factors that affect their costs:

- Discounts for quantity or repeat orders
- Deadlines that increase production or transportation costs
- Credit and payment terms
- Service
- Supply of promotional materials
- Training of sales personnel or customers[41]

Table 17.2 shows ways in which an exporter may deal more effectively in price negotiations.

The extent to which manufacturers can or must set prices at the retail level varies substantially by country. For instance, in Venezuela most consumer products must have prices printed on the label, whereas in Chile manufacturers are prohibited either from suggesting retail prices or putting prices on labels.[42] There also is substantial variation in whether consumers bargain in order to settle on an agreed price. For instance, bargaining takes place in about 60 percent of the stores in India and Kenya but in less than 5 percent of those in China and South Africa. Bargaining is much more prevalent in purchases from street vendors in India than in Singapore, whereas bargaining in high-priced specialty stores is more frequent in Singapore than in India.[43]

Countries also vary in companies' use of sale prices because of legal restrictions and custom. For example, German stores discount prices through sales for only a few days per year, and they all do so at the same time. Kmart found when entering the Czech Republic that customers were unaccustomed to and leery of price reductions, especially the company's "blue light" specials. This resulted from that country's history of communist control, during which time unsold merchandise would be stored and then brought back out in about five years.[44]

Countering International Competitors

As long as a company faces local competitors that lack resources to expand internationally, pricing decisions in one locale will have little potential impact elsewhere. However, when it faces the same potential competitors in more than one location, pricing decisions must be examined in terms of global competitive

Table 17.2
Preparations for Price Discussions
Note that the suggested approach for exporters is to delay a pricing commitment while discussing a whole package of other commitments.

Importer's reaction to price offer	Exporter's possible response
1. The initial price quoted is too high; a substantial drop is required.	Ask the buyer what is meant by too high; ask on what basis the drop is called for; stress product quality and benefits before discussing price.
2. Better offers have been received from other exporters.	Ask for more details on such offers; find out how serious such offers are; convince the buyer that the exporter has a better offer.
3. A counteroffer is required; a price discount is expected.	Avoid making a better offer without asking for something in return, but without jeopardizing loss of interest; when asking for something in return, make a specific suggestion, such as "If I give you a 5% price discount, would you arrange for surface transport including storage costs?"
4. The price of $___ is my last offer (the importer specifies a lower price).	Avoid accepting such an offer immediately; find out the quantities involved; determine if there will be repeat orders; ascertain who will pay for storage, publicity, after-sales service, and so on.
5. The product is acceptable, but the price is too high.	Agree to discuss details of the costing; promote product benefits, reliability as a regular supplier, timely delivery, unique designs, and so on.
6. The initial price quoted is acceptable.	Find out why the importer is so interested in the offer; recalculate the costing; check competition; contact other potential buyers to get more details on market conditions; review the pricing strategy; accept a trial order only.

Source: Claude Cellich, "Negotiating Strategies: The Question of Price," *International Trade Forum*, April–June 1991, p. 12.

strategy. For example, P&G was concerned about the possible U.S. entry of the large Japanese consumer-products company, Kao. By selling detergent at a low price in the Japanese market, P&G forced Kao to freeze its prices below P&G's for twelve years and delayed its entry into the United States.[45] A company also may face the same industrial consumer in more than one market; therefore the paint price to Toyota in Mexico may well affect the paint company's ability to sell to Toyota in other countries.

Promotion

Promotion is the process of presenting messages intended to help sell a product or service. The types and direction of messages and the method of presentation may be extremely diverse, depending on the company, product, and/or country of operation.

The Push-Pull Mix

Push is more likely when
• Self-service is not predominant
• Product price is a high portion of income
• Advertising is restricted

Promotion may be categorized as push, which involves direct selling techniques, or pull, which relies on mass media. An example of push is door-to-door selling of encyclopedias; an example of pull is magazine advertisements for a brand of cigarettes. Most companies use combinations of both strategies. For each product in each country, a company must determine its total promotional budget as well as the mix of the budget between push and pull.

Several factors necessitate differences in the relative mix of push and pull among countries:

• Type of distribution system
• Cost and availability of media to reach target markets
• Consumer attitudes toward sources of information
• Price of the product relative to incomes

Generally, the more tightly controlled the distribution system, the more likely a company is to emphasize a push strategy because a greater effort is required to get distributors to handle a product. This is true, for example, in Belgium, where distributors are small and highly fragmented, forcing companies to concentrate on making their goods available.[46] Also affecting promotion is the amount of contact between salespeople and consumers. In a self-service situation, in which there are no salespersons to whom customers can turn for opinions on products, it is more important for the company to advertise through mass media or at the point of purchase.

Because of diverse national environments, promotional problems are extremely varied. For example, in India the large number of languages, low literacy rate, and lack of reliable media information make it very difficult and expensive to reach the mass market. In many countries, government regulations pose an even greater barrier. For example, Scandinavian television has long refused to accept commercials. A less obvious effect of government on the promotional mix is the direct or indirect tax many countries place on advertising.

France and the United States present an interesting contrast of cultural factors that affect the push-pull mix.[47] U.S. homemakers spend more time watching television and reading magazines, and they rely more on friends and advertising before purchasing a new product. In contrast, French homemakers spend more time shopping, examining items on shelves, and listening to the opinions of retailers. Therefore it has been easier to presell U.S. homemakers, whereas in France discounts to distributors and point-of-purchase displays have been more effective.

Finally, the amount of consumer involvement in making a purchase decision varies by country because of income levels. When a product's price relative to consumers' income is high, the consumer usually will want more time and information before making a decision. Information is best conveyed in a personal selling situation where two-way communication is fostered. In LDCs, more products usually have to be pushed because incomes are low in relation to price.

Standardization of Advertising Programs

The economies from using the same advertising programs as much as possible, such as on a global basis or among a group of countries with shared consumer attributes, are not as great as those from product standardization. Nevertheless, they can be significant. For example, McCann-Erickson claims to have saved $90 million in production costs for the advertising program it developed for Coca-Cola by carrying over certain elements of the program on a global basis over a twenty-year period. Some savings also occur in hidden costs for executive time spent in supervising advertising campaigns.[48]

In addition to reducing costs, standardization may be implemented to improve the quality of advertising at the local level (since local agencies may lack expertise), to prevent internationally mobile consumers from being confused by different images, and to speed the entry of products into different countries. For example, Coca-Cola's ads for the 1992 Winter Olympics showed people singing in twelve different languages. This was a truly standardized campaign that reached 3.8 billion viewers in 131 countries.[49] But standardized advertising usually means a program that is recognizable from market to market rather than one that is identical in each. For example, Coca-Cola's print advertisements for the United States and France used the same concept of "refreshment" and showed young people who had been playing sports. In the United States, the slogan was "Coke is it!" and the ad showed a baseball player in action. In France, the slogan was "*Un Coca-Cola pour un sourire*" ("A Coca-Cola for a smile") and the ad showed soccer players. Some of the problems that hinder complete standardization of advertising relate to translation, legality, and message needs.

Translation   When media reach audiences in multiple countries, such as MTV programs aired throughout most of Europe, ads in those media cannot be translated. However, when a company is going to sell in a country with a different language, translation is usually necessary. For example, to market its motorcycles abroad, Harley-Davidson published its magazines in foreign languages and staged beer-and-band rallies.[50] The most visible problem in translation is dubbing, because words on an added sound track never quite correspond to lip movements. Dubbing problems can be avoided by using actors who do not speak, along with a voice and/or print overlay in the appropriate language. Levi Strauss has done this for its jeans ads.[51]

On the surface, translating a message would seem to be easy; however, some messages, particularly those involving a play on words, simply don't translate. One example is a Kellogg's U.S. ad: "What are you eating?" "Nut n' Honey." The number of ludicrous but costly mistakes companies have made attest to translation difficulties. Sometimes what is an acceptable word or direct translation in one place is obscene, misleading, or meaningless in another. For example, one company described itself as an "old friend" of China; however, it used the character for "old" that meant former instead of long-term.[52] Even within the same language, words can have different meanings in different countries. For example, United Airlines showed Paul Hogan, star of the *Crocodile Dundee* films, in the Australian outback on the cover of its inflight magazine. The caption was "Paul Hogan Camps It Up." In Australian slang, it meant "flaunts his homosexuality."[53]

Legality   What is legal in one place may not be elsewhere. The differences result mainly from varying national views on consumer protection, competitive protection, promotion of civil rights, standards of morality, and nationalism.[54] A few examples illustrate the vast differences that exist. In terms of consumer protection, policies differ on the amount of deception permitted, what can be advertised to children, whether warnings must be given of possible harmful effects, and the extent to which ingredients must be listed. The United Kingdom and the United States allow direct comparisons with competitive brands (for example, Pepsi versus Coca-Cola), whereas the Philippines prohibits them. Only a few countries regulate sexism in advertising. Advertising of some products (for example, contraceptives and feminine-hygiene products) has been restricted in some locales because of rationales based on morality and good taste. Elsewhere, restrictions have been placed on ads that might prompt children to misbehave or people to break laws (for example, advertising automobile speeds that exceed the speed limit) and those that show barely clad women. Finally, nationalism in several countries has caused them to restrict the use of foreign words, models, or themes in advertisements. A number of countries restrict the entry of foreign-produced films, tapes, mats, and other advertising materials through import duties, quotas, or embargos. In addition, union contracts sometimes disallow the use of foreign actors or crews in ads, thus forcing local production.[55]

Message needs   Because of competitive differences among countries, an advertising theme may not be appropriate everywhere. Recall from the discussions of gap analysis and product life cycles how conditions vary. For example, American Express's U.S. campaign "Do You Know Me?" aimed at gaining market share from other credit cards. However, in Europe the company needed to build credit-card usage.[56] Cultural differences are another factor. The theme for selling Pampers in the United States is convenience; however, this theme could not be used in Thailand because women there felt that using disposable diapers made them bad mothers who put their own comfort ahead of that of their babies. Instead, a theme of night-time use to keep babies drier was used.[57]

Ads also differ among countries because of consumers' expectations. For example, Japanese ads tend to be more informative than those in the United States. Japanese ads on television also wait longer to identify brands and mention them fewer times than do U.S. TV ads.[58]

Branding

MNEs must make four major branding decisions:

1. Brand versus no brand
2. Manufacturer's brand versus private brand
3. One brand versus multiple brands
4. Worldwide brand versus local brands[59]

Only the last of these is substantially affected by the international environment.

Some companies, such as Coca-Cola, have opted to use the same brand and logo globally. Doing this gives the product instant recognition and may save some promotional costs. Some other companies, for example, Nestlé, have associated many of their products under the same family of brands, such as the Nestea and Nescafé brands, in order to share in the good will that they have developed. Yet, there are a number of problems in trying to use uniform brands internationally.

Language Factors

One problem is that names may carry a different association in another language. For example, GM thought its Nova model could easily be called the same in Latin America, since the name means "star" in Spanish. However, people started pronouncing it "*no va,*" which is Spanish for "it does not go." Coca-Cola tries to use global branding wherever possible but discovered that the word "diet" in Diet Coke had a connotation of illness in Germany and Italy; consequently, the brand is called Coca-Cola Light outside the United States. Mars hesitated for years to change the name of its Marathon candy bar in Britain to Snickers in order to create an internationally known brand because of the closeness in pronunciation to "knickers," a British term for women's underwear.[60] And Mars has encountered problems in standardizing names for other candy bars because of longstanding product alterations. For example, the company has both Mars and Milky Way bars in both the United States and Europe. The Mars bar in Europe is the same as a Milky Way in the United States. The U.S. Mars bar is unlike any candy bar the company has in Europe, and the Milky Way in Europe is unlike any the company has in the United States.[61]

Pronunciation presents other problems, because either a foreign language or its alphabet may lack some of the sounds of a brand name or the pronunciation of the name may have a different meaning from the original. For example, McDonald's uses Donald McDonald in Japan because the Japanese have difficulty pronouncing the letter R. Marcel Bich dropped the H from his name when branding Bic pens because of the fear of mispronunciation in English. Perrier's popular French soft drink, Pschitt, has an unappetizing meaning when pronounced in English.

Criticisms have been leveled at MNEs for introducing and promoting products that have adverse effects on LDCs. So-called superfluous products and luxury goods are criticized for shifting spending away from necessities and contributing to the enhancement of elitist class distinctions.[62] For example, critics have questioned making soft drinks available to consumers who lack funds for pharmaceuticals. This criticism has been answered largely by arguments that consumers should make their own choices and by showing the positive side effects of seemingly unnecessary products. For example, soft-drink companies have argued that they are responsible for introducing the sanitary bottling operations essential for other industries, such as pharmaceuticals. Yet critics question if this is sufficient justification.

ETHICAL DILEMMAS

There are also questions as to whether companies have a similar ethical responsibility in industrial countries, in which consumers are more likely to have the educational level necessary to make informed choices. For example, as the Japanese economy has become more open, consumption of food additives, sugar, beef, and dairy products in Japan has grown to the point that diet-related heart disease, strokes, protein anemia, diabetes, and cancer have increased markedly.

MNEs also have been criticized for advertising products to people who are not equipped to understand those products' implications or their own needs. The most famous case involved sales of infant formula in LDCs, where infant mortality increased because the rate of bottle feeding increased over that of breast feeding. Because of low incomes and poor education, mothers frequently overdiluted formula so that it was no longer nutritious and gave it to their babies in unhygienic conditions. Critics argued that increased bottle feeding resulted from heavy promotion of formula. Companies countered by claiming increased bottle feeding resulted from factors other than promotion of formula—specifically, the rise in the number of working mothers and a resultant general trend toward fewer products and services being made in the home. The promotion, they argued, persuaded people to give up their "home brews" in favor of the most nutritious breast milk substitute available. Regardless, the World Health Organization overwhelmingly passed a voluntary code for restricting formula promotion in developing countries. The company hardest hit by criticism was Nestlé because it had the largest market share in LDCs and because organizing a boycott against it was easy because of its name-identified products. In 1984, the company agreed to cease advertising that could discourage breast feeding, limit free formula supplies at hospitals, and ban personal gifts to health officials.[63] Despite these events, governments have been slow and reluctant to prohibit infant formula promotion. For example, in Taiwan fewer than 10 percent of babies are breast-fed, but its government did not restrict formula promotion until 1993 and then only on TV advertisements.[64] In the absence of regulations, how far companies should go to protect consumers is unclear.

Unilever has successfully translated the brand name for its fabric softener, while leaving its brand symbol, a baby bear, intact on the packaging. The U.S. name "Snuggle" is "Kuschelweich" in Germany, "Cajoline" in France, "Coccolino" in Italy, and "Mimosin" in Spain. But "Snuggle" did not quite convey the same meaning in English-speaking Australia, where Unilever uses "Huggy."[65]

Acquisitions

Much international expansion takes place through acquisition of companies in foreign countries that already have branded products. For example, when Nestlé acquired Carnation, the Carnation name was so well-known in the United States that it was kept as an addition to the canned-milk brands Nestlé promotes elsewhere. Bic Pens acquired Waterman Pens as its entry into the U.S. market in order to benefit from the Waterman name; however, when the name turned out to have less value than anticipated, the Bic name was adopted in the United States as well. When Whirlpool, virtually unknown by consumers in Europe, acquired the appliance business of Philips, the brand name Philips-Whirlpool was used. In 1998, the Philips name will be dropped; by then Whirlpool expects to be well known.[66] Sunbeam has continued to use acquired brand names in Italy (Rowenta, Oster, Cadillac, Aircap, and Stewart) because they are well known and enjoy good will; however, Sunbeam has found that stretching the promotional budget over so many brands means that promotions are not as effective as they might be.[67]

Nationality Images

Images of products are affected by where they are made.

Companies should consider whether to create a local or a foreign image for their products. The products of some countries, particularly developed countries, tend to have a higher-quality image than do those from other countries. But images can change. Consider that for many years various Korean companies sold abroad under private labels or under contract with well-known companies. Some of these Korean companies, such as Samsung, now emphasize their own trade names and the quality of Korean products.[68]

There also are image differences concerning specific products from specific countries. For example, the French company BSN-Gervais Dannone brews Kroenenbourg, the largest-selling bottled beer in Europe, and the company's director general frankly admits that the Kroenenbourg trademark "sounds German."[69] Also, Czechs associate locally made products with poor quality, and so P&G has added German words to the labels of detergents it makes in the Czech Republic.[70]

Generic and Near-Generic Names

If a brand name is used for a class of product, the company may lose the trademark.

Companies want their product names to become household words but not so much so that trademarked brand names can be used by competitors to describe similar products. In the United States, the names Xerox and Kleenex are nearly synonymous with copiers and paper tissues but have remained proprietary brands. Some other names, such as cellophane, linoleum, and cornish hens, have become generic, or available for anyone to use.

In this context, companies sometime face substantial differences among countries that may either stimulate or frustrate their sales. For example, Roquefort cheese and champagne are proprietary names in France but generic in the United States, a situation that impairs French export sales of those products. Also, international sales of U.S., Canadian, Irish, and Japanese whiskeys are hindered by the fact that in much of the world, whisky is a synonym for Scotch whisky.

Distribution

Companies may have to devise ways to help distributors so that they give attention to the companies' products.

A company may accurately assess market potential, design products or services for that market, and promote to probable consumers; however, it will have little likelihood of reaching its sales potential if the goods or services are not conveniently available to customers. One aspect of this problem is getting goods to where people want to buy them. For example, does a man prefer to buy hair dressing in a grocery store, barber shop, drugstore, or some other type of outlet?

Distribution is the course—physical path or legal title—that goods take between production and consumption. In international marketing, a company must decide on the method of distribution among countries as well as the method within the country where final sale occurs. We already have discussed many considerations for distribution, including the distribution channels to move goods among countries, how the title to goods gets transferred, and the operating forms for foreign-market penetration. This section does not review these aspects of distribution; it discusses distributional differences and conditions within foreign countries that an international marketer should understand.

Difficulty of Standardization

Distribution reflects different country environments:
- **It may vary substantially among countries.**
- **It is difficult to change.**

Different systems Within the marketing mix, distribution is one of the most difficult functions to standardize internationally, for several reasons. Each country has its own distribution system. This usually is difficult to change because it has evolved over time and reflects the country's cultural, economic, and legal environments. Some of the factors that influence how goods will be distributed in a given country are the attitudes toward owning one's own store, the cost of paying retail workers, labor legislation differentially affecting chain stores and individually owned stores, legislation restricting the operating hours and size of stores, the trust that owners have in their employees, the efficacy of the postal system, and the financial ability to carry large inventories. For example, Hong Kong supermarkets, compared to those in the United States, carry a higher proportion of fresh goods, are smaller, sell smaller quantities per customer, and are located more closely to each other (see Table 17.3).

A few other examples should illustrate how distribution norms differ. Finland has few stores per capita because general-line retailers predominate there, whereas Italian distribution is characterized by a very fragmented retail and wholesale struc-

Table 17.3
Sociocultural Elements of Supermarket Technology in the United States and Hong Kong
Different conditions (columns 2 and 3) with respect to sociocultural elements (column 1) have caused supermarkets in Hong Kong to sell a high proportion of fresh foods, to handle customers more frequently, to sell in low quantities, and to be located closer to competitors.

Sociocultural elements	United States	Hong Kong
Dietary habits	Like meats Used to frozen foods	Like seafood and meats Used to fresh foods
Shopping patterns	Objective to save time Infrequent	Objective to preserve freshness of food More frequent
Living conditions	Better conditions Spacious	Conditions not as good Crowded
Size of refrigerator	Bigger	Smaller
Availability of car	More available	Less available
Population density	Less dense	Very dense
Urbanization	Low	High

Source: From "Development of Supermarket Technology: The Incomplete Transfer Phenomenon" by Suk-ching Ho and Ho-fuk Lau, *International Marketing Review,* Spring 1988, p. 27. Reprinted with permission.

ture. In the Netherlands, buyers' cooperatives deal directly with manufacturers; in Japan, there are cash-and-carry wholesalers for retailers that do not need financing or delivery. In Germany, mail-order sales are very important; however, in Portugal, they aren't.

How do these differences affect companies' marketing activities? One soft-drink company, for example, has targeted most of its European sales through grocery stores; however, the method for getting its soft drinks to those stores varies widely. In the United Kingdom, one national distributor has been able to gain sufficient coverage and shelf space so that the soft-drink company can concentrate on other aspects of its marketing mix. In France, a single distributor has been able to get good coverage in the larger supermarkets but not in the smaller ones; consequently, the soft-drink company has been exploring how to get secondary distribution without upsetting its relationship with the primary distributor. In Norway, regional distributors predominate; thus the soft-drink company has been challenged to get them to cooperate sufficiently that national promotion campaigns will be effective. In Belgium, the company could find no acceptable distributor, so it has had to assume that function itself.[71]

Most distributors are national rather than international.

Domestic rather than international distributors Most large advertising and public-relations firms have become international. However, even though wholesalers and retailers have expanded considerably overseas since the late 1980s, few have extensive foreign operations. Consequently, companies that are marketing abroad must rely mainly on the services of locally controlled distributors. It is extremely difficult to get these distributors to alter their accustomed practices to adhere to one the producer wants as a global standard, especially if initial sales expectations are not very high.

Choosing Distributors and Channels

Distribution may be handled internally
- **When volume is high**
- **When there is a need to deal directly with the customer due to the nature of the product**
- **When the customer is global**
- **To gain a competitive advantage**

Internal handling When sales volume is low, it usually is more economical for a company to handle distribution by contracting with an external distributor. By doing so, however, it may lose a certain amount of control. Management should reassess periodically whether sales have grown to the point that they can be effectively handled internally.

Circumstances conducive to the internal handling of distribution include not only high sales volume but also the following:

- When the product has the characteristic of high price, high technology, *or* need for complex after-sales servicing (such as aircraft), the producer probably will have to deal directly with the buyer. The producer may simultaneously use a distributor within the foreign country that will serve to identify sales leads.
- When the company deals with global customers, especially in business-to-business sales, such as an auto-parts manufacturer that sells original equipment to the same automakers in multiple countries, such sales may go directly from the producer to the global customer.
- When the company views its main competitive advantage to be its distribution methods, such as some food franchisors, it eventually may franchise abroad but maintain its own distribution outlet to serve as a "flagship." Amway is an example of a company that has successfully transferred its house-to-house distribution methods from the U.S. to the Japanese market under its own control. Also, Dell Computer has successfully handled its own mail-order sales in Europe.[72]

Some evaluative criteria for distributors include their
- **Financial capability**
- **Connections with customers**
- **Fit with a company's product**
- **Other resources**

Distributor qualifications A company usually can choose from a number of potential distributors. Common criteria for selecting a distributor include

- Its financial strength
- Its good connections
- Extent of its other business commitments
- Current status of its personnel, facilities, and equipment

The distributor's financial strength is important because of the potential long-term relationship between company and distributor and because of the assurance that money will be available for such things as maintaining sufficient inventory. Good connections are particularly important if sales must be directed to certain types of buyers, such as governmental procurement agencies. The amount of other business commitments can indicate whether the distributor has time for the company's product and whether it currently handles competitive or complementary products. Finally, the current status of the distributor's personnel, facilities, and equipment indicates not only its ability to deal with the product but also how quickly start-up can occur.

Spare parts and repair   Consumers are reluctant to buy products that may require spare parts and service in the future unless they feel assured these will be readily available in good quality and at reasonable prices. The more complex and expensive the product, the more important after-sales servicing is. In the 1950s, for example, some European automakers entered the U.S. market without sufficient consideration of this factor. After they made some initial sales, customer "horror stories" followed, such as having to wait weeks or months for parts and finding no trained mechanics. Sales dried up as a result. Volkswagen entered the market later and successfully invested heavily in parts depots and training, as well as promotion. When after-sales servicing is important, companies may need to invest in service centers for groups of distributors that serve as intermediaries between producers and consumers. Earnings from sales of parts and after-sales service sometimes may match that of the original product.

Gaining distribution   Companies must evaluate potential distributors, but distributors must choose which companies and products to represent and emphasize. Both wholesalers and retailers have limited storage facilities, display space, money to pay for inventories, and transportation and personnel to move and sell merchandise; therefore they try to carry only those products that have the greatest profit potential. In many cases, distributors are tied into exclusive arrangements with manufacturers that prevent new competitive entries. For example, there are about 25,000 Japanese outlets that sell only Shiseido's cosmetics.[73] A company that is new to a country and wants to introduce products that some competitors are already selling may find it difficult to convince distributors to handle its brands. Even established companies sometimes may find it hard to gain distribution for their new products, although they have the dual advantage of being known and of being able to use existing profitable lines as "bait" for the new merchandise.

A company wanting to use existing distribution channels may need to analyze competitive conditions carefully in order to offer effective incentives for those distributors to handle the product. It may need to identify problems distributors have in order to gain their loyalty by offering assistance. For example, Coca-Cola has held seminars for mom-and-pop stores abroad on how to operate more effi-

Spare parts and service are important for sales.

Distributors choose what they will handle. Companies
- *May need to give incentives*
- *May use successful products as bait for new ones*
- *Must convince distributors that product and company are viable*

ciently and to compete with larger distributors.[74] Companies alternatively may turn to several other possibilities, including offering higher margins, after-sales servicing, and promotional support, any of which may be offered on either a permanent or introductory basis. The type of incentive should also depend on the comparative costs within each market. In the final analysis, however, incentives will be of little help unless the distributors believe a company's products are viable. The company therefore must sell the distributors on its products as well as itself as a reliable company.

Distribution Segmentation

A company may enter a market gradually by limiting geographic coverage and emphasizing only certain types of intermediaries.

Many products and markets lend themselves to gradual development or to different distributional strategies in different areas. In many cases, geographic barriers divide countries into very distinct markets; for example, Colombia is divided by mountain ranges and Australia by a desert. In other countries, such as Zimbabwe and Zaire, very little wealth or few potential sales may lie outside the large metropolitan areas. In still others, advertising and distribution may be handled effectively on a regional basis. For example, when Kikkoman first began selling soy sauce in the United States, the company could not find intermediaries willing and able to get the sauce onto the shelves of supermarket chains nationally, and Kikkoman did not have the resources to bypass such intermediaries. However, it was able to target its first sales to the San Francisco area, where the product was already well known to much of the large Japanese-American population. Through a local food broker, Kikkoman gained access to distribution in neighborhoods with a large Asian population. By advertising the product to the general public on television and by showing sales results from the initial distribution, the company was able to gain distribution in other neighborhoods. Two years later, Kikkoman moved into Los Angeles and continued to expand gradually over the next seventeen years, using food brokers in all cases, until it achieved national distribution and over 50 percent of the soy-sauce market. It is not uncommon for a company to use one type of intermediary in one area and another elsewhere.

Hidden Costs

When companies consider launching products in foreign markets, they must consider what final consumer prices will be in order to estimate sales potential. Because of different national distribution systems, the cost of getting products to consumers varies widely from one country to another. Three factors that often contribute to cost differences in distribution are the number of levels in the distribution system, retail inefficiencies, and inventory stock-outs.

Many countries have multitiered wholesalers that sell to each other before the product reaches the retail level. For example, national wholesalers sell to regional ones, who sell to local ones, and so on. This sometimes occurs because wholesalers are too small to cover more than a small geographic area. Japan is an example of such a market: There are about the same number of wholesalers in Japan as in the

United States, despite the much smaller geographic area and population. Because each intermediary adds a markup, product prices are driven up.[75]

In some countries, particularly LDCs, low labor costs and a basic distrust by owners of all but family members result in retail practices that raise consumer prices. A typical situation involves counter service rather than self-service. In the former case, a customer waits to be served and shown merchandise. If the customer decides to purchase what is shown, the customer is given an invoice to take to a cashier's line in order to pay. Once the invoice is stamped as paid, the customer must go to another line to pick up the merchandise after presenting the stamped invoice. This procedure is followed for purchases as small as a pencil. The additional personnel add to retailing costs, and the added time people must be in the store means fewer people can be served in the given space. In contrast, most retailers in some (mainly industrialized) countries have equipment that improves the efficiency of handling customers and reports, such as electronic scanners, cash registers linked to inventory control records, and machines connecting purchases to credit card companies.

Where retailers are typically small, as is true of grocers in Spain, there is little space to store inventory. Wholesalers must incur the cost of making small deliveries to many more establishments and sometimes may have to visit each retailer more frequently because of stock outages.

COUNTERVAILING

FORCES

One trend that is most likely to have an impact on the future of international marketing is the continued improvement in transportation and communications, which influences global awareness of products and life-styles. Thus a continued trend toward standardized marketing programs on a worldwide basis is likely. This does not mean, however, that MNEs will be able to narrow their product lines or promotional activities. Instead, they may have to differentiate further in order to satisfy people's needs according to demographic, sociographic, and psychographic variables that cut across national boundaries. For example, companies may well find themselves defining a market segment as finely as "females, age 26 to 30, working, unmarried, three to four years of college, high achievement motivation, church members, with low dogmatic personalities." As discretionary income increases, not only do exotic products become so commonplace that they lose their attractiveness but also more products and services compete with each other (for example, cars, travel, jewelry, and furniture compete for the same discretionary spending). Thus increased segmentation probably will be necessary.

Greater standardization also does not imply that companies can disregard national differences. As companies from industrial countries have increasingly embraced the concept of global standardization, there is some evidence that they are losing market niches to companies from NICs that are more willing to make adaptations.

LOOKING TO THE FUTURE

Most projections are that disparities between the "haves" and "have-nots" will grow rather than diminish in the foreseeable future, both within and among countries. This probably will mean a simultaneous growth in affluent and poor market segments. Globally, the affluent sector will have the means of purchasing more goods and services and will not be likely to forgo purchases because of antimaterialistic sentiments. Because of rising educational levels within this sector, more of its members will be knowledgeable about slight differences in the end utility of products. It will be less possible to segment along national lines to reach these consumers.

The rise in affluence and leisure of the "haves" probably will result in changes in where they spend their money. As these consumers take at least a part of productivity increases in the form of leisure, they will spend a proportionately larger amount of their incomes on entertainment, sports clothes and equipment, organizational memberships, and travel. In addition, they probably will spend more on services than on products.

At the other extreme will be growing numbers of poor people who will have little disposable income to spend on nonnecessities. MNEs will face increasing pressures to develop standardized products to fit the needs of these people and to produce goods by labor-intensive methods so as to employ more of them. Accomplishing this will create operational problems because of conflicting competitive pressures to differentiate products and to cut costs through capital-intensive methods.

What products and services are likely to enjoy the major growth markets? It is generally agreed that data generation and storage will continue to be a major growth area during the next few decades. It also is probable that among the market-growth leaders will be companies making breakthroughs in process technologies to improve productivity, such as lasers, optics, and robotics, and those making breakthroughs in energy conservation, such as solar photovoltaics, fuel cells, and coal conversion.

Summary

- Although the principles for selling abroad are the same as those for selling domestically, the international businessperson must deal with a less familiar environment, which may change rapidly.

- Tools for broadly assessing foreign demand for products include analysis of consumption patterns, estimates based on what has happened in other countries, studies of historical trends, income elasticity, regression, and gap analysis. Some problems with these tools include changes in taste and technology that render observations from the past and observations from other countries invalid for specific countries.

- A standardized approach to marketing means maximum uniformity in products and programs among the countries in which sales occur. Although this ap-

- The most important trend was growing diet consciousness. Miller Brewing had had phenomenal success with its Lite beer. Because cyclamates had been banned in soft drinks, producers of low-calorie sodas had turned to saccharin, which many people found distasteful. Also, there was no popular low-calorie drink that was considered chic. The use of the adjective "diet" simply announced that the drinker had weight problems. If people could be persuaded that Perrier tasted good, it could become a preferred low-calorie alternative.

- A second trend Nevins observed was a movement toward natural foods for health reasons. Even tap water and the 75 percent of bottled water processed from tap water had become suspect because in the process of purification, suspected cancer-causing chlorine derivatives were added. Further, certain viruses, sodium, and heavy metals were still found in most purified water and soda water. Perrier came from natural springs and contained high levels of calcium, very little sodium, and no additives. It could be promoted as a natural drink with healthy properties, even though it was not completely natural because some of the bubbles were lost when the water was removed from the springs and replaced during the bottling process.

- There was a growing U.S. preference for imports, apparent not only in the rising ratio of imports to gross national expenditures but also in the acceptance of "foreignness." In terms of food, so-called gourmet restaurants, cookbooks, dinner clubs, ingredients, and wines were becoming commonplace, and French items were practically synonymous with the word "gourmet." Perrier might be able to capitalize successfully on these attitudes.

The U.S. marketing program began in 1977. The company first had to decide in which part of the market to position itself. The three trends just discussed clearly would lead to different pricing, promotional, and distributional strategies. In seeking the diet-conscious market segment, for example, Source Perrier would come face-to-face with Coca-Cola and Pepsi-Cola, which between them controlled 45 percent of the soft-drink market. These companies, along with many others, fought vigorously in the market by keeping prices fairly low, advertising heavily, and clamoring for shelf space in supermarket soft-drink sections. The difficulty of competing in this segment is evident from the experience of Schweppes, which despite establishing U.S. bottling facilities and engaging in heavy marketing outlays failed to get even 1 percent of the market. Competing in this mass-market segment also might cause Perrier to lose the snob appeal it held for high-income buyers.

Entering the natural or health-food segment would pit Perrier against other bottled waters and various tonics that contained healthful additives. This market in 1976 was only $189 million. Of this, 93 percent was from purified domestic still water, which was sold largely in five-gallon containers at low prices through home or commercial delivery. Less than 20 percent of bottled water was sold in retail stores, and there was little brand identification. To expand retail sales probably would mean concentrating on gaining shelf space in the health-food sections of stores. Since bottled-water sales were determined to be much more concentrated geographically (about 50 percent in California) than were soft-drink sales, it would be far easier for Source Perrier to target its promotion and distribution for this segment.

Although Source Perrier was already selling to the gourmet market, usage and distribution gaps undoubtedly existed in this market. The total sales of mineral water in 1976 were only $15 million. Primary demand might be increased and Perrier might be made more readily available through increased distribution to specialty stores and new distribution to the growing gourmet sections of supermarkets.

Source Perrier decided to stress the soft-drink market segment. However, price was a problem. Through massive distribution, the retail price could be cut about 30 percent from what it was when the company emphasized the gourmet segment of the market; however, the price was still about 50 percent higher than the average soft-drink price, partly due to the cost of transporting water across the Atlantic. Further, the price included a higher retail gross margin—27.6 percent compared to 22.6 percent on soft drinks—which was necessary in order to induce supermarkets to handle the product. The company kept its price at "rock bottom" not only to become more price competitive with domestic soft drinks but also to dissuade other European companies from exporting to the United States. To get people to pay what was still a high price, the company had to segment the soft-drink market differently than anyone had done so far—by aiming at an adult population and using the higher price to gain snob appeal.

The company felt distribution was the key to success and so hired a sales force of forty people who formerly worked with soft-drink companies. It initially targeted New York, San Francisco, and Los Angeles because they had consumers with the largest penchant for imported food items. The company made a film designed to convey to distributors and supermarket chains that Perrier had long-term viability. The film showed that the springs had been popular as far back as 218 B.C., when Hannibal partook of the waters, and that Source Perrier dated back to 1903, supplied 400 million bottles a year, and outsold the leading cola in Europe by two to one. Source Perrier sought out the most aggressive distributors, including soft-drink bottlers, alcoholic-beverage distributors, and food brokers in different areas. For the company's success, it was essential that distributors be able to get supermarket space in the soft-drink sections, replenish stocks frequently, and set up point-of-purchase displays. One of the first distributors, Joyce Beverage Management, bought fifty-five trucks and hired a hundred additional people to handle the Source Perrier account. During the introductory period, arrangements were made for secondary display stacks and in-store tastings. The company also gave cents-off coupons with purchases. Within a year, Source Perrier had moved from three into twenty major market areas; this latter figure doubled in the second year.

Source Perrier developed 11-ounce and 6.5-ounce bottles, the latter sold in multipacks. It also developed a modern logo on the bottles, which was later replaced by the original label design to be more in line with the old-world image the company wanted to project. With initial distribution assured, it was necessary to sell the bottles that were on the shelves. To do so necessitated advertising messages different from those the company used in Europe. In Europe, the company could make therapeutic claims; however, U.S. law strictly forbade this. In U.S. test marketing, Source Perrier tried such themes as "Formerly heavy drinkers such as Richard Burton and Ed McMahon are now 'hooked' on Perrier" and Perrier "contains no sodium which causes heartburn." These claims were abandoned in favor of messages emphasizing the water's qualities as a natural thirst-quencher with no calories and no additives.

The advertising budget was high. Initial promotion was regional and relied heavily on the print media. Food and beverage writers were courted at dinners and exhibitions so that they would write about Perrier. The company sponsored marathons so that the product would be associated both with "healthiness" and "thirst quenching." As distribution became national, Source Perrier switched to TV spots on major networks. It was able to maintain snob appeal by getting tidbits in gossip columns about celebrities being seen sipping Perrier in the "right places."

The resultant rapid increase in sales did not go unnoticed by competitors. In 1979, a bottling executive said, "Everyone with water seeping from a rock is buying glass, slapping a label on it, and marketing a new bottled water." One market-research group, SAMI, reported 104 brands of bottled waters in its territory. Some of the established bottled spring-water companies promoted blind tasting comparisons to emphasize that U.S. water was just as tasty as the imports. Deer Park issued a challenge with a spring water priced 35–40 percent below Perrier. Hincley and Schmitt introduced Premier in a bottle with a label that unashamedly copied Perrier. Its theme was "Let your guests think it's imported." Norton Simon's Canada Dry began repositioning its club soda to be more competitive with Perrier.

In 1980, Bruce Nevins believed the "U.S. market for sparkling water is in the process of maturing." Source Perrier's U.S. sales peaked in 1980 and then began falling along with overall imported water sales, largely because of competition from domestic seltzer (carbonated tap water) and domestic club soda (carbonated tap water to which mineral salts are usually added). To combat U.S. domestic competition, Source Perrier subsequently repurchased Poland Spring in 1980 for $10 million. After buying Poland Spring in 1976 for $1 million, that company's new owners had carbonated the still water, modernized the facilities, and captured 6 percent of the bottled-water market. In addition to the problem of domestic competition, the Perrier name was becoming practically generic as customers increasingly asked for Perrier when they simply wanted some kind of sparkling water.

In 1982 Source Perrier devised a new U.S. strategy. It decided to begin handling specialized imports that could be sold to market segments similar to those to which Perrier seemed to appeal. This segment was described by different company executives as "aspirant people who try to improve their quality of life," as "households with incomes of $30,000 or more," and as "the same people who tend to buy better fashions, better cars, and the like." Source Perrier took on Lindt chocolate from Switzerland and Bonne Maman preserves from France and substantially increased their U.S. sales. In 1985, in an attempt to shore up its U.S. water sales, the company began marketing the water with traces of lemon, lime, or orange flavoring.

But what had appeared to be a maturing of the U.S. bottled-water market turned out to be a mere blip. By the mid-1980s, industry sales were growing between 15 and 20 percent per year. Growing fastest was the imported mineral-water segment. But the U.S. market continued to be fragmented, for two reasons. First, the cost and technology to enter the market are low; thus new companies start up each year. Second, transportation costs lead to regional distribution. Perrier is distributed nationally because it is cheaper to ship the water from

France than to ship domestic waters across the United States by truck or rail. By the late 1980s, the following industry trends seemed apparent to Source Perrier's management:

- Growth in all sectors of the bottled-water market would be robust over the next ten years, especially in geographic areas not yet accounting for a large share of the sales.
- Big competitors increasingly would get involved. Coca-Cola, PepsiCo, Anheuser-Busch, and Japan's Suntory had recently become involved in some aspect of the market through ownership, bottling, and/or distribution.
- Because of the capital-intensive nature of distribution (for example, the cost of adding trucks), growth would more likely come from acquisitions by the bigger competitors than from new company start-ups.
- New importers would attack Source Perrier by targeting specific U.S. market niches. For example, Rambosa (Sweden) targeted snobbish consumers, Eau Canada Sparcal (Canada) played up its high calcium content to appeal to women fearful of developing weak bones, and Heart of Tuscany (Italy) promoted its low mineral content for therapeutic purposes.

Consequently, Source Perrier chose to reemphasize the bottled-water market in the United States as opposed to the handling of related products. It did this largely through acquisitions. However, the company has made no attempt to connect acquired brands to the Perrier name. Similarly, Nestlé has made no attempt to combine the Perrier brand with any of the other thirty-four bottled-water brands it now produces in ten different countries.

In 1990, Source Perrier was hit by two unforeseen events that had a negative impact on its U.S. sales. First, because of a bottling worker's error in France, some bottles reaching the U.S. were contaminated with benzene. A worldwide recall resulted. Second, the Federal Food and Drug Administration (FDA) required two changes in Perrier's labels: The terms "naturally sparkling water" and "calorie free" had to be dropped because carbonation was added and because "calorie free" implied that other water contains calories. Prior to the recall, Perrier held 5.7 percent of the U.S. bottled-water market and 44.8 percent of the imported market; afterward, sales fell 42 percent in 1990 and the company's major French competitor, BSN's nonbubbly Evian, became the number-one U.S. water import. Despite these problems, Source Perrier–owned brands, which at the time collectively held 18.2 percent of the U.S. bottled-water market, increased their sales so that their overall U.S. sales went up by 3 percent.

Many U.S. analysts openly questioned whether Perrier would ever regain the market share that had made it the best-selling bottled water in the United States. Although U.S. supermarket sales rebounded to their earlier level in the first year after the recall, sales in restaurants and bars, which earlier had accounted for 35 percent of Perrier sales in the United States, had not recovered completely. In contrast, Perrier regained its French market share for bubbly water (in number-two position after BSN's Badoit) almost immediately after the company relaunched the water in 1990.

In 1991 Source Perrier's new chairman, Jacques Vincent, announced a long-term strategic change for Perrier. The company planned to position the water as a more exclusive

product to be sold mainly in restaurants. Supermarket sales were to focus on locally produced, less expensive brands that are not readily associated with the Perrier name. To this
end, Perrier acquired Volvic and Contrex, two brands popular in Europe outside of France.
Through brand diversification, Perrier expected to be able to minimize problems with any
single brand. However, many analysts questioned Source Perrier's ability to carry out the
brand diversification strategy. They pointed out that Nestlé's acquisition of Perrier was
held up by the EU Commission on antitrust grounds until Perrier divested itself of several
European mineral-water producers.

Questions

1. Might Source Perrier have been better off if it had positioned itself in a segment other
   than the soft-drink market?
2. Should Perrier have tried a means other than exporting to penetrate the U.S. market?
3. What useful insights might be gained by applying the tools and concepts of this chapter
   to an analysis of Perrier?
4. What characteristics might account for Perrier's quicker recovery in the French market
   than in the U.S. market?
5. What options are open to Nestlé for its U.S. Perrier operations?

Chapter Notes

1. Data for the case were taken from "M & S
   Getting Their French Lessons Right," *The
   Times* (London), August 2, 1976, p. 16;
   Sandra Salmans, "Britain: How Marks &
   Spencer Lost Its Spark," *New York Times*,
   August 31, 1980, p. F3; Barbara Crossette,
   "British Store Shapes Up for Parisians,"
   New York Times, June 28, 1975, p. 14; "St.
   Michael Spreads the Gospel," *Economist*,
   September 1977, pp. 68–69; "Super Su-
   permarkets," *The Accountant*, June 26,
   1980, pp. 981–983; Carrie Dolan, "Marks
   & Spencer Finds No-Frills Policy in Retail-
   ing Suits the British Just Fine," *Wall Street
   Journal*, April 14, 1981, p. 35; Alan Free-
   man, "Marks & Spencer Canada Adheres
   to Parent's Principles Despite Losses,"
   Wall Street Journal, August 4, 1981, p. 39;
   Margaret de Miraval, "British Influence
   Aiding French Department Stores," *Chris-
   tian Science Monitor*, July 7, 1983, p. 15;
   "Marks & Spencer Tries Yet Again," *Finan-
   cial Times*, April 25, 1985, p. 16; Mina
   Williams, "St. Michael Chilled Foods In-
   troduced in Kings Stores," *Supermarket
   News*, December 11, 1989, p. 1+; Andrew
   Collier, "Marks & Spencer to Buy More
   Abroad," *Women's Wear Daily*, October 6,
   1989, p. 6; Stephen Dowdell, "Marks &
   Spencer Buys Kings in First U.S. Food
   Venture," *Supermarket News*, August 15,
   1988, p. 1+; Steven Weiner, "Low Marks,
   Few Sparks," *Forbes*, September 18, 1989,
   pp. 146–147; Isadore Barmash, "Brooks
   Brothers Stays the Course," *New York
   Times*, November 23, 1990, p. C1; John
   Thornhill, "A European Spark for Marks,"
   Financial Times, July 13, 1992, p. 12; Mike
   Sheridan, "British Values," *Sky*, October
   1992, pp. 69–74; Stephanie Strom, "A
   Quiet Updating for Brooks Bros.," *New
   York Times*, November 9, 1992, p. C1; and
   Maureen Whitehead, "International Fran-
   chising—Marks & Spencer: A Case Study,"
   *International Journal of Retail and Distribution
   Management*, Vol. 19, No. 2, March–April
   1991, pp. 10–12.
2. For a discussion of differences and simi-
   larities, see Hugh E. Kramer, "International Marketing: Methodological
   Excellence in Practice and Theory," *Management International Review*, Vol. 29,
   No. 2, 1989, pp. 59–65.
3. For a more extensive coverage of similar
   techniques, see Susan P. Douglas, C.
   Samuel Craig, and Warren J. Keegan,
   "Approaches to Assessing International
   Marketing Opportunities for Small- and
   Medium-sized Companies," *Columbia Journal of World Business*, Vol. 17, No. 3, Fall
   1982, pp. 26–32.
4. Bill Powell and Frederick Shaw Myers,
   "Death by Fried Chicken," *Newsweek*,
   September 24, 1990, p. 36.
5. "Food Spending Dominates in Japan,"
   Wall Street Journal, March 4, 1991, p. A6.
6. Houston H. Stokes and Hugh Neuburger,
   "The Box-Jenkins Approach—When Is It
   a Cost-Effective Alternative?" *Columbia
   Journal of World Business*, Winter 1976,
   pp. 78–86.
7. H. Youn Kim, "Estimating Consumer Demand in Korea," *Journal of Development Economics*, Vol. 20, No. 2, 1986, pp. 325–338.
8. Joann S. Lublin, "Slim Pickings," *Wall
   Street Journal*, May 15, 1990, p. A20.
9. J. A. Weber, "Comparing Growth Opportunities in the International Marketplace," *Management International Review*,
   No. 1, 1979, pp. 47–54.
10. "Chocolate Makers in Switzerland Try to
    Melt Resistance," *Wall Street Journal*, Janu-
    ary 5, 1981, p. 14.
11. Yumiko Ono, "Japanese Treating Them-
    selves to More Imported Chocolate,"
    Wall Street Journal, January 5, 1990, p. A4.
12. Bruce Siefert and John Ford, "Are Ex-
    porting Firms Modifying Their Product,
    Pricing and Promotion Policies?" *Interna-
    tional Marketing Review*, Vol. 6, No. 6,
    1989, pp. 53–68, discuss these points.
13. For a discussion of niche strategy, see
    James Leontiades, "Going Global—Global
    Strategies vs. National Strategies," *Long
    Range Planning*, Vol. 19, No. 6, December
    1986, pp. 96–104. For details on the bour-
    bon example, see Christopher Power and
    Robert Neff, "Sweet Sales for Sour Mash
    Abroad," *Business Week*, July 1, 1991, p. 62.

14. Sigurd Villads Troye and Van R. Wood, "A Conceptual Perspective of International Marketing: Meeting the Educational Challenges of the 1990s and Beyond," *1989 International Management Symposium* (Monterrey, CA: Monterrey Institute of International Studies, 1989), pp. 84–95.

15. Christopher Power, "Will It Sell in Podunk? Hard to Say," *Business Week,* August 10, 1992, pp. 46–47.

16. Michael J. McCarthy, "More Companies Shop Abroad for New Product Ideas," *Wall Street Journal,* March 14, 1990, p. B1+.

17. John D. Daniels, "Combining Strategic and International Business Approaches through Growth Vector Analysis," *Management International Review,* Vol. 23, 3, 1983, p. 11.

18. John Thackray, "Much Ado about Global Marketing," *Across the Board,* April 1985, pp. 38–46; Yves L. Doz, "Managing Manufacturing Rationalization within Multinational Companies," *Columbia Journal of World Business,* Fall 1978, pp. 82–93.

19. Troye and Wood, loc. cit.

20. John S. Hill and Richard R. Still, "Adapting Products to LDC Tastes," *Harvard Business Review,* Vol. 62, No. 2, March–April 1984, pp. 92–101.

21. "Abolishing Litter," *The Economist,* August 22, 1992, pp. 59–60; and Philippe Bruno and Bernd Graf, "The New EC Environmental Framework for Packaging," *Export Today,* March 1993, pp. 17–23.

22. Bob Davis, "Europe Defeats Japan's Proposal on TV Standard," *Wall Street Journal,* May 25, 1990, p. B4.

23. G. Pierre Goad, "In the U.S., They'll Probably Try Renaming It McGlop or Big Muck," *Wall Street Journal,* March 8, 1990, p. B1.

24. Andrew H. Malcolm, "On the Battlefield of Beauty," *New York Times,* May 22, 1977, p. 1.

25. William W. Locke, "The Fatal Flaw: Hidden Cultural Differences," *Business Marketing,* Vol. 7, No. 4, April 1986, p. 65+.

26. Siefert and Ford, loc. cit.

27. Adam Bryant, "GM Names President of Japan Unit," *New York Times,* June 18, 1992, p. C4.

28. Gabriella Stern, "Heinz Aims to Export Taste for Ketchup," *Wall Street Journal,* November 20, 1992, p. B1+.

29. Susan P. Douglas and C. Samuel Craig, "Evolution of Global Marketing Strategy: Scale, Scope and Synergy," *Columbia Journal of World Business,* Vol. 14, No. 3, Fall 1989, p. 54.

30. Joshua Levine, "The Rabbit Grows Up," *Forbes,* February 17, 1992, pp. 122–127.

31. Stephen Baker, Sally Gelston, and Jonathon Kapstein, "The Third World Is Getting Cellular Fever," *Business Week,* April 16, 1990, pp. 80–81; and "Dinosaur Brands," *Adweek's Marketing Week,* June 17, 1991, p. 17.

32. "The Bugs from Brazil," *The Economist,* August 21, 1993, p. 54.

33. Saeed Samiee, "Pricing in Marketing Strategies of U.S.- and Foreign-Based Companies," *Journal of Business Research,* Vol. 15, No. 1, February 1987, pp. 17–30.

34. Alicia Swasy, "Foreign Formula," *Wall Street Journal,* June 15, 1990, p. A7.

35. Mark Alpert and Aimety Dunlap Smith, "Nestlé Shows How to Gobble Markets," *Fortune,* Vol. 119, January 16, 1989, p. 76.

36. Andrea C. Rutherford, "Sea Urchin Industry Is Threatened By Its Own Growth," *Wall Street Journal,* July 11, 1992, p. B2; and "Japanese Snap Up Eye of Tuna," *Wall Street Journal,* April 7, 1994, p. A10.

37. Luis V. Dominguez and Carlos G. Sequeira, "Strategic Options for LDC Exports to Developed Countries," *International Marketing Review,* Vol. 8, No. 5, 1991, pp. 27–43.

38. Johny K. Johansson and Hans B. Thorelli, "International Product Positioning," *Journal of International Business Studies,* Vol. 16, No. 3, Fall 1985, pp. 57–75.

39. Swasy, loc. cit.

40. Ann Hughey, " 'Gray Market' in Camera Imports Starts to Undercut Official Dealers," *Wall Street Journal,* April 1, 1982, p. 29; and Douglas R. Sease, "Selling Abroad," *Wall Street Journal,* August 31, 1987, p. 1+.

41. Claude Collich, "Negotiating Strategies: The Question of Price," *International Trade Forum,* April–June 1991, pp. 10–13.

42. Hill and Still, op. cit., p. 95.

43. Laurence Jacobs, Reginald Worthley, and Charles Keown, "Perceived Buyer Satisfaction and Selling Pressures versus Pricing Policy: A Comparative Study of Retailers in Ten Developing Countries," *Journal of Business Research,* Vol. 12, No. 1, March 1984, p. 67.

44. Neil King, Jr., "Kmart's Czech Invasion Lurches Along," *Wall Street Journal,* June 8, 1993, p. A11.

45. Alicia Swasy and Jeremy Mark, "Japan Brings Its Packaged Goods to U.S.," *Wall Street Journal,* January 17, 1989, p. B1.

46. Seymour Banks, "Cross-National Analysis of Advertising Expenditures: 1968–1979," *Journal of Advertising Research,* Vol. 26, No. 2, April–May 1986, p. 21.

47. Robert T. Green and Eric Langeard, "A Cross-National Comparison of Consumer Habits and Innovator Characteristics," *Journal of Marketing,* July 1975.

48. John A. Quelch and Edward J. Hoff, "Customizing Global Marketing," *Harvard Business Review,* Vol. 64, No. 3, May–June 1986, p. 62; Dennis Chase, "Global Marketing: The New Wave," *Advertising Age,* June 25, 1984, p. 49+; and Joanne Lipman, "Ad Fad," *Wall Street Journal,* May 12, 1988, p. 1+.

49. Kevin Goldman, "Prof. Levitt Stands By Global-Ad Theory," *Wall Street Journal,* October 13, 1992, p. B7.

50. Kevin Kelly and Karen Lowry Miller, "The Rumble Heard Round the World: Harleys," *Business Week,* May 24, 1993, pp. 58–60.

51. Ken Wells, "Selling to the World," *Wall Street Journal,* August 27, 1992, pp. A1+.

52. Rene White, "Beyond Berlitz: How to Penetrate Foreign Markets through Effective Communications," *Public Relations Quarterly,* Vol. 31, No. 2, Summer 1986, p. 15.

53. John R. Zeeman, "What United Airlines Is Learning in the Pacific," speech before the Academy of International Business, Chicago, November 14, 1987.

54. Frank J. Prial, "Very, Very Bad, Pakistani Says as He Confiscates Lingerie Ad," *New York Times,* April 20, 1981, p. A11; Barry Newman, "Watchdogs Abroad," *Wall Street Journal,* April 8, 1980, p. 1+; J. J. Boddewyn, "Advertising Regulation in the 1980s: The Underlying Global Forces," *Journal of Marketing,* Vol. 46, Winter 1982, pp. 27–35; Damon Darlin, "Advertising," *Wall Street Journal,* April 19, 1989, p. B1; Michael Richardson, "Malaysia TV Debate: Beyond Skin-Deep," *International Herald Tribune,* June 28, 1989, p. 5; and "Breaking Britain's Speed Limit," *Wall Street Journal,* September 24, 1990, p. A10.

55. Jean J. Boddewyn, *Barriers to Trade and Investment in Advertising: Government Regulation and Industry Self-Regulation in 53 Countries* (New York: International Advertising Association, 1989).

56. John Marcom, Jr., "American Express's Ads in Europe Seek to Leap Borders," *Wall Street Journal,* April 1, 1988, p. 16.

57. "Full of Western Promise," *Economist,* November 14, 1992, pp. 84–85.

58. David R. Wheeler, "Content Analysis: An Analytical Technique for International Marketing Research," *International Marketing Review,* Vol. 5, No. 4, Winter 1988, pp. 34–40; and Gordon E. Miracle, Charles R. Taylor, and Kyu Yeol Chang, "Culture and Advertising Executions: A Comparison of Selected Characteristics of Japanese and U.S. Television Commercials," *Journal of International Consumer Marketing,* Vol. 4, No. 4, 1992, pp. 89–113.

59. Sak Onkvisit and John J. Shaw, "The International Dimension of Branding: Strategic Considerations and Decisions," *International Marketing Review,* Vol. 6, No. 3, 1989, pp. 22–34.

60. Steven Prokesch, " 'Eurosell' Pervades the Continent," *New York Times,* May 31, 1990, p. C1+.

61. E. S. Browning, "In Pursuit of the Elusive Euroconsumer," *Wall Street Journal,* April 23, 1992, p. B1.

62. Donald G. Howard, "Developing a Defensive Product Management Philosophy for Third World Markets," *International Marketing Review,* Vol. 5, No. 1, Spring 1988, pp. 31–40.

63. "Boycott against Nestlé over Infant Formula to End Next Month," *Wall Street Journal,* January 27, 1984, p. 19; and Alix M. Freedman, "Advertising," *Wall Street Journal,* April 25, 1989, p. B6.

64. "Baby-Formula TV Ads in Taiwan," *Wall Street Journal,* February 24, 1993, p. A8.

65. Shlomo Maital, "Transnational Teddies," *Across the Board,* Vol. 26, No. 10, October 1989, pp. 15–18.

66. "But Will It Wash?" *The Economist,* July 13, 1991, p. 70.

67. Myron M. Miller, "Sunbeam in Italy: One Success and One Failure," *International Marketing Review,* Vol. 7, No. 1, 1990, pp. 68–73.

68. "Marketing Korean as Korean," *Business Korea,* Vol. 3, No. 5, November 1985, p. 41.

69. William H. Flanagan, "Big Battle Is Brewing as French Beer Aims to Topple Heineken," *Wall Street Journal,* February 22, 1980, p. 16. For some Japanese examples, see Yumiko Ono, "Japan Eats Up 'U.S.' Food Never Tasted in America," *Wall Street Journal,* April 4, 1990, p. B1+.

70. E. S. Browning, "Eastern Europe Poses Obstacles for Ads," *Wall Street Journal,* July 30, 1992, p. B6.

71. John D. Daniels, "Bridging National and Global Marketing Strategies Through Regional Operations," *International Marketing Review,* Vol. 4, No. 3, Autumn 1987, pp. 29–44.

72. Yumiko Ono, "Amway Translates with Ease into Japanese," *Wall Street Journal,* September 21, 1990, p. B1+; and Patrick Oster and Igor Reichlin, "Breaking Into European Markets by Breaking the Rules," *Business Week,* January 20, 1992, pp. 88–89.

73. "Taking Aim," *The Economist,* April 24, 1993, p. 74.

74. Michael J. McCarthy, "The Real Thing," *Wall Street Journal,* December 19, 1989, p. A1+; and Bert Rosenbloom, "Motivating Your International Channel Partners," *Business Horizons,* Vol. 33, No. 2, March–April 1990, pp. 53–57.

75. Michael R. Czinkota, "Distribution in Japan: Problems and Changes," *Columbia Journal of World Business,* Vol. 20, No. 3, Fall 1985, p. 66.

76. Data for the case were taken from Louis Botto, "Straight from the Source," *New York Times Magazine,* June 26, 1977, pp. 68–72; Roger B. May, "French Bottler Tries to Replace U.S. Pop with a Natural Fizz," *Wall Street Journal,* April 12, 1978, p. 1+; "Deep Chic," *Wall Street Journal,* December 7, 1979, p. 24; Peter C. DuBois, "Perrier Going Flat?" *Barron's,* May 12, 1980, p. 71; "Perrier: Putting More Sparkle into Sales," *Sales & Marketing Management,* January 1979, pp. 16–17; Bob Lederer and Martin Westerman, "How Perrier Became a Soft Drink," *Beverage World,* May 1979, pp. 37–45; "Perrier: The Astonishing Suc-cess of an Appeal to Affluent Adults," *Business Week,* January 22, 1979, pp. 64–65; "Sales Boon for Bottled Water," *New York Times,* August 8, 1982, p. F27; Steven P. Galante, "Perrier's U.S. Marketing Know-How Put to Use for Other European Brands," *Wall Street Journal,* June 26, 1984, p. 30; Lawrence M. Fisher, "A New Zip to Bottled Water Sales," *New York Times,* May 23, 1986, p. F6; John Roussant, "Perrier's Unquenchable U.S. Thirst," *Business Week,* No. 3005, June 29, 1987, p. 46; Robert Alsop, "New Imports Aiming to Take the Fizz Out of Perrier's Sales," *Wall Street Journal,* December 24, 1987, p. 11; Anthony Ramirez, "Perrier Recall: How Damaging Is It?" *New York Times,* February 13, 1990, p. C1+; Barry Meier, "Perrier Will Bow to F.D.A. and Change Its Label," *New York Times,* April 19, 1990, p. C7; Alix M. Freedman, "Perrier Finds Mystique Hard to Restore," *Wall Street Journal,* December 12, 1990, p. B1+; Mark Landler, Lisa Driscoll, and Stewart Toy, "You Can Lead a Restaurateur to Perrier, But . . . ," *Business Week,* June 25, 1990, pp. 25–26; E. S. Browning, "Perrier Chief Serves Up New Formula," *Wall Street Journal,* February 14, 1991, pp. B1–B2; Charles Goldsmith, "Nestlé Now Finds Itself in a Crunch as Trouble Bubbles Up at Perrier," *Wall Street Journal,* August 13, 1992, p. B1; and Cara Appelbaum, *Adweek's Marketing Week,* January 27, 1992, pp. 4–6.

Chapter 18

Sourcing and Production Strategies

*Right mixture
makes good mortar.*
——English Proverb

Objectives

- To gain an overview of the different dimensions of a global production strategy

- To describe the major differences in the ways companies can source materials and components and manufacture and assemble products for international use

- To examine the important dimensions of quality for the manufacturing process, with special reference to ISO 9000

- To show how the just-in-time system is an important dimension of manufacturing strategy but also is more difficult to implement in a global manufacturing context

Case
Black & Decker (B&D)[1]

Black & Decker (B&D), once known almost exclusively as a manufacturer of power tools for professionals, is now involved in "the manufacturing, marketing, and servicing of a wide range of power tools, household products, and other labor-saving devices generally used in and around the home and by professional users."

In the 1970s, before broadening its base to include a larger segment of the household market, B&D was flying high. It had captured a large share of the world's power-tool market, and financial analysts were betting strongly on its future. By 1981, however, the picture began to change. Earnings had begun to slip, and a worldwide recession caused a significant downturn in the power-tools segment of B&D's business, which was its bread and butter. Other events in the world economy added to B&D's problems. For example, a strong U.S. dollar eroded the company's competitive position in export markets and made it vulnerable to foreign competition from companies such as Japan's Makita Electric Works Ltd. Makita adopted a global strategy for its products that allowed it to become the world's lowest-cost producer of power tools. It decided that consumers in different countries really did not need significantly different products. Then it combined its cost advantage with aggressive marketing and took advantage of the yen's relative weakness compared to the U.S. dollar and of B&D's problems to make serious inroads in the power-tool market. By the late 1970s and early 1980s, Makita was able to nearly equal B&D's 20 percent market share in professional tools worldwide.

B&D's problems were partly a result of its own strategy. By 1982, it operated twenty-five manufacturing plants in thirteen countries on six continents. It had three operating groups in addition to its Maryland headquarters. Each group had its own staff; this led to duplication and overstaffing. In addition, individual B&D companies, such as B&D of West Germany, operated autonomously in each of the more than fifty countries in which the company sold and serviced products. The parent company's philosophy had been to let each country company adapt products and product lines to fit its market's unique characteristics: The Italian company produced power tools for Italians, the British company made power tools for Britons, and so on.

As a result, companies in different countries did not communicate well with each other. Successful products in one country often took years to introduce in others. For example, the highly successful Dustbuster, introduced in the United States in the late 1970s, did not make it to Australia until 1983. When efforts were made to introduce B&D home products into European markets, the European managers balked. Despite stagnating sales, B&D still held a large percentage of the European power-tool market in the early 1980s—over 50 percent on the Continent and 80 percent in the United Kingdom. The managers felt that home appliances and products were uniquely American and would not do well outside of the United States.

Meeting the tailor-made specifications of different markets resulted in inefficient utilization of design centers. At one point eight design centers around the world had produced 260 different models of motors, even though B&D needed fewer than 10 models. Plant capacity utilization was low, employment levels were high, and output per employee was unacceptable. Further, B&D had begun to stagnate in new product development.

B&D's consumer-tool and professional-tool product lines operated in two different product groups. However, the groups did not work together to develop new product lines.

It appeared the company had decided to concentrate on its top lines and sell them aggressively. Thus Makita was able to spot a market niche that it could exploit—mid-priced tools.

As B&D moved into the mid-1980s, management realized it had to do something. One of the first things new CEO Nolan Archibald did was establish a global strategy. He then surrounded himself with the personnel necessary to effect it. His strategy included selling the same basic products worldwide with relatively minor modifications. Consequently, B&D had to improve its designs and reduce the number of parts per product.

Archibald's strategy also called for a cut-and-build program. Under this program, 3000 of the company's 23,000 employees were let go between 1985 and 1987, resulting in the closing of five plants worldwide and the downsizing of several others. This move enabled B&D to concentrate production in fewer plants, thus increasing economies of scale. At the same time, the sales force was almost doubled and the new-product and engineering departments were increased. As described in the company's 1992 *Annual Report,*

> Major design and manufacturing centers in North America and Europe provide a competitive advantage for Black & Decker. Global business teams help focus our worldwide engineering, manufacturing, and marketing resources to bring products and services to market quickly and efficiently. Our research and advanced technology, product development, and manufacturing planning reflect a global outlook. This approach gives us the broadest perspective on competitive and market developments and promotes worldwide economies of scale.

Acquisitions also became an important part of B&D's new global strategy. One area in which the Japanese had not made significant inroads was the housewares and small-appliances market. Japanese consumers were not fond of those items, so Makita and other competitors had not established a strong home market to use as an export base. B&D was having trouble introducing its own line of housewares because of its image as a power-tool manufacturer. As a result, B&D acquired the small-appliances division of GE in 1984 to give it more shelf space in housewares and also a large enough line of products to provide economies of scale in manufacturing.

In April 1989, B&D acquired Emhart Corporation, the worldwide manufacturer of such leading brands as Kwikset door locks and hardware, Price Pfister faucets, True Temper lawn and garden products, Molly bolts, POP rivets, and other consumer and commercial products. However, the added debt created problems, and B&D's management had to look for ways to cut costs and service the debt.

Will B&D be able to shine in the future? Part of its success will depend on its global manufacturing strategy and its ability to turn out high-quality products in sufficient numbers on a worldwide basis.

Introduction

Most companies can select where they want to source the purchase or manufacture of products they can sell worldwide. For any given market, a company can manufacture the product itself or buy it from someone else. If the company decides to manufacture the product itself, it can manufacture it either in the local market or in another country and then import it into the market.

Chapter 14 discussed importing and exporting strategies but not in the context of a globally integrated manufacturing system. This chapter discusses a manufacturing strategy that combines elements of importing and exporting of raw materials, intermediate components, and final goods. Chapters 5, 6, and 8 described why companies import, export, and invest abroad. Then, Chapters 15–17 covered collaborative strategies, control, and the site selection for foreign operations, issues that are germane to the discussion of manufacturing strategy. This chapter focuses more on the configuration of manufacturing operations worldwide and some of the important issues that affect manufacturing strategy, such as quality and outsourcing—having an unrelated company be a supplier of components.

Global Manufacturing Strategies

MNEs are involved in fairly sophisticated forms of production sharing in which they may produce and/or assemble components in one or several countries for worldwide markets. In the simplest form of production sharing, production occurs in the home country and goods are exported to final markets. Alternatively, an MNE could produce in different countries in order to serve those particular markets or third-country markets. However, during the past decade intermediate goods, such as components, are increasingly being produced in many countries and shipped to other countries for assembly and sale. The production and exporting functions are much more complex than they used to be under the simpler forms.

Global sourcing implies that companies need to determine where parts and components will be manufactured and where final products will be assembled.

For each particular market an MNE serves, the strategy of global sourcing implies that it needs to determine where parts and components will be manufactured and where the final products will be assembled. This was one of the first problems that Archibald had to solve when he took over the leadership of B&D.

Historically, companies tend to operate initially on a country-by-country basis. However, as they become more globally oriented, they find they can develop a definite competitive advantage by coordinating and integrating their operations across national borders.[2]

Global Sourcing and Production Options

Global sourcing and production strategies need to include consideration of location and stage in the production process.

From an international standpoint, the global sourcing and production strategies can be better understood by looking at Fig. 18.1. This figure illustrates the basic options available by country (the home country or any foreign country) and by stage in the production process (sourcing of raw materials and/or components and the manufacture and assembly of components and final products).

For example, Ford assembles cars in Hermosillo, Mexico, and ships them into the United States. The cars are designed by the Japanese company Toyo Kogyo Co. (Mazda) and use some Japanese parts. Ford can purchase components manufactured in Japan and ship them to the United States for final assembly and sale in the

**Figure 18.1
Global Sourcing and
Production Strategy**
Companies have many possibilities for sourcing raw materials and assembling them into final goods to serve worldwide markets. For example, a U.S. company could source components in the United States, assemble them in Mexico, and export the final product back to the United States or to other countries.

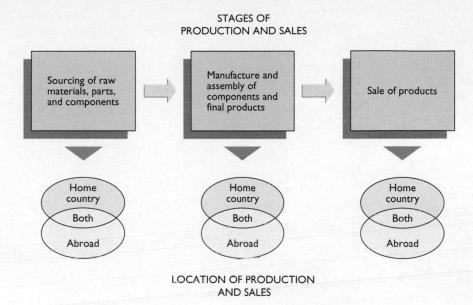

STAGES OF
PRODUCTION AND SALES

LOCATION OF PRODUCTION
AND SALES

U.S. market, or it can have Japanese- and U.S.-made components shipped to Mexico for final assembly and sale in the United States and Mexico. For Mexican assembly, some of the components come from the United States, some from Japan, and a small percentage from Mexico. If the components are manufactured in Japan, many of the raw materials are probably imported. When Ford decided to manufacture the Escort in Europe, it utilized the global sourcing of components from plants in fifteen different countries for final assembly in the United Kingdom and Germany. Figure 18.2 illustrates how that was accomplished.

An expansion of Fig. 18.1 would show sixty-four different combinations for manufacturing components and assembling them into final products for different markets. This expanded model would account for the facts that components can be manufactured internally in the company or purchased from external (unrelated) manufacturers and that final assembly also can be done internally or by external companies. Manufacture of components and final assembly may take place in the company's home country, the country in which it is trying to sell the product, a developed third country, or a developing third country.[3]

As an MNE establishes its manufacturing strategy, it must do so in the context of its competitive strategy. Competitive strategies are based on the following priorities:

Four elements of the competitive strategy that affect the manufacturing strategy:
• Efficiency/cost
• Dependability
• Quality
• Flexibility

- Efficiency/cost—reduction of manufacturing costs
- Dependability—degree of trust in a company's products and its delivery and price promises
- Quality—performance reliability, service quality, speed of delivery, and maintenance quality of the product(s)
- Flexibility—ability of the production process to make different kinds of products and/or to adjust the volume of output[4]

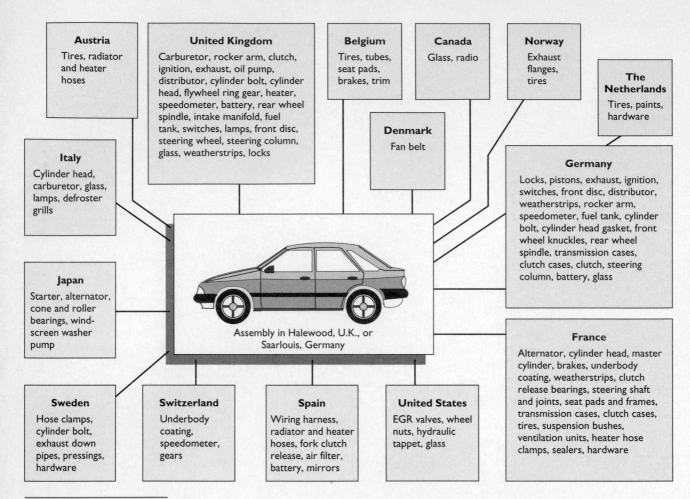

**Figure 18.2
The Global
Component Network
for Ford's European
Manufacturing of the
Escort**
Ford assembles Escorts in
only two facilities in Europe, but parts and components used in the
automobiles come from all
over the world.

*Source: World Development Report 1987 (New York: Oxford
University Press, 1987), p. 39.*

For example, cost-minimization strategies and the drive for global efficiencies tend to force MNEs to establish economies of scale in manufacturing, often by producing in areas with low-cost labor. On the other hand, the need for responsiveness or flexibility because of differences in national markets results in regional manufacturing to service local markets. As a company's competitive strategies change, so do its manufacturing strategies. In addition, MNEs may adopt different strategies for different product lines, depending on the competitive priorities of those products. This was one of the dilemmas B&D faced in the mid-1980s because it had always operated on the basis of local flexibility and yet it was losing market share because of high costs. This loss argued for a move to economies of scale in manufacturing.

The manufacturing strategy needs to take into account different activities. Of these, the most important are as follows:

• Location and scale of the manufacturing facilities
• Choice of manufacturing process

Manufacturing activities are
- **Location and scale**
- **Choice of process**
- **Control of the system**
- **Degree of vertical integration relative to outsourcing**
- **Coordination of R&D**
- **Licensing of technology**

- Control of the production system, including the assignment of activities to plants in a multiplant network
- Degree of vertical integration relative to outsourcing of each manufacturing facility
- Coordination of R&D units
- Licensing of technology[5]

International Manufacturing Configurations

Three basic manufacturing philosophies are multidomestic, regional, and global.

MNEs differ from smaller companies involved in international business in their sheer scale and geographic reach. There are three basic philosophies MNEs consider as they establish a global manufacturing strategy—that is, the pattern of decisions in manufacturing activities. Some MNEs have followed a multidomestic approach in which they manufacture products close to their customers, using country-specific manufacturing facilities to meet local needs—the old B&D approach. A variation on this approach is to use regional manufacturing facilities to serve customers within a specific region. Others have centralized manufacturing and offer a selection of standard, lower-priced products to different markets.[6] In reality, MNEs choose a combination of these approaches depending on their product strategies.

Major types of international manufacturing configurations are
- **Home-country production with exporting**
- **Autonomous regional plants**
- **Combination of regional and global focus**
- **Coordinated global focus**

Although MNEs must integrate their worldwide operations if they are to be globally competitive, there are a variety of international manufacturing configurations (IMC) that relate to different manufacturing strategies. These are the major types of IMCs:

- Home-country production with limited or extensive exporting
- Autonomous regional plants designed to serve the needs of specific foreign markets
- Combination of regional and global focus (configurations involving local or regional assembly of globally produced parts and components)
- Coordinated global focus (configurations involving international dispersal of stages of the production process to low-cost regions, with final assembly taking place at different locations)

These different configurations are not mutually exclusive but are often used simultaneously, depending on competitive demands.

Product strategies can be technology-driven, marketing-intensive, or low-cost.

In each of these configurations, the MNE is trying to balance conflicting objectives that relate to its product strategy. One product strategy is technology-driven. In this case, the plant-location strategy would be to position the plant in a high-income country that has a large market. This is basically a country-specific strategy. Although the parent company would influence manufacturing decisions, most would be made at the local level, unless there were significant intracompany transfers of components.[7]

If the product strategy is marketing-intensive, the key is to operate a marketing program that includes good product quality and prompt delivery. In this case, several manufacturing facilities are located close to local markets and controlled by local management. The company would adopt a country-specific or regional manufacturing strategy.

If the product strategy is low-cost, the manufacturing strategy is to use large-scale manufacturing to reduce unit costs or to rely on manufacturing in cheap-labor countries if labor is a significant component of total cost. There is significantly more central control in this situation than with a marketing-intensive strategy.[8] These possibilities are summarized in Table 18.1.

Selecting the number of plants and their locations depends on complex factors, such as transportation costs, duties on components versus those on finished goods, need for closeness to the market, foreign-exchange risk, economies of scale in the production process, technological requirements, and national image. In addition, a company's decision as to the specific location within a country for manufacturing is a function of external factors (such as market size and local government incentives) and internal strategic factors (such as the relative importance of product lines, location of markets, importance of cost, the improvement over time of knowledge of the country, and the perceptions of changes in risks).[9]

Manufacturing systems:
- **Single plant**
- **Multiple plants**
- **Manufacturing interchange**
- **Rationalization**

A company may choose one of many manufacturing systems. For example, it could try to serve all markets from one plant. However, transportation charges and tariffs could make this system infeasible. In addition, the scale of production may be so large in this case that the marginal cost of production would be higher than if smaller plant sizes were used to achieve economies of scale. A company also may specialize production by product or process so that a particular plant produces a product or range of products or produces all products using a particular process and serves all markets (rationalization). Or it may have several plants specializing in the same product or process so that it has a larger geographical spread. The process of manufacturing interchange involves plants producing a range of components and interchanging them so that all plants assemble the finished product for the local market. Obviously, there is no one best way to set up the production process. For a particular product or line of products, a company may use a single-plant strategy and depend on exports to serve world markets. This would be essentially a worldwide product and production strategy. For other products or groups of products, a multiplant strategy such as rationalization or manufacturing interchange may be best.

Table 18.1
Product and Manufacturing Strategies

	Product strategy		
Manufacturing strategy	**Technology-driven**	**Marketing-intensive**	**Low-cost**
Multidomestic, country-specific	✔	✔	
Regional		✔	
Centralized			✔

Offshore Manufacturing

Offshore manufacturing
often is done in low-cost locations and followed by importation into the home
market.

Offshore manufacturing—manufacturing outside of the borders of a particular country—has provided a useful means to avoid losing market share to low-cost foreign competitors. Worldwide, it escalated sharply in the 1960s and 1970s in the electronics industry as one company after another set up production facilities in the Far East, principally in Taiwan and Singapore. Those locations were chosen because of low labor costs, availability of cheap materials and components, and proximity to markets. Even the athletic shoe market left the United States for Korea. As wages rose in Korea, however, manufacturing began to shift to other low-cost countries, such as Indonesia, Malaysia, and Thailand.

Market conditions also can affect offshore manufacturing strategies. As B&D's operations in Europe continued to falter in the early 1990s due to the European recession, B&D found it had to close down some plants and cut back production in others. This move favored using U.S. production facilities to serve world markets for many products.

Maquiladora Industry

A maquiladora is an operation in Mexico to which components are shipped from
the United States duty-free
for assembly and the goods
re-exported to the United
States.

Recall from Chapter 7 that Mexico has become one of the most important centers for offshore production for U.S. companies through maquiladora operations. Under the Mexican maquiladora concept, U.S.-sourced components are shipped to Mexican border facilities duty-free and assembled by Mexican workers; the goods then are re-exported to the United States or other foreign markets under favorable tariff provisions. U.S. duties are levied on the imports only to the extent of the value added in Mexico. The benefits of establishing a maquiladora operation are especially strong for companies for which 30 percent or more of the product cost is labor. This condition applies to fewer and fewer companies because the average labor percentage for most products manufactured in the United States is less than 20 percent.

Many companies combine the maquiladora concept with the use of free-trade zones being established by many Caribbean Basin countries. These countries include Costa Rica, the Dominican Republic, El Salvador, Guatemala, Haiti, Honduras, Jamaica, Panama, and Puerto Rico. Their major attractions are low labor costs, tax incentives, tariff concessions, and access to U.S. markets through specially negotiated agreements or through provisions in the U.S. tariff schedule.

The problems with
maquiladoras include
• Pollution
• Social problems resulting
from population movement
• Enclaves of foreign
companies

However, there are problems with maquiladora operations. Many critics complain they are little more than foreign enclaves on Mexican soil. Given that the companies bring into Mexico 97 percent of the components, the value added in Mexico is practically nothing. Because the goods are produced for export rather than domestic consumption, local consumers do not benefit from the production. In addition, the growth in employment has created serious social problems along the border. People have streamed to the border for jobs because the jobless rate in the nearby area prior to the establishment of the maquiladoras was close to 40 percent. There is insufficient infrastructure to handle this influx. Living conditions are poor, and the largest component of the labor force is women.[10] In addition, there have been charges of severe environmental degradation, which Mexico's lax environmental standards have done nothing to impede.

NAFTA will change the nature of the maquiladora industry. A key condition underlying the maquiladora concept is the existence of tariffs on trade between the United States and Mexico and the fact that those tariffs are relaxed on maquiladora transactions. As tariff barriers between the United States and Mexico are eliminated, there still will be investment in border industries, but there will be no need for it to remain there exclusively. Investment in other parts of Mexico will be able to take advantage of good labor rates. In addition, the manufactured goods will serve the domestic Mexican market, and plants therefore will be located closer to the population centers.

Foreign Trade Zones

In recent years, **foreign trade zones (FTZs)** have become more popular as an intermediate step in the process between import and final use. Often, the final use is for export; however, these zones also are good for making use of foreign sourcing. FTZs are areas in which domestic and imported merchandise can be stored, inspected, and manufactured free from formal customs procedures until the goods leave the zones. The zones are intended to encourage companies to locate domestically by allowing them to defer duties, pay less duties, or avoid certain duties completely.[11]

FTZs can be general-purpose zones or subzones. A general-purpose zone usually is established near a port of entry, such as a shipping port, a border crossing, or an airport, and usually consists of a distribution facility or an industrial park. A subzone generally is physically separated from a general-purpose zone but is under the same administrative structure. Since 1982, the major growth in FTZs has been in subzones rather than general-purpose zones, although the latter must be established before the former. For example, the major growth in subzones in the United States has been in the automobile industry, especially in the Midwest.[12] In fact, 60 percent of all subzone activity in the United States is connected with that industry. These zones are available to foreign-owned as well as domestic companies. During trade negotiations between Japan and the United States in 1994, U.S. negotiators threatened to withdraw subzone eligibility for Japanese automakers if the Japanese government did not make progress in helping the United States reduce its trade deficit with Japan. It was hoped that the Japanese automakers would pressure their government. Subzone activity is spreading to other industries, especially shipbuilding, pharmaceuticals, and home appliances, and becoming more heavily oriented to manufacturing and assembly than was originally envisioned.[13]

FTZs are used worldwide. For example, in Japan, they are being established for the benefit of foreign companies exporting products to that country. Japanese zones serve as warehousing and repackaging facilities at which companies can display consumer goods for demonstration to Japanese buyers.[14]

FTZs are generally used to provide greater flexibility as to when and how customs duties are to be paid.

In the United States, FTZs have been used primarily as a means of providing greater flexibility as to when and how customs duties are paid. However, their use in the export business has been expanding. The exports for which these FTZs are used fall into one of the following categories:

- Foreign goods transshipped through U.S. zones to third countries
- Foreign goods processed in U.S. zones, then transshipped abroad
- Foreign goods processed or assembled in U.S. zones with some domestic materials and parts, then re-exported
- Goods produced wholly of foreign content in U.S. zones and then exported
- Goods produced from a combination of domestic and foreign materials and components in U.S. zones and then exported
- Domestic goods moved into a U.S. zone to achieve export status prior to their actual exportation[15]

An example of how an FTZ can be used occurs at a subzone in Texas, where a Coastal Corp. subsidiary refines imported oil. If the subsidiary exports the refined oil products, it pays no duty at all. If it sells the products domestically, it saves over $250,000 a year in interest on duties postponed until the products leave the zone.[16]

Smith Corona established an FTZ in order to import parts and components into the United States duty-free for its typewriter-manufacturing facilities. The U.S. Customs code provides that duties apply to parts but not to a final product.[17] Therefore Smith Corona's imported parts and components were subject to duty, but the imported finished typewriters of its major competitors in the United States—Brother, Panasonic, and others—were not.[18] Since establishing the FTZ, Smith Corona imports parts and components into the zone and assembles them into typewriters there. The finished typewriters then are officially imported into the United States duty-free.

Coordination of Research and Development
There is a growing trend among MNEs, both U.S.-based and non–U.S.-based, to engage in foreign-based R&D. The conditions leading to this increase in foreign R&D are as follows:

Increased global coordination of R&D is partly due to improved information and communications technologies.

- Improved information and communications technologies have facilitated international coordination and integration, thus creating a favorable environment for multinational R&D.
- Improved social, economic, and technological resources in many newly developed and developing countries have provided the necessary infrastructure for the establishment of R&D facilities.
- Increased uniformity in international patenting has made it easier for MNEs to protect inventions that result from foreign R&D.

An important countervailing force is the difference in the size of manufacturing operations abroad.

C O U N T E R V A I L I N G

F O R C E S

An issue touched on only indirectly in this chapter is company size. In discussing outsourcing by Japanese manufacturers, we noted that many Japanese suppliers are small. However, some suppliers—especially U.S. suppliers—have become large MNEs in their own right and are establishing components factories worldwide to supply their customers.

Another dimension of scale involves the size of manufacturing operations abroad. When an MNE employs a technology-driven product strategy, the key manufacturing strategy is flexibility to change products and processes quickly to take advantage of market trends. In this case, manufacturing facilities tend to start out small and grow as markets grow. With a marketing-intensive product strategy, manufacturing facilities tend to be located in or near local markets in order to respond more quickly to market needs. The size of the manufacturing facility is directly correlated to the size of the market and the degree to which the MNE uses the facility to serve markets nearby.

With a low-cost product strategy, for which the manufacturing strategy is to achieve economies of scale, the MNE tends to establish manufacturing facilities on a regional basis or in large markets (such as the United States) and to use large-scale operations. When the low-cost strategy is accomplished by using low-cost labor, MNEs are usually manufacturing mature products and components, so the scale is not very large. Thus you can see that product strategy can have an important impact on the location and size of manufacturing facilities.

Company and country strategies often conflict in the area of employment.

Company and country strategies often conflict in the area of employment. If the company uses a single-plant strategy with the home country as the plant's location, it will generate jobs in compatibility with the desires of the home-country government. However, if the company adopts a multidomestic or regional manufacturing strategy, then jobs will be lost in the home-country market. In addition, if it adopts a single-plant strategy that is compatible with a low-cost product strategy, then the plant may well be located in a country with low labor costs. In this case, the company's strategy will not be consistent with the home country's, and unemployment may ensue. The problem is that the company must adopt whatever manufacturing strategy is consistent with its product strategy, and it cannot make full employment in the home country a strategic objective. If it does, it runs the risk of going out of business altogether.

Most host countries prefer to have R&D facilities located locally rather than have all R&D take place abroad.

Another important issue relates to the centralization or decentralization of R&D, discussed earlier in this chapter. There are clear strategic differences between MNEs and countries concerning the location of R&D facilities. Although MNEs can benefit from the decentralization of such facilities, individual countries will always argue for local R&D facilities in order to develop products for global markets and to attract and retain a domestic scientific community. There also are tax implications of R&D location. For example, the IRS requires U.S. companies to allocate R&D expenditures to revenues from foreign sources. However, foreign governments are not inclined to allow the reallocation of U.S.-based expenses to revenues generated in their countries. This sets up a key conflict between governments.

LOOKING TO THE FUTURE In establishing manufacturing facilities to serve worldwide markets, MNEs started with large home-market plants and exported to foreign markets. As the importance of those markets increased, companies needed to establish manufacturing facilities abroad, almost in a multidomestic approach. Now, however, they are finding that they need much stronger control over manufacturing operations worldwide in order to take advantage of market differences and to drive down costs.

Improvements in communications technology will continue to facilitate the flow of information worldwide. This will be especially helpful in the design of new products. As the design time is cut down, MNEs will be able to get new products to market much more quickly.

An important trend is the movement of MNEs away from vertical integration and toward outsourcing as a way to cut costs. This movement will continue to accelerate, and MNEs will be forced to develop closer relationships with suppliers in order to increase quality and reduce costs.

Summary

- **Procedural considerations in importing refer to the rules and regulations of a country's customs agency.**

- **Strategic issues in importing refer to the long-term reasons why a company would rather buy products from foreign instead of domestic sources.**

- **FTZs are the sites of an intermediary step between the importation and assembly of parts and components and their eventual exportation to foreign markets or importation into the domestic market.**

- **A global production strategy involves the storage and movement of goods from the source of raw materials to the production of components, the assembly of goods, and finally the distribution to consumers.**

- **The MNE differs from the domestic company in that it may move goods in intermediate or final form from country to country rather than only within a particular country.**

- **For each particular market an MNE serves, global sourcing means that companies need to determine where parts and components will be manufactured and where the final products will be assembled.**

- **Competitive strategies are based on four priorities: efficiency/cost, dependability, quality, and flexibility.**

in its facilities in Korea, Malaysia, and Singapore. In addition, the company has contractual relationships with unaffiliated parties that conduct manufacturing and assembly operations on a contract-labor basis for it in China. The principal competitive factors in the markets that AM serves are price, technological sophistication, product performance and quality, product availability, and responsiveness to customers.

AMM manufactures a very technical product—read/write heads for hard-disk drives for the microcomputer market. The Malaysian workforce seems to be well suited to the manufacture of this type of product, which is why many U.S. high-tech companies have relocated to Malaysia.

AMM uses the JIT inventory management strategy that it learned from its U.S. counterpart. Although the strategy isn't implemented perfectly, it's getting there. Interestingly, in Malaysia only a few U.S. plants, and none of the Japanese plants, have implemented JIT, primarily because (according to the Japanese) they have had difficulty with organizing effective work teams. The United States is the second-largest investor in Malaysia, following Japan. The Japanese plants, and most of the other plants, tend to be based on Material Requirements Planning (MRP).

AMM has organized its production area into numerous production "lines" in an attempt to implement the lessons learned from management's experience at Motorola. These lines are a series of tables laid out in the sequence of the production process. They use table-space-defined KANBANs, where each KANBAN takes the form of a tape-defined location on the table rather than a card or a box. However, Ganesan was concerned:

> We also need to get our production lines balanced. There are large differences between capacity and workload on many of our lines. These differences are causing workload inefficiency, bottlenecks, and employee frustration. Some employees feel they are getting overworked when compared with their counterparts. I'm not sure which aspect is more important, the line balancing or the teaming.

AMM needs to integrate into the international marketplace. Specifically, the company is trying to make its mark in Europe. However, the European market has developed the ISO 9000 quality standards for all international suppliers. To effectively serve this marketplace, AMM needs to be ISO-certified. Of the several classifications within this certification, AMM is specifically focusing on ISO 9002 certification, which focuses on manufacturers.

AMM also is forward-looking in that it sees ISO-certification as only a stepping stone toward a total continuous quality improvement program. Management is hoping to implement TQM and the "Total Quality Control Philosophy" of the AM corporate office, based on TQM principles. For ISO certification, or even more importantly, for TQM to function effectively, teaming is critical.

Senior Quality Assurance Engineer Ridzwan Raja said, "We need to get the teaming working first. It's the teams that come up with the ideas that help in the line-balancing process. A large part of the problem behind our ineffective teaming is the cross-cultural mixture of employees within our factory." Like Ganesan, Raja is Malaysian born and a

Malaysian citizen, although of Indian descent. However, unlike Ganesan, who has maintained his Hindu faith, Ridzwan Raja recently converted from the Hindu to the Muslim faith and has changed his name to Raja Mohan, although his business cards still reflect his Hindi name.

AMM's workforce, like that of most Malaysian companies, was composed of about 60 percent Malays, 30 percent Chinese, and 10 percent Indians, all of which are Malaysian-born and Malaysian citizens (see Map 18.2). However, each group has its own culture and religion, and outside the workplace, each tends to be culturally isolated. AMM also had a few expatriates, such as Ken Lanshe, a quality manager, who was from corporate head-quarters in the United States.

Raja went on to explain:

What happens is that we will organize a team of employees based on the project we want the team to accomplish, selecting which employees would be the most appropriate. Then, when the team meets together, only that employee with the highest status will speak. Status can be defined by number of years on the job, job position, or even age. Somehow, status is nonverbally defined. Everyone just seems to know which individual has the most status. Out of respect for that individual, all the remaining members of the team will subordinate their comments to the ranking team member. No one will offer anything creative or innovative except this one individual.

Sri Shan, another quality manager, added:

Even if we carefully organize our team so that all the members of the team have relatively equal status, thereby allowing everyone to comment freely, we still have problems, isn't it. What happens is that no one is willing to criticize anyone else. They only pat each other on the back, la. How can we get them to improve if they are afraid to comment, la?

(The words "isn't it" and "la" are used in Malaysia to add emphasis, like the Canadian "aey.")

In Malaysia, it is considered bad taste to demean someone's "face." People should always try to respect and positively influence someone else's "face." This becomes especially important when mixing cultures. Cross-cultural understanding is often very weak, and employees look at each other as strangers, to some extent, not wanting to put themselves or their cultures in a bad light. The presence of the different ethnic groups mentioned above has created tensions in Malaysian society. Malays make up the most powerful group in Malaysian politics, but the Chinese control much of the nation's economy. Social, economic, and political differences between the Chinese and Malays have led to friction and—sometimes—violence between members of the two groups. After violent clashes in the early 1980s, those from different cultures, especially the Malay Bumi-Putras ("People of the Land" who are Muslims) and the Chinese, tend to "walk on eggs" when interacting with each other. No one wants the issues to pop out into the open again; they prefer to keep them "hidden."

The problem is that the company can't wait until it has the teams working in order to balance the production process. The balancing is an operations research process and requires the use of mathematical models. Once the line has been balanced as much as possible, then the team can start improving the process flow by eliminating the waste, which is part of the production process. The line balancing and the team building should go on simultaneously, since one involves the development of the employees and the other can be worked on by the operations research group.

From the standpoint of multi-ethnic work groupings, it is important to teach the employees to criticize the function, not the person. It also is important for members of the work group to become socially comfortable with each other. They need to be given opportunities to spend time together outside the work setting. Often the best ideas and suggestions occur during these informal settings. A social strategy of this nature takes longer to implement but has worked effectively in other U.S.-based, team-oriented companies functioning in Malaysia.

Another teaming strategy that has been effective is defining a set of goals that can be used as a measurement tool and a motivation tool for the teams. Often, the ineffectiveness of teams derives from their lack of understanding of what is needed and how to satisfy this need. No one wants to volunteer a suggestion or idea that may turn out to be off the mark.

"Training and cross training of team members would help a lot in the implementation of these suggestions," commented Lanshe. "If employees understand each other's job functions better, they would be more willing to offer suggestions and less concerned about making themselves look bad."

A consultant to AMM suggested the following:

Malaysians need to start looking at the benefits of their cultural mix. This mix offers them the opportunity to look at problems through several different perspectives. The synergy of this type of mix can make Malaysian industry leading-edge. Back in my home of the United States, we have teaming problems too, but nothing compared to the complexity that you are experiencing. However, in spite of its complexity the Malaysian culture offers enormous synergistic benefits, if you can only learn to cash in on them.

Ganesan wrapped up by saying, "We need to achieve the Total Quality Control Philosophy as stated by our corporate office. We need to do this through JIT, ISO certification, and TQM, all of which require effective teaming. We also need to work towards a greatly improved balance in our production process."

Questions
1. Describe AM's product and manufacturing strategies.
2. Discuss the cultural dimensions affecting AMM and their impact on AMM's ability to achieve its objectives in terms of quality and production scheduling.
3. How can culture influence manufacturing strategy and international manufacturing configurations?
4. Why do you think AM has a manufacturing facility in Malaysia? What advantages might Malaysia offer over another offshore site? Given the unique challenges AMM faces, under what conditions should AM move these facilities elsewhere?

Chapter Notes

1. Roy Furchgott, "Dateline: Towson, Md.," *The Houston Chronicle,* February 7, 1993; several issues of Black & Decker's *Annual Report;* Bill Saporito, "Black & Decker's Gamble on 'Globalization,' " *Fortune,* May 14, 1984, p. 40+; Christopher S. Eklund, "How Black & Decker Got Back in the Black," *Business Week,* July 13, 1987, pp. 86–90; "How Black & Decker Forged a Winning Brand Transfer Strategy," *Business International,* July 20, 1987, pp. 225–227; Mary Lu Carnevale, "Black & Decker Goes to Full-Court Press," *The Wall Street Journal,* November 10, 1988, p. A8; and Stuart Flack, "All Leverage Is Not Created Equal," *Forbes,* March 19, 1990, p. 39.

2. Michael E. Porter, ed., *Competition in Global Industries* (Boston: Harvard Business School Press, 1986).

3. Masaaki Kotabe and Glen S. Omura, "Sourcing Strategies of European and Japanese Multinationals: A Comparison," *Journal of International Business Studies,* Spring 1989, pp. 120-122.

4. S. C. Wheelwright, "Reflecting Corporate Strategy in Manufacturing Decisions," *Business Horizons,* Vol. 21, February 1978; S. C. Wheelwright, "Manufacturing Strategy: Defining the Missing Link, *Strategic Management Journal,* Vol. 5, 1984, pp. 77–91; and Frank DuBois, Brian Toyne, and Michael D. Oliff, "International Manufacturing Strategies of U.S. Multinationals: A Conceptual Framework Based on a Four-Industry Study," *Journal of International Business Studies,* Vol. 24, No. 2, Second Quarter 1993, pp. 313–314,

5. Robert Stobaugh and Piero Telesio, "Match Manufacturing Policies and Product Strategy," in *Transnational Management,* Christopher A. Bartlett and Sumantra Ghoshal, eds. (Homewood, Ill.: Richard D. Irwin, 1992), pp. 760–768.

6. Michael E. McGrath and Richard W. Hoole, "Manufacturing's New Economies of Scale," *Harvard Business Review,* May–June 1992, p. 94.

7. Stobaugh and Telesio, op. cit., p. 765.

8. Stobaugh and Telesio, op. cit., pp. 767–768.

9. Paul M. Swamidass, "A Comparison of the Plant Location Strategies of Foreign and Domestic Manufacturers in the U.S.," *Journal of International Business Studies,* Second Quarter 1990, p. 302.

10. Sonia Nazario, "Boom and Despair," *The Wall Street Journal,* September 22, 1989, p. R26.

11. Ibid.

12. David D. Weiss, "Foreign Trade Zones: Growth Amid Controversy," *Chicago Fed Letter,* Number 48, August 1991, pp. 1–2.

13. Peter Tirschwell, "Subzones: Vehicle of Choice?" *Journal of Commerce and Commercial,* August 2, 1993.

14. "World Becomes Smaller as Japan, Central Europe Catch Zone Fever," *The Journal of Commerce and Commercial,* October 1991, p. 6B.

15. John J. DaPonte, Jr., "Foreign-Trade Zones and Exports," *American Export Bulletin,* April 1978.

16. Ken Slocum, "Foreign-Trade Zones Aid Many Companies But Stir Up Criticism," *The Wall Street Journal,* September 30, 1987, p. 1.

17. Ibid.

18. Peter Trischwell, "Subzones: Vehicle of Choice?" *Journal of Commerce and Commercial,* May 15, 1992, p. 12B.

19. Joseph L.C. Cheng, "The Management of Multinational R&D: A Neglected Topic in International Business Research," *Journal of International Business Studies,* Volume 24, Number 1, First Quarter 1993, p. 4.

20. Karen Lowry Miller, Larry Armstrong, and David Woodruff, "A Car Is Born," *Business Week,* September 13, 1993, p 67.

21. Julie Edelson Halpert, "One Car, Worldwide, with Strings Pulled from Michigan," *New York Times,* August 29, 1993, p. F7.

22. G. H. Manoochehri, "Crucial Requirements for Effective Application of Just-in-Time System," unpublished paper, California State University, Fullerton, 1984.

23. Robert H. Hayes, Steven C. Wheelwright, and Kim B. Clark, *Dynamic Manufacturing* (New York: Free Press, 1988), p. 17.

24. Gerhard Plenert, "TQM—Clearing Away the Confusion to Find Out What's Compatible and What's Not," *PORG Newsletter,* Second Quarter, 1991 (Provo, UT: BYU Productivity and Quality Research Group).

25. Robert S. Kaplan, "Measuring Manufacturing Performance: A New Challenge for Managerial Accounting Research," *The Accounting Review,* Vol. 58, No. 4 (October 1983), pp. 690–691.

26. Jonathan B. Levine, "Want EC Business? You Have Two Choices," *Business Week,* October 19, 1992, p. 58.

27. Mary Saunders, "U.S. Firms Doing Business in EC Have Options in Registering for ISO 9000 Quality Standards," *Business America,* June 14, 1993, p. 7.

28. Paul M. Swamidass and Masaaki Kotabe, "Component Sourcing Strategies of Multinationals: An Empirical Study of European and Japanese Multinationals," *Journal of International Business Studies,* Volume 24, Number 1, First Quarter 1993, p. 84.

29. Mark L. Fagan, "A Guide to Global Sourcing," *The Journal of Business Strategy,* March–April 1991, p. 21.

30. Ibid., p. 22.

31. Alan S. Blinder, "A Japanese Buddy System That Could Benefit U.S. Business," *Business Week,* October 14, 1991, p. 32.

32. Ravi Venkatesan, "Strategic Sourcing: To Make or Not To Make," *Harvard Business Review,* November–December 1991, p. 98.

33. Ibid., pp. 101–102.

34. John McMillan, "Managing Suppliers: Incentive Systems in Japanese and U.S Industry," *California Management Review,* Summer 1990, p. 38.

35. Russell Johnston and Paul R. Lawrence, "Beyond Vertical Integration—The Rise of the Value-Adding Partnership," *Harvard Business Review,* July–August 1988, p. 98.

36. Miller, Armstrong, and Woodruff, op. cit., p. 68.

37. Johnston and Lawrence, op. cit., p. 94.

38. Joseph B. White, "Japanese Auto Makers Help Parts Suppliers Become More Efficient," *Wall Street Journal,* September 10, 1991, p. 1.

39. Ibid., p. 10.

40. Zachary Schiller, David Woodruff, Kevin Kelly, and Michael Schroeder, "GM Tightens the Screws," *Business Week,* June 22, 1992, p. 30.

41. Tom L. Beauchamp and Norman E. Bowie, *Ethical Theory and Business,* 4th Edition (Englewood Cliffs, N.J.: Prentice-Hall), pp. 21–22.

42. This case was created by Professor Gerhard Plenert of Brigham Young University based on his experiences in Malaysia in 1992–93; information also was found in Applied Magnetics' 1992 *Annual Report* and 1993 *Prospectus.*

Chapter 19

Multinational Accounting
and Tax Functions

Even between parents and children,
money matters make strangers.

—Japanese Proverb

Objectives

- To examine the major factors influencing the development of accounting practices in different countries and the worldwide harmonization of accounting principles

- To explain how companies account for foreign-currency transactions and translate foreign-currency financial statements

- To describe the impact of accounting methods on the evaluation of foreign operations

- To investigate the U.S. taxation of foreign-source income

- To examine some of the major non-U.S. tax practices and to show how international tax treaties can alleviate some of the impact of double taxation

Case
The Coca-Cola Company[1]

Between 1886, when Atlanta pharmacist J. S. Pemberton mixed up his first batch of Coca-Cola, and 1992, Coca-Cola's worldwide revenues increased from only $50 to more than $13 billion. Today, Coca-Cola operates two different product divisions: soft drinks (split into soft drinks U.S. and soft drinks international) and foods (see Fig. 19.1). In this sense, Coca-Cola is far less diversified than PepsiCo, its major competitor in the soft-drink industry, which has three product divisions: beverages, restaurants (KFC, Taco Bell, and Pizza Hut), and snack foods. However, according to its 1992 *Annual Report,* Coca-Cola is the world's largest manufacturer, marketer, and distributor of soft-drink concentrates and syrups, both of which it sells to bottling and canning operations. It also manufactures fountain/post-mix soft-drink syrups, which it sells to fountain wholesalers and some fountain retailers. Further, Coca-Cola has substantial equity investments in numerous soft-drink bottling and canning operations, and it owns and operates certain bottling and canning operations outside the United States. In its foods division, Coca-Cola processes and markets citrus and other juice and juice-drink products, primarily orange juice. It is the world's largest marketer of packaged citrus products.

The company averages a 45-percent worldwide market share in flavored carbonated soft drinks: Its market share is 41 percent in the United States and 47 percent internationally. In terms of total sales, Coca-Cola has four of the world's top five carbonated soft drinks: Coca-Cola and Coca-Cola Classic (number 1), Diet Coca-Cola and Coca-Cola Light (number 3), Fanta (number 4), and Sprite (number 5). Diet Coke is called Coke Light in many countries because the word "diet" has a connotation of illness in Germany and Italy, as noted in Chapter 17. Coca-Cola is the worldwide market leader in the three largest carbonated soft-drink segments: cola (61 percent of the world market), orange (32 percent), and lemon-lime (36 percent).

As Fig. 19.2 shows, Coca-Cola's domestic revenues and profits are only 33.3 percent and 19.4 percent of total revenues and profits, respectively. Although the United States is its largest market in terms of revenues, the EU is a close second. As a result of strong price competition in the United States, however, both the EU and the Pacific and Canadian regions are more profitable.

Coca-Cola truly operates worldwide. The Coca-Cola brand is sold in more than 195 countries, Diet Coke/Coke Light in 117 countries, Fanta in 164 countries, and Sprite in 164

Figure 19.1
Coca-Cola's Revenues and Profits by Product Division

Coca-Cola's major product divisions are soft drinks and foods. International sales of soft drinks provide 65.6 percent of the company's revenues and 80.2 percent of its profits.

REVENUES

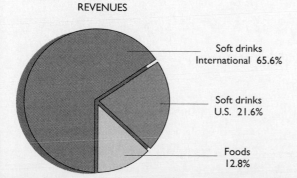

Soft drinks
International 65.6%

Soft drinks
U.S. 21.6%

Foods
12.8%

PROFITS

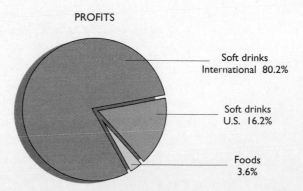

Soft drinks
International 80.2%

Soft drinks
U.S. 16.2%

Foods
3.6%

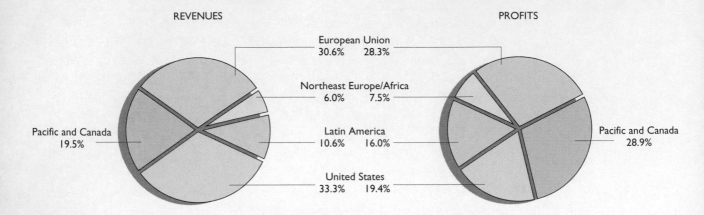

REVENUES   PROFITS

European Union
30.6%   28.3%

Northeast Europe/Africa
6.0%   7.5%

Pacific and Canada
19.5%

Latin America
10.6%   16.0%

Pacific and Canada
28.9%

United States
33.3%   19.4%

**Figure 19.2
Coca-Cola's Revenues
and Profits by
Geographical Area**
Coca-Cola generates 66.7
percent of its revenues and
80.6 percent of its profits
outside the United States.
The EU is the largest foreign market in terms of
revenues but ranks second
to the Pacific and Canadian
market in terms of profits.

countries. The company continues to expand internationally because of market growth and potential. Although the average annual growth rate of unit case volume for Coca-Cola in the five years ending in 1992 was only 3 percent in the United States, it was 7 percent internation-ally, although growth slowed to only 4 percent internationally in 1992. The United States leads the world with average per capita consumption of 296 cases of Coca-Cola's carbonated soft drinks (each case equals twenty-four 8-ounce drinks). The international average is only 40 cases; in China, for example, per capita consumption is only 1 case per year. Commenting on the value of the international market as the growth area of the future, company CEO Robert Goizueta noted, "We have really just begun reaching out to the 95 percent of the world's population that lives outside the United States. Today our top sixteen markets account for 80 percent of our volume, and those markets cover only 20 percent of the world's population."

Given its international growth, foreign exchange is a major issue for Coca-Cola. Balance sheets and income statements for all of the countries in which it operates must be translat-ed from the foreign currencies into U.S. dollars so that they can be combined with Coca-Cola's domestic dollar results.

In the mid-1980s, Coca-Cola's management saw that its international operations were increasing significantly and that the nature of its business had changed since its last account-ing manual had been written. It needed a comprehensive, easy-reference accounting manu-al to help it maintain strong financial controls over its operations. Management felt that a better accounting manual would help the company acquire reliable information about units all over the world in order to help local subsidiaries operate at peak efficiency and gener-ate corporate-wide reports consistently.

In addition, after Goizueta became CEO, he became concerned about the poor financial information he was getting. He also noticed that the company, in effect, was going out of business because it was investing equity capital at 16 percent but earning only 8–10 percent on some of its investments. He decided to evaluate the company's performance by type of business worldwide. Across the top of his financial chart, he identified Coca-Cola's lines of business. Down the side, he listed key financial measures, such as margins, cash-flow relia-bility, capital requirements, etc. But to make the concept work, Goizueta needed reliable information from operations worldwide.

A team consisting of a project manager and three senior accountants worked for eight months to develop an entirely new accounting manual. A universal chart of accounts was set up so that each account in the balance sheet and income statement would be shown consistently by Coca-Cola subsidiaries around the world. Based on the chart of accounts, the team wrote definitions of each account and developed policies and procedures governing the use of each and the flow of information into the financial statements. A separate section was written describing how to translate financial statements from local currencies into U.S. dollars. Drafts of the report were given to audit, legal, and tax managers for their comments, and other field accounting managers were asked for their input before a final draft was completed.

Introduction

The accountant is essential in providing information to financial decision makers.

Managers cannot make good decisions without the availability of adequate and timely information regarding accounting and taxation. Although accounting and information systems specialists provide the information, all managers need to understand which data are needed and the problems specialists face in gathering that data from around the world. The accounting and finance functions of any MNE such as Coca-Cola are very closely related. Each relies on the other in fulfilling its own responsibilities. The financial manager of any company, whether domestic or international, is responsible for procuring and managing the company's financial resources. That manager relies on the accountant to provide the information necessary to manage financial resources.

The actual and potential flow of assets across national boundaries complicates the finance and accounting functions. The MNE must learn to cope with differing inflation rates, exchange rate changes, currency controls, expropriation risks, customs duties, levels of sophistication, and local requirements.

The controller of an international company must be concerned about different currencies and accounting systems.

A company's accounting or controllership function is responsible for collecting and analyzing data for internal and external users. As noted in Chapter 16, foreign managers and subsidiaries are usually evaluated based on data provided by the controller's office. Reports must be generated for internal consideration, local governmental needs, creditors, employees, stockholders, and prospective investors. The controller must be concerned about the impact of many different currencies and inflation rates on the statements as well as being familiar with different countries' accounting systems.

Factors Influencing the Development of Accounting Around the World

Both the form and the substance of financial statements are different in different countries.

One problem that an MNE such as Coca-Cola faces is that accounting standards and practices vary around the world; for example, financial statements in France do not look the same as those in the United States. Some observers argue that this is a minor matter, a problem of form rather than substance. In fact, however, the substance also differs, in that assets are measured differently and income is determined differently in different countries.

A good example of this situation involves SmithKline Beecham plc, a British company that is the product of a merger between a U.S. company (SmithKline) and a British company (Beecham). When the new merged company tried to raise funds in the United States, it had to disclose its income according to both British and U.S. accounting standards and also to reconcile the difference. Because of differences in accounting policies, SmithKline Beecham reported a net income of £130 million according to British standards but a net income of only £87 million according to U.S. standards. There were several reasons for the difference; the major one was the different ways in which British and U.S. companies are allowed to account for mergers.[2]

These variations put the MNE in a difficult position because it needs to prepare and understand reports generated according to the local accounting standards as well as prepare financial statements consistent with **generally accepted accounting principles (GAAP)** in the home country in order to provide information for home-country users of financial statements. Each country develops its own GAAP, which are the accounting standards recognized by the profession as being required in the preparation of financial statements for external users. Each country's GAAP is a function of the factors discussed in the following sections. The more the GAAP differs from country to country, the more costly and difficult it is for an MNE to generate financial statements.

Accounting Objectives

Accounting is basically a process of identifying, recording, and interpreting economic events, and its goals and purposes should be clearly stated in the objectives of any accounting system. According to the Financial Accounting Standards Board (FASB), the private-sector body that establishes accounting standards in the United States, financial reporting should provide information useful in the following areas:

- Investment and credit decisions
- Assessment of cash-flow prospects
- Evaluation of enterprise resources, claims to those resources, and changes in them[3]

The users of this data identified by the board are primarily investors and creditors, although other users might be considered important. The **International Accounting Standards Committee (IASC),** a standard-setting organization composed of professional accounting organizations from over eighty countries, includes employees as well as investors and creditors as critical users. Also named as users of this information are suppliers, customers, regulatory and taxing authorities, and many others.

Generally accepted accounting principles are those established in each country that must be following by companies in generating their financial statements.

The FASB sets accounting standards in the United States.

The IASC is an international private-sector organization that sets accounting standards.

Critical users of information are creditors, investors, and employees. Additional users are suppliers, customers, and regulatory and tax authorities.

Equity markets are an important source of influence on accounting in the United States and the United Kingdom. Banks are more influential in Germany and Switzerland, and taxation is a major influence in Japan and France.

Former colonial relationships influence accounting.

Figure 19.3
Environmental Influences on Accounting Practices
The importance of any of these environmental influences on accounting practices varies by country.

Source: Lee H. Radebaugh, "Environmental Factors Influencing the Development of Accounting Objectives, Standards, and Practices—The Peruvian Case," *The International Journal of Accounting,* Fall 1975, p. 41.

Although the question of whether there should be a uniform set of accounting standards and practices for all classes of users worldwide, or even for one class of users, has been discussed widely, no consensus has been reached. To understand the different accounting principles and how they affect an MNE's operations, you must be aware of some of the forces leading to the development of accounting practices internationally (see Fig. 19.3). Although all the factors shown in the figure are important, they vary in importance by country. For example, investors are an important source of influence in the United States and the United Kingdom, but creditors—primarily banks—are more important in Germany and Switzerland. Also, taxation is a major source of influence on accounting standards and practices in Japan and France, but it is less important in the United States. Certain international factors also are important, such as former colonial influence and foreign investment. For example, most former members of the British Commonwealth have an accounting system similar to the United Kingdom's; former French colonies use the French model, and so forth.

Cultural Differences

A major source of influence on accounting standards and practices is culture. Of special interest to international investors are the differences in measurement and disclosure practices among countries. Measurement refers to such issues as how to

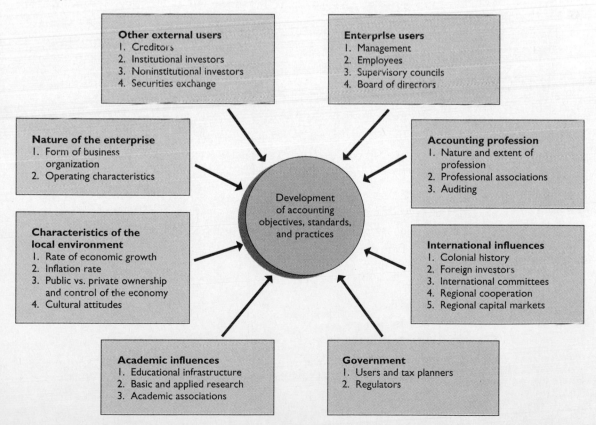

Culture influences measurement and disclosure practices. Measurement—how to value assets Disclosure—the presentation of information and discussion of results

Secrecy and transparency refer to the degree to which corporations disclose information to the public.

Optimism and conservatism refer to the degree of caution companies display in valuing assets and recognizing income.

British companies are very optimistic in recognizing income, and U.S. companies are slightly less optimistic. Japanese companies are even less optimistic than U.S. ones.

value assets, including inventory and fixed assets. Disclosure refers to the presentation of information and discussion of results in documents that are prepared for external users of financial data, such as the annual report.

Figure 19.4 depicts the possible locations of the accounting practices of various groupings of countries in a matrix of the cultural values of secrecy/transparency and optimism/conservatism. With respect to accounting, secrecy and transparency refer to the degree to which companies disclose information to the public. Countries such as Germany, Switzerland, and Japan tend to have less disclosure (illustrating the cultural value of secrecy) than do the United States and the United Kingdom—Anglo-Saxon countries—which are more transparent or open with respect to disclosure. This is illustrated by the more extensive footnotes in reports of the Anglo-Saxon countries than is the case elsewhere.

Optimism and conservatism (in an accounting, not a political, sense) refer to the degree of caution companies exhibit in valuing assets and recognizing income—an illustration of the measurement issues mentioned above. More conservative countries from an accounting point of view tend to understate assets and income, whereas optimistic countries tend to be more liberal in their recognition of income. The problem with comparing this cultural value is that accounting is inherently conservative, so we are really looking at the degree of conservatism.

For example, German companies are funded primarily by banks, and banks are concerned with liquidity. Therefore German companies tend to be very conservative in recording profits—which keeps them from paying taxes and declaring dividends—while piling up cash reserves that can be used to service their bank debt. In contrast, U.S. companies want to show optimistic earnings in order to attract in-

Figure 19.4
Cultural Differences in Measurement and Disclosure for Accounting Systems
Anglo-Saxon countries (such as the United Kingdom and the United States) have accounting systems that tend to be more transparent and optimistic. Systems in Germanic countries, in contrast, tend to be secretive and conservative.

Source: Lee H. Radebaugh and Sidney J. Gray, *International Accounting and Multinational Enterprises*, 3rd ed. (New York: John Wiley & Sons, 1993), p. 76.

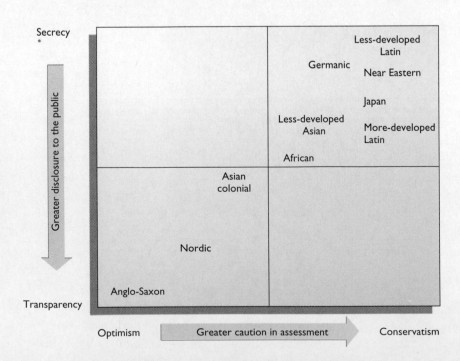

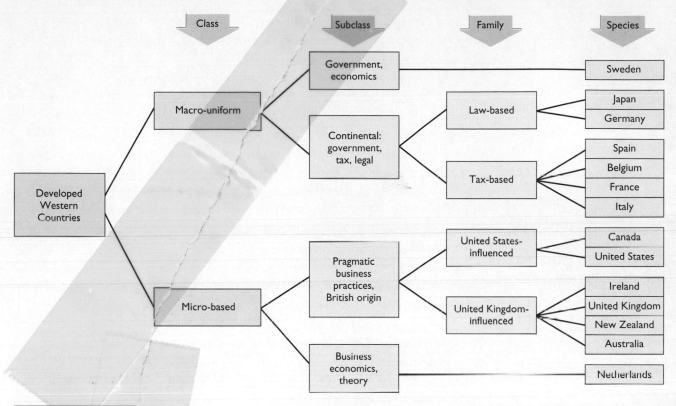

**Figure 19.5
Hypothetical
Classification of
Accounting Systems of
Developed Western
Countries**
Accounting systems can be
classified as macro-uniform
or micro-based depending
on how important govern-
mental influence is.

Source: From C. W. Nobes, "A
Judgmental International Classification of Financial Reporting
Practices," *Journal of Business Finance and Accounting,* Spring 1983,
p. 7. Reprinted with permission.

Macro-uniform accounting
systems are shaped more by
governmental influence,
whereas micro-based sys-
tems rely on pragmatic business practice.

vestors. Generally, British companies tend to be more optimistic in earnings recognition than U.S. companies, but U.S. companies are significantly more optimistic
than other European companies and Japanese ones. In a very subjective cross
national comparison of earnings that sets the index of earnings of U.S. companies
equal to 100, British earnings are at an index level of 125, German earnings are at a
level of 87, and Japanese earnings are at 66.[4] Thus there are significant worldwide
differences in accounting standards and practices that affect earnings measures.

Classification of Accounting Systems

Although accounting standards and practices differ significantly worldwide, systems
used in various countries can be grouped according to common characteristics. Figure 19.5 illustrates one approach to classifying accounting systems. This scheme
does not attempt to classify all countries but simply illustrates the concept using
several developed Western countries.

In the figure, accounting systems are initially divided into macro-uniform and
micro-based systems. Macro-uniform systems are shaped more by governmental
influence than are micro-based systems. Except for Sweden's system, macro-
uniform systems are influenced by tax law or just a strong legal system. These systems also tend to be more conservative and secretive about disclosure. Micro-based
systems, except for that of the Netherlands, include features that support pragmatic
business practice and have evolved from the British system. The U.S. system is clos-

er to the macro-uniform systems, however, because of the strong influence of the Securities and Exchange Commission (SEC), a federal government agency that regulates securities offerings within the United States.

The bottom line is that MNEs need to adjust to different accounting systems around the world. Thus the accounting function is made more complex and costly to perform. An MNE's parent company must gather data from far-flung subsidiaries and affiliates and convert those data into a format consistent with the home country's preferred accounting system.

An MNE expected to provide its annual report or at least its financial statements to foreign users has five major alternatives regarding presentation of financial data:

1. Do nothing to aid the user's understanding
2. Prepare convenience translations
3. Prepare convenience statements
4. Restate the data to a limited extent
5. Prepare secondary financial statements[5]

In the first case, the MNE offers its annual report or financial statement in its home-country language and currency and leaves the burden on the foreign user to try to figure out what the data mean. With the second, and most common, approach, the MNE provides a convenience translation into the language of the foreign user. The report or financial statement is still prepared according to home-country GAAP and in the home-country currency, however. With the third approach, the MNE provides the report or financial statement in the foreign user's language and currency. However, the MNE still uses its home country's GAAP rather than that of the foreign user's country. This approach is rarely used. Some companies, such as Philips, the Dutch electronics company, provide year-end exchange rates in their annual reports for several currencies so that users can make their own currency conversions. That way the company does not have to issue financial statements in several different currencies. The fourth and fifth approaches are more common for MNEs that want to list their stock on a foreign stock exchange and so must reconcile their GAAP to that of the foreign country. For example, the SEC requires any foreign corporation that wants to list its securities on a U.S. exchange either to provide a reconciliation to U.S. GAAP in a special filing called form 20-F or to recast its financial statements in terms of U.S. GAAP. Reconciliations are more common than entire recastings. Recasting, however, is typical of Japanese companies that list their stock in the United States.

Harmonization of Differences

Despite the many differences in accounting standards and practices, a number of forces are leading to harmonization:

Companies listing their stock overseas need to determine whether to adjust financial statements for language, currency, and accounting practices.

MNEs can choose from among the following alternatives in providing financial information for foreign investors:
- *Do nothing—make no adjustments to information prepared for domestic users*
- *Prepare convenience translations of the language of the report*
- *Prepare convenience statements, usually by translating the amounts into the foreign currency*
- *Restate financial information to a limited extent*
- *Prepare secondary financial statements*

Major forces leading to harmonization:
• Investor orientation
• Global integration of capital markets
• MNEs' need for foreign capital
• Regional political and economic harmonization
• MNEs' desire to reduce accounting and reporting costs

- A movement to provide information compatible with the needs of investors
- The global integration of capital markets, which means that investors have easier and faster access to investment opportunities around the world and therefore need financial information that is more comparable
- The need of MNEs to raise capital outside of their home-country capital markets while generating as few different financial statements as possible
- Regional political and economic harmonization, such as the efforts of the EU, which affects accounting as well as trade and investment issues
- Pressure from MNEs for more uniform standards to allow greater ease and reduced costs in general reporting in each country and in reporting to be used by investors in the parent company's country

The EU is harmonizing accounting in order to promote the free flow of capital.

Impelled by these developments, some countries and organizations are working to harmonize accounting standards on a regional as well as an international level. Regionally, the most ambitious and potentially most effective efforts are taking place in the EU. The European Commission is empowered to set directives, which are orders to member countries to bring their laws into line with EU requirements within a certain transition period. The initial accounting directives addressed the type and format of financial statements, the measurement bases on which the financial statements should be prepared, the importance of consolidated financial statements, and the requirement that auditors must ensure that the financial statements reflect a true and fair view of the operations of the company being audited.

Other countries in Europe, including those of Eastern Europe and the former Soviet Union, are following the lead of the EU.

The EU's influence is being felt beyond the borders of its members. The EFTA and Eastern European countries are attempting to adopt EU accounting directives in preparation for becoming members. In addition, Eastern European countries and those of the former Soviet Union are moving from centrally planned to market economies, and they need an accounting system that will aid in the transition. The EU directives provide some guidance in this area.

The IASC comprises professional accounting bodies and is attempting to harmonize accounting standards.

The International Accounting Standards Committee (IASC), organized in 1973 by the professional accounting bodies of Mexico and several primarily industrial countries, has worked toward harmonizing accounting standards. IASC member countries are shown on Map 19.1. The organization comprises over a hundred professional accounting organizations representing more than eighty countries and 900,000 accountants. Initially, the IASC wanted to develop standards that would have rapid and broad acceptance; thus it seemed to focus mostly on improved disclosure. More recently, it has been interested in tackling some more substantive issues. It also issued an **exposure draft** on narrowing the options present in the earlier standards in order to have standards that are much more precise. An exposure draft is the first draft of a standard, which is open to comment by parties other than the IASC itself.

The IASC has no legislative mandate like that of the EU, so it must rely on good will for acceptance of its standards. However, a number of countries have used the standards as models for their own legislation. For example, Singapore has success-

Map 19.1 Membership of the International Accounting Standards Committee

The IASC membership consists of 107 accountancy bodies from 81 countries. For example, the members from the United States are the American Institute of Certified Public Accountants, the National Association of State Boards of Accountancy, and the Institute of Management of Accountants, the Institute of Internal Auditors. The IASC board is made up of representatives of accountancy bodies from twelve countries, the Nordic Federation of Public Accountants, and up to four other organizations with an interest in financial reporting.

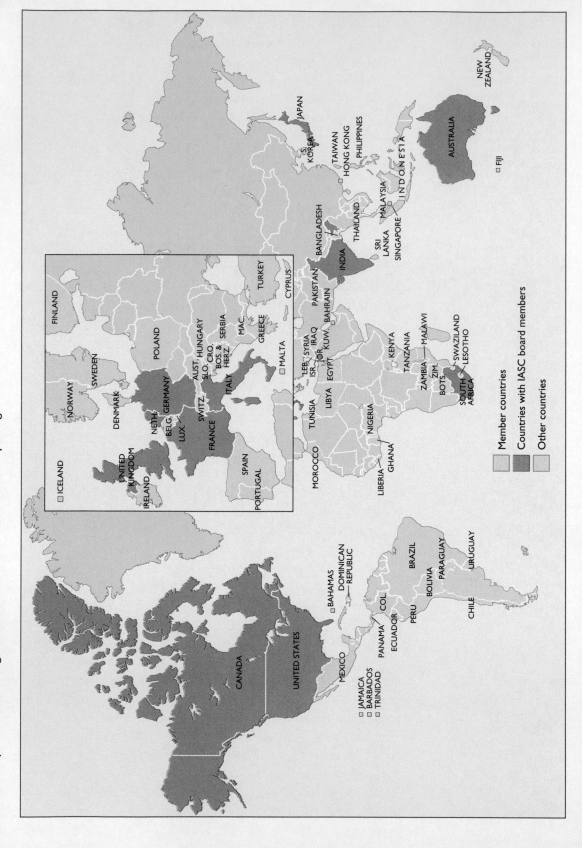

Member countries

Countries with IASC board members

Other countries

fully adopted IASC standards. Other countries have modified the standards as appropriate for their own national settings. In addition, the International Organization of Securities Commissions (IOSCO) is working with the IASC to ensure that the standards being developed can be adopted by companies that want to list securities on a variety of national stock exchanges.

Transactions in Foreign Currencies

A major accounting problem for international business arises from operating in different currencies. In addition to eliminating or minimizing foreign-exchange risk, a company must concern itself with the proper recording and subsequent accounting of assets, liabilities, revenues, and expenses that are measured or denominated in foreign currencies. These transactions can result from the purchase and sale of goods and services as well as the borrowing and lending of foreign currency.

Recording of Transactions

Foreign-currency receivables and payables give rise to gains and losses whenever the exchange rate changes.

Any time an importer is required to pay for equipment or merchandise in a foreign currency, it must trade its own currency for that of the exporter in order to make the payment. Assume Sundance Ski Lodge, a U.S. company, buys skis from a French supplier for 28,000 francs when the exchange rate is 0.1900 dollar per franc. Sundance records the following in its books:

Purchases	5320	
Accounts payable		5320
FF28,000 @ $0.1900		

If Sundance pays immediately, there is no problem. But what happens if the exporter extends thirty-days' credit to Sundance? The original entry would be the same as above, but during the next thirty days, anything could happen. If the rate changed to 0.1800 dollar per franc by the time the payment was due, Sundance would record a final settlement as follows:

Accounts payable	5320	
Gain on foreign exchange		280
Cash		5040

The merchandise stays at the original value of $5320, but there is a difference between the dollar value of the account payable to the exporter ($5320) and the actual number of dollars that the importer must come up with in order to purchase the French francs to pay the exporter ($5040). The difference between the two accounts ($280) is the gain on foreign exchange and is recognized as income.

These gains and losses arising from foreign-currency transactions must be recognized at the end of each accounting period even if the payable (in the case of a purchase) or receivable (in the case of a sale) has not been settled. For most U.S. companies, this adjustment is made monthly. For the example above, assume the end of the month has arrived and Sundance still has not paid the French exporter. The skis continue to be valued at $5320, but the payable has to be updated to the new exchange rate of 0.1800 dollar per franc. The journal entry would be as follows:

```
Accounts payable                    280
    Gain on foreign exchange                280
```

The liability now would be worth $5040. If settlement were to be made at the end of the next month and the exchange rate were to remain the same, the final entry would be as follows:

```
Accounts payable        5040
    Cash                        5040
```

If the U.S. company were an exporter and anticipated receiving foreign currency, the corresponding entries (using the same information as in the example above) would be as follows:

```
Accounts receivable        5320
    Sales                           5320


Cash                        5040
Loss on foreign exchange    280
    Accounts receivable             5320
```

In this case, a loss results because the company received less cash than if it had collected its money immediately.

Correct Procedures for U.S. Companies

The procedures that U.S. companies must follow to account for foreign-currency transactions are found in Financial Accounting Standards Board (FASB) Statement No. 52, "Foreign Currency Translation," which the board adopted in December 1981. Statement No. 52 requires companies to record the initial transaction at the spot-exchange rate in effect on the transaction date and record receivables and payables at subsequent balance-sheet dates at the spot-exchange rate on those dates. Any foreign-exchange gains and losses that arise from carrying receivables or payables during a period in which the exchange rate changes are taken directly to the income statement.[6]

Translation of Foreign-Currency Financial Statements

Even though U.S.-based MNEs receive reports originally developed in a variety of different currencies, they eventually must end up with one set of financial statements in U.S. dollars in order to help management and investors get an aggregate view of worldwide activities in a common currency. The process of restating foreign-currency financial statements into U.S. dollars is known as **translation.** The combination of all of these translated financial statements into one is known as **consolidation.**

Translation in the United States is a two-step process:

1. The foreign-currency financial statements are recast into statements consistent with U.S. GAAP.
2. All foreign-currency amounts are translated into U.S. dollars.

FASB Statement No. 52 describes how companies must translate their foreign-currency financial statements into dollars.

Translation Methods

Statement No. 52 allows either of two methods to be used to translate financial statements: the current-rate method or the temporal method. The method the company chooses depends on the **functional currency** of the foreign operation, which is the currency of the primary economic environment in which that entity operates. For example, one of Coca-Cola's largest operations outside the United States is in Japan. The primary economic environment of the Japanese subsidiary is Japan, and the functional currency is the Japanese yen. The FASB identifies several factors that are examined to determine whether the parent's currency or the foreign operation's currency is used the most, and thus is the functional currency. Among the major factors are cash flows, sales prices, sales market data, expenses, financing, and intercompany transactions. For example, if the cash flows and/or expenses are primarily in the foreign operation's currency, that is the functional currency. If they are in the parent's currency, that is the functional currency.

If the functional currency is that of the local operating environment, the company must use the **current-rate method.** The current-rate method provides that all assets and liabilities are translated at the current exchange rate, which is the spot exchange rate on the balance sheet date. All income statement items are translated at the average exchange rate, and owners' equity is translated at the rate in effect when capital stock was issued and retained earnings were accumulated. For example, Coca-Cola states in its *Annual Report* that it distributes its products in more than 195 countries and uses approximately 42 functional currencies. In Germany and the United Kingdom, the functional currency would be the mark and the

---

Translation is the process of restating foreign-currency statements into U.S. dollars.

Consolidation is the process of combining financial statements of different operations into one statement.

The functional currency is the currency of the primary economic environment in which the entity operates.

The current-rate method is used when the local currency is the functional currency.

The temporal method is used when the parent's reporting currency is the functional currency.

Table 19.1
Balance Sheet, December 31, 1993

	Pounds	Temporal method		Current-rate method	
		Rate	Dollars	Rate	Dollars
Cash	20,000	1.4900	29,800	1.4900	29,800
Accounts receivable	40,000	1.4900	59,600	1.4900	59,600
Inventories	40,000	1.5100	60,400	1.4900	59,600
Fixed assets	100,000	1.8000	180,000	1.4900	149,000
Accumulated dep.	(20,000)	1.8000	(36,000)	1.4900	(29,800)
Total	180,000		293,800		268,200
Accounts payable	30,000	1.4900	44,700	1.4900	44,700
Long-term debt	44,000	1.4900	65,560	1.4900	65,560
Capital stock	60,000	1.8000	108,000	1.8000	108,000
Retained earnings	46,000	*	75,540	*	76,480
Accum. trans. adj.					(26,540)
Total	180,000		293,800		268,200

*Retained earnings is the sum of all income earned in prior years and translated into dollars and this year's income. There is no single exchange rate used to translate retained earnings into dollars.

pound, respectively, because Coca-Cola's primary operating environments would be the local environments. Thus Coca-Cola would use the current-rate method to translate the financial statements of operations in Germany and the United Kingdom from marks and pounds to dollars.

Although the spot rate is used for translation purposes, which spot rate does a company select when multiple exchange rates exist? In general, the exchange rate used to translate foreign-currency financial statements is the rate that must be used for dividends sent back to the parent company. In some countries, this exchange rate also is called the financial rate.

If the functional currency is the parent's currency, the MNE must use the **temporal method.** The temporal method provides that only monetary assets (cash, marketable securities, and receivables) and liabilities are translated at the current exchange rate. Inventory and property, plant, and equipment are translated at the historical rate, that is, the exchange rate in effect when the assets were acquired. In general, net income also is translated at the average exchange rate, but cost of goods sold and depreciation expenses are translated at the appropriate historical exchange rate.

Tables 19.1 and 19.2 show a balance sheet and income statement developed under both approaches in order to compare the differences in translation methodologies. Some of the key assumptions are as follows:

Table 19.2
Income Statement, 1993

	Pounds	Temporal method		Current-rate method	
		Rate	Dollars	Rate	Dollars
Sales	230,000	1.5200	349,600	1.5200	349,600
Expenses					
CGS	(110,000)	1.5150	(166,650)	1.5200	(167,200)
Depreciation	(10,000)	1.8000	(18,000)	1.5200	(15,200)
Other	(80,000)	1.5200	(121,600)	1.5200	(121,600)
Taxes	(6,000)	1.5200	(9,120)	1.5200	(9,120)
	24,000		34,230		36,480
Transl. Gain (Loss)			1,310		
Net income	24,000		35,540		36,480

$1.8000	Historical exchange rate when fixed assets were acquired and capital stock was issued
$1.4900	Current exchange rate on December 31, 1993
$1.5200	Average exchange rate during 1993
$1.5100	Exchange rate during which ending inventory was acquired
$1.5150	Historical exchange rate for cost of goods sold

Also, the beginning balance in retained earnings for both methods is assumed to be $40,000. The British pound was falling in value between the time when the fixed assets were acquired and the end of the year, so the balance sheet reflects a negative accumulated translation adjustment under the current-rate method. This is consistent with the idea that assets were losing value in a weak currency.

Disclosure of Foreign-Exchange Gains and Losses

With the current-rate method, the translation gain or loss is taken to owners' equity.

With the temporal method, the translation gain or loss is taken to income.

A major difference between the two translation methods is the recognition of foreign-exchange gains and losses. Under the current-rate method, the gain or loss is called an accumulated translation adjustment and is taken directly to the balance sheet as a separate line item in owners' equity. Under the temporal method, the gain or loss is taken directly to the income statement and thus affects earnings per share. For example, Coca-Cola Company recorded a negative accumulated translation adjustment balance of $271.211 million on December 31, 1992. This is illustrated in Table 19.3, which is the owners' equity portion of the balance sheet for Coca-Cola for 1992. In its *Annual Report,* Coca-Cola also disclosed that it recognized in "other income" a foreign-exchange gain of $25 million in 1992. Although part of the gain shown in the table came from foreign-currency transactions, a portion of it came from the company's use of the temporal method of translation for some of its operations.

Table 19.3
Coca-Cola's Owners' Equity, December 31

	1992	1991 (restated)
Share-owners' equity		
Common stock, $.25 par value—		
Authorized: 2,800,000,000 shares; Issued: 1,696,202,840 shares in 1992;		
1,687,351,094 shares in 1991	424,051	421,838
Capital surplus	871,349	639,990
Reinvested earnings	8,165,024	7,238,643
Unearned compensation related to outstanding restricted stock	(99,631)	(114,909)
Foreign-currency translation adjustment	(271,211)	(4,909)
	9,089,582	8,180,653
Less treasury stock, at cost (389,431,622 common shares in 1992;		
358,390,928 common shares in 1991)	5,201,194	3,941,706
	3,888,388	4,238,947
	$11,051,934	$10,189,215

Source: Coca-Cola Company 1993 *Annual Report*

Performance Evaluation and Control

Chapter 16 discussed some of the reports MNEs use as part of the control process. Table 19.4 identifies the major financial measures these companies use to evaluate foreign subsidiaries and their managers. Budgets, profits, and return on investment (ROI) dominate the list. It is interesting to note how currency translation can affect the financial ratios. Using the information in Tables 19.1 and 19.2, it is possible to compute the ROI (net income/total assets) in British pounds, U.S. dollars under the current-rate method, and U.S. dollars under the temporal method. The ROI is 13.3 percent in pounds. However, in dollars it is 13.6 percent using the current-rate method but only 8.7 percent using the temporal method. Net income is lower and total assets are higher under the temporal method than under the current-rate method in this example. When evaluating subsidiaries' results, managers need to be sure to compare like measures.

Transfer Prices

A major impediment to performance evaluation is the extensive use of transfer pricing in international operations. A **transfer price** is a price on goods and services sold by one member of a corporate family to another, such as from a parent to its subsidiary in a foreign country. Because the price is between related entities, it is not necessarily an **arm's-length price,** that is, a price between two companies that do not have an ownership interest in each other. The assumption is that an arm's-length price is more likely than a transfer price to accurately reflect the market.

Table 19.4
Measures Used to Evaluate Foreign Subsidiaries and Their Managers

Financial measure	Percentage of the sixty-four MNEs using each measure	
	Foreign subsidiary	Foreign-subsidiary managers
Return-on-investment (ROI)	74	67
Profits	78	66
Budgeted ROI compared to actual ROI	66	64
Budgeted profit compared to actual profit	86	87
Other measures	36	36

Source: From Wagdy M. Abdallah and Donald E. Keller, "Measures Used to Evaluate Foreign Subsidiaries and Foreign Subsidiary Managers," *Management Accounting,* October 1985, p. 27. Reprinted with permission of the Institute of Management Accountants.

Companies establish arbitrary transfer prices primarily because of differences in taxation between countries. For example, if the corporate tax rate is higher in the parent company's country than in the subsidiary's country, the parent will set a low transfer price on products it sells the subsidiary in order to keep profits low in its country and high in the subsidiary's country. The parent also will set a high transfer price on products sold to it by the subsidiary.

Arbitrary transfer pricing affects performance evaluation.

Companies also set arbitrary transfer prices for competitive reasons or because of restrictions on currency flows. In the former case, if the parent ships products at a low transfer price to the subsidiary, the subsidiary will be able to sell the products to local consumers for less, thus improving its competitive position. In the latter case, if the subsidiary's country has currency controls on dividend flows, the parent can get more hard currency out of the country by shipping in products at a high transfer price or by receiving products at a low transfer price. Because prices are manipulated for reasons other than market conditions, arbitrary transfer pricing makes evaluating subsidiary and management performance difficult.

Budgets

Budgets may be established in the local currency, the parent currency, or both.

The most important financial measure is the budget. MNEs must determine the appropriate currency in which the budget should be prepared: the local currency of the country in which the subsidiary is established or the reporting currency of the parent company (the parent currency). Using the local currency is advantageous because the subsidiary's management operates in that currency and it is more indicative of the overall operating environment than is the parent currency. Another argument for using the local currency is that the exchange rate is something over which local management has no control, so it would not be wise to have a key uncontrollable item as part of the budgeting and evaluation process.

On the other hand, it is often difficult for top management in the parent's country to understand budgets generated in different currencies. This is especially true for a geographically diverse company such as Coca-Cola. Translating the budget into the parent currency enables top management to compare the performance of subsidiaries from all over the world and forces the subsidiaries' managers to think in terms of the parent currency.

Budgets and final results can be translated into dollars at the actual exchange rate when the budget was set, a projected exchange rate, or the actual rate at the end of the period.

Generally, the budget is translated into the parent currency and then compared with final results. However, there are many different exchange rates that can be used for establishing the budget and monitoring results. Table 19.5 identifies nine different combinations for establishing the budget and monitoring results using three different exchange rates:

- The actual exchange rate in effect when the budget was established
- A projected, or forecasted, rate that is a prediction of what the exchange rate is expected to be during the period being budgeted
- The exchange rate actually in effect when performance takes place

Of the possibilities identified in the table, the ones most likely to be used are A-3, P-2, and P-3. The advantage of P-2 and P-3 is that management is forced to forecast the exchange rate for budget purposes. Although this is very difficult to do, it is helpful for management in attempting to determine where the company might be at the end of the forecasting period. The difference between P-2 and P-3 is that under P-2, there is no foreign-exchange variance, only an operating variance, whereas under P-3, the foreign-exchange variance is the difference between the forecasted and actual exchange rates. For A-3, the foreign-exchange variance is the difference between the rate in effect when the budget was made and the actual rate at the end of the period. For both A-3 and P-3, performance is measured at the actual exchange rate at the end of the period.

Table 19.5
Possible Combinations of Exchange Rates for the Budget Process

Rate used for determining budget	Rate used to track performance relative to budget		
	Actual at time of budget	Projected at time of budget	Actual at end of period
Actual at time of budget	A-1	A-2	A-3
Projected at time of budget	P-1	P-2	P-3
Actual at end of period (through updating)	E-1	E-2	E-3

Source: From Donald R. Lessard and Peter Lorange, "Currency Changes in Management Control: Resolving the Centralization/Decentralization Dilemma," *The Accounting Review,* 52, July 1977, p. 630. Reprinted with permission.

Arbitrary transfer pricing can create legal and ethical problems. In the United States and many other countries, companies are expected to establish transfer prices on an arm's-length basis. Doing this ensures that taxes are paid on profits based on market decisions. However, when companies manipulate profits in order to minimize global tax payments and maximize cash flows, they may be breaking the law. Laws in this regard are much more rigid in Canada, France, Germany, the United Kingdom, and the United States. The U.S. government, for example, requires that companies use an arm's-length price on intracompany transactions between the United States and foreign countries; otherwise, the IRS will allocate profits between the two taxing jurisdictions. Sometimes foreign companies underinvoice shipments to the United States in order to minimize customs payments. In that case, the U.S. Customs Service can fine them and force them to correct the invoice so that the proper duty is paid.

Some countries, such as Italy, Japan, and Korea, are less interested in rigid transfer-pricing policies. Others, such as Ireland, Puerto Rico, and a few other tax-haven countries, have no transfer-pricing policies. Thus an MNE needs to determine whether it is ethical to transfer profits to low-tax countries through arbitrary transfer-pricing policies. By shifting profits to a low-tax country, the MNE is not harming tax collection in that country, but it is harming tax collection in the high-tax country from which the profits are shifted. In trying to maximize cash flows, management of an MNE is likely to assume that ethical means legal. If there are no legal requirements for transfer-pricing policies in a particular country, management is likely to assume that the absence of law implies permission to pursue the company's self-interest.

In some cases, an MNE might take advantage of transfer-pricing policies to transfer cash out of weak-currency developing countries. If a developing country has currency controls and does not allow cash to be shipped out in the form of dividends, a company might be tempted to charge a high transfer price on a product shipped to the country as a way of getting cash out. Doing this also results in lower taxable income in the developing countries and lower tax payments, which creates a problem for developing countries that desperately need hard currency. Such behavior by MNEs could be construed as unethical. Further, if a country has laws that establish the need for market-based transfer prices, the actions could be construed as illegal. It is doubtful that an MNE's home country would encourage the use of market-based transfer prices, because a high price on exports to developing countries would result in greater taxable income in the home country.

Taxation

Tax planning influences profitability and cash flow.

Tax planning is crucial for any business, since taxes can profoundly affect profitability and cash flow. This is especially true in international business. As complex as domestic taxation seems, it is relatively simple compared to the intricacies of international taxation. The international tax specialist must be familiar with both the home country's tax policy relating to foreign operations and the tax laws of each country in which the international company operates.

Taxation has a strong impact on several choices:

* Location of the initial investment
* Legal form of the new enterprise, such as branch or subsidiary
* Method of financing, such as internal versus external sourcing and debt versus equity
* Method of setting transfer prices[7]

This section examines taxation for the company with international operations, emphasizing U.S. tax policy because of the nature and extent of U.S. FDI. However, as any country finds domestic companies generating more and more foreign-source income, it must decide on the principles of accounting for that income. Therefore principles of taxation that U.S.-based MNEs face at home and abroad are, or could be, applicable to companies domiciled in other countries.

When a domestic company decides to sell its products internationally, it can do so directly through exportation of goods and services (including licensing agreements, management contracts, and so on), through foreign branch operations (a legal extension of the parent), and/or through foreign corporations in which it holds an equity interest that may vary from a small percentage to complete ownership.

Exports of Goods and Services

Many companies, such as public accounting firms, advertising agencies, banks, and management consulting firms, deal in services rather than products. Many manufacturing industries also find it easier and more profitable to sell expertise, such as patents or management services, than to sell goods. Generally, payment is received in the form of royalties and fees, and this payment usually is taxed by the foreign government. Because the sale of services is made by the parent, the sale also must be included in the parent's taxable income.

An FSC can be used by a U.S. exporter to shelter some of its income from taxation.

The FSC must be engaged in substantial business activity.

To gain tax advantages from exporting, a U.S. company can set up a **foreign sales corporation (FSC)** according to strict IRS guidelines. To qualify as an FSC, a company must be engaged in the exporting of either merchandise or services, such as engineering or architectural services. Also substantial economic activity must occur outside the United States. An FSC cannot be a mailbox company in Switzerland that simply passes documents from the United States to the importing country. It must engage in advertising and sales promotion, processing customer orders and arranging for delivery, transportation, determination and transmittal of final invoices or statements of account and receipt of payments, and the assumption of credit risk.[8] If a foreign corporation qualifies as an FSC, a portion of its income is exempt from U.S. corporate income tax. Also, any dividends distributed by the FSC to its parent company are exempt from U.S. income taxation as long as that income is foreign trade income.

Foreign Branch

Foreign branch income (or loss) is directly included in the parent's taxable income.

A foreign branch is an extension of the parent company rather than an enterprise incorporated in a foreign country. Therefore any income generated by the branch is taxable immediately to the parent, whether or not cash is remitted. However, if the branch suffers a loss, the parent is allowed to deduct that loss from its taxable income, thus reducing its overall tax liability.

Foreign Subsidiary

Tax deferral means that income is not taxed until it is remitted to the parent company as a dividend.

Income earned from a foreign corporation is either taxable or tax-deferred, that is, not taxed until it is remitted to the U.S. investor. Which tax status applies depends on whether the foreign corporation is a controlled foreign corporation and whether the income is active or passive. These factors are discussed next.

A **controlled foreign corporation (CFC)** is any foreign corporation that meets the following two tests:

In a CFC, more than 50 percent of the voting stock is held by U.S. shareholders.

1. More than 50 percent of its voting stock is held by "U.S. shareholders."
2. A "U.S. shareholder" is any U.S. person or company that holds 10 percent or more of the CFC's voting stock.

Table 19.6 shows how this might work. Foreign corporation A is a CFC because it is a wholly owned subsidiary of a U.S. parent company. Foreign corporation B also is a CFC because U.S. persons V, W, and X each own 10 percent or more of the voting

---

Table 19.6
Determination of Controlled Foreign Corporations
A controlled foreign corporation must have U.S. shareholders holding more than 50 percent of the voting shares.

	Percentages of the voting stock		
Shareholder	Foreign corporation A	Foreign corporation B	Foreign corporation C
U.S. person V	100%	45%	30%
U.S. person W		10	10
U.S. person X		20	8
U.S. person Y			8
Foreign person Z		25	44
Total	100%	100%	100%

stock, which means they qualify as U.S. shareholders and their combined voting stock is more than 50 percent of the total. Foreign corporation C is not a CFC because even though U.S. persons V and W qualify as U.S. shareholders, their combined stock ownership is only 40 percent. U.S. persons X and Y do not qualify as U.S. shareholders because their individual ownership shares are only 8 percent each.

If a foreign corporation qualifies as a CFC, the U.S. tax law requires the U.S. investor to divide the foreign-source income into two categories: active income, and Subpart F (or passive) income. **Active income** is income derived from the active conduct of a trade or business, such as from sales of products manufactured in the foreign country. **Subpart F income,** which is specifically defined in Subpart F of the U.S. Internal Revenue Code, is income from sources other than those connected with the active conduct of a trade or business. Subpart F income includes these major types:

- *Holding company income*—primarily dividends, interest, rents, royalties, and gains on sale of stocks
- *Sales income*—income from foreign sales corporations that are separately incorporated from their manufacturing operations, and the product is manufactured outside of and sold for use outside of the CFC's country of incorporation and the CFC has not performed significant operations on the product
- *Service income*—income from the performance of technical, managerial, or similar services for a company in the same corporate family as the CFC and outside the country in which the CFC is organized

Subpart F income usually derives from the activities of subsidiaries in tax-haven countries such as the Bahamas, the Netherlands Antilles, Panama, and Switzerland, as well as Hong Kong. The tax-haven subsidiary may act as an investment company, as a sales agent or distributor, as an agent for the parent in licensing agreements, or as a holding company of stock in other foreign subsidiaries, which are called grandchild, or second-tier, subsidiaries, as shown in Fig. 19.6. In the latter role, its purpose is to concentrate cash from the parent's foreign operations into the low-tax country and to use the cash for global expansion.

Figure 19.7 illustrates how the tax status of a subsidiary's income is determined. All non-CFC income—active and Subpart F—earned by the foreign corporation is deferred until remitted as a dividend to the U.S. shareholder (the parent company in this example). In contrast, a CFC's active income is tax-deferred to the parent, but its Subpart F income is taxable immediately to the parent as soon as it is earned by the CFC. If the income is earned by a foreign branch, it is immediately taxable to the parent company, whether it is active or Subpart F. There is an exception, however. If the foreign-source income is the lower of $1 million or 5 percent of the CFC's gross income, none of it is treated as Subpart F income. Or, if the foreign-source income is subject to a tax liability at least 90 percent of the U.S. tax liability, none of it is subject to U.S. tax.

Active income is that derived from the active conduct of a trade or business.

Passive income usually is derived from operations in a tax-haven country.

A tax-haven country is one with low taxes or no taxes on foreign-source income.

**Figure 19.6
A Tax-Haven
Subsidiary as a Holding
Company**
A parent company can
shelter income from U.S.
income taxation by utilizing
a tax-haven subsidiary located in a low-tax country,
such as Hong Kong.

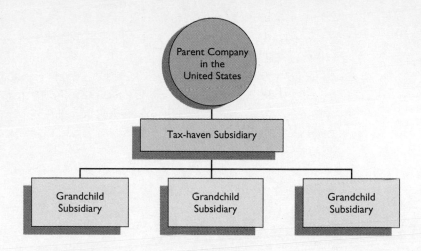

Tax Credit

The IRS allows a tax credit
for corporate income tax
paid to another country.

A tax credit is a dollar-for-
dollar reduction of tax liability and must coincide with
the recognition of income.

Every country has a sovereign right to levy taxes on all income generated within its borders. Problems arise when companies are owned by foreigners or are branches of foreign companies. This is an important issue for U.S. companies because of the magnitude of U.S. FDI.

A U.S. parent that defers recognition of active income until a dividend is declared to it gets credit for a portion of income taxes paid. For example, if 50 percent of the income of the foreign subsidiary is distributed as a dividend to the parent, the parent can claim no more than 50 percent of the tax as a creditable tax. Branch income cannot be deferred, but all branch foreign income taxes are eligible for inclusion in the tax credit. Credit also is allowed for taxes (called withholding taxes) paid by the parent to the foreign government on dividends paid by the foreign corporation to the parent.

**Figure 19.7
Tax Status of Active
and Subpart F Income
from Foreign
Subsidiaries of U.S.
Companies**
Different rules regarding
the tax status and deferra-
bility of income are in effect for CFCs, non-CFCs,
and foreign branches.

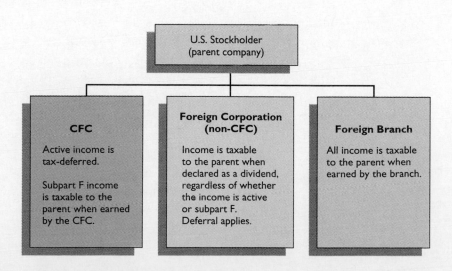

The total tax credit is subject to an upper limit—what the tax would have been in the United States.

After a U.S. company adds up its eligible credits, it finds that it is constrained by an upper limit imposed by the IRS. The upper limit is what it would have paid in taxes on that income in the United States. For example, if the foreign-source income is $1 million and the applicable U.S. tax rate is 35 percent, the upper limit is $350,000. If the tax credits exceed $350,000, the company can carry the excess credits back two years and recompute its tax burden or carry them forward five years and try to use them. If the credits total less than the upper limit, the company is allowed the full amount.

In reality, the computation of tax credits is significantly more complex. Foreign-source income must be divided into separate categories, or baskets: overall and passive. The overall category basically contains active income and probably will generate excess credits. The passive category basically contains Subpart F income and probably will use up all of its available credits and then some.

Taxation of U.S. Citizens Abroad

There are unique problems associated with compensating U.S. personnel working abroad. A company usually must offer employees a significant salary to entice them to move abroad. The total compensation usually consists of the base salary plus additional compensation in the form of a housing allowance, a hardship allowance, an education allowance for children, a cost-of-living differential, and so on. These additional allowances can escalate an employee's total compensation significantly and subject it to a higher income tax in the foreign country as well as in the United States.

U.S. citizens working abroad can exclude $70,000 of their income from U.S. taxation.

The U.S. policy of taxing such foreign income has changed significantly throughout history. The more lenient the tax treatment, the easier it is to send employees abroad. Under current law, U.S. expatriates (that is, U.S. citizens working abroad) are allowed to exclude up to $70,000 of their foreign-source income from U.S. taxation. This income is taken off the top; that is, income at higher marginal tax rates is excluded first, and the taxpayer ends up paying tax on income in the lowest tax brackets.[9]

U.S. employees working abroad can claim a housing exclusion for housing expenses in excess of a base amount determined by the IRS.

In addition to the foreign earned-income exclusion, an expatriate may elect to claim a housing exclusion. Housing expenses in excess of a base amount determined by the IRS can be excluded from the determination of income for tax purposes.

An expatriate might receive a significant amount of income that could be taxed by foreign and U.S. authorities. Income taxes paid to foreign governments can be treated as a credit or deduction, similar to the way in which corporate taxes are treated. However, companies sending expatriates abroad generally must make up the difference between what the expatriate would have paid in taxes in the United States and what must be paid because of the foreign assignment. The difference in tax liability is usually a result of the higher compensation earned by the expatriate as a result of allowances for housing, hardship, cost of living, etc. That tax-equalization practice can be quite expensive for the company.

Non-U.S. Tax Practices

Problems with different countries' tax practices are related to
- **Lack of familiarity with laws**
- **Loose enforcement**

Differences in tax practices around the world often cause problems for domestic companies operating overseas. Lack of familiarity with laws and customs can create confusion. In many countries, tax laws are loosely enforced. In others, taxes generally are negotiated between the tax collector and the taxpayer, if they are ever paid at all.

Variations among countries in GAAP can lead to differences in the determination of taxable income. This in turn may affect the cash flow required to settle tax obligations. For example, in France companies can depreciate assets very quickly and take additional depreciation for certain assets. In Sweden, companies can reduce the value of inventories, which tends to reduce taxable income.

In the separate entity approach, each taxable entity is taxed when it earns income.

Taxation of corporate income is accomplished through one of two approaches in most countries: the separate entity, or classical, approach, or the integrated system. In the **separate entity approach,** which is used in the United States, each separate unit—company or individual—is taxed when it earns income. For example, a corporation is taxed on its earnings and stockholders are taxed on the distribution of earnings (dividends). The result is double taxation.

An integrated system tries to avoid double taxation of corporate income through split tax rates or tax credits.

Most other industrial countries use an **integrated system** to eliminate double taxation. The British give a dividend credit to stockholders to shelter them from double taxation. In Germany, a split-rate system provides for a lower corporate income tax rate to be applied to distributed profits, since the stockholders are taxed also. A German stockholder must increase the value of the dividend by including the corporate tax that was paid and then pay the tax based on the individual tax rate. However, the stockholder is allowed to take a tax credit equal to what the corporation paid.

Countries also have unique systems for taxing the earnings of the foreign subsidiaries of domestic companies. Some, such as France, use a territorial approach and therefore tax only domestic-source income. Others, such as Germany and the United Kingdom, use a global approach; that is, they tax the profits of foreign branches and the dividends received from foreign subsidiaries. The United States is the only country to tax unremitted earnings in the form of Subpart F income.

Value-Added Tax

With a value-added tax, each company is taxed only on the value added to the product.

A **value-added tax (VAT)** has been used since 1967 by most Western European countries. A VAT is computed by applying a percentage rate on total sales less any purchases from other business entities that have already paid the VAT. As the name implies, VAT means that each independent company is taxed only on the value added at each stage in the production process. For a company that is fully integrated vertically, the tax rate applies to its net sales because it owned everything from raw materials to finished product.

The VAT rates vary significantly among European countries despite efforts by the EU toward harmonization among its members. However, the EU is narrowing differences in rates for specific categories of goods. The VAT does not apply to exports, since the tax is rebated (or returned) to the exporter and thus is not included in the final price to the consumer. This practice results in an effective stimulus for exports.

Tax Treaties: The Elimination of Double Taxation

The primary purpose of tax treaties is to prevent international double taxation or to provide remedies when it occurs. The United States has active tax treaties with more than thirty countries. The general pattern between two treaty countries is to grant reciprocal reductions on dividend withholding and to exempt royalties and sometimes interest payments from any withholding tax.

The United States has a withholding tax of 30 percent for owners (individuals and corporations) of U.S. securities that are from countries with which it has no tax treaty. However, interest on portfolio obligations and on bank deposits is normally exempted from withholding. When a tax treaty is in effect, the U.S. rate on dividends generally is reduced to 15 percent and the tax on interest and royalties either is eliminated or is reduced to a very low level.

A good example of a tax treaty is that between the United States and Canada. Canadian dividends, interest, and royalties remitted to U.S. citizens and companies normally would be subject to a 25-percent withholding tax rate by the Canadian government, but because of the tax treaty U.S. companies are subject to only a 15-percent tax rate.

Planning the Tax Function

Because taxes affect both profits and cash flow, they must be considered in the investment as well as the operational decision process. When a U.S. parent company decides to set up operations in a foreign country, it can do so through a branch or a foreign subsidiary. If the parent expects the foreign operations to show a loss for the initial years of operation, it should begin with a branch, since the parent can deduct branch losses against its current year's income. As the operations become profitable, the company should switch to a foreign subsidiary. If tax deferral applies to the subsidiary's income, then the income of the subsidiary will not be taxed until a dividend is declared.

Tied in with the initial investment decision as well as with continuing operations is the financing decision. Both debt and equity financing affect taxation. If loans from the parent are used to finance foreign operations, the repayment of principal is not taxable, but the interest income received by the parent is taxable. Also, the interest paid by the subsidiary is generally a business expense for that entity, which reduces taxable income in the foreign country. Dividends are taxable to the parent and are not a deductible business expense for the subsidiary. One reason why international finance subsidiaries are set up outside the United States is to escape withholding tax requirements.

The purpose of tax treaties is to prevent double taxation or to provide remedies when it occurs.

Companies should set up
- *Branches in early years to recognize losses*
- *Subsidiaries in later years to shield profits*

Debt and equity financing both have tax ramifications.

An MNE aiming to maximize its cash flow worldwide should concentrate profits in tax-haven or low-tax countries. This can be accomplished by carefully selecting a low-tax country for the initial investment, setting up companies in tax-haven countries to receive dividends, and carrying out judicious transfer pricing. Whenever possible, the parent company should utilize the 5-percent rule. This rule provides that if the parent has a profitable operating subsidiary in a relatively low-tax country, it can accumulate Subpart F income there without worrying about U.S. taxes, provided that income does not reach 5 percent of total subsidiary income. For example, because of its low-tax status and membership in the EU, Ireland can be used as both a manufacturing center to supply the EU with goods and a tax-haven country. The Subpart F income provisions require complicated tax planning, but opportunities still exist. Tax law is very involved, and a company needs the counsel of an experienced tax specialist.

National sovereignty is a major stumbling block to harmonization of accounting standards and practices.

The principle of mutual recognition means that securities regulators of one country are willing to accept a foreign company's financial statements if those statements are prepared according to the GAAP of the company's home country.

COUNTERVAILING FORCES

Although there are forces for harmonization of both accounting and taxation, national sovereignty is a major stumbling block. Accounting standards and practices are a function of each country's unique environment. As noted in this chapter, capital markets have a strong influence in countries such as the United States and the United Kingdom, whereas banks have a strong influence in countries such as Germany and Japan. Because of these differences, harmonizing accounting standards and practices worldwide is very difficult. Even the IASC is composed of organizations of accountants, such as the American Institute of Certified Public Accountants, rather than standards-setting bodies, such as the Financial Accounting Standards Board.

Some countries, such as Germany, prefer the principle of mutual recognition rather than harmonization. Under this principle, the securities regulators of one country are willing to accept a foreign company's financial statements, provided those statements are prepared according to the GAAP of the company's home country. However, the SEC has rejected this principle and instead requires foreign companies to adhere to U.S. GAAP in order to file in the United States. Thus the major forces of harmonization—the globalization of stock markets and the global interest of investors—directly conflict with national sovereignty, as both the German and the U.S. examples show.

The international harmonization of taxation is even more difficult because of the political nature of taxes. Although the EU has tried to narrow tax differences among its members in order to improve the flow of capital, it has not eliminated all differences. NAFTA deals only with trade issues and does not even refer to tax harmonization.

LOOKING TO THE FUTURE

Although accounting standards differ significantly by country, the differences are beginning to narrow. As capital markets become increasingly integrated and as companies increasingly move to list their stock on different national stock exchanges, accounting differences will continue to decrease. The stock exchanges will become an increasingly more important force in harmonizing accounting standards.

It is hard to predict what will happen in taxation, since tax policy is subject to the whim of governments. Certainly tax differences among countries in the EU will narrow in the years to come. Harmonization should take place in the determination of taxable income and the tax rates themselves. MNEs will need to be more creative in their tax planning worldwide as they seek to operate in such a way as to minimize their tax liabilities.

Summary

- **In performing its finance and accounting functions, an MNE must cope with differing inflation rates, exchange-rate changes, currency controls, risk of expropriation, customs duties, levels of sophistication, and local reporting requirements.**

- **A company's accounting or controllership function is responsible for collecting and analyzing data for internal and external users.**

- **Some of the major factors that influence the development of accounting standards and practices are finance and capital markets, taxation, legal systems, inflation, former colonial influence, and culture.**

- **Culture can have a strong influence on the accounting dimensions of measurement and disclosure. The cultural values of secrecy and transparency refer to the degree of disclosure of information. The cultural values of optimism and conservatism refer to the valuation of assets and the recognition of income. Conservatism results in the undervaluation of both assets and income.**

- **There are five major ways in which an MNE can alter financial data in its annual report or financial statements for users in other countries: do nothing, prepare convenience translations, prepare convenience statements, restate on a limited basis, or prepare secondary financial statements.**

- **The major forces for harmonization of accounting standards and practices are global investors and global capital markets.**

- **The EU is engaged in the most effective regional effort to harmonize accounting.**

- **The IASC is a global organization of public accountants from different countries that is trying to harmonize accounting standards.**

- **When transactions denominated in a foreign currency are translated into dollars, all accounts are recorded initially at the exchange rate in effect at the** time of the transaction. At each subsequent balance-sheet date, recorded dollar balances representing amounts owed by or to the company that are denominated in a foreign currency are adjusted to reflect the current rate.

- The translation of financial statements involves measuring and expressing in the parent currency and in conformity with parent country's **GAAP** the assets, liabilities, revenues, and expenses that are measured or denominated in a foreign currency.

- According to **FASB** Statement No. 52, the financial statements of foreign companies are translated into dollars by using the current-rate or temporal method. According to the more widely used current-rate method, all balance-sheet accounts except owners' equity are translated into dollars at the current exchange rate in effect on the balance-sheet date. All income statement accounts are translated at the average exchange rate in effect during the period.

- Foreign-exchange gains and losses arising from foreign-currency transactions are entered on the income statement during the period in which they occur. Gains and losses arising from translating financial statements by the current-rate method are entered as a separate component of owners' equity. Gains and losses arising from translating according to the temporal method are entered directly on the income statement.

- International tax planning has a strong impact on the choice of location for the initial investment, the legal form of the new enterprise, the method of financing, and the method of setting transfer prices.

- Tax deferral means that income earned by a subsidiary incorporated outside the home country is taxed only when it is remitted to the parent as a dividend, not when it is earned.

- A **CFC** must declare its Subpart F income as taxable to the parent in the year it is earned, whether or not it is remitted as a dividend.

- A tax credit allows a parent company to reduce its tax liability by the direct amount paid to foreign governments on dividends declared by a subsidiary to the parent as well as by the amount of the corporate income tax paid by the subsidiary to the foreign government.

- Policies of countries vary as to what is taxable income and how taxes are assessed. The United States taxes each separate unit (the separate entity approach), whereas most other industrial countries use an integrated system in which double taxation of dividends is minimized or eliminated.

• **The purpose of tax treaties is to prevent international double taxation or to provide remedies when it occurs.**

Case
Daimler-Benz and a
U.S. Listing[10]

In 1993, Daimler-Benz management decided to adjust its financial reporting in order to list shares of stock as American Depositary Receipts (ADRs), also known as American Depositary Shares, on the New York Stock Exchange (NYSE). This decision resulted from months of negotiations between Daimler-Benz, the NYSE, and the SEC.

An ADR is a negotiable certificate issued by a U.S. bank in the United States to represent the underlying shares of stock, which are held in a custodian bank. ADRs are sold, registered, and transferred in the United States in the same way as any share of stock.

Daimler-Benz is the large German MNE best known for its vehicles division, Mercedes-Benz. In 1992, Daimler-Benz saw profits fall by 25 percent from the previous year, and prospects for the future were not bright. The company relied historically on strong profits for cash flow, and thus its management realized that it would have to look to other sources of cash to fund future growth.

One way to raise cash is to borrow funds. Only 22.8 percent of the assets of Daimler-Benz in 1992 were funded by equity. Daimler-Benz has relied more on debt financing from banks—especially Deutsche Bank, the large German bank—than on equity financing. This strategy is typical of Germanic countries, such as Germany and Switzerland, and countries heavily influenced by the German tradition, such as Japan. When West Germany decided to absorb East Germany into a reunified country, there was a tremendous need on the part of the German government for money to fund the venture. Thus a significant amount of debt capital was pulled into the public sector, and interest rates rose to counter the inflationary effects of heavy governmental spending. Debt financing consequently became scarce and costly.

An alternate means of raising cash is to issue shares of stock. Daimler-Benz is a major player in the German stock market. In 1992, 11.5 percent of all shares traded on the eight German stock exchanges were Daimler-Benz shares, and 90 percent of Daimler-Benz share activity took place on the German exchanges, primarily Frankfurt but also Berlin, Bremen, Dusseldorf, Hamburg, Hanover, Munchen, and Stuttgart. About one third of Daimler-Benz's shares are held by approximately 400,000 stockholders, one half of whom live outside of Germany. Of the remaining shares, 28 percent are owned by Deutsche Bank, 25 percent by Mercedes AG Holding, and about 14 percent by the Emirate of Kuwait.

To gain access to non-German capital, Daimler-Benz has actively traded its shares in other markets, although such trading has made up only 10 percent of share activity. The company has been listed in Switzerland since the 1980s (Basel, Geneva, and Zurich), in Tokyo since September 1990, in Vienna since February 1991, and in Paris since October 1991. In addition, its shares are listed on the London Stock Exchange. Although Daimler-Benz had offered unlisted ADRs through the Bank of New York, until 1993 it had avoided the largest stock market in the world, the NYSE.

Why has Daimler-Benz avoided the NYSE for so many years? The major reason is the difference in accounting standards. The SEC has held fast to the idea that foreign companies must adhere to U.S. GAAP if they want to list in the United States. German companies tend to be much more conservative than are U.S. companies in reporting earnings and information in general. Company law is the predominant influence on accounting in Germany. The legal system in Germany is highly codified and prescriptive, since it is based on the Roman law system rather than the Anglo-Saxon common law system used in the United States and the United Kingdom. The tax laws also strongly influence the extent to which annual accounts form the basis for tax accounts. Thus any allowance or deduction claimed for tax purposes must be charged in the annual accounts.

The accounting tradition in Germany gives preference to the information needs of creditors and tax authorities. There is a very conservative approach to valuation in Germany, with strict application to historical cost accounting. Consistent with the emphasis on creditor interests, there also is a much more prudent interpretation of historical-cost accounting principles than usually occurs in the United States or the United Kingdom. To protect creditors, the law also requires German corporations to create a legal reserve. Depreciation rates are determined by the tax rules, and accelerated methods are widely used. With respect to inventories, the lower-of-cost-or-market rule is used but conservatively applied.

Provisions for future losses or expenses are a very important aspect of accounting in Germany. Traditionally, such provisions have been used to smooth or reduce profits. In good years, provisions may be made against the probability that the current results are unlikely to be maintained into the future; in bad years, these provisions will be called upon. This undervaluation of assets and overstatement of expenses and liabilities gives rise to hidden reserves that allow German companies to retain cash in the business to protect creditors, cash that is not available to stockholders because of the conservative determination of profits. Financial information is generally reported only annually, and footnote disclosures tend not to be extensive, leading to the charge that German financial statements are not very transparent.

When Daimler-Benz announced on March 25, 1993 that it was nearing an agreement with the SEC on the nature of its financial reporting for U.S. listing, it declared DM4 billion ($2.45 billion) in hidden reserves as an extraordinary profit on its 1992 balance sheet. These hidden reserves emerged as a result of applying uniform valuation methods throughout the company; different accounting methods had been used for different subsidiaries, so there was no uniformity in accounting. Since 1992, however, results have been provided on a uniform basis. The hidden reserves will be retained as an internal cash reserve rather than used for investment purposes. Daimler-Benz does not provide quarterly earnings reports and provides divisional results only annually. Even annual results are provided much later than would be the case for a U.S. company: 1992 results were not disclosed to the public until May 1993, and the results by division were not disclosed even then. This will have to change in order for Daimler-Benz to list in the United States. Another change in reporting, to be consistent with SEC requirements, is the need for a statement of cash flows divided into operating, investing, and financing activities, something that Daimler-Benz had not done prior to its 1992 *Annual Report.*

As the company's management negotiated with the SEC, it had two major options: It could offer one set of financial data to U.S. investors that meets SEC regulations and another set to German investors, or it could combine its financial data into one package acceptable to both groups. The German, U.S., and U.K. offices of KPMG Peat Marwick, a global public accounting firm, worked with Daimler-Benz to determine how results would be presented within the SEC's Form 20-F (the filing required for foreign companies listing in the United States).

Daimler-Benz issued a sponsored ADR on October 5, 1993 and is hoping that eventually 10 percent of its shares will be traded on the NYSE. Because of Daimler-Benz's high share price of DM760 (approximately $467) on October 5, ten ADRs equaled one share in order to make the price of the ADR more similar to share prices of other blue-chip companies in the United States. Other global service firms played an important role. For example, Citibank is the depositary bank for the ADR, and Deutsche Bank Capital Corporation of New York and Goldman, Sachs & Co. acted as investment bank advisors. The U.S.-based international law firm of Skadden, Arps, Slate, Meagher & Flom advised Daimler-Benz on matters relating to the registration and listing of the shares, and KPMG, mentioned above, prepared and audited the accounts to make sure that they conformed with U.S. GAAP.

Form 20-F includes a lot of information that provides insight into the differences between German and U.S. accounting practices and shows how difficult it is for an international investor to make investment decisions. Daimler-Benz provides financial information primarily in German marks, but it also provides some information in U.S. dollars. Its approach to translating information into dollars is as follows:

> Amounts stated in dollars, unless otherwise indicated, have been translated from marks at an assumed rate solely for convenience and should not be construed as representations that the mark amounts actually represent such dollar amounts or could be converted into dollars at the rate indicated. Unless otherwise stated, such dollar amounts have been translated from marks at the noon buying rate in New York City for cable transfers in foreign currencies as certified for customs purposes by the Federal Reserve Bank of New York (the "Noon Buying Rate") on June 30, 1993, which was DM1.706 per $1. Such rate may differ from the actual rates used in the preparation of the consolidated financial statements of Daimler-Benz. . . .

Regarding the differences in accounting practices, Form 20-F stated the following: "The statements in this Registration Statement are based on financial information prepared in accordance with the German Commercial Code, which represents . . . German GAAP. . . . These principles differ in certain significant respects from . . . U.S. GAAP."

Table 19.7 contains summary financial data provided by Daimler-Benz in Form 20-F (p. 58). Form 20-F identifies ten major differences between German and U.S. GAAP that influenced the numbers in the table. The major difference is appropriated retained earnings—provisions, reserves, and valuation differences. According to German GAAP, accruals or provisions may be recorded for uncertain liabilities and loss contingencies. The amount of such accruals or provisions represents the anticipated expense to the company. Application of German GAAP may also lead to higher accrual balances and reserves for possible asset risks than are allowed under U.S. GAAP.

Questions

1. What are some of the differences in philosophy and practice between German and U.S. accounting?
2. Why did Daimler-Benz decide to list ADRs on the NYSE?
3. Do you think Daimler-Benz would prefer that the SEC allow mutual recognition of accounting practices in approving listings on the NYSE? Explain.

Table 19.7
Summary Financial Data for Daimler-Benz, Year Ended December 31 (in millions, except per ordinary share and ADS amounts)

	Year					
	1992*	1992†	1991†	1990†	1989	1988
Income Statement Data						
Amounts in accordance with German GAAP						
Revenues	$57,766	DM98,546	DM95,010	DM85,500	DM76,392	DM73,495
Total output	59,132	100,879	98,566	88,340	80,552	75,637
Results from ordinary business activities	1,485	2,533	4,027	4,221	10,096‡	5,197
Extraordinary results§	—	—	(544)	—	—	—
Net income	851	1,451	1,942	1,795	6,809‡	1,702
Earnings per ordinary share	17.85	30.46	40.21	36.18	38.55**,††	39.58
Earnings per ADS‡‡	1.79	3.05	4.02	3.62	3.86	3.96
Dividends declared	354	604	603	557	555	504
Approximate amounts in accordance with U.S. GAAP						
Net income	$ 791§§	DM1,350§§	DM1,886	DM884	—	—
Earnings per ordinary share	17.00	29.00§§	40.52	18.99	—	—
Earnings per ADS‡‡	1.70	2.90§§	4.05	1.90	—	—
Balance Sheet Data						
Amounts in accordance with German GAAP						
Total assets	$50,518	DM86,184	DM75,714	DM67,339	DM62,737	DM51,931
Long-term borrowings	4,408	7,520	7,039	4,676	3,533	3,370
Stockholders' equity	11,559	19,719	19,448	17,827	16,966††	11,323
Approximate amounts in accordance with U.S. GAAP						
Total assets	$53,102	DM90,592	DM87,186	—	—	—
Stockholders' equity	16,181	27,604	26,745	—	—	—

* Amounts in this column are unaudited and have been translated solely for the convenience of the reader at an exchange rate of DM 1.706 = $1.00, the Noon Buying Rate on June 30, 1993.

† Deutsche Aerospace Airbus was consolidated beginning in 1992. Assuming Deutsche Aerospace Airbus had been consolidated since acquisition at the end of 1989, revenue and long-term debt in 1991 and 1990 would have been DM99,892 and DM7,044 and DM89,648 and DM14,727, respectively. . . . Under U.S. GAAP, Deutsche Aerospace Airbus would have been consolidated since acquisition.

‡ Includes nonrecurring expenses of DM1,370 and nonrecurring income credit of DM6,500 related to restructuring costs and changes in Group accounting methods principally relating to pensions and inventories of the Group.

§ Extraordinary result would be included as part of results from ordinary business activities under U.S. GAAP. . . .

** Excludes the effect of nonrecurring items discussed . . . above. Including such items, earnings per ordinary share would have been DM150.71.

†† Includes the effects of the issuance of approximately 4,200,000 ordinary shares in December 1989.

‡‡ Each ADS (American Depositary Share) represents one tenth of an ordinary share.

§§ Includes the cumulative effect of a change in accounting for postretirement benefits other than pensions of DM52 ($32), net of tax of DM33 ($19), or DM1.12 ($0.66) per ordinary share, or DM0.11 ($0.06) per ADS.

4. What impact do you think Daimler-Benz's experience might have on other German companies?
5. Was the SEC right in requiring Daimler-Benz to provide a reconciliation to U.S. GAAP as a precondition to listing on the NYSE? Explain.
6. What impact do the differences between German and U.S. accounting practices have on standard financial ratios, such as net income/sales, asset turnover (sales/average total assets), return on assets (net income/average total assets), and return on equity (net income/average stockholders' equity)?

Chapter Notes

1. Sources for the case were the 1989 *Annual Report* of the Coca-Cola Company; Timothy K. Smith and Laura Landro, "Profoundly Changed, Coca-Cola Co. Strives to Keep on Bubbling," *Wall Street Journal,* April 24, 1986, p. 1; Andrew L. Nodar, "Coca-Cola Writes an Accounting Procedures Manual," *Management Accounting,* October 1986, pp. 52-53; and John Huey, "The World's Best Brand," *Fortune,* May 31, 1993, p. 44+.
2. Lee H. Radebaugh and Sidney J. Gray, *International Accounting and Multinational Enterprises,* 3rd ed. (New York: John Wiley, 1993), pp. 257–258.
3. Financial Accounting Standards Board, *Statement of Financial Accounting Concepts No. 1—Objectives of Financial Reporting by Business Enterprises* (Stamford, Conn.: FASB, 1979), paragraphs 34-54.

4. Radebaugh and Gray, op. cit., pp. 389–390.
5. Gerhard G. Mueller, Helen Gernon, and Gary S. Meek, *Accounting: An International Perspective,* 3rd ed. (Burr Ridge, Ill.: Richard D. Irwin, 1994), p. 56.
6. Financial Accounting Standards Board, *Statement of Financial Accounting Standards No. 52: Foreign Currency Translation* (Stamford, Conn.: FASB, December 1981), pp. 6–7.
7. Albert J. Radler, "Taxation Policy in Multinational Companies," in *The Multinational Enterprise in Transition,* A. Kapoor and Philip D. Grub, eds. (Princeton: Darwin Press, 1972), p. 30.
8. Prentice-Hall, *A Complete Guide to the Tax Reform Act of 1984* (Englewood Cliffs, N.J.: Prentice-Hall, 1984), pp. 1791–1805.
9. Arthur Andersen & Co., *U.S. Taxation of Americans Abroad,* 4th ed. (Chicago: Arthur Andersen & Co., S.C., 1991).

10. Timothy Aeppel, "Daimler Says Mercedes Has Operating Loss," *Wall Street Journal,* May 7, 1993, p. A11; Timothy Aeppel, "Daimler-Benz Discloses Hidden Reserves of $2.45 Billion, Seeks Big Board Listing," *Wall Street Journal,* March 25, 1993, p. A10; "Daimler Plays Ball," *The Economist,* March 27, 1993, p. 76; Herbert Fromme, "Daimler Drives into Trouble," *World Accounting Report,* May 1993, pp. 2–3; Bernhard Harling, corporate communications of Daimler-Benz North America Corporation, New York; Christopher Parkes, "Daimler to Make New York Debut in October," *Financial Times,* July 28, 1993, p. 23; Radebaugh and Gray. op. cit., pp. 91–93 and 386–390; and Anita Raghavan and Christi Harlan, "Daimler-Benz's Listing Is Likely to Draw More Foreign Firms to the U.S. Market," *Wall Street Journal,* March 31, 1993, p. A4.

Chapter 20

The Multinational Finance Function

To have money is a good thing;
to have a say over the money is even better.
— Yiddish Proverb

Objectives

- To describe the multinational finance function and how it fits in the MNE's organizational structure

- To show how companies can acquire outside funds for normal operations and expansion

- To discuss the major internal sources of funds available to the MNE and show how these funds are managed globally

- To explain how companies protect against the major financial risks of inflation and exchange-rate movements

- To highlight some of the financial aspects of the investment decision

Case
NCR's
Risk-Management
Strategy[1]

In 1991, AT&T and NCR merged to form a $63-billion company (in sales revenues) with operations worldwide. However, foreign revenues of the new company were only 8.6 percent of total revenues, even though NCR's foreign revenues were 59.2 percent of total revenues prior to the merger.

NCR, one of five major business units of AT&T, develops, manufactures, markets, and services company-wide information systems for customers worldwide. It links departments, buildings, campuses, and global locations through servers and client computers—from pen-based notepad computers to massively parallel systems. It also offers hardware, software, and services for networking and imaging systems that convert paper-based information into electronic form.

NCR generated revenues in four different geographic segments (see Fig. 20.1) in 1990, the last year it issued an annual report before the merger. NCR notes in its annual report that transfer pricing between geographic divisions is done at market prices. It also emphasizes how interdependent its units are: "The methods followed in developing the geographic area data require the use of estimation techniques and do not take into account the extent to which NCR's product development, manufacturing, and marketing depend upon each other. Thus, the information may not be as indicative of results as it would be if the geographic areas were independent organizations."

Similar breakdowns are not found in the AT&T *Annual Report,* since foreign revenues are less than 10 percent of total revenues. AT&T provides revenues, operating income, and identifiable assets for only two geographic segments: United States and Foreign. FASB Statement No. 14 does not require the disclosure of geographic segment data if foreign revenues, earnings, and identifiable assets are less than 10 percent of total revenues. However, AT&T's *Annual Report* mentions that foreign revenues in its segment disclosures include only revenues from foreign-based operations. Revenues from all international activities, including the foreign-segment revenues and those from international telecommunications services and export sales, provided 24.3 percent of consolidated revenues in 1992. AT&T hopes to generate 50 percent of its revenues from abroad by the turn of the century. However, NCR, with nearly 60 percent of its revenues coming from abroad, is clearly more global than AT&T in general.

Prior to the merger, NCR took advantage of foreign capital markets to borrow money. In its 1990 *Annual Report,* NCR reported notes payable totaling $182 million, classified as short-term borrowings from banks, mainly denominated in foreign currencies. NCR also included long-term obligations denominated in Eurodollars (which will be explained more fully in this chapter) and in Japanese yen.

If AT&T uses foreign capital markets, it does not disclose that fact. AT&T's 1992 *Annual Report* describes its debt obligations but does not disclose whether any are in a foreign currency. However, AT&T lists its stock on exchanges in Brussels, Geneva, London, Paris, and Tokyo, in addition to several in the United States, so it is gaining access to equity capital abroad.

Although AT&T and NCR were joined in the merger, NCR has retained its foreign-currency risk-management responsibilities for foreign operations. The Latin America/Middle East/Africa geographic segment generates only 4.8 percent of total revenues for NCR, but it encompasses the world's most volatile regions. This segment is essentially a market-

**Figure 20.1
NCR's 1990 Revenues
by Geographic Area**
Less than half (40.2 percent) of NCR's 1990 revenues were from the United States, and only 4.8 percent were from the volatile regions of Latin America, the Middle East, and Africa. Europe (34 percent) and the Pacific (21 percent) were fairly significant sources of revenue. The Pacific region includes Australasia, the Far East, and Canada.

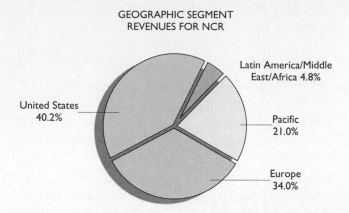

GEOGRAPHIC SEGMENT
REVENUES FOR NCR

Latin America/Middle East/Africa 4.8%

United States 40.2%

Pacific 21.0%

Europe 34.0%

ing unit that buys products at a discount from the company's production and development units and then sells the products in its own regions. To focus corporate resources and expertise internationally, the unit performs its own currency-risk management in coordination with corporate treasury staff.

The objective of NCR's risk-management strategy is to neutralize economic exposure from foreign-currency fluctuations, first through operational strategies and second with foreign-exchange contracts. To illustrate how significant those contracts are, on December 31, 1990, NCR had $1.271 billion in outstanding forward contracts, of which 60 percent were in European currencies and 40 percent were in Pacific currencies. There were no contracts in Latin American currencies, because those financial markets are not developed enough for forward contracts. This information was disclosed in NCR's 1990 *Annual Report* but not in AT&T's 1992 *Annual Report.*

From an organizational standpoint, NCR puts a lot of responsibility on the shoulders of group management. Each geographic unit has a group vice president and finance director responsible for the overall risk-management strategy of the group, subject to the approval of top management and corporate treasury. Each of the eight regions that compose the Latin America/Middle East/Africa group has a general manager and a finance director. Once the risk-management strategy has been determined, the execution of the strategy is left to the local level, where market conditions vary considerably.

As NCR further integrates with AT&T, it will be interesting to see whether it can maintain its separate risk-management strategy or will have to combine that function with those of AT&T. This question is especially interesting given AT&T's lack of international expertise compared with NCR's, and the fact that such a small part of AT&T's revenues have traditionally come from abroad. On the other hand, AT&T may be able to borrow expertise from NCR as it moves to generate an increasing percentage of its revenues from abroad. AT&T is currently organized not into geographic units like NCR, but into business units that have worldwide responsibility for their businesses. Should each division within AT&T be responsible for risk management or should that function be centralized in corporate treasury? As AT&T's foreign operations grow, will it be able to maintain its business-unit organizational structure, or will it have to shift to a geographic focus, and what would that mean to its risk-management policies?

Introduction

Why do you need to understand the nature of capital markets, cash management, and financial risk? Having a good product idea is not sufficient for success. MNEs need to get access to capital markets in different countries in order to finance expansion. Even though U.S. capital markets are the world's largest and most significant, many companies still choose to raise money in the markets in which they plan to expand.

The small company involved only tangentially in international business may be concerned primarily about the functions of the foreign-exchange section of its commercial bank and not global capital markets. However, the MNE investing and operating abroad usually is concerned about access to capital in local markets as well as in the large global markets. This chapter examines external sources of funds available to companies operating abroad, internal sources of funds that often arise from intercompany links, global cash management, risk-management strategies, and international dimensions of the capital investment decision.

The Finance and Treasury Functions

One of the most important people on the management team, crucial to a company's success, is the vice president of finance, also known as the chief financial officer (CFO). The functions of the CFO are often divided into the controllership and treasury functions. The responsibilities of the controller were discussed in Chapter 19. This chapter focuses on the most important global responsibilities of the CFO's treasury side.

The corporate finance function involves the acquisition and allocation of financial resources among the company's potential activities and projects.

The corporate finance function deals with the acquisition of financial resources and their allocation among the company's activities and projects. Acquiring resources (financing) involves generating funds either internally (within the company) or from sources external to the company at the lowest possible cost. Allocating resources (investing) involves increasing stockholders' wealth through the allocation of funds to different projects and investment opportunities.[2]

The CFO's job is more complex in a global environment than in the domestic setting because of forces such as foreign-exchange risk, currency flows and restrictions, different tax rates and laws pertaining to the determination of taxable income, and regulations on access to capital in different markets.

The capital structure is the permanent financing of a company through long-term debt, capital stock, and retained earnings.

MNEs clearly are looking for capital worldwide in order to ensure their long-term ability to survive. They may issue stock or borrow money in foreign markets for parent-company needs, or they may raise capital to fund subsidiaries in foreign countries. The choice between debt and equity funding is complex. The company's capital structure, or capitalization, is the permanent financing of its assets through long-term debt, capital stock, and retained earnings. Its leverage is the ratio of the book value of total debt to total assets. The CFO is responsible for ensuring that the total cost of capital (both debt and equity) is as low as possible.

The CFO must determine the degree to which a firm leverages its assets, which varies from country to country. Country-specific factors are a more important determinant of a company's capital structure than is any other factor. Even though leveraging is often perceived as the most cost-effective route to capitalization, it may not be the best approach in all countries, for two major reasons. First, excessive reliance on long-term debt increases financial risk and so requires a higher return for investors. Second, foreign subsidiaries of an MNE may have limited access to local capital markets, making it difficult for the MNE to rely on debt to fund asset acquisition.[3] In a study of foreign subsidiaries of U.S. MNEs, it was found that the debt/asset ratio of those studied averaged 0.54. The debt/asset ratio on average for companies in a few countries was as follows: the Netherlands (0.32), Brazil (0.37), Australia (0.49), Mexico (0.51), Canada (0.52), England (0.64), Japan (0.65), and Germany (0.69).[4]

In addition, different tax rates, dividend remission policies, and exchange controls may cause a company to rely more on debt in some situations and more on equity in others. The debt/equity ratio of the MNE will be a weighted average of the debt/equity ratios of all entities in its corporate structure. German, Japanese, and Swiss companies traditionally have relied on debt financing because of its relatively better availability compared to equity financing and because of low interest rates. However, a rise in interest rates and an improvement in equity markets in recent years have prompted them to consider changing their mix of debt and equity financing. It is important to understand that the different debt and equity markets discussed in this chapter have different levels of importance for companies worldwide.

Country-specific factors are a more important determinant of capital structure than is any other factor.

External Sources of Funds

Once an MNE has established an investment overseas—usually through investing assets in return for capital stock in the foreign entity—it can choose from many different ways for generating long-term sources of funds to ensure the investment's long-term ability to survive.

MNEs rely on local capital markets to fund subsidiary operations.

Local Capital Markets
After the initial investment, the parent company usually prefers to have the foreign subsidiary become self-sufficient through retained earnings and straight debt rather than relying on it for additional infusions of capital in order to survive.

Because each country has different business customs, MNEs must not attempt to impose the same operating procedures in all countries. For example, Caterpillar Tractor was accustomed to operating through one bank for all of its transactions. However, when it first entered Brazil, it quickly realized that the country's tight credit market required a different operating procedure. So it opened accounts at several Brazilian banks, thus enabling it to tap several different credit sources. Caterpillar liked this Brazilian policy so much that it exported it back to the United States.

Although domestic and international markets are becoming more and more like a single market—at least among industrial countries—local markets still are influenced a great deal by internal political and economic pressures. For example, Brazil's high inflation rates have made it difficult for MNEs to get access to funds on a consistent, ongoing basis. Further, interest rates are usually very high in order to ensure a real return for the lending institutions. Occasionally, the Brazilian government has excluded the subsidiaries of foreign-owned companies from the domestic credit markets in order to encourage those companies to bring in hard currency from abroad.[5]

In a back-to-back loan, the parent company in country A deposits cash in the local branch of a bank from country B, and the bank from country B loans funds to the parent's subsidiary in Country B.

Sometimes, foreign companies' subsidiaries can obtain credit easier than local companies can because of the former's access to hard currency. They can enter into **back-to-back loans** during periods when interest rates are high or credit is frozen. A back-to-back loan is one that involves a company in country A with a subsidiary in country B and a bank in country B with a branch in country A. For example, the Italian subsidiary of a U.S. food company can gain access to Italian loans if its U.S. parent provides dollars to the U.S. branch of an Italian bank. Under that condition, the Italian bank will lend money to the Italian subsidiary of the U.S. parent:

> A dollar deposit is made in the United States with a branch of a leading Italian bank. At the same time, the equivalent amount in lira is lent by the bank to the company's Italian subsidiary as a seven-year loan. The loan will be repaid in full to the bank at the end of the loan period. Once the loan is terminated, the parent will withdraw its deposit plus interest. The subsidiary pays Italian prime [the prime interest rate]. Every six months, the exchange rate is adjusted if it varies more than 5 percent from the contracted rate. Thus, the subsidiary shoulders the exchange risk.[6]

A good example of how an MNE can utilize local debt and markets for its operations was discussed in the Euro Disney case in Chapter 1. When Euro Disney was initially capitalized, the project cost 24 billion French francs (about $4.4 billion), and the funding came from both debt and equity sources. Disney purchased 49 percent of the capital stock at only 10 francs per share, compared with a price of 72 francs per share to other stockholders. Operating losses in 1992 and 1993 caused the price of the stock to fall, so Euro Disney could not raise additional funds through issuing capital stock. The operating losses prevented Euro Disney from generating enough cash to service existing debt and to expand. Most of the debt— 21 billion francs—had been raised from French banks by Euro Disney, not by Disney. Thus Disney had limited its own exposure by having its subsidiary raise funds from local French banks, with the debt to be serviced by franc revenues in France. In addition, this debt was not guaranteed by Disney, so the immediate exposure was limited to Euro Disney and the French banks, as well as the French government, which had backed some of the loans. Apparently, NCR also took advantage of local capital markets by borrowing Japanese yen through its subsidiary in Japan.

Eurocurrencies

The Eurocurrency market is an important source of debt financing for the MNEs. A **Eurocurrency** is any currency that is banked outside of its country of origin. Eurodollars, which constitute a fairly consistent 65–80 percent of the Eurocurrency market, are dollars banked outside of the United States. Dollars held by foreigners on deposit in the United States are not Eurodollars, but dollars held at branches of U.S. or other banks outside of the United States are. Smaller Eurocurrency market segments exist for Japanese yen (Euroyen), German marks (Euromarks), and other currencies, such as British pounds (Eurosterling), French francs, and Swiss francs.

The **Eurocurrency market,** which has a volume of approximately $6 trillion, is a market whose transactions take place worldwide.[7] Large transactions occur in Asia (Hong Kong and Singapore), Canada, and the Caribbean (the Bahamas and the Cayman Islands), as well as in London and other European centers. However, London is the key center for this market, with nearly 20 percent of all Eurocurrency transactions taking place there. Luxembourg is the center for Euromark deposits, and Brussels and Paris are the centers for Eurosterling deposits.[8]

The major sources of Eurocurrencies are

- Foreign governments or individuals who want to hold dollars outside of the United States
- Multinational corporations that have cash in excess of current needs
- European banks with foreign currency in excess of current needs
- Countries such as Germany, Japan, and Taiwan that have large balance-of-trade surpluses held as reserves.

The demand for Eurocurrencies comes from sovereign governments, supranational agencies such as the World Bank, companies, and individuals. Eurocurrencies exist partly for the convenience and security of the user and partly because of cheaper lending rates for the borrower and better yield for the lender.

The Eurocurrency market is a wholesale rather than a retail market, which means that transactions tend to be very large. Public borrowers such as governments, central banks, and public-sector corporations tend to be the major players. MNEs are involved in the Eurodollar market; for example, as noted in the opening case, NCR borrowed heavily there. However, nearly four fifths of the Eurodollar market is interbank; that is, the transactions occur between banks. The Eurocurrency market exists for savings and time deposits rather than demand deposits. That is, institutions that create Eurodollar deposits do not draw down those deposits into a particular national currency in order to buy goods and services.

The Eurocurrency market is both short- and medium-term. Short-term borrowing has maturities of less than one year. Anything over one year is considered a **Eurocredit,** which may be a loan, line of credit, or other form of medium- and

---

A Eurocurrency is any currency banked outside of its country of origin.

London is the key center of the Eurocurrency market.

A Eurocredit is a type of loan that matures in one to five years.

long-term credit, including **syndication,** in which several banks pool resources to extend credit to a borrower.

A major attraction of the Eurocurrency market is the difference in interest rates compared with those in domestic markets. Because of the large transactions and the lack of controls and their attendant costs, Eurocurrency deposits tend to yield more than domestic deposits do, and loans tend to be relatively cheaper than they are in domestic markets. Traditionally, loans are made at a certain percentage above the **London Inter-Bank Offered Rate (LIBOR),** which is the interest rate banks charge one another on loans of Eurocurrencies. How much above LIBOR the interest rate charged to a borrower is depends on the credit-worthiness of the customer and must be large enough to cover expenses and build reserves against possible losses. However, the Eurocurrency market's unique characteristics mean that the borrowing rate usually is less than it would be in the domestic market. Most loans are variable-rate, and the rate-fixing period generally is six months, although it may be one or three months.

International Bonds

Many countries have very active bond markets available to domestic and foreign investors. At the end of 1992, the total domestic bond market in terms of amounts outstanding worldwide was $14 trillion, of which $6.7 trillion was in U.S. dollars outstanding in the United States. The next largest domestic bond market was in Japan, with a dollar value of $2.9 trillion. This compares with only $1.7 trillion for the entire international bond market. However, the international bond market still fills an important niche in financing.

Foreign Bonds, Eurobonds, and Global Bonds

The international bond market can be divided into foreign bonds, Eurobonds, and global bonds. **Foreign bonds** are sold outside of the borrower's country but are denominated in the currency of the country of issue. For example, a French company floating a bond issue in Swiss francs in Switzerland would be selling a foreign bond. Foreign bonds typically make up about 18 percent of the international bond market. They also have creative names, such as Yankee bond (issues in the United States), Samurai bond (issued in Japan), and Bulldog bond (issued in England).

A **Eurobond** is usually underwritten (placed in the market for the borrower) by a syndicate of banks from different countries and sold in countries other than the one in whose currency the bond is denominated. For example, a bond issue floated by a French company in German marks in London, Luxembourg, and Switzerland is a Eurobond. Eurobonds make up approximately 75 percent of the international bond market, although that proportion was as high as 90 percent as recently as 1989.

The **global bond,** introduced by the World Bank in 1989, is a combination of domestic bond and Eurobond in that it must be registered in each national market according to that market's registration requirements. It also is issued simultaneously in several markets, usually those in Asia, Europe, and North America. Global bonds are a small but growing segment of the international bond market—currently less than 10 percent of the total.

The Eurobond Market

Although the Eurobond market is centered in Europe, it has no national boundaries. Unlike most conventional bonds, Eurobonds are sold simultaneously in several financial centers through multinational underwriting syndicates and are purchased by an international investing public that extends far beyond the confines of the countries of issue.

Eurobonds were first issued in 1963 as a means of avoiding U.S. tax and disclosure regulations. They are typically issued in denominations of $5000 or $10,000, pay interest annually, are held in bearer form, and are traded over the counter (OTC), most frequently in London.[9] Any investor who holds a bearer bond is entitled to receive the principal and interest payments. In contrast, for a registered bond, which is more typical in the United States, the investor is required to be registered as the bond's owner in order to receive payments. Obviously, there is more secrecy attached to a bearer bond. An OTC bond is traded with an investment bank rather than on a securities exchange, such as the London Stock Exchange.

Occasionally, Eurobonds may provide currency options, which enable the creditor to demand repayment in one of several currencies and thereby reduce the exchange risk inherent in single-currency foreign bonds. More frequently, however, both interest and principal on Eurobonds are payable to the creditor in U.S. dollars.

The European Currency Unit (ECU) has become an interesting "currency" of lending in the Eurobond market. Based on a basket composed of the currencies of the EU member countries, the ECU at one time accounted for nearly 10 percent of all international bond issues.[10] The ECU bond enables a borrower to diversify into different currencies and to use cash flows from different countries in which it has operations to pay back the investors. However, the crisis in the European Monetary System in 1992 and continued uncertainty about the system have caused ECU bonds to be less attractive.

Equity Securities

Another source of financing is the equity-capital market. The world's ten largest stock exchanges in terms of market capitalization (the total number of shares of stock listed on the exchange times the market price per share) are in what are considered developed countries (including Hong Kong). The world's three largest stock exchanges are the New York Stock Exchange (NYSE), Tokyo Stock Exchange, and London Stock Exchange (LSE).

Margin notes:

Eurobonds are typically issued in denominations of $5000 or $10,000, pay interest annually, are held in bearer form, and are traded over the counter.

Some Eurobonds have currency options, which allow the creditor to demand repayment in one of several currencies.

The ECU bond is based on a basket of currencies of the countries that are EU members.

The three largest stock markets in the world are in New York, Tokyo, and London.

Emerging-country stock
markets are an important
source of funds and are
growing on average more
rapidly than are the
developed-country stock
markets.

A major trend recently has been the increasing importance of stock markets in emerging nations. In 1983, the market capitalization of these emerging-country markets was only 2.5 percent of the total; by 1992, it was 7 percent (see Fig. 20.2). The emerging-country markets also are among the world's highest-performing. Taking advantage of this performance, institutional investors in the developed countries increased their holdings of stocks in emerging-country markets to 13 percent of their international funds in 1993, up from 10 percent in 1992 and only 2 percent in 1989.[11] Map 20.1 identifies the ten largest emerging-country stock exchanges and the ten largest developed-country stock exchanges.

The Euroequity Market

The Euroequity market is
the market for shares sold
outside the boundaries of
the issuing company's home
country.

Another significant event in the past decade is the creation of the **Euroequity market,** the market for shares sold outside the boundaries of the issuing company's home country. Prior to 1980, few companies thought of offering stock outside the national boundaries of their headquarters country. Since then, hundreds of companies worldwide have issued stock simultaneously in two or more countries.

Companies from twenty-two different countries are listed in the Euroequity market. Of the 300 stocks traded most actively in this market, Japanese and U.S. stocks dominate with 68 and 44 entries, respectively, followed by the United Kingdom (26), France (25), Canada (23), the Netherlands (19), Germany (15), and Sweden (13).[12]

In some cases, companies list on only one foreign exchange. It is expensive to list on foreign exchanges and so companies often list on one big one, such as the NYSE or the LSE. However, some companies list on several different exchanges, especially if they have foreign investments in several countries and are trying to raise capital in those countries. For example, AT&T lists its stock on exchanges in Brussels, Geneva, London, Paris, and Tokyo, in addition to the United States. Deutsche Bank of Germany lists on eight different exchanges, including Brussels, London, Paris, Tokyo, and several exchanges in Germany.[13]

The U.S. market is important for U.S. and foreign companies looking for equity capital and is popular for Euroequity issues partly because of the size of the market

---

**Figure 20.2
Growth of
Emerging-Country
Stock Markets**
The market capitalization
of emerging-country stock
markets rose from 2.5 percent of the world's total in
1983 to 7 percent in 1992.

Source: International Finance
Corporation, *Emerging Stock
Markets Factbook 1993* (Washington, D.C.: IFC, 1993), pp.
10–11, 13.

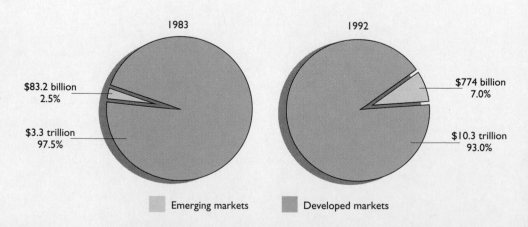

Map 20.1   Market Capitalization (in billions of U.S. dollars), 1992

Stock markets in the industrial countries far surpass those in developing countries in terms of market capitalization. Note that almost 43 percent of the world's market capitalization is in U.S. stock markets.

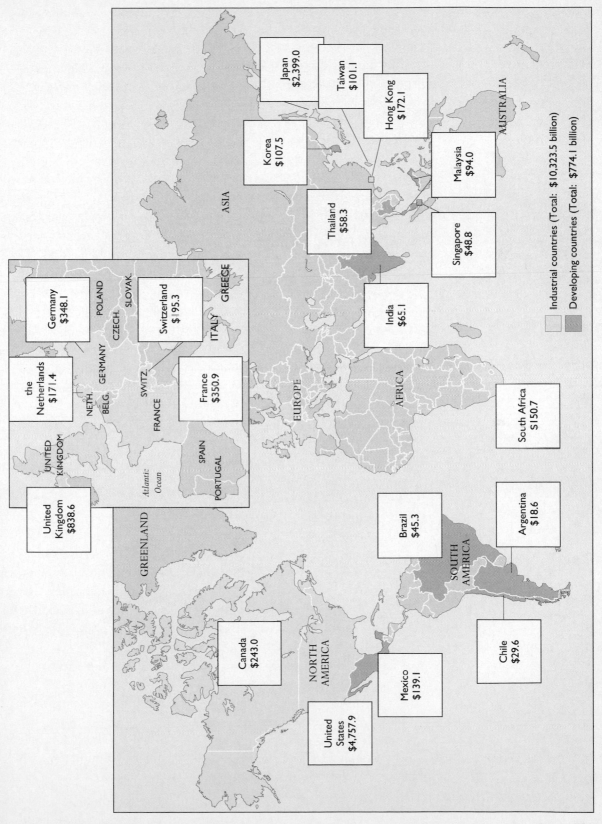

Japan $2,399.0	Taiwan $101.1
Korea $107.5	Hong Kong $172.1
Thailand $58.3	Malaysia $94.0
	Singapore $48.8
India $65.1	

ASIA

AUSTRALIA

Germany $348.1	the Netherlands $171.4
Switzerland $195.3	France $350.9
United Kingdom $838.6	

POLAND
CZECH.
SLOVAK.
GERMANY
BELG.
NETH.
SWITZ.
FRANCE
ITALY
GREECE
SPAIN
PORTUGAL
UNITED KINGDOM
GREENLAND
Atlantic Ocean
EUROPE
AFRICA

South Africa $150.7

NORTH AMERICA

United States $4,757.9	Canada $243.0
Mexico $139.1	Brazil $45.3
Chile $29.6	Argentina $18.6

SOUTH AMERICA

Industrial countries (Total: $10,323.5 billion)

Developing countries (Total: $774.1 billion)

721

and the speed with which offerings are taken. For example, the large pension funds in the United States can buy large blocks of stock at relatively low transaction costs. Pension-fund managers regard foreign stocks as a good form of portfolio diversification.

An ADR is a negotiable certificate issued by a U.S. bank and representing shares of stock of a foreign corporation.

The most popular way for a Euroequity to get a listing in the United States is to issue an ADR as Daimler-Benz did (see the opening case in Chapter 19). ADRs are traded like shares of stock, with each one representing some number of shares of the underlying stock; for example, ten ADRs equal one share of Daimler-Benz stock.

The listings of foreign shares in the United States have increased dramatically in recent years. For example, the most actively traded stock in 1992 in the United States was Glaxo Holdings, a British pharmaceuticals giant; more than 569 million shares changed hands on the NYSE through ADRs. In 1992, ADRs worth $125 billion were traded in the United States, a 33-percent increase over 1991. By mid-1993, 1000 different ADRs were available to U.S. investors.[14]

The United States is not the only market for Euroequities. A much larger percentage of the total shares traded on the LSE belong to foreign companies than is true for the NYSE, even though the total trading volume in the United States is quite large. Another example of Euroequity trading involves the nine Chinese companies that the Chinese Securities Regulatory Commission chose in 1993 to be listed on the Hong Kong Stock Exchange. The Maanshan Iron & Steel Company considered different alternatives to raise money for plant expansion and debt reduction, but it decided to list in Hong Kong. Although Maanshan could have listed B securities in Shenzhen, China (B securities are those that can be held by foreign investors), it considered the issue too large for that market to absorb.[15]

Offshore Financial Centers

Offshore financial centers provide large amounts of funds in currencies other than their own.

Offshore financial centers are cities or countries that provide large amounts of funds in currencies other than their own. Generally, the markets in these centers are regulated differently, and usually more flexibly, than the domestic markets are. These centers provide an alternative, and usually cheaper, source of funding for MNEs so that they don't have to rely strictly on their own national markets. In essence, offshore financial centers are the locations for Eurocurrency trading of all types and maturities and have one or more of the following characteristics:

- A large foreign-currency (Eurocurrency) market for deposits and loans (that in London, for example)
- A market that is a large net supplier of funds to the world financial markets (that in Switzerland, for example)
- A market that is an intermediary or pass-through for international loan funds (those in the Bahamas and the Cayman Islands, for example)
- Economic and political stability
- An efficient and experienced financial community

- Good communications and supportive services
- An official regulatory climate favorable to the financial industry, in the sense that it protects investors without unduly restricting financial institutions[16]

These centers can be considered as operational centers, where extensive banking activities are carried out, or booking centers, where little actual banking activity takes place but where transactions are recorded in order to take advantage of secrecy and low (or no) tax rates. London is an example of an operational center; the Cayman Islands is an example of a booking center. Although there are many offshore financial centers, the seven most important are Bahrain (for the Middle East), the Caribbean (servicing mainly Canadian and U.S. banks), Hong Kong, London, New York, Singapore, and Switzerland.

London is a crucial center because it offers a variety of services and has a large domestic as well as offshore market. The Caribbean centers (primarily the Bahamas, the Cayman Islands, and the Netherlands Antilles) are essentially offshore locations for New York banks. Switzerland has been a primary source of funds for decades, offering stability, integrity, discretion, and low costs. Singapore has been the center for the Eurodollar market in Asia (sometimes referred to as the Asiadollar market) since 1968, thanks to its strategic geographic location, its strong worldwide telecommunications links, and a variety of governmental regulations that have facilitated the flow of funds. Hong Kong is critical because of its unique status with respect to China and the United Kingdom and its geographic proximity to the rest of the Pacific Rim. Bahrain, an island country in the Persian Gulf, is the financial center of petrodollars (dollars generated from the sale of oil) in the Middle East.

Offshore financial centers are good locations for establishing finance subsidiaries that can raise capital for the parent company or its other subsidiaries. They allow the finance subsidiaries to take advantage of lower borrowing costs and tax rates.

Internal Sources of Funds

A company that wants to expand operations or needs additional working capital can look not only to the debt and equity markets, but also to sources within itself. For an MNE, the complexity of internal sources is magnified because of the number of its subsidiaries and the diverse environments in which they operate. Although the term *funds* usually means cash, it is used in a much broader sense in business and generally refers to working capital, that is, the difference between current assets and current liabilities.

Figure 20.3 illustrates a situation involving a parent company with two foreign subsidiaries. The parent, as well as the two subsidiaries, may be increasing funds through normal operations. These funds may be used on a company-wide basis. One possible way is through loans: The parent can loan funds directly to one subsidiary or guarantee an outside loan to the other.

Figure 20.3
Internal Sources of Working Capital for MNEs
There are many ways in which MNEs can use internal cash flow to fund worldwide operations.

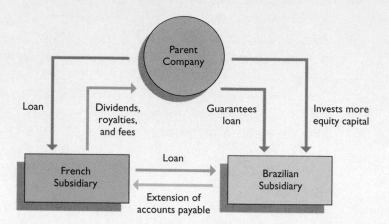

Equity capital from the parent is another source of funds for the subsidiary. Funds also can go from subsidiary to parent. The subsidiary could declare a dividend to the parent as a return on capital or could loan cash directly to the parent. If the subsidiary declared a dividend to the parent, the parent could lend the funds back to the subsidiary. The interest payment to the parent would be additional foreign-source income. There may be a withholding tax on the interest payment, which would reduce the cash flow to the parent. However, if the withholding tax is less than the tax on dividends, local management might be happy with the lower tax outflow.[17]

Intercompany financial links become extremely important as MNEs increase in size and complexity. Goods as well as loans can travel between subsidiaries, giving rise to receivables and payables. Companies can move money between and among related entities by paying quickly (leading payments) or can accumulate funds by deferring payment (lagging payments). They also can adjust the size of the payment by arbitrarily raising or lowering the price of intercompany transactions in comparison with the market price. (This strategy, called transfer pricing, was discussed more fully in Chapter 19.)

Thus cash is generated from debt and equity markets both domestically and overseas, from operations, and from internal sources. The problems of managing cash globally are complex. International cash management is complicated by differing inflation rates, changes in exchange rates, and governmental restrictions on the flow of funds.

Global Cash Management

Effective cash management is a chief concern of the MNE. The following three questions must be answered to ensure effective cash management:

1. What are the local and corporate system needs for cash?
2. How can the cash be withdrawn from subsidiaries and centralized?
3. Once the cash has been centralized, what should be done with it?

The general cash-flow cycle an MNE must deal with is illustrated in Fig. 20.4. The MNE must collect and pay cash in its normal operational cycle, and then it must deal with financial institutions, such as commercial and investment banks, in generating and investing cash.

Before any cash is remitted to a control center, whether on a regional or a headquarters level, local cash needs must be properly assessed through cash budgets and forecasts. Because the cash forecast projects the excess cash that will be available, the manager also will know how much cash can be invested for short-term profits.

Once local needs have been adequately provided for, the cash manager must decide whether to allow the local manager to invest the excess cash or to have it remitted to a central cash pool. If the cash is centralized, the manager must find a way of making the transfer. A cash dividend is the easiest way to distribute cash, but governmental restrictions may reduce the effectiveness of this means. For example, foreign-exchange controls may prevent the company from remitting as large a dividend as it would like. In some countries, the size of the dividend may be tied to the capital invested in the local operation. Cash also can be remitted through royalties, management fees, and repayment of principal and interest on loans.

Many developing countries with large foreign debt, such as Brazil, have made transferring money abroad difficult for companies operating within them because they want to curtail the outflow of foreign exchange. For example, one U.S. company with large operations in Brazil used dividends, loan repayments, and sales commissions to transfer funds out of Brazil. The Brazilian operation was treated as a manufacturing facility, and all export sales were made by a sales subsidiary of the U.S. parent. When the manufacturing facility was established in Brazil, it was financed primarily through debt rather than equity. The parent could get more cash out of Brazil by paying off principal and interest than it could by paying a dividend, which was subject to such large taxes. When foreign sales were made, the Brazilian manufacturer was permitted to pay a commission to the sales company in the United States, which allowed it to transmit more funds abroad. However, the Brazilian government constantly tried to lower the amount of the commission, whereas the parent company tried to increase it.

Cash budgets and forecasts are essential in assessing a company's cash needs.

Dividends are a good source of intercompany transfers, but governments often restrict their free movement.

Figure 20.4
The Cash-Flow Cycle
This cycle relates the generation of cash from sales to the payment of cash for inputs to the production process.

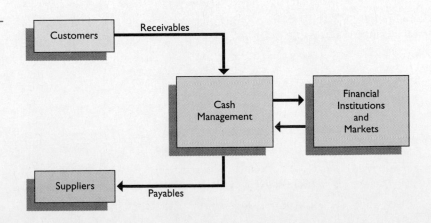

Multilateral Netting

Multilateral netting enables companies to reduce the amount of cash flow and move cash more quickly and efficiently.

An important cash-management strategy is netting cash flows internationally. For example, an MNE with operations in four European countries could have several different intercompany cash transfers resulting from loans, the sale of goods, licensing agreements, etc. In Fig. 20.5 for example, there are seven different transfers among the four subsidiaries. Table 20.1 identifies the total receivables, payables, and net position for each subsidiary. Rather than have each subsidiary settle its accounts independently with subsidiaries in other countries, many MNEs are establishing cash-management centers in one city (such as Brussels) to coordinate cash flows among subsidiaries from several countries. Figure 20.6 illustrates how each subsidiary in a net payable position transfers funds to the central clearing account. The manager of the clearing account then transfers funds to the accounts of the net receiver subsidiaries. Thus, in this example only four transfers need to take place. The clearing account manager receives monthly transactions information and computes the net position of each subsidiary. Then the manager orchestrates the settlement process. The transfers take place in the payor's currency, and the foreign-exchange conversion takes place centrally.

The multilateral netting process has several major advantages:

- Savings in foreign-exchange conversion costs, since the central manager can effect large exchanges
- Savings of transfer charges and commissions, again due to the large size and smaller number of transactions
- Quicker access to the funds

It sometimes can take five days for funds to be exchanged through wire transfer, so netting allows the company to get access to the cash much faster. Electronic transfers also enable the company to standardize and streamline payment routes and banking channels.[18]

**Figure 20.5
Multilateral Cash Flows**
Multilateral cash flows in the absence of netting require each subsidiary to settle intercompany obligations.

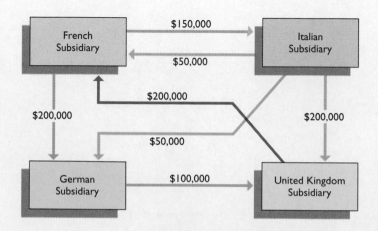

Table 20.1
Net Positions of Subsidiaries in Four Countries (in dollars)
Net positions show total receivables less total payables

Subsidiary	Total receivables	Total payables	Net position
French	250,000	350,000	(100,000)
German	250,000	100,000	150,000
Italian	150,000	300,000	(150,000)
U.K.	300,000	200,000	100,000

Coordination Centers

> Regional finance-coordination centers can be used to centralize cash-management strategies and practices.

The netting process just described is one of the functions that a regional finance-coordination center can perform. Other functions of such a center are:

- Centralization of financial transactions, including foreign-exchange dealings, pooling, and reinvoicing
- Centralization of administration, accounting, data processing, and information gathering and dissemination
- Advertising, insurance, and reinsurance
- Auxiliary services such as planning[19]

Europe is currently a favored location for these centers. Belgium (especially Brussels) is popular because it levies virtually no taxes on those operations and offers low rents and salaries, compared with European standards.

Figure 20.6
Multilateral Netting
Multilateral netting allows subsidiaries to transfer net intercompany flows to a cash center, or clearing account, which disburses cash to net receivers.

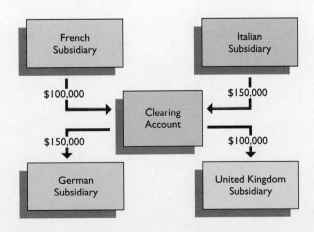

Financial-Risk Management

Major financial risks arise from inflation and exchange-rate changes.

Global cash-management strategy focuses on the flow of money for specific operating objectives. Another important objective of an MNE's financial strategy is to protect against the risks of investing abroad. The strategies that it adopts to do this may involve the internal movement of funds as well as the use of one or more of the foreign-exchange instruments described in Chapter 9, such as options and forward contracts.

Financial managers need to assess
• The nature of a financial risk
• Circumstances under which it can occur
• Its implications for the company
• Defensive strategies

In examining the risks encountered in international business, companies must consider the nature of a risk, the circumstances under which it can occur, the implications for the company, and the best defense against it. Major categories of risks are currency, commercial, and political. Currency risks include inflation and exchange-rate changes. Commercial risks arise from the problems of extending and receiving credit and the difficulties of collection or payment of accounts in different currencies. Political risks are extensive and include trade relations and expropriations.

Inflation

High inflation is often accompanied by a weak currency.

Inflation occurs in varying degrees in nearly every country in which MNEs operate. It can erode the value of financial assets and make financial liabilities more attractive, although the attractiveness of liabilities is softened somewhat by the high interest rates that often accompany loans in countries with high inflation.

High inflation rates often bring a variety of problems that influence the way MNEs operate. The following are the most important:

- Accelerated depreciation or devaluation of the local currency or a maxidevaluation
- Tighter capital controls and import restrictions
- Scarcer credit and higher borrowing costs
- A buildup of accounts receivable and lengthening of collection periods
- Price controls to help bring inflation under control
- Economic and political chaos and labor unrest
- Capital flight
- Greater difficulty in evaluating the performance of foreign subsidiaries[20]

Price controls can be circumvented by
• Modifying product strategies
• Reintroducing products with different brand names
• Changing packaging

Many companies faced with price controls need to get around them through imaginative product development and pricing strategies. This may involve slight product or packaging modifications and/or brand-name changes in order to effect price increases. Frequently, however, MNEs are so brand-conscious that they refuse to exploit this strategy. For example, Coca-Cola would never consider changing its product name in order to get a price increase. The importance of the brand name outweighs any advantage to be gained by changing it.

C ash-flow management gives rise to numerous ethical dilemmas. Many critics question the practice of setting up subsidiaries in tax-haven countries, especially when the legitimate use of offshore centers turns into illegal activity as a result of the underreporting of revenues or the overstating of expenses. MNEs have been known to transfer money illegally into tax-haven countries so that it can be used to pay bribes. This practice became common knowledge in the United States with the investigation of the Watergate break-in during the presidency of Richard Nixon. The secrecy possible in tax-haven countries makes them natural locations in which to hide cash for illegal purposes. However, not all use of tax havens is illegal. Although the governments of high-tax countries may criticize domestic companies that shelter income in tax-haven countries, those companies are simply taking advantage of differences in tax rates and are not necessarily acting unethically.

ETHICAL DILEMMAS

Many think that even when investing cash to yield a high return, MNEs should be concerned about the nature of investments. For example, prior to the all-race elections in South Africa in 1994, many pension-fund managers had eliminated from their portfolios the securities of South African companies and of foreign companies doing business in South Africa. Activists had put a lot of pressure, especially during the 1970s, on pension-fund managers for local and state governments, demanding that they get rid of South African investments. More recently, activists have argued that the U.S. government should impose sanctions against China because of human-rights violations by that country's government. However, there have been no attempts to boycott U.S. companies that do business in China or to pressure pension-fund managers to get rid of investments related to that country. An example of a value-based investment practice is that of Muslim-owned banks, which do not invest in business activities that are inconsistent with the tenets of Islam, such as the manufacture of alcoholic beverages.

Another ethical criticism of MNEs is that they are able to use their size and power to extract favorable borrowing terms in developing countries, leaving little capital for local companies and forcing them to pay higher rates than the MNEs pay.[21] However, this is true primarily of large MNEs, rather than medium-sized or small ones. Many smaller MNEs are not able to access local capital markets any differently than domestic companies do. Large MNEs that bring capital into a locale instead of getting it from local sources are behaving more ethically from the viewpoint of the host country. However, MNEs often employ local borrowing as a strategy for hedging against possible future losses, as Disney did when building Euro Disney. Further, it is easier to repay local-currency loans with local-currency revenues than it is to convert local-currency revenues into foreign currency to pay off foreign-currency loans.

One multinational cosmetics company operating in Brazil got around price controls by changing the container size of a brand-name product to a smaller container while listing the product at a significantly higher price. However, in order to attract sales it would sell the product for considerably less than list price. Then it could increase the price according to inflationary trends up to the upper price limit established by price-control authorities. A major problem the company faced was trying to estimate inflation correctly. If it predicted inflation at 200 percent and priced accordingly, it would be in serious trouble if inflation actually was 500 percent because it would have underpriced its products and sold them for less than the replacement cost of raw materials. On the other hand, if inflation ran at less than 200 percent, it risked pricing itself out of the market.

It is evident that a company operating in an inflationary environment needs to manage receivables and payables carefully. Receivables must be collected on a timely basis through a well-trained credit and collection department and a sophisticated and reliable reporting system.[22] Once receivables are collected, idle cash should be kept at a minimum. Funds should be remitted to the parent cash pool, as described earlier in this chapter, or invested in income-producing assets that provide a return in excess of inflation.

Exchange-Rate Changes

If all exchange rates were fixed in relation to one another, there would be no foreign-exchange risk. However, rates are not fixed, and currency values change frequently. Instead of infrequent one-way changes, currencies fluctuate often and both up and down. A change in the exchange rate can result in three different exposures for a company: translation exposure, transaction exposure, and economic exposure.

Translation exposure   Foreign-currency financial statements are translated into the reporting currency of the parent company (assumed to be U.S. dollars for U.S. companies) for a number of reasons, as noted in Chapter 19. Exposed accounts—those translated at the balance sheet rate or current exchange rate—either gain or lose command over dollars. For example, assume a subsidiary of a U.S. company operates in Mexico and has 350,000 pesos in a bank account there. If the Mexican peso, weakened by inflation, were to depreciate in relation to the dollar from 3.5 pesos per dollar to 4.0 pesos per dollar, the subsidiary's bank account would drop in value from $100,000 to $87,500 as a result of the depreciation.

The combined effect of the exchange-rate change on all exposed assets and liabilities is either a gain or a loss. However, whether the foreign-currency financial statements are translated according to the temporal method or the current-rate method, the gain or loss does not represent an actual cash-flow effect. For example, the cash in the Mexican bank is only translated, not converted, into dollars.

Transaction exposure   Denominating a transaction in a foreign currency represents foreign-exchange risk because the company has accounts receivable or payable

In countries with high inflation, payables should be stretched out, receivables collected quickly, and excess cash repatriated or invested.

Translation exposure arises because, as the exchange rate changes, the dollar value of the exposed asset or liability changes.

Transaction exposure arises because the receivable or payable changes in value as the exchange rate changes.

in foreign currency that must be settled eventually. For example, assume a U.S. exporter delivers merchandise to a British importer at a total price of $500,000 when the exchange rate is 1.5000 dollars per pound. If the exporter were to receive payment in dollars, there would be no immediate impact on the exporter if the dollar/pound exchange rate changed. If payment were to be received in pounds, however, the exporter could be exposed to a foreign-exchange gain or loss. For example, with the exchange rate at 1.5000 dollars per pound, the sale would be carried on the exporter's books at $500,000, but the underlying value in which the sale is denominated, as explained in Chapter 19, would be 333,333 pounds. If the rate moved to 1.4000 dollars per pound by the time the receivable was collected, the exporter would receive 333,333 pounds, but that payment would be worth $466,666, a loss of $33,334. This would be an actual cash-flow loss to the exporter.

Economic exposure arises from effects of exchange-rate changes on
- **Future cash flows**
- **Sourcing of parts and components**
- **Location of investments**
- **Competitive position of the company in different markets**

Economic exposure Economic exposure arises from, for example, the pricing of products, the sourcing and cost of inputs, and the location of investments. The economic impact on the company is difficult to measure, but that impact is crucial to its long-run viability. Pricing strategies have both an immediate and a long-term impact. For example, the inventory sold to the British importer probably was sold to final users before the exchange rate changed, but future sales would be affected by the rate change. Assume the exporter sold its most recent shipment of $500,000 at an exchange rate of 1.5000 dollars per pound for a cost to the importer of 333,333 pounds. If the British pound were to weaken to 1.4000 dollars per pound, the exporter would have two choices. The first alternative is to continue to sell the product to the British importer for $500,000, which would now cost the importer 357,143 pounds. At the higher price, the importer might lose market share. Or the importer could absorb the cost increase in its profit margin and continue to sell the product for a total of 333,333 pounds. The second alternative is to sell the inventory to the importer for fewer dollars so that the pound equivalent is still 333,333 pounds. At the new exchange rate, the sale price would have to be $466,666. Thus the exporter would end up with the lower profit margin. Exporters and importers must always determine the impact of a price change on volume.

Because of the strengthening yen, many Japanese companies have moved production facilities offshore, including to the United States, in order to avoid their high costs and take advantage of low-cost locations.

To protect assets from exchange-rate risk, management needs to
- **Define and measure exposure**
- **Establish a reporting system**
- **Adopt an overall policy on exposure management**
- **Formulate hedging strategies**

Exposure-Management Strategy

To protect assets adequately against risks from exchange-rate fluctuations, management must

- Define and measure exposure
- Organize and implement a reporting system that monitors exposure and exchange-rate movements

- Adopt a policy assigning responsibility for hedging exposure
- Formulate strategies for hedging exposure

Defining and measuring exposure   Most MNEs will be subject to all three types of exposure: translation, transaction, and economic. To develop a viable hedging strategy, a company must be able to forecast the degree of exposure in each major currency in which it operates. Because the types of exposure differ, the actual exposure by currency must be kept separate. For example, the translation exposure in Brazilian cruzeiros should be kept separate from the transaction exposure because the transaction exposure will result in an actual cash flow, whereas the translation exposure may not. Thus the company may adopt different hedging strategies for the different types of exposure.

A key aspect of measuring exposure involves forecasting exchange rates that apply to the identified exposure. Estimating future exchange rates is similar to using a crystal ball: Approaches range from gut feelings to sophisticated economic models, each having varying degrees of success. Whatever the approach used, a company should estimate ranges within which it expects a currency to vary over the forecasting period. Some companies develop in-house capabilities to monitor exchange rates, using economists who also try to obtain a consensus of exchange-rate movements from the banks with whom they deal. Their concern is to forecast the direction, magnitude, and timing of an exchange-rate change. Other companies contract out this work.

A reporting system   Once the company has decided how to define and measure exposure and estimate future exchange rates, it must design, organize, and implement a reporting system that will assist in protecting it against risk. To achieve this, substantial participation from foreign operations must be combined with effective central control. Foreign input is important in order to ensure the quality of information being used in forecasting techniques. Because exchange rates move frequently, the company must obtain input from those who are attuned to the pulse of the foreign country. In addition, the maximum effectiveness of hedging techniques will depend on the cooperation of personnel in the foreign operations.

Central control of exposure is needed to protect resources more efficiently. Each organizational unit may be able to define its own exposure, but the company also has an overall exposure. To set hedging policies on a separate-entity basis might not take into account the fact that exposures of several entities (that is, branches, subsidiaries, affiliates, and so on) could offset one another.

Management of an MNE should devise a uniform reporting system to be used by all units. The report should identify the exposed accounts the company wants to monitor, the exposed position by currency of each account, and the different time periods to be covered. Exposure should be separated into translation, transaction, and economic components, with the transaction exposure identified by cash inflows and outflows over time.

All three types of exposure must be monitored and measured separately.

Exchange-rate movements are forecasted using in-house or external experts.

The reporting system should utilize both central control and input from foreign operations.

The time periods to be covered depend on the company. One possibility is to look at long-term as well as short-term flows. For example, staggered periods (thirty, sixty, and ninety days; six months, nine months, and twelve months; or two, three, and four years) could be considered. The reason for the longer time frame is that operating commitments, such as plant construction and production runs, are fairly long-term decisions.[23]

Once each basic reporting unit has identified its exposure, the data should be sent to the next organizational level for preliminary consolidation. That level may be a regional headquarters (for Latin America or Europe, for example) or a product division, depending on the company's organizational structure. The preliminary consolidation enables the region or division to determine exposure by account and by currency for each time period. The resulting reports should be routine, periodic, and standardized to ensure comparability and timeliness in formulating strategies. Final reporting should be at the corporate level, where corporate exposure can be determined and strategies identified to reflect the best interests of the company as a whole.

Centralized exposure-management policy permits economies of scale and the specialization of experts.

A centralized policy   It is important for management to decide at what level hedging strategies will be determined and implemented. To achieve maximum effectiveness in hedging, a policy should be established at the corporate level. Having an overview of corporate exposure and the cost and feasibility of different strategies at different levels in the company, the corporate treasurer should be able to design and implement a cost-effective program for exposure management. As the company grows in size and complexity, it may have to decentralize some decisions in order to increase flexibility and speed of reaction to a more rapidly changing international monetary environment. However, such decentralization should stay within a well-defined policy established at the corporate level. This is the strategy GM uses. Some companies, such as Eastman Kodak, run their hedging operations more as profit centers and nurture in-house trading desks. Most MNEs, however, are very traditional and conservative in their approach, preferring to cover exposure rather than to extract huge profits or risk huge losses.

Hedging strategies can be operational or contractual.

Formulating hedging strategies   Effective management of foreign-exchange risk involves deciding which risks are important and then establishing a management structure that can manage the risk. Once a company has identified its level of exposure and determined which exposure is critical, it can hedge its position by adopting numerous strategies, each with cost/benefit implications as well as operational implications. The safest position is a balanced position in which exposed assets equal exposed liabilities. Achieving this involves operational strategies to hedge exposure, the principal ones being balance-sheet management and leads and lags in the transfer of funds. In addition, companies can enter into a number of contractual obligations to hedge exposure, such as forward-exchange contracts and currency options.

Operational strategies include
- **Using local debt to balance local assets**
- **Taking advantage of leads and lags for intercompany payments**

To reduce exposure through operational strategies, management must determine the working capital needs of a subsidiary. Although it may be wise to collect receivables as fast as possible in an inflationary country in which the local currency is expected to depreciate, the company must consider the competitive implications of not extending credit.

In reality, working-capital management under exchange risk assumes that currency values move in one direction. A weak-currency country generally (although not always) suffers from inflation. The approach to protecting assets in the face of currency depreciation also applies to protection against inflation. Inflation erodes the purchasing power of local currency, whereas depreciation erodes the foreign currency equivalent. In the weak-currency situation, subsidiaries' cash should be remitted to the parent as fast as possible or invested locally in something that appreciates in value, such as fixed assets. Accounts receivable should be collected as quickly as possible when they are denominated in the local currency and stretched out when denominated in a stronger currency. Liabilities should be treated in the opposite manner.

A policy for inventory is difficult to determine. If inventory is considered to be exposed, it should be kept at as low a working level as possible. However, because its value usually increases through price rises, it can be a successful hedge against inflation and exchange-rate moves. If the inventory is imported, it should be stocked before a depreciation, since it will cost more local currency after the change to purchase the same amount in foreign currency. When price controls are in effect or there is strong competition, the subsidiary may not be able to increase the price of inventory. In this case, inventory can be treated in the same way as cash and receivables. These principles can be reversed when an appreciation is predicted, that is, keep cash and receivables high and liquidate debt as rapidly as possible. The safest approach is to keep the net exposed position as low as possible.

The use of debt to balance exposure is an interesting strategy. Many companies have adopted a "borrow locally" strategy, especially in weak-currency countries. One problem with this strategy is that interest rates in weak-currency countries tend to be quite high, so there must be a trade-off between the cost of borrowing and the potential loss from exchange-rate variations. For example, Coca-Cola has a strategy whereby at least half of its net exposed asset position in foreign countries is offset by foreign currency borrowings.[24] B&D also uses local borrowings to hedge a net exposed asset position, but each exposure is considered on a case-by-case basis rather than automatically covered with local borrowing.[25]

Protecting against loss from transaction exposure becomes very complex. In dealing with foreign customers, it is always safest for the company to denominate the transaction in its own currency. Alternatively, it could denominate purchases in a weaker currency and sales in a stronger currency. If forced to make purchases in a strong currency and sales in a weak currency, it could resort to contractual measures or try to balance its inflows and outflows through more astute sales and purchasing strategies.

A lead strategy involves collecting or paying early.

Another operational strategy, known as leads and lags, often is used to protect cash flows among related entities, such as a parent and its subsidiaries. The **lead strategy** involves collecting foreign-currency receivables before they are due when

A lag strategy involves collecting or paying late.

the foreign currency is expected to weaken and paying foreign-currency payables before they are due when the foreign currency is expected to strengthen. With a **lag strategy,** a company delays collection of foreign-currency receivables if that currency is expected to strengthen and delays payables when the currency is expected to weaken. In other words, a company usually leads into and lags out of a hard currency and leads out of and lags into a weak currency.

Leads and lags are much easier to use among related entities when a central corporate financial officer can spot the potential gains and implement a policy. There are two problems with a lead or lag strategy. First, it may not be useful for the movement of large blocks of funds. If there are infrequent decisions involving small amounts of money, it is easy to manage the system, but as the number, frequency, and size of transactions increase, it becomes difficult to manage. Second, as mentioned earlier in this chapter, leads and lags are often subject to governmental control, since currency movements impact a country's balance of payments.

Forward contracts can be used to establish a fixed exchange rate for future transactions.

In addition to the operational strategies just mentioned, a company may hedge exposure through contractual arrangements, using derivatives such as forward contracts and options. The most common approach is to use a forward contract. For example, assume a U.S. exporter sells goods to a British manufacturer for 1 million pounds, with payment due in ninety days. The spot exchange rate is 1.5000 dollars per pound, and the forward rate is 1.4500 dollars per pound. At the time of the sale, it is recorded on the books of the exporter at $1.5 million, and a corresponding receivable is set up for the same amount. However, the exporter is concerned about the exchange risk. The exporter can enter into a forward contract, which will guarantee that the proceeds of the receivable can be converted into dollars at a rate of 1.4500 dollars per pound, no matter what the actual future exchange rate is. This move will yield $1.45 million, for a cost of protection of $50,000. Or the exporter could wait until the receivable is collected in ninety days and gamble on a better rate. If the actual rate at that time is 1.4700 dollars per pound, the exporter will receive $1.47 million, which is not as good as the initial receivable of $1.5 million but is better than the forward yield of $1.45 million. On the other hand, if the dollar strengthens to 1.4000 dollars per pound, the exporter would be much better off with the forward contract.

Currency options can be utilized to assure access to foreign currency at a fixed exchange rate for a specific period of time.

The foreign-currency option is a relatively recent foreign-exchange instrument. It is more flexible than the forward contract because it gives its purchaser the right, but not the obligation, to buy or sell a certain amount of foreign currency at a set exchange rate within a specified amount of time. For example, assume a U.S. exporter decides to sell merchandise to a British manufacturer for 1 million pounds when the exchange rate is 1.5000 dollars per pound. At the same time, the exporter goes to Goldman Sachs, its investment banker, and enters into an option to deliver pounds for dollars at an exchange rate of 1.5000 dollars per pound at an option cost of $25,000. That means that whether or not the exporter exercises the option, having it costs $25,000. When the exporter receives the 1 million pounds from the manufacturer, it must decide whether to exercise the option. If the exchange rate is above 1.5000 dollars per pound, it will not exercise the option, because it can get a better yield by converting pounds at the market rate. The only thing lost is the $25,000 cost of the option, which is like insurance. On the other hand, if the exchange rate is below 1.5000 dollars per pound, say at 1.4500, the exporter will exercise the option and trade pounds at the rate of 1.5000. The proceeds will be $1.5 million less the option cost of $25,000.

Historically, companies have preferred to use a forward contract when the amount and timing of the future cash flow are certain. Where there is high uncertainty, they prefer the flexibility of an option. Although options can be more expensive than forward contracts, especially in a highly volatile market, they sometimes can be very useful. Their flexibility has prompted corporate treasurers to use options increasingly since the mid-1980s.

Financial Aspects of the Investment Decision

The parent company needs to compare the net present value or internal rate of return of a foreign project with that of its other projects and with that of others available in the host country.

The parent company must compare the net present value or internal rate of return of a foreign project with that of its other projects and that of others available in the host country. Discounted cash flows often are used to compare and evaluate investment projects. Several aspects of capital budgeting are unique to foreign project assessment:

- Parent cash flows must be distinguished from project cash flows. Each flow contributes to a different view of value.
- Parent cash flows often depend on the form of financing. Thus cash flows cannot be clearly separated from financing decisions.
- Remittance of funds to the parent must be explicitly recognized because of differing tax systems, legal and political constraints on the movement of funds, local business norms, and differences in how financial markets and institutions function.
- Cash flows from subsidiaries to parent can be generated by an array of nonfinancial payments, including payment of license fees and payments for imports from the parent.
- Differing rates of national inflation must be anticipated because of their importance in causing changes in competitive position and thus in cash flows over time.
- The possibility of unanticipated exchange-rate changes must be considered because of their potential direct effects on the value of cash flows to the parent, as well as their indirect effects on the competitive position of the foreign subsidiary.
- Use of segmented national capital markets may create an opportunity for financial gains or may lead to additional financial costs.
- Use of loans subsidized by the host-country government complicates both capital structure and the ability to determine an appropriate weighted average cost of capital for discounting purposes.

- Political risk must be evaluated because political events can drastically reduce the value or availability of expected cash flows.
- Terminal value (the value of the project at the end of the budgeting period) is more difficult to estimate because potential purchasers from the host, home, or third countries or from the private or public sector may have widely divergent perspectives on the value of the project.[26]

Management must view cash flows from two perspectives: the total flows available to the local operations, and the cash available to the parent. The outflows to the parent are important to consider in light of the original investment made, especially if the investment was made with the parent's funds. Finally, the company must analyze foreign political and exchange risks. The best approach is for it to adjust forecasted cash outflows to different estimates representing different levels of risk.

C O U N T E R V A I L I N G

F O R C E S

To optimize the flow of funds worldwide, the MNE must determine the proper parent-subsidiary relationship with respect to the finance function. In addition, the finance function needs to be broken down into different elements, such as foreign-exchange risk management and long-term and short-term financing decisions, because the parent-subsidiary relationship may depend on the specific decision being considered.

Parent-subsidiary relationships are typically viewed as being of three types:

1. Complete decentralization at the subsidiary level
2. Complete centralization at the parent level
3. Varying degrees of decentralization, typically through regional financial centers[27]

However, general organizational structure complicates the choice of parent-subsidiary relationships. For example, if a company is organized along product lines as well as by geographic regions, does the finance function flow through the product chain of command or the regional one?

Some argue for decentralization of the finance function because country environments are so unique that they need to be treated differently. For example, in the 1980s when Argentina's annual inflation rate rose to 5000 percent, a U.S. pump manufacturing company with an Argentinean subsidiary found that it was generating lots of cash that it was able to invest at high interest rates. It was earning so much interest income that its net income actually exceeded sales. The company's U.S. management was having a difficult time understanding the problems of the local environment, so it gave local management the responsibility for managing liquid assets, to the great benefit of the company.

If an MNE's management regards overseas operations as a portfolio of independent businesses—basically a multidomestic strategy—the parent-subsidiary relationship is likely to be more informal, with very simple financial controls. If management thinks of overseas operations as appendages of the parent company, the financial control systems are likely to be much tighter, with information and excess cash being shipped back to the parent. Finally, if management treats overseas operations as delivery pipelines to a unified global market—a global strategy—financial controls are likely to be tight, but only so that financial resources can be used on a global basis as needed.[28]

In a decentralized situation, in which the subsidiary is relatively independent of the parent, the parent receives reports but generally issues only minor guidelines, especially when foreign sales comprise a small part of total sales and when the parent staff is relatively unfamiliar with the foreign environment. In a centralized situation, the parent staff dominates planning and decision making, and the subsidiary carries out orders. The idea behind this approach is that the more sophisticated parent staff understands the intricacies of moving funds across national boundaries in order to serve the needs of the whole company at the greatest profit.

However, truly global companies try to achieve high levels of sophistication at both parent and subsidiary levels. Because of this dual expertise, the parent staff is better suited to coordinate system activities and to monitor results, whereas the subsidiary staff is better able to act within specified guidelines. To maintain close proximity to foreign financial-information sources, many companies have organized regional financial decision-making centers. The parent staff continues to issue guidelines for decision making and coordinates the entire system, but financial organization and management functions are turned over to the regional organizations.

LOOKING TO THE FUTURE

It is difficult to forecast trends in global capital markets because of rapid economic changes worldwide. As world trade increases and global interdependence rises, the velocity of financial transactions also must increase. Financial markets will continue to be dominated by the world's largest—New York, Tokyo, and London. However, the action increasingly will take place in the emerging nations within Eastern Europe, Latin America, and Southeast Asia. As fund managers continue to diversify their portfolios to include securities of emerging countries and as investment advisors continue to recommend that their clients diversify their portfolios away from domestic to global funds, the interest in emerging-country markets will continue to rise. This will clearly benefit investors through high returns and also will help the emerging nations in capital formation.

Two events will significantly influence the cash-management and hedging strategies of MNEs in the future: the information and technology explosion, and the growing number and sophistication of hedging instruments (financial derivatives such as options and forwards). The information explosion will continue to enable companies to get information more quickly and cheaply. In addition, the advent of electronic data interchange (EDI) will allow them to transfer information and money instantaneously worldwide. Companies will significantly reduce paper flow and increase the speed of delivery of information and funds, enabling them to manage cash and to utilize intercompany resources much more effectively. Consequently, companies will be able to reduce not only the cost of producing information, but also interest and other borrowing costs.

The growing number and sophistication of financial derivatives, along with the growing expertise of providers and users of those instruments, should allow companies to identify and hedge their exposure much more effectively. Companies that previously did not hedge certain types of exposure will find that the availability of derivatives will increase and their cost will decrease, making risk protection much more possible.

Also, the centralization and regionalization of cash and exposure management will increase, not decrease, even though local finance staff will become much more sophisticated. The sheer volume of transactions and the resulting economies argue for more, not less, centralization. The speed and sophistication of communication should allow companies to manage assets much more quickly than in the recent past.

Summary

- **The corporate finance function deals with the acquisition of financial resources and their allocation among the company's present and potential activities and projects.**

- **Country-specific factors are the most important determination of the capital structure of a company.**

- **Local debt markets, which vary dramatically from country to country because of local business customs and practices, are important sources of funds for MNEs.**

- **A Eurocurrency is any currency banked outside of its country of origin, but primarily dollars banked outside the United States.**

- **A Eurobond is a bond issue sold in a currency other than that of the country of issue. A foreign bond is one sold outside the country of the borrower but denominated in the currency of the country of issue. A global bond is one issued simultaneously in North America, Asia, and Europe according to the listing requirements of each market.**

- **Although the three largest stock markets in the world are in New York, Tokyo, and London, the markets in emerging countries in Asia, Eastern Europe, and Latin America are among the world's most dynamic.**

- **Euroequities are shares listed on stock exchanges in countries other than the home country of the issuing company.**

- **Offshore financial centers such as Bahrain, the Caribbean, Hong Kong, London, New York, Singapore, and Switzerland deal in large amounts of foreign currency.**

- The major sources of internal funds for an MNE are dividends, royalties, management fees, intercompany loans, loans from parent to subsidiaries, purchases and sales of inventory, and equity flows from parent to subsidiaries.

- Global cash management is complicated by differing inflation rates, changes in exchange rates, and governmental restrictions on the flow of funds. A sound cash-management system for an MNE requires timely reports from affiliates worldwide.

- Management must protect corporate assets from losses due to inflation and exchange-rate changes. Exchange rates can influence the dollar equivalent of foreign-currency financial statements, the amount of cash that can be earned from foreign-currency transactions, and a company's production and marketing decisions.

- Foreign-exchange risk management involves defining and measuring exposure, setting up a good monitoring and reporting system, adopting a policy to assign responsibility for exposure management, and formulating strategies for hedging exposure.

- Forward contracts can lock the company into a specific exchange rate for future obligations, which could result in gains or losses, depending on what happens to the actual exchange rate. However, a forward contract eliminates exchange-rate uncertainty for the company.

- Foreign-currency options give the purchaser the option to buy or sell foreign currency in a certain amount, at a fixed exchange rate, during a specified time period. An option is more expensive than a forward contract but is more flexible.

- When deciding to invest abroad, a company must consider its optimal debt/equity ratio, evaluate local currency and parent currency rates of return, identify cash flows unique to the foreign investment, calculate a multinational cost of capital, and offset foreign political and exchange risks.

Case
LSI Logic Corp.[29]

In the late 1970s, Wilfred Corrigan, the British-born chairman and president of Fairchild Camera & Instrument Corp., sold Fairchild to Schlumberger Ltd. Approximately one year later, in November 1980, he started LSI Logic Corp., a manufacturer of custom-made microchips based in Malpitas, California. Although Corrigan's idea of manufacturing custom-made microchips sounded unconventional at the time, he was able to use his track record at Fairchild to convince some U.S. venture capitalists to invest nearly $7 million in the new company in January 1981. Corrigan's move was timely because U.S. chip manufacturers controlled 57.2 percent of the world's semiconductor market, compared with only 27.4 percent for Japanese companies.

The company began with only four employees, but because Corrigan had solved two key issues—the nature of the product and the initial infusion of cash—there was a solid foundation for growth. He next had to decide how LSI Logic should service its customers worldwide and how and where it would raise capital to keep expanding.

From his experience at Fairchild, Corrigan knew that a producer of microchips had to think globally in terms of the location of production and the consumer. He quickly decided that in order to be successful, he needed to concentrate on three key geographic areas—Asia, Europe, and the United States. He called this his "global triad strategy," defining the triad more specifically as Japan, Western Europe, and North America (see Map 20.2). His key organizational strategy was to incorporate companies in the producing and consuming countries that would be jointly owned by LSI Logic and local investors, with LSI Logic holding the controlling interest. Although the operations in each country would be relatively independent of each other, they would be linked by technology, money, and management. This setup would encourage the synergy of interdependence while permitting local freedom in meeting the demands of the market.

Once Corrigan got operations under way, he began to look for more cash. The key was to find the right amount, at the right price, with the least number of problems. In February 1982, LSI Logic turned to Europe in search of venture capital, which was found in a European investing community hungry for U.S. high-tech stock. The company subsequently was able to raise $10 million, mostly—but not exclusively—in the United Kingdom. At this point, LSI Logic was growing rapidly. In May 1983, Corrigan took the company public in the United States and raised over $162 million, an average of $21 a share. That demonstrated the size of the appetite in the United States for stock in new high-tech companies.

Despite the European and U.S. successes, Corrigan still had not been able to raise capital in Japan. However, he learned that the Japanese brokerage house Nomura Securities had purchased large blocks of LSI stock for its clients in Japan. Encouraged by this informa-

Map 20.2
Triad Strategy for LSI Logic Corp.
LSI Logic's global business and financing strategy focused on three of the world's largest markets: North America, Western Europe, and Japan.

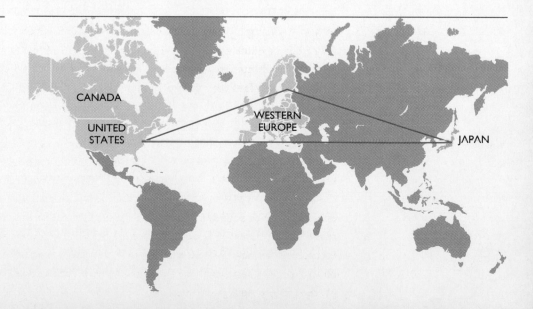

tion, Corrigan traveled to Japan to meet with Nomura officials and to try to decide what LSI Logic's next move should be. As a result of the visit, Corrigan decided the time was right for starting operations in Japan. Following the strategy he had used elsewhere, he established a Japanese subsidiary of LSI Logic (called LSI Logic Corp. K.K.), of which the parent company owned 70 percent and twenty-five Japanese investors together owned 30 percent. The new investment was just right for LSI Logic—it gained access not only to the Japanese consumer market but also to the Japanese capital market. As a Japanese company, LSI Logic Corp. K.K. and its manufacturing affiliate, Nihon Semiconductor Inc., could establish lines of credit with Japanese banks, and did so at only 6 percent, compared with 9 percent in the United States at the time.

Corrigan's move into Japan came at a time when Japanese semiconductor companies, especially Fujitsu Ltd., NEC Corp., and Toshiba Corp., were expanding rapidly. Relying on high-volume manufacturing techniques and aggressive marketing strategies, the Japanese had expanded their market share to 35.3 percent in 1982, compared with a shrinking U.S. market share of 51.4 percent.

When business in Japan was under way, Corrigan once more turned his attentions to Europe. He planned to set up a new European company and needed to decide on its structure. The company could be set up as a European company, or it could be set up as a branch of the U.S. parent that would use U.S. capital and be totally controlled and protected by the parent. Corrigan decided on the former and consequently used Morgan Stanley & Co., the large U.S.-based securities firm, to set up LSI Logic Ltd. Corrigan was convinced that by setting up a European company, he would be able to get more money by selling shares at a higher price than would be possible otherwise and that LSI Logic Ltd. would be better placed to serve European customers than would a branch of the parent company. The parent company retained an 82-percent ownership share in the new company and sold the rest in a private offering to European investors, one of which was the venture-capital arm of five German banks.

In 1985 and again in 1987, Corrigan returned to European capital markets; both times LSI Logic floated a bond issue. The first issue of $23 million was put together by Swiss Bank Corp., one of the world's largest banks. The second, a bond issue with securities convertible into common stock, was floated by Morgan Stanley and Prudential-Bache Capital Funding. LSI Logic was attracted to the Eurobond market for two main reasons: a decent price (lower interest rates than were being offered in the United States), and a quicker time frame. Because the company was issuing the bonds in Europe and so didn't have to worry about the more onerous regulations of the SEC, it was able to get the offering together and out to the investing public faster.

Although significant amounts of funds were raised by LSI Logic in foreign markets (over $200 million since 1982), there was no real foreign-exchange risk. The company's worldwide operations were earning revenues that could be used to pay off the financial obligations. In addition, its subsidiaries had access to local credit markets because they were organized as local corporations rather than as branches of a foreign corporation.

LSI Logic continued to expand to selected markets overseas. However, the U.S. semiconductor industry was being clobbered by the Japanese. By 1988, the Japanese had captured 51 percent of the market, and the U.S. market share had plummeted to only 36.5 percent. However, the U.S.-Japan Semiconductor Trade Agreement signed in 1986 required the Japanese chipmakers to cease pricing products below cost in the United States and to buy 20 percent of their semiconductors from non-Japanese suppliers, compared with only about 8 percent in 1986. This agreement enabled U.S. chipmakers, including LSI Logic, to make a comeback. By the end of 1992, U.S. market share had recovered to 41.5 percent, compared with 42.3 percent for the Japanese. A year later, U.S. market share surpassed the Japanese share, with the Koreans coming on strong in the high-volume, low-end chips.

Although LSI Logic suffered an operating loss in 1992, it turned things around in 1993. International revenues continued to be a significant percentage of its total revenues—17.1 percent of total revenues came from Europe, 16.8 percent from Japan, and 5.1 percent from Canada. As in its early years, LSI Logic continued to borrow abroad. One of its Japanese subsidiaries had ¥9.3 billion of loans outstanding at the end of 1992 (approximately $74.9 million). As noted in its 1992 *Annual Report,* the borrowing agreements were obtained to fund the construction of a manufacturing facility. The borrowings, which are secured by the facility and production equipment, have a weighted average variable interest rate of 5.4 percent and are payable in semi-annual installments through 2008. At the end of 1992, the company's European subsidiary had outstanding bank borrowings of approximately $24.3 million. These funds were used to finance operations, purchase equipment, and construct a German manufacturing facility. Interest rates on those loans varied from 6.5 to 10 percent.

Questions

1. In what different ways did LSI Logic use international capital markets to fund its expansion? Discuss specifically the nature of the financial instruments used.
2. Why did it use foreign capital markets rather than just the U.S. market?
3. How did the company's organizational strategy fit with its capital-acquisition strategy?
4. Given the nature of its international activities and FDI, what kind of foreign-exchange risk do you think LSI Logic faces?
5. How do the company's financing activities affect that risk?

Chapter Notes

1. Nilly Landau, "Volatility is the Common Thread," *Finance & Treasury,* May 10, 1993, pp. 5–6; NCR, 1990 *Annual Report;* and AT&T, 1992 *Annual Report.*
2. Alan C. Shapiro, *Modern Corporate Finance* (New York: Macmillan, 1988), p. 1.
3. "Theory versus the Real World," *Finance & Treasury,* April 26, 1993, p. 1.
4. Ibid., p. 2.
5. Rodrigo Briones, "Latin American Money Markets," in *International Finance Handbook,* Abraham M. George and Ian H. Giddy, eds. (New York: Wiley, 1983), p. 4.9.4.

6. "Italy," in *Financing Foreign Operations* (New York: Business International Corporation, June 1990), p. 13.
7. Bank for International Settlements, *63rd Annual Report* (Basle, Switz.: BIS, June 14, 1993), p. 99.
8. "The Euromarkets," in *Financing Foreign Operations* (New York: Business International Corporation, May 1990), p. 1.
9. Anant Sundaram, "International Financial Markets," in *Handbook of Modern Finance,* Dennis E. Logue, ed. (New York: Warren, Gorham, Lamont, 1994), pp. F3–4.

10. Ibid., p. 2.
11. "Emerging Equity Markets," *Euromoney,* December 1993, p. 68.
12. "How the Heavyweights Shape Up," *Euromoney,* May 1990, p. 56.
13. Ibid.
14. Steven Ramos, "Making Foreign Shares More Marketable," *Forbes,* July 19, 1993, p. 188.
15. "The Rise of the Red Chip," *Euromoney Supplement,* December 1993, p. 23.
16. Maximo Eng and Francis A. Lees, "Eurocurrency Centers," in *International Fi-*

nance Handbook, Abraham M. George and Ian H. Giddy, eds. (New York: Wiley, 1983), pp. 3.6.3 and 3.6.4.

17. Robert K. DeCelles and Anthony G. Alexandrou, "Relaxed U.S. Interest Allocation Rules Open Up Intercompany Debt for Foreign Funding," *Business International Money Report* (New York: Business International Corporation, February 6, 1989), pp. 34-35, 39.

18. William J. Bokos and Anne P. Clinkard, "Multilateral Netting," *Journal of Cash Management,* June–July 1983, pp. 24–34.

19. Bill Millar, "What Is a BCC?" *Business International Money Report* (New York: Business International Corporation, March 6, 1989), p. 67.

20. "Financial Strategies in Risky Markets," *Financing Foreign Operations* (New York: Business International Corporation, January 1987), pp. 1–2.

21. Richard T. De George, *Business Ethics,* 3rd ed. (New York: Macmillan, 1990), p. 403.

22. "Financial Strategies in Risky Markets," pp. 2–5.

23. Helmut Hagemann, "Anticipate Your Long-Term Foreign Exchange Risks," *Harvard Business Review,* March–April 1977, p. 82.

24. Bill Millar, "How Coca-Cola's Treasury Manages a Giant's Global Finances," *Business International Money Report* (New York: Business International Corporation, September 25, 1989), p. 311.

25. Susan Arterian, *Business International Money Report* (New York: Business International Corporation, December 18, 1989), p. 405.

26. David K. Eiteman and Arthur I. Stonehill, *Multinational Business Finance,* 6th ed. (Reading, Mass.: Addison-Wesley, 1992), pp. 493–494.

27. Sidney M. Robbins and Robert B. Stobaugh, *Money in the Multinational Enterprise* (New York: Basic Books, 1973), pp. 37–48.

28. Christopher A. Bartlett and Sumantra Ghoshal, *Managing Across Borders* (Boston: Harvard University Press, 1989), pp. 48–53.

29. LSI Logic, *Annual Report, 1992;* Ken Siegmann, "An American Tale of Semi-Success: How American Chip Companies Regained Lead," *The San Francisco Chronicle,* December 20, 1993, p. B1; Udayan Gupta, "Raising Money the New-Fangled Way," in "Global Finance & Investing: A Special Report," *Wall Street Journal,* September 18, 1987, p. 14D; Nick Arnett, "LSI Lands Former NEC Chief to Head Affiliated Company," *Business Journal* (San Jose), January 14, 1985, p. 17(1); and "LSI Gets a Circuit-Supply Pact," *Wall Street Journal,* January 6, 1987, p. 7.

Chapter 21

Human Resource Management

*If the leader is good,
the followers will be good.*
—Philippine Proverb

Objectives
- To explain the unique qualifications of international managers

- To evaluate the specific issues that occur when managers are transferred internationally

- To examine alternatives for recruitment, selection, compensation, and development of international managers

- To discuss how national labor markets can affect optimum methods of production

- To describe diversities in labor policies and practices on a country-to-country basis

- To highlight some major international pressures on how MNEs deal with labor worldwide

- To examine the effect of transnational operations on collective bargaining

Case
Dow's International
Management
Development[1]

Bulgarian-born Frank P. Popoff became CEO of U.S.-based Dow Chemical in 1992 when he replaced Italian-born Paul Oreffice, who had replaced Hungarian-born Zoltan Merszei as COO in 1979. Popoff, who had once headed Dow's European division, said, "I had a lot of international experience and I think, for a company that has over 50 percent of its sales outside the U.S., that's very important." As of 1990, Dow's 22-member top management committee included 10 who were non–U.S. born and 17 with foreign experience.

This placement of foreign-born and/or internationally experienced persons at the helm of the company might suggest the process of multinationalization. For example, Peter Drucker, a leading management authority, stated that a truly multinational company "demands of its management people that they think and act as international businessmen in a world in which national passions are as strong as ever." A company whose top management includes people from various countries and with varied country experiences presumably is less likely to place the interests of one country above those of others and supposedly will have a more worldwide outlook. Whether this is true is debatable. However, the experience of working abroad under some very different environmental conditions is very useful for grasping some problems that are not as prevalent in a purely domestic context. In 1980, Paul Oreffice described the importance of his foreign experience at Dow:

> I would never have risen as far as I have in Dow if it hadn't been for my foreign experience. What I learned in Brazil in the 1960s influenced and advanced my career. . . . In a high-inflation country . . . the only way we could get dollars to import goods from the U.S. was to go to the exchange and bid on how many cruzieros we would pay per dollar for imported goods. . . . I learned the maintenance of margins, or replacement cost pricing, which is the only way you can make sufficient profit to buy and build more plants.

In 1990, Oreffice reiterated the importance of this experience when he said:

> Our chief financial officer is Cuban, our treasurer is Brazilian, the next man at the top is Italian, and after him comes a Chilean. Native-born Americans seem to have fallen behind in Treasury simply because of the wider experience that financial people from other countries have had all over the world.

That most Dow top executives have had considerable foreign experience indicates that international operations are an integral part of the company's total commitment. To bring international operations to this level, Dow had to gain a dedication to international business from a broad spectrum of managers. The company estimates that it took about twenty years to bring this about. Until 1954, only about 6 percent of Dow's business was abroad, and of that, over 80 percent was from its one foreign subsidiary in Canada. The attitude in the late 1950s was expressed by a company historian:

> As for the overseas operations, a majority of the veterans regarded them as a sideline. The foreign market was all right as a place for getting rid of surplus products, but the only truly promising market was in the United States. They questioned the idea of the company becoming too deeply involved in countries whose politics, language, culture, monetary controls, and ways of doing business were strange to them.

Some of Dow's younger managers did not share this ethnocentric attitude, but dramatic steps were needed to convert the majority of managers to an international outlook. One method employed by the company's president in 1958 was to give international responsibilities to people who were widely perceived to be destined for top-level positions in the company. C. B. Branch, who was managing Dow's fastest-growing department, was appointed head of foreign operations. Herbert "Ted" Dow Doan, who at 31 was already a member of the board of directors, went to Europe on a fact-finding mission. (Ted Doan's father and grandfather both had been Dow presidents.) Both Branch and Doan quickly went on to become presidents of Dow. Thus the importance of international operations became readily apparent to the company's managers.

Although the discussion so far emphasizes the importance of international exposure for top-level managers in MNEs, this is not the only management consideration. Companies also must attract and retain high-quality personnel within each country in which they operate. These are largely local personnel. To attract them, Dow feels it must give people from all over the world the same opportunity to reach the top levels. Local needs also change as corporate strategies evolve. For instance, Dow had to hire many more non-U.S. scientists and technicians in the 1980s when the company was strengthening R&D in Europe and Asia.

Companies also must transfer people to foreign locations either when qualified local managers are not readily available or to upgrade the qualifications of the local managers. When Dow sends managers to foreign operations, what qualifications should they have? Robert Lundeen, a former Dow chairman who had served twelve years as president of the Pacific division and three years as president of the Latin American division, gave some indication of his philosophy. After speaking about the obvious technical needs, he said, "When I worked in Asia, I observed that many Americans seemed to delight in their insularity, and that attitude hurts the ability of the United States to do business in foreign countries."

For many years, Dow had difficulty in convincing people to take foreign assignments because of bad experience in repatriating them to acceptable positions. Dow has reacted to this problem by

- Sending some of its best people abroad so that "everybody will want them when they come back"
- Assigning higher-level supervisors to serve as "godfathers" by looking after the transferred employees' home-career interests
- Providing each transferee with a written guarantee of a job at the same or higher level on return from the foreign assignment

Because many managers have difficulty adjusting to foreign locations, Dow holds a briefing session with each prospective transferee to explain transfer policies and to provide an information package compiled by personnel in the host country. This is followed by a meeting between the transferee and that person's spouse and a recently repatriated employee or spouse to explain the emotional issues involved in the move's early stages. The couple is also given the option of attending a two-week language and orientation program.

Introduction

A company's international human resources efforts should complement its level of international development and grow with its international commitment. The Dow case highlights one company's experience in dealing with some international aspects of its personnel policies. Dow is an MNE already highly dependent on and committed to international operations. Its international human resource needs are more extensive than those of a company that merely exports or imports a small portion of its output or supplies. Such a company's primary need is for personnel that are technically trained or knowledgeable about trade documentation, foreign-exchange risk, and political-economic conditions that may affect trade flows. An MNE such as Dow shares this need but also needs a multinational workforce and managers who can integrate this workforce effectively. Most of this book deals with the technical aspects of international business, but this chapter focuses on the MNE's needs with respect to personnel.

Dow's international human resource efforts are more comprehensive than one finds within most other MNEs.[2] Although companies have taken various approaches to international human resource management, most agree on the importance of having qualified personnel in order to achieve foreign growth and operational objectives. For instance, at a roundtable discussion of chief executives on how the world is changing and what, if anything, management can do to keep change under control, the chairman of Unilever said, "The single most important issue for us has been, and will continue to be, organization and people."[3]

The need to have highly qualified people to staff the organization cannot be overemphasized. Any company must determine its personnel needs, hire people to meet those needs, motivate them to perform well, and upgrade their skills so that they can move to more demanding tasks. Several factors make the management of international human resources different from such management at the domestic level:

- *Different labor markets.* Each country has a different mix of available workers and a different mix of labor costs. MNEs may gain advantages by accessing these various human resource capabilities. For example, GM's Mexican upholstery operation employs low-cost production workers, and IBM's Swiss R&D facility hires skilled physicists. Whether companies seek resources or markets abroad, they may produce the same product differently in different countries, for example, substituting hand labor for machines because of diverse labor markets.

- *International mobility problems.* There are legal, economic, physical, and cultural barriers to overcome when moving workers to a foreign country. Yet MNEs benefit from moving people, especially when labor market differences result in shortages of needed skills. In such situations, companies often must develop special recruitment, training, compensation, and transfer practices.

- *Management styles and practices.* Attitudes toward different management styles vary from country to country; norms among management practices and labor-management relations testify to this. These differences may strain relations between headquarters and subsidiary personnel or make a manager less effective when working abroad than when working at home. At the same time, the experience of working with different national practices offers some opportunities for transferring successful practices from one country to another.

- *National orientations.* Although a company's goals may include attaining global efficiencies and competitiveness, its personnel (both labor and management) may emphasize national rather than global interests. Certain personnel practices can help overcome national orientations; other operating adjustments may be necessary when such orientations prevail.

- *Control.* Such factors as distance and diversity make it more difficult to control foreign operations than domestic ones, and personnel policies sometimes are used to gain more control over foreign operations. However, distance and diversity may inhibit a company's ability to conduct personnel policies as it would prefer and may cause its practices to vary from one country to another.

This chapter emphasizes these points, differentiating between managerial and labor personnel.

Management Qualifications and Characteristics

Headquarters-Subsidiary Relationship

Management must consider country and global needs.

International staffing is two-tiered: First, the subsidiary level must employ persons who are equipped to conduct the activities within the countries in which the company is operating. Second, people at corporate and/or regional headquarters must be equipped to coordinate and control the company's various worldwide and regional operations. These two staffing dimensions are closely related, particularly since headquarters personnel usually choose and evaluate those who direct the subsidiaries. Both headquarters and subsidiary personnel must be sufficiently aware of and willing to accept trade-offs between the need to adapt to local environmental differences and the need to gain global efficiencies.

Headquarters-subsidiary relationships are affected by
- **Polycentrism versus ethnocentrism**
- **Benefits of independence**

The balance of power for these trade-offs is complex and depends on such factors as the company's philosophy (for example, polycentric versus ethnocentric) and on how much its operations in different countries may benefit from independence as opposed to interdependence. Much less effort is needed to impose standard practices or a corporate culture abroad when a company's philosophy is polycentric and its foreign subsidiaries are a federation of highly independent operations than when its philosophy is ethnocentric and its foreign operations are internationally interdependent.[4] Regardless of where between these extremes the company lies, it may face dilemmas because the technology, policy, and managerial style it has developed in one place may be only partially applicable elsewhere. International managers, at headquarters and in subsidiaries, are responsible for introducing (or not introducing) practices to a country.

Top-Level Duties Abroad

Top managers in subsidiaries usually have broader duties than do managers of similar-sized home-country operations.

Subsidiary management   Although foreign subsidiaries usually are much smaller than their parents, their top managers often have to perform top-level management duties. This usually means being more of a generalist than a specialist and more of a leader than a follower, having responsibility for a wide variety of functions, and spending more time on the job, on external relations with the community, government, and general public, and on outside business meetings. Managers with comparable profit or cost responsibility in the home country may be performing middle-management tasks there and lack the breadth of experience necessary for a top-level management position in a foreign subsidiary.

Corporate managers abroad
- **Deal at top levels in many countries**
- **Experience the rigors of foreign travel**
- **Face difficulties if they have risen entirely through domestic divisions**

Headquarters travel   The corporate staff charged with responsibility for international business functions must interact frequently with very high-level authorities in foreign countries, for example, in negotiations for new or expanded plants, in the sale of technology, and in the assessment of monetary conditions. Their tasks are in many ways even more difficult than those of the subsidiary managers since they must be away from home for extended and indefinite periods while seeking the confidence and rapport of officials in many foreign countries rather than in just one. Further, they suffer *jet lag,* a condition in which one's biological clock (located in the bottom middle of the brain) tells the body the wrong time to sleep, eat, and feel alert or drowsy; this clock can adjust by only one or two hours a day.[5] Even if headquarters personnel are not faced with the rigors of foreign travel, they may be ill at ease with the foreign aspects of their responsibilities if their rise to the corporate level has been entirely through work in domestic divisions.

Communication Problems

International communications are complex and more likely to be misunderstood than domestic ones are.

Interpretation   International managers must communicate well to ensure that the intent of messages between headquarters and subsidiary operations is understood. Accomplishing this is somewhat complicated by the cost of overseas calls and faxes, the different time zones involved, and the longer time for international mail delivery.

Communication difficulties are further compounded when managers' native languages differ. Corporate communications, directives, and manuals may be translated, which takes time and expense. If they are not, the content may be understood perfectly abroad, but the comprehension time may be longer because people read more slowly in a second language. Likewise, communication problems may force a manager working abroad to work harder to do the same quality work as home-country counterparts.[6] Although these inherent inefficiencies are often over-looked by the parent, subsidiary management is held responsible.

Cultural differences color intents and perceptions of what is transmitted and received in formal communications; thus international managers may assume erroneously that foreigners will react the same way as their compatriots to such things as decision-making and leadership styles. This is a particular problem when various nationalities are grouped, such as on a team project. Some of these differences may be lessened through the development of a common corporate culture. A corporate culture may help little, however, when managers must work internationally in the growing number of cooperative business activities that include not just different nationalities but also different companies, such as joint ventures and licensing agreements.[7]

Use of English   Today, English is the international language of business because so much international business is conducted by companies from and in English-speaking countries. Further, when people learn a second language, English has become the most common choice worldwide. Managers cannot be expected to learn all the languages in every country in which their companies operate. Thus business between, for example, Mexico and Brazil or between Italy and Saudi Arabia may be conducted in English. Even some MNEs from non–English speaking countries have adopted English as their official language.[8]

A working knowledge of the host country's language nevertheless can help transplanted managers of a subsidiary adapt to the country as well as gain acceptance by its people. It also helps them assess potential changes in the external environment because they can read local newspapers and talk to nationals about politics and other conditions. Further, English may be spoken by upper-level managers but not necessarily by the staff, customers, and suppliers with whom the transplanted manager comes in contact. However, even those who are fully fluent in a local or common language should consider employing good interpreters when attempting serious discussions, such as negotiations with governmental officials.

Which foreign language should be learned by a native English speaker who wants a successful international business career in the twenty-first century? The choice depends largely on where one's employer does business and on one's geographic work preference. Nevertheless, one poll of U.S. companies put Spanish clearly in front with 44 percent of responses; Japanese followed at 33 percent. The only other languages receiving at least 1 percent of responses were French (8), Chinese (6), German (5), and Russian (1). Another poll predicted that Japanese, German, and Spanish will be the most important languages.[9]

Isolation

International managers are isolated and have less access to staff specialists.

A foreign-subsidiary manager must be able to work independently because many staff functions are eliminated abroad to reduce the costs of duplication. At headquarters, a manager can get advice from specialists by walking to the next office or floor or making a few telephone calls. The subsidiary manager, however, ends up relying much more heavily on his or her personal judgment.

Headquarters personnel traveling abroad also can face problems of isolation, with the added element of being isolated in their personal lives. Further, international trips are apt to be longer than domestic trips are because of the greater distances and the difficulty of returning home for weekends. As one international executive commented humorously:

> Often you won't be able to plan in advance when you are leaving on business or when you will return. Being present at birthdays, school plays, anniversaries, family reunions, and other events may become the exception instead of the rule. While you're away, mortgage payments will probably be due, the MasterCard bill will arrive, the furnace will fail, your child will get chicken pox, the IRS will schedule a full audit, the family car will be totaled, and your spouse will sue for divorce.[10]

International Managerial Transfers

Some Definitions

Managers are commonly categorized as **locals** (citizens of the countries in which they are working) or **expatriates** (noncitizens). Expatriates are either **home-country nationals** (citizens of the country in which the company is headquartered) or **third-country nationals** (citizens neither of the country in which they are working nor of the headquarters country). Locals or expatriates may be employed in the company's home country or in its foreign operations.

Expatriates: A Minority of Managers

Most managerial positions in both headquarters and foreign subsidiaries are filled by locals rather than expatriates. The one exception is for project management in some LDCs, such as Saudi Arabia, where there is an acute shortage of qualified local candidates.

Foreign managerial slots are difficult to fill because
- **Many people don't want to move**
- **There are legal impediments to using expatriates**

Mobility   Many people, regardless of nationality, do not want to work in a foreign country, particularly if an assignment is perceived to be very long-term or permanent. The most common reason for rejecting a foreign assignment is the negative effect on family life-style, such as unacceptable living conditions, inadequate educational opportunities for children, and the need to be near aged parents. Career considerations are also important, for two reasons: In many companies, a foreign assignment takes one outside the corporate mainstream for advancement; the spouse can rarely get a permit to work in a comparable job abroad.[11] There also are legal impediments for people willing to accept overseas assignments, such as licensing requirements that prevent the use of foreign-trained accountants and lawyers and immigration restrictions that cause delays and uncertainties in filling positions.

In many cases, companies have had to set up special operating units to employ people who cannot or will not work where a company would prefer; for example, R&D labs and regional staff offices have been established abroad when personnel refused to move to the country where global headquarters is located.

Local managers may help sales and morale.

Local needs   The greater the need for local adaptations, the more advantageous it is for companies to use local managers, since they presumably understand local conditions better than expatriates would. The need to adapt may arise because of unique environmental conditions, barriers to imports, or the existence of strong local competitors or large customers.

Sometimes it is useful for the company to create a local image for foreign operations, especially when there is animosity toward foreign-controlled operations. Local managers may be perceived locally as "better citizens" because they presumably put local interests ahead of the company's global objectives. This local image may play a role in employee morale as well, since many subsidiary employees prefer to work for someone from their own country.[12]

If top jobs are given only to expatriates, the company may find it difficult to attract and keep good locals.

Incentives to local personnel   The possibility of advancement provides an incentive to local employees to perform well; without this incentive, they may seek employment elsewhere. Practices that keep the best-qualified people, regardless of nationality, from top positions in foreign subsidiaries and at corporate headquarters may be even more damaging to employee motivation.

Expatriates may take shorter-term perspectives.

Long-term objectives   Because employees transferred to a subsidiary usually expect to be there for only a few years, they often are more anxious than local nationals to choose short-term projects that will materialize during their tenure in the foreign location.[13] In producing highly visible and measurable results that further their personal goals for advancement when the foreign assignment is terminated, they may not be best serving longer-range corporate goals. Local nationals who stay on longer therefore may take more heed of long-term objectives because of the probability of their continued employment after the practices are instituted.

Reasons for Using Expatriates

Although expatriate managers comprise a minority of total managers within MNEs, several hundred thousand are employed worldwide. Companies employ expatriates because of their competence to fill positions, their need to gain foreign experience, and their ability to control operations according to headquarters' preferences.

The most qualified person may be an expatriate.

Competence   Companies use expatriate managers primarily when they cannot find qualified local candidates. This is partly a function of the particular country's level of development; thus expatriates constitute a much smaller portion of subsidiary managers in industrial than in developing countries. It also is a function of the need to infuse new home-country developments abroad. For example, when new products or new production methods are to be transferred, especially in start-up operations, there usually is a need to transfer home-country personnel to subsidiaries or subsidiary personnel to the home country until the operation is running smoothly.

Management development   MNEs transfer foreigners to their home country or regional operations and home-country nationals to foreign subsidiaries to train them to understand the overall corporate system.[14] In companies with specialized activities only in certain countries (for example, extraction separated from manufacturing or basic R&D separated from applied R&D), long-term foreign assignments may be the only means of developing a manager's integrative competence. These moves also enhance a manager's ability to work in a variety of social systems and are therefore valuable training for ultimate corporate responsibility, involving both domestic and foreign operations.

The move of expatriates into top-level corporate positions has been slow, however, even though an increasing number of companies have become highly dependent on their foreign operations. For example, only about 10 percent of large U.S. companies have foreigners either as board members or in high corporate positions.[15] (Dow therefore represents a small minority of companies.) There are obvious international perspectives that foreigners can bring to a company. The founder of Compaq Computer said, "As more and more companies are forced to be global, you are going to see more mixing of nationalities at the top."[16]

Control   MNEs use transfers and visits to subsidiaries to control the foreign operations and coordinate organizational development. These goals are accomplished because the people who are transferred are used to doing things the headquarters way and because frequent transfers let them increase their knowledge of the company's global network.[17] Further, foreign nationals may spend time at worldwide or regional headquarters, thereby giving a foreign perspective to the company's global direction. Through the greater interchange brought about by moves of both home- and host-country nationals, a new hybrid corporate culture, or at least an understanding and acceptance of global corporate goals, can develop as a means of controlling the company's operations.[18]

A company that follows a more global strategy needs to use more expatriates for control purposes. They generally are or become more familiar with the complexities of the corporate system and tend not to see their own personal development in terms of what happens only in the country to which they are assigned.[19]

The use of expatriates for control is affected by the type of ownership of foreign operations. For example, an expatriate transferred abroad by a joint-venture partner may be in an ambiguous situation, not knowing for sure whether he or she represents and should report to both partners or just the partner making the transfer.

Multicountry experience gives upward-moving managers new perspectives.

People transferred from headquarters are more likely to know corporate policies.

People transferred to headquarters learn the headquarters' way.

Home-Country versus Third-Country Nationals

Most advances in technology, product, and operating procedures originate in the home country and are later transferred into foreign operations. Because the use of expatriates in foreign facilities is dictated in part by a desire to infuse new methods, personnel with recent home-country experience (usually home-country nationals) are apt to have the desired qualifications.

However, third-country nationals sometimes might have more compatible technical and personal adaptive qualifications than do home-country expatriates. For example, a U.S. company used U.S. personnel to design and manage a Peruvian plant until local managers could be trained. Years later, the company decided to manufacture in Mexico using a plant that more closely resembled the Peruvian operations than its U.S. operations in terms of size, product qualities, and factor inputs. The company's Spanish-speaking Peruvian managers were adaptive and were used effectively in the planning, start-up, and early operating phases in Mexico. When companies establish lead operations abroad, such as headquarters for a product division or a country operation that is larger than that in the home country, third-country nationals are more likely to have the competencies needed for the foreign assignments.

Some Individual Considerations for Transfers

Technical competence   Unless a foreign assignment is clearly intended for training an expatriate, local employees will resent someone coming in from a foreign country (usually at higher compensation) who, they feel, is no more qualified than they are. The opinions of corporate decision makers, expatriate managers, and local managers all confirm that job ability factors, usually indicated by past job performance that is not necessarily international, are determinants of success in overseas assignments.[20] Although various other skills are important for success in an overseas assignment, the expatriate must know the technical necessities of the tasks as they are performed in the home country and must be able to adapt to foreign variations, such as scaled-down plants and equipment, varying standards of productivity, lack of efficient infrastructure and internal distribution, nonavailability of credit, and restrictions on type of communications media selected. The expatriate also must be fully aware of corporate policies so that foreign decisions are compatible with them. For these reasons, managers usually have several years' work experience with a company before being offered a foreign assignment.

Adaptiveness   Although some companies rely only on technical competence as the criterion in the selection of expatriates for transfer, three types of adaptive characteristics are important for an expatriate's success when entering a new culture:

1. Those needed for self-maintenance, such as being self-confident and able to reduce stress

Third-country nationals may know more about
- **Language**
- **Operating adjustments**

Job-ability factors are a necessary attribute.

2. Those related to the development of satisfactory relationships with host nationals, such as flexibility and tolerance
3. Cognitive skills that help one to perceive correctly what is occurring within the host society[21]

An expatriate who lacks any of these may not be able to function effectively. At an extreme, the expatriate may leave, either by choice or by company decision.

Family adaptation is important.

Estimates vary widely on the percentage of expatriates transferred abroad who return home prematurely or perform ineffectively because of adjustment problems, either the employee's or the family's. Nevertheless, there is consensus that the costs to MNEs in the form of transfer expenses and lost performance are high.[22] An international move may greatly disrupt a family's current way of living, especially since most transfers send people from industrial countries to LDCs, and a major reason for failure in a foreign assignment is the family's inability to adjust.[23] A move means new living and shopping habits, new school systems, and unfamiliar business practices. In addition, close friends and relatives—the personal support system—are left behind. However, some individuals do enjoy and adapt easily to a foreign way of life; MNEs should use them if possible. Some companies even maintain a core international group of employees who are the only ones assigned abroad.

Fixed-term versus open-end assignments are viewed differently.

A distinction must be made between a foreign assignment of fixed duration and one that is open-ended. Many more people can cope with a position abroad if they know that they will return home after a specific time period.

Expatriates may meet with local prejudice.

Local acceptance Expatriates may encounter some acceptance problems regardless of who they are. For example, it usually takes time for managers to gain recognition of their personal authority, and expatriates may not be there long enough to achieve this. Local employees may feel that the best jobs are given to overpaid foreigners. Expatriates may have to make unpopular decisions in order to meet global objectives. Or local management may have had experiences with expatriates who made short-term decisions and then left before dealing with the longer-term implications.[24] If negative stereotypes are added to these attitudes, the expatriate may find it very difficult to succeed. Certain individuals may encounter insurmountable problems when dealing as an expatriate with employees, suppliers, and customers, for example, a Jewish manager in Libya, a very young manager in Japan, or a female manager in Saudi Arabia. The U.S. Civil Rights Act of 1991 extended the nondiscrimination provisions of the earlier civil rights law to cover the employment of U.S. citizens abroad, except where foreign law prohibits the employment of a certain class of individual. Because most discrimination problems abroad are cultural rather than legal, companies face challenges in handling the requirements of this act.[25]

But do companies overreact to these acceptance problems? Consider stereotypes of women: They should not give orders to men, they are temperamental, their place is in the home, clients will not accept them, employees will not take them seriously, they don't have the stamina to work in harsh areas, they will not be given work permits, they don't want to upset their husbands' careers. Partly because of these stereotypes, MNEs have given very few expatriate positions to women, especially to foreign women in the companies' home countries. Yet women have succeeded as expatriates, primarily in service rather than industrial products industries, in such places as India, Japan, and Thailand because they were seen first as foreigners and then as women.[26] Suggestions to improve the acceptability of women as expatriates may be applied as well to other groups. These include selecting very well-qualified older, mid-career women who could command more authority, disseminating in advance information concerning the person's high qualifications, placing expatriate women in locations where there are already some local women in management positions, and establishing longer than normal assignments in order to develop role models for acceptance.[27]

Post-Expatriate Situations

Coming home can require adaptation in many areas, including
- **Financial**
- **Job**
- **Social**

Repatriation problems Problems with repatriation from foreign assignments arise in three general areas: personal finances, readjustment to home-country corporate structure, and readjustment to life at home. Expatriates are given many financial benefits to encourage them to accept a foreign assignment. While abroad, they may live in the best neighborhoods, send their children to the best private schools, employ domestic help, socialize with the upper class, and still save more money than before the move. But this life-style is lost on their return home. Returning expatriates often find that many of their peers have been promoted above them in their absence, that they now have less autonomy in the job, and that they are now "little fish in a big pond." Many families that have successfully adjusted to a foreign life-style also have problems readjusting to schools and other aspects of life in their home countries. Some suggestions for smoothing the reentry include providing ample advance notice of when the return will occur, maximum information about the new job, housing assistance, and a reorientation program, as well as requiring frequent visits to headquarters and using a formal headquarters mentor to look after the manager's interests while that person is abroad.[28]

Career movements The significance of an overseas assignment to one's career varies widely. The opinions of repatriated employees reveal that a foreign assignment is most likely to have a neutral long-term effect on one's career. The accuracy of this opinion is confirmed in studies of career paths of top executives. However, for many, foreign assignments have had appreciable positive or detrimental effects.[29] Whether the experience is positive, negative, or neutral depends on individual differences and such factors as the company's commitment to foreign operations, the integration between domestic and international activities, and the communications linkages between headquarters and subsidiary personnel.

For companies with a very high commitment to global operations, multicountry experience may be as essential as multifunctional and multiproduct experience in reaching upper-echelon organizational levels. The Dow case illustrates such a situation. Nevertheless, some companies with a high international commitment so separate foreign and domestic operations that they function almost as two separate companies. If the domestic business dominates, there may be not only little interchange of personnel between domestic and foreign operations but also little advancement of personnel with international experience to top-level positions. For example, of GM's top executives, very few have been assigned abroad.[30] However, this has not daunted GM's foreign success: It is one of the largest U.S. exporters, and its overseas production, especially in the United Kingdom and Germany, is highly competitive. Its personnel and organizational policies are compatible because of its largely multidomestic strategy.

In any case, very few people reach the top rungs of large companies, with or without foreign work experience. Some companies, particularly those with international divisions, depend heavily on a cadre of specialists who may either rotate between foreign locations and international headquarters assignments or spend most of their careers abroad. Although not reaching the top management levels of the parent, they can reach plateaus above most domestic managers in terms of compensation and responsibility. Many people with a penchant for international living do not aspire to anything different.

Within some companies, foreign assignments carry a high career risk, regardless of corporate executives' statements to the contrary. A Ford vice president once said candidly, "For the vast majority of people [in middle and senior-middle management] at Ford, foreign assignments are a career negative." This type of situation may arise for two reasons. First, there may be little provision to fit someone into the domestic or headquarters organization on repatriation. One's old office simply does not stay vacant while one is abroad for several years; a repatriated employee cannot easily bump his or her replacement. Holding a position available while an employee is abroad is particularly difficult when the foreign assignment is of indefinite length, and such open-ended assignments are a significant portion of the total; at Hewlett-Packard such assignments constitute 25 percent of foreign transfers, for example.[31] A senior engineer working for Westinghouse in Belgium described finding a job with Westinghouse in the United States as being the same as when he first applied to the company while in college.[32] Second, some "out of sight, out of mind" may come into play. A General Dynamics executive said he would never have known about domestic openings if a friend had not kept him apprised of the organization's promotional pipeline.[33] Reentry is further complicated if the expatriate is on lengthy assignment in a location where older technologies and corporate policies are practiced.

When repatriated employees have career problems, it becomes more difficult to convince other people to take foreign assignments. Very few companies follow Dow's example and make written guarantees that repatriated employees will come back to jobs at least as good as those they left. (However, companies do not guarantee future positions to their domestic managers either.) Some companies simply explain the career risk and compensate employees so highly that they are enticed to become expatriates. Others integrate foreign assignments into career planning and are developing mentor programs to look after the expatriates' domestic interests.[34]

Foreign nationals who are transferred to headquarters sometimes confront a different problem. If the assignment is a promotion from a manager's subsidiary post rather than part of a planned rotation, then the move to headquarters may be permanent. For example, the Brazilian head of a Brazilian subsidiary may have performed so well that the MNE wants to give that manager multicountry responsibility at the corporate offices in New York or Frankfurt. Because the manager would not be able to return to Brazil without taking a demotion, he or she might refuse the transfer.

Expatriate Compensation

MNEs must pay enough to entice people to move but must not overpay.

If a U.S. company transfers its British finance manager, who is making $50,000 per year, to Italy, where the going rate is $60,000 per year, what should the manager's salary be? Or if the Italian financial manager is transferred to the United Kingdom, what pay should be offered? Should the compensation be in dollars, pounds, or lira? Whose holidays should apply? Which set of fringe benefits should apply? These are but a few of the many questions that must be solved when a company moves people abroad. On the one hand, it must keep costs down; on the other, it must maintain high employee morale.

The amount and type of compensation necessary to entice a person to move to another country vary widely by person and locale. Company practices also vary widely in terms of compensation for differences. Companies with very few expatriate employees may work out a foreign compensation package on an individual basis. As international activities grow, however, it becomes too cumbersome to handle each transfer in this way. As long as consistency is sought in transfer policy, some people inevitably will receive more than would be necessary to entice them to go abroad. Overall, the package may multiply the compensation cost in comparison with what the expatriate had been making domestically. Table 21.1 illustrates a typical package.

Living is more expensive abroad because
- *Habits change slowly*
- *People don't know how and where to buy*

MNEs use various cost-of-living indexes and
- *Increase compensation when foreign cost is higher*
- *Do not decrease compensation when foreign cost is lower*
- *Remove the differential when the manager is repatriated*

Cost of living Most people who move to another country encounter cost-of-living increases (sometimes called a goods-and-services differential), primarily because their accustomed way of living is expensive to duplicate in a new environment. Habits are difficult to change. Knowledge of the local country is a second consideration. Food and housing may be obtained at higher than the local rate because expatriates may not know the language well, where to buy, or how to bargain for reductions.

Most companies raise salaries by a differential to account for higher foreign-country costs. After the expatriate returns home, the differential is removed. A few companies reduce the cost-of-living differential over time, reasoning that as expatriates become better assimilated, they should be able to adjust more to local pur-

Table 21.1
Typical First-Year Cost for a U.S. Expatriate (Married, Two Children) in Tokyo, Japan
An expatriate's cost to the company may be several times what it would be for the same employee in his or her home country.

Direct compensation costs	
Base salary	$100,000
Foreign-service premium	15,000
Goods and services differential	73,600
Less: U.S. housing norm*	(15,400)
U.S. hypothetical taxes	(17,200)
Company-paid costs	
Schooling (two children)	15,000
Annual home leave	4,800
Housing*	150,000
Japanese income taxes†	84,000
Transfer/moving costs	38,000
Total company costs	**$447,800**

*Assumes company rents housing in its name and provides to expatriate. If company pays housing allowance instead, Japanese income taxes (and total costs) will be about $65,000 higher.
†Note that Japanese income taxes will increase each year as some company reimbursements, most notably for taxes, become taxable.

Source: Organization Resources Counselors, Inc.

chasing habits, for example, by buying vegetables from a native market instead of using imported packaged goods. When moves are to areas with a lower cost of living, few companies reduce an employee's pay because doing so might adversely affect the employee's morale; thus expatriates may receive a windfall. Companies that do reduce expatriates' pay, such as Hewlett-Packard, usually offer temporary bridging payments to ease the adjustment.[35]

Companies rely on estimates of cost-of-living differences, even though the differences do not fit everyone's situation perfectly. Some commonly used sources of such estimates are the U.S. State Department's cost-of-living index published yearly in *Labor Developments Abroad,* the *U.N. Monthly Bulletin of Statistics,* and surveys by the *Financial Times, Business International,* and the International Monetary Fund *Staff Papers.* In using any of these, companies must determine which items are included in order to adjust omitted ones separately. Some items commonly handled separately are housing, schooling, and taxes. Differences in inflation and exchange rates may quickly render surveys and indexes obsolete; thus cost-of-living adjustments must be updated frequently.

The ultimate objective of cost-of-living adjustments is to ensure that expatriates' after-tax income will not suffer as a result of a foreign assignment. Because taxes are usually assessed on the overseas premiums in addition to the base salaries, the premiums must be adjusted even further upward if the foreign tax rate is higher than the home country's. For example, in Sweden it is sometimes less expensive for an expatriate to commute daily by plane from Germany rather than be subjected to the Swedish personal income taxes, which are among the world's highest.

A transfer is more attractive if employees see it as an advancement.

Job-status payment Some employees may not accept a position abroad unless it is considered a promotion, and most people consider a promotion without a pay increase inequitable. Expatriates compare their compensation with that of other managers in both the foreign country and their home country. Thus where the going rate for the job is higher than that in the home country, companies also will normally raise an expatriate's salary temporarily while the person is working abroad.

Employees may encounter living problems for which extra compensation is given.

Foreign-service premiums and hardship allowances There are bound to be things expatriates will have to do without when living abroad. Such sacrifices range from nuisance to hardship. For example, expatriates may miss certain foods, a holiday celebration, television in the native language, or following particular sports results. Or their children may have to attend school away from home, perhaps even in another country. There also is the problem of adjusting to a new culture; such adjustments may cause adverse psychological effects and social frustrations. Further, in about 25 percent of countries, domestic help is deemed essential for expatriates because of unavailability of babysitters, unsanitary conditions that require more housework, such as boiling water and soaking vegetables, and security considerations that dictate always having someone in the residence.[36] Consequently, companies frequently give expatriates foreign-service premiums just for being posted in a foreign location. This practice appears to be dropping off, however, especially in so-called world capitals, in which there is assumed to be little deprivation and to which it is not difficult to get people to transfer.

Few would deny that living conditions in certain locales present particularly severe hardships, such as harsh climatic or health conditions or political insurrection or unrest that places the expatriate and family in danger. For instance, recently antigovernment groups kidnapped expatriates of such companies as Ford, Kodak, and Owens-Illinois. Companies have been hit by legal suits from victims' families that allege the companies mishandled ransom negotiations. Some MNEs have faced stockholder suits claiming the companies should not pay ransom.[37] Consequently, companies have had not only to rethink their hardship allowances but also to purchase ransom insurance and to provide training programs on safety for expatriates and families. Many companies also pay for home alarm systems and security guards.

Finally, a hardship may occur because of potential changes in total family income and status. In the home country, all members of the family may be able to work. Many companies now provide spouses of expatriates with job-search assistance, often through networks with other companies. For example, Eastman Kodak finds employment for about 25 percent of spouses.[38] However, people other than the transferred employee are seldom given permission to work in a foreign country. So the spouse (or live-in companion) of an expatriate may either have to give up well-paying and satisfying employment or be separated from the partner for long periods. Some companies increase the expatriate's compensation, and about one third of large U.S. companies assist couples with commuter marriages. For example, Stride Rite transferred a manager to Taiwan, while her husband continued working in the United States. Stride Rite paid for all their telephone calls to each other plus seven trips a year to reunite.[39]

Choice of currency   An expatriate's salary is usually (but not always) paid partly in local currency and partly in the currency of the expatriate's home country. This procedure allows the expatriate to save money in the home country and often to forgo host-country taxes on the home-country portion of income. Other factors that influence the preference for payment in home-country or host-country currency include whether hard-currency expenditures can be charged to the local operation, whether exchange control exists, and whether the expatriate can receive more local currency by exchanging the hard currency through a free market.

Remote areas   Many large-scale international projects are in areas so remote that MNEs would get few people to transfer there if the companies did not create an environment more like that at home or make other special arrangements. For example, Lockheed Aircraft set up its own color TV broadcasting station in Saudi Arabia for its expatriates there. Also, INCO built schools, hospitals, churches, supermarkets, a golf course, a yacht club, a motel, and a restaurant for its expatriates in Indonesia.[40]

Expatriates in remote areas often are handled very differently from employees elsewhere. To attract the large number of people necessary for construction and start-up, MNEs usually will offer fixed-term contract assignments at high salaries and hire most people from outside the company. Some people are attracted to these assignments and are willing to undergo difficult living conditions because they can save money at a rate that would be impossible to achieve at home.

Complications of nationality differences   As companies employ expatriates from both home and third countries, compensation issues have become very complex. There is no consensus among companies on how to deal with most of these. For example, salaries for similar jobs vary substantially among countries, as do the relationships of salaries within the corporate hierarchy. For example, in 1992 the head of human resources at an Italian company made about 37 percent more than that person's counterpart in a U.S. company; however, the typical U.S. CEO made 55 percent more than the typical Italian CEO. The method of payment also varies substantially. Long-term incentives, such as options on restricted stock, are popular in the United States but not in Germany. However, German managers often receive

Salaries usually are paid in a mixture of home- and host-country currencies.

MNEs may have to provide more fringe benefits to employees in remote areas.

compensation that U.S. managers do not, such as housing allowances and partial payment of salary outside Germany, neither of which are taxable. When sending people of different nationalities abroad to work, companies disagree on how to calculate home-country base incomes and whether to use a standard means of adjusting those incomes. However, there is nearly a consensus to maintain expatriates on their home-country retirement systems because of the complexities involved in standardization and the need to protect people in the locales in which they are most apt to retire.[41]

Management Recruitment and Selection

College Recruitment

College recruitment is used at home and abroad, but the biggest need abroad is for higher-level managers.

MNEs recruit through universities at home and abroad to find capable nationals of the countries in which they have foreign operations. They also recruit home-country nationals, usually to work in their domestic operations until they have gained technical experience and knowledge of the corporate culture.

Management Inventories

Foreign personnel are not easily encompassed in information inventories because
• Foreign operations may not be wholly owned
• There may be restrictions on cross-national data flows

Some companies have centralized personnel record systems, which include data on home- and foreign-country nationals. These data include not only the usual technical and demographic data but also information on adaptive capabilities such as foreign-language qualifications, willingness to accept foreign assignments, and results of company-administered tests. However, a company may encounter problems in bringing foreign managers into the system; if the company owns less than 100 percent of the foreign facility, the other stockholders may complain.[42] Also, restrictions on data flows among countries could inhibit future uses of centralized management inventories.

Adaptability Assessment

Companies usually know more about their employees' technical capabilities than about their adaptive ones; thus they must focus on measuring adaptability for foreign-transfer purposes. For example, people who have successfully adjusted to domestic transfers or have previous international experience are more likely to adapt abroad. In addition, some companies use a variety of testing mechanisms as assessment aids. One is the Early Identification Program, which assesses an individual's match with different environments. Many other tests assess personality traits that indicate a willingness to change basic attitudes. These include the Minnesota Multiphasic Personality Inventory, the Guilford-Zimmerman Temperament Survey, and the Allport-Vernon Study of Values.[43]

A few companies include spouses in tests and extensive interviews because a foreign assignment is usually more stressful for the spouse than for the transferred employee.[44] For example, a foreign assignment is generally (in most cases) an advancement for the husband, but the wife must start at the bottom in developing new social relations and learning how to carry out the day-to-day management of the home. The separation from friends, family, and career often makes her very lonely so that she turns to her husband for more companionship. But the husband may have less time because of his new working conditions. This may lead to marital stress which, in turn, affects work performance. Interviewers thus look not only at likely adaptiveness but also at whether the marriage is strong enough to weather the stress and not impede performance of employment duties.[45]

Although some companies follow a rigorous procedure of selecting and training people cross-culturally for foreign assignments, the adjustment and performance of their expatriates have been mixed. Nevertheless, the evidence supports a positive relationship between vigorous procedures and adjustment and performance.[46]

The Help of Local Companies

One way to staff foreign operations is by buying an existing foreign company and using the personnel already employed; however, companies should consider the possible efficiency problems of acquisitions. Companies also may tie in closely with local companies in the expectation that the latter will contribute personnel to the operation as well as hire new personnel. In countries such as Japan, where the labor market is tight and people are reluctant to move to new companies, the use of a local partner may be extremely important. However, if a local partner handles staffing arrangements, the employees may see their primary allegiance to that partner rather than to the foreign investor.

International Development of Managers

The Needs

To carry out global operations, companies need people with a variety of specialized skills; therefore, programs to develop managers internationally must be tailored to some extent to specific individuals and situations.[47] In some companies, operations are handled in a multidomestic manner, and there is a cadre of international specialists who go from country to country and perhaps never work in their home countries. The primary need in these situations is to develop competent specialists. In other companies, the primary need is to develop generalized international attitudes and skills so that the organization as a whole will move toward achieving its global objectives. Conclusions from recent studies conflict as to whether companies are utilizing primarily the specialized or the generalized development of international skills.[48] There is, however, agreement on two developmental needs:

I. Top executives must have a global mindset that is sufficiently free of national prejudices and sufficient knowledge about the global environment that they can exert the leadership necessary to attain a global mission.

Tests' ability to predict success in foreign assignments is not very high.

Acquisitions and joint ventures secure staff but the staff may be
- **Inefficient**
- **Hard to control**

2. Operating personnel, particularly those with direct international responsibility, must be able to effect a proper balance in well-being between corporate and national operations.

Preemployment Training

There is an increase in international studies in universities.

Managers need to be trained to understand how operating differences are brought about by international business activities. Managers with direct international responsibilities need specialized skills; those with indirect responsibilities need generalized skills. Business schools are increasing their international offerings and requirements, but there is no consensus as to what students should learn to help prepare them for international responsibilities. Two distinct approaches are to convey specific knowledge about foreign environments and international operating adjustments and to train in interpersonal awareness and adaptability. The former may tend to remove some of the fear and aggression that are aroused when dealing with the unknown. However, the understanding of a difference does not necessarily imply a willingness to adapt to it, particularly to a cultural difference. The Peace Corps uses sensitivity training, which is designed to develop attitudinal flexibility.[49] Although either approach generally helps a person adjust relative to those who lack training, there appears to be no significant difference in the effectiveness of the two approaches.[50]

Postemployment Training

Postemployment training may include
- Environment-specific information
- Adaptiveness training
- Training by an unaffiliated company abroad

Many employees may continue to place domestic performance objectives above global ones or feel ill-equipped to handle worldwide responsibilities as they move up in their organizations. To counter this, a company can train those people who are about to take a foreign assignment, such as through language and orientation programs. Or it could include international business components in external or internal programs for employees that may or may not work abroad. Examples of internal programs are those at PepsiCo International and Raychem, which bring foreign nationals to U.S. divisions for periods of six months to a year; IBM's regional training centers, in which managers from several countries are gathered for specific topics; P&G's training on globalization issues; and GE's and Honda of America's programs to teach foreign languages and cultural sensitivity.[51] Sometimes a company will train employees and families from an unaffiliated company, including those from abroad, as a means of amortizing training costs and broadening backgrounds of attendees.[52]

Transferees may find it difficult even to know which questions to ask; thus the most common predeparture training takes the form of an informational briefing. Topics covered typically include job design, compensation, housing, climate, education, health conditions, home sales, taxes, transport of goods, job openings after repatriation, and salary distribution. But such things as the foreign social structure, communications links, kidnapping precautions, and legal advice on the law of domicile are seldom considered before settlement abroad.[53] A suggestion is to follow predeparture training with cultural training about six months after arrival in a foreign country so that expatriates may relate better to issues covered.[54]

Labor-Market Differences

External Reference Points

MNEs should look to existing operations as references for planning manpower needs in new operations abroad.

Typically, a company setting up a new foreign operation is duplicating, perhaps on a small or slightly altered scale, a product, process, or function being performed at home. Past experience will have shown company officials which type and how many employees are needed for the size of operation being built. The company probably will have descriptions for each type of job to be filled and from past experience will know which types of people ideally fit into specific positions.

The Production Method

MNEs may shift labor or capital intensities if relative costs differ.

There is some danger in a company's attempting to duplicate organizational structures and job descriptions abroad, particularly in LDCs. Labor-saving devices that are economically justifiable at home, where wage rates are high, may be more costly than labor-intensive types of production in a country with high unemployment rates and low wages. Using labor-intensive methods also may ingratiate the company with governmental officials, who must cope with the host country's unemployment. Because of differences in labor skills and attitudes, the company also may find it advantageous to simplify tasks and use equipment that would be considered obsolete in a more advanced economy.

International Labor Mobility

There is pressure for labor to move from high-unemployment and low-wage areas to places of perceived opportunities.

Cause   At the same time that most LDCs and the countries of Eastern Europe have faced critical unemployment problems, many industrialized countries, under-populated oil-producing countries, and newly industrialized countries of Asia have been short of workers to run facilities. A great deal of pressure for increased immigration has resulted, which in turn has been tempered by legal restrictions to minimize the economic and social problems for the countries absorbing large numbers of immigrants.

There is incentive to hire immigrant workers because they often will work for a fraction of what domestic workers with comparable skills will demand. This is especially true of illegal immigrants who cannot afford to return to their own countries. In other cases, companies have sought specialists from abroad. For example, Computer Consulting Services, a small U.S.-based software company, has brought in 90 percent of its computer consultants from abroad. Alternatively, Software Services International has exported much of its software work to India.[55]

Reliable figures on the amount of international migration are unavailable because so many immigrants are illegal and therefore undocumented. However, the fragmentary evidence is rather startling. Estimates for the early 1990s indicate that about 1 million immigrants a year entered the United States and about half a million a year went to Western Europe.[56] Remittances home from workers from such countries as Egypt, Jordan, Pakistan, and the Republic of Yemen exceed the value of exports from those countries.[57]

Companies are less certain of labor supply when they depend on foreign laborers because
- **Countries become restrictive**
- **Workers return home**
- **Turnover necessitates more training**

Workforce stability problem   Migrant workers in many countries have permission to stay for only short periods, for example, three to six months for New Zealand's workers from Fiji and Tonga. In many other cases, workers leave their families behind in the hope of returning home after saving sufficient money while working in the foreign country; this creates workforce uncertainty for employers. In the mid-1970s, for example, France had a net loss in its workforce as large numbers of Spanish workers returned home, and in the late 1980s, the United States had a net loss of Korean scientists and engineers. Another uncertainty is the extent to which governmental authorities will restrict the number of foreign workers. All industrial countries are pressured to expel foreign workers in order to protect job opportunities for domestic workers or to promote a more homogeneous culture. Even if cutbacks are accomplished during a slack period in the economy, during which a company may switch to using local rather than foreign workers, the company then may face the costly process of training workers who may leave as soon as the economy improves.

MNEs must build infrastructure to operate in remote areas.

Employment adjustments   MNEs' ability to mobilize capital, technology, and management has fed the demand for migrant workers in remote parts of the world. To operate facilities where minerals are located or in previously unoccupied areas of oil-producing countries, companies have had to import many foreign skilled and unskilled workers. When doing this, they have had to construct housing and infrastructure and to develop social services to serve the new population. Even in populated areas, housing shortages might prevent the influx of temporary workers if a company did not make housing provisions.

The influx and use of foreign workers create additional workplace problems. For example, in parts of Western Europe today, certain nationality groups are relegated to less complex jobs because their language makes training them difficult. A result has been the development of homogeneous ethnic work groups at cross-purposes with other groups in the organization, as well as the emergence of go-betweens who can communicate with management and labor.

Labor Compensation

Importance of Differences
Labor-cost differences among companies and countries sometimes lead to competitive advantages and can influence where companies will establish production facilities. The amount of compensation people receive depends on their estimated

contributions to the business, supply of and demand for particular skills ("going wage") in the area, cost of living, government legislation, and collective-bargaining ability. The methods of payment (salaries, wages, commissions, bonuses, and fringe benefits) depend on customs, feelings of security, taxes, and governmental requirements.

MNEs usually pay slightly better than do their local counterparts in lower-wage countries, although the salary is still less than what would be paid in higher-wage countries. Some factors leading to higher wages paid by MNEs relate to their management philosophies and structures: The typical management philosophy, particularly in contrast to that of local, family-run companies, often is to attract high-level workers by offering higher relative wages. In addition, techniques that lead to greater efficiencies allow for higher employee compensation. Further, when a company first comes into a country, experienced workers may demand higher compensation because they have doubts about whether the new operation will succeed.

Fringe Benefits

Fringe benefits differ radically from one country to another. Direct-compensation figures therefore do not accurately reflect the amount a company must pay for a given job in a given country. The types of benefits that are either customary or have been required also vary widely. In Japan, for example, workers in large companies commonly receive such benefits as family allowances, housing loans and subsidies, lunches, children's education, and subsidized vacations; thus fringe benefits make up a much higher portion of total compensation in Japan than in the United States. In the United Kingdom, about 70 percent of automobiles are corporate-owned because of the personal tax advantages of using a company car rather than receiving income to buy a personal car. Also common in many countries are benefits such as end-of-the-year bonuses of up to three-months' pay, housing, payments based on the number of children, long vacations, and profit sharing.

Job-security benefits   In many countries, firing or laying off an employee may be either impossible or very expensive, resulting in unexpectedly higher costs for a company accustomed to the economies that can result from manipulating its employment figures. In the United States, for example, layoffs are not only permitted but have grown to be expected when demand falls seasonally or cyclically. In many countries, however, a company has no legal recourse except to fire workers—and then perhaps only if it is closing down its operations. For example, in Belgium, Italy, and Spain, a fired worker making $50,000 a year with twenty years of service would receive termination benefits ranging from $94,000 to $130,000.[58] To curtail operations in such countries, a company must come to an agreement with its unions and the government on such issues as extended benefits and the retraining and relocation of workers.

Liability for injuries   Company, worker, or third-party neglect may lead to various types of worker or company injury. The worker may be injured physically from, for example, negligent driving by transport workers, faulty maintenance of equipment, and/or lack of safety equipment. The company may be injured monetarily from, for example, careless handling of cash, embezzlement of funds, and breakage of product and equipment. There are widespread variances in the extent to which workers or companies are held responsible for injuries.[59] The determination of responsibility should dictate how companies handle these contingencies. The amount and allocation of expenditures for insurance, training, and safety equipment thus vary substantially by country.

How to compare   Too often, compensation expenses are compared on a per-worker basis, which may bear little relationship to the total employment expenditure. People's abilities and motivations vary widely; consequently, it is the output associated with cost that is important. Seemingly cheap labor actually may raise the total compensation expenditure because of the need for more supervision, added training expenses, and adjustments in the method of production. For example, Quality Coils, a small U.S. company, moved some operations to Mexico because hourly wages were only about one third of what it paid in Connecticut. However, the company later returned to Connecticut because of high absenteeism and low productivity in Mexico.[60]

Labor-Cost Dynamics

Differences among countries in amount and type of compensation change; salaries and wages (as well as other expenditures) may rise more rapidly in one locale than in another. Therefore, the relative competitiveness of operations in different countries may shift. For example, in the 1980s Korean workers made hundreds of thousands of shoes for Nike and Reebok; however, as Korean labor costs grew, most of these jobs shifted to China and Indonesia.[61] But the process of comparing costs is complex. An example will illustrate shifting capabilities. Assume U.S. productivity per worker in manufacturing increased by 2.8 percent, and hourly compensation rates went up by 10.2 percent. The result was a unit labor-cost increase of 7.2 percent (1.102 divided by 1.028). Meanwhile, in the United Kingdom productivity increased by 5.9 percent and hourly compensation by 16.2 percent, amounting to a unit labor-cost increase of 9.7 percent (1.162 divided by 1.059). This meant that labor costs were rising more rapidly in the United Kingdom than in the United States in terms of local currencies. But if the pound depreciated substantially in relation to the dollar, the unit labor cost measured in dollars could actually have become more favorable in the United Kingdom than in the United States.

Relative costs change, so MNEs must consider
- *Productivity change*
- *Labor-rate change*
- *Conversion of labor rate to competitor's currency*

Comparative Labor Relations

In each country in which an MNE operates, it must deal with a group of workers whose approach will be affected by the sociopolitical environment of the country and by the traditions and regulations concerning collective bargaining.

Sociopolitical Environment

There are striking international differences in how labor and management view each other. When there is very little mobility between the two groups and a marked class difference exists, considerable labor strife may result. Labor may perceive itself as involved in a class struggle, even though it may have been gaining in real and relative terms for some time.

In such countries as Brazil, Switzerland, and the United States, labor demands are largely met through an adversarial process between the directly affected management and labor.[62] The adversarial relationship in the United States has perhaps given employers an added incentive to oppose unions and set up nonunion operations: Between 1970 and 1989, the percentage of U.S. workers belonging to unions fell by about two thirds to only 16 percent, whereas union membership in the seventeen major industrialized competitors of the United States rose to slightly over half of their workforces.[63] Unions in the United States negligibly influence members' vote in political elections. In contrast, labor groups in many countries vote largely in blocs, resulting in a system in which demands are met primarily through national legislation rather than collective bargaining with management. Such mechanisms as strikes or slowdowns to effect changes also may be national in scope. In this situation a company's production or ability to distribute its product may be much more dependent on the way labor perceives conditions in the whole country.

The use of mediation by an impartial party to try to bring opposing sides together varies as well. In Israel, it is required by law; in the United States and the United Kingdom, it is voluntary. Among countries that have mediation practices, attitudes toward it are diverse; for example, there is much less enthusiasm for it in India than in the United States.[64] Not all differences are settled either through changes in legislation or through collective bargaining. Other means are the labor court and the government-chosen arbitrator. For example, in Austria wages in many industries are arbitrated semiannually.[65] Settlements may be highly one-sided if appointments to a country's labor courts have been made by political parties that are either pro- or anti-labor.

Union Structure

Companies in a given country may deal with one or several different unions. A union itself may represent workers in many different industries, in many different companies within the same industry, or in only one company. If it represents only one company, the union may represent all plants or just one plant. Although there are diversities within countries, one type of relationship is most prevalent within most countries. For example, unions in the United States tend to be national, representing certain types of workers (for example, airline pilots, coal miners, truck drivers, or university professors). Thus a company may deal with several different national unions. Each collective-bargaining process usually is characterized by a single company on one side rather than an association of different companies that deals with one of the unions representing a certain type of worker in all the companies' plants.

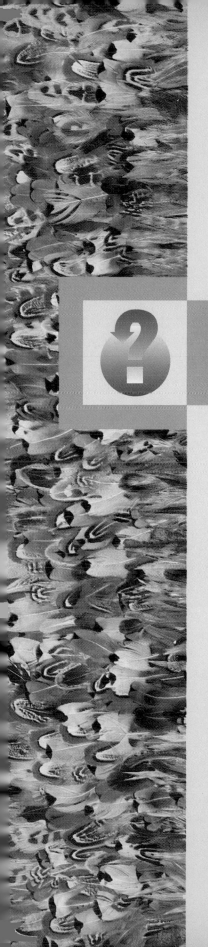

Critics have argued that MNEs have too often established capital-intensive rather than labor-intensive production methods, thus not contributing fully to decreasing unemployment in LDCs. **Appropriate technology** is the technology that best fits the factor endowment where it is used; however, the term usually is used to mean technology that is more labor-intensive than would be cost-effective in an industrial country.

Ethical dilemmas arise whether or not a labor-saving production method is more economical. For example, in India machine-made textiles are less expensive to produce than hand-woven ones are. However, hand-woven textiles employ about 7.5 million people in India, and their production represents a strong cultural value of self-reliance.[66] As the country's production of machine-made textiles has increased (some by MNEs), the number of unemployed weavers and reports of starvation deaths among them

ETHICAL DILEMMAS

have increased. On the one hand, critics have argued that the hand-loom industry should be subsidized and that on ethical grounds, companies should not establish production that will cause unemployment. On the other hand, others argue that the perpetuation of inefficient production merely condemns workers and their descendants to lifetimes of drudgery.

The evidence is very mixed on whether MNEs alter production to the extent that is cost-feasible. There are undoubtedly engineering biases toward duplicating facilities built to save labor in industrialized countries. Management control systems also may heavily emphasize output per person, which is more relevant to production needs in industrialized countries. Further, many governmental authorities within LDCs want showcase plants as symbols of modernization. However, case studies point to substantial alterations by MNEs, such as using human labor instead of mechanized loading equipment, because of local costs and availabilities.[67]

MNEs also are criticized for exploiting women in many LDCs, where they have had less formal education than men have, have been trained since childhood in tasks requiring manual dexterity, and are willing to accept lower wages than men will. Their qualifications are thus ideal for certain labor-intensive activities. Without the constraints of sex-discrimination legislation, companies advertise openly that they want female workers. Governments even encourage the practice. For example, Malaysia has advertised "the manual dexterity of the Oriental female" within its investment-promotion programs. But the ethical issue is broader. As women have been enticed into the workplace in LDCs, sometimes living in company-provided dormitories, critics argue that social costs have increased because of resultant instability within the family unit and increase in unemployment among the traditional male heads of households. Companies argue that these practices make more jobs and income available and that the employment gives women more independence from their traditional subservient roles.

In Japan, one union typically represents all workers in a given company and has only very loose affiliations with unions in other companies. This allegedly explains why Japanese unions are less militant than those in most other industrialized countries: They seldom strike, and when they do, they may stop working for only a short period of time or may continue working while wearing symbolic arm bands. Because of the workers' closer affiliation with the company, Japanese union leaders are hesitant to risk hurting the company's ability to compete in world markets.[68] In Sweden, bargaining tends to be highly centralized in that employers from numerous companies in different industries deal together with a federation of trade unions. In Germany, employers from associations of companies in the same industries bargain jointly with union federations.[69]

Protection from Closures and Redundancy

In response to proposed layoffs, shifts in production location, and cessation of operations, workers in many countries have physically moved into plants to prevent the transfer of machinery, components, and finished goods.[70] They have even continued to produce until they ran out of raw materials and components and then sold the output on the streets in order to prolong their ability to occupy the plants. The results of these efforts have been mixed, sometimes preventing the plant's closing and other times not.

The fact that workers will go so far to try to prevent a plant from closing indicates how important this issue is in some countries, particularly those in Western Europe where prenotification has been negotiated or legislated almost everywhere. The Western European situation contrasts with that in Canada and the United States, where fewer than one fifth of contracts require employers to give more than a week's notice of closure.[71]

The lifetime-employment custom in Japan offers some contrasts to labor practices in North America and Western Europe. Some Japanese employees, usually skilled male workers in large companies, enjoy lifetime employment. In turn, these employees voluntarily switch companies less frequently than do their counterparts in North America and Europe. Other Japanese workers are considered temporaries. The number of temporaries is large, constituting about 40 percent of the workforce even in a large company such as Toyota. In addition, there are many part-time workers. When business takes a downturn or when labor-saving techniques are introduced, Japanese companies keep the lifetime employees on the payroll by releasing the temporary workers, reducing the variable bonuses of lifetime employees, and transferring workers to other product divisions.

There is some evidence, although inconclusive, that this system has enabled Japanese companies to introduce automated systems more effectively than companies elsewhere can because unionized employees have little concern about job security. It also has helped Japanese companies to spend heavily on training because the lifetime employees have a strong moral commitment to stay with their employers. The temporary workers have tolerated the system because of the labor shortage

Workers' takeover of plants has been done to publicize their plight.

Prior notification of plant closings has been legislated in some countries.

Lifetime employment in Japan
- **Is a dual system**
- **Helps institute certain efficiency measures**

that has existed during recent decades in Japan and because many are women who, by cultural definition, are disinclined to engage in adversarial behavior.[72]

Codetermination

Some MNEs seek labor-management cooperation through sharing of leadership.

Particularly in Northern Europe, labor participates in the management of companies, a process known as **codetermination.** Most commonly, labor is represented on the board of directors, either with or without veto power.

Despite some voluntary moves toward codetermination, most existing examples have been mandated by legislation, such as that in Germany. These moves have been dictated not only by the philosophy of cooperative leadership but also by the feeling that labor has risks and stakes in the organization just as stockholders do. Because of a belief that the interests of blue-collar workers and white-collar workers differ, some effort has been made to ensure each group is represented. Although there are some early examples of workers deterring investment outflows, acquisitions, and plant closures, codetermination apparently has had little effect on either the types of decisions reached by companies or the speed with which those decisions have been reached. One reason given for this minimal effect is that workers are so divided in terms of what they want that it is hard for their representatives to take strong stances on issues. Where layoffs have been necessary, foreign workers have been given less protection than citizens have.[73]

For example, in Germany workers elect representatives to serve on the company's Works' Council.[74] This council makes decisions on social matters (such as employee conduct, hours of work, and safety), and when disputes arise between the Council and the company's Labor Director, they are settled by arbitration. In economic and financial matters, the Council is provided information and consulted in decisions. However, the workers do not have the greater strength on the Council. Although the stockholders and workers have an equal number of representatives, the chairman (elected by stockholders) has the tie-breaking vote. The Works' Council and the unions have different responsibilities. Collective bargaining takes place between employer associations and the unions and covers all workers within a German state or part of that state. The companies in the employer associations vary in size and ability to cover different possible wage rates, so the negotiated annual wage rates are minimums and can be negotiated upward at the company level. But the unions are barred by law from negotiating at the company or plant level; this is the task of the Works' Council.

Team Efforts

In some countries, particularly Japan, work teams have been emphasized in order to foster a group cohesiveness and involve workers in multiple rather than a limited number of tasks. In terms of group cohesiveness, it is not uncommon for a portion of the compensation to be based on the group output so that peer pressure is created to reduce absenteeism and increase efforts. In terms of worker involvement in multiple tasks, workers may rotate jobs within the group to reduce boredom and to develop replacement skills to use when someone is not present. Practices that allow workers' groups to control their own quality and repair their own equipment also have been included.[75]

International Pressures on National Practices

The ILO monitors labor conditions worldwide.

In 1919, the International Labor Organization (ILO) was set up on the premise that the failure of any country to adopt humane labor conditions is an obstacle to other countries that want to improve their conditions. Several associations of unions from different countries also support similar ideals. These include various international trade secretariats representing workers in specific industries, for example, the International Confederation of Free Trade Unions (ICFTU), the World Federation of Trade Unions (WFTU), and the World Confederation of Labour (WCL).[76] Through these organizations' activities and the general enhancement of communications globally, people increasingly are aware of differences in labor conditions among countries. Among the newsworthy reports have been legal proscriptions against collective bargaining in Malaysia and wages below minimum standards in Indonesia. The ILO also has brought attention to the prevalence of child labor in LDCs. Once such conditions have been noted, there has been pressure for changes through economic and political sanctions from abroad.

The most noteworthy example of these efforts involved pressures by various groups on MNEs operating in South Africa. For example, through church groups, resolutions were presented to stockholders proposing that companies cease, cut back, operate on a nondiscriminatory basis, or report more fully on their South African operations. These pressures led to a large exodus of FDI from South Africa in the late 1980s, the 1991 repeal of apartheid laws, and the subsequent return of many foreign companies.

Another area influencing MNE labor practices has been codes of conduct on industrial relations issued by the OECD and the ILO. Another is the Social Charter, a nonbinding statement of intent by EU heads of government. Although the codes and charter are voluntary, they may signal future transnational regulations of MNE activities. Trade unions have been anxious to get interpretations of the guidelines and make them legally enforceable.

Multinational Ownership and Collective Bargaining[77]

MNE Advantages

Job security   It is often argued that when the number of jobs is not growing, workers are concerned about employment stability rather than other work condi-

There is disagreement on home-country employment effects of FDI, but labor pushes to save home-country jobs.

tions. If MNEs have exported jobs from industrialized countries, then it should follow that labor demands in those countries have been tempered in the process. Yet it is difficult to conclude whether MNEs have increased or decreased home-country employment through FDI.

The workforce composition in industrial countries has increasingly emphasized white-collar jobs over blue-collar ones. Although some of this realignment may be inevitable with or without MNE activities, the result is nevertheless a shrinking of *traditional* bargaining units made up of blue-collar workers. White-collar workers have been less prone to join unions in the United States than in other industrial countries. But even when these workers are organized by unions, they may not be as adverse to management as blue-collar workers are, since they may look forward to moving into management positions themselves. MNEs may set up production facilities in countries that have low wages and high unemployment, while simultaneously concentrating such functions as accounting, R&D, and staff support in industrialized countries. To the extent they do this, they contribute to workforce composition changes that weaken the size of traditional bargaining units in industrialized countries.

Labor may be at a disadvantage in MNE negotiations because the
- Country bargaining unit is only a small part of MNE activities
- MNE may continue serving customers with foreign production or resources

Product and resource flows   If, during a strike in one country, an MNE can divert output from facilities in other countries to the consumers in the country in which the strike is occurring, there is less pressure due to lost revenues for the MNE to reach an agreement. Further, since the operations in a given country usually comprise a small percentage of an MNE's total worldwide sales, profits, and cash flows, a strike in that country may have minimal effect on the MNE's global performance. The MNE's geographic diversification therefore is argued to be to its advantage when bargaining with labor in a given country. Some analysts contend an MNE simply may hold out longer and be less affected in a strike situation than a domestic company would be.

MNE limitations come from capacity, legal restrictions, shared ownership, integrated production, and differentiated products.

Several factors moderate the MNE's ability to continue supplying customers in the struck country. The MNE may divert output to other markets only if it has excess capacity and only if an identical product is produced in more than one country. If these two conditions are present, the MNE still would confront the cost and trade barriers that led to the initial establishment of multiple production facilities. If the struck operation is only partially owned by the MNE, partners or even minority stockholders may be less willing and able to sustain a lengthy work stoppage. Further, if the idle facilities normally produce components needed for integrated production elsewhere, then a strike may have far-reaching effects. This is particularly important as companies seek to decrease production costs by instituting JIT inventory systems. For example, during a U.K. strike at Ford, Belgian facilities were shut down almost immediately because they needed British components; this may have hastened Ford's agreement to a settlement.[78] Thus there appear to be advantages of international diversification for the collective-bargaining process, but only in limited circumstances.

MNEs may threaten workers with the prospect of moving production abroad.

Production switching   There are documented examples of threats by companies to move production units to other countries if labor conditions and demands in one country result in changes in the least-cost location of production. For example, the president of Monroe Manufacturing, in a speech to U.S. workers, said, "Listen, if I can't compete in America with American workers, I'll take your jobs overseas where we can be competitive."[79] But such threats are not limited to international operations. When GM announced that either a plant in Michigan or one in Texas would be closed, the Texans flouted the union and agreed to cut costs by moving to three shifts without overtime pay.[80] Further, production shifts may be inevitable as the least-cost location changes, regardless of labor actions.

Even domestic companies face threats of losing jobs to workers abroad.

Although sometimes production shifts would seem more plausible when a company has facilities in more than one country, at other times they would seem more plausible when facilities in different countries are owned by different companies. For example, a Korean company producing only in Korea and exporting to the Canadian market may not worry much about what happens as a result to employment at a competitor's Canadian-owned plant in Canada. However, if the Canadian and Korean facilities were both owned by the same MNE, management would have to weigh the cost-saving advantages of moving its production location against the losses in terms of cutting back at existing facilities, creating bad will, and becoming vulnerable through decreased diversification.

Labor claims it is disadvantaged in dealing with MNEs because
• Decision making is far away
• It is hard to get full data on MNEs' global operations

Structural problems   Observers often contend it is difficult for labor unions to deal with MNEs because of the complexities in the location of decision making and the difficulties involved in interpreting financial data. It often is assumed that when the real decision makers are far removed from the bargaining location, at home-country headquarters, for example, arbitrarily stringent management decisions will result. Conceivably, the opposite might happen, particularly if the demands abroad seem low in comparison with those being made at home. In reality, labor relations usually are delegated to subsidiary management.

The question of interpreting MNEs' financial data is complex because of disparities among managerial, tax, and disclosure requirements in home and host countries. Labor has been particularly leery of the possibility that artificial transfer pricing may be used to give the appearance that a given subsidiary is unable to meet labor demands. These concerns seem to place an overreliance on a company's ability to pay rather than on the seemingly more important going wage rates in the industry and geographic area. Although MNEs may have more complex data, at least one set of financial statements must satisfy local authorities. This set should be no more difficult to interpret than that of a purely local company. In terms of transfer pricing, it is very doubtful that MNEs set artificial levels to aid in collective-bargaining situations. To understate profits in one place would imply overstating elsewhere, which would negate the advantage, unless changes were made to reflect different contract periods. Tax authorities would not be likely to approve sudden price changes before contract negotiation. Further, any decision to set artificial prices also would have to consider income taxes, tariffs, and opinions of minority stockholders.

Labor Responses and Initiatives

Labor might strengthen its position relative to MNEs through cross-national cooperation.

Information sharing   The most common form of cooperation among unions in different countries is exchanging information, which helps them refute company claims as well as cite precedents from other countries when bargaining issues seem transferable. The information exchange is carried out by international confederations of unions representing different types of workers and ideologies, by trade secretariats composed of unions in a single industry or in a complex of related industries, and by company councils that include representatives from an MNE's plants around the world.[81] Councils represent trade unions in the European countries in which MNEs have operations. They meet two or three times a year for consultation and are involved with about thirty MNEs, including Volkswagen, Bayer, Unilever, and the Allianz insurance group.[82]

Assistance to foreign bargaining units   Labor groups in one country may support their counterparts in other countries in several ways. These include refusing to work overtime when that output would supply the market normally served by striking workers' production, sending financial aid to workers in other countries, and presenting demands to management through other countries. Although there are examples of these types of assistance actually being used, they must still be classified as potential rather than actual initiatives. There are more examples of refusals to cooperate in these matters than of successful collaborations.

Simultaneous actions   There have been a few examples of simultaneous negotiations and strikes. The concept appeals to labor, particularly in Europe, where the single market has caused companies to merge, consolidate multicountry facilities, and shift production among countries.[83] A major problem for labor's cooperation across borders is national differences in terms of union structures and demands. The percentage of workers in unions is much higher in some countries than others; for example, it is much higher in Belgium than in the Netherlands. About half of organized workers in France and Portugal belong to communist unions that do not get along with unions representing the bulk of workers elsewhere in Europe. In addition, both wage rates and workers' preferences differ widely among EU countries. For instance, Spanish workers are more willing to work on weekends than are German workers. Further, there undoubtedly has been a growing nationalism among workers as their fear of foreign competition has grown.

National approaches   Unions' conflicts with MNEs have been primarily on a national basis. There is little enthusiasm on the part of workers in one country to incur costs to support workers in another, since they tend to view each other as competitors. Even in Canada and the United States, which have long shared a common union membership, there has been a move among Canadian workers to form unions independent of those in the United States. One Canadian organizer summed up much of the attitude by saying, "An American union is not going to fight to protect Canadian jobs at the expense of American jobs." The logic is that international unions will adopt policies favoring the bulk of their membership, which in any joint Canadian-U.S. relationship is bound to be American.[84]

National legislation in some countries has provided for worker representation on boards of directors, regulated the entry of foreign workers, and limited imports and foreign investment outflows. It is probable that most future regulations will be at the national rather than international level.

C O U N T E R V A I L I N G

F O R C E S

Managers are challenged to break down nationalistic barriers that impair the achievement of global corporate cultures and integrated global strategies. To balance a company's global and national needs, managers must be neither too ethnocentric nor too polycentric (recall the discussion in Chapter 2). MNEs are challenged to find managers who are committed to the operations at which they work, to the parent company if they happen to be working in a foreign subsidiary, and to the company's global well-being. However, even a dual allegiance (local operation and parent company) is rarely found.

Expatriate managers may be classified into one of four categories, as shown in Fig. 21.1: free agent, heart at home, going native, and dual citizen.[85] There are two types of "free agent." The first consists of people whose commitment to career is higher than their commitment to either the parent company or the foreign operation where they are working. They often are highly effective, but they will move with little warning from one company to another in foreign assignments, may serve their own short-term interests at the expense of the company's long-term ones, and do not want to return to their home country. The second type of "free agent" includes people whose careers have plateaued at home and who take a foreign assignment only for the paycheck. The "heart at home" type is overly ethnocentric and is usually eager to be repatriated. When there is a need for strong headquarters control, this type of person may be very effective. The "going native" type learns the local way of doing business very well and wants to stay in the foreign location and be left alone by headquarters. This type of person may be very appropriate for situations in which multidomestic practices are followed. The "dual citizen" type has a clear understanding both of why he or she is needed there and of local realities that may cause operations to deviate from home-country practices. This person usually finds mechanisms by which to work out differences between headquarters and subsidiary and is overall the most effective type of expatriate manager.

To counterbalance a "heart at home," the company may send younger managers abroad and do everything possible to facilitate cultural adjustment. To counterbalance "going native," the company may send people abroad who have strong ties to the company, limit their time away from headquarters, keep in close contact with them (perhaps through a

Figure 21.1
Allegiance of
Expatriate Managers
The "dual citizen" type of manager is most effective at balancing global and local needs; however, each of the other types can be very effective for specific types of foreign operations.

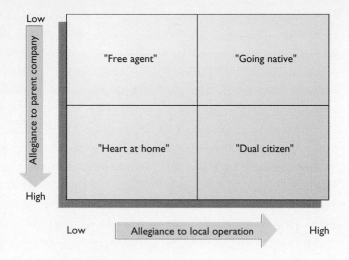

mentor program), and provide them with assistance in repatriation. In either situation, the international transfer should be handled so that the expatriate understands why he or she is being sent to the post, how the performance will be measured, the objectives of the parent company and local unit, and the location of control. These suggestions also may be applied to other than expatriate employees. For example, local managers in foreign subsidiaries may be less apt to be a "heart at home" if they have closer contact with headquarters and see their own future as tied more to global than to local interests. To accomplish increased interactions, more cross-national interchange may be necessary, although the traditional problems of cost and governmental regulations continue to impede these interchanges.

LOOKING TO THE FUTURE As capital and technology continue to become more mobile, among countries and among companies, human resource development should account increasingly for competitive differences. Consequently, the access to and retention of ever more qualified personnel should gain in importance. This does not mean there will be a lack of employee mobility. In fact, the highly skilled, highly valued worker will likely be more difficult to retain in the future.[86]

Personal adaptation probably will be a continuing problem. The head of international human resources at Campbell Soup Company said, "There is too much emphasis on executives' technical abilities and too little on their cultural skills and family situation."[87] This does not mean that technical skills will be less important to success in foreign assignments but rather that this dimension is already well understood and taken into account. But management still knows far too little about the identification and training of successful personnel for overseas assignments. Further, such factors as two-career families and international terrorism may make managers even more reluctant to accept foreign assignments.

Demographers are nearly unanimous in projecting that populations will grow much faster in LDCs (China being an exception) than in industrial countries, at least up to the year 2030.[88] At the same time, in industrial countries the number of elderly people as a percentage of the population will grow, as will the need to be educated for more years to get the so-called "better jobs" and the tendency to retire at earlier ages. Overall, these industrial-country trends indicate that there will be fewer people to do the productive work within society. Adjustments may come about in any of several ways or combinations of them, and each way has a number of social and economic consequences. MNEs must adapt their production to these changing conditions.

One reaction might be to encourage immigration to industrial countries from LDCs, which neither have now nor are expected to generate enough jobs for their potential workers. In Canada, the United States, and parts of Western Europe there has been a fairly long-term entry of foreign workers, both legally and illegally. During the late 1980s, both Italy and Japan had to seek foreign workers, perhaps for the first time ever. Such movements generate assimilation costs within receiving countries and, if they involve highly qualified personnel, charges of a brain drain from LDCs. Further, in economic downturns, foreign workers are likely to be blamed for unemployment. If such movements develop, companies will have to spend more efforts on paperwork required for work permits and develop means of incorporating different groups into the workforce.

Another potential reaction is a continued push toward adoption of robotics and development of other labor-saving equipment. Although this may help solve some of the shortages in industrial countries, average work-skill levels may increase so much that less educated members of the workforce may be either unemployable or forced to take lesser-paying jobs in the service sector. Gaps between haves and have-nots thus may widen, and unemployment problems of LDCs will not be solved. From a company standpoint, this alternative may necessitate some shifts in technology spending, possibly away from natural resource–saving and new product development toward labor-saving.

A third possible reaction is the acceleration of industry migration to LDCs to tap ample supplies of labor. Such moves would enhance the international division of labor but may amplify the distinctions between developed countries and LDCs and the dilemma of what to do with marginal workers in industrial countries. Companies sourcing more heavily in LDCs will have to expend more efforts on logistics to ensure that supplies flow among countries. They also will have to concern themselves more with efforts to minimize the political and monetary risks of operating in LDCs.

Summary

- **The tasks of international managers differ from those of purely domestic managers in several ways, including needing to know how to adapt home-country practices to foreign locales and being more likely to deal with high-level governmental officials.**

- **The top-level managers of foreign subsidiaries normally perform much broader duties than do domestic managers with similar cost or profit responsibilities. They must cope with communications problems between corporate headquarters and the subsidiaries, usually with less staff assistance.**

- **MNEs employ more local than expatriate managers** because the locals understand regional operating conditions and may focus more on long-term operations and goals. Doing so also demonstrates that opportunities are available for local citizens, shows consideration for local interests, avoids the red tape of cross-national transfers, and usually is cheaper.

- **MNEs transfer people abroad** in order to infuse technical competence and home-country business practices, to control foreign operations, and to develop managers.

- **MNEs that transfer personnel abroad** should consider how well the people will be accepted, how to treat them when the foreign assignment is over, and how well they will adapt.

- **When transferred abroad,** an expatriate's compensation usually is adjusted because of hardship and differences in cost of living and job status.

- **Companies frequently acquire personnel abroad** by buying existing companies. They also may go into business with local companies, which then assume most staffing responsibilities.

- **Two major international training functions** are to build a global awareness among managers in general and to equip managers to handle the specific situations entailed in a foreign assignment.

- **When setting up a new operation in a foreign country,** a company may use existing facilities as guides for determining labor needs. However, it should adjust to compensate for different labor skills, costs, and availabilities.

- **For some areas,** a substantial portion of the labor supply is imported, which creates special stability, supervision, and training problems for companies operating there.

- **Because of the enormous variation in fringe benefits,** direct-compensation figures do not accurately reflect the amount a company must pay for a given job. In addition, job-security benefits (no layoffs, severance pay, etc.) add substantially to compensation costs.

- **Although per-worker comparisons are useful indicators of labor-cost differences,** it is the output associated with total costs that is relevant for international competitiveness. These costs may shift over time, thus changing relative international competitive positions.

- A country's sociopolitical environment will determine to a great extent the type of relationship between labor and management and affect the number, representation, and organization of unions.

- Codetermination is a type of labor participation in a company's management and usually is intended to cultivate a cooperative rather than an adversarial environment.

- In recent years, there have been efforts to get companies to follow internationally accepted labor practices regardless of where they are operating or whether the practices conflict with the norms and laws of the countries in which they are operating.

- MNEs often are blamed for weakening the position of labor in the collective-bargaining process because of those companies' international diversification, threats to export jobs, and complex structures and reporting mechanisms.

- Cooperation between labor groups in different countries in conflicts with MNEs is minimal. Strategies include information exchanges, simultaneous negotiations or strikes, and refusals to work overtime if the intent is to compensate for a striking company in another country.

Case
Office Equipment
Company (OEC)

In 1994, the managing director (a U.S. national) of the Office Equipment Company (OEC) in Lima, Peru (see Map 21.1), announced suddenly that he would leave within one month. The company had to find a replacement. OEC manufactures a wide variety of small office equipment (such as copying machines, recording machines, mail scales, and paper shredders) in eight different countries and distributes and sells products worldwide. It has no manufacturing facilities in Peru but has been selling and servicing there since the early 1970s. OEC first tried selling in Peru through independent importers but quickly became convinced that in order to make sufficient sales it needed to have its own staff there. Despite Peru's political turmoil, which over the last few years has bordered on being a full-scale civil war, OEC's operation there (with about 100 employees) has enjoyed good and improving sales and profitability.

OEC is constructing its first factory in Peru that is scheduled to begin operations in early 1996. This factory will import components for personal computer printers and assemble them locally. Peru offers an abundant supply of cheap labor, and the assembly operation will employ approximately 150 people. The government will allow up to 10 percent of the output to be sold locally. By assembling locally and then exporting, OEC expects to be able to ward off trade restrictions on the other office equipment it imports for sale within Peru. This plant's construction is being supervised by a U.S. technical team, and a U.S. expatriate will be assigned to direct the production. This director will report directly to OEC's U.S. headquarters on all production and quality-control matters but will report

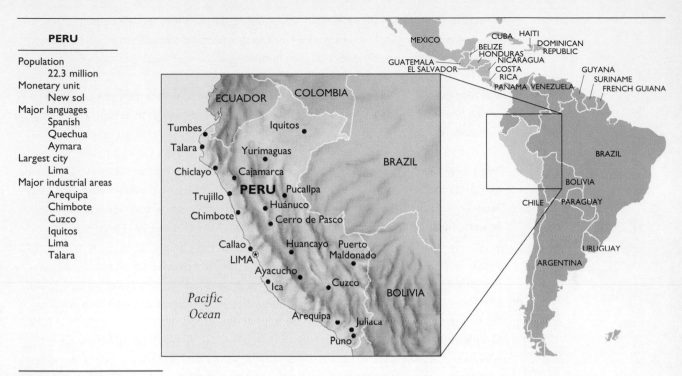

PERU

Population
  22.3 million
Monetary unit
  New sol
Major languages
  Spanish
  Quechua
  Aymara
Largest city
  Lima
Major industrial areas
  Arequipa
  Chimbote
  Cuzco
  Iquitos
  Lima
  Talara

Map 21.1
Peru

to the managing director in Peru on all other matters, such as accounting, finance, and labor relations.

OEC, by policy, will replace the exiting managing director with an internal candidate. The company employs a combination of home-, host-, and third-country nationals in top positions in foreign countries, and managers commonly rotate among foreign and U.S. locations. In fact, it has been increasingly evident to OEC that international experience is an important factor in deciding who will be appointed to top corporate positions. The sales and service facility in Peru reports to a Latin American regional office located in Coral Gables, Florida. A committee at this office, charged with selecting the new managing director, quickly narrowed its choice to five candidates.

Tom Zimmerman A thirty-year OEC veteran, Zimmerman is well versed in all the technical and sales aspects required in the job. He has never worked abroad for OEC but has visited various of the company's foreign facilities as part of sales teams. He is considered competent and will retire in about four and a half years. Neither he nor his wife speak Spanish. Their children are grown and living with their own children in the United States. Zimmerman currently is in charge of an operation that is about the size of that in Peru after the new factory begins operating. However, Zimmerman's present position will become redundant because the operation he heads is being merged with another.

Brett Harrison Harrison, 40, has spent fifteen years at OEC. Considered highly competent and capable of moving into upper-level management within the next few years, he has never been based abroad but has worked for the last three years in the Latin American regional office and frequently travels to Latin America. Both he and his wife speak Spanish adequately, and their two children, ages 14 and 15, are just beginning to study the language. His wife holds a responsible marketing position with a pharmaceuticals company.

Carolyn Moyer   Moyer joined OEC twelve years ago after getting her MBA from a prestigious university. At 37, she has already moved between staff and line positions of growing responsibility. For two years, she was second in command of a product group that was about the size of the newly expanded one in Peru. Her performance in that post was considered excellent. Currently, she works on a planning staff team. When she joined OEC, she indicated her interest in eventual international responsibilities because of her undergraduate major in international affairs. She has recently expressed interest in international duties because of a belief it will help her advancement. She speaks Spanish well and is unmarried.

Francisco Cabrera   Cabrera, 35, currently is an assistant managing director in the larger Mexican operation, which produces and sells for the Mexican market. A Mexican citizen, he has worked for OEC in Mexico for all his twelve years with the company. He holds an MBA from a Mexican university and is considered to be a likely candidate to head the Mexican operation when the present managing director retires in seven years. He is married with four children (ages 2 to 7) and speaks English adequately. His wife does not work outside the home or speak English.

Juan Moreno   At 27, Moreno is assistant to the present managing director in Peru. He has held that position since joining OEC upon his U.S. college graduation four years ago. Unmarried, he is considered competent, especially in employee relations, but lacking in experience. He had been successful in increasing OEC's sales, in part because he is well connected with local families who can afford to buy new office equipment for their businesses.

Questions

1. Which candidate should the committee choose for the assignment, and why?
2. What problems might each candidate encounter in the position?
3. How might OEC go about minimizing the problems that each candidate would have in managing the Peruvian operations?
4. Calculate an estimated compensation package for each candidate based on the following additional information:
   - Present annual salaries: Zimmerman, US$70,000; Harrison, US$75,000; Moyer, US$65,000; Cabrera, M$124,000; Moreno, S57,000
   - Exchange rates: $1 = M$3.1 (Mexican pesos); $1 = S1.9 (Peruvian new sols)
   - U.S. Department of State cost-of-living index based on items covering 35 percent of income for a family of one, 40 percent for a family of two, 45 percent for a family of four, and 50 percent for a family of five or more: Washington, D.C. = 100; Lima = 86; Mexico City = 77
   - U.S. Department of State foreign-service premiums for Peru: hardship = 15 percent; danger = 15 percent

- Housing allowance (nontaxable): single = US$12,100; family = US$15,000
- Schooling allowance: age 6–12 = US$5000; age 13–18 = US$9000
- Average tax rates: Mexico = 20 percent; United States = 25 percent; Peru = 30 percent

Chapter Notes

1. The data for the case were taken from Edwin McDowell, "Making It in America: The Foreign-Born Executive," *New York Times,* June 1, 1980, Section 3, p. 1+; Don Whitehead, *The Dow Story* (New York: McGraw-Hill, 1968); "Dow's Shifts in R&D Presage Overseas Work," *Chemical Week,* Vol. 128, No. 13, April 1, 1981, p. 17; "Lundeen Urges More Aid for Universities," *Chemical Marketing Reporter,* Vol. 224, No. 19, November 7, 1983, p. 3+; John Bussey, "Dow Chemical's Popoff Named President," *Wall Street Journal,* May 15, 1987, p. 49; Paul L. Blocklyn, "Developing the International Executive," *Personnel,* Vol. 66, March 1989, pp. 44–47; "Globesmanship," *Across the Board,* Vol. 27, Nos. 1, 2, January–February 1990, pp. 24–34; and William Storck, "Dow Chemical Changes Executive Lineup," *Chemical and Engineering News,* September 14, 1992, p. 5.

2. Gary R. Oddou and Mark E. Mendenhall, "Succession Planning for the 21st Century: How Well Are We Grooming Our Future Business Leaders?" *Business Horizons,* January–February 1991, pp. 26–34.

3. "Globesmanship," *Across the Board,* Vol. 27, Nos. 1, 2, January–February 1990, p. 26, quoting Michael Angus.

4. Daniel Ondrack, "International Transfers of Managers in North American and European MNEs," *Journal of International Business Studies,* Vol. 16, No. 3, Fall 1985, pp. 1–19.

5. Katarzyna Wandycz, "Resetting the Internal Clock," *Forbes,* August 30, 1993, p. 74.

6. Bob Masterson and Bob Murphy, "Internal Cross-Cultural Management," *Training and Development Journal,* Vol. 40, No. 4, April 1986, pp. 56–60.

7. Peter Lorange, "Human Resource Management in Multinational Cooperative Ventures," *Human Resource Management,* Vol. 25, No. 1, Spring 1986, pp. 133–148; Wayne E. Cascio and Manuel G. Serapio, Jr., "Human Resources Systems in an International Alliance: The Undoing of a Done Deal?" *Organizational Dynamics,* Winter 1991, pp. 63–75; and Heinz-Dieter Meyer, "The Cultural Gap in Long-Term International Work Groups: A German-American Case Study," *European Management Journal,* Vol. 11, No. 1, March 1993, pp. 93–101.

8. Jean Ross-Skinner, "English Spoken Here," *Dun's Review,* March 1977, pp. 56–57; and David A. Weeks, *Recruiting and Selecting International Managers,* Report No. 998 (New York: The Conference Board, 1992).

9. "When in Rome?" *Wall Street Journal,* September 28, 1989, p. 1; and Stuart Feldman, "Losing the Home Field Advantage," *Management Review,* September 1991, pp. 7–8.

10. David C. Waring, "Doing Business Overseas," *Cornell Enterprise,* Fall–Winter 1988, p. 29.

11. Weeks, loc. cit.

12. Dafna N. Izraeli, Moshe Banai, and Yoram Zeira, "Women Executives in MNC Subsidiaries," *California Management Review,* Vol. 23, No. 1, Fall 1980, pp. 53–63; Yves Doz and C. K. Prahalad, "Controlled Variety: A Challenge for Human Resource Management in the MNC," *Human Resource Management,* Vol. 25, No. 1, Spring 1986, pp. 55–57; and Peter Coy and Neil Gross, "When the Going Gets Tough, Yanks Get Yanked," *Business Week,* April 26, 1993, p. 30.

13. Yoram Zeira and Ehud Harari, "Structural Sources of Personnel Problems in Multinational Corporations: Third-Country Nationals," *Omega,* Vol. 5, No. 2, 1977, pp. 167–168.

14. Anders Edström and Jay R. Galbraith, "Alternative Policies for International Transfers of Managers," *Management International Review,* No. 2, 1977, pp. 13–14; and Asya Pazy and Yoram Zeira, "Training Parent-Country Professionals in Host-Country Organizations," *Academy of Management Review,* Vol. 8, No. 2, 1983, pp. 262–272.

15. Joann S. Lublin, "More U.S. Companies Venture Overseas for Directors Offering Fresh Perspectives," *Wall Street Journal,* January 27, 1992, p. B1; and Joann S. Lublin, "Foreign Accents Proliferate in Top Ranks as U.S. Companies Find Talent Abroad," *Wall Street Journal,* May 21, 1992, p. B1.

16. Ibid.

17. Anders Edström and Jay R. Galbraith, "Transfer of Managers as a Coordination and Control Strategy in Multinational Organizations," *Administrative Science Quarterly,* June 1977, pp. 248–261; and A. B. Sim, "Decentralized Management of Subsidiaries and Their Performance," *Management International Review,* No. 2, 1977, p. 48.

18. Alfred Jaeger, "Organization Development and National Culture: Where's the Fit?" *Academy of Management Review,* Vol. 11, No. 1, 1986, pp. 178–190; and "The Elusive Euro-Manager," *The Economist,* November 7, 1992, p. 83.

19. Anders Edström and Peter Lorange, "Matching Strategy and Human Resources in Multinational Companies," *Journal of International Business Studies,* Fall 1984, pp. 125–137; Stephen J. Kobrin, "Expatriate Reduction and Strategic Control in American Multinational Corporations," *Human Resource Management,* Vol. 27, No. 1, Spring 1988, pp. 63–75; and Louis Uchitelle, "Only the Bosses Are American," *New York Times,* July 24, 1989, p. 21+.

20. Duerr and Greene, *The Problems Facing International Management,* Managing International Business, No. 1 (New York: National Industrial Conference Board, 1968), p. 18; see also Richard D. Hays, "Behavioral Determinants of Success-Failure among U.S. Expatriate Managers," *Journal of International Business Studies,* Spring 1971, pp. 40–46; Martine Gertsen, "Intercultural Competence and Expatriates," Working Paper No. 1, 1990, Copenhagen School of Economics and Business Administration, Institute of International Economics and Management; Moran, Stahl & Boyer, Inc., *International Human Research Management* (Boulder, Colo.: Moran, Stahl & Boyer, 1987); and Weeks, loc. cit.

21. J. Stewart Black and Mark Mendenhall, "Cross-Cultural Training Effectiveness: A Review and a Theoretical Framework for Future Research," *Academy of Management Review,* Vol. 15, No. 1, January 1990, p. 117; and Mark Mendenhall and Gary Oddou, "The Dimensions of Expatriate Acculturation: A Review," *Academy of Management Review,* Vol. 10, No. 1, January 1985, pp. 39–47.

22. Philip R. Harris and Robert L. Moran, *Managing Cultural Differences* (Houston: Gulf, 1979), p. 164; J. Stewart Black and Gregory K. Stephens, "The Influence of the Spouse on American Expatriate Adjustment and

Intent to Stay in Pacific Rim Overseas Assignments," *Journal of Management*, Vol. 15, No. 4, 1989, pp. 529–530; and Alicia Kitsuse, "At Home Abroad," *Across the Board*, September 1992, pp. 34–39.

23. Karen Dawn Stuart, "Teens Play a Role in Moves Overseas," *Personnel Journal*, March 1992, pp. 72–78.

24. Izraeli et al., loc. cit.

25. Patricia Feltes, Robert K. Robinson, and Ross L. Fink, "American Female Expatriates and the Civil Rights Act of 1991: Balancing Legal and Business Interests," *Business Horizons*, March–April 1993, pp. 82–86.

26. Mariann Jelinek and Nancy J. Adler, "Women: World Class Managers for Global Competition," *Academy of Management Executive*, Vol. II, No. 1, February 1988, pp. 11–19; Jolie Solomon, "Women, Minorities and Foreign Postings," *Wall Street Journal*, June 2, 1989, p. B1; and Weeks, loc. cit.

27. Izraeli et al., loc. cit. For some suggestions on how women may make themselves more acceptable, see Gladys L. Symons, "Coping with the Corporate Tribe: How Women in Different Cultures Experience the Managerial Role," *Journal of Management*, Vol. 12, No. 3, 1986, pp. 379–389; and Marlene L. Rossman, *The International Businesswoman* (New York: Praeger, 1986).

28. David M. Noer, "Integrating Foreign Service Employees to Home Organization: The Godfather Approach," *Personnel Journal*, January 1974, pp. 45–50; William F. Cagney, "Executive Reentry: The Problems of Repatriation," *Personnel Journal*, September 1975, pp. 487–488; J. Alex Murray, "Repatriated Executives: Culture Shock in Reverse," *Management Review*, November 1973, pp. 43–45; Philip R. Harris, "Employees Abroad: Maintain the Corporate Connection," *Personnel Journal*, Vol. 65, No. 8, August 1986, pp. 107–110; Oddou and Mendenhall, loc. cit.; and Jodi Zurawski, "Plan for Expatriates: 'Welcome Home' before They Say 'Bon Voyage,'" *Human Resources Professional*, Summer 1992, pp. 42–44.

29. Oddou and Mendenhall, loc. cit., found that foreign assignments helped careers in 29 percent of cases. Moran, Stahl & Boyer, as reported in the *New York Times*, June 17, 1990, Sec. 3, p. 1, found that of the MNEs studied, 44 percent perceived foreign assignments as being advantageous or essential to careers, whereas 56 percent viewed them as immaterial or detrimental.

30. "Fast-Trackers Fight," *Wall Street Journal*, November 8, 1988, p. 1, shows that three out of eighteen had such tours.

31. Amanda Bennett, "What's an Expatriate?" *Wall Street Journal*, April 21, 1993, p. R5.

32. Thomas F. O'Boyle, "Little Benefit to Careers Seen in Foreign Stints," *Wall Street Journal*, December 11, 1989, p. B4.

33. Claudia H. Deutsch, "Getting the Brightest to Go Abroad," *New York Times*, June 17, 1990, p. C1.

34. Ibid. Most indications are that these involve a minority of companies; however, Weeks, loc. cit., found the inclusion of international experience in succession plans of 61 percent of large companies.

35. Bennett, loc. cit.

36. "Domestic Help for Expatriates," *Wall Street Journal*, September 9, 1991, p. A10.

37. Sam Passow, "Manager's Journal," *Wall Street Journal*, June 18, 1984, p. 18; Rod Willis, "Corporations vs. Terrorists," *Management Review*, Vol. 75, No. 11, November 1986, pp. 16–27; Jonathan Dahl, "Firms Warn Workers Traveling Abroad," *Wall Street Journal*, April 10, 1989, p. B1; Don Dunn, "A Baedeker for Travel in a Tense World," *Business Week*, September 10, 1990, p. 105; David D. Medina and Carolyn Phillips, "Companies with Hostages in Persian Gulf Struggle to Help Stateside Families Cope," *Wall Street Journal*, September 26, 1990, p. B1+; Larry Light and Jeffrey Ryser, "The Miniboom in Kidnapping Coverage," *Business Week*, March 19, 1990, p. 100; and "Expatriate Protection Boosted," *Wall Street Journal*, June 21, 1993, p. A8.

38. Gilbert Fuchsberg, "As Costs of Overseas Assignments Climb, Firms Select Expatriates More Carefully," *Wall Street Journal*, January 9, 1992, p. B1.

39. Joann S. Lublin, "Spouses Find Themselves Worlds Apart as Global Commuter Marriages Increase," *Wall Street Journal*, August 19, 1992, p. B1+.

40. "Global Report," *Wall Street Journal*, July 11, 1977, p. 6; and Barry Newman, "Mine over Matter," *Wall Street Journal*, August 25, 1977, p. 1.

41. Bennett, loc. cit.; Amanda Bennett, "Managers' Incomes Aren't Worlds Apart," *Wall Street Journal*, October 12, 1992, p. B1; and Richard Morais et al., "The Global Boss' Pay: Where and How the Money Is," *Forbes*, June 7, 1993, pp. 90–98.

42. Samir M. Youssef, "The Integration of Local Nationals into the Managerial Hierarchy of American Overseas Subsidiaries: An Exploratory Study," *Academy of Management Journal*, March 1973, p. 29; and Oded Shenkar and Yoram Zeira, "Human Resources Management in International Joint Ventures: Directions for Research," *Academy of Management Review*, Vol. 12, No. 3, July 1987, pp. 546–557.

43. Rosalie L. Tung, "Selection and Training of Personnel for Overseas Assignments," *Columbia Journal of World Business*, Vol. 16, No. 1, Spring 1981, p. 72; Canadian International Development Agency (CIDA), "Going Abroad with CIDA"; Bureau of Naval Personnel, *Overseas Diplomacy: Guidelines for United States Navy: Trainer* (Washington, D.C.: U.S. Government Printing Office, 1973); M. H. Tucker, D. Raik Rossiter, and M. Uhes, *Improving the Evaluation of Peace Corps Training Activities*, Vol. 3 (Denver: Center for Research and Education, June 4, 1973); and J. Stewart Black, "Work-role Transitions: A Study of American Expatriate Managers in Japan," *Journal of International Business Studies*, Vol. 19, 1988, pp. 277–294.

44. Weeks, loc. cit., found that 32 percent of companies interview families and 16 percent use psychological tests for either the employee or the employee and family.

45. Michael G. Harvey, "The Executive Family: An Overlooked Variable in International Assignments," *Columbia Journal of World Business*, Spring 1985, pp. 84–92; and Black and Stephens, loc. cit.

46. Black and Mendenhall, op. cit., pp. 118–119; and J. Stewart Black, Mark Mendenhall, and Gary Oddou, "Toward a Comprehensive Model of International Adjustment: An Integration of Multiple Theoretical Perspectives," *Academy of Management Review*, March–April 1991.

47. Christopher A. Bartlett and Sumantra Ghoshal, "What Is a Global Manager?" *Harvard Business Review*, September–October 1992, pp. 124–132.

48. Bennett ("What's An Expatriate?") refers to studies by Organization Resources Counselors that indicate a trend toward reliance on specialists. Weeks, loc. cit., indicates an opposite trend.

49. R. Lynn Barnes, "Across Cultures: The Peace Corps Training Model," *Training and Development Journal*, Vol. 39, No. 10, October 1985, pp. 46–49.

50. P. Christopher Early, "Intercultural Training for Managers: A Comparison of Documentary and Interpersonal Methods," *Academy of Management Journal*, Vol. 30, No. 4, December 1987, pp. 685–698.

51. F. T. Murray and Alice Haller Murray, "SMR Forum: Global Managers for Global Businesses," *Sloan Management Review*, Vol. 27, No. 2, Winter 1986, pp. 75–80; and Joann S. Lublin, "Younger Managers Learn Global Skills," *Wall Street Journal*, March 31, 1992, p. B1.

52. Alicia Kitsuse, "At Home Abroad," *Across the Board*, September 1992, pp. 34–39; and Yoram Zeira and Asya Pazy, "Crossing National Borders to Get Trained," *Training and Development Journal*, Vol. 39, No. 10, October 1985, pp. 53–57.

53. Frank L. Acuff, "Awareness Levels of Employees Considering Overseas Relocation," *Personnel Journal*, November 1974, pp. 809–812. Kenneth Darrow and Bradley Palmquist, eds., *Trans-Cultural Study*

Guide, 2nd ed. (N.P.: Volunteers in Asia, 1975) lists pertinent questions to ask.

54. Kitsuse, loc. cit., referring to suggestions by Stewart Black.

55. Brent Bowers, "Tapping Foreign Talent Pool Can Yield Lush Growth," *Wall Street Journal,* March 23, 1992, p. B2.

56. Igor Reichlin, Sabrina Kiefer, Charles Hoots, and Jacek Dobrowlski, "Long Days, Low Pay, and a Moldy Cot," *Business Week,* January 27, 1992, pp. 44–45; and Michael J. Mandel, Christopher Farrell, Dori Jones Yang, Gloria Lau, Christina Del Valle, and S. Lynne Walker, "The Immigrants," *Business Week,* July 13, 1992, pp. 114–122.

57. R. Aggarwal and I. Khera, "Exporting Labor: The Impact of Expatriate Workers on the Home Country," *International Migration,* Vol. 25, No. 4, 1987, pp. 415–424.

58. "In Europe, Cash Eases the Pain of Getting Fired," *Business Week,* March 16, 1992, p. 26.

59. Felice Morgenstern, "The Civil Liability of Workers for Injury or Damage Caused in Their Employment," *International Labour Review,* May–June 1976, pp. 317–328.

60. Bob Davis, "Illusory Bargain," *Wall Street Journal,* September 15, 1993, p. A1+.

61. Steve Glain, "Korea Is Overthrown as Sneaker Champ," *Wall Street Journal,* October 7, 1993, p. A12.

62. Efrin Cordova, "A Comparative View of Collective Bargaining in Industrialised Countries," *International Labour Review,* July–August 1978, p. 423; and Eduardo B. Gentil, "Brazil's Labor Movement," *Wall Street Journal,* November 11, 1980, p. 34.

63. Gene Koretz, "Why Unions Thrive Abroad—But Wither in the U.S.," *Business Week,* September 10, 1990, p. 26, referring to a study by David Blanchflower and Richard Freeman for the National Bureau of Economic Research.

64. Joseph Krislov, "Supplying Mediation Services in Five Countries: Some Current Problems," *Columbia Journal of World Business,* Vol. 18, No. 2, Summer 1983, pp. 55–63.

65. Frances Bairstow, "The Trend Toward Centralized Bargaining—A Patchwork Quilt of International Diversity," *Columbia Journal of World Business,* Spring 1985, pp. 75–83.

66. Edward A. Gargan, "As Hand Looms of India Fall Silent, the Country's Social Fabric Frays," *New York Times,* October 7, 1992, p. A4.

67. For a good survey of the various studies, see Peter Enderwick, *Multinational Business & Labor* (New York: St. Martin's Press, 1985), pp. 55–58.

68. Masayoshi Kanabayashi, "Japan's Unions, Anxious to Avoid Fight, Again Likely to Accept a Modest Pay Raise," *Wall Street Journal,* February 9, 1984, p. 31.

69. Bairstow, loc. cit.

70. Donna Bridgeman, "Worker Take-Overs," ICCH Case 9-475-093, Harvard Business School, 1975; "Bulova Watch Plant Is Occupied to Protest Closing," *Wall Street Journal,* January 19, 1976; "ICL Workers Say They Took Over Plant to Prevent Closing," *Wall Street Journal,* November 11, 1980, p. 34; and Barbara Ehrenreich and Annette Fuentes, "Life on the Global Assembly Line," *Ms.,* January 1981, pp. 53–71.

71. Bennett Harrison, "The International Movement for Prenotification of Plant Closures," *Industrial Relations,* Fall 1984, pp. 387–409.

72. Mourdoukoutas and S. N. Sohng, "The Japanese Industrial System: A Study in Adjustment to Automation," *Management International Review,* Vol. 27, No. 4, 1987, pp. 46–55; John Hoerr and Wendy Zellner, "A Japanese Import That's Not Selling," *Business Week,* February 26, 1990, pp. 86–87; Masayoshi Kanabayashi, "Bucking Tradition," *Wall Street Journal,* October 11, 1988, p. 1+; Masayoshi Kanabayashi, "Japanese Workers Aren't All Workaholics," *Wall Street Journal,* May 8, 1989, p. A10; and D. H. Whittaker, *Managing Innovation: A Study of British and Japanese Factories* (Cambridge, Eng.: Cambridge University Press, 1990).

73. For early operational problems, see "Sweden: Worker Participation Becomes the Law," *Business Week,* June 21, 1976, pp. 42–46; G. McIsaac and H. Henzler, "Co-Determination: A Hidden Noose for MNCs," *Columbia Journal of World Business,* Winter 1974, pp. 67–74; and M. Warner and R. Peccei, "Worker Participation and Multinationals," *Management International Review,* No. 3, 1977, pp. 93–98. For recent evidence on overall effects, see Wolfgang Scholl, "Codetermination and the Ability of Firms to Act in the Federal Republic of Germany," *International Studies of Management & Organization,* Vol. XVII, No. 2, Summer 1987, pp. 27–37; and Giuseppe Benelli, Claudio Loderer, and Thomas Lys, "Labor Participation in Corporate Policy-making Decisions: West Germany's Experience with Codetermination," *Journal of Business,* Vol. 60, No. 4, October 1987, pp. 553–575.

74. Much of the information on codetermination in Germany is taken from Trevor Bain, "German Codetermination and Employment Adjustments in the Steel and Auto Industries," *Columbia Journal of World Business,* Vol. 18, No. 2, Summer 1983, pp. 40–47.

75. For two discussions of these efforts, see Duane Kujawa, "Technology Strategy and Industrial Relations: Case Studies of Japanese Multinationals in the United States," *Journal of International Business Studies,* Vol. 14, No. 3, Winter 1983, pp. 9–22; and Wolf Reitsperger, "British Employees: Responding to Japanese Management Philosophies," *Journal of Management Studies,* Vol. 23, No. 5, September 1986, pp. 563–586.

76. "Child-Worker Abuses in Third World Draw Fire of Labor Group," *Wall Street Journal,* June 8, 1988, p. 26.

77. Unless otherwise noted, information in this section is taken largely from the following treatises: Gerald B. J. Bomers and Richard B. Peterson, "Multinational Corporations and the Industrial Relations: The Case of West Germany and the Netherlands," *British Journal of Industrial Relations,* March 1977, pp. 45–62; Duane A. Kujawa, "Collective Bargaining and Labor Relations in Multinational Enterprise: A U.S. Policy Perspective," paper presented at New York University Conference on Economic Issues of Multinational Firms, November 1976; Duane Kujawa, "U.S. Manufacturing Investment in the Developing Countries: American Labour's Concerns and the Enterprise Environment in the Decade Ahead," *British Journal of Industrial Relations,* Vol. 19, No. 1, March 1981, pp. 38–48; and Roy B. Helfgott, "American Unions and Multinational Enterprises: A Case of Misplaced Emphasis," *Columbia Journal of World Business,* Vol. 18, No. 2, Summer 1983, pp. 81–86.

78. Richard L. Hudson, "Strike at Ford Shows Problems of New Methods," *Wall Street Journal,* February 10, 1988, p. 14; and Barbara Toman, "Ford, Unions Agree on Contract Offer in Breakthrough in 9-Day U.K. Strike," *Wall Street Journal,* February 17, 1988, p. 2.

79. Ron Suskind, "Tough Vote," *Wall Street Journal,* July 28, 1992, p. A1.

80. Gregory A. Patterson, "New Rules," *Wall Street Journal,* March 6, 1992, p. A1.

81. Martin C. Seham, "Transnational Labor Relations: The First Steps Are Being Taken," *Law and Policy in International Business,* Vol. 6, 1974, pp. 347–354.

82. Thomas Werres, "Trade Unions Struggle to Discover a Common Path for a United Europe," *The German Tribune,* December 4, 1992, p. 7.

83. For examples, see I. A. Litvak and C. J. Maule, "The Union Response to International Corporations," *Industrial Relations,* February 1972, pp. 66–67; and Duane A. Kujawa, "International Labor Relations: Trade Union Initiatives and Management Responses," *Personnel Administrator,* February 1977, p. 50.

84. Douglas Martin, "A Canadian Split on Unions," *New York Times,* March 12, 1984, p. D12.

85. J. Stewart Black and Hal B. Gregersen, "Serving Two Masters: Managing the Dual Allegiance of Expatriate Employ-

ees," *Sloan Management Review,* Summer 1992, pp. 61–71, covers the typologies of expatriates.

86. For a good discussion of the changing power of employees, see Frank P. Doyle,

"The Changing Workplace: People Power: The Global Human Resource Challenge for the 1990s," *Columbia Journal of World Business,* Vol. 25, Nos. 1 and 2, Spring–Summer 1990, pp. 36–45.

87. Blocklyn, op. cit., p. 44, quoting Roger Herod.

88. For a short summary, see Kenneth H. Bacon, "The Outlook," *Wall Street Journal,* June 6, 1988, p. 1.

Glossary

Absolute advantage: A theory first presented by Adam Smith, which holds that because certain countries can produce some goods more efficiently than other countries can, they should specialize in and export those things they can produce more efficiently and trade for other things they need.

Acceptable quality level: A concept of quality control whereby managers are willing to accept a certain level of production defects, which are dealt with through repair facilities and service centers.

Accounting: The process of identifying, recording, and interpreting economic events.

Acquired advantage: A form of trade advantage due to technology rather than the availability of natural resources, climate, etc.

Acquired group memberships: Affiliations not determined by birth, such as religions, political affiliations, and professional and other associations.

Acquisition: The purchase of one company by another company.

Active income: Income of a CFC that is derived from the active conduct of a trade or business, as specified by the U.S. Internal Revenue Code.

Ad valorem duty: A duty (tariff) assessed as a percentage of the value of the item.

Administratively guided market economy: An economic system in which there is a great deal of cooperation among government, management, and workers to achieve growth and full employment with low job turnover on a nonmandated basis.

ADR: *See* American Depositary Receipt.

AFTA: *See* ASEAN Free Trade Area.

ALADI: *See* Latin American Integration Association.

American Depositary Receipt (ADR): A negotiable certificate issued by a U.S. bank in the United States to represent the underlying shares of a foreign corporation's stock held in trust at a custodian bank in the foreign country.

American system: *See* U.S. terms.

Andean Group (ANCOM): A South American form of economic integration involving Bolivia, Colombia, Ecuador, Peru, and Venezuela.

Appropriability theory: The theory that companies will favor foreign direct investment over such non-equity operating forms as licensing arrangements so that potential competitors will be less likely to gain access to proprietary information.

Appropriate technology: Technology that best fits the local factor endowment; often used to mean a more labor-intensive technology than would be cost-efficient in a developing country.

Arbitrage: The process of buying and selling foreign currency at a profit resulting from price discrepancies between or among markets.

Area division: *See* Geographic division.

Arm's-length price: A price between two companies that do not have an ownership interest in each other.

Arrangement Regarding International Trade in Textiles: An agreement among governments establishing rules on textile trade; also known as the Multifibre Arrangement (MFA).

Ascribed group memberships: Affiliations determined by birth, such as those based on gender, family, age, caste, and ethnic, racial, or national origin.

ASEAN: *See* Association of South East Asian Nations.

ASEAN Free Trade Area (AFTA): A free-trade area formed by the ASEAN countries on January 1, 1993, with the goal of cutting tariffs on all intrazonal trade to a maximum of 5 percent by January 1, 2005.

Association of South East Asian Nations (ASEAN): A free-trade area involving the Asian countries of Brunei, Indonesia, Malaysia, the Philippines, Singapore, and Thailand.

Back-to-back loan: A loan that involves a company in Country A with a subsidiary in Country B, and a bank in Country B with a branch in Country A.

Balance of payments: Statement that summarizes all economic transactions between a country and the rest of the world during a given period of time.

Balance-of-payments deficit: An imbalance of some specific component within the balance of payments, such as merchandise trade or current account, that implies that a country is importing more than it exports.

Balance-of-payments surplus: An imbalance in the balance of payments that exists when a country exports more than it imports.

Balance of trade: The value of a country's exports less the value of its imports ("trade" can be defined as merchandise trade, services, unilateral transfers, or a combination of these).

Balance on goods and services: The value of a country's exports of merchandise trade and services minus imports.

Bank for International Settlements (BIS): A bank in Basel, Switzerland that facilitates transactions among central banks, effectively the central banks' central bank.

Bargaining school theory: A theory holding that the negotiated terms for foreign investors depend on how much investors and host countries need each other's assets.

Barter: The exchange of goods for goods instead of for money.

Base currency: The currency whose value is implicitly 1 when a quote is made between two currencies; for example, if the cruzeiro is trading at 2962.5 cruzeiros per dollar, the dollar is the base currency and the cruzeiro is the quoted currency.

Basic balance: The net current account plus long-term capital within a country's balance of payments.

Bid (buy): The amount a trader is willing to pay for foreign exchange.

Bill of exchange: *See* Commercial bill of exchange.

Bill of lading: A document that is issued to a shipper by a carrier, listing the goods received for shipment.

BIRPI: *See* International Bureau for the Protection of Industrial Property Rights.

BIS: *See* Bank for International Settlements.

Black market: The foreign-exchange market that lies outside the official market.

Body language: The way people move their bodies, gesture, position themselves, etc., to convey meaning to others.

Bonded warehouse: A building or part of a building used for the storage of imported merchandise under supervision of the U.S. Customs Service and for the purpose of deferring payment of customs duties.

Booking center: An offshore financial center whose main function is to act as an accounting center in order to minimize the payment of taxes.

Branch (foreign): A foreign operation of a company that is not a separate entity from the parent that owns it.

Brand: A particular good identified with a company by means of name, logo, or other method, usually protected with a trademark registration.

Bretton Woods Agreement: An agreement among IMF countries to promote exchange-rate stability and to facilitate the international flow of currencies.

Broker (in foreign exchange): Specialists who facilitate transactions in the interbank market.

Buffer-stock system: A partially managed system that utilizes stocks of commodities to regulate their prices.

Bundesbank: The German central bank.

Buy local legislation: Laws that are intended to favor the purchase of domestically sourced goods or services over imported ones, even though the imports may be a better buy.

CACM: *See* Central American Common Market.

Canada-U.S. Free Trade Agreement: An agreement, enacted in 1989, establishing a free-trade area involving the United States and Canada.

Capital account: A measure of transactions involving previously existing rather than currently produced assets.

Capital market: The market for stocks and long-term debt instruments.

Capitalism: An economic system characterized by private ownership, pricing, production, and distribution of goods.

Caribbean Community and Common Market (CARICOM): A customs union in the Caribbean region.

CARICOM: *See* Caribbean Community and Common Market.

Central American Common Market (CACM): A customs union in Central America.

Central bank: A governmental "bank for banks," customarily responsible for a country's monetary policy.

Centralization: The situation in which decision making is done at the home office rather than the country level.

Centrally planned economy (CPE): *See* Command economy.

Certificate of origin: A shipping document that determines the origin of products and is usually validated by an external source, such as a chamber of commerce; it helps countries determine the specific tariff schedule for imports.

CFC: *See* Controlled foreign corporation.

Chicago Mercantile Exchange: The largest commodity exchange in the world, dealing primarily in agricultural products, U.S. treasury bills, coins, and some metals.

CIA: The Central Intelligence Agency, a U.S. governmental agency charged with gathering intelligence information abroad.

Civil law system: A legal system based on a very detailed set of laws that are organized into a code; countries with a civil law system, also called a codified legal system, include Germany, France, and Japan.

Civil liberties: The freedom to develop one's own views and attitudes.

COCOM: *See* Coordinating Committee on Multilateral Exports.

Code of conduct: A set of principles guiding the actions of MNEs in their contacts with societies.

Codetermination: A process by which both labor and management participate in the management of a company.

Codified legal system: *See* Civil law system.

COMECON: *See* Council for Mutual Economic Assistance.

Command economy: An economic system in which resources are allocated and controlled by government decision.

Commercial bill of exchange: An instrument of payment in international business that instructs the importer to forward payment to the exporter.

Commercial invoice: A bill for goods from the buyer to the seller.

Commission agent: A type of intermediary that sells a manufacturer's goods for commission without taking title.

Commission on Transnational Corporations: A United Nations agency that deals with multinational enterprises.

Commodities: Basic raw materials or agricultural products.

Commodity agreement: A form of economic cooperation designed to stabilize and raise the price of a commodity.

Common Agricultural Policy (CAP): An EU policy aimed at free trade, price supports, and modernization programs in agriculture.

Common law system: A legal system based on tradition, precedent, and custom and usage, in which the courts interpret the law based on those conventions; found in the United Kingdom and former British colonies.

Common market: A form of regional economic integration in which countries abolish internal tariffs, use a common external tariff, and abolish restrictions on factor mobility.

Communism: A form of totalitarianism initially theorized by Karl Marx in which the political and economic systems are virtually inseparable.

Comparative advantage: The theory that there may still be global efficiency gains from trade if a country specializes in those products that it can produce more efficiently than other products.

Compound duty: A tax placed on goods traded internationally, based on value plus units.

Concentration strategy: A strategy by which an international company builds up operations quickly in one or a few countries before going to another.

Confirmed letter of credit: A letter of credit to which a bank in the exporter's country adds its guarantee of payment.

Conservatism: A characteristic of accounting systems that implies that companies are hesitant to disclose high profits or profits that are consistent with its actual operating results; more common in Germanic countries.

Consolidation: An accounting process in which financial statements of related entities, such as a parent and its subsidiaries, are combined to yield a unified set of financial statements; in the process, transactions among the related enterprises are eliminated so that the statements reflect transactions with outside parties.

Consortium: The joining together of several entities, such as companies or governments, in order to strengthen the possibility of achieving some objective.

Consular invoice: A document that covers all the usual details of the commercial invoice and packing list, prepared in the language of the foreign country for which the goods are destined, on special forms obtainable from the consulate or authorized commercial printers.

Consumer-directed market economy: An economy in which there is minimal government participation while growth is promoted through the mobility of production factors, including high labor turnover.

Consumer price index: A measure of the cost of typical wage-earner purchases of goods and services expressed as a percentage of the cost of these same goods and services in some base period.

Consumer sovereignty: The freedom of consumers to influence production through the choices they make.

Continental terms: *See* European terms.

Control: The planning, implementation, evaluation, and correction of performance to ensure that organizational objectives are achieved.

Controlled foreign corporation (CFC): A foreign corporation of which more than 50 percent of the voting stock is owned by U.S. shareholders (taxable entities that own at least 10 percent of the voting stock of the corporation).

Convertibility: The ability to exchange one currency for another currency without restrictions.

Coordinating Committee on Multilateral Exports (COCOM): An agreement among Western industrial nations to limit militarily useful exports to communist countries; disbanded in 1991 after the former Soviet Union broke up.

Copyright: The right to reproduce, publish, and sell literary, musical, or artistic works.

Corporate culture: The common values shared by employees in a corporation, which form a control mechanism that is implicit and helps enforce other explicit control mechanisms.

Correspondent (bank): A bank in which funds are kept by another, usually foreign, bank to facilitate check clearing and other business relationships.

Cost-of-living adjustment: An increase in compensation given to an expatriate employee when foreign living costs are more expensive than those in the home country.

Council for Mutual Economic Assistance (CMEA or COMECON): A regional form of economic integration that involved essentially those communist countries considered to be within the Soviet bloc; terminated in 1991.

Council of Ministers: One of the five major institutions of the EU; composed of one member from each country in the EU and entrusted with making major policy decisions.

Countertrade: A reciprocal flow of goods or services valued and settled in monetary terms.

Country analysis: A process of examining the economic strategy of a nation state, taking a holistic approach to understanding how a country, and in particular its government, has behaved, is behaving, and may behave.

Country-similarity theory: The theory that a producer, having developed a new product in response to observed market conditions in the home market, will turn to markets that are most similar to those at home.

Country size theory: The theory that larger countries are generally more self-sufficient than smaller countries.

Court of Justice: One of the five major institutions of the EU; composed of one member from each country in the EU and serves as a supreme appeals court for EU law.

CPE (centrally planned economy): *See* Command economy.

Creolization: The process by which elements of an outside culture are introduced.

Cross-licensing: The exchange of technology by different companies.

Cross rate: An exchange rate between two currencies used in the spot market and computed from the exchange rate of each currency in relation to the U.S. dollar.

Cultural relativism: The belief that behavior has meaning and can be judged only in its specific cultural context.

Culture: The specific learned norms of a society, based on attitudes, values, and beliefs.

Culture shock: A generalized trauma one experiences in a new and different culture because of having to learn and cope with a vast array of new cues and expectations.

Current-account balance: Exports minus imports of goods, services, and unilateral transfers.

Current-rate method: A method of translating foreign-currency financial statements that is used when the functional currency is that of the local operating environment.

Customs duties: Taxes imposed on imported goods.

Customs union: A form of regional economic integration that eliminates tariffs among member nations and establishes common external tariffs.

Customs valuation: The value of goods on which customs authorities charge tariffs.

Debt-service ratio: The ratio of interest payments plus principal amortization to exports.

Decentralization: The situation in which decisions tend to be made at lower levels in a company or at the country-operating level rather than at headquarters.

Deferral: The postponing of taxation of foreign-source income until it is remitted to the parent company.

Democracy: A political system that relies on citizens' participation in the decision-making process.

Democratic socialism: The belief that economics and politics are so closely connected that the voters should rely on their elected governments to control the economic system.

Dependencia theory: The theory holding that LDCs have practically no power when dealing with MNEs as host countries.

Dependency: A state in which a country is too dependent on the sale of one primary commodity and/or too dependent on one country as a customer and supplier.

Derivative: A foreign-exchange instrument such as an option or futures contract that derives its value from some underlying financial instrument.

Derivatives market: Market in which forward contracts, futures, options, and swaps are traded in order to hedge or protect foreign-exchange transactions.

Devaluation: A formal reduction in the value of a currency in relation to another currency; the foreign-currency equivalent of the devalued currency falls.

Developing country: A poor country, also known as a Third-World country or a less developed country.

Direct foreign investment: *See* Foreign direct investment.

Direct identification drawback: A provision that allows U.S. firms to use imported components in the manufacturing process without having to include the duty paid on the imported goods in costs and sales prices.

Direct investment: *See* Foreign direct investment.

Direct quote: A quote expressed in terms of the number of units of the domestic currency given for one unit of a foreign currency.

Direct selling: A sale of goods by an exporter directly to distributors or final consumers rather than to trading companies or other intermediaries in order to achieve greater control over the marketing function and to earn higher profits.

Directive: A proposed form of legislation in the EU.

Discount (in foreign exchange): A situation in which the forward rate for a foreign currency is less than the spot rate, assuming that the domestic currency is quoted on a direct basis.

Distribution: The course—physical path or legal title—that goods take between production and consumption.

Distributor: A merchant in a foreign country that purchases products from the manufacturer and sells them at a profit.

Diversification: A process of becoming less dependent on one or a few customers or suppliers.

Diversification strategy: A strategy by which an international company produces or sells in many countries to avoid relying on one particular market.

Divestment: Reduction in the amount of investment.

Drawback: A provision allowing U.S. exporters to apply for refunds of 99 percent of the duty paid on imported components, provided they are used in the manufacture of goods that are exported.

Dumping: The underpricing of exports, usually below cost or below the home-country price.

Duty: A governmental tax (tariff) levied on goods shipped internationally.

Economic Community of West African States (ECOWAS): A form of economic integration among certain countries in West Africa.

Economic exposure: The foreign-exchange risk that international businesses face in the pricing of products, the source and cost of inputs, and the location of investments.

Economic integration: The abolition of economic discrimination between national economies, such as within the EU.

Economic system: The system concerned with the allocation of scarce resources.

Economics: A social science concerned chiefly with the description and analysis of the production, distribution, and consumption of goods and services.

Economies of scale: The lowering of cost per unit as output increases because of allocation of fixed costs over more units produced.

ECOWAS: *See* Economic Community of West African States.

ECU: *See* European Currency Unit.

EEC: *See* European Economic Community.

EEC Patent Convention: An important cross-national patent convention that involves the members of the EU.

Effective tariff: The real tariff on the manufactured portion of developing countries' exports, which is higher than indicated by the published rates because the ad valorem tariff is based on the total value of the products, which includes raw materials that would have had duty-free entry.

EFTA: *See* European Free Trade Association.

Elastic (product demand): A condition in which sales are likely to increase or decrease by a percentage that is more than the percentage change in income.

Electronic data interchange (EDI): The electronic movement of money and information via computers and telecommunications equipment.

Embargo: A specific type of quota that prohibits all trade.

EMC: *See* Export management company.

EMS: *See* European Monetary System.

Entente Council: A regional economic group in Africa that includes the nations of Benin, Burkina Faso, Côte d'Ivoire, Niger, and Togo.

Enterprise of the Americas: A proposed series of bilateral trade relationships between the United States and Latin American countries, based on a "hub and spokes" concept and eventually resulting in one huge multilateral relationship involving the Americas.

Entrepôt: A country that is an import/export intermediary; for example, Hong Kong is an entrepôt for trade between China and the rest of the world.

Environmental climate: The external conditions in host countries that could significantly affect the success of a foreign business enterprise.

Environmental scanning: The systematic assessment of external conditions that might affect a company's operations.

EPC: *See* European Patent Convention.

Essential-industry argument: The argument holding that certain domestic industries need protection for national security purposes.

ETC: *See* Export trading company.

Ethnocentrism: A belief that one's own group is superior to others; also used to describe a company's belief that what worked at home should work abroad.

Eurobond: A bond sold in a country other than the one in whose currency it is denominated.

Eurocredit: A loan, line of credit, or other form of medium- or long-term credit on the Eurocurrency market that has a maturity of more than one year.

Eurocurrency: Any currency that is banked outside of its country of origin.

Eurocurrency market: An international wholesale market that deals in Eurocurrencies.

Eurodollars: Dollars banked outside of the United States.

Euroequity market: The market for shares sold outside the boundaries of the issuing company's home country.

Europe 1992: Legislation enacted by the EU and designed to eliminate most key barriers to trade of goods and services by December 31, 1992.

European Commission: One of the five major institutions of the EU; composed of a president, six vice presidents, and ten other members whose allegiance is to the EU and serving as an executive branch for the EU.

European Community (EC): The predecessor of the European Union.

European Council: One of the five major institutions of the European Union; made up of the heads of state of each of the EU members.

European Currency Unit (ECU): A unit of account based on currency basket composed of the currencies of the members of the EU.

European Economic Community (EEC): The predecessor of the European Community.

European Free Trade Association (EFTA): A free-trade area among a group of European countries that are not members of the EU.

European Monetary System (EMS): A cooperative foreign-exchange agreement involving most of the members of the EU and designed to promote exchange-rate stability within the EU.

European Parliament: One of the five major institutions of the EU; its representatives are elected directly in each member country.

European Patent Convention (EPC): A European agreement allowing companies to make a uniform patent search and application which is then passed on to all signatory countries.

European terms: The practice of using the indirect quote for exchange rates.

European Union (EU): A form of regional economic integration among countries in Europe that involves a free-trade area, a customs union, and the free mobility of factors of production that is working toward political and economic union.

Exchange rate: The price of one currency in terms of another currency.

Eximbank: *See* Export-Import Bank.

Exotic currencies: The currencies of developing countries; also called *exotics*.

Expatriates: Noncitizens of the country in which they are working.

Experience curve: The relationship of production-cost reductions to increases in output.

Export-Import Bank (Eximbank): A U.S. federal agency specializing in foreign lending to support exports.

Export-led development: An industrialization policy emphasizing industries that will have export capabilities.

Export license: A document that grants government permission to ship certain products to a specific country.

Export management company (EMC): A company that buys merchandise from manufacturers for international distribution or sometimes acts as an agent for manufacturers.

Export packing list: A shipping document that itemizes the material in each individual package and indicates the type of package.

Export tariff: A tax on goods leaving a country.

Export trading company (ETC): A form of trading company sanctioned by U.S. law to become involved in international commerce as independent distributors to match up foreign buyers with domestic sellers.

Exports: Goods or services leaving a country.

Exposure: A situation in which a foreign-exchange account is subject to a gain or loss if the exchange rate changes.

Exposure draft: The first draft of an accounting standard, which is open to comment by parties other than the IASC.

Expropriation: The taking over of ownership of private property by a country's government.

External convertibility: *See* Nonresident convertibility.

Externalities: External economic costs related to a business activity.

Extraterritoriality: The extension by a government of the application of its laws to foreign operations of companies.

Factor mobility: The free movement of factors of production, such as labor and capital, across national borders.

Factor-proportions theory: The theory that differences in a country's proportionate holdings of factors of production (land, labor, and capital) explain differences in the costs of the factors and that export advantages lie in the production of goods that use the most abundant factors.

FASB: *See* Financial Accounting Standards Board.

Fatalism: A belief that events are fixed in advance and human beings are powerless to change them.

Favorable balance of trade: An indication that a country is exporting more than it imports.

FCPA: *See* Foreign Corrupt Practices Act.

FDI: *See* Foreign direct investment.

Fees: Payments for the performance of certain activities abroad.

Financial Accounting Standards Board (FASB): The private-sector organization that sets financial accounting standards in the United States.

FIRA: *See* Foreign Investment Review Act.

First-in advantage: Any benefit gained in terms of brand recognition and lining up of the best suppliers, distributors, and local partners because of entering a market before competitors do.

First-mover advantage: A cost-reduction advantage due to economies of scale attained through moving into a foreign market ahead of competitors.

First-World countries: The nonsocialist industrialized countries.

Fisher Effect: The theory about the relationship between inflation and interest rates; for example, if the nominal interest rate in one country is lower than that in another, the first country's inflation should be lower so that the real interest rates will be equal.

Fixed price: A method of pricing in which bargaining does not take place.

Flexible exchange rate: An exchange rate determined by the laws of supply and demand and with minimal governmental interference.

Floating currency: A currency whose value responds to the supply of and demand for that currency.

Foreign bond: A bond sold outside of the borrower's country but denominated in the currency of the country of issue.

Foreign Corrupt Practices Act (FCPA): A law that criminalizes certain types of payments by U.S. companies, such as bribes to foreign governmental officials.

Foreign direct investment (FDI): An investment that gives the investor a controlling interest in a foreign company.

Foreign exchange: Checks and other instruments for making payments in another country's currency.

Foreign-exchange control: A requirement that an importer of a product must apply to governmental authorities for permission to buy foreign currency to pay for the product.

Foreign freight forwarder: A company that facilitates the movement of goods from one country to another.

Foreign investment: Direct or portfolio ownership of assets in another country.

Foreign Investment Review Act (FIRA): A Canadian law intended to limit foreign control of that country's economy.

Foreign sales corporation (FSC): A special type of corporation established by U.S. tax law that can be used by a U.S. exporter to shelter some of its income from taxation.

Foreign trade zone (FTZ): A government-designated area in which goods can be stored, inspected, or manufactured without being subject to formal customs procedures until they leave the zone.

Forward contract: A contract between a company or individual and a bank to deliver foreign currency at a specific exchange rate on a future date.

Forward discount: *See* Discount.

Forward premium: *See* Premium.

Forward rate: A contractually established exchange rate between a foreign-exchange trader and the trader's client for delivery of foreign currency on a specific date.

Franchising: A specialized form of licensing in which one party (the franchisor) sells to an independent party (the franchisee) the use of a trademark that is an essential asset for the franchisee's business and also gives continual assistance in the operation of the business.

Free-trade area (FTA): A form of regional economic integration in which internal tariffs are abolished, but member countries set their own external tariffs.

Freight forwarder: *See* Foreign freight forwarder.

Fringe benefit: Any employee benefit other than salary, wages, and cash bonuses.

FSC: *See* Foreign sales corporation.

FTZ: *See* Foreign trade zone.

Functional currency: The currency of the primary economic environment in which an entity operates.

Functional division: An organizational structure in which each function in foreign countries (e.g., marketing or production) reports separately to a counterpart functional group at headquarters.

Futures contract: A foreign-exchange instrument that specifies an exchange rate, an amount of currency, and a maturity date in advance of the exchange of the currency.

G-7 countries: *See* Group of 7.

GAAP: *See* Generally accepted accounting principles.

Gap analysis: A tool used to discover why a company's sales of a given product are less than the market potential in a country; the reason may be a usage, competitive, product line, or distribution gap.

GATT: *See* General Agreement on Tariffs and Trade.

General Agreement on Tariffs and Trade (GATT): A multilateral arrangement aimed at reducing barriers to trade, both tariff and nontariff ones; at the signing of the Uruguay round, the GATT was designated to become the World Trade Organization (WTO).

Generalized System of Preferences (GSP): Preferential import restrictions extended by industrial countries to developing countries.

Generally accepted accounting principles (GAAP): The accounting standards accepted by the accounting profession in each country as required for the preparation of financial statements for external users.

Generic: Any of a class of products, rather than the brand of a particular company.

Geographic division: An organizational structure in which a company's operations are separated for reporting purposes into regional areas.

Geography: A science dealing with the earth and its life, especially with the description of land, sea, air, and the distribution of plant and animal life.

Global bond: A combination of domestic bond and Eurobond that is issued simultaneously in several markets and must be registered in each national market according to that market's registration requirements.

Global company: A company that integrates operations located in different countries.

Global sourcing: The acquisition on a worldwide basis of raw materials, parts, and subassemblies for the manufacturing process.

Globally integrated company: *See* Global company.

Go–no-go decision: A decision, such as on foreign investments, that is based on minimum-threshold criteria and does not compare different opportunities.

Grandchild subsidiary: An operation that is under a tax-haven subsidiary; also called a second-tier subsidiary.

Grass-roots campaign: A method of influencing governmental action from the bottom up.

Gray market: The handling of goods through unofficial distributors.

Gross domestic product (GDP): The total of all economic activity in a country, regardless of who owns the productive assets.

Gross national product (GNP): The total of incomes earned by residents of a country, regardless of where the productive assets are located.

Group of 7 (G-7): A group of developed countries that periodically meet to make economic decisions; this group consists of Canada, France, Germany, Italy, Japan, the United Kingdom, and the United States.

GSP: *See* Generalized System of Preferences.

Hard currency: A currency that is freely traded without many restrictions and for which there is usually strong external demand; often called a freely convertible currency.

Hardship allowance: A supplement to compensate expatriates for working in dangerous or adverse conditions.

Hedge: To attempt to protect foreign-currency holdings against an adverse movement of an exchange rate.

Hetarchy: An organizational structure in which management of an alliance of companies is shared by so-called equals rather than being set up in a superior-subordinate relationship.

Hickenlooper Amendment: A U.S. act requiring cessation of aid to a country that nationalizes assets of U.S. citizens or has moved to abrogate contracts without taking appropriate means of settlement within a reasonable period of time.

Hierarchy of needs: A well-known motivation theory stating that there is a hierarchy of needs and that people must fulfill the lower-order needs sufficiently before they will be motivated by the higher-order ones.

High-need achiever: One who will work very hard to achieve material or career success, sometimes to the detriment of social relationships or spiritual achievements.

High-value activities: Activities that either produce high profits or are done by high-salaried employees such as managers.

Historically planned economy (HPE): The World Bank's term for Second-World countries in transition to market economies.

History: A branch of knowledge that records and explains past events.

Home country: The country in which an international company is headquartered.

Home-country nationals: Expatriate employees who are citizens of the country in which the company is headquartered.

Horizontal expansion: Any foreign direct investment by which a company produces the same product it produces at home.

Host country: Any foreign country in which an international company operates.

HPE: *See* Historically planned economy.

Hyperinflation: A rapid increase (at least 1 percent per day) in general price levels for a sustained period of time.

IASC: *See* International Accounting Standards Committee.

Idealism: Trying to determine principles before settling small issues.

Ideology: The systematic and integrated body of constructs, theories, and aims that constitute a society.

IFC: *See* International Finance Corporation.

IFE: *See* International Fisher Effect.

ILO: *See* International Labor Organization.

IMF: *See* International Monetary Fund.

Imitation lag: A strategy for exploiting temporary monopoly advantages by moving first to those countries most likely to develop local production.

Import broker: An individual who obtains various governmental permissions and other clearances before forwarding necessary paperwork to the carrier that will deliver the goods from the dock to the importer.

Import deposit requirement: Governmental requirement of a deposit prior to the release of foreign exchange.

Import licensing: A method of governmental control of the exchange rate whereby all recipients, exporters, and others who receive foreign exchange are required to sell to the central bank at the official buying rate.

Import substitution: An industrialization policy whereby new industrial development emphasizes products that would otherwise be imported.

Import tariff: A tax placed on goods entering a country.

Imports: Goods or services entering a country.

In-bond industry: Any industry that is allowed to import components free of duty, provided that the components will be re-exported after processing.

Independence: An extreme situation in which a country would not rely on other countries at all.

Indigenization: The process of introducing elements of an outside culture.

Indirect quote: An exchange rate given in terms of the number of units of the foreign currency for one unit of the domestic currency.

Indirect selling: A sale of goods by an exporter through another domestic company as an intermediary.

Individually validated license (IVL): A special export license under which certain restricted products need to be shipped.

Industrialization argument: A rationale for protectionism that argues that the development of industrial output should come about even though domestic prices may not become competitive on the world market.

Inelastic (product demand): A condition in which sales are likely to increase or decrease by a percentage that is less than the percentage change in income.

Infant-industry argument: The position that holds that an emerging industry should be guaranteed a large share of the domestic market until it becomes efficient enough to compete against imports.

Infrastructure: The underlying foundation of a society, such as roads, schools, and so forth, that allows it to function effectively.

Input-output table: A tool used widely in national economic planning to show the resources utilized by different industries for a given output as well as the interdependence of economic sectors.

Intangible property: *See* Intellectual property rights.

Integrated system: A system for taxation of corporate income aimed at preventing double taxation through the use of split rates or tax credits.

Intellectual property rights: Ownership rights to intangible assets, such as patents, trademarks, copyrights, and know-how.

Interbank market: The market for foreign-exchange transactions among commercial banks.

Interbank transactions: Foreign-exchange transactions that take place between commercial banks.

Interdependence: The existence of mutually necessary economic relations among countries.

Interest aggregation: The collection of interests in the political system.

Interest arbitrage: Investing in debt instruments in different countries and earning a profit due to interest-rate and exchange-rate differentials.

Interest articulation: The process by which politicians, individuals, businesses, and interest groups make their desires known in the political process.

Interest rate differential: An indicator of future changes in the spot exchange rate.

Internalization: Control through self-handling of foreign operations, primarily because it is less expensive to deal within the same corporate family than to contract with an external organization.

International Accounting Standards Committee (IASC): The international private-sector organization that sets financial accounting standards for worldwide use.

International Bureau for the Protection of Industrial Property

Rights (BIRPI): A multilateral agreement to protect patents, trademarks, and other property rights.

International business: All business transactions involving private companies or governments of two or more countries.

International division: An organizational structure in which virtually all foreign operations are handled within the same division.

International Fisher Effect (IFE): The theory that the relationship between interest rates and exchange rates implies that the currency of the country with the lower interest rate will strengthen in the future.

International Labor Organization (ILO): A multilateral organization promoting the adoption of humane labor conditions.

International Monetary Fund (IMF): A multigovernmental association organized in 1945 to promote exchange-rate stability and to facilitate the international flow of currencies.

International Monetary Market (IMM): A specialized market located in Chicago and dealing in select foreign-currency futures.

International Organization of Securities Commissions (IOSCO): An international organization of securities regulators that wants the IASC to establish more comprehensive accounting standards.

International standard of fair dealing: The concept that investors should receive prompt, adequate, and effective compensation in cases of expropriation.

International Trade Administration (ITA): A branch of the U.S. Department of Commerce offering a variety of services to U.S. exporting companies.

Intervention currencies: The currencies in which a particular country trades the most.

Intrazonal trade: Trade among countries that are part of a trade agreement, such as the EU.

Investment Canada: A Canadian act whose intent is to persuade foreign companies to invest in Canada.

Invisibles: *See* Services.

IOSCO: *See* International Organization of Securities Commissions.

Irrevocable letter of credit: A letter of credit that cannot be canceled or changed without the consent of all parties involved.

Islamic law: A system of theocratic law based on the religious teachings of Islam; also called Muslim law.

ISO 9000: A quality standard developed by the International Standards Organization in Geneva that requires companies to document their commitment to quality at all levels of the organization.

IVL: *See* Individually validated license.

Jamaica Agreement: A 1976 agreement among countries that permitted greater flexibility of exchange rates, basically formalizing the break from fixed exchange rates.

JIT: *See* Just-in-time system.

Joint venture: A direct investment of which two or more companies share the ownership.

Just-in-time (JIT) system: A system that decreases inventory costs by having components and parts delivered as they are needed in production.

Keiretsu: A corporate relationship linking certain Japanese companies, usually involving a noncontrolling interest in each other, strong high-level personal relationships among managers in the different companies, and interlocking directorships.

Key industry: Any industry that might affect a very large segment of a country's economy or population by virtue of its size or influence on other sectors.

Labor market: The mix of available workers and labor costs available to companies.

Labor union: An association of workers intended to promote and protect the welfare, interests, and rights of its members, primarily by collective bargaining.

LAFTA: *See* Latin American Free Trade Association.

Lag strategy: An operational strategy that involves delaying collection of foreign-currency receivables if the currency is expected to strengthen or delays payment of foreign-currency payables when the currency is expected to weaken; the opposite of a lead strategy.

Laissez-faire: The concept of minimal governmental intervention in a society's economic activity.

Latin American Free Trade Association (LAFTA): A free-trade area formed by Mexico and the South American countries in 1960; it was replaced by ALADI in 1980.

Latin American Integration Association (ALADI): A form of regional economic integration involving most of the Latin American countries.

Law: A binding custom or practice of a community.

Lead country strategy: A strategy of introducing a product on a test basis in a small-country market that is considered representative of a region before investing to serve larger-country markets.

Lead strategy: An operational strategy that involves collecting foreign-currency receivables early when the currency is expected to weaken or paying foreign-currency payables early when the currency is expected to strengthen; the opposite of a lag strategy.

Learning curve: A concept used to support the infant industry argument for protection; it assumes that costs will decrease as workers and managers gain more experience.

Leontief paradox: A surprising finding by Wassily Leontief that overall U.S. exports were less capital-intensive and more labor-intensive than U.S. imports.

Less developed country (LDC): *See* Third-World country.

Letter of credit: A precise document by which the importer's bank extends credit to the importer and agrees to pay the exporter.

LIBOR: *See* London Inter-Bank Offered Rate.

License: Formal or legal permission to do some specified action; a governmental method of fixing the exchange rate by requiring all recipients, exporters, and others that receive foreign exchange to sell it to the central bank at the official buying rate.

Licensing agreement: Agreement whereby one company gives rights to another for the use, usually for a fee, of such assets as trademarks, patents, copyrights, or other know-how.

Licensing arrangement: A procedure that requires potential importers or exporters to secure permission from governmental authorities before they conduct trade transactions.

Lifetime employment: The Japanese custom that workers are effectively guaranteed employment with the company for their working lifetime and that workers seldom leave for employment opportunities with other companies.

LIFFE: *See* London International Financial Futures Exchange.

Liquidity preference: A theory that helps explain capital budgeting and, when applied to international operations, means that investors are willing to take less return in order to be able to shift the resources to alternative uses.

Lobbyist: An individual who participates in advancing or otherwise securing passage of legislation by influencing public officials before and during the legislation process.

Local content: Costs incurred within a given country, usually as a percentage of total costs.

Locally responsive company: Synonym for *multidomestic company.*

Locals: Citizens of the country in which they are working.

London Inter-Bank Offered Rate (LIBOR): The interest rate for large interbank loans of Eurocurrencies.

London International Financial Futures Exchange (LIFFE): An exchange dealing in futures contracts for several major currencies.

London Stock Exchange (LSE): A stock exchange located in London and dealing in Euroequities.

Maastricht (Treaty of): The treaty approved in December 1991 that was designed to bring the EU to a higher level of integration and is divided into Economic and Monetary Union (EMU) and political union.

Management contract: An arrangement whereby one company provides management personnel to perform general or specialized management functions to another company for a fee.

Manufacturing interchange: A process by which various plants produce a range of components and exchange them so that all plants assemble the finished product for the local market.

Maquiladora: An industrial operation developed by the Mexican and U.S. governments in which U.S.-sourced components are shipped to Mexico duty-free, assembled into final products, and re-exported to the United States.

Marginal propensity to import: The tendency to purchase imports with incremental income.

Market capitalization: A common measure of the size of a stock market, which is computed by multiplying the total number of shares of stock listed on the exchange by the market price per share.

Market economy: An economic system in which resources are allocated and controlled by consumers who "vote" by buying goods.

Market environment: The environment that involves the interactions between households (or individuals) and companies to allocate resources, free from governmental ownership or control.

Matrix: A method of plotting data on a set of vertical and horizontal axes, in order to compare countries in terms of risk and opportunity.

Matrix structure: An organizational structure in which foreign units report (by product, function, or area) to more than one group, each of which shares responsibility over the foreign unit.

Mentor: A person at headquarters who looks after the interests of an expatriate employee.

Mercantilism: An economic philosophy based on the beliefs that a country's wealth is dependent on its holdings of treasure, usually in the form of gold, and that countries should export more than they import in order to increase wealth.

Merchandise exports: Goods sent out of a country.

Merchandise imports: Goods brought into a country.

Merchandise trade account: The part of a country's current account that measures the trade deficit or surplus; its balance is the net of merchandise imports and exports.

MERCOSUR: A major subregional group comprised of Argentina, Brazil, Paraguay, and Uruguay, which spun off

from ALADI in 1991 with the goal of setting up a customs union and common market.

MFA: *See* Multifibre Arrangement.

MFN: *See* Most-favored-nation clause.

Ministry of International Trade and Industry (MITI): The Japanese governmental agency responsible for coordinating overall business direction and helping individual companies take advantage of global business opportunities.

Mission statement: A long-range strategic intent.

Mixed economy: An economic system characterized by some mixture of market and command economies and public and private ownership.

Mixed venture: A special type of joint venture in which a government is in partnership with a private company.

MNE: *See* Multinational enterprise.

Monopoly advantage: The perceived supremacy of foreign investors in relation to local companies, which is necessary to overcome the perceived greater risk of operating in a different environment.

Most-favored-nation (MFN) clause: A GATT requirement that a trade concession that is given to one country must be given to all other countries.

Multidomestic company: A company with international operations that allows operations in one country to be relatively independent of those in other countries.

Multifibre Arrangement (MFA): *See* Arrangement Regarding International Trade in Textiles.

Multilateral agreement: An agreement involving more than two governments.

Multilateral Investment Guarantee Agency (MIGA): A member of the World Bank Group that encourages equity investment and other direct investment flows to developing countries by offering investors a variety of different services.

Multinational corporation (MNC): A synonym for *multinational enterprise.*

Multinational enterprise (MNE): A company that has an integrated global philosophy encompassing both domestic and overseas operations; sometimes used synonymously with multinational corporation or transnational corporation.

Multiple exchange-rate system: A means of foreign-exchange control whereby the government sets different exchange rates for different transactions.

Muslim law: *See* Islamic law.

National responsiveness: Readiness to implement operating adjustments in foreign countries in order to reach a satisfactory level of performance.

Nationalism: The feeling of pride and/or ethnocentrism focused on an individual's home country or nation.

Nationalization: The transfer of ownership to the state.

Natural advantage: Climatic conditions, access to certain natural resources, or availability of labor, which gives a country an advantage in producing some product.

Need hierarchy: *See* Hierarchy of needs.

Neomercantilism: The approach of countries that apparently try to run favorable balances of trade in an attempt to achieve some social or political objective.

Net capital flow: Capital inflow minus capital outflow, for other than import and export payment.

Net export effect: Export stimulus minus export reduction.

Net import change: Import displacement minus import stimulus.

Netting: The transfer of funds from subsidiaries in a net payable position to a central clearing account and from there to the accounts of the net receiver subsidiaries.

Newly industrializing country (NIC): A Third-World country in which the cultural and economic climate has led to a rapid rate of industrialization and growth since the 1960s.

Nonmarket economy: *See* Command economy.

Nonmarket environment: Public institutions (such as government, governmental agencies, and government-owned businesses) and nonpublic institutions (such as environmental and other special-interest groups).

Nonpublic institutions: Special interest groups, such as environmentalists.

Nonresident convertibility: The ability of a nonresident of a country to convert deposits in a bank to the currency of any other country; also known as external convertibility.

Nontariff barriers: Barriers to imports that are not tariffs; examples include administrative controls, "Buy America" policies, and so forth.

Normal quote: Synonym for *direct quote*.

North American Free Trade Agreement (NAFTA): A free-trade agreement involving the United States, Canada, and Mexico that went into effect on January 1, 1994 and will be phased in over a period of fifteen years.

OAU: *See* Organization of African Unity.

OECD: *See* Organization for Economic Cooperation and Development.

OEEC: *See* Organization for European Economic Cooperation.

Offer rate: The amount for which a foreign-exchange trader is willing to sell a currency.

Official reserves: A country's holdings of monetary gold, Special Drawing Rights, and internationally acceptable currencies.

Offset: A form of barter transaction in which an export is paid for with other merchandise.

Offset trade: A form of countertrade in which an exporter sells goods for cash but then helps businesses in the importing country find opportunities to earn hard currency.

Offshore financial centers: Cities or countries that provide large amounts of funds in currencies other than their own and are used as locations in which to raise and accumulate cash.

Offshore manufacturing: Manufacturing outside the borders of a particular country.

Oligopoly: An industry in which there are few producers or sellers.

OPEC: *See* Organization of Petroleum Exporting Countries.

Open account: Conditions of sale under which the exporter extends credit directly to the importer.

Operational centers: Offshore financial centers that perform specific functions, such as the sale and servicing of goods.

OPIC: *See* Overseas Private Investment Corporation.

Opinion leader: One whose acceptance of some concept is apt to be emulated by others.

Optimism: A characteristic of an accounting system that implies that companies are more liberal in recognition of income.

Optimum-tariff theory: The argument that a foreign producer will lower its prices if an import tax is placed on its products.

Option: A foreign-exchange instrument that gives the purchaser the right, but not the obligation, to buy or sell a certain amount of foreign currency at a set exchange rate within a specified amount of time.

Organization of African Unity (OAU): An organization of African nations that is more concerned with political than economic objectives.

Organization for Economic Cooperation and Development (OECD): A multilateral organization of industrialized and semi-industrialized countries that helps formulate social and economic policies.

Organization for European Economic Cooperation (OEEC): A sixteen-nation organization established in 1948 to facilitate the utilization of aid from the Marshall Plan; it evolved into the EU and EFTA.

Organization of Petroleum Exporting Countries (OPEC): A producers' alliance among twelve petroleum-exporting countries that attempt to agree on oil production and pricing policies.

Organizational structure: The reporting relationships within an organization.

Outright forward: A forward contract that is not connected to a spot transaction.

Outsourcing: The use by a domestic company of foreign suppliers for components or finished products.

Overseas Private Investment Corporation (OPIC): A U.S. government agency that provides insurance for companies involved in international business.

Over-the-counter (OTC) market: Trading in stocks, usually of smaller companies, that are not listed on one of the stock exchanges; also refers to how government and corporate bonds are traded, through dealers who quote bids and offers to buy and sell "over the counter."

Par value: The benchmark value of a currency, originally quoted in terms of gold or the U.S. dollar and now quoted in terms of Special Drawing Rights.

Parliamentary government: A form of government that involves the election of representatives to form the executive branch.

Passive income: Income from investments in tax-haven countries or sales and services income that involves buyers and sellers in other than the tax-haven country, where either the buyer or the seller must be part of the same organizational structure as the corporation that earns the income; also known as Subpart F income.

Patent: A right granted by a sovereign power or state for the protection of an invention or discovery against infringement.

Patent cooperation treaty: A multilateral agreement to protect patents.

Peg: To fix a currency's exchange rate to some benchmark, such as another currency.

Penetration strategy: A strategy of introducing a product at a low price to induce a maximum number of consumers to try it.

Philadelphia Stock Exchange (PSE): A specialized market dealing in select foreign-currency options.

Piggyback exporting: Use by an exporter of another exporter as an intermediary.

Piracy: The unauthorized use of property rights that are protected by patents, trademarks, or copyrights.

Planning: The meshing of objectives with internal and external constraints in order to set means to implement, monitor, and correct operations.

PLC: *See* Product life cycle theory.

Pluralistic societies: Societies in which different ideologies are held by various segments rather than one ideology being adhered to by all.

Political freedom: The right to participate freely in the political process.

Political risk: Potential changes in political conditions that may cause a company's operating positions to deteriorate.

Political science: A discipline that helps explain the patterns of governments and their actions.

Political system: The system designed to integrate a society into a viable, functioning unit.

Polycentrism: Characteristic of an individual or organization that feels that differences in a foreign country, real and imaginary, great and small, need to be accounted for in management decisions.

Porter diamond: A diagram showing four conditions—demand, factor endowments, related and supporting industries, and firm strategy, structure, and rivalry—that usually must all be favorable for an industry in a country to develop and sustain a global competitive advantage.

Portfolio investment: An investment in the form of either debt or equity that does not give the investor a controlling interest.

Power distance: A measurement of preference for consultative or autocratic styles of management.

PPP: *See* Purchasing-power parity.

Pragmatism: Settling small issues before deciding on principles.

Premium (in foreign exchange): The difference between the spot and forward exchange rates in the forward market; a foreign currency sells at a premium when the forward rate exceeds the spot rate and when the domestic currency is quoted on a direct basis.

Pressure group: A group that tries to influence legislation or practices to foster its objectives.

Price escalation: The process by which the lengthening of distribution channels increases a product's price by more than the direct added costs, such as transportation, insurance, and tariffs.

Prior informed consent (PIC): The concept of requiring each exporter of a banned or restricted chemical to obtain, through the home-country government, the expressed consent of the importing country to receive the banned or restricted substance.

Privatizing: Selling of government-owned assets to private individuals or companies.

Product division: An organizational structure in which different foreign operations report to different product groups at headquarters.

Product life cycle (PLC) theory: The theory that certain kinds of products go through a cycle consisting of four stages (introduction, growth, maturity, and decline) and that the location of production will shift internationally depending on the stage of the cycle.

Production switching: The movement of production from one country to another in response to changes in cost.

Promotion: The process of presenting messages intended to help sell a product or service.

Protestant ethic: A theory that there is more economic growth when work is viewed as a means of salvation and when people prefer to transform productivity gains into additional output rather than into additional leisure.

Pull: A promotion strategy that sells consumers before they reach the point of purchase, usually by relying on mass media.

Purchasing power: What a sum of money actually can buy.

Purchasing-power parity (PPP): A theory that explains exchange-rate changes as being based on differences in price levels in different countries.

Push: A promotion strategy that involves direct selling techniques.

Quantity controls: Government limitations on the amount of foreign currency that can be used for specific purposes.

Quota: A limit on the quantitative amount of a product allowed to be imported into or exported out of a country in a year.

Quota system: A commodity agreement whereby producing and/or consuming countries divide total output and sales in order to stabilize the price of a particular product.

Quoted currency: The currency whose value is not 1 when an exchange rate is quoted by relating one currency to another.

Rationalization: *See* Rationalized production.

Rationalized production: The specialization of production by product or process in different parts of the world to take advantage of varying costs of labor, capital, and raw materials.

Reciprocal quote: The reciprocal of the direct quote; also known as the *indirect quote.*

Regression: A statistical method showing relationships among variables.

Reinvestment: The use of retained earnings to replace depreciated assets or to add to the existing stock of capital.

Relationship enterprises: Networks of strategic alliances among big companies, spanning different industries and countries.

Renegotiation: A process by which international companies and governments decide on a change in terms for operations.

Repatriation: An expatriate's return to his or her home country.

Representative democracy: A type of government in which individual citizens elect representatives to make decisions governing the society.

Return on investment (ROI): The amount of profit, sometimes measured before and sometimes after the payment of taxes, divided by the amount of investment.

Revaluation: A formal change in an exchange rate by which the foreign-currency value of the reference currency rises, resulting in a strengthening of the reference currency.

Revocable letter of credit: A letter of credit that can be changed by any of the parties involved.

Rio Declaration: The result of the Rio Earth Summit, which sets out fundamental principles of environmentally responsive behavior.

Rio Earth Summit: A meeting held in Rio de Janeiro in June 1992 that brought together people from around the world to discuss major environmental issues.

ROI: *See* Return on investment.

Rounds: Conferences held by GATT to establish multilateral agreements to liberalize trade.

Royalties: Payments for the use of intangible assets abroad.

SADCC: *See* Southern African Development Co-ordination Conference.

Sales representative (foreign): A representative that usually operates either exclusively or nonexclusively within an assigned market and on a commission basis, without assuming risk or responsibility.

Sales response function: The amount of sales created at different levels of marketing expenditures.

SDR: *See* Special Drawing Right.

Second-tier subsidiaries: Subsidiaries that report to a tax-haven subsidiary.

Second-World countries: Socialist countries, often referred to as historically planned economies, centrally planned economies, or communist countries.

Secondary boycott: The boycotting of a company that does business with a company being boycotted.

Secrecy: A characteristic of an accounting system that implies that companies do not disclose much information about accounting practices; more common in Germanic countries.

Secular totalitarianism: A dictatorship not affiliated with any religious group or system of beliefs.

Securities and Exchange Commission (SEC): A U.S. government agency that regulates securities brokers, dealers, and markets.

Separate entity approach: A system for taxation of corporate income in which each unit is taxed when it receives income, with the result being double taxation.

Service exports: International received earnings other than those derived from the exporting of tangible goods.

Service imports: International paid earnings other than those derived from the importing of tangible goods.

Services: International earnings other than those on goods sent to another country; also referred to as invisibles.

Services account: The part of a country's current account that measures travel and transportation, tourism, and fees and royalties.

Settlement: The actual payment of currency in a foreign-exchange transaction.

Shipper's export declaration: A shipping document that controls exports and is used to compile trade statistics.

Sight draft: A commercial bill of exchange that requires payment to be made as soon as it is presented to the party obligated to pay.

Silent language: The wide variety of cues other than formal language by which messages can be sent.

Single European Act: A 1987 act of the EU (then the EC) allowing all proposals except those relating to taxation, workers' rights, and immigration to be adopted by a weighted majority of member countries.

Smithsonian Agreement: A 1971 agreement among countries that resulted in the devaluation of the U.S. dollar, revaluation of other world currencies, a widening of exchange-rate flexibility, and a commitment on the part of all participating countries to reduce trade restrictions; superseded by the Jamaica Agreement of 1976.

Social market economy: An economic system in which there is heavy governmental spending and high taxation to pay for such social services as health care, education, subsidized housing for the poor, and unemployment benefits but the prices of products are determined by supply and demand rather than by government fiat.

Society: A broad grouping of people having common traditions, institutions, and collective activities and interests, the term *nation-state* is often used in international business to denote a society.

Soft budget: A financial condition in which an enterprise's excess of expenditures over earnings is compensated for by some other institution, typically a government or a state-controlled financial institution.

Soft currency: *See* Weak currency.

Sogo shosha: Japanese trading companies that import and export merchandise.

Sourcing strategy: The strategy that a company pursues in purchasing materials, components, and final products; sourcing can be from domestic and foreign locations and from inside and outside the company.

Southern African Development Co-ordination Conference (SADCC): A regional economic group in Africa that involves Angola, Botswana, Lesotho, Malawi, Mozambique, Swaziland, Tanzania, Zambia, and Zimbabwe.

Sovereignty: Freedom from external control, especially when applied to a body politic.

Special Drawing Right (SDR): A unit of account issued to countries by the International Monetary Fund to expand their official reserves bases.

Specific duty: A duty (tariff) assessed on a per-unit basis.

Speculation: The buying or selling of foreign currency with the prospect of great risk and high return.

Speculator: A person who takes positions in foreign exchange with the objective of earning a profit.

Spillover effects: Situations in which the marketing program in one country results in awareness of the product in other countries.

Spot market: The market in which an asset is traded for immediate delivery, as opposed to a market for forward or future deliveries.

Spot rate: An exchange rate quoted for immediate delivery of foreign currency, usually within two business days.

Spread: In the forward market, the difference between the spot rate and the forward rate; in the spot market, the difference between the bid (buy) and offer (sell) rates quoted by a foreign-exchange trader.

Stakeholders: The collection of groups, including stock-holders, employees, customers, and society at large, that a company must satisfy to survive.

Stereotype: A standardized and oversimplified mental picture of a group.

Strategic alliance: An agreement between companies that is of strategic importance to one or both companies' competitive viability.

Strategic intent: An objective that gives an organization cohesion over the long term while it builds global competitive viability.

Strategic plan: A long-term plan involving major commitments.

Subpart F income: Income of a CFC that comes from sources other than those connected with the active conduct of a trade or business, such as holding company income.

Subsidiarity: A principle that implies that EU interference should take place only in areas of common concern and that most policies should be set at the national level.

Subsidiary: A foreign operation that is legally separate from the parent company, even if wholly owned by it.

Subsidies: Direct or indirect financial assistance from governments to companies, making them more competitive.

Substitution drawbacks: A provision allowing domestic merchandise to be substituted for merchandise that is imported for eventual export, thus allowing the U.S. firm to exclude the duty paid on the merchandise in costs and in sales prices.

Super 301: A clause in U.S. tariff legislation permitting U.S. trade negotiators to threaten more restrictive import regulations to get other countries to lower their restrictions against U.S.-made products or services.

Swap: A simultaneous spot and forward foreign-exchange transaction.

Syndication: Cooperation by a lead bank and several other banks to make a large loan to a public or private organization.

Tariff: A governmental tax levied on goods, usually imports, shipped internationally; the most common type of trade control.

Tax treaty: A treaty between two countries that generally results in the reciprocal reduction on dividend withholding taxes and the exemption of taxes or royalties and sometimes interest payments.

Tax-haven countries: Countries with low income taxes or no taxes on foreign-source income.

Tax-haven subsidiary: A subsidiary of a company established in a tax-haven country for the purpose of minimizing income tax.

Technology: The means employed to produce goods or services.

Temporal method: A method of translating foreign-currency financial statements used when the functional currency is that of the parent company.

Terms of trade: The quantity of imports that can be bought by a given quantity of a country's exports.

Theocratic law system: A legal system based on religious precepts.

Theocratic totalitarianism: A dictatorship led by a religious group.

Third-country nationals: Expatriate employees who are neither citizens of the country in which they are working nor citizens of the country where the company is headquartered.

Third-World countries: Developing countries or those not considered socialist or nonsocialist industrial countries.

Time draft: A commercial bill of exchange calling for payment to be made at some time after delivery.

Time series: A statistical method of illustrating a pattern over time, such as in demand for a particular product.

TNC: *See* Transnational corporation.

Tort: A civil wrong independent of a contract.

Total quality management (TQM): The process that a company uses to achieve quality, where the goal is elimination of all defects.

Totalitarianism: A political system characterized by the absence of widespread participation in decision making.

TQM: *See* Total quality management.

Trade diversion: A situation in which exports shift to a less efficient producing country because of preferential trade barriers.

Trademark: A name or logo distinguishing a company or product.

Transaction exposure: Foreign-exchange risk arising because a company has outstanding accounts receivable or accounts payable that are denominated in a foreign currency.

Transfer price: A price charged for goods or services between entities that are related to each other through stock ownership, such as between a parent and its subsidiaries or between subsidiaries owned by the same parent.

Transit tariff: A tax placed on goods passing through a country.

Translation: The restatement of foreign-currency financial statements into U.S. dollars.

Translation exposure: Foreign-exchange risk that occurs because the parent company must translate foreign-currency financial statements into the reporting currency of the parent company.

Transnational corporation (TNC): A company owned and managed by nationals in different countries; also may be synonymous with multinational enterprise.

Transparency: A characteristic of an accounting system that implies that companies disclose a great deal of information about accounting practices; more common in Anglo-Saxon countries (United States, United Kingdom).

Triad strategy: A strategy proposing that an MNE should have a presence in Europe, the United States, and Asia (especially Japan).

Turnkey operation: An operating facility that is constructed under contract and transferred to the owner when the facility is ready to begin operations.

Underemployed: Those people who are working at less than their capacity.

Unfavorable balance of trade: An indication of a trade deficit—that is, imports are greater than exports.

Unilateral transfer: A transfer of currency from one country to another for which no goods or services are received; an example is foreign aid to a country devastated by earthquake or flood.

Unit of account: A benchmark on which to base the value of payments.

United Nations (UN): An international organization of countries formed in 1945 to promote world peace and security.

United Nations Conference on Trade and Development (UNCTAD): A UN body that has been especially active in dealing with the relationships between developing and industrialized countries with respect to trade.

Universal Copyright Convention: A multilateral agreement to protect copyrights.

Unrequited transfer: *See* Unilateral transfer.

U.S.-Canada Free Trade Agreement: *See* Canada-U.S. Free Trade Agreement.

U.S. shareholder: For U.S. tax purposes, a person or company owning at least 10 percent of the voting stock of a foreign subsidiary.

U.S. terms: The practice of using the direct quote for exchange rates.

Value-added tax (VAT): A tax that is a percentage of the value added to a product at each stage of the business process.

Value chain: The collective activities that occur as a product moves from raw materials through production to final distribution.

Variable price: A method of pricing in which buyers and sellers negotiate the price.

VAT: *See* Value-added tax.

VER: *See* Voluntary export restrictions.

Vertical integration: The control of the different stages as a product moves from raw materials through production to final distribution.

Visible exports: *See* Merchandise exports.

Visible imports: *See* Merchandise imports.

Voluntary export restraint (VER): A negotiated limitation of exports between an importing and an exporting country.

Weak currency: A currency that is not fully convertible.

West African Economic Community: A regional economic group involving Benin, Burkina Faso, Côte d'Ivoire, Mali, Mauritania, Niger, and Senegal.

WIPO: *See* World Intellectual Property Organization.

World Intellectual Property Organization (WIPO): A multilateral agreement to protect patents.

Zaibatsu: Large, family-owned Japanese businesses that existed before World War II and consisted of a series of financial and manufacturing companies usually held together by a large holding company.

Zero defects: The elimination of defects, which results in the reduction of manufacturing costs and an increase in consumer satisfaction.

Company Index and Trademarks

Name Index

Map Index

This map index refers to the maps on pages 35–42.

Country/Territory	Pronunciation	Map 1	Map 2	Map 3	Map 4	Map 5	Map 6	Map 7
Afghanistan	af-ˈgan-ə-ˌstan	E6	—	—	E4	—	—	—
Albania	al-ˈbā-nē-ə	D5	—	H6	—	—	—	—
Algeria	al-ˈjir-ē-ə	E5	B3	—	—	—	—	—
Andorra	an-ˈdȯr-ə	—	—	H2	—	—	—	—
Angola	aŋ-ˈgō-lə	F5	G4	—	—	—	—	—
Antigua & Barbuda	an-ˈtē-g(w)ə / bär-ˈbüd-ə	—	—	—	—	H3	—	—
Argentina	ˌär-jən-ˈtē-nə	G3	—	—	—	—	G4	—
Armenia	är-ˈmē-nē-ə	D6	—	—	D3	—	—	—
Australia	ȯ-ˈstrāl-yə	G8	—	—	—	—	—	E4
Austria	ˈȯs-trē-ə	D5	—	G5	—	—	—	—
Azerbaijan	ˌaz-ər-ˌbī-ˈjän	E6	—	—	D3	—	—	—
Bahrain	bä-ˈrān	—	—	—	E3	—	—	—
Bangladesh	ˌbäŋ-glə-ˈdesh	E7	—	—	F5	—	—	—
Barbados	bär-ˈbād-əs	—	—	—	—	I3	—	—
Belarus	ˌbē-lə-ˈrüs	D6	—	E6	—	—	—	—
Belgium	ˈbel-jəm	D5	—	F3	—	—	—	—
Belize	bə-ˈlēz	E3	—	—	—	I6	—	—
Benin	bə-ˈnin	E5	D3	—	—	—	—	—
Bermuda	(ˌ)bər-ˈmyüd-ə	—	—	—	—	G8	—	—
Bhutan	bü-ˈtan	E7	—	—	F5	—	—	—
Bolivia	bə-ˈliv-ē-ə	F3	—	—	—	—	E4	—
Bosnia & Herzegovina	ˈbäz-nē-ə / ˌhert-sə-gō-ˈvē-nə	D5	—	G5	—	—	—	—
Botswana	bät-ˈswän-ə	F5	H5	—	—	—	—	—
Brazil	brə-ˈzil	F4	—	—	—	—	D6	—
Bulgaria	ˌbəl-ˈgar-ē-ə	D6	—	H6	—	—	—	—
Burkina Faso	bůr-ˈkē-nə-ˈfä-sō	E5	D2	—	—	—	—	—
Burundi	bů-ˈrün-dē	F6	E6	—	—	—	—	—
Cambodia	kam-ˈbōd-ē-ə	E8	—	—	G6	—	—	—
Cameroon	ˌkam-ə-ˈrün	F5	D4	—	—	—	—	—
Canada	ˈkan-əd-ə	C2	—	—	—	D5	—	—
Central African Republic	—	F5	D5	—	—	—	—	—
Chad	ˈchad	E5	C5	—	—	—	—	—
Chile	ˈchil-ē	G3	—	—	—	—	G3	—
China	ˈchī-nə	E7	—	—	E6	—	—	—
Colombia	kə-ˈləm-bē-ə	F3	—	—	—	—	B3	—
Congo Republic	ˈkäŋ(ˌ)gō	F5	E4	—	—	—	—	—
Costa Rica	ˌkäs-tə-ˈrē-kə	F3	—	—	—	I7	—	—
Côte d'Ivoire	ˌkōt-dēv-ˈwär	F5	D2	—	—	—	—	—
Croatia	krō-ˈā-sh(ē)ə	D5	—	G5	—	—	—	—
Cuba	ˈkyü-bə	E3	—	—	—	H7	—	—
Curaçao	ˈk(y)ür-ə-ˌsō	—	—	—	—	—	A4	—
Cyprus	ˈsī-prəs	—	—	I8	—	—	—	—
Czech Republic	ˌchek	D5	—	F5	—	—	—	—

Country/Territory	Pronunciation	Map 1	Map 2	Map 3	Map 4	Map 5	Map 6	Map 7
Denmark	ˈden-ˌmärk	D5	—	E4	—	—	—	—
Djibouti	jə-ˈbüt-ē	E6	D7	—	—	—	—	—
Dominica	ˌdäm-ə-ˈnē-kə	—	—	—	—	I3	—	—
Dominican Republic	də-ˌmin-i-kən	E3	—	—	—	H8	—	—
Ecuador	ˈek-wə-ˌdȯ(ə)r	F3	—	—	—	—	C2	—
Egypt	ˈē-jəpt	E6	B6	—	—	—	—	—
El Salvador	el-ˈsal-və-ˌdȯ(ə)r	E3	—	—	—	I6	—	—
Eritrea	ˌer-ə-ˈtrē-ə	E6	C7	—	—	—	—	—
Estonia	e-ˈstō-nē-ə	D5	—	D6	—	—	—	—
Ethiopia	ˌē-thē-ˈō-pē-ə	F6	D7	—	—	—	—	—
Falkland Islands	ˈfȯ(l) klənd	—	—	—	—	—	I5	—
Finland	ˈfin-lənd	C6	—	C6	—	—	—	—
France	ˈfran(t)s	D5	—	G3	—	—	—	—
French Guiana	gē-ˈan-ə	F4	—	—	—	—	B6	—
Gabon	ga-ˈbōⁿ	F5	E4	—	—	—	—	—
Gambia	ˈgam-bē-ə	E5	C1	—	—	—	—	—
Georgia	ˈjȯr-jə	D6	—	—	—	—	—	—
Germany	ˈjerm-(ə-)nē	D5	—	F4	—	—	—	—
Ghana	ˈgan-ə	F5	D2	—	—	—	—	—
Greece	ˈgrēs	E5	—	H6	—	—	—	—
Greenland	ˈgrēn-lənd	B4	—	—	—	A6	—	—
Guatemala	ˌgwät-ə-ˈmäl-ə	E3	—	—	—	I6	—	—
Guinea	ˈgin-ē	F5	E4	—	—	—	—	—
Guinea-Bissau	ˌgin-ē-bis-ˈaů	F4	D1	—	—	—	—	—
Guyana	gı-ˈan-ə	F3	—	—	—	—	—	—
Haiti	ˈhāt-ē	E3	—	—	—	H8	—	—
Honduras	hän-ˈd(y)ůr-əs	E3	—	—	—	I6	—	—
Hong Kong	ˈhäŋ-ˌkäŋ	E8	—	—	F7	—	—	—
Hungary	ˈhəŋ-g(ə)rē	D5	—	G5	—	—	—	—
Iceland	ˈī-slənd	C4	—	B1	—	—	—	—
India	ˈin-dē-ə	E7	—	—	F4	—	—	—
Indonesia	ˌin-də-ˈnē-zhə	F8	—	—	H7	—	—	A3
Iran	i-ˈrän	E6	—	—	E3	—	—	—
Iraq	i-ˈräk	E7	—	—	D3	—	—	—
Ireland	ˈī(ə)r-lənd	D5	—	E2	—	—	—	—
Israel	ˈiz-rē-əl	E6	—	—	D2	—	—	—
Italy	ˈit-ᵊl-ē	D5	—	H5	—	—	—	—
Jamaica	jə-ˈmā-kə	E3	—	—	—	H7	—	—
Japan	jə-ˈpan	E8	—	—	D8	—	—	—
Jordan	ˈjȯrd-ᵊn	E6	—	—	D2	—	—	—
Kazakhstan	kə-ˌzak-ˈstan	D6	—	—	D4	—	—	—
Kenya	ˈken-yə	F6	E7	—	—	—	—	—
Korea, North	kə-ˈrē-ə	E8	—	—	D7	—	—	—

Country/Territory	Pronunciation	Map 1	Map 2	Map 3	Map 4	Map 5	Map 6	Map 7
Korea, South	kə-ˈrē-ə	E8	—	—	E7	—	—	—
Kuwait	kə-ˈwät	E6	—	—	E3	—	—	—
Kyrgyzstan	kîr-gē-stänˈ	D7	—	—	D4	—	—	—
Laos	ˈlaŭs	E7	—	—	F6	—	—	—
Latvia	ˈlat-vē-ə	D6	—	E6	—	—	—	—
Lebanon	ˈleb-ə-nən	E6	—	—	D2	—	—	—
Lesotho	lə-ˈsō-(ˌ)tō	G6	I5	—	—	—	—	—
Liberia	lī-ˈbir-ē-ə	F5	D1	—	—	—	—	—
Libya	ˈlib-ē-ə	E5	B4	—	—	—	—	—
Lithuania	ˌlith-(y)ə-ˈwā-nē-ə	D6	—	E6	—	—	—	—
Luxembourg	ˈlək-səm-ˌbərg	D5	—	F3	—	—	—	—
Macedonia	ˌmas-ə-ˈdō-nyə	D5	—	H6	—	—	—	—
Madagascar	ˌmad-ə-ˈgas-kər	F6	G8	—	—	—	—	—
Malawi	mə-ˈlä-wē	F6	G6	—	—	—	—	—
Malaysia	mə-ˈlā-zh(ē-)ə	F7	—	—	G6	—	—	—
Mali	ˈmäl-ē	E5	C2	—	—	—	—	—
Malta	ˈmȯl-tə	—	—	I5	—	—	—	—
Mauritania	ˌmȯr-ə-ˈtā-nē-ə	E4	C1	—	—	—	—	—
Mexico	ˈmek-si-ˌkō	E2	—	—	—	H4	—	—
Moldova	mäl-ˈdō-və	D6	—	G7	—	—	—	—
Mongolia	män-ˈgōl-yə	D7	—	—	D6	—	—	—
Morocco	mə-ˈräk-(ˌ)ō	E5	A2	—	—	—	—	—
Mozambique	ˌmō-zəm-ˈbēk	G6	G6	—	—	—	—	—
Myanmar	ˈmyän-ˌmär	E7	—	—	F6	—	—	—
Namibia	nə-ˈmib-ē-ə	G5	H4	—	—	—	—	—
Nepal	nə-ˈpȯl	E7	—	—	F5	—	—	—
Netherlands	ˈneth-ər-lən(d)z	D5	—	F3	—	—	—	—
New Caledonia	ˌkal-ə-ˈdō-nyə	—	—	—	—	—	—	D9
New Zealand	ˈzē-lənd	G9	—	—	—	—	—	H8
Nicaragua	ˌnik-ə-ˈräg-wə	E3	—	—	—	I7	—	—
Niger	ˈnī-jər	E5	C3	—	—	—	—	—
Nigeria	nī-ˈjir-ē-ə	F5	D3	—	—	—	—	—
Norway	ˈnȯ(ə)r-ˌwā	C5	—	C4	—	—	—	—
Oman	ō-ˈmän	E6	—	—	F3	—	—	—
Pakistan	ˌpak-i-ˈstan	E6	—	—	E4	—	—	—
Panama	ˈpan-ə-ˌmä	F3	—	—	—	J7	—	—
Papua New Guinea	ˈpap-yə-wə	F8	—	—	—	—	—	B6
Paraguay	ˈpar-ə-ˌgwī	G3	—	—	—	—	F5	—
Peru	pə-ˈrü	F3	—	—	—	—	D3	—
Philippines	ˌfil-ə-ˈpēnz	F8	—	—	—	—	—	—
Poland	ˈpō-lənd	D5	—	F5	—	—	—	—
Portugal	ˈpōr-chi-gəl	D5	—	H1	—	—	—	—
Puerto Rico	ˌpȯrt-ə-ˈrē(ˌ)kō	E3	—	—	—	H2	—	—
Qatar	ˈkät-ər	E6	—	—	E3	—	—	—
Romania	rō-ˈmā-nē-ə	D5	—	G6	—	—	—	—
Russia	ˈrəsh-ə	C7	—	C8	C6	—	—	—
Rwanda	rů-ˈän-də	F6	E6	—	—	—	—	—

Country/Territory	Pronunciation	Map 1	Map 2	Map 3	Map 4	Map 5	Map 6	Map 7
St. Kitts & Nevis	'kits / 'nē-vəs	—	—	—	—	I3	—	—
St. Lucia	sānt-'lü-shə	—	—	—	—	I3	—	—
Saudi Arabia	,saud-ē	E6	—	—	E2	—	—	—
Senegal	,sen-i-'gȯl	E4	C1	—	—	—	—	—
Serbia	'sər-bē-ə	D5	—	G6	—	—	—	—
Sierra Leone	sē-,er-ə-lē-'ōn	F5	D1	—	—	—	—	—
Singapore	'siŋ-(g)ə-,pō(ə)r	F8	—	—	H6	—	—	—
Slovakia	slō-'väk-ē-ə	D5	—	F6	—	—	—	—
Slovenia	slō-'vēn-ē-ə	D5	—	G5	—	—	—	—
Solomon Islands	'säl-ə-mən	—	—	—	—	—	—	B8
Somalia	sō-'mäl-ē-ə	F6	D8	—	—	—	—	—
South Africa	'a-fri-kə	G5	I5	—	—	—	—	—
Spain	'spān	E5	—	H2	—	—	—	—
Sri Lanka	(')srē-'läŋ-kə	F7	—	—	G5	—	—	—
Sudan	sü-'dan	F6	D6	—	—	—	—	—
Suriname	,sur-ə-'näm-ə	F3	—	—	—	—	B5	—
Swaziland	'swäz-ē-,land	G6	H6	—	—	—	—	—
Sweden	'swēd-ᵊn	C5	—	C5	—	—	—	—
Switzerland	'swit-sər-lənd	D5	—	G4	—	—	—	—
Syria	'sir-ē-ə	E6	—	—	D2	—	—	—
Taiwan	'tī-'wän	E8	—	—	F7	—	—	—
Tajikistan	tä-,ji-ki-'stan	D7	—	—	E4	—	—	—
Tanzania	,tan-zə-'nē-ə	F6	F7	—	—	—	—	—
Thailand	'tī-,land	F7	—	—	G6	—	—	—
Togo	'tō-(,)gō	F5	D3	—	—	—	—	—
Trinidad & Tobago	'trin-ə-,dad / tə-'bā-(,)go	—	—	—	—	J3	—	—
Tunisia	t(y)ü-'nē-zh(ē-)ə	E5	A4	—	—	—	—	—
Turkey	'tər-kē	E6	—	H7	D2	—	—	—
Turkmenistan	tûrk'-mĕn-ĭ-stăn'	E6	—	—	D3	—	—	—
Uganda	(y)ü-'gan-də	F6	E6	—	—	—	—	—
Ukraine	yü-'krān	D6	—	F7	—	—	—	—
United Arab Emirates	yo͞o-nī'tĭd ăr'əb ĭ-mîr'its	E6	—	—	F3	—	—	—
United Kingdom	kĭng'dəm	D5	—	E2	—	—	—	—
United States	yü-,nīt-əd-'stāts	D2	—	—	—	G5	—	—
Uruguay	'(y)ur-ə-gwī	G3	—	—	—	—	G5	—
Uzbekistan	(,)uz-,bek-i-'stan	E6	—	—	D4	—	—	—
Vanuatu	van-ə-'wät-(,)ü	—	—	—	—	—	—	C9
Venezuela	,ven-əz(-ə)-'wā-lə	F3	—	—	—	—	B4	—
Vietnam	vē-'et-'näm	F8	—	—	F6	—	—	—
Western Sahara	sə-hâr'ə	E4	B1	—	—	—	—	—
Yemen	'yem-ən	F6	—	—	F2	—	—	—
Zaire	'zī(ə)r	F5	E5	—	—	—	—	—
Zambia	'zam-bē-ə	F5	G5	—	—	—	—	—
Zimbabwe	zim-'bäb-wē	F5	G6	—	—	—	—	—

Subject Index